A People and A Nation

A HISTORY OF THE UNITED STATES

Brief Eighth Edition

MARY BETH NORTON
Cornell University

CAROL SHERIFF
College of William and Mary

DAVID M. KATZMAN
University of Kansas

DAVID W. BLIGHT
Yale University

HOWARD P. CHUDACOFF
Brown University

FREDRIK LOGEVALL
Cornell University

BETH BAILEY
Temple University

DEBRA MICHALS
Merrimack College

WADSWORTH
CENGAGE Learning

Australia • Brazil • Japan • Korea • Mexico • Singapore • Spain • United Kingdom • United States

WADSWORTH
CENGAGE Learning™

A People and A Nation: A History of the United States, **Brief Eighth Edition**

Mary Beth Norton, Carol Sheriff, David M. Katzman, David W. Blight, Howard P. Chudacoff, Fredrik Logevall, Beth Bailey, Debra Michals

Sponsoring Editor: Ann West

Development Manager: Jeffrey Greene

Assistant Editor: Megan Curry

Editorial Assistant: Megan Chrisman

Senior Editor: Lisa Ciccolo

Senior Marketing Manager:
    Katherine Bates

Marketing Coordinator:
    Lorreen Pelletier

Marketing Communications Manager:
    Christine Dobberpuhl

Content Project Manager, Editorial
    Production: Aimee Chevrette Bear

Art and Design Manager: Jill Haber

Print Buyer: Miranda Klapper

Senior Rights Acquisition Account
    Manager: Katie Huha

Text Designer: Cia Boynton

Senior Photo Editor:
    Jennifer Meyer Dare

Photo Researcher: Bruce Carson

Cover Design Manager: Tony Saizon

Cover Image: Julianita by Robert Henri,
    ca. 1917

Cover Credit: Private Collection,
    courtesy Gerald Peters Gallery,
    New York and John G. Hagan

Compositor: Macmillan Publishing
    Solutions

For product information and technology assistance, contact us at
Cengage Learning Academic Resource Center,
1-800-423-0563
For permission to use material from this text or product,
submit all requests online at **www.cengage.com/permissions.**
Further permissions questions can be e-mailed to
permissionrequest@cengage.com

Library of Congress Control Number: 2008933839

Student Edition:

ISBN-13: 978-0-547-17558-4

ISBN-10: 0-547-17558-2

Wadsworth
25 Thomson Place
Boston, MA 02210
USA

Cengage Learning products are represented in Canada by Nelson Education, Ltd.

For your course and learning solutions, visit
www.cengage.com.

Purchase any of our products at your local college store or at our preferred online store **www.ichapters.com.**

Printed in the United States of America
2 3 4 5 6 7 14 13 12 11 10

Brief Contents

Maps   *xii*

Figures   *xiii*

Tables   *xiv*

Preface to the Brief Eighth Edition   *xv*

Preface to the Full-Length Eighth Edition   *xvii*

1 Three Old Worlds Create a New, 1492–1600   *1*

2 Europeans Colonize North America, 1600–1650   *28*

3 North America in the Atlantic World, 1650–1720   *55*

4 American Society Transformed, 1720–1770   *80*

5 Severing the Bonds of Empire, 1754–1774   *107*

6 A Revolution, Indeed, 1774–1783   *131*

7 Forging a National Republic, 1776–1789   *154*

8 The Early Republic: Conflicts at Home and Abroad, 1789–1800   *181*

9 Defining the Nation, 1801–1823   *203*

10 The Rise of the South 1815–1860   *230*

11 The Modernizing North, 1815–1860   *261*

12 Reform and Politics in the Age of Jackson 1824–1845   *289*

13 The Contested West, 1815–1860   *315*

14 Slavery and America's Future: The Road to War, 1845–1861   *346*

15 Transforming Fire: The Civil War, 1861–1865   *373*

16 Reconstruction: An Unfinished Revolution, 1865–1877   *409*

17 The Development of the West, 1877–1900   *439*

18 The Machine Age, 1877–1920   *465*

19 The Vitality and Turmoil of Urban Life, 1877–1920   *493*

20 Gilded Age Politics, 1877–1900   *522*

21 The Progressive Era, 1895–1920   *548*

22 The Quest for Empire, 1865–1914   *575*

23 Americans in the Great War, 1914–1920   *600*

24 The New Era 1920–1929   *627*

25 The Great Depression and the New Deal, 1929–1941   *655*

26 The United States in a Troubled World, 1920–1941   *684*

27 The Second World War at Home and Abroad, 1941–1945   *707*

28 The Cold War and American Globalism, 1945–1961   *733*

29 America at Midcentury, 1945–1960   *762*

30 The Tumultuous Sixties, 1960–1968   *792*

31 Continuing Divisions and New Limits, 1969–1980   *821*

32 Conservatism Revived, 1980–1992   *850*

33 Into the Global Millennium: America Since 1992   *878*

Appendix   *A-1*

Index   *I-1*

Contents

Maps   *xii*

Figures   *xiii*

Tables   *xiv*

Preface to the Brief Eighth Edition   *xv*

Preface to the Full-Length Eighth Edition   *xvii*

1

Three Old Worlds Create a New, 1492–1600   1

▍ American Societies   *3*

▍ North America in 1492   *5*

▍ African Societies   *8*

▍ European Societies   *10*

▍ Early European Explorations   *12*

▍ Voyages of Columbus, Cabot, and Their Successors   *13*

▍ Spanish Exploration and Conquest   *17*

▍ The Columbian Exchange   *19*

▍ Europeans in North America   *20*

Links to the World: Maize   *21*

▍ Summary   *23*

Legacy for a People and a Nation: Kennewick Man/Ancient One   *24*

2

Europeans Colonize North America, 1600–1650   28

▍ Spanish, French, and Dutch North America   *30*

▍ The Caribbean   *33*

Links to the World: Wampum   *34*

▍ English Interest in Colonization   *35*

▍ The Founding of Virginia   *37*

▍ Life in the Chesapeake   *41*

▍ The Founding of New England   *44*

▍ Life in New England   *48*

▍ Summary   *51*

Legacy for a People and a Nation: Blue Laws   *51*

3

North America in the Atlantic World, 1650–1720   55

▍ The Growth of Anglo-American Settlements   *57*

▍ A Decade of Imperial Crises: The 1670s   *62*

▍ The Atlantic Trading System   *65*

▍ Slavery in North America and the Caribbean   *68*

▍ Imperial Reorganization and the Witchcraft Crisis   *72*

Links to the World: Exotic Beverages   *76*

▍ Summary   *77*

Legacy for a People and a Nation: Americans of African Descent   *77*

4

American Society Transformed, 1720–1770   80

▍ Population Growth and Ethnic Diversity   *82*

▍ Economic Growth and Development   *86*

▍ Colonial Cultures   *91*

Links to the World: Smallpox Inoculation   *93*

▍ Colonial Families   *96*

▍ Politics: Stability and Crisis in British America   *99*

▍ A Crisis in Religion   *101*

▍ Summary   *103*

Legacy for a People and a Nation: "Self-Made Men"   *103*

5

Severing the Bonds of Empire, 1754–1774   107

▍ Renewed Warfare Among Europeans and Indians   *109*

▍ 1763: A Turning Point   *112*

Links to the World: The First Worldwide War   *113*

▍ The Stamp Act Crisis   *116*

■ Resistance to the Townshend Acts *120*
■ Confrontations in Boston *122*
■ Tea and Turmoil *125*
■ Summary *127*
Legacy for a People and a Nation: Women's Political Activism *127*

6

A Revolution, Indeed, 1774–1783   131

■ Government by Congress and Committee *133*
■ Contest in the Backcountry *135*
■ Choosing Sides *136*
■ War and Independence *138*
Links to the World: New Nations *139*
■ The Struggle in the North *143*
■ Life in the Army and on the Home Front *145*
■ Victory in the South *147*
■ Summary *150*
Legacy for a People and a Nation: Revolutionary Origins 150

7

Forging a National Republic, 1776–1789   154

■ Creating a Virtuous Republic *156*
Links to the World: Novels *158*
■ The First Emancipation and the Growth of Racism *160*
■ Designing Republican Governments *163*
■ Trials of the Confederation *165*
■ Order and Disorder in the West *169*
■ From Crisis to the Constitution *170*
■ Opposition and Ratification *175*
■ Summary *177*
Legacy for a People and a Nation: The Township and Range System *177*

8

The Early Republic: Conflicts at Home and Abroad, 1789–1800   181

■ Building a Workable Government *182*
■ Domestic Policy Under Washington and Hamilton *184*
■ The French Revolution and the Development of Partisan Politics *188*
■ Partisan Politics and Relations with Great Britain *190*
■ John Adams and Political Dissent *192*
■ The West in the New Nation *194*
■ "Revolutions" at the End of the Century *196*
Links to the World: Haitian Refugees *198*
Legacy for a People and a Nation: Dissent During Wartime *199*
■ Summary *200*

9

Defining the Nation, 1801–1823   203

■ Political Visions *205*
■ National Expansion Westward *208*
■ The Nation in the Orbit of Europe *212*
■ The War of 1812 *215*
Links to the World: Industrial Piracy *219*
■ The Nationalist Program *220*
■ Sectionalism Exposed *223*
■ Summary *225*
Legacy for a People and a Nation: States' Rights and Nullification *226*

10

The Rise of the South 1815–1860   230

■ The "Distinctive" South? *232*
■ Southern Expansion, Indian Resistance, and Removal *235*
Links to the World: The Amistad Case *237*

■ Limits of Mobility in a Hierarchical Society   *242*

■ The Planters' World   *246*

■ Slave Life and Labor   *249*

■ Slave Culture and Resistance   *252*

■ Summary   *257*

Legacy for a People and a Nation: Reparations for Slavery   *257*

11

The Modernizing North, 1815–1860   261

■ Or Is It the North That Was Distinctive?   *262*

■ The Transportation Revolution   *265*

■ Factories and Industrialization   *269*

Links to the World: The United States as a Developing Nation   *270*

■ Consumption and Commercialization   *273*

■ Families in Flux   *276*

■ The Growth of Cities   *277*

■ Summary   *285*

Legacy for a People and a Nation: A Mixed Economy   *285*

12

Reform and Politics in the Age of Jackson, 1824–1845   289

■ From Revival to Reform   *291*

■ Communitarian Experiments   *294*

■ Abolitionism   *296*

Links to the World: The International Antislavery Movement   *298*

■ Women's Rights   *300*

■ Jacksonianism and Party Politics   *301*

■ Federalism at Issue: The Nullification and Bank Controversies   *304*

■ The Whig Challenge and the Second Party System   *307*

■ Summary   *310*

Legacy for a People and a Nation: The Bible Belt   *311*

13

The Contested West, 1815–1860   315

■ The West in the American Imagination   *317*

■ Expansion and Resistance in the Old Northwest   *320*

■ The Federal Government and Westward Expansion   *325*

Links to the World: Gold In California   *327*

■ The Southwestern Borderlands   *330*

■ Migration to the Far West   *335*

■ The Politics of Territorial Expansion   *340*

■ Summary   *342*

Legacy for a People and a Nation: Descendants of Early Latino Settlers   *343*

14

Slavery and America's Future: The Road to War, 1845–1861   346

■ The War with Mexico and Its Consequences   *348*

■ 1850: Compromise or Armistice?   *352*

■ Slavery Expansion and Collapse of the Party System   *357*

Links to the World: Annexation of Cuba   *360*

■ Slavery and the Nation's Future   *362*

■ Disunion   *364*

■ Summary   *370*

Legacy for a People and a Nation: Terrorist or Freedom Fighter?   *370*

15

Transforming Fire: The Civil War, 1861–1865   373

■ America Goes to War, 1861-1862   *375*

■ War Transforms the South   *380*

■ Wartime Northern Economy and Society   *383*

■ The Advent of Emancipation   *387*

The Soldiers' War   *391*

1863: The Tide of Battle Turns   *393*

Disunity: South, North, and West   *394*

1864–1865: The Final Test of Wills   *399*

Links to the World: The Civil War in Britain   *400*

Summary   *404*

Legacy for a People and a Nation: "Big Government"   *405*

16

Reconstruction: An Unfinished Revolution, 1865–1877   **409**

Wartime Reconstruction   *411*

The Meanings of Freedom   *413*

Johnson's Reconstruction Plan   *416*

The Congressional Reconstruction Plan   *418*

Reconstruction Politics and Economy in the South   *425*

Retreat from Reconstruction   *429*

Links to the World: The Grants' Tour of the World   *431*

Summary   *435*

Legacy for a People and a Nation: The Lost Cause   *436*

17

The Development of the West, 1877–1900   **439**

The Economic Activities of Native Peoples   *441*

The Transformation of Native Cultures   *443*

The Extraction of Natural Resources   *447*

Irrigation and Transportation   *452*

Links to the World: The Australian Frontier   *454*

Farming the Plains   *456*

The Ranching Frontier   *459*

Summary   *461*

Legacy for a People and a Nation: The Myth of the Cowboy   *462*

18

The Machine Age, 1877–1920   **465**

Technology and the Triumph of Industrialization   *468*

Links to the World: The Atlantic Cable   *469*

Mechanization and the Changing Status of Labor   *472*

Labor Violence and the Union Movement   *476*

Standards of Living   *480*

The Corporate Consolidation Movement   *485*

The Gospel of Wealth and Its Critics   *487*

Summary   *488*

Legacy for a People and a Nation: Technology of Recorded Sound   *489*

19

The Vitality and Turmoil of Urban Life, 1877–1920   **493**

Growth of the Modern City   *495*

Urban Neighborhoods   *500*

Living Conditions in the Inner City   *503*

Managing the City   *505*

Family Life   *509*

The New Leisure and Mass Culture   *512*

Links to the World: Japanese Baseball   *514*

Summary   *518*

Legacy for a People and a Nation: Ethnic Food   *518*

20

Gilded Age Politics, 1877–1900   **522**

The Nature of Party Politics   *524*

Issues of Legislation   *525*

Tentative Presidents   *528*

Discrimination, Disfranchisement, and Responses   *529*

▌ Agrarian Unrest and Populism *532*

Links to the World: Russian Populism *536*

▌ The Depression and Protests of the 1890s *537*

▌ The Silver Crusade and the Election of 1896 *541*

▌ Summary *543*

Legacy for a People and a Nation: Interpreting a Fairy Tale *544*

21

The Progressive Era, 1895–1920   548

▌ The Varied Progressive Impulse *550*

Links to the World: Workers' Compensation *553*

▌ Government and Legislative Reform *554*

▌ New Ideas in Social Institutions *557*

▌ Challenges to Racial and Sexual Discrimination *559*

▌ Theodore Roosevelt and the Revival of the Presidency *564*

▌ Woodrow Wilson and the Extension of Progressive Reform *569*

▌ Summary *571*

Legacy for a People and a Nation: Margaret Sanger, Planned Parenthood, and the Birth-Control Controversy *571*

22

The Quest for Empire, 1865–1914   575

▌ Imperial Dreams *578*

Links to the World: National Geographic *581*

▌ Ambitions and Strategies *582*

▌ Crises in the 1890s: Hawai'i, Venezuela, and Cuba *583*

▌ The Spanish-American War and the Debate over Empire *587*

▌ Asian Encounters: War in the Philippines, Diplomacy in China *589*

▌ TR's World *591*

▌ Summary *596*

Legacy for a People and a Nation: Guantánamo Bay *596*

23

Americans in the Great War, 1914–1920   600

▌ Precarious Neutrality *602*

▌ The Decision for War *605*

▌ Winning the War *607*

Links to the World: The Influenza Pandemic of 1918 *611*

▌ Mobilizing the Home Front *612*

▌ Civil Liberties Under Challenge *615*

▌ Red Scare, Red Summer *617*

▌ The Defeat of Peace *619*

▌ Summary *622*

Legacy for a People and a Nation: Freedom of Speech and the ACLU *623*

24

The New Era, 1920–1929   627

▌ Big Business Triumphant *629*

▌ Politics and Government *630*

▌ A Consumer Society *632*

▌ Cities, Migrants, and Suburbs *634*

Links to the World: Pan American Airways *636*

▌ New Rhythms of Everyday Life *638*

▌ Lines of Defense *641*

▌ The Age of Play *644*

▌ Cultural Currents *646*

▌ The Election of 1928 and the End of the New Era *648*

▌ Summary *650*

Legacy for a People and a Nation: Intercollegiate Athletics *651*

25

The Great Depression and the New Deal, 1929–1941   655

▌ Hoover and Hard Times: 1929–1933 *657*

▌ Franklin D. Roosevelt and the Launching of the New Deal *662*

▌ Political Pressure and the Second New Deal   *666*

▌ Labor   *671*

▌ Federal Power and the Nationalization of Culture   *673*

Links to the World: The 1936 Olympic Games   *676*

▌ The Limits of the New Deal   *677*

▌ Summary   *680*

Legacy for a People and a Nation: Social Security   *681*

26

The United States in a Troubled World, 1920–1941   684

▌ Searching for Peace and Order in the 1920s   *686*

▌ The World Economy, Cultural Expansion, and Great Depression   *688*

▌ U.S. Dominance in Latin America   *691*

▌ The Course to War in Europe   *693*

▌ Japan, China, and a New Order in Asia   *696*

▌ U.S. Entry into World War II   *698*

Links to the World: Radio News   *700*

▌ Summary   *703*

Legacy for a People and a Nation: Presidential Deception of the Public   *704*

27

The Second World War at Home and Abroad, 1941–1945   707

▌ The United States at War   *709*

▌ The Production Front and American Workers   *712*

▌ Life on the Home Front   *715*

▌ The Limits of American Ideals   *718*

Links to the World: War Brides   *719*

▌ Life in the Military   *721*

▌ Winning the War   *723*

▌ Summary   *728*

Legacy for a People and a Nation: Nuclear Proliferation   *729*

28

The Cold War and American Globalism, 1945–1961   733

▌ From Allies to Adversaries   *735*

▌ Containment in Action   *740*

▌ The Cold War in Asia   *744*

▌ The Korean War   *745*

▌ Unrelenting Cold War   *747*

Links to the World: The People-to-People Campaign   *750*

▌ The Struggle for the Third World   *751*

▌ Summary   *757*

Legacy for a People and a Nation: The National Security State   *758*

29

America at Midcentury, 1945–1960   762

▌ Shaping Postwar America   *764*

▌ Domestic Politics in the Cold War Era   *768*

▌ Cold War Fears and Anticommunism   *770*

▌ The Struggle for Civil Rights   *773*

▌ Creating a Middle-Class Nation   *776*

▌ Men, Women, and Youth at Midcentury   *780*

Links to the World: Barbie   *784*

▌ The Limits of the Middle-Class Nation   *785*

▌ Summary   *788*

Legacy for a People and a Nation: The Pledge of Allegiance   *788*

30

The Tumultuous Sixties, 1960–1968   792

▌ Kennedy and the Cold War   *794*

▌ Marching for Freedom   *798*

▌ Liberalism and the Great Society   *801*

▌ Johnson and Vietnam   *805*

▌ A Nation Divided   *810*

Links to the World: The British Invasion   *814*

▌ 1968   *815*

▌ Summary   *817*

Legacy for a People and a Nation: The Immigration Act of 1965   *817*

31

Continuing Divisions and New Limits, 1969–1980   821

▌ The New Politics of Identity   *823*
▌ The Women's Movement and Gay Liberation   *826*
▌ The End in Vietnam   *828*
▌ Nixon, Kissinger, and the World   *831*
Links to the World: OPEC and the 1973 Oil Embargo   *833*
▌ Presidential Politics and the Crisis of Leadership   *834*
▌ Economic Crisis   *838*
▌ An Era of Cultural Transformation   *841*
▌ Renewed Cold War and Middle East Crisis   *843*
▌ Summary   *846*
Legacy for a People and a Nation: The All-Volunteer Force   *846*

32

Conservatism Revived, 1980–1992   850

▌ Reagan and the Conservative Resurgence   *852*
▌ Reaganomics   *855*
▌ Reagan and the World   *860*
▌ American Society in the 1980s   *864*
▌ The End of the Cold War and Global Disorder   *869*
Links to the World: CNN   *873*
▌ Summary   *875*
Legacy for a People and a Nation: The Americans with Disabilities Act   *875*

33

Into the Global Millennium: America Since 1992   878

▌ Social Strains and New Political Directions   *880*
▌ The New Economy and Globalization   *883*
▌ Paradoxes of Prosperity   *887*
▌ September 11 and the War on Terrorism   *891*
▌ War and Occupation in Iraq   *894*
▌ Americans in the First Decade of the New Millennium   *898*
Links to the World: The Global AIDS Epidemic   *903*
Legacy for a People and a Nation: The Internet   *905*
▌ Summary   *906*

Appendix A-1
Index I-1

Maps

Map 1.1 Native Cultures of North America *6*

Map 1.2 European Explorations in America *14*

Map 2.1 European Settlements and Indian Tribes in Eastern North America, 1650 *32*

Map 3.1 The Anglo-American Colonies in the Early Eighteenth Century *58*

Map 3.2 Atlantic Trade Routes *66*

Map 4.1 Major Origins and Destinations of Africans Enslaved in the Americas *83*

Map 5.1 European Settlements and Indians, 1754 *111*

Map 6.1 The War in the North, 1775–1777 *143*

Map 6.2 The War in the South *148*

Map 7.1 African American Population, 1790: Proportion of Total Population *162*

Map 7.2 Western Land Claims and Cessions, 1782–1802 *166*

Map 9.1 Louisiana Purchase *209*

Map 9.2 Missouri Compromise and the State of the Union, 1820 *225*

Map 10.1 Removal of Native Americans from the South, 1820–1840 *241*

Map 11.1 Major Roads, Canals, and Railroads, 1850 *268*

Map 11.2 Major American Cities in 1830 and 1860 *278*

Map 12.1 Presidential Election, 1824 *302*

Map 12.2 Presidential Election, 1828 *303*

Map 13.1 Westward Expansion, 1800–1860 *318*

Map 13.2 Settlement in the Old Southwest and Old Northwest, 1820 and 1840 *321*

Map 13.3 Western Indians and Routes of Exploration *326*

Map 13.4 Mexico's Far North *330*

Map 13.5 The California Gold Rush *339*

Map 14.1 The Kansas-Nebraska Act and Slavery Expansion, 1854 *354*

Map 14.2 The Divided Nation—Slave and Free Areas, 1861 *368*

Map 15.1 Battle of Gettysburg *394*

Map 15.2 Sherman's March to the Sea *402*

Map 16.1 The Reconstruction *422*

Map 16.2 Presidential Election of 1876 and the Compromise of 1877 *434*

Map 17.1 The Development and Natural Resources of the West *448*

Map 17.2 The United States, 1876–1912 *452*

Map 17.3 Agricultural Regions of the United States, 1890 *457*

Map 18.1 Industrial Production, 1919 *467*

Map 19.1 Urbanization, 1880 and 1920 *497*

Map 20.1 Presidential Election, 1896 *543*

Map 21.1 Woman Suffrage Before 1920 *563*

Map 22.1 Imperialism in Asia: Turn of the Century *590*

Map 22.2 U.S. Hegemony in the Caribbean and Latin America *592*

Map 23.1 American Troops at the Western Front, 1918 *610*

Map 26.1 Japanese Expansion Before Pearl Harbor *697*

Map 26.2 The German Advance *699*

Map 27.1 The Pacific War *711*

Map 27.2 The Allies on the Offensive in Europe, 1942–1945 *724*

Map 28.1 Divided Europe *742*

Map 28.2 The Rise of the Third World: Newly Independent Nations Since 1943 *752*

Map 29.1 Rise of the Sunbelt, 1950–1960 *778*

Map 30.1 Southeast Asia and the Vietnam War *807*

Map 31.1 The Continued Shift to the Sunbelt in the 1970s and 1980s *840*

Map 32.1 The United States in the Caribbean and Central America *861*

Map 32.2 The End of the Cold War in Europe *871*

Map 33.1 The Middle East *896*

Map 33.2 Mapping the United States's Diversity *899*

Figures

Figure 1.1 Major Items in the Columbian Exchange *19*

Figure 2.1 Population of Virginia, 1625 *43*

Figure 4.1 Regional Trading Patterns: New England *88*

Figure 4.2 Regional Trading Patterns: Middle Colonies *89*

Figure 4.3 Regional Trading Patterns: The Chesapeake *90*

Figure 4.4 Regional Trading Patterns: The Lower South *91*

Figure 7.1 Depreciation of Continental Currency, 1777–1780 *167*

Figure 11.1 Major Sources of Immigration to the United States, 1831–1860 *281*

Figure 14.1 Voting Returns of Counties with Few Slaveholders, Eight Southern States, 1860 and 1861 *369*

Figure 15.1 Comparative Resources, Union and Confederate States, 1861 *376*

Figure 18.1 Distribution of Occupational Categories Among Employed Men and Women, 1880–1920 *474*

Figure 18.2 Children in the Labor Force, 1880–1930 *475*

Figure 20.1 Consumer Prices and Farm Product Prices, 1865–1913 *533*

Figure 22.1 The Rise of U.S. Economic Power in the World *579*

Figure 23.1 The Federal Budget, 1914–1920 *612*

Figure 24.1 Changing Dimensions of Paid Female Labor, 1910–1930 *640*

Figure 24.2 Sources of Immigration, 1907 and 1927 *643*

Figure 25.1 The Economy Before and After the New Deal, 1929–1941 *667*

Figure 25.2 Distribution of Total Family Income Among the American People, 1929–1944 (percentage) *671*

Figure 29.1 Birth Rate, 1945–1964 *766*

Figure 29.2 Marital Distribution of the Female Labor Force, 1944–1970 *781*

Figure 30.1 Poverty in America for Whites, African Americans, and All Races, 1959–1974 *805*

Figure 32.1 The United States's Rising National Debt, 1974–1989 *857*

Figure 32.2 Poverty in America by Race. *859*

Figure 32.3 Poverty in the United States by Race, 1974–1990 *866*

Figure 33.1 The Growth of the U.S. Hispanic Population *898*

Figure 33.4 The Changing American Family *900*

Tables

Table 2.1 The Founding of Permanent European Colonies in North America, 1565–1640   *31*

Table 2.2 Tudor and Stuart Monarchs of England, 1509–1649   *37*

Table 3.1 Restored Stuart Monarchs of England, 1660–1714   *57*

Table 3.2 The Founding of English Colonies in North America, 1664–1681   *59*

Table 4.1 Who Moved to America from England and Scotland in the Early 1770s, and Why?   *85*

Table 5.1 The Colonial Wars, 1689–1763   *109*

Table 5.2 British Ministries and Their American Policies   *120*

Table 14.1 New Political Parties   *352*

Table 14.2 The Vote on the Kansas-Nebraska Act   *357*

Table 14.3 Presidential Vote in 1860 (by State)   *366*

Table 16.1 Plans for Reconstruction Compared   *422*

Table 17.1 Summary: Government Land Policy   *459*

Table 18.1 American Living Standards, 1890–1910   *481*

Table 24.1 Consumerism in the 1920s   *633*

Table 25.1 New Deal Achievements   *666*

Table 29.1 Geographic Distribution of the U.S. Population, 1930–1970 (in percentages)   *767*

Table 30.1 Great Society Achievements, 1964–1966   *804*

Table 33.1 U.S. Military Personnel on Active Duty in Foreign Countries, 2005   *904*

Preface to the Brief Eighth Edition

CREATION OF THE BRIEF EDITION

Nearly three decades have passed since the publication of the first brief edition of *A People and a Nation*. In that initial brief edition, as well as each subsequent one, the intent was to preserve the uniqueness and integrity of the complete work while condensing it. This Brief Eighth Edition once again reflects the scholarship, readability, and comprehensiveness of the full-length version. It also maintains the integration of social, cultural, political, economic, and foreign relations history that has been a hallmark of *A People and a Nation*.

Starting with this edition, a new editor, Dr. Debra Michals, has worked with us, ensuring that the changes in content and organization incorporated in the full-length Eighth Edition were retained in the condensation. The authors attained reductions by paring down details rather than deleting entire sections. The Brief Eighth Edition thus contains fewer statistics, fewer quotations, and fewer examples than the unabridged version. A sufficient number of quotations and examples are retained, however, to maintain the richness in style created by the authors.

The Brief Eighth Edition is available in both one-volume and two-volume formats. The two-volume format is divided as follows: Volume 1 contains Chapters 1 through 16, beginning with a discussion of three cultures—American, African, and European—that intersected during the exploration and colonization of the New World and ending with a discussion of the Reconstruction era. Volume 2 contains Chapters 16 through 33, beginning its coverage at Reconstruction and extending the history of the American people to the present. The chapter on Reconstruction appears in both volumes to provide greater flexibility in matching a volume to the historical span covered by a specific course.

CHANGES IN THIS EDITION

While the following Preface to the full-length Eighth Edition elaborates on specific content changes, we note here that the authors paid increased attention to the following: the history of children and childhood; the environment, including the past impact of hurricanes; the American West, subject of a completely new chapter; and the social and religious diversity of America's population, developed through territorial incorporation as well as through immigration. We have further widened our lens to include more coverage of America's place in the world. These emphases as well as the updated scholarship on which they are based, are fully retained in the Brief Eighth Edition. New to this edition are focus questions that follow each chapter's introduction to call students' attention to key issues in the chapter. These questions are answered at the end of each chapter.

Although each author feels answerable for the whole of *A People and a Nation*, we take primary responsibility for particular chapters: Mary Beth Norton, Chapters 1–8; Carol Sheriff, Chapters 9, 11–13; David Blight, Chapters 10, 14–16;

Howard P. Chudacoff, Chapters 17–21 and 24; Fredrik Logevall, Chapters 22, 23, 26, 28, and shared responsibility for 30–33; Beth Bailey, Chapters 25, 27, 29, and shared responsibility for 30–33.

LEARNING AND TEACHING AIDS

This edition of *A People and a Nation* includes a number of useful learning and teaching aids. These ancillaries are designed to help students get the most from the course and to provide instructors with useful course management and presentation tools.

Website Tools

The **Instructor Website** features the **Instructor's Resource Manual** written by George C. Warren of Central Piedmont Community College. For each chapter, there is a brief list of learning objectives, a comprehensive chapter outline, ideas for classroom activities, discussion questions and several suggested paper topics, and a lecture supplement. Also available on the Instructor Website are primary sources with instructor notes in addition to hundreds of maps, images, audio and video clips, and PowerPoint slides for classroom presentation created by Barney Rickman of Valdosta State University. The **HM Testing™** CD-ROM provides flexible test-editing capabilities for the Test Items written by George Warren.

HistoryFinder, a new Houghton Mifflin technology initiative, helps instructors create rich and exciting classroom presentations. This online tool offers thousands of online resources, including art, photographs, maps, primary sources, multimedia content, Associated Press interactive modules, and ready-made PowerPoint slides. HistoryFinder's assets can easily be searched by keyword, or browsed from pull-down menus by topic, media type, or by textbook. Instructors can then browse, preview, and download resources straight from the website.

The **Student Website** contains a variety of tutorial resources including the **Study Guide** written by George Warren, ACE quizzes with feedback, interactive maps, primary sources, chronology exercises, flashcards, and other interactivities. The Website for this edition of *A People and a Nation* features **Audio Summaries,** audio files that are downloadable as MP3 files. These audio summaries help students review each chapter's key points.

Please contact your local Houghton Mifflin sales representative for more information about these learning and teaching tools in addition to the **Rand McNally Atlas of American History,** WebCT and Blackboard cartridges, and transparencies for United States History.

ACKNOWLEDGMENTS

Author teams rely on review panels to help create and execute successful revision plans. For the revision of this Brief Eighth Edition, we were guided by the many historians whose thoughtful insights and recommendations helped us with the preparation of the full-length Eighth Edition. Their names appear in the preface to that edition that follows.

Finally, we want to thank the many people who have contributed their thoughts and labors to this work, especially the talented staff at Houghton Mifflin.

For the authors, Mary Beth Norton, coordinating author.

Preface to the Full-Length Eighth Edition

In this eighth edition, *A People and a Nation* has undergone both reorganization and revision, while still retaining the narrative strength and focus that have made it so popular with students and teachers alike. In the years since the publication of the seventh edition, new materials have been uncovered, new interpretations advanced, and new themes have come to the forefront of American historical scholarship. All the authors—joined by one new member, Carol Sheriff—have worked diligently to incorporate those findings into this text.

Like other teachers and students, we are always re-creating our past, restructuring our memory, and rediscovering the personalities and events that have influenced us, injured us, and bedeviled us. This book represents our continuing rediscovery of America's history—its diverse people and the nation they created and have nurtured. As this book demonstrates, there are many different Americans and many different memories. We have sought to present as many of them as possible, in both triumph and tragedy, in both division and unity.

ABOUT A PEOPLE AND A NATION

A People and a Nation, first published in 1982, was the first major textbook in the United States to fully integrate social and political history. From the outset, the authors have been determined to tell the story of *all* the people of the United States. This book's hallmark has been its melding of social and political history, its movement beyond history's common focus on public figures and events to examine the daily life of America's people. All editions of the book have stressed the interaction of public policy and personal experience, the relationship between domestic concerns and foreign affairs, the various manifestations of popular culture, and the multiple origins of America and Americans. We have consistently built our narrative on a firm foundation in primary sources—on both well-known and obscure letters, diaries, public documents, oral histories, and artifacts of material culture. We have long challenged readers to think about the meaning of American history, not just to memorize facts. Both students and instructors have repeatedly told us how much they appreciate and enjoy our approach to the past.

As has been true since the first edition, each chapter opens with a dramatic vignette focusing on an individual or a group of people. These vignettes introduce key themes, which then frame the chapters in succinct introductions and summaries. Numerous maps, tables, graphs, and charts provide readers with the necessary geographical and statistical context for observations in the text. Carefully selected illustrations—many of them unique to this book—offer readers visual insight into the topics under discussion, especially because the authors have written the captions. In this edition, as in all previous ones, we have sought to incorporate up-to-date scholarship, readability, a clear structure, critical thinking, and instructive illustrative material on every page.

THEMES IN THIS BOOK

Several themes and questions stand out in our continuing effort to integrate political, social, and cultural history. We study the many ways Americans have defined themselves—gender, race, class, region, ethnicity, religion, sexual orientation—and the many subjects that have reflected their multidimensional experiences. We highlight the remarkably diverse everyday lives of the American people—in cities and on farms and ranches, in factories and in corporate headquarters, in neighborhoods and in legislatures, in love relationships and in hate groups, in recreation and in work, in the classroom and in military uniform, in secret national security conferences and in public foreign relations debates, in church and in voluntary associations, in polluted environments and in conservation areas. We pay particular attention to lifestyles, diet and dress, family life and structure, labor conditions, gender roles, migration and mobility, childbearing, and child rearing. We explore how Americans have entertained and informed themselves by discussing their music, sports, theater, print media, film, radio, television, graphic arts, and literature, in both "high" culture and popular culture. We study how technology has influenced Americans' lives, such as through the internal combustion engine and the computer.

Americans' personal lives have always interacted with the public realm of politics and government. To understand how Americans have sought to protect their different ways of life and to work out solutions to thorny problems, we emphasize their expectations of governments at the local, state, and federal levels; governments' role in providing answers; the lobbying of interest groups; the campaigns and outcomes of elections; and the hierarchy of power in any period. Because the United States has long been a major participant in world affairs, we explore America's participation in wars, interventions in other nations, empire-building, immigration patterns, images of foreign peoples, cross-national cultural ties, and international economic trends.

WHAT'S NEW IN THIS EDITION

Planning for the eighth edition began at a two-day authors' meeting at the Houghton Mifflin headquarters in Boston. There we discussed the most recent scholarship in the field, the reviews of the seventh edition solicited from instructors, and the findings of our own continuing research. For this edition, we added a new colleague, Carol Sheriff, who experienced the intellectual exhilaration and rigor of such an authors' meeting for the first time. Sheriff, a member of the History Department at the College of William and Mary, has written extensively on antebellum America, especially in the north, and she has taken on the responsibility for those chapters in the eighth edition.

This edition builds on its immediate predecessor in continuing to enhance the global perspective on American history that has characterized the book since its first edition. From the "Atlantic world" context of European colonies in North and South America to the discussion of international terrorism, the authors have incorporated the most recent globally oriented scholarship throughout the volume. Significantly, the eighth edition includes an entirely new chapter on the American west in the years before the Civil War and the discussion of the west has been expanded throughout. The treatment of the history of children and childhood has been increased, as has the discussion of environmental history, including the devastating impact of hurricanes in North America and the Caribbean from the earliest days of European settlement. As in the seventh edition, we have worked to strengthen our treatment of the diversity of America's people by examining differences within the broad ethnic categories commonly employed and by paying greater attention to immigration, cultural and intellectual infusions from around the world, and America's growing religious diversity. We have also stressed the incorporation of different peoples into the United States through territorial acquisition as well as through immigration. At the same time, we have integrated the discussion of such diversity into our narrative, so as not to artificially isolate any group from the mainstream. We have added three probing questions at the end of each chapter's introduction to guide students' reading of the pages that follow.

As always, the authors reexamined every sentence, interpretation, map, chart, illustration, and caption, refining the narrative, presenting new examples, and bringing to the text the latest findings of scholars in many areas of history, anthropology, sociology, and political science. More than one-third of the chapter-opening vignettes are new to this edition.

"Legacies" and "Links to the World"

Each chapter contains two brief feature essays: "Legacies" (introduced in the sixth edition) and "Links to the World" (introduced in the seventh edition). Legacies follow chapter summaries and offer compelling and timely answers to students who question the relevance of historical study by exploring the historical roots of contemporary topics. New subjects of Legacies are: Kennewick Man/Ancient One, Blue Laws, women's political activism, the township and range system, descendants of early Latino settlers, "Big Government," the Lost Cause, the Cowboy myth, recorded music, Guantanamo Bay, atomic proliferation, and the all-volunteer military. Numerous other Legacies have been updated.

"Links to the World" examine both inward and outward ties between America (and Americans) and the rest of the world. The "Links" appear at appropriate places in each chapter to explore specific topics at considerable length. Tightly constructed essays detail the often little-known connections between developments here and abroad. The topics range broadly over economic, political, social, technological, medical, and cultural history, vividly demonstrating that the geographical region that is now the United States has never lived in isolation from other peoples and countries. New to this edition are Links on smallpox inoculations, the Amistad case, Russian Populism, European influence on American workers' compensation, and *National Geographic*. Each Link highlights global interconnections with unusual and lively examples that will both intrigue and inform students.

Section-by-Section Changes in This Edition

Mary Beth Norton, who had primary responsibility for Chapters 1 through 8 and served as coordinating author, augmented her discussion of the age of European expansion with new information on Muslim power and the allure of exotic spices; she also expanded the treatment of Spanish colonization and settlements in the Caribbean. She incorporated extensive new scholarship on early Virginia into Chapter 2. In addition to reorganizing part of Chapter 3 to bring more coherence to the discussion of the origins of slavery in North America, she added demographic information about enslaved people (both Indians and Africans) and those who enslaved and transported them, stressing in particular the importance of African women in South Carolina rice cultivation. She added material on transported English convicts, Huguenot immigrants, Acadian exiles, iron-making, land riots, the Stono Rebellion, the Seven Years' War in western Pennsylvania, the experiences of common soldiers in the Revolution, Shays's Rebellion, and the Jay Treaty debates. In Chapter 8 she created new sections on Indians in the new nation and on revolutions at the end of the century, including among them the election of Thomas Jefferson.

Carol Sheriff completely reorganized the contents of Chapters 9, 11, and 12, clarifying chronological developments and including much new material. Chapter 9 now covers politics through 1823 in order to emphasize the impact of the War of 1812 in accelerating regional divisions. It has expanded coverage of popular political practice (including among non-voters), the separation of church and state, the Marshall Court, the First and Second Barbary Wars, and the incorporation of the Louisiana Territory and its residents into the United States. Chapter 11, retitled "The Modernizing North," consolidates information previously divided between two chapters and augments it with new discussions of daily life before commercial and industrial expansion, rural-urban contrasts, children and youth culture, male and female common laborers, and the origins of free-labor ideology. Chapter 12 focuses on reform and politics in the age of Jackson, with expanded attention to communitarian experiments, abolitionism (including African Americans in the movement), women's rights, and religion, including revivalism in general and the Second Great Awakening in particular. The entirely new Chapter 13, "The Contested West," combines material that was previously scattered in different locations with a great deal of recent scholarship on such topics as the disjunction between the ideal and reality of the West, exploration and migration, cultural diversity in the West, cooperation and conflict among the West's peoples, and the role of the federal government in regional development. In all her reorganized chapters she relied on a base created by David M. Katzman, an original member of the author team who had responsibility for this section in the seven earlier editions.

David W. Blight, who had primary responsibility for Chapters 10 and 14 through 16, extensively reorganized Chapter 10 (previously Chapter 13), on the South, in part to reflect its new chronological placement in the book. The chapter now covers material beginning in 1815 rather than 1830 and contains a section on Southern expansion and Indian removal. In his chapters he has added material on the Taos revolt, enslaved children, "Bleeding Kansas," Harriet Scott, Louisa May Alcott, union sentiment in the South, the conduct of the war, and economic and social conditions in the postwar North and South. He has revised Chapter 16 to emphasize economic as well as political change in the era of Reconstruction.

Howard P. Chudacoff, responsible for Chapters 17 through 21 and 24, has increased the coverage of Indians, Exodusters, and Hispanics in the West, and of western Progressivism. His treatment of popular culture now stresses its lower-class, bottom-to-top origins. He added information on the history of childhood, vaudeville, and the movies; and he revised discussions of monetary policy, Progressivism, Populism, and urban and agrarian protests. He also has included more coverage of racism and those who combated it, such as Ida B. Wells, and on women and the Ku Klux Klan. Business operation and regulation receive new attention in his chapters, as do Calvin Coolidge, consumerism, and baseball.

Fredrik Logevall, with primary responsibility for Chapters 22, 23, 26, and 28, continued throughout his chapters to work to establish the wider international context for U.S. foreign affairs. He added considerable new material on the Middle East (especially in Chapter 28) and incorporated recent scholarship on the Vietnam War. He also updated the treatment of the Spanish-American War with new information on the sinking of the *Maine* and on the Philippine insurrection. His discussion of World War I now includes consideration of the antagonistic relationship of Woodrow Wilson and V.I. Lenin; and he has given more attention to American economic and cultural expansion in the 1920s and 1930s. He has furthermore expanded his treatment of American reactions to the Spanish Civil War.

Beth Bailey, primarily responsible for Chapters 25, 27, and 29, added information on women, the left, and popular culture (especially film and the production code) during the 1930s. She expanded coverage of the European front in World War II and of divisions within the United States during the war. In Chapter 29, she thoroughly reorganized the section on civil rights to clarify the chronology and key points of development, and she also included new information on emerging countercultures and the beats, union activities, and the Eisenhower administration.

Bailey and Logevall shared responsibility for Chapters 30 through 33. In Chapter 30 Freedom Summer is given enhanced attention and the section on civil rights has been reorganized to emphasize a clear chronology. These chapters contain new material on the women's movement and the barriers women faced before 1970s reforms, recent immigration, neoconservatism, anti-Vietnam War protests, Nixon's presidency, the Supreme Court, the 1982 Israeli invasion of Lebanon, and the 1991 Iraq War. Chapter 33 in particular has been thoroughly revised to include the latest demographic data on Americans and their families, along with discussions of the struggles over science and religion, hurricane Katrina, the Bush administration's domestic policies, and especially the Iraq War.

TEACHING AND LEARNING AIDS

The supplements listed here accompany the Eighth Edition of *A People and a Nation*. They have been created with the diverse needs of today's students and instructors in mind.

FOR THE INSTRUCTOR

- Houghton Mifflin's **HistoryFinder** is a new online tool developed to help instructors create rich and exciting presentations for the U.S. history survey class. HistoryFinder offers thousands of online resources, including art, photographs, maps, primary sources, multimedia content, Associated Press interactive modules, and ready-made PowerPoint slides. HistoryFinder's assets can easily be searched by keyword topic, media type, or by textbook chapter. It is then possible to browse, preview, and download resources straight from the website into the instructor's own PowerPoint collection.

- **The Instructor Website**, at HM HistorySPACE(tm), includes a variety of resources that will help instructors engage their students in class and assess their understanding inside and outside the classroom. The Instructor Website includes the **Instructor's Resource Manual,** written by George C. Warren, of Central Piedmont Community College. For each chapter, there is a brief list of learning objectives, a comprehensive chapter outline, ideas for classroom activities, discussion questions and several suggested paper topics, and a lecture supplement. Also available on the Instructor Website is a complete set of PowerPoint slides created by Barney Rickman of Valdosta State University, to assist in instruction and discussion of key topics and materials for each chapter.
- The **HM Testing™ CD-ROM** provides flexible test-editing capabilities for the Test Items written by George Warren of Central Piedmont Community College. Included in the Test Bank are multiple choice, identification, geography, and essay questions.
- Houghton Mifflin's **Eduspace Course** for *A People and a Nation* offers a customizable course management system powered by Blackboard along with homework assignments that engage students and encourage in-class discussion. Assignments include gradable homework exercises, writing assignments, primary sources with questions, and Associated Press Interactives. Eduspace also provides a gradebook and communication capabilities, such as live chats, threaded discussion boards, and announcement postings. The Eduspace course also includes an interactive version of *A People and a Nation* with direct links to relevant primary sources, quizzes, and more.

FOR THE STUDENT

- The **Student Website,** at HM HistorySPACE™, contains a variety of review and self-assessment resources to help students succeed in the U.S. history survey course. ACE quizzes with feedback, interactive maps, primary sources, chronology exercises, flashcards, and other activities are available for each chapter. Audio files provide chapter summaries in MP3 format for downloading and listening to at any time.
- **Study Guides** (Volumes I and II), written by George Warren, provide learning objectives, vocabulary exercises, identification suggestions, skill-building activities, multiple choice questions, essay questions, and map exercises in two volumes.

Please contact your local Houghton Mifflin sales representative for more information about these learning and teaching tools in addition to the **Rand McNally Atlas of American History,** WebCT and Blackboard cartridges, and transparencies for United States History. Your sales representative can also provide more information about **BiblioBase for U.S. History,** a database of hundreds of primary sources from which you can create a customized course pack.

Acknowledgments

The authors would like to thank the following persons for their assistance with the preparation of this edition: Shawn Alexander, Marsha Andrews, Edward Balleisen, Philip Daileader, Katherine Flynn, John B. Heiser, Danyel Logevall, Daniel Mandell, Clark F. Norton, Mary E. Norton, Anna Daileader Sheriff, Benjamin Daileader Sheriff, Selene Sheriff, Seymour Sheriff.

At each stage of this revision, a sizable panel of historian reviewers read drafts of our chapters. Their suggestions, corrections, and pleas helped guide us through this momentous revision. We could not include all of their recommendations, but the book is better for our having heeded most of their advice. We heartily thank:

Marynita Anderson, Nassau Community College/SUNY
Stephen Aron, UCLA and Autry National Center
Gordon Morris Bakken, California State University, Fullerton
Todd Forsyth Carney, Southern Oregon University
Kathleen S. Carter, High Point University
Robert C. Cottrell, California State University, Chico
Lawrence Culver, Utah State University
Lawrence J. DeVaro, Rowan University
Lisa Lindquist Dorr, University of Alabama
Michelle Kuhl, University of Wisconsin, Oshkosh
Martin Halpern, Henderson State University
John S. Leiby, Paradise Valley Community College
Edwin Martini, Western Michigan University
Elsa A Nystrom Kennesaw State University
Chester Pach, Ohio University
Stephen Rockenbach, Northern Kentucky University
Joseph Owen Weixelman, University of New Mexico

The authors once again thank the extraordinary Houghton Mifflin people who designed, edited, produced, and nourished this book. Their high standards and acute attention to both general structure and fine detail are cherished in the publishing industry. Many thanks, then, to Patricia Coryell, vice president, publisher, history and social science; Suzanne Jeans, publisher, history and political Science; Sally Constable and Ann West, senior sponsoring editors; Ann Hofstra Grogg, freelance development editor; Jeff Greene, senior development editor; Jane Lee, senior project editor, Katherine Bates, senior marketing manager; Pembroke Herbert, photo researcher; Jill Haber, art and design manager, Charlotte Miller, art editor; and Evangeline Bermas, editorial assistant.

M.B.N.
C.S.
D.B.
H.C.
F.L.
B.B.

CHAPTER 1

Three Old Worlds Create a New

CHAPTER OUTLINE

American Societies

North America in 1492

African Societies

European Societies

Early European Explorations

Voyages of Columbus, Cabot, and Their Successors

Spanish Exploration and Conquest

The Columbian Exchange

Europeans in North America

LINKS TO THE WORLD:
Maize

Summary

LEGACY FOR A PEOPLE AND A NATION: Kennewick Man/Ancient One

F ive years later, Alvar Nuñez Cabeza de Vaca still recalled the amazement he encountered in northern Mexico in mid-February 1536. "I reached four Christians on horseback who registered great surprise at seeing me so strangely dressed and in the company of Indians. They . . . neither spoke to me nor dared to ask anything."

Cabeza de Vaca, two Spaniards, and an enslaved North African named Estevan had just walked across North America. They, along with about six hundred others, left Spain in June 1527 on an ill-fated expedition. After exploring near Tampa Bay, eighty of the men, including Cabeza de Vaca, were shipwrecked in late 1528 on the coast of modern Texas. Most of the survivors—alternately abused, aided, and enslaved by local Indians—died. Cabeza de Vaca reached the mainland, where he survived as a traveling trader, exchanging seashells for hides and flint.

In January 1533 he stumbled on the other three. Guided by Indians, they walked south in September 1534; turned inland and headed north, exploring the upper reaches of the Rio Grande; then walked almost to the Pacific before turning south once more. Vaca described the diets, living arrangements, and customs of many villages, thus providing modern historians and anthropologists with an invaluable record of native cultures as they first encountered Europeans. For thousands of years before 1492, human societies in the Americas developed in isolation from the rest of the world. That ended in the Christian fifteenth century. As Europeans sought treasure and trade, peoples from different cultures came into contact for the first time and were profoundly changed. Their interactions over the next 350 years involved cruelty and kindness, greed and deception, trade and theft, sickness and enslavement. The history of the

This icon will direct you to interactive activities and study materials on A People And A Nation, Brief Edition website: **www.cengage.com/history/norton/peoplenationbrief8e**

Chronology

12,000–10,000 B.C.E.	Paleo-Indians migrate from Asia to North America across the Beringia land bridge.
7000 B.C.E.	Cultivation of food crops begins in America.
ca. 2000 B.C.E.	Olmec civilization appears.
ca. 300–600 C.E.	Height of influence of Teotihuacán.
ca. 600–900 C.E.	Classic Mayan civilization exists.
1000 C.E.	Ancient Pueblos build settlements in modern states of Arizona and New Mexico.
1001	Norse establish a settlement in Vinland.
1050–1250	Height of influence of Cahokia. Prevalence of Mississippian culture in modern midwestern and southeastern United States.
1300s	Aztecs rise to power.
1450s–80s	Portuguese explore and colonize islands in the Mediterranean Atlantic and São Tomé in Gulf of Guinea.
1477	Publication of Marco Polo's *Travels*, describing China.
1492	Columbus reaches the Bahamas.
1494	Treaty of Tordesillas divides land claims between Spain and Portugal in Africa, India, and South America.
1496	Last Canary Island falls to Spain.
1497	Cabot reaches North America.
1513	Ponce de León explores Florida.
1518–30	Smallpox epidemic devastates the Indian population of the West Indies and Central and South America.
1519	Cortés invades Mexico.
1521	Tenochtitlán surrenders to Cortés; Aztec Empire falls to Spaniards.
1524	Verrazzano sails along Atlantic coast of the United States.
1534–35	Cartier explores the St. Lawrence River.
1534–36	Vaca, Estevan, and two companions walk across North America.
1539–42	de Soto explores the southeastern United States.
1540–42	Coronado explores the southwestern United States.
1587–90	Raleigh's Roanoke colony vanishes.
1588	Harriot publishes *A Briefe and True Report of the New Found Land of Virginia.*

colonies that would become the United States must be seen in this context of European exploration and exploitation.

The continents that European sailors reached in the late fifteenth century had their own histories, which the intruders largely ignored. The residents of the Americas were the world's most skillful plant breeders; they developed vegetable crops more nutritious and productive than in Europe, Asia, or Africa. They invented systems of writing and mathematics. As in Europe, their societies rose and fell as leaders succeeded or failed in expanding their power. But the arrival of Europeans immeasurably altered Americans' struggles with one another.

After 1400 European nations tried to acquire valuable colonies and trading posts around the world. Initially interested in Asia and Africa, Europeans eventually focused on the Americas. Even as Europeans slowly achieved dominance, their fates were shaped by Americans and Africans. In the Americas of the fifteenth and sixteenth centuries, three old worlds came together to produce a new.

- **What were the key characteristics of the three worlds that met in the Americas?**
- **What impact did their encounter have on each of them?**
- **What were the crucial initial developments in that encounter?**

AMERICAN SOCIETIES

Human beings originated on the continent of Africa, where humanlike remains about 3 million years old have been found in what is now Ethiopia. Over many millennia, the growing population dispersed to other continents. Because the climate was far colder than it is now, much of the earth's water was concentrated in huge rivers of ice called glaciers. Sea levels were lower, and land masses covered a larger proportion of the earth's surface. Scholars long believed that the earliest inhabitants of the Americas crossed a land bridge known as Beringia (at the site of the Bering Strait) approximately 12,000 to 14,000 years ago. Yet new archaeological discoveries suggest that parts of the Americas may have been settled earlier, possibly in three successive waves beginning 30,000 years ago. When, about 12,500 years ago, the climate warmed and sea levels rose, Americans were separated from the connected continents of Asia, Africa, and Europe.

Ancient America

The first Americans are called Paleo-Indians. Nomadic hunters of game and gatherers of wild plants, they spread throughout North and South America, probably as bands of extended families. By about 11,500 years ago the Paleo-Indians were making stone projectile points, which they attached to wooden spears to kill and butcher bison (buffalo), woolly mammoths, and other large mammals. But as the Ice Age ended and the human population increased, all the large American mammals except the bison disappeared.

Consequently, by approximately 9,000 years ago, the residents of what is now central Mexico began cultivating food crops, especially maize (corn), squash, beans, avocados, and peppers. As knowledge of agricultural techniques improved, vegetables proved a more reliable food source than hunting and gathering. Most Americans adopted a sedentary life so they could tend fields regularly. Some established permanent settlements; others moved several times a year among fixed sites. They cleared forests through controlled burning, which created cultivable lands by killing trees and fertilizing the soil with ashes and also opened meadows for deer and other wildlife. Although they traded such items as shells, flint, salt, and copper, none of the American cultures became dependent on other groups for survival.

Wherever agriculture dominated, civilizations flourished. With steady supplies of grains and vegetables, such societies could broaden their focus from subsistence to trade, accumulating wealth, producing ornamental objects, and creating elaborate rituals. In North America, the cultivation of nutritious crops seems to have led to the development of all the major civilizations: first the large city-states of Mesoamerica (modern Mexico and Guatemala) and then the urban clusters known collectively as the Mississippian culture (in present-day United States). Each later collapsed after reaching the limits of its food supply.

Mesoamerican Civilizations

Scholars know little about the first major Mesoamerican civilization, the Olmecs, who about 4,000 years ago lived in cities near the Gulf of Mexico. The Mayas and Teotihuacán, which developed approximately 2,000 years later, are better recorded. Teotihuacán, founded in the Valley of Mexico about 300 B.C.E. (Before the Common

Era), became one of the largest urban areas in the world with 100,000 people in the fifth century C.E. (Common Era). Pilgrims traveled long distances to visit Teotihuacán's impressive pyramids and the great temple of Quetzalcoatl—the feathered serpent, primary god of central Mexico.

On the Yucatán Peninsula, in today's eastern Mexico, the Mayas built urban centers containing pyramids and temples, studied astronomy, and created an elaborate writing system. Their city-states engaged in near-constant warfare with one another, which, combined with inadequate food supplies, caused the collapse of the most powerful cities by 900 C.E. and ended the classic era of Mayan civilization.

| **Pueblos and Mississippians** | Ancient native societies in what is now the United States learned to grow maize, squash, and beans from Mesoamericans. The Hohokam, Mogollon, and ancient |

Pueblo peoples of the modern states of Arizona and New Mexico subsisted by combining hunting and gathering with agriculture in an arid region with unpredictable rainfall. Hohokam villagers constructed extensive irrigation systems, but relocated when water supplies failed. Between 900 and 1150 C.E., Chaco Canyon, at the juncture of perhaps 400 miles of roads, served as a trading and processing center for turquoise. Yet aridity caused the Chacoans to migrate to other sites.

Almost simultaneously, the unrelated Mississippian culture flourished in what is now the midwestern and southeastern United States. Relying largely on maize, squash, nuts, pumpkins, and venison, the Mississippians lived in settlements organized hierarchically. Their largest urban center was the City of the Sun (now called Cahokia), near modern St. Louis. Located on rich farmland near the confluence of the Illinois, Missouri, and Mississippi Rivers, Cahokia was a focal point for religion and trade. At its peak (in the eleventh and twelfth centuries C.E.), the City of the Sun covered more than 5 square miles and had a population of about twenty thousand—small by Mesoamerican standards but larger than other northern communities or London.

The sun-worshipping Cahokians developed an accurate calendar. The city's main pyramid, today called Monks Mound, remains the largest earthwork ever built in the Americas. Yet following 1250 C.E. the city was abandoned, and archaeologists believe that climate change and the degradation of the environment, caused by overpopulation and the destruction of nearby forests, contributed to its collapse.

| **Aztecs** | Aztec histories tell of its peoples' migration into the Valley of Mexico during the twelfth century. They record that their primary deity, Huitzilopochtli—a war god represented |

by an eagle—directed them to establish their capital on an island where they saw an eagle eating a serpent. That island city became Tenochtitlán, the center of a society composed of hereditary classes of warriors, merchants, priests, common folk, and slaves.

The Aztecs (who called themselves Mexica) conquered their neighbors, forcing them to pay tribute in textiles, gold, foodstuffs, and human sacrifices to Huitzilopochtli. They also engaged in ritual combat for further sacrificial victims. In the Aztec year Ten Rabbit (1502), at the coronation of Motecuhzoma II (the Spaniards mispronounced his name as Montezuma), thousands were sacrificed by having their hearts torn from their bodies.

NORTH AMERICA IN 1492

Over the centuries, the Americans who lived north of Mexico adapted their once-similar ways of life to different climates and terrains, thus creating the diverse culture areas that the Europeans encountered (see Map 1.1). Scholars often refer to such culture areas by language group (such as Algonquian or Iroquoian). Bands that lived in environments not suited to agriculture followed a nomadic lifestyle typified by the Paiutes and Shoshones, who inhabited the Great Basin (now Nevada and Utah). Because finding sufficient food was difficult, hunter-gatherer bands were small, usually composed of one or more related families. Where large game was plentiful, as in present-day central and western Canada and the Great Plains, bands were somewhat larger.

In favorable environments, larger groups like the Chinooks of present-day coastal Washington and Oregon combined agriculture with gathering, hunting, and fishing. Residents of the interior (for example, the Arikaras of the Missouri River valley) hunted large animals while cultivating maize, squash, and beans. The peoples of contemporary eastern Canada and the northeastern United States combined hunting, fishing, and agriculture.

Gendered Division of Labor

Societies that relied primarily on hunting large animals, such as deer and bison, assigned that task to men, allotting food preparation and clothing production to women. Before acquiring horses from the Spaniards, women—occasionally assisted by dogs—carried the family's belongings whenever their band relocated. The sexual division of labor was universal among hunting peoples. Yet agricultural societies assigned work in divergent ways. The Pueblo peoples defined agricultural labor as men's work. In the east, clusters of peoples speaking Algonquian, Iroquoian, and Muskogean languages allocated most agricultural chores to women, although men cleared the land. In farming societies, women gathered wild foods and prepared food for consumption or storage, where men were responsible for hunting.

Almost universally, women cared for young children, while older youths learned adult skills from their same-sex parent. Children enjoyed a lot of freedom. Young people chose their own marital partners, and in most societies couples could easily divorce. Infants and toddlers were nursed until the age of two or older, and taboos prevented couples from having sexual intercourse during that period.

Social Organization

Similarly, southwestern and eastern agricultural peoples lived in villages, sometimes with a thousand or more inhabitants. The Pueblos resided in multistory buildings constructed on terraces along the sides of cliffs or other easily defended sites. Northern Iroquois villages (in modern New York State) were composed of large, rectangular, bark-covered structures, or long houses; the name Haudenosaunee, which the Iroquois called themselves, means "People of the Long House." In the present-day southeastern United States, Muskogeans and southern Algonquians lived in large thatched houses. Most of the eastern villages were surrounded by wooden palisades and ditches to fend off attackers.

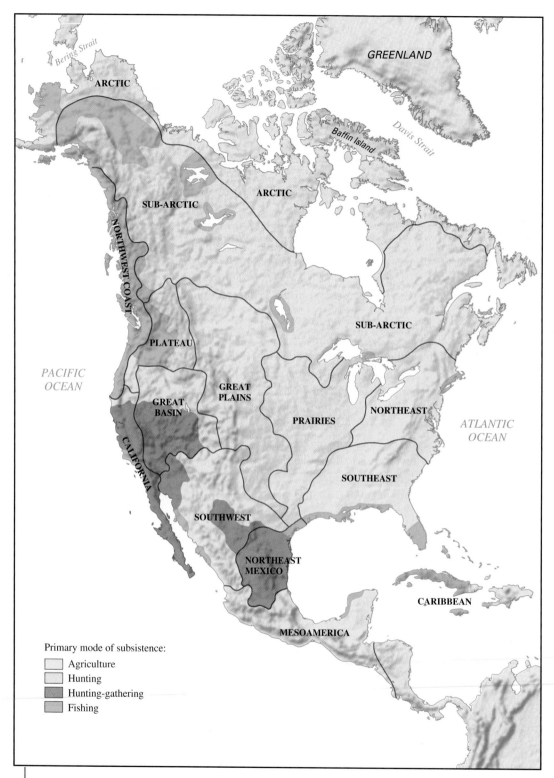

Primary mode of subsistence:
- Agriculture
- Hunting
- Hunting-gathering
- Fishing

Map 1.1   Native Cultures of North America

The natives of the North American continent effectively used the resources of the regions in which they lived. As this map shows, coastal groups relied on fishing, residents of fertile areas engaged in agriculture, and other peoples employed hunting (often combined with gathering) as their primary mode of subsistence.

Jacques Le Moyne, an artist accompanying the French settlement in Florida in the 1560s, produced some of the first European images of North American peoples. His depiction of native agricultural practices shows the gendered division of labor: men breaking up the ground with fish-bone hoes before women drop seeds into the holes. But Le Moyne's version of the scene cannot be accepted uncritically: Unable to abandon a European view of proper farming methods, he erroneously drew plowed furrows in the soil.   (Collection of Mary Beth Norton)

In all agricultural societies, each dwelling housed an extended family defined matrilineally (through a female line of descent). Mothers, their married daughters, and their daughters' husbands and children lived together. Matrilineal descent did not imply matriarchy, or the wielding of power by women, but denoted kinship and linked extended families into clans. The nomadic bands of the Prairies and Great Plains were most often related patrilineally (through the male line).

War and Politics

Long before Europeans arrived, residents fought one another for control of the best hunting and fishing territories, the most fertile agricultural lands, or the sources of essential items, such as salt (for preserving meat) and flint (for making knives and arrowheads). Bands of Americans protected by wooden armor literally stood face to face in battle, because their clubs and throwing spears were only effective at close quarters. They began to shoot arrows from behind trees only when they confronted

European guns. Captives were sometimes enslaved, but slavery was never an important labor source in pre-Columbian America.

Political structures varied considerably. Among Pueblos, the village council, composed of ten to thirty men, was the highest political authority; no government structure connected the villages. The Iroquois had an elaborate system incorporating villages into nations and nations into a confederation. A council comprising representatives from each nation made the crucial decisions of war and peace. Women more often assumed leadership roles among agricultural peoples than among nomadic hunters. Female sachems (rulers) led Algonquian villages in what is now Massachusetts, but women never became heads of hunting bands. Iroquois women did not become chiefs, yet older women chose the village chief and could both start wars (by calling for the capture of prisoners to replace dead relatives) and stop them (by refusing to supply warriors with foodstuffs).

Religion

All the American peoples were polytheistic, worshiping a multitude of gods. The major deities of agricultural peoples like the Pueblos and Muskogeans were associated with cultivation, and festivals centered on planting and harvest. The important gods of hunters like those on the Great Plains and Prairies were associated with animals. Women held the most prominent religious positions in agricultural societies where they were also the chief food producers, whereas in hunting societies men took the lead in religious and political affairs.

A variety of cultures, comprising more than 10 million people speaking over one thousand different languages, inhabited America north of Mexico when Europeans arrived. The hierarchical kingdoms of Mesoamerica bore little resemblance to the nomadic hunting societies of the Great Plains or to the agriculturalists of the Northeast or Southwest. They did not consider themselves one people, nor did they think of uniting to repel European invaders.

AFRICAN SOCIETIES

Fifteenth-century Africa housed a variety of cultures. In the north, along the Mediterranean Sea, lived the Berbers, who were Muslims, or followers of the Islamic religion. On the east coast of Africa, Muslim city-states engaged in extensive trade with India, the Moluccas (part of modern Indonesia), and China. Sustained contact and intermarriage among Arabs and Africans created the Swahili language and culture. Waterborne commerce passed between the eastern Mediterranean and East Asian city-states; land commerce followed the Silk Road, the long land route across Central Asia.

South of the Mediterranean coast in the African interior lie the great Saharan and Libyan Deserts. The introduction of the camel in the fifth century C.E. made long-distance travel possible, and as Islam expanded after the ninth century, commerce controlled by Muslim merchants helped spread similar religious and cultural ideas throughout the region. Below the deserts, the continent is divided between tropical rain forests (along the coasts) and grassy plains (in the interior). South of the Gulf of Guinea, the grassy landscape came to be dominated by Bantu-speaking peoples, who left their homeland in modern Nigeria about two thousand years ago.

West Africa (Guinea)

West Africa was a land of tropical forests and savanna grasslands where fishing, cattle herding, and agriculture supported the inhabitants for at least ten thousand years before Europeans arrived in the fifteenth century. The northern region of West Africa, or Upper Guinea, was heavily influenced by the Islamic culture of the Mediterranean. Trade via camel caravans between Upper Guinea and the Muslim Mediterranean was sub-Saharan Africa's major connection to Europe and West Asia. In return for salt, dates, silk, and cotton cloth, Africans exchanged ivory, gold, and slaves.

Upper Guinea runs northeast-southwest from Cape Verde to Cape Palmas. The people of its northernmost region, the so-called Rice Coast (present-day Gambia, Senegal, and Guinea), fished and cultivated rice in coastal swamplands. The Grain Coast, the next region to the south, was thinly populated and, with only one good harbor (modern Freetown, Sierra Leone), was not easily accessible from the sea. Its people concentrated on farming and raising livestock.

In Lower Guinea, south and east of Cape Palmas, most Africans were farmers who practiced traditional religions. Believing that spirits inhabited particular places, they developed rituals intended to ensure good harvests. With individual villages linked into hierarchical kingdoms, decentralized political and social authority characterized the region at the time of initial European contact.

Complementary Gender Roles

Like American society, West African societies assigned different tasks to men and women. In general, the sexes shared agricultural duties. Men also hunted, managed livestock, and did most of the fishing. Women were responsible for childcare, food preparation, manufacture, and trade. They managed local and regional networks through which families, villages, and small kingdoms exchanged goods.

Lower Guinea had similar social systems organized on the basis of what anthropologists have called the dual-sex principle. Each sex handled its own affairs: male political and religious leaders governed men; females ruled women. Many West African societies practiced polygyny (one man's having several wives, each of whom lived separately with her children). Thus few adults lived permanently in marital households, but the dual-sex system ensured that their actions were scrutinized by their own sex.

Throughout Guinea, religious beliefs stressed complementary male and female roles. Both women and men served as heads of the cults and secret societies that directed village spiritual life. Young women were initiated into the Sandé cult, young men into Poro. Although West African women rarely held formal power over men, female religious leaders governed their sex within the Sandé cult, enforcing conformity to accepted norms.

Slavery in Guinea

West African law recognized individual and communal land ownership, but men seeking wealth needed labor—wives, children, or slaves—who could work the land. West Africans enslaved for life were vital to the economy. Africans could be enslaved for criminal acts, but more often slaves were enemy captives or people who enslaved themselves or their children in payment for debts. An African slave owner had the right to the products of a slave's labor, although slave status did not always descend to the next generation. Some slaves were held as chattel, and whatever they produced belonged entirely to slave owners; others could trade in products raised in their spare time, retaining a portion of their profits; and still others achieved prominent political or military positions. All, however, could be traded at the will of their owners.

West Africans were agricultural peoples, skilled at tending livestock, hunting, fishing, and manufacturing cloth. Both men and women enjoyed an egalitarian relationship and worked communally in family groups or with members of their sex. Carried as captives to the Americas, they became essential laborers for European settlers who showed little respect for their traditions.

EUROPEAN SOCIETIES

In the fifteenth century, European society was also largely agricultural. In the hierarchical European societies, a few families wielded autocratic power over the majority. English society was organized as a series of interlocking hierarchies; that is, each person (except those at the very top or bottom) was superior to some, inferior to others. At the bottom were people held in bondage. Although Europeans were not subjected to perpetual slavery, Christian doctrine permitted the enslavement of "heathens" (non-Christians) and serfdom, which tied some Europeans to the land or to specific owners. In short, Europe's kingdoms resembled those of Africa or Mesoamerica but differed from the more egalitarian societies found in America north of Mexico.

Work, Politics, and Religion

Most Europeans, like most Africans and Americans, lived in small villages. European farmers, called peasants, owned or leased separate landholdings but worked the fields communally. Because fields had to lie unplanted every second or third year to regain fertility, a family could not be assured of food unless all villagers shared the work and the crops. Men did fieldwork; women helped at planting and harvest. In some regions men concentrated on herding livestock. Women's duties consisted primarily of childcare and household tasks, including preserving food, milking cows, and caring for poultry. If a woman's husband was a city artisan or storekeeper, she might assist him in business. Because Europeans kept domesticated animals (pigs, goats, sheep, and cattle) for meat, hunting had little economic importance and was primarily a sport for male aristocrats.

Men dominated European society. A few women—notably Queen Elizabeth I of England—achieved power by birthright, but most were excluded from positions of political authority. They also held inferior social, religious, and economic positions, yet wielded power over children and household servants. European children were tightly controlled and subjected to harsh discipline.

Christianity was the dominant European religion. In the West, authority rested in the Catholic Church, based in Rome and led by the pope, who directed a male clergy. Although Europeans were nominally Catholic, many adhered to local belief systems that the church deemed heretical. Still, Europe's Christian nations from the twelfth century on publicly united to drive nonbelievers (especially Muslims) from their domains and from the holy city of Jerusalem, triggering a series of wars known as the Crusades. Nevertheless, in the fifteenth century Muslims dominated the commerce and geography of the Mediterranean, especially after they conquered Constantinople (capital of the Christian Byzantine empire) in 1453. Few would have predicted that Christian Europeans would ever pose a challenge.

Effects of Plague and Warfare

When the fifteenth century began, European nations were recovering from the devastating Black Death epidemic, which seems to have reached Europe from China, brought by traders. The disease recurred with severity in the 1360s and 1370s. Although the impact of the Black Death varied regionally, the best estimate is that one-third of Europe's people died. A precipitous economic decline followed, as did severe social, political, and religious disruption.

As plague ravaged the population, England and France waged the Hundred Years' War (1337–1453), initiated because English monarchs claimed the French throne. The war interrupted overland trade routes connecting England and Antwerp (in modern Belgium) to Venice, a Christian trading center, and thence to India and China. Needing a new way to reach their northern trading partners, eastern Mediterranean merchants forged a maritime route to Antwerp. Using a triangular, or lateen, sail (rather than square rigging) improved ships' maneuverability, enabling vessels to sail from the Mediterranean and north around the European coast. The perfection of navigational instruments like the astrolabe and the quadrant allowed sailors to estimate their position (latitude) by measuring the relationship of the sun, moon, or certain stars to the horizon.

Political and Technological Change

After the Hundred Years' War, European monarchs consolidated their political power and raised revenues through increased taxation of an already hard-pressed peasantry. In England, Henry VII in 1485 founded the Tudor dynasty and began uniting a previously divided land. In France, Charles VII's successors unified the kingdom. Most successful were Ferdinand of Aragón and Isabella of Castile; in 1492 they defeated the Muslims, who had lived in Spain and Portugal for centuries, and established a strongly Catholic Spain by expelling Jews and Muslims.

The fifteenth century also brought technological change to Europe. Movable type and the printing press, invented in Germany in the 1450s, made information more accessible, including information in books about fabled lands across the seas. The most important was Marco Polo's *Travels*, published in 1477, which recounted a Venetian merchant's adventures in thirteenth-century China and described that nation as bordered on the east by an ocean. That led Europeans to believe they could reach China by sea. A transoceanic route, if it existed, would allow northern Europeans to circumvent the Muslim and Venetian merchants who controlled their access to Asian goods.

Motives for Exploration

Technological advances and newly powerful national rulers made possible the European explorations of the fifteenth and sixteenth centuries. Each country craved easy access to African and Asian goods—silk, dyes, perfumes, jewels, sugar, gold, and especially spices, which were desirable for seasoning food and as possible medicines.

Their allure stemmed largely from their rarity, their extraordinary cost, and their mysterious origins. They passed through so many hands en route to London or Seville that no European knew exactly where they came from. Acquiring products directly would improve a country's income and its standing relative to other countries.

Spreading Christianity around the world supplemented the economic motive. Fifteenth-century Europeans saw no conflict between materialistic and spiritual goals. Explorers and colonizers—especially Roman Catholics—sought to convert "heathen" peoples and also hoped to increase their nation's wealth via direct trade with Africa, China, India, and the Moluccas.

EARLY EUROPEAN EXPLORATIONS

To reach Asia, seafarers also required knowledge of the sea, its currents and winds. Wind would power their ships. But where would Atlantic breezes carry their square-rigged ships, which needed the wind directly behind the vessel?

Sailing in the Mediterranean Atlantic The answers would be found in the Mediterranean Atlantic, the expanse of the Atlantic Ocean south and west of Spain and bounded by the Azores (on the west) and the Canaries (on the south), with the Madeiras in their midst. Europeans reached all three sets of islands during the fourteenth century. Sailing to the Canaries from Europe was easy because strong Northeast Trade winds blew southward along the Iberian and African coastlines. The voyage took just a week.

The Iberian sailor attempting to return home from the Canaries, however, faced a major obstacle: the winds now blew directly at him. Rowing and tacking back and forth against the wind were tedious and ineffectual. So, mariners began sailing "around the wind"—literally, sailing as directly against the wind as possible without being forced to tack. In the Mediterranean Atlantic, a mariner would head northwest into the open ocean until—weeks later—he reached the winds that would carry him home, the so-called Westerlies.

This solution became the key to successful exploration of both the Atlantic and the Pacific Oceans. Faced with a contrary wind, a sailor just sailed around it until he found a wind to carry him in the proper direction.

Islands of the Mediterranean Atlantic During the fifteenth century, Iberian sailors regularly visited the three island groups. The uninhabited Azores were settled by Portuguese migrants who raised wheat for sale in Europe and sold livestock to passing sailors. By the 1450s Portuguese colonists who settled the uninhabited Madeiras were employing slaves (probably Jews and Muslims brought from Iberia) to grow sugar for export. By the 1470s Madeira had developed into a colonial plantation economy. For the first time in history, a region had been settled explicitly to cultivate a valuable crop—sugar—for sale elsewhere. Because the work was so backbreaking, only a supply of enslaved laborers (who could not quit) could ensure the system's success.

The Canaries had indigenous residents—the Guanche people, who traded animal skins and dyes with Europeans. After 1402 the French, Portuguese, and Spanish sporadically attacked the islands. The Guanches resisted but were weakened by

European diseases. The seven islands fell to Europeans, who carried Guanches as slaves to the Madeiras or the Iberian Peninsula. Spain conquered the last island in 1496 and devoted it to sugar plantations.

Portuguese Trading Posts in Africa

For other Europeans, the islands of the Mediterranean Atlantic were stepping-stones to Africa. In 1415 Portugal seized control of Ceuta, a Muslim city in North Africa (see Map 1.2). Prince Henry the Navigator, son of King John I of Portugal, dispatched ships southward along the African coast, attempting to discover an oceanic route to Asia. Not until after his death did Bartholomew Dias round the southern tip of Africa (1488) and Vasco da Gama finally reach India (1498), where at Malabar he located the richest source of peppercorns in the world.

Although West African states resisted European penetration of the interior, they let the Portuguese establish trading posts along their coasts. The African kingdoms charged the traders rent and levied duties on imports. The Portuguese gained, too, profiting from transporting African gold, ivory, and slaves to Europe. By bargaining with African masters to purchase slaves and carrying those bondspeople to Iberia, the Portuguese introduced black slavery to Europe.

Lessons of Early Colonization

In the 1480s the Portuguese colonized São Tomé, an island in the Gulf of Guinea. With Madeira at its sugar-producing capacity, the soil of São Tomé proved ideal, and plantation agriculture there expanded rapidly. Planters imported large numbers of slaves to work the cane fields, thus creating the first economy based primarily on the bondage of black Africans.

By the 1490s, Europeans had learned three key colonization lessons in the Mediterranean Atlantic. First, they learned how to transplant crops and livestock to exotic locations. Second, they discovered that native peoples could be conquered (like the Guanches) or exploited (like the Africans). Third, they developed a model of plantation slavery and a system for supplying many such workers. The stage was set for a pivotal moment in world history.

VOYAGES OF COLUMBUS, CABOT, AND THEIR SUCCESSORS

Christopher Columbus understood the lessons of the Mediterranean Atlantic. Born in 1451 in the Italian city-state of Genoa, this self-educated son of a wool merchant was by the 1490s an experienced sailor and mapmaker. Drawn to Portugal and its islands, especially Madeira, he voyaged at least once to the Portuguese outpost on the Gold Coast, where he became obsessed with gold and witnessed the economic potential of the slave trade.

Like all accomplished seafarers, Columbus knew the world was round. But he thought that China lay only 3,000 miles from the southern European coast. Thus, he argued, it would be easier to reach Asia by sailing west. Experts scoffed, accurately predicting that the two continents lay 12,000 miles apart. When Columbus in 1484 asked the Portuguese rulers to back his plan, they rejected what appeared to be a crazy scheme.

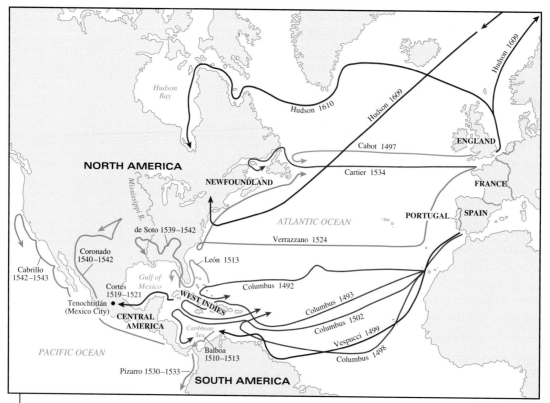

Map 1.2   European Explorations in America

In the century following Columbus's voyages, European adventurers explored the coasts and parts of the interior of North and South America.

Columbus's Voyage

Jealous of Portugal's successes in Africa, Ferdinand and Isabella of Spain agreed to finance Columbus's risky voyage. In part they hoped the profits would pay for a new expedition to conquer Muslim-held Jerusalem. On August 3, 1492, in command of three ships—the *Pinta,* the *Niña,* and the *Santa Maria*—Columbus sailed from the Spanish port of Palos.

Just over two months later, the vessels found land approximately where Columbus had predicted (see Map 1.2). On October 12, he and his men landed on an island in the Bahamas, which its inhabitants called Guanahaní but he renamed San Salvador. Later he explored the islands now known as Cuba and Hispaniola, which their residents, the Taíno people, called Colba and Bohío. Because he thought he had reached the East Indies, Columbus referred to the inhabitants as Indians.

Columbus's Observations

Three themes predominate in Columbus's log. First, he insistently asked the Taínos where he could find gold, pearls, and spices. They replied (via signs) that such products were on other islands, on the mainland, or in interior cities. He came to mistrust such answers, noting, "They will tell me anything I want to hear."

Second, Columbus wrote about the strange and beautiful plants and animals. His interest was not soley aesthetic. "There are many plants and trees here that could be worth a lot in Spain for use as dyes, spices, and medicines," he observed and planned to carry home "a sample of everything I can" for experts to examine.

Third, Columbus described the people, seizing some to take back to Spain. The Taínos were, he said, handsome, gentle, and friendly, though they told him of fierce people on nearby islands who raided their villages. Columbus believed the Taínos to be likely converts to Catholicism and potentially "good and skilled servants." Thus the records of the first encounter between Europeans and America revealed themes that would be of enormous significance for centuries. Europeans wanted to extract profits from the Americas by exploiting natural resources—plants, animals, and people. Columbus made three more voyages to the region, and until his death in 1506, he mistakenly believed he had reached Asia. Because the Florentine Amerigo Vespucci, who explored the South American coast in 1499, was the first to publish the idea that a new continent had been discovered, Martin Waldseemüller in 1507

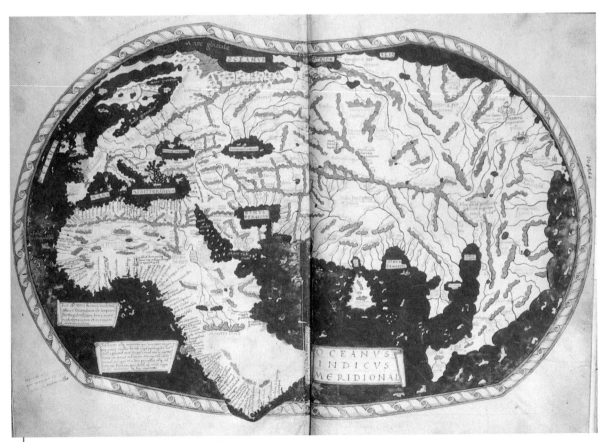

This map, produced in 1489 by Henricus Marcellus, represents the world as Christopher Columbus knew it, for it incorporates information obtained after Bartholomew Dias, a Portuguese sailor, rounded the Cape of Good Hope at the southern tip of Africa in 1488. Marcellus did not try to estimate the extent of the ocean separating the west coast of Europe from the east coast of Asia.   (© British Library Board. All Rights Reserved, Add. 15760, f.68–f69v)

labeled the land America in his map (reproduced on page 00). By then, Spain, Portugal, and Pope Alexander VI had signed the Treaty of Tordesillas (1494), confirming Portugal's dominance in Africa—and later Brazil—in exchange for Spanish preeminence in the rest of the Americas.

Norse and Other Northern Voyagers

About the year 1001, Leif Ericsson and other Norse people sailed to North America across the Davis Strait, which separated their Greenland villages from Baffin Island (located northeast of Hudson Bay; see Map 1.1) by 200 nautical miles, settling at a site they named Vinland. Attacks by residents forced them out after a few years. In the 1960s, archaeologists determined that the Norse had established an outpost at what is now L'Anse aux Meadows, Newfoundland, but Vinland was probably located farther south.

Some historians argue that in the 1480s European sailors probably located the rich fishing grounds off the Newfoundland coast but kept the information secret. Fifteenth-century seafarers voyaged between the European continent, England, Ireland, and Iceland. The mariners who explored the region that would become the United States and Canada built on their knowledge.

The winds that the northern sailors confronted posed problems on their outbound journeys. But mariners soon learned that the strongest winds shifted southward during the winter and that, by departing from northern ports in spring, they could steer northward to catch easterly breezes. Thus, those taking the northern route usually reached America along the coast of what is now Maine or the Canadian Maritime Provinces.

John Cabot's Explorations

The European generally credited with "discovering" North America is Zuan Cabboto, known today as John Cabot. More precisely, Cabot brought to Europe the first formal knowledge of the northern continental coastline and claimed the land for England. Like Columbus, Cabot was a master mariner from the Italian city-state of Genoa. Calculating that England, which traded with Asia through a network of intermediaries, would be eager to sponsor exploratory voyages for a possible alternative route, he gained financial backing from King Henry VII. He sailed from Bristol in late May 1497, reaching his destination about a month later. Scholars disagree about the location of Cabot's landfall but recognize the importance of his month-long exploration of the coast of modern Newfoundland.

The voyages of Columbus, Cabot, and others brought the Eastern and Western Hemispheres together. The Portuguese explorer Pedro Álvares Cabral reached Brazil in 1500; Cabot's son Sebastian landed in North America in 1507; France financed Giovanni da Verrazzano in 1524 and Jacques Cartier in 1534; and in 1609 and 1610 Henry Hudson explored the North American coast for the Dutch West India Company. All were hoping to find the legendary, nonexistent "Northwest Passage" through the Americas, an easy route to Asia's riches. Although they did not plant colonies in the Western Hemisphere, their discoveries interested European nations in exploring North and South America.

SPANISH EXPLORATION AND CONQUEST

Only Spain began colonization immediately. On his second voyage in 1493, Columbus brought to Hispaniola seventeen ships loaded with twelve hundred men, seeds, plants, livestock, chickens, and dogs. The settlement named Isabela (in the modern Dominican Republic) and its successors became the staging area for the Spanish invasion of America.

Cortés and Other Explorers

At first, Spanish explorers fanned out around the Caribbean basin. In 1513 Juan Ponce de León reached Florida, and Vasco Núñez de Balboa crossed the Isthmus of Panama to the Pacific Ocean, followed by Pánfilo de Narváez and others who traced the Gulf of Mexico. In the 1530s and 1540s, conquistadores explored other regions claimed by Spanish monarchs. Francisco Vásquez de Coronado journeyed through the southwestern portion of what is now the United States while Hernán de Soto explored the Southeast. Francisco Pizarro, who ventured into western South America, acquired the richest silver mines in the world by conquering the Incas. But the most important conquistador was Hernán Cortés, who in 1521 seized control of the Aztec Empire.

Cortés landed a force on the Mexican mainland in 1519 to search for rumored wealthy cities. Near the coast, local Mayas presented him with young enslaved women. One of them, Malinche (whom the Spaniards baptized as a Christian and renamed Doña Marina), became Cortés's translator, bore him a son, Martín—one of the first *mestizos,* or mixed-blood children—and eventually married one of his officers.

Capture of Tenochtitlán

Traveling toward the Aztec capital, Cortés, with Malinche's help, recruited peoples whom the Aztecs had long subjugated. The Spaniards' strange beasts (horses, livestock) and noisy weapons (guns, cannon) awed their new allies. Yet the Spaniards, too, were awed. Years later, Bernal Díaz del Castillo recalled his first sight of Tenochtitlán: "We were amazed . . . on account of the great towers and cues [temples] and buildings rising from the water, and all built of masonry."

The Spaniards also brought smallpox to Tenochtitlán, transporting an epidemic that had begun on Hispaniola. The disease peaked in 1520, fatally weakening Tenochtitlán's defenders. Largely as a consequence, Tenochtitlán surrendered in 1521, and the Spaniards built Mexico City on its site while Cortés seized a treasure of gold and silver. Thus, the Spanish monarchs controlled the richest, most extensive empire Europe had known since ancient Rome.

Spanish Colonization

Spain established the model of colonization based on three major elements that other countries would later imitate. First, the Crown sought tight control over the colonies, imposing a hierarchical government that allowed little autonomy to American jurisdictions. That included carefully vetting and limiting prospective emigrants and insisting that colonies import all manufactured goods from Spain. Roman Catholic priests attempted to ensure their religious conformity.

Second, men constituted most of the first colonists. Although some Spanish women later immigrated to America, the men took primarily Indian—and later, African—women as wives or concubines, a development often encouraged by colonial administrators. They thereby began the racially mixed population that characterizes much of Latin America today.

Third, the colonies' wealth was based on the exploitation of the native population and slaves from Africa. Spaniards took over the autocratic rule once assumed by native leaders, who exacted labor and tribute from their subjects. Cortés established the *encomienda* system, which granted Indian villages to conquistadors as a reward for service, thus legalizing slavery in all but name.

In 1542, after an outcry from sympathetic Spaniards, a new legal code forbade the conquerors from enslaving Indians while still allowing them to collect money and goods from tributary villages. That, combined with the declining Indian population, led the *encomenderos* to import Africans as their controlled labor force. They employed Indians and Africans primarily in gold and silver mines, on sugar plantations, and on horse, cattle, and sheep ranches. African slavery was more common in the Greater Antilles (the major Caribbean islands) than on the mainland.

Many demoralized residents of Mesoamerica accepted the Christian religion brought to New Spain by Franciscan and Dominican friars. Spaniards leveled cities, constructing Roman Catholic cathedrals and monasteries on sites once occupied by Aztec, Incan, and Mayan temples. Indians were exposed to European customs and religious rituals designed to assimilate Catholic and pagan beliefs. Friars juxtaposed the cult of the Virgin Mary with that of the corn goddess, and the Indians melded aspects of their world-view with Christianity, in a process called syncretism. Thousands of Indians embraced Catholicism, at least partly because it was the religion of their new rulers.

Gold, Silver, and Spain's Decline

The New World's gold and silver, initially a boon, ultimately brought about the decline of Spain as a major power. China gobbled up roughly half of the total output of New World mines. In the 1570s, the Spanish dispatched silver-laden galleons annually from Acapulco (on Mexico's west coast) to trade at their new settlement at Manila, in the Philippines, which gained them easy access to luxury Chinese goods, such as silk and spices.

This unprecedented wealth led to rapid inflation, which caused Spanish products to be overpriced in international markets and imported goods to become cheaper in Spain. The once-profitable Spanish textile-manufacturing industry collapsed, as did many other businesses. The seemingly endless income from American colonies emboldened Spanish monarchs to spend lavishly on wars against the Dutch and the English.

Late-sixteenth- and early-seventeenth-century monarchs repudiated the state debt, wreaking havoc on national finances. When the South American gold and silver mines faltered in the mid-seventeenth century, Spain's economy crumbled, ending its international importance.

THE COLUMBIAN EXCHANGE

A mutual transfer of diseases, plants, and animals (called the Columbian Exchange by historian Alfred Crosby; see Figure 1.1) resulted directly from the European voyages of the fifteenth and sixteenth centuries and Spanish colonization. Many large mammals, such as cattle and horses, were native to the connected continents of Europe, Asia, and Africa, but the Americas had no domesticated beasts larger than llamas. Vegetable crops of the Americas—particularly maize, beans, squash, cassava, and potatoes—were more nutritious and produced higher yields than those of Europe and Africa. In time, native peoples learned to raise and consume European livestock, and Europeans and Africans planted and ate American crops. The diets of all three peoples were enriched, helping the world's population to double over the next three hundred years. About three-fifths of all crops cultivated worldwide today were first grown in the Americas.

Smallpox and Other Diseases

Diseases carried from Europe and Africa devastated the Americas. Indians fell victim to microbes that had long infested other continents, killing hundreds of thousands of Europeans but leaving survivors with some immunity. When Columbus landed on

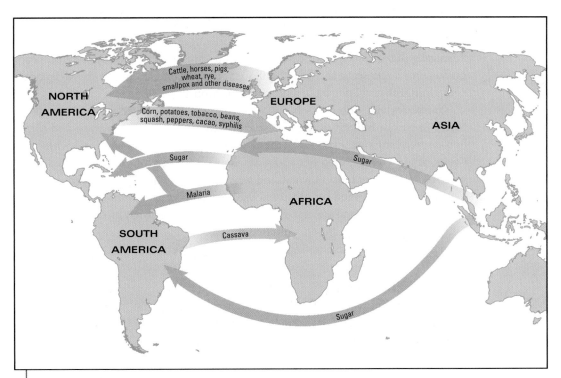

Figure 1.1   Major Items in the Columbian Exchange
As European adventurers traversed the world in the fifteenth and sixteenth centuries, they initiated the Columbian Exchange of plants, animals, and diseases. These events changed the lives of the peoples of the world forever, bringing new foods and new pestilence to both sides of the Atlantic.

Hispaniola in 1492, approximately half a million people resided there. Fifty years later, there were fewer than two thousand native inhabitants.

Although measles, typhus, influenza, malaria, and other illnesses severely afflicted native peoples, the greatest killer was smallpox. Historians estimate that over time, alien diseases could have reduced the precontact American population by as much as 90 percent. The epidemics recurred at twenty- to thirty-year intervals, appearing either in tandem or in quick succession. Large numbers of deaths further strained native societies, rendering them more vulnerable to droughts, crop failures or other challenges. A great epidemic, probably viral hepatitis, swept through the coastal villages north of Cape Cod from 1616 to 1618, wiping out up to 90 percent of the population. Because of this dramatic depopulation, a few years later English colonists were able to establish settlements virtually unopposed.

The Americans, however, probably gave the Europeans syphilis, a virulent venereal disease. The first recorded European case occurred in Barcelona, Spain, in 1493, after Columbus's return from the Caribbean. Although less likely than smallpox to be fatal, syphilis was debilitating. Carried by soldiers, sailors, and prostitutes, it spread through Europe and Asia, reaching China by 1505.

Sugar, Horses, and Tobacco

The exchange of three commodities significantly altered Europe and the Americas. The ravenous European demand for sugar, a luxury foodstuff, led Columbus to take Canary Island sugar canes to Hispaniola in 1493. By the 1520s, plantations in the Greater Antilles worked by African slaves regularly shipped sugar to Spain. Half a century later, Portugal's Brazil colony (founded in 1532) was producing sugar for the European market on a larger scale, and after 1640, sugar cultivation became the crucial component of English and French Caribbean colonization.

Horses—which Columbus brought to America in 1493—fell into the hands of North American Indians during the seventeenth century. Through trade and theft, horses spread among the peoples of the Great Plains by 1750. Lakotas, Comanches, and Crows, among others, used horses for transportation and hunting, calculated their wealth in number of horses owned, and waged war primarily on horseback. After acquiring horses, their mode of subsistence shifted from hunting various animals, combined with gathering and agriculture, to one based almost entirely on buffalo hunting.

In America, Europeans encountered tobacco, which at first they believed to be medicinal. Smoking and chewing the "Indian weed" became a European fad after it was planted in Turkey in the sixteenth century. Despite the efforts of King James I of England, who in 1604 pronounced smoking "hatefull to the Nose, harmfull to the brain, [and] dangerous to the Lungs," tobacco's popularity climbed.

EUROPEANS IN NORTH AMERICA

Europeans were initially more interested in exploiting North America's natural resources than in establishing colonies. John Cabot reported that fish were plentiful near Newfoundland, so the French, Spanish, and Portuguese rushed to take advantage of abundant codfish, which were prized in European markets. In the early 1570s, the English joined the Newfoundland fishery, selling salt cod to the Spanish

Maize

Maize, to Mesoamericans, was a gift from Quetzalcoatl, the plumed serpent god. Cherokees told of an old woman whose blood produced the prized stalks after her grandson buried her body in a field. For the Abenakis, the crop began when a beautiful maiden ordered a youth to drag her by the hair through a burned-over field. The long hair turned into silk, the flower on corn stalks. Both tales' symbolic association of corn and women supports archaeologists' recent suggestion that—in eastern North America at least—female plant breeders were responsible for substantial improvements in the productivity of maize.

Sacred to the Indian peoples who grew it, maize was a main part of their diet. They dried the kernels; ground into meal, maize was cooked as a mush or baked as flat cakes, the forerunners of modern tortillas. Although European invaders initially disdained maize, they soon learned that it could be cultivated under many conditions—from sea level to twelve thousand feet, from regions with abundant rainfall to dry lands. So Europeans, too, came to rely on corn, growing it in their American settlements and their homelands.

Maize cultivation spread to Asia and Africa. Today China is second only to the United States in corn production, and corn is more widely grown in Africa than any other crop. Still, the United States produces 45 percent of the world's corn, and it is the nation's single largest crop. More than half of American corn is consumed by livestock. Much of the rest is processed into syrup used as a sweetener or into ethanol, a gasoline additive that reduces both pollution and dependence on fossil fuels. Of the ten thousand products in a modern American grocery store, about one-fourth rely on corn. Currently this crop provides one-fifth of all the calories consumed by the earth's peoples.

The earliest known European drawing of maize, the American plant that was to have such an extraordinary impact on the entire world. (Typ 565.42.409 F[B], Department of Printing and Graphic Arts, Houghton Library, Harvard University Library)

in exchange for Asian goods. The English became dominant in the region, which by century's end was the focal point of valuable European commerce.

Trade Among Indians and Europeans

Fishermen quickly realized that they could increase profits by exchanging cloth and metal goods, such as pots and knives, for native trappers' beaver pelts, used to make fashionable hats in Europe. Initially, Europeans traded from ships along the coast. Later, male adventurers set up outposts on the mainland.

Indians similarly desired European goods that could make their lives easier and establish their tribal superiority. Some bands concentrated entirely on trapping for the European market and abandoned their traditional economies. The Abenakis of Maine, for example, trapped beaver to sell to French traders and became partially dependent on food supplied by their southern neighbors, the Massachusett tribe. In exchange, the Massachusetts sought European metal tools which they preferred over their handmade stone implements. The pelt trade wiped out beaver in some regions. The disappearance of their dams led to soil erosion, which later increased when European settlers cleared forests for farmland.

A watercolor by John White, an artist with Raleigh's second preliminary expedition (and who later was governor of the ill-fated 1587 colony). He identified his subjects as the wife and daughter of the chief of Pomeioc, a village near Roanoke. Note the woman's elaborate tattoos and the fact that the daughter carries an Elizabethan doll, obviously given to her by one of the Englishmen.   (© Trustees of the British Museum)

Contest Between Spain and England

In the mid-sixteenth century, English "sea dogs" like John Hawkins and Sir Francis Drake raided Spanish treasure fleets from the Caribbean. Their actions helped foment a war that in 1588 culminated in the defeat of the Spanish Armada off the English coast. English leaders started to consider planting colonies in the Western Hemisphere, thereby gaining better access to trade goods while preventing Spain from dominating the Americas.

The first English colonial planners hoped to reproduce Spanish successes by dispatching to America men who would exploit the native peoples for their nation's benefit. In the mid-1570s, a group that included Sir Walter Raleigh promoted a scheme to establish outposts that could trade with the Indians and provide bases for attacks on New Spain. Approving the idea, Queen Elizabeth I authorized Raleigh to colonize North America.

Roanoke

After two preliminary expeditions, in 1587 Sir Walter Raleigh sent 117 colonists to the territory he named Virginia, after Elizabeth, the Virgin Queen. They established a settlement on Roanoke Island, in what is now North Carolina, but in 1590 a resupply ship found the colonists had vanished, leaving only the word *Croatoan* (the name of a nearby island) carved on a tree. Recent tree-ring studies have shown that the North Carolina coast experienced a severe drought between 1587 and 1589 that may have led colonists to abandon Roanoke.

Harriot's *Briefe and True Report*

The reason becomes clear in Thomas Harriot's *A Briefe and True Report of the New Found Land of Virginia,* published in 1588. Harriot, a noted scientist traveling with the second voyage to Roanoke, revealed that, although explorers depended on villagers for food, they needlessly antagonized them by killing some of them for what Harriot admitted were unjustifiable reasons.

Harriot advised later colonizers to treat the native peoples more humanely. But his book's description of America's economic potential demonstrated why that advice would rarely be followed. Harriot stressed three points: the availability of familiar European commodities, such as grapes, iron, copper, and fur-bearing animals; the potential profitability of exotic American products, such as maize and tobacco; and the relative ease of manipulating the native population. Should the Americans resist, Harriot asserted, England's disciplined soldiers and superior weaponry would quickly deliver victory.

Harriot's *Briefe and True Report* depicted for English readers a bountiful land of profitable opportunities. The people residing there would, he thought, "in a short time be brought to civilitie" through conversion to Christianity, admiration for European superiority, or conquest—if they did not die from disease. But European dominance of North America was never fully achieved as Harriot and his compatriots intended.

Summary

Initial contact among Europeans, Africans, and Americans that ended near the close of the sixteenth century began approximately 250 years earlier when Portuguese sailors explored the Mediterranean Atlantic and the West African coast. Those seamen established commercial ties that brought African slaves first to Iberia and then to the islands the Europeans conquered and settled. The Mediterranean Atlantic and its island sugar plantations nurtured the mariners. Except for the Spanish, early explorers regarded the Americas primarily as a barrier blocking them from their goal of an oceanic route to the riches of China and the Moluccas. European fishermen were the first to realize that the northern coasts had valuable products of fish and furs to offer.

The Aztecs experienced hunger after Cortés's invasion, and their great temples were destroyed as the Spaniards used their stones (and Indian laborers) to construct cathedrals. The conquerors employed first American and later, enslaved African workers, to till the fields, mine the precious metals, and herd the livestock that generated immense profits.

The initial impact of Europeans on the Americas proved devastating in just decades. Europeans' diseases killed millions, and their livestock, along with other imported animals and plants, irrevocably modified the American environment. Europe, too, was changed: American foodstuffs like corn and potatoes improved nutrition, and American gold and silver first enriched, then ruined, the Spanish economy.

By the late sixteenth century, fewer people resided in North America than had lived there before Columbus's arrival. The Indians, Africans, and Europeans who lived there inhabited a new world that combined in unprecedented ways foods, religions, economies, ways of life, and political systems that had developed separately for millennia. Understandably, conflict permeated that process.

Kennewick Man/Ancient One

On July 28, 1996, Will Thomas, a college student wading in the Columbia River near Kennewick, Washington, felt a skull underfoot. Shocked, Thomas initially believed he had found a recent murder victim. Soon the skeleton was determined to be about 9,200 years old. During the next decade, the skeleton, dubbed Kennewick Man (by the press) or Ancient One (by local Indian tribes), was featured on television news shows and in magazines.

The oldest nearly complete skeleton found in the United States, the remains became the subject of a major federal court case. At issue was the interpretation of the Native American Graves Protection and Repatriation Act (NAGPRA), adopted by Congress in 1990 to prevent the desecration of Indian gravesites and to provide for the return of bones and sacred objects to native peoples. It defined the term *Native American* as "of, or relating to, a tribe, people, or culture that is indigenous to the United States." Led by the Umatillas, area tribes prepared to reclaim and rebury the remains. But eight anthropologists filed suit in federal court, contending that bones of such antiquity were unlikely to be linked to modern tribes and requesting access to them for scientific study.

Although the U.S. government supported the tribes' claims, in late August 2002 a federal judge ruled in favor of the anthropologists, in a decision upheld on appeal two years later. He declared that the Interior Department had erred in concluding that all pre-1492 remains found in the United States should automatically be considered Native American. The Umatillas protested, contending that he clearly contradicted Congress's intent in enacting NAGPRA. In June 2006 Umatilla leaders visited the bones at a Seattle museum to honor and pray for them.

The debate over the skeleton reveals one facet of the continuing legacy of the often-contentious relationship between the nation's indigenous inhabitants and later immigrants.

Chapter Review

AMERICAN SOCIETIES

What led to the development of major North American civilizations in the centuries before Europeans arrived?

Paleo-Indians were the first known people on the North American continent about 11,000 years ago. When the Ice Age ended, and the prevalence of mammals decreased, many native peoples in what is now central Mexico began cultivating food crops for survival, including maize (corn), squash, beans, avocados, and peppers. As agricultural methods improved, vegetables became a more reliable and nutritious food source, leading most early Americans to abandon nomadic ways and settle to tend crops. Agricultural success facilitated the rise of civilizations, since with steady food supplies, people could broaden their focus from farming to trade to accumulating wealth. Food supply, however, was so keenly linked to a civilization's success that the first large city-states of MesoAmerica and Mississippian culture later collapsed from lack of adequate food.

NORTH AMERICA IN 1492

What were the gender dimensions of native cultures?

Like Europeans, Native American societies assigned various tasks and responsibilities to members along gender lines. Societies that were predominantly hunting assigned women to making food and clothing. Agricultural peoples varied in their gendered division of labor; some, like the Pueblos, defined farming as men's work, while others, like the Algonquian, Iroquoian, and Muskogean, gave women most agricultural chores, and men hunted and cleared the land. Women just about everywhere raised children. Agricultural families were defined matrilineally, through the female line of descent, and women assumed more leadership roles than in nomadic hunter peoples. They never became chiefs, but older women chose chiefs and could start or stop wars.

[Handwritten margin notes: Hunting society / Women - clothing, food / Agricultural / Men - farming / Women - chores / women - Children / Agricultural women more leadership / Chose chiefs]

AFRICAN SOCIETIES

What was the nature of slavery in Africa?

Slavery enabled upwardly mobile farmers to expand their labor force and potentially gain wealth. People became enslaved due to criminal acts, or more typically, either because they were captured by enemies or agreed to enslave themselves or family members to repay debts. Unlike the form of slavery that would develop in America, slave status did not always pass to the next generation. African slavery varied from complete chattel to allowing slaves to participate in trade or even achieve prominent military or political posts.

EUROPEAN SOCIETIES

What were the motives behind fifteenth and sixteenth century European explorations?

While technological advances and powerful rulers facilitated explorations, the driving force behind them was the quest for a transoceanic trade route that would provide direct access to African and Asian goods such as silks, dyes, jewels, sugar, gold, and spices. This would allow northern Europeans to bypass the Muslim and Venetian merchants who served as middle men for these items. Rulers also believed that the more they controlled access to these much-desired products, the better their nation's standing would be relative to other countries. The other motivation was to spread Christianity and convert those they considered to be heathen peoples.

EARLY EUROPEAN EXPLORATIONS

What lessons learned during early colonization would influence future European settlement in the sixteenth century?

By the end of the fifteenth century, Europeans learned how to transport crops and livestock to their exotic new world conquests. They recognized that native peoples could be conquered, exploited, and forced to labor. The Portuguese colony of Madeira was the first in history to be settled to cultivate a cash crop—

sugar—for exportation. This experience, and others like it, led to the creation of the plantation slavery model, as well as a system for supplying slave labor to do the backbreaking work of cultivating crops, without the ability to quit.

VOYAGES OF COLUMBUS, CABOT, AND THEIR SUCCESSORS

How did the voyages of Columbus, Cabot, and others inspire further exploration and settlement of what became America?

Explorers initially launched their expeditions partly seeking a northwest passage to Asia and partly hoping to discover gold, spices, and other riches they could claim for their sponsoring nations. Columbus, for example, found plants and trees that he envisioned Spain might use for dyes, spices, and medicines. He and many other explorers looked to America as a source of future profits, and their discoveries did indeed inspire further exploration by European nations, though for most, colonization would lag for generations.

SPANISH EXPLORATION AND CONQUEST

What model of colonization did Spain establish that other nations would later follow?

Spain sought immediately to colonize America and developed a model based on three key concepts that would later be adopted by other European colonizing nations. First, Spain's monarchy maintained firm control over its colonies with virtually no autonomy granted to American colonies. Second, men made up the majority of early colonists, taking first Indian, and later African, women as wives or concubines. Third, the development of the colonies and its subsequent wealth was based on exploiting native people and African slaves as labor.

THE COLUMBIAN EXCHANGE

What were the results of contact between native populations and European settlers and explorers?

Native Americans and Europeans exchanged diseases, plants, and animals when they came into contact on the North American continent in the fifteenth and sixteenth centuries. Native American vegetable crops were more nutritious than those in Europe and Africa, while Europeans brought livestock that helped enrich Indians' diets, too. The Spanish also brought horses to their American territories, which aided the shift in native society from hunting various animals combined with some farming and gathering, to almost exclusively hunting buffalo as their main form of subsistence. The exchange of diseases, however, had severe consequences. Europeans brought many diseases from typhus to malaria to hepatitis, all of which devastated tribal populations, but none as much as small pox. Dramatic Indian depopulation in what became New England enabled settlers to claim land and establish colonies almost uncontested. Europeans, meanwhile acquired syphilis from Native Americans, which was debilitating, but not usually fatal.

EUROPEANS IN NORTH AMERICA

What were the reasons behind the failure of England's, Portugal's, and France's initial attempts at colonization?

In a nutshell, all three failed because colonists were unable to be self-sustaining and at the same time, did little to diminish the hostility of native peoples. In fact, while many colonists relied on Indians for food, they also heightened animosities by antagonizing them or, as one British scientist wrote, killing some with little cause. Ironically, the solution this scientist, Thomas Harriot, proposed was on the one hand to treat native people with greater humanity, but on the other hand, to take advantage of the fact that they are easily manipulated toward whatever ends Europeans sought. And if they resisted, he recommended the use of military force, and he hoped conversion to Christianity would civilize them and make such conquest unnecessary.

SUGGESTIONS FOR FURTHER READING

Alfred W. Crosby, *The Columbian Exchange: Biological and Cultural Consequences of 1492* (1972)

John H. Elliott, *Empires of the Atlantic World: Britain and Spain in America, 1492–1830* (2006)

Alvin Josephy Jr., ed., *America in 1492* (1992)

Charles C. Mann, *1491: New Revelations of the Americas Before Columbus* (2005)

D. W. Meinig, *Atlantic America, 1492–1800* (1986)

Samuel Eliot Morison, *The Southern Voyages, A.D. 1492–1616* (1974); *The European Discovery of America: The Northern Voyages, A.D. 1500–1600* (1971)

John Thornton, *Africa and Africans in the Making of the Atlantic World, 1400–1680* (1992)

CHAPTER 2

Europeans Colonize North America

CHAPTER OUTLINE

Spanish, French, and Dutch North America

The Caribbean

LINKS TO THE WORLD: Wampum

English Interest in Colonization

The Founding of Virginia

Life in the Chesapeake

The Founding of New England

Life in New England

LEGACY FOR A PEOPLE AND A NATION: Blue Laws

Summary

Captain William Rudyerd seemed like the sort of man Puritan colonies in the Americas would prize, so when his older brother urged planners of a new settlement to appoint him master general, they agreed. Rudyerd followed the dissenting English faith and vigorously trained the settlers to defend themselves. But he also vigorously defended his status and wreaked havoc in the fragile community. He beat to death a servant suffering from scurvy (who he thought was merely lazy) and quarreled with settlers, whom he believed failed to show him the respect due to a gentleman of noble birth.

One of Rudyerd's antagonists was the Reverend Lewis Morgan, with whom the captain argued about religious books and church services. Their disagreements escalated into insults. "Your foul-mouthed answer deserves rather sharp retribution than any equal respect from a gentleman," the captain once haughtily told the minister.

Similar conflicts occurred elsewhere, as gentlemen accustomed to unquestioning deference learned that in the colonies their social standing could be challenged. But in Rudyerd and Morgan's colony the disputes were especially dangerous because they lived on Providence Island, an isolated Puritan outpost off the coast of modern Nicaragua.

Providence Island, founded by Puritan adventurers in 1630—the same year as the Massachusetts Bay colony—sought to establish an English beachhead in the tropics as an entrée to colonizing the Central American mainland. Yet its perilous location amid Spanish settlements, failure to establish a local economy, and, ultimately, its desperate attempts to stay afloat by serving as a base for English privateers caused its downfall. The latter riled the Spaniards, who attacked in 1635 and 1640. In May 1641 a Spanish fleet of seven ships carrying two thousand

This icon will direct you to interactive activities and study materials on *A People And A Nation*, Brief Edition website: **www.cengage.com/history/norton/ peoplenationbrief8e**

Chronology

1533	Henry VIII divorces Catherine of Aragón. English Reformation begins.	1622	Powhatan Confederacy attacks Virginia.
1558	Elizabeth I becomes queen.	1624	Dutch settle on Manhattan Island (New Amsterdam).
1565	St. Augustine (Florida), the oldest permanent European settlement in present-day United States, is founded.		English colonize St. Kitts, the first island in Lesser Antilles to be settled by Europeans.
			James I revokes the Virginia Company's charter.
1598	Oñate conquers the Pueblos in New Mexico for Spain.	1625	Charles I becomes king.
		1630	Massachusetts Bay colony is founded.
1603	James I becomes king.	1634	Maryland is founded.
1607	Jamestown, the first permanent English settlement in North America, is founded.	1636	Williams is expelled from Massachusetts Bay and founds Providence, Rhode Island.
1608	Quebec is founded by the French.		Connecticut is founded.
1610	Santa Fe, New Mexico, is founded.	1637	Pequot War occurs in New England.
1611	First Virginia tobacco crop is harvested.	1638	Hutchinson is expelled from Massachusetts Bay and goes to Rhode Island.
1614	Fort Orange (Albany) is founded by the Dutch.		
1619	Virginia House of Burgesses, the first representative assembly in the English colonies, is established.	ca. 1640	Sugar cultivation begins on Barbados.
		1642	Montreal is founded by the French.
1620	Plymouth colony, the first permanent English settlement in New England, is founded.	1646	Treaty ends hostilities between Virginia and Powhatan Confederacy.

soldiers and sailors captured the island, and survivors scattered to other Caribbean settlements, English mainland colonies, or back to England.

By this time, Spain no longer predominated in the Americas, and by the 1640s, France, the Netherlands, and England had permanent colonies in North America. The French and Dutch colonies, like the Spanish outposts, were settled largely by European men who interacted with indigenous peoples, using their labor or seeking to convert them to Christianity. Like the conquistadors, French and Dutch merchants (on the mainland) and planters (in the Caribbean) hoped to make a quick profit and perhaps return home. The English were similarly interested in profiting from North America, but pursued profits differently.

Unlike other Europeans, most English settlers came to stay. In the area that would later be known as New England, they arrived in family groups and re-created the European agricultural economy and family life to an extent impossible in colonies where single men predominated.

The first permanent English colonies survived because of contacts with nearby Indians. The settlers learned to grow such unfamiliar American crops as maize and squash. They also developed extensive trading relationships with native peoples and with other colonies. Needing field laborers, they first used English indentured servants, then African slaves. Thus the early history of the region that became the United States and the English Caribbean is best understood as a series of complex interactions among various European, African, and American peoples and environments.

The *history companion* *powered by Eduspace*® Your primary source for interactive quizzes, exercises, and more to help you learn efficiently. http://history.college.cengage.com/students

- Why did different groups of Europeans choose to migrate to the Americas?
- How did different native peoples react to their presence?
- In what ways did the English colonies in the Chesapeake and New England differ, and in what ways were they alike?

Spanish, French, and Dutch North America

Spaniards established the first permanent European settlement within the modern United States, but others had tried earlier. Twice in the 1560s Huguenots (French Protestants) escaping persecution planted colonies on the southern Atlantic coast. A passing ship rescued the starving survivors of the first, located in present-day South Carolina. The second, near modern Jacksonville, Florida, was destroyed in 1565 by a Spanish expedition commanded by Pedro Menéndez de Avilés, who sought Spanish domination of the strategically important region. Menéndez set up a small outpost, which he named St. Augustine—now the oldest continuously inhabited European settlement in the United States.

The local Guale and Timucua nations initially allied with the powerful newcomers and welcomed Franciscan friars. The relationship fractured quickly, as natives resisted Spanish authority. Still, the Franciscans offered the Indians spiritual solace for the diseases and troubles besetting them after the Europeans' invasion. Eventually they gained numerous converts across Florida and the islands along the Atlantic coast.

New Mexico

In 1598, drawn by rumors of rich cities, Juan de Oñate, a Mexican-born adventurer, led about five hundred soldiers and settlers to New Mexico. At first, the Pueblo peoples greeted them cordially. But when the Spaniards used torture, murder, and rape to extort food and clothing from the villagers, the residents of Acoma killed several soldiers, including Oñate's nephew, Juan de Zaldívar. The invaders responded ferociously, killing more than eight hundred people and capturing the remainder. All the captives above age twelve were enslaved for twenty years, and men older than twenty-five had one foot amputated. Other Pueblo villages surrendered.

Oñate's bloody victory proved illusory. New Mexico held little wealth and was too far from the Pacific coast to help protect Spanish sea-lanes. Many Spaniards returned to Mexico, and officials considered abandoning the isolated colony, which was 800 miles north of the nearest Spanish settlement. Instead, they maintained a small military outpost and a few Christian missions there, with the capital at Santa Fe (founded in 1610). As in southern regions, Spanish leaders were granted *encomiendas* guaranteeing them control over Pueblo villagers' labor. But in the absence of mines or fertile agricultural lands, such grants yielded little profit.

Quebec and Montreal

On the Atlantic coast, the French focused on the area that Jacques Cartier had explored in the 1530s. They tried to establish permanent bases along the Canadian coast but failed until 1605, when they founded Port Royal. In 1608 Samuel de Champlain set

TABLE 2.1   The Founding of Permanent European Colonies in North America, 1565–1640

Colony	Founder(s)	Date	Basis of Economy
Florida	Pedro Menéndez de Avilés	1565	Farming
New Mexico	Juan de Oñate	1598	Livestock
Virginia	Virginia Co.	1607	Tobacco
New France	France	1608	Fur trading
New Netherland	Dutch West India Co.	1614	Fur trading
Plymouth	Separatists	1620	Farming, fishing
Maine	Sir Ferdinando Gorges	1622	Fishing
St. Kitts, Barbados, et al.	European immigrants	1624	Sugar
Massachusetts Bay	Massachusetts Bay Company	1630	Farming, fishing, fur trading
Maryland	Cecilius Calvert	1634	Tobacco
Rhode Island	Roger Williams	1636	Farming
Connecticut	Thomas Hooker	1636	Farming, fur trading
New Haven	Massachusetts migrants	1638	Farming
New Hampshire	Massachusetts migrants	1638	Farming, fishing

up a trading post at an interior site that the Iroquois called Stadacona, which he renamed Quebec. It was the most defensible spot in the St. Lawrence River valley, a stronghold that controlled access to the continent's heartland. In 1642 the French established a second post, Montreal, at the falls of the St. Lawrence.

Previously, fishermen were the major transporters of North American beaver pelts to France, but the new posts quickly took over (see Table 2.1). Only a few Europeans resided in New France; most were men, and some married Indian women. The colony's leaders gave land grants along the river to wealthy seigneurs (nobles), who imported tenants to work their farms. A few Frenchmen brought their wives and took up agriculture; still, more than twenty-five years after Quebec's founding, it had just sixty-four resident families along with traders and soldiers. Northern New France never grew much beyond the river valley between Quebec and Montreal (see Map 2.1). Thus it differed from New Spain, characterized by scattered cities and direct supervision of Indian laborers.

Jesuit Missions in New France

Missionaries of the Society of Jesus (Jesuits), a Roman Catholic order dedicated to converting nonbelievers to Christianity, first arrived in Quebec in 1625. The Jesuits, whom the Indians called Black Robes, tried to persuade indigenous peoples to live near French settlements and adopt European agricultural methods. Failing that, they tried to introduce Catholicism without insisting that Indians fundamentally alter their traditions. Accordingly, the Black Robes learned Indian languages and traveled to remote regions, where they lived among hundreds of potential converts.

Jesuits sought to gain the confidence of influential men and to undermine the authority of village shamans, the traditional religious leaders. Immune to smallpox

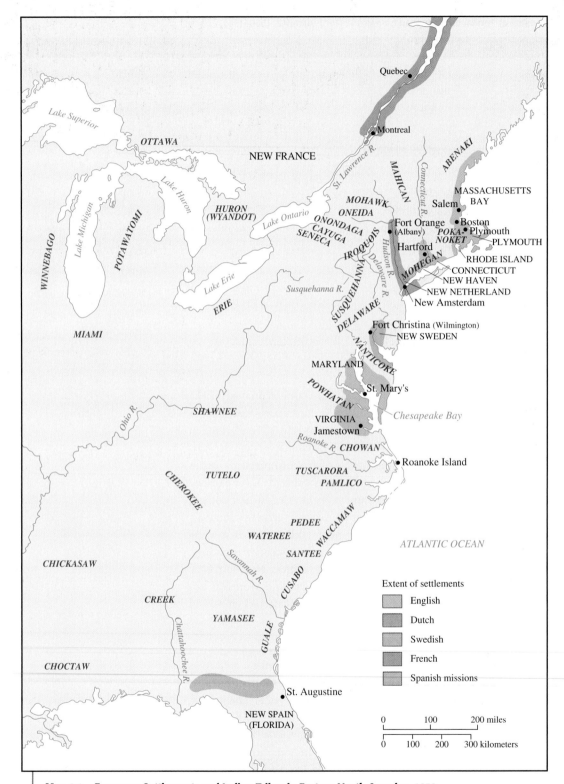

Map 2.1   European Settlements and Indian Tribes in Eastern North America, 1650

The few European settlements established in the East before 1650 were widely scattered, hugging the shores of the Atlantic Ocean and the banks of its major rivers. By contrast, America's native inhabitants controlled the vast interior expanse of the continent, and Spaniards had begun to move into the West.

(having survived it already), Jesuits explained epidemics among the Indians as God's punishment for sin. It helped that shamans' traditional remedies proved ineffective against the new pestilence. Perhaps most important, they amazed the villagers by communicating with each other over long distances through marks on paper (letters). The Indians' desire to harness the extraordinary power of literacy made them receptive to the missionaries' spiritual message.

Over time, the Jesuits gained thousands of converts. Catholicism offered women the inspiring role model of the Virgin Mary, personified in Montreal and Quebec by communities of nuns who taught and ministered to Indian women and children. Many converts altered the native customs of premarital sexual relationships and easy divorce because Catholic doctrine prohibited both. Yet they resisted strict European child-rearing practices. Jesuits recognized that aspects of native culture could be compatible with Christianity. Their conversion efforts were further aided by their lack of interest in labor tribute or land.

New Netherland

Jesuit missionaries had little competition from other Europeans, but French fur traders faced direct challenges. In 1614, only five years after Henry Hudson explored the river that now bears his name, his sponsor, the Dutch West India Company, established an outpost (Fort Orange) at the site of present-day Albany, New York. The Dutch, too, sought beaver pelts, and their presence close to Quebec threatened French regional domination. The Netherlands, at the time the world's greatest commercial power, sought trade rather than colonization. Thus New Netherland remained small. The colony's southern anchor was New Amsterdam, founded in 1624 on Manhattan Island.

New Netherland was the small outpost of the Dutch West India Company's vast commercial empire extending to Africa, Brazil, the Caribbean, and modern-day Indonesia. Autocratic directors-general ruled the colony, garnering little loyalty. Even an offer in 1629 of large land grants, or patroonships, to anyone bringing fifty settlers to the province failed to attract takers. (Only one such tract—Rensselaerswyck, near Albany—was ever developed.) As late as the mid-1660s, New Netherland had only about five thousand inhabitants. Some were Swedes and Finns in the former colony of New Sweden (founded in 1638 on the Delaware River; see Map 2.1), which the Dutch took over in 1655.

Indian allies of New France and New Netherland clashed partly because of fur-trade rivalries. In the 1640s the Iroquois, who traded chiefly with the Dutch and lived in modern upstate New York, went to war against the Hurons, who traded primarily with the French and lived in present-day Ontario. The Iroquois wanted to become the major pelt supplier and safeguard their hunting territories. With guns supplied by the Dutch, they virtually exterminated the Hurons, whose population was already decimated by smallpox. The Iroquois thus established themselves as a major force in the region.

THE CARIBBEAN

In the first half of the seventeenth century, the Spanish concentrated on colonizing the Greater Antilles—Cuba, Hispaniola, Jamaica, and Puerto Rico. They ignored many smaller islands, partly because of resistance from inhabitants and partly

Wampum

Native North Americans highly valued small cylindrical beads made from whelk and quahog shells, known as wampum. For centuries, the white and purple beads were strung to make necklaces and ornamental belts, but with the Europeans' arrival, wampum became a currency.

Wampum's transformation occurred not only because the Indians would trade deerskins and beaver pelts for the beads but also because Dutch and English settlers lacked access to currency from their homelands. Wampum filled a need as a handy medium of exchange, especially in the early settlement decades.

Whelk (white) and quahog (purple) shells were found primarily along the shores of Long Island Sound, where Narragansetts, Montauks, Niantics, and other local peoples gathered them in summer. In winter, women fashioned the hard shells into beads, a time-consuming and skilled task. But Europeans' metal tools allowed a rapid increase in the quantity and quality of wampum. Some villages abandoned hunter-gatherer modes of subsistence and settled permanently in shell-rich areas to focus on the manufacture of wampum year-round.

Wampum played a key role in the early economies of New Netherland and New England. Dutch settlers in Manhattan traded such manufactured goods as guns, kettles, axes, or knives with the wampum makers, then used wampum to purchase furs and skins from the Iroquois. In 1627 Isaac de Rasière, a Dutch trader, introduced wampum to English colonists at Plymouth. Ten years later, the Massachusetts Bay colony made wampum legal tender for paying debts under 12 pennies, at a rate of six white beads or three purple beads to 1 penny. Wampum were often strung on thin cords in set amounts worth English equivalents from 1 penny to 5 shillings (60 pennies) in white beads, or 2 pennies to 10 shillings (120 pennies) in purple beads. Wampum became an initial, indispensable link in the commerce between Europe and North America.

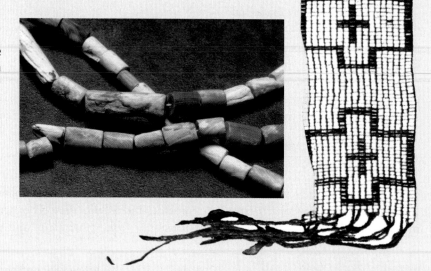

Before Europeans arrived in North America, wampum—which required great skill to make—served primarily ceremonial purposes for native peoples, as in the Four Huron Nations wampum belt presented to Samuel de Champlain in 1611 to signify the alliance of France and the Hurons. But several decades later, after Dutch and English colonists came to rely on it as a medium of exchange and European tools made it easier to manufacture, wampum became far more utilitarian in design and appearance. (Right: Time LifePictures/GettyImages; below: Image #18491 Wampum Beads by Craig Chesek, courtesy the Library, American Museum of Natural History)

because the mainland offered greater wealth for less effort. But the tiny islands attracted other European powers as bases from which to attack Spanish vessels loaded with American gold and silver and as sources of valuable tropical products such as dyes and fruits.

Warfare and Hurricanes

England was the first northern European nation to establish a permanent foothold in the smaller Caribbean islands (the Lesser Antilles), settling on St. Christopher (St. Kitts) in 1624, then on other islands, such as Barbados (1627) and Providence (1630). France colonized Guadeloupe and Martinique by defeating the Caribs, whereas the Dutch easily gained control of tiny St. Eustatius (strategically located near St. Kitts). Along with indigenous inhabitants, Europeans worried about conflicts with Spaniards and each other. Many colonies changed hands during the seventeenth century: the English drove the Spanish out of Jamaica in 1655, and the French soon assumed over half of Hispaniola, creating the colony of St. Domingue (modern Haiti).

Great windstorms, called *hurakán* by the Taíno people (hurricanes in English), also posed a danger. Almost every year in late summer one or two islands suffered significant hurricane damage. Survivors expressed awe at the destructive storms, which repeatedly forced them to rebuild and replant.

Sugar Cultivation

Sugar was the main reason Europeans sought control of these imperiled volcanic islands. Europeans loved sugar with its sweet taste and quick energy boost. Sugar entered Europe at approximately the same time as coffee and tea—the stimulating, addictive, and bitter Asian drinks improved by sweetening.

After experimenting with tobacco, cotton, and indigo, English residents of Barbados discovered in the early 1640s that the island's soil and climate were ideal for sugar cane. At the time, sugar came primarily from the Madeiras, the Canaries, São Tomé, and Brazil. Barbadians initially copied the Brazilians' machinery and small-scale production methods, which used servants and slaves. But by the mid-1650s, substantial planters increased the size of their landholdings, built sugar mills, and purchased more laborers.

Sugar remained the most valuable American commodity for more than a century. In the 1700s, sugar grown by slaves in British Jamaica and French St. Domingue dominated the world market. Yet, the future economic importance of the American colonies lay on the mainland, not the Caribbean.

ENGLISH INTEREST IN COLONIZATION

After Raleigh's Roanoke colony failed, it was two decades before the English attempted to settle North America again. When they tried in 1606, they found success using a settlement model unlike those of other European powers. England sent large numbers of men and women to set up agriculturally-based colonies on the mainland. Two major developments prompted approximately 200,000 English people to move to North America in the seventeenth century.

Social and Economic Change

The first was dramatic social and economic change. In the 150 years after 1530, largely as a result of nutritious American crops, England's population doubled. More people competed for food, clothing, and other goods; this led to inflation. Wages also fell as the supply of workers increased. Some English people—especially those with sizable landholdings that could produce food and clothing fibers for the growing population—gained substantially. Others, particularly landless laborers and those with small land holdings, fell into poverty. When landowners raised rents, seized lands that peasants had long used in common (enclosure), or combined small holdings into large units, they forced tenants out. Consequently, the population of cities swelled. London more than tripled in size to 375,000 by 1650.

Landless and homeless people filled the streets. Fearing overcrowding, officials concluded that colonies established in North America could siphon off England's "surplus population." Likewise, many English people hoped to improve their circumstances by migrating to a land-rich, apparently empty continent and its nearby islands. Similarly attracted were younger sons of gentlemen who were excluded from inheriting land by wealthy families' practice of primogeniture, which reserved all real estate for the eldest son.

English Reformation

The sixteenth century also witnessed a religious transformation that eventually led many English dissenters to leave. In 1533 Henry VIII, wanting a male heir and infatuated with Anne Boleyn, sought to annul his twenty-year marriage to Spanish-born queen Catherine of Aragón, despite the birth of a daughter. When the pope refused, Henry founded the Church of England and—with Parliament's concurrence—proclaimed himself its head. English people welcomed the schism, for many disliked the English Catholic Church. Initially, the reformed Church of England differed little from the Catholic Church, but under Henry's daughter Elizabeth I (child of his later marriage to Anne Boleyn), new currents of religious belief affected the English church.

These currents were the Protestant Reformation, led by Martin Luther, a German monk, and John Calvin, a French cleric and lawyer. Challenging the Catholic doctrine that priests were intermediaries between laypeople and God, Luther and Calvin insisted that people could interpret the Bible for themselves. They rejected Catholic rituals and the elaborate church hierarchy. They also asserted that the key to salvation was faith in God, rather than the Catholic combination of faith and good works. Calvin went further, stressing the need for total submission to God's will.

Puritans and Separatists

Elizabeth I tolerated diverse forms of Christianity as long as she was acknowledged as head of the Church of England. During her reign (1558–1603), Calvin's ideas gained influence. By the late sixteenth century, many English Calvinists—those who came to be called Puritans, because they wanted to purify the church, or Separatists, because they wanted to leave it—believed that the English Reformation had not gone far enough. Henry had simplified the church hierarchy; they wanted to abolish it. Henry had subordinated the church to the state; they wanted a church free from political interference. Puritans and Separatists wanted to confine church membership to persons they believed God had selected for salvation before birth.

Paradoxically, a key article of their faith insisted that people could not know if they were "saved" because mortals could not comprehend or affect their predestination to heaven or hell. Thus pious Puritans and Separatists daily confronted serious dilemmas: If one was predestined and could not alter one's fate, why attend church or do good works? They admitted that their judgments as to eligibility for church membership only approximated God's unknowable decisions. And they reasoned that God gave the elect the ability to accept salvation and lead a good life. Therefore, piety and good works could indicate one as saved.

Stuart Monarchs

Elizabeth I's Stuart successors, her cousin James I (1603–1625) and his son Charles I (1625–1649), exhibited less tolerance for Puritans and Separatists. As Scots, they also had little respect for the representative government that developed in England under the Tudors (see Table 2.2). Wealthy landowners in Parliament had grown accustomed to having considerable influence on government policies. But James I publicly declared the divine right of kings, the notion that a monarch's power came from God and that his subjects had a duty to obey him.

TABLE 2.2   Tudor and Stuart Monarchs of England, 1509–1649

Monarch	Reign	Relation to Predecessor
Henry VIII	1509–1547	Son
Edward VI	1547–1553	Son
Mary I	1553–1558	Half-sister
Elizabeth I	1558–1603	Half-sister
James I	1603–1625	Cousin
Charles I	1625–1649	Son

Both James I and Charles I sought to enforce religious conformity. Because Puritans, Separatists, and the remaining English Catholics challenged many important precepts of the English church, the Stuart monarchs authorized the removal of dissenting clergy. In the 1620s and 1630s, some English Puritans, Separatists, and Catholics decided to move to America, where they hoped to practice their religion freely. Some fled to avoid arrest and imprisonment.

THE FOUNDING OF VIRGINIA

The motivation for England's first permanent colony in the Western Hemisphere was, however, economic. A group of merchants and wealthy gentry in 1606 obtained a royal charter for the Virginia Company, organized as a joint-stock company. Such enterprises pooled the resources of many small investors through stock sales, spreading out the risks and typically providing quick returns. But colonies required significant capital and commonly suffered from a shortfall in financing. Although investors anticipated great profits, the joint-stock company, then as later, proved a poor vehicle for establishing colonies.

Jamestown and Tsenacomoco

In 1607 the Virginia Company dispatched 104 men and boys to a region near the Chesapeake Bay called Tsenacomoco by its native inhabitants. In May they established a settlement called Jamestown on a swampy peninsula in a river. Ill equipped for survival, the colonists fell victim to dissension and disease. The gentlemen and soldiers at Jamestown expected to rely on local Indians for food and tribute, but they refused. Moreover, the settlers arrived in the midst of a severe drought (now known to be the worst for 1,700 years), which persisted until 1612.

The weroance (chief) of Tsenacomoco, Powhatan, had inherited the rule over six Algonquian villages and subsequently controlled twenty-five others (see Map 2.1). In late 1607 negotiations with colonial leader Captain John Smith, the weroance tentatively agreed to an alliance with the Englishmen. In exchange for foodstuffs, Powhatan wanted guns, hatchets, and swords which would give him a technological advantage over his people's enemies.

The fragile relationship soon foundered on mutual mistrust. The wereoance relocated his primary village in early 1609 to a place the newcomers could not access easily. Without Powhatan's assistance, the settlement experienced a "starving time" (winter 1609–1610). Many died, and at least one colonist resorted to cannibalism. In spring 1610 the survivors left on a newly arrived ship but en route encountered a new governor, more settlers, and supplies, so they returned to Jamestown. To gain the upper hand, settlers in 1613 kidnapped Powhatan's daughter, Pocahontas. In captivity, she converted to Christianity and married colonist John Rolfe. He had fallen in love, but she probably married him for diplomatic reasons; their union initiated peace between the English and Powatans. Funded by the Virginia Company, she and Rolfe sailed to England to promote the colony. She died at Gravesend in 1616, leaving an infant son who returned to Virginia as a young adult.

Although their royal charter claimed a wider territory, the Jamestown settlers saw their Virginia as corresponding to Tsenacomoco. Beyond that lay the Powhatans' enemies. English people relied on the Powhatans as guides and interpreters in trading with the Powhatans' partners. For more than half a century, settlement in Virginia was confined to Tsenacomoco.

Algonquian and English Cultural Differences

In Tsenacomoco and elsewhere on the North American coast, English settlers and local Algonquians focused on their cultural differences, although both groups similarly held deep religious beliefs, subsisted primarily through agriculture, accepted social and political hierarchy, and observed well-defined gender roles. English men regarded Indian men as lazy because they did not cultivate crops and spent much of their time hunting (a sport, not work, in English eyes). Indian men thought English men effeminate because they did woman's work of cultivation.

Among Algonquians like Powhatans, political power and social status did not pass through the male line, instead flowing through sisters' sons. English gentlemen inherited their position from their father. English political and military leaders tended to rule autocratically, whereas Algonquian leaders (even Powhatan) had limited authority over their people. Accustomed to powerful kings, the English overestimated the chiefs' ability to make treaties that would bind their people.

Furthermore, Algonquians and English had different notions of property ownership. Most Algonquian villages held their land communally. It could not be bought or sold absolutely. English villagers had once used land in common, but in the previous century had become accustomed to individual farms. The English also refused to accept Indians' claims to traditional hunting territories, insisting that only cultivated land could be owned or occupied. Ownership of such "unclaimed" property, the English believed, lay with the English monarchy, in whose name John Cabot had claimed North America in 1497.

In the early years of colonization, English settlers often anticipated living peacefully alongside indigenous peoples, but on English terms. They expected native peoples to adopt English customs and convert to Christianity. They showed little

A comparison of the portrait of Sir Walter Raleigh and his son (left), with that of an Algonquian Indian drawn by John White, from Raleigh's Roanoke expedition (right), shows a dramatic difference in standard dress styles which for many must have symbolized the apparent cultural gap between Europeans and Americans. Yet the fact that both men (and the young boy) were portrayed in similar stances, with arms akimbo, demonstrated that all were high-status individuals. In Europe, only aristocrats were represented in such a domineering pose. (Left: National Portrait Gallery, London; right: © Trustees of the British Museum)

respect for the Indians when English interests were at stake, as demonstrated once settlers found a salable commodity in Virginia.

Tobacco Cultivation

That commodity was tobacco. In 1611 John Rolfe planted seeds of a tobacco strain from the Spanish Caribbean, which was superior to the strain Indians grew. Nine years later, Virginians exported 40,000 pounds of cured leaves, and by the late 1620s shipments jumped to 1.5 million pounds. Escalating demand from Europe and Africa meant high prices and substantial profits. The price later fell sharply and fluctuated annually in response to increasing supply and international competition.

Tobacco cultivation made Virginia prosper and immeasurably altered life for everyone. It required abundant land because a field could produce only about three satisfactory crops before needing to lie fallow for several years to regain its fertility. Thus applicants asked the Virginia Company for large land grants. Virginians established farms some distance from one another along the riverbanks—a settlement pattern convenient for tobacco cultivation but dangerous for defense.

Indian Assaults

Opechancanough, Powhatan's brother and successor, watched the English colonists' expansion and attempts to convert natives to Christianity. Recognizing the danger, he attacked along the James River on March 22, 1622. By day's end, 347 colonists (about one-quarter) lay dead. Only a timely warning from two Christian converts saved Jamestown from destruction.

Reinforced by shipments of men and arms from England, Virginia's settlers repeatedly attacked Opechancanough's villages. A peace treaty was signed in 1632, but in April 1644 the elderly Opechancanough assaulted the invaders one last time; then in 1646, survivors formally subordinated themselves to England.

End of the Virginia Company

The 1622 assault killed the Virginia Company, which remained unprofitable due to internal corruption and the heavy cost of supporting the settlers. Before its demise, the company developed two precedent-setting policies. First, to attract settlers, in 1617 it established the headright system, giving each arrival who paid his or her own way a land grant of 50 acres; those who financed the passage of others received similar headrights. To English farmers who owned little or no land, the headright system offered a powerful incentive to move to Virginia. To wealthy gentry, it promised the possibility of vast agricultural enterprises. Two years later, the company authorized landowning men of major Virginia settlements to elect representatives to an assembly called the House of Burgesses. This was similar to their long-held English right of electing members of Parliament and controlling local governments.

When James I revoked the charter in 1624, transforming Virginia into a royal colony, he continued the headright policy but abolished the assembly. Virginians protested, and by 1629 the House of Burgesses was functioning again. Two decades after the first permanent English settlement in North America, the colonists successfully insisted on governing themselves locally. Thus England's American possessions differed from the autocratic rule in the Spanish, Dutch, and French colonies.

LIFE IN THE CHESAPEAKE

Tobacco quickly became as important in the second English Chesapeake colony: Maryland. Given by Charles I to George Calvert, first Lord Baltimore, as a personal possession (proprietorship), it was settled in 1634. (Virginia and Maryland border the Chesapeake Bay—see Map 2.1—and are referred to collectively as the Chesapeake.) The Calvert family envisioned the colony as a haven for their persecuted fellow Catholics. Cecilius Calvert, second Lord Baltimore, became the first colonizer to offer religious freedom to all Christian settlers, codified in 1649 in Maryland's Act of Religious Toleration.

In everything but religion the two Chesapeake colonies resembled each other. Tobacco planters spread out along the riverbanks because the rivers offered dependable water transportation. Each farm or group of farms had its own wharf where oceangoing vessels could load or discharge cargo.

Demand for Laborers Planting, cultivation, harvesting, and curing tobacco were repetitive, time consuming, and labor intensive. Above all, successful Chesapeake farms required workers, but with their numbers reduced by war and disease, Indians could not supply such needs. Nor were enslaved Africans available: traders could more easily and profitably sell slaves to Caribbean sugar planters. By 1650 barely three blacks, some of them free, lived in Virginia.

Chesapeake tobacco farmers thus looked primarily to England for labor. Because of the headright system (which Maryland adopted in 1640), a tobacco farmer could obtain land and labor by importing English workers. He could use his profits to pay for the passage of more workers and thereby gain more land. Success could even move him into the region's new planter gentry.

Male laborers, along with a few women, immigrated to America as indentured servants; that is, in return for their passage, they contracted to work from four to seven years. Indentured servants accounted for 75 to 85 percent of the approximately 130,000 English immigrants to Virginia and Maryland during the seventeenth century. The rest were young couples with one or two children.

Roughly three-quarters of servants were males aged fifteen to twenty-four; only one in five or six was female. Most young men came from farming or laboring families, often from areas experiencing severe social disruption. Some had moved several times within England before relocating to America. Often they came from the middling ranks—what their contemporaries called the "common sort."

Conditions of Servitude From a distance, America seemed to offer opportunities for advancement unavailable in England. Servants who fulfilled their indenture earned freedom dues consisting of clothes, tools, livestock, casks of corn and tobacco, and sometimes land. Yet servants typically worked six days a week, ten to fourteen hours a day, in sweltering climates. Masters could discipline or sell them, and they faced severe penalties for running away. Laws did offer some protection. Masters were to supply them with sufficient food, clothing, and shelter and not beat them excessively. Cruelly treated servants could seek court assistance, sometimes winning verdicts directing their transfer to more humane masters or release from indenture.

Immigrants first had to survive "seasoning," a bout with disease (probably malaria) that usually occurred during colonists' first Chesapeake summer. They often endured recurrences of malaria, along with dysentery, typhoid fever, and other illnesses. About 40 percent of male servants did not survive to become freedmen. Even men of twenty-two who survived their seasoning could expect to live only about another twenty years.

For those who endured, opportunities were real. Until the late seventeenth century, former servants often became independent farmers (freeholders), living a modest but comfortable existence. But in the 1670s tobacco prices entered a fifty-year period of stagnation and decline, while land grew increasingly scarce and expensive. In 1681 Maryland dropped its requirement that servants receive land with their freedom dues, forcing many freed servants to live as wage laborers or tenant farmers. By 1700 the Chesapeake was no longer a land of opportunity.

Standard of Living

Life in the early Chesapeake was hard. Farmers (and sometimes their wives) toiled in the fields alongside servants. Because hogs needed little tending, Chesapeake households subsisted mainly on pork and corn, a filling but not sufficiently nutritious diet. Families supplemented by eating fish, shellfish, wildfowl, and vegetables they grew, such as lettuce and peas. The difficulty of safely preserving food for winter consumption magnified the health problems caused by epidemic disease.

Few households had more than farm implements, bedding, and basic cooking and eating utensils. Chairs, tables, candles, and knives and forks were luxury items. The ramshackle houses commonly had just one or two rooms. Colonists devoted their income to their farms and imported necessities such as cloth or tools from England.

Chesapeake Families

The predominance of males (see Figure 2.1), the incidence of servitude, and the high mortality rates produced unusual patterns of family life. Female servants normally could not marry while indentured because masters feared pregnancies would deprive them of workers. Many male ex-servants could not marry at all because of the scarcity of women. In contrast, nearly every free Chesapeake woman married, and widows usually remarried within months of a husband's death. Because of high infant mortality and marriages delayed by servitude or broken by death, Chesapeake women commonly reared only one to three healthy children, where English women normally had at least five.

Thus Chesapeake families were few, small, and short lived. In one Virginia county, more than three-quarters of the children had lost at least one parent by age twenty-one. Those children were put to work as soon as possible on the farms of parents, stepparents, or guardians. Their schooling, if any, was haphazard; whether Chesapeake-born children learned to read or write depended largely on whether their parents were literate and took the time to teach them.

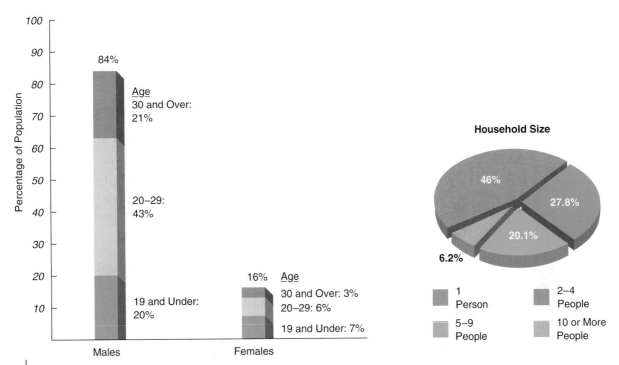

Figure 2.1   Population of Virginia, 1625

The only detailed census taken in the English mainland North American colonies during the seventeenth century was prepared in Virginia in 1625. It listed a total of 1,218 people, constituting 309 households living in 278 dwellings, so some houses contained more than one family. The chart shows, on the left, the proportionate age and gender distribution of the 765 individuals for whom full information was recorded, and on the right, the percentage variation in the sizes of the 309 households. The approximately 42 percent of the residents of the colony who were servants were concentrated in 30 percent of the households. Nearly 70 percent of the households had no servants at all.

(*Source of data:* Robert V. Wells, *The Population of the British Colonies in America Before 1776: A Survey of Census Data* [Princeton: Princeton University Press, 1975], Tables V-5 and V-6 and pp. 165–166)

Chesapeake Politics

Throughout the seventeenth century, immigrants composed a majority of the Chesapeake population. Most members of Virginia's House of Burgesses and Maryland's House of Delegates (established in 1635) were immigrants; they also dominated the governor's council, which simultaneously served as the highest court, part of the legislature, and executive adviser to the governor. A cohesive, native-born ruling elite emerged only in the early eighteenth century.

In the seventeenth-century Chesapeake, most property-owning white males could vote and chose as their legislators (burgesses) the local elites who seemed to be the natural leaders. But because most such men were immigrants lacking strong ties to one another or to the colonies, the assemblies did not create political stability, and were instead contentious.

THE FOUNDING OF NEW ENGLAND

Economic motives also drew men and women to New England, known as North Virginia before Captain John Smith renamed it in 1616. Due to environmental factors and the Puritans' organization of the New England colonies, the northern settlements turned out vastly different than their southern counterparts.

Contrasting Regional Demographic Patterns   In late 1634, royal bureaucrats ordered London's port officials to collect information on travelers departing for the colonies. The records for 1635 document the departure of fifty-three vessels—twenty to Virginia, seventeen to New England, eight to Barbados, five to St. Kitts, two to Bermuda, and one to Providence Island. Almost five thousand people set sail, two thousand for Virginia, about twelve hundred for New England, and the rest for island destinations. Nearly three-fifths were between the ages of fifteen and twenty-four.

But among those bound for New England, such youths constituted less than one-third of the total; nearly 40 percent were older, and another third were younger. Whereas women made up just 14 percent of those going to Virginia, they composed almost 40 percent of the passengers to New England. New England migrants often traveled in family groups, brought more goods and livestock, and often journeyed with others from the same region. Their lives in North America must have been less lonely than those of their southern counterparts.

Contrasting Regional Religious Patterns   Many New England colonists were inspired to migrate by religion. Puritan congregations became key institutions in colonial New England, whereas neither the Church of England nor Catholicism had much impact on the early development of the Chesapeake. Catholic and Anglican bishops in England largely ignored their coreligionists in America, and Chesapeake congregations languished. Not until the 1690s did the Church of England take firmer root in Virginia; by then it also replaced Catholicism as Maryland's established church.

Pious Puritans regularly reassessed the state of their souls. Many devoted themselves to self-examination and Bible study, and families prayed together daily under the guidance of the husband and father. Yet because even the most pious could never be certain that they were among the elect, anxiety troubled Puritans. It lent a special intensity to their beliefs and their concern with proper behavior—their own and that of others.

Separatists   Separatists who thought the Church of England too corrupt to be salvaged became the first religious dissenters to move to New England. In 1609 a Separatist congregation relocated to Leiden, in the Netherlands, where they found religious freedom as well as tolerance for faiths and behaviors they abhorred. Hoping to isolate their families from corrupting influences, these people, who came to be known as Pilgrims, received permission from the Virginia Company to colonize its northern territory.

In September 1620 more than one hundred people, only thirty of them Separatists, sailed from England on the crowded *Mayflower*. In December they landed in

America, farther north than intended. They moved into the empty dwellings of an Indian village whose inhabitants perished in the epidemic of 1616–1618, at a harbor named Plymouth by John Smith in 1616.

Pilgrims and Pokanokets

Because they landed outside the jurisdiction of the Virginia Company, some non-Separatists aboard questioned the authority of the colony's leaders. In response, the Mayflower Compact, which substituted for a charter, was signed in November 1620 on shipboard to establish a Civil Body Politic which bound all settlers to the colony's leaders and laws . Male settlers elected a governor and made all decisions at town meetings. Later, Plymouth created an assembly to which landowning male settlers elected representatives.

The residents of Plymouth were poorly prepared to subsist in the new environment. Only half of the *Mayflower's* passengers lived to spring. The survivors owed much to the Pokanokets (a branch of the Wampanoags), who controlled the area. Pokanoket villages suffered terrible losses in a recent epidemic, so to protect themselves from the powerful Narragansetts of the southern New England coast, the Pokanokets allied themselves with the newcomers. In spring 1621, their leader, Massasoit, agreed to a treaty, and during the colony's first difficult years the Pokanokets supplied settlers with foodstuffs. The colonists also relied on Squanto, an Indian who served as a conduit between native peoples and Europeans. Captured by fishermen in the early 1610s and taken to Europe, Squanto learned to speak English. After returning, he became the settlers' interpreter and taught them about the environment.

Massachusetts Bay Company

Before the 1620s ended, another group of Puritans (Congregationalists, who hoped to reform the Church of England from within) launched the colonial enterprise that would dominate New England. Under the leadership of Charles I, who became king in 1625, the Church of England attempted to suppress Puritan practices. Some Congregationalist merchants, concerned about their prospects in England, sent colonists to Cape Ann (north of Cape Cod) in 1628. The following year the merchants obtained a royal charter, constituting themselves as the Massachusetts Bay Company.

The new joint-stock company quickly attracted Puritans of the "middling sort" who feared they could no longer practice their religion freely in their homeland. The Congregationalist merchants transferred the Massachusetts Bay Company's headquarters to New England. The settlers would then be able to handle their affairs, secular and religious, as they pleased. Like Plymouth settlers, they expected to profit from cod fishing and additionally from timber exports.

Governor John Winthrop

In October 1629, the Massachusetts Bay Company elected John Winthrop, a member of the lesser English gentry, as its governor. (Until his death twenty years later, he served continuously in one leadership post or another.) Winthrop organized the initial segment of the great Puritan migration. In 1630 over one thousand English men and women moved to Massachusetts, most to Boston. By 1643 nearly twenty thousand more followed.

On board the *Arbella,* en route to New England in 1630, John Winthrop preached a sermon, "A Model of Christian Charity," outlining his expectations for the colony. He stressed the communal nature of the endeavor where differences in status or wealth—although retained—would not imply worth. Instead, he explained that God had planned the world so that "every man might have need of other, and from hence they might be all knit more nearly together." In America, Winthrop asserted, "we shall be as a city upon a hill—the eyes of all people are upon us."

Winthrop foresaw in Puritan America a true commonwealth in which each person put the good of the whole ahead of his or her own. Although that society would be characterized by social inequality and hierarchies of status and power, Winthrop hoped its members would live by the precepts of Christian love. Early New England and its Caribbean counterpart, Providence Island, had some bitter quarrels and unchristian behavior, though remarkably, in New England the ideal persisted for generations.

Covenant Ideal

Puritans embraced the doctrine of the covenant, believing God had made a contract with them when they were chosen for their special mission to America. In turn they covenanted with one another to work together. The founders of churches, towns, and colonies in Anglo America often drafted formal documents outlining the principles on which their institutions would be based. The Pilgrims' Mayflower Compact was a covenant as was the Fundamental Orders of Connecticut (1639), which defined the basic law for settlements along the Connecticut River valley in 1636.

The leaders of Massachusetts Bay likewise transformed their company charter into the basis for a covenanted community based on mutual consent. Under pressure from landowning male settlers, they gradually changed the General Court—officially the company's small governing body—into a colonial legislature. They also granted the status of freeman, or voting member, to all property-owning, adult, male church members. Less than two decades after the Puritans arrived in Massachusetts Bay, the colony had a functioning system of self-government composed of a governor and a two-house legislature. The General Court also established a judicial system modeled on England's, although with very different laws.

New England Towns

The colony's method of distributing land furthered the communal ideal. In Massachusetts groups of men—often from the same English village—applied together for grants of land on which to establish towns (novel governance units that did not exist in England). Receiving a grant, these men then determined how the land would be distributed. Understandably, they copied their home villages, first laying out lots for houses and a church. They then gave each family parcels of land around the town center and reserved the best and largest plots for the most distinguished among them, including the minister. People with low status in England received smaller, less desirable allotments. Still, every man and even a few single women obtained land.

Towns developed quickly, evolving in three distinct ways. Some, chiefly isolated agricultural settlements in the interior, tried to sustain Winthrop's vision of community life based on diversified family farms. A second group, the coastal towns like Boston and Salem, became bustling seaports, focal points for trade and places of entry for new immigrants. The third category, commercialized agricultural towns, grew up in the Connecticut River valley, where easy water transportation enabled farmers to sell surplus goods.

Pequot War and Its Aftermath

Migration into the Connecticut valley ended the Puritans' relative freedom from clashes with nearby Indians. Relocating under the direction of their minister, Thomas Hooker, their new settlements were far from other English towns, although the wide river promised ready access to the ocean. The site, however, fell within territory controlled by the powerful Pequots.

The Pequots' dominance stemmed from their role as primary intermediaries in the trade between the New England Algonquians and the Dutch in New Netherland. With the arrival of the English, however, previously subordinate bands could now trade directly with Europeans. Clashes between Pequots and English colonists began earlier, but the establishment of settlements in the Connecticut valley pushed them toward war. After two English traders were killed (not by Pequots), the English raided a Pequot village. The Pequots then attacked the new town of Wethersfield in April 1637, killing nine and capturing two. To retaliate, a Massachusetts Bay expedition attacked and burned the main Pequot town on the Mystic River. The Englishmen and their Narragansett allies slaughtered at least four hundred Pequots, mostly women and children, capturing and enslaving most of the survivors.

For the next four decades, the New England Indians accommodated themselves to the European invasion. They traded with newcomers and sometimes worked for them, but resisted incorporation into English society. Native Americans persisted in using traditional farming methods, which did not employ plows or fences, and women continued to be the chief cultivators. When Indian men learned European trades, they chose those—like broom making, basket weaving, and shingle splitting—that most resembled their customary occupations and ensured independence. The one European practice they adopted was keeping livestock, for domesticated animals provided excellent sources of meat once hunting territories became English farms and wild game disappeared.

Missionary Activities

Most colonists showed little interest in converting the Algonquians to Christianity. Only a few Massachusetts clerics, notably John Eliot and Thomas Mayhew, seriously undertook missionary work. Eliot insisted that converts reside in towns, farm the land in English fashion, assume English names, wear European-style clothing and shoes, cut their hair, and stop observing a wide range of their own customs. He met with little success. Only eleven hundred Indians (out of many thousands) lived in the fourteen "Praying Towns" Eliot established, and just 10 percent were formally baptized.

The missions in New France, however, were more successful. Puritan services lacked Catholicism's beautiful ceremonies and special appeal for women, and Calvinist Puritans could not offer assurances of a heavenly afterlife. Yet on the island of Martha's Vineyard, Thomas Mayhew converted substantial numbers of Indians to Calvinist Christianity, partly by allowing Wampanoag Christians to lead traditional lives and by training their men as ministers.

While conversion often alienated new Christians from their relatives and traditions, many Indians hoped to use the Europeans' religion to cope with the dramatic changes the intruders had wrought. The combination of disease, alcohol, new trading patterns, and loss of territory disrupted customary ways of life. Shamans had little success in restoring tradition. Many Indians must have concluded that the Europeans' ideas could help them survive.

John Winthrop's description of a great smallpox epidemic that swept through southern New England in the early 1630s reveals the relationship among smallpox, conversion to Christianity, and English land claims. "Divers of them, in their sickness, confessed that the Englishmen's God was a good God; and that if they recovered, they would serve him," he noted in his diary in 1633. But by July, Winthrop observed that most Indians within a 300-mile radius of Boston had died of the disease, declaring "the Lord hath cleared our title to what we possess."

LIFE IN NEW ENGLAND

New England's colonizers lived differently than their Algonquian neighbors and Chesapeake counterparts. Algonquian bands usually moved four or five times annually to fully utilize their environment. In spring, women planted the fields, and once crops were established, they gathered wild foods while men hunted and fished. Villagers returned for harvest, separated for fall hunting, and wintered together in a sheltered spot. Women probably determined the timing of these moves because their activities used the environment more intensively than did men's.

English people lived year-round in the same location. Household furnishings resembled those of Chesapeake residents, but New Englanders' diets were somewhat more varied. They replowed fields, believing it was less arduous to employ manure as fertilizer than to clear new fields every few years. Furthermore, they fenced their croplands to keep out the cattle, sheep, and hogs that were their chief sources of meat. Animal crowding more than human crowding caused New Englanders to spread out across the countryside.

New England Families Because Puritans commonly moved in family groups, the age range in early New England was wide; and because many more women migrated to New England than to the tobacco colonies, the population could immediately reproduce itself. Lacking tropical diseases, New England was, after the difficult early years, healthier than the Chesapeake and the mother country. Adult male migrants to the Chesapeake lost about a decade from their English life expectancy of fifty to fifty-five years; their Massachusetts counterparts gained five or more years.

Consequently, New England families were numerous, large, and long lived. Most men married; immigrant women married young (at age twenty, on the average); and marriages lasted longer and produced more children likely to live to maturity. Seventeenth-century New England women raised five to seven children compared to one to three for Chesapeake women.

The presence of many children, combined with the Puritans' stress on reading the Bible, led to concern for the education of youth. That people lived in towns meant small schools could be established; girls and boys were taught basic reading by their parents or a school "dame," and boys could then learn writing and eventually arithmetic and Latin. Whereas early Chesapeake parents commonly died before their children married, New England parents exercised much control over their adult offspring. Young men could not marry without acreage and depended on their fathers for that land. Daughters, too, needed a dowry of household goods from their parents. Parents relied on their children's labor and often seemed reluctant to see them marry. These needs sometimes led to generational conflicts, though children generally obeyed their parents' wishes.

Impact of Religion

Puritans controlled the governments of Massachusetts Bay, Plymouth, Connecticut, and other early northern colonies. Congregationalism was the only officially recognized religion; except in Rhode Island, founded by Massachusetts dissenters, other sects had no freedom of worship. In Massachusetts Bay and New Haven, church membership was a prerequisite for voting. Early colonies taxed residents to build meetinghouses and pay ministers' salaries, but only in New England were provisions of criminal codes based on the Old Testament. Massachusetts's first bodies of law (1641 and 1648) incorporated regulations drawn from scriptures; New Haven, Plymouth, New Hampshire, and Connecticut later copied those codes. Colonists were required to attend religious services, and people who expressed contempt for ministers or their preaching could be punished with fines or whippings.

Strict Puritan codes of conduct meant colonists could be tried for drunkenness, card playing, dancing, or idleness, although frequent prosecutions suggest that New Englanders often enjoyed such activities. Couples who had sex during their engagement (as revealed by the birth of a baby less than nine months after their wedding) were fined and publicly humiliated. Men, and a handful of women, who engaged in behaviors that today would be called homosexual were seen as especially sinful, and some were executed.

In New England, church and state were thus intertwined. Puritans objected to secular interference in religious affairs yet expected the church to influence politics and social life. They also believed that the state was obliged to support and protect their one true church. Although they came to America seeking religious freedom, they saw no contradiction in refusing that freedom to others.

Roger Williams

Roger Williams, a Separatist who migrated to Massachusetts Bay in 1631, quickly ran afoul of Puritan orthodoxy. He told fellow settlers that the king of England had no right to grant them land already occupied by Indians, that church and state should be kept separate, and that Puritans should not impose their beliefs on others. In October 1635, the Massachusetts General Court tried Williams for challenging the validity of the colony's charter and for maintaining that New England Congregationalists had not separated sufficiently from England's corrupt institutions and practices.

Convicted and banished, Williams journeyed in early 1636 to the head of Narragansett Bay, where he founded the town of Providence on land he obtained from the Narragansetts and Wampanoags. Providence and other towns in what became Rhode Island tolerated all religions, including Judaism. Along with Maryland, Williams' tiny colony presaged the religious freedom that eventually became a hallmark of the United States.

Anne Hutchinson

Mistress Anne Hutchinson presented a more sustained challenge to Massachusetts' leaders. A skilled medical practitioner popular with Boston women, she admired John Cotton, a minister who stressed the covenant of grace, or God's free gift of salvation. Most Massachusetts clerics emphasized the need for good works, study, and reflection to receive God's grace. (In its most extreme form, such a doctrine could verge on the covenant of works, or the idea that people could earn their salvation.) Mistress Hutchinson began holding women's meetings in her home. She emphasized the covenant of grace and asserted that the elect could be assured of salvation and communicate directly with God, which lessened the importance of the institutional church.

In November 1637, Puritan officials charged Hutchinson with maligning the colony's ministers by accusing them of preaching the covenant of works. For two days she defended herself, matching scriptural references with John Winthrop. But then Hutchinson boldly declared that God had spoken to her and would curse the Puritans if they harmed her. Excommunicated, she was exiled to Rhode Island in 1638, along with her family and some faithful followers. Several years later, after moving to New Netherland, she and most of her children were killed by Indians.

Authorities in Massachusetts perceived Anne Hutchinson as a threat to religious orthodoxy and traditional gender roles. Puritans believed in the equality before God of all souls, but they considered actual women inferior to men. The magistrates' comments during Hutchinson's trial reveal that they were almost as outraged by her masculine behavior as by her religious beliefs. A minister told her, "You have stepped out of your place, you have rather been a Husband than a Wife and a preacher than a Hearer."

To New England authorities, an orderly society required the submission of wives to husbands as well as the obedience of subjects to rulers and ordinary folk to gentry. English people intended to make many changes by colonizing North America, but not to the gendered division of labor, the assumption of male superiority, or the maintenance of social hierarchies.

Blue Laws

Seventeenth-century New England colonies enacted statutes, now referred to as *blue laws*, preventing residents from working or engaging in recreation on Sundays, when they were supposed to attend church. Colonists were fined for plowing their fields, pursuing wandering livestock, drinking in taverns, or playing such games as shuffleboard. More harshly treated were thieves who took advantage of church attendance to break into homes.

The term *blue laws* appears to have been coined by the Reverend Samuel Peters, a loyalist, in his *General History of Connecticut*, published in 1781. Peters used *blue laws* to refer to Connecticut's early legal code in general, defining it as "bloody Laws; for they were all sanctified with whippings, cutting off the ears, burning the tongue, and death." Eventually, *blue laws* acquired its current meaning of legislation regulating behavior on Sundays. States continued to enact such statutes throughout the nineteenth century, but as in the colonial period, enforcement varied.

Still, they remained on the books. A 1961 Supreme Court decision, *McGowan v. Maryland*, upheld that state's law restricting what could be sold on Sundays because of its secular purpose—promoting the "health, safety, recreation, and general well-being" of the populace. Whereas colonial legislators were attempting to prevent Sunday work, modern Americans seem more concerned about halting Sunday shopping. Not until 1991 did the last state (North Dakota) repeal a law requiring stores to be closed on Sundays, and only in May 2003 did New York State remove its ban on Sunday liquor sales.

Today a website, *www.BlueLaws.net*, urges readers to join its "Keep Sunday Special Campaign," arguing that Sunday closing laws are "pro-family, pro-environment and pro-labor." Its plea to "restore the observance of the Lord's Day in our nation" shows the continuing legacy of the seventeenth century.

Summary

By the mid-seventeenth century, Europeans came to North America and the Caribbean to stay and indelibly altered their lives and those of native peoples. Europeans killed Indians with weapons and diseases and had varying success in converting them to Christianity. Contacts with indigenous peoples taught Europeans to eat new foods and recognize—however reluctantly—other cultural patterns. The survival and prosperity of many European colonies depended heavily on the cultivation of American crops (maize and tobacco) and an Asian crop (sugar), thus attesting to the importance of post-Columbian ecological exchange.

To a greater extent than their European counterparts, the English transferred the society and politics of their homeland to a new environment. Their sheer numbers, coupled with their need for vast quantities of land for cultivating crops and raising livestock, inevitably led to conflict with Indian neighbors. New England and the Chesapeake differed in the sex ratio and age range of their immigrant populations, their diverse economies, their settlement patterns, and the impact of their religious beliefs. Yet their expansions engendered similar internal and external conflicts. Both regions would become embroiled in increasingly fierce rivalries besetting the European powers that would affect Americans of all races until after the mid-eighteenth century, when the Anglo-American colonies won their independence.

Chapter Review

SPANISH, FRENCH, AND DUTCH NORTH AMERICA

How did the Jesuits' treatment of Native Americans differ from that of explorers and other settlers?

Spanish and other settlers typically sought to dominate the native populations, controlling their labor and often enslaving them, sometimes through the use of violence. The French Jesuits who settled New France (Montreal and Quebec) tried to convert Indians to Christianity while not insisting that they abandon their traditions. These missionaries learned Indian languages and lived among potential converts, and Indians' desire for literacy made them willing to listen to spiritual messages. And while they tried to undermine the authority of shamans and encouraged converts to abandon premarital sex and easy divorce, Jesuits also recognized the compatibility of some aspects of native culture with Christianity. This somewhat flexible approach, combined with their lack of interest in land or tribute, made at least some Indians receptive to conversion.

THE CARIBBEAN

What made the Caribbean islands initially desirable for colonization?

While Spain focused on larger islands that offered the potential for greater wealth with less effort, other countries explored smaller islands, initially as a base to attack Spanish vessels transporting gold, silver, and other valuable commodities from the Americas. The second reason for settling on the smaller islands was sugar cultivation. Sugar was in high demand in Europe, particularly since the sweetener improved the taste of coffee and tea and provided a sweet, yet quick, energy boost. Soil on volcanic islands such as Barbados proved ideal for sugar cane and later mills added an additional, and British-controlled, source of sugar.

ENGLISH INTEREST IN COLONIZATION

What two developments prompted England to make a second attempt at colonization in the early seventeenth century?

First, dramatic population growth in England, partly as a result of more nutritious American food exports, increased competition for food, clothing, shelter, and jobs. That, in turn, spurred inflation, reduced wages, and made upward mobility increasingly impossible for those at the lower end of the socioeconomic spectrum. Officials looked to the prospect of colonizing North America as a way to reduce England's population and related woes. Second, the Protestant Reformation sparked new forms of Christianity that diverged from the Church of England, and while Elizabeth I tolerated such dissent, her successors, the Stuart monarchs, did not. Ultimately, seeking to practice freely their religious beliefs (and avoid imprisonment), some English Puritans, Separatists, and Catholics fled to America.

THE FOUNDING OF VIRGINIA

How did English cultural traditions clash with those of Native Americans in Virginia?

While both were deeply religious, Englishmen considered Indian men lazy because they let women cultivate crops while they hunted, which the British regarded as a sport and not work. Native Americans thought Englishmen were effeminate because they farmed, which Indians considered women's work. Political power in Algonquian culture passed through sisters' sons rather through the father, as was the custom in England. Because the British were used to powerful kings, they assumed Indian chiefs held the same autocratic control and ability to make treaties, where in reality, they had limited authority. Most importantly, where the English believed in individual farms and private land ownership, the Algonquians held land communally as a village.

LIFE IN THE CHESAPEAKE

What were the myths and realities of indentured servitude in the Chesapeake?

Chesapeake tobacco farmers filled their extensive demand for labor with indentured servants from England—typically young men who worked for four to seven years in exchange for their passage. Indentured servitude for these young men represented a slim chance at upward mobility. Most gained "freedom dues" at the completion of their contract, including clothes, tools, livestock, casks of corn and tobacco, and sometimes land. But they worked long hours, six or seven days a week, doing intense physical labor in hot climates. Masters could discipline or sell them, and if indentured servants fled, they faced extreme penalties, although some did win verdicts against cruel masters calling for their transfer or release from indenture. Exposure to disease combined with intense labor so that only 60 percent of indentured men lived to become freedmen, and many who did, lived only another twenty years.

THE FOUNDING OF NEW ENGLAND

What were John Winthrop's expectations for the Massachusetts Bay Company colony?

First elected governor in 1629, John Winthrop was instrumental in organizing the first Puritan migration from England to the colony. While in transit, he delivered his famous sermon, calling for the new colony to serve as a moral and spiritual example for the rest of the world, a "city upon a hill." He urged colonists to mediate status differences and unite around their communal interests. He envisioned a true commonwealth, where people put the common good ahead of their own and be governed by Christian brotherhood.

LIFE IN NEW ENGLAND

What was the impact of religion on colonial life in New England?

Although Puritans fled England to practice their faith freely, in New England, they offered no such freedom of worship to those who dissented from their beliefs.

Puritans controlled the government in many early northern colonies and made Congregationalism the only recognized religion, with church membership and voting rights linked. Colonists were punished with fines or whippings for missing religious services. In addition, strict behavioral codes meant colonists were tried for drunkenness, card playing, dancing, or idleness. Couples who had sex during their engagement (as revealed by the birth of a baby less than nine months after their wedding) were fined and publicly humiliated. People who behaved in ways that today would be called homosexual were sometimes executed. Separatists such as Roger Williams or Anne Hutchinson, who challenged Puritan orthodoxy, were tried and banished—Williams founded Providence based on religious tolerance and was subsequently joined by Hutchinson. Beyond challenging church authority, Hutchinson violated gender norms by preaching.

SUGGESTIONS FOR FURTHER READING

Virginia DeJohn Anderson, *Creatures of Empire: How Domestic Animals Transformed Early America* (2004)

Richard S. Dunn, *Sugar and Slaves: The Rise of the Planter Class in the English West Indies, 1624–1713* (1972)

Alison Games, *Migration and the Origins of the English Atlantic World* (1999)

David D. Hall, *Worlds of Wonder, Days of Judgment: Popular Religious Belief in Early New England* (1989)

Karen O. Kupperman, *Indians & English: Facing off in Early America* (2000)

Mary Beth Norton, *Founding Mothers & Fathers: Gendered Power and the Forming of American Society* (1996)

Helen C. Rountree, *Pocahontas, Powhatan, Opechancanough: Three Indian Lives Changed by Jamestown* (2005)

David J. Weber, *The Spanish Frontier in North America* (1992)

Keith Wrightson, *English Society, 1580–1680* (1982)

CHAPTER 3

North America in the Atlantic World

CHAPTER OUTLINE

The Growth of Anglo-American Settlements

A Decade of Imperial Crises: The 1670s

The Atlantic Trading System

Slavery in North America and the Caribbean

Imperial Reorganization and the Witchcraft Crisis

LINKS TO THE WORLD:
Exotic Beverages

LEGACY FOR A PEOPLE AND A NATION: Americans of African Descent

Summary

She was starving. Offered a piece of boiled horse's foot by a compassionate neighbor, the slave gulped it down and seized another piece from a child. Later, she recalled, "Thus the Lord made that pleasant refreshing, which another time would have been an abomination." But Mary Rowlandson's mistress then threatened to kill her, saying she disgraced the household by begging for food.

What brought the wife of the Reverend Joseph Rowlandson of Lancaster, Massachusetts, to such distress? On February 10, 1676, in the conflict that New Englanders called King Philip's War, a force of Wampanoags, Narragansetts, and Nipmucks killed fourteen townspeople (including her daughter) and captured twenty-three others. Carried away, she endured their hardships in the wintry countryside of western Massachusetts and southern New Hampshire. She became the slave of Quinnapin, a Narragansett sachem, and his three wives, one of whom, Weetamoo, was herself a sachem and her mistress. Both were eventually killed by the colonists after the death of their leader, the Wampanoag known as King Philip, in August 1676. Months earlier, in May, Mary Rowlandson had been ransomed for £20—roughly equivalent to $500 today.

Mary Rowlandson's famous 1682 narrative, *The Sovereignty and Goodness of God,* exposes the sufferings she shared with her captors and her inability to understanding or sympathize with them. When Weetamoo's baby died, she remarked coldly that "there was one benefit in it, that there was more room" in the wigwam. Her narrative illustrates the contentious relationships between Anglo New Englanders and their native neighbors.

Much of the tension was related to the mainland colonies' involvement in a growing international network. North America, like England, was becoming embedded in a worldwide matrix

This icon will direct you to interactive activities and study materials on A People And A Nation, Brief Edition
website: **www.cengage.com/history/norton/ peoplenationbrief8e**

Chronology

1642–46	English Civil War occurs.	**1688–89**	James II is deposed in the Glorious Revolution. William and Mary ascend to the throne.
1649	Charles I is executed.	**1689**	Glorious Revolution in America: Massachusetts, New York, and Maryland overthrow colonial governors.
1651	First Navigation Act is passed to regulate colonial trade.		
1660	Stuarts are restored to throne. Charles II becomes king.	**1688–99**	King William's War is fought on northern New England frontier.
1663	Carolina is chartered.	**1691**	New Massachusetts charter is issued.
1664	English conquer New Netherland. New York is founded. New Jersey is established.	**1692**	Witchcraft crisis in Salem: nineteen people are hanged.
1670s	Marquette, Jolliet, and La Salle explore the Great Lakes and Mississippi valley for France.	**1696**	Board of Trade and Plantations is established to coordinate English colonial administration. Vice-admiralty courts are established in America.
1675–76	Bacon's Rebellion disrupts Virginia government. Jamestown is destroyed.	**1701**	Iroquois adopt neutrality policy toward France and England.
1675–78	King Philip's War devastates New England.	**1702–13**	Queen Anne's War is fought by French and English.
1680–1700	The Pueblo revolt temporarily drives the Spaniards from New Mexico.		
1681	Pennsylvania is chartered.	**1711–13**	Tuscarora War (North Carolina) leads to capture or migration of most Tuscaroras.
1685	James II becomes king.	**1715**	Yamasee War nearly destroys South Carolina.
1686–88	Dominion of New England is established, superseding all charters of colonies from Maine to New Jersey.	**1718**	New Orleans is founded in French Louisiana.

of trade and warfare. Oceangoing vessels now crisscrossed the globe, carrying European goods to America and Africa, Caribbean sugar to New England and Europe, Africans to the Americas, and New England fish and wood products—and occasionally Indian slaves—to the Caribbean. North American colonies expanded their territorial claims and diversified their economies after the mid-seventeenth century.

Three developments shaped life in mainland English colonies between 1640 and 1720: escalating conflicts with Indians and other European colonies, the expansion of slavery, and changes in the colonies' political and economic relationships with England.

The explosive growth of the slave trade significantly altered the Anglo-American economy. Mariners and ship owners transporting human cargoes profited handsomely, as did planters who could afford slaves. Initially the slave trade involved Indians and already enslaved Africans from the Caribbean, but it soon focused on cargoes from Africa. The large influx of West African slaves expanded agricultural productivity, fueled the international trading system, and dramatically reshaped colonial society.

The burgeoning North American economy attracted new attention from colonial administrators. After the Stuarts were restored to the throne in1660 (having lost it briefly because of the English Civil War), London bureaucrats attempted to supervise American settlements to ensure the mother country benefited from their economic growth.

As English settlements expanded, they came into violent conflict with powerful Indian nations, the Dutch, the Spanish, and the French. All European colonies confronted significant crises during the 1670s. By 1720, war—between Europeans and Indians, among Europeans, and among Indians allied with colonial powers—had become a familiar feature of American life. No longer isolated, the people and products of the North American colonies had become integral to the world trading system and enmeshed in its conflicts.

- **What were the consequences of the transatlantic slave trade in North America and Africa?**
- **How did English policy toward the colonies change from 1650 to 1720?**
- **What were the causes and results of new friction between Europeans and native peoples?**

THE GROWTH OF ANGLO-AMERICAN SETTLEMENTS

Between 1642 and 1646 civil war between supporters of King Charles I and the Puritan-dominated Parliament engulfed England. Parliament triumphed, leading to the execution of the king in 1649 and interim rule by the parliamentary army's leader, Oliver Cromwell, during the so-called Commonwealth period. But after Cromwell's death, Parliament decided to restore the monarchy if Charles I's son agreed to restrictions on his authority (see Table 3.1). Assuming the throne in 1660, Charles II rewarded nobles and other supporters with huge land tracts on the North American mainland, thereby establishing six of the thirteen polities that would form the American nation: New York, New Jersey, Pennsylvania (including Delaware), and North and South Carolina (see Map 3.1). These became known as the Restoration colonies. All were proprietorships, where one man or several men owned the soil and controlled the government.

TABLE 3.1   Restored Stuart Monarchs of England, 1660–1714

Monarch Reign	Relation to Predecessor
Charles II 1660–1685	Son
James II 1685–1688	Brother
Mary 1688–1694	Daughter
William 1688–1702	Son-in-law
Anne 1702–1714	Sister, sister-in-law

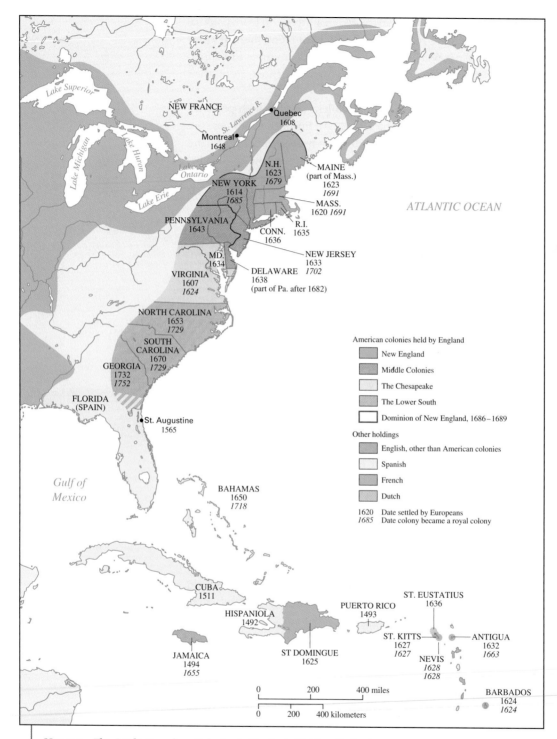

Map 3.1   The Anglo-American Colonies in the Early Eighteenth Century

By the early eighteenth century, the English colonies nominally dominated the Atlantic coastline of North America. But the colonies' formal boundary lines are deceiving because the western reaches of each colony were still largely unfamiliar to Europeans and because much of the land was still inhabited by Native Americans.

TABLE 3.2   **The Founding of English Colonies in North America, 1664–1681**

Colony	Founder(s)	Date	Basis of Economy
New York (formerly New Netherland)	James, duke of York	1664	Farming, fur trading
New Jersey	Sir George Carteret, John Lord Berkeley	1664	Farming
North Carolina	Carolina proprietors	1665	Tobacco, forest products
South Carolina	Carolina proprietors	1670	Rice, indigo
Pennsylvania (incl. Delaware)	William Penn	1681	Farming

New York

In 1664 Charles II gave his brother James, the duke of York, the region between the Connecticut and Delaware Rivers, including the Hudson valley and Long Island. That the Dutch had settled there mattered little; the English and the Dutch were engaged in sporadic warfare. In August James's warships anchored off Manhattan Island, demanding and achieving New Netherland's surrender. Although in 1672 the Netherlands briefly retook the colony, the Dutch permanently ceded it in 1674.

In 1664 a significant minority of English people (mostly Puritans who had come to Long Island from New England) already lived in the territory James renamed New York, along with the Dutch, Indians, Africans, Germans, Scandinavians, and other Europeans (see Table 3.2). The Dutch West India Company had imported slaves, intending some for resale in the Chesapeake, although many remained in New Netherland as laborers. At the time of the English conquest, almost one-fifth of Manhattan's approximately fifteen hundred inhabitants were of African descent.

Recognizing the population's diversity, James's representatives moved cautiously in establishing English authority. The Duke's Laws, a 1665 legal code, applied solely to English settlements on Long Island and was only later extended to the entire colony. James initially maintained Dutch local government, confirmed Dutch land titles, and allowed Dutch residents to maintain customary legal practices. Each town could decide which church (Dutch Reformed, Congregational, or Church of England) to support with its taxes. Much to the dismay of English residents, there was no provision for a representative assembly. James distrusted legislative bodies, and not until 1683 did he agree to an elected legislature. The English takeover thus had little immediate effect. The colony's population barely reached eighteen thousand by 1698. Until the 1720s, New York City remained a commercial backwater within Boston's orbit.

New Jersey

In 1664, the duke of York regranted the land between the Hudson and Delaware Rivers—East and West Jersey—to his friends Sir George Carteret and John Lord Berkeley. That left the duke's own colony hemmed in between Connecticut to the east and the Jerseys to the west and south, hindering its economic growth. He failed to promote migration, while the Jersey proprietors quickly attracted settlers by promising generous land grants, limited freedom of religion, and—without the Crown's authorization—a representative assembly. Many Puritan New Englanders migrated to the Jerseys, along with Barbadians and Dutch New Yorkers. By 1726, New Jersey had 32,500 inhabitants, only 8,000 fewer than New York.

Within twenty years, the Society of Friends, also called Quakers, purchased Carteret's share (West Jersey) and portions of Berkeley's (East Jersey). Rejecting religious hierarchies, Quakers believed that anyone could be saved by receiving God's "inner light" and that all people were equal in God's sight. With no formally trained clergy, this new, small sect allowed men and women to speak in meetings or become a "public Friend" and spread God's word. Quakers proselytized throughout the Atlantic world in the 1650s. Authorities rejected their radical egalitarianism, and Quakers encountered persecution everywhere.

Pennsylvania

In 1681, Charles II granted the region between Maryland and New York to his friend William Penn, a prominent Quaker. Penn held the colony as a personal proprietorship, one that earned profits for his descendants until the American Revolution. Penn also saw his province as a haven for persecuted coreligionists. He offered land to settlers on liberal terms, promised religious toleration (although only Christians could vote), guaranteed English liberties, and pledged to establish a representative assembly. He also publicized the availability of land in Pennsylvania through promotional tracts in German, French, and Dutch.

By mid-1683, more than three thousand people—among them Welsh, Irish, Dutch, and Germans—had already moved to Pennsylvania, and within five years the population reached twelve thousand. Philadelphia, situated on the navigable Delaware River, drew merchants and artisans from throughout the English-speaking world. Quakers seeking religious freedom arrived from mainland and Caribbean colonies, bringing experience on American soil and trade connections. Pennsylvania's fertile lands enabled residents to export surplus flour and other foodstuffs to the West Indies. Philadelphia acquired more than two thousand citizens and challenged Boston's commercial dominance.

Penn attempted to treat native peoples fairly. He learned to speak the language of the Delawares (or Lenapes), from whom he bought land to sell to European settlers. Penn also established strict trade regulations and forbade the sale of alcohol to Indians. His policies attracted native peoples who moved to Pennsylvania in the late seventeenth century to escape clashes with English colonists in Maryland, Virginia, and North Carolina. Ironically, the same toleration that attracted Native Americans also brought non-Quaker Europeans—notably the Scots-Irish, Germans, and Swiss— who showed little respect for Indian claims to the soil.

Carolina

Granted by Charles II in 1663, the southernmost proprietary colony stretched from the southern boundary of Virginia to Spanish Florida. Strategically, a successful English settlement there would prevent Spaniards from pushing farther north. The fertile, semitropical land also promised to produce such exotic and valuable commodities as figs, olives, wines, and silk. The proprietors named their new province Carolina in honor of Charles. The Fundamental Constitutions of Carolina, which they asked political philosopher John Locke to draft, outlined a colony governed by landholding aristocrats and characterized by a structured distribution of political and economic power.

Carolina quickly developed two distinct population centers, which in 1729 split into separate colonies under royal rule. Virginia planters settled the Albemarle region that became North Carolina and established a society like their own, based on cultivating tobacco and exporting forest products. The other population center, which eventually formed South Carolina, developed at Charles Town, founded in 1670. Many of its early residents were sugar planters from overcrowded Barbados who expected to reestablish plantation agriculture and escape hurricanes. They were disappointed: sugar would not grow in Carolina, and they experienced a destructive hurricane in 1686.

The settlers raised corn and cattle, which they sold to Caribbean planters. They also depended on trade with nearby Indians for commodities they could sell elsewhere, mostly deerskins and Indian slaves, which were shipped to the Caribbean and northern colonies. Indians sold captured enemies to the English settlers. During the first decade of the eighteenth century, South Carolina exported approximately 54,000 deerskins annually, which peaked at 160,000 a year. Before 1715, Carolinians exported 30,000 to 50,000 Indian slaves.

The Chesapeake

The English Civil War retarded the development of the earlier English settlements. Struggles between supporters of the king and Parliament caused military clashes in Maryland and political upheavals in Virginia. Once the war ended and immigration resumed, the colonies expanded again. Some settlers, especially those on the Virginia coast and southern border, raised grain, livestock, and flax to be sold to English and Dutch merchants. Tobacco growers began importing increasing numbers of English indentured servants as farms grew into plantations. No longer fearing Indian attacks after the defeat of the Powhatan Confederacy in 1646, they eagerly sought to enlarge their landholdings.

Chesapeake tobacco planters also started to acquire slaves. Most came from a population that historian Ira Berlin has termed *Atlantic creoles*—people (perhaps of mixed race) who came from other European Atlantic settlements, primarily Iberian outposts. Not all Atlantic creoles who came to the Chesapeake were bondspeople; some were free or indentured. With their arrival, the Chesapeake became a society with slaves, where slavery coexisted with other labor systems.

New England

In New England, migration ceased after the English Civil War began in 1642. While Puritans were challenging the king and then governing England as a commonwealth, they had little incentive to leave their homeland. Yet the Puritan colonies' population grew dramatically by natural increase. By the 1670s, New England's population more than tripled to approximately seventy thousand, putting pressure on available land. Colonial settlement spread into the Massachusetts and Connecticut interior, and many later generations migrated—north to New Hampshire or Maine, south to New York or New Jersey, west beyond the Connecticut River—to find sufficient farmland. Others learned such skills as blacksmithing or carpentry to support themselves in the growing towns.

Those who remained in the small, densely populated older New England communities experienced witchcraft accusations and trials after 1650. The accused allies of the Devil were thought to harness spirits for good or evil. A witch might engage in fortunetelling, prepare healing potions or charms, or cause the death of a child or animal. Only New England witnessed many witch trials (about one hundred before 1690). Most of the accused were middle-aged women who had angered their neighbors. Historians have concluded that daily interactions in close-knit communities fostered quarrels that led some colonists to believe others had diabolically caused certain misfortunes. Even so, judges and juries were skeptical: only a few of the accused were convicted, and fewer were executed.

Colonial Political Structures

By the last quarter of the seventeenth century, almost all Anglo-American colonies had well-established political and judicial structures. In New England, property-holding men or the legislature elected the governors; in other regions, the king or proprietor appointed them. A council, elected or appointed, advised the governor, as well as serving as the upper legislative house and the appeals court. Each colony also had local justices of the peace and county courts, and most jurisdictions elected local governing bodies.

A DECADE OF IMPERIAL CRISES: THE 1670S

Between 1670 and 1680, New France, New Mexico, New England, and Virginia experienced bitter conflicts as their interests collided with those of America's original inhabitants.

New France and the Iroquois

In the mid-1670s Louis de Buade de Frontenac, the governor-general of Canada, decided to expand New France south and westward to establish a trade route to Mexico and gain control of the valuable fur trade. Accordingly, he encouraged the explorations of Father Jacques Marquette, Louis Jolliet, and René-Robert Cavelier de La Salle in the Great Lakes and Mississippi valley regions. His goal led to conflict with the powerful Iroquois Confederacy, composed of five Indian nations—the Mohawks, Oneidas, Onondagas, Cayugas, and Senecas. (In 1722 the Tuscaroras became the sixth.)

Under the terms of a unique defensive alliance forged early in the sixteenth century, a representative council made war decisions for the entire Iroquois Confederacy. Before the arrival of Europeans, the Iroquois waged wars primarily for captives to replenish their population. Foreigners brought ravaging disease by 1633, intensifying the need for captives. Simultaneously, Europeans inspired a new economic motive for warfare: the desire to dominate the fur trade and gain unimpeded access to European goods. The war with the Hurons in the 1640s initiated a series of conflicts with other Indians known as the Beaver Wars, in which the Iroquois fought to control the lucrative peltry trade. Iroquois did not trap beaver; instead, they raided other villages for pelts or attacked Indians carrying furs to European outposts. The

Iroquois then traded that booty for European-made blankets, knives, guns, alcohol, and other items.

In the mid-1670s, and for the next twenty years, the French repeatedly attacked Iroquois villages, seeing them as a threat to France's plans to trade with western Indians. Depleted by constant warfare, the confederacy in 1701 negotiated a neutrality treaty with France and other Indians. For the next half-century the Iroquois maintained their power through trade and diplomacy, especially focusing on a covenant chain alliance with New York.

French Expansion

The wars against the Iroquois in the 1670s were crucial to French Canada's plan to penetrate the North American heartland. Unlike the Spaniards, French adventurers did not subjugate the Indians they encountered or initially claim large territories. Still, when France decided to strengthen its presence near the Gulf of Mexico by founding New Orleans in 1718, the Mississippi posts became the glue of empire. *Coureurs de bois* (literally, "forest runners") used the interior waterways to carry French goods between Quebec and Louisiana to outposts such as Michilimackinac (at the junction of Lakes Michigan and Huron), Kaskaskia (in present-day Illinois), and Fort Rosalie (Natchez) on the lower Mississippi River.

Indians, such as the Choctaws, Chickasaws, and Osages, gained access to valuable trade goods by tolerating the minimal European presence. The largest French settlements in the region, known as *le pays de Illinois* ("the Illinois country"), barely totaled three thousand in population. Located south of modern St. Louis and north of Fort Chartres, the settlements produced wheat for export to New Orleans. The shortage of European women led to interracial unions between French men and Indian women and created a mixed-race people known as *metís*.

Pueblo Peoples and Spaniards

In New Mexico, too, events of the 1670s led to a crisis with long-term consequences. Under Spanish domination, Pueblo peoples added Christianity to their beliefs while retaining traditional rituals. But as decades passed, Franciscans adopted brutal and violent tactics to erase the native religion. Priests and colonists who held *encomiendas* also placed heavy labor demands on the population. In 1680, the Pueblos revolted under the leadership of Popé, a respected shaman, driving the Spaniards out of New Mexico. Although Spain restored its authority by 1700, Spanish governors now stressed cooperation with native peoples, no longer violating their cultural integrity or enslaving them. The Pueblo revolt constituted the most successful and longest-sustained Indian resistance in colonial North America.

Contemporary engraving of John Verelst's 1710 portrait of the Mohawk chief known as Hendrick to Europeans (his Indian name was rendered as "Dyionoagon" or "Tee Yee Neen Ho Ga Row"). Hendrick and three other Iroquois leaders visited London in 1710, symbolically cementing the Covenant Chain negotiated in 1677. His primarily European dress and the wampum belt in his hand accentuate his identity as a cross-cultural diplomatic emissary.   (Anne S.K. Brown Military Collection, Brown University Library)

When Spaniards expanded their territorial claims to the east and north, they followed the strategy they used in New Mexico, establishing military outposts (presidios) and Franciscan missions. The army maintained order among the subject Indians—to protect them from attack and ensure the availability of their labor—and guarded the boundaries of New Spain from possible incursions, especially by the French. The friars concentrated on conversions and allowed religious syncretism. By the late eighteenth century, Spain claimed a vast territory that stretched from California (first colonized in 1769 to prevent Russian sea-otter trappers from taking over the region) through Texas (settled after 1700) to the Gulf Coast. Throughout that region, the Spanish presence consisted of a mixture of missions and presidios dotting the countryside, sometimes at considerable distances from one another.

King Philip's War

In the 1670s in the densely settled English colonies, hostilities developed as the expanding Anglo-American population sought more land. In both New England and Virginia settlers began to encroach on territories that belonged to Native Americans.

By the early 1670s the growing settlements in southern New England surrounded Wampanoag ancestral lands on Narragansett Bay. The local chief, Metacom, or King Philip, was troubled by territorial loss and the impact of European culture and Christianity on his people. Philip led attacks on nearby communities in June 1675. Other Algonquian peoples, among them Nipmucks and Narragansetts, joined King Philip's forces. In the fall, they attacked settlements in the northern Connecticut River valley, and the war spread to Maine when the Abenakis joined the conflict. In early 1676 the Indian allies devastated villages like Lancaster, where they captured Mary Rowlandson and others, and attacked Plymouth and Providence; later, Abenaki assaults forced the abandonment of most Maine settlements. Altogether, the alliance wholly or partially destroyed twenty-seven of ninety-two towns and attacked forty others, pushing the line of English settlement back toward the east and south.

In summer 1676, the Indian coalition ran short of food and ammunition. On June 12, the Mohawks—ancient Iroquois enemies of New England Algonquians—devastated a major Wampanoag encampment while most of the warriors were attacking an English town. After King Philip was killed that August, the southern alliance crumbled. Fighting continued on the Maine frontier for another two years until the English and Abenakis agreed to end the conflict in 1678.

In addition to the Wampanoags, Nipmucks, Narragansetts, and Abenakis who were captured and sold into slavery, still more died of starvation and disease. New Englanders had broken the power of the southern coastal tribes. Thereafter southern Indians lived in small clusters, subordinated to the colonists and often working as servants or sailors. Only on Martha's Vineyard did Christian Wampanoags preserve their cultural identity.

The settlers may have won King Philip's War, but an estimated one-tenth of the adult male population was killed or wounded. Proportional to population, it was the most costly conflict in American history. New Englanders did not fully rebuild abandoned interior towns for thirty years, and not until the American Revolution did the region's per capita income reach pre-1675 levels.

Bacon's Rebellion

In the early 1670s, ex-servants unable to acquire land avidly eyed the territory reserved by treaty for Virginia's Indians. Governor William Berkeley resisted starting a war, and dissatisfied colonists rallied behind a recent immigrant, the gentleman Nathaniel Bacon, who shared their frustrations about the lack of available land. Using as a pretext the July 1675 killing of an indentured servant by Doeg Indians, settlers attacked the Doegs and the Susquehannocks, a more powerful nation. In retaliation, Susquehannocks raided outlying farms early in 1676.

The governor outlawed Bacon and his men; the rebels held Berkeley hostage until they won authorization to attack the Indians. As the chaotic summer of 1676 wore on, Bacon alternately pursued Indians and battled the governor. In September Bacon's forces burned Jamestown to the ground. But when Bacon died of dysentery the following month, the rebellion collapsed. Even so, in 1677 a new treaty opened much of the disputed territory to settlement. The end of Bacon's Rebellion pushed most of Virginia's Indians west beyond the Appalachians.

THE ATLANTIC TRADING SYSTEM

In the 1670s and 1680s, the Chesapeake's prosperity rested on tobacco, which required an ample labor supply. But fewer English men and women proved willing to indenture themselves. Population pressures had eased in England, and the Restoration colonies gave migrants other settlement options. Furthermore, fluctuating tobacco prices and the scarcity of land made the Chesapeake less appealing. Wealthy Chesapeake tobacco growers found the answer to their labor problem in the Caribbean sugar islands, where Dutch, French, English, and Spanish planters were accustomed to purchasing African slaves.

Why African Slavery?

Slavery had been practiced in Europe and Islamic lands for centuries. European Christians justified enslaving heathen peoples, especially those of exotic origin, in religious terms, arguing it might lead to their conversion. Muslims, too, enslaved infidels and imported tens of thousands of black African bondspeople into North Africa and the Middle East. Others believed that wartime prisoners could be enslaved. Consequently, when Portuguese mariners encountered African societies holding slaves, they purchased bondspeople. Starting in the 1440s, Portugal imported large numbers of slaves into the Iberian Peninsula; by 1500, enslaved Africans composed about one-tenth of the population of Lisbon, Portugal, and Seville, Spain. In 1555 some were taken to England, and soon residents of London and Bristol became accustomed to black slaves on the streets.

Iberians exported African slavery to New Spain and Brazil. Because the Catholic Church prevented the formal enslavement of Indians in those domains and free laborers would not do difficult jobs in mines or on sugar plantations, African bondspeople became mainstays of the Caribbean and Brazilian economies. The first African slaves in the Americas were imported from Angola, Portugal's early trading partner, and the Portuguese word *Negro* came into use as a descriptor.

English people had few moral qualms about enslaving other humans. Slavery was sanctioned in the Bible and widely practiced by contemporaries. Yet their early attempts to define slave status indicate that seventeenth-century English colonists lacked clear conceptual categories for race or slave. For example, the 1670 Virginia law that first tried to define the enslaveable declared that "all servants not being christians imported into this colony by shipping shall be slaves for their lives." Such nonracial phrasing reveals that Anglo-American settlers had not fully developed the meaning of *race* and *slave;* that would come over time.

Atlantic Slave Trade

North American mainland planters could not have obtained enslaved workers without the rapid development of an Atlantic trading system. Although this elaborate Atlantic economic system has been called the triangular trade, people and products did not move across the ocean in easily diagrammed patterns. Rather, a complex web of exchange inextricably tied the peoples of the Atlantic world together (see Map 3.2).

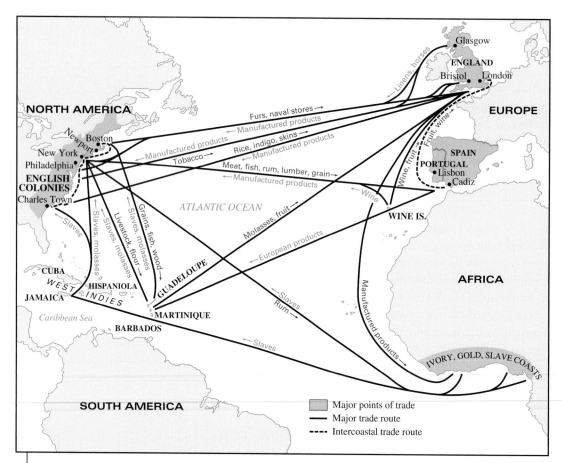

Map 3.2   Atlantic Trade Routes

By the late seventeenth century, an elaborate trade network linked the countries and colonies bordering the Atlantic Ocean. The most valuable commodities exchanged were enslaved people and the products of slave labor.

The expanding trade network between Europe and its colonies was fueled by the sale and transport of slaves, the exchange of commodities produced by slave labor, and the need to feed and clothe bound laborers. By the late seventeenth century, the basis of the European economy shifted from the Mediterranean and Asia to the Atlantic, with commerce in slaves and the products of slave labor as its core.

Chesapeake tobacco and Caribbean and Brazilian sugar were shipped to Europe, where they were in demand. The profits paid for African laborers and European manufactured goods. The African coastal rulers received their payment for slave cargoes in European manufactures and East Indian textiles. Europeans purchased slaves from Africa for resale in their colonies and acquired sugar and tobacco from America and dispatched their manufactures everywhere.

Europeans fought bitterly to control the lucrative trade. The Portuguese, who first dominated it, were supplanted by the Dutch in the 1630s. In the Anglo-Dutch wars, the Dutch lost to the English, who controlled the trade through the Royal African Company. Holding a monopoly on English trade with sub-Saharan Africa until 1712, the company maintained forts and trading posts, dispatched to West Africa hundreds of ships and transported about 100,000 slaves to England's Caribbean colonies. After the company's monopoly expired, independent traders carried most of the Africans imported into the colonies.

West Africa and the Slave Trade

Most of the enslaved people carried to North America originated in West Africa, some from the Rice and Grain Coasts, many others from the Gold and Slave Coasts and the Bight of Biafra (modern Nigeria) and Angola (see Map 1.2). Certain coastal rulers served as intermediaries, allowing permanent slave-trading posts and supplying resident Europeans with slaves. Such rulers simultaneously controlled inland peoples' access to desirable trade goods, such as textiles, iron bars, alcohol, tobacco, guns, and cowry shells from the Maldive Islands (in the Indian Ocean), used as currency. At least 10 percent of all slaves exported to the Americas passed through Ouidah, Dahomey's slave-trading port.

The slave trade's centralizing tendencies helped create such powerful eighteenth-century kingdoms as Dahomey and Asante (formed from the Akan States). Yet rulers in parts of Upper Guinea, especially modern Gambia and Senegal, resisted involvement. Traffic in slaves destroyed smaller polities and disrupted economic and demographic patterns. Agricultural production intensified, especially in rice-growing areas, to supply slave ships with foodstuffs. Because prisoners of war constituted most of the exported slaves, successful traders were also successful warriors. Some nations even initiated conflicts specifically to acquire captives.

New England and the Caribbean

New England produced only one item England wanted: tall trees for masts on sailing vessels. To buy English manufactures, New Englanders needed profits earned elsewhere, especially in the Caribbean. By the late 1640s, decades before the Chesapeake became dependent on *production* by slaves, New England already relied on *consumption* by slaves and owners. The sale of cheap foodstuffs (primarily corn and salt fish) to feed the slave population and wood products for barrels to Caribbean sugar planters provided New England farmers and merchants with a major source of income.

Shopkeepers in the New England interior and the middle colonies bartered with local farmers for grains, livestock, and barrel staves, then traded those items to merchants in port towns. Such merchants dispatched ships to the Caribbean, where they exchanged their cargoes for molasses, sugar, fruit, dyestuffs, and slaves. Fully reloaded, the ships then returned to Boston, Newport, New York, or Philadelphia. Americans distilled molasses into rum, the only part of the trade that could be termed triangular. Rhode Islanders took rum to Africa and traded it for slaves, whom they carried to Caribbean islands to exchange for more molasses to produce more rum.

Slaving Voyages   Tying the system together was the voyage (commonly called the middle passage) that brought Africans to the Americas. That voyage could be fatal for the enslaved. About 10 to 20 percent of the captives died en route; on long or disease-ridden voyages, mortality rates could be higher. Another 20 percent died either before the ships left Africa or shortly after arriving in the Americas. Europeans in the trade also died at high rates, chiefly through exposure to such diseases as yellow fever and malaria. One in every four or five European sailors died on voyages, and just 10 percent of the men sent to the Royal African Company's forts in Lower Guinea lived to return to England.

Sailors signed on to slaving voyages reluctantly. Slave merchants were notoriously greedy and captains brutal—to sailors and slaves. Unfortunately, sailors, often the subject of abuse, in turn abused bondspeople. Yet through contact with the enslaved, they learned the value of freedom, and sailors became known for their fierce attachment to independence.

Slavery in North America and the Caribbean

Barbados, America's first slave society (an economy wholly dependent on enslavement), spawned others. As the island's population expanded, about 40 percent of the early English residents dispersed to other colonies, carrying their laws, commercial contacts, and slaveholding practices with them. A large proportion of the first Africans imported into North America came via Barbados. In addition to the many Barbadians who settled in Carolina, others moved to the southern regions of Virginia, New Jersey, and New England.

African Enslavement in the Chesapeake   Newly arrived Africans in the Chesapeake were typically assigned to outlying parts of plantations (called quarters) until they learned some English and the routines of tobacco cultivation. Such Africans—primarily men—lived with ten to fifteen workers housed together in one or two buildings, supervised by an Anglo-American overseer. Each man was expected to cultivate two acres of tobacco a year. Their lives must have been filled with toil and loneliness, for few spoke the same language, and all were expected to work six days a week. Many used their Sunday off to cultivate gardens or to hunt or fish to supplement their meager diet. Only rarely could they form families, because of the scarcity of women.

Slaves usually cost about two and a half times more than indentured servants, but they supplied a lifetime of service, assuming they survived—which large numbers, weakened by the voyage and sickened by new diseases, did not. Those with enough money could acquire slaves, accumulate greater wealth, and establish large plantations worked by hundreds of bondspeople, whereas the less affluent could not even buy indentured servants. Anglo-American society in the Chesapeake thus became increasingly stratified, as the gap between rich and poor planters steadily widened.

So many Africans were imported into Virginia and Maryland that by 1710 people of African descent composed one-fifth of the population. Even with continuing imports, a decade later American-born slaves outnumbered their African-born counterparts in the Chesapeake, a trend that continued thereafter.

In 1726, William Smith, an employee of the Royal African Company, sketched this musician playing a traditional marimba-like instrument called a *balafo*. Later in the eighteenth century, Virginians described slaves playing the same instrument, thus showing that African music came to North America with the enslaved multitudes.   (University of Chicago Library, Special Collections Research Center)

African Enslavement in South Carolina

Africans who came with their masters from Barbados to South Carolina in 1670 composed one-quarter to one-third of Carolina's early population. The Barbadian slaveowners quickly discovered that African-born slaves' skills were well suited to South Carolina's semitropical environment. African-style dugout canoes became the chief means of transportation in the colony, which was crossed by rivers with large islands offshore. Fishing nets copied from African models proved more efficient. Baskets that enslaved laborers wove and gourds that they hollowed out came into general use as food and drink containers. Finally, Africans adapted their cattle herding techniques in America. Because meat and hides initially constituted a chief export, Africans contributed significantly to South Carolina's prosperity.

After 1700 South Carolinians began importing slaves directly from Africa. By 1710 African-born slaves outnumbered those born in the Americas, and they made up a majority of the enslaved population in South Carolina until midcentury. The similarity of the South Carolinian and West African environments, coupled with the substantial African-born population, ensured the survival of more aspects of West African culture than elsewhere. Only in South Carolina did enslaved parents give their children African names and develop a dialect that combined English and African terms. (Known as Gullah, it has survived to the present in isolated areas.) And in South Carolina African women became the primary petty traders, dominating the markets of Charles Town as they did in Guinea.

Rice and Indigo

Slave importation coincided with the successful introduction of rice in South Carolina. English people knew nothing about rice production, but people from Africa's Rice Coast had spent their lives working with the crop. Rice-growing techniques from West Africa, especially cultivation in inland swamps and tidal rivers, were widely adopted. South Carolinians preferred slaves from the Rice Coast, and they preferred women. That was possibly due to women's crucial role in cultivating rice in West Africa, where they sowed and weeded the crop, pounded harvested rice with a mortar and pestle to remove the hulls and bran, and then winnowed to separate the grains from the chaff. South Carolinians utilized the West African system of pounding rice by hand until the late eighteenth century.

Every field worker on rice plantations was expected to cultivate three to four acres a year. Most were female, because many enslaved men were assigned to jobs like blacksmithing or carpentry. Planters also expected slaves to grow part of their own food. Under the task system of predefined work assignments, experienced slaves could complete their tasks by early afternoon; after that and on Sundays, they were free to work their gardens or rest. One scholar has suggested this unique task system in South Carolina in the early eighteenth century resulted from negotiations between slaves familiar with rice cultivation and masters who desperately needed their expertise.

Developers of South Carolina's second cash crop—indigo—also used the task system and drew on slaves' specialized skills. Indigo, the only source of blue dye for the growing English textile industry, was much prized. Eliza Lucas, who managed her father's plantations, experimented with indigo cultivation during the early 1740s. Drawing on the knowledge of slaves and overseers from the Caribbean, she developed the planting and processing techniques later adopted colony-wide. South Carolina indigo never matched the quality of that from the Caribbean, but indigo plantations flourished because Parliament offered a bounty on every pound exported to Great Britain.

Indian Enslavement in North and South Carolina

In 1708 enslaved Indians composed about 14 percent of the South Carolina population. The lucrative traffic in Indian slaves significantly affected South Carolina's relationship with its indigenous neighbors. Native Americans knew they could find a ready market for captive enemies in Charles Town and used it to rid themselves of potential rivals. Yet as settlers and traders shifted their priorities, first one set of former allies, then another, found themselves enslaved.

The trade in Indian slaves began when the Westos (originally known as the Eries), migrated south from the Great Lakes in the mid-1650s, fleeing their Iroquois enemies after the Beaver Wars. The Westos raided Spain's lightly defended Florida missions and sold Indian captives to Virginians. With the establishment of Carolina, the proprietors monopolized trade with the Westos, which infuriated settlers shut out of the commerce in slaves and deerskins. The planters secretly financed attacks on the Westos, wiping them out by 1682. Southeastern Indians protected themselves from these slave raids—continued by other native peoples—by subordination to either the English or Spanish or by coalescing into larger political units, such as those later known as Creeks, Chickasaws, or Cherokees.

At first the Carolinians did not directly conflict with neighboring Indians. But in 1711 the Tuscaroras, an Iroquoian people, attacked a Swiss-German settlement at New Bern, North Carolina, which had expropriated their lands. South Carolinians and their Indian allies combined to defeat the Tuscaroras. Afterward, more than a thousand Tuscaroras were enslaved, and the remainder drifted northward, where they joined the Iroquois Confederacy.

Four years later, the Yamasees, who helped overcome the Tuscaroras, turned on their English allies. In what seems a long-planned retaliation for abuses by traders and threats to their lands, the Yamasees enlisted the Creeks and other Muskogean peoples to attack outlying English settlements. In spring and summer 1715, English and African refugees by the hundreds streamed into Charles Town. The Yamasee-Creek offensive was thwarted when reinforcements arrived from the north, colonists hastily armed African slaves, and Cherokees joined the fight. Afterward, Carolinian involvement in the Indian slave trade ceased because their native neighbors moved away for self-protection. Then, the native peoples of the Carolinas could regroup and rebuild, for they were no longer subjected to slavers' raids.

Slaves in Spanish and French North America

Few Indians or Africans were enslaved in any of Spain's North American territories, which had no plantations or cash crops. In 1693, Florida officials offered freedom to Carolina fugitives who converted to Catholicism. Hundreds of runaways accepted the offer, although not all won their liberty. Many settled in a town founded for them near St. Augustine, Gracia Real de Santa Teresa de Mose, headed by former slave Francisco Menéndez.

In early Louisiana, too, slaves—some Indians, some Atlantic creoles—at first composed only a tiny proportion of the residents. But a growing European population demanded more, and after 1719 French officials dispatched more than six thousand Africans. The residents failed to develop a plantation economy, but they angered the Natchez Indians by taking their lands. In 1729 the Natchez, assisted by newly arrived slaves, attacked, killing more than 10 percent of the European population. The French struck back, slaughtering the Natchez and their allies. Throughout the century, Louisiana remained a society with slaves rather than a slave society.

Enslavement in the North

Bondspeople in the northern mainland colonies were Atlantic creoles from the Caribbean, native peoples from the Carolinas and Florida, and local Indians sentenced to slavery for crime or debt. The intricate involvement of northerners in the commerce surrounding the slave trade ensured that many people of African descent lived north of Virginia, and that "Spanish Indians" became part of the New England population. Some bondspeople resided in urban areas, especially New York, which in 1700 had a larger black population than any mainland city. Women tended to work as domestic servants, men as unskilled laborers on the docks.

Yet even in the North most bondspeople worked in the country doing agricultural tasks. Dutch farmers in the Hudson Valley and northern New Jersey were likely to rely on enslaved Africans, as were the owners of large landholdings in the Rhode Island's Narragansett region. Some toiled in new enterprises, such as ironworks, alongside hired laborers and indentured servants. While slavery did not greatly contribute to the northern economy, individual slaveholders benefited from the institution and wanted to preserve it.

Slave Resistance

As slavery increased, so did slaves' resistance. Typically that meant malingering or running away, but occasionally bondspeople planned rebellions. Seven times before 1713 the English Caribbean experienced major revolts. The first mainland slave revolt occurred in New York in 1712. The rebels set a fire and ambushed anyone trying to put it out, killing eight and wounding twelve. Of the rebels caught and tried, eighteen were executed, with their decapitated bodies left rotting outdoors as a warning.

IMPERIAL REORGANIZATION AND THE WITCHCRAFT CRISIS

English officials seeking new sources of revenue focused on the expanding Atlantic trade in slaves and the products of slave labor. Parliament and the Stuart monarchs drafted laws to harness proceeds of the trade for the benefit of the mother country.

Mercantilism and the Navigation Acts

Like other European nations, England based its commercial policy on mercantilism, the theory that viewed the economic world as a collection of national states, whose governments competed for shares of a finite amount of wealth. What one nation gained, another lost. Each nation sought economic self-sufficiency and a favorable balance of trade by exporting more than it imported. Colonies played an important role, supplying the mother country with valuable raw materials and its market for the mother country's manufactured goods.

Parliament's Navigation Acts—passed between 1651 and 1673—established three principles that accorded with mercantilist theory. First, only English or colonial merchants could legally trade in the colonies. Second, certain valuable American products could be sold only in the mother country or other English colonies. Initially, these enumerated goods included wool, sugar, tobacco, indigo, ginger, and dyes, and later, rice, naval stores (masts, spars, pitch, tar, and turpentine), copper, and furs. Third, foreign goods for sale in the colonies had to be shipped through England, with English import duties paid. Years later, new laws established a fourth principle: the colonies could not export items (such as wool clothing or iron) that competed with English products.

These laws adversely affected Chesapeake planters, who were barred from seeking foreign markets for their staple crops. The statutes initially helped sugar producers of the English Caribbean by driving Brazilian sugar from the home market, but later prevented English planters from selling sugar elsewhere. The laws, however, stimulated a lucrative colonial shipbuilding industry, especially in New England. And the northern and middle colonies produced many unenumerated goods—fish, flour, meat and livestock, and barrel staves—that could be traded directly to the French, Spanish, or Dutch Caribbean islands if they were carried in English or American ships.

English authorities soon learned that enforcing mercantilist laws would be difficult. The American coast's many harbors were havens for smugglers, and colonial officials often looked the other way when illegally imported goods were sold. Because American juries had already demonstrated a tendency to favor local smugglers, Parliament in 1696 established American vice-admiralty courts, which operated without juries and adjudicated violations of the Navigation Acts.

Colonial Autonomy Challenged

By the early 1680s Massachusetts, Plymouth, Connecticut, and Rhode Island operated independently, subject neither to the direct authority of the king nor to a proprietor. Whereas Virginia was a royal colony and New Hampshire (1679) and New York (1685) gained that status, all other mainland settlements were proprietorships, over which England exercised little control. In all English colonies, free adult men who owned property expected to have an influential voice in their government, especially about decisions concerning taxation.

When James II became king in 1685, he and his successors sought to tighten the reins of colonial government and reduce the colonies' political autonomy. English officials were convinced that New England was a hotbed of smuggling. Moreover, Puritans denied religious freedom to non-Congregationalists and maintained laws incompatible with English practice. The charters of all the colonies from New Jersey to Maine were revoked, and a Dominion of New England was established in 1686 (see Map 3.1). Sir Edmund Andros, the governor, had immense power: Parliament dissolved all the assemblies, and Andros needed only the consent of an appointed council to make laws and levy taxes.

Glorious Revolution in America

New Englanders endured Andros's autocratic rule for more than two years. Then, James II's power crumbled when he angered his subjects by levying taxes without parliamentary approval and by converting to Catholicism. In April 1689, Boston's leaders jailed Andros and his associates. The following month they received news of the bloodless coup known as the Glorious Revolution, in which James was replaced in late 1688 by his daughter Mary and her husband, the Dutch prince William of Orange. With Protestants William and Mary in power, the Glorious Revolution affirmed the supremacy of Parliament and Protestantism.

In other colonies, the Glorious Revolution inspired revolt. In Maryland the Protestant Association overturned the government of the Catholic proprietor, and in New York a militia officer of German origin, Jacob Leisler, assumed control of the government. Bostonians, Marylanders, and New Yorkers saw themselves as carrying out the colonial phase of the English revolt.

But William and Mary also believed that England should exercise tighter control over its unruly American possessions. Consequently, only the Maryland rebellion received royal sanction, primarily because of its anti-Catholic thrust. In New York, Leisler was hanged for treason, and Massachusetts became a royal colony with an appointed governor. The province retained its town meeting system and continued to elect its council, but the 1691 charter eliminated the religious test for voting and holding office. A parish of the Church of England appeared in Boston.

King William's War

A war with the French and their Algonquian allies compounded New England's difficulties. King Louis XIV of France allied himself with the deposed James II, and England declared war on France in 1689. (In Europe, this conflict was known as the War of the League of Augsburg, but the colonists called it King William's War.) Even before war broke out in Europe, Anglo-Americans and Abenakis clashed over English settlements in Maine that had been reoccupied after the 1678 truce and were expanding. Attacks wholly or partially destroyed several towns, and colonial expeditions against Montreal and Quebec in 1690 failed miserably. Even the Peace of Ryswick (1697), which ended the war in Europe, did not bring peace to the northern frontiers. Maine could not be resettled for decades because of the continuing conflict.

The 1692 Witchcraft Crisis

For eight months in 1692, witchcraft accusations spread through rural Essex County, Massachusetts—the area most threatened by the Indian attacks in southern Maine and New Hampshire. Before the crisis ended, 14 women and 5 men were hanged, 1 man was pressed to death with stones, 54 people confessed to being witches, and more than 140 people were jailed. The crisis began in late February when several children and young women in Salem Village formally charged older female neighbors with torturing them in spectral form. Other accusers and confessors chimed in, among them some female domestic servants orphaned in the Maine war. These young women offered fellow New Englanders a compelling explanation for the troubles afflicting them: their province was under direct assault not only by the Indians and their French allies but also by the Devil and his allied witches.

Among others, the afflicted people accused prominent men from the Maine frontier who had traded with or failed to defeat the Indians. Their leader, accusers declared, was the Reverend George Burroughs, a Harvard graduate who had ministered in Maine and Salem Village and was suspected of bewitching soldiers sent to combat the Abenakis. The colony's magistrates, who were also its political and military leaders, were willing to believe such accusations because it freed them from any responsibility for New England's troubles.

In October, the worst phase of the crisis ended when the governor dissolved the special court established to try the suspects. He and prominent clergymen regarded the descriptions of spectral torturers as "the Devil's testimony," and the Devil could not be trusted. Most critics did not think the afflicted were faking, that confessions were false or that witches did not exist. Rather, they questioned whether guilt could be legally established by the evidence. During the final trials in 1693, almost all the defendants were acquitted, and the governor pardoned the few found guilty.

New Imperial Measures

In 1696 England created the fifteen-member Board of Trade and Plantations, the chief government organ concerned with the American colonies. The board gathered information, reviewed Crown appointments, scrutinized legislation passed by colonial assemblies, supervised trade policies, and advised ministries on colonial issues.

The Wonders of the Invisible World.

OBSERVATIONS

As well *Historical* as *Theological*, upon the NATURE, the NUMBER, and the OPERATIONS of the

DEVILS.

Accompany'd with,

I. Some Accounts of the Grievous Molestations, by DÆMONS and WITCHCRAFTS, which have lately annoy'd the Countrey; and the Trials of some eminent *Malefactors* Executed upon occasion thereof: with several Remarkable *Curiosities* therein occurring.

II. Some Counsils, Directing a due Improvement of the terrible things, lately done, by the Unusual & Amazing Range of EVIL SPIRITS, in Our Neighbourhood: & the methods to prevent the *Wrongs* which those *Evil Angels* may intend against all sorts of people among us; especially in Accusations of the Innocent.

III. Some Conjectures upon the great EVENTS, likely to befall, the WORLD in General, and NEW-ENGLAND in Particular; as also upon the Advances of the TIME, when we shall see BETTER DAYES.

IV A short Narrative of a late Outrage committed by a knot of WITCHES in *Swedeland*, very much Resembling, and so far Explaining, *That* under which our parts of *America* have laboured!

V. THE DEVIL DISCOVERED: In a Brief Discourse upon those TEMPTATIONS, which are the more Ordinary *Devices* of the Wicked One.

By **Cotton Mather.**

Boston Printed by *Benj. Harris* for *Sam. Phillips*. 1693.

The Reverend Cotton Mather of Boston, twenty-nine years old in 1692 at the time of the Salem witchcraft crisis, rushed this book—*The Wonders of the Invisible World*—into print shortly after the trials ended. He tried to explain to his fellow New Englanders the "Grievous Molestations by Daemons and Witchcrafts which have lately annoy'd the Countrey" by providing both brief trial narratives and examples of similar recent occurrences elsewhere, most notably in Mohra, Sweden.   (Image courtesy of The Massachusetts Historical Society)

It had no powers of enforcement and shared jurisdiction with the customs service, the navy, and a member of the ministry. Although this reform improved colonial administration, supervision of the American provinces remained decentralized and haphazard.

Most colonists resented alien officials who arrived to implement the policies of king and Parliament, but they adjusted to them and to the Navigation Act's trade restrictions. They fought another of Europe's wars—the War of the Spanish Succession, called Queen Anne's War in the colonies—from 1702 to 1713, without enduring the stresses of the first, despite the heavy economic burdens the conflict imposed. Colonists who allied with the royal government were given offices and land grants and made up court parties that supported English officials. Others, who were without well-placed friends or who defended colonial autonomy, formed the opposition, or country interest. By the end of the first quarter of the eighteenth century, most men in both groups were American born. They were from elite families whose wealth derived in the South from staple-crop production and in the North from commerce.

Exotic Beverages

Seventeenth-century colonists developed a taste for tea (from China), coffee (from Arabia), chocolate (from Mesoamerica), and rum. Demand for these once-exotic beverages helped reshape the world economy after the mid-seventeenth century. Approximately two-thirds of the people who migrated across the Atlantic before 1776 were involved, primarily as slaves, in the production of tobacco, calico, and these four drinks. These exotic beverages profoundly affected culture, too, as they moved from luxury to necessity.

Each beverage had its own pattern of consumption. Chocolate, brought to Spain from Mexico and consumed hot at intimate gatherings, became the drink of aristocrats. Coffee became the morning beverage of English and colonial businessmen, who praised its caffeine for keeping drinkers alert. Coffee was served in new public coffeehouses, patronized by men, which opened first in London in the late 1660s and then in Boston in the 1690s. By the mid-eighteenth century, tea, consumed at home in the afternoon at tea tables presided over by women, supplanted coffee in England and America. In contrast, rum was the drink of the masses, made possible by new technology and the increasing production of sugar.

Cacao plantations in the South American tropics multiplied to meet the rising chocolate demand. Rum involved Americans in every phase of its production and consumption. The sugar grown on Caribbean plantations was transported to the American mainland in barrels and ships made from North American wood. There the syrup was turned into rum at 140 distilleries. Americans drank an estimated four gallons per person annually, but exported much of the rum to Africa, where it could purchase more slaves to produce more sugar to make more rum.

Thus these beverages linked the colonies to the world and altered their economic and social development.

The frontispiece of Peter Muguet, *Tractatus De Poto Caphe, Chinesium The et de Chocolata,* 1685. Muguet's treatise visually linked the three hot, exotic beverages recently introduced to Europeans. The drinks are being consumed by representatives of the cultures in which they originated: a turbaned Turk (with coffeepot in the foreground), a Chinese man (with teapot on the table), and an Indian drinking from a hollowed, handled gourd (with a chocolate pot and ladle on the floor in front of him).

(Library of Congress)

Americans of African Descent

After the 1670s, the rise of southern economies based on the enslavement of Africans, coupled with employment of enslaved Africans in northern colonies, dramatically altered the American population. By 1775, more than a quarter-million Africans had been imported into the territory that later became the United States, constituting about 20 percent of the population at the time of the Revolution.

According to the 2000 census, 12.5 percent of Americans today claim descent from African ancestors. Because the legal importation of African slaves ended in 1808 and because the United States attracted few voluntary African migrants until the late twentieth century, most of today's African Americans have colonial ancestors. Conversely, most European Americans are descended from the massive European migrations of the nineteenth and early twentieth centuries.

The modern African American population includes people with various skin colors, reflecting many past interracial sexual relationships, coerced and voluntary. African Americans, free and enslaved, have had children with Europeans and Indians since the colonial period; more recently, they have intermarried with Asian immigrants. State miscegenation laws, enacted from the early American republic until 1967—when they were struck down by the Supreme Court—forbade legal marriages between people of European descent and those of other races. That forced the non-European groups to seek marital partners among themselves.

The 2000 census allowed Americans to define themselves as members of more than one race. African American leaders opposed this change, fearing a diminution of political clout. Previous laws defined people with any African ancestry as black; on census forms people of African descent have now proved less willing to define themselves as multiracial. Their racial self-definition thus continues to be influenced by a legacy of discrimination.

Summary

The seventy years from 1650 to 1720 established the basic economic and political patterns in mainland colonial society. In 1650 two isolated centers of English population, New England and the Chesapeake, existed along the seaboard, along with the tiny Dutch colony of New Netherland. In 1720 nearly the entire North American east coast was in English hands and Indian control east of the Appalachian Mountains had largely been broken by King Philip's War, Bacon's Rebellion, the Yamasee and Tuscarora wars, and Queen Anne's War. West of the mountains, the Iroquois reigned supreme. Most of the population was American born, except for African-born people in South Carolina and the Chesapeake. Economies originally based on trade in fur and skins had become more complex and linked with the mother country; and political structures had become more uniform. Yet the adoption of large-scale slavery and production of tobacco, rice, and indigo in the Chesapeake and Carolinas differentiated them from northern colonies. They had become slave societies, heavily reliant on a system of perpetual servitude.

The northern colonies, too, counted on profits from the Atlantic trading system, the key element of which was traffic in slaves, primarily Africans. New England sold corn, salt fish, and wood products to the West Indies, where slaves consumed the foodstuffs and from where planters shipped sugar and molasses in barrels made from staves crafted by northern farmers. Pennsylvania and New York also found the Caribbean islands a ready market for their livestock, grains, and wheat flour.

Meanwhile, the Spanish expanded their influence throughout the Gulf Coast and, after midcentury, north to California. The French moved to dominate the length of the Mississippi River and the Great Lakes region. Both Spanish and French colonists lived near Indian nations and depended on their labor and goodwill. The extensive Spanish and French presence to the south and west of English settlements made future conflicts among European powers in North America inevitable.

By 1720, key elements of the imperial administrative structure that would govern the English colonies until 1775 were in place. Anglo-Americans' commitment to autonomous local government would later lead them into conflict with Parliament and the king.

Chapter Review

THE GROWTH OF ANGLO-AMERICAN SETTLEMENTS

Why did New York's development lag behind that of other British colonies in the seventeenth century?

Several factors were critical to a colony's growth. Leaders who encouraged migration and settlement, often through land grants and freedom of religion as well as the prospect of a representative assembly, typically had the best results. Granted to James the Duke of York in 1664, New York remained a shadow of Boston until well into the 1720s largely because James, unlike William Penn of Pennsylvania and other proprietors, made none of these moves. Instead, his colony remained hemmed in by Connecticut and New Jersey, which each made successful overtures to draw populations helpful to development. Instead, James retained Dutch local government, land title, and legal practices that had been in place when he came to power and refused a legislative assembly—which many English colonists wanted—until 1683.

A DECADE OF IMPERIAL CRISES: THE 1670S

How did settlers' interests collide with those of Native Americans?

Settlers' and Native Americans' interests clashed in two pivotal areas: control of trade and desire for more land. New France and the Iroquois Confederacy clashed over control of the valuable fur trade, which the Iroquois had fought hard to attain. Bitter battles and attacks lasted for twenty years, before culminating in a neutrality treaty. Similarly, in the densely settled New England colonies in the 1670s, hostilities developed as Anglo-Americans sought more land and tried to grab it away from Native Americans, fueling the deadly and destructive King Phillips' War. And in Virginia, Bacon's Rebellion also focused on seizing desirable interior land from Indians, ultimately attacking them and pushing them further west.

THE ATLANTIC TRADING SYSTEM

How was slavery at the center of the expanding trade network between Europe and the colonies?

First, the Chesapeake developed around tobacco farming, which required a vast supply of workers. Fewer English workers were available as population pressures in England eased and Restoration colonies offered land and other opportunities to would-be settlers. Tobacco growers instead turned to slave labor, as did other plantation colonies, thereby expanding the sale and transport of slaves. In addition, commodities produced by slave labor helped boost exports and trade networks, while the need to feed and clothe slaves stimulated new business opportunities for other colonies, particularly New England, which grew economically by selling cheap foodstuffs to feed slaves. And the slave trade itself created a global economic network and tensions among European nations seeking to control the lucrative trade.

SLAVERY IN NORTH AMERICA AND THE CARIBBEAN

What skills did African slaves bring to America that proved vital to the development of colonial South Carolina?

African-born slaves had several skills that were crucial to the economic development of South Carolina. From a similarly semi-tropical climate, these slaves adapted dugout canoes from their homeland that became a key means of transportation in the many rivers of the Carolinas. Their fishing nets also proved more efficient. African cattle herding techniques aided in producing the meat and hides that were an early export from the region. Slaves, particularly women, also knew how to cultivate rice, which was rapidly becoming a staple crop in South Carolina. The area's other crash crop—indigo (the only source of blue dye for the growing English textile industry)—similarly drew on the knowledge of slaves transported to South Carolina from the Caribbean, where indigo plantations flourished.

IMPERIAL REORGANIZATION AND THE WITCHCRAFT CRISIS

How did mercantilism benefit some colonies economically and hurt others?

Mercantilism was grounded in the notion that the world contained a finite amount of wealth, and that if one nation gained, another had to lose. For England, that meant exporting more than it imported and using the colonies to facilitate its prosperity. England controlled colonial trade through the Navigation Acts (passed between 1651 and 1673), which allowed only English merchants to trade in the colonies, permitted American products to be sold only to England or other English colonies, and required foreign goods bound for the colonies to ship through England and pay related duties. Later, it additionally prevented colonists from exporting anything that competed with English goods. For Chesapeake planters, these policies had a negative affect, preventing them from selling staple crops in foreign markets. English sugar producers in the Caribbean were initially helped, as their Brazilian competitors were driven from the market, but later hurt when they were prevented from selling their sugar elsewhere. New England benefitted from the emergence of a lucrative shipbuilding industry, while the northern and middle colonies gained from trading goods not outlined in the Navigation Acts, including fish, flour, meat, livestock, and barrels.

SUGGESTIONS FOR FURTHER READING

Wesley Frank Craven, *The Colonies in Transition, 1660–1713* (1968)

David Eltis, *The Rise of African Slavery in the Americas* (1998)

Alan Gallay, *The Indian Slave Trade: The Rise of the English Empire in the American South, 1670–1717* (2002)

Andrew Knaut, *The Pueblo Revolt of 1680* (1995)

Jill Lepore, *The Name of War: King Philip's War and the Origins of American Identity* (1998)

David S. Lovejoy, *The Glorious Revolution in America* (1972)

Edmund S. Morgan, *American Slavery, American Freedom: The Ordeal of Colonial Virginia* (1975)

Jennifer L. Morgan, *Laboring Women: Reproduction and Gender in New World Slavery* (2004)

Mary Beth Norton, *In the Devil's Snare: The Salem Witchcraft Crisis of 1692* (2002)

Betty Wood, *The Origins of American Slavery* (1997)

CHAPTER 4

American Society Transformed

CHAPTER OUTLINE

Population Growth and Ethnic Diversity

Economic Growth and Development

Colonial Cultures

   LINKS TO THE WORLD:
   Smallpox Inoculation

Colonial Families

Politics: Stability and Crisis in British America

A Crisis in Religion

   LEGACY FOR A PEOPLE AND A NATION: "Self-Made Men"

Summary

"I f god Spers [spares] you in this Cuntrie but a few years you will blis the day you left" Alexander McAllister told his cousin in late 1770. McAllister, who as a youth moved to North Carolina with his parents, urged friends and family in his Scottish Highlands hometown in Argyleshire to come to North America. He noted that at his adopted home at Cross Creek (near modern Fayetteville, North Carolina) anyone could easily grow corn, wheat, barley, rye, oats, potatoes, and tobacco, and other immigrants had harvested "plenty of Corn for them Selves and famile and seemes to be very well Satisfied."

McAllister's letters were central to a network of correspondents that brought five thousand Scots to North America in the two decades after the mid-1750s. When Scots arrived in North Carolina with letters of introduction, McAllister helped them find land and supplies, even while knowing that "the best [land] is taken up many years ago" and that newcomers' early years would be hard. McAllister's own prosperity illustrated what some might achieve: by the late 1780s, having fathered numerous children by two wives, he owned forty slaves and more than 2,500 acres. He served as an elder of the Presbyterian church, a member of the colonial assembly, and a state senator.

Highland Scots were part of a massive eighteenth-century migration of Europeans and Africans that by 1770 had changed the American population and landscape. The British colonies south of New England drew the most newcomers, who swelled the population, altered political balances, and introduced new sects. Unwilling immigrants (slaves and transported convicts), too, clustered in the middle and southern colonies.

Several key themes marked colonial development in the mid-eighteenth century: the new ethnic diversity, the increasing importance of urban centers, the creation of a prosperous urban

This icon will direct you to interactive activities and study materials on A People And A Nation, Brief Edition
website: **www.cengage.com/history/norton/peoplenationbrief8e**

Chronology

1690	Locke's *Essay Concerning Human Understanding,* a key example of Enlightenment thought, is published.
1721–22	Smallpox epidemic in Boston leads to the first widespread adoption of inoculation in America.
1732	Georgia is founded.
1733	John Peter Zenger is tried for and acquitted of seditious libel in New York.
1739	Stono Rebellion (South Carolina) leads to increased white fears of slave revolts.
	George Whitefield arrives in America; Great Awakening broadens.
1739–48	King George's War disrupts the American economy.
1740s	Black population of the Chesapeake begins to grow by natural increase, contributing to the rise of large plantations.
1741	New York City conspiracy reflects whites' continuing fears of slave revolts.
1747	Princeton University is founded, joining Harvard, Yale, and other earlier institutions of higher learning.
1751	Franklin's *Experiments and Observations on Electricity,* an important American contribution to Enlightenment science, is published.
1760s	Baptist congregations take root in Virginia.
1760–75	This is the peak of eighteenth-century European and African migration to the English colonies.
1765–66	Hudson River land riots pit tenants and squatters against large landlords.
1767–69	Regulator movement (South Carolina) tries to establish order in the backcountry.
1771	North Carolina Regulators are defeated by the eastern militia at Battle of Alamance.

elite, rising consumption, and the new significance of internal markets. Where exports continued to dominate French and British mainland colonies, settlers along the Atlantic and Gulf coasts were tied to an international commercial system that fluctuated wildly, as expanding populations demanded greater quantities and types of goods and Europe could not keep up. Consequently, colonists increasingly depended on their own resources.

Intermarried networks of wealthy families developed in Europe's American possessions by the 1760s. Most colonists of the "lesser sort" worked with their hands from dawn to dusk and could neither read nor write. Well-off, educated elites, however, participated in transatlantic intellectual life, such as the Enlightenment, lived in comfortable houses, and enjoyed leisure activities. Divisions were most pronounced in British America, the largest and most prosperous settlement, where by the last half of the century, social and economic distance among different ranks of Anglo-Americans had widened and sparked new conflicts.

In 1720 much of North America remained under Indian control. But by 1770, settlements of Europeans and Africans ruled by Great Britain filled most of the region between the Appalachian Mountains and the Atlantic Ocean. After defeating France in the Seven Years' War (see pages 112–113), the British dominated North America's extensive rivers and lakes. Spanish missions extended from present-day northern California to the Gulf Coast. Such changes transformed Europe's North American possessions.

- **What were the effects of demographic and economic changes in the mainland colonies?**
- **What were the key elements of eighteenth-century colonial culture?**
- **What developments at midcentury began the process of political and religious change?**

POPULATION GROWTH AND ETHNIC DIVERSITY

Dramatic population growth characterized British mainland colonies in the eighteenth century. About 250,000 European and African Americans resided in the colonies in 1700. Thirty years later, that number more than doubled, reaching 2.5 million by 1775. Only modest population changes occurred in French and Spanish North America. At the end of the eighteenth century, Texas had just 2,500 Spanish residents, and the largest Spanish colony, New Mexico, included only 20,000. The total European population of the mainland French colonies expanded from 15,000 in 1700 to about 70,000 in the 1760s, but concentrations of French settlers existed only along the St. Lawrence River between Quebec and Montreal and in New Orleans.

Migration was important, but most of the population growth in Anglo America resulted from natural increase. Once the difficult early decades of settlement passed and the sex ratio evened out in the South (after 1700), the American population doubled every twenty-five years. Because of women's youthful age at the onset of childbearing (early twenties for European Americans, late teens for African Americans), married women became pregnant every two or three years and bore five to ten children. With a large proportion of children reaching maturity, about half of the American population was under sixteen years old in 1775. (By contrast, only about one-quarter of the American population was under sixteen in 2005.)

Involuntary Migrants from Africa

More Africans than Europeans came to the Americas, the overwhelming majority as slaves. Of at least 11 million slaves brought to the Americas during slavery, by 1775 only 260,000 were imported into the region that became the United States. The height of the trade occurred in the eighteenth century, when about half of all slaves crossed the Atlantic, primarily in British or Portuguese vessels. Furthermore, in the slaveholding South America and Caribbean, a surplus of males and appallingly high mortality rates meant that only a continuing influx of slaves could maintain a consistent work force. On the mainland, only South Carolina, where rice cultivation was difficult and unhealthful (chiefly because malaria-carrying mosquitoes bred in the rice swamps), required a similar influx of slaves.

The involuntary migrants came from various ethnic groups and regions of Africa (see Map 4.1). More than 40 percent embarked from West Central Africa (modern Congo and Angola), nearly 20 percent from the Bight of Benin (modern Togo, Benin, and southwestern Nigeria), about 13 percent from the Bight of Biafra (today's Cameroon, Gabon, and southeastern Nigeria), and approximately 9 percent from the Gold Coast (modern Ghana and neighboring countries). Smaller proportions came from East Africa and the Windward and Rice Coasts (modern Senegal, Gambia, and Sierra Leone).

Standard slave-trading practice of loading an entire cargo at one port and selling them in another meant that people from the same area were often taken to the Americas together. That was heightened by planter partiality for particular ethnic groups. Virginians favored Igbos from the Bight of Biafra, whereas South Carolinians and Georgians selected Senegambians and people from West Central Africa. Louisiana planters first chose slaves from the Bight of Benin but later bought many from West Central Africa.

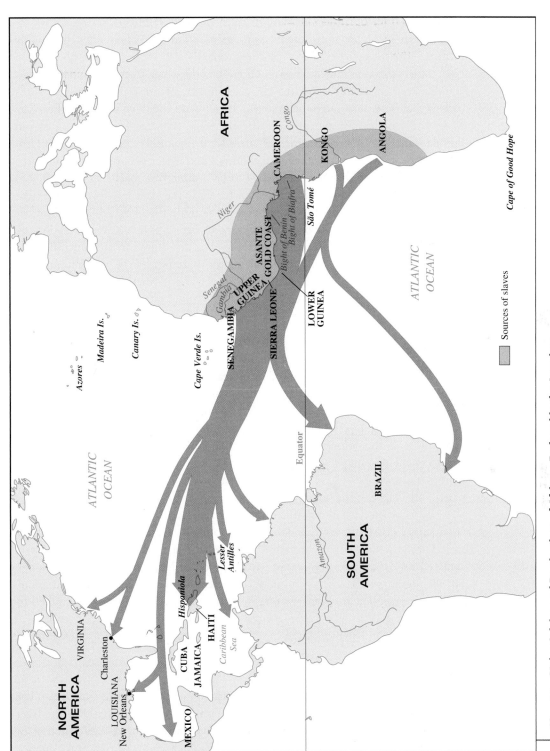

Map 4.1 Major Origins and Destinations of Africans Enslaved in the Americas

As this schematic map shows, enslaved Africans were drawn from many regions of western Africa (with some coming from the interior of the continent) and were shipped to areas throughout the Americas.

Possibly tens of thousands of enslaved Africans were Muslims, some of whom were literate in Arabic and came from aristocratic families. The discovery of noble birth could lead to slaves' being returned home. For example, Job Ben Solomon, a slave trader from Senegal, had been captured by raiders while selling bondspeople in Gambia and sent to Maryland in 1732. A letter he wrote in Arabic so impressed his owners that he was liberated the next year. Despite the 260,000 slaves brought to the mainland, American-born people of African descent came to dominate the enslaved population because of natural increase after 1740. Although about 40 percent of imported Africans were male, women and children composed a majority of slave imports. Females were valued for their productive and reproductive capacities. A planter who owned female slaves could watch his labor force expand steadily through the births of their children, designated as slaves in every colony. In the Chesapeake, the number of bondspeople rose rapidly because the imports were added to an enslaved population that also grew through natural increase. Work routines involved in cultivating tobacco, coupled with a roughly equal sex ratio, reduced slave mortality and increased fertility. Even in unhealthful South Carolina, American-born slaves outnumbered the African born as early as 1750.

Newcomers from Europe

About 500,000 Europeans moved to British North America during the eighteenth century, most after 1730. Influenced by mercantilist thought, British authorities regarded an industrious population at home as an asset. They deported undesirables—vagabonds and Jacobite rebels (supporters of the deposed Stuart monarchs)—but otherwise discouraged emigration. Instead they recruited German and French Protestants to the colonies by promising free land and religious toleration, even financing the passage of some groups. After 1740 they relaxed citizenship requirements to a small fee, seven years' residence, adherence to Protestant beliefs, and an oath of allegiance to the king.

The most successful migrants came prepared, having learned from their correspondents like McAllister that land and resources were abundant and that they would need capital. People who arrived penniless did less well; approximately 40 percent fell into that category, immigrating as bound laborers. Worse off were the 50,000 migrants who came as criminals convicted of offenses such as theft and murder. Many unskilled and perhaps one-third female, they were often dispatched to Maryland, where they worked in tobacco fields or as ironworkers or household servants. Little is known about their fate, but some who committed further crimes in the colonies became notorious in newspaper accounts.

Scots-Irish, Scots, and Germans

One of the largest immigrant groups came from Ireland or Scotland, largely in family units. About 70,000 Scots-Irish descendants of Presbyterian Scots who had settled in Northern Ireland during the seventeenth century joined 35,000 who came to America from Scotland (see Table 4.1). Another 45,000, both Protestants and Catholics, migrated from southern Ireland. High rents, poor harvests, and religious discrimination (in Ireland) pushed people from their homeland. Such immigrants usually landed in Philadelphia or New Castle, Delaware, and moved to the Pennsylvania

TABLE 4.1   Who Moved to America from England and Scotland in the Early 1770s, and Why?

	English Emigrants	Scottish Emigrants	Free American Population
Destination			
13 British colonies	81.1%	92.7%	—
Canada	12.1%	4.2%	—
West Indies	6.8%	3.1%	—
Age Distribution			
Under 21	26.8%	45.3%	56.8%
21–25	37.1%	19.9%	9.7%
26–44	33.3%	29.5%	20.4%
45 and over	2.7%	5.3%	13.1%
Sex Distribution			
Male	83.8%	59.9%	—
Female	16.2%	40.1%	—
Unknown	4.2%	13.5%	—
Traveling with Families or Alone			
With families	20.0%	48.0%	—
Alone	80.0%	52.0%	—
Known Occupation or Status			
Gentry	2.5%	1.2%	—
Merchandising	5.2%	5.2%	—
Agriculture	17.8%	24.0%	—
Artisanry	54.2%	37.7%	—
Laborer	20.3%	31.9%	—
Why They Left			
Positive reasons (e.g., desire to better one's position)	90.0%	36.0%	—
Negative reasons (e.g., poverty, unemployment)	10.0%	64.0%	—

Note: Between December 1773 and March 1776, the British government questioned individuals and families leaving ports in Scotland and England for the American colonies to learn who they were, where they were going, and why they were leaving. This table summarizes just a few of the findings of the official inquiries, which revealed a number of significant differences between the Scottish and English emigrants.

Source of data: Bernard Bailyn, *Voyagers to the West* (New York: Knopf, 1986), Tables 4.1, 5.2, 5.4, 5.7, 5.23, and 6.1.

backcountry along the Susquehanna River. Later migrants moved to the backcountry of Maryland, Virginia, and the Carolinas. Frequently unable to afford land, they lived illegally on acreage belonging to Indians, land speculators, or colonial governments and gained a reputation for lawlessness, hard drinking, and fighting.

Migrants from Germany and German-speaking areas of Switzerland numbered about 85,000 between 1730 and 1755. They, too, usually came in family groups and landed in Philadelphia. By century's end, they accounted for one-third of Pennsylvania's residents. Many Germans moved west and then south into the backcountry of Maryland and Virginia, as well as of Charles Town and the southern interior. The Germans belonged to a wide variety of Protestant sects, adding to the already substantial religious diversity of Pennsylvania. So many Germans had arrived by

In December 1729, probably in New York's Hudson Valley, an unknown artist portrayed J. M. Stolle, the son of a Palatine immigrant who came to North America from Germany in 1709. The young man's fancy clothing and the column and balustrade in the background suggest that the artist wanted to convey an image of the family's economic success, though whether that image was accurate is unknown. (National Gallery of Art, Washington, D.C. Gift of Edgar William and Bernice Chrysler Garbisch)

1751 that Benjamin Franklin feared they would Germanize Pennsylvania. They "will never adopt our Language or Customs," he predicted, inaccurately.

The most concentrated period of colonial migration fell between 1760 and 1775, when more than 220,000 free and enslaved people arrived—nearly 10 percent of the population of British North America. Tough economic times led many to seek a better life in America; simultaneously, the slave trade burgeoned. Late-arriving free immigrants had little choice but to remain in cities or move to the edges of settlement; land elsewhere was fully occupied. In the settlement periphery, they became the tenants of, or bought property from, land speculators.

Maintaining Ethnic and Religious Identities

Half of the colonial population south of New England had non-English origins by 1775. Assimilation into Anglo-American culture depended on settlement patterns, group size, and the migrants' cultural ties. The French Protestants (Huguenots) who migrated to Charles Town or New York City were unable to sustain either their language or religious practices for more than two generations, whereas Huguenots settling in the Hudson Valley remained recognizably French and Calvinist for a century. By contrast, the equally small group of colonial Jews maintained a distinct identity wherever they settled. In places like New York and Newport, Rhode Island, they established synagogues and preserved their religion.

Members of larger migrant groups (Germans, Irish, and Scots) found it easier to sustain European ways. Some ethnicities dominated certain localities. When migrants from different countries settled the same region, ethnic antagonisms surfaced. One German clergyman in Pennsylvania, for example, claimed that Scots-Irish were "lazy, dissipated and poor." Anglo-American elites fostered antagonisms to maintain their political and economic power and frequently subverted naturalization laws to deprive even long-resident immigrants a voice in government.

Ultimately, elites would need the support of non-English Americans. When they moved toward revolution in the 1770s, they quite deliberately began speaking of the rights of man, rather than English liberties, to enlist recruits.

ECONOMIC GROWTH AND DEVELOPMENT

The dramatic population increase in Anglo America caused its economies to grow, despite the vagaries of international markets. By contrast, the population and economy of New Spain's northern Borderlands stagnated. The isolated settlements produced few exports (notably, hides); residents typically exchanged goods illegally with French and English colonies rather than with Spanish Mexico or the Caribbean.

French Canada exported large quantities of furs and fish, but the government's trade monopoly ensured that most of the profits ended up in the home country. The Louisiana colony required substantial government subsidies, despite its active internal trade. Of France's American possessions, only the Caribbean islands flourished.

Population and Economic Growth

In British North America, the rising population increasingly demanded more goods and services; this led to the development of small-scale colonial manufacturing and a complex internal trade network. Roads, bridges, mills, and stores were built to serve new settlements. A lively coastal trade developed; more than half of the vessels leaving Boston by the late 1760s sailed to other mainland colonies, collecting exports and distributing imports and American-made goods. For the first time, the American population generated sufficient demand to encourage manufacturing enterprises, enabling the colonies to move away from dependence on European goods.

Iron making became the largest indigenous industry, surpassing England's by 1775. Located primarily in New Jersey, Pennsylvania, and the Chesapeake, ironworks required large investments and substantial work forces—usually indentured servants, convicts, and slaves—who dug the ore, chopped and hauled trees, then burned them to make charcoal, which was used to smelt and refine the ore. The work was dirty, dangerous, and difficult; convicts and servants often fled, but enslaved men gained valuable skills and could accumulate property because supervisors compensated them for extra work above assigned tasks. Colonial prosperity nevertheless depended chiefly on overseas demand for tobacco, rice, indigo, fish, and timber products. By selling these items, colonists earned credit to purchase English and European imports. If demand for American exports slowed, the colonists' income dropped.

Wealth and Poverty

Despite fluctuations, the American economy grew during the eighteenth century, in part due to higher earnings from exports. That, in turn produced better standards of living for property-owning Americans. Early in the century, as the price of British manufactures fell, households began acquiring amenities such as chairs and earthenware dishes. Diet also improved as trade brought more varied foodstuffs. After 1750, luxury items like silver plate could be found in wealthy homes, and the middling sort purchased imported English ceramics and teapots. Even the poorest property owners had more and better household goods.

Wealthy Americans improved their position relative to other colonists. Native-born elite families who dominated America by 1750 had begun the century with sufficient capital to take advantage of the changes caused by population growth. They were the urban merchants who exported raw materials and imported luxury goods, the large landowners who rented small farms to immigrant tenants, the slave traders, and the owners of rum distilleries. The rise of this moneyed group made mid-eighteenth-century America more socially and economically stratified.

New arrivals did not have the same opportunities for advancement as their predecessors. Still, at least two-thirds of rural householders owned their own land by 1750. But in cities, laboring families lived on the edge of destitution. By the 1760s, applicants for assistance overwhelmed public, urban poor-relief systems, and some cities established workhouses or almshouses to accommodate the growing number of poor, among them recent immigrants, the elderly and infirm, and widows, especially those with small children.

New England and King George's War

In New England, three elements influenced economic development: the landscape, shipping, and the impact of imperial wars. New England's farms produced little to sell other than livestock and timber; the region also had the lowest average wealth per freeholder in the colonies. But there were wealthy merchants who profited from trade with the Caribbean in salt fish and molasses (see Figure 4.1).

Boston, by the 1730s a major shipbuilding center, was greatly affected when British vessels clashed with Spanish ships in the Caribbean in 1739, sparking what became known in America as King George's War (Europeans called it the War of the Austrian Succession). The war initially energized Boston's economy, for ships—and sailors—were in great demand. Merchants profited by supplying military expeditions. But costly losses in Caribbean battles against Canada and an expensive victory in capturing the French Louisbourg fortress (in modern Nova Scotia) led to heavy

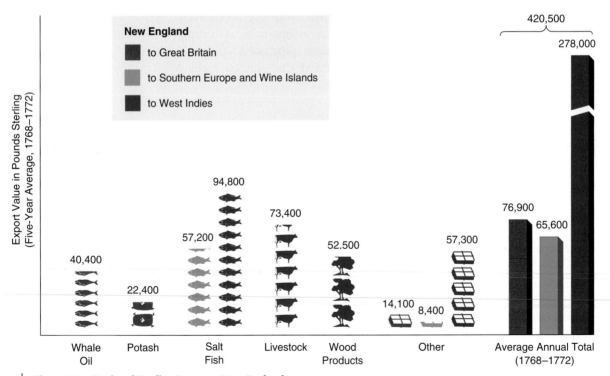

Figure 4.1   Regional Trading Patterns: New England

New England's major exports—salt fish, livestock, and wood products—were sold primarily in the West Indies.

(*Source:* James F. Shepherd and Gary M. Walton, *Shipping, Maritime Trade, and the Economic Development of Colonial North America* [Cambridge: Cambridge University Press, 1972]. Copyright 1972. Used by permission of Cambridge University Press.)

taxation of Massachusetts residents. After the war, the shipbuilding boom ended, the economy stagnated, taxes remained high, and widows and children crowded Boston's relief rolls. Britain even returned Louisbourg to France in the Treaty of Aix-la-Chapelle (1748).

Middle Colonies and the Chesapeake

King George's War affected the middle colonies and the Chesapeake more positively, thanks to the prevalence of commercial farming in the region's fertile soil. An average Pennsylvania farm family consumed only 40 percent of what it produced, selling the rest. New York and New Jersey both had many tenant farmers who leased acreage, often paying rent by sharing crops with landlords. Prosperous landlords and farmers profited from wartime demand for grain and flour, especially from the Caribbean (see Figure 4.2). After the war, several poor harvests in Europe caused flour prices to skyrocket. Philadelphia and New York, with grain- and livestock-producing areas, led the foodstuffs trade. Some Chesapeake planters began to convert tobacco fields to wheat and corn (see Figure 4.3). Tobacco remained the largest single export from mainland colonies, yet grain cultivation significantly changed Chesapeake settlement by encouraging the development of port towns (like Baltimore), where merchants and shipbuilders would handle the new trade.

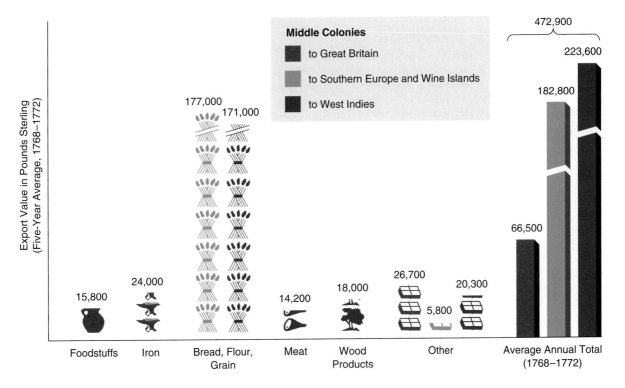

Figure 4.2   Regional Trading Patterns: Middle Colonies

The middle colonies' major trading partners were the West Indies, the Wine Islands, and southern Europe. Bread, flour, and grains were the region's most valuable exports.

(*Source:* James F. Shepherd and Gary M. Walton, *Shipping, Maritime Trade, and the Economic Development of Colonial North America* [Cambridge: University Press, 1972]. Used by permission of Cambridge University Press.)

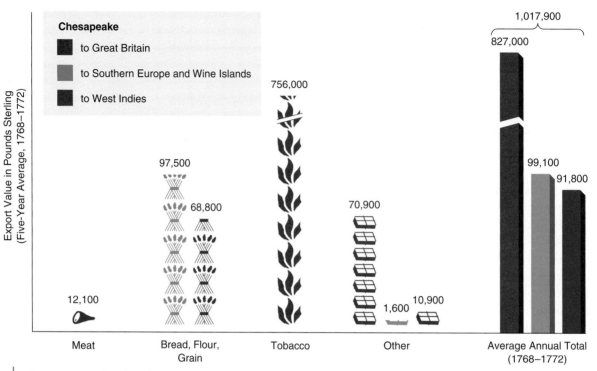

Figure 4.3   Regional Trading Patterns: The Chesapeake

Tobacco—legally exported only to Great Britain under the terms of the Navigation Acts—was the Chesapeake's dominant product. Grain made up an increasing proportion of the crops this region sold to other destinations.

(*Source:* James F. Shepherd and Gary M. Walton, *Shipping, Maritime Trade, and the Economic Development of Colonial North America* [Cambridge: Cambridge University Press, 1972]. Copyright 1972. Used by permission of Cambridge University Press.)

Carolina and Georgia

The Lower South, too, depended on staple crops and an enslaved labor force but had a distinctive pattern of economic growth. After Parliament in 1730 removed rice from the list of enumerated products, South Carolinians traded directly with Europe. Rice prices doubled by the late 1730s (see Figure 4.4). But the outbreak of King George's War disrupted trade. Rice prices plummeted, and South Carolina entered a decade-long depression. Rising European demand for South Carolina's exports restored prosperity by the 1760s. But throughout the century the colony's rice and indigo crops—and sugar cane in the Caribbean islands—were periodically devastated by hurricanes that caused some overextended planters to go bankrupt. Still, the Lower South grew faster than other regions and had the highest average wealth per freeholder in mainland Anglo America by the American Revolution.

The newest mainland settlement, Georgia, was chartered in 1732 as a haven for previously imprisoned English debtors; its founder, James Oglethorpe, envisioned Georgia as a garrison where farmers would defend the southern flank of English settlement against Spanish Florida. The charter prohibited slavery, but neighboring Carolina rice planters had the restriction removed in 1751. Thereafter, Georgia developed into a rice-planting slave society resembling South Carolina.

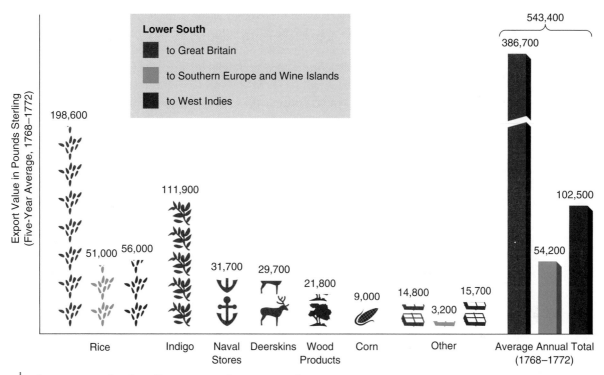

Figure 4.4   Regional Trading Patterns: The Lower South

Rice and indigo, sold primarily in the mother country, dominated the exports of the Lower South.

(*Source:* James F. Shepherd and Gary M. Walton, *Shipping, Maritime Trade, and the Economic Development of Colonial North America* [Cambridge: Cambridge University Press, 1972]. Copyright 1972. Used by permission of Cambridge University Press.)

Regional economic variations show that the British mainland colonies were not a unified whole. Despite increasing coastal trade, individual colonies' fortunes depended on the shifting markets of Europe and the Caribbean. Without an unprecedented crisis in the British imperial system (discussed in Chapter 5), it seems unlikely they could have been persuaded to join in a common endeavor. Even with that impetus, unity proved difficult to maintain.

COLONIAL CULTURES

By 1750, Britain's American possessions were marked by a denser, more diverse population than a half-century earlier, as well as by visible extremes of wealth and poverty, especially in cities. Native-born colonial elites sought to distinguish themselves from ordinary folk as they consolidated their hold on local power.

Genteel Culture

Colonists who acquired wealth through trade, agriculture, or manufacturing spent their money ostentatiously, dressing fashionably, traveling in horse-drawn carriages, and hosting lavish parties. They built large houses with rooms for dancing, cardplaying, or drinking tea. Sufficiently well-off to enjoy leisure time (a first for North America), they attended concerts and the theater, gambled at horse races, and played billiards and other games. They also cultivated polite manners. Although the effects of accumulated wealth were most pronounced in Anglo America, elite families in New Mexico, Louisiana, and Quebec as well set themselves off from the lesser sort. Together these wealthy families deliberately constructed a genteel culture quite different from that of ordinary colonists.

Men from such families prided themselves on their possessions, their positions in colonial society, their education, and their intellectual connections to Europe. Many had been tutored by private teachers; some attended college. (Harvard, the first colonial college, founded in 1636, was joined by William and Mary in 1693 and Yale in 1701.) In the seventeenth century, only aspiring clergymen attended college, but by the mid-eighteenth century, as colleges broadened their curricula to include mathematics, science, law, and medicine, young men from elite or upwardly mobile families enrolled. American women were mostly excluded from advanced education, except those tutored at nunneries in Canada or Louisiana.

The Enlightenment

The intellectual current known as the Enlightenment deeply affected the clergymen who headed colonial colleges and their students. Around 1650, European thinkers analyzed nature to determine the laws governing the universe. They employed experimentation and abstract reasoning to discover general principles behind phenomena like the motions of planets. Enlightenment philosophers emphasized acquiring knowledge through reason, challenging unquestioned assumptions. John Locke's *Essay Concerning Human Understanding* (1690) disputed the notion that human beings were imprinted with innate ideas at birth. All knowledge, Locke asserted, derived from observations. Belief in witchcraft, astrology, and similar phenomena thus came under attack.

The Enlightenment supplied educated, wealthy people in Europe and America with a common vocabulary and unified world-view—one that believed the enlightened eighteenth century was better and wiser than previous ages. It joined them in the common endeavor of making sense of God's creation. Thus American naturalists like John and William Bartram supplied European scientists with information about New World plants and animals for newly formulated classification systems. A prime example of America's participation in the Enlightenment was Benjamin Franklin, who retired from a successful printing business in 1748 at age forty-two, devoting himself to scientific experimentation and public service. His *Experiments and Observations on Electricity* (1751) established the basic theory of electricity still used today.

Enlightenment rationalism affected politics, too. Locke's *Two Treatises of Government* (1691) and works by French and Scottish philosophers challenged a divinely sanctioned, hierarchical political order originating in the power of fathers over families. Men created governments and could alter them, Locke declared. A ruler who broke the social contract and failed to protect people's rights could legitimately be ousted from power by peaceful—or violent—means. Enlightenment theorists proclaimed God's natural laws governed even the power of monarchs.

Smallpox Inoculation

Smallpox, the world's greatest killer of human beings, repeatedly ravaged North American colonists and Indians. Thus, when the vessel *Seahorse* arrived in Boston from the Caribbean in April 1721 with smallpox-infected people on board, New Englanders feared the worst and quarantined the ship. It was too late: smallpox escaped into the city, and by June several dozen people were infected.

But the Reverend Cotton Mather, a member of London's Royal Society (an Enlightenment organization), had read years earlier of a medical technique previously unknown to Europeans but widely employed in North Africa and the Middle East. Called inoculation, it involved taking pus from the pustules (or poxes) of an infected person and inserting it into a cut on the arm of a healthy individual. With luck, that person would experience a mild case and gain lifetime immunity. Mather's interest was further piqued by his slave Onesimus, a North African who had been inoculated as a youth and who described the procedure in detail.

With the disease coursing through the city, Mather promoted inoculation to the local medical community. But nearly all the city's doctors ridiculed his ideas, except Zabdiel Boylston, a physician and apothecary. The two men inoculated their children and about two hundred others. After the epidemic ended, Bostonians could see the results: of those inoculated, just 3 percent had died; among the thousands of others who contracted the disease, mortality was 15 percent. Even Mather's most vocal opponents supported inoculation thereafter.

Thus, through transatlantic links forged by the Enlightenment and enslavement, American colonists learned to combat the deadliest disease. Although Americans feared smallpox might be used as a biological weapon by its enemies after the attacks of September 11, 2001, no such incident has occurred. Today, thanks to a campaign by the World Health Organization, smallpox has been eradicated.

An Historical

ACCOUNT

OF THE

SMALL-POX

INOCULATED

IN

NEW ENGLAND,

Upon all Sorts of Persons, *Whites*, *Blacks*, and of all Ages and Constitutions.

With some Account of the Nature of the Infection in the NATURAL and INOCULATED Way, and their different Effects on HUMAN BODIES.

With some short DIRECTIONS to the UNEXPERIENCED in this Method of Practice.

Humbly dedicated to her Royal Highness the Princess of WALES, by *Zabdiel Boylston*, Physician.

LONDON:

Printed for S. CHANDLER, at the Cross-Keys in the Poultry. M.DCC.XXVI.

Several years after he and Cotton Mather combated a Boston smallpox epidemic by employing inoculation, Zabdiel Boylston published this pamphlet in London to spread the news of their success. The dedication to the Princess of Wales was designed to indicate the royal family's support of the procedure.
(Picture Research Consultants and Archives)

Oral Cultures

The world in which such ideas were discussed was small. Books and newspapers were scarce until the 1750s, and many Anglo-Americans could not read or write. Youngsters who learned to read were usually taught at home by parents, older siblings, or local widows who needed extra income. More fortunate boys (and genteel girls after the 1750s) might learn to write in private schools. Few Americans other than some Church of England missionaries in the South tried to instruct enslaved children. And only the most zealous Indian converts learned Europeans' literacy skills.

Thus the cultures of colonial North America were primarily oral, communal, and local. Face-to-face conversation was the major means of communication. Different locales developed divergent cultural traditions, and racial and ethnic variations heightened those differences.

Religious and Civic Rituals

Church attendance was perhaps the most important ritual. In early New England Congregational (Puritan) churches, men and women sat on opposite sides of a central aisle, arranged by age, wealth, and church membership. By the mid-eighteenth century, wealthy husbands and wives sat in privately owned pews; their children, servants, slaves, and the less fortunate still sat in sex-segregated fashion at the rear, sides, or balcony of the church. In eighteenth-century Virginia, planter families purchased pews, and in some parishes landed gentlemen strode into church as a group just before the service, deliberately drawing attention to their exalted position. In Quebec City, formal processions of men into the parish church celebrated Catholic feast days; each participant's rank determined his place in the procession. By contrast, Quaker meetinghouses in Pennsylvania and elsewhere used an egalitarian but sex-segregated seating system. The various seating and entrance rituals symbolized social rank and local values.

Communal culture also centered on civic involvement. In New England, governments proclaimed official days of thanksgiving (for good harvests, military victories, etc.) and days of fasting and prayer (during difficulties such as droughts or epidemics). Everyone was expected to participate. Because able-bodied men between ages sixteen and sixty were required to serve in local militias, monthly musters also brought the community together.

In the Chesapeake, important rituals occurred on court and election days. When the county court met, men came to file lawsuits, appear as witnesses, or serve as jurors. Court attendance provided civic education; from the proceedings men learned what behavior was expected of them. Elections served the same purpose, for property-holding men voted in public. An election official, often flanked by the candidates for office, would call each voter forward to declare his preference. Voters would then be thanked by the gentleman selected, often treated later to rum at nearby taverns.

Throughout colonial North America, the public punishment of criminals served to both humiliate the offender and remind the community of proper behavioral standards. Public hangings, whippings, and sitting in the stocks expressed community outrage and restored harmony. Judges often assigned penalties that shamed miscreants. When a New Mexico man assaulted his father-in-law, he was directed to pay medical expenses and kneel before him publicly to beg his forgiveness.

Even after being pardoned of capital offenses, New Englanders were frequently ordered to wear nooses around their necks for years, as a reminder to all of their violation of community norms.

Rituals of Consumption

By 1770 Anglo-American households allocated roughly one-quarter of their spending to consumer goods, which fostered new rituals centered on consumption and created what historians have termed an empire of goods. In the seventeenth century, settlers acquired necessities by bartering with neighbors or ordering from a home-country merchant. By the middle of the eighteenth century, specialized shops selling nonessentials proliferated in cities like Philadelphia and New Orleans. In 1770 Boston had more than five hundred stores, offering millinery, sewing supplies, tobacco, gloves, tableware, and the like. Even small towns had one or two retail establishments. Colonists would set aside time to go shopping, a novel and pleasurable leisure activity that marked the beginning of consumption rituals.

Colonists took pleasure in owning and displaying lovely objects for neighbors and kin to see: hanging a mirror prominently, displaying a ceramic bowl on a table, turning fabric into special clothing. A rich man might hire an artist to paint his family using the objects, thereby creating a record to be displayed.

Tea and Madeira

Tea drinking, a consumption ritual dominated by women, played an important role in Anglo America. Households with aspirations to genteel status sought the necessary items for the proper tea consumption: pots, cups, strainers, sugar tongs, bowls, and special tables. Tea provided a focal point for socializing and, because of its cost, served as a status symbol. Wealthy women regularly entertained friends at afternoon tea parties. Because tea also appeared healthful, even poor households consumed it, although without the fancy equipment of their wealthier neighbors.

Another genteel drink was Madeira wine, imported from the Portuguese islands. By 1770 Madeira had become the favored drink of the elite, expensive to purchase and consume properly. Opening the bottle, letting it breathe, decanting and serving it with appropriate glassware were all accomplished with elaborate ceremony. After the 1750s, urban dwellers could buy wines at specialized stores. Much of it must have been smuggled, because more wines were advertised than were recorded in customs records.

Rituals on the Middle Ground

Other rituals provided an opportunity for the disparate cultures of colonial North America to interact. Particularly important rituals developed on what the historian Richard White has termed the *middle ground*—the psychological and geographical space in which Indians and Europeans encountered each other, primarily via trade or warfare.

When Europeans sought to trade with Indians, they encountered an indigenous exchange system that stressed gift giving over buying and selling. Successful bargaining required French and English traders to present Indians with gifts (cloth, rum, gunpowder, and other items) before negotiating with them for pelts and skins. Only after those gifts were reciprocated could formal trading begin. Rum became a crucial component, as traders concluded that drunken Indians would sell their furs more cheaply, and some Indians refused to hunt or trade unless they first received rum. Alcohol abuse hastened the deterioration of villages already devastated by disease and dislocation.

Intercultural rituals also developed to deal with murders. Where Europeans sought primarily to punish the murderer, Indians regarded Europeans' eye for an eye revenge as only one possible response. Compensation could also be accomplished by capturing another Indian or a colonist to take the dead person's place or by "covering the dead"—providing the deceased's family with compensatory goods. Eventually, the French and the Algonquians evolved an elaborate ritual borrowed from both societies' traditions: murders were investigated and murderers identified, but deaths were covered by trade goods rather than blood revenge.

COLONIAL FAMILIES

Families constituted the basic units of colonial society, serving as the mechanism for production and consumption. Never-married adults were extremely rare. Yet family forms varied widely, and not all were headed by couples.

Indian and Mixed-Race Families As Europeans consolidated their hold on North America, Indians had to adapt. Bands reduced by disease and warfare recombined into new units; for example, the Catawbas emerged in the 1730s in the western Carolinas by merging several earlier peoples including the Yamasees and Guales. Likewise, European authorities reshaped Indian family forms. Whereas many Indian societies had permitted easy divorce, European missionaries frowned on it; and societies that had allowed polygynous marriages (including New England Algonquians) redefined them to designate one wife as legitimate and others as concubines.

With continued high mortality rates, extended kin took on new importance in Indian societies, with other relatives—even occasionally nonkin—assuming child-rearing responsibilities when parents died. Once Europeans established dominance in any region, Indians were unable to pursue traditional modes of subsistence, pushing them into unusual family structures and new economic strategies. In New England, for instance, Algonquian husbands and wives survived by working separately and often living apart (perhaps wives as domestic servants, husbands as sailors). Some native women married African American men, due to sexual imbalances in both populations. In New Mexico, detribalized Navajos, Pueblos, and Apaches employed as servants by Spanish settlers clustered in the small Borderlands towns. Known as *genizaros,* they lost contact with Indian cultures, instead living on the fringes of Latino society.

Wherever the population contained relatively few European women, sexual liaisons occurred between European men and Indian women. The resulting mixed-race population of *mestizos* and *métis* worked as a familial middle ground to ease other cultural interactions. In New France and the Anglo-American backcountry, such families resided in Indian villages, and their children sometimes became prominent

Native American leaders. By contrast, in the Spanish Borderlands the offspring of Europeans and *genizaros* were shunned. Largely denied legal marriage, they bore generations of illegitimate children of various racial mixtures, giving rise in Latino society to multiple labels describing degrees of skin color with a precision unknown in English or French America.

European American Families

To eighteenth-century Anglo-Americans, the word *family* meant everyone in one household (including servants and slaves). In 1790 the average home in the United States contained 5.7 free people; few included extended kin, such as grandparents. Family members worked together to produce goods for consumption or sale. The head of the household represented it to the outside world, voting in elections, managing the finances, and holding legal authority over the rest of the family—his wife, his children, and his servants and slaves.

In English, French, and Spanish America, the vast majority of European families supported themselves by cultivating crops and raising livestock. While the work differed by region and crop produced, household tasks were allocated by sex.

The mistress oversaw her female helpers in what Anglo-Americans called indoor affairs, preparing food, cleaning the house, doing laundry, and often making clothes. Along with cooking, food preparation involved cultivating a garden, harvesting and preserving vegetables, salting and smoking meat, drying apples and pressing cider, milking cows, and making butter and cheese. The head of the household and his male helpers, managed outdoor affairs, cultivating the fields, building fences, chopping wood, harvesting and marketing crops, caring for livestock, and butchering cattle and hogs. Farm work was so extensive that a married couple could not do it alone; if childless, they needed servants or slaves.

African American Families

Most African American families lived as components of European American households. More than 95 percent of colonial African Americans were held in perpetual bondage, sometimes on farms with only a few other slaves. In South Carolina, a majority of the population was of African origin; in Georgia, about half; and in the Chesapeake, 40 percent. Portions of the Carolina low country were nearly 90 percent African American by 1790.

Where African Americans lived determined the shape of their families. In the North, the scarcity of other blacks made it difficult for bondspeople to form stable households. In the Chesapeake, men and women who regarded themselves as married (slaves could not legally wed) frequently lived on different quarters or different

In eighteenth-century Spain, the existence of mixed-race North American families aroused great curiosity, creating a market for so-called *casta* paintings, which illustrated different sorts of multiracial households. In 1763 the Mexican artist Miguel Cabrera depicted a Spanish father and an Indian mother, who have produced a *mestiza* daughter. Real families resembling this idealized picture would have been seen in New Mexico.
(© The Gallery Collection / Corbis)

plantations. Children generally resided with their mothers. On large Carolina and Georgia rice plantations, enslaved families usually lived together and accumulated property by working for themselves after completing daily tasks. Some Georgia slaves sold surplus produce, earning money for nice clothing or such luxuries as tobacco, but rarely enough for their freedom.

Forms of Resistance   Because all British colonies legally permitted slavery, bondspeople had few options for escaping servitude other than fleeing to Florida, where the Spanish offered protection. Some recently arrived Africans stole boats or ran off to join Indians or establish independent communities on the frontier. Among American-born slaves, family ties strongly affected such decisions. As one South Carolina planter wrote, slaves "love their families dearly and none runs away from the other." Consequently, many owners sought to keep families together. In the Chesapeake, where family members often lived separately, affectionate ties could cause slaves to run away, especially if family members were sold.

Although colonial slaves rarely rebelled collectively, they resisted in other ways. Bondspeople rejected owners' attempts to commandeer their labor on Sundays without compensation. Extended-kin groups protested excessive punishment of relatives and sought to live near one another. If parents and children were separated by sale, other relatives helped with child rearing. Just as among Indians, the extended family served a more important function for African Americans than for European Americans.

Most slave families carved out some autonomy, especially in their working and spiritual lives, and particularly in the Lower South. Some African Americans preserved traditional beliefs or Islamic faith, while others converted to Christianity, comforted by its assurances that everyone would be free and equal in heaven. South Carolina and Georgia slaves jealously guarded their ability to control their time after completing their tasks. Even on Chesapeake tobacco plantations, slaves planted gardens and trapped or fished to supplement their meager diet. Late in the century, some Chesapeake planters began to hire slaves out, often allowing the workers to keep some of their earnings.

City Life   In cities, African and European Americans resided together in unsegregated neighborhoods. (In 1760s Philadelphia, one-fifth of the work force was enslaved, and by 1775 blacks composed nearly 15 percent of New York City's population.) Such cities were tiny by today's standards. In 1750 the largest cities, Boston and Philadelphia, had just seventeen thousand and thirteen thousand inhabitants, respectively. Unlike their rural counterparts, city dwellers purchased food and wood, and men's jobs frequently took them away from their household, giving them greater contact with the broader world.

By the 1750s, most major cities had at least one weekly newspaper. Anglo-American newspapers mixed local reports with the latest advices from London (usually two to three months old). People who could not afford to buy newspapers could either read them (or listen to them read aloud) at taverns and coffeehouses. Urban contact with the outside world, however, meant sailors sometimes brought deadly diseases into port. Boston, New York, Philadelphia, and New Orleans endured small-pox and yellow fever epidemics, which Europeans and Africans in the countryside largely escaped.

POLITICS: STABILITY AND CRISIS IN BRITISH AMERICA

Early in the eighteenth century, Anglo-American political life exhibited new stability. Despite substantial immigration, most mainland residents were born in America. Men from genteel families dominated the political structures, for voters (free male property holders) typically deferred to their well-educated betters in elections.

Colonial Assemblies   Throughout the Anglo-American colonies, political leaders sought to increase the powers of elected assemblies relative to that of governors and other appointed officials. Assemblies began to claim privileges associated with the British House of Commons, such as initiating tax legislation and controlling the militia. Assemblies also influenced British appointees by threatening to withhold their salaries. In some colonies (Virginia and South Carolina, for example), elite assemblymen presented a united front to royal officials, but in others (such as New York), they fought among themselves bitterly. To win hotly contested elections, New York's genteel leaders began competing for commoners' votes. Yet in 1733 the New York government imprisoned a newspaper editor, John Peter Zenger, who had criticized it, on the charge of seditious libel. Arguing that the truth could not be defamatory, his lawyer helped establish the free-press principle in American law.

Assemblymen saw themselves as acting to prevent encroachments on the colonists' liberties, for example, by preventing governors from imposing oppressive taxes. By midcentury, they were comparing the structure of their governments to Britain's balanced polity, equating their governors with the monarch, their councils with the aristocracy, and their assemblies with the House of Commons. All three were believed essential to good government, but Anglo-Americans viewed governors and appointed councils as Britain's representatives and potential threats to colonial ways of life. Many colonists saw the assemblies, however, as the people's protectors. And the assemblies regarded themselves as the people's representatives.

In reality, the assemblies, controlled by dominant families whose members were reelected year after year, rarely responded to poorer constituents' concerns. They also did not reapportion themselves to provide representation for new settlements; this led to grievances among backcountry dwellers, especially non-English ethnic groups. The colonial ideal of the assembly as the defender of liberty was a myth. In truth, the most ably represented were wealthy male colonists, particularly the assembly members themselves.

At midcentury, the political structures that had stabilized in a period of relative calm confronted a series of crises—ethnic, racial, economic, and regional—that exposed internal tensions and foreshadowed the disorder of the revolutionary era. They demonstrated that the political accommodations achieved after the Glorious Revolution could no longer adequately govern Britain's American empire.

Slave Rebellions in South Carolina and New York

Early on Sunday, September 9, 1739, about twenty enslaved men, most likely Catholics from Kongo, gathered near the Stono River south of Charles Town. September fell in the midst of the rice harvest (and thus a stressful time for male Africans, less accustomed than women to rice cultivation), and September 8 was, to Catholics, the birthday of the Virgin Mary. Seizing guns and ammunition, the slaves killed storekeepers and nearby planter families. Then, joined by other slaves, they headed toward Florida in hopes of finding refuge. By midday, however, the militia attacked the nearly one hundred fugitives, killing some and dispersing the rest. A week later, most of the remaining conspirators were captured and executed. But for two years rumors about escaped renegades haunted the colony.

After the Stono Rebellion, laws governing African Americans were stiffened throughout British America. In New York City, the site of the first mainland slave revolt in 1712, the Stono news combined with fears of Spain generated by the outbreak of King George's War to set off a reign of terror in the summer of 1741. Colonial authorities suspected a biracial gang of thieves and arsonists of fomenting a slave uprising under the guidance of a white schoolteacher thought to be a Spanish priest. By summer's end, thirty-one blacks and four whites had been executed for participating in the alleged plot. The Stono Rebellion and the New York conspiracy confirmed Anglo-Americans' deepest fears about the dangers of slaveholding and revealed the assemblies' inability to prevent internal disorder.

Rioters and Regulators

By midcentury, with most fertile land east of the Appalachians purchased or occupied, conflicts over land titles and conditions of landholding increased. In 1746, for example, violence erupted when the East proprietors claimed farmers' land as theirs and demanded annual payments, called quit-rents. The most serious land riots occurred along the Hudson River in 1765–1766. Late in the seventeenth century, the governor of New York had granted huge tracts in the lower Hudson valley to prominent families. They then divided these estates into small farms, which they rented to poor Dutch and German migrants who regarded tenancy as a step toward independence.

After 1740, though, New Englanders increasingly migrated to the region, resisting tenancy and often squatting. In the mid-1760s the Philipse family sued farmers who had lived on Philipse land for two decades. The courts ordered squatters to make way for tenants with valid leases. Instead, a diverse group of farmers rebelled, terrorizing proprietors and tenants and on one occasion battling a county sheriff and his posse. The rebellion lasted nearly a year, ending when British troops captured its leaders.

Violent conflicts erupted in the Carolinas as well when the Regulator movements of the late 1760s (South Carolina) and early 1770s (North Carolina) pitted backcountry farmers against wealthy eastern planters who controlled colonial governments. In South Carolina, Scots-Irish settlers protested their lack of an adequate voice in political affairs. For months they policed the countryside in vigilante bands known as Regulators, complaining of lax and biased law enforcement. North Carolina Regulators, who objected to heavy taxation, lost a battle with eastern militiamen at Alamance in 1771.

A CRISIS IN RELIGION

The most widespread crisis was religious. From the mid-1730s through the 1760s, waves of religious revivalism—today known as the First Great Awakening—swept over various colonies, primarily New England (1735–1745) and Virginia (1750s–1760s). Orthodox Calvinists sought to combat Enlightenment rationalism, which denied innate human depravity. The economic and political uncertainty accompanying King George's War made colonists receptive to evangelists' messages. With no prior religious affiliation, many recent immigrants and backcountry residents became potential converts.

The Great Awakening began in New England, where descendants of the Puritan founding generation still composed the membership of Congregational churches. While church members were predominantly female, men and women responded with equal fervor. In the mid-1730s, the Northampton, Massachusetts, preacher and theologian Reverend Jonathan Edwards gained new youthful adherents with a Calvinist-based message that individuals could attain salvation, only by recognizing their depraved nature and surrendering completely to God's will.

George Whitefield The effects of such conversions remained isolated until 1739, when George Whitefield, a Church of England clergyman, who led celebrated revivals in England, arrived in America. A gripping orator, Whitefield toured the British colonies for fifteen months, effectively generating the Great Awakening by preaching to large audiences from

Reverend George Whitefield, the charismatic evangelist who sparked the First Great Awakening in the mainland British colonies, attracted harsh critics as well as avid admirers. Here an English cartoonist satirizes him as a money-grubbing charlatan who hoodwinks his gullible followers into believing that he is a "Pious Churchman" motivated by "Holy Zeal." Whitefield's crossed eyes, obvious in this image as in others, played a prominent role in contemporary depictions of him. (The Granger Collection, New York)

Georgia to New England. The historian Harry Stout has termed him *the first modern celebrity* because of his skillful self-promotion and clever manipulation of both listeners and the newspapers. Everywhere he traveled, his fame preceded him. Readers snapped up books by and about him, among the first colonial bestsellers. Thousands of free and enslaved folk from Boston to Savannah heard him speak and experienced conversion. Whitefield's journey created new interconnections among the previously distinct colonies.

Regular clerics initially welcomed Whitefield and his American-born imitators, but soon concluded that the revived religion ran counter to their own doctrine. They disliked the emotional style of the revivalists, who lured churchgoers away from their usual church services. Particularly troublesome to the orthodox were the female exhorters who publicly proclaimed their right to expound God's word.

Impact of the Awakening

Opposition to the Awakening heightened rapidly, further splintering the already fragmented American Protestantism. Major denominations split into Old Lights—traditional clerics and their followers—and New Lights—the evangelicals. New sects such as Methodists and Baptists also gained adherents. Paradoxically, the angry fights and the rapid rise in the number of distinct denominations eventually inspired an American willingness to tolerate religious diversity. Since no single sect could make an unequivocal claim to orthodoxy, they had to coexist if they were to exist at all.

Most significantly, the Awakening challenged traditional social patterns, in particular the colonial tradition of deference. Itinerant preachers, only a few of whom were ordained, claimed they understood God's will better than elite college-educated clerics. They and their followers divided the world into the saved and the damned, without respect to gender, age, or status. New Lights also defended the rights of individuals to dissent from a community consensus, thereby challenging fundamental tenets of colonial political life. The egalitarian themes of the Awakening simultaneously attracted ordinary folk and repelled the elite.

Virginia Baptists

By the 1760s Baptists gained a foothold in Virginia, but their beliefs clashed with genteel lifestyles. They rejected as sinful the horseracing, gambling, and dancing that occupied the gentry's leisure time. They dressed plainly, in contrast to the gentry's opulence. They addressed one another as Brother and Sister regardless of social status, and they elected their congregation's leaders. Their monthly great meetings, which attracted hundreds of people, introduced new public rituals that rivaled weekly Anglican services.

Strikingly, almost all the Virginia Baptist congregations included free and enslaved members, and some had African American majorities. Church rules applied equally to all members; interracial sexual relationships, divorce, and adultery were forbidden. Congregations forbade masters from breaking up slave couples through sale. Biracial committees investigated complaints about members' misbehavior. Churches excommunicated slaves for stealing from their masters and masters for physically abusing their slaves.

By injecting an egalitarian strain into Anglo-American life at midcentury, the Great Awakening had important social and political consequences, calling into question habitual modes of behavior in the secular as well as the religious realm.

"Self-Made Men"

Americans universally celebrate the ideal of the self-made man (always someone explicitly *male*) of humble origins who gains wealth through extraordinary efforts. Most commonly cited as examples are nineteenth-century businessmen such as Andrew Carnegie (a poor immigrant from Scotland) and John D. Rockefeller (born on a hardscrabble farm in upstate New York).

The initial exemplars, though, lived in the eighteenth century. Benjamin Franklin's *Autobiography* chronicled his method for achieving success after beginning life as the seventeenth child of a Boston candle maker. From such humble origins Franklin became a wealthy, influential man active in science, politics, education, and diplomacy. Yet Franklin's tale is rivaled by that of a man apparently born a slave in South Carolina. He acquired literacy, worked as a sailor, purchased his freedom, became an influential abolitionist, married a wealthy Englishwoman, and published a popular autobiography that predated Franklin's. His first master called him Gustavus Vassa, but when publishing his *Interesting Narrative* in 1789, he called himself Olaudah Equiano.

In his *Narrative*, Equiano said he was born in Africa in 1745, kidnapped at the age of eleven, and transported to Barbados and then to Virginia, where a British naval officer purchased him. For years, scholars and students have relied on that account for its insights into the experience of the middle passage. But evidence recently uncovered by Vincent Carretta, although confirming much of Equiano's autobiography, shows that Equiano twice identified his birthplace as Carolina and was three to five years younger than he claimed. Carretta speculates that the *Narrative* gained its credibility from Equiano's African birth and that admitting his real age would have raised questions about his early life.

Equiano, or Vassa, thus truly made himself, just as Benjamin Franklin and many others have done. (Franklin tended to omit, rather than alter, inconvenient parts of his personal history, for example, his having fathered an illegitimate son.) Equiano used information undoubtedly gleaned from acquaintances who *had* experienced the middle passage to craft an accurate depiction of its horrors. In the process he became one of the first Americans to explicitly reinvent himself.

Summary

Over the half-century before 1770, British North America was transformed, partly by the many newcomers from Germany, Scotland, Ireland, and Africa, who brought their languages, customs, and religions with them. The European immigrants were concentrated in the growing cities and backcountry. By contrast, enslaved migrants from Africa lived and worked within 100 miles of the Atlantic coast. In many colonial South areas, 50 to 90 percent of the population was of African origin.

The economic life of Europe's North American colonies proceeded on two levels. On the farms, plantations, and ranches where most colonists resided, arduous labor dominated people's lives while providing the goods for consumption or sale. Simultaneously, an intricate international trade network affected the economies of the British, French, and Spanish colonies. The bitter wars fought by European nations during the eighteenth century both created new opportunities for overseas sales and disrupted traditional markets. The few who reaped the profits of international commerce were the wealthy class of merchants and landowners who dominated colonial life. A century and a half after Europeans first settled in North America, the colonies mixed diverse European, American, and African traditions into a novel cultural blend.

Europeans who interacted regularly with peoples of African and American origin—and with Europeans from other nations—developed new methods of accommodating intercultural differences while also creating ties within their own potentially fragmenting communities. Initially, many colonists continued to identify themselves as French, Spanish, or British rather than as Americans, but in the 1760s some Anglo-Americans began to realize that their interests did not necessarily coincide with those of Great Britain.

Chapter Review

POPULATION GROWTH AND ETHNIC DIVERSITY

What spurred population growth in the thirty years before 1775?

Immigration—particularly Scots-Irish and Germans—contributed to some of the population growth among European Americans, but the largest single factor was natural increase (live births). Once the difficult years of early settlement passed and the sex ratio evened out in the South, the population doubled every twenty-five years. Natural increase also boosted the African American enslaved population after 1740, and in some regions the slave population was further augmented by new imports.

[handwritten margin notes: Immigration — Scots-Irish and Germans — live births — doubled every 25 yrs. — boosted Af. Am. enslaved pop.]

ECONOMIC GROWTH AND DEVELOPMENT

How were the colonies' economic fate increasingly linked to world markets?

Simply put, as colonial population grew, the increased demand for goods and products sparked the development of small-scale American manufacturing and broader trade networks. Moreover, selling tobacco, rice, indigo, fish, and timber overseas provided the resources for colonists to import what they did not produce and to prosper individually and regionally. But as colonies became more entwined in overseas trade, their fortunes were increasingly tied to the ups and downs of those economies. The outbreak of King George's War, for example, disrupted the rice trade and caused prices to plummet.

COLONIAL CULTURES

How did rituals function in colonial America?

Cultural rituals played a central role in colonial life, both to create community and reinforce social status. Church rituals were among the most important, but also the most revealing, with seating arrangements often made by sex, class, age, or wealth. Civic rituals likewise generated community involvement and revealed what society expected of its members. In New England, everyone was expected to participate in official holidays or local militia musters; in the Chesapeake, rituals centered on court or election days; and public punishment of criminals throughout North America was a ritual designed to reinforce behavioral standards.

Even simple rituals, such as tea-drinking, reinforced gender norms but also distinctions of wealth and status. Finally, colonists created middle ground rituals to facilitate trade with Indians, who had vastly different customs. Europeans seeking to trade with Indians engaged in the gift-giving system typical of native cultures before trade could begin.

COLONIAL FAMILIES

How did European American families differ from those of Indians or African Americans?

Anglo Americans used the word "family" to describe everyone in a household: parents, children, extended kin, and slaves. Families typically supported themselves by farming, with each member assigned a task according to gender norms. (Women did indoor work and related tasks; men did outdoor work.) Indian families were more fluid; before contact with Europeans, they permitted divorce, for example. After contact, extended kin became more important, particularly as families were decimated by disease. Shortages of European women in some colonies fueled increased inter-marriages, with children raised in Indian villages rather than among settlers. Most African Americans were enslaved, and their families subsumed under European American households. In the Chesapeake, slaves who considered themselves married (despite laws prohibiting slave marriage) often lived in different quarters or plantations with children residing with mothers (and potentially sold off at any time.) On large Georgia or Carolina rice plantations, slave families often lived together.

POLITICS: STABILITY AND CRISIS IN BRITISH AMERICA

What were the myths and realities of colonial assemblies?

Anglo-American assemblymen believed they safeguarded colonists' liberties from encroachments by the British government, such as oppressive taxation. Regarding Britain's appointed councils and governors as potential threats, colonists looked to assemblies as their protectors. In truth, elite, wealthy families dominated the assemblies and paid little regard to constituents' concerns, nor did they reapportion themselves so that new settlements would gain representatives, which angered backcountry residents and non-English immigrants.

A CRISIS IN RELIGION

What was the social and political impact of the Great Awakening?

Socially, the Great Awakening challenged traditional norms and patterns. Women, for example, began to claim an equal right to preach, and Protestant denominations further split into the "Old Lights"—who followed traditional teachings and ministers—and the "New Light" evangelicals. In the end, the rise of new denominations promoted greater tolerance for religious diversity, but at the time, it sparked animosity. The Great Awakening's egalitarianism also challenged the colonial tradition of deference, in which people knew their place and respected their so-called "betters." New Lights attracted ordinary people as followers and preachers, and argued that the world was divided into the saved and the damned without respect to gender, age or status.

SUGGESTIONS FOR FURTHER READING

Marilyn Baseler, *"Asylum for Mankind": America 1607–1800* (1998)

Richard R. Beeman, *The Varieties of Political Experiences in Eighteenth-Century America* (2004)

James F. Brooks, *Captives and Cousins: Slavery, Kinship, and Community in the Southwest Borderlands* (2002)

William E. Burns, *Science and Technology in Colonial America* (2005)

Richard Bushman, *The Refinement of America: Persons, Houses, Cities* (1992)

Rhys Isaac, *The Transformation of Virginia, 1740–1790* (1982)

Jill Lepore, *New York Burning: Liberty, Slavery, and Conspiracy in Eighteenth-Century Manhattan* (2005)

John J. McCusker and Russell R. Menard, *The Economy of British America, 1607–1789* (1985)

Harry S. Stout, *The Divine Dramatist: George Whitefield and the Rise of Modern Evangelicalism* (1991)

Stephanie G. Wolf, *As Various as Their Land: The Everyday Lives of 18th Century Americans* (1992)

CHAPTER 5

Severing the Bonds of Empire

CHAPTER OUTLINE

Renewed Warfare Among Europeans and Indians

1763: A Turning Point

LINKS TO THE WORLD: The First Worldwide War

The Stamp Act Crisis

Resistance to the Townshend Acts

Confrontations in Boston

Tea and Turmoil

LEGACY FOR A PEOPLE AND A NATION: Women's Political Activism

Summary

The well-born Scotswoman Janet Schaw chose an inopportune time to visit her older brother in North America. Sailing from Edinburgh in October 1774, she arrived in the West Indies in January 1775, where she visited Scottish planter families and did some shopping before sailing on to meet her brother in North Carolina. There she encountered "rusticks" who had, in her opinion, a "rooted hatred" for the mother country and were forming "schemes" detrimental to Britain and America.

Janet Schaw soon learned that an American congress had forbidden "every kind of diversion, even card-playing." When Wilmington residents held a ball before the ban took effect, she compared it to seventeenth-century Dutch paintings of comic, carousing peasants. She also reported that "the Ladies have burnt their tea in a solemn procession," but added, "the sacrifice was not very considerable, as I do not think any one offered above a quarter of a pound." All the "genteel" merchants, she observed, "disapprove of the present proceedings," and were planning to leave. She concluded that the trouble in the colonies had been caused by "mistaken notions of moderation" in parliamentary policy. Janet returned to Scotland within the year; her brother's property was later confiscated by the state for refusing an oath of allegiance, but he remained in his new homeland until his death.

In retrospect, John Adams identified 1760 to 1775 as the era of the true American Revolution. The Revolution, Adams declared, ended before the fighting started, for it was "in the Minds of the people," involving not the actual wartime victory but a shift of allegiance from Britain to America. Today, not all historians would concur. But none would deny the importance of the events of those crucial years, which divided Americans politically and pointed the colonies toward independence.

This icon will direct you to interactive activities and study materials on A People And A Nation, Brief Edition website: **www.cengage.com/history/norton/peoplenationbrief8e**

Chronology

1754	Albany Congress meets to try to forge colonial unity.	**1766**	Stamp Act is repealed.
	Fighting breaks out with Washington's defeat at Fort Necessity.		Declaratory Act insists that Parliament can tax the colonies.
1756	Britain declares war on France; Seven Years' War officially begins.	**1767**	Townshend Acts lay duties on trade within the empire and sends new officials to America.
1759	British forces take Quebec.	**1768**	Fort Stanwix treaty opens Kentucky to Anglo-American settlement.
1760	American phase of war ends with fall of Montreal to British troops.	**1768–70**	Townshend duties are resisted; boycotts and public demonstrations divide merchants and urban artisans.
	George III becomes king.		
1763	Treaty of Paris ends Seven Years' War.	**1770**	Lord North becomes prime minister.
	Pontiac's allies attack British forts in the West.		Townshend duties are repealed, except for tea tax.
	Proclamation of 1763 attempts to close land west of the Appalachians to English settlement.		Boston Massacre kills five colonial rioters.
1764	Sugar Act lays new duties on molasses and tightens customs regulations.	**1772**	Boston Committee of Correspondence is formed.
		1773	Tea Act aids the East India Company.
	Currency Act outlaws paper money issued by the colonies.		Boston Tea Party protests the Tea Act.
1765	Stamp Act requires stamps on all printed materials in the colonies.	**1774**	Coercive Acts punish Boston and Massachusetts as a whole.
	Sons of Liberty is formed.		Quebec Act reforms government of Quebec.
			First Continental Congress is called.

During the 1760s and early 1770s, an ever-widening split occurred between Great Britain and Anglo America. In the long history of British settlement in the Western Hemisphere, tension had occasionally marred the relationship between individual provinces and the mother country. Still, it rarely persisted for long and was not widespread, except during the crisis following the Glorious Revolution in 1689. In the 1750s, however, a series of events beginning with the Seven Years' War drew the colonists' attention toward their relations with Great Britain.

Britain's overwhelming victory in that war, confirmed by treaty in 1763, forever altered the balance of power in North America. France was ousted from the continent and Spain from Florida, with major consequences for interior indigenous peoples and British colonists. Indians, who were expert at playing European powers against one another, lost a major diplomatic tool. Anglo-Americans no longer feared the French on their northern and western borders or the Spanish in the Southeast. The coastal British colonies would never have risked breaking with their mother country, some historians contend, had France still controlled the Mississippi River and the Great Lakes.

The British victory in 1763 left Great Britain with a massive war debt that needed to be repaid. Consequently, Parliament for the first time imposed revenue-raising taxes on the colonies in addition to the customs duties that had long regulated trade. That exposed differences in the political thinking of Americans and Britons that had previously been obscured by a shared political vocabulary.

During the 1760s and early 1770s, Anglo-American men and women resisted new tax levies and Britain's attempts to tighten controls over provincial governments. The colonies' elected leaders became increasingly suspicious of Britain's motives. They laid aside old antagonisms to coordinate their responses to these measures. As late as summer 1774, though, most were seeking a solution within the empire; few harbored thoughts of independence.

- What were the causes and consequences of the Seven Years' War?
- What British policies did Americans protest, and what theories and strategies did they develop to support those protests?
- Was a war for independence inevitable by the end of 1773? Why or why not?

RENEWED WARFARE AMONG EUROPEANS AND INDIANS

In the mid-eighteenth century, British colonies along the Atlantic seaboard were surrounded by potentially hostile neighbors: Indians everywhere, the Spanish in Florida and the Gulf of Mexico, the French along the rivers and lakes stretching from the St. Lawrence to the Mississippi. Spanish outposts posed little threat, since Spain was no longer a major power. However, France's forts and settlements dominated the North American interior. In all three Anglo-French wars between 1689 and 1748 Britain could not shake France's hold on the American frontier. Under the Peace of Utrecht, which ended Queen Anne's War in 1713, England won control of such peripheral northern areas as Newfoundland, Hudson's Bay, and Acadia (Nova Scotia). But Britain made no territorial gains in King George's War (see Table 5.1).

Iroquois Neutrality

During Queen Anne's War and King George's War, the Iroquois Confederacy maintained a neutrality policy first developed in 1701. While British and French forces vied for nominal control of North America, the confederacy skillfully manipulated the Europeans, refusing to commit warriors to either side despite gifts from both. The Iroquois continued a long-standing conflict with Cherokees and Catawbas in the South, thus giving young warriors combat experience and replacing population

TABLE 5.1   The Colonial Wars, 1689–1763

American Name	European Name	Dates	Participants	American Sites	Dispute
King William's War	War of the League of Augsburg	1689–97	England, Holland versus France, Spain	New England, New York, Canada	French power
Queen Anne's War	War of the Spanish Succession	1702–13	England, Holland, Austria versus France, Spain	Florida, New England	Throne of Spain
King George's War	War of the Austrian Succession	1739–48	England, Holland, Austria versus France, Spain, Prussia	West Indies, New England, Canada	Throne of Austria
French and Indian War	Seven Years' War	1756–63	England versus France, Spain	Ohio country, Canada	Possession of Ohio country

losses with new captives. They also cultivated peaceful relationships with Pennsylvania and Virginia, partly to obtain the colonists' imprimatur for their domination of the Shawnees and Delawares. And they forged ties with Algonquians of the Great Lakes region, thereby making themselves indispensable go-betweens for commerce between the Atlantic coast and the West. Thus the Iroquois consolidated their control over the interior north of Virginia and south of the Great Lakes.

But the region inhabited by the Shawnees and Delawares (now western Pennsylvania and Virginia, and eastern Ohio) provided the spark that set off a major war. In a significant reversal of previous patterns, that conflict spread from America to Europe, decisively resolving the contest for North America.

Trouble began in the 1740s, when at two treaty conferences Iroquois negotiators, claiming to speak for the Delawares and Shawnees, ceded large land tracts to Pennsylvania officials. Squatters (mainly Scots-Irish and Germans, but also some Anglo-Americans) had negotiated individual agreements with the Delawares for settlement rights; some paying rent to native "landlords." But the agreements reached by agents of the Penn family and the Iroquois ignored local Indians and squatters, all of whom were told to move. Disgruntled Delawares and Shawnees migrated west, where they joined other displaced eastern Indians.

The region to which they moved, claimed by both Virginia and Pennsylvania, was coveted by wealthy Virginians, who, organized as the Ohio Company, received a huge land grant in 1749. The company's agents established trading posts in the west, hoping to control the crucial area where the Allegheny and Monongahela Rivers join to form the Ohio (see Map 5.1). But the French relied on the Ohio River for direct access to its posts on the Mississippi. Thus, in the early 1750s, Pennsylvania fur traders, Ohio Company representatives, the French military, squatters, Iroquois, Delawares, and Shawnees jostled for position in the region. A 1752 raid by the French and their native allies on a trading outpost situated at modern Cleveland rid the region of Pennsylvanians, but the Virginians posed a challenge. Accordingly, in 1753 the French pushed southward, building fortified outposts at strategic points.

Albany Congress

In response to the French threat, delegates from seven northern and middle colonies gathered in Albany, New York, in June 1754. They sought two goals: to persuade the Iroquois to abandon their neutrality and to coordinate colonial defense. The Iroquois saw no reason to change a policy that served them well for half a century. And although the Albany Congress adopted a Plan of Union (which would have established an elected intercolonial legislature with the power to tax), their provincial governments rejected the plan, fearing a loss of autonomy.

While the Albany Congress delegates deliberated, the war began. Virginia Governor Robert Dinwiddie sent a small militia troop to build a palisade at the forks of the Ohio. When a substantial French force arrived there, the Virginia militia surrendered and left. The French then constructed the more elaborate Fort Duquesne. Learning of the confrontation, the inexperienced young officer who commanded Virginia reinforcements pressed on, attacking a French detachment and becoming trapped in his crudely built Fort Necessity at Great Meadows, Pennsylvania. After a day-long battle (on July 3, 1754), during which more than one-third of his men were killed or wounded, twenty-two-year-old George Washington surrendered.

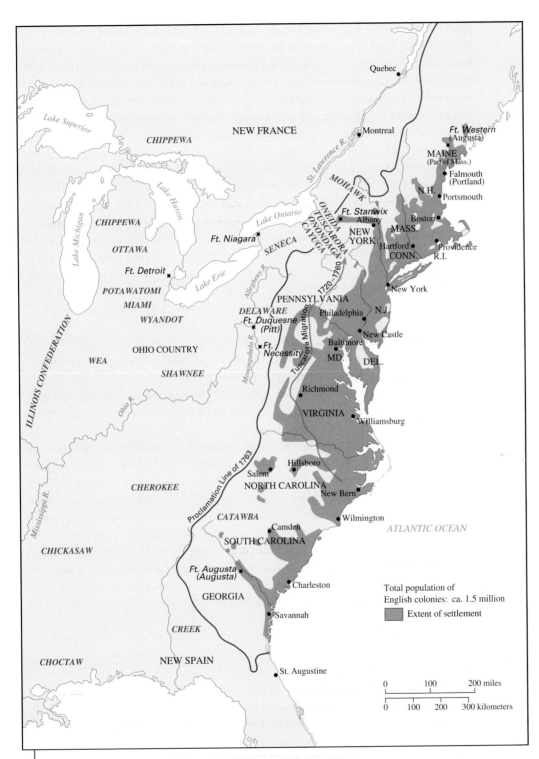

Map 5.1   European Settlements and Indians, 1754

By 1754 Europeans had expanded the limits of the English colonies to the eastern slopes of the Appalachian Mountains. Few independent Indian nations still existed in the East, but beyond the mountains they controlled the countryside. Only a few widely scattered English and French forts maintained the Europeans' presence there.

Seven Years' War

Washington's blunder helped ignite a war that would encompass nearly the entire world. In July 1755, a few miles south of Fort Duquesne, the French and Indians jointly attacked British and colonial troops. In the devastating defeat, General Edward Braddock was killed. The Pennsylvania frontier was repeatedly attacked by Delawares for two more years. Settlers felt betrayed because the Indians attacking them—their former neighbors—had once been (an observer noted) "allmost dayly familiars at their houses."

Britain declared war on France in 1756, thus formally beginning the Seven Years' War. Even before then, Britons and New Englanders feared that France would try to retake Nova Scotia, where most of the population was descended from seventeenth-century French settlers who had intermarried with local Mikmaqs. Afraid that the approximately twelve thousand French Nova Scotians would abandon their neutrality policy, British commanders in 1755 forced about seven thousand from their homeland—the first large-scale modern deportation, now called ethnic cleansing. Ships crammed with Acadians sailed to each mainland colony. Many families were separated, some forever. After 1763 the survivors relocated, some to Canada, others to France or its Caribbean islands. Many settled in Louisiana, where they became known as Cajuns (derived from *Acadian*).

British officers tried unsuccessfully to coerce the colonies into supplying men and materiel to the army. When William Pitt, the civilian official spearheading the war effort in 1757, agreed to reimburse the colonies' wartime expenditures and placed recruitment in local hands, he gained American support. Many colonial militiamen served alongside red-coated regulars from Britain; the two groups maintained an antagonistic relationship, however.

In July 1758, British forces recaptured the fortress at Louisbourg, winning control of the entrance to the St. Lawrence River. In the fall, the Delawares and Shawnees accepted British peace overtures, and the French abandoned Fort Duquesne. Then, in September 1759, General James Wolfe's regulars defeated the French and took Quebec. Sensing a British victory, the Iroquois abandoned neutrality, hoping to gain a postwar advantage by allying with Britain. A year later, the British captured Montreal, the last French stronghold, and the American phase of the war ended.

In the Treaty of Paris (1763), France ceded its major North American holdings to Britain. Spain, an ally of France toward war's end, gave Florida to the victors. France ceded Louisiana west of the Mississippi to Spain, in partial compensation for its ally's losses elsewhere. The British thus gained control of the continent's fur trade. No longer would the English seacoast colonies have to worry about the threat to their existence posed by France's extensive North American territories.

1763: A TURNING POINT

Indigenous peoples of the interior first felt the impact of Britain's victory. After Britain gained the upper hand in the American war in 1758, Creeks and Cherokees lost their ability to force concessions by threatening to turn to France or Spain. In desperation, and retaliation for British atrocities, Cherokees attacked the Carolina and Virginia frontiers in 1760. Though initially victorious, the Indians were defeated the following year. Late in 1761, a treaty allowed the construction of British forts in Cherokee territories and opened a large tract to European settlement.

The First Worldwide War

Today we call two twentieth-century conflicts world wars, but the contest that historians term the *Great War for the Empire* was actually the first worldwide war. It began in spring 1754 in southwestern Pennsylvania, over whether Britain or France would build a fort at the forks of the Ohio. That it eventually involved combatants around the world attests to the growing importance of European nations' overseas empires and the increasing centrality of North America to their struggles for dominance.

The contest at the forks of the Ohio helped to reinvigorate a conflict between Austria and Prussia that sent European nations scrambling for allies. Eventually England, Hanover, and Prussia lined up against France, Austria, Russia, Sweden, Saxony, and, later, Spain. The war in Europe would last seven years. In 1763 these nations signed a peace treaty that returned the continent to its prewar status, but in the rest of the world, Britain vanquished France and Spain.

In the Caribbean, Britain seized the French islands of Guadeloupe and Martinique, and took Havana from Spain. In North America, the British recaptured the French fortress of Louisbourg and conquered Quebec. In Africa, Britain overwhelmed France's slave-trading posts in Senegambia. In India, British forces won control of Bengal by defeating a local ruler and French soldiers. Three years later, the British beat a French army at Pondicherry; four months after France lost Canada, its influence in India was also extinguished. At the very end of the war, a British expedition took Manila in the Philippines from Spain.

Thus the war that started in the American backcountry revealed the steadily growing links between North America and the rest of the world. Winners and losers had to pay for this first worldwide war. Financial struggles in Britain and France, produced revolutions abroad (for Britain, in America) and at home (for France).

In 1771 the artist Dominic Serres, the Elder, depicted British naval vessels attacking the French fortress at Chandernagore in India in 1757 (at left in background). Cannon fire from the warships was critical to the British victory, one of the keys to the conquest of India during the Seven Years' War.

(© National Maritime Museum, Greenwich, London)

Neolin and Pontiac

In the Ohio country, the Ottawas, Chippewas, and Potawatomis reacted angrily when Great Britain, no longer facing French competition, raised prices on trade goods and ended traditional gift-giving practices. As settlers moved into the Monongahela and Susquehanna valleys, a shaman named Neolin urged Indians to oppose European settlement and influence on their culture. Contending that Indian peoples were destroying themselves by dependence on European goods (especially alcohol), Neolin advocated peaceful, armed, and unified resistance. If Indians west of the mountains collectively rejected the invaders, Neolin declared, the Master of Life would replenish the depleted deer herds and look kindly on his people.

Heeding Neolin's call, in spring 1763 Ottawa war chief Pontiac forged an unprecedented alliance among Hurons, Chippewas, Potawatomis, Delawares, Shawnees, and Mingoes (Pennsylvania Iroquois). Pontiac then besieged Fort Detroit while war parties attacked other British outposts in the Great Lakes. Detroit withstood the siege, but by late June the forts west of Niagara and north of Fort Pitt had fallen. Indians then raided the Virginia and Pennsylvania frontiers throughout the summer, but failed to take Niagara, Fort Pitt, or Detroit. In early August, colonial militiamen defeated a combined Indian force at Bushy Run, Pennsylvania. Pontiac concluded the Detroit siege in late October; a treaty ending the war was negotiated three years later.

For nearly eighty years European settlers and Indians in Penn's Woods avoided major conflicts. But the Indian attacks and the settlers' response—especially the massacre of several defenseless Conestoga Indian families in December 1763 by fifty Scots-Irish men known as the Paxton Boys—revealed that violence in the region would become endemic.

Proclamation of 1763

London officials had no experience managing an area as vast as the territory it acquired from France, which included French settlers along the St. Lawrence and many Indian communities. In October the ministry issued the Proclamation of 1763, designating the headwaters of rivers flowing into the Atlantic from the Appalachians as the temporary western boundary for colonial settlement (see Map 5.1). Its promulgators expected to prevent clashes by forbidding colonists to move onto Indian lands. But it infuriated colonists who had squatted west of the line and land speculation companies from Pennsylvania and Virginia.

After 1763, the latter groups (which included such men as George Washington, Thomas Jefferson, Patrick Henry, and Benjamin Franklin) lobbied vigorously to have their claims validated by colonial governments and London administrators. At a treaty conference at Fort Stanwix, New York, in 1768, they negotiated with Iroquois representatives to push the boundary farther west and south. The Iroquois, still claiming to speak for the Delawares and the Shawnees, agreed to the deal, which yielded valuable trade goods and did not affect their own territories. While the Virginia land companies eventually gained the support of the House of Burgesses, they never made headway in London because administrators worried that western expansion would require funds they did not have.

Benjamin West, the first well-known American artist, engraved this picture of a prisoner exchange at the end of Pontiac's Uprising, with Colonel Henry Bouquet supervising the return of settlers abducted during the war. In the foreground, a child resists leaving the Indian parents he had grown to love. Many colonists were fascinated by the phenomenon West depicted—the reluctance of captives to abandon their adoptive Indian families. (Ohio Historical Society)

George III

Financing Britain's debt from the Seven Years' War—and defending the newly acquired territories—bedeviled King George III, who in 1760 succeeded his grandfather, George II. During the crucial years between 1763 and 1770, when the rift with the colonies widened and various political crises beset England, the twenty-two-year-old king replaced ministries rapidly. Although determined to assert the power of the monarchy, George III stubbornly regarded adherence to the status quo as the hallmark of patriotism.

Selected as prime minister in 1763, George Grenville confronted a financial crisis: England's indebtedness had nearly doubled since 1754, from £73 million to £137 million. Pre-war annual expenditures amounted to no more than £8 million; now the yearly interest on the debt came to £5 million. Grenville's ministry needed funds, but the British people were already heavily taxed. Because the colonists benefited from wartime expenditures, Grenville concluded that Anglo-Americans should pay a larger share of the empire's costs.

Theories of Representation

Americans believed that they could be represented only by men who lived nearby and for whom they or their property-holding neighbors voted. Grenville and his English contemporaries, however, believed that Parliament—king, lords, and Commons acting together—represented all British subjects, even overseas, whether or not they could vote.

In Parliament, the particular constituency that chose a member of the House of Commons had no special claim on that member's vote, nor did the member have to live near his constituents. According to this theory, called virtual representation, all Britons—including colonists—were represented in Parliament. Thus their consent to acts of Parliament could be presumed. In the colonies, however, members of the assemblies' lower houses were viewed as specifically representing the regions that elected them. Before Grenville proposed to tax the colonists, the two notions coexisted. But events of the 1760s revealed their incompatibility.

Real Whigs

Colonists had become accustomed to a central government with limited authority. Consequently, they believed that a good government was one that largely left them alone, a view matching the theories of British writers known as the Real Whigs. Drawing on a tradition of dissent reaching back to John Locke, the Real Whigs stressed the dangers inherent in a powerful government, particularly a monarchy. Some favored republicanism, which proposed to eliminate monarchs and rest power more directly on the people. Real Whigs warned the people to guard against government's attempted encroachments on their liberty and property.

As Britain tightened the reins in the 1760s and early 1770s, many Americans saw parallels in their circumstances and the Real Whigs' ideology. Excessive and unjust taxation, they believed, could destroy their freedoms, and they saw oppressive designs behind the actions of Grenville and his successors. In the mid-1760s, however, colonial leaders merely questioned the wisdom of Grenville's proposed laws.

Sugar and Currency Acts

In 1764 Parliament passed the Sugar and Currency Acts. The Sugar Act (also known as the Revenue Act) revised existing customs regulations and laid new duties on some foreign imports into the colonies. Its key provisions, advocated in London by influential Caribbean planters, aimed at discouraging American rum distillers from smuggling French West Indian molasses, thereby improving the market for British sugar. Although the Sugar Act resembled the Navigation Acts, it broke with tradition by deliberately seeking to raise revenue rather than channel American trade through Britain. The Currency Act outlawed most colonial issues of paper money, because British merchants had complained that Americans paid debts in inflated local currencies.

The Sugar and Currency Acts were imposed on an already depressed economy. A business boom accompanied the Seven Years' War, but prosperity ended in 1760 when the war shifted overseas. Atlantic trade routes were disrupted, merchants found few buyers for imported goods, and the loss of the military's demand for foodstuffs hurt American farmers. The bottom dropped out of the European tobacco market, threatening the livelihood of Chesapeake planters. Sailors and artisans had little work. Thus, the prospect of increased import duties and inadequate currency aroused merchants' hostility.

Without precedent for a united campaign against acts of Parliament, Americans in 1764 took uncoordinated steps. Eight colonial legislatures sent petitions to Parliament requesting the Sugar Act's repeal. They argued that its commercial restrictions would hurt Britain as well as the colonies and that they had not consented to its passage. The law remained in force.

THE STAMP ACT CRISIS

The Stamp Act (1765), Grenville's most important revenue proposal, required tax stamps on most printed materials, placing the heaviest burden on merchants and the colonial elite, who used printed matter more than ordinary folk. Anyone who purchased a newspaper, made a will, accepted a government appointment, or borrowed money would have to pay the tax. Never before had a revenue measure of such scope been proposed for the colonies. The act also required that tax stamps be purchased with scarce sterling coin. Violators would be tried by vice-admiralty courts, where judges rendered decisions, leading Americans to fear the loss of their right to trial by a jury of their peers. Finally, such a law broke with the colonial tradition of self-imposed taxation.

James Otis's *Rights of the British Colonies*

The young Massachusetts attorney James Otis Jr., penned the most important pamphlet protesting the Sugar Act and proposed Stamp Act: *The Rights of the British Colonies Asserted and Proved*. Otis exposed the dilemma that confounded the colonists for the next decade. How could they oppose certain acts of Parliament without questioning Parliament's authority over them? On the one hand, Otis asserted, Americans were "entitled to all the natural, essential, inherent, and inseparable rights" of Britons, including the right not to be taxed without their consent. On the other, Otis admitted that, under the British system after the Glorious Revolution, "the power of parliament is uncontrollable but by themselves, and we must obey . . . till they will be pleased to relieve us."

Otis's first contention implied that Parliament could not constitutionally tax the colonies because Americans were not represented in its ranks. Yet his second point accepted the prevailing theory of British government: that Parliament was the sole, supreme authority in the empire. Otis tried to find a middle ground by proposing colonial representation in Parliament, but the British believed that colonists were already virtually represented in Parliament, and colonists realized that a handful of colonial delegates to London would be outvoted. When Americans learned of the act's adoption in the spring of 1765, they reacted indecisively. Few colonists publicly favored the law, but petitions failed to prevent its adoption. Perhaps Otis was correct: the only course was to pay the stamp tax, reluctantly but loyally.

Patrick Henry and the Virginia Stamp Act Resolves

A twenty-nine-year-old lawyer serving his first term in the Virginia House of Burgesses, Patrick Henry was appalled by his fellow legislators' unwillingness to oppose the Stamp Act. "Alone, unadvised, and unassisted, on a blank leaf of an old law book," he took action and wrote the Virginia Stamp Act Resolves.

Little in Henry's earlier life foreshadowed his political success. The son of a prosperous Scots immigrant to western Virginia, Henry had little formal education. After marrying at eighteen, he failed at farming and storekeeping before turning to the law to support his wife and six children. Henry lacked legal training, but his oratorical skills made him an effective advocate first for his clients and later for his political beliefs.

In 1795 the artist Lawrence Sully painted the only known life portrait of Patrick Henry. The old man's fierce gaze reflects the same intensity that marked his actions thirty years earlier, when he introduced the Virginia Stamp Act Resolves in the House of Burgesses.   (Mead Art Museum, Amherst College. Bequest of Herbert L. Pratt, Class of 1985, Acc. No. AC1945.115)

Patrick Henry introduced his seven proposals near the end of the legislative session, when many burgesses had already departed. The few remaining burgesses adopted five of Henry's resolutions by a bare majority. But some colonial newspapers printed Henry's seven original resolutions as if they had been uniformly passed by the House. One was rescinded and two others were never debated or voted on.

The four propositions adopted by the burgesses asserted that colonists had never forfeited their rights as British subjects, which included consent to taxation. The other resolutions went further. The repealed resolution claimed the burgesses had the exclusive right to tax Virginians, and the two never considered asserted that Virginians need not obey tax laws passed by other legislative bodies (namely, Parliament).

Continuing Loyalty to Britain

Though vying for their rights, the colonists did not seek independence. Maryland lawyer Daniel Dulany, whose *Considerations on the Propriety of Imposing Taxes on the British Colonies* was the most widely read pamphlet of 1765, expressed the consensus: "The colonies are dependent upon Great Britain, and the supreme authority vested in the king, lords, and commons, may justly be exercised to secure, or preserve their dependence." But, warned Dulany, there was a crucial distinction between "dependence and inferiority" and "absolute vassalage and slavery."

Over the next ten years, America's political leaders searched for a way to control their internal affairs, especially taxation, but remain under British rule. The notion that Parliament could exercise absolute authority over colonial possessions inhered in the British theory of government. Even Britain's harshest critics of the 1760s and 1770s questioned only the wisdom of specific policies, not the principles on which they rested. In effect, the Americans (perhaps unrealistically) wanted British leaders to revise their fundamental understanding of their government.

Anti–Stamp Act Demonstrations

In August, the Loyal Nine, a Boston social club of printers, distillers, and other artisans, organized an anti–Stamp Act demonstration. Hoping to show that people from all ranks opposed the act, they approached leaders of the city's rival laborers' associations, based in Boston's North End and South End neighborhoods. The two gangs, composed of unskilled workers and poor tradesmen, were often at odds, but the Loyal Nine convinced them to lay aside their differences for the demonstration.

On August 14, the demonstrators hung an effigy of Andrew Oliver, the province's stamp distributor, from a tree on Boston Common. That night a crowd led by about fifty well-dressed tradesmen paraded the effigy around the city. The crowd tore down a small building they thought was intended as the stamp office, making a bonfire near Oliver's house and tossing the beheaded effigy onto the flames. Demonstrators broke Oliver's windows and threw stones at officials. During the melee, the North End and South End leaders toasted their union. Oliver publicly promised not to fulfill the duties of his office.

But another crowd action twelve days later, aimed at Oliver's brother-in-law, Lieutenant Governor Thomas Hutchinson, drew no praise from respectable Bostonians. On the night of August 26, a mob attacked the homes of several customs officers and destroyed Hutchinson's elaborately furnished townhouse. But Hutchinson took some comfort in the fact that "the encouragers of the first mob never intended matters should go this length and the people in general express the utmost detestation of this unparalleled outrage."

Americans' Divergent Interests

Few colonists sided with Britain during the 1760s, but groups had divergent goals. The skilled craftsmen who composed the Loyal Nine and merchants, lawyers, and other educated elites preferred orderly demonstrations. For the city's laborers, economic grievances may have been paramount. Certainly, their "hellish Fury" as they wrecked Hutchinson's house suggests resentment against his display of wealth.

Colonists, like Britons, had a long tradition in which disfranchised people took to the streets to redress grievances. But the Stamp Act controversy for the first time drew ordinary urban folk into transatlantic politics, including recent non-English-speaking immigrants targeted by the double taxation of foreign-language newspapers. Matters that previously concerned only the gentry or colonial legislators were now discussed everywhere.

The entry of unskilled workers, slaves, and women into imperial politics threatened and aided elite men who wanted to oppose British measures. Anti–Stamp Act demonstrations occurred in areas stretching from Halifax in the north to the Caribbean island of Antigua in the south. They were so successful that, by November 1, when the law was to take effect, not one stamp distributor would carry out his duties. But wealthy men recognized that mobs composed of the formerly powerless could endanger their own dominance of the society.

Sons of Liberty

They therefore attempted to channel resistance into acceptable forms through a newly created intercolonial association, the Sons of Liberty. Composed of merchants, lawyers, and prosperous tradesmen, the Sons of Liberty by early 1766 linked protest leaders from New York to those in Charleston, South Carolina, to those in Portsmouth, New Hampshire. With taverns as key settings for exchanging news and opinions, many members were tavern owners.

In Charleston (formerly Charles Town) in October 1765, a crowd shouting, "Liberty Liberty and stamp'd paper" forced the resignation of the South Carolina stamp distributor. But the Charleston chapter of the Sons of Liberty was horrified when in January 1766 local slaves paraded through the streets similarly crying, "Liberty!" Freedom from slavery was not what elite slave owners had in mind.

In Philadelphia, resistance leaders were dismayed when an angry mob threatened to attack Benjamin Franklin's house. The city's laborers believed Franklin to be partly responsible for the Stamp Act because he obtained the post of stamp distributor for a friend. But Philadelphia's artisans—the foundation of the opposition there and elsewhere—were loyal to Franklin, considered one of their own, and protected his home. The resulting split between Philadelphia's better-off tradesmen and common laborers prevented an alliance as successful as Boston's.

Opposition and Repeal During fall and winter 1765–1766, Stamp Act opposition mounted. Colonial legislatures petitioned Parliament to repeal the hated law, and courts closed because they could not obtain the stamps needed for legal documents. In October, nine colonies sent delegates to a general congress, the Stamp Act Congress, in New York to draft a protest statement stressing the law's adverse economic effects rather than its rights violations. Meanwhile, the Sons of Liberty held mass meetings to rally public support. Finally, American merchants organized nonimportation associations to pressure British exporters, expecting that since one-quarter of all exports went to the colonies by 1760, London merchants might lobby for repeal, especially if sales suffered.

In March 1766, Parliament repealed the Stamp Act. The nonimportation agreements had the anticipated effect of allying wealthy London merchants to the colonies. But the main factor in winning repeal than was the appointment of a new prime minister. Lord Rockingham, who replaced Grenville in summer 1765, opposed the Stamp Act as an unwise and divisive law. But Rockingham linked repeal to passage of a Declaratory Act, which asserted Parliament's authority to tax and legislate for Britain's American possessions.

News of the repeal arrived in Newport, Rhode Island, in May, and the Sons of Liberty dispatched messengers throughout the colonies. They organized celebrations, stressing unwavering loyalty to Britain. Their goal achieved, the Sons of Liberty dissolved.

RESISTANCE TO THE TOWNSHEND ACTS

In summer 1766, another ministry change in London revealed how fragile the colonists' victory had been. The new prime minister, William Pitt, fostered cooperation between the colonies and Britain during the Seven Years' War. But when Pitt fell ill, Charles Townshend became the dominant force in the ministry. An ally of Grenville, Townshend renewed efforts to obtain funds from Britain's American possessions (see Table 5.2).

The duties Townshend proposed in 1767 seemed to extend the existing Navigation Acts by focusing on trade goods like paper, glass, and tea. But they differed first, by

TABLE 5.2   British Ministries and Their American Policies

Head of Ministry	Major Acts
George Grenville	Sugar Act (1764)
	Currency Act (1764)
	Stamp Act (1765)
Lord Rockingham	Stamp Act repealed (1766)
	Declaratory Act (1766)
William Pitt/Charles Townshend	Townshend Acts (1767)
Lord North	Townshend duties (except for the tea tax) repealed (1770)
	Coercive Acts (1774)
	Quebec Act (1774)

applying to British imports, not those from foreign countries. Second, the revenues would pay some royal officials in the colonies, thereby eliminating assemblies' ability to threaten to withhold salaries from uncooperative officials. Additionally, Townshend's scheme established an American Board of Customs Commissioners and vice-admiralty courts at Boston, Philadelphia, and Charleston. This angered merchants, whose profits would be threatened by more vigorous enforcement of the Navigation Acts.

John Dickinson's Farmer's Letters

Passage of the Townshend Acts drew a quick response from the colonies. One series of widely published essays, *Letters from a Farmer in Pennsylvania,* by prominent lawyer John Dickinson, expressed a broad consensus. Dickinson contended that Parliament could regulate colonial trade but could not raise revenue. By distinguishing between trade regulation and taxation, Dickinson avoided the sticky issue of consent and colonial subordination to Parliament. But his argument obligated the colonies to assess Parliament's motives in passing trade laws before deciding whether to obey them.

The Massachusetts assembly responded to the Townshend Acts by circulating a letter calling for unity among colonial legislatures and a joint petition of protest. When Lord Hillsborough, recently named secretary of state for America, learned of the letter, he ordered Massachusetts governor Francis Bernard to insist that the assembly recall it and directed other governors to prevent their assemblies from discussing it. Hillsborough's order motivated colonial assemblies to unite in opposing this new threat to their prerogatives. In late 1768, the Massachusetts legislature resoundingly rejected recall by a vote of 92 to 17. Bernard immediately dissolved the assembly, and other governors followed suit.

Rituals of Resistance

The number of votes cast against recalling the circular letter—92—assumed ritual significance for the resistance. The number 45 was already symbolic because John Wilkes, a radical Londoner sympathetic to the American cause, had been jailed for publishing an essay entitled *The North Briton,* No. 45. In Boston, the silversmith Paul Revere made a punchbowl weighing 45 ounces that held 45 gills (half-cups). Charleston's tradesmen decorated a tree with 45 lights, set off 45 rockets, and carrying 45 candles, met at a tavern where 45 tables were set with 45 bowls of wine, 45 bowls of punch, and 92 glasses.

Such public rituals taught illiterate Americans about the reasons for resistance. When Boston's revived Sons of Liberty invited hundreds of residents to dine with them each August 14 to commemorate the first Stamp Act demonstration, crowds listened. Likewise, the public singing of songs supporting the American cause helped to spread the word.

The Sons of Liberty and other American leaders made a deliberate effort to involve ordinary folk in the campaign against the Townshend duties. Most important, they urged colonists of all ranks and both sexes to sign agreements not to purchase or consume British products. The new consumerism that had linked colonists economically now supplied them with a ready method of displaying their allegiance.

Daughters of Liberty

As the primary purchasers of textiles and household goods, women played a central role in the nonconsumption movement. More than three hundred Boston matrons publicly promised not to buy or drink tea, "Sickness excepted." As Janet Schaw later noted, the women of Wilmington, North Carolina, burned their tea after walking through town in a solemn procession. Women exchanged recipes for tea substitutes or drank coffee instead. The best known of the protests, the so-called Edenton Ladies Tea Party, was actually a meeting of prominent North Carolina women who pledged to work for the public good and support resistance to British measures.

In many towns, young women calling themselves Daughters of Liberty met to spin in public squares to persuade other women to make homespun and wear homespun clothing, thereby ending the colonies' dependence on British cloth. These patriotic displays served the same purpose as the male rituals involving the numbers 45 and 92. When young ladies from well-to-do families sat outdoors at spinning wheels all day, eating only American food, drinking local herbal tea, and listening to patriotic sermons, they served as political instructors, a role they accepted with pride.

Divided Opinion Over Boycotts

Colonists were by no means united in support of nonimportation and nonconsumption. Resistance to the Townshend Acts exposed new splits in American ranks. The most significant rifts divided urban artisans and merchants, allies in 1765.

The Stamp Act boycotts helped revive a depressed economy by stimulating demand for local products and reducing merchants' inventories. But in 1768 and 1769, merchants enjoyed boom times and had no incentive to support a boycott. Artisans, however, supported nonimportation, recognizing that the absence of British goods would create a market for their own manufactures. Thus tradesmen formed the core of the crowds that coerced both importers and their customers by picketing stores, publicizing offenders' names, and sometimes destroying property.

Such tactics were effective: colonial imports from England dropped dramatically in 1769, especially in New York, New England, and Pennsylvania. But these tactics also aroused heated opposition. Some Americans who supported resistance questioned the use of violence to force others to join the boycott. The threat to private property inherent in the campaign frightened wealthier and more conservative men and women. Political activism by ordinary colonists challenged the ruling elite's domination, as many feared in 1765.

Disclosures that leading merchants had violated the nonimportation agreement caused dissension in the ranks of boycotters, so Americans were relieved when news arrived in April 1770 that the Townshend duties had been repealed, except the tea tax. A new prime minister, Lord North, persuaded Parliament that duties on trade within the empire were ill advised. The other Townshend Acts remained in force, but provisions for paying officials' salaries and tightening customs enforcement now appeared less objectionable.

CONFRONTATIONS IN BOSTON

On the day Lord North proposed repeal of the Townshend duties, a confrontation between civilians and soldiers in Boston led to five Americans' deaths. The decision to base the American Board of Customs Commissioners in Boston ultimately caused the confrontation that patriots called the Boston Massacre.

Mobs targeted the customs commissioners on their arrival in November 1767. In June 1768 their seizure of the patriot leader John Hancock's sloop *Liberty* on suspicion of smuggling caused a riot in which prominent customs officers' property was destroyed. The ministry brought in troops to maintain order. The assignment of two regiments to their city confirmed Bostonians' worst fears about the oppressive potential of British power. Guards on Boston Neck, the entrance to the city, checked travelers and their goods. Redcoat patrols roamed the city, questioning and sometimes harassing passersby. Parents feared for the safety of daughters, who were subjected to soldiers' coarse sexual insults. Additionally, many redcoats sought off-duty employment, competing for unskilled jobs with the city's workingmen. The two groups brawled repeatedly in taverns and on the streets.

Boston Massacre

On the evening of March 5, 1770, a crowd of laborers threw snowballs at soldiers guarding the Customs House. Against orders, the sentries fired on the crowd, killing four and wounding eight, one of whom died days later. Reportedly the first to die was Crispus Attucks, a sailor of mixed Nipmuck and African origins. Resistance leaders idealized Attucks and the other dead rioters as martyrs for liberty, holding a solemn funeral and later commemorating March 5 annually.

Despite the political benefits patriots derived from the massacre, they probably did not approve the crowd action that provoked it. Since the destruction of Hutchinson's house in August 1765, men allied with the Sons of Liberty supported orderly demonstrations. Thus, when the soldiers were tried in November, John Adams and Josiah Quincy Jr., both unwavering patriots, acted as their defense attorneys. Almost all were acquitted, and the two convicted were released after being branded on the thumb. Undoubtedly this favorable outcome persuaded London officials not to retaliate against the city.

A British Plot?

For more than two years after the Boston Massacre, a superficial calm emerged. In June 1772, Rhode Islanders angry with overzealous customs enforcement by the British naval schooner *Gaspée* attacked and burned it in Narragansett Bay near Providence. Because the perpetrators were never identified, there were no adverse consequences for the colony. The most outspoken newspapers, such as the *Boston Gazette,* the *Pennsylvania Journal,* and the *South Carolina Gazette,* published essays drawing on Real Whig ideology and accusing Great Britain of scheming to oppress the colonies. After the Stamp Act's repeal, the protest leaders praised Parliament; following repeal of the Townshend duties, they warned of impending tyranny. The single ill-chosen stamp tax now seemed part of a plot against American liberties. Essayists pointed to the stationing of troops in Boston and the growing number of vice-admiralty courts as evidence of plans to enslave the colonists. Indeed, patriot writers repeatedly used the word *enslavement.* Most free colonists had direct knowledge of slavery, and the threat of enslavement by Britain must have had peculiar force.

Although some colonists were increasingly convinced that they should seek freedom from parliamentary authority, they continued to acknowledge their British identity and allegiance to George III. They began to envision a system that would enable

Shortly after the Boston Massacre, Paul Revere printed this illustration of the confrontation near the Customs House on March 5, 1770. Offering visual support for the patriots' version of events, it showed the British soldiers firing on an unresisting crowd (instead of the aggressive mob described at the soldiers' trial) and—even worse—a gun firing from the building itself, which has been labeled Butchers Hall. (Anne S.K. Brown Military Collection, Brown University Library)

them to be ruled by their own elected legislatures while remaining subordinate to the king. But any such scheme violated Britons' conception of their government, which posited that Parliament (which they believed encompassed the king as well as lords and commons) wielded sole, undivided sovereignty over the empire. Then, in fall 1772, the North ministry implemented the Townshend Act that would pay governors and judges from customs revenues. In early November, voters at a Boston town meeting established a Committee of Correspondence to publicize the decision by exchanging letters with other Massachusetts towns. Heading the committee was Samuel Adams.

Samuel Adams and Committees of Correspondence

Fifty-one in 1772, Samuel Adams was about a decade older than other American resistance leaders. He had been a Boston tax collector, a member and clerk of the Massachusetts assembly, an ally of the Loyal Nine, and one of the Sons of Liberty. Adams drew a sharp contrast between a corrupt, vice-ridden Britain and the colonies, peopled by simple, liberty-loving folk. An experienced political organizer, Adams' Committee of Correspondence sought to create an informed consensus among Massachusetts residents.

Until 1772, the protest movement was confined largely to the seacoast and major cities and towns. Adams wanted to widen the movement's geographic scope. Accordingly, the Boston town meeting directed the Committee of Correspondence "to state the Rights of the Colonists and of this Province in particular"; to list "the Infringements and Violations thereof that have been, or from time to time may be made"; and to send copies to other towns. The statement of colonial rights declared that Americans had absolute rights to life, liberty, and property. The idea that "a British house of commons, should have a right, at pleasure, to give and grant the property of the colonists" was "irreconcileable" with "the first principles of natural law and Justice . . . and of the British Constitution." They complained of taxation without representation, unnecessary troops and customs officers on American soil, the use of imperial revenues to pay colonial officials, and the expanded jurisdiction of vice-admiralty courts.

The document, which was printed as a pamphlet for distribution to the towns, exhibited none of the hesitation of 1760s' claims against Parliament. No longer were resistance leaders—at least in Boston—preoccupied with defining the limits of parliamentary authority, nor did they mention obedience to Parliament. They placed American rights first, loyalty to Great Britain a distant second.

The towns' response to the pamphlet must have thrilled Samuel Adams. While some disagreed with Boston's assessment, most aligned with the city. The town of Holden declared that "the People of New England have never given the People of Britain any Right of Jurisdiction over us." The citizens of Petersham commented that resistance to tyranny was "the first and highest social Duty of this people." Beliefs like these made the next crisis in Anglo-American affairs the last.

TEA AND TURMOIL

The tea tax was the sole Townshend duty in effect by 1773. After 1770, some Americans continued to boycott English tea; others resumed drinking it. As explained in Chapter 4, tea figured prominently in the colonists' diet and social lives, so the boycott meant giving up a favorite beverage and altering habitual forms of socializing.

Reactions to the Tea Act

In May 1773, Parliament passed the Tea Act to save the East India Company from bankruptcy. The company, which held a monopoly on British trade with the East Indies, was important to the British economy and to the prominent British politicians who invested in it. Under the act, only the East India Company's agents could legally sell tea in America. That enabled the company to avoid intermediaries and lower its prices to compete with smugglers. Resistance leaders, however, interpreted the measure as designed to make them admit Parliament's right to tax them, since the less expensive tea would still be taxed. Others saw the Tea Act as the first step in an East India Company monopoly on all colonial trade. Residents of the four cities to receive the first tea shipments prepared to respond to this perceived threat to their freedom.

In New York City, tea ships never arrived. In Philadelphia, Pennsylvania's governor persuaded the captain to return to Britain. In Charleston, the tea was unloaded; some was destroyed, the rest sold in 1776 by the new state government. The only confrontation occurred in Boston, where both sides—the town meeting and Governor Thomas Hutchinson, two of whose sons were tea agents—rejected compromise.

The first of three tea ships, the *Dartmouth,* entered Boston harbor on November 28. Customs laws required cargo to be landed and the duty paid within twenty days of arrival; otherwise, it would be seized and sold at auction. After several mass meetings, Bostonians voted to post guards to prevent the tea from being unloaded. Hutchinson refused to permit the vessels to leave the harbor.

On December 16, one day before the cargo would have been confiscated, more than five thousand people (nearly a third of the city's population) crowded into Old South Church. Chaired by Samuel Adams, the meeting hoped to convince Hutchinson to send the tea back. But he refused. In the early evening Adams reportedly announced "that they had now done all they could for the Salvation of their Country." Cries rang out from the crowd: "Boston harbor a tea-pot tonight!" Within minutes, about sixty men crudely disguised as Indians assembled at the wharf, boarded the ships, and dumped the cargo into the harbor. By 9 P.M. 342 chests of tea worth approximately £10,000 floated on the water.

Among the "Indians" were many Boston artisans, including the silversmith Paul Revere. Five masons, eleven carpenters and builders, three leatherworkers, a blacksmith, two barbers, a coachmaker, a shoemaker, and twelve apprentices have been identified as participants. That their ranks also included four farmers from outside Boston, ten merchants, two doctors, a teacher, and a bookseller illustrated the resistance movement's widespread support.

Coercive and Quebec Acts

Responding to the Tea Party, in March 1774, Parliament adopted the first of four laws that became known as the Coercive, or Intolerable, Acts. It ordered Boston's port closed until the tea was paid for, prohibiting all but coastal trade in food and firewood. Later that spring, Parliament passed three other punitive measures. The Massachusetts Government Act altered the province's charter, substituting an appointed council for the elected one, increasing the governor's powers, and forbidding most town meetings. The Justice Act provided that a person accused of committing murder while suppressing a riot or enforcing the laws could be tried outside the colony. Finally, the Quartering Act allowed military officers to commandeer privately owned buildings to house troops.

Parliament then turned to reforming Quebec's government. Intended to ease strains emerging since the British conquest of the French colony, the Quebec Act granted greater religious freedom to Catholics—alarming Protestant colonists, who equated Roman Catholicism with despotism. It also reinstated French civil law, which had been replaced by British procedures in 1763, and it established an appointed council (rather than an elected legislature). Finally, to protect northern Indians against Anglo-American settlement, the act annexed to Quebec the area west of the Appalachians, east of the Mississippi River, and north of the Ohio River—thereby

Women's Political Activism

In the twenty-first century, female citizens of the United States participate at every level of American politics. But before the 1760s, American women were seen as having no political role; they often apologized for even talking about political issues. A male essayist expressed the consensus in the mid-1730s: "the Governing Kingdoms and Ruling Provinces are Things too difficult and knotty for the fair Sex, it will render them grave and serious, and take off those agreeable Smiles that should always accompany them."

But that changed when colonists resisted new British taxes and laws in the mid- to late 1760s. Because women made purchasing decisions for American households and because in the case of spinning and cloth manufacture their labor could replace imported clothing, it was vital for them to participate in the resistance. For the first time in American history, women of all ranks took political stands, deciding whether to boycott British goods. The groups they established to promote home manufactures—dubbed *Daughters of Liberty*—constituted the first American women's political organizations.

Since then, American women have taken part in many political movements, among them antislavery societies, suffrage organizations, the Women's Christian Temperance Union, and the civil rights movement. The legacy of revolutionary-era women continues today in such groups as the National Women's Political Caucus and Concerned Women for America. Contemporary Americans would find it impossible to imagine their country without female activists of all political affiliations.

removing the region from the jurisdiction of the seacoast colonies. Wealthy colonists who hoped to develop the Ohio country now faced the prospect of dealing with officials in Quebec.

To resistance leaders, the Coercive Acts and the Quebec Act proved what they had feared since 1768: that Britain had a deliberate plan to oppress them. If Boston's port could be closed, why not Philadelphia's or New York's? If the royal charter of Massachusetts could be changed, why not that of South Carolina? If the Catholic Church could receive favored status in Quebec, why not everywhere?

The Boston Committee of Correspondence urged all colonies to boycott British goods. But Rhode Island, Virginia, and Pennsylvania suggested that another intercolonial congress be convened to consider an appropriate response, and in mid-June 1774 Massachusetts acquiesced. Even the most ardent patriots remained loyal Britons and hoped for reconciliation. Americans were approaching the brink of confrontation, but had yet to reach an irrevocable break. So the colonies agreed to send delegates to a Continental Congress in Philadelphia in September.

Summary

Twenty years earlier, at the outbreak of the Seven Years' War in the western Pennsylvania wilderness, no one could have predicted such a dramatic change for Britain's mainland colonies. Yet that conflict simultaneously removed France from North America and created a huge debt for Britain, developments with major implications for the imperial relationship.

After the war ended in 1763, the number of colonists who defined themselves as political actors increased substantially. Once linked unquestioningly to Great Britain, they began to develop an American identity. Their concept of the political process differed from that of the mother country, and they held a different definition of what constituted representation and consent to government actions. After a long train of events, they understood that their economic interests did not necessarily coincide with those of Great Britain. Parliamentary acts such as the Stamp and Townshend Acts elicited colonial responses that produced further responses from Britain. Tensions escalated and climaxed when Bostonians destroyed the East India Company's tea. From then on, there would be no turning back.

In late summer 1774, Americans were committed to resistance but not independence. During the next decade, they would forge the bonds of a new American nationality.

Chapter Review

RENEWED WARFARE AMONG EUROPEANS AND INDIANS

What was at stake in the Seven Years' War?

The Seven Years' War was ultimately a contest over land between the British, French, Native Americans, and some settlers. All parties vied for control of large tracts of western land. The Iroquois, believing themselves the voice of the Delawares and Shawnees, negotiated to cede the land to Pennsylvania; the two tribes then moved west onto land claimed by Virginia and Pennsylvania, while France sought to hold and expand its possessions along the Ohio River, which it relied on for trade. After battling with Indians, the French continued to push southward in its land grabbing, and Anglo-American colonists gathered to address the French threat. England declared war and, after winning the protracted battle, the issue of land between European nations was settled when France ceded most of its North American territories to Britain.

1763: A TURNING POINT

How did colonists' ideas about government differ from those of the British in the 1760s?

British authorities believed that Parliament—which included the king, lords, and Commons—represented all British subjects regardless of where they lived and voting status. In this system of virtual representation, the people's consent to Parliament's actions was assumed. Americans, on the other hand, increasingly believed in direct representation, that they could only be represented by men who lived nearby and whom they elected. Moreover, the lower houses were specifically linked to the interests and needs of the regions that elected them. Living on the other side of the ocean, colonists were also accustomed to a central government with limited authority, and embraced the Real Whig notion that good government was one that left them alone to manage their affairs. As England imposed taxes and greater control over the colonies beginning in 1763, many Americans felt their freedom was endangered and questioned whether authority should lie with the monarchy or the people.

THE STAMP ACT CRISIS

How did the Stamp Act raise issues that would lead to the American Revolution?

Angry about the heavy taxes and questioning Britain's right to impose them, colonists began to wonder how they might resist Parliament yet remain British subjects. At issue for essayists such as James Otis was that as British subjects, they were entitled to the right to consent to taxation—which had not been granted under the Stamp Act. On the other hand, Parliament was a supreme authority to which they must give complete consent. Other leaders, such as Patrick Henry and the Virginia House of Burgesses, were unwilling to relinquish the right to consent to taxation, and some sought representation in Parliament. For ten years, Americans struggled with how to control their internal affairs yet remain under British rule. Protests led to the act's repeal in 1766, but questions about government nonetheless remained.

RESISTANCE TO THE TOWNSHEND ACTS

How did the Sons of Liberty politicize ordinary Americans during resistance to the Townshend Acts?

Ordinary Americans were not accustomed to being involved in political affairs, which they understood as matters handled by elites. But the Sons of Liberty made a conscious effort to draw people from all ranks into their anti-Townshend campaign, partly because they needed widespread participation for their boycott of British products designed in protest to the act. To rally a wider populace, they created rituals that would teach illiterate Americans about the reasons for resistance, including commemorating previous demonstrations with elaborate public celebrations including singing. Women helped, too, by spinning their own textiles outdoors in public, symbolically displaying their patriotism and pride for all to see.

CONFRONTATIONS IN BOSTON

How do Samuel Adams's Committees of Correspondence mark a turning point in Americans' political thinking?

An original member of the Sons of Liberty, Adams wanted to widen the movement's scope beyond its stronghold in New England cities and seacoast towns and create consensus among Massachusetts residents for the cause of liberty. The pamphlet he produced for the Boston Committee of Correspondence in 1772 was widely distributed. It stated the rights of colonists to life, liberty, and property, and it outlined complaints against England for taxation without representation, unnecessary troops and customs officers on American soil, the use of imperial revenues to pay colonial officials, and the expanded jurisdiction of vice-admiralty courts. Far more radical than earlier documents, this one did not seek to define the limits of Parliamentary authority but instead declared colonists' allegiance to America first and England a distant second. This new articulation, along with the pamphlet's widespread popularity, marked an important ideological moment.

TEA AND TURMOIL

How did the Tea Act push the country to the brink of revolution?

When Parliament imposed the Tea Act on the colonies in May 1773, it was attempting to save the East India Tea Company from bankruptcy, but colonists interpreted the move as an effort to make them admit Parliament's right to tax them. Citizens in several cities wanted to prevent the tea from being unloaded from ships; in Boston that effort led to a protest in which the tea was dumped in the harbor by men dressed as Indians. In response, Parliament adopted punitive laws, known as the Coercive or Intolerable Acts, ordering the city to pay for the tea and closing the port to food and other shipments until it did. Other acts reorganized the state's government and forbade town meetings, and allowed officers to commandeer private buildings to house troops. Colonists saw such measures as proof that Britain would oppress them. They considered boycotts and other measures, with colonies sending delegates to a Continental Congress in Philadelphia in 1774 to consider what to do next.

SUGGESTIONS FOR FURTHER READING

Fred Anderson, *The War That Made America: A Short History of the French and Indian War* (2005)

Bernard Bailyn, *The Ideological Origins of the American Revolution* (1967)

T. H. Breen, *The Marketplace of Revolution: How Consumer Politics Shaped American Independence* (2004)

Gregory Dowd, *War Under Heaven: Pontiac, the Indian Nation, and the British Empire* (2002)

Marc Egnal, *A Mighty Empire: The Origins of the American Revolution* (1988)

Merrill Jensen, *The Founding of a Nation: A History of the American Revolution, 1763–1776* (1968)

Pauline R. Maier, *From Resistance to Revolution: Colonial Radicals and the Development of American Opposition to Britain, 1765–1776* (1972)

Gary B. Nash, *The Unknown American Revolution: The Unruly Birth of Democracy and the Struggle to Create America* (2005)

William A. Pencak and Daniel K. Richter, eds., *Friends & Enemies in Penn's Woods: Indians, Colonists, and the Racial Construction of Pennsylvania* (2004)

Timothy Shannon, *Indians and Colonists at the Crossroads of Empire: The Albany Congress of 1754* (1999)

CHAPTER 6

A Revolution, Indeed | 1774–1783

CHAPTER OUTLINE

Government by Congress and Committee

Contest in the Backcountry

Choosing Sides

War and Independence

LINKS TO THE WORLD:
New Nations

The Struggle in the North

Life in the Army and on the Home Front

Victory in the South

LEGACY FOR A PEOPLE AND A NATION: Revolutionary Origins

Summary

The Shawnee chief Blackfish named his new captive Sheltowee, or Big Turtle, and adopted him as his son. In February 1778, Blackfish's warriors had caught the lone hunter, Daniel Boone, who then persuaded his fellow frontiersmen to surrender to the Shawnees (British allies). Boone had moved his family from North Carolina to Kentucky three years earlier as the Revolutionary War began. His contemporaries and some historians have questioned Boone's allegiances during the Revolution. His encounter with the Shawnees highlights ambiguities of revolutionary-era loyalties.

The Shawnees sought captives to cover the death of their chief, Cornstalk, killed months earlier while a prisoner of American militiamen in the Ohio country. Half of the twenty-six men taken were adopted into Shawnee families; those less willing to conform to Indian ways were dispatched as prisoners to the British fort at Detroit. Boone, who assured Blackfish that in the spring he would negotiate the surrender of women and children at his Boonesborough settlement, watched and waited. In June 1778 he escaped to warn the Kentuckians of an impending attack.

When Shawnees and their British allies appeared outside the Boonesborough stockade in mid-September, Boone agreed to negotiate. Although the settlers refused to move back across the mountains, fragmentary evidence suggests that they promised allegiance to the British to avert a battle. But discussions dissolved into a melee, with Indians besieging the fort for a week before withdrawing. That threat gone, Boone was charged with treason and court-martialed by the Kentucky militia. Although he was later cleared, questions about the incident and its aftermath haunted him for the rest of his life.

This icon will direct you to interactive activities and study materials on A People And A Nation, Brief Edition website: **www.cengage.com/history/norton/ peoplenationbrief8e**

Chronology

1774	First Continental Congress meets in Philadelphia, adopts Declaration of Rights and Grievances.
	Continental Association implements economic boycott of Britain; committees of observation are established to oversee boycott.
1774–75	Provincial conventions replace collapsing colonial governments.
1775	Battles of Lexington and Concord, first shots of war are fired.
	Second Continental Congress begins.
	Washington is named commander-in-chief.
	Dunmore's proclamation offers freedom to patriots' slaves who join British forces.
1776	Paine publishes *Common Sense*, advocating independence.

	British evacuate Boston.
	Declaration of Independence is adopted.
	New York City falls to British.
1777	British take Philadelphia.
	Burgoyne surrenders at Saratoga.
1778	French alliance brings vital assistance to America.
	British evacuate Philadelphia.
1779	Sullivan expedition destroys Iroquois villages.
1780	British take Charleston.
1781	Cornwallis surrenders at Yorktown.
1782	Peace negotiations begin.
1783	Treaty of Paris, granting independence to the United States, is signed.

Where did Boone's loyalties lie? To the British, the Americans, or other Kentuckians? His actions made all three seem possible. Had he betrayed the settlers to Shawnees, seeking to establish British authority in Kentucky? Had he, as he claimed, twice deceived the Shawnees? Or was the survival of the fragile settlements his highest priority? Kentucky was a borderland where British, Indians, and American settlers vied for control. Boone and other Appalachian backcountry residents did not always face clear-cut choices as they struggled under precarious circumstances.

The American Revolution uprooted thousands of families, disrupted the economy, reshaped society by forcing many colonists into permanent exile, led Americans to develop new conceptions of politics, and created a nation from thirteen separate colonies. The struggle for independence required revolutionary leaders to accomplish three separate but related tasks. First, they had to transform a consensus favoring loyal resistance into a coalition supporting independence. They pursued various measures (ranging from persuasion to coercion) to enlist European Americans in the patriot cause, while seeking neutrality from Indians and slaves.

Second, to win independence, patriot leaders needed international recognition and aid, particularly from France. Thus they dispatched to Paris the most experienced American diplomat, Benjamin Franklin, who skillfully negotiated the Franco-American alliance of 1778, crucial to gaining independence.

Only the third task directly involved the British. George Washington, commander-in-chief of the American army, soon recognized that his primary goal should be not to win battles but to survive to fight another day. The British military concentrated on winning battles, as they had in other European wars, and did not consider the difficulties of their main goal, retaining the colonies' allegiance.

- **What choices of allegiance confronted residents of North America after 1774? Why did people of various descriptions make the choices they did?**
- **What military strategies did the British and American forces adopt?**
- **Why did the Americans win the war?**

GOVERNMENT BY CONGRESS AND COMMITTEE

When the fifty-five delegates to the First Continental Congress convened in Philadelphia in September 1774, they knew that any measures they adopted would likely enjoy widespread support. That summer, participants at well-publicized open meetings throughout the colonies promised (in the words of Johnson County, North Carolina, freeholders) to "strictly adhere to, and abide by, such Regulations and Restrictions as the Members of said General Congress shall agree to." Most congressional delegates were selected by extralegal provincial conventions whose members were chosen at local gatherings, because governors had forbidden regular assemblies to conduct formal elections. By designating delegates to the Congress, Americans openly defied British authority.

First Continental Congress

The colonies' leading political figures—mostly lawyers, merchants, and planters representing every colony but Georgia—attended the Philadelphia Congress. The Massachusetts delegation included Samuel Adams, the Boston resistance organizer, and his younger cousin John, an ambitious lawyer. Among others, New York sent the talented, young attorney John Jay. Virginia elected Richard Henry Lee, Patrick Henry, and George Washington. These men became the chief architects of the new nation.

The congressmen faced three tasks when they convened at Carpenters' Hall on September 5: defining American grievances, developing a resistance plan, and articulating their constitutional relationship with Great Britain. Radical congressmen, like Lee of Virginia, argued that colonists owed allegiance only to George III and that Parliament had no legitimate authority over them. Conservatives, like Pennsylvania's Joseph Galloway and his allies, proposed a union requiring Parliament and a new American legislature to consent jointly to all laws pertaining to the colonies. After heated debate, delegates narrowly rejected Galloway's proposal, but did not embrace the radicals' position either.

Finally, they accepted wording proposed by John Adams. The crucial clauses in the Congress's Declaration of Rights and Grievances declared that Americans would obey Parliament, but only voluntarily, and would resist all taxes in disguise, like the Townshend duties. Remarkably, this position, which would have seemed radical years before, represented a compromise in fall 1774.

Continental Association

The delegates agreed on the laws they wanted repealed (notably the Coercive Acts) and implemented an economic boycott while petitioning the king for relief. They adopted the Continental Association, which called for nonimportation of British goods (effective December 1, 1774), nonconsumption of British products (effective March 1, 1775), and nonexportation of American goods to Britain and the British West Indies (effective September 10, 1775).

More comprehensive than previous economic measures, the provisions of the association appealed to different groups and regions. The nonimportation agreement's inclusive language banned commerce in slaves and manufactures; this accorded with the Virginia gentry's desire to halt or slow the arrival of enslaved Africans. (Leading Virginians believed slave importations discouraged free Europeans with useful skills from immigrating.) Delaying nonconsumption until three months after implementing nonimportation allowed northern urban merchants time to sell items they acquired legally before December 1. The novel tactic of nonexportation and its postponement for nearly a year served other interests. In 1773 small farmers in Virginia already vowed to stop exporting tobacco to raise prices in the glutted market. The next year, the association accomplished the same end while letting them profit from higher prices for their 1774 crop. It similarly benefited northern exporters of wood products and foodstuffs to the Caribbean with a final sales season before the embargo.

Committees of Observation

To enforce the Continental Association, the Congress recommended the election of committees of observation and inspection in every American locality. By specifying that committee members be chosen by all men qualified to vote, the Congress guaranteed them a broad popular base. The seven thousand to eight thousand committeemen became local leaders of the American resistance.

Initially charged with overseeing implementation of the boycott, within six months these committees became de facto governments. They examined merchants' records, publishing the names of those who continued importing British goods. They promoted home manufactures, encouraging simple modes of dress and behavior that symbolized Americans' commitment to liberty. Because expensive leisure-time activities were believed to reflect vice and corruption, the Congress urged Americans to forgo dancing, gambling, horseracing, cardplaying, and cockfighting.

The committees gradually extended their authority. They attempted to identify opponents of American resistance, developing spy networks, circulating copies of the Continental Association for signatures, and investigating questionable remarks and activities. Suspected dissenters were urged to support the colonial cause publicly; if they refused, the committees had them watched, restricted their movements, or tried to force them to move away. People engaging in casual political exchanges one day could find themselves charged with treasonable conversation the next.

Provincial Conventions

Meanwhile, during the winter and early spring of 1775, colonial governments were collapsing. Only a few legislatures met without challenges to their authority. In most colonies, popularly elected provincial conventions took over the government, sometimes replacing legislatures or holding concurrent sessions. In late 1774 and early 1775, these conventions approved the Continental Association, elected delegates to the Second Continental Congress (scheduled for May), organized militias, and gathered arms.

Royal officials suffered constant humiliation. Courts were prevented from meeting; taxes were paid to the conventions' agents rather than to provincial tax collectors; and militiamen would muster only when committees ordered. During the six months preceding the battles at Lexington and Concord, independence was being won at the local level. Not many Americans fully realized what was happening. Most continued to proclaim loyalty to Great Britain.

CONTEST IN THE BACKCOUNTRY

While the committees of observation consolidated their authority in the East, some colonists headed west. Ignoring the Proclamation of 1763, pronouncements by colonial governors, and the threat of Indian attacks, land-hungry folk—many of them recent immigrants from Ireland and soldiers who demobilized in North America after the Seven Years' War—swarmed onto lands along the Ohio River and its tributaries after the mid-1760s. Sometimes they purchased property from opportunists with dubious grants; often, they claimed land as squatters. Britain's 1771 decision to abandon (and raze) Fort Pitt removed final restraints on settlement there and rendered the Proclamation of 1763 unenforceable. By late 1775, thousands of new homesteads dotted the backcountry from western Pennsylvania south through Virginia and eastern Kentucky into western North Carolina.

Distrust and Warfare Few backcountry folk viewed the region's native peoples positively. Frontier dwellers had little interest in the small-scale trade that had once sustained an uneasy peace; they wanted land for crops and livestock pastures.

Headed by a new governor, Lord Dunmore, in 1774 Virginia asserted its title to the developing backcountry. During spring and early summer, tensions mounted as Virginians surveyed Kentucky land on the south side of the Ohio River—territory claimed by the Shawnees. Lord Dunmore's war consisted of one large-scale confrontation between Virginia militia and some Shawnee warriors. Neither won, but in the immediate aftermath thousands of settlers—including Daniel Boone and his associates—flooded across the mountains.

When the Revolutionary War began, the loyalties of Indians and settlers in the backcountry remained fluid and uncertain. Hostile to each other, the side each would take in the imperial struggle might depend on which could better serve their interests. Understanding that, the Continental Congress moved to reoccupy Fort Pitt and establish other garrisons in the Ohio country. With this protection, up to twenty thousand settlers poured into Kentucky and western Pennsylvania by 1780.

Native Americans' grievances against the European American newcomers predisposed many to ally with Great Britain. Yet some chiefs urged caution: the British abandonment of Fort Pitt (and them) suggested that Britain might not protect them in the future. Furthermore, Britain hesitated to make immediate use of its potential native allies and initially sought from the Indians only a promise of neutrality.

Patriots also sought the Indians' neutrality. In 1775 the Second Continental Congress sent a message to Indian communities, describing the war as "a family quarrel between us and Old England" and requesting that they "not join on either side." The Iroquois pledged neutrality. But the Cherokees led by Chief Dragging Canoe hoped to use the family quarrel to regain land. In summer 1776, they attacked settlements in western Virginia and the Carolinas. After a militia campaign destroyed many Cherokee towns, Dragging Canoe and some followers fled to the West, establishing new villages. Other Cherokees agreed to a treaty that ceded more of their land.

Frontier Hostilities   Shawnees and Cherokees continued to attack backcountry settlements throughout the war, but dissent within their ranks crippled these efforts. The British victory over France in 1763 destroyed the Indians' ability to maintain independence by playing European powers against one another. Only a few communities (among them the Stockbridge Indians of New England and the Oneidas in New York) unwaveringly supported the American revolt; most others either remained neutral or sporadically aligned with the British. In 1778 and early 1779 a frontier militia force under George Rogers Clark captured British posts in modern Illinois (Kaskaskia) and Indiana (Vincennes). The revolutionaries could never overtake the redcoats' stronghold at Detroit. Backcountry warfare between settlers and Indians persisted long after the Revolution ended. Indeed, the Revolutionary War itself constituted a brief chapter in the ongoing struggle for control of the region west of the Appalachians, which began in 1763 and continued into the next century.

CHOOSING SIDES

In 1765 Stamp Act protests were supported by most colonists in the Caribbean, Nova Scotia, and the future United States. Although provisions of the 1764 Sugar Act benefited Britain's Caribbean possessions, the Stamp Act levied higher duties on them than on the mainland colonies. When the act took effect, though, islanders loyally paid the duties. Eventually many colonists in North America and the West Indies questioned the aims and tactics of the resistance movement.

Nova Scotia and the Caribbean   Northern mainland and southern island colonies depended on Great Britain militarily and economically. Despite the British victory in the Seven Years' War, they felt vulnerable to French counterattack. Additionally, sugar planters—on some islands outnumbered by their bondspeople twenty-five to one—feared potential slave revolts. Neither region had a large population of European descent or strong political structures. Fewer people lived in Halifax in 1775 than in the late 1750s, and with successful men heading to England, the sugar islands had just a few resident planters to provide leadership.

Nova Scotians and West Indians had economic reasons for supporting the mother country. In the mid-1770s the northerners finally broke into the Caribbean market with their dried and salted fish. They also began to reduce New England's domination of the northern coastal trade, and they benefited from Britain's retaliatory measures against the rebels' commerce. British sugar producers relied on their trade monopoly within the empire, for more efficient French planters could sell sugar for one-third less. Further, the West Indian planters' lobbyists in London won the islands' exclusion from some Townshend Act provisions.

Patriots

Many residents of the thirteen colonies supported resistance, then independence. Active revolutionaries accounted for about two-fifths of the European American population and included small and middling farmers, members of dominant Protestant sects, Chesapeake gentry, merchants, city artisans, elected officeholders, and people of English descent. Wives usually adopted their husbands' political beliefs, but not always. Although all supported the Revolution, they pursued divergent goals within the broader coalition. Some sought limited political reform; others, extensive political change; and still others, social and economic reforms. (The ways their concerns interacted are discussed in Chapter 7.)

Loyalists

About one-fifth of the European American population remained loyal to Great Britain, firmly rejecting independence. Most loyalists long opposed the men who became patriot leaders for varying reasons. British-appointed government officials; Anglican clergy and lay Anglicans in the North; tenant farmers; members of persecuted religious sects; backcountry southerners who rebelled against eastern rule in the late 1760s and early 1770s; and non-English ethnic minorities, especially Scots—all feared the power of those who controlled the colonial assemblies and who had previously shown little concern for their welfare. Joined by merchants whose trade depended on imperial connections and by former British military men who settled in America after 1763, they formed a loyalist core.

During the war, loyalists congregated in cities held by the British army. When those posts were evacuated at war's end, loyalists scattered throughout the British Empire—Britain, the Bahamas, and especially Canada. In Nova Scotia, New Brunswick, and Ontario roughly seventy thousand former Americans laid the foundations of British Canada.

Neutrals

Between patriots and loyalists, there remained in the middle perhaps two-fifths of the European American population. Some, like the Quakers, were sincere pacifists. Others opportunistically shifted their allegiance to whichever side happened to be winning. Still others cared little about politics and obeyed whoever was in power. Such colonists resisted British and Americans alike when their demands seemed too heavy—when taxes became too high or when calls for militia service were too frequent. They made up a large proportion of the backcountry population, where Scots-Irish settlers had little love for either the patriot gentry or English authorities.

To patriots, apathy or neutrality was as heinous as loyalism. By winter 1775–1776, the Second Continental Congress recommended that "disaffected" persons be disarmed and arrested. State legislatures passed laws prescribing severe penalties for suspected loyalists or neutrals. Many began to require voters (or, in some cases, all free adult men) to take oaths of allegiance; refusal usually meant banishment to England or extra taxes. After 1777 many states confiscated the property of banished persons, using it to fund the war. The patriots' policies ensured that their scattered and persecuted opponents could not band together against the revolutionary cause.

Slaves

In New England, with few resident bondspeople, revolutionary fervor was widespread, and free African Americans enlisted in patriot militias. The middle colonies, where slaves constituted a small but substantial proportion of the population, were more divided but largely revolutionary. In Virginia and Maryland, where free people constituted a slender majority, the potential for slave revolts raised occasional but not disabling fears. By contrast, South Carolina and Georgia, where slaves composed more than half of the population, were less enthusiastic about resistance. Georgia sent no delegates to the First Continental Congress and reminded representatives at the second to consider its circumstances, "with our blacks and tories [loyalists] within us," when voting on independence.

Bondspeople faced a dilemma during the Revolution. Their goal was *personal* independence, but how best could they escape from slavery? To most slaves, supporting the British held promise. In late 1774 and early 1775, slaves offered to assist the British army in return for freedom.

Slaveowners' worst fears were realized in November 1775, when Virginia's royal governor, Lord Dunmore, offered to free slaves and indentured servants willing to join the British forces. About one thousand African Americans rallied to the British; although many perished in a smallpox epidemic, three hundred survived to reach occupied New York City under British protection. Because other commanders renewed Dunmore's proclamation, tens of thousands of runaway slaves eventually joined the British. At war's end, at least nine thousand left with the redcoats.

Although slaves did not pose a serious threat early on, patriots turned rumors of slave uprisings to their advantage. In South Carolina, resistance leaders argued that the Continental Association could protect masters from their slaves. Undoubtedly many wavering Carolinians were drawn into the revolutionary camp by fear that divisiveness among free people would encourage rebellion by the bondspeople.

Patriots could never completely ignore threats posed by loyalists, neutrals, slaves, and Indians. Occasionally backcountry militiamen refused to turn out for duty on the seacoast because they feared Indian attacks in their absence. Sometimes southern troops refused to serve in the North because they would not leave their regions unprotected against a slave insurrection. But the unlikelihood of a large-scale slave revolt, coupled with dissension in Indian communities and the patriots' successful campaign to disarm and neutralize loyalists, ensured that the revolutionaries would control the countryside.

WAR AND INDEPENDENCE

On January 27, 1775, Lord Dartmouth, secretary of state for America, wrote to General Thomas Gage in Boston, urging decisive action. On April 14, Gage responded by sending an expedition to confiscate colonial military supplies stockpiled at Concord.

New Nations

The American Revolution not only created the United States but led to the formation of three other nations: English-dominated Canada, Sierra Leone, and Australia.

In northern North America before the Revolution, only Nova Scotia had a sizable number of English-speaking settlers. Largely New Englanders, they were recruited after 1758 to repopulate the region forcibly taken from exiled Acadians. During and after the Revolution, loyalist families, especially from northern and middle colonies, moved to the region that is now Canada, which remained under British rule. Some exiles settled in Quebec as well. In a few years, loyalist refugees transformed the sparsely populated former French colony, laying the foundation for the modern bilingual (but majority English-speaking) Canadian nation.

Sierra Leone, too, was founded by colonial exiles—African Americans who had fled to the British army during the war, many of whom ended up in London. Seeing the refugees' poverty, charitable merchants—calling themselves the Committee for Relief of the Black Poor—developed a plan to resettle the African Americans elsewhere. The refugees rejected the Bahamas, fearing reenslavement there. They accepted a return to the land of their ancestors. In early 1787, vessels carrying about four hundred settlers reached Sierra Leone in West Africa, where representatives of the Black Poor Committee acquired land. The first years were difficult, and many newcomers died of disease and deprivation. But in 1792 they were joined by several thousand other loyalist African Americans who originally moved to Nova Scotia. The influx ensured the colony's survival; it remained a part of the British Empire until its independence in 1961.

At the Paris peace negotiations in 1782, American diplomats rejected British suggestions that the United States continue to serve as a dumping ground for convicts. Britain thus needed another destination for people sentenced for crimes such as theft, assault, and manslaughter. It sent them halfway round the world to Australia, which Captain James Cook claimed in 1770. Britain continued this practice until 1868, but voluntary migrants also arrived. The modern nation was created from a federation of separate colonial governments on January 1, 1901.

Thus the founding event in the history of the United States links the nation to the formation of its northern neighbor and to new nations in West Africa and the Asian Pacific.

The New York Public Library / Art Resource, NY

National Library of Australia

Battles of Lexington and Concord

Bostonians dispatched two messengers, William Dawes and Paul Revere (later joined by Dr. Samuel Prescott), to rouse the countryside. When the British vanguard of several hundred men approached Lexington at dawn on April 19, they found just seventy militiamen—about half of the town's adult male population—mustered on the common. Realizing they could not halt the redcoats, the Americans' commander ordered his men to withdraw. But as they dispersed, a shot rang out; British soldiers then fired. When they stopped, eight Americans lay dead, and another ten wounded. The British moved on to nearby Concord.

There the militia contingents, joined by men from nearby towns, were larger. At the North Bridge three British men were killed and nine wounded. Thousands fired from houses and from behind trees as British forces retreated to Boston. By day's end, the redcoats suffered 272 casualties, including 70 deaths. The arrival of reinforcements and the American militia's lack of coordination prevented heavier British losses. The patriots suffered just 93 casualties.

First Year of War

By the evening of April 20, thousands of American militiamen gathered around Boston, summoned by local committees. Many did not stay long, but those who remained were organized into formal units. Officers under the command of General Artemas Ward of the Massachusetts militia ordered that latrines be dug, the water supply protected, supplies purchased, military discipline enforced, and defensive fortifications constructed.

For nearly a year the two armies stared at each other across siege lines. The redcoats attacked only once, on June 17, when they drove the Americans from trenches atop Breed's Hill in Charlestown. In that misnamed Battle of Bunker Hill, the British incurred their greatest wartime losses: over 800 wounded and 228 killed. The Americans lost less than half that number.

During the same eleven-month period, patriots captured the British Fort Ticonderoga on Lake Champlain, acquiring much-needed cannon. Trying to bring Canada into the war, patriots also mounted a northern campaign that ended in disaster at Quebec in early 1776 when troops were ravaged by smallpox. But the long lull in fighting between the main armies at Boston during the war's first year gave both sides time to regroup and strategize.

British Strategy

Lord North and his new American secretary, Lord George Germain, made three central assumptions about the war. First, they concluded that patriot forces could not withstand assaults by trained British regulars. Convinced that the 1776 campaign would begin and end the war, they dispatched Great Britain's largest force ever: 370 transport ships carrying 32,000 troops and tons of supplies, accompanied by 73 naval vessels and 13,000 sailors. Among the troops were thousands of German mercenaries, soldiers who hired out to the highest bidder.

Second, British officials and officers adopted a conventional strategy of capturing major American cities and defeating the rebel army with minimal casualties. Third, they assumed that military victory would retain the colonies' allegiance.

All three assumptions proved false. London officials also missed the significance of the American population's dispersal over an area 1,500 miles long and more than 100 miles wide. Although Britain would control each of America's largest ports at some time during the war, less than 5 percent of the population lived in those cities. Furthermore, with a vast coastline, commerce was easily rerouted. Hence, the loss of cities did little to damage the American cause.

Most of all, London officials did not initially understand that military triumph would not necessarily lead to political victory. Securing the colonies would require Americans to return to their original allegiance. After 1778 the ministry adopted a strategy to achieve that through the expanded use of loyalist forces and the restoration of civilian authority in occupied areas. But the policy came too late.

Second Continental Congress

Great Britain had a bureaucracy to supervise the war. Americans had only the Second Continental Congress. The delegates who convened in Philadelphia on May 10, 1775, had to assume the mantle of intercolonial government. As summer passed, Congress organized the colonies for war. It authorized the printing of money, established a committee to supervise foreign relations, and strengthened the militia. Most important, it created the Continental Army.

Until Congress met, the Massachusetts provincial congress supervised Ward and the militiamen encamped at Boston. But that army, composed of men from all over New England, heavily drained local resources. Consequently, Massachusetts asked the Continental Congress to direct the army and choose a commander-in-chief. John Adams proposed the appointment of a Virginian "whose Skill and Experience as an Officer, whose independent fortune, great Talents and excellent universal Character, would command the Approbation of all America": George Washington. Congress unanimously concurred.

George Washington

Washington had not participated prominently in the pre-revolutionary agitation. Devoted to the American cause, he was dignified, conservative, and respectable—a man of unimpeachable integrity. The younger son of a Virginia planter, Washington did not expect to inherit substantial property and planned to work as a surveyor. But the early death of his older brother and his marriage to the wealthy widow Martha Custis made George Washington one of Virginia's largest slaveholders. After his mistakes early in the Seven Years' War, he repaired his reputation by rallying the troops and maintaining calm during Braddock's defeat in 1755.

Washington had remarkable stamina and leadership ability. More than six feet tall (when most men were five inches shorter), he displayed a commanding presence. Even a loyalist admitted that Washington could "atone for many demerits by the extraordinary coolness and caution which distinguish his character."

British Evacuate Boston

Washington took command of the army outside Boston in July 1775. By March 1776, when the arrival of cannon from Ticonderoga enabled him to pressure the redcoats, his army was prepared. Yet an assault on Boston proved unnecessary. Sir William Howe, the new commander, wanted to transfer his men to New York City. The patriots' cannon decided the matter. On March 17, the British and their loyalist allies abandoned Boston forever.

Although at war for months, American leaders denied seeking a break with Great Britain until a pamphlet published in January 1776 advocated that step.

Common Sense

Thomas Paine's *Common Sense* exploded, quickly selling tens of thousands of copies. The author, a radical English printer who had lived in America only since 1774, called for independence and challenged many common American assumptions about government and the colonies' relationship to Britain. He advocated the establishment of a republic, a government by the people with no king or nobility. Paine insisted that Britain had exploited the colonies. And for the frequent assertion that an independent America would be weak and divided, he substituted unlimited confidence in America's strength once freed from European control.

By late spring, independence had become inevitable. On May 10, the Second Continental Congress recommended that individual colonies form new governments, replacing colonial charters with state constitutions. On June 7, Richard Henry Lee of Virginia, seconded by John Adams of Massachusetts, introduced the crucial resolution: "that these United Colonies are, and of right ought to be, free and independent States, . . . and that all political connection between them and the State of Great Britain is, and ought to be, totally dissolved." Congress did not immediately adopt Lee's resolution, postponing a vote until early July. Meanwhile, a five-man committee—including Thomas Jefferson, John Adams, and Benjamin Franklin—was directed to draft a declaration of independence.

Jefferson and the Declaration of Independence

The committee assigned primary responsibility for writing the declaration to Thomas Jefferson, who was known for his eloquence. The thirty-four-year-old Virginia lawyer and member of the House of Burgesses was educated at the College of William and Mary and in the law offices of a prominent attorney. His knowledge of history and political theory was evident in the declaration and his draft of the Virginia state constitution. While Jefferson wrote and debated in Philadelphia, his beloved wife Martha suffered a miscarriage at their home, Monticello. Not until after her 1782 death from complications following the birth of their sixth (but only third surviving) child, did Jefferson fully commit to public service.

The draft of the declaration reached Congress on June 28, 1776. The delegates voted for independence four days later, then debated the declaration's wording for two days, adopting it with changes on July 4. The Declaration of Independence concentrated on George III (see the appendix), accusing the king of attempting to destroy representative government in the colonies and of oppressing Americans.

The declaration's chief long-term importance lay in the ringing statements of principle that have since served as the American ideal: "We hold these truths to be self-evident: That all men are created equal; that they are endowed by their Creator with certain unalienable rights; that among these are life, liberty and the pursuit of happiness; that, to secure these rights, governments are instituted among men, deriving their just powers from the consent of the governed; that whenever any form of government becomes destructive of these ends, it is the right of the people to alter or to abolish it, and to institute new government."

When the delegates in Philadelphia voted to accept the Declaration of Independence, they were committing treason. Therefore, when they concluded with the assertion that they "mutually pledge[d] to each other our lives, our fortunes, and our sacred honor," they spoke the truth.

THE STRUGGLE IN THE NORTH

In late June 1776, ships carrying Sir William Howe's troops from Halifax appeared off the New York coast (see Map 6.1). On July 2, redcoats landed on Staten Island. Washington marched his army of seventeen thousand from Boston to defend Manhattan. Because Howe waited until more troops arrived from England, Americans could prepare to defend the city.

New York and New Jersey

Still inexperienced, Washington and his men made major mistakes, losing battles at Brooklyn Heights and on Manhattan Island. The city fell to the British, who captured nearly three thousand American soldiers. Washington retreated into Pennsylvania, and British forces took most of New Jersey. Occupying troops met little opposition; the revolutionary cause appeared in disarray. "These are the times that try men's souls," wrote Thomas Paine in his pamphlet *The Crisis*.

The British then forfeited their advantage as redcoats in New Jersey went on a rampage of rape and plunder. Determined to strike back, Washington crossed the Delaware River at night to attack a Hessian encampment at Trenton early on December 26. The patriots captured more than nine hundred Hessians and killed another thirty; only three Americans were wounded. Days later, Washington attacked

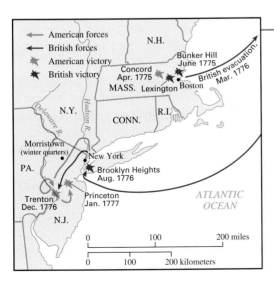

Map 6.1   The War in the North, 1775–1777

The early phase of the Revolutionary War was dominated by British troop movements in the Boston area, the redcoats' evacuation to Nova Scotia in the spring of 1776, and the subsequent British invasion of New York and New Jersey.

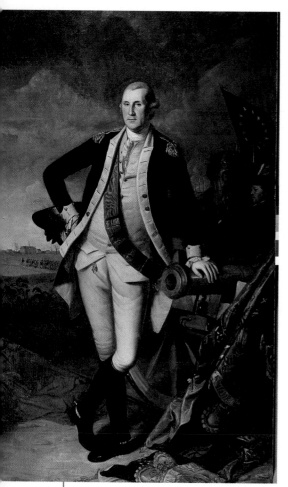

George Washington at the Battle of Princeton, 1779, by Charles Willson Peale. Two years after the battle, Peale created this heroic image of the Continental Army's commander, intended (as were all his portraits of revolutionary leaders) to instill patriotic sentiments and pride in its viewers.   (Courtesy of the Pennsylvania Academy of the Fine Arts, Philadelphia. Gift of Maria McKean Allen and Phebe Warren Downs through the bequest of their mother, Elizabeth Wharton McKean)

at Princeton. Gaining command of the field, Washington set up winter quarters at Morristown, New Jersey.

Campaign of 1777

British strategy for 1777 aimed to isolate New England from the other colonies. General John Burgoyne would lead an invading force down the Hudson River from Canada to rendezvous near Albany with a similar force moving east. The combined forces would then link up with Howe's troops in New York City. But Howe was planning to capture Philadelphia. In 1777 the British armies in America operated independently; the result was disaster.

Howe took Philadelphia, but he delayed before beginning the campaign, took six weeks to transport his troops by sea, and ended up only 40 miles closer to Philadelphia than when he started. This gave Washington time to prepare a defense. At Brandywine Creek and Germantown, the two armies clashed. Although the British won both engagements, the Americans handled themselves well. The redcoats captured Philadelphia in late September but to little effect. The campaign season was nearly over; the revolutionary army had gained confidence in itself and its leaders; and, far north, Burgoyne was going down to defeat.

Burgoyne and his men set out from Montreal in mid-June. An easy triumph at Fort Ticonderoga in July was followed in August by two setbacks—the redcoats and Indians marching east along the Mohawk River turned back after a battle at Oriskany, New York; and in a clash near Bennington, Vermont, American militiamen nearly wiped out eight hundred of Burgoyne's German mercenaries. After several skirmishes, Burgoyne was surrounded near Saratoga, New York. On October 17, 1777, he surrendered his force of more than six thousand men.

Iroquois Confederacy Splinters

The August 1777 battle at Oriskany divided the Iroquois Confederacy. Although the Six Nations had pledged neutrality, two influential Mohawk leaders, siblings Mary and Joseph Brant, believed the Iroquois should ally with the British to protect their territory from land-hungry colonists. The Brants won over the Senecas, Cayugas, and Mohawks, but the Oneidas preferred the Americans and brought the Tuscaroras with them. The Onondagas split into three factions, one on each side and one supporting neutrality. At Oriskany, some Oneidas and Tuscaroras joined patriot militiamen in fighting their Iroquois brethren, shattering three-hundred years of friendship.

The collapse of Iroquois unity had significant consequences. In 1778 Iroquois warriors allied with the British raided frontier villages in Pennsylvania and New York. The following summer, the Americans dispatched an expedition to burn Iroquois crops and settlements. The devastation led many bands to seek food and shelter north of the Great Lakes during the winter of 1779–1780. Many Iroquois settled permanently in Canada.

Burgoyne's surrender at Saratoga brought joy to patriots, discouragement to loyalists and Britons. Most important, the American victory at Saratoga drew France into the conflict. The American Revolution gave the French an opportunity to avenge their defeat in the Seven Years' War. Even before Benjamin Franklin arrived in Paris in late 1776, France covertly supplied the revolutionaries with military necessities. Indeed, 90 percent of the gunpowder Americans used during the war's first two years came from France, transported via the French Caribbean island of Martinique.

Franco-American Alliance of 1778

Benjamin Franklin worked tirelessly to strengthen ties between the two nations. Adopting a plain style of dress, Franklin played on the French image of Americans as virtuous farmers. In 1778 the countries signed two treaties. In the Treaty of Amity and Commerce, France recognized American independence and established trade ties. In the Treaty of Alliance, France and the United States promised—assuming that France would declare war on Britain, which it soon did—that neither would negotiate peace without consulting the other. France also abandoned claims to Canada and to North American territory east of the Mississippi River. The most visible symbol of Franco-American cooperation was the Marquis de Lafayette, a young nobleman who volunteered for service with George Washington in 1777 and fought with American forces.

With the alliance, France aided Americans openly, sending troops, naval vessels, arms, ammunition, clothing, and blankets. And Britain now had to fight France in the Caribbean and elsewhere, in addition to its battles on the American mainland. Spain's entry into the war in 1779 as an ally of France (but not of the United States) transformed the Revolution into a global war. The French aided Americans throughout the conflict, but in its last years that assistance proved vital.

Joseph Brant, the Iroquois leader who helped to persuade the Mohawks, Senecas, and Cayugas to support the British in the latter stages of the Revolution, as painted by Charles Willson Peale in 1797.
(Independence National Historic Park Collection)

LIFE IN THE ARMY AND ON THE HOME FRONT

Only in the first months of the war was the revolutionaries' army manned primarily by the semimythical citizen-soldier, who exchanged his plow for a gun. After a few months, early arrivals went home. They reenlisted only briefly when the contending armies neared their farms and towns. In such militia units, elected officers and the soldiers who chose them reflected social hierarchies in their regions of origin, yet also retained a flexibility absent from the Continental Army, composed of men in formally organized statewide units led by appointed officers.

Continental Army

Continental soldiers, unlike militiamen, were primarily young, single, or propertyless men who enlisted for long periods or for the war's duration, partly for monetary bonuses or land. They saw in military service an opportunity to assert their masculinity and claim postwar citizenship and property-owning rights. As the fighting dragged on,

Barzillai Lew, a free African American born in Groton, Massachusetts, in 1743, served in the Seven Years' War before enlisting with patriot troops in the American Revolution. An accomplished fifer, Lew fought at the Battle of Bunker Hill. Like other freemen in the north, he cast his lot with the revolutionaries, in contrast to southern bondspeople, who tended to favor the British. (Courtesy of Mae Theresa Bonitto)

bonuses grew larger. To meet quotas, towns and states recruited everyone, including recent immigrants; about 45 percent of Pennsylvania soldiers were of Irish origin and about 13 percent were German.

Dunmore's proclamation led Congress in January 1776 to modify an earlier policy prohibiting African Americans in the regular army. Recruiters in northern states turned increasingly to slaves, who were often promised freedom after the war. Southern states initially resisted, but later all except Georgia and South Carolina enlisted black soldiers. Approximately five thousand African Americans served in the Continental Army, typically in racially integrated units where they were assigned tasks that others shunned, such as burying the dead, foraging for food, and driving wagons. Overall, they composed about 10 percent of the regular army, although rarely serving in militia units.

American wives and widows of poor soldiers came to the army with their menfolk because they were too impoverished to survive alone. Such camp followers—roughly 3 percent of the total number of troops—worked as cooks, nurses, and launderers for rations and low wages. The women, along with civilian commissaries and militiamen who floated in and out at irregular intervals, were difficult to manage, especially since they were not subject to military discipline.

Officer Corps

The officers of the Continental Army developed intense pride and commitment to the revolutionary cause. The realities of warfare were often messy and corrupt, but officers drew strength from a developing image of themselves as professionals who sacrificed for the nation. When Benedict Arnold, an officer who fought heroically for the patriot cause early in the war, defected to the British, they made his name a metaphor for villainy.

Unlike poor women, officers' wives did not travel with the army but made extended visits while the troops were in camp (usually during winter). They brought food, clothing, and household furnishings to make their stay more comfortable, and they entertained each other and their menfolk at teas, dinners, and dances. Socializing created friendships later renewed when some of their husbands became the new nation's leaders.

Hardship and Disease

Ordinary soldiers endured more hardships than officers. Wages were small, and often the army could not meet the payroll. Rations (a daily allotment of bread, meat, vegetables, milk, and beer) did not always appear, and men had to forage for food. Clothing and shoes were often poor quality. When conditions deteriorated, troops threatened mutiny (though only a few followed through) or, more often, simply deserted. Punishments for desertion or offenses such as theft and assault were harsh; convicted soldiers were sentenced to hundreds of lashes, whereas officers were publicly humiliated, deprived of their commission, and discharged in disgrace.

Endemic disease in the camps—dysentery, various fevers, and, early in the war, smallpox—made matters worse. Most native-born colonists had neither been exposed to smallpox nor been inoculated and were vulnerable when smallpox spread through the northern countryside in early 1774. The disease ravaged Bostonians during the British occupation, troops attacking Quebec in 1775–1776, and African Americans who fled to join Lord Dunmore (1775) or Lord Cornwallis (1781). Most British soldiers had already survived smallpox (which was endemic in Europe), so it posed little threat to redcoat troops.

Recognizing smallpox's potential to decimate the revolutionaries' ranks, Washington ordered that the regular army be inoculated in Morristown in early 1777. Some would die from the risky procedure and survivors would be incapacitated for weeks. Yet inoculation, coupled with the increasing numbers of foreign-born (and mostly immune) enlistees, helped protect Continental soldiers later in the war, contributing to the eventual American victory.

Home Front

Men who enlisted in the army or served in Congress were away from home for long periods of time. In their absence their womenfolk, who previously had handled only the indoor affairs of the household, shouldered outdoor affairs as well. John and Abigail Adams took pride in Abigail's developing skills as a "farmeress." Like other female contemporaries, Abigail Adams stopped calling the farm *yours* in letters to her husband and began referring to it as *ours*. Most women did not work in the fields, but they supervised field workers and managed their families' resources.

Wartime disruptions affected all Americans. People suffered from shortages of necessities like salt, soap, and flour. Severe inflation added to the country's woes. Soldiers on both sides plundered farms and houses, looking for food or salable items; they burned fence rails in fires and took horses and oxen for their wagons. Moreover, they carried smallpox and other diseases wherever they went. Women had to decide whether to deliberately risk their children's lives by inoculating them with smallpox or to chance youngsters' contracting the disease "in the natural way." Many chose the former and were relieved when their children survived.

VICTORY IN THE SOUTH

In early 1778, in the wake of the Saratoga disaster, British military leaders reassessed their strategy. Loyalist exiles in London persuaded them to shift the field of battle southward, contending that loyal southerners would welcome the redcoat army as liberators. The South could then serve as a base for attacking the middle and northern states.

South Carolina and the Caribbean

Sir Henry Clinton oversaw the regrouping of British forces in America. He ordered the evacuation of Philadelphia in June 1778 and sent a convoy that captured the French Caribbean island of St. Lucia, thereafter a key British base. He also dispatched a small expedition to Georgia. When Savannah and then Augusta fell into British hands, Clinton became convinced that a southern strategy would

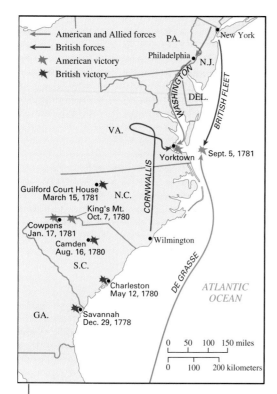

Map 6.2 The War in the South

The southern war—after the British invasion of Georgia in late 1778—was characterized by a series of British thrusts into the interior, leading to battles with American defenders in both North and South Carolina. Finally, after promising beginnings, Cornwallis's foray into Virginia ended with disaster at Yorktown in October 1781.

succeed. In late 1779 he sailed down the coast from New York to besiege Charleston, the most important city in the South (see Map 6.2). Although afflicted by smallpox, Americans trapped there held out for months. On May 12, 1780, General Benjamin Lincoln surrendered the entire southern army—5,500 men. The redcoats then spread through South Carolina, establishing garrisons at key points. Hundreds of South Carolinians proclaimed renewed loyalty to the Crown.

Success of the southern campaign depended on controlling the seas, for the British armies were widely dispersed and travel by land was difficult. The Royal Navy dominated the American coastline, but French naval power posed a threat. American privateers infested Caribbean waters, seizing cargoes to and from the British islands. Furthermore, after late 1778 France picked off those islands one by one, including Grenada—second only to Jamaica in sugar production. In early 1781 the British captured St. Eustatius (the Dutch island that was the main conduit for moving military supplies from Europe to America). But the victory might well have cost them the war, for Admiral Sir George Rodney failed to pursue the French fleet under Admiral François de Grasse when it subsequently sailed from the Caribbean to Virginia, where it played a major role in the battle at Yorktown.

The redcoats never established control of the areas they seized in South Carolina or Georgia. Patriot bands operated freely, and the fall of Charleston spurred them to greater exertions. Patriot women in four states formed the Ladies Association, raising funds to purchase shirts for needy soldiers. Recruiting efforts were stepped up.

Nevertheless, the war in South Carolina went badly for the patriots throughout 1780. At Camden in August, forces under Lord Cornwallis, the new British commander, crushed a reorganized southern army led by Horatio Gates. Thousands of enslaved African Americans joined the redcoats. Running away from their patriot masters individually and as families, they disrupted farming in the Carolinas and Georgia in 1780 and 1781. Tens of thousands of slaves were lost to their owners. Not all of them won their freedom. Many served the redcoats as scouts and guides or as laborers in camps or occupied cities like New York.

Greene and the Southern Campaign

After the Camden defeat, Washington (who remained in the North to contain the British army occupying New York) appointed General Nathanael Greene to command the southern campaign. Greene was appalled by conditions in South Carolina. His troops needed clothing, blankets, and food. He told a friend that incessant guerrilla warfare had "so corrupted the principles of the people that they think of nothing but plundering one another."

Greene moved cautiously. He adopted a conciliatory policy toward the many Americans who had switched sides, a wise choice in a region where people changed their allegiance up to seven times in less than two years. He ordered his troops to treat captives fairly and not loot loyalist property. He helped the shattered provincial congresses of Georgia and South Carolina reestablish civilian authority in the interior—a goal the British were never able to accomplish. With only sixteen hundred regulars, Greene could not afford to have frontier militia companies occupied in defending their homes from Indian attack. He accordingly pursued diplomacy to keep Indians out of the war. Although royal officials initially won some Indian allies, by war's end, only the Creeks remained allied with Great Britain.

Even before Greene took command in December 1780, the tide was turning. In October, at King's Mountain, a backcountry force defeated a large party of redcoats and loyalists. Then in January 1781 Greene's trusted aide Daniel Morgan brilliantly routed the British regiment Tarleton's Legion at Cowpens. Greene confronted the main body of British troops under Lord Cornwallis at Guilford Court House, North Carolina, in March. Although Cornwallis controlled the field at day's end, most of his army was destroyed. Greene returned to South Carolina, where he forced the redcoats to abandon their interior posts and retire to Charleston.

Surrender at Yorktown Cornwallis headed north into Virginia, where he joined forces with redcoats commanded by the American traitor Benedict Arnold. He then withdrew to the peninsula between the York and James Rivers, where he fortified Yorktown. Washington moved more than seven thousand French and American troops south from New York City. When De Grasse's fleet arrived in time to defeat the Royal Navy vessels sent to relieve Cornwallis, the British general was trapped (see Map 6.2). On October 19, 1781, Cornwallis surrendered.

When news of the defeat reached London, Parliament voted to cease offensive operations in America, authorizing peace negotiations. Washington returned with the main army to the environs of New York, where in March 1783, his underpaid—and, they thought, underappreciated—officers threatened to mutiny unless Congress guaranteed them adequate compensation. Washington, warned in advance of the so-called Newburgh Conspiracy, defused the crisis with a well-reasoned and patriotic speech. At the end of the year, he resigned as commander-in-chief. Still, Washington established an enduring precedent: civilian control of the American military.

The war had been won but at terrible cost. More than 25,000 American men died, about one-quarter of them from battle. The rest were declared missing or died of disease or as prisoners of war. In the South, years of guerrilla warfare and the loss of thousands of runaway slaves shattered the economy. Indebtedness soared, and local governments were crippled, as few people could pay taxes. Some formerly wealthy planters descended into insolvency.

Treaty of Paris Yet Americans all rejoiced when they learned of the signing of the preliminary peace treaty at Paris in November 1782. American diplomats—Benjamin Franklin, John Jay, and John Adams—ignored their instructions from Congress to be guided by France and negotiated directly with Great Britain. Their instincts were sound: the French government was more an enemy to Britain than a friend to the United States. French ministers worked secretly to try to prevent the establishment of a strong, unified

Revolutionary Origins

Many historians today would contend that the American Revolution was not truly revolutionary, if *revolution* means overturning an earlier power structure. The United States won its independence and established a republic, both radical events in the eighteenth century, but essentially the same men who led the colonies also led the new country (with the exception of British officials and appointees). In contrast, the nearly contemporary French Revolution witnessed the execution of the monarch and many aristocrats, and a significant redistribution of authority. So the legacy of the American Revolution appears radical and conservative by comparison.

Throughout the more than two hundred years since the Revolution, varying groups have frequently declared that they are acting in the spirit of the Revolution. People protesting discriminatory policies against women and minorities (usually liberals) invoke the created-equal language of the Declaration of Independence. Left-wing organizations rail against concentrations of wealth and power in a few hands. Those protesting higher taxes (usually conservatives wanting a reduced role for government) often adopt the symbolism of the Boston Tea Party. Right-wing militias arm themselves, preparing to defend their homes against a malevolent government, just as they believe the minutemen did in 1775. In 2006 so-called minutemen formed vigilante groups to guard the United States– Mexico border against illegal aliens. The message of the Revolution can be invoked to support extralegal demonstrations of any description, from invasions of military bases by antiwar protesters to demonstrations outside abortion clinics. But the Revolution can also be invoked to oppose such street protests, because—some would argue—in a republic, change should come peacefully, via the ballot box.

Just as Americans in the eighteenth century disagreed over the meaning of their struggle, so the legacy of revolution remains contested early in the twenty-first century.

government in America. Spain's desire to lay claim to the region between the Appalachian Mountains and the Mississippi River further complicated the negotiations. But the American delegates proved adept at power politics, achieving their main goal: independence as a united nation. Weary of war, the new British ministry made so many concessions that Parliament ousted it shortly after peace terms were approved.

The treaty, signed on September 3, 1783, granted independence to a nation named the United States of America. Generous boundaries delineated that new nation: to the north, approximately the present-day boundary with Canada; to the south, the 31st parallel (about the modern northern border of Florida); to the west, the Mississippi River. Florida, which Britain had acquired in 1763, reverted to Spain (see Map 7.2). The Americans also gained unlimited fishing rights off Newfoundland. In ceding so much land, Great Britain ignored the territorial rights of its Indian allies. British diplomats also poorly served loyalists and British merchants. The treaty's ambiguously worded clauses regarding prewar debts and postwar treatment of loyalists proved impossible to enforce.

Summary

The victorious Americans could reflect on their achievement with satisfaction. Having unified the mainland colonies, they claimed their place in the family of nations and forged a successful alliance with France. With an inexperienced army, they defeated the world's greatest military power. They won only a few actual victories—most notably at Trenton, Saratoga, and Yorktown—but their army survived to fight again. Ultimately, the Americans simply wore their enemy down.

In winning the war, Americans abandoned their British identity, excluding from their new nation loyalist neighbors unwilling to break with the mother country. They established republican governments at state and national levels and created new national loyalties. They also claimed most of the territory east of the Mississippi River and south of the Great Lakes, thereby greatly expanding land open to settlement and threatening traditional Indian dominance of the interior.

In the future Americans faced new challenges: ensuring the survival of their republican polity in a world dominated by bitter rivalries among Britain, France, and Spain.

Chapter Review

GOVERNMENT BY CONGRESS AND COMMITTEE

How did the first Continental Congress redefine America's relationship to England?

Congressmen meeting at the First Continental Congress in September 1774 were not ready for a complete break from England, but they did outline America's grievances, develop a resistance plan, and define America's relationship to Great Britain. Debate covered the spectrum of opinion from the radical call to obey only the king and not Parliament to the more conservative view that would have Parliament and a new American legislature jointly enacting colonial laws. In the end, the group compromised and agreed in the Declaration of Rights and Grievances to obey Parliament on a voluntary basis (rather than as subjects) and resist all taxes.

CONTEST IN THE BACKCOUNTRY

Where did backcountry Indians' loyalties lay at the onset of the Revolution?

Initially, Indians were inclined to ally with Great Britain, given the hostility they experienced from European American settlers in the backcountry. But other chiefs had their doubts: England had abandoned them in vacating Fort Pitt years earlier. Both the Americans and the British sought a pledge of neutrality, and while some, such as the Iroquois, agreed, others, such as the Cherokees and Shawnees, attacked backcountry settlements in western and the Carolinas hoping to use the conflict to regain lost land. A few Indian communities supported the Americans, but most others remained neutral or sporadically sided with the British.

CHOOSING SIDES

How did people choose sides in the conflict with England?

Not everyone supported complete and total independence from Great Britain. In fact, only two-fifths of the European American population of the thirteen colonies were Patriots seeking to separate from England—among them small and middling farmers, Chesapeake gentry, merchants, city artisans, elected officeholders—and even then, their specific goals varied. Loyalists who opposed the break with England represented one-fifth of the population, and included Anglican clergy parishioners in the North; tenant farmers; members of persecuted religious sects; backcountry southerners; ethnic minorities, especially Scots; and merchants who relied on British trade. Two-fifths of the population remained neutral, including pacifist groups such as the Quakers. Finally, free blacks in the North and slaves in the middle colonies took the Patriots' side, while southern bondspeople thought they'd have a better chance at personal freedom by allying with the British, and some offered to join the British in exchange for their freedom.

WAR AND INDEPENDENCE

How did Thomas Paine's *Common Sense* potentially reshape the war's purpose?

While Americans had been at war with Great Britain for months, most leaders denied seeking a complete break from England and focused on achieving some autonomy and a redress for various grievances. In January 1776, Paine's widely popular pamphlet called for independence and the establishment of a republic (a government by the people with no king or nobility). He argued that once America broke from European control, it would become strong and prosperous. Within months of its publication, the Second Continental Congress passed a resolution that the colonies should be free and all ties to Great Britain dissolved, and they charged several men, among them Thomas Jefferson, to write a Declaration of Independence.

THE STRUGGLE IN THE NORTH

What was France's role in the American Revolution?

Initially, France secretly sent military supplies to the Americans and regarded the revolution as a chance to avenge its defeat to Britain in the Seven Years' War. Once Americans won the Battle of Saratoga, the French openly supported them, sending naval vessels, ammunition, and troops. France's assistance proved vital to American victory in the final years of the war. Americans and the French signed two treaties in 1778, the Treaty of Amity and Commerce, which recognized American independence and set up trade relations; and the Treaty of Alliance, which promised neither side would negotiate peace (in conflicts with Britain) without consulting the other. France also abandoned claims to Canada and to North American territory east of the Mississippi River.

LIFE IN THE ARMY AND ON THE HOME FRONT

How was the Continental Army staffed?

Only in the war's earliest months were battlefields filled by militia men, who left their fields to fight. After that, American leaders organized an army comprising young, single, often propertyless men who enlisted for a period of time for money or land. Towns were required to send their quota of soldiers and did so by enlisting everyone, including recent immigrants. Initially, African Americans were banned from the army, but by 1776, that prohibition was lifted, as northern recruiters promised slaves their freedom after the war. About five thousand enlisted, composing 10 percent of the army, though they were typically in segregated units and often given tasks others rejected, such as burying the dead. Wives and widows of poor soldiers often followed the camps, too, working as cooks, nurses, and launderers for rations or low wages.

VICTORY IN THE SOUTH

How did the decision to ignore the Treaty of Alliance prove wise in negotiating the peace with England after the American Revolution?

In the 1778 Treaty of Alliance, Americans agreed not to make peace with England without consulting France first (and vice versa). During the signing of a preliminary peace treaty in Paris in 1782 ending the American Revolution, diplomats Benjamin Franklin, John Jay, and John Adams ignored Congress's instructions to let Paris lead the way and trusted their instincts about France's true motives. French ministers had secretly tried to prevent a strong government from taking hold in America. War-weary Britain not only gave America its independence, but also ceded vast tracts of land and unlimited fishing rights off Newfoundland.

SUGGESTIONS FOR FURTHER READING

Robert McCluer Calhoon, *The Loyalists in Revolutionary America, 1760–1781* (1973)

Colin Calloway, *The American Revolution in Indian Country* (1995)

Stephen Conway, *The War of American Independence, 1775–1783* (1995)

Sylvia Frey, *Water from the Rock: Black Resistance in a Revolutionary Age* (1991)

Pauline Maier, *American Scripture: Making the Declaration of Independence* (1997)

Charles Niemeyer, *America Goes to War: A Social History of the Continental Army* (1997)

Mary Beth Norton, *Liberty's Daughters: The Revolutionary Experience of American Women, 1750–1800* (2d ed., 1996)

Cassandra Pybus, *Epic Journeys of Freedom: Runaway Slaves of the American Revolution and their Global Quest for Liberty* (2006)

Charles Royster, *A Revolutionary People at War: The Continental Army and American Character, 1775–1783* (1980)

Richard W. Van Alstyne, *Empire and Independence: The International History of the American Revolution* (1965)

CHAPTER 7

Forging a National Republic

1776–1789

CHAPTER OUTLINE

Creating a Virtuous Republic

LINKS TO THE WORLD:
Novels

The First Emancipation and the Growth of Racism

Designing Republican Governments

Trials of the Confederation

Order and Disorder in the West

From Crisis to the Constitution

Opposition and Ratification

LEGACY FOR A PEOPLE AND A NATION: The Township and Range System

Summary

On December 26, 1787, a group of Federalists— supporters of the proposed Constitution—gathered in the frontier town of Carlisle, Pennsylvania. The men planned to fire a cannon in celebration of their state convention's ratification vote two weeks earlier, but a crowd of Antifederalists stopped them. First, the Antifederalists blocked the cannon. Then, they attacked the Federalists, who fled as the angry Antis burned a copy of the Constitution.

The next day, Federalists fired their cannon and read the ratification proclamation. Antifederalists paraded and burned effigies of two Federalists. When Federalist officials arrested several demonstrators for rioting, the Antifederalist-dominated militia broke them out of jail. For weeks, participants argued in the Carlisle newspaper about what the demonstrations meant. Federalists proclaimed that the respectable celebrants acted with "good order." Replying, Antifederalists pronounced the Federalists "an unhallowed riotous mob," claiming that the Constitution's supporters declared themselves "friends of government" but, through advocacy of a government that aimed to suppress people's liberties, they revealed they were secretly aristocrats.

The Carlisle riots presaged violent disputes over the new Constitution in Albany, New York; Providence, Rhode Island; and other cities. In a struggle that began in 1775 and persisted until century's end, Americans argued over how to implement republican principles and who best represented the people. In a world where relatively few property-holding men had the right to vote, people often expressed their political opinions in the streets.

Republicanism—the idea that governments should be based on the consent of the people—originated with political theorists in ancient Greece and Rome. Republics, theorists declared, were

This icon will direct you to interactive activities and study materials on A People And A Nation, Brief Edition
website: **www.cengage.com/history/norton/ peoplenationbrief8e**

Chronology

1776	Second Continental Congress directs states to draft constitutions.	**1786**	Annapolis Convention meets and discusses reforming government.
	Abigail Adams advises her husband to "Remember the Ladies."	**1786–87**	Shays's Rebellion in western Massachusetts raises questions about the future of the republic.
1777	Articles of Confederation are sent to states for ratification.	**1787**	Royall Tyler's *The Contrast*, the first successful American play, is performed.
	Vermont becomes first jurisdiction to abolish slavery.		Northwest Ordinance organizes the territory north of Ohio River and east of Mississippi River.
1781	Articles of Confederation are ratified.		Constitutional Convention drafts a new form of government.
1783	Treaty of Paris is signed, formalizing American independence.	**1788**	Hamilton, Jay, and Madison write *The Federalist* to urge ratification of the Constitution by New York.
1784	Diplomats sign treaty with Iroquois at Fort Stanwix, but Iroquois repudiate it two years later.		Constitution is ratified.
1785	Land Ordinance of 1785 provides for surveying and sale of national lands in Northwest Territory.	**1789**	William Hill Brown publishes *The Power of Sympathy*, the first American novel.
1785–86	United States negotiates treaties at Hopewell, South Carolina, with Choctaws, Chickasaws, and Cherokees.		Massachusetts orders towns to support public schools.
		1800	Weems publishes his *Life of Washington*.

desirable yet fragile government forms. Unless citizens were virtuous—that is, sober, moral, and industrious—and agreed on key issues, republics were doomed. When Americans left the British Empire, they abandoned the idea that the best system of government balanced participation by a king, the nobility, and the people. Instead, they embraced republicanism, in which the people were sovereign. Still, during and after the war, Americans wondered how to ensure political stability, how to foster consensus, and how to create and sustain a virtuous republic.

Leaders attempted to inculcate virtue in their fellow American countrymen and countrywomen. After 1776, literature, theater, art, architecture, and education pursued moral goals. Women's education became important, for mothers of the republic's children were responsible for ensuring the nation's future. Almost all white men assumed that women, African Americans, and Indians should have no role in politics; the first two groups were regarded as household dependents, the last as outside the polity. Still, they disagreed on how many of their number should be included in the political process and how their new governments should be structured.

Then there were Thomas Jefferson's words in the Declaration of Independence: "all men are created equal." Given that statement of principle, how could white republicans justify holding African Americans in perpetual bondage? Some freed their slaves or voted for state laws abolishing slavery. Others denied that blacks were men in the same sense as whites.

The most important task facing Americans was constructing a unified national government. Before 1765, many circumstances divided the British mainland colonies: diverse economies, varying religious traditions and ethnic compositions, competing western land claims, and different polities. But the Revolutionary War brought them together, creating a new nationalistic spirit that replaced loyalties to state and region.

However, America's first national government, under the Articles of Confederation, proved weak and decentralized. Political leaders tried another approach in drafting the Constitution in 1787. Some historians have argued that the Articles of Confederation and the Constitution reflect opposing political philosophies, the Constitution representing an aristocratic counterrevolution against the democratic Articles. The two documents are more accurately viewed as successive attempts to solve the same problems—the relationship of states and nation and the extent to which authority should be centralized. Both applied theories of republicanism to questions of governance; neither was entirely successful in resolving those difficulties.

- **What were the elements of the new national identity? How did women, Indians, and African Americans fit into that identity?**
- **What problems confronted the new nation's leaders as they attempted to establish the first modern republic?**
- **How and why were those problems resolved differently at different times?**

CREATING A VIRTUOUS REPUBLIC

When the colonies declared independence, John Dickinson recalled, many years later, "there was no question concerning forms of Government, no enquiry whether a Republic or a limited Monarchy was best. . . . We knew that the people of this country must unite themselves under some form of Government and that this could be no other than the republican form"—in short, self-government by the people. But how should that goal be implemented?

Varieties of Republicanism

Three definitions of republicanism emerged in the new United States. Ancient history and political theory informed the first, held chiefly by the educated elite (such as the Adamses of Massachusetts). The histories of popular governments in Greece and Rome suggested that republics could succeed only if they were small and homogeneous. According to classical republican theory, unless a republic's citizens were virtuous men willing to forgo personal profit for the best interests of the nation, the government would collapse. In return for sacrifices, a republic offered equality of opportunity. Rank would be based on merit rather than inherited wealth and status. Society would be governed by members of a "natural aristocracy," men whose talent elevated them from possibly humble beginnings to positions of power.

A second definition, advanced by other elites and some skilled craftsmen, drew on economic theory. Instead of perceiving the nation as composed of people nobly sacrificing for the common good, this version of republicanism followed Scottish theorist Adam Smith in emphasizing individuals' pursuit of rational self-interest. When republican men sought to improve their own economic and social circumstances, the nation would benefit. Republican virtue would be achieved through the pursuit of private interests, rather than through subordination to communal ideals.

The third notion of republicanism was less influential but more egalitarian than the others. Men who advanced the third version of republicanism, among them Thomas Paine, called for widening men's political participation. They wanted government to respond directly to the needs of ordinary folk, rejecting that the "lesser sort" should defer to their "betters." They were democrats in the modern sense. For them, the untutored wisdom of the people embodied republican virtue.

All three strands of republicanism contrasted America's industrious virtue with the corruption of Britain and Europe. In the first version, that virtue manifested itself in frugality and self-sacrifice; in the second, it would prevent self-interest from becoming vice; in the third, it was the justification for including propertyless free men as voters. Most agreed that a virtuous country would be composed of hardworking citizens who would dress and live simply, elect wise leaders, and forgo conspicuous consumption of luxury goods.

Virtue and the Arts

As citizens of the United States constructed their republic, they expected to replace the vices of monarchical Europe—immorality, selfishness, and lack of public spirit—with the virtues of republican America. They sought to embody republican principles in their governments and in their culture, expecting painting, literature, drama, and architecture to convey nationalism and virtue.

Americans faced a crucial contradiction, however. To some republicans, fine arts were manifestations of vice, signaling luxury and corruption. Why did a frugal farmer need a painting or a novel? Why should anyone spend hard-earned wages to see a play in a lavish theater? The first American artists and authors wanted to produce works embodying virtue, but many viewed those works as corrupting, regardless of their content.

Still, authors and artists tried. In Royall Tyler's *The Contrast* (1787), the first successful American play, Colonel Manly's virtuous conduct was contrasted with Billy Dimple's reprehensible behavior. The era's most popular book, Mason Locke Weems's *Life of Washington,* published in 1800 after George Washington's death, was intended to "hold up his great Virtues . . . to the imitation of Our Youth." The famous tale Weems invented—six-year-old George bravely admitting cutting down his father's favorite cherry tree—ended with George's father exclaiming, "Such an act of heroism in my son, is worth more than a thousand trees."

Painting and architecture were also expected to exemplify moral standards and instill patriotism. The period's most prominent artists, Gilbert Stuart and Charles Willson Peale, painted portraits of upstanding republican citizens. John Trumbull's canvases depicted historical milestones such as the Battle of Bunker Hill and Cornwallis's surrender at Yorktown. When the Virginia government asked Thomas Jefferson, then minister to France, for advice on designing the state capitol in Richmond, Jefferson recommended copying a simple but noble Roman building, the Maison Carrée at Nîmes. Ideals he set forth would guide American architecture for a generation: simplicity of line, harmonious proportions, a feeling of grandeur.

Despite the artists' efforts (or perhaps because of them), some Americans detected signs of luxury and corruption by the mid-1780s. The resumption of European trade after the war brought imported fashions for men and women. Elite

Novels

In novels, poems, paintings, plays, and histories, citizens of the United States explored their new national identity. Ironically, the standards against which they measured themselves and the models they followed were primarily British.

This was especially true of the most widely read literary form: the novel. In the mid-eighteenth century, the Englishman Samuel Richardson composed the first fictional works that today are called novels. Richardson's novels—*Pamela* (1740), *Clarissa* (1748), and *Sir Charles Grandison* (1753)—revolved around the courtship and sexual relationships of young adults. Those themes permeated the most popular early American novel, Susanna Haswell Rowson's *Charlotte: A Tale of Truth*, and other novels. Changing mores in the late eighteenth century freed English and American youth from parental supervision of their marital decisions. That freedom also rendered girls vulnerable to new dangers of deception and seduction by unscrupulous suitors. Young women were the most avid readers of novels, especially as women's literacy rates increased.

One of the best-selling novels of its time, *Charlotte*, had the subtitle *A Tale of Truth* despite no known factual basis. First published in London in 1791, Rowson's novel was reprinted in Philadelphia three years later and went through more than 160 editions. *Charlotte* focuses on a naive young woman who elopes, pregnant and unmarried, with her seducer, only to be deserted when a beautiful, rich, and virtuous rival appears. After giving birth, Charlotte dies in her father's arms. "Oh my dear girls," Rowson cautions readers, "pray for fortitude to resist the impulses of inclination, when it runs counter to the precepts of religion and virtue."

Generations of young American women sobbed over Charlotte's fate, visiting Trinity churchyard in lower Manhattan, where a real-life counterpart of the fictional heroine was reputed to be buried. Their tears and women's preference on both sides of the Atlantic for such sentimental novels linked the young readers and their nation to the former mother country from which they were nominally so eager to separate.

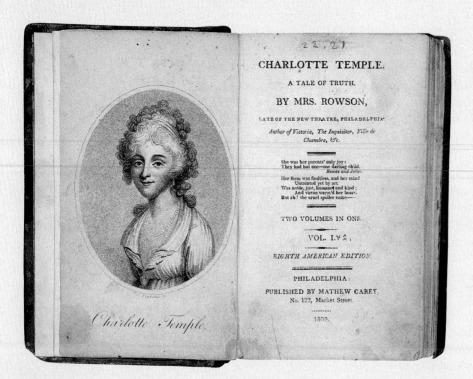

This "Eighth American Edition" (such statements on the title pages of early novels can rarely be trusted because some printings were pirated) of Susanna Rowson's *Charlotte Temple* included a "portrait" of its entirely fictional heroine. That engraving thus reinforced the subtitle, *A Tale of Truth.* (AC7.R7997.791c 1804, Houghton Library, Harvard University Library)

families again attended balls and concerts. Parties no longer seemed complete without gambling and cardplaying. Social clubs for young people multiplied. Especially alarming was the establishment in 1783 of the Society of the Cincinnati, a hereditary association for Revolutionary War officers and their firstborn sons. Although organizers hoped to advance the citizen-soldier, opponents feared that the group would become the nucleus of a native-born aristocracy. All these developments challenged the United States' self-image as a virtuous republic.

Educational Reform

Americans' concern for the infant republic's future focused their attention on children. Education was previously seen as the concern of individual families. Now schooling would serve a public purpose. If young people were to resist vice and become useful citizens, they would need education. The nation's survival depended on it. The 1780s and 1790s thus witnessed two major changes in educational practice.

First, some northern states began using tax money to support public elementary schools. In 1789 Massachusetts became one of the first states to require towns to offer free public elementary education. Second, since mothers would have to be educated if they were to instruct children adequately, Massachusetts insisted that elementary schools teach girls as well as boys. Throughout the United States, private academies were founded to provide advanced schooling to teenage girls from well-to-do families. Colleges remained closed to women, but a few fortunate girls could study history, geography, rhetoric, and mathematics.

Judith Sargent Murray

Judith Sargent Murray of Gloucester, Massachusetts, became the chief theorist of women's education in the early republic. Murray argued that women and men had equal intellectual capacities, but inadequate education might make women seem less intelligent. Therefore, concluded Murray, boys and girls should be offered equivalent schooling. She further contended that girls should be taught to support themselves: "Independence should be placed within their grasp."

Murray's views were part of a general rethinking of women's position that resulted from the Revolution. Men and women realized that female patriots had made important contributions toward independence. Consequently, Americans considered new ideas about women's roles in republican society.

Women and the Republic

The best-known expression of those ideas appeared in a letter Abigail Adams addressed to her husband in March 1776. "In the new Code of Laws which I suppose it will be necessary for you to make I desire you would Remember the Ladies," she wrote.

Judith Sargent Stevens (later Murray), by John Singleton Copley, ca. 1770–1772. The eventual author of tracts advocating improvements in women's education sat for this portrait two decades earlier, during her first marriage. Her clear-eyed gaze suggests both her intelligence and her seriousness of purpose. (Terra Foundation for American Art, Chicago / Art Resource, NY)

"Remember all Men would be tyrants if they could. . . . If perticuliar [sic] care and attention is not paid to the Laidies [sic] we are determined to foment a Rebelion, and will not hold ourselves bound by any Laws in which we have no voice, or Representation." With these words, Abigail Adams deliberately applied the ideology developed to combat parliamentary supremacy. She argued that, because men were "Naturally Tyrannical," the United States should reform marriage laws, which subordinated wives to their husbands, giving men control of family property and denying wives the right to independent legal action.

Abigail Adams did not ask for woman suffrage, but others claimed that right. In 1776, the New Jersey state constitution defined voters as "all free inhabitants" who met property qualifications. They thereby unintentionally gave the vote to property-holding white spinsters and widows and free black landowners. Qualified women and African Americans regularly voted in New Jersey's local and congressional elections until 1807, when they were disfranchised by the state legislature. That women voted at all was evidence of their altered perception of their place in the nation's political life.

Even after the war, European Americans still viewed women in traditional terms, affirming their primary function as wives, mothers, and mistresses of households. Because wives could not own property or participate directly in economic life, women came to be seen as the embodiment of self-sacrificing republicanism. Through new female-run charitable associations, better-off women assumed public responsibilities, among them caring for poor widows and orphans. Thus men were freed to pursue their economic self-interests, while wives and daughters fulfilled the family's obligation to the common good. The ideal republican man was an individualist, seeking advancement for himself and his family. The ideal republican woman always put the well-being of others first.

THE FIRST EMANCIPATION AND THE GROWTH OF RACISM

Revolutionary ideology exposed a primary contradiction in American society. There were 700,000 African Americans residing in the new nation, roughly 20 percent of the population. European and African Americans saw the irony in slaveholders' claims that they sought to prevent Britain from "enslaving" them. In 1773 Dr. Benjamin Rush called slavery "a vice which degrades human nature," warning ominously that "the plant of liberty is of so tender a nature that it cannot thrive long in the neighborhood of slavery."

African Americans used revolutionary ideology to their advantage. In 1779 slaves from Portsmouth, New Hampshire, asked the state legislature "from what authority [our masters] assume to dispose of our lives, freedom and property?" The same year, several bondsmen in Fairfield, Connecticut, petitioned the legislature for their freedom, characterizing slavery as a "dreadful Evil." How could men who were "nobly contending in the Cause of Liberty," they asked, continue "this detestable Practice?"

Emancipation and Manumission

Both legislatures responded negatively, but the postwar years witnessed the gradual abolition of slavery in the North. Vermont banned slavery in its 1777 constitution. Responding to lawsuits filed by enslaved men and women, Massachusetts courts ruled in 1783 that the state constitution prohibited slavery. Other states north of Maryland adopted emancipation laws between 1780 (Pennsylvania) and 1804 (New Jersey). New Hampshire did not abolish slavery, but only eight slaves were reported on the 1800 census and none in 1810. Although no southern state adopted emancipation laws, the legislatures of Virginia (1782), Delaware (1787), and Maryland (1790 and 1796) loosened earlier laws restricting slaveowners' ability to free their bondspeople. South Carolina and Georgia never considered any such acts, and North Carolina insisted that manumissions (emancipations of individual slaves) be approved by county courts.

Revolutionary ideology thus had limited impact on the economic interests of large slaveholders. Only in northern states—societies with slaves, not slave societies—could state legislatures abolish slavery. Even there, legislators' concern for the property rights of slave owners led them to favor gradual over immediate emancipation. For example, New York's law freed children born into slavery after July 4, 1799, but only once they reached their mid-twenties. Laws failed to emancipate the existing slave population. Although emancipation laws forbade the sale of slaves to jurisdictions where slavery remained legal, slaveowners regularly circumvented such provisions. As late as 1840 the census recorded the presence of slaves in several northern states.

A sailor of African descent posed proudly for this portrait around 1790. Unfortunately, neither the name of the sailor nor the name of the artist is known today.   (Private collection, photograph courtesy of Hirschl and Adler Galleries, New York)

Growth of Free Black Population

The number of free people of African descent in the United States grew dramatically in the initial post-Revolution years. Most slaves emancipated before the war were mulattos, born of unions between bondswomen and their masters, who manumitted the children. Wartime escapees from plantations, slaves who served in the American army, and those emancipated by owners or by state laws contributed to the nearly 60,000 free people of color by 1790. Ten years later they numbered more than 108,000, nearly 11 percent of the total African American population.

In the Chesapeake, manumissions were speeded by economic changes, such as declining soil fertility and the shift from tobacco to grain production. Because grain cultivation was less labor-intensive than tobacco growing, planters had excess slaves. They occasionally solved that problem by freeing less productive or more favored bondspeople. The enslaved also negotiated agreements with owners allowing them to live and work independently until they could purchase themselves. Virginia's free black population more than doubled between 1790 and 1810; also by 1810, nearly one-quarter of Maryland's African American population was no longer in bondage.

Freedpeople's Lives

Beginning in the 1780s, rural freedpeople headed to northern port cities, such as Boston and Philadelphia. With better employment opportunities, especially in domestic service, women outnumbered male migrants by three to two. Some freedmen also worked in domestic service, but larger numbers were unskilled laborers and sailors. A few women and many men (nearly one-third of those in Philadelphia in 1795) were skilled workers or retailers. They exchanged the surnames of former masters for names like Newman or Brown and established independent two-parent families. They also began to occupy distinct neighborhoods, probably due to discrimination.

Even whites who recognized African Americans' right to freedom were unwilling to accept them as equals. Laws discriminated against freedpeople as they had against slaves. Several states—among them Delaware, Maryland, and South Carolina—adopted laws denying property-owning black men the vote. South Carolina forbade free blacks from testifying against whites in court. New Englanders used indenture contracts to control freed youths, who were often denied public education. Freedmen found it difficult to purchase property and find good jobs.

Gradually, freedpeople developed their own institutions. In Charleston, mulattos formed the Brown Fellowship Society, which provided insurance for them, financed a school, and helped support orphans. In 1794 former slaves in Philadelphia and Baltimore, led by the Reverend Richard Allen, founded societies that eventually formed the African Methodist Episcopal (AME) denomination. AME churches sponsored schools and, along with African Baptist, African Episcopal, and African Presbyterian churches, became cultural centers for free blacks.

Development of Racist Theory

Before the revolution, European Americans regarded slaves as inferior. Influential writers argued that African slaves' seemingly debased character derived from their enslavement, rather than enslavement's being the consequence of inherited inferiority.

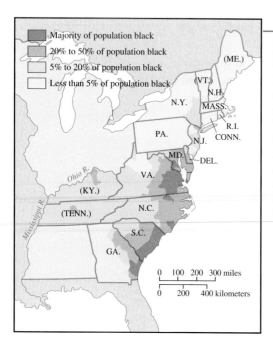

Majority of population black
20% to 50% of population black
5% to 20% of population black
Less than 5% of population black

0   100   200   300 miles
0   200   400 kilometers

Map 7.1   African American Population, 1790: Proportion of Total Population

The first census clearly indicated that the African American population was heavily concentrated in just a few areas of the United States, most notably in coastal regions of South Carolina, Georgia, and Virginia. Although there were growing numbers of blacks in the backcountry—presumably taken there by migrating slaveowners—most parts of the North and East, with the exception of the immediate vicinity of New York City, had few African American residents. (*Source:* From Lester J. Cappon et al., eds., *Atlas of Early American History: The Revolutionary Era, 1760–1790.* Copyright © 1976 by Princeton University Press. Reprinted by permission of Princeton University Press.)

In the Revolution's aftermath, slaveowners needed to defend human bondage against the proposition that "all men are created equal." Consequently, they argued that people of African descent were less than fully human and that the principles of republican equality applied only to European Americans.

Egalitarian thinking among European Americans downplayed status distinctions within their own group and differentiated all whites from people of color—Indians and African Americans. Decades earlier, Indians began referring to themselves as *red*. Experience as slaves on American soil forged the identity African or black from the various ethnic and national affiliations of people who survived the transatlantic crossing. Among the first to term themselves *Africans* were oceanic sailors—men whose contacts with Europeans caused them to construct a unified, separate identity. Thus in the revolutionary era whiteness, redness, and blackness—along with the superiority of the first and the inferiority of the latter two—developed as contrasting concepts.

With this racism came first the assertion that, as Thomas Jefferson insisted in 1781, blacks were "inferior to the whites in the endowments both of body and mind." (He was less certain about Indians.) There followed the belief that blacks were congenitally lazy, even though owners often argued that slaves were natural workers. Third was the notion that blacks were sexually promiscuous and that African American men lusted after European American women. The specter of interracial sexual intercourse involving black men and white women haunted early American racist thought. Significantly, the more common sexual exploitation of enslaved women by their masters aroused little concern.

African Americans challenged these racist notions. In 1791 Benjamin Banneker, a free black mathematical genius, sent Thomas Jefferson a copy of his latest almanac (including astronomical calculations) to show blacks' mental powers. Jefferson admitted Banneker's intelligence, but said Banneker was exceptional and he needed more evidence before he would change his mind about the inferiority of people of African descent.

A White Men's Republic

Laws from the 1770s on linked whiteness and male citizenship rights. Some historians have argued that the subjugation of blacks, Indians, and women was a necessary precondition for theoretical equality among white men. Identifying common racial antagonists helped create white solidarity and lessen the threat to gentry power posed by the enfranchisement of poorer men. Moreover, excluding women from politics reserved power for men, specifically the "better sort." After the Revolution the division of American society between slave and free was transformed into a division between blacks—some of whom were free—and whites.

DESIGNING REPUBLICAN GOVERNMENTS

In May 1776, the Second Continental Congress directed states to devise new republican governments to replace the provincial conventions and committees that had met since colonial governments collapsed in 1774 and 1775. Thus American men devoted little attention to their national government—an oversight they would later remedy.

State Constitutions

At the state level, political leaders had trouble defining a constitution and concluded that legislative bodies should not draft their constitutions. Following Vermont in 1777 and Massachusetts in 1780, they elected conventions exclusively to draft constitutions. Thus states sought authorization from the people—the theoretical sovereigns in a republic—before establishing new governments. After preparing new constitutions, delegates submitted them to voters for ratification.

Framers of state constitutions concerned themselves with outlining the distribution of and limitations on government power. If authority was not confined within reasonable limits, states might become tyrannical, as Britain had.

Under colonial charters, Americans learned to fear the power of the governor—usually the appointed agent of the king or proprietor—and to see the legislature as their defender. Accordingly, the first state constitutions typically provided for the governor to be elected annually (commonly by the legislature), limited the number of terms he could serve, and gave him little independent authority. Simultaneously, they expanded the legislature's powers. Every state except Pennsylvania and Vermont retained a two-house structure, with members of the upper house having longer terms and meeting higher property-holding standards than members of the lower house. They also redrew electoral districts to reflect population patterns. Finally, most states lowered property qualifications for voting. Thus the revolutionary era witnessed the first deliberate attempt to broaden the base of American government.

Limiting State Governments

But the state constitutions' authors worried about what might happen if tyrants were elected. They consequently included limitations on government authority to protect the inalienable rights of citizens. Seven constitutions contained a bill of rights, and others had similar clauses. Most guaranteed freedom of the press, rights to fair trials, and protection against general search warrants. An independent judiciary was charged with upholding such rights. Most states also guaranteed freedom of religion but with restrictions. For example, seven states required that officeholders be Christians, and some supported churches with tax money.

In general, constitution makers put greater emphasis on preventing state governments from becoming tyrannical than on making them effective wielders of political authority. Establishing such weak political units, especially in wartime, practically ensured that the constitutions would need revision in the 1780s.

Revising State Constitutions

The revised constitutions increased the powers of the governor and reduced those of the legislature. By the mid-1780s, some political leaders concluded that the best way to limit government power was to balance legislative, executive, and judicial powers, a design called checks and balances. The national Constitution drafted in 1787 also embodied that principle.

Yet the constitutional theories applied at the state level did not immediately influence Americans' conception of national government. Because American officials initially focused on the war, the Continental Congress evolved by default. Not until late 1777 did Congress send the Articles of Confederation—which outlined a national government—to the states for ratification, and those Articles simply made law the unplanned arrangements of the Continental Congress.

Articles of Confederation

The chief organ of national government was a unicameral (one-house) legislature in which each state had one vote. Its powers included conducting foreign relations, mediating interstate disputes, controlling maritime affairs, regulating Indian trade, and valuing state and national coinage. The United States was described as a "league of friendship" in which each state "retains its sovereignty, freedom and independence, and every Power, Jurisdiction and right, which is not by this confederation expressly delegated to the United States, in Congress assembled."

The Articles required unanimous consent of state legislatures for ratification or amendment. A clause concerning western lands proved troublesome. The draft accepted by Congress allowed states to retain land claims from their original charters. But states with definite western boundaries (such as Maryland and New Jersey) wanted other states to cede to the national government their landholdings west of the Appalachian Mountains. They feared states with large claims could expand and overpower smaller neighbors. Maryland refused to accept the Articles until 1781, when Virginia surrendered its western holdings to national jurisdiction (see Map 7.2). Other states followed, establishing the principle that unorganized lands would be held by the nation.

The unicameral legislature, whether it was called the Second Continental Congress (until 1781) or the Confederation Congress (thereafter), was too inefficient to govern effectively. The Articles' authors had not given adequate thought to the distribution of power within the national government or to the relationship between the Confederation and the states. Congress was a legislative body and a collective executive (there was no judiciary), but it had no independent income and no authority to compel the states to accept its rulings. Under the Articles, national government lurched from crisis to crisis. (See the appendix for the text of the Articles of Confederation.)

TRIALS OF THE CONFEDERATION

Finance posed the most persistent problem. Because legislators levied taxes reluctantly, Congress and the states first tried to finance the war by printing currency. Although the money was backed only by good faith, it circulated freely and without excessive depreciation during 1775 and most of 1776. Demand for military supplies and civilian goods was high, stimulating trade and local production.

Financial Affairs

But in late 1776, as the American army suffered reverses in New York and New Jersey, prices rose and inflation set in. State governments fought inflation by controlling wages and prices and requiring acceptance of paper currency equally with specie (coins). States also borrowed funds, established lotteries, and levied taxes. Their efforts were futile, as was Congress's attempt to stop printing currency and rely on state

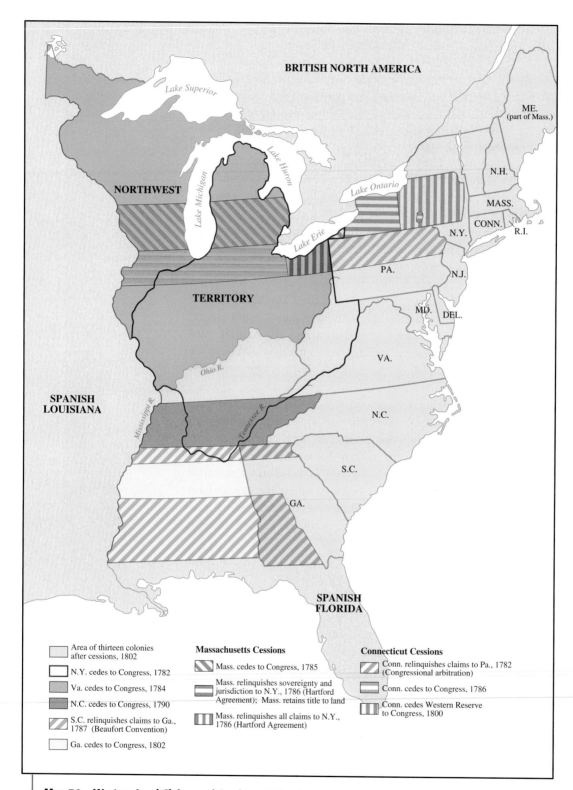

Map 7.2   Western Land Claims and Cessions, 1782–1802

After the United States achieved independence, states competed with one another for control of valuable lands to which they had possible claims under their original charters. That competition led to a series of compromises among the states or between individual states and the new nation, indicated on this map.

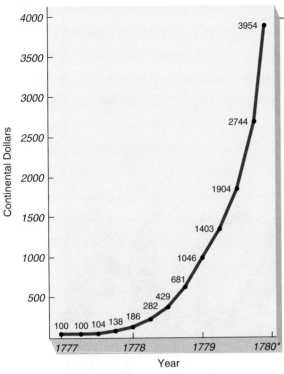

Figure 7.1 Depreciation of Continental Currency, 1777–1780

The depreciation of Continental currency accelerated in 1778, as is shown in this graph measuring its value against 100 silver dollars. Thereafter, its value dropped almost daily.

(*Source for data:* John J. McCusker, "How Much Is That in Real Money? A Historical Price Index for Use as a Deflator of Money Values in the Economy of the United States," *Proceedings of the American Antiquarian Society* 101, pt. 2 [1991], Table C-1.)

* Currency abandoned in April 1780

contributions. By early 1780 it took 40 paper dollars to purchase 1 silver dollar. Continental currency was worthless (see Figure 7.1).

In 1781, faced with the collapse of the monetary system, Congress undertook ambitious reforms. After establishing a department of finance under the wealthy Philadelphia merchant Robert Morris, it asked states to amend the Articles of Confederation to allow a national duty of 5 percent on imported goods. Morris put national finances on a solid footing, but the customs duty was never adopted. The states' resistance reflected fear of a powerful central government.

Foreign Affairs

Because the Articles denied Congress the power to establish a national commercial policy, foreign trade exposed the new government's weaknesses. After the war, Britain, France, and Spain restricted American trade with their colonies. Congress watched helplessly as British goods flooded the United States while American produce could not be sold in the British West Indies, once its prime market. Although Americans reopened commerce with other European countries and started a profitable trade with China in 1784, neither substituted for access to closer and larger markets.

Congress furthermore had difficulty dealing with the Spanish on the nation's southern and western borders. Spain in 1784 closed the Mississippi River to American navigation. Congress, through its Department of Foreign Affairs, opened negotiations with Spain in 1785, but talks collapsed the following year after Congress divided: southerners and westerners insisted on navigation rights, whereas

A British cartoon ironically reflected Americans' hopes for postwar trade, hopes that were dashed after 1783. The Indian woman symbolizing America sits on a pile of tobacco bales, with rice and indigo casks bound for Europe nearby. The artist was satirizing the failed 1778 British peace commission and Britons' willingness to make concessions to the rebellious colonies, but his image captured Americans' belief in the importance of their produce. (Chicago History Museum / Chicago Historical Society)

northerners were willing to abandon that claim for commercial concessions in the West Indies.

Peace Treaty Provisions

Provisions of the 1783 Treaty of Paris, too, caused problems. Article four, which promised payment of prewar debts (most owed by Americans to British merchants), and Article five, which recommended that states allow loyalists to recover their confiscated property, aroused opposition. States passed laws denying British subjects the right to sue for recovery of debts or property in American courts. Another reason for state opposition was that sales of loyalists' property and possessions had helped finance the war. Because many purchasers were prominent patriots, states hesitated to question the legitimacy of their property titles.

The refusal of state and local governments to comply with Articles four and five gave Britain an excuse to maintain military posts on the Great Lakes. Furthermore, Congress's inability to enforce the treaty disclosed its lack of power, even in an area—foreign affairs—in which it had authority under the Articles. Concerned nationalists argued that failure to enforce the treaty challenged the republic's credibility.

ORDER AND DISORDER IN THE WEST

Although British and American diplomats did not discuss tribal claims, the United States assumed that the Treaty of Paris cleared its title to all land east of the Mississippi except that held by Spain. Recognizing that land cessions should be obtained from the most powerful tribes, Congress initiated negotiations with northern and southern Indians.

Indian Relations

At Fort Stanwix, New York, in 1784, American diplomats negotiated a treaty with chiefs who claimed to represent the Iroquois; and at Hopewell, South Carolina, in late 1785 and early 1786, they negotiated with emissaries from the Choctaw, Chickasaw, and Cherokee nations. In 1786 the Iroquois repudiated the Fort Stanwix treaty, denying that the negotiators were authorized to speak for the Six Nations. The confederacy threatened new attacks on frontier settlements, but the treaty stood by default. By 1790 the once-dominant confederacy was confined to a few scattered reservations. In the South, too, the United States took the treaties as confirmation of its sovereignty. European Americans poured over the southern Appalachians, provoking the Creeks to declare war. In 1790, they came to terms with the United States.

Western nations, such as the Shawnees, Chippewas, Ottawas, and Potawatomis, rejected Iroquois hegemony as early as the 1750s. After Iroquois power collapsed, they formed a confederacy and demanded negotiations with the United States. As a united front, they hoped to avoid the piecemeal surrender of land by individual bands and villages. But in the postwar world, Indian nations could no longer play European and American powers against one another. France was gone, Spanish territory lay far to the west and south, and British power was confined to Canada. Only the United States remained.

Ordinance of 1785

Shortly after state land cessions were completed, Congress organized the Northwest Territory, bounded by the Mississippi River, the Great Lakes, and the Ohio River (see Map 7.2). Ordinances passed in 1784, 1785, and 1787 outlined the process through which the land could be sold and governments organized.

To ensure orderly development, Congress in 1785 wanted the land surveyed into townships 6 miles square, each divided into thirty-six sections of 640 acres (1 square mile). Revenue from the sale of the sixteenth section of each township would support public schools—the first federal aid to education in American history. One dollar was the minimum price per acre; the minimum sale was one section. The resulting minimum outlay, $640, was unaffordable for ordinary Americans, except veterans who received part of their army pay in land warrants. Proceeds from western land sales constituted the first independent revenues available to the national government.

Northwest Ordinance

The most important of the three land policies—the Northwest Ordinance of 1787—contained a bill of rights guaranteeing freedom of religion and the right to a jury trial, forbidding cruel and unusual punishments, and nominally prohibiting slavery.

Eventually, that prohibition became an important symbol for antislavery northerners, but at the time it had little effect. Some residents already held slaves, and Congress would not deprive them of their property. The ordinance also allowed slaveowners to reclaim runaways who took refuge in the territory—the first national fugitive slave law. It prevented slavery from taking deep root by discouraging slaveholders from moving into the territory, but enslavement was not abolished until 1848.

The ordinance of 1787 also specified how territorial residents could organize state governments and seek admission to the Union. Early in the nation's history, therefore, Congress established a policy of admitting new states on the same basis as the old. Having suffered under the rule of a colonial power, congressmen understood the importance of preparing the new nation's first "colony" for eventual self-government.

In 1787 the ordinance was largely theoretical. Miamis, Shawnees, and Delawares refused to acknowledge American sovereignty and attacked pioneers who ventured too far north of the Ohio River. In 1788 the Ohio Company, to which Congress had sold a large tract of land at reduced rates, established the town of Marietta at the juncture of the Ohio and Muskingum Rivers. But Indians prevented the company from extending settlement into the interior.

Not until after the Articles of Confederation were replaced with a new constitution could the United States muster sufficient force to implement the Northwest Ordinance. Thus, although the ordinance is often viewed as one of the few lasting accomplishments of the Confederation Congress, it existed within a context of political impotence.

FROM CRISIS TO THE CONSTITUTION

Under the Articles of Confederation, Congress could not levy taxes, force states to establish a uniform commercial policy, or enforce treaties. Partly as a result, the economy slid into a depression within a year after the war's end. Exporters of staple crops (especially tobacco and rice) and importers of manufactured goods suffered from postwar restrictions that European powers imposed on American commerce. Although recovery began by 1786, some estimates suggest that between 1775 and 1790 America's per capita gross national product declined by nearly 50 percent.

Economic Change and Commercial Reform   The near-total cessation of foreign commerce in nonmilitary items during the war stimulated domestic manufacturing. Despite the influx of European goods after 1783, the postwar period witnessed stirrings of American industrial development. Because of continuing population growth, the domestic market assumed greater economic importance. Moreover, foreign trade patterns shifted from Europe toward the West Indies. Foodstuffs to the French and Dutch Caribbean islands became America's largest export, replacing tobacco (and thus accelerating the Chesapeake's conversion to grain). South Carolina resumed large-scale slave importation, as planters sought to replace workers lost to wartime disruptions. Yet without British subsidies, American indigo could not compete with Caribbean indigo, and rice planters struggled to find new markets.

Representatives of Virginia and Maryland met at Mt. Vernon (George Washington's plantation) in March 1785 to negotiate an agreement about trade on the Potomac River, which divided the two states. The successful meeting led to an invitation to other states to discuss trade policy at a convention in Annapolis, Maryland. Nine states named representatives to the meeting in September 1786; only five delegations attended. Consequently, they issued a call for another convention in Philadelphia nine months later "to devise such further provisions as shall . . . appear necessary to render the constitution of the federal government adequate to the exigencies of the Union."

Shays's Rebellion

An armed rebellion in Massachusetts convinced doubting states that reform was needed. Men from several western counties, many of them veterans from leading families, violently opposed the high taxes levied by the eastern-dominated legislature to pay war debts. Such obligations consisted largely of securities issued during the war to soldiers in lieu of pay and to others for supplies and loans. During the hard times following the war, many veterans and creditors sold the securities at heavy discounts. The state legislature nevertheless levied taxes to pay off the securities (plus interest) at full price in specie by decade's end. Men with little prospect of obtaining specie without selling their land responded furiously when the state moved to collect the taxes.

Daniel Shays, a former Continental Army officer, led the disgruntled westerners. On January 25, 1787, about fifteen hundred of Shay's troops assaulted the Springfield federal armory. The militiamen defending the armory fired on their former comrades-in-arms, who withdrew after suffering twenty-four casualties. Some (including Shays) fled the state; two were hanged; and most escaped punishment by paying small fines and taking oaths of allegiance to Massachusetts. The state legislature reduced the burden on landowners with new import duties and by easing tax collections.

Terming Massachusetts *tyrannical* and styling themselves *Regulators,* Shaysites insisted that "whenever any encroachments are made either upon the liberties or properties of the people, if redress cannot be had without, it is virtue in them to disturb government." Thus they linked their rebellion to the earlier independence struggle.

Constitutional Convention

To political leaders, the rebellion confirmed the need for a stronger federal government. After most states appointed delegates, the Confederation Congress belatedly endorsed the convention, "for the sole and express purpose of revising the Articles of Confederation." In mid-May 1787, fifty-five men, representing every state but Rhode Island, assembled in Philadelphia.

Most delegates to the Constitutional Convention were substantial men of property: merchants, planters, physicians, generals, governors, and especially lawyers. They wanted to give the national government new authority over taxation and foreign commerce, but also sought to advance their states' interests. Many had been state legislators, and some helped draft state constitutions. Most were born in America; many came from families that arrived a century earlier. More than half had attended college. The youngest delegate was twenty-six, the oldest—Benjamin

Franklin—eighty-one. George Washington was elected presiding officer. A dozen men did the bulk of the convention's work; among them, Virginia's James Madison deserves the title *Father of the Constitution*.

Madison and the Constitution

The shy James Madison was thirty-six years old in 1787. A Princeton graduate raised in western Virginia, he served on the local Committee of Safety and was elected to the provincial convention, the state's lower and upper houses, and the Continental Congress (1780–1783). Although Madison returned to serve in the Virginia state legislature in 1784, he kept up with national politics, partly through correspondence with his friend Thomas Jefferson.

Madison systematically prepared for the Philadelphia meeting. He bought more than two hundred books on history and government, analyzing their accounts of past confederacies and republics. He summed up his research in a paper entitled "Vices of the Political System of the United States." After listing the flaws he perceived in the current government (among them "encroachments by the states on the federal authority" and lack of unity), Madison revealed his guiding belief that government had to be constructed so that it could not become tyrannical or fall under the influence of a particular faction. Rejecting the notion that republics had to be small, Madison asserted that a large, diverse republic was preferable. Because the nation would include many factions, no one of them could control the government. Political stability would result from compromises among contending parties.

Virginia and New Jersey Plans

The so-called Virginia Plan, introduced on May 29 by Edmund Randolph, embodied Madison's conception of national government. The plan provided for a two-house legislature, the lower house elected directly by the people and the upper house selected by the lower; representation in both houses proportional to property or population; an executive elected by Congress; a national judiciary; and congressional veto over state laws. Had it been adopted intact, it would have created a government in which national authority reigned unchallenged and state power was diminished. Proportional representation in both houses would also have given large states a dominant voice in national government.

Many delegates believed the Virginia Plan went too far toward national consolidation. After two weeks of debate, disaffected delegates—particularly those from small states—united under William Paterson of New Jersey. On June 15 Paterson presented an alternative, the New Jersey Plan, calling for strengthening the Articles rather than overhauling the government. Paterson proposed retaining a unicameral Congress in which each state had an equal vote, but giving Congress new powers of taxation and trade regulation. Although the convention initially rejected Paterson's position, he and his allies won several victories in subsequent months.

Debates over Congress

The delegates agreed that the new national government should have a two-house (bicameral) legislature. Further, they concurred that the people should be directly represented in at least one house. But they differed on three key questions: Should representation in both houses of Congress be proportional to population? How was representation to be apportioned among the states? How were the members of the two houses to be elected?

The last issue proved the easiest to resolve. Delegates thought it "essential" that the lower branch of Congress be elected directly by the people and "expedient" that members of the upper house be chosen by state legislatures. If the convention had not agreed to allow state legislatures to elect senators, the Constitution would have run into significant opposition among state leaders. The plan also placed the election of one house of Congress one step removed from the "lesser sort," whose judgment wealthy convention delegates did not wholly trust.

The delegates accepted without much debate the principle of representation proportional to population in the House of Representatives. But small states wanted equal representation in the Senate, which would give them relatively more power at the national level. Large states supported a proportional plan that would give them more votes in the upper house. For weeks the convention deadlocked. A committee appointed to devise a compromise recommended equal representation in the Senate, with a proviso that all appropriation bills originate in the lower house. A breakdown was only averted when the convention accepted a suggestion that a state's two senators vote as individuals rather than as a unit.

Slavery and the Constitution

The remaining question of how to apportion representation in the lower house divided the nation along sectional lines. Delegates concurred that a census should be conducted every decade to determine the nation's population and that Indians who paid no taxes should be excluded. Delegates from states with large slave populations wanted African and European inhabitants counted equally; delegates from states with few slaves wanted only free people counted. Slavery thus became linked to the new government. Delegates resolved the dispute with a formula developed by the Confederation Congress in 1783 to allocate financial assessments among states: three-fifths of slaves would be included in population totals. (The formula reflected delegates' judgment that slaves were less efficient producers of wealth than free people, not that they were 60 percent human and 40 percent property.)

Although the words *slave* and *slavery* do not appear in the Constitution (the framers used such euphemisms as "other persons"), the document contained direct and indirect protections for slavery. The three-fifths clause, for example, assured white southern male voters congressional representation out of proportion to their numbers and a disproportionate influence on the selection of the president, because the number of each state's votes in the electoral college (see below) was determined by the size of its congressional delegation. In return for southerners' agreement that commercial regulations could be adopted by a simple majority vote (rather than two-thirds), New Englanders agreed that Congress could not end the importation of slaves for twenty years. The fugitive slave clause required states to return runaways to their masters. By guaranteeing national assistance to states threatened with "domestic violence," the Constitution promised aid in putting down future slave revolts and incidents like Shays's Rebellion.

Congressional and Presidential Powers

With the questions of slavery and representation resolved, delegates concurred that the national government needed the authority to tax and to regulate foreign and interstate commerce. But instead of giving Congress the wide latitude of the Virginia Plan, delegates enumerated congressional powers and then granted Congress the "necessary and proper" authority to carry them out. Discarding the Virginia Plan's congressional veto, the convention implied but did not explicitly authorize a national judicial veto of state laws. The Constitution plus national laws and treaties would constitute "the supreme law of the land; and the judges in every state shall be bound thereby," Article VI declared ambiguously. Delegates drafted a long list of actions forbidden to states, and—contrary to many state constitutions—they provided that religious tests could never be required of U.S. officeholders.

The convention placed primary responsibility for foreign affairs with a new official, the president, who was also designated commander-in-chief of the armed forces. That raised the question, unspecified in the Constitution's text, of whether the president (or Congress) acquired special powers in wartime. With the Senate's consent, the president could appoint judges and other federal officers. To select the president, delegates established the electoral college, whose members would be chosen in each state by legislatures or voters. If a majority of electors failed to unite behind one candidate, the House of Representatives (voting as states, not as individuals) would choose the president. The chief executive would serve for four years but be eligible for reelection.

The key to the Constitution was the distribution of political authority, that is, the separation of powers among executive, legislative, and judicial branches of the national government and the division of powers between states and nation (called *federalism*). Two-thirds of Congress and three-fourths of the states had to concur on amendments. The branches balanced one another, their powers deliberately entwined to prevent each from acting independently. The president could veto congressional legislation, but that veto could be overridden by two-thirds majorities in both houses, and his treaties and major appointments required the Senate's consent. Congress could impeach the president and federal judges, but courts would have the final say on interpreting the Constitution. These checks and balances would keep the government from becoming tyrannical, but at times, they prevented the government from acting quickly and decisively. Furthermore, the Constitution drew such a vague line between state and national powers that the United States fought a civil war in the next century over that issue.

The convention held its last session on September 17, 1787. Of the forty-two delegates present (others left weeks earlier), three refused to sign the Constitution, two partly because it lacked a bill of rights. Benjamin Franklin urged unity, admitting, "I confess that there are several parts of this constitution which I do not at present approve." Yet he encouraged its acceptance "because I expect no better, and because I am not sure, that it is not the best." Only then was the Constitution made public. (See the appendix for the full text of the Constitution.)

OPPOSITION AND RATIFICATION

Later that month, the Confederation Congress submitted the Constitution to the states. The ratification clause provided for the new system to take effect after approval by special conventions in at least nine states. Thus the national Constitution, unlike the Articles of Confederation, would rest directly on popular authority.

As states elected delegates to the special conventions, newspaper essays and pamphlets defended or attacked the Philadelphia convention's decisions. Every newspaper in the country printed the Constitution, and most supported its adoption. Although most citizens concurred that the national government should have more power over taxation and foreign and interstate commerce, some believed that the proposed government held the potential for tyranny. As happened in Carlisle, Pennsylvania, the debate frequently spilled into the streets.

Federalists and Antifederalists

The Constitution's supporters called themselves Federalists. Building on classical republicanism, they envisioned a virtuous, self-sacrificing republic led by a manly aristocracy of talent. They argued that when good men drawn from the elite were in charge, the carefully structured government would prevent tyranny. A republic could be large if the government's design kept any one group from controlling it. The separation of powers among legislative, executive, and judicial branches and the division of powers between states and nation would accomplish that.

The Federalists termed those who opposed the Constitution Antifederalists, thus casting them in a negative light. While recognizing the need for a national source of revenue, Antifederalists feared a too-powerful central government. They saw the states as the chief protectors of individual rights; consequently, weakening the states could bring the onset of arbitrary power. Antifederalist arguments often listed potential abuses of government authority.

Heirs of the Real Whig ideology of the late 1760s and early 1770s, Antifederalists stressed the need for constant popular vigilance to avert oppression. Indeed, some Antifederalists promulgated those ideas prior to the centralizing, nationalistic Revolution—Samuel Adams, Patrick Henry, and Richard Henry Lee led the opposition to the Constitution. Joining them were small farmers preoccupied with guarding their property against excessive taxation, backcountry Baptists and Presbyterians, and upwardly mobile men who would benefit from an economic and political system less tightly controlled than that the Constitution envisioned.

Bill of Rights

Antifederalists focused on the Constitution's lack of a bill of rights. Even if the new system weakened the states, critics believed, people could be protected from tyranny by specific guarantees of rights. The Constitution did contain some prohibitions on congressional power. For example, the writ of habeas corpus, which prevented arbitrary imprisonment, could not be suspended except in "cases of rebellion or invasion." But Antifederalists found such constitutional provisions to be few and inadequate. They wanted a bill of rights.

Letters of a Federal Farmer, perhaps the most widely read Antifederalist pamphlet, listed the rights that should be protected: freedom of the press and religion, trial by jury, and guarantees against unreasonable searches. From Paris, Thomas Jefferson added his voice to the chorus, declaring, "A bill of rights is what the people are entitled to against every government on earth."

Ratification

Many state conventions were persuaded when Federalists promised that a national government with the power to tax foreign commerce would lessen the financial burdens that prompted Shays's Rebellion and protests in other states. Four of the first five states to ratify did so unanimously, but serious disagreements then surfaced. Massachusetts, where Antifederalist forces were bolstered by a backlash against the state's heavy-handed treatment of the Shays rebels, ratified by a majority of only 19 of 355 votes and recommended amendments identifying rights. In June 1788, when New Hampshire ratified, the requirement of nine states was satisfied. But New York and Virginia had not yet voted, and everyone realized the new Constitution could not succeed without those key states.

Pro-Constitution forces won by ten votes in the Virginia convention, which recommended adding rights specifications. In New York, James Madison, John Jay, and Alexander Hamilton, writing collectively as Publius, published *The Federalist,* eighty-five essays explaining the theory behind the Constitution and answering its critics. Their arguments, coupled with Federalists' promise to add a bill of rights, helped win the battle. On July 26, 1788, New York ratified the Constitution by just three votes. Although the last states—North Carolina and Rhode Island—did not join the Union until November 1789 and May 1790, respectively, the new government was a reality.

Celebrating Ratification

Americans in many cities celebrated ratification with parades on July 4, 1788, linking the acceptance of the Constitution to the adoption of the Declaration of Independence. The processions dramatized the history and unity of the new nation, seeking to counteract the dissent that had engulfed such towns as Carlisle, Pennsylvania. The processions aimed to educate people about the significance of the new Constitution and instruct them about leaders' hopes for industry and frugality on the part of a virtuous public.

About five thousand people participated in the Philadelphia parade. Floats portraying such themes as "The Grand Federal Edifice" stretched for a mile and a half. More than forty groups of tradesmen sponsored floats. Marchers representing the first pioneers and Revolutionary War troops paraded with farmers and artisans, followed by lawyers, doctors, clergymen, and congressmen. Symbolizing the nation's future, students from the University of Pennsylvania and other schools bore a flag labeled *The Rising Generation.*

The Township and Range System

Anyone flying over the American countryside west of the Appalachians today can see the township and range system inscribed on the landscape. Roads cross the land in straight lines, meeting at 90-degree angles, carving the terrain into a checkerboard. Originated in the Land Ordinance of 1785, that system organized land sales in the Northwest Territory.

English and native peoples traditionally bounded their lands by natural landmarks such as hills, streams, large trees, and rock outcroppings. That system was known as *metes and bounds.* Some early colonial settlers employed surveyors, who created lots of varying sizes divided by lines laid out abstractly on the soil. Sometimes those lines related to natural features, such as the long, narrow lots in French Canada that fronted on the St. Lawrence River. But because North America was settled piecemeal, no one system dominated until the Land Ordinance of 1785. Thereafter, the ordinance's system became the template for the U.S. government's land distribution.

After a surveyor established an east-west baseline and a north-south meridian on a particular tract, he laid out rectangular townships composed of thirty-six numbered square-mile sections. He ignored natural features; potential buyers would learn for themselves which sections had rivers, hills, or assets like salt licks. The initial policy of selling equally priced sections broadened by 1832 to allow individuals to purchase as few as 40 acres and, after 1854, included price variations. As the United States expanded westward, the township and range system followed, democratizing access to land and opening land for settlement.

The legacy of the Land Ordinance of 1785 for the American people and nation still marks the landscape west of the Ohio River.

Summary

During the 1770s and 1780s the nation began to develop an economy independent of Britain and attempted to protect the national interest, defend its borders, and promote trade. Some Americans outlined artistic and educational goals for a properly virtuous people. The formulation of American racist thought was also an integral part of the developing Union. Emphasizing race (rather than status as slave or free) as a determinant of African Americans' standing allowed men who now termed themselves *white* to define republicanism to exclude most men but themselves. White women, viewed primarily as household dependents, had a limited role in the republic, as mothers of the next generation and selfless contributors to the nation's welfare.

In 1775 most Americans believed that "that government which governs best governs least," but by the late 1780s many changed their minds. Drafters and supporters of the Constitution concluded that a more powerful central government was needed. During ratification debates, they contended that their proposals were just as republican as the Articles of Confederation.

Both sides adhered to republican principles, but Federalists embraced classical republicanism, stressing the community over the individual. Antifederalists wanted a weak central government, protection of individual rights, and a loosely regulated economy. The Federalists won when the Constitution was adopted, however narrowly. The 1790s, the first decade under the Constitution, would witness hesitant steps toward creating a true nation, the United States of America.

Chapter Review

CREATING A VIRTUOUS REPUBLIC

How were notions of republican virtue gendered in post-revolutionary America?

Leaders wanted the new United States to be a republican form of government, and while they debated the specifics, they agreed that in a republic, citizens were virtuous men willing to forgo personal profit for the best interests of the nation. The notion of virtue—the absence of vice or corruption—became increasingly important and inspired educational reform to help children become useful citizens. Some argued that since childrearing was women's role, they, too, would need education to help raise virtuous future citizens. Since women could not own property or participate in politics, their role was as the embodiment of self-sacrificing republicanism, using their nurturing skills to run charitable associations aiding the poor and others. This, in turn, conveyed virtue on their families and freed men to pursue their economic self-interests. The ideal republican male sought upward mobility for himself and his family, while the ideal republican woman put the needs of others first.

THE FIRST EMANCIPATION AND THE GROWTH OF RACISM

What contributed to the growing number of free blacks in America after the revolution?

Northern states, which were less reliant on slave labor, increasingly freed slaves after court challenges from blacks about the contradictions between forced bondage and the Declaration of Independence. Other former slaves obtained their freedom by escaping during the war, by enlisting, or by state emancipation laws. Some slaveholders also manumitted slaves. Postwar economic changes also spurred manumissions, particularly in the Chesapeake, where the shift from tobacco to grain production meant far fewer slaves were required.

DESIGNING REPUBLICAN GOVERNMENTS

How did Americans' former experience as British subjects influence the state governments they established?

Americans feared tyranny as well as the power of the governor, and as such, early state constitutions sought to limit governors' power through annual elections and term limitations. They further provided little independent authority for governors while expanding that granted to legislatures, typically in a two-house structure. And states put more power in the hands of the people by redrawing election districts to reflect the population and reducing property requirements for voting. To protect citizens' rights, several states included a bill of rights guaranteeing freedom of the press, rights to fair trials and sometimes freedom of religion even if officeholders had to be Christians. Ultimately, the emphasis on preventing tyranny made states weak politically. Subsequent revisions to state constitutions in the mid-1780s increased the power of the governor and reduced that of the legislature via a system of checks and balances.

TRIALS OF THE CONFEDERATION

How did fears of a strong central government ultimately tie the hands of the Confederation Congress?

The Articles of confederation limited congressional power in a number of areas that, in turn, led to policy problems for the new nation. First, because of state resistance to a large central government, a much-needed customs duty was never adopted. Second, Congress's limited ability to establish a national commercial policy left it unable to take action when Britain, France, and Spain restricted American trade. Third, Congress had little power to enforce the 1783 Treaty of Paris promising payment of prewar debts (owed by Americans to British merchants) and allowing loyalists to recover confiscated property. States passed various laws prohibiting both, which gave the British an excuse to maintain military posts on the Great Lakes. Worse, the inability to enforce the treaty hurt the republic's credibility in foreign affairs.

ORDER AND DISORDER IN THE WEST

What was the significance of the Northwest Ordinance?

One of the lasting accomplishments of the First Continental Congress, the Northwest Ordinance of 1787 effectively outlined how territories west of the Mississippi would be organized, how land could be divided and sold, how new states would be admitted to the Union, as well as the rights of people living there. It included a bill of rights guaranteeing freedom of religion and the right to a jury trial, and it forbade cruel and unusual punishments and nominally prohibited slavery. While the ordinance did not deprive those with slaves of their property and included the first fugitive slave law, it did discourage slaveholders from moving into the territory and prevented slavery from taking hold on a large scale.

FROM CRISIS TO THE CONSTITUTION

How did the question of slavery become linked to the new U.S. Constitution?

Slavery came into play at the Constitutional Convention as states debated how their populations should be counted in determining the number of representatives each would get in the lower house of Congress. Slave states wanted their bondsmen fully counted, while those from states with few slaves wanted only free people counted. The dispute was resolved by a formula known as the three-fifths compromise, noting that three-fifths of slaves would be included in population totals in censuses conducted every decade. While the words *slave* and *slavery* are not used in the Constitution, it nonetheless included direct and indirect protections for slavery, among them assistance in putting down revolts, returning fugitive slaves to masters, and agreeing not to end the importation of slaves for twenty years.

OPPOSITION AND RATIFICATION

What were the differences between Federalists and Antifederalists in the Constitution debate?

Federalists supported ratification of the Constitution and believed a strong national government led by a talented elite would prevent tyranny. Moreover, they agued that dividing power between the legislative, executive, and judicial branches, as well as between states and the nation, would prevent a tyrant from rising up. Antifederalists, so dubbed by their opponents, feared a too-powerful central government and saw states as protectors of individual rights. As such, they supported state sovereignty, and while they agreed on the need for central currency and taxation, Antifederalists were concerned that the Constitution did not include a bill of rights to safeguard people's individual rights.

SUGGESTIONS FOR FURTHER READING

Richard Beeman et al., eds., *Beyond Confederation: Origins of the Constitution and American National Identity* (1987)

Carol Berkin, *A Brilliant Solution: Inventing the American Constitution* (2002)

Ira Berlin and Ronald Hoffman, eds., *Slavery and Freedom in the Age of the American Revolution* (1983)

Cathy N. Davidson, *Revolution and the Word: The Rise of the Novel in America* (1987)

Edith Gelles, *Portia: The World of Abigail Adams* (1992)

Peter S. Onuf, *Statehood and Union: A History of the Northwest Ordinance* (1987)

Jack N. Rakove, *Original Meanings: Politics and Ideas in the Making of the Constitution* (1996)

Leonard L. Richards, *Shays's Rebellion: The American Revolution's Final Battle* (2002)

David Waldstreicher, *In the Midst of Perpetual Fetes: The Making of American Nationalism, 1776–1820* (1997)

Gordon S. Wood, *The Creation of the American Republic, 1776–1787* (1969)

The Early Republic: Conflicts at Home and Abroad

CHAPTER 8

1789–1800

CHAPTER OUTLINE

Building a Workable Government

Domestic Policy Under Washington and Hamilton

The French Revolution and the Development of Partisan Politics

Partisan Politics and Relations with Great Britain

John Adams and Political Dissent

The West in the New Nation

"Revolutions" at the End of the Century

LINKS TO THE WORLD: Haitian Refugees

LEGACY FOR A PEOPLE AND A NATION: Dissent During Wartime

Summary

In late 1798, the wealthy Philadelphia matron Deborah Norris Logan became the target of widespread criticism. Her husband, Dr. George Logan, who supported Jefferson, had undertaken a personal peace mission to France, fearing war between the United States and its former ally. When Logan's wife defended him, she endured a campaign unlike anything experienced by an American woman. Her treatment suggests the political symbolism now embodied by women, the growing division between the Federalist and Republican factions, and the significance of foreign affairs in the early republic.

First to attack was the Federalist newspaper editor William Cobbett, who observed with sly sexual innuendo in his *Porcupine's Gazette* in July that "it is said that JEFFERSON went to his friend Doctor Logan's farm and spent three days there, soon after the Doctor's departure for France. *Query:* What did he do there?" Later Cobbett suggested that George and Deborah Logan should be publicly shamed—him, presumably, for treason and her, Cobbett implied, for adultery. Republican newspapers leaped to Deborah's defense, attacking the vulgarity of suggestions about her and Vice President Jefferson.

At first Deborah Logan secluded herself at her country estate, but on Jefferson's advice she returned to Philadelphia to prove she was "not afraid nor ashamed to meet the public eye." As reports emerged that her husband had some success in quelling hostilities, she reveled in the praise subsequently showered on him. George Logan was enthusiastically welcomed home by Jeffersonian partisans. However, in January 1799, Congress, controlled by Federalists, adopted the so-called Logan Act, still in effect, which forbids private citizens from undertaking diplomatic missions.

The Logan controversy was one of many battles in the 1790s. The fight over ratifying the Constitution presaged wide divisions

This icon will direct you to interactive activities and study materials on A People And A Nation, Brief Edition
website: **www.cengage.com/history/norton/peoplenationbrief8e**

Chronology

1789	Washington is inaugurated as first president.
	Judiciary Act of 1789 organizes the federal court system.
	French Revolution begins.
1790	Hamilton's *Report on Public Credit* proposes the assumption of state debts.
1791	First ten amendments (Bill of Rights) are ratified.
	First national bank is chartered.
1793	France declares war on Britain, Spain, and the Netherlands.
	Washington's neutrality proclamation keeps the United States out of war.
	Democratic and Republican societies, the first grassroots political organizations, are founded.
1794	Wayne defeats the Miami Confederacy at Fallen Timbers.
	Whiskey Rebellion in western Pennsylvania protests taxation.
1795	Jay Treaty with England resolves issues remaining from the Revolution.

	Pinckney's Treaty with Spain establishes the southern boundary of the United States.
	Treaty of Greenville with the Miami Confederacy opens Ohio to settlement.
1796	First contested presidential election: Adams is elected president, Jefferson vice president.
1798	XYZ affair arouses American opinion against France.
	Sedition Act penalizes dissent.
	Virginia and Kentucky Resolutions protest suppression of dissent.
1798–99	Quasi-War with France occurs.
	Fries's Rebellion in Pennsylvania protests taxation.
1800	Franco-American Convention ends the Quasi-War.
	Gabriel's Rebellion threatens Virginia slaveowners.
1801	Thomas Jefferson is elected president by the House of Representatives after a stalemate in the electoral college.

over the major political, economic, and diplomatic questions confronting the young republic: the extent to which authority should be centralized, the relationship between national power and states' rights, the formulation of foreign policy in an era of continual warfare in Europe, and the limits of dissent. Americans had not anticipated the acrimonious disagreements that rocked the 1790s or the difficulties that would develop as the United States attempted to deal with Indian nations within its borders.

Most important, Americans could not understand the division of citizens into two competing factions. In republics, they believed, the rise of such factions signified decay and corruption. Yet on numerous occasions, Federalist and Republican leaders sought to mobilize their supporters, thereby reworking the nation's political practice if not its theory. As the decade closed, Americans were still grappling with the implications of partisan politics, as evidenced by the 1800 election.

- What major challenges confronted the new republic?
- What issues caused disputes among the nation's citizens?
- How did Americans react to those disputes?

BUILDING A WORKABLE GOVERNMENT

At first, consensus appeared possible, as the nation's celebratory mood after the Constitution's ratification carried into Congress's first session. Only a few Antifederalists ran for office in 1788, and even fewer were elected. Thus the First Congress consisted chiefly of men who supported a strong national government. The drafters of the Constitution deliberately left key issues undecided, so the nationalists' domination of Congress meant that their views prevailed.

First Congress

Congress faced four immediate tasks when it convened in April 1789: raising revenue, responding to states' calls for a bill of rights, setting up executive departments, and organizing the judiciary.

James Madison, representing Virginia in the House of Representatives, became influential in Congress. He persuaded Congress to adopt the Revenue Act of 1789, imposing a 5 percent tariff on certain imports. Thus the First Congress achieved an effective national tax law.

Bill of Rights

Madison opposed additional limitations on the national government and believed it unnecessary to guarantee people's rights explicitly given the government's limited powers. But he recognized that Congress should respond to amendments proposed in state ratifying conventions. Accordingly, he introduced nineteen amendments; the states ratified ten, which became part of the Constitution on December 15, 1791 (see the appendix for the Constitution and all amendments). Their adoption defused Antifederalist opposition.

The First Amendment prohibited Congress from passing laws restricting the right to freedom of religion, speech, press, peaceable assembly, or petition. The Second Amendment guaranteed the right "to keep and bear arms" because of the need for a "well-regulated Militia." It was based on the expectation that most able-bodied men would serve as citizen-soldiers, eliminating the need for a permanent army. The Third Amendment limited the conditions under which troops could be quartered in private homes. The next five pertained to judicial procedures. The Fourth Amendment prohibited "unreasonable searches and seizures"; the Fifth and Sixth established the rights of accused persons; the Seventh specified the conditions for jury trials in civil (as opposed to criminal) cases; and the Eighth forbade "cruel and unusual punishments." The Ninth and Tenth Amendments reserved to the people and the states other unspecified rights and powers.

Executive and Judiciary

Congress also considered the organization of the executive branch. It agreed to continue the three administrative departments established under the Articles of Confederation: War, Foreign Affairs (renamed State), and Treasury. Congress instituted two lesser posts: the attorney general—the nation's official lawyer—and the postmaster general. Controversy arose over whether the president alone could dismiss officials whom he appointed with Senate approval. Ultimately, the House and Senate agreed that he had such authority. That established the principle that heads of executive departments are accountable solely to the president.

The far-reaching Judiciary Act of 1789 defined the jurisdiction of the federal judiciary and established a six-member Supreme Court, thirteen district courts, and three circuit courts of appeal. Its most important provision, Section 25, allowed appeals from state to federal courts when cases raised certain constitutional questions. It presumed that Article VI of the Constitution, which stated that federal statutes and treaties were "the supreme Law of the Land," implied the right of appeal from state to federal courts, yet the Constitution did not explicitly permit such actions. In the nineteenth century, judges and legislators committed to states' rights would challenge Section 25's constitutionality.

During its first decade, the Supreme Court handled few cases of any importance, and several members resigned. But in a 1796 decision, *Ware v. Hylton,* the Court for the first time declared a state law unconstitutional. That same year it also reviewed the constitutionality of an act of Congress, upholding its validity in the case of *Hylton v. U.S.* The most important case of the decade, *Chisholm v. Georgia* (1793), established that states could be sued in federal courts by citizens of other states. Five years later, the Eleventh Amendment to the Constitution overturned that decision.

Debate over Slavery

Constitutional provisions forbade Congress from prohibiting the importation of slaves for twenty years, but in 1790 three Quakers groups petitioned Congress to end slavery. Southerners asserted that had they thought that the federal government would consider interfering with slavery, they would never have ratified the Constitution. Southern legislators insisted, as they would for the next seven decades, that slavery was integral to the Union and that abolition would cause bigger problems, primarily how to deal with a sizable population of freed people.

Some northern congressmen—and Benjamin Franklin—contested the southerners' position. But Congress accepted a committee report denying it the power to halt slave importations before 1808 or emancipate slaves at any time, that authority "remaining with the several States alone."

DOMESTIC POLICY UNDER WASHINGTON AND HAMILTON

George Washington did not seek the presidency. In 1783 he returned to Mount Vernon as a Virginia planter. But his fellow countrymen never regarded Washington as just another citizen. Americans concurred that only Washington had sufficient stature to serve as the republic's first president, an office designed with him in mind. The unanimous vote of the electoral college formalized that consensus. Washington could not ignore his country's call and headed to New York City, the nation's capital.

Washington's First Steps

Washington acted cautiously during his first months in office in 1789, knowing he would set future precedents. When the title by which he should be addressed aroused controversy (Vice President John Adams favored His Highness, the President of the United States of America, and Protector of their Liberties), Washington said nothing. The accepted title became simply Mr. President. By using the heads of executive departments as chief advisers, he created the cabinet. Washington also exercised his veto power over congressional legislation sparingly—only if he believed a bill was unconstitutional.

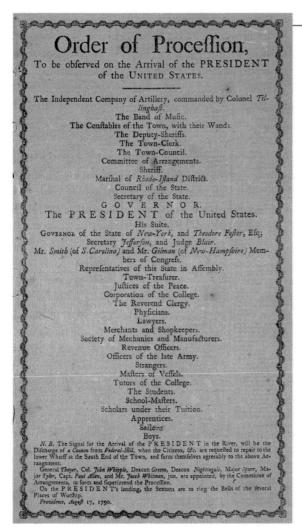

Order of Procession,

To be observed on the Arrival of the PRESIDENT of the UNITED STATES.

The Independent Company of Artillery, commanded by Colonel *Tillinghaft.*
The Band of Music.
The Constables of the Town, with their Wands.
The Deputy-Sheriffs.
The Town-Clerk.
The Town-Council.
Committee of Arrangements.
Sheriff.
Marshal of *Rhode-Island* District.
Council of the State.
Secretary of the State.
G O V E R N O R.
The P R E S I D E N T of the United States.
His Suite.
Governor of the State of *New-York*, and *Theodore Fofter*, Efq;
Secretary *Jefferfon*, and Judge *Blair.*
Mr. *Smith* (of *S. Carolina*) and Mr. *Gilman* (of *New-Hampfhire*) Members of Congrefs.
Reprefentatives of this State in Affembly.
Town-Treafurer.
Juftices of the Peace.
Corporation of the College.
The Reverend Clergy.
Phyficians.
Lawyers.
Merchants and Shopkeepers.
Society of Mechanics and Manufacturers.
Revenue Officers.
Officers of the late Army.
Strangers.
Mafters of Veffels.
Tutors of the College.
The Students.
School-Mafters.
Scholars under their Tuition.
Apprentices.
Sailors.
Boys.

N. B. The Signal for the Arrival of the P R E S I D E N T in the River, will be the Difcharge of a *Cannon* from *Federal-Hill*, when the Citizens, &c. are requested to repair to the lower Wharff at the South End of the Town, and form themfelves agreeably to the above Arrangement.

General *Thayer*, Col. *John Whipple*, Deacon *Greene*, Deacon *Nightingale*, Major *Spurr*, Major *Tyler*, Capt. *Paul Allen*, and Mr. *Jacob Whitman*, jun. are appointed, by the Committee of Arrangements, to form and fuperintend the Proceffion.

On the P R E S I D E N T's landing, the Sextons are to ring the Bells of the feveral Places of Worfhip.

Providence, Auguft 17, 1790.

When George Washington toured the nation during his first term in office, he was greeted by local leaders in elaborately orchestrated rituals. The organizers of the ceremony at Providence, Rhode Island, on August 17, 1790, issued this broadside to inform participants of their plans for a formal procession. While some Americans gloried in such displays of pomp, others feared they presaged the return of monarchy.   (The Huntington Library and Art Collections, San Marino, California)

Washington's first major task was to choose the heads of the executive departments. For the War Department he selected Henry Knox of Massachusetts, who was his artillery general during the Revolution. For the State Department, he selected fellow Virginian Thomas Jefferson, who had been minister to France. For secretary of the treasury, Washington chose the brilliant, ambitious Alexander Hamilton.

Alexander Hamilton

The illegitimate son of a Scottish aristocrat and a woman whose husband divorced her for adultery and desertion, Hamilton was born in the British West Indies in 1757. He spent his early years in poverty, working as a mercantile clerk after his mother's death when he was eleven. In 1773 Hamilton enrolled at King's College (later Columbia University) in New York City. In late 1774, the seventeen-year-old contributed a pamphlet to the prerevolutionary publication wars. A devoted patriot, Hamilton volunteered for the American army, where in 1777, Washington appointed him as an aide, and they developed great mutual affection.

At twenty-three, Hamilton wed Elizabeth Schuyler, daughter of a wealthy New York family. After the war, he practiced law in New York City and served as a delegate to the Annapolis Convention and the Constitutional Convention. His contributions to *The Federalist* in 1788 made him one of the republic's chief political thinkers.

As treasury secretary and presidential adviser, Hamilton's primary loyalty lay with the nation. With no natal ties to any state, Hamilton neither sympathized with nor fully understood demands for local autonomy. His fiscal policies aimed at consolidating national power, and he openly favored close ties with Britain.

Second, Hamilton cynically believed people to be motivated by self-interest. He placed no reliance on people's capacity for virtuous, self-sacrificing behavior. This set him apart from those Americans who believed that public-spirited citizens would pursue the common good rather than private gain. Hamilton's beliefs influenced the way he tackled the new nation's tangled finances.

National and State Debts

Congress ordered the new treasury secretary to assess the public debt. The country's war debts fell into three categories: those owed by the nation to foreign governments and investors, mostly France (about $11 million); those owed by the national government to merchants, soldiers, and revolutionary bondholders (about $27 million); and, finally, those owed by state governments (roughly $25 million). Regarding the national debt, Americans recognized that, if their new government were to succeed, it would have to repay financial obligations incurred while winning independence.

State debts were another matter. Some—notably, Virginia, Maryland, North Carolina, and Georgia—had already paid off most war debts by levying taxes and handing out land grants in lieu of money. They opposed taxing their citizens so the national government could assume other states' debts. Massachusetts, Connecticut, and South Carolina still had sizable unpaid debts and welcomed national assumption. Consolidating state debt in the hands of the national government would help concentrate power at the national level.

Hamilton's Financial Plan

In his first *Report on Public Credit* in January 1790, Hamilton proposed that Congress assume outstanding state debts, combine them with national obligations, and issue new securities covering principal and accumulated unpaid interest. Hamilton hoped to ensure that holders of the public debt—many of them wealthy merchants and speculators—had a stake in the new government's survival. Opposition coalesced around James Madison, whose state of Virginia had mostly eliminated its war debt and who wanted to avoid rewarding wealthy speculators who purchased debt certificates at a fraction of their value from needy veterans and farmers.

The House initially rejected the assumption of state debts, but the Senate adopted Hamilton's plan largely intact. Compromises followed, in which the assumption bill became linked to another major issue: location of the permanent national capital. Deals were struck. A site on the Potomac River became the capital, and the first part of Hamilton's program became law in August 1790.

First Bank of the United States

Four months later, Hamilton submitted to Congress a second report on public credit, recommending the chartering of a national bank modeled on the Bank of England. The Bank of the United States, to be chartered for twenty years, was to be capitalized at $10 million. Just $2 million would come from public funds; private investors would supply the rest. The bank would act as collecting and disbursing agent for the Treasury, and its notes would become the nation's currency. But did the Constitution give Congress the power to establish such a bank?

Interpreting the Constitution

James Madison thought not. He pointed out that Constitutional Convention delegates rejected a clause authorizing Congress to issue corporate charters. President Washington sought other opinions. Attorney General Edmund Randolph and Secretary of State Thomas Jefferson agreed with Madison. Jefferson referred to Article I, Section 8, of the Constitution, which gave Congress the power "to make all Laws which shall be necessary and proper." The key word, Jefferson argued, was *necessary:* Congress could do what was needed, but not what was merely desirable. Thus Jefferson formulated the strict-constructionist interpretation of the Constitution.

Hamilton's *Defense of the Constitutionality of the Bank,* presented in February 1791, expounded a broad-constructionist view of the Constitution. Hamilton argued that Congress could choose any means not specifically prohibited by the Constitution to achieve a constitutional end. He reasoned: if the end was constitutional and the means was not *un*constitutional, then the means was constitutional.

Washington concurred, and the bill became law. The bank proved successful, as did the debt program. The new nation's securities became desirable investments for citizens and wealthy foreigners, especially those in the Netherlands. The influx of new capital, coupled with the high prices that American grain now commanded in European markets, eased farmers' debt burdens and contributed to a new prosperity.

Report on Manufactures

In December 1791, Hamilton presented to Congress his *Report on Manufactures,* his third and final economic prescription. Hamilton argued that the nation could never be truly independent as long as it relied heavily on Europe for manufactured goods. He urged Congress to promote the immigration of technicians and laborers and to support industrial development through limited use of protective tariffs. Many of Hamilton's ideas were implemented in later decades, but congressmen in 1791 believed that America's future lay in agriculture and the carrying trade. Congress rejected Hamilton's report.

That year Congress tried another of Hamilton's suggestions, an excise tax on whiskey distilled within the United States. Although proceeds from the Revenue Act of 1789 covered the interest on the national debt, the national government required additional income to fund state debts. A whiskey tax affected few westerners—farmers who grew corn and distillers who turned it into whiskey—and might also reduce whiskey consumption. (Eighteenth-century Americans, notorious for their heavy drinking, consumed about twice as much alcohol per capita as Americans do today.) Moreover, western farmers and distillers were Jefferson's supporters, and Hamilton saw the benefits of taxing them rather than his merchant allies.

Whiskey Rebellion

News of the tax sparked protests on Pennsylvania's frontier. Residents were upset that the government that protected them inadequately from Indian attacks was proposing to tax them disproportionately. Unrest continued for two years on the frontiers of Pennsylvania, Maryland, and Virginia. Large groups drafted petitions protesting the tax, deliberately imitated 1760s' crowd actions, and occasionally harassed tax collectors.

President Washington stayed restrained until violence erupted in July 1794, when western Pennsylvania farmers resisted two excise tax collectors. When about seven thousand rebels convened on August 1 to plot the destruction of Pittsburgh, Washington took action to prevent a repeat of Shays's Rebellion. On August 7, he told insurgents to disperse and summoned nearly thirteen thousand militia from Pennsylvania and neighboring states. By the time federal forces marched westward in October and November, the disturbances ceased. Troops met no resistance and arrested only twenty suspects. Two were convicted of treason, but Washington pardoned both.

The importance of the Whiskey Rebellion lay in the forceful message it conveyed. The national government, Washington demonstrated, would not allow violent resistance to its laws. In the republic, people dissatisfied with laws should peacefully try to amend or repeal them.

THE FRENCH REVOLUTION AND THE DEVELOPMENT OF PARTISAN POLITICS

By 1794 some Americans were beginning to seek change through electoral politics. In a monarchy, formal opposition groups, commonly called factions, were expected. In a government of the people, however, sustained factional disagreement was taken as a sign of corruption, but that did not halt partisanship.

Republicans and Federalists

Jefferson and Madison became convinced as early as 1792 that Hamilton's policies favoring wealthy commercial interests over agriculture aimed at imposing a corrupt, aristocratic government on the United States. Characterizing themselves as the true heirs of the Revolution, they charged that Hamilton was plotting to subvert republican principles and began calling themselves and their followers Republicans. Hamilton likewise accused Jefferson and Madison of attempting to destroy the republic. Hamilton and his supporters called themselves Federalists to link themselves with the Constitution.

Washington tried to remain aloof from the political dispute dividing his chief advisers. The growing controversy persuaded him to promote political unity by seeking office again in 1792. But beginning in 1793, developments in foreign affairs magnified the disagreements, for France (America's wartime ally) and Great Britain (America's most important trading partner) resumed the periodic hostilities that originated a century earlier.

French Revolution

In 1789 Americans welcomed news of the French Revolution. The French people's success in limiting, and then overthrowing, an oppressive monarchy enabled Americans to see themselves as the vanguard of an inevitable trend that would reshape the world in republican terms. But by the early 1790s violence in France continued, and political leaders rapidly succeeded each other. Executions mounted; the king was beheaded in early 1793. Although many Americans, including Jefferson and Madison, retained sympathy for the revolution, others, among them Alexander Hamilton, cited France as an example of the perversion of republicanism.

Debates within the United States intensified when the newly republican France became enmeshed in conflict with other European nations. Seeking to keep neighboring monarchies from intervening, and hoping to spread republicanism, French leaders declared war on Austria and then, in 1793, on Britain, Spain, and Holland. That posed a dilemma for Americans. The 1778 Treaty of Alliance with France bound them as allies "forever." Yet the United States was connected to Great Britain through a shared history and language and renewed economic ties. Americans still purchased most of their manufactured goods from Great Britain, and because U.S. revenues depended heavily on import tariffs, the nation's economic health required uninterrupted trade with England.

Edmond Genêt

The situation intensified in April 1793, when Edmond Genêt, a representative of the French government, arrived in Charleston, South Carolina. As he traveled to New York City, he recruited Americans for expeditions against British and Spanish colonies. Washington wondered: Should he receive Genêt, thus officially recognizing the French revolutionary government? Or should he proclaim neutrality?

Washington resolved his dilemma by receiving Genêt but also issuing a proclamation that the United States would adopt "a conduct friendly and impartial toward the belligerent powers." Federalist newspapers defended the proclamation, while Republicans only reluctantly accepted the enormously popular neutrality policy.

Genêt's faction fell from power in Paris, and he sought political asylum in the United States. But the domestic divisions Genêt helped to widen were perpetuated by clubs called Democratic societies, formed by Americans sympathetic to the French Revolution and worried about the Washington administration.

Democratic Societies

More than forty Democratic societies organized between 1793 and 1800. Members saw themselves as heirs of the Sons of Liberty with the same goal: protecting people's liberties against encroachments by corrupt, self-serving rulers. They protested government fiscal and foreign policy and proclaimed their belief in the equal rights of man, particularly free speech, free press, and free assembly. The Democratic societies comprised chiefly artisans and craftsmen, although professionals, farmers, and merchants also joined. They communicated through newspapers and allied with congressional Republicans.

The rapid spread of citizens' groups outspokenly critical of the administration disturbed Hamilton and Washington. Calling them dangerously subversive, the groups' "real design," a Federalist newspaper asserted, was "to involve the country in war, to assume the reins of government and tyrannize over the people." The counter-attack climaxed in the fall of 1794, when Washington accused the societies of fomenting the Whiskey Rebellion. As the first organized political dissenters in the United States, the Democratic societies alarmed officials, who had not yet accepted that organized loyal opposition was one component of a free government.

PARTISAN POLITICS AND RELATIONS WITH GREAT BRITAIN

In 1794 George Washington dispatched Chief Justice John Jay to London to negoti-ate unresolved questions in Anglo-American relations. The United States wanted to establish freedom of the seas and to assert its right, as a neutral nation, to trade freely with both combatants. Further, Great Britain still held posts in the American Northwest, thus violating the 1783 peace treaty. Settlers there believed that the British were responsible for renewed warfare with neighboring Indians. The Americans also hoped for a commercial treaty and sought compensation for the slaves who left with the British army after the war.

Jay Treaty Debate   Britain agreed to evacuate western forts and ease restric-tions on American trade to England and the West Indies. The treaty established two arbitration commissions—one to deal with prewar debts Americans owed to British creditors and the other to hear claims for captured American merchant ships—but Britain refused slaveowners com-pensation for lost bondspeople. Most Americans, including the president, expressed dissatisfaction with some treaty clauses.

The Senate debated the Jay Treaty in secret, and the public only learned its pro-visions after ratification in late June 1795. Protests followed, in newspaper essays and popular gatherings that asked Washington to reject the treaty. Southern planters criticized the lack of compensation for runaway slaves and objected to the commis-sion on prewar debts, which might make them pay debts dating back to the 1760s. Federalists countered with their own meetings and publications, contending that the Jay Treaty would prove preferable to no treaty at all. The president signed the treaty in mid-August. One opportunity remained to prevent it from taking effect: Congress had to appropriate funds, and, according to the Constitution, appropria-tion bills had to originate in the House of Representatives.

Washington delayed submitting the treaty to the House until March 1796, fu-tilely hoping that opposition would have dissipated. During the debate, Republicans argued against the appropriations, and they asked Washington to give the House all negotiation documents. In resisting the request, Washington established a power still used today—executive privilege, in which the president may withhold informa-tion from Congress if he deems it necessary.

The treaty's opponents initially commanded a congressional majority, but soon pressure mounted for appropriating the necessary funds, fostered by a Federalist campaign targeting middle-state congressmen whose districts would benefit from approval. Petitions contended that failure to fund the treaty would lead to war with Britain, thus endangering Pennsylvania frontier settlements and New York and

New Jersey commercial interests. Further, Federalists linked the Jay Treaty with the more popular Pinckney's Treaty. In 1795 Thomas Pinckney of South Carolina negotiated a treaty with Spain giving the United States navigation privileges on the Mississippi River and the right to land and store goods at New Orleans tax free. The overwhelming support for Pinckney's Treaty helped to overcome opposition to the Jay Treaty. In late April, the House appropriated the money by 51 to 48. The vote divided along partisan and regional lines: all but two southerners opposed the treaty; all but three congressional Federalists supported it; and a majority of middle-state representatives also voted yes. Despite the Federalists' success, their campaign to sway public opinion ironically violated their fundamental government philosophy—that ordinary people should defer to the judgment of elected leaders. The Federalists had won the battle, but in the long run they lost the war, for Republicans ultimately proved far more effective in appealing to the citizenry at large.

Bases of Partisanship

The terms used by Jefferson and Madison (the people versus the aristocrats) or by Hamilton and Washington (true patriots versus subversive rabble) do not adequately explain growing divisions in the electorate. Differences between agrarian and commercial interests do not cover it either, since more than 90 percent of Americans lived in rural areas. Nor did the divisions in the 1790s simply echo the Federalist-Antifederalist debate of 1787–1788. Although most Antifederalists became Republicans, the party's leaders, Madison and Jefferson, had supported the Constitution.

Republicans, especially prominent in the southern and middle states, were confident and optimistic about politics and the economy. Southern planters foresaw a prosperous future based partly on westward expansion, which they expected to dominate. Republicans employed democratic rhetoric to win over small farmers south of New England and non-English ethnic groups, especially Irish, Scots, and Germans. Artisans also joined the coalition. Republicans emphasized developing America's resources and remained sympathetic to France.

Federalists, concentrated among New England commercial interests, came mostly from English stock. They stressed the need for order, hierarchy, and obedience to authority. Wealthy New England merchants aligned with the Federalists, as did the region's farmers who, prevented from expanding production because of New England's poor soil, gravitated toward the more conservative party. To Federalists, potential enemies—internal and external—threatened the nation, requiring an ongoing alliance with Great Britain for protection. Given the dangers posed by European warfare, the Federalists' vision of international affairs may have been accurate. But because the Federalist view held little hope of a better future, Republicans ultimately prevailed.

Washington's Farewell Address

After the treaty debate, wearied by criticism, George Washington decided to retire. In September Washington published his Farewell Address, most of which Hamilton wrote. In it Washington outlined two principles that guided American foreign policy until the late 1940s: to maintain commercial but not political ties to other nations and to enter no permanent alliances. He also stressed America's uniqueness—its exceptionalism—and the need for independent action in foreign affairs, today called unilateralism.

Some historians have interpreted Washington's call for an end to partisan strife as the statement of a man who focused on the good of the whole. But given the impending presidential election, the Farewell Address appears as an attack on the Republican opposition. Washington advocated unity behind the Federalist banner. Both Federalists and Republicans saw themselves as the true heirs of the Revolution and regarded their opponents as misguided, unpatriotic troublemakers.

Election of 1796

The presidential election of 1796 saw the first serious contest for the position. Federalists in Congress put forward Vice President John Adams, with the diplomat Thomas Pinckney as his running mate. Congressional Republicans chose Thomas Jefferson as their presidential candidate; the lawyer, Revolutionary War veteran, and politician Aaron Burr of New York agreed to run for vice president.

In most states, legislatures appointed electors, and the method of voting in the electoral college did not account for the possibility of party slates. The Constitution's drafters had not foreseen the development of competing political organizations, so there was no way to support one person for president and another for vice president. The electors voted for two people. The man with the highest total became president; the second highest, vice president.

This proved to be the Federalists' undoing. Adams won the presidency with seventy-one votes, but Thomas Jefferson won sixty-eight votes, nine more than Pinckney, to become vice president. The incoming administration was thus politically divided. The president and vice president, once allies, eventually became enemies.

JOHN ADAMS AND POLITICAL DISSENT

As president, John Adams never abandoned the outdated notion that the president should be above politics and factionalism. Thus Adams kept Washington's cabinet intact, despite its key members' allegiance to his chief Federalist rival, Alexander Hamilton. Adams was often passive, letting others (usually Hamilton) lead when he should have. But Adams's detachment did enable him to weather the greatest international crisis yet: the Quasi-War with France.

XYZ Affair

The Jay Treaty improved America's relationship with Great Britain, but it provoked the French government to retaliate by ordering its ships to seize American vessels carrying British goods. In response, Congress authorized ship building and stockpiling weapons and ammunition. President Adams also sent three commissioners to Paris to negotiate a settlement. For months, the commissioners sought talks with Talleyrand, the French foreign minister, but Talleyrand's agents demanded a bribe of $250,000 first. The Americans refused. Adams informed Congress of the impasse and recommended increases in defense appropriations.

Convinced that Adams deliberately sabotaged negotiations, congressional Republicans insisted that the commissioners' reports be turned over to Congress.

Adams complied, aware that releasing these dispatches would work to his advantage. He withheld only the names of French agents, referring to them as X, Y, and Z. The revelation that the Americans were treated with contempt stimulated anti-French sentiment in the United States. Cries for war resounded. Congress abrogated the Treaty of Alliance and authorized American ships to seize French vessels.

Quasi-War with France Thus began an undeclared war with France fought in Caribbean waters between warships of the U.S. Navy and French privateers. Although Americans initially suffered heavy merchant shipping losses, by early 1799 the U.S. Navy established its superiority. Its ships captured eight French privateers and naval vessels, easing the threat to America's Caribbean trade.

The Republicans, who opposed war and sympathized with France, could not quell anti-French feelings. Because Agent Y boasted of a "French party in America," Federalists accused Republicans of traitorous designs. A New York newspaper declared that anyone who remained "lukewarm" after reading the XYZ dispatches "must have a soul black enough to be fit for treason Strategems and spoils."

Alien and Sedition Acts Now that the country seemed to see the truth of what Federalists argued since the Whiskey Rebellion in 1794—that Republicans were subversive foreign agents—Federalists sought to codify that belief into law. In 1798 the Federalist-controlled Congress adopted four laws known as the Alien and Sedition Acts, intended to suppress dissent and prevent the growth of the Republican faction.

Three of the acts targeted recent immigrants, whom Federalists accurately suspected of having Republican sympathies. The Naturalization Act lengthened the residency period required for citizenship and ordered resident aliens to register with the federal government. The two Alien Acts provided for the detention of enemy aliens in wartime and gave the president authority to deport any alien he deemed dangerous to national security.

The fourth statute, the Sedition Act, outlawed conspiracies to prevent enforcement of federal laws, punishable with five years in prison and a $5,000 fine. And writing, printing, or uttering "false, scandalous and malicious" statements against the government or the president "with intent to defame . . . or to bring them or either of them, into contempt or disrepute" became a crime punishable by up to two years' imprisonment and a fine of $2,000. Today, laws punishing speech alone would be unconstitutional. But in the eighteenth century, when organized political opposition was suspect, many Americans supported the Sedition Act's free speech restrictions. The Sedition Act led to fifteen indictments and ten convictions, including one congressman, Matthew Lyons of Vermont, and several outspoken Republican newspaper editors. One was James Callender, a Scots immigrant and scandalmonger, who relentlessly attacked Federalists while being subsidized by Thomas Jefferson. Callender's exposé forced Alexander Hamilton to admit to an extramarital affair. After turning his attention to President Adams, Callender was convicted, fined, and jailed for nine months, but he continued to produce pro-Jeffersonian writings from the Richmond prison.

Virginia and Kentucky Resolutions

Faced with prosecutions of their allies, Jefferson and Madison sought to combat the acts. Petitioning the Federalist-controlled Congress to repeal the laws would fail. Furthermore, Federalist judges refused to allow accused individuals to question the Sedition Act's constitutionality. Accordingly, the Republican leaders turned to the state legislatures. Concealing their role to avoid being indicted for sedition, Jefferson and Madison drafted resolutions that were introduced into the Kentucky and Virginia legislatures in the fall of 1798. Because a compact among the states created the Constitution, the resolutions contended, people speaking through their states had a right to judge the constitutionality of federal measures. Both pronounced the Alien and Sedition Acts unconstitutional, and thus advanced the doctrine later known as nullification.

Although they stood alone, the Virginia and Kentucky Resolutions had considerable influence. First, they rallied Republican opinion nationwide and placed the opposition party in the revolutionary tradition of resistance to tyrannical authority. Second, the theory of union that they proposed inspired the Hartford Convention of 1814 and southern states' rights advocates in the 1830s and thereafter. Jefferson and Madison identified a key constitutional issue: How far could states go in opposing the national government? The question would not be definitively answered until the Civil War.

Convention of 1800

Federalists split over France. Hamilton and his supporters called for a declaration legitimizing the undeclared naval war. Adams, though, received private signals—among them George Logan's report—that the French government regretted its treatment of the American commissioners.

Adams dispatched William Vans Murray as envoy to Paris to negotiate with Napoleon Bonaparte, France's new leader. The United States sought compensation for ships the French had seized since 1793 and abrogation of the treaty of 1778. The Convention of 1800, which ended the Quasi-War, provided the latter but not the former. Still, it freed the United States to follow the independent diplomatic course Washington urged in his Farewell Address.

THE WEST IN THE NEW NATION

By the end of the eighteenth century, the nation added three states (Vermont, Kentucky, and Tennessee) and more than 1 million people to the nearly 4 million in the 1790 census. It also nominally controlled the land east of the Mississippi River and north of Spanish Florida. Control of the land north of the Ohio River was achieved only after considerable bloodshed, for the land was dominated by a powerful western confederacy of eight Indian nations led by the Miamis.

War in the Northwest Territory

General Arthur St. Clair, first governor of the Northwest Territory, tried to open more land to settlement through treaty negotiations with the western confederacy in early 1789, but negotiations failed. Subsequently, Little Turtle, the confederacy's war

The two chief antagonists at the Battle of Fallen Timbers and negotiators of the Treaty of Greenville (1795). On the left, Little Turtle, the leader of the Miami Confederacy; on the right, General Anthony Wayne. Little Turtle, in a copy of a portrait painted two years later, appears to be wearing a miniature of Wayne on a bear-claw necklace.
(Left: Chicago History Museum / Chicago Historical Society / Neg #ICHi-35980 / Painter, Ralph Dille; right: Independence National Historic Park)

chief, defeated forces led by General Josiah Harmar (1790) and by St. Clair (1791) in battles near the present Indiana and Ohio border. More than six hundred of St. Clair's men died, and more were wounded, in the United States' worst defeat in frontier history.

In 1793 the Miami Confederacy declared that peace would come only if the United States recognized the Ohio River as its northwestern boundary. But the national government refused. A reorganized army under the Revolutionary War hero General Anthony Wayne defeated the confederacy in August 1794 at the Battle of Fallen Timbers (near present-day Toledo, Ohio).

In August 1795, Wayne and the Miami Confederacy agreed to the Treaty of Greenville. The United States gained the right to settle much of what would become Ohio. Indians received the acknowledgment they long sought: the United States accepted the principle of Indian sovereignty, by virtue of residence, over lands native peoples had not ceded. Never again would the U.S. government claim that it acquired Indian territory solely through negotiation with a European or North American country.

Pinckney's Treaty with Spain that year established the 31st parallel as the boundary between the United States and Florida. Spanish influence in the Old Southwest raised questions about the loyalty of American settlers in the region, much of it still unceded and occupied by Creeks, Cherokees, and other Indians. A Southwest Ordinance (1790) attempted to organize the territory; by permitting slavery, it made the region attractive to slaveholders.

"Civilizing" the Indians

Increasingly, even Indian peoples came within the orbit of U.S. influence. The nation's stated goal was to "civilize" them. Henry Knox, Washington's secretary of war, contended in 1789, the government should "impart our knowledge of cultivation and the arts to the aboriginals of the country." The first step, Knox suggested, should be to introduce Indians to "a love for exclusive property" by giving livestock to individual Indians. The Indian Trade and Intercourse Act of 1793 codified Knox's plan, promising that the federal government would supply Indians with animals, agricultural implements, and instructors.

The plan incorrectly posited that Indians' traditional commitment to communal landowning could be overcome, and it ignored their centuries-long agricultural experience. Policymakers focused on Indian men: because they hunted, male Indians were "savages" who should be "civilized" by learning to farm. That women traditionally farmed was irrelevant because, to officials, Indian women—like those of European descent—should confine themselves to child rearing, household chores, and home manufacturing.

Iroquois and Cherokees

The Iroquois Confederacy was devastated by the war. Restricted to small reservations increasingly surrounded by Anglo-American farmlands in the 1790s, men could no longer hunt and often spent their days in idle carousing. Quaker missionaries started a demonstration farm among the Senecas to teach men to plow, but women showed greater interest. The same was true among the Cherokees of Georgia. As their southern hunting territories were reduced, Cherokee men did begin to raise cattle and hogs, but they startled reformers by treating livestock like wild game, allowing the animals to run free and shooting them when needed. Men also started to plow fields, although women continued to handle cultivation and harvest.

Iroquois men became more receptive to the Quakers' lessons after the spring of 1799, when a Seneca named Handsome Lake experienced a series of visions. Like earlier prophets, Handsome Lake preached that Indian peoples should renounce alcohol, gambling, and other destructive European customs. He directed followers to reorient men's and women's work assignments as the Quakers advocated, as he recognized that only by adopting this European sexual division of labor could the Iroquois retain an autonomous existence.

"Revolutions" at the End of the Century

Three events at the end of the eighteenth century were real or potential revolutions: Fries's Rebellion, Gabriel's Rebellion, and the election of Thomas Jefferson. Each mirrored the tensions and uncertainties of the young republic. The Fries rebels resisted national authority to tax. Gabriel and his followers challenged the slave system crucial to the Chesapeake economy. And the venomous presidential election of 1800 exposed a structural flaw in the Constitution that had to be corrected.

Fries's Rebellion

The tax resistance movement named for Revolutionary War veteran John Fries arose in Pennsylvania's Lehigh Valley in 1798–1799 among German American farmers. To finance the Quasi-War, Congress enacted taxes on land, houses, and legal documents. German Americans, imbued with revolutionary ideals (at least two-fifths were veterans like Fries), regarded the taxes as a threat to their liberties and livelihoods. Asserting their right to resist unconstitutional laws, they raised liberty poles, signed petitions to Congress, and nonviolently prevented assessors from evaluating their homes.

A federal judge ordered the arrest of twenty resisters. In response, in March 1799 Fries led 120 militiamen to Bethlehem, where they surrounded the tavern temporarily housing the prisoners. Fearing a violent confrontation, a federal marshal eventually let the men go. Fries and many of his neighbors were arrested and tried; he and two others were convicted of treason; thirty-two more, of violating the Sedition Act. Although Fries and the other "traitors" were sentenced to hang, Adams pardoned them two days before their scheduled execution, concluding they were rioters rather than traitors. But the region's residents remained Republican partisans.

Gabriel's Rebellion

Like their white compatriots, African Americans became familiar with concepts of liberty and equality during the Revolution. They, too, witnessed the benefits of fighting collectively for freedom. Buoyed by news of the successful slave revolt in St. Domingue in 1793, Gabriel, an enslaved Virginia blacksmith, planned the second end-of-the-century revolution.

For months, Gabriel visited Sunday services at black Baptist and Methodist congregations, where bondspeople gathered free of their owners. Gabriel first recruited other skilled African Americans who like himself lived in semifreedom with minimal supervision. Next he enlisted rural slaves. The rebels planned to attack Richmond on the night of August 30, 1800, set fire to the city, seize the state capitol, and capture the governor, James Monroe. At that point, Gabriel believed, other slaves and perhaps poor whites would join in.

Heavy rain forced a postponement. Several planters then learned of the plot. Gabriel avoided arrest for weeks, but militia troops apprehended and interrogated other rebel leaders. Twenty-six rebels, including Gabriel, were hanged. Ironically, only slaves who betrayed their fellows won freedom as a result of the rebellion.

At his trial, one of Gabriel's followers told his judges that, like George Washington, "I have adventured my life in endeavouring to obtain the liberty of my countrymen, and am a willing sacrifice in their cause." Southern state legislatures responded by increasing the severity of slavery laws. Talk of emancipation ceased in the South, and slavery became more firmly entrenched.

Election of 1800

The third end-of-the-century revolution was a Republican takeover—the election of Thomas Jefferson as president and a Congress dominated by Republicans. Prior to November 1800, Federalists and Republicans campaigned for congressional seats and maneuvered to control the electoral college. Both sides wanted to avoid reproducing the divided results of 1796. Republicans again nominated Thomas

Haitian Refugees

Less than a decade after winning independence, the United States confronted its first immigration crisis when in 1789 a slave rebellion broke out in the French colony of St. Domingue (later Haiti). Among the approximately 600,000 residents of St. Domingue in the early 1790s were about 100,000 free people, almost all slave-owners; half were whites, the rest mulattos. When in the wake of the French Revolution those free mulattos sought greater social and political equality, slaves seized the opportunity to revolt. By 1793 they triumphed, led by former slave Toussaint L'Ouverture. In 1804 they ousted the French, establishing the republic of Haiti. Thousands of whites and mulattos, accompanied by as many slaves as they could transport, sought asylum in the United States.

American political leaders feared the consequences of the refugees' arrival. Southern plantation owners worried that slaves so familiar with ideas of freedom and equality would mingle with their bondspeople. Many were uncomfortable with the immigration of numerous free people of color. Most southern states adopted laws forbidding the entry of Haitian slaves and free mulattos, but they were difficult to enforce, as was a similar congressional act. More than 15,000 refugees—white, black, and of mixed-race origins—flooded into the United States and Spanish Louisiana. Many ended up in Virginia or the cities of Charleston, Savannah, and New Orleans.

In New Orleans and Charleston, the influx of mulattos aroused a heightened color consciousness that placed light-skinned people at the top of a hierarchy of people of color. After the United States purchased Louisiana in 1803, the number of free people of color there almost doubled in three years, largely because of a final surge of immigration from Haiti. In Virginia, the revolt inspired local slaves in 1800 to plan the incident now known as Gabriel's Rebellion.

The Haitian refugees thus linked European and African Americans to events in the West Indies.

A free woman of color in Louisiana early in the nineteenth century, possibly one of the refugees from Haiti. Esteban Rodriguez Miró, named governor of Spanish Louisiana in 1782, ordered all slave and free black women to wear head wraps rather than hats—which were reserved for whites—but this woman and many others subverted his order by nominally complying, but nevertheless creating elaborate headdresses.

(Louisiana State Museum)

Dissent During Wartime

The Quasi-War with France in 1798 and 1799 brought the first attempt to suppress dissent. By criminalizing dissenting speech, the Sedition Act of 1798 tried to quiet Republicans' criticism of the war and President John Adams. Fifteen men (including a congressman) were fined and jailed after being convicted under the statute's provisions.

Although Americans might assume that their right to free speech under the First Amendment, now more fully accepted than two centuries ago, protects dissenters during wartime, history suggests otherwise. Every conflict has stimulated efforts by government and individuals to suppress dissenters. During the Civil War, the Union jailed civilian Confederate sympathizers; during the First World War, the government deported immigrant aliens who too vocally criticized the war effort. World War II brought the silencing of isolationists' voices, denying those who opposed American entry into the war public outlets for their ideas.

Americans remain divided over whether the proper course of action during the Vietnam War of the 1960s and 1970s was dissent from, or acquiescence to, government policy. The USA PATRIOT Act, adopted after the September 11, 2001, attacks, removed long-standing restrictions on federal government surveillance of citizens, controversially granting access to library records. Criticism of the Iraq war has raised heated questions: Do newspapers that publish classified information or pictures of abused prisoners overstep their bounds? Can a political figure censure the conduct of the war without seeming unpatriotic?

Freedom of speech is never easy to maintain, and wartime conditions make it harder. When the nation comes under attack, many patriotic Americans argue that dissent should cease. Others contend that people must always have the right to speak freely. Events in the United States since the 9/11 attacks suggest that this legacy remains contentious for the American people.

Jefferson and Aaron Burr; Federalists named John Adams, with Charles Cotesworth Pinckney of South Carolina as vice president. Jefferson and Burr tied with 73 votes, while Adams had 64 and Pinckney 63. Under Article II, Section 1, of the Constitution, the election had to be decided in the existing House of Representatives.

Balloting continued for six days and thirty-five ballots, with Federalists uniformly supporting Burr, and Republicans holding for Jefferson. Finally, James Bayard, a Federalist and the sole congressman from Delaware, brokered a deal that gave Jefferson the presidency on the thirty-sixth ballot. A crucial consequence of the election was the adoption of the Twelfth Amendment, which provided that electors would henceforth cast separate ballots for president and vice president.

The defeated Federalists turned to strengthening their hold on the judiciary. President Adams named his secretary of state, John Marshall, chief justice; Marshall would serve for thirty-four years, leaving a lasting imprint on constitutional interpretation. Adams spent his last hours in office on March 3, 1801, appointing so-called midnight justices to new positions created in the hastily adopted Judiciary Act of 1801, which also reduced the number of Supreme Court justices from six to five. The fiercely partisan Federalists thus hoped to prevent Jefferson from exerting immediate influence on the judicial branch, despite Republican control of the presidency and Congress.

Summary

The first eleven years of government under the Constitution established many enduring precedents for congressional, presidential, and judicial action—among them the establishment of the cabinet, interpretations of key clauses of the Constitution, and stirrings of judicial review of state and federal legislation. Building on successful negotiations with Spain (Pinckney's Treaty), Britain (the Jay Treaty), and France (the Convention of 1800), the United States developed its diplomatic independence.

Yet the 1790s spawned debates over foreign and domestic policy and saw the beginnings of organized factionalism and grassroots politicking, if not yet formal parties. The Whiskey and Fries Rebellions showed that regional conflicts persisted. The waging of an undeclared war against France proved extremely contentious. In 1801, the Jeffersonian ideal of agrarian, decentralized republicanism prevailed over Alexander Hamilton's vision of a powerful centralized economy and strong national government.

Chapter Review

BUILDING A WORKABLE GOVERNMENT

What was the purpose behind the Bill of Rights?

Even after the Constitution was ratified, leaders recognized that tensions still existed over a strong national government versus. the rights of states. While nationalism prevailed, James Madison and others thought that Congress should not ignore amendments proposed in state ratifying conventions that sought to safeguard the rights of the people. As such, he introduced nineteen amendments—ten of which the states ratified—that were added to the Constitution as the Bill of Rights on December 15, 1791. Adopting the Bill of Rights eased Antifederalist concerns about the unwieldy power of the central government and its potential to tyrannize or oppress the people.

DOMESTIC POLICY UNDER WASHINGTON AND HAMILTON

How did the chartering of the Bank of the United States provoke an early constitutional debate?

Treasury Secretary Alexander Hamilton asked Congress to charter a national bank, modeled on England's, which would act as a collecting and disbursing agent for the treasury and the source for national currency. Congress was unsure if the Constitution gave it the power to set up a bank. Some, like Madison and Jefferson, took a strict-constructionist interpretation of the Constitution, arguing that it allowed Congress only to make laws deemed "necessary"—not merely what was desirable. Hamilton took a broad-constructionist view, stating that Congress could use any means not prohibited by the Constitution to achieve a constitutional end. President Washington agreed, and the bill establishing the Bank of the United States became law.

THE FRENCH REVOLUTION AND THE DEVELOPMENT OF PARTISAN POLITICS

Why did U.S. leaders find the rise of political factions disturbing?

In the new republic, leaders had not yet come to understand or embrace dissent as a natural part of democratic government. Factions were seen as linked to monarchies and deemed a sign of corruption in republics. That explains why Washington tried to smooth over discord when Jefferson and Madison critiqued treasury secretary Alexander Hamilton's policies for favoring commercial interests over agriculture. Both sides accused the other of trying to subvert republican principles or destroy the new republic. Similarly, when dozens of Democratic Societies sprang up in the 1790s to protect people's liberties from corrupt rulers, Washington and Hamilton feared their rapid growth as subversive and dangerous.

PARTISAN POLITICS AND RELATIONS WITH GREAT BRITAIN

What fueled the growing partisanship in the new republic at the end of the eighteenth century?

Several different factors divided people and leaders. Debates over who the true patriots were fueled some discord, as did growing differences between agrarian and commercial interests. Republicans optimistically put their faith in the nation's future prosperity, enticing southerners, small farmers, and artisans to ally with them. Federalists, on the other hand, were often New England merchants who sought order and organized authority. Federalists also thought an ongoing alliance with Great Britain would protect their interests from internal and external enemies.

JOHN ADAMS AND POLITICAL DISSENT

What was the underlying purpose of the Alien and Sedition Acts of 1798?

Adopted by the Federalist-controlled Congress, these acts were designed to suppress dissent—still seen as dangerous and subversive rather than a natural part of a republic—and weaken the competing Republican faction. Hence, the acts targeted recent immigrants, typically Republican supporters, by lengthening the residency requirement for citizenship among other rules, as well as allowing the president to detain or deport any alien considered dangerous to national security. The Sedition Act outlawed antigovernment conspiracies and curbed free speech by making the writing or uttering of false or scandalous statements against the government illegal. Both acts enabled Federalists to weaken, silence, and ultimately indict those with whom they disagreed.

THE WEST IN THE NEW NATION

How did the new nation begin to expand its boundaries westward?

The United States controlled the land east of the Mississippi and north of Spanish Florida, and later, through warfare and treaty, managed to extend its

northernmost boundary to the Ohio River. Initially, leaders attempted to negotiate for the land; when that failed, war with eight Indian nations ensued, culminating in 1795 with the Treaty of Greenville. This agreement allowed the
United States to settle most of what would become Ohio in exchange for ac-
knowledging the principle of Indian sovereignty—by virtue of residence—over
lands that had not been ceded.

"REVOLUTIONS" AT THE END OF THE CENTURY

**What gave rise to new potential revolutions in America at the end
of the eighteenth century?**

Three events revealed unresolved issues—and growing tensions—in the new republic. First, Fries's Rebellion questioned the power of the central government to
tax, seeing it—much as early revolutionaries had—as a threat to personal liberties
and livelihoods. Second, Gabriel's Rebellion of semifree blacks sought to challenge
the slave system in the Chesapeake (but ended up inspiring stricter slave laws in the
South). And finally the hotly contested 1800 presidential election revealed a structural flaw in the Constitution that would need to be addressed for the new nation
to survive. It led to the Twelfth Amendment, which provided that electors cast
separate ballots for presidential and vice presidential candidates.

SUGGESTIONS FOR FURTHER READING

Joyce Appleby, *Capitalism and a New Social Order: The Republican
Vision of the 1790s* (1984)

Douglas Egerton, *Gabriel's Rebellion: The Virginia Slave Conspiracies
of 1800 and 1802* (1993)

Stanley Elkins and Eric McKitrick, *The Age of Federalism,
1788–1800* (1993)

Joseph J. Ellis, *Founding Brothers: The Revolutionary Generation* (2000)

Ronald Hoffman and Peter J. Albert, eds., *Launching the "Extended
Republic": The Federalist Era* (1998)

James Horn, Jan Ellen Lewis, and Peter S. Onuf, eds., *The Revolution of 1800: Democracy, Race, and the New Republic* (2002)

Thomas P. Slaughter, *The Whiskey Rebellion* (1986)

CHAPTER 9

Defining the Nation | 1801–1823

CHAPTER OUTLINE

Political Visions

National Expansion Westward

The Nation in the Orbit of Europe

The War of 1812

LINKS TO THE WORLD:
Industrial Piracy

The Nationalist Program

Sectionalism Exposed

Summary

LEGACY FOR A PEOPLE AND A NATION: States' Rights and Nullification

E ager to stand apart from the allegedly aristocratic ways of his Federalist predecessors, President Thomas Jefferson displayed impatience for ceremony. But on his first New Year's Day in office, he awaited the presentation of a tribute to his commitment, as one gift's bearer put it, to "defend Republicanism and baffle all the arts of Aristocracy." Crafted in Massachusetts, the belated inaugural gift weighed more than twelve hundred pounds and measured four feet in diameter, bearing the inscription "THE GREATEST CHEESE IN AMERICA— FOR THE GREATEST MAN IN AMERICA."

The mammoth cheese was born the previous July and made by the "Ladies" of Cheshire, Massachusetts, a farming community as resolutely Jeffersonian-Republican as it was Baptist. As members of a religious minority in New England, where Congregationalists dominated the pulpits and statehouses, the Cheshire Baptists celebrated a president whose vision featured both agrarianism and separation of church and state.

Federalist editors said the mammoth cheese's semi-rotten, maggot-infested condition on delivery symbolized the nation under Republican rule. Its existence and size resulted from the excesses of democracy, in which even women and backwoods preachers had roles. Federalists' derision of the mammoth cheese may have backfired, inspiring additional showy expressions of democratic pride. A Philadelphia baker sold Mammoth Bread, while in Washington, a Mammoth Eater consumed forty-two eggs in ten minutes. Two years later, in 1804, a mammoth loaf was served in the Capitol building to a crowd of Federalist-disparaging Republicans, including President Jefferson. Behind such symbolism lay serious political ideologies. Jeffersonsians believed that virtue derived from agricultural endeavors. They thus delighted in the acquisition of the Louisiana Territory, but

This icon will direct you to interactive activities and study materials on A People And A Nation, Brief Edition website: **www.cengage.com/history/norton/ peoplenationbrief8e**

Chronology

1801	Marshall becomes chief justice of the United States. Jefferson is inaugurated as first Democratic-Republican president.
1801–05	United States defeats the Barbary states in Tripoli War.
1803	*Marbury v. Madison* establishes judicial review. United States purchases the Louisiana Territory from France.
1804	Burr kills Hamilton in a duel. Jefferson is reelected president, Clinton vice president.
1804–06	Lewis and Clark explore the Louisiana Territory.
1805	Tenskwatawa emerges as a Shawnee leader.
1807	*Chesapeake* affair almost leads to war with Great Britain. Embargo Act halts foreign trade.
1808	Congress bans the importation of slaves to the United States. Madison is elected president, Clinton vice president.
1808–13	Tenskwatawa and Tecumseh organize Native American resistance.
1808–15	Embargoes and the War of 1812 secure American sovereignty and stimulate economic development.
1811	Work begins on the federally financed National Road from Cumberland, Maryland, to Wheeling, Virginia.
1812	Madison is reelected president, Gerry vice president.
1812–15	United States and Great Britain fight the War of 1812.
1813	Death of Tecumseh ends effective pan-Indian resistance. Boston Manufacturing Company starts a textile mill in Waltham, Massachusetts.

1814	Jackson's defeat of the Red Stick Creeks at the Battle of Horseshoe Bend begins Indian removal from the South. Treaty of Ghent ends the War of 1812.
1814–15	Hartford Convention undermines the Federalists.
1815	Battle of New Orleans makes Jackson a national hero. First upriver voyage on the Mississippi River by a steamboat occurs.
1815-17	United States experiences a postwar economic boom and Congress-led economic nationalism.
1817	Rush-Bagot Treaty limits British and American naval forces on Lake Champlain and the Great Lakes.
1817–25	The New York State–funded Erie Canal is constructed.
1819	*McCulloch v. Maryland* establishes the supremacy of federal over state law. Adams-Onís Treaty with Spain gives Florida to the United States and defines the Louisiana territorial border. Missouri applies for statehood with a constitution permitting slavery. Financial panic occurs when the Second Bank of the United States calls in debts.
1819–early 20s	United States undergoes its first major depression.
1820–21	Missouri Compromise lays out the rules governing the admission of future slave states carved from the Louisiana Territory.
1823	Monroe Doctrine declares that European nations should stay out of American affairs and that the United States will stay out of European conflicts that do not occur in the Americas.

efforts to expand their agriculturally based "empire of liberty" westward were resisted by Native Americans and their European allies, and sometimes by Federalists. With the War of 1812, the United States began its expansion west. Although that war ended with few issues resolved, it had profound consequences for American development. It secured the United States' status as a sovereign nation, opened up the West for settlement by European Americans and their slaves, and helped spur revolutions in transportation and industry.

Contemporary observers described postwar nationalism as an Era of Good Feelings, but when economic boom turned to bust, nationalistic optimism and unity faded. No issue proved more divisive than slavery in the West, as Missouri's petition to be admitted to the Union revealed.

- What characterized the two main competing visions for national development?
- How did America's relationship with Europe influence political and economic developments?
- In what ways did nonvoting Americans—most blacks, women, and Native Americans—take part in defining the new nation?

POLITICAL VISIONS

In his inaugural address, Jefferson appealed to the electorate not as party members but as citizens with common beliefs: "We are all republicans, we are all federalists. . . . A wise and frugal government, which shall restrain men from injuring one another, which shall leave them free to regulate their pursuits of industry and improvement, and shall not take from the mouth of labor the bread it had earned. This is the sum of good government."

Outgoing president John Adams had already left Washington and did not hear Jefferson's call for unity. Former friends, the two men now disliked each other intensely. Despite Jefferson's inaugural address, the Democratic-Republicans—as the Republicans of the 1790s called themselves—and the Federalists bitterly differed on how society and government should be organized. The Federalists advocated a strong national government to promote economic development. The Democratic-Republicans believed that limited government would foster republican virtue. Nearly two decades later, Jefferson would refer to his election as "the revolution of 1800."

This portrait of President Thomas Jefferson was painted by Rembrandt Peale in 1805. Charles Willson Peale (Rembrandt's father) and his five sons helped establish the reputation of American art in the new nation. Rembrandt Peale achieved fame for his presidential portraits; here he has captured Jefferson in a noble pose without the usual symbols of office or power, befitting the Republican age. (© Collection of The New-York Historical Society)

Separation of Church and State

In part, the mammoth cheese represented Cheshire farmers' gratitude for Jefferson's commitment to the separation of church and state. A core component of his vision of limited government, Jefferson believed that the Constitution's First Amendment supported a "wall of separation between church and state" and that "religion is a matter which lies solely between Man & his God." New England Baptists hailed Jefferson as a hero, but New England Federalists' worst fears were confirmed. During the election of 1800, Federalists waged a venomous campaign against Jefferson, incorrectly labeling him an atheist. Their rhetoric proved so effective that some New England women hid their Bibles in gardens and wells to foil Democratic-Republicans allegedly bent on confiscating them.

Jefferson took office during a period of religious revivalism, particularly among Methodists and Baptists, whose democratic preaching—all humans, they said, were equal in God's eyes—fed into a growing democratic political culture. Thus, the Cheshire Baptists informed the president that their cheese was made "without a single slave to assist."

Political Mobilization

The revolution of 1800, which gave the Democratic-Republicans majorities in both houses of Congress and the presidency, resulted from an electorate that was limited largely to property-holding men. Under the Constitution, states regulated voting. Nowhere but in New Jersey could women vote, a right granted inadvertently and later revoked. In 1800 free black men who met property qualifications could vote in all states but Delaware, Georgia, South Carolina, and Virginia, but local custom often kept them from exercising that right. Candidates rallied support locally on militia training grounds, in taverns and churches, at court gatherings, and during holiday celebrations. Voters and nonvoters expressed their views by marching in parades, signing petitions, singing, and debating. Perhaps most important, they devoured a growing print culture of pamphlets, broadsides (posters), almanacs, and newspapers.

The Partisan Press

Read aloud in taverns, artisans' workshops, and homes, newspapers gave national importance to local events. In 1800 the nation had 260 newspapers; by 1810 it had 396, virtually all of which were unabashedly partisan.

The parties adopted official organs. After his election, Jefferson persuaded the *National Intelligencer* to move from Philadelphia to Washington, where it became the voice of the Democratic-Republicans. In 1801 Alexander Hamilton launched the *New-York Evening Post* to promote Federalists. Published six or seven times a week, party papers helped feed the growing obsession with partisan politics.

Limited Government

To bring into his administration men who shared his vision of individual liberty, an agrarian republic, and limited government, Jefferson rejected appointments that Adams made during his final days as president and dismissed Federalist customs collectors. He awarded vacant treasury and judicial offices to Republicans. Jefferson, his cabinet, and Congress worked to make the government leaner. If Alexander Hamilton viewed national debt as the engine of economic growth, Jefferson saw it as the source of government corruption. Secretary of the Treasury Albert Gallatin halved the army budget and reduced the 1802 navy budget by two-thirds. He moved to decrease the national debt from $83 million to $57 million, and retire it altogether by 1817. Jefferson closed two of five diplomatic missions abroad, at The Hague and in Berlin. And the Democratic-Republican–controlled Congress oversaw the repeal of all internal taxes, including the despised whiskey tax of 1791.

Along with frugality, ideas of liberty distinguished Democratic-Republicans from Federalists. Opposition to the Alien and Sedition Acts of 1798 united

Republicans. Jefferson now declined to use the acts against opponents and pardoned those convicted under the provisions. Congress let the Sedition Act expire in 1801 and the Alien Act in 1802. Congress also repealed the Naturalization Act of 1798, which required fourteen years of residency for citizenship. The 1802 act that replaced it required five years of residency, loyalty to the Constitution, and the forsaking of foreign allegiances and titles. It would remain the basis of naturalized American citizenship into the twentieth century.

Judicial Politics

To many Democratic-Republicans, the judiciary represented a centralizing and undemocratic force, since judges were appointed rather than elected and served for life. At Jefferson's prompting, the House impeached (indicted) and the Senate convicted Federal District Judge John Pickering of New Hampshire, whose alleged alcoholism made him an easy mark. The House impeached Supreme Court Justice Samuel Chase for judicial misconduct in 1803. A staunch Federalist, Chase pushed for prosecutions under the Sedition Act, campaigned for Adams in 1800, and denounced Jefferson's administration. But Democratic-Republicans failed to muster the two-thirds Senate majority necessary for conviction. The failure to remove Chase preserved the Court's independence and established the precedent that criminal actions, not political disagreements, justified impeachment.

The Marshall Court

Although Jefferson appointed three new Supreme Court justices, the Court remained a Federalist stronghold under his distant cousin John Marshall. Even after Democratic-Republicans achieved a majority of Court seats in 1811, Marshall remained influential as chief justice (1801–1835). Under Marshall, the Supreme Court consistently upheld federal supremacy over the states while protecting the interests of commerce and capital.

Marshall made the Court an equal branch of government. Previously regarded lightly, judicial service became a coveted honor for talented men. Marshall strengthened the Court by having it speak with a unified voice; rather than issuing individual concurring judgments, justices now issued joint majority opinions. From 1801 through 1805, Marshall wrote twenty-four of the Court's twenty-six decisions; through 1810 he wrote 85 percent of the opinions.

Judicial Review

In his last hours in office, Adams named the Federalist William Marbury as justice of the peace in the District of Columbia. Jefferson's secretary of state, James Madison, declined to certify the appointment, so the new president could appoint a Democratic-Republican. Marbury sued for a writ of mandamus (a court order forcing the president to appoint him). If the Supreme Court ruled in Marbury's favor in *Marbury v. Madison,* the president probably would not comply, and the Court had no means to make him. Yet, if the Federalist-dominated bench refused to issue the writ, it would hand the Democratic-Republicans a victory.

Marshall recast the issue to avoid both pitfalls. He ruled that Marbury had a right to his appointment but that the Supreme Court could not compel Madison to honor it because the Constitution did not grant the Court power to issue a writ of mandamus. Without any specific mention in the Constitution, Marshall ruled, the section of the Judiciary Act of 1789 that authorized the Court to issue writs was unconstitutional. Thus the Supreme Court denied itself the power to issue writs of mandamus but established its far greater power to judge the constitutionality of laws. In doing so, Marshall fashioned the theory of judicial review. Because the Constitution was "the supreme law of the land," Marshall wrote, any federal or state act contrary to the Constitution must be null and void. This power of the Supreme Court to determine the constitutionality of legislation and presidential acts enhanced the independence of the judiciary and breathed life into the Constitution.

Election of 1804

In the first election after the Twelfth Amendment's ratification, Jefferson dropped Burr as his running mate and, to have a North-South balance, chose George Clinton of New York. They swamped their opponents—South Carolinian Charles Cotesworth Pinckney and New Yorker Rufus King—in the electoral college by 162 votes to 14, carrying fifteen of the seventeen states.

That 1804 election escalated animosity between Burr and Hamilton, who supported Burr's rival in the New York gubernatorial election. When Hamilton called Burr a liar, Burr challenged him to a duel. Because New York outlawed dueling, the encounter happened in New Jersey. Hamilton decided not to fire, and it cost him his life. New York and New Jersey prosecutors indicted Burr for murder.

Burr fled to the West, where he and Brigadier General James Wilkinson planned to create a new empire by militarily taking what is now Texas and by persuading western territories to leave the United States. Wilkinson, fearful of negative repercussions, revealed the scheme to Jefferson. The president assisted the prosecution in Burr's 1807 trial for treason, which was overseen by Chief Justice Marshall. Prompted by Marshall to use a narrow interpretation of treason, the jury acquitted Burr, who fled to Europe.

NATIONAL EXPANSION WESTWARD

By 1800 hundreds of thousands of white Americans settled in the rich Ohio River and Mississippi River valleys, intruding on Indian lands. In the Northwest they raised foodstuffs, primarily wheat, and in the Southwest they cultivated cotton. During the revolutionary era, cotton production was profitable only for Sea Island planters in South Carolina and Georgia, who grew the long-staple variety. Short-staple cotton, which grew in the interior, was unmarketable because its sticky seeds could be removed only by hand. After the New England inventor Eli Whitney designed a cotton gin in 1793, allowing one person to remove the same number of seeds that previously required fifty people, cultivation of short-staple cotton spread rapidly into Louisiana, Mississippi, Alabama, Arkansas, and Tennessee. The cotton gin greatly increased the demand for slaves, who seeded, tended, and harvested cotton fields.

American settlers depended on free access to the Mississippi River and its Gulf port, New Orleans. "The Mississippi," wrote Secretary of State James Madison, "is to them [western settlers] everything."

Spain, which acquired France's territory west of the Mississippi after the Seven Years' War (1763), secretly transferred it back to France in 1800 and 1801. American officials discovered the transfer only in 1802, when Napoleon seemed poised to re-build a French empire in the New World. American concerns intensified when Spanish officials, on the eve of ceding control to the French, violated Pinckney's treaty by denying Americans the privilege of storing their products at New Orleans prior to transshipment to foreign markets. Western farmers and eastern merchants thought Napoleon had closed the port; they talked war.

To ease the pressure for war and win western farmers' support, Jefferson urged Congress to authorize the call-up of eighty thousand militiamen. He also sent Virginia governor James Monroe to join Robert Livingston in France to buy the port of New Orleans and as much of the Mississippi valley as possible. Arriving in Paris in April 1803, Monroe learned that France had already offered to sell Louisiana to the United States for a mere $15 million. With St. Domingue torn from French control, Napoleon abandoned dreams of a New World empire. He urgently needed money to wage war against Britain. On April 30, Monroe and Livingston signed a treaty buy-ing the 827,000-square-mile territory (see Map 9.1).

The Louisiana Purchase ensured that the United States would control the Mississippi's mouth, pleasing western settlers who relied on the river to market their

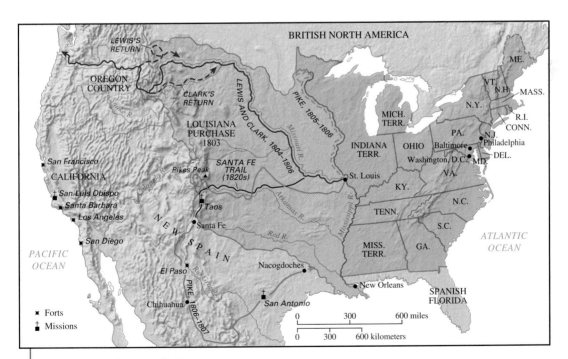

Map 9.1 Louisiana Purchase
The Louisiana Purchase (1803) doubled the area of the United States and opened the trans-Mississippi West for American settlement.

goods. It also inspired those who imagined the United States as the nexus of international trade between Europe and Asia. Louisiana promised to fulfill easterners' dreams of cheap, fertile lands. Its vast expanse meant, too, that land could be reserved for Indians displaced by white settlers and their black slaves. But some doubted the purchase's constitutionality, others worried that it belied the Democratic-Republicans' commitment to debt reduction, and some New England Federalists complained that it undermined their commercial interests and threatened the republic by spreading the population beyond where it could be controlled. Overall, though, the Louisiana Purchase was the most popular achievement of Jefferson's presidency.

Louisiana was not, however, a vast wilderness. When the United States acquired the territory, hundreds of thousands of people living there became American subjects, including Native Americans from various nations, as well as people of European and African descent—or, often, a mixture of the two. Around New Orleans, Louisiana's colonial heritage was reflected in its people: creoles of French and Spanish descent; slaves of African descent; free people of color; and Acadians, or Cajuns (descendants of French settlers in eastern Canada), and some Germans and English. The 1810 census reported that 97,000 non-Indians lived in the area. Although Jefferson imagined the West as an "empire of liberty," the free blacks and slaves lost some rights accorded them under French and Spanish law.

Lewis and Clark Expedition

Jefferson had a long-standing interest in the trans-Mississippi West and feared that, if Americans did not claim it, the British, who still controlled present-day Canada and parts of the Pacific Northwest, would. He launched a military-style mission to chart the region's commercial possibilities—its water passages to the Pacific and trading opportunities with Indians—while cataloguing its geography, flora, and fauna.

The expedition, headed by Meriwether Lewis and William Clark, began in May 1804 and lasted for more than two years; it traveled up the Missouri River, across the Rockies, and down the Columbia to the Pacific Ocean—and back. Expedition's members "discovered" (as they saw it) dozens of previously unknown Indian tribes. Although the Corps of Discovery, as the expedition came to be called, was prepared for possible Indian conflict, its goal was peaceable: to foster trade relations, win political allies, and tap into Indians' knowledge of the landscape. Lewis and Clark brought twenty-one bags of gifts for Native American leaders to establish goodwill and stimulate interest in trade. Most interactions were cordial, but when Indians were unimpressed by the gifts, tensions arose.

The Corps of Discovery proved democratic in seating enlisted men on courts-martial and allowing Clark's black slave York and the expedition's female guide and translator, Sacagawea, to vote on where to locate winter quarters in 1805. But, unlike other expedition members, neither York nor Sacagawea drew wages, and when York later demanded his freedom, Clark later wrote to his brother that he gave York "a severe trouncing."

Lewis and Clark failed to discover a Northwest Passage to the Pacific, and the route they mapped across the Rockies proved perilous. But their expedition set the stage for additional government-sponsored exploration.

In their quest for land, white Americans mostly ignored the presence of Native Americans. Although Jefferson displayed more sympathy toward Indians than did many contemporaries—he took interest in their cultures and believed them intellectually equal to whites—he lobbied, unsuccessfully, for a constitutional amendment that would transport them west of the Mississippi into the Louisiana Territory. He became involved in efforts to pressure the Chickasaws to sell their land, and if legal methods failed, he advocated trickery. Traders, he suggested, might run them into debt, which they would have to repay "by a cessation of lands."

Divisions Among Indian Peoples

Some Indian nations adopted white customs as a means of survival and often agreed to sell their lands and move west. These "accommodationists" (or "progressives") were opposed by "traditionalists," who urged adherence to native ways and refused to relinquish their lands. Distinctions between accommodationists and traditionalists were not always so clear-cut, however.

In the early 1800s, two Shawnee brothers, Tenskwatawa (1775–1837) and Tecumseh (1768–1813), led a traditionalist revolt against American encroachment by fostering a pan-Indian federation centered in the Old Northwest and parts of the South. By the 1800s, the Shawnees lost most of their Ohio land, occupying scattered sites there and in the Michigan and Louisiana territories. Despondent, Lalawethika—Tenskwatawa's name as a youth—turned to whiskey and later became a shaman in 1804. When European diseases ravaged his village, he despaired.

Tenskwatawa and Tecumseh

Lalawethika emerged from a battle with illness in 1805 a new man, renamed Tenskwatawa ("The Open Door") or, by whites, the Prophet. Claiming to have died and been resurrected, he traveled in the Ohio River valley as a religious leader, attacking the decline of moral values among Native Americans, warning against whiskey, and condemning intertribal battles. He urged Indians to return to the old ways: to hunt with bows and arrows, not guns; to stop wearing hats; and to give up bread for corn and beans.

By 1808 Tenskwatawa and his older brother Tecumseh talked more about resisting American aggression. They invited all Indians to settle in pan-Indian towns in Indiana, first at Greenville (1806–1808) and then at Prophetstown (1808–1812). This challenged the treaty-making process by denying the claims of Indians who were given the same land under the 1795 Treaty of Greenville. Younger Indians flocked to Tecumseh, the more political of the two brothers.

Convinced that only an Indian federation could stop increasing white settlement, Tecumseh sought to unify northern and southern Indians from Canada to Georgia. Among southern Indians, only one Creek faction welcomed him, but his efforts nonetheless alarmed white settlers and government officials. In November 1811, while Tecumseh was in the South, the Indiana governor William Henry Harrison moved against Tenskwatawa's followers. During the battle of Tippecanoe, the army burned their town; as they fled, the Indians exacted revenge on white settlers. With the stakes raised, Tecumseh entered an alliance with the British. This alliance, along with American neutrality rights on the high seas, propelled the United States toward war with Britain.

THE NATION IN THE ORBIT OF EUROPE

The republic's economy relied heavily on fishing and the carrying trade, in which the American merchant marine transported commodities between nations. Merchants in Boston, Salem, and Philadelphia traded with China, sending cloth and metal to swap for furs with Chinook Indians on the Oregon coast, and then sailing to China to trade for porcelain, tea, and silk. The slave trade lured American ships to Africa. Not long after Jefferson's first inaugural address, the United States was at war with Tripoli—a state along North Africa's Barbary Coast—over a principle that would become a cornerstone of American foreign policy: freedom of the seas. That is, outside national territorial waters, the high seas should be open for free transit.

First Barbary War In 1801 the bashaw (pasha) of Tripoli declared war on the United States for refusing to pay tribute for safe passage of its ships through the Mediterranean. After two years of stalemate, Jefferson declared a blockade of Tripoli, but when the American frigate *Philadelphia* ran aground in the harbor, its three hundred officers and sailors were imprisoned. Jefferson refused to ransom them, and a small American force accompanied by Arab, Greek, and African mercenaries marched from Egypt to the shores of Tripoli to seize the port of Derne. A treaty ended the war in 1805, but the United States continued to pay tribute to three other Barbary states—Algiers, Morocco, and Tunis—until 1815. In the intervening years, the United States became embroiled in European conflicts.

At first Jefferson distanced the nation from the European turmoil in the wake of the French Revolution. After the Senate ratified the Jay Treaty in 1795, the United States and Great Britain reconciled: Britain withdrew from its western forts on American soil and interfered less in American trade with France. Then, in May 1803, two weeks after Napoleon sold Louisiana to the United States, France was at war against Britain and, later, Britain's allies, Prussia, Austria, and Russia. The United States initially benefited as merchants gained control of most of the West Indian trade. After 1805, however, when Britain defeated French and Spanish fleets at Trafalgar, Britain's Royal Navy tightened its control of the oceans. Two months later, Napoleon crushed the Russian and Austrian armies at Austerlitz. Stalemated, France and Britain launched a commercial war, blockading trade and costing the United States dearly.

Threats to American Sovereignty To replenish their supply of sailors, British vessels stopped American ships and impressed (forcibly recruited) British deserters, British-born naturalized American seamen, and other sailors suspected of being British. Perhaps six to eight thousand Americans were seized between 1803 and 1812. Alleged deserters—many of them American citizens—faced British courts-martial. Americans saw impressment as an assault on their nation's independence. Americans also resented the British interfering with their West Indian trade and seizing American vessels within U.S. territorial waters.

In April 1806 Congress responded with the Non-Importation Act, barring British manufactured goods from American ports. Because the act exempted most cloth and metal articles, it had little impact on British trade. In November Jefferson suspended the act while the Baltimore lawyer William Pinkney joined James Monroe in London to negotiate a settlement. The treaty they carried home did not mention impressments; hence, the president never submitted it for ratification.

Tense Anglo-American relations came to a head in June 1807 when the USS *Chesapeake*, sailing from Norfolk for the Mediterranean, was stopped by the British frigate *Leopard*, whose officers demanded to search the ship. Refused, the *Leopard* opened fire, killing three Americans and wounding eighteen others. The British then seized four deserters, three of whom held American citizenship; one was hanged. The incident outraged Americans and exposed American military weakness.

The Embargo of 1807

With poor military preparedness, Jefferson responded to the incident with what he called peaceable coercion. In July, the president closed American waters to British warships and increased military and naval expenditures. In December 1807, Jefferson increased economic pressure on Great Britain by invoking the Non-Importation Act, followed by the Embargo Act. The embargo, which forbade all exports from the United States to any country, was designed as a short-term means to avoid war by pressuring Britain and France to respect American rights.

The embargo's biggest economic impact, however, fell on the United States. Exports declined by 80 percent in 1808, squeezing New England shippers and their workers as economic depression set in. Manufacturers fared well as the domestic market became theirs exclusively. Merchants began to shift from shipping to manufacturing. In 1807 there were twenty cotton and woolen mills in New England; by 1813 there were more than two hundred. Merchants willing to engage in smuggling profited enormously.

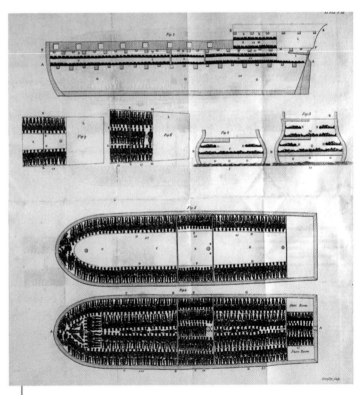

In an effort to win support for measures to end the international slave trade and slavery itself, abolitionists published drawings of the inhumanely cramped slave ships, where each person was allotted a space roughly the size of a coffin. Disease spread rapidly under such conditions, causing many slaves to die before reaching American shores. (The Huntington Library and Art Collections, San Marino, California)

International Slave Trade

With Jefferson's encouragement, Congress voted in 1807 to abolish the international slave trade as of January 1, 1808—the earliest date permissible under the Constitution. South Carolina alone still allowed the legal importation of slaves, but most of the state's planters favored a ban, fearful of adding to the black population of a state where whites were outnumbered. Congressional debate focused on what should become of Africans imported illegally.

The final bill provided that smuggled slaves would be sold in accordance with the laws of the state or territory in which they arrived, underscoring that even illegal slaves were property. Had the bill not done so, threatened one Georgia congressman, the result might have been "resistance to the authority of the Government," even civil war.

During the last four months of 1807, sixteen thousand African slaves arrived at Gadsden Wharf in Charleston, where they were detained by merchants eager to wait out the new law's January 1 deadline and net higher prices for their human cargo. Although possibly thousands died in the disease-ridden holding pens before they could be sold, merchants calculated that the increased value of those who survived would outweigh losses. After January 1, 1808, a brisk—and profitable—illegal slave trade took over. In 1819 Congress authorized the president to use force to intercept slave ships along the African coast, but the small American navy could not halt the illicit trade.

Election of 1808

As the 1808 presidential election approached, debate over the embargo heated up. Democratic-Republicans suffered from factional dissent and dissatisfaction in seaboard states hobbled by the trade restrictions. Although nine state legislatures passed resolutions urging Jefferson to run again, the president declined a third term. He supported James Madison, his secretary of state, as the Democratic-Republican candidate. Madison won the endorsement of the party's congressional caucus, and Madison and Clinton headed the ticket. Charles Cotesworth Pinckney and Rufus King again ran on the Federalist ticket.

The younger Federalists, led by Harrison Gray Otis and other Bostonians, played up the widespread disaffection with Democratic-Republican policy, especially the embargo. Pinckney received only forty-seven electoral votes to Madison's 122, but he carried all of New England, except Vermont, and won Delaware. Federalists also gained seats in Congress and captured the New York State legislature. Still, the transition from one Democratic-Republican administration to the next went smoothly.

Women and Politics

Wives eased the transition of newly elected and appointed officials by encouraging political and diplomatic negotiation. This often occurred in social settings, even private homes. As such, personal relationships helped people with divergent interests bridge their ideological divides. Women fostered conversation, providing an ear or a voice for unofficial messages and—in the case of international affairs—standing as surrogates for their nation. Wives' interactions among themselves served political purposes, too: when First Lady Dolley Madison visited congressmen's wives, she cultivated goodwill for her husband while collecting recipes so she could serve regional cuisine at White House functions.

Jeffersonians appealed for women's support of their embargo. Sympathetic women responded by spurning imported fabric and making (or directing their slaves to make) homespun clothing. Federalists, however, encouraged women to keep commerce alive, and sympathetic women bought smuggled goods.

Failed Policies

Under intense domestic opposition, the embargo collapsed. Instead, the Non-Intercourse Act of 1809 reopened trade with all nations except Britain and France and authorized the president to resume trade with those nations once they respected American neutrality rights. In June 1809, President Madison reopened trade with Britain after its minister offered assurances that Britain would repeal restrictions on American trade. His Majesty's government in London, though, repudiated the minister's assurances, and Madison reverted to nonintercourse.

When the Non-Intercourse Act expired in 1810, Congressed substituted Macon's Bill Number 2, which reopened trade with Great Britain and France but provided that, when one nation stopped violating American commercial rights, the president would suspend American commerce with the other. When Napoleon accepted, Madison declared nonintercourse on Great Britain in 1811. Although the French continued to seize American ships, Britain became the focus of American hostility because it dominated the seas.

In spring 1812, the British admiralty ordered its ships not to stop, search, or seize American warships, and in June Britain reopened the seas to American shipping. But before word of this policy change reached America, Congress declared war.

Mr. Madison's War

The House voted 79 to 49 for war; the Senate, 19 to 13. Democratic-Republicans favored war by 98 to 23; Federalists opposed it 39 to 0. Those who favored war, including President Madison, pointed to impressment, violation of neutral trading rights, British alliances with western Indians, and affronts to American independence. Others saw an opportunity to annex British Canada. Most militants were land-hungry southerners and westerners—the War Hawks—led by John C. Calhoun of South Carolina and first-term congressman and House Speaker Henry Clay of Kentucky. Most representatives from the coastal states, especially the Northeast, feared trade disruption and opposed Mr. Madison's War.

Federalists benefited from antiwar sentiment about the War of 1812. They joined renegade Democratic-Republicans in supporting New York City mayor DeWitt Clinton for president in 1812. Clinton lost to Madison by 128 to 89 electoral votes, but Federalists gained some congressional seats and carried many local elections. The pro-war South and the West remained solidly Democratic-Republican.

THE WAR OF 1812

The War of 1812 lasted until 1815, unfolding in skirmishes for which the U.S. armed forces, kept lean by Jeffersonian fiscal policies, were ill prepared. Officers executed campaigns poorly, and the U.S. Navy was no match for the Royal Navy. By 1812 the ten-year-old U.S. Military Academy at West Point produced only eighty-nine regular officers. Senior army officers were aged Revolutionary War veterans or political appointees.

The government's efforts to lure recruits—with sign-up bonuses and promises of three months' pay and rights to purchase 160 acres of western land—met with mixed success. At first, recruitment went well among westerners, motivated by the desire for land, strong anti-Indian sentiment, and fears of Tecumseh's pan-Indian organization. But with pay delays and inadequate supplies, recruitment dwindled. In New England, Federalists discouraged enlistments. Militias in New England and New York often refused to fight outside their own states. Desperate, New York offered freedom to slaves who enlisted, and compensation to their owners, and the U.S. Army made the same offer to slaves in the Old Northwest and Canada. But in the Deep South, fear of arming slaves kept them out of the military except in New Orleans, where a free black militia dated back to the Spanish. The British recruited slaves by promising freedom in exchange for service. In the end, British forces outnumbered American.

Invasion of Canada

Still, Americans expected to take Canada easily. Canada's population was sparse, its army small, and the Great Lakes inaccessible to the Royal Navy. American strategy aimed to split Canadian forces and isolate pro-British Indians, especially Tecumseh, to whom the British promised an Indian nation in the Great Lakes. In July 1812, the U.S. general William Hull, territorial governor of Michigan, marched his troops into Upper Canada. Although his forces outnumbered the British, Hull retreated more than he attacked. He abandoned Mackinac Island and Fort Dearborn and surrendered Fort Detroit, leaving the Midwest exposed. The only bright spot was the September 1812 defense of Fort Harrison in Indiana Territory by Captain Zachary Taylor, who secured the first American land victory. By winter 1812–1813, the British controlled about half of the Old Northwest.

Naval Battles

Despite victories on the Atlantic by the USS *Constitution* (nicknamed Old Ironsides), the USS *Wasp*, and the USS *United States*, the American navy—which began the war with just seventeen ships—could not match the powerful Royal Navy. By 1814, the Royal Navy blockaded nearly all American ports along the Atlantic and Gulf coasts. After 1811, American trade overseas declined by nearly 90 percent, and the loss of customs duties threatened to bankrupt the federal government and prostrate New England.

The contest over the Great Lakes, the key to the war in the Northwest, evolved as a shipbuilding race. Under Master Commandant Oliver Hazard Perry and the shipbuilder Noah Brown, the United States outbuilt the British on Lake Erie and defeated them at the bloody Battle of Put-in-Bay on September 10, 1813, gaining control of Lake Erie.

Burning Capitals

A ragged group of Kentucky militia volunteers, armed with swords and knives, marched 20 to 30 miles a day to join General William Henry Harrison's forces in Ohio. Now 4,500 strong, Harrison's force took Detroit before crossing into Canada, where at the Battle of the Thames they defeated British, Shawnee, and Chippewa forces in October 1813. Among the fallen was Tecumseh. The Americans then razed the Canadian capital of York (now Toronto).

After defeating Napoleon in Europe in April 1814, the British launched a land counteroffensive against the United States, concentrating on Chesapeake Bay. Royal troops occupied Washington, D.C., in August and set it ablaze, leaving the presidential mansion and parts of the city burning all night. The president and cabinet fled. Dolley Madison stayed to oversee the removal of cabinet documents and save a Gilbert Stuart portrait of George Washington.

The British intended the attack as a diversion. The major battle occurred in September 1814 at Baltimore, where Americans held firm. Francis Scott Key, detained on a British ship, watched the bombardment of Fort McHenry and wrote "The Star-Spangled Banner" (which became the national anthem in 1931). The British inflicted heavy damage, but achieved little militarily; their offensive on Lake Champlain also failed. The war reached a stalemate.

War in the Old Southwest

The war's final campaign began with an American attack on the Red Stick Creeks along the Gulf of Mexico and the British around New Orleans. Responding to Tecumseh's call to resist U.S. expansion, in 1813 the Red Sticks attacked Fort Mims, outside Mobile, killing hundreds of white men, women, and children. General Andrew Jackson of Tennessee rallied his militiamen and Indian opponents of the Red Sticks and crushed the Red Sticks at Horseshoe Bend (in present-day Alabama) in March 1814. In the 1814 Treaty of Fort Jackson, the Creeks ceded 23 million acres, about half of their holdings, and withdrew to the southern and western part of Mississippi Territory.

Jackson became a major general, and after seizing Pensacola (in Spanish Florida) and then securing Mobile, Jackson's forces continued to New Orleans. Three weeks later, on January 8, 1815, Jackson's poorly trained army held its ground against two British frontal assaults. At day's end, more than two thousand British soldiers lay dead or wounded, while Americans suffered only twenty-one casualties.

The Battle of New Orleans occurred two weeks after the war's official conclusion: word had not reached the United States that British and American diplomats signed the Treaty of Ghent on December 24, 1814. Still, the Battle of New Orleans catapulted General Andrew Jackson to national prominence.

Treaty of Ghent

The Treaty of Ghent essentially restored the prewar status quo. It provided for an end to hostilities, release of prisoners,

Americans rejoiced that the War of 1812 had reaffirmed their independence from the British monarchy. The sailor's foot here steps on the crown while broken chains of bondage lie nearby. (Picture Research Consultants and Archives)

restoration of conquered territory, and arbitration of boundary disputes. But the United States received no satisfaction on impressment, blockades, or maritime rights for neutrals, and British demands for territorial cessions from Maine to Minnesota went unmet. The British dropped their promise of an independent Indian nation.

Napoleon's defeat allowed the United States to discard its prewar demands, because peace in Europe made impressment and interference with American commerce moot issues. Similarly, war-weary Britain—its treasury nearly depleted—stopped pressing for military victory.

American Sovereignty Reasserted

The War of 1812 affirmed the independence of the American republic and ensured Canada's independence from the United States. Although conflict with Great Britain over trade and territory continued, it never again led to war. The return of peace with Europe also allowed the United States to again focus on the Barbary Coast, where the dey (governor) of Algiers declared war on the United States. In the Second Barbary War, U.S. forces held hundreds of Algerians captive while negotiating a treaty in summer 1815 that forever freed the United States from paying tributes for passage in the Mediterranean. The Second Barbary War reaffirmed America's commitment to freedom of the seas.

Domestic Consequences

With its economy shattered and the War of 1812 stalemated, New England delegates met in Hartford, Connecticut, for three weeks in winter 1814–1815 to discuss revising the national compact or pulling out of the republic. Moderates prevented a resolution of secession—withdrawal from the Union—but delegates condemned the war and the embargo while endorsing constitutional changes to weaken the South and make it harder to declare war. When news arrived of Jackson's New Orleans victory and the Treaty of Ghent, the Hartford Convention made the Federalists look wrong, if not treasonous. By the 1820s, the party faded from the national scene.

With Tecumseh's death, midwestern Indians lost their powerful political and military leader; with the British withdrawal, they lost their strongest ally. Some accommodationists, such as the Cherokees, temporarily flourished in the war's aftermath, but it disarmed traditionalists bent on resisting American expansion. Although the Treaty of Ghent pledged the United States to end hostilities with Indians and restore their prewar "possessions, rights, and privileges," Indians lacked the power to make the United States honor the agreement.

The war's end accelerated three trends that would dominate future decades: westward expansion, industrial takeoff, and the entrenchment of slavery. It opened vast tracts of formerly Indian land for American cotton cultivation in the Old Southwest and for growing wheat in the Old Northwest. The war also stimulated industry as Americans could no longer rely on overseas imports, particularly textiles. The War of 1812 thus fueled the demand for raw cotton, and the newly acquired lands in the Southwest beckoned southerners who migrated either with slaves or with expectations of someday owning slaves.

Industrial Piracy

Great Britain, which in the late eighteenth century pioneered mechanical weaving and power looms, knew the value of its head start in the industrial revolution and prohibited the export of textile technology. But the British-born brothers Samuel and John Slater, their Scottish-born power-loom-builder William Gilmore, and the Bostonians Francis Cabot Lowell and Nathan Appleton evaded British restrictions to establish America's first textile factories.

As an apprentice and then supervisor in a British cotton-spinning factory, Samuel Slater mastered the machinery and the process. To get around British technology laws, Slater emigrated to the United States disguised as a farmer. In 1790 in Pawtucket, Rhode Island, he opened the first water-powered spinning mill in America, rebuilding the machines from memory. With his brother John and Rhode Island partners Moses and Obadiah Brown and William Almy, Slater later built mills in Rhode Island and Massachusetts. In 1815 he hired the recent immigrant William Gilmore to build a water-powered loom like those in Britain. In the 1820s, the Slaters introduced British steam-powered looms.

In 1810, while vacationing in Edinburgh, Scotland, Francis Cabot Lowell met fellow Bostonian Nathan Appleton. Impressed by the British textile mills, they planned to introduce water-powered mechanical weaving into the United States. Lowell went to Britain's textile center in Manchester, visiting and observing the factories by day. At night he sketched from memory the power looms and processes he viewed. Back in the United States, he and others formed the Boston Associates, which created the Waltham-Lowell Mills based on Lowell's industrial piracy. Within a few years, textiles would be a major American industry, and the Boston Associates would dominate it.

Thus the modern American industrial revolution began with international links, not homegrown inventions.

This contemporary painting shows the Boston Manufacturing Company's 1814 textile factory at Waltham, Massachusetts. All manufacturing processes were brought together under one roof, and the company built its first factories in rural New England to tap roaring rivers as a power source.
(Gore Place Society, Waltham, Massachusetts)

THE NATIONALIST PROGRAM

In his last year as president, James Madison and the Democratic-Republicans absorbed the Federalist idea that the federal government should encourage economic growth. His agenda, which Henry Clay later called the American System, included a national bank, improved transportation, and a protective tariff—a tax on imported goods to protect American manufacturers from foreign competition. Yet true to his Jeffersonian roots, Madison argued that only a constitutional amendment could authorize the federal government to build local roads and canals.

American System

Clay and other congressional leaders, such as Calhoun of South Carolina, thought the American System would unify the expanding nation, bridging sectional divides. The tariff would stimulate New England industry; those goods would find markets in the South and West. Agricultural products of the South and West—cotton and foodstuffs—would feed New England mills and workers. Manufactured and agricultural products would move along roads and canals which tariff revenues would fund. A national bank would handle the transactions.

In 1816 Congress chartered the Second Bank of the United States (the first bank's charter expired in 1811) to serve as a depository for federal funds and to issue currency, collect taxes, and pay government debts. The Second Bank was responsible, too, for overseeing state and local banks, ensuring that their paper money had backing in specie (precious metals). Like its predecessor, the bank mixed public and private ownership; the government provided one-fifth of the bank's capital and appointed one-fifth of its directors.

Congress also passed the Tariff of 1816, which taxed imported woolens and cottons, iron, leather, hats, paper, and sugar. The tariff divided rather than unified the nation. New England and the western and Middle Atlantic states would benefit from it and so supported it, whereas the southern states would face increased prices on goods they purchased and the possibility that Britain would retaliate with a tariff on cotton and so opposed it.

Southerners such as Calhoun promoted roads and canals to "bind the republic together." However, on March 3, 1817, the day before he left office, President Madison, citing constitutional scruples, vetoed Calhoun's Bonus Bill, which would have authorized federal funding for such public works.

Early Internal Improvements

Federalists and Democratic-Republicans agreed that internal improvements would promote prosperity. Federalists saw roads and canals as a way to spur the nation's commercial development; Jeffersonians, as the route to western expansion and agrarian growth. In 1806 Congress passed (and Jefferson signed into law) a bill authorizing federal funding for the Cumberland Road (later, the National Road) running between Cumberland, Maryland, and Wheeling, Virginia (now West Virginia). In 1820 Congress authorized a survey for the National Road to Columbus, Ohio, which was funded in 1825 and completed in 1833.

Most transportation initiatives were funded by states, private investors, or both. In 1817 New York began construction on the Erie Canal, linking the Great Lakes to the Atlantic seaboard; it was completed in 1825. The South relied mostly on rivergoing steamboats that dominated river trade following Robert Fulton's successful trial of a steam-powered vessel in 1807. By 1817, steamboats made regular trips on the Mississippi. Canals and steamboats greatly reduced the time and cost of transporting western agricultural products to market and fueled westward expansion. Canals expanded commercial networks into regions without natural waterways and would reorient midwestern commerce through the North.

The Era of Good Feelings

Madison's successor, James Monroe, was the third Virginian elected president since 1801. A former senator and twice governor of Virginia, he served under Madison as secretary of state and of war and used his association with Jefferson and Madison to attain the presidency. In 1816 he and his running mate, Daniel Tompkins, trounced the last Federalist presidential nominee, Rufus King, garnering all the electoral votes except those of Federalist strongholds Massachusetts, Connecticut, and Delaware. A Boston newspaper dubbed this one-party period the Era of Good Feelings.

Led by Federalist chief justice John Marshall, the Supreme Court became the bulwark of the nationalist point of view. In *McCulloch v. Maryland* (1819), the Court struck down a Maryland law taxing banks that were not chartered by the Maryland legislature—a law aimed at hindering the Baltimore branch of the Second Bank of the United States. At issue was state versus federal jurisdiction. Writing for a unanimous Court, Marshall asserted the supremacy of the federal government over the states. The Court also unanimously ruled that Congress had the power to charter banks. The Marshall Court thus provided a bulwark for the Federalist view that the federal government could promote interstate commerce.

Government Promotion of Market Expansion

Later Supreme Court cases validated government promotion of economic development and encouraged business enterprise. In *Gibbons v. Ogden* (1824), the Supreme Court overturned the New York law that granted Robert Fulton and Robert Livingston a monopoly on the New York–New Jersey steamboat trade. Chief Justice John Marshall ruled that the federal power to license new enterprises took precedence over New York's grant of monopoly rights and declared that Congress's power under the commerce clause of the Constitution extended to "every species of commercial intercourse." Within two years, the number of steamboats in New York increased from six to forty-three. A later ruling under Chief Justice Roger Taney, *Charles River Bridge v. Warren Bridge* (1837), encouraged new enterprises and technologies by favoring competition over monopoly.

Federal and state courts, in conjunction with state legislatures, also encouraged the proliferation of corporations—organizations holding property and transacting business as if they were individuals. Corporation owners, called shareholders, were granted limited liability, or freedom from personal responsibility for the company's debts beyond their original investment. The government assisted commercial development by expanding the number of U.S. post offices from three thousand in 1815 to fourteen thousand in 1845 and by protecting inventions and domestic industries. Patent laws gave inventors a seventeen-year monopoly on their inventions, and tariffs protected American industry from foreign competition.

Boundary Settlements Monroe's secretary of state, John Quincy Adams, managed foreign policy from 1817 to 1825, stubbornly pushing for expansion, American fishing rights in Atlantic waters, political distance from Europe, and peace. An ardent expansionist, this son of John and Abigail Adams believed that newly acquired territories must come via negotiations, not war, and must bar slavery.

Under Adams's leadership, in 1817 the United States and Great Britain signed the Rush-Bagot Treaty, limiting them to one naval ship each on Lake Champlain and Lake Ontario, and to two ships each on the remaining Great Lakes. This first modern disarmament treaty led to the demilitarization of the United States-Canada border. Adams then pushed for the Convention of 1818, which fixed the U.S.-Canadian boundary from Lake of the Woods in Minnesota westward to the Rockies along the 49th parallel. When they could not agree on the boundary west of the Rockies, the two countries settled on joint occupation of Oregon for ten years (renewed indefinitely in 1827).

Adams's negotiations acquired Florida for the United States. Although the Louisiana Purchase omitted reference to Spanish-ruled West Florida, the United States claimed the territory as far east as the Perdido River (the present-day Florida-Alabama border). During the War of 1812, the United States seized Mobile and the remainder of West Florida, and after the war, Adams claimed East Florida. In 1819 Don Luís de Onís, the Spanish minister to the United States, agreed to cede Florida without payment if the United States renounced its dubious claims to northern Mexico (Texas) and assumed $5 million of claims by American citizens against Spain. The Adams-Onís (or Transcontinental) Treaty also defined the southwestern boundary of the Louisiana Purchase and set the line between Spanish Mexico and Oregon Country at the 42nd parallel.

But Adams's greatest achievement was the Monroe Doctrine. Between 1808 and 1822, the United Provinces of Río de la Plata (present-day northern Argentina, Paraguay, and Uruguay), Chile, Peru, Colombia, and Mexico broke from Spain. In 1822, the United States became the first nation outside Latin America to recognize the new states. But with reactionary regimes ascending in Europe and France now occupying Spain, the United States feared that continental powers would attempt to return the Latin American states to colonial rule.

Monroe Doctrine Monroe's message to Congress in December 1823 became known as the Monroe Doctrine. He announced that the American continents "are henceforth not to be considered subjects for future colonization by any European power." This addressed American anxiety about Latin America and Russian expansion beyond Alaska and its settlements in California. Monroe demanded nonintervention by Europe in the affairs of independent New World nations, and he pledged U.S. noninterference in European affairs, including Europe's existing New World colonies. European nations stayed out of New World affairs because they feared the British Royal Navy, not the United States' proclamations.

SECTIONALISM EXPOSED

The embargo, the War of 1812, and postwar internal improvements helped southern and northern economies develop in different but interrelated ways. While the South would become more dependent on cotton, the North saw an acceleration of industrial development. Although Jeffersonians did not promote industry, a few entrepreneurs did.

Early Industrial Development

Americans relied on British technology to combine the many steps of textile manufacturing—carding (or disentangling) fibers, spinning yarn, and weaving cloth—in one factory. The first American water-powered spinning mill was established in 1790 by Samuel Slater, a British immigrant who reconstructed from memory the complex machines he used in England. But Slater's mill only carded and spun yarn; handweaving it into cloth was often done by farm women seeking extra cash. In 1810 the Bostonian Francis Cabot Lowell visited the British textile center of Manchester, touring factories and later sketching what he had seen. In 1813 he and his business associates founded the Boston Manufacturing Company, uniting all textile manufacturing phases under one roof in Waltham, Massachusetts. A decade later, the Boston Manufacturing Company established a model industrial village—named for its then-deceased founder—along the banks of the Merrimack River. At Lowell, Massachusetts, there would be boarding houses for workers, a healthy alternative to Manchester's tenements and slums.

When the British flooded America with cheap textiles after the War of 1812, Lowell realized the domestic market required protection. He lobbied hard to include cotton textiles in the Tariff of 1816, helping persuade reluctant South Carolinians to support it.

The growth of northern industry was linked to slavery. Much of the capital behind early industrialization came from merchants who partly made their fortunes through the slave trade. Two of the most prominent industries—textiles and shoes—expanded with a growing southern cotton economy. Southern cotton fed northern textile mills, and northern shoe factories sold "Negro brogans" (work shoes) to southern planters.

Panic of 1819

Immediately after the war, the international demand for (and price of) American commodities reached new heights. Poor weather in Europe led to crop failures, which sparked the demand for northern agricultural exports and the South's raw cotton. The demand for American wheat and cotton touched off western land speculation. Speculators raced to buy large tracts of land at modest, government prices and then resell them at a hefty profit to settlers.

Prosperity proved short-lived. By the late 1810s Europeans could grow their own food, and Britain's new Corn Laws established high tariffs on imported foodstuffs—lessening the demand for American agricultural exports. Cotton prices fell in England. Wars in Latin America interfered with mining and reduced the supply of precious metals. European nations hoarded specie; in response, American banks printed paper money and expanded credit. Fearful of inflation, the Second Bank of the United States demanded in 1819 that state banks repay loans in specie. State banks called in the loans and mortgages they made to individuals and companies. Falling prices meant farmers could not pay their mortgages, and plummeting land values—from 50 to 75 percent in portions of the West—meant they could not meet their debts even by selling their farms. The nation's banking system collapsed, triggering a financial panic.

Foreclosures soared. Unemployment skyrocketed, reaching 75 percent in Philadelphia. Workers and their families often could not make it through the winter without charity for food, clothing, and firewood.

Americans everywhere contemplated the virtues and hazards of rapid market expansion, disagreeing on what to blame for its shortcomings. Even as the nation's economy rebounded in the early 1820s, amid a flurry of internal improvement projects, no one could predict in what region or sector the nation's fortunes would lie.

Missouri Compromise

The nation also faced a political crisis in 1819 about slavery's westward expansion. Residents of the Missouri Territory petitioned Congress for admission to the Union with a constitution permitting slavery. Missouri's admission would give slaveholding states a two-vote majority in the Senate and would surely set a precedent for new western states created from the vast Louisiana Purchase. After the War of 1812, the American population surged westward, leading five new states to join the Union: Louisiana (1812), Indiana (1816), Mississippi (1817), Illinois (1818), and Alabama (1819). Of these, Louisiana, Mississippi, and Alabama permitted slavery. Because Missouri was on the same latitude as free Illinois, Indiana, and Ohio, its admission as a slave state would thrust slavery farther northward.

For two and a half years the issue dominated Congress. When Representative James Tallmadge Jr. of New York proposed gradual emancipation in Missouri, some southerners accused the North of threatening to destroy the Union. The House, which had a northern majority, passed the Tallmadge Amendment, but the Senate rejected it.

House Speaker Henry Clay—himself a western slaveholder—suggested a compromise in 1820. Maine, carved out of Massachusetts, would enter as a free state, followed by Missouri as a slave state, maintaining the balance between slave and free states. In the rest of the Louisiana Territory north of Missouri's southern border of 36°30′, slavery would be prohibited forever (see Map 9.2). Thus, the compromise divided the United States into northern and southern regions.

The compromise carried but almost unraveled when Missouri submitted a constitution barring free blacks from entering the state. Opponents contended it violated the federal constitutional provision that citizens of each state were "entitled to all privileges and immunities of citizens in the several States." Proponents countered that many states already barred free blacks. In 1821 Clay proposed a second compromise: Missouri would guarantee that its laws would not discriminate against citizens of other states. (Once admitted to the Union, Missouri twice adopted laws barring free blacks.)

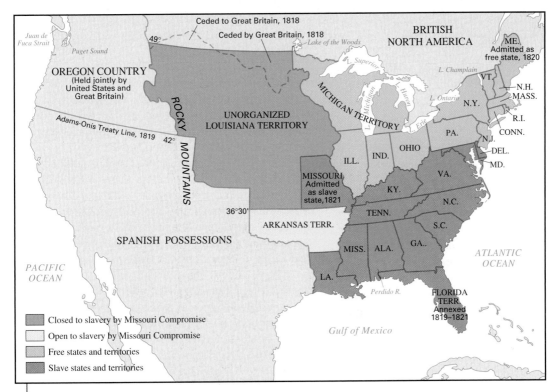

Map 9.2   Missouri Compromise and the State of the Union, 1820

Map labels:

Juan de Fuca Strait

Ceded to Great Britain, 1818
Ceded by Great Britain, 1818

49°

Lake of the Woods

BRITISH NORTH AMERICA

Puget Sound

L. Superior

ME. Admitted as free state, 1820

OREGON COUNTRY (Held jointly by United States and Great Britain)

L. Champlain

VT.

N.H.

MASS.

ROCKY MOUNTAINS

UNORGANIZED LOUISIANA TERRITORY

L. Michigan

L. Huron

MICHIGAN TERRITORY

L. Ontario

N.Y.

R.I.

Adams-Onis Treaty Line, 1819   42°

L. Erie

PA.

CONN.

N.J.

OHIO

DEL.

ILL.

IND.

MD.

MISSOURI Admitted as slave state, 1821

VA.

KY.

36°30'

ARKANSAS TERR.

TENN.

N.C.

SPANISH POSSESSIONS

S.C.

MISS.   ALA.   GA.

ATLANTIC OCEAN

PACIFIC OCEAN

LA.

Perdido R.

FLORIDA TERR. Annexed 1819–1821

Gulf of Mexico

Legend:
- Closed to slavery by Missouri Compromise
- Open to slavery by Missouri Compromise
- Free states and territories
- Slave states and territories

Summary

The partisanship of the 1790s made the early republic a period of vigorous political engagement. With a vision of an agrarian nation that protected individual liberty, Jeffersonians promoted a limited national government—one that stayed out of religious affairs and spent little on military forces, diplomatic missions, and economic initiatives. The rival Federalists, who exerted their influence through the judiciary, declared federal supremacy over the states even as the judiciary affirmed its supremacy over other government branches. Federalists hoped a strengthened federal government would help promote commerce and industry.

Jefferson considered the acquisition of the Louisiana Territory and the Corps of Discovery his greatest presidential accomplishments. Americans soon streamed into the Louisiana Territory. More would have gone if not for Indians (and their British allies) and poorly developed transportation routes.

With its economy focused on international shipping, the greatest threats to the United States came from abroad. In its wars with the Barbary states, the United States sought to guard its commerce and ships on the high seas. Although the second war with Britain—the War of 1812—was a military stalemate, it helped inspire a new sense of nationalism and launch an era of American development.

States' Rights and Nullification

The exact nature of the relationship between the states and the federal government was ambiguous under the Constitution, because Constitutional Convention delegates could not agree on whether states or nation should prevail in an irreconcilable conflict. The Tenth Amendment offered a slight clarification: powers not delegated to the central government, it said, were reserved to the states or the people.

When New England Federalists met in Hartford in late 1814 to prepare a list of grievances against Mr. Madison's War, they drew on the doctrine of nullification, first announced sixteen years earlier in the Kentucky and Virginia Resolutions, written by Thomas Jefferson and James Madison. Opposing the Alien and Sedition Acts, these founding fathers asserted that, if the national government assumed powers not delegated to it by the Constitution, states could individually nullify federal actions. Federalist representatives of New England states discussed taking nullification further by seceding. Their formulation of states' rights to nullify federal authority left a legacy that was reinvoked in crises up to the present.

In the following decade, South Carolina nullified federal tariffs, and in 1861 southern states threatened by Abraham Lincoln's election as president claimed the right of secession. Although the Civil War supposedly settled the issue—states could neither nullify federal law nor secede—southern states opposing the Supreme Court's 1954 ruling in favor of school integration again claimed the right to nullify "unauthorized" federal policy within their borders. In the early twenty-first century, as the U.S. Congress failed to muster a two-thirds majority to propose a constitutional amendment banning gay marriage, dozens of states ratified their own such constitutional amendments. The Hartford Convention's legacy provides Americans who dissent from national policy with a model for using state governments as vehicles for protest.

The Treaty of Ghent reaffirmed American independence; thereafter the nation settled disputes with Great Britain at the bargaining table. The war also dealt a serious blow to Indian resistance in the Midwest and Southwest, while accelerating American industrial growth. Federalists' opposition to the war undermined their political credibility, and their party faded from the national political scene by 1820. The absence of well-organized partisan conflict created what contemporaries called an Era of Good Feelings.

Still, competing visions of America's route to prosperity endured. Under Chief Justice John Marshall, the Supreme Court supported the Federalist agenda, issuing rulings that stimulated commerce and industry. The Democratic-Republicans looked, instead, toward the vast and fertile Louisiana Territory. Fearful of European intentions to reassert their influence in the Americas and emboldened by the Louisiana Purchase and acquisition of Florida, President Monroe proclaimed that the United States would not tolerate European intervention in American affairs. But even as its expanding boundaries strengthened the United States' international presence, it threatened new-found political unity at home.

Tensions mounted in 1819, when the postwar economic boom came to a halt and congressmen sharply divided over whether to admit Missouri as a slave state. The compromise brokered by Henry Clay quelled the issue of slavery's expansion, but it did not permanently settle the issue.

Chapter Review

POLITICAL VISIONS

> **Was Jefferson's election and political vision truly "the revolution of 1800"?**

Jefferson considered his election in 1800 a revolution, since it also gave his Democratic-Republican Party a majority in both houses of Congress. That made it easier to enact his vision of limited government, individual liberty (which required the separation of church and state) and an agrarian (versus commercial) republic. While Federalists bitterly opposed Jefferson where they could, he replaced Hamilton with a treasury secretary who would cut the federal budget and decrease the national debt—both signs of corruption to Jefferson and Democratic-Republicans (and Federalists' tools to stimulate the economy). Jefferson also pardoned those convicted under the Alien and Sedition Acts, which he saw as a violation of liberties, and attempted to remove from court appointments people opposed to his brand of politics (but was ultimately unsuccessful, maintaining the Court's independence).

NATIONAL EXPANSION WESTWARD

> **Why was the Louisiana Purchase among Jefferson's most popular decisions as president?**

The purchase of 827,000 square miles of land west of the Mississippi from France doubled the size of the United States, secured American interests from potential European incursion at its inland borders, and opened more land for American settlement (even though Native Americans were already living there). Moreover, by purchasing the land on the other side of the river, the United States controlled access to the Mississippi, which appealed to western settlers who relied on it to get their goods to market. Finally, it fed dreams of cheap, fertile lands for would-be settlers.

THE NATION IN THE ORBIT OF EUROPE

> **What led to the War of 1812?**

Freedom of the seas was the main cause. Ongoing hostilities between European nations spilled over onto American ships, as Great Britain often stopped and seized US ships and forced those aboard into military service. Trade embargoes did little to stop the practice and ultimately hurt American merchants and the U.S. economy. Madison pointed to violation of neutral trading rights, British alliances with western Indians, and affronts to American independence as additional causes, while others saw war as an opportunity to annex British Canada. Although Britain reopened the seas and ordered its ships not to disturb American warships by June of 1812, news of the policy change did not reach America until long after Congress declared war.

THE WAR OF 1812

What were the consequences of the War of 1812?

Although the Treaty of Ghent ended the fighting and restored the prewar status quo, the United States did not get the results it wanted on impressments, blockades, and maritime rights for neutral parties. The war did, however, affirm American independence and guarantee no future battles with Britain over trade or territory. On the home front, the war shattered the U.S. economy and led some New England Federalists to threaten secession, which led to the party's demise when the war soon ended. Indians who had supported the British lost a major ally. And while Indians had their land and rights restored by the Treaty of Ghent, they had no power to enforce it. With the end of war, three trends emerged that were pivotal for the nation's future: westward expansion, the entrenchment of slavery, and industrial development.

THE NATIONALIST PROGRAM

How did the American System mark the triumph of Federalist economic policy?

Long opposed to big government, Democratic-Republicans amended this philosophy to adopt the Federalist notion that the central government should aid economic growth. Their program was dubbed the American System, and included a national bank, development of transportation networks, and a protective tariff that would tax imported goods to protect American products from foreign competitors. Advocates of the American System, such as South Carolina leader John C. Calhoun, believed it could bridge sectional divides and expand the nation. Both parties embraced internal improvements for different reasons: Federalists saw them as spurring commercial development, while Jeffersonians (Democratic-Republicans) thought they would lead to western and agrarian expansion.

SECTIONALISM EXPOSED

How did the admission of new states after the War of 1812 ultimately divide the nation?

The question of slavery's westward expansion sparked controversy in 1819 when the Missouri Territory asked to be admitted as a slave state. Many feared it would give slaveholding states a two-vote congressional majority and would set a precedent for admitting other western states. And since Missouri was on the same latitude as free Illinois, Indiana, and Ohio, its admission as a slave state would move slavery northward. House Speaker Henry Clay suggested the winning compromise: to maintain the balance between free and slave states, Maine would enter as a free state, Missouri as a slave state, and all future new states north of Missouri's 36°30′ border would prohibit slavery. As such, the Missouri Compromise divided the nation into two regions, north and south, according to the politics of slavery.

SUGGESTIONS FOR FURTHER READING

Catherine Allgor, *A Perfect Union: Dolley Madison and the Creation of the American Nation* (2006)

Stephen Aron, *American Confluence: The Missouri Frontier from Borderland to Border State* (2006)

David Edmunds, *Tecumseh and the Quest for Indian Leadership* (2006)

Morton J. Horowitz, *The Transformation of American Law, 1780–1860* (1977)

Reginald Horsman, *The Diplomacy of the Early Republic* (1985)

John Lauritz Larson, *Internal Improvement: National Public Works and the Promise of Popular Government in the United States* (2001)

Peter Onuf and Leonard J. Sadosky, *Jeffersonian America* (2002)

Jeffrey Ostler, *The Plains Sioux and U.S. Colonialism from Lewis and Clark to Wounded Knee* (2004)

Jeffrey Pasley, Andrew Robertson, and David Waldstreicher, eds., *Beyond the Founders: New Approaches to the Political History of the Early American Republic* (2004)

CHAPTER 10

The Rise of the South | 1815–1860

CHAPTER OUTLINE

The "Distinctive" South?

Southern Expansion, Indian Resistance, and Removal

LINKS TO THE WORLD:
The Amistad Case

Limits of Mobility in a Hierarchical Society

The Planters' World

Slave Life and Labor

Slave Culture and Resistance

LEGACY FOR A PEOPLE AND A NATION: Reparations for Slavery

Summary

Aslaveholder in debt was a dangerous man, and Pierce Butler was broke. In late winter 1859, fear of disunion dominated national life, and Butler's slave auction had coastal Georgia and South Carolina talking. Butler was the grandson of Major Pierce Butler, a South Carolina senator, wealthy planter, and framer of the Constitution. Butler the younger moved between the family's ostentatious Philadelphia home and fifteen hundred acres of cotton plantations, worked by eight hundred slaves, on Butler Island and St. Simons Island in Georgia. His marriage to famous British actress Fanny Kemble ended in divorce, partly over differences about slavery. By 1859 Butler had squandered $700,000 through speculation and gambling. Most of Butler's Philadelphia properties and possessions were sold to satisfy creditors. Then came the largest slave auction in American history: four hundred thirty-six Butler slaves were taken to Savannah by railroad and steamboat in late February. People of all ages—infants, husbands, wives, children, grandparents—fearfully huddled in horse-and-carriage sheds at the Ten Broeck racetrack. Joseph Bryan, a slave broker and auctioneer, managed the sale. An undercover *New York Tribune* reporter left a detailed account of the auction, held over two days in a driving rainstorm.

If possible, families were sold intact for group prices. Some families of four brought only $1,600 together, while a "prime young man," Abel, netted $1,295 alone. At the end of the second day of what blacks called the weeping time, Butler amassed $303,850 by selling 436 human beings.

In 1815, southern states and territories, with fertile soil and a growing slave labor force to cultivate it, was poised for prosperity and power. New lands were settled, new states were peopled,

This icon will direct you to interactive activities and study materials on A People And A Nation, Brief Edition website: **www.cengage.com/history/norton/peoplenationbrief8e**

Chronology

1810–20	One lakh thirty-seven thousand slaves are forced to move from the Upper South to Alabama, Mississippi, and other western regions.
1822	Vesey's insurrection plot is discovered in South Carolina.
1830s	Vast majority of African American slaves are native-born in America.
1830s–40s	Cotton trade grows into the largest source of commercial wealth and America's leading export.
1831	Turner leads a violent slave rebellion in Virginia.
1832	Virginia holds the last debate in the South about the future of slavery; gradual abolition is voted down.
	Dew's proslavery tract *Abolition of Negro Slavery* is published.
1836	Arkansas gains admission to the Union as a slave state.
1839	Mississippi's Married Women's Property Act gives married women some property rights.
1845	Florida and Texas gain admission to the Union as slave states.
	Douglass's *Narrative of the Life of Frederick Douglass, an American Slave, Written by Himself* is published.
1850	Planters' share of agricultural wealth in the South is 90 to 95 percent.
1850–60	Of some 300,000 slaves who migrate from the Upper to the Lower South, 60 to 70 percent go by outright sale.
1857	Hinton R. Helper's *The Impending Crisis,* denouncing the slave system, is pubished.
	George Fitzhugh's *Southern Thought,* an aggressive defense of slavery, is pubished.
1860	There are 405,751 mulattos in the United States, 12.5 percent of the African American population.
	Three-quarters of all southern white families own no slaves.
	South produces the largest cotton crop ever.

and the South emerged as the world's most extensive commercial agricultural economy, linked to an international cotton trade and textile industry. The Old South's wealth came from export crops, land, and slaves, and its population was almost wholly rural. Beyond economics, racial slavery also affected values, customs, laws, class structure, and the region's relationship to the nation and the world. As slaves were increasingly defined as chattel, they struggled to survive and resist, sometimes overtly, but more often in daily life and culture. By 1860 white southerners not only asserted the moral and economic benefits of slavery, but also sought to advance their power over the national government.

- How and why was the Old South a slave society, with slavery permeating every class and group within it, free or unfree?
- How and why did white southerners come to see cotton as "king" of a global economy, and how did the cotton trade's international reach shape southern society from 1815 to 1860?
- How did African American slaves build and sustain a meaningful life and a sense of community amid the potential chaos and destruction of their circumstances?
- How would you weigh the comparative significance of the following central themes in the history of the Old South: class, race, migration, power, liberty, and wealth?

THE "DISTINCTIVE" SOUTH?

Not until the first half of the 1800s did slaveholding states from the Chesapeake and Virginia to Missouri and from Florida across to Texas come to be designated as the South. Today many consider it America's most distinctive region. Historians have long examined how the Old South was like and unlike the rest of the nation. Because of its unique history, has the South, in the words of poet Allen Tate, always been "Uncle Sam's other province"? Analyzing why the South seems more religious, conservative, or tragic than other regions has been an enduring practice in American culture and politics.

American values, such as materialism, individualism, and faith in progress, have been associated with the North and tradition, honor, and family loyalty, with the South. Stereotypes also label the South as static, even backward, and the North as dynamic in the decades before the Civil War. In truth, there were many Souths: low-country rice and cotton regions with dense slave populations, mountainous regions of small farmers, semitropical wetlands in the Southeast, plantation culture in the Cotton Belt and Mississippi valley, tobacco- and wheat-growing regions in Virginia and North Carolina, bustling port cities, and wilderness areas with rare hillfolk homesteads.

South-North Similarity The South shared much in common with the rest of the nation. The geographic sizes of the South and the North were roughly the same. In 1815 white southerners and free northerners shared heroes and ideology from the American Revolution and the War of 1812. They worshiped the same Protestant God as northerners, lived under the same Constitution, and similarly combined nationalism and localism in their attitudes toward government. But as slavery and the plantation economy expanded, the South did not become a land of individual opportunity in the same manner as the North.

Research has shown that, despite enormous cruelties, slavery was a profitable labor system. Southerners and northerners shared an expanding capitalist economy. As it grew, the slave-based economy of money-crop agriculture reflected planters' rational choices. More land and slaves generally converted into more wealth.

By the Civil War in 1860, the distribution of wealth and property in the two sections was almost identical: 50 percent of free adult males owned only 1 percent of real and personal property, and the richest 1 percent owned 27 percent of the wealth. Both North and South had ruling classes. Entrepreneurs in both sections sought their fortunes in an expanding market economy. The southern master class was more likely than propertied northerners to move west in search of profits.

South-North Dissimilarity In terms of differences, the South's climate and longer growing season gave it a rural and agricultural destiny. Many great rivers provided rich soil and transportation routes. The South developed as a biracial society of brutal inequality, where the liberty and wealth of one race depended on the enslavement of another.

Cotton growers spread out over large areas to maximize production and income. Consequently, population density in the South was low; by 1860 there were only 2.3 people per square mile in vast and largely unsettled Texas, 15.6 in Louisiana, and 18.0 in Georgia. The Northeast averaged 65.4 people per square mile. Massachusetts had 153.1 people per square mile, and New York City compressed 86,400 people into each square mile.

Where people were scarce, it was difficult to finance and operate schools, churches, libraries, and even inns and restaurants. Similarly, the South's rural character and sense of the plantation as self-sufficient meant that the region spent little on public health. Southerners were strongly committed to their churches, and some embraced universities, but all such institutions were far less developed than in the North. Factories were rare, because planters invested their capital primarily in slaves. The largest southern industry was lumbering, and the largest factories used slaves to make cigars. The South was slower than the North to develop a unified market economy and a regional transportation network and had only 35 percent of the nation's railroad mileage in 1860.

The Old South never developed its own banking and shipping capacity to any degree, and relied heavily on the North for both. Most southern bank deposits were in the North, and as early as 1822, one-sixth of all southern cotton cleared for Liverpool or Le Havre from the port of New York. With cotton constituting two-fifths of New York's exports, merchants and bankers there became interested in the fate of slavery and cotton prices. In economic conventions from 1837 to 1839, southern delegates debated foreign trade, dependence on northern importers and financiers, and other alleged threats to their commercial independence. But nothing came of these conventions.

The South lagged far behind the North in industrial growth. Its urban centers were mostly ports like New Orleans and Charleston, which became crossroads of commerce and small-scale manufacturing. In the interior were small market towns dependent on agricultural trade. As a system of racial control, slavery did not work well in cities. Lacking manufacturing jobs, the South did not attract immigrants as readily as the North. By 1860 only 13 percent of the nation's foreign-born population lived in slave states.

Like most northerners, antebellum southerners embraced evangelical Christianity. Americans from all regions believed in a personal God and in conversion and piety as the means to salvation. But southern evangelical Baptists and Methodists concentrated on personal rather than social improvement. By the 1830s in the North, evangelicalism was a wellspring of reform movements; but in states where blacks were numerous and unfree, religion, as one scholar has written, preached "a hands-off policy concerning slavery." Moreover, distance and sparse population prevented reform-minded women from developing associations with each other. The reform movements that emerged in the South, such as temperance, focused on personal behavior, not social reform.

A Southern World-View and the Proslavery Argument

In the wake of the American Revolution, Enlightenment ideas of natural rights and equality stimulated antislavery sentiment in the Upper South, produced a brief flurry of manumissions, and inspired hope for gradual emancipation. But that confidence waned in the new nation. As slavery spread, southerners vigorously defended it. In 1816 George Bourne, a Presbyterian minister exiled from Virginia for his antislavery sermons and for the expulsion of slaveholders from his church, charged that, whenever southerners were challenged on slavery, "they were fast choked, for they had a Negro stuck fast in their throats."

By the 1820s, white southerners justified slavery as a positive good, not merely a necessary evil. They used the antiquity of slavery, as well as the Bible's references to

America, 1841, Edward Williams Clay. An idealized portrayal of loyal and contented slaves, likely distributed by northern apologists for slavery. All is well on the plantation as well-dressed slaves dance and express their gratitude to their master and his perfect family. The text includes the old slave saying: "God bless you master! You feed and clothe us. When we are sick you nurse us, and when too old to work, you provide for us!" The master replies piously: "These poor creatures are a sacred legacy from my ancestors and while a dollar is left me, nothing shall be spared to increase their comfort and happiness."   (Library of Congress)

slaveholding, to foster a historical argument for bondage. But at the heart of the proslavery argument was a deep and abiding racism. Whites were the more intellectual race, they deemed, and blacks more inherently physical and therefore destined for labor. In a proslavery tract written in 1851, John Campbell declared that "there is as much difference between the lowest tribe of negroes and the white Frenchman, Englishman, or American, as there is between the monkey and the negro."

Some southerners defended slavery in practical terms; their bondsmen were economic necessities. In 1845 James Henry Hammond of South Carolina argued that slaveholding was a matter of property rights, protected by the Constitution because slaves were legal property. The deepest root of the proslavery argument was a hierarchical view of the social order with slavery prescribed by God or nature. Southerners cherished tradition, believing social change should come slowly, if at all. As Nat Turner's slave rebellion compelled the Virginia legislature to debate the gradual abolition of slavery in 1831–1832, Thomas R. Dew, a slaveholder and professor at the College of William and Mary, contended that "that which is the growth of *ages* may require *ages* to remove." Dew's widely read work, *Abolition of Negro Slavery* (1832), sparked an outpouring of proslavery writing that would intensify over the next thirty years. As slavery expanded westward and fueled national prosperity, Dew cautioned that gradual abolition threatened the South's "irremediable ruin." Dew declared black slavery the basis of the "well-ordered, well-established liberty" of white Americans.

Proslavery advocates invoked natural-law doctrine, arguing that the natural state of humankind was inequality of ability and condition, not equality. Proslavery writers believed that people were born to certain stations in life; they stressed dependence over autonomy and duty over rights as the human condition. As the Virginia writer George Fitzhugh put it in 1854, "Men are not born entitled to equal rights. It would be far nearer the truth to say, that some were born with saddles on their backs, and others booted and spurred to ride them."

Many slaveholders saw themselves in a paternal role, as guardians of a familial relationship between masters and slaves. Although contradicted by countless examples of slave resistance and escape, and slave sales, planters needed to believe in and exerted great energy in constructing the idea of the contented slave.

A Slave Society

In the Old South, whites and blacks grew up, were socialized, married, reared children, worked, conceived of property, and honed even basic habits under the influence of slavery. This was true of slaveholding and nonslaveholding whites, as well as slave and free blacks. Slavery shaped the social structure of the South, fueled its economy, and dominated its politics. The South was interdependent with the North, West, and even Europe in a growing capitalist market system. For its cotton trade, southerners relied on northern banks, northern steamship companies, and northern merchants. But there were elements of that system that southerners increasingly rejected, especially urbanism, wage labor, a broadening right to vote, and threats to their racial and class order.

Americans have long struggled to define what one historian called the "Dixie difference." "The South is both American and something different," writes another historian, "at times a mirror or magnifier of national traits and at other times a counterculture." Distinctive and national, the South's story begins in what we have come to call the *Old South*, a term only conceivable after native peoples were evicted from the region.

SOUTHERN EXPANSION, INDIAN RESISTANCE, AND REMOVAL

When the trans-Appalachian frontier opened after the War of 1812, some 5 to 10 percent of the population moved annually, usually westward. In the first two decades of the century, they poured into the Ohio valley; by the 1820s, they were migrating into the Mississippi River valley and beyond. By 1850 two-thirds of Americans lived west of the Appalachians.

A Southern Westward Movement After 1820 the heart of cotton cultivation and the slave-based plantation system shifted from southern coastal states to Alabama and the newly settled Mississippi valley—Tennessee, Louisiana, Arkansas, and Mississippi. Slaveholders initiated the move to newer areas of the South, and yeoman farmers followed, also hoping for wealth through cheap land and slaves.

A wave of migration was evident across the Southeast. As early as 1817, a Charleston, South Carolina, newspaper reported that migration out of that state had reached "unprecedented proportions." Almost half of the white people born in South Carolina after 1800 left the state, most for the Southwest. The way to wealth for southern seaboard planters was to go west to grow cotton for the booming world markets, purchasing more land and slaves. The population of Mississippi soared from 73,000 in 1820 to 607,000 in 1850, with African American slaves in the majority. Across the Mississippi River, the population of Arkansas went from 14,000 in 1820 to 210,000 in 1850. By 1835 the American immigrant population in Texas reached 35,000, including 3,000 slaves, outnumbering Mexicans two to one. American settlers declared Texas's independence from Mexico in 1836, spurring further American immigration into the region. By 1845 Texas fever boosted the Anglo population there to 125,000. Statehood that year opened the floodgates to more immigrants and to a confrontation with Mexico that would lead to war.

As the cotton kingdom grew to what southern political leaders dreamed would be national and world dominion, this westward migration, fueled initially by optimistic nationalism, ultimately made migrant planters more sectional and more southern. In time, political dominance in the South migrated westward into the Cotton Belt. By the 1840s and 1850s, capitalist planters, fearful that their slave-based economy was under attack, sought to protect and expand their system. Increasingly, they saw themselves, as one historian has written, less as "landowners who happened to own slaves" than as "slaveholders who happened to own land."

But other Americans already occupied much of the desired land. Before 1830 large swaths of upper Georgia belonged to the Cherokees, and huge regions of Alabama and Mississippi were Creek, Choctaw, or Chickasaw land. Indians were also on the move, but in forced migrations. For most white Americans, Indians were in the way of their growing empire. Taking Indian land, so the reasoning went, reflected the natural course of history and progress: the "civilizers" had to displace the "children of the forest." National leaders provided the rhetoric and justification needed. As president in 1830, Andrew Jackson spoke with certainty about why the Indians must go. "What good man would prefer a country," he asked, "covered with forests and ranged by a few thousand savages to our extensive Republic, studded with cities, towns, and prosperous farms?"

Indian Treaty Making

In theory, under the U.S. Constitution, the federal government recognized Indian sovereignty and treated Indian peoples as foreign nations. Agreements between Indian nations and the United States were signed and ratified like other international treaties. In practice, however, fraud dominated the government's approach to treaty making and Indian sovereignty. As the country expanded, new treaties replaced old ones, shrinking Indian land holdings.

Although Indian resistance persisted against such pressure after the War of 1812, it only delayed their ultimate removal. In the 1820s, native peoples in the middle West, Ohio valley, Mississippi valley, and other parts of the cotton South ceded lands totaling 200 million acres for a pittance.

Indian Accommodation

Increasingly, Indian nations east of the Mississippi sought to survive through accommodation. In the first three decades of the century, the Choctaw, Creek, and Chickasaw peoples in the lower Mississippi became suppliers and traders. Under treaty provisions, trading posts and stores provided Indians with supplies and purchased or bartered Indian-produced goods. The trading posts extended credit to chiefs, who increasingly fell into debt that they could pay off to the federal government only by selling their land.

By 1822 the Choctaw nation sold 13 million acres yet still carried a $13,000 debt. The Indians struggled, increasing agricultural production and hunting, working as farmhands and craftsmen, and selling produce at market stalls in Natchez and New Orleans. As the United States expanded westward, white Americans promoted their assimilation, through education and conversion to Christianity. In 1819, in response to missionary lobbying, Congress appropriated $10,000 annually for "civilization of the tribes adjoining the frontier settlements."

Within five years, thirty-two boarding schools administered by Protestant missionaries enrolled Indian students. They substituted English for Indian languages

The Amistad Case

In April 1839 a Spanish slave ship, *Tecora*, sailed from Lomboko, the region of West Africa that became Sierre Leone. On board were Mende people, captured and sold by their African enemies. In June they arrived in Havana, Cuba, a Spanish colony. Two Spaniards purchased fifty-three of the Mende and sailed aboard *La Amistad* for their plantations elsewhere in Cuba. After three days, the Africans revolted. Led by a man the Spaniards called Joseph Cinque, they killed the captain and seized control of the vessel. They ordered the two Spaniards to take them back to Africa, but the slaveholders tried to reach the American South. Far off course, the *Amistad* was seized by the USS *Washington* in Long Island Sound and brought ashore in Connecticut.

The Amistad Africans soon became a cause for abolitionists and slaveholders, as well as in U.S.-Spanish relations. The Africans were imprisoned in New Haven, and a dispute ensued: Were they slaves and murderers and the property of their Cuban owners, or were they free people exercising their natural rights? Were they Spanish property, seized on the high seas in violation of a 1795 treaty? If a northern state could "free" captive Africans, what did it mean for enslaved African Americans in the South? Connecticut abolitionists went to court, where a U.S. Circuit Court judge dismissed the mutiny and murder charges but refused to release the Africans because their Spanish owners claimed them as property.

Meanwhile, a Yale professor of ancient languages, Josiah Gibbs, visited the captives and learned their words for numbers. In New York he walked along the docks repeating the Mende words until an African seaman, James Covey, responded. Covey journeyed to New Haven, conversed with the jubilant Africans, and soon their tale garnered sympathy throughout New England.

In a new trial, the judge ruled that the Africans were illegally enslaved and ordered them returned to their homeland. Slave trade between Africa and the Americas was outlawed in a treaty between Spain and Great Britain. Spain's lawyers demanded the return of their "merchandise." Needing southern votes to win reelection, President Martin Van Buren supported Spanish claims and advocated the Africans' return to a likely death in Cuba.

The administration appealed to the Supreme Court in February 1841. Arguing the abolitionists' case, former president John Quincy Adams pointed to a copy of the Declaration of Independence on the court wall, invoked the natural rights to life and liberty, and chastised the Van Buren administration. In a 7-to-1 decision, the Court ruled that the Africans were "freeborn."

Fund-raising and speaking tours featuring Cinque financed the return voyage. On November 27, 1841, thirty-five survivors and five American missionaries disembarked for Africa, arriving in Sierre Leone on January 15, 1842. The Amistad case showed how intertwined slavery was with freedom, and the United States with the world. It poisoned diplomatic relations between America and Spain for a generation, and stimulated Christian mission work in Africa.

Amistad Mutiny
(The Granger Collection, New York)

and taught agriculture alongside Christian gospel. But teaching the value of private property did not deter settlers from eyeing Indian land. Wherever native peoples lived, illegal settlers disrupted their lives. The federal government only halfheartedly enforced treaties, as legitimate Indian land rights gave way to the advance of white civilization.

With loss of land came dependency. The Choctaws relied on white Americans for manufactured goods and even food. Disease further facilitated removal of American Indian peoples to western lands. While other groups increased rapidly, the Indian population fell, some nations declining by 50 percent in three decades. The French traveler and author Alexis de Tocqueville concluded, after observing the tragedy of forced Indian removal in 1831, "as they give way or perish, an immense and increasing people fill their place. There is no instance upon record of so prodigious a growth or so rapid a destruction." As many as 100,000 eastern and southern Indian peoples were removed between 1820 and 1850; about 30,000 died in the process.

Removal had a profound impact on all Shawnees, the people of the Prophet and Tecumseh. After giving up 17 million acres in Ohio in a 1795 treaty, the Shawnees scattered to Indiana and eastern Missouri. Many moved to the Kansas territory in 1825. By 1854 Kansas was open to white settlement, and the Shawnees had to cede seven-eighths of their land, or 1.4 million acres. Shawnee men lost their traditional role as providers; their hunting methods and knowledge of woodland animals were useless on the Kansas prairies. As grain became the tribe's dietary staple, Shawnee women played a greater role as providers, supplemented by government aid under treaty provisions. Remarkably, the Shawnees preserved their language and culture despite these devastating dislocations.

Indian Removal as Federal Policy

Cherokees, Creeks, Choctaws, Chickasaws, and Seminoles aggressively resisted white encroachment after the War of 1812 and maintained much of their land. In his last annual message to Congress in late 1824, President James Monroe proposed that all Indians be moved west of the Mississippi River. Monroe considered this an honorable proposal that would protect Indians from invasion and provide them with independence for "improvement and civilization." He believed Indians would willingly accept western land free from white encroachment.

The Cherokees, Creeks, Choctaws, and Chickasaws unanimously rejected Monroe's proposition. In 1789 and 1825 the four nations negotiated thirty treaties with the United States, and they reached their limit. Most wished to remain on what little was left of their ancestral land.

Pressure from Georgia prompted Monroe's policy. In the 1820s, the state accused the federal government of not fulfilling its 1802 promise to remove the Cherokees and Creeks from northwestern Georgia in return for the state's renunciation of its claim to western lands. Georgia remained unsatisfied by Monroe's removal messages and by the Creeks' recalcitrance. In 1826, under federal pressure, the Creek nation ceded all but a small strip of its Georgia acreage, but for Georgians, only their complete removal to the West could resolve the conflict.

In an unsuccessful attempt to hold fast to the remainder of their traditional lands, which were in Alabama, the Creeks radically altered their political structure. In 1829, they abandoned village autonomy for centralized tribal authority and forbade any chief from ceding land. In the end, they lost both their land and their social and political traditions. In 1830, after extensive debate and a narrow vote, Congress passed the Indian Removal Act, authorizing the president to negotiate removal treaties with all tribes east of the Mississippi. The bill, which provided federal funds for relocations, would likely not have passed the House without the additional representation afforded slave states due to the Constitution's three-fifths clause.

Cherokees

No people met the challenge of assimilating to American standards more thoroughly than the Cherokees, whose traditional home centered on eastern Tennessee and northern Alabama and Georgia. Between 1819 and 1829 the tribe became economically self-sufficient and politically self-governing; during this Cherokee renaissance, the nearly fifteen thousand adult Cherokees considered themselves a nation, not a collection of villages. In 1821 and 1822, Sequoyah, a self-educated Cherokee, devised an eighty-six-character phonetic alphabet that made possible a Cherokee-language Bible and a bilingual newspaper, *Cherokee Phoenix* (1828). Between 1820 and 1823, the Cherokees created a formal government with a bicameral legislature and a court system, and in 1827 they adopted a constitution modeled after the United States'.

The Cherokee nation, however, collectively owned all tribal land and forbade land sales to outsiders. Nonetheless, many became individual farmers and slaveholders; by 1833 they held fifteen hundred black slaves. They transformed their economy from hunting, gathering, and subsistence agriculture to commodity trade based on barter, cash, and credit.

But Cherokees' political and economic changes failed to win respect from white southerners. In the 1820s, Georgia pressed them to sell the 7,200 square miles of land they held in the state for $30,000 appropriated by Congress. The Cherokees resisted. Impatient, Georgia annulled the Cherokees' constitution, extended the state's sovereignty over them, prohibited the Cherokee National Council from meeting except to cede land, and ordered their lands seized. The discovery of gold on Cherokee land in 1829 further whetted Georgia's appetite for Cherokee territory.

Cherokee Nation v. Georgia

The Cherokees under Chief John Ross turned to the federal courts to defend their treaty with the United States. In *Cherokee Nation v. Georgia* (1831), Chief Justice John Marshall ruled that under the Constitution an Indian tribe was neither a foreign nation nor a state. Indians' relationship with the United States was "marked," said Marshall, "by cardinal and peculiar distinctions which exist nowhere else." They were deemed "domestic, dependent nations" that were in but not of the United States. Nonetheless, said Marshall, the Indians had an unquestionable right to their lands; they could lose title only by voluntarily giving it up.

A year later, in *Worcester v. Georgia*, Marshall declared that the Indian nation was a distinct political community in which "the laws of Georgia can have no force" and into which Georgians could not enter without permission or treaty. The *Cherokee Phoenix* editor Elias Boudinot called the decision "glorious news." However, President Jackson, whose reputation was built as an Indian fighter, tried to usurp the court's action. Newspapers widely reported that Jackson had said, "John Marshall has made his decision: now let him enforce it." To open up new lands for settlement, Jackson favored expelling the Cherokees.

Georgians, too, refused to comply, and they refused to hear Indians' pleas to share their American dream. A Cherokee census indicated that they owned 33 gristmills, 13 sawmills, 1 powder mill, 69 blacksmith shops, 2 tanneries, 762 looms, 2,486 spinning wheels, 172 wagons, 2,923 plows, 7,683 horses, 22,531 cattle, 46,732 pigs, and 2,566 sheep. "You asked us to form a republican government," declared the Cherokee leader, John Ridge, in 1832. "We did so—adopting your own as a model. You asked us to cultivate the earth, and learn the mechanic arts: We did so. You asked us to learn to read: We did so. You asked us to cast away our idols, and worship your God: We did so." But neither the plow nor the Bible earned the Cherokees respect in the face of the economic, imperial, and racial quests of fellow southerners (see Map 10.1).

Trail of Tears

The Choctaws made the first forced journey from Mississippi and Alabama to the West in the winter of 1831 and 1832. Alexis de Tocqueville was visiting Memphis when they passed through: "The wounded, the sick, newborn babies, and the old men on the point of death. . . . I saw them embark to cross the great river," he wrote. "Neither sob nor complaint rose from that silent assembly." The Creeks in Alabama resisted removal until 1836; a year later the Chickasaws followed.

Some Cherokees believed that further resistance was hopeless and accepted removal, agreeing in 1835 to exchange their southern home for western land in the Treaty of New Echota. Most wanted to stand firm. John Ross, with petitions signed by fifteen thousand Cherokees, lobbied the Senate against ratification of the treaty. He lost. But when evacuation came in 1838, most Cherokees refused to move. President Martin Van Buren sent federal troops; about twenty thousand Cherokees were evicted, held in detention camps, and marched under military escort to Indian Territory in present-day Oklahoma. Nearly one-quarter died of disease and exhaustion on what came to be known as the Trail of Tears.

When the forced march ended, the Indians swapped about 100 million acres east of the Mississippi for 32 million acres west of the river plus $68 million. Forced removal had a disastrous impact on the Cherokees and other displaced Indian nations. In the West they encountered an alien environment. Unable to live off the land, many became dependent on government payments. The Cherokees struggled over their tribal government. In 1839 followers of John Ross assassinated leaders of the protreaty faction. Violence continued sporadically until a new treaty in 1846 imposed a temporary truce. In time the Cherokees reestablished their political institutions and a governing body in Tahlequah, in northeastern Oklahoma.

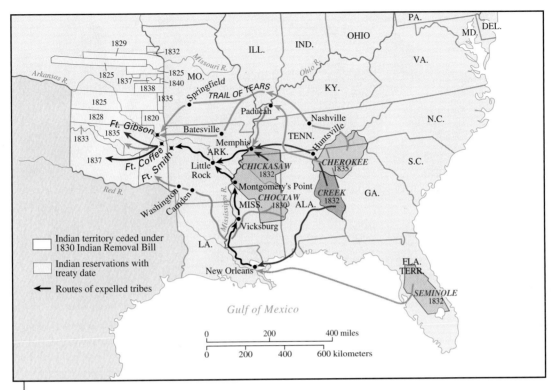

Map 10.1 Removal of Native Americans from the South, 1820–1840

Over a twenty-year period, the federal government and southern states forced Native Americans to exchange their traditional homes for western land. Some tribal groups remained in the South, but most settled in the alien western environment.   (Acknowledgment is due to Martin Gilbert and George Weidenfeld and Nicholson Limited for permission to reproduce this map, taken from *American History Atlas*)

Seminole Wars   In Florida some Seminole leaders agreed in the 1832 Treaty of Payne's Landing to relocate to the West within three years, but others opposed the treaty. A minority under the charismatic leader Osceola refused to vacate and fought the protreaty group. When federal troops were sent to impose removal in 1835, Osceola waged a fierce guerrilla war against them.

The Florida Indians were a varied group that included many Creeks and mixed Indian–African Americans (ex-slaves or descendants of runaway slaves). The U.S. Army, however, considered them all Seminoles. General Thomas Jesup believed that the runaway slave population was the key to the war. "And if it be not speedily put down," he wrote a friend in 1836, "the South will feel the effects of it on their slave population before the end of the next season."

Osceola was captured and died in an army prison in 1838, but Seminoles fought on under Chief Coacoochee (Wild Cat) and other leaders. In 1842 the United States abandoned removal. Most of Osceola's followers agreed to move west to Indian Territory after another war in 1858, but some remained in the Florida Everglades, proud of having resisted.

The Trail of Tears, by twentieth-century Pawnee artist Brummet Echohawk. About twenty thousand Cherokees were evicted in 1838–1839, and about one-quarter of them died on the forced march to present-day Oklahoma.   (Gilcrease Museum, Tulsa, Oklahoma)

LIMITS OF MOBILITY IN A HIERARCHICAL SOCIETY

A large majority of white southerners (three-quarters in 1860) owned no slaves. Some lived in towns and ran stores or businesses, but most were yeoman farmers who owned land and grew their own food. The social distance between poorer whites and the planter class could be great. Still greater was the distance between whites and free blacks. White yeomen, landless whites, and free blacks occupied the broad base of the social pyramid in the Old South.

Yeoman Farmers

After the War of 1812, white farmers, many with no slaves, moved in successive waves down the southern Appalachians into the Gulf lands or through the Cumberland Gap into Kentucky and Tennessee. In large sections of the South, especially inland from the coast and away from large rivers, small, self-sufficient farms were the norm. Lured by stories of good land, many men repeatedly uprooted their wives and children. These farmers were individualistic and hard working. Their status as a numerical majority did not mean that they set the political or economic direction of the slave society. Self-reliant and often isolated, they operated both apart from and within the slave-based staple-crop economy.

On the southern frontier, men cleared fields, built log cabins, and established farms, while their wives labored in the household and patiently re-created the social ties—to relatives, neighbors, fellow churchgoers—that enriched everyone's experience. Women typically dreaded the isolation and loneliness that came with moving to the frontier.

Some yeomen acquired large tracts of level land, purchased slaves, and became planters. They forged part of the new wealth of the cotton-boom states of Mississippi and Louisiana, where mobility into the slaveowning class was possible. Others clung to familiar mountainous areas or sought self-sufficiency. As one historian has written, though they owned no slaves, yeomen were jealous of their independence, and "the household grounded their own claims to masterhood."

Yeoman Folk Culture Yeomen enjoyed a folk culture based on family, church, and local region. Their speech patterns and inflections recalled their Scots-Irish and Irish backgrounds. They flocked to religious revivals called camp meetings and got together for house-raisings, logrollings, quilting bees, corn-shuckings, and hunting. Such occasions combined work with fun and fellowship, offering food and liquor in abundance.

Demanding work and family responsibilities shaped women's lives. They worked in the fields, but the preparation of food consumed much of women's time. Household tasks continued during frequent pregnancies and childcare. Nursing and medical care also fell to mothers, who relied on folk wisdom. Women, too, wanted to be masters of their household, although it came at the price of their health.

Yeomen's Livelihoods At age eighteen in 1841, the North Carolinian John F. Flintoff went to Mississippi to seek his fortune. Like other aspiring yeomen, he worked as a slave overseer. Finding it impossible to please his employers, he returned to North Carolina, married, and lived in his parents' house. "Impatient to get along in the world," Flintoff tried Louisiana next and then Mississippi again.

In the Gulf region, routinely first-rate employment alternated with "very low wages." His uncle and other employers found fault with his work, and in 1846 Flintoff concluded that "managing negroes and large farms is soul destroying."

At twenty-six, even before he owned land, Flintoff bought his first slave, "a negro boy 7 years old." Soon he purchased two more children, the cheapest slaves available. Conscious of his status as a slaveowner, Flintoff resented the low wages he was paid. In 1853, with nine young slaves and a growing family, Flintoff was fired by his uncle. He returned to North Carolina, sold some of his slaves, and purchased 124 acres with help from his in-laws. By 1860 he owned animal stock and several slaves and was paying off his debts. As the Civil War approached, he hoped to free his wife from labor and possibly send his sons to college. Although Flintoff demonstrated that a farmer could move in and out of the slave-holding class, he never achieved cotton planter status (owning roughly twenty or more slaves).

Probably more typical of the southern yeoman was Ferdinand L. Steel, who as a young man moved from North Carolina to Tennessee to work as a river boatman but eventually took up farming in Mississippi. Steel rose every day at 5 A.M. and worked until sundown. He and his family raised corn and wheat, though cotton was his cash product: he sold five or six bales (about two thousand pounds) a year to obtain money for sugar, coffee, salt, calico, gunpowder, and a few other store-bought goods. He picked his own cotton and complained that it was brutal and unprofitable work. When cotton prices fell, a small grower like Steel could be driven into debt and lose his farm.

Steel's life in Mississippi in the 1840s survived on a household economy. He made the family's shoes; his wife and sister sewed dresses, shirts, and pantaloons. As the nation fell deeper into crisis over slave labor, this independent southern farmer never came close to owning a slave.

The focus of Steel's life was family and religion. Family members prayed together daily, and he studied Scripture for an hour after lunch. Steel borrowed histories, Latin and Greek grammars, and religious books from his church. Eventually he became a traveling Methodist minister.

Landless Whites

A sizable minority of white southern workers—from 25 to 40 percent—were hired hands who owned no land and worked for others. Their property consisted of a few household items and some animals—usually pigs. The landless included some immigrants, especially Irish, who did heavy and dangerous work, such as building railroads and digging ditches.

In the countryside, white farm laborers struggled to purchase land in the face of low wages or, if they rented, unpredictable market prices for their crops. Scrimping, some climbed into yeomen ranks. When James and Nancy Bennitt of North Carolina succeeded in their ten-year struggle to buy land, they avoided unstable cotton and raised extra corn and wheat for cash.

Herdsmen with pigs and other livestock had a desperate struggle. By 1860, as the South anticipated war to preserve its society, between 300,000 and 400,000 white people in Virginia, North and South Carolina, and Georgia—approximately one-fifth of the total white population—lived in poverty. Land and slaves determined wealth in the Old South, and many whites possessed neither.

Yeomen's Demands and White Class Relations

Class tensions emerged in the western, nonslaveholding parts of the seaboard states by the 1830s. There, yeoman farmers resented their underrepresentation in state legislatures and the corruption in local government. Voters in more recently settled states of the Old Southwest adopted white manhood suffrage and other reforms, including the popular election of governors, legislative apportionment based on white population only, and locally chosen county government. Slaveowners with new wealth, however, knew that a more open government could permit troubling class conflicts and were determined to hold the reins of power.

Historians have offered several explanations why these tensions did not fuel greater conflict between slaveholders and nonslaveholders. One of the most important factors was race. The South's racial ideology stressed the superiority of all whites to blacks. Thus slavery became the basis of equality among whites, and white privilege inflated the status of poor whites, giving them a common interest with the rich. The dream of upward mobility also blunted class conflict. The Old South was a somewhat fluid society in which some people rose in status by acquiring land or slaves and others wished that they could.

Most important, before the Civil War yeomen worked their farms and avoided debt, largely unhindered by slaveholding planters. Likewise, slaveholders pursued their goals independent of yeomen. Suppression of dissent also played an increasing role. After 1830 white southerners who criticized the slave system were intimidated, attacked, legally prosecuted, or rendered politically powerless in a society held together by white racial solidarity.

Still, there were signs that the relative lack of conflict was ending in the late antebellum period. As cotton lands filled up, nonslaveholders faced narrower economic prospects; meanwhile, wealthy planters enjoyed expanding profits. The risks of entering cotton production were becoming too great and the cost of slaves too high for many yeomen to rise in society. From 1830 to 1860 the percentage of white southerners holding slaves declined from 36 to 25 percent. Although slaveowners were a minority in the white population, the planters' share of the South's agricultural wealth remained at 90 to 95 percent.

Anticipating secession and the prospect of a war, slaveowners expressed growing fear about the loyalty of nonslaveholders during the late antebellum years. But in the 1850s slaveowners occupied from 50 to 85 percent of the seats in state legislatures and a similarly high percentage of the South's congressional seats. And planters' interests controlled all other major social institutions, such as churches and colleges.

Free Blacks

The nearly quarter-million free blacks in the South in 1860 often fared little better than slaves. Upper South free blacks were usually descendants of people manumitted by their owners in the 1780s and 1790s. A remarkable number of slaveholders in Virginia and the Chesapeake freed their slaves because of religious principles and revolutionary ideals in the wake of American independence (see Chapter 7). Many blacks also became free as runaways, especially by the 1830s.

Some free blacks worked in towns or cities, but most lived in rural areas and struggled to survive. They usually did not own land and labored in someone else's fields, often beside slaves. By law, free blacks could not own guns, buy liquor, violate curfew, assemble except in church, testify in court, or (throughout the South after 1835) vote. Despite obstacles, a minority bought land, and others found jobs as skilled craftsmen, especially in cities.

A few free blacks prospered and bought slaves. In 1830 there were 3,775 free black slaveholders in the South; 80 percent lived in Louisiana, South Carolina, Virginia, and Maryland, and approximately half of the total lived in New Orleans and Charleston. Most purchased their own wives and children, whom they could not free because laws required newly emancipated blacks to leave their state. To free the family members they purchased, hundreds of black slaveholders petitioned for exemption from the antimanumission laws. At the same time, a few mulattos in New

Orleans were active slave traders. Although rare in the United States, the greed and quest for power that lay at the root of slavery could cross any racial or ethnic barrier.

Free Black Communities

In the Cotton Belt and Gulf regions, a large proportion of free blacks were mulattos, the privileged offspring of wealthy white planters. Not all planters freed their mixed-race offspring, but those who did often gave their children a good education and financial backing. In cities like New Orleans, Charleston, and Mobile, extensive interracial sex, as well as migrations from the Caribbean, produced a mulatto population that was recognized as a distinct class.

Free black communities formed in many southern cities by the 1840s, especially around churches. By the late 1850s, Baltimore had fifteen churches, Louisville nine, and Nashville and St. Louis four each—most of them African Methodist Episcopal. Class and race distinctions were important to southern free blacks, but outside a few cities, most mulattos experienced hardship. In the United States, "one drop" of black "blood" made them black, and potentially enslaveable.

THE PLANTERS' WORLD

At the top of the southern social pyramid were slaveholding planters. Most lived in comfortable farmhouses, not in the opulence legend suggests. The grand plantation mansions with outlying slave quarters, are an enduring symbol of the Old South. But statistics tell the fuller story: in 1850, 50 percent of southern slaveholders had fewer than five slaves, 72 percent had fewer than ten, and 88 percent had fewer than twenty. Thus the average slaveholder was not a wealthy aristocrat but an aspiring farmer.

The Newly Rich

The newly rich Louisiana cotton planter Bennet Barrow was preoccupied in the 1840s with moneymaking. He worried about his cotton crop, yet to overcome his worries, he hunted frequently and had a passion for racing horses and raising hounds. He could report the loss of a slave without feeling, but became emotional when illness afflicted his sporting animals. His strongest feelings surfaced when his horse Jos Bell—equal to "the best Horse in the South"—"broke down running a mile . . . ruined for Ever." The same day, Barrow gave his human property a "general Whipping." In 1841 diary entries he worried about a rumored slave insurrection. When a slave named Ginney Jerry "sherked" his cotton-picking duties and was rumored "about to run off," Barrow whipped him one day and the next.

The richest planters used their wealth to model genteel sophistication. Extended visits, parties, and balls to which women wore the latest fashions provided opportunities for friendship, courtship, and display. These entertainments were important diversions for plantation women, who relished social events to break the monotony of their domestic lives. Yet such socializing also sustained a rigidly gendered society.

Most of the planters in the cotton-boom states of Alabama and Mississippi were newly rich by the 1840s. As one historian put it, "a number of men mounted from log cabin to plantation mansion on a stairway of cotton bales, accumulating slaves as they climbed." But many did not live like rich men. They put their new wealth into cotton acreage and slaves even as they sought refinement and high social status.

The cotton boom in the Mississippi valley created one-generation aristocrats. A case in point is Greenwood Leflore, a Chocktaw chieftain who owned a plantation in Mississippi with four hundred slaves. After selling his cotton on the world market, he spent $10,000 in France to furnish one room of his mansion with hand-woven carpets, furniture upholstered with gold leaf, tables and cabinets ornamented with tortoise-shell inlay, mirrors, paintings, and a clock and candelabra of brass and ebony.

Social Status and Planters' Values

Slave ownership was the main determinant of wealth in the South, and slave labor was the primary means of cultivating cotton and other cash crops on a large scale. Slaves were a commodity and an investment, much like gold; people bought them on speculation, hoping for a steady rise in their market value. Wealth in slaves also translated into political power: a majority of political officeholders were slaveholders, and the most powerful were usually large-scale planters.

The availability of slave labor tended to devalue free labor: where strenuous work under supervision was reserved for an enslaved race, few free people relished it. When Alexis de Tocqueville crossed from Ohio into Kentucky on his travels of 1831, he observed, "On the right bank of the Ohio [River] everything is activity, industry; labor is honoured; there are no slaves. Pass to the left bank and the scene changes so suddenly that you think yourself on the other side of the world; the enterprising spirit is gone. There, work is not only painful; it is shameful." Aristocratic values—lineage, privilege, pride, honor, and refinement of person and manner—commanded respect throughout the South. Many of those qualities were in short supply in the recently settled portions of the cotton kingdom, where frontier values of courage and self-reliance ruled during the 1820s and 1830s. By the 1850s, a settled aristocratic group of planters did predominate in much of the Mississippi valley.

Instead of disappearing, as it had in the North, the Code Duello, which required men to defend their honor through violence, endured in the South. In North Carolina in 1851, wealthy planter Samuel Fleming sought to settle disputes with lawyer William Waightstill Avery by "cowhiding" him in public. Under the code, Avery could redeem his honor violently or brand himself a coward through inaction. Three weeks later, he shot Fleming dead at point-blank range. A jury took ten minutes to find Avery not guilty, and the spectators gave him a standing ovation.

Aristocratic planters expected to wield power and receive deference from poorer whites. But the sternly independent yeoman class resented infringements of their rights, and many belonged to evangelical faiths that exalted simplicity and condemned the planters' wealth. Yeomen sometimes challenged planters' political pretensions. Much of the planters' power and claims to leadership, after all, were built on their assumption of a monopoly on world cotton and a foundation of black slave labor.

King Cotton in a Global Economy

The American South so dominated the world's supply of cotton that southern planters gained enormous confidence that the cotton boom was permanent and that the industrializing nations of England and France would always bow to King Cotton. American cotton production doubled in yield each decade after 1800 and provided three-fourths of the world's supply by the 1840s. Southern staple crops were three-fifths of American exports by 1850, and one of every seven workers in England depended on American cotton for his job. Cotton production made slaves the most valuable financial asset in the United States—greater than banks, railroads, and manufacturing combined. In 1860 dollars, the slaves' total value as property equaled an estimated $3.5 billion ($70 billion in early-twenty-first-century dollars).

"Cotton is King," the *Southern Cultivator* declared in 1859, "and wields an astonishing influence over the world's commerce." Until 1840 the cotton trade furnished much of the export capital that financed northern economic growth. After, the northern economy expanded without dependence on cotton profits. Nevertheless, southern planters and politicians continued to boast of King Cotton's supremacy. "No power on earth dares . . . to make war on cotton," James Hammond lectured the U.S. Senate in 1858. Although the South produced 4.5 million bales in 1861, its greatest crop ever, its world dominance was about to collapse. Thereafter, cotton became a shackle to the South.

Paternalism

Slaveholding men often embraced a paternalistic ideology that justified their dominance over black slaves and white women. They stressed their obligations, viewing themselves as custodians of society and of the black families they owned. The paternalistic planter saw himself not as an oppressor but as the benevolent guardian of an inferior race.

This comforting self-image let rich planters obscure the harsh dimensions of slave treatment. And slaves—accommodating to the realities of power—encouraged their masters to think their benevolence was appreciated. Paternalism also served as a defense against abolitionist criticism. In reality, paternalism grew as a give-and-take relationship between masters and slaves—owners took labor from the bondsmen, while slaves obligated masters to provide them a measure of autonomy and living space.

Relations between men and women in the planter class were similarly defined by paternalism. The upper-class southern woman was raised and educated to be a wife, mother, and subordinate companion to men. South Carolina's Mary Boykin Chesnut wrote of her husband, "He is master of the house. . . . All the comfort of my life depends upon his being in a good humor." Women found it difficult to challenge society's rules on sexual or racial relations.

Planters' daughters usually attended one of the South's rapidly multiplying boarding schools. Typically, the young woman could entertain suitors whom her parents approved, but she quickly had to choose a husband and commit herself to a man whom she generally had known only briefly. Young women had to follow the wishes of their family, especially their father, even if it left them emotionally empty.

On marriage, a planter-class woman ceded to her husband most of her legal rights, becoming part of his family. She was isolated on a large plantation, where she oversaw the cooking and preserving of food, managed the house, supervised the children, and attended sick slaves. These realities were more confining on the frontier, where isolation was greater. Men on plantations could occasionally escape into the public realm—to town, business, or politics. Women could retreat from rural plantation culture only into kinship and associations with other women.

Marriage and Family Among Planters

A perceptive white woman sometimes approached marriage with anxiety. Lucy Breckinridge, a wealthy Virginia girl of twenty, lamented the autonomy she surrendered at the altar. In her diary she recorded: "If [husbands] care for their wives at all it is only as a sort of servant, a being made to attend to their comforts and to keep the children out of the way."

Childbearing often involved grief, poor health, and death. In 1840 the birth rate for white southern women was almost 30 percent higher than the national average. The average southern white woman would bear eight children in 1800; by 1860 the figure decreased to six. Childbirth complications were a major cause of death, occurring twice as often in the hot South as in the Northeast.

Sexual relations between planters and slaves were another problem white women endured but were not supposed to notice. "Violations of the moral law . . . made mulattos as common as blackberries," protested a woman in Georgia, but wives had to play "the ostrich game." In the 1840s and 1850s, as abolitionist attacks on slavery increased, southern men published a barrage of articles stressing that women should not discuss the slavery issue. The *Southern Quarterly Review* declared, "The proper place for a woman is at home. One of her highest privileges, to be politically merged in the existence of her husband."

But a study of women in Petersburg, Virginia, a large tobacco-manufacturing town, revealed behavior that valued financial autonomy. Over several decades before 1860, the proportion of women who never married or did not remarry after a spouse's death grew to exceed 33 percent. Likewise, the number of women who worked for wages, controlled their own property, and ran dressmaking businesses increased. In managing property, these and other women benefited from legal changes enacted to protect families from the husband's indebtedness during business panics and recessions. These reforms gave married women some property rights.

SLAVE LIFE AND LABOR

Slaves provided the physical strength and much of the know-how to build an agricultural empire, but their lives were marked by poverty, coercion, toil, and resentment. They embodied the nation's most basic contradiction: in the world's model republic, slaves were on the wrong side of a brutally unequal power relationship.

Slaves' Everyday Conditions

Beyond bare necessities, southern slaves enjoyed few material comforts. Although they generally had enough to eat, their diet was monotonous and nonnutritious. Clothing was coarse and inexpensive. Few slaves received more than one or two changes of clothing for hot and cold seasons, and one blanket each winter. Children of both sexes ran naked in hot weather and wore long cotton shirts in winter. Many slaves went without shoes until December. Conditions were generally better in cities, where slaves frequently lived in the same dwelling as their owners and were regularly hired out, enabling them to accumulate their own money.

The average slave lived in a crude, one-room cabin. Each dwelling housed one or two families. Crowding and lack of sanitation fostered the spread of infection and such contagious diseases as typhoid fever, malaria, and dysentery. White plantation doctors were hired to care for sick slaves, but some "slave doctors" attained a degree of power in the quarters and with masters by healing through herbalism and spiritualism.

Slave Work Routines

Long hours and large work gangs characterized Gulf Coast cotton districts. Overseers rang the morning bell before dawn, and black people, tools in hand, walked toward the fields. Slaves who cultivated tobacco in the Upper South worked long hours picking the sticky, sometimes noxious, leaves under harsh discipline. As one woman recalled when interviewed in the 1930s, "it was way after sundown fore they could stop that field work. Then they had to hustle to finish their night work [such as watering livestock or cleaning cotton] in time for supper, or go to bed without it."

Working from sun to sun became a norm in much of the South. Profit took precedence over paternalism. Slave women did heavy fieldwork, often as much as the men and even during pregnancy. Old people cared for children, did light chores or carded, ginned, and spun cotton.

By the 1830s planters in the South Carolina and Georgia low country used a task system whereby slaves were assigned measured amounts of work to be performed in a given amount of time. So much cotton on a daily basis was to be picked from a designated field, so many rows hoed or plowed in a specified section. On completion, slaves' time was their own for working garden plots, tending hogs, even hiring out their own labor. From this experience, many slaves developed a sense of property ownership.

Of the 1860 population of 4 million slaves, half were under the age of sixteen. "A child raised every two years," wrote Thomas Jefferson, "is of more profit than the crop of the best laboring man." And in 1858 a slaveowner writing in an agricultural magazine calculated that a slave girl he purchased in 1827 for $400 had borne three sons now worth $3,000 as his working field hands. Slave children gathered kindling, carried water to the fields, swept the yard, lifted cut sugar-cane stalks into carts, stacked wheat, chased birds away from sprouting rice plants, and labored in cotton and tobacco production.

As slave children matured, they faced psychological traumas, including powerlessness and an awareness that their parents could not protect them. They had to fight to keep from internalizing what whites labeled their inferiority. Many former slaves resented their denial of education. And for girls reaching maturity, the potential trauma of sexual abuse loomed over their lives.

Violence and Intimidation Against Slaves

Whites throughout the South believed that slaves "can't be governed except with the whip." One South Carolinian explained to a northern journalist that he whipped his slaves regularly; "the fear of the lash kept them in good order." Evidence suggests that whippings were less frequent on small farms than on large plantations. But beatings symbolized authority to the master and tyranny to slaves, who used them to evaluate a master. Former slaves said a good owner was one who did not "whip too much," whereas a bad owner "whipped till he's bloodied you and blistered you."

The master wielded virtually absolute authority on his plantation. Slaveholders rarely had to answer to the law or state, and courts did not recognize the word of chattel. Pregnant women were whipped, and there were burnings, mutilation, torture, and murder. Yet physical cruelty may have been less prevalent in the United States than in other slaveholding parts of the New World, especially some of the sugar islands of the Caribbean, where death rates were so high that the heavily male slave population shrank in size. In the United States, the slave population experienced a steady natural increase, as births exceeded deaths.

The worst evil of American slavery was the nature of slavery itself: coercion, belonging to another person, virtually no hope for mobility or change. Recalling their time in bondage, some former slaves emphasized the physical abuse, but memories focused on the tyranny of whipping as much as the pain. Delia Garlic made the essential point: "It's bad to belong to folks that own you soul an' body. . . . you couldn't guess the awfulness of it." To be a slave was to be the object of another person's will and material gain, as the saying goes, from the cradle to the grave.

Most American slaves retained their self-respect despite their bondage. They had to be subservient to their masters, but they talked and behaved differently among themselves. In *Narrative of the Life of Frederick Douglass, an American Slave, Written by Himself* (1845), Douglass wrote that most slaves, when asked about "their condition and the character of their masters, almost universally say they are contented, and that their masters are kind." Slaves did this, said Douglass, because they were governed by the maxim that "a still tongue makes a wise head." Slaves often quarreled over who had the best master, but, Douglass remarked, when one had a bad master, he sought a better master; and when he had a better one, he wanted to "be his own master."

Slave-Master Relationships

Some former slaves remembered warm feelings between masters and slaves, but the prevailing attitudes were distrust and antagonism. One woman said her mistress was "a mighty good somebody to belong to" but only "'cause she was raisin' us to work for her." Slaves also resented being used as beasts of burden. One man observed that his master "fed us reg'lar on good, 'stantial food, just like you'd tend to your horse, if you had a real good one."

Slaves were alert to the daily signs of their degraded status. One man recalled the general rule that slaves ate corn bread and owners ate biscuits. If blacks did get biscuits, "the flour that we made the biscuits out of was the third-grade sorts." If the owner took his slaves' garden produce to town to sell, slaves often suspected him of pocketing part of the profits.

Suspicion often grew into hatred. When a yellow fever epidemic struck in 1852, many slaves saw it as God's retribution. An elderly ex-slave named Minnie Fulkes cherished the conviction that God was going to punish white people for their cruelty to blacks. On the plantation, of course, slaves kept such thoughts to themselves and created ways to survive and to sustain their humanity in this world of repression.

SLAVE CULTURE AND RESISTANCE

The resource that enabled slaves to maintain such defiance was their culture: beliefs, values, and practices born of their past and maintained in the present. As best they could, they built a community knit together by stories, music, a religious world-view, leadership, the smells of their cooking, the sounds of their own voices, and the tapping of their feet. "The values expressed in folklore," wrote the African American poet Sterling Brown, provided a "wellspring to which slaves . . . could return in times of doubt to be refreshed."

African Cultural Survival

Slave culture changed significantly after 1808, when Congress banned further importation of slaves and the generations born in Africa died out. For a few years South Carolina reopened the international slave trade, but by the 1830s, the vast majority of slaves in the South were native-born Americans. Yet African influences remained strong. Some slave men plaited their hair into rows and designs; slave women often wore their hair tied in small bunches secured by string or cloth. A few men and many women wrapped their heads in kerchiefs of the styles and colors of West Africa. Some remembered the names of African ancestors passed on by family lore.

Music, religion, and folktales were part of daily life for most slaves. Borrowing from their African background and forging new American folkways, they developed what scholars have called a sacred world-view, which affected work, leisure, and self-understanding. Slaves made musical instruments with carved motifs that resembled African stringed instruments. One visitor to Georgia in the 1860s described a ritual dance of African origin known as the ring shout: "A ring of singers is formed. . . . They then utter a kind of melodious chant, which gradually increases in strength, and in noise, until it fairly shakes the house, and it can be heard for a long distance."

Many slaves continued to believe in spirit possession. While whites believed in ghosts and charms, slaves' beliefs resembled the African concept of the living dead—deceased relatives visit the earth for years until the process of dying is complete. Slaves also practiced conjuration and quasi-magical root medicine. By the 1850s noted conjurers and root doctors were reputed to live in South Carolina, Georgia, Louisiana, and isolated coastal areas with high slave populations.

Slaves increasingly developed a racial identity. In the colonial period, Africans arrived in America from many states and kingdoms, represented in distinctive languages and traditions. Africans arrived in the New World with virtually no concept of race; by the antebellum era, their descendants learned through bitter experience that race was now the defining feature of their lives.

Slaves' Religion and Music

Over time, more and more slaves adopted Christianity, fashioning it into an instrument of support and resistance. Theirs was a religion of justice and deliverance, quite unlike their masters' religious propaganda. "You ought to have heard that preachin'," said one man. "'Obey your master and mistress, don't steal chickens and eggs and meat,' but nary a word about havin' a soul to save." Slaves believed that Jesus cared about their souls and their plight.

Devout men and women worshiped every day, in the field or by the side of the road. Some slaves held secret prayer meetings that lasted far into the night. Many nurtured an unshakable belief that God would end their bondage. This faith—and the emotional release that accompanied worship—sustained them.

Slaves also adapted Christianity to African practices. In West African belief, devotees are possessed by a god so thoroughly that the god's own personality replaces the human personality. In the late antebellum era, Christian slaves experienced possession by the Protestant Holy Spirit. The combination of shouting, singing, and dancing that seemed to overtake black worshipers formed the heart of their religious faith. "The old meeting house caught fire," recalled an ex-slave preacher. "The spirit was there. . . . God saw our need and came to us." Out in brush arbors or in meetinghouses, slaves thrust their arms to heaven, made music with their feet, and sang away their woes.

Rhythm and physical movement were crucial to slaves' religious experience. In black preachers' chanted sermons, which pulled the sinner into a narrative of meanings and cadences en route to conversion, an American tradition was born. The chanted sermon was a scriptural and patterned form that required audience response punctuated by "yes sirs!" and "amens!" But it was in song that slaves left their most sublime gift to American culture.

Through spirituals, slaves tried to impose order on the chaos of their lives. Often referred to later as the *sorrow songs,* slave lyrics covered many themes, especially imminent rebirth. Sadness could immediately give way to joy: "Oh, Freedom": "Oh, Oh, Freedom / Oh, Oh, Freedom over me— / But before I'll be a slave, / I'll be buried in my grave, / And go home to my Lord, / And Be Free!"

Many songs also express intimacy and closeness with God. Some display a rebelliousness, such as the enduring "He said, and if I had my way / If I had my way, if I had my way, / I'd tear this building down!" And some spirituals reached for collective hope in the black community.

> O, gracious Lord! When shall it be,
> That we poor souls shall all be free;
> Lord, break them slavery powers—
> Will you go along with me?
> Lord break them slavery powers,
> Go sound the jubilee!

In many ways, American slaves converted the Christian God to themselves. They sought an alternative world—a home other than the one fate had given them on earth. In variations on the Br'er Rabbit folktales—in which the weak survive by wit and power is reversed—and in songs, they fashioned survival and resistance from their cultural imagination.

The Black Family in Slavery

Although American law did not recognize slave families, slaveowners expected slaves to form families and have children. As a result, there was a normal ratio of men to women, young to old. Studies have shown that, on some of the largest cotton plantations of South Carolina, when masters gave their slaves increased autonomy through the task system, the property accumulation in livestock, tools, and garden produce thus fostered led to more stable and healthier families.

Following African kinship traditions, African Americans avoided marriage between cousins (commonplace among aristocratic slaveowners). By naming their children after relatives of past generations, African Americans emphasized family history. Kinship networks and extended families held life together in many slave communities.

For slave women, sexual abuse and rape by white masters were ever-present threats. By 1860 there were 405,751 mulattos in the United States, making up 12.5 percent of the African American population. White planters were sometimes open with their behavior toward slave women, but not in the way they talked about it. Buying slaves for sex was common at the New Orleans slave market. In what was called the

This photograph of five generations of a slave family, taken in Beaufort, South Carolina, in 1862, is silent but powerful testimony of the importance that enslaved African Americans placed on their ever-threatened family ties.   (Library of Congress)

fancy trade (a fancy was a young, attractive slave girl or woman), females were sold for prices as much as 300 percent higher than the average. At such auctions, slaveholders exhibited some of the ugliest values at the heart of the slave system by paying $3,000 to $5,000 for female "companions."

The Domestic Slave Trade

Slave families most feared and hated separation by violence from those they loved, sexual appropriation, and sale. Many struggled to keep their children together and, after emancipation, to reestablish contact with loved ones lost by forced migration and sale. Between 1820 and 1860, an estimated 2 million slaves were moved into the region from western Georgia to eastern Texas. When the Union Army registered thousands of black marriages in Mississippi and Louisiana in 1864 and 1865, 25 percent of the men over forty reported that they had been forcibly separated from a previous wife. Thousands of black families were disrupted annually to serve the needs of the expanding cotton economy. Many antebellum white southerners made their living from the slave trade. In South Carolina by the 1850s, there were over one hundred slave-trading firms selling approximately 6,500 slaves annually to southwestern states. One estimate from 1858 indicated that slave sales in Richmond, Virginia, netted $4 million that year. A market guide to slave sales that same year in Richmond listed prices for "likely ploughboys," ages twelve to fourteen, at $850 to $1,050; "extra number 1 fieldgirls" at $1,300 to $1,350; and "extra number 1 men" at $1,500.

At slave pens in cities like New Orleans, traders promoted "a large and commodious showroom . . . prepared to accommodate over 200 Negroes for sale." Traders made slaves appear young, healthy, and happy, cutting gray whiskers off men, using paddles as discipline to avoid scarring their merchandise, and forcing people to dance and sing as buyers arrived. When transported to the southwestern markets, slaves were often chained together, making journeys of 500 miles or more on foot.

The complacent mixture of racism and business among traders is evident in their own language. "I refused a girl 20 year[s] old at 700 yesterday," one trader wrote in 1853. "She is very badly whipped but good teeth." Some sales were transacted at owners' requests, often for tragically inhumane reasons. "Bought a cook yesterday that was to go out of state," wrote a trader; "she just made the people mad that was all."

Strategies of Resistance

Slaves brought to their resistance efforts the common sense and determination that characterized their struggle to secure families. The scales weighed against overt revolution, but they seized opportunities to alter work conditions. They sometimes slacked off when they were not watched. Daily discontent and desperation were also manifest in equipment sabotage; carelessness about work; theft of food, livestock, or crops; or getting drunk on stolen liquor. Some slaves who were hired out might hoard their earnings or become recalcitrant. A woman named Ellen, hired as a cook in Tennessee in 1856, quietly put mercury poison into a roasted apple for her unsuspecting mistress. And some slave women resisted by trying to control their own pregnancy, either by avoiding it or by seeking it to improve conditions.

Many male and some female slaves violently attacked overseers or owners. They were customarily secured and flogged, sold away, or hanged. Southern court records and newspapers contain accounts of resistant slaves who disproved the image of the docile bondsman or woman.

Many slaves attempted to run away to the North, and some received assistance from the loose network known as the Underground Railroad. But it was more common for slaves to run off temporarily and hide in the woods. Approximately 80 percent of runaways were male; children prevented women from fleeing as readily. Fear, disgruntlement over treatment, or family separation might motivate slaves to flee. Only a minority ever made it to freedom in the North, but these fugitives made slavery an insecure institution by the 1850s.

American slavery produced some fearless revolutionaries. Gabriel's Rebellion involved as many as a thousand slaves when it was discovered in 1800, just before it would have exploded in Richmond, Virginia. According to controversial court testimony, a similar conspiracy existed in Charleston in 1822, led by a free black named Denmark Vesey. Born a slave in the Caribbean, Vesey won a lottery of $1,500 in 1799, bought his freedom, and became a religious leader. According to one long-argued interpretation, Vesey was a heroic revolutionary determined to free his people. But, in a recent challenge, the historian Michael Johnson points out that court testimony is the only reliable source on the alleged insurrection. Might the testimony reveal less of reality than of white South Carolina's fears of slave rebellion? The court, says Johnson, built its case on rumors and intimidated witnesses, and "conjured into being" an insurrection that was not truly about to occur. Whatever the facts, thirty-seven "conspirators" were executed, and more than three dozen others were banished from the state.

Nat Turner's Insurrection

The most famous rebel, Nat Turner, struck for freedom in Southampton County, Virginia, in 1831. Turner was a precocious child who learned to read. Encouraged by his first owner to study the Bible, he enjoyed privileges but also endured hard work and changes of masters. Young Nat eventually became a preacher known for eloquence and mysticism. After planning for years, Turner led rebels from farm to farm in the predawn darkness of August 22, 1831. The group severed limbs and crushed skulls with axes or killed victims with guns. Before alarmed planters stopped them, Turner and his followers had in forty-eight hours slaughtered sixty whites. In retaliation whites randomly killed slaves across the region. Turner was caught and hanged. As many as two hundred African Americans, lost their lives as a result of the rebellion.

Nat Turner remains a haunting symbol in America's unresolved history with slavery and discrimination. While in jail, Turner was interviewed by the Virginia lawyer and slaveholder Thomas R. Gray. Their intriguing creation, *The Confessions of Nat Turner,* became a bestseller within a month of Turner's hanging. Gray called the rebel a gloomy fanatic in a manner that made him fascinating and produced one of the most remarkable documents of American slavery. After Turner's insurrection, many states passed stiffened legal codes against black education and religious practice.

Most importantly, in 1832 a shocked Virginia held a legislative and public debate over gradual emancipation. The plan would not have freed any slaves until 1858 and provided that eventually all blacks would be colonized outside Virginia. When the House of Delegates voted, gradual abolition lost, 73 to 58. Virginia merely reinforced its defense of slavery. It was the last time white southerners would debate emancipation.

Reparations for Slavery

How should the United States come to terms with 250 years of racial slavery? Is this period best forgotten as a terrible passage, or does the nation owe a long-overdue debt to black people for their oppression? After emancipation in 1865 and rooted in vague federal promises, many former slaves believed they were entitled to forty acres and a mule, but these never materialized.

In 1897 Callie House, a poor mother of four born in 1865 in a contraband camp for ex-slaves, organized the National Ex-Slave Pension and Bounty Association, modeled after the soldiers' pension system. House traveled across the South, recruiting 250,000 members at 10-cent dues. Her lobbying of the federal government for slave pensions failed; she was accused of mail fraud and imprisoned for one year in 1916.

More recently, a widespread debate over reparations for slavery has emerged. In the rewriting of slavery's history since the 1960s, Americans have learned a great deal about how slave labor created American wealth: how insurance companies insured slaves, how complicit the U.S. government was in slavery's defense and expansion, and how slaves built the U.S. Capitol while their owners received $5 a month for their labor.

The debate is fueled by analogies: reparations paid to Japanese Americans interned during World War II, reparations paid to Native American tribes for stolen land, reparations paid Holocaust survivors and victims of forced labor, and a suit settled in 1999 that will pay roughly $2 billion to some twenty thousand black farmers for discrimination by the Agriculture Department in the early twentieth century.

Some argue that, because there are no living former slaves or slaveholders, reparations can never take the form of money. But in 2002 a lawsuit was filed against three major corporations who allegedly profited from slavery, and the National Reparations Coordinating Committee promises a suit against the U.S. government. Some city councils passed resolutions forcing companies in their jurisdictions to investigate any possible complicity with slave trading or ownership, prompting some firms to establish scholarship programs for African Americans.

Critics argue that resources would be better spent "making sure black kids have a credible education" and rebuilding inner cities. Advocates contend that, when "government participates in a crime against humanity," it is "obliged to make the victims whole." The movement for reparations has sparked broad public debate. The legacy of slavery for a people and a nation promises to become America's most traumatic test of how to reconcile its history with justice.

Summary

During the four decades before the Civil War, the South grew in land, wealth, and power along with the rest of the country. Although southern states were enmeshed in the nation's heritage and political economy, they also developed as a distinctive region, ideologically and economically, because of slavery. More than the North, the antebellum South was a biracial society; whites grew up influenced by black folkways and culture, and blacks, the vast majority of whom were slaves, became cobuilders of a rural, agricultural society.

With the sustained cotton boom, as well as state and federal Indian removal policies, the South grew into a slave society. The coercive influence of slavery affected southern life and politics and increasingly produced a leadership determined to preserve a hierarchical social and racial order. Despite their shared white supremacy, the democratic values of yeomen often clashed with the profit motives of aristocratic planters. The benevolent self-image and paternalistic ideology of slaveholders was tested by slaves' own judgments. African American slaves responded by fashioning a rich folk culture and a religion of deliverance. By 1850, white southerners built one of the last profitable, expanding slave societies on earth. The North, though deeply intertwined with southerners nationally, economically, and through a shared constitutional system and history, grew along different lines, through industrialism and free labor. The clash of these two connected yet divided societies would soon explode over the nation's future.

Chapter Review

THE "DISTINCTIVE" SOUTH

What made the antebellum South different from the North?

Both regions were capitalist and Christian (largely Protestant), and embraced the heroes and causes of the American Revolution. But they differed in their economic development: because of its climate and longer growing season, the South's development was agricultural and rural, whereas the North became increasingly urban and industrial. With a comparatively low population density and people spread out from each other, the South's commercial, educational and health-related institutions lagged. The South was also slower to develop a regional transportation network or market economy and relied on slaves for labor and the North for banking and other financial institutions. The South had fewer urban areas, and those that existed were primarily port cities such as Charleston that provided a link for commerce and small manufacturing. With few labor opportunities, the South also did not attract as many immigrants as the North.

SOUTHERN EXPANSION, INDIAN RESISTANCE, AND REMOVAL

How did Native Americans living in western territories deal with increasing migration by southern whites?

Indians dealt with white encroachment on their land in several ways. Some embraced accommodation, establishing trading posts to exchange supplies with settlers, ultimately falling into heavy debt that could only be repaid by selling their land. Others resisted, rejecting removal/relocation plans that whites offered, and holding fast to their land. The Creeks and Cherokees assimilated to American standards—even changed their political structure to more closely resemble that of whites—in an effort to keep their land. When Congress narrowly passed the Indian Removal Act in 1830, which provided funds to relocate Indians to territory further west, the Cherokees refused to leave and sued the state of Georgia in federal court. While the courts found them entitled to their land, President Jackson sent in troops to evacuate thousands of Cherokees and march them from Georgia to present-day Oklahoma. Many refused to go and were imprisoned; others died of disease and exhaustion on the trek known as the Trail of Tears.

LIMITS OF MOBILITY IN A HIERARCHICAL SOCIETY

| What class tensions emerged in the antebellum South?

| Although they were fewer in number, the slave-holding planter class occupied the highest rungs of southern society and dominated its political life (controlling up to 85 percent of legislative posts), as well as churches and colleges. Before the 1830s, the vast socioeconomic differences between rich planters and small, independent, nonslaveholding yeomen farmers were mediated by their shared racial status as white. However tensions emerged as yeomen began to resent their underrepresentation in state government and the corruption of local governments. They sought universal manhood suffrage and other reforms, including popular election of governors and legislative apportionment based solely on the white population—all of which planters resisted. Moreover, as cotton farming made land less and less available, nonslaveholders faced fewer opportunities to improve their station, while planters enjoyed greater and greater profits.

THE PLANTERS' WORLD

| How did paternalism function on southern plantations?

| Paternalism was a belief system that enabled slaveholders to justify their dominance over slaves and white women. In this view, slave owners portrayed themselves as benevolent guardians over their slaves and families—which put them at the helm and required submission of those beneath them. Paternalism denied the truth of slavery's brutality and inhumanity, while providing a counter to abolitionism. As the system developed, it functioned as an exchange in which slaves labored and obligated their owners to provide them with necessities and some autonomy. Between husbands and wives, paternalism gave men control of women's legal rights in marriage—her property became his to manage—and she became his subordinate in every way.

SLAVE LIFE AND LABOR

| What was the true nature of the master-slave relationship?

| Generally speaking, distrust and antagonism were at the core of most master-slave relationships. For slaves, the vulnerability and frustration of being owned, ruled, and at the mercy of another human being, along with being used as a work-animal, sparked much resentment. Slaves did not trust masters to deal fairly with them in their exchanges. There was also much cruelty and brutality—rather than paternalism—on the part of many owners, including whippings and beatings. Slave families were often separated, as one or more members were sold away to other plantations.

SLAVE CULTURE AND RESISTANCE

| How did slaves adapt Christianity and make it their own?

| While many slaves maintained and adapted aspects of the African heritage to their new circumstances, they also embraced and remade Christianity

as a form of resistance. In secret prayer meetings, slaves focused on justice and deliverance, believing God would liberate them from their servitude and exact retribution from those who unjustly enslaved or abused them. They also merged their Christianity with African practices, adding shouting, singing, dancing, and other rituals to their religious meetings, along with chanted sermons, which were regarded as vital for the conversion experience. Their religious rituals not only attempted to restore order and meaning to their lives but also establish closeness with God and hope for the future. Finally, while prayer meetings were often held in secret, they helped forge relationships and community in slave quarters.

SUGGESTIONS FOR FURTHER READING

Ira Berlin, *Generations of Captivity: A History of African American Slaves* (2003)

David Brion Davis, *Inhuman Bondage: The Rise and Fall of Slavery in the New World* (2006)

Steven Deyle, *Carry Me Back: The Domestic Slave Trade in American Life* (2005)

Drew G. Faust, ed., *The Ideology of Slavery: Proslavery Thought in the Antebellum South, 1830–1860* (1981)

Walter Johnson, *Soul by Soul: Life Inside the Antebellum Slave Market* (1999)

Charles Joyner, *Down by the Riverside: A South Carolina Slave Community* (1984)

James D. Miller, *South by Southwest: Planter Emigration and Identity in the Slave South* (2002)

James Oakes, *Slavery and Freedom: An Interpretation of the Old South* (1991)

Michael O'Brien, *Conjectures of Order: Intellectual Life and the American South, 1810–1860* (2004)

Daniel H. Usner Jr., *American Indians in the Lower Mississippi Valley* (1998)

Jean Fagan Yellin, *Harriet Jacobs: A Life* (2004)

CHAPTER 11

The Modernizing North | 1815–1860

CHAPTER OUTLINE

Or Is It the North That Was Distinctive?

The Transportation Revolution

Factories and Industrialization

> **LINKS TO THE WORLD:**
> The United States as a Developing Nation

Consumption and Commercialization

Families in Flux

The Growth of Cities

> **LEGACY FOR A PEOPLE AND A NATION:** A Mixed Economy

Summary

After twenty-five days at sea, Mary Ann and James Archbald and their four children arrived in New York on April 17, 1807. The couple left their ancestral homeland in Scotland reluctantly, hoping for a bright future in which their children would be beholden to no one, neither landlord nor employer. They sought the Jeffersonian dream of republican independence.

The Archbalds bought a farm in central New York, along a Hudson River tributary, where they raised sheep, grew hay and vegetables, skinned rabbits for meat and fur, and sold whatever they did not need. Twenty-one years after leaving Scotland, Mary Ann Archbald, in anticipation of their last mortgage payment, declared "being out of debt is, in my estimation, being rich." By then, her sons were young adults with visions of wealth that centered on water, not land.

On April 17, 1817—a decade after the Archbalds arrived on American shores—the New York State legislature authorized construction of a canal connecting Lake Erie to the Hudson River, and surveyors mapped a route through the Archbalds' farm. The sons (one in his early twenties, the other a teenager) helped dig the canal, while Mary Ann and her daughters cooked and cleaned for the twenty Irish laborers whom the sons hired. The Archbald sons tried commercial speculation, borrowing money to buy wheat and lumber in western New York to resell hopefully for substantial profits to merchants in Albany and New York City. As early as 1808 Mary Ann reached an unpleasant conclusion about her new home: "We are a nation of traders in spite of all Mr. Jefferson can say or do."

After the War of 1812, the market economy took off in unanticipated ways. In the North, steamboats, canals, and then

This icon will direct you to interactive activities and study materials on A People And A Nation, Brief Edition
website: **www.cengage.com/history/norton/ peoplenationbrief8e**

Chronology

1825	Erie Canal is completed.	**1837**	Panic of 1837 begins economic downturn.
1830	Railroad era begins.	**1839–43**	Economic depression occurs.
1830s–50s	Urban riots are commonplace.	**1842**	*Commonwealth v. Hunt* declares strikes lawful.
1834	Women workers strike at Lowell textile mills.	**1844**	Federal government grant sponsors first telegraph line.
1835	Arkansas passes first women's property law.		Lowell Female Reform Association is formed.
1836	Second Bank of the United States closes.		

railroads remapped the young republic's geography and economy, setting off booms in westward migration, industry, commerce, and urban growth.

Even after the War of 1812, the United States' financial connections to Europe, particularly Britain, remained profound. When Europeans suffered hard times, so did American merchants, manufacturers, farmers, and workers. For wage-earning Americans, economic downturns often meant unemployment and destitution.

Some worried that rapid market expansion threatened the nation's moral fiber. It upset traditional family patterns and relied heavily on unskilled workers—many of whom were immigrants and free African Americans—who seemed unfit for republican citizenship. Commercially minded Americans saw cities as at once exemplars of civilization and breeding grounds of depravity and conflict. Only through strong faith in progress and upward mobility could Americans remain hopeful that the nation's future greatness lay in commercial expansion. They did so partly by articulating a free-labor ideology that rationalized the negative aspects of market expansion while promoting the northern labor system as superior to the South's.

- **What factors contributed to the commercialization of northern society, and why did they have less of an influence on the South?**
- **How did the daily lives—work, family, leisure—of northerners change between 1815 and 1860?**
- **What factors contributed to rapid urbanization, and how did urban and rural life in the North compare with that in the South?**

OR IS IT THE NORTH THAT WAS DISTINCTIVE?

The historian James McPherson has questioned whether it was the *North*—New England, the Middle Atlantic, and the Old Northwest—and not the South that diverged from the norm. At the republic's birth, the two regions had much in common: slavery, ethnic homogeneity, a majority of the population engaged in agriculture, and a small urban population. But that changed with economic development after the War of 1812. State and local governments as well as private entrepreneurs engaged in development, which happened more extensively and rapidly in the North. As the North embraced economic progress, it diverged from the international norm, and, writes McPherson, "hurtled forward toward a future that many Southerners found distasteful if not frightening."

While the South expanded as a slave society, during and after the War of 1812, the North transformed into a market society. With European trade largely cut off during the war, entrepreneurs invested in domestic factories. More men, women, and children began working for wages—rather than on family farms—making the domestic demand for foodstuffs soar. Consequently, farming became commercialized, with farmers abandoning self-sufficiency and specializing in crops that would yield cash on the market. Farmers then used the cash to buy goods they once made for themselves, such as cloth, candles, and soap, as well as some luxuries. In the North, market expansion altered virtually every aspect of life. Some historians see these rapid and pervasive changes as a market revolution.

Preindustrial Farms At the beginning of the nineteenth century, few yeoman farmers, North or South, were entirely independent. Most practiced mixed agriculture, raising a variety of crops and livestock. When they produced more than they needed, they traded the surplus with neighbors or sold it to local storekeepers. Such transactions often transpired without money; farmers might trade eggs for shoes, or they might labor in a neighbor's fields in exchange for hay. Farmers like James and Mary Ann Archbald engaged in long-distance market exchange, selling farm goods for cash to merchants, who then sent the goods to people hundreds of miles away. Although families like the Archbalds indulged in the occasional luxury, security and debt elimination mattered more than profit.

Family members provided most farm labor, though some yeoman farmers, North and South, relied on slaves or indentured servants. Men and boys worked in the fields, herded livestock, chopped firewood, fished, and hunted. Women and girls tended gardens, milked cows, spun and wove, processed and preserved food, prepared meals, washed clothes, and looked after infants and toddlers.

In their quest for independence, farmers cooperated with one another, lending each other tools, harvesting each other's fields, bartering goods, raising their neighbors' barns, and husking each other's corn. Little cash exchanged hands, mostly because money was scarce. Still, New England farmers kept elaborate account books listing what they owed and were owed, whereas Southern farmers simply made mental notes of debts. In both regions, years might pass without debts being repaid.

In the local economy—where farmers exchanged goods with people they knew—a system of just price prevailed, in which value was calculated on the basis of the amount of labor involved. When the same farmers engaged in long-distance trade—selling goods through a network of merchants who eventually resold them as far away as Europe—they set prices according to what the market would bear.

Preindustrial Artisans Farmers who lived near towns or villages often purchased crafted goods from local cobblers, saddlers, blacksmiths, gunsmiths, silversmiths, and tailors. Most artisans, though, lived in the nation's seaports, where master craftsmen (businessmen who owned their own shops and tools) employed apprentices and journeymen. Although the vast majority of craftsmen, North and South, were white, free blacks were well represented in some cities' trades, such as tailoring and carpentry in Charleston,

Although separating flax fibers from their woody base could be arduous work, flax-scutching bees—much like corn-husking bees—brought together neighbors for frivolity as well as work.   (National Gallery of Art, Washington, D.C. Gift of Edgar William and Bernice Chrysler Garbisch)

South Carolina. Teenage apprentices lived with masters, who trained, lodged, and fed them in exchange for labor. The master's wife and daughters, cooked, cleaned, and sewed for the workers. When their apprenticeship expired, apprentices became journeymen who earned wages, hoping to save money to open their own shops. The workplace had little division of labor or specialization. For example, a tailor measured, designed, and sewed an entire suit.

Men, women, and children worked long days on farms and in workshops, but the pace was uneven and unregimented. During busy periods, they worked dawn to dusk; work slowed after the harvest or after a large order was completed. Husking bees and barn raisings brought people together to shuck corn and raise buildings, but also to eat, drink, and flirt. Busy periods did not stop artisans from taking grog breaks or reading the newspaper aloud; they might even close their shops to attend a political meeting. Journeymen craftsmen often staggered in late on Monday mornings, if they showed up at all, after carousing on their day off. In this way, workers exerted influence over the workplace.

Early Industrialization   Early industry in the United States reorganized daily work routines and market relationships. In the late eighteenth and early nineteenth centuries, a putting-out system developed in the Northeast, particularly Massachusetts, New Jersey, and Pennsylvania. Women and children continued to produce household goods but now a merchant supplied them with raw materials, paid them a wage (usually a price for each piece they produced), and sold their wares in distant markets, pocketing the profits himself. Outwork, as it is sometimes called, appealed to women eager for cash to secure economic independence or save for additional land where their children could set up farms. Particularly in New England—where population density and tired soil constricted farming prospects—the putting-out system provided opportunities to earn money with which to buy cheaper, more fertile western lands.

The earliest factories grew in tandem with the putting-out system. Samuel Slater helped set up the first American water-powered spinning mill in Rhode Island in 1790, using children to card and spin raw cotton into thread. He sent the spun thread to nearby farm families who were paid to weave it into cloth. Although the work remained familiar, women now operated their looms for wages and produced cloth for the market.

THE TRANSPORTATION REVOLUTION

Before the War of 1812, natural waterways provided the most readily available and inexpensive transportation routes for people and goods, but they had limitations. Boatmen poled bateaux (cargo boats) down shallow rivers or floated flatboats down deep ones. Cargo generally moved in one direction—downstream—and most boats were destroyed for lumber at their destination. Upstream commerce was limited.

Roads

Although some roads were built during the colonial and revolutionary eras, they often became obstructed by fallen trees, soaked by mud, or clouded in dust, thereby restricting overland transport. To reduce mud and dust, some turnpike companies built corduroy roads, whose tightly lined-up logs resembled the ribbed fabric. But passengers complained of nausea from being continually jolted, and merchants remained wary of transporting fragile wares by wagon. Land transportation was slow and expensive. In 1800, it cost as much to ship a ton of goods 30 miles into the interior as to ship the same goods from New York to England. The lack of cheap, quick transportation impeded westward expansion and industrial growth.

After the American Revolution, some northern states chartered private stock companies to build turnpikes (toll roads), which expanded commercial possibilities in southern New England and the Middle Atlantic. But during the War of 1812 the lack of a road system in more northerly and southerly reaches constrained the movement of troops and supplies, prompting renewed interest in building roads. Aside from the National Road, financing fell on the states and private investors. The new turnpike companies that emerged did sometimes adopt improvements, such as laying hard crushed-stone surfaces, but many of the newly built roads suffered from the old problems. With natural water routes unpredictable and roads predictably bad, an urgent need arose for better transportation.

Steamboats

The first major innovation was the steamboat. In 1807 Robert Fulton's *Clermont* traveled between New York and Albany on the Hudson River in thirty-two hours, demonstrating the feasibility of steam engines to power boats. After the Supreme Court's 1814 ruling against monopolies in *Gibbons v. Ogden* (1824), steamboat companies flourished on eastern rivers and, to a lesser extent, the Great Lakes. They transported settlers to the Midwest, where they would grow grain and raise pigs. Along western rivers like the Mississippi and the Ohio, steamboats carried midwestern timber and grain and southern cotton to New Orleans, where they were transferred to oceangoing vessels destined for northern and international ports. Privately operated, steamboats became subject to federal regulations after frequent and deadly accidents in which boilers exploded, fires ignited, and boats collided.

Canals

In the late eighteenth and early nineteenth centuries, private companies (sometimes with state subsidies) built small canals to transport goods to and from interior locations. These projects rarely reaped the profits investors sought, making it difficult to court investors for other projects. In 1815 only three canals measured more than 2 miles long; the longest was 27 miles. After Madison's veto of the Bonus Bill dashed New Yorkers' hopes for a canal connecting Lake Erie to the port of New York, Governor DeWitt Clinton pushed successfully for a state-sponsored initiative. The Erie Canal was to run 363 miles between Buffalo and Albany, and was to be 4 feet deep.

Erie Canal

Construction began on July 4, 1817. The canal, its promoters emphasized, would demonstrate how American ingenuity and hard work could overcome any obstacle, including the combined ascent and descent of 680 feet between Buffalo and Albany. Building the canal would help unify the nation and secure its commercial independence from Europe.

Over the next eight years, nearly nine thousand laborers felled forests, shoveled dirt, blasted rock, hauled boulders, rechanneled streams, and molded the canal bed. Stonemasons and carpenters built aqueducts and locks. The work was dangerous, often taking place in malaria- and rattlesnake-infested swamps. Gunpowder explosions blew up some workers along with the rock. Collapsing canal beds smothered others, while some fell to their deaths from aqueducts and locks.

The canal's promoters celebrated the waterway as the work of "republican free men." Although farmers and artisans provided important labor, unskilled laborers—including immigrants and convicts—outnumbered them. Once completed, the Erie Canal relied heavily on child labor. Boys led the horses who pulled the canal boats between the canal's eighty-three locks, while girls cooked and cleaned on the boats. When the canal froze shut during winter, many workers had neither employment nor shelter.

After its completion in November 1825, the Erie Canal became an immediate commercial success. Horse-drawn boats, stacked with bushels of wheat, barrels of oats, and piles of logs, streamed eastward from western New York and Buffalo, where shipments were transferred to canal boat. Forty thousand passengers in 1825 alone traveled on the new waterway. The canal shortened the journey between Buffalo and New York City from twenty to six days and reduced freight charges by nearly 95 percent, thus securing New York City's position as the nation's preeminent port. Goods that were previously unavailable in the nation's interior now could be had easily and cheaply.

By 1840 canals crisscrossed the Northeast and Midwest, and total canal mileage reached 3,300. Fewer canals were dug in the South, where the region's navigable rivers made them less necessary. None of the new canals enjoyed the Erie's financial success. As the high cost of construction combined with economic contraction, investment in canals slumped in the 1830s. Several midwestern states could not repay their canal loans, leading them to bankruptcy or near-bankruptcy. By mid-century the canal era had ended. The Erie Canal (by then twice enlarged and rerouted) continued to prosper and operate until the late twentieth century.

Railroads

The future belonged to railroads. Trains moved faster than canal boats and could operate year-round. Railroads could connect the most remote locations to national markets. By 1860 the United States had 60,000 miles of track, mostly in the North, and railroads dramatically reduced the cost and time of shipping goods by land.

The United States railroad era began in 1830 when Peter Cooper's locomotive, Tom Thumb, steamed along 13 miles of Baltimore & Ohio Railroad track. Not until the 1850s did railroads offer long-distance service at reasonable rates. Even then, lack of a common standard for track width thwarted development of a national system. A journey from Philadelphia to Charleston involved eight different gauges; this meant that passengers and freight had to change trains seven times. Only at Bowling Green, Kentucky, did northern and southern railroads connect. As such, the nation's canals and railroads did little to unite the regions and promote nationalism, as proponents had hoped.

Government Promotion of Internal Improvements

Northern state and local governments and private investors spent substantially more on internal improvements than southerners. Pennsylvania and New York together accounted for half of all state monies invested. Southern states invested in railroads, but—with smaller free populations—they collected fewer taxes and had less to spend.

For capitalists seeking dividends, southern railroads seemed a poor bet. To be profitable for investors and affordable for shippers, trains had to be filled in both directions, transporting southern agricultural goods north and sending northern manufactured goods south. Although planters bought northern ready-made clothes and shoes for slaves, such purchases—made on an annual basis—did not constitute a regular source of incoming freight. Because the wealthiest men lived along rivers and could send their cotton to market on steamboats, they sometimes saw little need for railroads.

The North and South laid roughly the same amount of railroad track per person before the Civil War, but when measured in mileage, the more populous North had tracks that stretched considerably farther, forming an integrated system of local

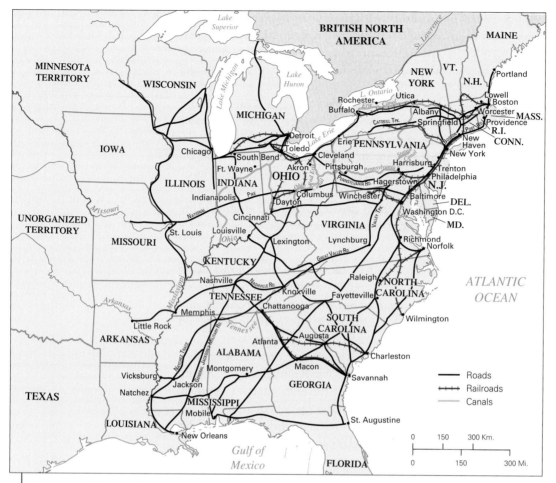

Map 11.1 Major Roads, Canals, and Railroads, 1850

A transportation network linked the seaboard to the interior. Settlers followed those routes westward, and they sent back grain, grain products, and cotton to the port cities.

lines branching off major trunk lines. In the South, railroads remained local. Neither people nor goods moved easily across the South, unless they traveled via steamboat or flatboat along the Mississippi River system, and even then, flooded banks disrupted passage for weeks.

Regional Connections   The North's frenzy of canal and railroad building expanded transportation networks far into the hinterlands. In 1815 nearly all produce from the Old Northwest floated down the Mississippi to New Orleans, tying that region's fortunes to the South. By the 1850s, though, canals and railroads strengthened economic, cultural, and political links between the Old Northwest—particularly the densely populated northern regions—and the Northeast.

Internal improvements hastened westward migration, making western settlement more appealing by providing easy access to eastern markets and the comforts of home. News, visitors, and luxuries now traveled regularly to previously remote areas of the Northeast and Midwest.

With Samuel F. B. Morse's invention of the telegraph in 1844, news traveled almost instantaneously. By 1852 more than 23,000 miles of lines were strung across the nation. The telegraph facilitated the birth of modern business practices involving the coordination of market conditions, production, and supply across great distances.

Ambivalence Toward Progress

Many northerners hailed internal improvements as symbols of progress. Northerners proclaimed that, by building canals and railroads, they had completed God's design for the North American continent. On a more practical level, canals and railroads enabled them to seek better opportunities in the West.

But many northerners worried about the costs of progress. Mary Ann Archbald savored the fresh seafood that now reached her but regretted that her sons turned to speculation. Others decried the enormous numbers of Irish canal diggers and railroad tracklayers, whom they deemed depraved and racially inferior. Still others worried that, by promoting urban growth, transportation innovations fostered social ills.

The degradation of the natural world proved worrisome, too. When streams were rerouted, swamps drained, and forests felled, natural habitats were disturbed, even destroyed. Deprived of waterpower, mills no longer ran. Without forests, wild animals—on which many rural people (Native and European American) had relied for protein—sought homes elsewhere. Fishermen, too, found their sources of protein (and cash) dried up when natural waterways were dammed or rerouted to feed canals.

FACTORIES AND INDUSTRIALIZATION

By dramatically lowering transportation costs, internal improvements facilitated the Northeast's rapid manufacturing and commercial expansion. With the trans-Appalachian West open for settlement, western farmers supplied raw materials and foodstuffs for northeastern factories and workers. They also expanded the domestic market for Northeastern manufactured goods. Focused on cultivating their lands, western settlers preferred to buy rather than make cloth, shoes, and other goods. They needed northeastern iron, too, for farm implements (plows, pitchforks, scythes), nails, and railroad tracks.

One of the oldest industries in North America, iron was centered in Middle Atlantic states, especially Pennsylvania, but stretched to Richmond and Albany. Iron forges, typically small enterprises, flourished wherever ore deposits and fuel sources abounded. During the 1840s, ironworks increasingly shifted from charcoal to coal and then steam to heat their furnaces. But production methods and daily work remained unchanged, with smaller firms remaining more efficient than larger ones.

Factory Work

In other industries, daily life changed dramatically. Much early industrialization involved processing raw materials—milling flour, turning hogs into packaged meat, or sawing lumber. The pork-packing industry illustrates how specialization turned skilled craftsmen into laborers. Traditionally, each butcher cut up an entire pig. Under industrial organization, each worker was assigned a particular task, such as cutting

The United States as a Developing Nation

In the early nineteenth century, the United States was a developing nation, as its economy slowly shifted from agriculture and raw materials to producing manufactured goods. To develop, the United States imported capital to finance international trade, internal improvements, and factories.

American political and economic leaders in the early nineteenth century talked as if they were masters of their own fate. Despite the political independence the United States established after the Revolutionary War and the War of 1812, in many ways, the United States remained economically dependent on Great Britain. Following the War of 1812, 90 percent of all U.S. foreign capital came from Britain, and around 60 percent of British capital exports flowed to the United States. Americans used British capital to develop the canals and railroads. The British invested $7 million in New York State bonds to finance the Erie Canal. Altogether, European investors provided 80 percent of the money to build the Erie.

The United States imported more goods than it exported. Imported capital balanced the trade deficit. As in most developing countries, exports were primarily agricultural commodities; 50 percent of all exports were cotton. British credit financed cotton sales.

U.S. dependency on international capital was highlighted during the Panics of 1819 and 1837. Although these financial crises began in the United States, they were intensified when economic problems in England led investors to pull capital from the United States while merchants demanded that Americans pay their debts to British creditors. Money became tight, and the economy declined.

Thus both economic development and hard times revealed the significance of international capital links to the United States, a developing nation.

Workers near the entrance of the Erie Canal into the Hudson River prepare to ship agricultural products from western New York and the Midwest to the international port of New York.

(© Collection of the New-York Historical Society)

off the right front leg or scooping out the entrails, as the pig moved down a "disassembly line."

The impersonal nature and formal rules of factory work contrasted with the informality of artisan shops and farm households. In large factories, laborers never saw owners, working instead under paid supervisors, nor did they see the final product of their labor. Factory workers lost their sense of autonomy as the bell, steam whistle, or clock governed their day. Jobs were insecure, as competition—particularly from the steady stream of European immigrants, who started arriving in the 1840s—frequently led to replacement by cheaper, less-skilled workers or children. Opportunities for advancement were virtually nil.

At first Americans imported the machines that would make mass production possible or copied British designs. Soon, they built their own. The American System of manufacturing, as the British called it, used precision machinery to produce interchangeable parts. Eli Whitney, the cotton gin's inventor, promoted interchangeable parts in 1798, when he contracted with the federal government to make ten thousand rifles in twenty-eight months. The American System quickly became the machine-tool industry—the manufacture of machines for mass production. With the time and skill involved in manufacturing greatly reduced, the new system permitted mass production of inexpensive but high-quality household items.

Textile Mills

In no industry was mechanization more dramatic than textiles, whose production was centered in New England, near sources of water to power spinning machines and looms. After 1815, New England's rudimentary cotton mills developed into modern factories where machines mass-produced goods. Cotton cloth production rose from 4 million yards in 1817 to 323 million in 1840, and in the mid-1840s, the cotton mills employed approximately eighty thousand operatives; more than half were women.

This young mill girl at Waltham or Lowell, probably in the late 1840s, posed for an early daguerreotype. Her swollen and rough hands contrast with her youth, neat dress, and carefully tied, beribboned hair. Her hands suggest that she worked, as did most twelve- and thirteen-year-olds, as a warper, straightening the strands of cotton or wool as they entered the looms.   (© Mary Evans Picture Library/ The Image Works)

Unable to find enough laborers near mills, managers recruited New England farm daughters, whom they housed in boarding houses in what became known as the Waltham or Lowell plan. People who lived off the land were often suspicious of those who did not—particularly in the young United States, where an agrarian lifestyle was associated with virtue. To ease concerns, mill owners offered paternalistic oversight; they enforced curfews, prohibited alcohol, and required church attendance. Still, the Waltham system offered farm girls opportunities to socialize with other women and gain a sense of independence.

Working conditions in textile mills—the deafening roar of the power looms, long hours, and regimentation—made young women cling to notions their stints were temporary. They used their wages to help their families buy land or send a brother to college, to save for their dowries or education, or to spend on personal items, such as clothing. The average girl arrived at sixteen and stayed five years, usually leaving to get married, often to men they met in town rather than farm boys at home.

Although the Waltham plan drew international attention, more common was the Rhode Island (or Fall River) plan employed by Samuel Slater, among others. Mills hired entire families, whom they lodged in boarding houses. Men often worked farm plots nearby while wives and children worked in the mills, though as the system developed, men worked in the factories, supervising wives and children in family-based work units.

Labor Protests

Life in the textile mills got harder over time. To increase productivity, managers sped up machines and required each worker to operate more machines. Between 1836 and 1850 the number of spindles and looms in Lowell increased 150 and 140 percent, respectively, whereas the number of workers increased by only 50 percent. To boost profits, owners lengthened hours, cut wages, and packed boarding houses.

Workers organized, and in 1834, responding to a 25 percent wage cut, they unsuccessfully turned out (struck) against the Lowell mills. As conditions worsened and strikes failed, workers resisted in new ways. In 1844 Massachusetts mill women formed the Lowell Female Reform Association and joined with other workers to press, unsuccessfully, for state legislation mandating a ten-hour instead of fourteen-hour day.

Women aired their complaints in worker-run newspapers: in 1842, the *Factory Girl* appeared in New Hampshire, the *Wampanoag and Operatives' Journal* in Massachusetts. Two years later, mill workers founded the *Voice of Industry,* nicknamed "the factory girl's voice." The owner-sponsored *Lowell Offering* faced controversy when workers charged that its editors suppressed articles criticizing working conditions.

Worker turnover weakened women's organizational efforts. Few militant native-born mill workers stayed to fight managers and owners, and gradually, fewer New England daughters entered the mills, replaced in the 1850s by Irish immigrants. Technological improvements made the work less skilled and more routine, reducing wages.

Male workers, too, protested changes wrought by the market economy. As voters, they formed labor political parties first in Pennsylvania, New York, and Massachusetts in the 1820s and later elsewhere. They advocated free public education and an end to imprisonment for debt and opposed banks and monopolies. Still aspiring to own land, some advocated for free homesteads.

Labor Unions

Organized labor's greatest achievement came through the courts. When journeyman shoemakers organized during the early 1800s, employers accused them of criminal conspiracy. The cordwainers' (shoemakers') cases between 1806 and 1815 left labor organizations in an uncertain position. Although the courts acknowledged journeymen's right to organize, judges viewed strikes as illegal until a Massachusetts case, *Commonwealth v. Hunt* (1842), ruled that Boston journeyman boot makers could strike "to subserve their own interests."

The first unions arose among urban journeymen in printing, woodworking, shoemaking, and tailoring. Typically local, the strongest sought protection against competition from inferior workmen by regulating apprenticeships and establishing minimum wages. Umbrella organizations of individual craft unions, like the National Trade Union (1834), arose in several cities in the 1820s and 1830s. But the movement fell apart amid wage reductions and unemployment in the hard times of 1839–1843.

Permanent labor organizations were difficult to sustain. Skilled craftsmen looked down on unskilled and semiskilled workers. Moreover, workers divided along ethnic, religious, racial, and gender lines.

CONSUMPTION AND COMMERCIALIZATION

Before the 1820s, women sewed most clothing at home, and some people purchased used clothing. Tailors and seamstresses made wealthy men's and women's clothing to order. By the 1820s and 1830s, much clothing was mass-produced for sale in clothing stores. Measuring was replaced by standard sizes. And now, instead of a tailor's performing every task, the process was divided so one worker cut patterns, another sewed hems, and another fixed buttons. The invention of the sewing machine in 1846 sped the process, especially after it became widely available in the 1850s. Many farm families continued to make their own clothing, but when they could afford to, they bought clothes.

The Garment Industry

Market expansion created a demand for mass-produced clothing. Girls working in factories no longer had time to sew clothes. Young immigrant men, separated from mothers and sisters, had to buy the crudely made, loose-fitting clothing. But the biggest market for ready-made clothes initially was the cotton South. With the success of the textile industry driving up the demand and price for raw cotton, planters bought ready-made shoes and clothes for slaves.

Retailers often bought goods wholesale, though many manufactured shirts and trousers in their own factories. Lewis and Hanford of New York City boasted of cutting more than 100,000 garments in winter 1848–1849. The New York firm did business mostly in the South and owned a retail outlet in New Orleans. While southerners and westerners became involved in the clothing trade, its center remained in New York.

Specialization of Commerce

Commercial specialization transformed some urban traders, especially in New York, into merchant princes. After the Erie Canal opened, New York City became a stop on every major trade route from Europe, southern ports, and the West. Traders sometimes invested in factories, further stimulating urban manufacturing. Some cities specialized: Rochester became a milling center (the Flour City), and Cincinnati (Porkopolis) became the first meatpacking center.

Merchants who engaged in complex commercial transactions required large—mostly male—office staffs. At the bottom were messenger boys, often preteens, who delivered documents. Above them were copyists, who hand-copied documents. Clerks processed documents and did translations. Above them were the bookkeeper and the confidential chief clerk. Those seeking employment in such countinghouses took a course from a writing master. All hoped to rise to partner, although their chances were increasingly slim.

Specialization lagged in small towns, where merchants continued to exchange goods with local farm women, and craftsmen continued to sell finished goods, such as shoes. In some rural areas, peddlers acted as general merchants. But as transportation improved and towns grew, small-town merchants began to specialize.

Commercial Farming

Even amid the manufacturing and commercial boom, agriculture remained the backbone of the economy, North and South. But while the expansion of cotton production in the Southwest brought limited economic change to the rest of the South, in the North, the transportation revolution and market expansion transformed formerly semi-subsistence farms into commercial enterprises. Many families stopped practicing mixed agriculture and began to specialize in cash crops.

By the 1820s, eastern farmers had cultivated nearly all available land, and the uneven terrains did not lend themselves to the new labor-saving farm implements introduced in the 1830s, such as mechanical sowers, reapers, and threshers. Consequently, many northern farmers either moved west or gave up farming for jobs in merchants' houses and factories. Those who remained, however, proved adaptable, their efforts encouraged by state governments that promoted agricultural innovation.

In 1820 about one-third of northern produce was intended for the market, but by 1850 it surpassed 50 percent. As farmers shifted toward market-oriented production, they invested in additional land (buying farms of neighbors who moved west), new equipment, and new labor sources (hired hands). Many New England and Middle Atlantic farm families faced steep competition from midwestern farmers after the Erie Canal's opening, and they began abandoning wheat and corn and turning toward vegetables, fruit, and livestock, especially cattle. Much of what they produced fed the North's growing urban and manufacturing populations.

Farmers financed innovations through land sales and debts. Indeed, increasing land values promised the greatest profit. Farm families who owned land flourished, but by the 1840s it took more than ten years for a laborer in the Northeast to save enough to buy a farm. The number of tenant farmers and hired hands increased, and farmers who previously relied mostly on unpaid family members and enslaved workers now leased portions of their farms or hired waged labor.

Farm Women's Changing Labor

As the commercial economy expanded, rural women added new responsibilities to their substantial chores. Some took in outwork. Many increased production of eggs, dairy products, and garden produce for sale; others raised bees or silkworms.

With New England textile mills producing more finished cloth, farm women and children often abandoned time-consuming spinning and weaving and instead bought factory-produced cloth. With the time saved, women made butter and cheese in large quantities for the market. Some mixed-agriculture farms converted entirely to dairy production, with men taking over formerly female tasks. Canals and railroads carried cheese to eastern ports, where wholesalers sold it worldwide.

Rural Communities

Despite pressure to manage their farms like time-efficient businesses, some farmers clung to old practices of gathering at market, general stores, taverns, and church. They continued barn raisings and husking bees, but by the 1830s, with young women working in textile mills and young men laboring as clerks or factory hands, there were fewer young people at such events.

Farmers continued to swap labor and socialize with neighbors, but they began to reckon debts in dollars. They watched national and international markets more closely. When financial panics hit, cash shortages almost halted business activity, casting many farmers further into debt, even bankruptcy. Faced with potentially losing their land, farmers called in neighbors' debts, sometimes rupturing long-established relationships.

Cycles of Boom and Bust

With market expansion came boom and bust cycles. Prosperity stimulated demand for finished goods, such as clothing and furniture, which led to higher prices and still higher production and to speculation in land. Investment money was plentiful as Americans saved and foreign, mostly British, investors bought U.S. bonds and securities. Then production surpassed demand. Prices and wages fell; land and stock values collapsed, and investment money left the United States. This boom-and-bust cycle touched the whole country, but particularly the Northeast.

Although the 1820s and 1830s were boom times, financial panic triggered a bust in 1837, the year after the Second Bank of the United States closed. Economic contraction remained severe through 1843. Many banks could not repay depositors, and states, facing deficits, defaulted on bonds. European, especially British, investors became suspicious of U.S. loans and withdrew money from the United States.

Hard times had come. "The streets seemed deserted," Sidney George Fisher observed of Philadelphia in 1842. "The largest [merchant] houses are shut up and to rent, there is no business . . . no money, no confidence." New York countinghouses closed their doors. The hungry formed bread lines at soup societies, and beggars crowded the sidewalks. Crowds of laborers demanding their deposits gathered at closed banks. Sheriffs sold seized property at one-quarter of pre–hard-time prices. In smaller cities like Lynn, Massachusetts, shoemakers weathered hard times by fishing and tending gardens, while laborers dug for clams and harvested dandelions. Congress passed the Federal Bankruptcy Law of 1841; by the time the law was repealed two years later, forty-one thousand bankrupts sought protection under its provisions.

FAMILIES IN FLUX

Sweeping changes in the household economy, rural as well as urban, led to new family ideals. In the preindustrial era, families were primarily economic units; now they became a moral and cultural institution. In reality few families could live up to this ideal.

The Ideal Family

In the North, the market economy increasingly separated the home from the workplace, leading to a new middle-class ideal in which men functioned in the public sphere, while women oversaw the private or domestic sphere. The home became, in theory, an emotional retreat from the competitive, selfish business world. Men provided and protected, while women nurtured and guarded the family's morality, ensuring that capitalism's excesses stayed outside the home. Childhood expanded: children remained at home until their late teens or early twenties, and education became important.

This ideal came to be known as separate-sphere ideology, the cult of domesticity, or the cult of true womanhood. Although it rigidly separated male and female spheres, this ideology elevated domestic responsibilities. In her widely read *Treatise on Domestic Economy* (1841), Catharine Beecher approached housekeeping as a science while trumpeting mothers' role as moral guardians. Beecher maintained that women's natural superiority as moral, nurturing caregivers suited them for teaching (when single) and parenting (once married). Beecher insisted that the private sphere be elevated to the same status as the public.

Shrinking Families

These new domestic ideals depended on smaller families, enabling parents, particularly mothers, to give children better attention, education, and financial help. Urban families produced fewer household goods, and commercial farmers, unlike self-sufficient ones, relied on hired laborers rather than family members. Although smaller families resulted partly from first marriages' occurring at a later age, they also resulted from planning, made easier when cheap rubber condoms became available in the 1850s. Some women chose, too, to end accidental pregnancies with abortion.

In 1800 American women bore seven or eight children; by 1860 they had five or six. This decline occurred even though immigrants with large-family traditions were settling in the United States; thus the birth rate among native-born women declined more sharply.

Few northern women could fulfill the middle-class ideal of separate spheres. Most wage-earning women provided essential income for their families and could not stay home. Yet middle-class reformers mistook poverty for immorality, condemning working mothers for letting their children work or scavenge rather than attend school. Middle-class women could stay home, but new standards of cleanliness and comfort drained their time. Women's contributions to their families were assessed in moral, not economic, terms. Working inside their homes, women could not devote themselves primarily to childrearing, making the ideals of the cult of domesticity impossible for even middle-class families.

Women's Paid Labor

In working-class families, women left home as early as age twelve, earning wages most of their lives, with short respites for bearing and rearing children. Unmarried girls and women worked primarily as domestic servants or in factories; married and widowed women worked as laundresses, seamstresses, and cooks. Some hawked food and wares on city streets, others did piecework, and some became prostitutes. Few could support themselves or a family comfortably.

If middle-class girls left home to work—in New England's textile mills, in new urban stores as clerks—it was only briefly, before marriage. Otherwise, teaching was the only occupation consistent with genteel femininity. In 1823 Catharine and Mary Beecher established the Hartford Female Seminary, adding history and science to the traditional women's curriculum of domestic arts and religion. A decade later, Catharine Beecher successfully campaigned for teacher-training schools for women. Single, these women would not need to earn as much as their male counterparts, whom she presumed to be married. Unmarried women earned half the salary of male teachers. By 1850 schoolteaching had become a woman's profession.

The proportion of single women in the population increased significantly in the nineteenth century. As more young men headed west, some eastern communities had a disproportionate number of young women. Other women chose to remain independent. Because women's work was often poorly paid, those who forswore marriage faced serious challenges; many single women could not support themselves without charitable or family assistance.

THE GROWTH OF CITIES

The most rapid urbanization occurred between 1820 and 1860. The percentage of people living in urban areas (defined by a population of 2,500 or more) grew from 7 percent in 1820 to nearly 20 percent in 1860. The greatest growth took place in the Northeast and the Midwest. Although most northerners continued to live on farms or in small villages, cities boomed. Many urban residents were temporary—soon moving to another city or the countryside—and many were immigrants.

Urban Boom

In 1820 the United States had thirteen places with a population greater than 10,000; in 1860 it had ninety-three (see Map 11.2). New York City, already the nation's largest city in 1820, saw its population grow from 123,709 people to 813,669 in 1860. Philadelphia, the nation's second-largest city, saw its population multiply ninefold in that forty-year period. In 1815 Rochester, New York, had just 300 residents. By 1830, the Erie Canal turned the sleepy agricultural town into the nation's twenty-fifth-largest city, with a population of just over 9,000.

Cities expanded geographically, too. Until 1830, New Yorkers could walk the entire length of the city in an hour. In 1825 Fourteenth Street was the city's northern boundary. By 1860, Forty-second Street was the city's northern limit. Public transit made city expansion possible. By the 1850s, all big cities had horse-drawn streetcars, allowing wealthier residents who could afford the fare to settle on the cities' outskirts.

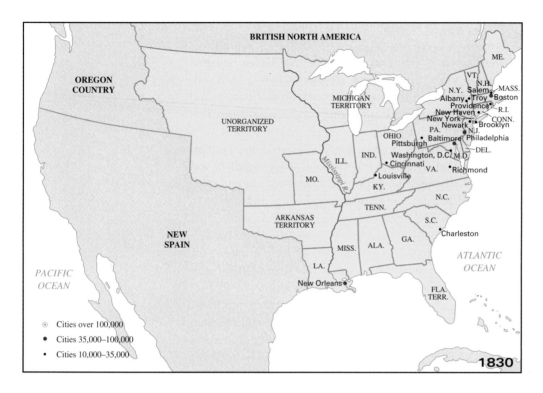

Map 11.2   Major American Cities in 1830 and 1860

The number of Americans who lived in cities increased rapidly between 1820 and 1860, and the number of large cities grew as well. In 1820 only New York City had a population exceeding 100,000; forty years later, eight more cities had surpassed that level.

Cities sustained the North's market revolution by serving as transportation hubs, commercial centers, and sometimes manufacturing sites. Some cities grew up with manufacturing. The Boston Manufacturing Company selected the site for Lowell, Massachusetts, because of its proximity to the Merrimack River, which could power the company's textile mill. Incorporated in 1826, by the 1850s it was the second-largest city in New England. Although most early manufacturing took place in rural areas, some cities, such as New York, experienced what historians call metropolitan industrialization. Most early ready-made clothing, for example, was produced as outwork by women in tenements throughout New York City. In 1860, 25,000 women worked in manufacturing jobs in New York City, constituting a quarter of the labor force; two-thirds worked in the garment industry.

Municipal Services

Northern cities developed elaborate municipal services but lacked taxing power to provide them for everyone. At best, they could tax property adjoining new sewers, paved streets, and water mains. New services and basic sanitation depended on residents' ability to pay. Another solution was to charter private companies to sell basic services. Baltimore first chartered a private gas company for lights in 1816. By midcentury every major city was lit by a private gas supplier. Private firms lacked the capital to build adequate water systems and laid pipe only in commercial and well-to-do residential areas. Supplying water ultimately fell to city governments.

Extremes of Wealth

Wealth was increasingly concentrated in fewer hands. By 1860 the top 5 percent of American families owned more than half of the nation's wealth, and the top 10 percent

This gouache, attributed to Nicholino Calyo, depicts the Haight family in their drawing room in 1848. Richard K. Wright was a wealthy New York City merchant, trading internationally, as the globe in the foreground suggests. Sarah Rogers Haight was a famous beauty and socialite, and the family's clothing, art, library, and furniture all stand in sharp contrast to the poverty, homelessness, and orphans found on the city's streets. (Museum of the City of New York, Bequest of Elizabeth Cushing Iselin)

owned nearly three-quarters. In the South, income extremes were most apparent on rural plantations, but in the North, economic inequities were most evident in cities.

A number of factors contributed to widespread poverty in America's industrial cities: poor wages, the lack of full-time employment, and the increasingly widespread employment of women and children, which further drove down wages for everyone. Women and children did not need a living wage because they were—employers rationalized—dependent, meaning that they could rely on men to support them. In reality, not all women or children had men to support them, nor did men's wages always prove adequate.

New York provides a striking example. Houses built for two families often held four. Some families took in lodgers to pay the rent; such crowding encouraged poorer New Yorkers to head outdoors. But poor neighborhoods were filthy. Excess sewage from outhouses drained into ditches that carried urine and fecal matter into the streets. People piled garbage into gutters, backyards, or alleys. Pigs, geese, dogs, and vultures scavenged the streets, while rats roamed under wooden side-walks and through large buildings. Typhoid, dysentery, malaria, and tuberculosis regularly visited the poorer sections of cities. Cholera epidemics struck in 1831, 1849, and 1866.

Just beyond poor neighborhoods, the wealthy lived in lavish mansions and escaped to country estates during summer's brutal heat or epidemics. Much of this wealth was inherited. Rich New Yorkers increased their fortunes by investing in commerce and manufacturing.

The middle class was larger than the wealthy elite but substantially smaller than the working classes. They were businessmen, traders, and professionals, and the rapid turn toward industrialization and commercial specialization made them a larger presence in northern cities than in southern ones. Middle-class families en-joyed new consumer items: wool carpeting, fine wallpaper, and rooms full of furni-ture. Houses were large, often from four to six rooms. By the 1840s and 1850s, middle-class families used indoor toilets that were mechanical, though not yet flush-ing. These families formed the backbone of urban clubs, filled the family pews in church, and sent their sons to college.

Immigration

Many of the urban poor were immigrants. The 5 million immigrants to the United States between 1830 and 1860 outnumbered the country's population in 1790. During peak pre–Civil War immigration (1847–1857), 3.3 million immigrants entered the United States, including 1.3 million Irish and 1.1 million Germans (see Figure 11.1). By 1860, 15 percent of the white population was foreign-born, with 90 percent of im-migrants living in northern states.

Various factors pushed Europeans from their homes and pulled them to the northern United States. In Ireland, the potato famine (1845–1850)—a period of widespread starvation caused by a diseased potato crop—drove millions from their homeland. Although economic conditions pushed most Germans, some were polit-ical refugees—liberals, freethinkers, Socialists, communists, and anarchists. Employ-ers, states, and shipping companies promoted opportunities in the United States to Europeans, with the message: work and prosper in America or starve in Europe.

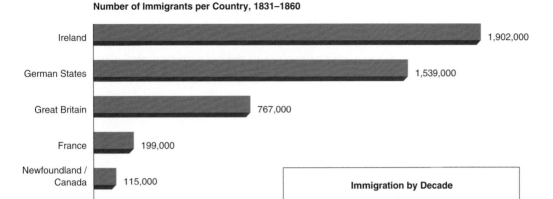

Number of Immigrants per Country, 1831–1860

Ireland	1,902,000
German States	1,539,000
Great Britain	767,000
France	199,000
Newfoundland / Canada	115,000
China	41,000
West Indies	36,000
Sweden / Norway	36,000
Switzerland	34,000
Netherlands	20,000
Mexico	13,000

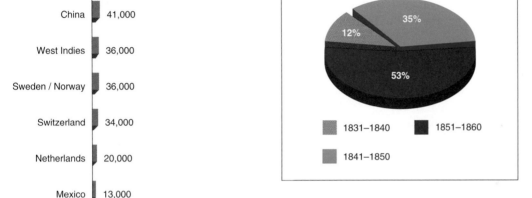

Immigration by Decade

35%
12%
53%

1831–1840   1851–1860
1841–1850

Figure 11.1   Major Sources of Immigration to the United States, 1831–1860

Most immigrants came from two areas: Great Britain, of which Ireland was a part, and the German states. These two areas sent more immigrants between 1830 and 1860 than the inhabitants of the United States enumerated at the first census in 1790. By 1860, 15 percent of the white population was of foreign birth.   (Data from Stephan Thernstrom, ed., *Harvard Encyclopedia of American Ethnic Groups* [Cambridge, MA, and London: Harvard University Press, 1980], 1047)

Once in the United States, immigrants often became disillusioned, and hundreds of thousands returned home.

Many early immigrants lived or worked in rural areas. Like the Archbalds, a few settled on farms and bought land. Others worked as hired farmhands, canal diggers, or railroad tracklayers, often hoping to buy land later. But by the 1840s and 1850s—when record numbers of immigrants arrived—the prospects of buying land became more remote.

By 1860 most immigrants settled in cities, often the port at which they arrived. The most destitute could not afford the fare to places farther inland. Others had resources but fell victim to swindlers. Cities' ethnic flair induced some to stay put. In 1855, 52 percent of New York's 623,000 inhabitants were immigrants, 28 percent from Ireland and 16 percent from German states. Throughout the 1850s about 35 percent of Boston was foreign-born; more than two-thirds were Irish.

Most of the new Irish immigrants were young, poor, Roman Catholics from rural districts. Women found work as domestic servants or millhands, while men worked in construction or transportation. Most Germans came with enough resources to head to states such as Ohio, Illinois, Wisconsin, and Missouri. Although some southern cities like Charleston and Savannah had Irish immigrants, European immigrants, with aversions to slavery and semitropical heat, settled in the Northeast or Midwest.

Ethnic Tensions

Anxieties over the era's economic changes fueled tension between native-born Americans and immigrants, particularly Irish Catholics. Native-born workers blamed immigrants for scarce jobs and low wages. Middle-class whites blamed them for poverty and crime and believed immigrants' moral depravity—not poor wages—led to poverty.

White northerners often portrayed Irish immigrants as nonwhite, as African in appearance. But Irish and African Americans did not develop a sense of solidarity. Instead, some of the era's most virulent riots erupted between Irish immigrants and African Americans.

Anti-Catholicism also became strident in the 1830s. In Boston, anti-Catholic riots occurred frequently. Nearby Charlestown, Massachusetts, saw a mob burn a convent in 1834. In Philadelphia a crowd attacked priests and nuns and vandalized churches in 1844, and in Lawrence, Massachusetts, a mob leveled the Irish neighborhood in 1854. Riots between native-born and Irish Catholic workers also erupted along canals and railroads, but urban riots attracted more newspaper attention, fueling fears that cities were depraved places.

Protestant German immigrants fared better than the Irish. Because Germans generally arrived with resources and skills, Americans stereotyped them as hard working. But non-Protestant Germans—Catholics and Jews (whom white Americans considered a separate race)—frequently encountered racial and religious prejudice.

Irish Catholics usually lived in their own neighborhoods, where they set up churches and schools. In larger cities, immigrants from the same German states clustered together. Immigrants set up social clubs and mutual-aid societies.

People of Color

African Americans also forged their own communities and culture. As late as the 1830s, many remained enslaved in New York and New Jersey, but the numbers of free African Americans grew steadily, and by 1860 nearly 250,000 (many of them refugees from southern slavery) lived in the urban North. African Methodist Episcopal churches and preachers helped foster a sense of community among African Americans.

White racism impinged on northern African Americans' lives. Streetcars, hotels, restaurants, and theaters could turn away African Americans without legal penalty. City laws barred African Americans from public buildings. Even where laws were liberal, whites' attitudes constrained African Americans' opportunities. In Massachusetts, for example, African Americans enjoyed more legal rights than anywhere else. But laws protecting civil and political rights could not make whites shop at black businesses.

African Americans were excluded from factory and clerical jobs. Women worked as house servants, cooks, washerwomen, and child nurses. Most African American men worked as construction workers, porters, longshoremen, or day laborers—all jobs subject to frequent unemployment. Others took lower-paying but more stable service industry jobs as servants, waiters, cooks, barbers, and janitors. Many African American men hired on as sailors and merchant seamen, jobs offering regular employment and advancement, though not protection from racial taunts.

In the growing cities, African Americans turned service occupations into businesses, opening restaurants, hotels, barber shops, and employment agencies for domestic servants. Some sold used clothing or were junk dealers. A few became wealthy, invested in real estate, and loaned money. With professionals—ministers, teachers, physicians, dentists, lawyers, and newspaper editors—they formed a small but expanding African American middle class.

African Americans became targets of urban violence. Philadelphia experienced five major riots in the 1830s and 1840s. White rioters clubbed and stoned African Americans and destroyed their houses, churches, and businesses. By 1860 hundreds died in urban riots.

Urban Culture

Living in cramped, squalid conditions, working-class families spent little time indoors. In the 1840s, a working-class youth culture developed on the Bowery, one of New York's entertainment strips. Lined with theaters, dance halls, and cafés, it became an urban midway. The Bowery boys' greased hair, distinctive clothing, and swagger frightened middle-class and elite New Yorkers, as did the Bowery girls' colorful costumes. Equally scandalous were the middle-class clerks who succumbed to the city's temptations, notably prostitution.

Gangs of garishly dressed young men and women—flaunting their sexuality and drinking to excess—drove self-styled respectable citizenry to establish private clubs. Some men joined the Masonic order, which offered members an elaborate code of deference between ranks, while women organized literary clubs and benevolent societies.

Increasingly, urban recreation and sports became commodities. Horseracing, walking races, and, in the 1850s, baseball began to attract urban men. Some Wall Street office workers formed the Knickerbocker Club in 1842 and in 1845 drew up rules for playing baseball. Large cities boasted two or more theaters catering to different classes. Some plays cut across class lines; Shakespeare was so widely performed that even illiterate theatergoers knew his plays. In the 1840s, singing groups, theater troupes, and circuses traveled from city to city. Particularly popular were minstrel shows, in which white men (often Irish) in makeup imitated African Americans in song and dance. In the early 1830s, Thomas D. Rice of New York became famous for his role as Jim Crow, an old southern slave. Minstrel performers told jokes mocking economic and political elites and evoked nostalgia for preindustrial work habits and morality. But blackface actors also encouraged a racist stereotype of African Americans as sensual and lazy.

Cities as Symbols of Progress

To many northerners, cities represented economic advancement and nurtured churches, schools, governments, and museums—all signs of civilization and culture. As canals and railroads opened the West for settlement, many white northerners applauded the appearance of civilization—church steeples, public buildings—in areas that been savage wilderness, that is, controlled by Native Americans. To many nineteenth-century white Americans, cities represented the moral triumph of civilization over savagery and heathenism.

Yet some middle-class observers also deplored the character of the nation's largest cities, which they saw as havens of disease, poverty, crime, and vice—all signs of moral decline. They considered epidemics to be divine scourges, which struck the filthy, intemperate, and immoral. Theft and prostitution provided evidence of moral vice, and wealthy observers perceived these crimes not as by-products of poverty but as signs of individual failing. They pressed for laws against vagrancy and pushed city officials to establish police forces. Boston hired uniformed policemen in 1837, and New York launched its police force in 1845.

If disease was divine punishment—rather than an offshoot of cramped conditions—then it was within Americans' power to fix things. Middle-class reformers tried to convince the urban working classes that—unlike southern slaves—they could improve their condition through hard work and virtuous habits. This belief in upward mobility became central to many northerners' ideas about progress.

The concept that, in a competitive marketplace, those who worked hard and lived virtuously could improve their status appealed to manufacturers and merchants eager to take credit for their own success. Likewise, they hoped this free-labor ideology with its promise of upward mobility would encourage factory hands and clerks to work hard, live virtuously, and remain optimistic despite hardships. Many laborers initially rejected free-labor ideology as a veiled attempt to tout industrial work habits, rationalize poor wages, and quell worker protest. But by the 1850s, when the question of slavery's westward expansion returned to the political foreground, many northerners embraced free-labor ideology and regarded slavery as antithetical to the modernizing, free-labor ideology of the North.

Thomas D. Rice playing Jim Crow in blackface at the Bowery Theater in New York City, 1833. The rowdy audience climbed on the stage, leaving Rice little room to perform. In representing African Americans on stage, Rice and other minstrels contributed to establishing black and white as racial categories. (© Collection of The New-York Historical Society)

A Mixed Economy

Should the U.S. government run, regulate, or leave to the market system healthcare, Social Security and private pensions, corporate concentration, and stock trading and investments? To what degree should the government be responsible for the well-being of the economy and individuals?

In the early nineteenth century, government played an active role as federal and state governments built roads and canals, developed harbors, and operated post offices and the early telegraph. Government stimulated and regulated the private sector. In chartering corporations and banks and in land sales and grants, the United States created an infrastructure that paved the way for the market economy and industrialization.

In the late nineteenth century, advocates of laissez-faire, or hands-off government, challenged the pre–Civil War active government. Laissez-faire dominated until the 1880s and 1890s, when large corporations and trusts accumulated so much power that governments stepped in to regulate railroads and business concentration. After the turn of the century, the federal government extended regulation to food, drugs, working conditions, and fair business practices. Federal regulation and private initiative were innovatively combined in the Federal Reserve System, created in 1913, as a public system for overseeing currency and banking which left control in private hands. After a revival of laissez-faire in the 1920s, the Great Depression of the 1930s and World War II led the federal government to establish the modern welfare state, which operates through a mixed public and private structure.

Americans today still debate the appropriate role of government. Conservatives argue that regulation hampers individual freedom and distorts supply and demand. Advocates of an activist government argue that only government has the power to check economic concentration and protect health, safety, and the environment. This debate is a legacy from antebellum America.

Summary

During the first half of the nineteenth century, the North became enmeshed in commercial culture, as northern states and capitalists invested heavily in internal improvements. Most northerners shifted toward commercial farming or, in smaller numbers, industrial wage labor. Farmers specialized in cash crops, while their children often worked in factories or countinghouses.

To many northerners, the market economy symbolized progress, bringing easier access to cheap western lands, employment for surplus farm laborers, and the commercial availability of goods that had once been time-consuming to produce. But the market economy also led to increased specialization, a depersonalized workplace, and a sharper divide between work and leisure. The market economy tied northerners more directly to fluctuating national and international markets, and during economic downturns, many northern families experienced destitution.

With less need for children's labor, northerners began producing smaller families. Even as working-class children worked, middle-class families created a model of childhood that had parents shielding children from the world's dangers. Mothers, in theory, became moral guardians, keeping the home safe from the new economy's competitiveness and selfishness. In reality, few women could devote themselves entirely to nurturing children and husbands.

Immigrants and free African Americans generally performed the lowest-paying work, and many native-born whites blamed them for problems spurred by rapid economic change. Anti-immigrant (especially anti-Catholic) and antiblack riots became commonplace. Immigrants and African Americans responded by forming their own communities.

Cities came to symbolize the possibilities and limits of market expansion. Urban areas were marked by extremes of wealth, vibrant working-class cultures as well as poverty and crime. To reconcile these seeming contradictions, middle-class northerners articulated a free-labor ideology, touting the possibility for upward mobility in a competitive marketplace. This ideology would become central to northern regional identity.

Chapter Review

OR IS IT THE NORTH THAT WAS DISTINCTIVE?

What happened to the North and South economically after the War of 1812?

The South continued as an agricultural region and expanded its slave system, while the North transformed quickly into a market economy. With the war cutting off European trade, northern entrepreneurs invested in domestic production and factories. Former artisans and farmers increasingly shifted from producers to wage workers. Commercial farming emerged in the North to meet the growing demand for foodstuffs that was created when people shifted from farming to factory jobs. Those farmers who remained in agriculture shifted to cash crops. Early forms of market changes came from piece work or outwork, where manufacturers hired women and children in their homes to produce goods, often paying them for each piece produced. By 1790, the first spinning mills were opened in Rhode Island.

THE TRANSPORTATION REVOLUTION

Why did the canal era end after just a few decades?

Initially, canals were hailed for transporting goods to and from interior regions at much lower costs and faster timetables than overland routes, with the Erie Canal the largest of its kind and the greatest success story. But by the mid-nineteenth century, the canal heyday was over, as high construction costs combined with economic downturns to make them less desirable. The focus of transportation development shifted to railroads, which were quicker, easier, and cheaper to build; could move far more people and goods for far less money; and unlike canals, could operate year-round.

FACTORIES AND INDUSTRIALIZATION

How was factory work different from the work life people previously knew?

The artisan shops and family farms that pre-dated factories had fewer formal rules and less structure than the factories that arose in the late eighteenth and early nineteenth centuries. Artisans and farmers saw themselves as producers, in charge of their labor and its outcome and working side-by-side with hired helpers. In factories, workers never saw owners, and worked for wages under the watchful eye of supervisors with strict rules and a clock governing their day. There was no job security, and factory workers were often replaced by cheaper immigrant and women workers. Whereas artisan apprentices worked to learn a trade with the hope of setting up their own businesses, there was little or no opportunity for advancement in factories.

CONSUMPTION AND COMMERCIALIZATION

How did farm women's work change as the commercial economy expanded?

Along with their regular farm and household duties, rural women took on new responsibilities to help pay for some of the items they now bought (such as textiles) instead of bartering for or making on their own. Some took in outwork; others increased production of eggs, milk, butter, and produce and other items for sale in the market. Daughters were often sent to work in textile mills, sending part of their wages home to aid their families.

FAMILIES IN FLUX

What roles did families play in the new industrial era?

Before the rise of the market economy, families were the center of production and economic activity. As industrialization took hold, however, new ideals transformed families into moral and cultural institutions. Men, particularly middle-class men, occupied the public sphere, providing for and protecting their families. In this new "separate spheres" ideology, women's roles were confined to the home, and they were charged with making it a retreat for husbands and children from the harshness of economic life. This ideology, which elevated women's domestic roles, was later dubbed *the cult of domesticity* or *the cult of true womanhood*.

THE GROWTH OF CITIES

What contributed to increasing poverty in new urban areas of the Northeast and Midwest?

There were several causes for widespread poverty in industrial cities: poor wages, the lack of full-time employment, and the increasing employment of women and children, which drove down wages for everyone. Massive immigration between 1830 and 1860 also swelled the ranks of the poor, who often began their life in U.S. cities, such as New York. In urban areas, the poor doubled up in apartments or rented out rooms to lodgers to make ends meet. Without the ability to pay for city services, garbage and excess human waste piled high, contributing to disease and epidemics through the middle of the nineteenth century.

SUGGESTIONS FOR FURTHER READING

Hal Barron, *Those Who Stayed Behind: Rural Society in Nineteenth-Century New England* (1984)

Jeanne Boydston, *Home and Work: Housework, Wages, and the Ideology of Labor in the Early Republic* (1990)

Christopher Clark, *The Roots of Rural Capitalism: Western Massachusetts, 1780–1860* (1990)

Nancy Cott, *The Bonds of Womanhood: "Women's Sphere" in New England, 1780–1835* (1977)

Bruce Laurie, *Artisans into Workers: Labor in Nineteenth-Century America* (1989)

Winifred Barr Rothenberg, *From Market-Places to Market Economy: The Transformation of Rural Massachusetts, 1750–1850* (1994)

Mary Ryan, *Cradle of the Middle Class: The Family in Oneida County, New York, 1790–1865* (1981)

Carol Sheriff, *The Artificial River: The Erie Canal and the Paradox of Progress, 1817–1862* (1996)

Christine Stansell, *City of Women: Sex and Class in New York, 1789–1860* (1986)

George Rogers Taylor, *The Transportation Revolution, 1815–1860* (1951)

Reform and Politics in the Age of Jackson

CHAPTER OUTLINE

From Revival to Reform

Communitarian Experiments

Abolitionism

LINKS TO THE WORLD:
The International Antislavery Movement

Women's Rights

Jacksonianism and Party Politics

Federalism at Issue: The Nullification and Bank Controversies

The Whig Challenge and the Second Party System

Summary

LEGACY FOR A PEOPLE AND A NATION: The Bible Belt

The twenty-eight-year-old millhand steadied himself atop a cliff in Paterson, New Jersey; peered down the seventy-foot precipice to the river below; then leapt into the water. He resurfaced to cheers for his death-defying stunt and what it symbolized. It was September 1827, and Sam Patch—who had worked in mills since he was eight years old—was making a point.

Jumping from waterfalls had long been a pastime among boys working in textile mills. But Patch considered it an art imbued with political meaning. He timed his Paterson leap to steal the show from Timothy B. Crane, an entrepreneur who dreamed up Forest Garden, a pleasure park offering respectable ladies and gentlemen a respite from the mill town. To reach the park, which was formerly open to everyone, visitors now had to cross a toll bridge. The toll would raise revenue to sustain the park, but, more important, as Crane saw it, it would keep out the riffraff.

Patch and the mill hands understood that the riffraff meant *them*. Forest Garden symbolized a world in which manual labor was devalued, in which artisans became workers, in which industrialists and entrepreneurs increasingly held themselves as morally superior to wage earners. In previous months, town residents attacked (physically and verbally) the park, its workers, its buildings, and Crane. When Crane planned elaborate celebrations marking the toll bridge's completion, Patch determined to assert the pride of workers who made the industrial revolution possible.

In the two years following his Paterson leap—before his last, fatal jump at the 125-foot Genesee Falls in Rochester, New York—Sam Patch became a professional waterfall jumper. Even as some dismissed his leaps as drunken stunts, he costumed

This icon will direct you to interactive activities and study materials on A People And A Nation, Brief Edition website: **www.cengage.com/history/norton/ peoplenationbrief8e**

Chronology

1790s–1840s	Second Great Awakening spreads religious fervor.	1832	Jackson vetoes rechartering the Second Bank of the United States.
1820s	Reformers in New York and Pennsylvania establish model penitentiaries.		Jackson is reelected president.
1824	No presidential candidate wins a majority in the electoral college.	1832–33	South Carolina nullifies the Tariffs of 1828 and 1832, prompting a nullification crisis.
1825	House of Representatives elects Adams president.	1836	Specie Circular ends the credit purchase of public lands.
1826	American Society for the Promotion of Temperance is founded.		Van Buren is elected president.
1828	Tariff of Abominations is passed.	1837	*Caroline* affair sparks tension with Britain.
	Jackson is elected president.		Financial panic ends the boom of the 1830s.
1830s–40s	Democratic-Whig competition gets in the second party system.	1838–39	United States and Canada mobilize militias over Maine–New Brunswick border dispute.
		1839–43	Hard times spread unemployment and deflation.
1831	Garrison begins the abolitionist newspaper *The Liberator*.	1840	Whigs win the presidency under Harrison.
		1841	Tyler assumes the presidency after Harrison's death.
	Antimasons are the first political party to hold a national convention.	1848	Woman's Rights Convention at Seneca Falls, New York, calls for woman suffrage.

himself in the symbolic clothing of the textile spinner and associated socially and politically with a raucous crowd of skilled operatives. His flaunting of middle-class values caught the attention of the political press, organs for the era's two main political parties—the Whigs and Jacksonian Democrats. To Whigs, Patch exemplified what was, in one editor's words, "wrong with democracy," whereas Jacksonians labeled him a heroic artisan. In 1833 Philadelphia presented President Andrew Jackson with a horse, which he named Sam Patch.

Like Patch, many Americans sought to reaffirm control over their lives in an era of rapid economic and social changes. The market economy, growing wealth and inequality, immigration, the westward thrust of slavery, and territorial expansion contributed to Americans' hopes and fears. But Americans often divided over what defined progress, what constituted a social ill, and how those ills should be remedied.

To quell anxieties, many turned to evangelical religion and, in the North, reform movements. Believing in human perfectibility, reformers worked to free individuals and society from sin. In the Northeast and Midwest, people organized to end prostitution and alcohol abuse, improve prison and asylum conditions, and establish public schools. Other reformers created utopian communities. Opponents of slavery and proponents of women's rights, meanwhile, sought to radically alter the application of the revolutionary declaration that "all men are created equal."

Evangelical reformers generally aligned with the Whig Party, but Jacksonian Democrats, too, were concerned with social problems, mostly class inequities. They disliked middle-class reformers who told working-class men and women how to live, and they opposed privileges bestowed by government policies and institutions, such as the Second Bank of the United States. Yet when it came to slavery, the national parties often remained silent to keep sectional conflict submerged.

Democrats and Whigs held distinct positions on most other issues. Democrats emphasized that the best government is that which governs least, whereas Whigs championed a strong federal government. Democrats focused on the nation's agricultural expansion west, whereas Whigs promoted industrial and commercial growth in the East. They hoped to bring growth through high protective tariffs, centralized banking, and federal funding for internal improvements. Together, Democrats and Whigs constituted what is often called the second party system.

- What were the evils in society that reformers hoped to eliminate, and what motivated them to do so?
- What was the relationship between reform and politics?
- What were the main issues dividing Democrats and Whigs?

FROM REVIVAL TO REFORM

Religious revivals in the late eighteenth and early nineteenth centuries—sometimes called the Second Great Awakening for their resemblance to the eighteenth-century Great Awakening—raised people's hopes for the Second Coming of the Christian messiah and the establishment of God's kingdom on earth. Revivalists resolved to speed the millennium, or the thousand years of peace on earth that would accompany Christ's Second Coming, by combating sin. They urged individuals to renounce sins, such as drinking, swearing, and licentiousness, and aid in combating social evils, including slavery. Not until all Americans were converted would Christ make his Second Coming.

Revivalists strove for large-scale conversions. Rural women, men, and children traveled to camp meetings, where they listened to fiery sermons day and night delivered from hastily constructed platforms and tents in forests or fields. In cities, women in particular attended daily church services and prayer meetings, sometimes for months. Converts vowed to live sanctified lives and help others see the light.

Revivals

The most famous revival was at Cane Ridge, Kentucky, in August 1801. An estimated twenty-five thousand people attended at a time when Kentucky's largest city, Lexington, had barely two thousand inhabitants. The call to repentance and conversion invigorated southern Protestantism. Although laws often restricted or outlawed black churches and preachers, particularly after Nat Turner's 1831 revolt, black and mixed churches flourished locally. During the 1840s and 1850s, though, as slavery was publically debated, southern Presbyterian, Baptist, and Methodist churches seceded from their denominations' national conferences. For these churches' leaders, slavery did not impede human perfectibility but ensured it, as benevolent masters guided Africans to Christ.

Revivalists believed in individual self-improvement, but northern revivalists also emphasized communal improvement. Wherever they preached, northern evangelists generated new religious groups and voluntary reform societies. Preachers like Lyman

Samuel Waldo and William Jewett's oil portrait of Charles Finney around 1834 captures Finney at his peak. The charismatic Finney mesmerized his audiences, and contemporaries credited him with converting 500,000 people.   (Oberlin College Archives, Oberlin, Ohio)

Beecher, who began in New England before moving to Cincinnati, and Charles Finney, who traveled the canals and roads linking the Northeast to the Midwest, argued that "God has made man a moral free agent," that Christians were not doomed by original sin, and that anyone could achieve salvation. Revivalism had a strong base among Methodists and Baptists, whose denominational structures maximized democratic participation and drew ministers from ordinary folk.

Finney achieved his greatest successes in those parts of western New York experiencing rapid changes in transportation and industrialization—what he called the Burned-Over District because of the region's intense evangelical fires. Rapid change raised fears of the social evils that might accompany economic progress. Many individuals worried, too, about their economic fate in an era of booms and busts.

When northern revivalist preachers emphasized good works—that is, good deeds and piety—they helped ignite social reform movements, which began in the Burned-Over District and spread to New England, the Middle Atlantic, and the upper Midwest. These associations shared a commitment to human perfectibility and often turned to the same wealthy men for financial resources and advice.

Moral Reform

Those resources allowed them to use the era's new technologies—steam presses and railroads. By mass-producing pamphlets and newspapers for distribution far into the nation's interior, reformers spread their message throughout the Northeast and Midwest. With canals and railroads making travel easier, reformers could attend annual conventions and host speakers from distant places. Most reform organizations sponsored weekly newspapers, creating a virtual reform community.

While industrialists and merchants provided financial resources for evangelical reform, wives and daughters solicited new members and circulated petitions. Women, more than men, felt responsible for counteracting the expanding market economy's social evils. Evangelical reformers broadened the cult of domesticity's role for women as moral guardians beyond the home into the public realm. Women would help run reformatories for wayward youth or establish orphan asylums. Participation in reform movements gave some women a sense of purpose outside the home. Although some elite women in Upper South cities formed and joined reform societies, moral reform was primarily a northeastern and midwestern phenomenon.

For women and some men, particularly non-property owners who could not vote, reform led to political action. In 1830, as female reformers in New York City organized a shelter for prostitutes, they publicized the names of brothel clients to shame men who contributed to the women's waywardness. They then organized themselves into the Female Moral Reform Society, and by 1840 the society had

555 affiliated chapters nationwide. It soon lobbied successfully for criminal sanctions in New York State against men who seduced women into prostitution.

Penitentiaries and Asylums

Rather than simply punishing criminals, reformers tried to transform them into productive members of society. Their model penitentiaries aimed to rehabilitate criminals through disciplined regimens.

Other reformers sought to improve treatment of the mentally ill, who were frequently imprisoned, put in cages or dark dungeons, chained to walls, brutalized, or held in solitary confinement. The leader of this crusade, Dorothea Dix, exemplifies the reformer who started with a religious belief in human perfectibility and moved into social, then political action. Investigating asylums, petitioning the Massachusetts legislature, and lobbying other states and Congress, Dix pushed twenty-eight states to build institutions for the mentally ill by 1860.

Temperance

Temperance advocates, who railed against alcoholic beverages, likewise crossed from the personal into the political sphere. Drinking was widespread in the early nineteenth century, when men like Sam Patch gathered in public houses and inns to drink whiskey, rum, and hard cider. Respectable women did not drink in public, but many tippled alcohol-based patent medicines promoted as cure-alls.

Evangelicals considered drinking sinful, and in many denominations, forsaking alcohol was part of conversion. Preachers condemned alcohol for violating the Sabbath—workers' one day off, which some spent at the public house. Factory owners claimed alcohol made workers unreliable. Civic leaders connected alcohol with crime. Middle-class reformers, often women, condemned it for diverting men from family responsibilities and making them more likely to be abusive. In the early 1840s, thousands of women formed Martha Washington societies to reform alcoholics, raise children as teetotalers, and spread the temperance message.

As the temperance movement grew, its goal shifted from moderation to abstinence to prohibition. By the mid-1830s, five thousand state and local temperance societies touted teetotalism, and more than a million people had pledged abstinence. Per capita consumption of alcohol fell from five gallons per year in 1800 to below two gallons in the 1840s. The American Society for the Promotion of Temperance, organized in 1826, pushed for legislation ending alcohol manufacture and sale. In 1851 Maine became the first state to ban alcohol except for medicinal purposes, and by 1855 similar laws were enacted throughout New England, New York, Pennsylvania, and the Midwest.

The temperance campaign had an anti-immigrant and anti-Catholic strain to it. Along the nation's canals, reformers lamented the hundreds of taverns catering to Irish workers, and in the cities, they expressed outrage at the Sunday tradition of German families' gathering at beer gardens. Their efforts had some success, as Catholics pledged abstinence and formed organizations such as the St. Mary's Mutual Benevolence Total Abstinence Society in Boston.

But many workers—Protestants as well as Catholics—rejected middle-class temperance campaigns. Workers agreed that poverty and crime were problems but blamed poor wages, not drinking habits. Even some who abstained from alcohol opposed prohibition, believing that drinking should be a matter of self-control, not state coercion.

Public Schools   Protestants and Catholics differed over education as well. Public education almost always included religious education, but when teachers taught Protestant beliefs and used the King James Bible, Catholics established their own schools. Some Protestants feared that Catholics would never be assimilated into American culture and charged Catholics with plotting to impose papal control. Still, public education touched more Americans than any other reform movement.

Horace Mann, a Massachusetts lawyer and reformer from humble beginnings, advocated free, tax-supported education to replace church and private schools. Universal education, Mann proposed, would end crime and help Americanize immigrants.

During Mann's tenure as secretary of the Massachusetts Board of Education from 1837 to 1848, Massachusetts led the common school movement which established teacher training, lengthened the school year, and raised teachers' salaries to make the profession more attractive. Adhering to notions that women had special claims to morality and could be paid less than men, Mann envisioned a system in which women educated future clerks, farmers, and workers with a practical curriculum that stressed geography, arithmetic, and science. Education reformers believed that individuals could educate themselves out of their circumstances.

With the expansion of public education, by 1850 the majority of native-born white Americans were literate. Power printing presses and better transportation enabled a wide distribution of religious and secular publications.

COMMUNITARIAN EXPERIMENTS

Some idealists dreamed of an entirely new social order. They established dozens of utopian communities based on religious principles, a resistance to the market economy's excessive individualism, or both. Some groups, like the Shakers, originated in eighteenth-century Europe, while others, like the Mormons, arose from the Second Great Awakening. Utopian communities attempted to recapture what they perceived as the communal nature of the past, even while offering radical departures from marriage and child-rearing practices.

Utopian Communities   The Shakers, the largest of the communal utopian experiments, reached their peak between 1820 and 1860, when six thousand members lived in twenty settlements in eight states. Shaker communities emphasized agriculture and handcrafts, contrasting with the new factory regime. Many were profitable enterprises. But the Shakers were essentially a spiritual community. Founded in England in 1772 by Mother Ann Lee, their name derived from their worship service, which included shaking their bodies. Ann Lee's children died in infancy, and she believed their deaths were retribution for her sin of intercourse; thus she advocated celibacy. After imprisonment in England in 1773–1774, she settled in America.

Shakers lived communally, with men and women in separate quarters; individual families were abolished. Leadership was shared equally between men and women. Many Shaker settlements became temporary refuges for orphans, widows, runaways, abused wives, and unemployed workers. Their settlements depended on new recruits, not only because celibacy meant that they could not reproduce themselves but also because some members soon left, unsuited to communal living or the Shakers' spiritual message.

Other influential utopian communities also sought to resist social change. John Humphrey Noyes, a lawyer converted by Finney's revivals, established two perfectionist communities, first in Putney, Vermont, in 1835, and then—after being indicted for adultery—in Oneida, New York, in 1848. Noyes advocated communal property ownership, communal child rearing, and "complex marriage," in which all men were married to all women but women were free to reject sexual propositions. In the Oneida colony, pregnancies were to be planned; couples would apply to Noyes for permission to have a child, or Noyes would assign two people to reproduce. Robert Dale Owen's community in New Harmony, Indiana (1825–1828), abolished private property and advocated communal child rearing. The Fourierists, named after French philosopher Charles Fourier, established more than two dozen northeastern and midwestern communities that resisted the individualism of market society and promoted sexual equality.

The most famous Fourier community was Brook Farm in West Roxbury, Massachusetts. Inspired by transcendentalism—the belief that the physical world is secondary to the spiritual realm, which humans can reach only by intuition—Brook Farm's rural communalism combined spirituality, manual labor, intellectual life, and play. Founded in 1841 by Unitarian minister George Ripley, a literary critic and friend of transcendentalist essayist Ralph Waldo Emerson, Brook Farm attracted farmers, craftsmen, and writers, among them novelist Nathaniel Hawthorne. In 1845 Brook Farm's hundred members organized into phalanxes (working-living units) following Fourier's model. As regimentation replaced individualism, membership dropped. A year after a disastrous fire in 1846, the experiment collapsed.

American Renaissance Though short-lived, Brook Farm was crucial to the flowering of national literature. During these years, Hawthorne, Emerson, Margaret Fuller, Henry David Thoreau, Herman Melville, and others launched a literary outpouring known today as the American Renaissance. Their work was distinctively American and an outgrowth of the European romantic movement. Themes were universal, their settings and characters American. Hawthorne, for instance, used Puritan New England as a backdrop.

Essayist Ralph Waldo Emerson was the prime mover of the American Renaissance and a pillar of transcendentalism. Emerson followed his father and grandfather into the ministry but quit his Boston Unitarian pulpit in 1831. After a two-year sojourn in Europe, he returned to lecture and write, preaching individualism and self-reliance. Widely admired, he influenced Thoreau, Fuller, Hawthorne, and other members of Brook Farm.

Mormons

No communitarian experiment had a more lasting influence than the Church of Jesus Christ of Latter-Day Saints, whose members were known as Mormons. During the religious ferment of the 1820s in western New York, Joseph Smith, a young farmer, reported that an angel called Moroni had given him divinely engraved gold plates. Smith published his revelations as the *Book of Mormon* and organized a church in 1830. The next year, the community moved to Ohio to build a New Jerusalem and await the Second Coming of Jesus.

But angry mobs drove the Mormons from Ohio, and they settled in Missouri. Anti-Mormons charged that Mormonism was a scam by Joseph Smith. Opponents feared Mormon economic and political power. In 1838 Missouri's governor charged Smith with fomenting insurrection and gathered evidence to indict him and other leaders for treason.

Smith and his followers resettled in Nauvoo, Illinois. The state legislature gave them a city charter that made them self-governing. But again the community met antagonism, especially after Smith introduced polygamy in 1841, allowing men several wives. The next year Smith became mayor, and this consolidation of power further antagonized opponents, including former Mormons. In 1844, after Smith and his brother were charged with treason and jailed, then murdered, the Mormons left Illinois to seek security in the western wilderness. Under Brigham Young's leadership, they set up a cooperative community in the Great Salt Lake valley.

There, the Mormons distributed agricultural land according to family size. An extensive irrigation system transformed the arid valley into a rich oasis. As the colony developed, church elders gained control of water, trade, industry, and the territorial government of Utah.

ABOLITIONISM

Like reformers and utopians, evangelical abolitionists tried to eradicate a communal sin suffusing American society: slavery. Inspired by the Second Great Awakening, their efforts built on an earlier generation of antislavery activists.

Early Abolitionism and Colonization

From the nation's earliest days—in places like Philadelphia, New York, Albany, Boston, and Nantucket—free blacks formed societies to petition legislatures, seek judicial redress, stage public marches, and publish tracts chronicling the horrors of bondage. African American abolitionists wrote about slavery's devastating impact on black and white families, advocated an end to slavery, assisted fugitive slaves, and promoted legal equality for free blacks. By 1830 there were fifty African American abolitionist societies in the United States. David Walker, a southern-born free African American, captured white Americans' attention with his *Appeal . . . to the Colored Citizens* (1829). He advocated the violent overthrow of slavery, triggering fear throughout the white South and the North.

Early white antislavery advocates pressed for gradual abolition and an end to the international slave trade. After the American Revolution, abolitionists united in places like Boston and Philadelphia, with its large population of Quakers, whose religious beliefs emphasized human equality. Although they aided African Americans seeking freedom through judicial decisions, their assumptions about blacks' racial inferiority made them stop short of advocating equal rights. Early white abolitionists were typically wealthy men who excluded women, African Americans, and nonelites from their societies.

Elites often supported colonization, which crystallized in 1816 with the organization of the American Colonization Society. Its members planned to purchase and relocate American slaves and free blacks to Africa or the Caribbean. Supporters included Thomas Jefferson, James Madison, James Monroe, and Henry Clay. In 1824 the society founded Liberia, on Africa's west coast, and established a settlement for willing African Americans, resettling nearly twelve thousand by 1860. Some colonizationists aimed to strengthen slavery by ridding the South of troublesome slaves or to purge the North of African Americans. Although some African Americans supported the movement, black abolitionists generally denounced it.

In the early 1830s, a new group of more radical white abolitionists—most prominently, William Lloyd Garrison—demanded immediate, complete, and uncompensated emancipation. Garrison began publishing his abolitionist newspaper, *The Liberator,* in 1831, two years before founding the American Antislavery Society, the era's largest abolitionist organization.

Immediatism

Immediatists believed slavery was a sin needing urgent eradication. They were influenced by African American abolitionist societies and by evangelicals' notion that humans, not God, determined their spiritual fate by opting for good or evil. When all humans had chosen good over evil, the millennium would come. For every day that slavery continued, then, the millennium was delayed.

Because the millennium depended on *all* hearts having been won over to Christ, Garrison's brand of abolitionism focused on moral suasion. He and his followers hoped to bring about emancipation by winning over slaveowners and other white Americans who supported or tolerated slavery. Evangelical abolitionism depended, then, on large numbers of ministers and laypeople spreading the word nationwide.

The Lane Debates

In 1829 Congregationalists and Presbyterians founded the Lane Seminary in Cincinnati to train ministers. With Lyman Beecher as president, it drew students from North and South and encouraged "people of color" to apply. After Theodore Weld, one of Charles Finney's converts, arrived at Lane in 1833, he organized the Lane Debates, eighteen days of discussion among students and faculty about colonization and immediatism. Immediatism won.

Led by Weld, the Lane students and faculty founded an antislavery society and reached out to the growing African American population of Cincinnati. Fearful of disorder, white business leaders protested the antislavery society. Lane's trustees responded by banning antislavery organizations on campus and barring further debate on slavery. Beecher supported the trustees. Weld and the other Lane Rebels left and the following year enrolled in a new seminary at Oberlin, a northern Ohio town founded as a Christian perfectionist settlement. The new seminary would become the first college to admit women and one of the first to admit African Americans.

The International Antislavery Movement

The heart of the international antislavery movement had been Great Britain, but in the 1830s many of Britain's antislavery societies thought that their work was finished and disbanded. The international slave trade greatly diminished, and in 1833 Parliament ended slavery in the British Empire. Abolitionism in the United States was growing, and American abolitionists revived the international antislavery movement.

American abolitionism in the 1830s was invigorated by the militancy of black abolitionists and by William Lloyd Garrison's conversion to immediatism. Seeking to raise money and to pressure the United States to abolish slavery, African American abolitionists in the 1840s toured Britain regularly. Ex-slaves recounted their experiences of slavery and bared their scarred bodies.

After the fugitive slave Moses Gandy toured England, he published his autobiography, the first of dozens of slave narratives published in London. The next year, 1845, Frederick Douglass began a nineteen-month tour, giving three hundred lectures in Britain.

In 1849 the black abolitionists William Wells Brown, Alexander Crummell, and J. W. C. Pennington were among twenty American delegates at the international Paris Peace Conference. Brown's lecture tour in Britain became a five-year exile because, after passage of the 1850 Fugitive Slave Law, he feared being sent back to slavery if he returned to the United States. In 1854 he became free when British abolitionists purchased his freedom.

Gandy, Douglass, Brown, and other former slaves energized the British and Foreign Anti-Slavery Society, founded in 1839, and hundreds of militant local societies. By the early 1850s, abolitionists helped abolish slavery in Colombia, Argentina, Venezuela, and Peru. In the United States, black abolitionists were instrumental in reviving the worldwide antislavery movement and, as advocates of women's rights, international peace, temperance, and other reforms, linking Americans to other worldwide reform movements.

William Wells Brown's autobiography stirred abolitionists in the United States and England. In 1849 Brown was among the American delegates to the Paris Peace Conference, then spent the next five years as an exile in Britain, fearing being sent back to slavery under the 1850 Fugitive Slave Act. He returned to the United States only after British abolitionists purchased his freedom from his former master.

(Documenting the American South [http://docsouth.unc.edu], The University of North Carolina at Chapel Hill Libraries)

The American Antislavery Society

By 1838, at its peak, the society had 2,000 local affiliates and over 300,000 members. In contrast to earlier white abolitionists, the immediatists welcomed men and women of all races and classes. Lydia Maria Child, Maria Chapman, and Lucretia Mott served on its executive committee; Child edited its official paper, the *National Anti-Slavery Standard*, from 1841 to 1843, and Chapman coedited it from 1844 until 1848.

With the great postal campaign in 1835, the society flooded the mails with antislavery tracts. Women went door to door in northern and midwestern communities collecting signatures on antislavery petitions; by 1838 more than 400,000 petitions were sent to Congress. Abolitionist-minded women met in sewing circles, where they made clothes for fugitive slaves while organizing activities, such as antislavery fairs at which they sold goods—often hand-made items—donating the proceeds to antislavery causes.

African American Abolitionists

Even as white abolitionist societies included African Americans and sponsored speaking tours by former slaves, African Americans continued independent efforts to end slavery and improve free African Americans' status into the 1840s and 1850s. Former slaves—most famously, Frederick Douglass, Henry Bibb, Harriet Tubman, and Sojourner Truth—fought slavery through speeches, publications, and participation in a secret network known as the Underground Railroad, which spirited enslaved men, women, and children to freedom. By the thousands, African Americans established churches, founded moral reform societies, published newspapers, created schools and orphanages, and held conventions.

Opposition to Abolitionism

The immediatists' success at winning converts gave rise to a virulent opposition. In the South, mobs blocked the distribution of antislavery tracts. The state of South Carolina intercepted and burned abolitionist literature, and in 1835 proslavery assailants killed four abolitionists in South Carolina and Louisiana, as well as forty people allegedly plotting a slave rebellion in Mississippi and Louisiana.

White northerners who opposed abolition recognized cotton's vital role in the nation's economy and feared that emancipation would prompt an influx of freed slaves into their region. They believed blacks to be inherently inferior and incapable of the virtue and diligence required of freedom and citizenship.

The North saw its share of antiabolitionist violence. In Boston, David Walker died under mysterious circumstances in 1830, after a bounty was put on his head. Of northerners who despised abolitionists, most were commercial and political elites with strong connections to the southern cotton economy and political connections to leading southerners. Northern gentlemen incited antiabolitionist riots. Mob violence peaked in 1835, with more than fifty riots aimed

Women played an activist role in reform, especially in abolitionism. A rare daguerreotype from August 1850 shows women and men, including Frederick Douglass, on the podium at an abolitionist rally in Cazenovia, New York. (Collection of J. Paul Getty Museum, Los Angeles, California)

at abolitionists or African Americans. In 1837 in Alton, Illinois, a mob murdered the abolitionist editor Elijah P. Lovejoy and rioters sacked his printing office, and in 1838, Philadelphia rioters hurled stones at three thousand black and white women attending the Anti-Slavery Convention of American Women at the new Pennsylvania Hall, constructed to house abolitionist meetings and an abolitionist bookstore, before torching the building itself.

Moral Suasion Versus Political Action

Violence made some immediatists question moral suasion as a tactic. James G. Birney, the son of a Kentucky slave-owner, embraced immediatism but sought to elect abolitionists who would push for antislavery legislation. Those who favored a political solution saw little room for women within the movement. To involve women violated the natural order of things while detracting from the ultimate goal: freedom for slaves.

Thus, when William Lloyd Garrison, an ardent women's rights supporter, endorsed Abby Kelly's appointment to the business committee of the American Anti-Slavery Society in 1840, he provoked an irreparable split in the abolitionist movement. Arthur Tappan and Theodore Weld led a dissident group that formed the new American and Foreign Anti-Slavery Society. That society established a new political party: the Liberty Party, which nominated Birney for president in 1840 and 1844.

Although committed to immediate abolitionism, Liberty Party members doubted the federal government had the authority to abolish slavery. It was up to the states to determine the legality of slavery. They felt the government could act in the western territories, however, and demanded that new territories prohibit slavery. Prominent black abolitionists, including Frederick Douglass, endorsed the party, whose leaders also emphasized combating northern prejudice.

WOMEN'S RIGHTS

At the first World Anti-Slavery Convention in London in 1840, abolitionists Lucretia Mott and Elizabeth Cady Stanton were dismayed when female abolitionists were denied seats in the convention's main hall; eight years later, the two helped organize the first American women's rights convention. Born to a South Carolina slaveholding family, Angelina and Sarah Grimké moved north and became active in abolitionism. After critics attacked them for speaking to audiences that included men, the sisters began advocating for women's legal and social equality.

Religious revivals helped women see themselves as inherently equal to men, and reform movements brought middle-class women into the public sphere. Female reformers' lobbying helped to effect legal change, and some women believed the next step was citizenship rights for women.

Legal Rights

After independence, American states carried over traditional English marriage law, which gave husbands familial control. Men owned their wives' property, were legal guardians of their children, and owned whatever family members produced or earned.

A father had the legal authority to oppose his daughter's choice of husband, though by 1800 most women chose their spouses.

Married women made modest gains in property and spousal rights after 1830. Arkansas in 1835 passed the first married women's property law, and by 1860 sixteen more states followed. In those states, women could own and convey property and write wills. When a wife inherited property, it was hers, though money she earned still belonged to her husband. Such laws were popular among wealthy Americans who hoped to protect family fortunes during economic downturns; property in a woman's name was safe from her husband's creditors. In the 1830s, states also added cruelty and desertion as grounds for divorce.

Radical reformers argued that marriage constituted a form of bondage. Lucy Stone, an outspoken critic of marriage, consented to wed fellow abolitionist Henry Blackwell only if she could eschew a vow of obedience and keep her own name.

Political Rights The women's movement was launched in July 1848, when Elizabeth Cady Stanton, Lucretia Mott, Mary Ann McClintock, Martha Wright, and Jane Hunt organized the first Woman's Rights Convention at Seneca Falls, New York, where three hundred women and men demanded women's social and economic equality. Their Declaration of Sentiments, modeled on the Declaration of Independence, broadcast the injustices suffered by women and proclaimed "All men and women are created equal." The similarities between abolitionism and women's rights led reformers, including Stone and Blackwell, and former slaves like Sojourner Truth, to work for both movements. Some men supported women's rights, notably William Lloyd Garrison and Frederick Douglass, but most men opposed female suffrage. The Seneca Falls' suffrage resolution passed only after Frederick Douglass passionately defended it. In 1851 Elizabeth Cady Stanton joined with temperance advocate Susan B. Anthony to advocate persistently for women's voting rights.

Jacksonianism and Party Politics

Like reformers, politicians sought to control the direction of the expanding nation. As suffrage laws changed, they reached out to an increasingly broad-based electorate. Hotly contested elections drew the interest and participation of voters and non-voters alike.

Expanding Political Participation Property restrictions for voters remained in only seven of twenty-six states by 1840. Some states even allowed foreign nationals who officially declared their intention of becoming American citizens to vote. The net effect was that between 1824 and 1828 the number of votes cast in presidential elections tripled, from 360,000 to over 1.1 million. The proportion of eligible voters who cast ballots also grew, from about 27 percent in 1824 to more than 80 percent in 1840.

The selection of presidential electors also became more democratic. Previously a caucus of party leaders in most states picked them, but by 1824 eighteen out of twenty-four states chose electors by popular vote. Consequently, politicians augmented

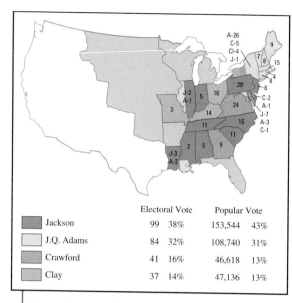

	Electoral Vote		Popular Vote	
Jackson	99	38%	153,544	43%
J.Q. Adams	84	32%	108,740	31%
Crawford	41	16%	46,618	13%
Clay	37	14%	47,136	13%

Map 12.1   Presidential Election, 1824

Andrew Jackson led in both electoral and popular votes but failed to win a majority of electoral college votes. The House elected John Quincy Adams president.

Presidential candidate Andrew Jackson is portrayed on a trinket or sewing box in 1824. This is an example both of how campaigns entered popular culture and of the active role of women, excluded from voting, in politics. (Collection of David J. and Janice L. Frent)

appeals to voters, and the 1824 election saw the end of the congressional caucus, when House and Senate members of the same political party united to select their candidate.

Election of 1824

As a result, five Democratic-Republican candidates ran for president in 1824. The poorly attended Republican caucus chose William H. Crawford of Georgia, secretary of the treasury, as its candidate. Instead of Congress, state legislatures now nominated candidates, offering the expanded electorate a slate of sectional candidates. John Quincy Adams drew support from New England, while westerners backed House Speaker Henry Clay of Kentucky. Some southerners at first supported Secretary of War John C. Calhoun, who later ran for the vice presidency instead. The Tennessee legislature nominated military hero Andrew Jackson.

Jackson led in electoral and popular votes, but no candidate received a majority in the electoral college. Adams finished second. Under the Constitution, the House of Representatives, voting by state delegation, one vote to a state, would select the next president from among the three electoral vote leaders. With the fewest votes, Clay was dropped. Crawford, disabled by a stroke, never received consideration. Clay backed Adams, who won with thirteen of the twenty-four state delegations and became president (see Map 12.1). Adams appointed Clay as secretary of state, the steppingstone to the presidency.

Angry Jacksonians denounced the election as a corrupt bargain, claiming that Adams had stolen the presidency by promising Clay a cabinet position for his votes. The Republican Party split. The Adams wing emerged as the National Republicans, and the Jacksonians became the Democrats.

Adams proposed a strong nationalist policy incorporating Clay's American System of protective tariffs, a national bank, and internal improvements. Adams believed the federal government's active role should extend to education, science, and the arts. He proposed a national university in Washington, D.C. Brilliant as a diplomat and secretary of state, Adams fared less well as chief executive.

Election of 1828

The 1828 election pitted Adams against Jackson. Andrew Jackson was born in South Carolina in 1767 and rose from humble beginnings to become a wealthy Tennessee planter and slaveholder. Jackson was the first American president from the West. Having served in the Revolution as a boy, Jackson claimed a connection to the founding generation. In the Tennessee militia, General Jackson led the campaign to remove Creeks from the Alabama and Georgia frontier. He burst onto the national scene in 1815 as the hero of the Battle of New Orleans and enhanced his glory in an 1818 expedition against Seminoles in Spanish Florida. Jackson served as congressman and senator from Tennessee and the first territorial governor of Florida (1821).

Jackson's proponents accused Adams of stealing the 1824 election and, when he was envoy to Russia, of securing prostitutes for the czar. Anti-Jacksonians published reports that Jackson's wife, Rachel, married Jackson before her divorce from her first husband was final. In 1806, while defending Rachel's integrity, Jackson killed a man during a duel, and the cry of "murderer!" haunted the election.

Although Adams held the states he won in 1824, his opposition was now unified behind a single candidate, and Jackson swamped him, polling 56 percent of the popular vote and winning the electoral college by 178 to 83 votes (see Map 12.2). Through a lavishly financed coalition of state parties, political leaders, and newspaper editors, a popular movement had elected the president. The Democratic Party became the first well-organized national political party in the United States.

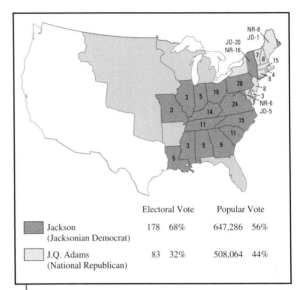

Map 12.2   Presidential Election, 1828
Andrew Jackson avenged his 1824 loss of the presidency, sweeping the election in 1828.

	Electoral Vote		Popular Vote	
Jackson (Jacksonian Democrat)	178	68%	647,286	56%
J.Q. Adams (National Republican)	83	32%	508,064	44%

Democrats

Democrats shared a commitment to the Jeffersonian concept of an agrarian society. They viewed a strong central government as the enemy of individual liberty and believed government intervention in the economy benefited special-interest groups and created corporate monopolies. They sought to end federal support of banks and corporations and restrict paper currency. Jackson and his supporters also opposed reform movements as interfering with individual liberty. When it came to westward expansion, though, Jackson and his followers wanted federal intervention. It was Jackson who initiated Indian removal despite northeastern reformers' protests.

By restraining government and emphasizing individualism, Jacksonians sought to restore traditional republican virtues, such as self-discipline and self-reliance, undermined by economic and social change. Jackson advocated for popular government and declared that sovereignty resided with the people, not with the states or courts.

Like Jefferson, Jackson strengthened the executive branch even as he advocated limited government. In combining the roles of party leader and chief of state, he centralized power in the White House. He relied on political friends, his Kitchen Cabinet, for advice, only rarely consulting his official cabinet. Rotating officeholders, Jackson claimed, made government more responsive to the public and allowed him to appoint loyal Democrats, a practice his critics called the spoils system, in which the victor rewards supporters. The spoils system, opponents charged, corrupted the government because appointments were based on loyalty, not competency.

King Andrew

Opponents mocked Jackson as King Andrew I, charging him with abuse of power by ignoring the Supreme Court's ruling on Cherokee rights, sidestepping his cabinet, and replacing experienced officeholders with his cronies.

Jackson frequently used the veto to promote limited government. In 1830 he vetoed the Maysville Road bill, which would have funded construction of a 60-mile turnpike from Maysville to Lexington, Kentucky. A federally subsidized internal improvement in one state was unconstitutional, he insisted; states should handle such projects. The veto undermined Clay's American System and embarrassed Clay because the project was in his home district.

The first six presidents vetoed nine bills; Jackson vetoed twelve. Previous presidents believed that vetoes were justified only on constitutional grounds; Jackson considered policy disagreements legitimate grounds. He made the veto a weapon for controlling Congress, because representatives and senators had to weigh the prospect of a veto as they deliberated.

FEDERALISM AT ISSUE: THE NULLIFICATION AND BANK CONTROVERSIES

The slave South feared federal power and no state more so than South Carolina, where the planter class was strongest and slavery most concentrated. Southerners resented protectionist tariffs, which in 1824 and 1828 protected manufactures by imposing import duties on manufactured cloth and iron. In protecting northern factories, the tariff raised the costs of manufactured goods to southerners, who labeled the 1828 tariff the Tariff of Abominations.

Nullification

South Carolina's political leaders rejected the 1828 tariff, invoking the doctrine of nullification, which proffered that states had the right to overrule, or nullify, federal legislation. Nullification was based on the Virginia and Kentucky Resolutions of 1798, stating that states, representing the people, have a right to judge the constitutionality of federal actions. Jackson's vice president, John C. Calhoun of South Carolina, argued in his unsigned *Exposition and Protest* that, in any disagreement between the federal government and a state, a special state convention should decide the conflict by either nullifying or affirming federal law.

As Jackson's running mate in 1828, Calhoun avoided endorsing nullification and embarrassing the Democratic ticket; he also hoped to win Jackson's support as the Democratic presidential heir apparent. Thus, in early 1830, Calhoun presided silently over the Senate when Massachusetts Senator Daniel Webster and South Carolina Senator Robert Y. Hayne debated states' rights. The debate started over a resolution to restrict western land sales but soon touched on the tariff. Hayne charged that the North was threatening to bring disunity. Webster defended New England and the republic, keeping nullification supporters on the defensive.

Though sympathetic to states' rights and distrustful of the federal government, Jackson rejected state sovereignty. Believing in the Union, he shared Webster's dread of nullification. The president made his position clear at a Jefferson Day dinner with the toast "Our Federal Union, it must and shall be preserved." Vice President Calhoun toasted "The Federal Union—next to our liberty the most dear," revealing his adherence to states' rights. Calhoun and Jackson grew apart, and Jackson looked to Secretary of State Martin Van Buren as his successor.

Tension resumed when Congress passed a new tariff in 1832, reducing some duties but retaining high taxes on imported iron, cottons, and woolens. Although a majority of southern representatives supported the new tariff, South Carolinians refused to go along. They feared the act could set a precedent for legislation on slavery. In November 1832 a South Carolina state convention nullified the 1828 and the 1832 tariffs, declaring it unlawful for federal officials to collect duties in the state.

The Force Act

In December Jackson issued a proclamation opposing nullification. He moved troops to federal forts in South Carolina and prepared U.S. marshals to collect the duties. At Jackson's request, Congress passed the Force Act, authorizing the president to call up troops but offering a way to avoid force by collecting duties before foreign ships reached Charleston's harbor. Jackson extended an olive branch by recommending tariff reductions.

Calhoun, disturbed by South Carolina's drift toward separatism, resigned as vice president and was soon elected to represent South Carolina in the U.S. Senate. There he worked with Henry Clay on the compromise Tariff of 1833. Quickly passed by Congress and signed by the president, the new tariff lengthened the list of duty-free items and reduced duties over nine years. Satisfied, South Carolina repealed its nullification law.

Nullification offered a genuine debate on the nature and principles of the republic. Each side believed it was upholding the Constitution. South Carolina opposed the tyranny of the federal government and manufacturing interests. Jackson fought the tyranny of South Carolina, which threatened to split the republic. It took the crisis over a central bank to define federal government's powers more clearly.

Second Bank of the United States

The Second Bank of the United States' twenty-year charter was scheduled to expire in 1836. The bank served as a depository for federal funds and provided business credit. Its bank notes circulated as currency nationwide; they could be readily exchanged for gold. Through its twenty-five branch offices, the Second Bank acted as a clearinghouse for state banks, refusing bank notes from state banks lacking sufficient gold reserves. But by presenting a state bank's notes for redemption all at once, the Second Bank could ruin a state bank. Moreover, with less money in reserve, state banks found themselves unable to compete with the Second Bank.

Many state governments regarded the national bank as unresponsive to local needs. Westerners and urban workers bitterly remembered the bank's conservative credit policies during the Panic of 1819. As a private, profit-making institution, its policies reflected its owners' interests, especially the president, Nicholas Biddle. The bank became the prime issue in the 1832 presidential campaign.

Antimasonry

The national political convention was the innovation of the Antimason Party, which started in upstate New York in the mid-1820s as a grassroots movement against Freemasonry, a secret male fraternity of middle- and upper-class men prominent in commerce and civic affairs. Opponents claimed Masons colluded to bestow business and political favors on each other. Evangelicals considered Masons sacrilegious, claiming that Masonry encouraged men to neglect their families for alcohol and ribald entertainment. In the 1828 presidential election, the Antimasons opposed Jackson, himself a Mason. They held the first national political convention in Baltimore in 1831, nominating William Wirt of Maryland for president and Amos Ellmaker of Pennsylvania for vice president.

Election of 1832

Following the Antimasons' lead, the Democrats and National Republicans also held conventions. Democrats reaffirmed Jackson for president and nominated Martin Van Buren of New York for vice president. The National Republican convention selected Clay and John Sergeant of Pennsylvania. The Independent Democrats ran John Floyd and Henry Lee of Virginia.

Jacksonians denounced the bank as a vehicle for special privilege, while Republicans supported it within their plan for economic nationalism. The bank's charter was valid until 1836, but Clay persuaded Biddle to ask Congress to approve an early rechartering. If Jackson signed the rechartering bill, then Clay could attack the president's inconsistency. If Jackson vetoed it, Clay hoped voters would favor him instead. The plan backfired. The president vetoed the bill with a message appealing to voters who feared that rapid economic development spread advantages undemocratically. Jackson took a strong stand against special interests that tried to use the government to their own unfair advantage and won 54 percent of the popular vote to Clay's 37 percent; in the electoral college, he captured 76 percent of electors. The Antimasons won only Vermont.

Jackson's Second Term

Jackson moved in 1833 to dismantle the Second Bank and deposited federal funds in state-chartered banks. Without federal money, the Second Bank shriveled, becoming a Pennsylvania-chartered private bank in 1836. Five years later it closed.

Congress passed the Deposit Act of 1836 with Jackson's support. It authorized the secretary of the treasury to designate one bank per state and territory to provide services formerly performed by the Bank of the United States. The act provided that federal surpluses over $5 million be distributed to states as interest-free loans beginning in 1837. These loans were never repaid.

The surplus derived from wholesale speculation in public lands: speculators borrowed money to purchase public land, used the land as collateral for credit to buy additional acreage, and repeated the cycle. Between 1834 and 1836, federal receipts from land sales rose from $5 million to $25 million. State banks providing the loans issued bank notes. Jackson feared that the speculative craze threatened the stability of state banks and undermined settlers, who could not compete with speculators for the best land.

Specie Circular

With his opposition to paper currency, the president ordered Treasury Secretary Levi Woodbury to issue the Specie Circular. It provided that after August 1836 only specie—gold or silver—or Virginia scrip (paper money) would be accepted as payment for land. By ending credit sales, it significantly reduced purchases of public land and the federal budget surplus. Consequently, the government suspended payments to states.

The policy was a disaster. Although federal land sales fell, speculation continued. The increased demand for specie squeezed banks, and many suspended the redemption of bank notes for specie. Credit contracted further as banks issued fewer notes and made fewer loans. More important, the Specie Circular was similar to a bill defeated in the Senate three months earlier, so Jackson used presidential powers to override legislative will. In the waning days of Jackson's administration, Congress voted to repeal the circular, but the president pocket-vetoed the bill by holding it unsigned until Congress adjourned. In May 1838, a joint resolution of Congress overturned the circular. Sales of land resumed, and speculative fervor ended.

THE WHIG CHALLENGE AND THE SECOND PARTY SYSTEM

In the 1830s, the Democrats' opponents, including remnants of the National Republican and Antimason Parties, joined to become the Whig Party. Resentful of Jackson's domination of Congress, Whigs borrowed the name of the eighteenth-century British party that opposed the tyranny of Hanoverian monarchs. They, too, were the loyal opposition. From 1834 through the 1840s, the Whigs and the Democrats competed on nearly equal footing, and each drew supporters from all regions. The second party system was more intense and better organized than what scholars have labeled as the first party system of Democratic-Republicans versus Federalists.

Whigs and Reformers

Whigs favored economic expansion through an activist government. They supported corporate charters, a national bank, and paper currency; Democrats opposed all three. Whigs professed a strong belief in progress and perfectibility, and favored public schools, prison and asylum reform, and temperance. Whigs did not object to helping special interests if it promoted the general welfare. The chartering of corporations, they argued, expanded economic opportunity for everyone. Democrats, distrustful of concentrated economic power, held to the Jeffersonian principle of limited government.

Whigs stressed a harmony of interests among all classes as well as equal opportunity. Democrats saw society divided into the haves and have nots and embraced equal rights. They championed heroic artisans like Sam Patch, whereas Whigs preferred to see society ruled from the top down. Whigs believed in free-labor ideology and thought that society's wealthy and powerful had risen by their own merits.

Whigs' support for moral reform won over evangelical Protestants. Methodists and Baptists were overwhelmingly Whigs, as were the small number of free black voters. In many locales the membership rolls of reform societies overlapped those of the party. Whigs' rallies resembled camp meetings, their speeches employed pulpit rhetoric, and their programs embodied perfectionist beliefs.

By appealing to evangelicals, Whigs alienated other faiths. The evangelicals' ideal Christian state had no room for nonevangelical Protestants, Catholics, Mormons, or religious freethinkers. Those groups opposed Sabbath laws and temperance legislation and preferred to keep religion and politics separate. Consequently, more than 95 percent of Irish Catholics, 90 percent of Reformed Dutch, and 80 percent of German Catholics voted Democratic.

Thus, Whigs appealed to those who benefited from the era's economic changes, whereas Democrats remained committed to agrarian expansion. Whigs drew antislavery supporters as well northern businessmen and workers pledged to good relations with the South. Well-settled slaveowners, especially in the Upper South, voted Whig, as did black New Englanders. Both favored halting slavery's westward expansion. Democrats' promises to open additional lands for settlement attracted yeoman farmers, wage earners, frontier slaveowners, and immigrants. With such broad voter coalitions, there was room within each party for a spectrum of beliefs, particularly about slavery.

Some politicians went to extremes to keep slavery out of the national debate. In response to the American Anti-Slavery Society's petitioning campaign, the House of Representatives in 1836 adopted what abolitionists labeled *the gag rule,* which automatically tabled abolitionist petitions. Defending the right of petition, former president John Quincy Adams, now a representative from Massachusetts, spoke against the gag rule, which was repealed in 1844.

Election of 1836

Vice President Martin Van Buren headed the Democratic ticket in the 1836 presidential election. Van Buren was a career politician who built a political machine—the Albany Regency—in New York and then joined Jackson's cabinet in 1829, first as secretary of state and then as American minister to Great Britain.

Not yet a national party, in 1836 Whigs entered three sectional candidates: Daniel Webster (New England), Hugh White (the South), and William Henry Harrison (the West). Van Buren comfortably captured the electoral college even though he had only a twenty-five thousand–vote lead. No vice-presidential candidate received a majority of electoral votes, and for the only time, the Senate decided a vice-presidential race, selecting Democratic candidate Richard M. Johnson of Kentucky.

Van Buren and Hard Times

Van Buren took office weeks before the American credit system collapsed. In response to the Specie Circular, New York banks stopped redeeming paper currency with gold in mid-1837. Soon all banks suspended payments in hard coin. A downward economic spiral began. Credit contraction made things worse. After a brief recovery, hard times persisted from 1839 until 1843.

Van Buren cut federal spending, causing prices to drop further, and he opposed a national bank, which would have expanded credit. The president proposed a new regional treasury system for government deposits that became law in 1840. Treasury branches would accept and disperse only gold and silver coin. Increasing the demand for hard coin accelerated price deflation. Whigs favored new banks, more paper currency, and readily available corporate and bank charters. As the party of hard money, Democrats favored eliminating paper currency, and by the mid-1840s most favored eliminating bank corporations.

Anglo-American Tensions

Amid hard times came renewed Anglo-American tensions. After the privately owned steamer *Caroline* carried supplies to aid an unsuccessful Canadian uprising against Great Britain, British loyalists burned the ship, killing an American. Britain refused to apologize, and American newspapers called for revenge. Fearing war, President Van Buren posted troops at the border to discourage vigilante retaliation. Tensions subsided in late 1840 when New York arrested a Canadian deemed responsible for the American's death. The alleged murderer was acquitted. Had the verdict gone otherwise, Lord Palmerston, the British foreign minister, might have sought war.

An old border dispute between Maine and New Brunswick also disrupted Anglo-American relations. When Canadian lumbermen cut trees in the disputed region in winter 1838–1839, a Maine posse assembled to expel them. The lumbermen captured the posse, both sides mobilized militias, and Congress authorized a call-up of fifty thousand men. General Scott was dispatched to Aroostook, Maine, where he arranged a truce. The Webster-Ashburton Treaty (1842) settled the boundaries between Maine and New Brunswick and along the Great Lakes.

William Henry Harrison and the Election of 1840

With the nation facing hard times, Whigs felt confident about the 1840 election. Their strategy was to maintain loyal supporters and win independents by blaming hardship on Democrats. Whigs rallied behind military hero, General William Henry Harrison, conqueror of the Shawnees at Tippecanoe Creek in 1811. Democrats renominated President Van Buren, and the Liberty Party ran James Birney.

Harrison and his running mate, John Tyler of Virginia, ran a people's crusade against the aristocratic president in the Palace. Although from a Virginia plantation family, Harrison presented

Even as the Whigs opposed the Democrats, they adopted many of the Democrats' campaign techniques, appealing to the common man with their log cabin and cider campaign of 1840. The band in this street scene is riding a wagon decorated with a log-cabin painting. The campaign's excitement appealed to voters and nonvoters alike, and 80 percent of eligible voters cast ballots.   (Franklin D. Roosevelt Library, Hyde Park, New York)

himself as an ordinary farmer. Whigs wooed voters with huge rallies, parades, songs, posters, campaign mementos, and a party newspaper, *The Log Cabin*. Roughly 80 percent of eligible voters cast ballots. Harrison won the popular vote by a narrow margin but swept the electoral college by 234 to 60.

Immediately after taking office in 1841, President Harrison convened a special session of Congress to pass the Whig program: repealing the independent treasury system, creating a new national bank, and passing a higher protective tariff. But sixty-eight-year-old Harrison caught pneumonia and died within a month of his inauguration. The Constitution did not stipulate what should happen, but Tyler took possession of executive powers and set a precedent that would not be codified in the Constitution until the twentieth century with the Twenty-fifth Amendment.

President Tyler Tyler became more a Democrat than a Whig. He repeatedly vetoed Clay's protective tariffs, internal improvements, and bills aimed at reviving the Bank of the United States. Two days after Tyler's second veto of a bank bill, the entire cabinet except Secretary of State Daniel Webster resigned, and he left after negotiating the Webster-Ashburton treaty. Disgusted Whigs referred to Tyler as His Accidency.

Like Jackson, Tyler expanded presidential powers and emphasized westward expansion. During his presidency, the United States negotiated its first treaties with China, and Tyler expanded the Monroe Doctrine to include Hawaii. More than anything else, Tyler's vision fixed on Texas and the westward expansion of slavery.

Summary

Religion and reform shaped politics from 1824 through the 1840s. Driven by a belief in human perfectibility, many evangelicals, especially women, worked to right the wrongs of American society. They hoped to trigger the millennium, the thousand years of peace on earth that would accompany Christ's Second Coming. Some utopians joined experimental communities that modeled radical alternatives to existing society. Abolitionists worked to perfect American society through the eradication of slavery. As women entered the public sphere as reformers and abolitionists, some embraced women's rights.

Struggles between the National Republicans and Democrats, then between Democrats and Whigs, stimulated interest in political issues. Both parties built strong organizations and favored economic expansion but by different means: Whigs advocated centralized government, whereas Democrats advocated limited government and agricultural expansion. Controversies over the Second Bank of the United States and nullification exposed different interpretations of the nation's founding principles.

The late 1830s and early 1840s would be a period of uncertainty: the economy experienced a period of bust; tensions with the British resurfaced; and a president died in office. John Tyler's vision of American greatness depended on westward expansion.

The Bible Belt

Had an eighteenth-century visitor to North America asked for the Bible belt, she would have been directed to New England, whose colonies were founded for religious purposes. By the 1830s, the South was the most churched and devout region. The Second Great Awakening, beginning in 1801, spread quickly through the South. By the 1830s, more than half of white and one-quarter of black southerners had a conversion experience. Embracing the Bible as God's word revealed, the South became known as the Bible belt.

Southern Protestant liturgy and cadences were as much African as European; thus southern and northern denominations grew apart. They separated in the 1840s, when Southern Baptists and Methodists withdrew from the national organizations that had barred slaveowners from church offices. Presbyterians withdrew later.

Protestantism dominated, making the South more religiously homogeneous than other regions. Mostly evangelical, southern religion emphasized conversion and a personal battle against sin. By the twentieth century, fundamentalism, which stressed a literal reading of the Bible, reinforced resistance to modernism. Yet southern Protestantism lost ground in opposing evolution and by allying with anti-immigrant groups.

Evangelicalism rose again in the 1960s, especially after the Catholic John F. Kennedy won the Democratic presidential nomination. Many evangelicals moved to the Republican Party, and in 1964 the Republican Barry Goldwater won the Bible belt states. His conservative rhetoric resonated with southerners concerned about desegregation and eroding religious values. *Time* called 1976 the Year of the Evangelical when the born-again Southern Baptist Jimmy Carter became president.

In the 1980s and 1990s, the Bible belt became the base of evangelical political action led by the Moral Majority. Religious and cultural issues rallied southern evangelicals defending the traditional family; advocating prayer in schools; and opposing abortion, the Equal Rights Amendment, and gay rights legislation. In the 2006 midterm elections, dissatisfaction with the Iraq war cost Republicans control of both houses of Congress, but most Bible belt states stuck with the party. Thus the revivals that began in Kentucky in 1801 have rippled across the South for two centuries, shaping the distinctive southern blend of culture and politics.

Chapter Review

FROM REVIVAL TO REFORM

How did religious revival movements lead to social reform?

Ministers and preachers in the Second Great Awakening focused on the importance of good works in gaining salvation in the afterlife. The more they told listeners that how they lived would make a difference in whether they entered God's Kingdom, the more they inspired social and moral reform. Women were often a major force in reform movements, expanding their domestic roles in the home into efforts to counteract the evils of the market economy. Reform goals included reformatories for wayward youth, orphan asylums, rehabilitation for criminals, temperance, and improvements in education.

COMMUNITARIAN EXPERIMENTS

What were the goals of utopian communities?

Often inspired by religious revivalism, the utopian movement sought to hold the line on the rapid social change that members found disturbing, in particular, the rising market economy's excessive individualism. They wanted to recapture the so-called communal nature of the past, and at the same time reshape marriage, child rearing, and other social arrangements. The Shakers, for example, built a profitable community around agriculture and handcrafts, but also abolished individual families in favor of men and women living in separate quarters and sharing leadership. The Oneida community centered on communal property ownership, communal child-rearing, and "complex marriage" in which all men were married to all women. The Fourierists included writers and intellectuals who inspired an American renaissance in literature and the arts, with Brook Farm in West Roxbury, Massachusetts, its most famous community. During its brief existence, the community embraced transcendentalism, the notion that the physical world is secondary to the spiritual realm.

ABOLITIONISM

How did the Second Great Awakening transform the antislavery movement?

Abolitionism dates back to the nation's earliest days, when efforts to end slavery were initiated by both free blacks and elite whites. After 1830, however, evangelical abolitionists seeking to eradicate America's sins focused on slavery with renewed vigor. The activist and newspaper editor William Lloyd Garrison led a new, more radical strain of abolitionism known as "immediatism," which called for the immediate and complete end of slavery without compensating slave owners. Immediatists shared the evangelical belief that people determined their spiritual fate through good or evil acts and that by ending slavery, they could bring about the millennium, or Christ's return to earth. Unlike earlier movements, these abolitionists relied on participation of ministers and many others, and as such encouraged women to not only join but serve on executive committees.

WOMEN'S RIGHTS

What inspired the rise of the women's movement in the mid-nineteenth century?

The religious revivals of the Second Great Awakening provided the first impetus for a later women's movement by encouraging women to see themselves as equal spiritually to men and urging them to take part in reforming society. Women's growing participation in the antislavery movement had many seeing parallels between slave bondage and marriage as a form of bondage, as well as their own lack of citizenship rights. Traditional marriage law, borrowed from the English, gave husbands control over the family, including wives' property and earnings. Eight years after being denied a seat at the World Anti-Slavery Convention because of their sex, Elizabeth Cady Stanton and Lucretia Mott joined others in holding the first Woman's Rights Convention in 1848 at Seneca Falls, N.Y. There, three hundred participants outlined their demands for political and social equality, including the right to vote, in their Declaration of Rights and Sentiments, a document that paralleled the Declaration of Independence.

JACKSONIANISM AND PARTY POLITICS

How did changing demographics influence the outcome of the 1824 presidential election and the future of political parties?

As suffrage laws changed to eliminate land requirements and allow immigrants to vote, the number of eligible voters tripled from 1824 to 1828. Politicians broadened their outreach to these new voters and successfully urged states to shift from appointing presidential electors to the more democratic popular vote. That, combined with the end of candidate selection by congressional caucus, meant that five Democratic-Republican candidates ran for president in 1824. Although Andrew Jackson led in both electoral and popular vote, no one had a clear majority, leaving the House of Representatives to choose the president. Its members chose second place John Quincy Adams, which led to charges of election-stealing and divided the party into the National Republicans (behind Adams) and the Democrats (behind Jackson). With two parties and only two candidates in the 1828 election, Jackson handily won the presidency, and the Democratic Party became the first well-organized national political party in the United States.

FEDERALISM AT ISSUE: THE NULLIFICATION AND BANK CONTROVERSIES

What was at issue in the Nullification Controversy?

At the core of the Nullification Controversy were differing interpretations of the Constitution regarding federal power and states' rights. The doctrine of nullification, which stated that states could overrule federal legislation, was based on the Virginia and Kentucky Resolutions of 1798, which argued that states could judge whether federal actions were constitutional, and ultimately nullify federal laws that did not pass the test. President Jackson rejected state sovereignty and saw nullification as leading to disunion. When South Carolina nullified a federal tariff, Jackson moved troops in to collect the duties. As a compromise, the tariff was reduced and South Carolina withdrew its nullification. But the debate on the nature of the republic and of federal power continued.

THE WHIG CHALLENGE AND THE SECOND PARTY SYSTEM

How did the Whigs and Democrats differ on the role of government in the economy?

Unlike the Democrats, Whigs embraced an activist government and had no problem with government aiding special interests as long as the public benefited as well. Democrats believed in the Jefferson model of limited government. Whigs thought government should be ruled from the top-down, and they embraced the notion of a meritocracy—that the wealthy obtained their status and power through their own hard work. Democrats saw the world divided into "haves" and "have nots" and sought equal rights for all to restore some form of balance. Whigs supported corporate charters, a national bank, and paper currency; Democrats opposed all three.

SUGGESTIONS FOR FURTHER READING

Michael F. Holt, *The Rise and Fall of the American Whig Party: Jacksonian Politics and the Onset of the Civil War* (1999)

Julie Roy Jeffrey, *The Great Silent Army of Abolitionism: Ordinary Women in the Antislavery Movement* (1998)

Curtis D. Johnson, *Redeeming America: Evangelicals and the Road to Civil War* (1993)

Paul E. Johnson, *Sam Patch, the Famous Jumper* (2003)

Steven Mintz, *Moralists and Modernizers: America's Pre–Civil War Reformers* (1995)

Richard S. Newman, *The Transformation of American Abolitionism: Fighting Slavery in the Early Republic* (2002)

Harry L. Watson, *Liberty and Power: The Politics of Jacksonian America* (1990)

Sean Wilentz, *The Rise and Fall of American Democracy: Jefferson to Lincoln* (2005)

CHAPTER 13

The Contested West   1815–1860

CHAPTER OUTLINE

The West in the American Imagination

Expansion and Resistance in the
Old Northwest

The Federal Government and Westward
Expansion

> **LINKS TO THE WORLD:**
> Gold in California

The Southwestern Borderlands

Migration to the Far West

The Politics of Territorial Expansion

Summary

> **LEGACY FOR A PEOPLE
> AND A NATION:** Descendants
> of Early Latino Settlers

To eight-year-old Henry Clay Bruce, moving west was an adventure. In April 1844, the Virginia boy began a 1,500-mile, two-month trip to his new home in Missouri. Henry marveled at the beautiful terrain, impressive towns, and the steamboat ride from Louisville to St. Louis. Once in Missouri, Henry noticed how much the West differed from the East. Farms were far apart, and the countryside abounded with wild fruits, game, and fish. But rattlesnakes, wolves, and vicious hogs kept Henry and his playmates from straying far from home.

A slave boy, Henry made the trip with his mother and siblings after the plantation owner Jack Perkinson decided to seek a new beginning in the West. Pettis Perkinson (Jack's brother and Henry's owner) and three other white Virginians crammed their families, slaves, and belongings into three wagons. In Missouri, Pettis took up residence with Jack Perkinson, who—according to Henry—yelled at and whipped his slaves.

Henry's first year in Missouri was as carefree as a slave child's life could be. The boy fished, hunted (with dogs, not guns), and gathered prairie chicken eggs. But by age nine, Henry was hired out, first to a brick maker, then to a tobacco factory. He worked sunup to sundown, and when he did not meet his bosses' expectations, he was whipped.

Meanwhile, Pettis Perkinson decided to return to Virginia, later sending for some of his slaves, including Henry. The slaves' work would be less arduous in Virginia, but that was small compensation for having to leave behind loved ones in Missouri.

Again Pettis Perkinson grew weary of Virginia and renewed his quest for opportunity in the West, this time in Mississippi. But cotton plantation life suited neither Henry nor his master, who now decided—to his slaves' joy—to give Missouri another chance.

This icon will direct you to interactive activities and study materials on *A People And A Nation*, Brief Edition website: **www.cengage.com/history/norton/ peoplenationbrief8e**

Chronology

1812	Congress establishes the General Land Office.
1820	Congress lowers the price of public lands.
1821	William Becknell charts the Santa Fe Trail.
	Mexico becomes an independent nation.
1823	Mexico allows Stephen Austin to settle U.S. citizens in Mexico.
1824	Congressional General Survey Act empowers the military to chart transportation routes.
	Jedediah Smith publicizes the South Pass to the Far West.
	Indian Office (later Bureau of Indian Affairs) is established.
1825–32	*Empresario* contracts are signed for American settlement of Texas.
1826	Fredonia rebellion fails in Texas.
1830	Indian Removal Act is passed (see Chapter 10).
1832	Black Hawk War occurs.
1834	Cyrus McCormick patents the mechanical reaper.
1836	Lone Star Republic is founded.
	U.S. Army Corps of Topographical Engineers is established.

1840–60	250,000 to 500,000 migrants travel overland to the Far West.
1841	Log Cabin Bill allows settlers to claim 160 acres of public land on credit.
1844	Presidential campaign features annexation of Texas.
1845	Democratic editor coins the term *manifest destiny*.
	Texas is annexed by joint resolution of Congress (March 1) and becomes twenty-eighth state (December 29).
1846–48	War occurs with Mexico.
1847	Mormons settle in Great Salt Lake valley.
1848	Gold is discovered in California.
1849–50s	Farmers and prospectors stream into the Great Plains and Far West.
1855	Massacre of Indians at Ash Hollow triggers warfare between the Sioux and the United States.
1857–58	Mormons and the U.S. Army engage in armed conflict.
1862	Homestead Act allots 160 acres of free land to those who improve it.

Two years later, the restless Perkinson set his eyes farther west, on Texas. Henry, now in his late teens, and his brothers refused to go. Although livid, Pettis Perkinson preferred to abandon his plans than deal with recalcitrant slaves. Henry became the foreman on Perkinson's Missouri farm, where he remained until escaping amid the Civil War to the free state of Kansas in 1864. More than twenty years after leaving Virginia, Henry Clay Bruce finally found the freedom and opportunity that led so many to the West.

In 1820 about 20 percent of the nation's population lived west of the Appalachian Mountains. By 1860 nearly 50 percent did. Most whites and free blacks moved west seeking better opportunities. They envisioned enormous tracts of fertile and uncultivated land or, beginning in the late 1840s, gold or silver mines that promised quick riches. Some saw opportunities for lumbering or ranching or selling goods or services to farmers, miners, lumbermen, and cattlemen.

Men often decided to head west without consulting their wives and children, and slaves' wishes received even less consideration. Nor did western settlers consider the Indian peoples already living there.

The federal government sponsored westward exploration, made laws regulating settlement and the establishment of territorial governments, surveyed and fixed prices on public lands, and sold land. It also invested in transportation routes and established a military presence to assist white settlers.

In the 1820s, the Mexican government, too, aided westward expansion by encouraging Anglo-American settlement in its northern borderlands—something it would later regret. U.S. settlers vied with the region's other inhabitants—Indians, Hispanics, and people of mixed heritage—for land and natural resources. A decade later, Mexico's northern province of Texas declared its independence and sought annexation by the United States. Thus began heightened tensions between the United States and Mexico and within the United States, as Texas's future became entangled with slavery.

For some white Americans, mostly southerners, the ability to own slaves in the West represented freedom. For others, from both the North and the South, slavery's westward expansion frustrated dreams for a new beginning in a region free from slavery's degrading influence on white labor. Even as political parties tried to avoid the slavery issue, they took distinct stands on westward expansion's role in the nation's economic development. Once the spotlight trained on Texas, political leaders would find it increasingly difficult to disentangle westward expansion and slavery.

With each passing decade, conflict—between expectations and reality, between people with different aspirations and world-views—increasingly defined life in the West. By the mid-1840s, western events would aggravate long-simmering discord between southern and northern political interests.

- How did tensions in the modernizing North and the slave South influence western migration and settlement?
- How did public, private, and individual initiatives work together to shape the West's development?
- What motivated cooperation in the West, and what spurred conflict?

THE WEST IN THE AMERICAN IMAGINATION

For historian Frederick Jackson Turner, writing in the late nineteenth century, the western frontier, with its abundant free land, was the "meeting point between savagery and civilization." It bred American democracy, shaped the American character, and made the United States exceptional. Modern historians generally eschew the notion of American exceptionalism, stressing instead the complex connections between the United States and the world. Although today's scholars reject the racialist assumptions of Turner's definition of *frontier*, some see value in the term when understood as a meeting place of different cultures. Others see the West as a place, not a process, though they disagree about what delineates it.

Defining the West For early-nineteenth-century Americans of European descent, the West included anything west of the Appalachian Mountains. It represented the future—a place where they might seek economic and social betterment, typically through land ownership. The West seemed to have so much land that even the poor might acquire a farm. Men who already owned land, like Pettis Perkinson, looked westward for cheaper, bigger, and more fertile landholdings. With the discovery of gold in California in 1848, the West became a place to strike it rich. Other people, though, went west only under

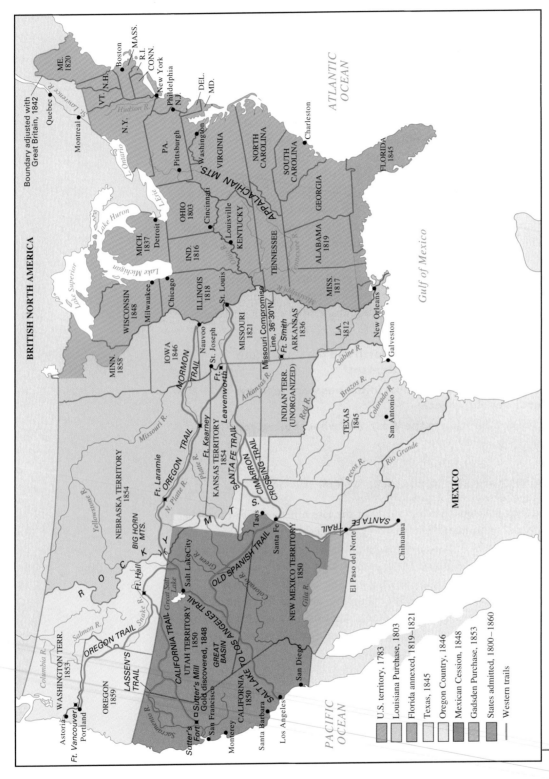

Map 13.1   Westward Expansion, 1800–1860
Through exploration, purchase, war, and treaty, the United States became a continental nation, stretching from the Atlantic to the Pacific.

the threat of force, including enslaved persons as well as Indians removed from their eastern homelands by the U.S. military.

To many, the concept of the West would have been baffling. Emigrants from Mexico and Central or South America traveled northward to reach what European Americans called the West. The twenty-five thousand or so Chinese who went to California during the 1850s traveled eastward from Asia. Some Indians and French Canadians journeyed southward to the West. All arrived in the western portion of the North American continent because of factors that pushed and pulled them.

Frontier Literature

For European Americans, Daniel Boone became the archetypical frontiersman, a man whose daring individualism opened the Eden-like West for virtuous and hardworking freedom lovers. Through biographies, Boone became a familiar figure in American and European households. The mythical Boone lived in the wilderness and shrank from society. He single-handedly overpowered bears and Indians but also became the pathfinder for civilization. As a friend wrote, he blazed a trail for millions "to a Land flowing with milk and honey." By borrowing Biblical language—the land of milk and honey referred to the Promised Land that God promised beleaguered Israelites—Boone's friend suggested he was a Moses leading his people to a land of abundance.

With the invention of the steam press in the early 1830s, western adventure stories were cheap and widely read. Davy Crockett, another real-life figure turned into mythical hero, was featured in many of them. Crockett first fought the Creeks under Andrew Jackson but later championed Indian rights. After he died defending the Alamo mission during Texas's fight for independence (1836), Crockett appeared in stories portraying the West as a place where one escaped from civilized society and fought Indians and Mexicans. But even in this western myth, the American West symbolized what white Americans saw as their nation's core value: freedom.

Western Art

In artists' renderings, the West was sometimes an untamed wilderness inhabited by savages (noble or otherwise) and sometimes a cultivated garden, a land of milk and honey where the Jeffersonian agrarian dream was realized. Either way, artwork often revealed more about white Americans' ideals that about the West itself.

The first Anglo-American artists to travel west were Samuel Seymour and Titian Ramsay Peale, whom the federal government hired to accompany explorer Stephen H. Long to the Rocky Mountains in 1820. They pioneered an influential genre: facsimiles in government reports. Between 1840 and 1860, Congress published nearly sixty works on western exploration, featuring hundreds of lithographs and engravings of the region's plants, animals, and people. Some of these reports became bestsellers.

Although government reports often faithfully reproduced original paintings, they sometimes made telling alterations. When Richard Kern accompanied explorer James H. Simpson in 1849 to the Southwest, for example, he painted a Navajo man

In one of his most famous portraits, George Catlin painted Wi-Jun-Jon, an Assiniboine Indian, both before and after he had mingled with white men. In the before stance, the Indian is a dignified, peace-pipe-bearing warrior; in the after portrait, the corrupted Indian has abandoned dignity for vanity and his peace pipe for a cigar.   (Smithsonian American Art Museum, Washington, D.C./Art Resource, NY)

in a submissive pose. The reproduction transformed the man's pose into a rebellious one. In other cases, the government reports changed artists' depictions of Indian-occupied landscapes into empty terrain free for the taking.

Artists portrayed their subjects through the lens of their own cultural assumptions, and commercial artists produced what they thought the public craved. When George Catlin traveled west in the immediate aftermath of the 1830 Indian Removal Act, Catlin painted with a moral in mind. Indians came in two varieties—those who preserved their original, almost noble qualities of freedom and moderation and those who, after coming in contact with whites, had become dissolute. Indians, he implied, would benefit from removal from white Americans' corrupting influence.

Countering the Myths   Western reality often clashed with promoters' promises, and disappointed settlers sometimes tried to clarify matters for future migrants. Rebecca Burlend and her family, for example, were lured to Illinois by a fellow Englishman's letters extolling "a land flowing with milk and honey." Later Burlend wrote with her son *A True Picture of Emigration* (1831), which described Illinois's hardships—intemperate weather, difficult working conditions, and swindlers. The Burlends did not discourage emigration, but substituted a realistic for a rosy description.

EXPANSION AND RESISTANCE IN THE OLD NORTHWEST

In the 1820s and 1830s, settlers streamed into the Old Northwest and the Old Southwest by foot, horseback, wagon, canal boat, steamboat, or a combination of means. Many people, like Pettis Perkinson and his slaves, moved several times, and when opportunities failed to materialize, some returned home.

In the first federal census of 1790, the Northwest Territory's white population numbered a few hundred people. By 1860 nearly 7 million people called it home. Between 1810 and 1830, the population of Ohio more than quadrupled, while Indiana and Illinois grew fourteenfold and thirteenfold, respectively. Michigan's population multiplied fiftyfold between 1820 and 1850. Migration accounted for most of this growth. Once in the Old Northwest, people did not stay put. Geographic mobility, the search for better opportunities, and connections to the market economy came to define the region that became the Midwest.

Map 13.2   Settlement in the Old Southwest and Old Northwest, 1820 and 1840
Removal of Indians and a growing transportation network opened up land to white and black settlers in the regions known as the Old Southwest and the Old Northwest, as the U.S. population grew from 9.6 million in 1820 to 17.1 million in 1840.

Deciding Where to Move

Moving west meant leaving behind worn-out soil and areas where little land was available for purchase, but it also meant leaving behind family, friends, and communities. The trip promised to be arduous, as did the backbreaking labor of clearing land for cultivation. But what if the soil proved less fertile than anticipated? What if neighbors proved unfriendly, or worse? What if homesickness became unbearable?

Settlers tried to control as many variables as possible. Like Pettis Perkinson, people often relocated to where they had relatives or friends and traveled with people they knew. They sought areas with familiar climates. The legal status of slavery also

In 1834 Karl Bodmer painted a farm on the Illinois Prairie, depicting the more permanent, if still modest, structures that farmers built after the initial urgency to clear fields for cultivation had subsided.   (© Collection of The New-York Historical Society)

influenced where people settled. Some white southerners, tired of the social and political power of the planter elite, sought areas free from slavery—or at least where plantations did not dominate. Many others went west to increase their chances of owning slaves or of owning more slaves. White northerners mostly hoped to distance themselves from slavery, not out of sympathy for slaves but because they, too, detested the economic and political power of elite slaveowners. Many northerners hoped to settle in areas free of *any* black people. In the 1850s, many midwestern states passed "black laws" prohibiting African Americans, free or enslaved, from living within their boundaries. Ironically, many free blacks migrated west believing that the region would be less prejudiced than the East.

Between 1815 and 1860, few western migrants settled on the Great Plains, a region reserved for Indians until the 1850s, and few easterners risked the journey to California and Oregon before the completion of the transcontinental railroad in 1869. At first the Southwest appealed most to settlers, but after 1820, the Midwest—with its better-developed transportation routes, democratic access to economic markets, smaller African American population, cheaper average landholding, and climatic similarity to New England and northern Europe—drew more settlers. The Midwest's thriving transportation hubs also made good first stops for western migrants lacking cash to purchase land. They found work unloading canal boats, planting and harvesting wheat, grinding wheat into flour, sawing trees into lumber, or, more often, a combination of these seasonal jobs. With the Old Northwest's population growing fast, white southerners became increasingly worried about congressional representation and slavery laws.

Indian Removal and Resistance

In the Midwest and the Southwest, white settlement depended on the removal of Indians. Even as the U.S. Army escorted Indians out of the Old Southwest, the federal government arranged eighty-six treaties between 1829 and 1851 in which northeastern

Indian nations relinquished land titles in exchange for lands west of the Mississippi River.

Some northern Indians evaded removal, including the Miamis in Indiana, the Ottawas and Chippewas in the upper Midwest, and the Winnebagos in southern Wisconsin. In 1840, chiefs of the Miamis acceded to pressure to exchange 500,000 acres of land in Indiana for 500,000 acres in Indian Country. Under the treaty, their people had five years to move or be escorted west by federal troops. But about half of the Miami nation dodged the soldiers, and many of those who made the trek later returned. In Wisconsin, some Winnebagos eluded removal or returned to Wisconsin after being escorted west of the Mississippi.

Black Hawk War

In a series of treaties between 1804 and 1830, Sauks (or "Sacs") and Fox leaders exchanged tribal lands in northwestern Illinois and southwestern Wisconsin for lands across the Mississippi River in Iowa Territory. The Sauk warrior Black Hawk disputed the validity of the treaties, and in 1832 he led Sauk and Fox families to Illinois, panicking white settlers. The state's governor called up the militia, who were joined by militia units from surrounding states and territories and U.S. Army regular soldiers. Over the next several months, hundreds of Indians and dozens of whites died under often-gruesome circumstances in the Black Hawk War. As the Sauks and Fox tried to flee across the Mississippi, they were fired on by American soldiers. Those who survived the river crossing were met with gunfire by Lakota (Sioux) warriors allied with the Americans.

Black Hawk surrendered, and U.S. officials undertook to impress on him and other leaders the futility of resistance. After being imprisoned, then sent to Washington, D.C., along a route meant to underscore the immense size and population of the United States, and imprisoned again, the Indians were returned to their homes. The Black Hawk War marked the end of militant Indian uprisings in the Old Northwest.

Selling the West

Land speculators, developers of "paper towns" (towns that existed on paper only), steamboat companies, and manufacturers of farming implements promoted the Midwest as tranquil place of unbounded opportunity. Land proprietors emphasized the region's connections to eastern ways of life and markets. They knew that, when families relocated in the West, they did not seek to escape civilization. Settlement in the West generally followed connections to national and international markets. Eastern farmers, hoping to escape tired soil or tenancy, sought fertile lands on which to grow commercial crops. Labor-saving devices, such as Cyrus McCormick's reaper (1834) and John Deere's steel plow (1837), made the West more alluring. McCormick, a Virginia inventor, patented a horse-drawn reaper that allowed two men to harvest the same number of acres of wheat that previously required between four and sixteen men. The reaper's efficiency achieved its greatest payoffs on the large, flat prairie lands, so McCormick relocated his factory to Chicago in 1847. Without John Deere's steel plow, which could break through tough grass and roots without constant cleaning, "breaking the plains" might not have been possible.

In his advertisements, Cyrus McCormick portrayed his reapers as turning the West into a place of prosperity and leisure.   (The Center for American History, The University of Texas at Austin)

MC CORMICKS MACHINES.

Clearing the Land

After locating a suitable land claim, settlers constructed a rudimentary cabin if one did not exist. Time did not permit more elaborate structures, because first they had to clear the land. At the rate of five to ten acres a year, the average family needed ten years to fully clear a farm. Prairie land took less time, though throughout the 1850s, many farmers considered lands free of timber to be deserts, unfit for cultivation.

Whereas farming attracted families, lumbering and mining appealed mostly to single young men. By the 1840s, as forests became depleted in the eastern United States and Canada, northeastern lumber companies and laborers migrated to Wisconsin, Michigan, and Minnesota. Recently arrived Scandinavians and French Canadians also worked in the lumber industry. As Great Lakes' forests thinned, lumbermen moved on again—some to the Gulf states' pine forests, some to Canada, and some to the Far West, where Mexicans in California and British in Canada had already established flourishing lumber industries. With the rapid growth of California's cities following the 1849 Gold Rush, timber demand soared, drawing midwestern lumbermen farther west.

Midwestern cities nurtured the settlement of the surrounding countryside. Steamboats turned river settlements like Louisville and Cincinnati into commercial centers, while Chicago, Detroit, and Cleveland grew up on the banks of the Great Lakes. By the mid-nineteenth century, Chicago, with its railroads, stockyards, and grain elevators, was positioned to dominate the region's economy; western farmers transported livestock and grain by rail to that city, where pigs became packed meat and grain became flour before being shipped east. The promise of future flour and future pigs gave rise to commodities markets. Some of the world's most sophisticated and speculative economic practices started in Chicago.

THE FEDERAL GOVERNMENT AND WESTWARD EXPANSION

Few white Americans considered settling in the West before the region had been explored, surveyed, and civilized, which meant Indian removal and the establishment of churches, businesses, and American legal structures. Wide-scale settlement became possible only with the sponsorship of the federal government.

Artist Alfred Jacob Miller portrayed a marriage *à la façon du pays* ("in the custom of the country") in which an Indian woman is given in marriage by her father to a *métis* man at a Rocky Mountain *rendezvous* in 1837. (Library of Congress)

The Fur Trade

Fur trappers were among the first white Americans in the trans-Appalachian West, but their lives bore faint resemblance to their mythical representation as mountain men who lived off the land, trapped beaver, cast off civilization, and dared to go where whites never trod. Although many had little contact with American society, fur trappers lived among Indians, became multilingual, and often married Indian women, who became their business partners, finishing pelts and helping smooth trade relations between their husbands and their native communities. The children of such marriages—*métis* or *mestizos* (people of mixed Indian and European heritage)—added to the cultural complexity of the West.

The fur trade was an international business, with many pelts from the American interior reaching Europe and Asia. Beginning in the 1820s, trappers and traders came together annually for a *rendezvous*—a multiday gathering at which they traded fur for guns, tobacco, and beads that they could later exchange with Indians while also sharing stories and alcohol and gambling. Modeled on similar Indian gatherings that had occurred for generations, the rendezvous brought together Americans, Indians, Mexicans, and people of mixed heritage from all over the West—from as far north as Canada and as far south as Mexico. Rendezvous took place in remote mountain locations, but they were cosmopolitan affairs.

By the 1840s, the American fur trade was in decline. Beavers had been overhunted, and fashions shifted toward silk rather than fur for hat making. One legacy of the fur trade was the devastating effect on native peoples of diseases introduced by mountain men. Another was the development of trails that crossed the trans-Mississippi West.

Transcontinental Exploration

A desire for quicker and safer routes for transporting furs and other goods to trading posts drove much early exploration. In 1821, the merchant William Becknell helped chart the Santa Fe Trail running between Missouri and Santa Fe, New Mexico, where it connected to the Chihuahua Trail running into Mexico, allowing American and

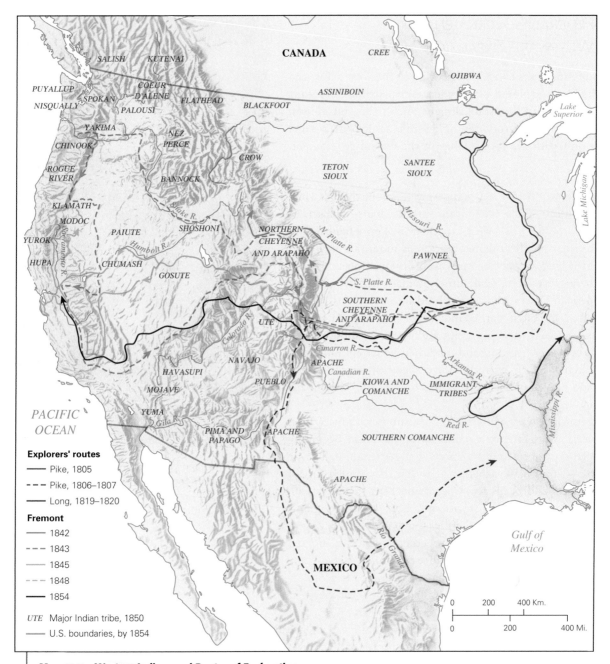

Map 13.3 Western Indians and Routes of Exploration

Although western explorers believed they were discovering new routes and places, Indians had long lived in most of the areas through which explorers traveled.

Mexican merchants to develop a vibrant trade. In 1824, the fur trader Jedediah Smith rediscovered the South Pass, a 20-mile break in the Rocky Mountains in present-day Wyoming previously known only to Native Americans and some Pacific Fur Company trappers. The South Pass became the route followed by most people headed overland to California and Oregon.

Gold in California

When James Marshall discovered gold in Sutter's Mill, California, in January 1848, word spread quickly worldwide. Within a year, tens of thousands of adventurers from other countries rushed to California, making it one of the most cosmopolitan places in North America.

In an era before the telegraph crossed the oceans, it is surprising how fast the news traveled. Mexicans heard of the gold strike first. Next, word spread to Chile, Peru, and throughout South America; then across the Pacific to Hawai'i, China, and Australia; and on to Europe—Ireland, France, and the German states. Overland travelers brought the news south to Baja California and Sonora in Mexico. By spring 1849 some six thousand Mexicans were panning for gold; many came seasonally, spreading news of California every trip home.

Sailing ships brought news of California gold to Hawai'i. The newspaper *Honolulu Polynesian* announced it in the kingdom on June 24, 1848. Gold seekers and merchants sailed to California, and regular steamship service between Hawai'i and California began in 1853.

A ship brought news of California gold discoveries to Valparaiso, Chile, in August 1848. People in Chile's cities talked feverishly about gold, and newspapers kept pace. Before year's end, two thousand Chileans left for California.

Word of gold reached Australia in December 1848, and by 1850 every ship in Sydney Harbour was destined for California. News reached China in mid-1848. After the upheavals of the Taiping Revolution in 1850, Chinese migration soared. By the mid-1850s, one in five gold miners was Chinese.

In 1850 the new state of California had nearly 40 percent foreign-born inhabitants, the majority non-European. Through word of mouth, rumor, letters home, and newspaper reports, the 1848 gold discovery linked California to millions of people around the globe.

This 1855 Frank Marryat drawing of a San Francisco saloon dramatizes the international nature of the California gold rush. Like theater performers, the patrons of the saloon dress their parts as Yankees, Mexicans, Asians, and South Americans.
(© Collection of the New York Historical Society)

Lewis and Clark's Corps of Discovery was only the first of many federally sponsored expeditions to chart the trans-Mississippi West. Some expeditions sought to establish cordial relations with Indian groups with whom Americans might trade or enter military alliances; others were scientific, exploring native inhabitants, flora, and fauna. But they were always also commercial. Like Lewis and Clark, later explorers hoped to locate land, water, and rail routes that would allow American businessmen and farmers to engage in national and international trade.

In 1805 the U.S. Army dispatched Zebulon Pike to find the source of the Mississippi and a navigable route west. Along the way, he was to research natural resources and native peoples and foster diplomatic relationships with Indian leaders. Before the Supreme Court ruled in *Johnson v. M'Intosh* (1823) that Indians did not own land but merely had a "right of occupancy," government officials instructed Pike and other explorers to purchase lands for military garrisons.

Although Pike failed to identify the Mississippi's source and had only limited success in cultivating relationships and purchasing land, he gathered important information about the terrain. When Pike and his men wandered into Spanish territory to the south, military officials held him captive for months in Mexico, inadvertently showing him areas he might not have explored himself. After his release, Pike wrote about a potential market in southwestern cities. The province of Tejas (Texas), with its fertile soil and rich grasslands, enchanted him. But Pike dismissed the other northern provinces of Mexico, whose boundaries stretched to present-day Nevada and Utah, as unsuitable for cultivation by civilized people. In 1820 the army explorer Stephen Long similarly branded modern-day Oklahoma, Kansas, and Nebraska as the Great American Desert, incapable of cultivation. Until the 1850s, when a transcontinental railroad was planned, this desert was reserved for Indian settlement.

In 1838 Congress established the U.S. Army Corps of Topographical Engineers to systematically explore the West. As a second lieutenant in that corps, John C. Frémont undertook three expeditions to the region between the upper Mississippi and Missouri rivers, the Rockies, the Great Basin, Oregon, and California. He helped

Charles Koppel portrayed the Colorado Desert and Signal Mountain for the *Pacific Railway Reports* (1853). The desert appears vast and unlimited, and those who travel through it are advancing into the unknown.   (The Center for American History, The University of Texas at Austin)

survey the Oregon Trail. Aided by his wife, Jessie Benton Frémont, Frémont published bestselling accounts of his explorations. The Corps of Topographical Engineers' most significant contributions came in the 1850s with its surveying of possible routes for a transcontinental railroad.

A Military Presence

The army also helped ready the West for settlement. With the General Survey Act of 1824, Congress empowered the military to chart transportation improvements vital to the nation's military protection or commercial growth. Army engineers helped design state- and privately sponsored roads, canals, and railroads, and soldiers cleared forests and laid roadbeds. A related bill in 1824 authorized the army to improve the Ohio and Mississippi Rivers, and a later amendment did the same for the Missouri.

By the 1850s, 90 percent of the U.S. military was stationed west of the Mississippi River. When Indians refused to relinquish their lands, the army escorted them westward; when they harmed whites or their property, the army waged war. The army sometimes destroyed the crops and buildings of white squatters who refused to vacate lands they did not own. But, primarily, the army presence assisted overland migration. Army forts intimidated Indians, defended settlers from Indian attacks, and supplied information and provisions. In theory, the army was also supposed to protect Indians by driving settlers off Indian lands and enforcing laws prohibiting alcohol sales to Indians. Yet the army's small size made it impossible to enforce such policies even when officers were disposed to do so.

The Office of Indian Affairs handled the government's other interactions with Indians, including negotiating treaties, managing schools, and overseeing trade. Created in 1824 as part of the War Department, the Indian Office cooperated with the military in removing Indians from lands needed for American expansion and in protecting citizens who relocated. In 1849 the Indian Office became part of the newly established Department of the Interior, and it soon shifted from removal to civilization, through a reservation system. Whereas some Indians accepted reservations as protection from white incursion, others rejected them, sometimes setting off deadly intratribal disagreements.

Public Lands

The federal government controlled vast tracts of land, procured either from the states' cessions of their western claims after the Revolution or through treaties with foreign powers, including Indian nations. The General Land Office, established in 1812 as part of the Treasury Department, handled the distribution of those lands. Its earliest policies divided western lands into 640-acre tracts to be auctioned at a minimum $2 an acre. These policies favored speculators—who bought up millions of acres—over individual, cash-poor farmers. Many settlers became squatters, prompting Congress in 1820 to lower land prices to $1.25 per acre and sell tracts as small as 80 acres. Twelve years later, it sold 40-acre tracts. Yet it also demanded that the land be bought outright; few would-be western settlers (particularly in the aftermath of the Panic of 1819) had enough cash to purchase government land. Because speculators sold land on credit, many small-time farmers bought from them at inflated prices.

Farmers pressed for a federal policy of preemption—the right to settle on land without obtaining title, improve it, and buy it later at the legal minimum price ($1.25). Some states offered land through preemption, and Congress occasionally authorized preemption of federal land in the 1820s and 1830s. But there was no general preemption law until the so-called Log Cabin Bill in 1841, and that applied to surveyed land only. Preemption extended to unsurveyed lands with the Homestead Act of 1862, which deemed that land would be provided free to any U.S. citizen (or foreigner who declared the intention of becoming a citizen) after residing on it for five years and improving it. Alternatively, settlers could buy land outright at $1.25 an acre after six months of living on it, which allowed them to use the land as collateral for loans for additional land, farming supplies, or machinery.

THE SOUTHWESTERN BORDERLANDS

Along the southwestern border of the Louisiana Territory were vast provinces under the domain of first Spain and then, after 1821, the newly independent nation of Mexico. New Mexico, with commercial centers in Albuquerque and Santa Fe, remained under

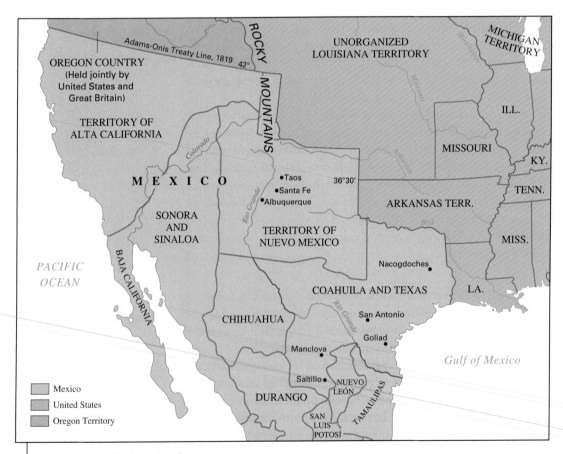

Map 13.4   Mexico's Far North

What is now considered the American Southwest was made up of the northern provinces of Mexico until the United States conquered the territory during the Mexican War (1846–1848).

Mexican control until the United States conquered the territory during its War with Mexico. Texas became an autonomous state in 1824, giving it greater independence from federal authorities in Mexico City than New Mexico enjoyed. This situation helped foster Texas's struggle for national independence and then annexation to the United States; this returned the divisive issue of slavery to the center of American politics.

Southwestern Slavery   Slavery existed in the Southwest for centuries. As practiced by Spaniards and indigenous peoples—the Apaches, Comanches, Kiowas, Navajos, Utes, and Pueblos—slavery centered on capturing women and children, who were then assimilated into their captors' communities, where they provided labor and status while aiding economic and diplomatic exchanges with their former communities.

This system was built on racial mixing, which was anathema to most white Americans. As white slaveholders from the Southeast pushed into Mexican territory during the 1820s and 1830s, they often justified their conquest in racial terms. The region's Hispanic settlers, they reasoned, had been rendered lazy and barbarous by racial intermixing and were thus destined to be supplanted.

The New Mexican Frontier   When Mexico gained independence from Spain in 1821, New Mexico's Hispanic population outnumbered indigenous Pueblo peoples by three to one. There were 28,000 Hispanics, including people born in Spain and *criollos*, people born in New Spain to parents of Spanish descent. Most New Mexicans engaged in irrigated agriculture. To the north of Santa Fe, they worked small plots of land, but to the south, larger farms and ranches predominated. Rancheros became wealthy by selling wool and corn in distant markets and by using unpaid laborers, often relatives, bound by debt. Threatened by the province's raiding Indian tribes—the Apaches, Utes, Navajos, and sometimes the Comanches—Hispanics, Pueblos, and *mestizos* sometimes united in defense. But their numerical superiority allowed Hispanics to take over many Pueblo villages and lands in the rich northern river valleys.

The Santa Fe Trail caused a commercial explosion in New Mexico, doubling the value of imports in two years. Whereas the Spanish tried to keep foreigners out, the Mexican government offered enormous land grants to Anglo-American and French entrepreneurs, hoping they would develop the region's industry and agriculture, and strengthen commercial ties with the United States.

While commercial relationships grew, few Americans settled in New Mexico during the 1820s and 1830s. The best lands were occupied by Indians and Hispanics. And Americans seeking cheap, fertile land could find it in Texas.

The Texas Frontier   In 1821, indigenous Indians remained the dominant group in Texas, although there were also immigrant Indians, Hispanics, Anglos, and *mestizos*. Of the thirty thousand indigenous people, most were Comanches. To identify distinctive Indian groups, though, belies the intermarriage and cultural exchange among them. Indians married Indians from other nations, as well as Europeans and African Americans.

As Indian groups competed for the region's resources, intermittent warfare resulted. Comanches hunted bison or stole horses, livestock, and crops from their enemies, the Pawnees, Arapahos, and Cheyennes. Smaller groups such as the Wichitas and Caddos grew corn, beans, squash, and pumpkin. When crops failed, these Indian farmers turned to bison hunting, sometimes triggering conflict with the Comanches.

Tensions increased around the time of Mexican independence, when the first of another ten thousand Indians migrated into the region. From the Old Northwest came Shawnees and Kickapoos—former members of Tecumseh's confederacy. From the Old Southwest came Cherokees, Creeks, Choctaws, Chickasaws, and Seminoles. As Indian newcomers competed for land and animals, they came into conflict with established Indian groups, such as the Comanches. Many immigrant Indians had adopted European clothing and European ideas about land and race. They saw land as a commodity, and some owned African American slaves. They often dismissed as savage the indigenous Indians who hunted bison and wore their skins. But such contempt did not guarantee an affinity for Anglo-Americans; many immigrant Indians resented those who had evicted them from their homelands.

Tejanos

Hispanic peoples had been in Texas since the 1500s, establishing missions and presidios, but by 1820 they numbered only five thousand. Most raised livestock on ranches, while others traded with Indians. Because they were so distant from the Spanish colonial capital in Mexico City, they formed a distinctive identity, seeing themselves as *Tejanos* (or Texans). Many intermarried with Indians.

In the years after the War of 1812, Anglo-Americans began entering Texas. They traded manufactured goods—guns, ammunition, and kettles—for animal hides,

This depiction of San Antonio residents going to a ball, circa 1848, represents the vibrant cultural life in early Texas society.   (Daughters of the Republic of Texas Library)

horses, and mules. Although some Anglos settled in Texas, more came and went along the Santa Fe and Chihuahua Trails. These Anglo newcomers largely supplanted the Tejanos as the Indians' trading partners, and the economic fortunes of the region's tribes became increasingly oriented toward the United States.

American *Empresarios*

In the 1820s, Americans began settling in Texas under an *empresario* system. The first arrangement was made by Moses Austin, a Missouri miner and trader, who approached Spanish authorities in Mexico City in January 1821 with a settlement plan. The Spanish considered Texas a buffer between hostile Indians and the United States and wanted it populated. They gave Austin a land grant of approximately 200,000 acres along the Brazos River in exchange for his promise to bring three hundred Catholic families and no slaves. Before Austin could act, he died. Mexico won its independence from Spain in September 1821.

Austin's son, Stephen, took up his father's scheme and pressed the new Mexican government to honor the grant, which it did in 1823, provided that Austin give up his American citizenship and become a Mexican national. By 1825 Stephen Austin brought two thousand white people and four hundred contract laborers of African descent. With ninety-nine-year contracts, these African Americans were slaves by another name. Still, Austin's success encouraged the Mexican government to contract with Austin to bring nine hundred families.

Satisfied with the Austin experiment, in 1824 Mexico passed a Colonization Law providing land and tax incentives to future foreign settlers. Details were left up to individual Mexican states. Coahuila y Texas specified that the head of a family could obtain 4,428 acres of grazing or 177 acres of farming land. The land was cheap, and could be paid in installments over six years, with nothing due until the fourth year. To be eligible, foreigners had to be upstanding Christians and had to establish permanent residency. The Coahuila y Texas government provided additional land to settlers who married Mexican women.

Most U.S. citizens who settled in Mexico did so under an *empresario,* or immigration agent, who selected moral colonists, distributed lands, and enforced regulations. In exchange, he received nearly twenty-five thousand acres of grazing land and one thousand acres of farming land for every hundred families he settled. Between 1825 and 1832, approximately twenty-four *empresario* contracts (seventeen of which went to Anglo-Americans) were signed covering eight thousand families total. The land grants enveloped almost all of present-day Texas.

Some Anglo-Americans who emigrated to Texas in the 1820s were pushed from the United States by the Panic of 1819 and pulled to Texas by cheap land and, especially, generous credit terms. Despite Mexican efforts to encourage assimilation with Mexicans of Spanish origin in Texas, Americans tended to settle in separate communities. Anglo-Americans outnumbered the Tejanos two to one. Authorities worried that transplanted Americans would try to make Texas part of the United States.

Texas Politics

In 1826 an *empresario* named Haden Edwards called for an independent Texas, which he named the Fredonia Republic. Other *empresarios,* seeing advantages in peaceful relations with the Mexican government, resisted Edwards's movement. Although the Fredonia revolt failed, Mexican authorities dreaded what it might foreshadow.

Consequently, in 1830, Mexican authorities terminated legal immigration from the United States while encouraging immigration from Europe and other parts of Mexico. They also prohibited American slaves from entering Texas, a provision that brought Texas in line with the rest of Mexico, where slavery had been outlawed the previous year. These laws did not keep Americans and their slaves from coming; soon they controlled most of the Texas coastline and Texas's U.S. border. Mexican authorities repealed the anti-immigration law in 1833, reasoning that it discouraged upstanding settlers without deterring undesirables. By 1835 the population of Texas was nearly thirty thousand, with Americans outnumbering Tejanos seven to one.

Among white Texans, some, like Stephen Austin, favored staying in Mexico and demanding more autonomy, the legalization of slavery, and free trade with the United States. Others pushed for Texas to secede from Mexico and request annexation by the United States. In 1835 the secessionists overtook a Mexican military installation charged with collecting taxes at Galveston Bay. Austin advocated a peaceful resolution, but, suspicious, Mexican authorities jailed him for eighteen months, which converted him to the independence cause.

The Lone Star Republic   With discontent over Texas increasing throughout Mexico, the Mexican president General Santa Anna declared himself dictator and marched his army toward Texas. Fearing that Santa Anna would free their slaves, Texans rebelled. After initial defeats at the Alamo mission in San Antonio and at Goliad in March 1836, the Texans won the conflict by year's end. They declared themselves the Lone Star Republic and elected Sam Houston as president. The Texas constitution legalized slavery and banned free blacks.

Texas then faced the challenge of nation building, which to its leaders involved Indian removal. When Indians refused to leave, Mirabeau Lamar, the nation's second

Like George Allen, many Texas settlers relied on slave labor to work their fields and maintain their households. (Texas Memorial Museum, University of Texas at Austin)

president, mobilized the Texas Rangers—mounted nonuniformed militia—to drive them out through terror. The Rangers raided Indian villages, where they robbed, raped, and murdered. This "ethnic cleansing," as one historian labeled it, ultimately cleared native settlers out to make room for white Americans and their African American slaves.

MIGRATION TO THE FAR WEST

In the following decade, more Americans moved to the Far West, even though California and Utah were part of Mexico. Some sought religious freedom or Christian converts, but most sought fertile farmland.

Western Missionaries Catholic missionaries—Americans, Europeans, and converted Indians—maintained a strong presence in the Far West even after a Mexican law secularized the California missions in 1833, using them to organize Indian labor. The missionaries ministered to Catholic immigrants, worked—with some success—to convert Indians and encouraged specifically Roman Catholic colonies.

In the Pacific Northwest, Catholics vied directly with Protestant missionaries for Indian souls. Under the auspices of the American Board of Commissioners for Foreign Missions, two missionary couples—credited as being the first white migrants along the Oregon Trail—traveled to the Pacific Northwest in 1836. Narcissa and Marcus Whitman built a meetinghouse for Cayuse Indians in Waiilatpu, near present-day Walla Walla, Washington, while Eliza and Henry Spalding worked to convert the Nez Percé at Lapwai, in what is now Idaho. With their air of cultural superiority, the Whitmans were unable to convert the Cayuses and focused instead on the white migrants flowing into Oregon in the 1840s.

Tensions escalated when a devastating measles epidemic struck in 1847, and the Cayuses saw it as a calculated assault on their people. They retaliated by murdering the Whitmans and twelve other missionaries. The Spaldings abandoned their successful mission, blamed Catholics for inciting the massacre, and became farmers in Oregon, not returning to Lapwai for another fifteen years.

Mormons Persecuted in Missouri and Illinois, the Mormons followed Brigham Young to their Promised Land in the Great Salt Lake valley. The region was still under Mexican control but about to become part of the U.S. territory of Utah. As non-Mormons began to settle in Utah, Young diluted their influence by attracting new Mormon settlers to what he called the state of Deseret.

Mormons prospered by providing services and supplies to California-bound settlers and miners. Young discouraged *gentiles* (his term for non-Mormons) from settling in Deseret and advocated boycotts of gentile businesses. When in 1852 the Mormons openly sanctioned polygamy, animosity toward them increased nationwide. In June 1857, President James Buchanan dispatched twenty-five hundred federal troops to suppress an alleged Mormon rebellion.

Anxious over their own safety and eager to maintain peace with neighboring Indians, some Mormons joined Paiutes in attacking a passing wagon train of non-Mormon migrants from Arkansas and Missouri. Approximately 120 men, women, and children died in the so-called Mountain Meadows Massacre in August 1857. In the next two years, the U.S. Army and the Mormons engaged in armed conflict, though there were no fatalities.

Oregon and California Trails

In the twenty years after 1840, between 250,000 and 500,000 men, women, and children walked across much of the continent, usually taking seven months. Although they traveled armed, most of their encounters with Indians were peaceful, if tense.

Overlanders began their journeys at one of the so-called jumping-off points—towns such as Independence, St. Joseph, and Westport Landing—along the Missouri River, where they bought supplies for the 2,000-mile trip. While miners frequently traveled alone or with other fortune-seeking young men, farmers traveled with their families, often in wagon trains of relatives, neighbors, church members, and other acquaintances.

They tried to time their departures to be late enough to find forage grass for their oxen and livestock, but not so late that they would encounter the treacherous snows of the Rockies and Sierra Nevada. They trudged alongside their wagons on average 15 miles a day, in weather from freezing cold to blistering heat. Men generally tended livestock, while women set up camp, prepared meals, and tended children.

Indians were usually peaceful, and during the trails' early days, they provided food and information or ferried migrants across rivers. In exchange, migrants offered blankets, knives, metal pots, tobacco, ornamental beads, and other items. When exchanges went bad—due to misunderstanding or attempts to swindle one or the other—tensions mounted.

This rare stereocard shows an emigrant train, including two women and possibly a child, dwarfed by the natural landscape in Strawberry Valley, California, in the 1860s. (Library of Congress)

Livestock theft persistently aggravated migrants, who blamed Indians even though white thieves stole livestock, too. Indians who took livestock often did so when whites failed to offer gifts in exchange for grazing rights. The so-called Mormon Cow Incident (or the Grattan Massacre) forever altered relationships along the Oregon Trail.

In August 1854, a Lakota in present-day Wyoming slaughtered a cow that strayed from a nearby Mormon camp. When Lakota leaders offered compensation for the cow, U.S. Army Lieutenant John Grattan, seeking to set an example, refused. Grattan ordered his men to shoot, and when a Lakota chief fell dead, Indians returned fire, killing Grattan and his twenty-nine men. The following year General William Harney led six hundred soldiers to a village near Ash Hollow, where migrants and Indians traded for many years. When Indian leaders refused to surrender anyone to Harney, he ordered his men to fire. Thirty minutes later, eighty-seven Indians lay dead, and seventy women and children were taken prisoner. The event disrupted peace along the trail and ignited nearly two decades of warfare between the Lakotas and the U.S. Army.

Indian Treaties

Still, the Indian Office negotiated treaties to keep Indians—and their intertribal conflicts—from interfering with western migration and commerce. The Fort Laramie Treaty of 1851 (or the Horse Creek Council Treaty) was signed by the United States and eight northern Plains tribes—the Lakotas, Cheyennes, Arapahos, Crows, Assinaboines, Gros-Ventres, Mandans, and Arrickaras—who occupied the Platte River valley through which the three great overland routes westward—the Oregon, California, and Mormon Trails—all passed. Two years later, in 1853, the United States signed a treaty with three southwestern nations, the Comanches, Kiowas, and Apaches, who lived

Established in 1834, Fort Laramie—pictured here three years later by Alfred Jacob Miller—served as a fur-trading site, where Indians and trappers of European or mixed heritage came together not only to exchange goods but also to socialize. In 1849, as interactions between Indians and overland migrants to Oregon grew increasingly tense, the U.S. Army took over the fort, now designed to protect overland emigrants. Located in eastern Wyoming, the fort stood at the beginning of the Oregon Trail.   (The Walters Art Museum, Baltimore)

near the Santa Fe Trail. Under both treaties, Indians agreed to maintain intertribal peace, recognize government-delineated tribal boundaries, allow the United States to construct roads and forts within those boundaries, refrain from depredations against western migrants, and issue restitution for any depredations committed. In return, they would receive annual allotments from the U.S. government for ten years, paid with provisions, domestic animals, and agricultural implements.

Contrary to U.S. expectations, Indian chiefs did not believe treaties were perpetually binding. Government officials, meanwhile, promised allotments but did little to ensure their timely arrival, often leaving Indians starving. Treaties did not end intertribal warfare, nor did they fully secure overlanders' safety. Instead, they represented the U.S. government's effort to promote expansion and protect its westward-bound citizens.

Ecological Consequences of Cultural Contact

Armed conflict took relatively few lives compared to cholera, smallpox, and other maladies. The trails' jumping-off points bred disease, which migrants carried with them, inadvertently infecting Indians with whom they traded. Fearful of infection, Indians and migrants increasingly shied away from trading relationships.

The bison provided protein to Plains Indians and held spiritual significance. Many Native Americans blamed the migrants for the bison's disappearance, even though most overlanders never laid eyes on a buffalo. By the time the overland migration reached its peak in the late 1840s and 1850s, the herds had already been overhunted, partly by Native Americans. The surviving bison scattered to areas where the grass was safe from the appetites and trampling feet of overlanders' livestock. On rare occasions when wagon trains stumbled on bison herds, men rushed to live out frontier fantasies and shot the animals. Overlanders hunted other animals for sport, too, leaving behind rotting carcasses of antelopes, wolves, bears, and birds—animals that held spiritual significance for many Native Americans.

The vibrant trade in bison hides prompted both Indians and whites to overhunt the American bison, leading to near extinction for the animal by the latter part of the nineteenth century.   (Library of Congress)

Gold Rush

In January 1848, John Wilson Marshall discovered gold in a shallow tributary to the American River near present-day Sacramento, California. During the next year, tens of thousands of forty-niners rushed to California, where they practiced placer mining, panning and dredging for gold in the hope of instant riches.

Some did make fortunes. Peter Brown, a black man from St. Genevieve, Missouri, wrote his wife in 1851 that "California is the best country in the world to make money. It is also the best place for black folks on the globe." He had earned $300 in two months. Most forty-niners, however, never found enough gold to pay their expenses. With their dreams dashed, many forty-niners took wage-paying jobs with large mining companies that used dangerous machinery to cut deep into the earth's surface.

As a remote Mexican province, California had a chain of small settlements surrounded by military forts (presidios) and missions. It was inhabited mostly by Indians, with a small number of Mexican *rancheros,* who raised cattle and sheep on enormous landholdings worked by coerced Indians. With the arrival of the forty-niners came the great California agricultural boom. Wheat became the preferred crop; it required minimal investment, was easily planted, and offered a quick return. Unlike the family farms of the Midwest and Oregon, California's large-scale wheat farming relied largely on bonded Indian laborers.

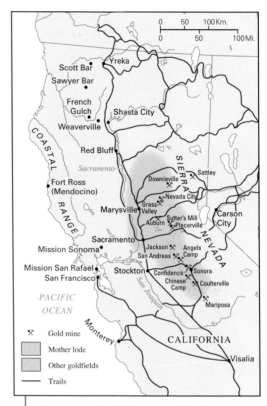

Map 13.5   The California Gold Rush
Gold was discovered at Sutter's Mill in 1848, sparking the California gold rush that took place mostly along the western foothills of the Sierra Nevada mountains.

Mining Settlements

Mining areas experienced a commercial and industrial boom, as enterprising merchants rushed to supply, feed, and clothe new settlers. Among them was Levi Strauss, a German Jewish immigrant, whose tough mining pants found a ready market among the prospectors. Because men greatly outnumbered women, women's skills were in demand. Even as men set up all-male households and performed traditionally female tasks, women received high fees for cooking, laundering, and sewing. Women also ran boarding houses, hotels, and brothels.

Cities sprang up. In 1848 San Francisco had been a small mission settlement of about one thousand Mexicans, Anglos, soldiers, friars, and Indians. With the gold rush, it became a city, ballooning to thirty-five thousand people in 1850. It was the West Coast gateway to the interior, and ships bringing people and supplies jammed the harbor. Although California was admitted into the Union as a free state in 1850, its legislature soon passed "An Act for the Government and Protection of Indians" that essentially legalized the enslavement of Indians. The practice of using enslaved Indians in the California mines between 1849 and 1851 ended only when newly arrived miners brutally attacked Indian workers, believing they degraded white labor and gave an unfair advantage to established miners. Those slaves who survived the violence became field workers and house servants. Between 1821 and 1860, the Indian population of California fell from 200,000 to 30,000, as Indians died from disease, starvation, and violence. Because masters separated male and female workers, Indians failed to reproduce in large numbers.

The Politics of Territorial Expansion

With Americans moving west in numbers that would shift the locus of political power, Democratic and Whig politicians tried, unsuccessfully, to keep the slavery issue out of the politics of territorial expansion. Westward expansion was central to Democratic ideology, which saw the West's fertile and abundant lands as essential for creating a society in which white men could establish independent livelihoods and receive equal rights, freed from the undue influence of established slaveholders or urban elites. Whigs were more suspicious of rapid westward expansion, though they welcomed the commercial opportunities it might bring. Instead, they pushed harder for industrial and commercial development within the nation's current boundaries.

The Texas issue made it impossible for politicians to disentangle westward expansion and slavery. Soon after establishing the Lone Star Republic, Sam Houston approached American authorities to propose annexation as a state. But a new slave state would upset the balance of slave and free states in the Senate. Neither Whigs nor Democrats, wary of causing sectional divisions within their ranks, were inclined to confront the issue. In the 1830s, Democratic presidents Andrew Jackson and Martin Van Buren—one a strong slavery proponent, the other a mild opponent—sidestepped the issue. But by the mid-1840s—with cotton cultivation expanding—some Democratic politicians equated Texas annexation with the nation's manifest destiny.

Manifest Destiny The belief that American expansion westward and southward was inevitable, just, and divinely ordained dated to the nation's founding but was first labeled manifest destiny in 1845 by John L. O'Sullivan, editor of the *United States Magazine and Democratic Review*. O'Sullivan claimed that Texas annexation would be "the fulfillment of our manifest destiny to overspread the continent allotted by Providence for the free development of our yearly multiplying millions." Manifest destiny implied that Americans had a God-given right, perhaps even an obligation, to expand their republican and Christian institutions to less fortunate and less civilized peoples. Implicit in the idea of manifest destiny was the belief that American Indians and Hispanics, much like people of African descent, were inferior peoples best controlled or conquered. Manifest destiny motivated few Americans to pack their wagons and head westward. It did, however, provide a political rationale for territorial expansion.

In June 1846, expansionists, including John C. Frémont, staged an armed rebellion and declared California an independent republic. Because the U.S. military soon conquered California in its War with Mexico, the Bear Flag Rebellion—so named for the symbol on the revolutionaries' flag—was short-lived but inflamed racial tensions in California.

Fifty-Four Forty or Fight Britain and the United States had jointly occupied the disputed Oregon Territory since 1818. Beginning with John Quincy Adams's administration, the United States tried

This 1845 portrayal of Oregon City, the western terminus of the Oregon Trail, was provided by a British army officer sent to investigate the influence of large-scale American immigration into a territory jointly occupied by Great Britain and the United States. After the Oregon Treaty (1846) drew the boundary between British and American territory at the forty-ninth parallel, Oregon City became the capital of the Oregon Territory from 1848 to 1851.   (Library of Congress)

to fix the boundary at the 49th parallel, but Britain wanted access to Puget Sound and the Columbia River. In the early 1840s, expansionists demanded the entire Oregon Country for the United States, up to its northernmost border at latitude 54°40′. Soon "fifty-four forty or fight" became their rallying cry.

President Tyler wanted both Oregon and Texas, but Texas was his obsession. He argued that slavery's expansion would spread the nation's black population more thinly, allowing for the institution's gradual demise. But when word leaked out that Secretary of State John Calhoun had written to the British minister in Washington justifying Texas annexation as a way of protecting slavery, the Senate rejected annexation in 1844 by a vote of 35 to 16.

Polk and the Election of 1844

Worried southern Democrats persuaded their party's 1844 convention to require that the presidential nominee receive two-thirds of the convention votes, effectively giving the southern states a veto and allowing them to block the nomination of Martin Van Buren, an opponent of annexation. Instead, the party ran Young Hickory, House Speaker James K. Polk, an avid expansionist and slaveholding cotton planter from Tennessee. The Democratic platform, designed to appeal to voters across regional lines, called for occupation of the entire Oregon Territory and annexation of Texas. The Whigs, who nominated Henry Clay, argued that the Democrats' belligerent nationalism would lead to war with Great Britain, Mexico, or both. Clay favored expansion through negotiation, whereas many northern Whigs opposed annexation altogether, fearful that it would add slave states and strain relations with vital trading partners. Polk won the election by 170 electoral votes to 105, though with a margin of just 38,000 out of 2.7 million popular votes.

Annexation of Texas

Interpreting Polk's victory as a mandate for annexation, President Tyler proposed that Texas be admitted to the Union by joint resolution of Congress. The usual method of annexation, by treaty negotiation, required a two-thirds vote in the Senate, which differences over slavery prevented. A joint resolution required only a simple majority in each house. On March 1, 1845, the resolution passed the House by 120 to 98 and the Senate by 27 to 25. Three days before leaving office, Tyler signed the measure. Mexico, which had never recognized Texas independence, broke relations with the United States. In October Texas citizens ratified annexation, and Texas joined the Union, with a constitution permitting slavery, in December 1845. The nation was on the brink of war with Mexico. That conflict—like none other before it—would expose the inextricable relationships among westward expansion, slavery, and sectional discord.

Summary

Encouraged by literary and artistic images of the frontier as a place of natural abundance and opportunity, easterners by the millions poured into the Old Southwest and Old Northwest in the early decades of the nineteenth century. The federal government promoted westward expansion via support for transportation improvements, surveying, cheap land, and protection from Indians. Still, western migrants did not always find what they were seeking. Some returned home, some moved to new locations, and some stayed in the West, where they reluctantly abandoned their dreams of economic independence.

African American slaves were moved westward by their owners in enormous numbers between 1820 and 1860. Native Americans saw their lands and livelihoods constricted and their environments altered dramatically, threatening their economic and spiritual lives. Some Indians responded to white incursion through accommodation and peaceful overtures; others resisted. For Indians in Texas and California, white incursions brought devastation.

While beliefs about Native Americans' supposed inferiority allowed many white Americans to rationalize the Indians' fate, the white Americans' attitudes toward black people and slavery drove where they settled in the West. Those who believed that slavery degraded white labor headed along a northern trajectory, whereas those who dreamed of slave ownership headed southward, where they clashed with yet another group they deemed racially inferior: Mexicans. When American settlers in Texas achieved their independence from Mexico, legalized slavery, and applied for annexation by the United States, they brought the divisive issue of slavery's westward expansion to the surface of American politics. Although Democratic politicians at first tried to maintain a geographic equilibrium by proposing an ambitious territorial agenda in Oregon as well, it would be Texas's annexation that set the stage for military conflict, the addition of vast territories in the Southwest, and reinvigorated sectional conflict.

Descendants of Early Latino Settlers

Current census figures identify Latinos as the largest racial or ethnic minority in the United States. The news media focus on such topics as the growing number of documented and undocumented Latino immigrants, their increasing social impact, and their occasionally difficult relationships with African Americans. Yet all the attention surrounding recent arrivals overlooks the sizable number who are descended from people whose residency in North America predated the existence of the United States.

When the region stretching from eastern Texas to California was acquired by the United States in the 1840s, its population included not only indigenous Indian nations but also thousands of people with at least partial European ancestry, primarily Spanish or Portuguese. Their descendants have included such U.S. legislators as Senator Dennis Chávez (who served from 1936 to 1962) and Congressman Manuel Luján (1969–1988). Their families have resided in what is now U.S. territory for up to fourteen generations.

Persuasive evidence suggests that many of the early Iberian settlers in New Mexico were *conversos,* or of New Christian descent, that is, people whose Jewish ancestors converted to Catholicism in the fifteenth century to avoid religious persecution. After Jews were expelled from Spain and Portugal in 1492, many fled throughout the Spanish empire. Some participated in Juan de Oñate's 1598 expedition to New Mexico. There, many secretly maintained such Jewish customs as Sabbath observances and food restrictions. Today, some Latino residents of New Mexico have acknowledged their *converso* roots and reclaimed a Jewish identity.

All long-standing Latino citizens of the United States, not just those of *converso* descent, have given the nation an important multicultural legacy.

Chapter Review

THE WEST IN THE AMERICAN IMAGINATION

What were the myths that helped shape American perceptions of the West?

In dime store novels, artists' paintings, and materials recruiting settlers, the West was depicted as a place of abundant land where anyone could seek to better themselves. It was also seen as untamed, and frontiersmen like Daniel Boone were portrayed as having the courage and independent spirit needed to tame and open the West to other freedom lovers. The mythical Daniel Boone overpowered Indians and civilized the terrain for settlement. The West effectively symbolized core American values of freedom, independence, and the opportunity.

EXPANSION AND RESISTANCE IN THE OLD NORTHWEST

What made the Midwest appealing to white settlers?

Migrants who headed west in search of a better life often chose the Midwest because they wanted a region with the same features and conveniences they had come to know. The Midwest, unlike the Plains and Southwest, had better-developed transportation routes, easier access to markets, a smaller African American population, and cheaper landholdings, and were similar to New England in climate. The region proved a good first stop for those who did not yet have enough cash to purchase land; in the Midwest they could obtain jobs unloading canal boats, or working in farms or mills, before moving on.

THE FEDERAL GOVERNMENT AND WESTWARD EXPANSION

How did the federal government sponsor and speed up westward expansion?

Federal Indian and land policies, particularly Indian removal from desirable lands, did much to encourage white movement into the West. Many whites, in fact, awaited government efforts to clear lands before moving there. The government funded exploration of the West in search of the best location for a transcontinental railroad. Army engineers helped design roads, canals, and railroads, while soldiers cleared forests and did other work. The military also removed Indians from lands that whites desired, defended settlers from Indian attacks, or pushed squatters from land they did not own. Sales of government-controlled land also encouraged settlement.

THE SOUTHWESTERN BORDERLANDS

What factors led Texas to break away from Mexico?

For decades prior to 1836, Americans moved into Texas, and their numbers increased in 1824 when a newly-independent Mexico encouraged further settlement by offering tax incentives and land grants to foreigners—who need be Christians willing to establish permanent residences to qualify. The land grants given covered most of present-day Texas and were populated by U.S. citizens pushed from their homeland by depressed economic conditions. Most were unwilling to assimilate, and Mexican officials rightly feared that the transplanted Americans would seek to annex Texas to the United States. Beginning in 1826, there were calls for an independent Texas under the name "Fredonia Republic"; and as the proportion of Americans to Tejanos reached 7 to 1 in 1835, calls for secession heightened, culminating in battles and the eventual declaration of Texas as the Lone Star Republic in 1836.

MIGRATION TO THE FAR WEST

How did the gold rush impact the development of the Far West?

As miners flooded into California seeking gold, an agricultural boom emerged, with wheat becoming the main crop often farmed by Indian slaves. Wherever mining areas sprung up, a commercial and industrial boom usually followed, as merchants rose to provide necessities and other goods to new settlers. Cities also grew up fast; San Francisco went from one thousand people in 1848 to thirty-five thousand two years later. While California was admitted as a free state that year, it quickly legalized the enslavement of Indians, using them to work the mines and later in fields or homes.

THE POLITICS OF TERRITORIAL EXPANSION

How was Manifest Destiny a factor in the U.S. War with Mexico?

Manifest Destiny was the belief that U.S. westward expansion was not only inevitable but divinely ordained as the nation's mission to spread its Christian and republican institutions as widely as possible. First articulated in 1845, its proponents saw the annexation of Texas as part of a broader mission to occupy the entire continent. The subtext of Manifest Destiny was the superiority of whites over Indians, Hispanics, and people of African descent, and as such, conquering land occupied by Mexico—such as Texas and California—was seen as just. When President Tyler sought annexation of Texas via joint resolution of Congress and a vote by Texans, Mexico broke off relations with the United States and the two nations moved toward war.

SUGGESTIONS FOR FURTHER READING

Gary Clayton Anderson, *The Conquest of Texas: Ethnic Cleansing in the Promised Land, 1820–1875* (2005)

Stuart Banner, *How the Indians Lost Their Land: Law and Power on the Frontier* (2005)

James F. Brooks, *Captives and Cousins: Slavery, Kinship, and Community in the Southwest Borderlands* (2002)

Andrew R. L. Cayton and Peter S. Onuf, *The Midwest and the Nation: Rethinking the History of an American Region* (1990)

Robert V. Hine and John Mack Faragher, *The American West: A New Interpretive History* (2000)

Albert L. Hurtado, *Indian Survival on the California Frontier* (1998)

Susan L. Johnson, *Roaring Camp: The Social World of the California Gold Rush* (2000)

Andrés Reséndez, *Changing National Identities at the Frontier: Texas and New Mexico, 1800–1850* (2005)

Michael L. Tate, *Indians and Emigrants: Encounters on the Overland Trails* (2006)

Richard White, *"It's Your Misfortune and None of My Own": A New History of the American West* (1991)

CHAPTER 14

Slavery and America's Future: The Road to War

CHAPTER OUTLINE

The War with Mexico and Its Consequences

1850: Compromise or Armistice?

Slavery Expansion and Collapse of the Party System

LINKS TO THE WORLD: Annexation of Cuba

Slavery and the Nation's Future

Disunion

LEGACY FOR A PEOPLE AND A NATION: Terrorist or Freedom Fighter?

Summary

On a stiflingly hot evening, June 16, 1858, Abraham Lincoln, a former one-term congressman, stepped onto the platform of the legislative chamber in the Springfield, Illinois, state house to accept the Republican Party's nomination for the U.S. Senate, running against America's leading Democrat, the incumbent Stephen A. Douglas. At six feet, four inches, Lincoln towered over the packed hall. The nation was at a historic crossroads, and he worked on this speech for weeks, delivering his poetic prose with intellectual power. "Slavery agitation" had convulsed American politics and exploded in guerrilla war in Kansas. "It will not cease," ventured Lincoln, "until a crisis shall have been reached, and passed." Then, in familiar biblical imagery, he gave the crisis its unforgettable metaphor:

> "A house divided against itself cannot stand." I believe this government cannot endure permanently half slave and half free.... It will become *all* one thing, or *all* the other. Either the *opponents* of slavery will arrest the further spread of it, and place it where the public mind shall rest in the belief that it is in the course of ultimate extinction; or its *advocates* will push it forward, till it shall become alike lawful in *all* the States, *old* as well as *new*—North as well as South.

Lincoln contended that a conspiracy—a "design" led by the Democratic Party's "chief bosses"—sought to make slavery a *national* institution. He charged Douglas with not caring "whether slavery be voted down or voted up."

In the ensuing campaign, Lincoln and Douglas squared off over the issues dividing the country: the westward expansion of slavery, the character of federal authority over property in slaves, whether the Declaration of Independence signaled racial equality, and ultimately the moral integrity and future of the American republic. Reluctantly, Douglas agreed to seven debates,

This icon will direct you to interactive activities and study materials on A People And A Nation, Brief Edition website: **www.cengage.com/history/norton/peoplenationbrief8e**

Chronology

1846	War with Mexico begins. Oregon Treaty is negotiated. Wilmot Proviso inflames sectional divisions.
1847	Cass proposes the idea of popular sovereignty.
1848	Treaty of Guadalupe Hidalgo gives the United States new territory in the Southwest. Free-Soil Party is formed. Taylor is elected president. Gold is discovered in California, which later applies for admission to Union as a free state.
1850	Compromise of 1850, containing the controversial Fugitive Slave Act, passes.
1852	Stowe publishes *Uncle Tom's Cabin*. Pierce is elected president.
1854	"Appeal of the Independent Democrats" is published. Kansas-Nebraska Act wins approval and ignites controversy. Republican Party is formed. Return of the fugitive Burns to slavery in Virginia.
1856	Bleeding Kansas troubles nation. Brooks attacks Sumner in Senate chamber. Buchanan is elected president, but the Republican Frémont wins most northern states.
1857	*Dred Scott v. Sanford* endorses southern views on black citizenship and slavery in the territories. Economic panic and widespread unemployment begin.
1858	Kansas voters reject the Lecompton Constitution. Lincoln-Douglas debates attract attention. Douglas contends popular sovereignty prevails over the *Dred Scott* decision in the territories.
1859	Brown raids Harpers Ferry.
1860	Democratic Party splits in two; southern Democrats demand a constitutional guarantee for the territories. Lincoln is elected president in a divided, sectional election. Crittenden Compromise fails. South Carolina secedes from the Union.
1861	Six more Deep South states secede. Confederacy is established at Montgomery, Alabama. Attack on Fort Sumter begins the Civil War. Four states in the Upper South join the Confederacy.

one in each congressional district of Illinois, except Chicago and Springfield, where the candidates had already appeared.

The Lincoln-Douglas debates were three-hour marathons of confrontation, political analysis, and theater, with the candidates speaking in long addresses and rebuttals. Tens of thousands of people attended these outdoor events, arriving by foot, wagon, or train and accompanied by brass bands. Perhaps never before or since have Americans demonstrated such an appetite for democratic engagement. As Douglas accused his opponent and all Republicans of being abolitionists and favoring racial equality, Lincoln was forced to admit that he opposed social equality between whites and blacks. He embraced, however, the natural-rights doctrine of the Declaration of Independence and condemned slavery as an evil that must be constrained. Lincoln insisted on stopping slavery's expansion, while maintaining that the federal government could not legally end it in the South. A foot shorter than Lincoln, better dressed, and resplendent in oratorical manner, Douglas appealed to racial prejudice and to a vague unionism. Lincoln cast the election as a moral choice between free-labor–Free-Soil doctrine and a republic ultimately dominated by slaveholders and their abettors, determined to erase ordinary citizens' liberties.

Of the quarter-million votes cast, Lincoln received four thousand more than Douglas. But senators were elected by state legislatures, and with an outdated apportionment, Democrats maintained a 54-to-46 margin to return Douglas to the U.S. Senate. Lincoln would be heard from again, however.

Well before 1858, conflict and violence were enveloping the nation. In the Kansas Territory, open warfare exploded between proslavery and antislavery settlers. On the floor of the U.S. Senate, a southern representative had beaten a northern senator senseless. A new fugitive slave law sent thousands of free and fugitive blacks fleeing into Canada in fear for their lives. The Supreme Court issued a dramatic decision about slavery's constitutionality in westward expansion, as well as the status of African American citizenship, to the delight of most southerners and the dread of many northerners. And the abolitionist John Brown was planning a raid into Virginia to start a slave rebellion.

As the 1850s advanced, divergent economic and political aims, which had long been held in check, now flew apart over the issue of slavery. Political parties fractured, replaced by a realignment that reinforced sectional interests. Each time the nation expanded, it confronted a thorny issue: should new territories and states be slave or free?

North and South, a feeling grew that America's future was at stake—the character of its economy, its labor system, its definition of constitutional liberty, and its racial self-definition. Blacks could take heart that political strife over slavery might lead to their liberation. In 1855 Frederick Douglass spoke for the enslaved when he wrote that "the thought of only being a creature of the present and the past, troubled me, and I longed to have a future—a future with hope in it."

- **After 1845, how and why did westward expansion become so intertwined with the future of slavery and freedom?**
- **During the 1850s, why did Americans (white males, virtually all of whom could vote, and blacks, few of whom had the franchise) seem to care so deeply about electoral politics?**
- **What were the long-term and immediate causes of the Civil War?**

THE WAR WITH MEXICO AND ITS CONSEQUENCES

In the 1840s, territorial expansion surged forward under President James K. Polk of North Carolina. The annexation of Texas just before his inauguration did not make war with Mexico inevitable, but several of Polk's decisions did. Mexico broke off relations with the United States, and during the annexation process, Polk urged Texans to seize all the land to the Rio Grande and claim the river as their southern and western border. Mexico held that the Nueces River was the border; hence, the stage was set for conflict. In his determination to fulfill the nation's manifest destiny over the continent, Polk wanted Mexico's territory to the Pacific and all of the Oregon Country. He and his expansionist cabinet achieved their goals but were largely unaware of the cost in domestic harmony.

Oregon

During the 1844 campaign, Polk's supporters threatened war with Great Britain to gain Oregon. Not wanting to fight Mexico and Great Britain at the same time, Polk sought diplomacy in the Northwest, where America and Britain had jointly occupied disputed territory since 1819. Dropping the demand for a boundary at latitude 54°40′, he convinced the British to accept the 49th parallel. In 1846, the Oregon Treaty gave the United States present-day Oregon, Washington, and Idaho, and parts of Wyoming and Montana. Thus a new era of land acquisition and conquest began under the eleventh president, who was the sixth to be a slaveholder and who, through an agent, secretly bought and sold slaves from the White House.

Mr. Polk's War

Toward Mexico Polk was more aggressive. In early 1846 he ordered American troops under Old Rough and Ready, General Zachary Taylor, to defend the contested border of the Rio Grande across from the town of Matamoros, Mexico. Polk saw California as the prize, and he attempted to buy from Mexico a huge tract of land extending to the Pacific, to no avail. After a three-week standoff, on April 24, 1846, Mexican cavalry ambushed a U.S. cavalry unit on the north side of the river; eleven Americans were killed, and sixty-three were captured. On April 26, Taylor sent a dispatch to Washington, D.C., announcing, "Hostilities may now be considered as commenced."

Polk then drafted a message to Congress: Mexico had "passed the boundary of the United States, invaded our territory and shed American blood on American soil." Polk deceptively declared that "war exists by the act of Mexico itself." Two days later, on May 13, the House recognized a state of war with Mexico by a vote of 174 to 14, and the Senate, by 40 to 2. Because Polk withheld key facts, the reality of what happened on the Rio Grande was not known. Manifest destiny launched the United States into its first major war on foreign territory.

Foreign War and the Popular Imagination

The idea of war unleashed public celebrations in southern cities, such as Richmond and Louisville, and northern cities, such as Philadelphia and New York. After news came of General Taylor's first victories at Palo Alto and Resaca de la Palma, volunteers swarmed recruiting stations. The New York writer Herman Melville remarked that "nothing is talked of but the 'Halls of the Montezumas.'" Publishers rushed books about Mexican geography into print. And new daily newspapers boosted sales by giving the war a romantic appeal.

Here was an adventurous war of conquest, the fulfillment of an Anglo-Saxon–Christian destiny to possess the North American continent and to civilize the semi-Indian Mexicans. Racism fueled the expansionist spirit. In 1846 an Illinois newspaper justified the war by labeling Mexicans as "reptiles in the path of progressive democracy." Because of newspapers, the War with Mexico became the first national event experienced with immediacy. War correspondents reported on battles, and ships from Vera Cruz on the Gulf Coast of Mexico carried news dispatches to New Orleans. Near war's end, news traveled by telegraph in only three days from New Orleans to Washington, D.C.

The war spawned an outpouring of poetry, song, drama, travel literature, and lithographs that glorified the conflict. But not everyone cheered. The abolitionist James Russell Lowell considered the war a "national crime committed in behoof of slavery, our common sin." Even the proslavery spokesman John C. Calhoun feared expansionism's perils.

Conquest

Early in the war, U.S. forces made significant gains. In May 1846 Polk ordered Colonel Stephen Kearny and a small detachment to invade the remote provinces of New Mexico and California. Taking Santa Fe, Kearny pushed into California, where he joined forces with two U.S. naval units and American settlers led by Captain John C. Frémont. General Zachary Taylor's forces attacked Monterrey, which surrendered in September, securing northeastern Mexico.

New Mexico did not prove easy for U.S. forces. In January 1847, in Taos, northwest of Santa Fe, Hispanics and Indians led by Pablo Montoya and Tomás Romero rebelled against the Americans and killed government officials. In what became known as the Taos Revolt, some 500 Mexican and Indian insurgents laid siege to a mill in Arroyo Hondo, outside Taos. The U.S. command swiftly suppressed the revolt, and the insurgents retreated to a thick-walled church in Taos Pueblo. With cannon, the U.S. Army killed 150 and captured 400 rebels. After many arrests, approximately twenty-eight insurgent leaders were hanged in the Taos plaza, ending bloody resistance to U.S. occupation.

Before the end of 1846, American forces also established dominion over California. Because losses on the periphery had not broken Mexican resistance, General Winfield Scott carried the war to the enemy's heartland. He led fourteen thousand men toward Mexico City in what proved to be the war's decisive campaign. Outnumbered and threatened by yellow fever, Scott's men repeatedly discovered flanking routes around their foes. After several hard-fought battles, U.S. troops captured the Mexican capital.

Treaty of Guadalupe Hidalgo

Representatives of both countries signed the Treaty of Guadalupe Hidalgo in February 1848. The United States gained California and New Mexico (including present-day Nevada, Utah, and Arizona, and parts of Colorado and Wyoming) and recognition of the Rio Grande as Texas's southern boundary. The American government agreed to settle the claims of its citizens (mostly Texans) against Mexico ($3.2 million) and to pay Mexico a mere $15 million. The costs of the war included the deaths of thirteen thousand Americans (mostly from disease) and fifty thousand Mexicans. Enmity between Mexico and the United States endured into the twentieth century. Domestically, southwesterners and most southern planters embraced the war; New Englanders opposed it. Whigs in Congress charged that Polk, a Democrat, provoked an unnecessary war and usurped the power of Congress. Abolitionists and a minority of antislavery Whigs charged that the war was a plot to extend slavery.

Slave Power Conspiracy

These charges fed northern fear of the Slave Power. Abolitionists had long warned of a slaveholding oligarchy that would dominate the nation through its hold on federal power. Slaveholders gained control of the South by suppressing dissent, and they forced a gag rule on Congress in 1836. To many white northerners, even those who had no problem with slavery, this battle over free speech made the idea of a Slave Power credible. The War with Mexico deepened such fears, as antislavery northerners wondered if it had been launched to acquire vast, new slave territory.

At first, some southern Whigs attacked the Democratic president for causing the war, and few southern congressmen saw slavery as the paramount issue. Many whites North and South feared that large land seizures would bring nonwhite Mexicans into the United States and upset the racial order. An Indiana politician did not want "any mixed races in our Union, nor men of any color except white, unless they be slaves."

Wilmot Proviso

In August 1846, David Wilmot, a Pennsylvania Democrat, proposed an amendment, or proviso, to a military appropriations bill: that "neither slavery nor involuntary servitude shall ever exist" in any territory gained from Mexico. Although the proviso was never passed, its repeated introduction by northerners transformed the debate over slavery's expansion. Southerners intensified efforts to protect slavery's future. John C. Calhoun insisted that the territories belonged to all the states, and the federal government could not limit slavery there.

This position, often called state sovereignty, was a radical reversal of history. In 1787 the Confederation Congress discouraged if not fully excluded slavery from the Northwest Territory (see pages 169–70?), Article IV of the U.S. Constitution authorized Congress to make "all needful rules and regulations" for the territories, and the Missouri Compromise barred slavery from most of the Louisiana Purchase. Now, southern leaders demanded future guarantees for slavery.

In the North, the Wilmot Proviso became a rallying cry for abolitionists. While fourteen state legislatures endorsed it, not all of its supporters were abolitionists. David Wilmot was neither an abolitionist nor an antislavery Whig. Instead, his goal was to defend "the rights of white freemen" and to obtain California "for free white labor."

As Wilmot demonstrated, it was possible to be a racist and an opponent of slavery. The vast majority of white northerners were not active abolitionists, and their desire to keep the West slavery-free was often matched by their desire to keep blacks from settling there. At stake was the free individual's access to social mobility through acquisition of land in the West. Slave labor, thousands of northerners soon believed, would degrade the toil of free men and render them unemployable. The West must therefore be kept free of slaves.

The Election of 1848 and Popular Sovereignty

The divisive slavery question infested national politics. After Polk renounced a second term as president, the Democrats nominated Senator Lewis Cass of Michigan for president and General William Butler of Kentucky for vice president. In 1847 Cass, a party loyalist who had served in Jackson's cabinet, devised the idea of popular sovereignty, letting residents in the western territories decide the slavery question for themselves. His party's platform declared that Congress lacked the power to interfere with slavery's expansion. The Whigs nominated General Zachary Taylor, a southern slaveholder and war hero; the New York Congressman Millard Fillmore was his running mate. The Whig convention similarly denied congressional power over slavery in the territories.

TABLE 14.1 New Political Parties

Party	Period of Influence	Area of Influence	Outcome
Liberty Party	1839–1848	North	Merged with other antislavery groups to form Free-Soil Party
Free-Soil Party	1848–1854	North	Merged with Republican Party
Know-Nothings (American Party)	1853–1856	Nationwide	Disappeared, freeing most to join Republican Party
Republican Party	1854–present	North (later nationwide)	Became rival of Democratic Party and won presidency in 1860

Many southern Democrats distrusted Cass and voted for Taylor because he was a slaveholder. New York Democrats committed to the Wilmot Proviso rebelled against Cass and nominated former president Martin Van Buren. Antislavery Whigs and former Liberty Party supporters joined them to form the Free-Soil Party (see Table 14.1). This party, which sought to restrict slavery's expansion to western territories and whose slogan was "Free Soil, Free Speech, Free Labor, and Free Men," won almost 300,000 northern votes. Taylor polled 1.4 million votes to Cass's 1.2 million and won the White House, but the results were ominous.

Like politics, religious denominations split into northern and southern wings. Many Protestants feared that God would either destroy the national sin of slavery or help the South defend it as part of the divine order. As the 1850s dawned, the legacies of the War with Mexico and the conflicts of 1848 threatened the nature of the Union.

1850: COMPROMISE OR ARMISTICE?

More than eighty thousand Americans flooded into California during the 1849 gold rush. With Congress unable to agree on a governing formula for the territories, President Taylor urged settlers to apply for admission to the Union. They did, proposing a state constitution that banned slavery. Because California's admission as a free state would upset the sectional balance in the Senate (the ratio of slave to free states was fifteen to fifteen), southern politicians wanted to postpone admission and make California a slave territory or at least extend the Missouri Compromise.

Debate over Slavery in the Territories

Twice before—in 1820 and 1833—Henry Clay, the venerable Whig leader and Great Pacificator, had shaped sectional compromise; now he struggled one last time to preserve the nation. In winter 1850, Clay and Senator Stephen A. Douglas of Illinois, the Little Giant, steered their compromise package through Senate debate and amendment.

The problems were numerous. Would California or part of it become a free state? How should the territory acquired from Mexico be organized? Texas, which allowed slavery, claimed areas extending as far west as Santa Fe. Southerners complained that fugitive slaves were not being returned as the Constitution required, and northerners objected to the sale of human beings in the nation's capital. Eight years earlier, in *Prigg v. Pennsylvania* (1842), the Supreme Court ruled that enforcement of the Constitution's fugitive slave clause was a federal obligation. The Court further ruled that states could not exact measures, often called personal liberty laws, banning the seizure and removal of a fugitive. Most troublesome, however, was the status of slavery in the territories.

Clay and Douglas discovered in Lewis Cass's idea of popular sovereignty what one historian called a "charm of ambiguity." Ultimately Congress would have to approve statehood for a territory, but "in the meantime," said Cass, it should allow the people living there "to regulate their own concerns in their own way."

To avoid dissension within their party, northern and southern Democrats explained Cass's statement to constituents in incompatible ways. Southerners claimed that neither Congress nor a territorial legislature could bar slavery. Northerners, however, insisted that Americans living in a territory were entitled to self-government and thus could outlaw slavery.

The cause of compromise gained a powerful supporter when on March 7 Senator Daniel Webster committed his prestige and eloquence to Clay's bill. Abandoning his earlier support for the Wilmot Proviso, Webster urged northerners not to "taunt or reproach" the South with antislavery measures. He warned southern firebrands that disunion inevitably would cause violence and destruction. Many of Webster's former abolitionist friends in New England condemned him for his compromise efforts and accused him of going over to the Devil.

Only three days earlier, with equal drama, Calhoun was carried from his sickbed to advocate against the compromise. With Calhoun unable to speak, Senator James Mason of Virginia read his address, which predicted disunion if southern demands went unanswered, frightening some into supporting compromise.

Months later, when Clay and Douglas brought their legislative package to a vote, it lost. With Clay sick, Douglas reintroduced the compromise measures one at a time. Douglas realized that because southerners favored some bills and northerners the rest, the small majority for compromise could be achieved only on each distinct issue. The strategy worked and the Compromise of 1850 became law.

Compromise of 1850   The compromise had five essential measures.

1. California became a free state.
2. The Texas boundary was set at its then-current limits (see Map 14.1), and the United States paid Texas $10 million for the loss of New Mexico Territory.
3. The territories of New Mexico and Utah were organized on the basis of popular sovereignty.
4. The fugitive slave law was strengthened.
5. The slave trade was abolished in the District of Columbia.

At best, the Compromise of 1850 was an artful evasion. Douglas found a way to pass the five proposals without convincing northerners and southerners to agree on fundamentals. The compromise bought time for the nation, but it did not resolve territorial questions.

The compromise had two flaws. The first concerned the ambiguity of popular sovereignty. Southerners insisted on no prohibition of slavery during the territorial

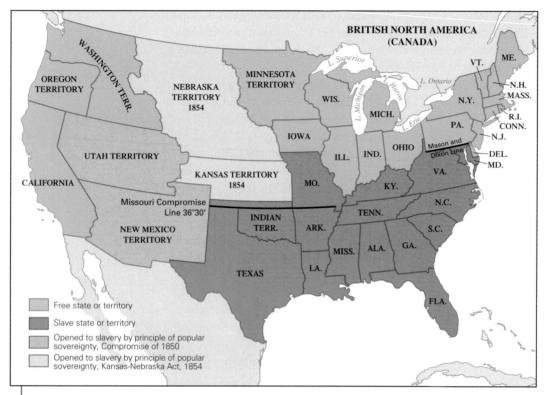

Map 14.1   The Kansas-Nebraska Act and Slavery Expansion, 1854

The vote on the Kansas-Nebraska Act in the House of Representatives (see also Table 14.2 on page 357) demonstrates the sectionalization of American politics due to the slavery question.

stage, and northerners declared that settlers could bar slavery whenever they wished. The compromise allowed for the appeal of a territorial legislature's action to the Supreme Court.

Fugitive Slave Act

The second flaw lay in the Fugitive Slave Act, which gave new—and controversial—protection to slavery. The law empowered slaveowners to go into state courts to present evidence that a slave had escaped. The resulting transcript and description of the fugitive would serve as legal proof of slave status, even in free states and territories. Court officials adjudicated the identity of the person described, not whether he or she was indeed a slave. The law made it a felony to harbor fugitives and stated that northern citizens could be summoned to hunt fugitives. U.S. marshals received $10 if the alleged fugitive was returned, $5 if not returned.

Abolitionist newspapers attacked the Fugitive Slave Act as a violation of American rights. Why were alleged fugitives denied a trial by jury? Why would northerners be arrested if they harbored runaways? These questions convinced some northerners that free blacks were vulnerable to kidnapping and enslavement. An estimated twenty thousand blacks fled to Canada.

Between 1850 and 1854, protests and violent resistance to slave catchers occurred in northern towns. Sometimes a captured fugitive was broken out of jail by abolitionists, as in the 1851 Boston case of Shadrach Minkins, who was spirited by wagons and trains to Montreal, Canada. That same year, the small black community in Lancaster County, Pennsylvania, defended four escaped slaves from a federal posse charged with reenslaving them. At this Christiana riot, fugitives shot and killed Edward Gorsuch, the Maryland slaveowner who sought the return of his property. A headline reporting the Christiana affair screamed, "Civil War, The First Blow Struck!"*

Many abolitionists became convinced that violence was a legitimate means of opposing slavery. In an 1854 column, Frederick Douglass said that the only way to make the fugitive slave law a dead letter was to make a "few dead slave catchers."

Uncle Tom's Cabin

Around this time, Harriet Beecher Stowe, whose New England family produced prominent ministers, wrote a novel portraying the humanity and suffering of slaves. Her story, *Uncle Tom's Cabin,* was serialized in 1851 and published as a book in 1852. It touched millions of northerners with its tale of a slave mother's dash to freedom with her child across the frozen Ohio River. Stowe also portrayed slavery's evil effects on slaveholders, indicting the institution more harshly than southerners caught in its web. Moreover, Stowe exposed northern racism and complicity with slavery by making the worst slaveholder a man of New England birth.

By mid-1853, the book sold over 1 million copies. Its popularity alarmed southern whites, who saw their way of life threatened. Behind the South's claims about territorial rights lay the fear that, if nearby areas outlawed slavery, they would become bases from which abolitionism would spread into slave states.

Some twenty proslavery novels were published in the 1850s as responses to *Uncle Tom's Cabin.* Most paled in comparison to Stowe's masterpiece, but southern writers defended their system as more humane than wage labor. In awkward stories, such as J. W. Page's *Uncle Robin in His Cabin and Tom Without One in Boston,* slaves were induced to run away by visiting abolitionists, and then starved in northern cities.

The Underground Railroad

By the 1850s, slaveholders were especially disturbed about the Underground Railroad, a loose, illegal network that spirited runaways to freedom. Thousands of slaves escaped by these often disorganized routes, but largely through their own wits and courage, with assistance from blacks in northern cities. Lewis Hayden in Boston; David Ruggles in New York; William Still in Philadelphia; John Parker in Ripley, Ohio; and Jacob Gibbs in Washington, D.C. were among the many black abolitionists who managed fugitive slave escapes through their regions.

Harriet Tubman, herself an escapee in 1848, returned to her native Maryland and Virginia at least a dozen times and secretly helped as many as three hundred slaves, some her family members, to freedom. Outraged Maryland planters offered a $40,000 reward for her capture.

In Ohio, white abolitionists, often Quakers, joined with blacks to help slaves cross the river to freedom. The Underground Railroad also had numerous maritime routes, as coastal slaves escaped aboard ships from Virginia, the Carolinas, or New

---

*A headline from the Lancaster, Pennsylvania, *Saturday Express,* reporting on the Christiana Affair screamed "Civil War! The first blow struck!"

In *Still Life of Harriet Tubman with Bible and Candle*, we see the youthful, calm, determined leader of the Underground Railroad. Appearing gentle, Tubman was in her own way a revolutionary who liberated nearly three hundred of her people.
(© psihoyos.com / Science Faction)

Orleans and ended up in northern port cities, the Caribbean, or England. Many slaves from the Lower South and Texas escaped to Mexico, which abolished slavery in 1829. Some joined Seminole communities in Florida, where they fought with them against the U.S. Army in the Seminole Wars of 1835–1842 and 1855–1858.

Slave escapes were a testament to human courage and the will for freedom. They never reached the scale believed by angry slaveholders or bragged about by northern towns and local historical societies today. But, in reality and legend, the Underground Railroad applied pressure to the institution of slavery and gave slaves hope.

Election of 1852 and the Collapse of Compromise

The 1852 election gave southern leaders hope that under a new president, slavery would be secure. Franklin Pierce, a New Hampshire Democrat, won easily over the Whig presidential nominee, General Winfield Scott. Pierce defended each section's rights as essential to national unity, and southerners hoped that his support for the Compromise of 1850 might end the ongoing crisis.

President Pierce's embrace of the compromise appalled many northerners. His enforcement of the Fugitive Slave Act provoked fear of the Slave Power, especially in the case of the fugitive slave Anthony Burns, who fled Virginia in 1852. In Boston, thinking he was safe, Burns began a new life. But in 1854 federal marshals placed him under guard in Boston's courthouse. An interracial crowd of abolitionists attacked the courthouse, killing a jailer while attempting to free Burns.

Pierce telegraphed local officials to "incur any expense to insure the execution of the law" and sent troops to Boston. Soldiers marched Burns to Boston harbor, while Burns's supporters draped the streets in black and hung American flags at half-mast. At a cost of $100,000, a single black man was returned to slavery.

This demonstration of federal support for slavery radicalized opinion, even among conservatives. Juries refused to convict the abolitionists who stormed the Boston courthouse, and New England states passed personal liberty laws that absolved local judges from enforcing the Fugitive Slave Act, in effect nullifying federal authority. What northerners now saw as evidence of a dominating Slave Power, slaveholders saw as legal defense of their rights.

Pierce confronted sectional conflict at every turn. His proposal for a transcontinental railroad stalled when congressmen fought over its location, North or South. An annexation treaty with Hawai'i failed because southern senators would not vote for another free state, while efforts to acquire slaveholding Cuba angered northerners. Events in the Pacific fueled debate over just how far American expansion should extend. With two orchestrated landings in the Bay of Tokyo, in 1853 and 1854, Commodore Matthew Perry established U.S. intentions to trade with Japan, whether that country wanted it or not. Offended, the Japanese were nonetheless impressed with Perry's steam-powered warships, the first they had seen. Perry's Treaty of Kanagawa in March 1854 negotiated two ports as coaling stations for American ships, but the sought-after trading arrangements were slow in coming.

Back home, another territorial bill threw Congress and the nation into greater turmoil, and the Compromise of 1850 collapsed.

SLAVERY EXPANSION AND COLLAPSE OF THE PARTY SYSTEM

The new controversy began in a surprising way. Stephen A. Douglas introduced a bill to establish the Kansas and Nebraska Territories. Ambitious for the presidency, Douglas did not think slavery would be a problem and was willing to risk some controversy to economically aid his home state of Illinois. A transcontinental railroad would encourage Great Plains settlement and stimulate the Illinois economy, but no company would build a railroad before Congress organized the territories it would cross. Thus interest in promoting a railroad drove Douglas to introduce a bill that inflamed sectional passions.

Kansas-Nebraska Act   The Kansas-Nebraska Act exposed conflicting interpretations of popular sovereignty. Douglas's bill left "all questions pertaining to slavery in the Territories . . . to the people residing therein." Northerners and southerners, however, still disagreed over what territorial settlers could constitutionally do. Moreover, the Kansas and Nebraska Territories lay within the Louisiana Purchase, and the Missouri Compromise prohibited slavery there from latitude 36°30′ north to the Canadian border. If popular sovereignty were applied in Kansas and Nebraska, it would mean that the Missouri Compromise was no longer valid.

Southern congressmen, anxious to establish slaveholders' right to take slaves into any territory, pressed Douglas for an explicit repeal of the 36°30′ limitation in exchange for their support. During a carriage ride with the Kentucky senator Archibald Dixon, Douglas conceded: "I will incorporate it in my bill, though I know it will raise a hell of a storm."

Douglas may have hoped that climate and soil conditions would keep slavery out of Kansas and Nebraska; nonetheless, his bill allowed slavery on land from which it had been prohibited for thirty-four years. Many Free-Soilers and antislavery forces considered this turn of events a betrayal of trust. The bill became law in May 1854 by a vote that demonstrated the dangerous sectionalization of American politics (see Map 14.1 and Table 14.2).

TABLE 14.2   The Vote on the Kansas-Nebraska Act

	Aye	Nay
The vote was 113 to 100 in favor.		
Northern Democrats	44	42
Southern Democrats	57	2
Northern Whigs	0	45
Southern Whigs	12	7
Northern Free-Soilers	0	4

Opposition to the Fugitive Slave Act grew; between 1855 and 1859, Connecticut, Rhode Island, Massachusetts, Michigan, Maine, Ohio, and Wisconsin passed personal-liberty laws. These laws enraged southerners by providing counsel for alleged fugitives and requiring trial by jury. The Kansas-Nebraska Act had a devastating impact on political parties. The weakened Whig Party broke into northern and southern wings. The Democrats survived, but their support in the North plummeted in the 1854 elections. Northern Democrats lost sixty-six of their ninety-one congressional seats and lost control of all but two free-state legislatures.

Birth of the Republican Party

The beneficiary of northern voters' wrath was a new political party. During debate on the Kansas-Nebraska Act, six congressmen—most prominently, Joshua Giddings, Salmon Chase, and Charles Sumner—published an "Appeal of the Independent Democrats." In it, they attacked Douglas's legislation as a violation of the Missouri Compromise and a "criminal betrayal of precious rights" that would make free territory a "dreary region of despotism." Their appeal tapped a reservoir of northern concerns, cogently expressed by Illinois's Abraham Lincoln.

Although Lincoln did not condemn southerners, he exposed the meaning of the Kansas-Nebraska Act. Lincoln argued that the founders, from love of liberty, banned slavery from the Northwest Territory, kept the word *slavery* out of the Constitution, and treated it as a cancer on the republic. Rather than encouraging liberty, the Kansas-Nebraska Act promised to extend slavery. America's future, Lincoln warned, was being mortgaged to slavery.

Thousands of white northerners agreed. During summer and fall 1854, antislavery Whigs and Democrats, Free-Soilers, and reformers throughout the Old Northwest formed the new Republican Party, dedicated to keeping slavery from the territories. Republicans' influence rapidly spread to the East. They won a stunning victory in the 1854 elections, capturing a majority of northern House seats and leading roughly a quarter of northern Democrats to desert their party.

For the first time, too, a sectional party gained power in the political system. The Whigs were gone, and Democrats struggled to maintain national membership. The emergence of the Republican coalition of antislavery interests is the most rapid transformation in party allegiance in American history.

Know-Nothings

Republicans drew into their coalition a growing nativist movement that called itself the American Party, or Know-Nothings (because initial members kept their purposes secret, answering "I know nothing" to questions). This group exploited fear of foreigners and Catholics. Between 1848 and 1860, nearly 3.5 million immigrants entered the United States—proportionally the heaviest influx of foreigners in American history. Democrats courted these new citizens, but many native-born Anglo-Saxon Protestants feared that Irish and German Catholics would owe primary allegiance to the pope in Rome.

In 1854 anti-immigrant fears made the Know-Nothings successful in some northern states, particularly Massachusetts, where they elected 11 congressmen, a governor, all state officers, all state senators, and all but 2 of 378 state representatives.

The temperance movement also gained ground early in the 1850s with promises to stamp out the evils associated with liquor and immigrants (a pointedly anti-Irish campaign). The Know-Nothings strove to reinforce Protestant morality and restrict voting and office holding to the native-born. As the Whig Party vanished, the Know-Nothings filled the void, but, like the Whigs, the Know-Nothings could not keep their northern and southern wings together due to the slavery expansion issue. They dissolved after 1856. Instead, Republicans wooed nativists with temperance ordinances and laws postponing suffrage for naturalized citizens (see Table 14.1).

Party Realignment and the Republicans' Appeal

The Whig Party's demise ensured a major realignment of the political system. Immigration, temperance, homestead bills, the tariff, and internal improvements were crucial issues for voters during the 1850s. Commercial agriculture was booming in the Ohio-Mississippi-Great Lakes area, but residents desired more canals, roads, and river and harbor improvements. Because credit was scarce, a homestead program—the idea that western land should be free to individuals who would farm it and make a home on it—attracted many voters. Republicans appealed strongly to those interested in the economic development of the West, promising internal improvements and land grants, as well as higher tariffs to protect industry.

Partisan ideological appeals became the currency of the realigned political system. As Republicans preached "Free Soil, Free Labor, Free Men," they conveyed many northerners' self-image. These phrases resonated with traditional ideals of equality, liberty, and opportunity under self-government—the heritage of republicanism. Invoking that heritage also undercut charges that the Republican Party was radical and abolitionist.

The northern economy was booming, and thousands of migrants moved west to establish farms and communities. Midwesterners multiplied their yields using new machines, such as mechanical reapers. Railroads were carrying crops to urban markets. And industry was making available goods that had recently been unaffordable for most people.

Republican Ideology

To many people, especially northerners, the key to progress appeared to be free labor—the dignity of work and prospect of opportunity. Any hard-working and virtuous man, it was thought, could improve his condition and achieve economic independence. Republicans argued that the South, with little industry and slave labor, was backward by comparison.

Traditional republicanism hailed the virtuous common man as the nation's backbone. In Abraham Lincoln, a man of humble origins who became a successful lawyer and political leader, Republicans had a symbol of that tradition. They portrayed their party as the guardian of economic opportunity, giving individuals a chance to work, acquire land, and attain success.

At stake in the crises of the 1850s were two competing definitions of liberty: southern planters' claims of their liberty to own and transport their slaves nationwide, and northern workers' and farmers' claims of their liberty to seek a new start on free land, unimpeded by a system that defined labor as slave and black.

Annexation of Cuba

One of the most contentious issues in antebellum American foreign relations was the annexation of Cuba. As a strategic bulwark against Britain and France in the Western Hemisphere, for its sugar wealth, and as a slave society that might reinforce southern slavery, the Spanish-controlled island fired the imagination of manifest destiny. In the early republic, Presidents Thomas Jefferson and James Madison explored acquisition. John Quincy Adams, as secretary of state in 1823, considered Cuba "indispensable to the continuance . . . of the Union."

Until the 1840s, the United States supported Spanish rule for stability and the preservation of slavery. Southerners feared a second Haiti if Cuba became independent through revolution. The prospect of slave insurrection and the spread of abolitionism throughout the upper Caribbean and the Deep South drove many southerners and three Democratic administrations to pursue acquisition of Cuba. Slaveholding politicians viewed Cuba as critical to expansion.

In 1848 President Polk authorized $100 million to purchase Cuba. The Spanish foreign minister, however, told Polk's emissary that his government would rather see Cuba "sunk in the ocean" than sell it to the United States. During the Kansas-Nebraska Act crisis in 1854, as President Pierce revived the annexation scheme, some southerners planned to seize Cuba by force. Although the expedition never embarked, its prospect outraged antislavery Republicans eager to halt slavery's expansion and protect free labor.

Yet another aggressive American design on Cuba emerged in the Ostend Manifesto in October 1854. Written after a meeting among the American foreign ministers to Britain, France, and Spain, the document advocated conquest of Cuba if it could not be purchased. But antislavery northerners saw schemes of the Slave Power. The Ostend controversy forced temporary abandonment of annexation efforts, but as the fires in Bleeding Kansas subsided in 1858, President Buchanan reignited Cuba fever. A fierce Senate debate over another purchase offer in early 1859 ended in bitter division over the extension of slavery's domain.

The failure of Cuban annexation was intertwined with the meaning of the United States as a slaveholding republic. "I want Cuba . . . for the planting or spreading of slavery," said the Mississippian Albert G. Brown in 1858. In America's links to the world—90 miles from the Florida coast—just as in domestic affairs, the expansion of slavery poisoned the body politic.

Despite the failure of filibustering expeditions, the effort to annex Cuba continued throughout James Buchanan's presidential administration. This cartoon portrays Sam Houston, the famed Texan and proponent of American expansion, rowing the boat for a harpoonist in quest of the whale, Cuba. The dream of appropriating Cuba to the United States died very hard in the antebellum era. *Vanity Fair,* June 1860.

(© Bettmann/Corbis)

Opposition to the extension of slavery helped create the Republican Party, but members carefully broadened their appeal by adopting other causes. Their coalition ideology consisted of several elements: resentment of southern political power, devotion to unionism, opposition to slavery based on a belief in free-labor, and moral revulsion to slavery and racial prejudice. As the *New York Tribune* editor Horace Greeley wrote in 1860, "an Anti-Slavery man per se cannot be elected." But, "a Tariff, River-and-Harbor, Pacific Railroad, Free Homestead man, may succeed although he is Anti-Slavery."

Southern Democrats

In the South, the disintegration of the Whig Party left many at loose ends politically, including wealthy planters, smaller slaveholders, and urban businessmen. In the tense atmosphere of sectional crisis, southerners were highly susceptible to strong states' rights positions and the defense of slavery. Hence, most formerly Whig slaveholders joined the Democratic Party.

Since Andrew Jackson's day, however, nonslaveholding yeomen had been the heart of the Democratic Party. Democratic politicians, though often slaveowners, lauded the common man and claimed to advance his interests. According to the southern version of republicanism, white citizens in slave society enjoyed liberty and equality because black people were enslaved. Jefferson Davis explained in 1851 that in the South, slavery elevated every white to "stand upon the broad level of equality with the rich man." To retain the support of ordinary whites, southern Democrats appealed to racism, asking: "Shall negroes govern white men, or white men govern negroes?"

Racial fears and traditional political loyalties kept the political alliance between yeoman farmers and planters intact through the 1850s. Across class lines, white southerners united against what they perceived as the Republican Party's capacity to cause slave unrest. In the South, no viable party emerged to replace the Whigs, and political realignment sharpened sectional identity.

Political leaders of both sections used race in their arguments about opportunity. The *Montgomery* (Alabama) *Mail* warned southern whites in 1860 that Republicans intended "to free the negroes and force amalgamation between them and the children of the poor men of the South." Republicans warned northern workers that if slavery entered the territories, the reservoir of opportunity would be poisoned.

Bleeding Kansas

The Kansas-Nebraska Act spawned violence as land-hungry partisans clashed in Kansas Territory. Abolitionists and religious groups sent armed Free-Soil settlers; southerners sent reinforcements to establish slavery and prevent "northern hordes" from stealing Kansas. Conflicts led to bloodshed, and soon the nation was talking about Bleeding Kansas.

Politics in the territory resembled war more than democracy. During 1855 elections for a territorial legislature, thousands of proslavery Missourians—known as Border Ruffians—invaded the polls and ran up a fraudulent majority for proslavery candidates. They murdered and intimidated free-state settlers. The resulting legislature legalized slavery. Free-Soilers responded with an unauthorized convention at which they created their own government and constitution.

In May, a proslavery posse sent to arrest Free-Soil leaders sacked the town of Lawrence, Kansas, killing several people and destroying a hotel. In revenge, the radical abolitionist John Brown and his followers murdered five proslavery settlers living along Pottawatomie Creek. The victims' heads and limbs were hacked by heavy broadswords. Brown did not wield a sword, but he fired a fatal shot into the head of one foe. Soon, armed bands of guerrillas battled over land claims and slavery.

Violence touched the U.S. Senate in May 1856, when Charles Sumner of Massachusetts denounced "the Crime against Kansas." Radically opposed to slavery, Sumner assailed the president, the South, and Senator Andrew P. Butler of South Carolina. Butler's cousin, Representative Preston Brooks, approached Sumner, raised his cane in defense of his kin's honor, and beat Sumner on the head.

Shocked northerners recoiled from another seeming case of wanton southern violence and assault on free speech. William Cullen Bryant, editor of the *New York Evening Post*, asked, "Has it come to this, that we must speak with bated breath in the presence of our southern masters?" Popular opinion in Massachusetts supported Sumner; South Carolina voters reelected Brooks.

Election of 1856

The election of 1856 reflected extreme polarization. For their nominee, Democrats chose James Buchanan of Pennsylvania, who, as ambassador to Britain for four years, was uninvolved in territorial controversies. Superior organization helped Buchanan win 1.8 million votes and the election, but he owed his victory to southern support. Hence, he was labeled "a northern man with southern principles."

Eleven of sixteen free states voted against Buchanan, and Democrats did not regain those states for decades. The Republican candidate, John C. Frémont, won those eleven free states and 1.3 million votes; Republicans became the dominant party in the North after only two years of existence. The coming battle would pit a sectional Republican Party against an increasingly divided Democratic Party, with voter turnouts as high as 75 to 80 percent in many states.

SLAVERY AND THE NATION'S FUTURE

For years Congress tried to settle the slavery issue. In 1857 the Supreme Court attempted to definitively silence controversy.

Dred Scott Case

A Missouri slave named Dred Scott and his wife, Harriet Robinson Scott, sued for their freedom. Scott argued that his former owner, an army surgeon, had taken him into and kept him for years in Illinois, a free state, and taken him to Fort Snelling in the Minnesota Territory, from which slavery was banned by the Missouri Compromise. Scott first won and then lost his case on appeal in the Supreme Court.

Harriet and Dred Scott were legally married at Fort Snelling in 1836 when Dred was forty and Harriet seventeen. She had lived as a slave on free soil for about five years and had four children, also born on free soil: two sons who died in infancy and two daughters, Eliza and Lizzie, who lived. The quest for freedom papers through a lawsuit—begun in 1846 as two cases, one in his name and one in hers—possibly came as much from Harriet's desire to protect her teenage daughters from potential sale as from the aging Dred. Indeed, her legal case may have been stronger than Dred's, but lawyers subsumed her case into his during the eleven-year appeal process.

With hesitation, the Supreme Court agreed to hear *Dred Scott v. Sanford*. Two northern justices indicated that they would dissent from the assigned opinion and argue for Scott's freedom and the constitutionality of the Missouri Compromise. Their decision emboldened southerners on the Court, who were eager to declare the 1820 geographical restriction on slavery unconstitutional. Several justices felt they should resolve sectional strife once and for all.

In March 1857, Chief Justice Roger B. Taney of Maryland delivered the majority opinion of a divided Court (the vote was 7 to 2). Taney declared that Scott was not a citizen of the United States or Missouri, that residence in free territory did not make Scott free, and that Congress had no power to bar slavery from any territory. The decision not only overturned a thirty-seven year-old sectional compromise, it also invalidated the Wilmot Proviso and popular sovereignty.

The Slave Power seemed to have won a major constitutional victory. African Americans were especially dismayed, for Taney's decision asserted that the founders never intended for blacks to be citizens. Taney was mistaken, however. African Americans had been citizens in several original states and had voted.

Nevertheless, the ruling seemed to shut the door permanently on black hopes for justice. In northern black communities, rage and despair prevailed. Many fugitive slaves sought refuge in Canada; others considered the Caribbean or even Africa. One black abolitionist said that the *Dred Scott* decision made slavery "the supreme law of the land." In this state of social dislocation and fear, blacks contemplated whether they had any future in the United States.

Northern whites who rejected the decision were suspicious of the circumstances that produced it. Five of the nine justices were southerners; three northern justices dissented or refused to concur in parts of the decision. The only northerner who supported Taney's opinion, Justice Robert Grier of Pennsylvania, was close to President Buchanan. In fact, Buchanan secretly applied improper but effective influence on him.

The decision seemed to confirm every northern charge against the aggressive Slave Power. The *Cincinnati Freeman* asked, "What security have the Germans and the Irish that their children will not, within a hundred years, be reduced to slavery in this land of their adoption?"

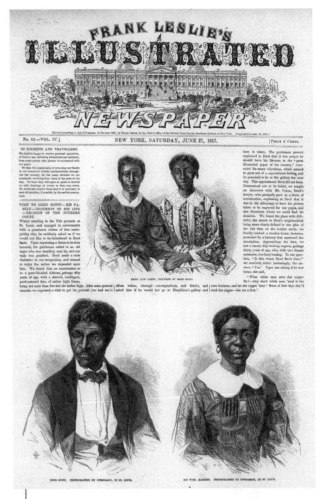

Dred Scott and his wife, from Frank Leslie's Illustrated Newspaper.
(Library of Congress)

Abraham Lincoln and the Slave Power

Republican politicians used these fears to strengthen their antislavery coalition. Abraham Lincoln declared as early as 1854 that the nation wanted the territories put to best use as "homes of free white people. This they cannot be, to any considerable extent, if slavery shall be planted within them."

More important, Lincoln warned of slavery's increasing control over the nation. While the founders recognized slavery's existence, the public, Lincoln argued in the "House Divided" speech of 1858, believed that slavery would die naturally or by legislation. The next step in the unfolding Slave Power conspiracy, Lincoln alleged, would be a Supreme Court decision "declaring that the Constitution does not permit a State to exclude slavery from its limits." Indeed, lawsuits soon challenged state laws that freed slaves brought within their borders.

By endorsing the South's doctrine of state sovereignty, the Court had in effect declared that the Republican Party's central position—no extension of slavery—was unconstitutional. Republicans could only repudiate the decision, appealing to a higher law or hope to change the personnel of the Court. They did both and gained politically as fear of the Slave Power grew.

Lecompton Constitution and Disharmony Among Democrats

Northern voters were alarmed by the prospect that the territories would be opened to slavery. To retain their support, northern Democrats like Stephen Douglas had to reassure these voters. Yet, given his presidential ambitions, Douglas could not alienate southern Democrats.

Douglas chose to stand by popular sovereignty, even if the result angered southerners. In 1857 Kansans voted on a proslavery constitution drafted at Lecompton. It was defeated by more than ten thousand votes in a referendum boycotted by most proslavery voters. Kansans did not want slavery, yet President Buchanan tried to force the Lecompton Constitution through Congress to hastily organize the territory.

Never had the Slave Power's influence over the government seemed more blatant; the Buchanan administration and southerners demanded a proslavery outcome, contrary to majority will in Kansas. Douglas threw his weight against the Lecompton Constitution, infuriating southern Democrats like Senator Albert G. Brown of Mississippi. Increasingly, though, many southerners believed that their sectional rights would be safe only in a separate nation. And northern Democrats, led by Douglas, found it harder to support the territorial protection for slavery that southern Democrats insisted was a constitutional right.

DISUNION

But in the late 1850s, most Americans were not always caught up in the slavery crisis. Daily, they were preoccupied with personal affairs, especially the economic panic that began in spring 1857. In the Midwest, clerks, mechanics, domestics, railroad hands, and lumber camp workers lost jobs by the thousands. Bankers did not know what to do about a weak credit system caused by frenzied western land speculation earlier in the decade. In parts of the South, such as Georgia, the panic intensified class divisions between upcountry yeomen and coastal slaveholding planters. Farmers blamed the tight money policies of Georgia's budding commercial banking system on wealthy planters who controlled the state's Democratic Party.

The panic was caused by several shortcomings of the unregulated American banking system, by speculation in western lands and railroads, and by a weak and overburdened credit system. By 1858 Philadelphia had 40,000 unemployed workers and New York City, nearly 100,000. Fear of bread riots and class warfare gripped many northern cities. Blame for the crisis became sectionalized, as southerners saw their system justified by the temporary collapse of industrial prosperity and northerners feared further incursions of the Slave Power on an insecure future.

John Brown's Raid on Harpers Ferry

Born in Connecticut in 1800, John Brown was raised by staunchly religious antislavery parents. Between 1820 and 1855, he engaged in some twenty business ventures, failing in nearly all of them. In his abolitionism, Brown relied on an Old Testament conception of justice—"an eye for an eye"—and he believed that slavery was an unjustifiable state of war conducted by one group against another. He also believed that violence in a righteous cause was a holy act. To Brown, the destruction of slavery in America required revolutionary ideology and revolutionary acts.

On October 16, 1859, Brown led a small band of eighteen whites and blacks in an attack on the federal arsenal at Harpers Ferry, Virginia. Hoping to trigger a slave rebellion, Brown failed and was quickly captured. In a celebrated trial in November and a widely publicized execution in December in Charles Town, Virginia, Brown became one of the most enduring martyrs, as well as villains, of American history. White southerners' outrage intensified when they learned first that Brown received financial backing from several prominent abolitionists, and second that such northern intellectuals as Ralph Waldo Emerson and Henry David Thoreau praised Brown as a holy warrior. The South almost universally interpreted Brown's attack at Harpers Ferry as an act of terrorism and the fulfillment of their dread of abolition emissaries who would infiltrate the region to incite slave rebellion. When Brown went to the gallows, he handed a note to his jailer with the famous prediction "I John Brown am now quite certain that the crimes of this guilty land will never be purged away, but with blood."

Election of 1860

Many Americans believed that the election of 1860 would decide the Union's fate. Until that election the Democratic Party was the only party that was truly national in scope, often, as one Mississippi editor wrote, waving "the olive branch over the troubled waters of politics." But, at its 1860 convention in Charleston, South Carolina, the Democratic Party split.

Stephen Douglas wanted his party's presidential nomination, but he feared alienating northern voters by accepting the southern position on the territories. Southern Democrats, however, insisted on recognition of their rights, as defined by the *Dred Scott* decision. When Douglas obtained a majority for his version of the platform, delegates from the Deep South walked out. Compromise attempts failed, and the Democrats presented two nominees: Douglas for the northern wing and Vice President John C. Breckinridge of Kentucky for the southern.

Republicans nominated Abraham Lincoln, a reflection of the Midwest's growing power. Lincoln was also perceived as more moderate on slavery than the early front runner, Senator William H. Seward of New York. A Constitutional Union Party nominated John Bell of Tennessee.

Bell's only issue in the campaign was preserving the Union, appealing to history, sentiment, and moderation to hold the country together. Douglas sought to unite his northern and southern supporters, while Breckinridge backed away from the appearance of extremism, and his supporters in several states stressed his unionism. Although Lincoln and the Republicans denied any intent to interfere with slavery where it existed, they stood firm against its extension into the territories.

The 1860 election was sectional in character, and the only one in American history in which the losers refused to accept the result. Lincoln won, but Douglas, Breckinridge, and Bell together received a majority of the votes. Douglas had broad-based support but won few states. Breckinridge carried nine southern states in the Deep South. Bell won pluralities in Virginia, Kentucky, and Tennessee. Lincoln prevailed in the North, but in the four slave states that remained loyal to the Union (Missouri, Kentucky, Maryland, and Delaware—the border states) he gained only a plurality (see Table 14.3). Lincoln's victory was won in the electoral college. He polled only 40 percent of the total vote and was not even on the ballot in ten slave states.

Opposition to slavery's extension was the core issue for Lincoln and the Republican Party. And abolitionists and Free-Soil supporters in the North held them to it. Meanwhile, in the South, proslavery advocates and secessionists whipped up public opinion and demanded that state conventions assemble to consider secession.

Lincoln did not soften his party's position on the territories. Although many conservative Republicans—eastern businessmen and former Whigs who did not feel strongly about slavery—hoped for a compromise, the original and most committed Republicans—old Free-Soilers and antislavery Whigs—held firm on slavery expansion.

In winter 1860–1861, the Kentucky senator John J. Crittenden offered a late-hour compromise. Hoping to avert disunion, Crittenden proposed that the two sections divide the territories between them at the Missouri Compromise line, 36°30′. When Lincoln ruled out concessions on the territorial issue, Crittenden's peacemaking effort collapsed.

TABLE 14.3   Presidential Vote in 1860 (by State)

Lincoln (Republican)*	Carried all northern states and all electoral votes except three in New Jersey
Breckinridge (Southern Democrat)	Carried all slave states except Virginia, Kentucky, Tennessee, Missouri
Bell (Constitutional Union)	Carried Virginia, Kentucky, Tennessee
Douglas (Northern Democrat)	Carried only Missouri

*Lincoln received only 26,000 votes in the entire South and was not even on the ballot in ten slave states. Breckinridge was not on the ballot in three northern states.

R. H. Howell, after Henry Cleenewerck, *The First Flag of Independence Raised in the South*. Lithograph, Savannah, Georgia, 1860. On the night of November 8, 1860, a huge crowd gathered in Johnson Square, Savannah, to protest Lincoln's election victory. The special banner on the obelisk reads "Our Motto Southern Rights, Equality of the States, Don't Tread on Me," drawing on traditions from the Revolutionary War.
(Library of Congress)

Secession and the Confederate States of America

Meanwhile, on December 20, 1860, South Carolina passed an ordinance of secession. Secession strategists concentrated on the most extreme proslavery state, hoping that South Carolina's move would induce other states to follow toward disunion.

No longer was secession unthinkable; secessionists now argued that other states should follow suit and that those favoring compromise could make a better deal outside the Union than in it.

Southern extremists called separate state conventions and passed secession ordinances in Mississippi, Florida, Alabama, Georgia, Louisiana, and Texas. By February 1861 these states joined South Carolina to form a new government in Montgomery, Alabama: the Confederate States of America. The delegates at Montgomery chose Jefferson Davis of Mississippi as their president, and the Confederacy began to function independently of the United States.

This apparent unanimity of action was deceiving. Many southerners who voted in the 1860 U.S. presidential election stayed home a few months later rather than vote for delegates who would decide on secession. And in some state conventions the secession vote was close—decided by overrepresentation of plantation districts. Four Upper South states—Virginia, North Carolina, Tennessee, and Arkansas—rejected secession and did not join the Confederacy until after fighting commenced. In the border states, popular sentiment was divided; minorities in Kentucky and Missouri tried to secede, but these slave states ultimately came under Union control, along with Maryland and Delaware (see Map 14.2).

Secession posed new and troubling issues for southerners, especially the possibility of war. Analysis of election returns from 1860 and 1861 indicates that slaveholders and nonslaveholders were beginning to part company politically.

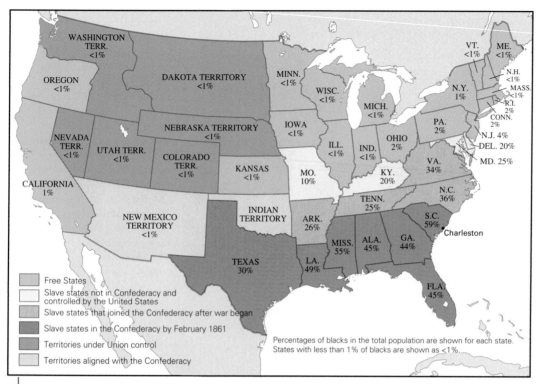

WASHINGTON TERR. <1%

OREGON <1%

DAKOTA TERRITORY <1%

MINN. <1%

WISC. <1%

MICH. <1%

VT. <1%

ME. <1%

N.H. <1%

N.Y. 1%

MASS. <1%

R.I. 2%

CONN. 2%

NEVADA TERR. <1%

UTAH TERR. <1%

NEBRASKA TERRITORY <1%

IOWA <1%

ILL. <1%

IND. <1%

OHIO 2%

PA. 2%

N.J. 4%

DEL. 20%

MD. 25%

COLORADO TERR. <1%

KANSAS <1%

MO. 10%

KY. 20%

VA. 34%

CALIFORNIA 1%

NEW MEXICO TERRITORY <1%

INDIAN TERRITORY

ARK. 26%

TENN. 25%

N.C. 36%

S.C. 59%

Charleston

TEXAS 30%

LA. 49%

MISS. 55%

ALA. 45%

GA. 44%

FLA. 45%

Free States

Slave states not in Confederacy and controlled by the United States

Slave states that joined the Confederacy after war began

Slave states in the Confederacy by February 1861

Territories under Union control

Territories aligned with the Confederacy

Percentages of blacks in the total population are shown for each state. States with less than 1% of blacks are shown as <1%.

Map 14.2 The Divided Nation–Slave and Free Areas, 1861

After fighting began, the Upper South joined the Deep South in the Confederacy. How does the nation's pattern of division correspond to the distribution of slavery and the percentage of blacks in the population?

Slaveholding counties strongly supported secession. But most counties with few slaves took an antisecession position or were staunchly Unionist (see Figure 14.1). With war looming, yeomen were beginning to ask themselves how far they would go to support slavery and slaveowners.

In speeches and writings, secession commissioners from the seven seceded states revealed why the Deep South broke away. Repeatedly they stressed independence as the only way to preserve white racial security and the slave system. On "slavery," said the Alabama commissioner, Stephen Hale, to the Kentucky legislature, rested "the wealth and prosperity of the southern people." Only secession, Hale contended, could sustain the "heaven-ordained superiority of the white over the black race."

Fort Sumter and Outbreak of War

The dilemma facing President Lincoln on inauguration day in March 1861 was how to maintain the authority of the federal government without provoking war. His solution: by holding onto forts in the states that left the Union, he could assert federal sovereignty while waiting for a restoration. But Jefferson Davis could not claim to lead a sovereign nation if the Confederate ports were under foreign (that is, U.S.) control. The two sides collided in the early morning of April 12, 1861, at Fort Sumter in Charleston harbor. When a federal garrison there ran low on food, Lincoln notified South Carolinians that he was sending a supply ship. For the

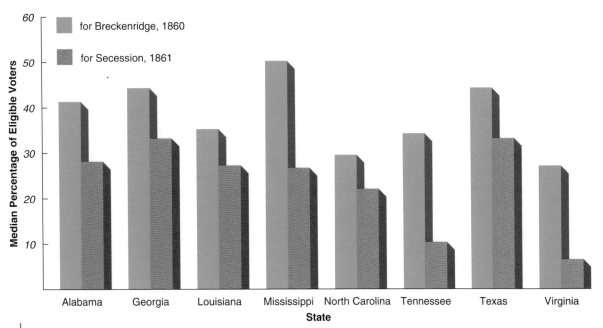

Figure 14.1   Voting Returns of Counties with Few Slaveholders, Eight Southern States, 1860 and 1861
This graph depicts voting in counties whose percentage of slaveholders ranked them among the lower half of the counties in their state. How does voters' support for secession in 1861 compare with support for John Breckinridge, the southern Democratic candidate in 1860? Why was their support for secession so weak? At this time counties with many slaveholders were giving increased support to secession.

Montgomery government, the alternatives were to attack the fort or acquiesce to Lincoln's authority. The secretary of war ordered local commanders to obtain a surrender or attack the fort. After two days of heavy bombardment, the federal garrison surrendered. Confederates permitted U.S. troops to sail away on unarmed vessels while Charlestonians celebrated. The Civil War—the bloodiest war in America's history—had begun.

Causation

Historians have long debated the causes of the Civil War. Some have interpreted it as the clash of two civilizations on divergent historical trajectories. But the issues dividing Americans in 1861 were fundamental to the republic's future. Republican ideology tended toward abolishing slavery, even though Republicans denied such intentions. Southern ideology led to establishing slavery everywhere, though southern leaders, too, denied such motives.

These positions hardened in American political life during the decade and a half before secession. In a postelection letter to his friend Alexander Stephens of Georgia, soon to be vice president of the Confederacy, Lincoln stated, "You think slavery is right and ought to be expanded; while we think it is wrong and ought to be restricted. That I suppose is the rub." Without slavery, there would have been no war. Many Americans still believe that the war was about states' rights. But the significance of states' rights is always in the cause in which it is employed. To borrow from Douglass, it is the meaning within the fight that we must understand.

Terrorist or Freedom Fighter?

The greatest significance of John Brown's 1859 raid on Harpers Ferry rests in its hold on American memory. Brown has been at once one of the most beloved and loathed figures in American history. In the song that bears his name, "John Brown's Body," a popular marching tune during the Civil War, his "soul goes marching on."

In the wake of his execution, in painting, song, and poetry people constructed a John Brown mythology. Was he a Christ-like figure who died for the nation's sins, who had to commit crimes to expose the nation's larger crime? Or was he a terrorist, who murdered according to his vision of God's will? Brown can be inspiring and disturbing, a warrior saint and a monster. He represents the highest ideals and the most ruthless deeds. He killed for justice and was hanged as a traitor. Over the years many organizations have adopted John Brown as their justifying symbol, from left-wing students opposing American foreign policy to current anti-abortion groups who target clinics and doctors. In today's world, terrorism and revolutionary violence are often in the news. Suicide bombers attack buses in Israel; a federal building exploded in Oklahoma City; Al Qaeda operatives blew up trains in Madrid; American embassies are attacked in Africa and Europe; on September 11, 2001, four hijacked passenger airplanes became weapons of death that brought terrorism to American soil as never before; and in Iraq an insurgency resists American occupation, as a country falls into sectarian civil war between Shi'ites and Sunnis. The story of John Brown's 1859 raid forces us to ask when and how revolutionary violence—for political or spiritual end—is justified. That is his legacy for a people and a nation.

Summary

The War with Mexico fostered massive land acquisition, which forced a debate about slavery in the West. The Compromise of 1850 attempted to settle the dispute but only exacerbated sectional tensions, leading to the fateful Kansas-Nebraska Act of 1854, which tore asunder the political party system and gave birth to an antislavery coalition. With Bleeding Kansas and the *Dred Scott* decision by 1857, Americans faced clear and dangerous choices about the future of labor and the meaning of liberty in an expanding society. Finally, by 1859, when the radical abolitionist John Brown attacked Harpers Ferry to foment a slave insurrection, southerners and northerners began viewing each other in conspiratorial terms. Meanwhile, African Americans, slave and free, fled from slave catchers and expected violent resolutions to their dreams of freedom in America.

Throughout the 1840s and 1850s, many able leaders worked to avert disunion. Secession dismayed northern editors and voters and plunged some planters into depression. Paul Cameron, the largest slaveowner in North Carolina, confessed to being "very unhappy. I love the Union." Many blacks, however, shared Frederick Douglass's outlook. "The contest must now be decided," he wrote in March 1861, "and decided forever, which of the two, Freedom or Slavery, shall give law to this Republic."

Why had all efforts to prevent war failed? The emotions bound up in attacking and defending slavery's future were too powerful, and the interests it affected too vital for compromise. During the 1850s, every southern victory in territorial expansion increased fear of the Slave Power, and each new expression of Free-Soil sentiment prompted slaveholders to harden their demands. In the profoundest sense, slavery was the root of the war. As a people and a nation, Americans reached the most fateful turning point in their history. Resolution would come from the battlefield.

Chapter Review

THE WAR WITH MEXICO AND ITS CONSEQUENCES

How did Polk make the war with Mexico inevitable?

President Polk wanted to expand America's borders into territory occupied by Great Britain and Mexico. He negotiated with Great Britain, securing for America the Oregon territory it desired, but he was aggressive in his dealings with Mexico. He supported annexation of Texas and contested the U.S. border with Mexico. Finally, Polk attempted to buy a tract of land extending into California, but when Mexico refused, he sent in troops. A three-day stand-off resulted in the temporary retreat of U.S. cavalry, but also the onset of war with Mexico.

1850: COMPROMISE OR ARMISTICE?

What were the two troubling flaws inherent in the Compromise of 1850?

The Compromise of 1850 attempted to resolve the debate between the North and South over slavery in the territories. In the end it only furthered controversy. First, it left the definition of popular sovereignty unclear so that southerners could interpret it to mean that a region could not ban slavery during the territorial stage, whereas northerners believed it was up to the people to decide. Second, the Fugitive Slave Act enabled slave owners to present evidence in state courts that a slave had escaped, which would then serve as proof of slave status even in free states and territories—and without investigation into its truth. Abolitionists feared that free blacks would be vulnerable to kidnapping and enslavement. Moreover, the law made it a felony to harbor fugitives and said northerners could be compelled to hunt runaway slaves.

SLAVERY EXPANSION AND COLLAPSE OF THE PARTY SYSTEM

How did slavery fuel the collapse of the party system?

It came in the form of the Kansas-Nebraska Act, which ultimately eroded the 1850 Compromise, and prompted sectional divisions within the political parties that led to each party's breakdown. The act established the Kansas and Nebraska territories, but it applied popular sovereignty to let the territories decide what to do about slavery. Northerners argued that since the territories were within the Louisiana Purchase, they were subject to the Missouri Compromise (which prohibited slavery from latitude 36°30′ north to the Canadian border). When the Act was passed in 1854, sectional divisions intensified. The weakened Whig Party split into northern and southern wings. Democrats' support in the North plummeted, costing them most of their congressional seats and control of all but two state legislatures. In late 1854, antislavery Whigs and Democrats, Free-Soilers, and reformers throughout the Old Northwest formed the new Republican Party to keep slavery from the territories.

SLAVERY AND THE NATION'S FUTURE

How did the issue of slavery—and the Dred Scott decision—further divide the nation?

The Dred Scott decision validated northern fears of a southern slave power, and inspired new fears about the territories being open to slavery. The Supreme Court was ultimately stacked in favor of the southern position on slavery and its extension into the new territories. Five of the nine justices were southerners. The court's decision in the Dred Scott case—that Scott was a slave despite the fact that he lived in the free territory of Missouri and that Congress could not make any laws that barred slavery—invalidated popular sovereignty, the Wilmot Proviso, and the Missouri Compromise.

DISUNION

What were the final straws leading to secession and the dissolution of the Union?

Lincoln's contested election by his Democratic rivals, along with the inability to reach a compromise on the extension of slavery in the territories, ultimately fueled the movement to secede. When Lincoln rejected a compromise that would divide the territories into slave and free at the Missouri Compromise line (36°30'), hopes for preventing secession collapsed. South Carolina passed the first secession ordinance in December 1860; Mississippi, Florida, Alabama, Georgia, Louisiana, and Texas followed. A month after Lincoln's inauguration, these states established their own national capitol in Montgomery, Alabama, dubbing themselves the Confederate States of America.

SUGGESTIONS FOR FURTHER READING

Edward L. Ayers, *What Caused the Civil War: Reflections on the South and Southern History* (2005)

Richard J. Carwardine, *Lincoln* (2003)

Charles Dew, *Apostles of Disunion: Southern Secession Commissioners and the Causes of the Civil War* (2001)

Nicole Etcheson, *Bleeding Kansas: Contested Liberty in the Civil War Era* (2004)

Don E. Fehrenbacher, *The Slaveholding Republic: An Account of the United States Government's Relations to Slavery* (2001)

Eric Foner, *Free Soil, Free Labor, Free Men: The Ideology of the Republican Party* (1970)

Robert W. Johannsen, *To the Halls of the Montezumas: The Mexican War and the American Imagination* (1985)

Michael A. Morrison, *Slavery and the American West: The Eclipse of Manifest Destiny and the Coming of the Civil War* (1997)

David S. Reynolds, *John Brown, Abolitionist: The Man Who Killed Slavery, Sparked the Civil War, and Seeded Civil Rights* (2005)

Richard H. Sewell, *Ballots for Freedom: Antislavery Politics in the United States* (1976)

CHAPTER 15

Transforming Fire: The Civil War

CHAPTER OUTLINE

America Goes to War, 1861–1862

War Transforms the South

Wartime Northern Economy
and Society

The Advent of Emancipation

The Soldiers' War

1863: The Tide of Battle Turns

Disunity: South, North, and West

1864–1865: The Final Test of Wills

> **LINKS TO THE WORLD:**
> The Civil War in Britain

Summary

> **LEGACY FOR A PEOPLE
> AND A NATION:** "Big
> Government"

Slave pens were the ugly crossroads of American history. Wallace Turnage, a seventeen-year-old slave from a cotton plantation in Pickens County, Alabama, entered wartime Mobile in December 1862 through the slave traders' yard; he would leave Mobile from that same yard twenty months later.

Turnage was born on a tobacco farm near Snow Hill, North Carolina, in 1846. In mid-1860, as the nation teetered on disunion, he was sold to a Richmond, Virginia, slave trader named Hector Davis. Turnage worked in Davis's three-story slave jail, organizing daily auctions until he was sold for $1,000 in 1861 to a cotton planter from Pickens County, Alabama. Frequently whipped, the desperate teenager tried four times over the next two years to escape to Mississippi. He was captured each time and returned to his owner.

Frustrated, his owner sold Turnage for $2,000 at the Mobile slave traders' yard to a wealthy merchant in the port city. During 1864, as Mobile came under siege, its slaves were enlisted to build trenchworks. Turnage did many urban tasks for his new owner's family, including driving their carriage on errands.

In early August, Turnage crashed the old carriage on a Mobile street. In anger, his owner took him to the slave pen, hiring the jailer to administer thirty lashes in the whipping house. Stripped naked, his hands tied in ropes, Turnage was hoisted up on a hook on the wall. When it was over, his owner instructed Wallace to walk home. Instead, Turnage "took courage," as he wrote in his postwar narrative, and walked southwest through the Confederate encampment. The soldiers mistook the bloodied and tattered black teenager for one among hundreds of slaves who did camp labor.

For the next three weeks, Turnage crawled and waded for 25 miles through the snake-infested swamps of the Foul River estuary, down the west edge of Mobile Bay. Nearly starved and

This icon will direct you to interactive activities and study materials on A People And A Nation, Brief Edition
website: **www.cengage.com/history/norton/
peoplenationbrief8e**

Chronology

1861	Battle of Bull Run occurs.
	McClellan organizes the Union Army.
	Union blockade begins.
	U.S. Congress passes the first confiscation act.
	Trent affair occurs.
1862	Union captures Fort Henry and Fort Donelson.
	U.S. Navy captures New Orleans.
	Battle of Shiloh shows the war's destructiveness.
	Confederacy enacts conscription.
	McClellan's Peninsula Campaign fails to take Richmond.
	U.S. Congress passes the second confiscation act, initiating emancipation.
	Confederacy mounts an offensive in Maryland and Kentucky.
	Battle of Antietam ends Lee's drive into Maryland in September.
	British intervention in the war on the Confederate side is averted.
1863	Emancipation Proclamation takes effect.
	U.S. Congress passes the National Banking Act.
	Union enacts conscription.
	African American soldiers join the Union Army.
	Food riots occur in southern cities.
	Battle of Chancellorsville ends in Confederate victory but Jackson's death.

	Union wins key victories at Vicksburg and Gettysburg.
	Draft riots take place in New York City.
	Battle of Chattanooga leaves the South vulnerable to Sherman's march into Georgia.
1864	Battles of the Wilderness and Spotsylvania produce heavy casualties on both sides in the efforts to capture and to defend Richmond.
	Battle of Cold Harbor continues the carnage in Virginia.
	Lincoln requests a Republican Party plank abolishing slavery.
	Sherman captures Atlanta.
	Confederacy begins to collapse on the home front.
	Lincoln wins reelection, eliminating any Confederate hopes for a negotiated end to war.
	Jefferson Davis proposes emancipation within the Confederacy.
	Sherman marches through Georgia to the sea.
1865	Sherman marches through the Carolinas.
	U.S. Congress approves the Thirteenth Amendment.
	Lee abandons Richmond and Petersburg.
	Lee surrenders at Appomattox Court House.
	Lincoln is assassinated.
	Death toll in war reaches 620,000.

narrowly escaping Confederate patrols, Turnage made it to Cedar Point, where he could see Dauphin Island, now occupied by Union forces. Alligators swam nearby, as Turnage hid from Confederates in a swampy den. He remembered: "It was death to go back and it was death to stay there and freedom was before me."

Then, Turnage noticed an old rowboat that rolled in with the tide. The veteran runaway began to row out into the bay. He suddenly "heard the crash of oars and behold there was eight Yankees in a boat." Turnage jumped into the Union gunboat. For a stunning few moments, he remembered, the oarsmen "were struck with silence" by the frail young black man crouched before them. Turnage looked back at Confederate soldiers on the shore. Then he took his first breaths of freedom.

The Civil War brought astonishing changes to individuals and daily life, North and South. Millions of men were swept into training camps and regiments. Armies numbering in the hundreds of thousands marched over the South, devastating the countryside. Families struggled to survive without men; businesses tried to cope with fewer workers. Women took on extra responsibilities and moved into new workforce jobs, with many becoming nurses and hospital workers.

But southerners also experienced utter defeat. For most, wealth changed to poverty as countless farms were ruined. Late in the war, many southerners yearned only for an end to inflation, shortages, slave escapes, and the death that touched most families. Southern slaves did not always encounter sympathetic liberators such as those who aided Turnage, fed and clothed him, and took him before a Union general, where the freedman could either join a black regiment or become a white officer's camp servant. Until war's end, Turnage cooked for a Maryland captain.

In the North, farm boys and mechanics would be asked for heretofore unimagined sacrifices. Businessmen, however, found new profits in war. The conflict ensured vast government expenditures and lucrative federal contracts. "The battle of Bull Run," predicted an eminent financier in *Harper's Monthly*, "makes the fortune of every man in Wall Street who is not a natural idiot."

Change was most drastic in the South, where secessionists launched a conservative revolution for their section's national independence. Born of states' rights doctrine, the Confederacy had to be transformed into a centralized nation to fight a vast war. Southern whites feared that a peacetime government of Republicans would interfere with slavery and ruin plantation life. Instead, their actions led to a war that turned southern society upside down and imperiled the existence of slavery.

The war created social strains in both North and South. To the alarm of many, the powers of the federal government and of the president increased during the war. Dissent flourished in the North, and antiwar sentiment occasionally erupted into violence. Disaffection was strongest, though, in the Confederacy, where poverty and class resentment threatened the South from within as federal armies assailed it from without.

The Civil War forced a social and political revolution regarding race. It compelled leaders and citizens to finally face the question of slavery. And blacks embraced the most fundamental turning point in their experience as Americans.

- **How and why did the Civil War bring social transformations to both South and North?**
- **How did the war to preserve the Union or for southern independence become the war to free the slaves?**
- **By 1865, when Americans on all sides searched for the *meaning* of the war they had just fought, what might some of their answers have been?**

AMERICA GOES TO WAR, 1861–1862

The onset of hostilities sparked patriotic sentiments, speeches, and ceremonies across the North and South. Northern communities raised companies of volunteers eager to save the Union. Southern recruits boasted of whipping the Yankees and returning home before Christmas. Southern women sewed dashing uniforms for men who would soon be lucky to wear drab gray or butternut homespun. Americans went to war in 1861 filled with romantic notions.

First Battle of Bull Run Through spring 1861, both sides scrambled to organize and train their undisciplined armies. On July 21, 1861, the first battle took place outside Manassas Junction, Virginia, near a stream called Bull Run. General Irvin McDowell and thirty thousand Union troops attacked General P. G. T. Beauregard's twenty-two thousand southerners. Federal forces gained ground, until they ran into a line of Virginia troops under General Thomas "Stonewall" Jackson. Jackson's line held, and the arrival of nine thousand Confederate reinforcements won the day for the South. Union troops fled to Washington.

The unexpected rout at Bull Run proved that although the United States enjoyed an enormous advantage in resources, victory would not be easy. Pro-Union feeling was growing in western Virginia, and loyalties were divided in the four border slave states—Missouri, Kentucky, Maryland, and Delaware. But the rest of the Upper South—the states of North Carolina, Virginia, Tennessee, and Arkansas—joined the Confederacy. Half a million southerners volunteered to fight—so many that the Confederate government could hardly arm them all. The United States therefore undertook a massive mobilization of troops around Washington, D.C.

Lincoln gave command of the army to General George B. McClellan, who proved better at organization and training than fighting. McClellan devoted fall and winter 1861 to readying a force of a quarter-million men to take Richmond, the Confederate capital.

Grand Strategy

While McClellan prepared, the Union began to implement other parts of its strategy, which called for a blockade of southern ports and capture of the Mississippi River. Like a constricting snake, this Anaconda plan would strangle the Confederacy. The Union Navy initially had too few ships to patrol 3,550 miles of coastline. Gradually, the navy increased the blockade's effectiveness, though it never stopped southern commerce completely.

The Confederate strategy was essentially defensive, given the South's claim of independence and the North's resource advantage (see Figure 15.1). But Jefferson Davis called the southern strategy an offensive defensive, taking advantage of opportunities to attack and using its interior transportation lines to concentrate troops at

Union States   **Confederate States**

Total Population, 2.5 to 1

Naval Ship Tonnage, 25 to 1

Farm Acreage, 3 to 1

Free Men 18–60 Yrs., 4.4 to 1

Factory Production Value, 10 to 1

Draft Animals, 1.8 to 1

44%   90%

Free Men in Military Service, 1864

Textile Goods Production, 14 to 1

Railroad Mileage, 2.4 to 1

Figure 15.1   Comparative Resources, Union and Confederate States, 1861
The North had vastly superior resources. Although the North's advantages in manpower and industrial capacity proved very important, the South still had to be conquered, its society and its will crushed. (*The Times Atlas of World History.* Time Books, London, 1978. Used with permission.)

crucial points. The Confederacy did not need to conquer the North; the Union, however, required conquest of the South.

Both sides slighted the importance of the West, that vast expanse between Virginia and the Mississippi River and beyond. Guerrilla warfare broke out in 1861 in politically divided Missouri, and key locations along the Mississippi and other western rivers would prove crucial prizes in the North's eventual victory. Beyond the Mississippi, the Confederacy hoped to gain an advantage by negotiating treaties with the Creeks, Choctaws, Chickasaws, Cherokees, Seminoles, and smaller groups of Plains Indians. Meanwhile, the Republican U.S. Congress carved the West into territories in anticipation of state making. For most Indians west of the Mississippi, the Civil War launched nearly three decades of an enveloping strategy of conquest, relocation, and slaughter.

Union Naval Campaign The last half of 1861 brought no major land battles, but in late summer, Union naval forces captured Cape Hatteras and Hilton Head, one of the Sea Islands off Port Royal, South Carolina. A few months later, federal naval operations established significant beachheads along the Confederate coastline, including vital points in North Carolina, as well as Fort Pulaski, which defended Savannah.

The coastal victories off South Carolina foreshadowed a revolution in slave society. As federal gunboats approached, planters abandoned their land and fled. The Confederate cavalry tried to round up slaves and move them to the interior. But thousands of slaves greeted what they hoped to be freedom with rejoicing and broke the hated cotton gins. Some entered their master's homes and took clothing and furniture. Many runaways poured into Union lines. Unwilling at first to wage a war against slavery, the federal government did not acknowledge the slaves' freedom, though it used their labor. These emancipated slaves, defined by Union officers as war contraband (confiscated enemy property), forced first a debate within the Union Army and government over how to treat the freedmen, and then an attempt to harness their labor and military power.

Spring 1862 brought southerners stronger evidence of the war's gravity. In March, two ironclad ships—the *Monitor* (a Union warship) and the *Merrimack* (a Union ship seized by the Confederacy)—fought off the coast of Virginia. Their battle, though indecisive, ushered in a new era in naval design. In April, Union ships commanded by Admiral David Farragut smashed through log booms blocking the Mississippi River and moved upstream to capture New Orleans. The South's greatest seaport and slave-trading center was now in federal hands.

War in the Far West Farther west, three Confederate regiments were organized, mostly of Cherokees, but a Union victory at Elkhorn Tavern, Arkansas, shattered southern control of the region. Thereafter, dissension within Native American groups and a Union victory the following year at Honey Springs, Arkansas, reduced Confederate operations in Indian Territory to guerrilla raids.

In the westernmost campaign of the war, from February to May 1862, some three thousand Confederate and four thousand Union forces fought to control New Mexico Territory. The Confederate invasion aimed to seize the trade riches of the

Santa Fe Trail and take possession of gold mines in Colorado and California. But Colorado and New Mexico Unionists fought back, and in a series of battles at Glorieta Pass, 20 miles east of Santa Fe, on March 26 through 28, they blocked the Confederates. By May 1, Confederate forces straggled down the Rio Grande River into Texas, abandoning efforts to take New Mexico.

Grant's Tennessee Campaign and the Battle of Shiloh

Meanwhile, in February 1862, forces in northern Tennessee won significant victories for the Union. A Union commander named Ulysses S. Grant saw the strategic importance of Fort Henry and Fort Donelson, the Confederate outposts guarding the Tennessee and Cumberland Rivers. In just ten days he seized the forts, completely cutting off the Confederates and demanding unconditional surrender of Fort Donelson. A path into Tennessee, Alabama, and Mississippi was now open to the Union Army.

Grant moved into southern Tennessee and the first of the war's shockingly bloody encounters, the Battle of Shiloh. On April 6, Confederate general Albert Sidney Johnston caught federal troops with their backs to the Tennessee River awaiting reinforcements. The Confederates attacked and inflicted heavy damage all day. Close to victory, General Johnston was killed. Union reinforcements arrived that night. The next day the battle turned, and after ten hours of combat, the Confederates withdrew.

Neither side won a decisive victory at Shiloh, yet losses were staggering and the Confederates were forced to retreat into northern Mississippi. Northern troops lost thirteen thousand men (killed, wounded, or captured) out of sixty-three thousand; southerners sacrificed eleven thousand out of forty thousand. Total casualties in this battle exceeded those in all three of America's previous wars combined. Before Shiloh, Grant hoped that southerners would soon tire of the conflict. After Shiloh, he recalled in his 1885 memoir, he "gave up all idea of saving the Union except by complete conquest." Memories of the Shiloh battlefield would haunt the surviving soldiers for the rest of their lives.

McClellan and the Peninsula Campaign

On the Virginia front, President Lincoln had problems with General McClellan. Only thirty-six, McClellan had achieved success as an army officer and railroad president. Habitually overestimating the size of enemy forces, he called repeatedly for reinforcements and ignored Lincoln's directions to advance. McClellan advocated a war of limited aims that would lead to a quick reunion. He intended neither disruption of slavery nor war on noncombatants. McClellan finally sailed his troops down the Chesapeake, landing them on the peninsula between the York and James Rivers, and advanced on Richmond.

After a bloody battle at Fair Oaks from May 31 through June 1, the federal armies moved to within 7 miles of the Confederate capital. The Confederate commanding general, Joseph E. Johnston, was badly wounded at Fair Oaks, and President Jefferson Davis placed his chief military adviser, Robert E. Lee, in command. The fifty-five-year-old Lee was an aristocratic Virginian, a lifelong military officer, and a veteran of distinction from the War with Mexico. Although he initially opposed secession, Lee gave his allegiance to his state and became a staunch Confederate. He soon foiled McClellan's legions.

First, Lee sent Stonewall Jackson's corps of seventeen thousand northwest into the Shenandoah valley behind Union forces, where they threatened Washington, D.C., and drew some federal troops away from Richmond to protect their own capital. Further, in mid-June, in an extraordinary four-day ride around the Union Army, Confederate cavalry under J. E. B. Stuart confirmed the exposed position of McClellan's army north of the Chickahominy River. In the Seven Days Battles from June 26 through July 1, Lee struck at McClellan's army. Lee's daring move of taking the majority of his army northeast and attacking the Union right flank, while leaving only a small force to defend Richmond, forced McClellan to retreat toward the James River.

During the sustained fighting of the Seven Days, Union forces suffered 20,614 casualties and the Confederates, 15,849. By August 3, McClellan withdrew his army to the environs of Washington. Richmond remained safe for almost two more years.

In October 1862 in New York City, photographer Mathew Brady opened an exhibition of photographs from the Battle of Antietam. Although few knew it, Brady's vision was very poor, and this photograph of Confederate dead was actually made by his assistants, Alexander Gardner and James F. Gibson.   (Library of Congress)

Confederate Offensive in Maryland and Kentucky

Buoyed by these results, Jefferson Davis conceived an ambitious plan to gain wartime advantage and recognition by European nations. He ordered a general offensive, sending Lee north into Maryland and Generals Kirby Smith and Braxton Bragg into Kentucky. Calling on residents of Maryland and Kentucky, still slave states, to make peace with his government, Davis also invited northwestern states like Indiana, which sent much of their trade down the Mississippi to New Orleans, to leave the Union. This was a coordinated effort to take the war to the North and force both a military and a political turning point.

The plan was promising, but the offensive ultimately failed. Lee's forces achieved a striking success at the battle of Second Bull Run, August 29 through 30. The entire Union army retreated to the federal capital. Thousands of wounded occupied schools and churches, and two thousand suffered on cots in the U.S. Capitol rotunda.

But in the bloodiest day of the war, September 17, 1862, McClellan turned Lee back from Sharpsburg, Maryland. In this Battle of Antietam, five thousand men died and another eighteen thousand were wounded. McClellan intercepted a battle order, wrapped around cigars for each Confederate corps commander and lost by a courier. But McClellan moved slowly, failed to use his larger forces in simultaneous attacks, and allowed Lee's stricken army to retreat across the Potomac. Lincoln removed McClellan from command.

In Kentucky, Generals Smith and Bragg secured Lexington and Frankfort, but their effort to force the Yankees back to the Ohio River was stopped at the Battle of Perryville on October 8. Bragg's army retreated into Tennessee, where from December 31, 1862, to January 2, 1863, they fought an indecisive but bloody battle at Murfreesboro. Casualties exceeded even those of Shiloh.

Outnumbered and disadvantaged, the South could not continue the offensive. Davis admitted to Confederate representatives that southerners were entering "the darkest and most dangerous period we have yet had."

But 1862 also brought painful lessons to the North. On December 13, Union general Ambrose Burnside, now in command of the Army of the Potomac, unwisely ordered his soldiers to attack Lee's army, which held fortified positions at Fredericksburg, Virginia. Lee's men performed efficiently in killing northerners, and Burnside's repeated assaults up Marye's Heights shocked his opponents, killing 1,300 and wounding 9,600 Union soldiers. The scale of carnage now challenged people on both sides to question the meaning of the war and what they would endure to win it.

War Transforms the South

One of the first traditions to fall was the southern preference for local and limited government. States' rights had been a formative ideology for the Confederacy, but state governments were weak operations. To withstand the North's massive power, Jefferson Davis saw the necessity of centralization and moved to thwart the separate aims of states.

The Confederacy and Centralization

Davis brought all arms, supplies, and troops under his control. But by early 1862 the scope and duration of the conflict required more recruits. Tens of thousands of Confederate soldiers volunteered for just one year's service, planning to return home in spring to plant their crops. Faced with a critical troop shortage, in April 1862 the Confederate government enacted the first national conscription (draft) law in American history.

Davis adopted a firm leadership role toward the Confederate Congress, which raised taxes and later passed a tax-in-kind—a tax paid in farm products. Nearly 4,500 agents dispersed to collect the tax. Where opposition arose, the government suspended the writ of habeas corpus (which prevented individuals from being held without trial) and imposed martial law. Still, this tax system proved inadequate for the South's war effort.

To replace the food that men in uniform would have grown, Davis exhorted state governments to require farmers to switch from cash crops to food crops. But army food and labor shortages continued. The War Department impressed slaves to work on fortifications, and after 1861, officers raided farms and carted away grain, meat, wagons, and draft animals to feed the troops. Such raids caused increased hardship and resentment for women managing farms without husbands and sons.

Soon the Confederate administration in Richmond gained control over the southern economy. The Confederate Congress also gave the central government almost complete control of the railroads. A large bureaucracy of over seventy thousand civilians administered these operations. By the war's end, the southern bureaucracy was larger in proportion to population than its northern counterpart.

Confederate Nationalism

Historians have long argued over whether the Confederacy itself was a rebellion, a revolution, or the creation of a genuine nation. Whatever the label, Confederates created a culture and ideology of nationalism. In flags, songs, language, seals, school readers, and other national characteristics, Confederates created their own story and identity.

Southerners believed that the Confederacy was the true legacy of the American Revolution—a bulwark against centralized power that was in keeping with the war for independence. To southerners, theirs was a continuing revolution against the excesses of Yankee democracy, and George Washington (a Virginian) on horseback formed the center of the Confederacy's official seal.

Also central to Confederate nationalism was a refurbished defense of slavery as a benign, protective institution, complete with the image of the faithful slave. In wartime schoolbooks, children were instructed in the divinely inspired, paternalistic character of slavery. A poem popular among whites captured an old slave's rejection of the Emancipation Proclamation.

> Now, Massa, dis is berry fine, dese words
> You've spoke to me,
> No doubt you mean it kindly, but ole Dinah
> Won't be free . . .
> Ole Massa's berry good to me—and though I am
> His slave,
> He treats me like I'se kin to him—and I would
> Rather have
> A home in Massa's cabin, and eat his black
> Bread too,
> Dan leave ole Massa's children and go and
> Lib wid you.

This and other forms of Confederate nationalism collapsed in the war's final year. But it would reappear in the postwar period.

Southern Cities and Industry

Clerks and subordinate officials crowded towns and cities where Confederate departments had offices. Clerks had always been males, but now government girls staffed the Confederate bureaucracy. The sudden migration overwhelmed the housing supply and stimulated new construction. Richmond's population increased 250 percent. Mobile's population jumped from twenty-nine thousand to forty-one thousand; and ten thousand people poured into war-related industries in little Selma, Alabama.

As the Union blockade disrupted imports, the traditionally agricultural South forged new industries. Many planters shared Davis's hope that industrialization would bring "deliverance . . . from all commercial dependence" on the North or the world. Indeed, the Confederacy achieved tremendous industrial development. Chief of Ordnance Josiah Gorgas increased the capacity of Richmond's Tredegar Iron Works and other factories so that by 1865 his Ordnance Bureau was supplying all

Confederate small arms and ammunition. The government constructed new railroad lines and ironworks, using slaves relocated from farms and plantations.

Changing Roles of Women

White women, restricted to narrow roles in antebellum society, gained new responsibilities in wartime. The wives and mothers of soldiers now headed households and performed men's work, including raising crops and tending animals. Women in nonslaveowning families cultivated fields, while wealthier women acted as overseers and managed fieldwork. In cities, white women—previously all but excluded from the labor force—found respectable paying jobs, often in the Confederate bureaucracy. And female schoolteachers appeared in the South for the first time.

Patriotic sacrifice appealed to some women; others resented their new burdens. A Texas woman who struggled to discipline slaves pronounced herself "sick of trying to do a man's business." Others grew angry over shortages and resented contact with lower-class women. Some scorned the war and demanded that their men return to provide for their families.

Human Suffering, Hoarding, and Inflation

For millions of southerners, the war brought privation and suffering. Mass poverty descended on a large minority of the white population, as many yeoman families lost their breadwinners to the army. Women sought help from relatives, neighbors, friends, anyone. Sometimes they pleaded with the Confederate government to discharge their husbands.

The South was in many places so sparsely populated that the conscription of one craftsman could wreak hardship on an entire county. Often people begged together for the exemption or discharge of the local miller, neighborhood tanner, wheelwright, or physician. Most serious, however, was the loss of a blacksmith, who could repair farming tools.

The blockade of Confederate shipping created shortages of important supplies—salt, sugar, coffee, nails—and speculation and hoarding made shortages worse. Greedy businessmen cornered the supply of some commodities; prosperous citizens stocked up on food. The *Richmond Enquirer* criticized a planter who purchased so many supplies that his "lawn and paths looked like a wharf covered with a ship's loads."

Inflation raged out of control, fueled by the Confederate government's heavy borrowing and inadequate taxes, until prices increased almost 7,000 percent. Inflation particularly imperiled urban dwellers without their own food sources. As early as 1861 and 1862, officials predicted that "women and children are bound to come to suffering if not starvation." Hoarding continued, and a rudimentary relief program organized by the Confederacy failed to meet the need.

Inequities of the Confederate Draft

Not all classes sacrificed equally. The Confederate government's policies decidedly favored the upper class. Until the last year of the war, for example, prosperous southerners could avoid military service by hiring substitutes. Well over fifty thousand upperclass southerners purchased substitutes, despite skyrocketing prices that reached

$5,000 or $6,000 per man. Mary Boykin Chesnut knew of one aristocrat who "spent a fortune in substitutes. . . . He is at the end of his row now, for all able-bodied men are ordered to the front."

Anger at such discrimination exploded in October 1862, when the Confederate Congress exempted from military duty anyone who was supervising at least twenty slaves. Protests poured in from across the Confederacy, and North Carolina's legislators condemned the law. Its defenders argued, however, that exemption preserved order and aided food production, and the statute remained on the books.

This Twenty Negro law is indicative of the racial fears many Confederates felt as the war threatened to overturn southern society. But it also fueled desertion and stimulated Unionism in nonslaveholding regions of the South. In Jones County, Mississippi, a wooded area with few slaves or plantations, Newt Knight, a Confederate soldier, led renegades who took over the county, declared allegiance to the Union, and called their district the Free State of Jones. They held out for the remainder of the war as an enclave of Union sympathizers.

The bitterness of letters to Confederate officials suggests the depth of the dissension and class anger. One woman swore to the secretary of war that, unless help was provided to poverty-stricken wives and mothers, "an allwise god . . . will send down his fury . . . [on] those that are in power."

WARTIME NORTHERN ECONOMY AND SOCIETY

War brought change in the North as well. Factories and citizens' associations geared up to support the war, and the federal government and its executive branch gained new powers. Idealism and greed flourished together, and the northern economy proved its awesome productivity. Unlike the South, northern farms and factories weathered the war unharmed.

Northern Business, Industry, and Agriculture

At first the war was a shock to business. Northern firms lost southern markets, and many companies changed their products and found new customers. Southern debts became uncollectible, jeopardizing northern merchants and western banks. In farming regions, families struggled with an aggravated labor shortage caused by army enlistments. Cotton mills lacked cotton, construction declined, and shoe manufacturers sold few of the cheap shoes that planters bought for slaves. Some businesses never recovered.

Certain entrepreneurs, such as wool producers, benefited from shortages of competing products, and soaring demand for war-related goods swept some businesses to new success. The Treasury issued $3.2 billion in bonds and paper money called greenbacks, and the War Department spent over $360 million in revenues from new taxes, including the first income tax. Government contracts soon totaled more than $1 billion.

Secretary of War Edwin M. Stanton's list of the supplies needed by the Ordnance Department indicates the scope of government demand: "7,892 cannon, 11,787 artillery carriages, 4,022,130 small-arms, . . . 1,022,176,474 cartridges for small-arms, 1,220,555,435 percussion caps, . . . 26,440,054 pounds of gunpowder, . . . and

90,416,295 pounds of lead." The government also purchased huge quantities of uniforms, boots, food, camp equipment, saddles, ships, and other necessities. War-related spending revived business in many northern states and saved Massachusetts shoe manufacturers from ruin.

The story of Jay Cooke, a wealthy New York financier, best illustrates the wartime partnership between business and government. Cooke earned hefty commissions marketing government bonds to finance the war. But the financier's profit served the Union cause, as the interests of capitalism and government merged in American history's first era of big government.

War aided heavy industries in the North as well, especially iron and steel production. Although new railroad construction slowed, the manufacture of rails actually increased with demand for repairs. Of future significance was the railroad industry's adoption of a standard gauge (width) for track, which created a unified transportation system.

The northern economy also grew because of a complementary relationship between agriculture and industry. Wartime recruitment and conscription gave western farmers an added incentive to purchase labor-saving machinery. The shift from human labor to machines created new markets for industry and expanded the food supply. Cyrus and William McCormick built an industrial empire in Chicago from the sale of their reapers. Between 1862 and 1864, the manufacture of mowers and reapers doubled to 70,000 yearly; by war's end, 375,000 reapers were in use, triple the number in 1861. Thus northern farm families whose breadwinners went to war did not suffer as much their counterparts in the South.

Northern Workers' Militancy

Northern industrial and urban workers did not fare as well. After the initial slump, jobs became plentiful, but inflation ate up much of a worker's paycheck. The price of coffee tripled; the price of rice and sugar doubled; and between 1860 and 1864, consumer prices rose at least 76 percent, while daily wages rose only 42 percent. Workers' families consequently suffered a substantial decline in their standard of living.

Industrial workers also lost job security. To increase production, some employers replaced workers with labor-saving machines. Others urged the government to promote immigration to secure cheap labor. Workers responded by forming unions and sometimes striking. Indeed, thirteen occupational groups—including tailors, coal miners, and railway engineers—formed national unions during the Civil War, and the number of strikes climbed.

Manufacturers viewed labor activism as a threat and formed statewide or craft-based associations to pool information. They shared blacklists of union members and required new workers to sign yellow dog contracts (promises not to join a union). To put down strikes, they hired strikebreakers from among blacks, immigrants, and women, and sometimes used federal troops.

Labor militancy, however, had little impact on employer profits or profiteering on government contracts. With an immense demand for army supplies, unscrupulous businessmen sold clothing and blankets made of "shoddy"—wool fibers reclaimed from rags or worn cloth. Shoddy goods often came apart in the rain; most of the shoes purchased early in the war were worthless. Contractors sold inferior guns for double the usual price and passed off tainted meat as good. Rampant corruption led to a year-long investigation by the House of Representatives.

Economic Nationalism and Government-Business Partnership

Legitimate enterprises also made healthy profits. The output of woolen mills increased so dramatically that industry dividends nearly tripled. Some cotton mills made record profits, even while reducing output. Brokerage houses earned unheard-of commissions. Railroads increased their business so much that railroad stocks skyrocketed.

Railroads were a leading beneficiary of government largesse. With southern representatives absent from Congress, the northern route of the transcontinental railroad prevailed. In 1862 and 1864, Congress chartered two corporations, the Union Pacific Railroad and the Central Pacific Railroad, and assisted them in connecting Omaha, Nebraska, with Sacramento, California. For each mile of track laid, the railroads received a loan of from $16,000 to $48,000 in government bonds plus 20 square miles of land along a free 400-foot-wide right of way. Overall, the two corporations gained approximately 20 million acres and nearly $60 million in loans.

Other businessmen benefited handsomely from the Morrill Land Grant Act (1862). To promote public education in agriculture, engineering, and military science, Congress granted each state thirty thousand acres of federal land for each of its congressional districts. The law eventually fostered sixty-nine colleges and universities, and early on enriched a few prominent speculators. Similarly, the Homestead Act of 1862 offered cheap and sometimes free land to people who would settle the West and improve their property.

Before the war, banks operating under state charters issued seven thousand different kinds of currency notes, which were difficult to distinguish from forgeries. During the war, Congress and the Treasury Department established a national banking system to issue national bank notes, and by 1865 most state banks were forced by a prohibitive tax to join the national system. This created sounder currency but also inflexibility in the money supply and an eastern-oriented financial structure.

In the excitement of wartime moneymaking, an eagerness to display one's wealth flourished in the largest cities. *Harper's Monthly* reported that "the men button their waistcoats with diamonds . . . and the women powder their hair with gold and silver dust." The *New York Herald* noted: "This war has entirely changed the American character. . . . The individual who makes the most money—no matter how—and spends the most—no matter for what—is considered the greatest man."

The Union Cause

In the first two years of the war, northern morale remained remarkably high for a cause that today may seem abstract—the Union—but at the time meant preservation of a social and political order that people cherished.

Secular and church leaders supported the Union, and many churches endorsed it as God's cause. One Methodist newspaper described the war as a contest between "equalizing, humanizing Christianity" and "disunion, war, selfishness, [and] slavery." Abolitionists campaigned to turn the war into a crusade against slavery. Free black communities and churches both black and white sent clothing, ministers and teachers to aid slaves who flocked to the Union lines. Indeed, thousands of northern blacks volunteered to join the war effort in spite of the initial rejection they received from the Lincoln administration. Thus in wartime northern society, materialism and greed flourished alongside idealism, religious conviction, and self-sacrifice.

Northern Women on Home Front and Battlefront

Northern women, like their southern counterparts, took on new roles. They organized over ten thousand soldiers' aid societies, rolled bandages, and raised $3 million for injured troops. Women pressed for the first trained ambulance corps in the Union Army, and they formed the backbone of the U.S. Sanitary Commission, a civilian agency recognized by the War Department in 1861, which provided nutritional and medical aid to soldiers. Although most of its officers were men, the bulk of the volunteers who ran its seven thousand auxiliaries were women. Women organized elaborate sanitary fairs all across the North to raise money and awareness for soldiers' health and hygiene.

Approximately 3,200 women also served as nurses in frontline hospitals. Yet women had to fight to serve; the professionalization of medicine since the Revolution created a medical system dominated by men, who often did not want women's aid. Even Clara Barton, famous for her working in the worst hospitals at the front, was ousted from her post in 1863. But women such as Dorothea Dix, who sought to reform asylums for the insane, and the Illinois widow Mary Ann Bickerdyke, who served in Sherman's army in the West, established a heroic tradition for Civil War nurses. They also advanced the professionalization of nursing, as several nursing schools were established in northern cities during or after the war.

Women also wrote sentimental war poetry, short stories, novels, and songs that reached thousands of readers in illustrated weeklies, monthly periodicals, and special story papers. In many stories, female characters seek recognition for their loyal service to the Union, while others probe the suffering and death of loved ones. Louisa May Alcott, arrived at her nursing job in Washington, D.C., after the horrific Union defeat at Fredericksburg in December 1862. From her six weeks' experience (she quit because of illness), she later wrote *Hospital Sketches* (1863), providing northern readers a view of the hospitals where loved ones agonized and perished.

By 1863 many women found the liberation of slaves an inspiring subject, as Julia Ward Howe did in her "Battle Hymn of the Republic": "As He died to make men holy/Let us die to make men free."

Walt Whitman's War

The poet Walt Whitman recorded his experiences as a volunteer nurse in Washington, D.C. As he dressed wounds and comforted suffering men, Whitman found "the marrow of the tragedy concentrated in those Army Hospitals." But he also found inspiration in such suffering and a deepening faith in American democracy. In "The Wound Dresser," Whitman meditated unforgettably on the deaths he witnessed:

On, on I go, (open doors of time! open hospital doors!)
The crush'd head I dress, (poor crazed hand tear not the bandage away,)

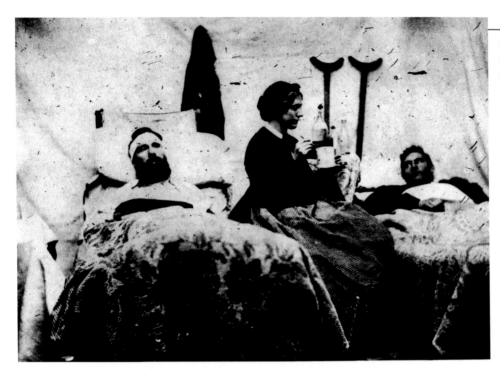

Nurse Anne Bell.
(U.S. Army Center of Military History)

The neck of the cavalry-man with the bullet through and through I examine,
Hard the breathing rattles, quite glazed already the eye, yet life struggles hard,
(Come sweet death! be persuaded O beautiful death! In mercy come quickly.)

Indeed, the scale of death in this war shocked many Americans into believing that
the conflict had to be for purposes larger than themselves.

THE ADVENT OF EMANCIPATION

Soldiers and civilians on both sides may have possessed fierce loyalty to their respective wartime cause, but the governments of the United States and the Confederacy
lacked clarity about the war's purpose. Throughout the war's early months, Davis
and Lincoln avoided references to slavery. Davis realized that emphasis on the issue
could increase class conflict in the South. Instead, he told southerners that they were
fighting for constitutional liberty: northerners betrayed the founders' legacy, and
southerners seceded to preserve it.

Lincoln had his reasons for avoiding slavery. It was crucial at first not to antag-
onize the Union's border slave states, whose loyalty was tenuous. Lincoln also
hoped that a pro-Union majority would assert itself in the South and help coax the
South back into the Union. And there were powerful political considerations. Some
Republicans burned with moral outrage over slavery; others were frankly racist,
dedicated to protecting free whites from the Slave Power and the competition of
cheap slave labor. No Republican or northern consensus on slavery existed early in
the war.

Lincoln and Emancipation

Lincoln's compassion, humility, and moral anguish during the war were evident in his speeches and writings. But as a politician, Lincoln distinguished between his convictions and his official acts. The latter were calculated for maximum advantage.

Many blacks attacked Lincoln furiously during the war's first year because of his refusal to convert the struggle into an abolition war. When Lincoln countermanded General John C. Frémont's order of liberation for slaves owned by disloyal masters in Missouri in September 1861, the *Anglo-African* declared that the president "hurls back into the hell of slavery thousands . . . rightfully set free." As late as July 1862, Frederick Douglass characterized administration policy as reconstruction of "the old union on the old and corrupting basis of compromise, by which slavery shall retain all the power that it ever had." Douglass wanted slavery destroyed and the Constitution rewritten in the name of human equality. Within a year, just such a profound result began to take place.

Lincoln first substantively broached the subject of slavery in March 1862, when he proposed that states consider emancipation. He asked Congress to promise aid to any state that emancipated, appealing especially to border state representatives. What Lincoln proposed was gradual emancipation, with compensation for slaveholders and colonization of freed slaves outside the United States.

Until well into 1864, Lincoln's administration promoted an impractical scheme to colonize 4.2 million freed slaves in Central America or the Caribbean. He was as yet unconvinced that America could become a biracial society, and he feared that white northerners might not support a war for black freedom. Black abolitionists vehemently opposed the Lincoln administration's machinations.

A group of congressional Republicans known as the Radicals—led by George Julian, Charles Sumner, and Thaddeus Stevens—dedicated themselves to a war for emancipation. They were instrumental in creating a special House-Senate committee on the conduct of the war, which investigated Union reverses, sought to improve wartime efficiency war effort, and prodded the president to take stronger measures against slavery.

Confiscation Acts

In August 1861, at the Radicals' instigation, Congress passed its first confiscation act. Designed to punish Confederates, the law confiscated all property used for "insurrectionary purposes." A second confiscation act (July 1862) confiscated the property of anyone who supported the rebellion, even those who merely resided in the South and paid Confederate taxes. Their slaves were declared "forever free of their servitude."

In summer 1862, Lincoln stood by his proposal of voluntary gradual emancipation and made no effort to enforce the second confiscation act. In protest, Horace Greeley, editor of the powerful *New York Tribune,* published an open letter to the president entitled "The Prayer of Twenty Millions." Greeley declared, "Mr. President, there is not one . . . intelligent champion of the Union cause who does not feel that all attempts to put down the Rebellion and at the same time uphold its inciting cause are preposterous and futile." Lincoln offered a calculated reply. He disagreed with those who would make slavery the paramount issue of the war and said,

"If I could save the Union without freeing any slave I would do it, and if I could save it by freeing all the slaves I would do it; and if I could save it by freeing some and leaving others alone I would also do that. What I do about slavery, and the colored race, I do because I believe it helps to save the Union."

But Lincoln had already decided to issue a presidential Emancipation Proclamation. He was waiting for a Union victory so it would not appear an act of desperation. The letter to Greeley was an integral part of Lincoln's approach to the future of slavery. Lincoln was concerned with conditioning public and international opinion for the coming social revolution.

Emancipation Proclamations

On September 22, 1862, shortly after Union success at the Battle of Antietam, Lincoln issued the first part of his two-part proclamation. Invoking his powers as commander-in-chief, he announced that on January 1, 1863, he would emancipate the slaves in the states "in rebellion" (those lacking legitimate representatives in the U.S. Congress by January). Thus his September 1862 proclamation was less a declaration of the right of slaves to be free than a threat to southerners: unless they put down their arms and returned to Congress, they would lose their slaves. Lincoln had little expectation that southerners would give up, but he carefully offered them the option.

In the fateful January 1, 1863, proclamation, Lincoln declared that "all persons held as slaves" in areas in rebellion "shall be then, thenceforward, and forever free." But he excepted every Confederate county or city that had fallen under Union control. Those areas, he declared, "are, for the present, left precisely as if this proclamation were not issued." Nor did Lincoln liberate slaves in the border slave states that remained in the Union. "The President . . . has proclaimed emancipation only where he has notoriously no power to execute it," charged the anti-administration *New York World*.

But Lincoln was worried about the constitutionality of his acts, and he anticipated that after the war, southerners might sue for restoration of their property. Making the liberation of the slaves "a fit and necessary war measure" raised a variety of legal questions: Would it expire with the suppression of a rebellion? The proclamation did little to clarify the status of freed slaves, but it did open the possibility of military service for blacks.

If as a legal document the Emancipation Proclamation was wanting, as a moral and political document it had great meaning. Because the proclamation defined the war as a war against slavery, congressional Radicals could applaud it. Yet at the same time it protected Lincoln's position with conservatives, enabling him to retreat and forcing no immediate changes on the border slave states.

Most important, though, thousands of slaves had already reached Union lines across the South. They voted with their feet for emancipation well before the proclamation. And now, every advance of federal forces into slave society was a liberating step.

Across the North and in Union-occupied sections of the South, blacks and their white allies celebrated the Emancipation Proclamation. At a large contraband camp in Washington, D.C., some six hundred black men, women, and children gathered at the superintendent's headquarters on New Year's Eve and sang through the night. In chorus after chorus of "Go Down, Moses," they announced the magnitude of their painful but beautiful exodus.

African American Recruits

The need for men soon convinced the administration to recruit northern and southern blacks for the Union Army. By the spring of 1863, African American troops were answering the call of a dozen or more black recruiters in northern cities and towns. Lincoln came to see black soldiers as "the great available and yet unavailed of force for restoring the Union."

African American leaders hoped that military service would secure equal rights for their people. Once the black soldier had fought for the Union, wrote Frederick Douglass, "there is no power on earth which can deny that he has earned the right of citizenship in the United States."

In June 1864, with thousands of former slaves in blue uniforms, Lincoln gave his support to a constitutional ban on slavery. On the eve of the Republican national convention, Lincoln called on the party to "put into the platform as the keystone, the amendment of the Constitution abolishing and prohibiting slavery forever." The party promptly called for the Thirteenth Amendment, which passed in early 1865 and went to the states for ratification. The war to save the Union had become a war to free the slaves.

Who Freed the Slaves?

It has long been debated whether Abraham Lincoln deserved the label (one he never claimed for himself) of Great Emancipator. Was Lincoln ultimately a reluctant emancipator, following rather than leading Congress and public opinion? Or did Lincoln give essential presidential leadership by going slow but, once moving, never backpedaling on black freedom? Once he focused on the unconditional surrender of the Confederates, Lincoln made slavery's destruction central to the war's purpose.

Others have argued, however, that the slaves were central in achieving their own freedom. When they were in proximity to war zones, slaves fled by the thousands. Some worked as camp laborers for the Union armies, and eventually more than 180,000 black men served in the Union Army and Navy. Some found freedom as individuals in 1861, and some not until 1865, as refugees trekking to contraband camps.

Nonetheless, emancipation was a historical confluence of a policy directed by and dependent on the military authority of the president; and the will and courage for self-emancipation. Wallace Turnage's escape in Mobile Bay in 1864 shows how emancipation could result from both a slave's own heroism and Union forces. Most blacks comprehended their freedom as given and taken, but also as their human right. "I now dreaded the gun and handcuffs . . . no more," recalled Turnage. "I could now speak my opinion . . . to men of all grades and colors."

A Confederate Plan of Emancipation

Before the war was over, the Confederacy, too, addressed emancipation. Late in the war Jefferson Davis was willing to sacrifice slavery to achieve independence. He proposed that the Confederate government purchase 40,000 slaves to work as army laborers, with a promise of freedom at the end of their service. He then called for the recruitment and arming of slaves as soldiers, who likewise would gain their freedom at war's end, as would their wives and children. Bitter debate over Davis's plan resounded through the Confederacy. When the Confederate Congress finally approved slave enlistments in March 1865, owners had to comply only on a voluntary basis. With manpower shortages, General Lee supported the idea of slave soldiers, while most Confederate slaveholders and editors vehemently opposed the enlistment plan. Supporters hoped to fight to a stalemate, achieve independence, and control the postwar racial order through their limited wartime emancipation schemes, but it was too late. By contrast, Lincoln's Emancipation Proclamation stimulated a vital infusion of forces into the Union armies; 134,000 former slaves (and 52,000 free blacks) fought for freedom and the Union. Their participation was pivotal in the northern victory.

THE SOLDIERS' WAR

Military service altered soldiers' lives. Enlistment submerged young men in large organizations whose military discipline ignored their individuality. It molded men on both sides so thoroughly that they came to resemble one another more than civilians back home. Many soldiers forged bonds with their fellows and a connection to a noble purpose that they cherished for years afterward.

Union soldiers may have sensed most clearly the massive scale of modern war. The average soldier was between eighteen and twenty-one, joining large armies with extensive bureaucracies. By late 1861 there were 640,000 volunteers, a stupendous increase over the regular army of 20,000 men.

Hospitals and Camp Life Soldiers benefited from certain new products, such as canned condensed milk, but blankets, clothing, and arms were often of poor quality. Hospitals were badly managed at first. Rules of hygiene in large camps were scarcely enforced. Water supplies were unsafe and typhoid common. About 57,000 men died from dysentery and diarrhea; 224,000 Union troops died from disease or accidents, double the 110,100 who died from battle. Confederate troops were less well supplied, and they had no sanitary commission. Still, an extensive hospital network, aided by white female volunteers and black female slaves, sprang up.

On both sides, troops quickly learned that soldiering was far from glorious. Fighting, wrote a North Carolina volunteer in 1863, taught him "the realities of a soldier's life.... Without time to wash our clothes or our persons ... the whole army became lousy more or less with body lice." Union troops skirmished against lice by boiling their clothes, but to little avail.

War soon exposed them to the blasted bodies of their friends and comrades. "It is a sad sight to see the dead and if possible more sad to see the wounded—shot in every possible way you can imagine."

Still, as campaigns dragged on, most soldiers who did not desert grew determined to see the struggle through. "We now, like true Soldiers go determined not to yield one inch," wrote a New York corporal. When at last the war was over, "it seemed like breaking up a family to separate," one man observed.

The Rifled Musket

Advances in technology made the Civil War particularly deadly. The most important were the rifle and the minié ball. Bullets fired from a smoothbore musket were not accurate at distances over eighty yards. Cutting spiraled grooves inside the barrel gave the projectile greater accuracy, but rifles remained difficult to use until the Frenchman Claude Minié and the American James Burton developed a new bullet that expanded on firing and flew accurately. With these bullets, rifles were deadly at four hundred yards and useful up to one thousand yards.

This meant that soldiers assaulting a position defended by riflemen were in greater peril. While artillery now fired from a safe distance, there was no substitute for the infantry assault or the popular turning movements aimed at an enemy's flank. Thus advancing soldiers exposed themselves repeatedly to accurate rifle fire. With only rudimentary medical knowledge, even minor wounds often led to amputation and death through infection. Never before in Europe or America had such massive forces pummeled each other with weapons of such destructive power.

The Black Soldier's Fight for Manhood

At the outset of the war, racism in the Union Army was strong. Most white soldiers wanted nothing to do with black people and regarded them as inferior. For many, acceptance of black troops grew only because they could do heavy labor and "stop Bullets as well as white people." A popular song celebrated "Sambo's Right to Be Kilt" as the only justification for black enlistments.

But white officers who volunteered to lead segregated black units to gain promotion found that experience altered their opinions. After one month with black troops, a white captain informed his wife, "I have a more elevated opinion of their abilities than I ever had before. I know that many of them are vastly the superiors of those . . . who would condemn them all to a life of brutal degradation." Black troops had a mission to destroy slavery and demonstrate their equality. "When Rebellion is crushed," wrote a black volunteer from Connecticut, "who will be more proud than I to say, 'I was one of the first of the despised race to leave the free North with a rifle on my shoulder.'" Corporal James Henry Gooding of Massachusetts's black Fifty-fourth Regiment explained that his unit intended "to live down all prejudice against its color, by a determination to do well in any position it is put."

Indeed, blacks and whites of the Fifty-fourth Massachusetts forged deep bonds. Just before the regiment launched its costly assault on Fort Wagner in Charleston harbor in July 1863, a black soldier called to abolitionist Colonel Robert Gould Shaw, who would perish that day, "Colonel, I will stay by you till I die." The Fort Wagner assault was celebrated for demonstrating the valor of black men, but this bloody chapter in the history of American racism also proved that black men had to die in battle to be acknowledged as men.

Such valor emerged despite persistent discrimination. Off-duty black soldiers were sometimes attacked by northern mobs; on duty, they did most of the heavy labor. The Union government, moreover, paid white privates $13 per month plus a clothing allowance of $3.50, whereas black privates earned only $10 per month less $3 for clothing. Outraged, several regiments refused to accept any pay, and Congress eventually remedied the inequity.

1863: THE TIDE OF BATTLE TURNS

The fighting in spring and summer of 1863 did not settle the war, but it suggested the outcome. The campaigns began in a deceptively positive way for Confederates, as Lee's army performed brilliantly in battles in central Virginia.

Battle of Chancellorsville

On May 2 and 3, west of Fredericksburg, Virginia, some 130,000 members of the Union Army of the Potomac bore down on fewer than 60,000 Confederates. Boldly, Lee and Stonewall Jackson divided their forces, ordering 30,000 men under Jackson on a day-long march westward to prepare a flank attack.

Arriving at their position in late afternoon, Jackson's seasoned foot cavalry found unprepared Union troops smoking and playing cards. The Confederate attack drove the right side of the Union Army back. Eager to press his advantage, Jackson rode forward with a few officers to study the ground. Returning at twilight, southern troops mistook them for federals and fired, fatally wounding their commander. The next day, Union forces left in defeat. Southern forces won at Chancellorsville, but it cost them Stonewall Jackson, who would remain a legend in Confederate memory.

Siege of Vicksburg

July brought crushing defeats for the Confederacy in two critical battles—Vicksburg and Gettysburg—that damaged Confederate hopes for independence. Vicksburg was the last major fortification on the Mississippi River in southern hands. General Ulysses S. Grant laid siege to Vicksburg in May, bottling up the defending army of General John Pemberton. If Vicksburg fell, Union forces would control the river, cutting the Confederacy in two and gaining an open path into its interior. To stave off such a result, Jefferson Davis put General Joseph E. Johnston in charge there and beseeched him to aid Pemberton. Meanwhile, General Robert E. Lee proposed a Confederate invasion of the North, which, though it would not relieve Vicksburg, could stun the North and possibly lead to peace. By invading the North a second time, Lee hoped to move from war-weary Virginia, garner civilian support in Maryland, win a vital victory on northern soil, threaten major cities, and thereby force a Union capitulation.

As Lee's emboldened army advanced through western Maryland and into Pennsylvania, Confederate prospects along the Mississippi darkened. Davis repeatedly wired General Johnston, urging him to attack Grant's army. Johnston, however, considered "saving Vicksburg hopeless." Grant's men, meanwhile, were supplying themselves from the abundant crops of the Mississippi River valley and could continue their siege indefinitely.

Battle of Gettysburg

On July 4, 1863, Vicksburg's commander surrendered. The same day, a battle that had been raging for three days concluded at Gettysburg, Pennsylvania (see Map 15.1). On July 1, Confederate forces hunting for a supply of shoes collided with the Union Army. Heavy fighting on the second day left federal forces in possession of high

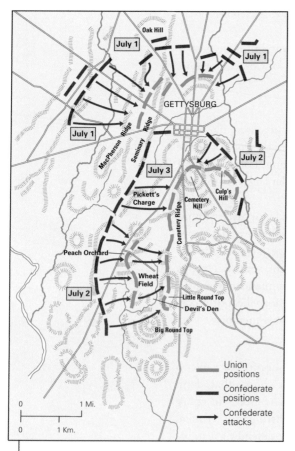

Map 15.1   Battle of Gettysburg

In the war's greatest battle, fought around a small market town in southern Pennsylvania, Lee's invasion of the North was repulsed. Union forces had the advantage of high ground, shorter lines, and superior numbers. The casualties for the two armies—dead, wounded, and missing—exceeded fifty thousand men.

ground along Cemetery Ridge, where they were shielded by a stone wall and had a clear view of their foe across almost a mile of open field.

Undaunted, Lee believed his reinforced troops could break the Union line, and on July 3 he ordered an assault. Virginians under General George E. Pickett and North Carolinians under General James Pettigrew marched up the slope in a doomed assault known as Pickett's Charge. They breached the enemy's line briefly, but most fell in heavy slaughter. On July 4 Lee withdrew, having suffered almost four thousand dead and about twenty-four thousand missing and wounded. The Confederate general blamed himself and offered to resign, but President Davis refused. The Confederacy had reached what many consider its high water mark at Gettysburg.

After Gettysburg and Vicksburg, the Confederacy was split; west of the Mississippi, General E. Kirby Smith had to operate on his own, independent of Richmond. Moreover, the heartland of Louisiana, Tennessee, and Mississippi lay exposed to invasion. Lee's northern defeat ended major southern offensive actions. Severely weakened, the Confederacy thenceforth relied on a prolonged defense. By wearing down northern morale, the South might yet win, but its prospects were darker than before.

DISUNITY: SOUTH, NORTH, AND WEST

Northern and southern governments waged the final two years of the war with increasing opposition at home. The gigantic costs of a civil war fed the unrest. But protest also arose from stresses in the regions' various social structures.

Union Occupation Zones

Wherever Union forces invaded, they imposed a military occupation consisting of three zones: garrisoned towns, with many troops in control of civilian and economic life; the Confederate frontier, areas still under southern control but with some federal military penetration; and no man's lands, regions between the two armies, beyond Confederate authority and under frequent Union patrols.

As many as one hundred southern towns were garrisoned, causing severe social disruption. Large sections of Tennessee, Virginia, Louisiana, Mississippi, and Georgia were occupied and suffered food shortages, crop and property destruction, disease, roadway banditry, guerrilla warfare, summary executions, and the random flow of escaped slaves. After two years of occupation, a southern white woman wrote to a kinsman about their native Clarksville, Tennessee: "It is nothing but a dirty hole filled . . . with niggers and Yankees."

Disintegration of Confederate Unity

Vastly disadvantaged in industrial capacity, natural resources, and labor, southerners felt the cost of the war more painfully than northerners. And internally, the southern class system threatened the Confederate cause.

Planters were increasingly opposed to their own government. Along with new taxation, Confederate military authorities impressed slaves to build fortifications. And when Union forces advanced, Confederate commanders burned cotton stores that lay in the enemy's path, enraging planters about such losses to their agricultural production and finances.

The increasing size and power of the Richmond government also alarmed planters. The Confederate constitution granted substantial powers to the central government, especially in war time. But many planters took the position articulated by R. B. Rhett, editor of the *Charleston Mercury,* that the Confederate constitution "leaves the States untouched in their Sovereignty, and commits to the Confederate Government only a few simple objects, and a few simple powers to enforce them."

Confused and embittered planters struck out at Jefferson Davis. Conscription, thundered Georgia's Governor James E. Brown, was "subversive of [Georgia's] sovereignty, and at war with all the principles for the support of which Georgia entered into this revolution." To frustrate the law, Brown ordered local enrollment officials not to cooperate with the Confederacy. Southern courts ultimately upheld Davis's power to conscript. Though Davis was devoted to southern independence, some of Davis's actions earned him the hatred of influential citizens.

Food Riots in Southern Cities

Widespread hunger and suffering sparked food riots in spring 1863 in Atlanta, Macon, Columbus, and Augusta, Georgia, and in Salisbury and High Point, North Carolina. On April 2 a crowd assembled in Richmond to demand relief. A passerby asked a young girl, "Is there some celebration?" "We are starving," replied the girl. "We are going to the bakeries and each of us will take a loaf of bread." That action fueled a riot that Davis ordered quelled at gunpoint.

Throughout the rural South, ordinary people resisted more quietly—by refusing to cooperate with conscription, tax collection, and impressments of food. Farmers who did provide food for the army refused to accept payment in certificates of credit or government bonds, as required by law. Conscription officers increasingly found no one to draft, and in some areas, tax agents were killed.

Austere and private by nature, Jefferson Davis was ill equipped to deal with such discontent. Often he buried himself in military affairs or administrative details. His class perspective also distanced him from common people's suffering. While his social circle in Richmond dined on duck and oysters, ordinary southerners went hungry. Failing to connect with plain folk, Davis thus lost their support.

Desertions from the Confederate Army

Such discontent affected the Confederate armies. Worried about their loved ones and resentful of what they saw as a rich man's war, large numbers of men abandoned the armies, supported by friends and neighbors. Mary Chesnut observed a man being dragged back to the army as his wife looked on. "Desert again, Jake!" she cried.

Desertion did not become a serious problem for the Confederacy until mid-1862, and stiffer policing solved the problem that year. But from 1863 on, the number of men on duty fell rapidly. By mid-1863, John A. Campbell, the South's assistant secretary of war, estimated that 40,000 to 50,000 troops were absent without leave and that 100,000 were evading duty. By November 1863, one-third of the army could not be accounted for.

The defeats at Gettysburg and Vicksburg dealt a heavy blow to Confederate morale. Desperate, President Davis and several state governors resorted to racial scare tactics to drive southern whites to further sacrifice. Defeat, Davis warned, would mean "extermination of yourselves, your wives, and children." Mississippi governor Charles Clark predicted "elevation of the black race to a position of equality—aye, of superiority, that will make them your masters and rulers."

Internal disintegration of the Confederacy quickened. A few newspapers began to call openly for peace. Similar proposals, presented as plans for independence on honorable terms, were made in several state legislatures. Confederate leaders were losing the people's support. It is remarkable how long and effectively the Confederacy sustained a military effort facing such internal division.

Antiwar Sentiment, South and North

In North Carolina, William W. Holden, a popular Democratic politician and editor, led a growing peace movement. Over one hundred public meetings supporting peace negotiations took place during summer 1863. In Georgia early in 1864, Governor Brown and Alexander H. Stephens, vice president of the Confederacy, led a similar effort. Ultimately, the lack of a two-party system made questionable the legitimacy of any government criticism.

In the 1863 congressional elections, secessionists and supporters of the administration lost seats to men not identified with the government. In the last years of the war, Davis's support in the Confederate Congress dwindled. Some newspaper editors and soldiers, especially in Lee's Army of Northern Virginia, kept the Confederacy alive despite disintegrating popular support.

By 1864 southerners everywhere were giving up the struggle. Deserters dominated whole towns and counties. Active dissent was particularly common in upland and mountain regions, where Union support always held fast.

Opposition to the war, though less extreme, existed in the North as well. Alarm intensified over the growing centralization of government. The draft sparked protest, especially among poor citizens, and the Union Army struggled with a troubling desertion rate. But with vast human resources, the Union government's effectiveness was never threatened. Fresh recruits were always available, especially after black enlistments in 1863.

Moreover, unlike Davis, Lincoln knew how to connect with ordinary citizens. The daily carnage, tortuous political problems, and ceaseless criticism weighed heavily on him, and he communicated his suffering in public letters to newspapers and private ones to soldiers' families. His moving words helped contain northern discontent, though they could not stop it.

Peace Democrats

Much of the wartime protest in the North was political. The Democratic Party fought to regain power by blaming Lincoln for the war's death toll, the expansion of federal powers, inflation, the high tariff, and the emancipation of blacks. Its leaders called for an end to the war and reunion on the basis of "the Constitution as it is and the Union as it was." Democrats denounced conscription and martial law and defended states' rights. They charged that Republican policies were designed to flood the North with blacks, depriving white males of their status, their jobs, and their women. In the 1862 congressional elections, Democrats made a strong comeback, with peace Democrats wielding influence in New York State and majorities in the legislatures of Illinois and Indiana.

Led by outspoken men like Representative Clement L. Vallandigham of Ohio, the peace Democrats became highly visible. Vallandigham criticized Lincoln as a dictator who suspended the writ of habeas corpus without congressional authority and arrested thousands of innocent citizens. He urged voters to depose King Abraham. Vallandigham's attacks seemed so damaging to the war effort that military authorities arrested him for treason. Lincoln wisely decided against punishment—and martyr's status—for the Ohioan and exiled him to the Confederacy. (Eventually Vallandigham returned to the North through Canada.)

Lincoln believed that antiwar Democrats were linked to secret organizations harboring traitorous ideas, and encouraged draft resistance, discouraged enlistment, sabotaged communications, and plotted to aid the Confederacy. Republicans sometimes branded them—and by extension the peace Democrats—as Copperheads, after the poisonous snake. Although Confederate agents were active in the North and Canada, they never genuinely threatened the Union war effort.

New York City Draft Riots

Although many soldiers risked their lives willingly, others sought to avoid service. Under the 1863 draft law, a draftee could stay home by providing a substitute or paying a $300 commutation fee. Many wealthy men chose these options, and with demand high, clubs, cities, and states provided the money for others to escape conscription. In all, 118,000 substitutes were provided and 87,000 commutations paid before Congress ended the commutation system in 1864.

Urban poor and immigrants in strongly Democratic areas were especially hostile to conscription. The North's poor viewed the system as discriminatory, and many immigrants suspected (wrongly, on the whole) that they were disproportionately called. (Approximately 200,000 men born in Germany and 150,000 born in Ireland served in the Union Army.)

As a result, enrolling officers received rough treatment in many northern areas, and riots occurred in New Jersey, Ohio, Indiana, Pennsylvania, Illinois, and Wisconsin. The most serious violence happened in New York City in July 1863. The war was unpopular there, and racial, ethnic, and class tensions ran high. Shippers had recently broken a longshoremen's strike by hiring black strikebreakers. Working-class New Yorkers feared an inflow of black labor from the South and regarded blacks as the cause of the war. Poor Irish resented being forced to serve in place of others who could afford to avoid the draft.

Military police officers were attacked first; then mobs crying, "Down with the rich" looted wealthy homes and stores. But blacks became the special target, as mobs ransacked African American neighborhoods, beating and murdering people in the streets and burning an orphan asylum. At least seventy-four people died during the three days of violence. Army units dispatched from Gettysburg ended this tragic event.

War Against Indians in the Far West

A civil war of another kind raged on the Great Plains and in the Southwest. By 1864 U.S. troops under the command of Colonel John Chivington waged full-scale war against the Sioux, Arapahos, and Cheyennes to eradicate Indian title to eastern Colorado. Indian chiefs sought peace, but American commanders had orders to "burn villages and kill Cheyennes." A Cheyenne chief, Lean Bear, was shot as he rode toward U.S. troops, holding papers he received from President Lincoln during a visit to Washington, D.C. Another chief, Black Kettle, was told by the U.S. command that his people would find safe haven in Sand Creek, Colorado. Instead, on November 29, 1864, 700 cavalrymen, many drunk, attacked the Cheyenne village. With many Indian men absent hunting, the slaughter at the Sand Creek Massacre included 105 Cheyenne women and children and 28 men. American soldiers scalped and mutilated victims, carrying women's body parts on their saddles or hats back to Denver.

In the New Mexico and Arizona Territories, an authoritarian and brutal commander, General James Carleton, waged war on the Apaches and the Navajos. For generations both tribes raided the region's Pueblo and Hispanic peoples to maintain their security and economy. During the Civil War years, Anglo-American farms also became Indian targets. In 1863 the New Mexico Volunteers, commanded by former mountain man Kit Carson, defeated the Mescalero Apaches and forced them onto a reservation at Bosque Redondo in the Pecos River valley.

But the Navajos resisted. Carson destroyed their livestock, orchards, and crops, causing the starving Navajos to surrender for food in January 1864. Three-quarters of the 12,000 Navajos were forced to march 400 miles (the Long Walk) to the Bosque Redondo Reservation, suffering malnutrition and death along the way. Permitted to return to a fraction of their homelands later in 1868, the Navajos never forgot the federal government's ruthless policies of removal and eradication of Indian peoples.

Election of 1864

Back east, war-weariness reached a peak in summer 1864, when the Democratic Party nominated popular general George B. McClellan for president and inserted a peace plank into its platform. Written by Vallandigham, it called for an armistice and spoke vaguely about preserving the Union. Democrats made racist appeals to white insecurity, calling Lincoln Abe the nigger-lover. No incumbent president had been reelected since 1832, and some Republicans worked to dump Lincoln from their ticket, favoring Salmon P. Chase or John C. Frémont, although little came of either effort.

With the fall of Atlanta and Union victories in the Shenandoah valley by early September, Lincoln's prospects rose. A decisive factor: eighteen states allowed troops to vote at the front. Lincoln received 78 percent of the soldier vote. With 55 percent of the popular vote, Lincoln's reelection—a referendum on the war and emancipation—crushed southern morale. Without this political outcome, a Union military victory and a redefined nation might never have happened.

1864–1865: THE FINAL TEST OF WILLS

The Confederates could still have won their version of victory in the war's final year if military stalemate and northern antiwar sentiment had forced a negotiated settlement. But northern determination prevailed.

Northern Diplomatic Strategy

From the outset, the North pursued one paramount goal: to prevent recognition of the Confederacy by European nations. Foreign recognition would belie Lincoln's claim that the United States was fighting an illegal rebellion and might lead to the financial and military aid that could ensure Confederate independence. Both England and France stood to benefit from a divided and weakened America. Thus, Lincoln and Secretary of State Seward needed to avoid serious military defeats and controversies with European powers.

Since the textile industry employed one-fifth of the British population, southerners banked on British recognition of the Confederacy. But at the beginning of the war, British mills had a 50 percent surplus of cotton, and they later found new supplies in India, Egypt, and Brazil. The British government flirted with recognition of the Confederacy but awaited southern battlefield successes. France was unwilling to act without Britain. Confederate agents purchased arms and supplies in Europe and obtained loans from European financiers, but they never achieved a diplomatic breakthrough.

An acute crisis occurred in 1861 when the overzealous commander of an American frigate stopped the British steamer *Trent* and moved two Confederate ambassadors, James Mason and John Slidell, to a Boston prison. The British interpreted the capture as a violation of freedom of the seas and demanded the prisoners' release. Lincoln and Seward waited until northern public opinion cooled before releasing them. The incident strained U.S.-British relations.

Then the sale to the Confederacy of warships constructed in England sparked protest from U.S. ambassador Charles Francis Adams. Over twenty-two months, the English-built ship, the *Alabama,* destroyed or captured more than sixty U.S. ships.

Battlefield Stalemate and a Union Strategy for Victory

On the battlefield, northern victory was far from won in 1864. General Nathaniel Banks's Red River campaign to capture more of Louisiana and Texas fell apart, and the capture of Mobile Bay in August did not cause the city to fall. Union general William Tecumseh Sherman soon brought total war to the southern heartland. On the eastern front during winter 1863–1864, the two armies in Virginia settled into a stalemate awaiting another northern spring offensive.

Military authorities have historically agreed that deep invasion is risky: the farther an army penetrates enemy territory, the more vulnerable its communications and

The Civil War in Britain

Because of the direct reliance of the British textile industry on southern cotton (cut off by the war), the American war was significant in Britain's economy and domestic politics. The British aristocracy and most cotton mill owners were pro-Confederate and proslavery, whereas clergymen, shopkeepers, artisans, and radical politicians worked for the causes of Union and emancipation. Most British workers saw their future at stake in a war for slave emancipation. Freedom to the huge British working class (who could not vote) meant basic political and civil rights, as well as secure jobs in an industrializing economy.

English aristocrats saw Americans as untutored and took satisfaction in America's troubles. Conservatives believed in the superiority of the British system of government and looked askance at America's leveling tendencies. And some aristocratic British Liberals sympathized with the Confederacy's demand for order and independence. English racism also intensified, exemplified by the popularity of minstrelsy and the employment of science in racial theory.

The British propaganda war over the American conflict was intensely debated: public meetings organized by both sides were huge affairs, with competing banners, carts and floats, orators, and resolutions. In a press war the British argued over when rebellion is justified, whether secession was right or legal, whether slavery was at the heart of the conflict, and especially over the democratic image of America. This bitter debate became a test of reform in Britain: those eager for a broadened franchise and increased democracy there were pro-Union, and those who preferred Britain's class-ridden political system favored the Confederacy.

The nature of the internal British debate was symbolized by the dozens of African Americans who served as pro-Union agents in England. The most popular was William Andrew Jackson, Confederate president Jefferson Davis's former coachman, who escaped from Richmond in September 1862. At British public meetings, Jackson countered pro-Confederate arguments that the war was not about slavery.

In the end, the British government did not recognize the Confederacy, and by 1864 English cotton lords found new sources in Egypt and India. But in this link between America and its English roots at its time of greatest travail, we can see the Civil War's international significance.

KING COTTON BOUND;
OR, THE MODERN PROMETHEUS.

Some southern leaders pronounced that cotton was king and would bring Britain to their cause. This British cartoon shows King Cotton brought down in chains by the American eagle, anticipating the cotton famine to follow and the intense debate in Great Britain over the nature and meaning of the American Civil War.
(The Granger Collection, New York)

supply lines become. Moreover, observed the Prussian expert Karl von Clausewitz, if the invader encounters a truly national resistance, his troops will be "everywhere exposed to attacks by an insurgent population."

General Grant, by now in command of the entire federal army, tested southern will with massive raids. Grant proposed to use armies to destroy Confederate railroads, thus ruining the enemy's transportation and economy. Union troops would live off the land while destroying resources useful to the Confederate military and to the civilian population. After General George H. Thomas's troops won the Battle of Chattanooga in November 1863, Georgia's heartland lay open. Grant entrusted General Sherman with 100,000 men for an invasion toward Atlanta's rail center.

Fall of Atlanta

Jefferson Davis positioned General Joseph E. Johnston's army in Sherman's path. Davis's political strategy for 1864 was to demonstrate Confederate military strength and defend Atlanta. When General Johnston slowly but steadily fell back toward Atlanta, Davis anxiously sought assurances that Atlanta would be held. From a military viewpoint, Johnston maneuvered skillfully. But when Johnston fell silent and continued to retreat, Davis replaced him with the one-legged General John Hood, who knew his job was to fight.

Hood attacked but was beaten, and Sherman's army occupied Atlanta on September 2, 1864. The victory buoyed northern spirits and ensured Lincoln's reelection. Davis exhorted southerners to fight on. Hood's army marched north to cut Sherman's supply lines and force him to withdraw, but Sherman marched sixty thousand of his men to the sea (see Map 15.2).

Sherman's March to the Sea

Sherman's army was formidable, composed almost entirely of battle-tested veterans and officers who rose through the ranks from the midwestern states. Before the march, army doctors weeded out men who were weak or sick. Although many harbored racist attitudes, most now supported emancipation because, as one said, "Slavery stands in the way of putting down the rebellion."

As Sherman's men moved across Georgia, they cut a path 50 to 60 miles wide and more than 200 miles long. The destruction they caused was awesome; indeed, it was Sherman's campaign that later prompted historians to deem this the first modern total war. A Georgia woman described the Burnt Country this way: "The fields were trampled down and the road was lined with carcasses of horses, hogs, and cattle that the invaders, unable either to consume or to carry with them, had wantonly shot down to starve our people."

After reaching Savannah in December, Sherman marched his armies into the Carolinas. To soldiers, South Carolina was the root of secession. They burned and destroyed as they marched, encountering little resistance. The opposing army of General Johnston was small, but Sherman's men should have faced guerrilla raids and attacks by local defense units. The absence of both led South Carolina's James Chesnut Jr. (a politician and the husband of Mary Chesnut) to write that

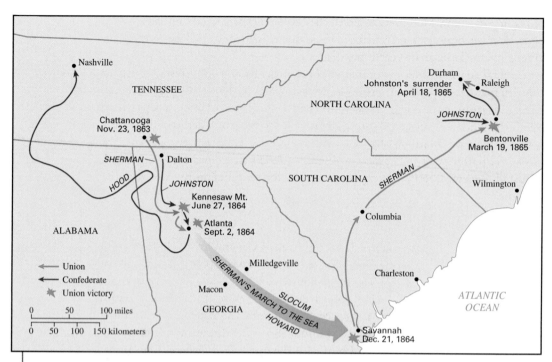

Map 15.2   Sherman's March to the Sea

The Deep South proved a decisive theater at the end of the war. From Chattanooga, Union forces drove into Georgia, capturing Atlanta. Following the fall of Atlanta, General Sherman embarked on his march of destruction through Georgia to the coast and then northward through the Carolinas.

his state "was shamefully and unnecessarily lost." Southerners lost the will to continue.

In Georgia, as many as nineteen thousand slaves followed the marauding Union troops. Others remained on the plantations to await the war's end, because of either wariness of whites or negative experiences with federal soldiers. The destruction of food harmed slaves along with white rebels, and many blacks lost livestock, clothing, crops, and other valuables to their liberators.

Virginia's Bloody Soil   Throughout spring and summer 1864, intent on capturing Richmond, Grant hurled his troops at Lee's army and suffered appalling losses: almost eighteen thousand casualties in the Battle of the Wilderness, more than eight thousand at Spotsylvania, and twelve thousand in only a few hours at Cold Harbor.

Before the assault at Cold Harbor, Union troops pinned scraps of paper bearing their names and addresses to their backs, certain they would be mowed down as they rushed Lee's trenches. In four weeks in May and June, Grant lost as many men as were enrolled in Lee's entire army. From early May until July, when Union forces fought from forests west of Fredericksburg to Petersburg, south of Richmond, the two armies engaged each other nearly every day. Wagon trains carrying thousands of Union wounded crawled back toward Washington.

Undaunted, Grant kept up the pressure. Although costly, these battles enabled eventual victory: Lee's army shrank until offensive action was no longer possible, while Grant's army kept replenishing itself with new recruits. The siege of Petersburg, with the armies facing each other in miles of trenches, lasted throughout winter 1864–1865.

Surrender at Appomattox

With the numerical superiority of Grant's army now greater than two to one, Confederate defeat was inevitable. On April 2, 1865, Lee abandoned Richmond and Petersburg. On April 9, he surrendered at Appomattox Court House. Grant treated his rival respectfully and paroled the defeated troops, allowing cavalrymen to keep their horses. Within weeks, Johnston surrendered to Sherman in North Carolina, and Davis, who had fled Richmond, was captured in Georgia. The war was over; the North rejoiced, and most southerners fell into despair.

Lincoln lived to see but a few days of the war's aftermath. On the evening of April 14, he accompanied his wife to Ford's Theatre in Washington. There, John Wilkes Booth, an embittered southern sympathizer, shot the president in the head at point-blank range. Lincoln died the next day. Twelve days later, troops tracked down and killed Booth. Relief at the war's end mingled with a renewed sense of loss and anxiety about the future.

Financial Tally

U.S. loans and taxes during the conflict totaled almost $3 billion, and interest on the war debt was $2.8 billion. The Confederacy borrowed over $2 billion but lost far more in the destruction of homes, crops, livestock, and other property. Union troops looted factories and put two-thirds of the South's railroad system out of service.

THE FUNERAL OF PRESIDENT LINCOLN, NEW YORK, APRIL 25TH 1865.
PASSING UNION SQUARE.
The magnificent Funeral Car was drawn by 16 gray horses richly caparisoned with ostrich plumes and cloth of black trimmed with silver bullion.

The death of President Lincoln caused a vast outpouring of grief in the North. As this Currier and Ives print shows, his funeral train stopped at several cities on its way to Illinois, to allow local services to be held.
(Anne S.K. Brown Military Collection, Brown University Library)

Estimates of the total cost of the war exceed $20 billion—five times the total expenditures of the federal government from its creation until 1861. By 1865 the federal government's spending soared to twenty times the prewar level and accounted for over 26 percent of the gross national product. Many changes were more or less permanent, as wartime measures left the government deeply involved in manufacturing, banking, and transportation.

Death Toll

More men died in the Civil War than in all other American wars combined until Vietnam. The total number of casualties exceeded 1 million—frightfully high for a nation of 31 million people. Approximately 360,000 Union soldiers died, 110,000 of them from battle wounds. Another 275,175 Union soldiers were wounded but survived. On the Confederate side, an estimated 260,000 lost their lives, and almost as many suffered wounds. Of an estimated 194,743 northerners in southern prisons, 30,218 died; of 214,865 southerners in northern prisons, 25,976 died. The prison story fueled mutual accusations for decades over starvation and brutal treatment.

Summary

The Civil War altered American society forever. Although precise figures are unavailable, it appears that 700,000 to 800,000 men served in the Confederate armies. Far more, possibly 2.3 million, served in the Union armies. All were taken from home and family; their lives, if they survived, were permanently altered. During the war, northern and southern women took on new roles to support the war effort.

Industrialization and economic enterprises grew exponentially with the war. Ordinary citizens' futures were increasingly tied to huge organizations. Under Republican leadership, the federal government expanded its power to preserve the Union and extend freedom. A social revolution and government authority emancipated the slaves.

It was unclear at war's end how or whether the nation would use its power to protect former slaves' rights. The war left many unanswered questions: How would white southerners, embittered and impoverished, respond to efforts to reconstruct the nation? How would the country care for the maimed, the orphans, the farm widows? What would be the place of black men and women in America?

In the West, a second civil war resulted in a conquest of southwestern Indians by U.S. troops and land-hungry settlers. On the diplomatic front, the Union government managed to keep Great Britain and other foreign powers out of the war. Dissent played a crucial role in the Confederacy's collapse, where the Union was only marginally affected by sabotage and draft riots.

In the Civil War, Americans underwent a dramatic transformation. White southerners experienced defeat that few other Americans ever faced. Blacks were moving proudly but anxiously from slavery to freedom. White northerners were self-conscious victors in a massive war for the nation's existence and for new definitions of freedom. The war would leave a compelling memory in American hearts and minds for generations.

"Big Government"

In 1995 President Bill Clinton declared that "the era of big government is over." Before him, President Ronald Reagan achieved considerable political success denouncing big-government programs. Whether the federal government ought to be the agent of social change, citizen welfare, and legal protection has been among the most polarizing questions in American political culture since at least the New Deal of the 1930s. But when did big government really begin?

One answer is with the Lincoln administration and Republican policies during the Civil War. Facing the demands of war, Republicans created an activist federal government, rooted in the harmony of interests among capitalism, free labor, and government power. Indeed, with agricultural legislation, an income tax, land grant colleges, higher tariffs, the Homestead Act, and railroad subsidies, the federal government permanently entered the nation's economy.

The powers of the federal government and the president grew steadily during the crisis. In one striking exercise of executive power, Lincoln suspended the writ of habeas corpus for everyone living between Washington, D.C., and Philadelphia. The president sought to ensure the loyalty of Maryland, which surrounded the capital on three sides. Later, with congressional approval, Lincoln repeatedly suspended habeas corpus and invoked martial law. Between fifteen and twenty thousand U.S. citizens were arrested on suspicion of disloyal acts and speech. Through such measures Lincoln expanded the powers of wartime presidents.

Above all, the Emancipation Proclamation and the Union military's prosecution of a war to destroy slavery was the most aggressive use of federal power. The Republicans' push for the Thirteenth Amendment to abolish slavery also stood as evidence of the advance of federal over state authority.

Today, Lincoln's legacy is richly controversial because of his exercise of such power. His admirers have honored him for his vision in taking the nation to a new birth of freedom in the crucible of total war. But critics have attacked him as the great centralizer, the father of big government. Ironically, twenty-first-century conservative Republicans crave the mantle of the party of Lincoln while denouncing the activist, regulatory government that Lincoln championed. As long as Americans debate the size and function of their federal government, they are replaying a chief Civil War legacy.

Chapter Review

AMERICA GOES TO WAR, 1861–1862

How did the North's naval victories trigger a revolution in slave society?

As federal gunboats drew near the South Carolina coast, planters fled their land. Confederate soldiers were unable to round up slaves, who, in their hopes that this signaled their freedom, broke cotton gins, stole clothing and furniture from masters' homes, and ran away to join the Union army. While the Union at first did not acknowledge the slaves as free, it did put them to work for the Union army.

WAR TRANSFORMS THE SOUTH

What happened to the South's embrace of state sovereignty during the war?

State power ultimately succumbed to a central authority. To maintain the war effort, the Confederacy centralized its operations, troops, and supplies, seeing the efforts of individual states as likely to fragment the greater cause. President Jefferson Davis took a firm leadership role toward the Confederate Congress and urged state governments to require farmers to switch from cash crops to food production. The central government assumed control of the southern economy and nearly complete control of the railroads. The Southern bureaucracy ironically became larger than its northern counterpart and provided new opportunities for women to work in government jobs.

WARTIME NORTHERN ECONOMY AND SOCIETY

How did the war affect workers in the North?

While many businesses weathered the initial slump and saw profits soar, northern industrial and urban workers enjoyed more job opportunities and higher wages but saw inflation devour much of their earnings. Consumer price hikes were nearly twice the rate of workers' salary increases, and workers' families saw their standard of living decline. Industrial workers were often replaced by labor-saving machines or cheap immigrant workers. While workers in several industries often went out on strike, manufacturers responded with blacklists or by requiring workers to sign "yellow dog" contracts promising not to join a union.

THE ADVENT OF EMANCIPATION

Why did Lincoln and Davis both avoid discussing slavery in the early days of the war?

Davis feared that the issue would increase class conflict in the South and preferred to point out that they were fighting to preserve their constitutional liberties against northerners. Lincoln avoided the topic of slavery to keep from antagonizing the Union's border states, whose loyalty he sought. He also hoped to inspire a pro-Union majority in the South that might bring the region back to the Union. Avoiding the topic was also politically expedient, since no Republican or northern consensus on slavery existed early in the war. When Lincoln first addressed emancipation in March 1862, he proposed gradual emancipation with payment for slaveholders and colonization for freed slaves outside the United States. Even the Emancipation Proclamation only promised freedom to slaves within confederate borders and exempted confederate cities that had fallen to Union control.

THE SOLDIERS' WAR

What changed white military leaders' minds about black soldiers?

Simply witnessing the bravery and determination of black units was enough to change white officers' opinions of the segregated black units they led. Black soldiers, too, felt they were fighting prejudice by their actions and proving their legitimate claim to freedom. In truth, black soldiers' willingness to die in battle was what earned the respect of white men. Many black and white soldiers who fought together did forge deep ties, especially those of the ill-fated 54th Massachusetts regiment.

1863: THE TIDE OF BATTLE TURNS

What turned the tide of war toward Union victory?

Battles at Vicksburg and Gettysburg changed the course of war from a possible Confederate victory to one assured for the Union. Vicksburg was the last major fortification on the Mississippi River in southern hands, while Gettysburg marked Lee's attempts to break the Union line and invade the North. Both battles produced heavy losses, but also left the Confederate army divided, so that west of the Mississippi General E. Kirby Smith operated alone, while Louisiana, Tennessee, and Mississippi were vulnerable to invasions. After Gettysburg, there were no more Confederate offensive moves; severely weakened, the Confederate army could only act defensively.

DISUNITY: SOUTH, NORTH, AND WEST

What were the causes of wartime dissent in the South?

Class divisions in the South fueled opposition to Confederate authority and its wartime operations. Planters opposed new taxation and the impressments of their slaves to build fortifications. They also disliked the fact that Confederate commanders burned planters' cotton stores as Union soldiers advanced. In addition, they rejected the increasing size and power of the central government in Richmond and conscription for military service. Outside the planter class, many people refused to comply with conscription, taxation, or the demand to provide food for soldiers. The ability of wealthy people to buy their way out of military service by hiring substitutes fueled resentment among soldiers, some of whom abandoned the army.

1864–1865: THE FINAL TEST OF WILLS

Why was it so crucial to northern military strategy that Europe remain neutral during the Civil War?

Lincoln felt that if foreign countries recognized the Confederacy, it would legitimize what Lincoln considered to be an illegal rebellion. He also feared it could lead to military and financial aid that would facilitate a Confederate victory and its ultimate independence. The president knew that both England and France would gain by a divided America, but France would not act without Britain, and Britain wasn't making a move until there were major southern battlefield successes. While England's relationship with southern textile mills made the confederacy hopeful for an alliance, Britain's large cotton surplus and new supplies in India, Egypt, and Brazil kept them from doing more than selling arms and supplies or offering loans.

SUGGESTIONS FOR FURTHER READING

Stephen V. Ash, *When the Yankees Came: Conflict and Chaos in the Occupied South* (1995)

Edward L. Ayers, *In the Presence of Mine Enemies: War in the Heart of America, 1859–1863* (2002)

Ira Berlin et al., eds., *Freedom: A Documentary History of Emancipation, 1861–1867*, 3 vols. (1979–1982)

David W. Blight, *Frederick Douglass' Civil War: Keeping Faith in Jubilee* (1989)

Alice Fahs, *The Imagined Civil War: Popular Literature of the North and South* (2001)

Drew G. Faust, *Mothers of Invention: Women of the Slaveholding South in the Civil War* (1996)

William W. Freehling, *The South vs. the South* (2001)

Gary W. Gallagher, *The Confederate War* (1997)

Bruce Levine, *Confederate Emancipation: Southern Plans to Free and Arm Slaves During the Civil War* (2006)

James M. McPherson, *Battle Cry of Freedom: The Civil War Era* (1987)

Philip S. Paludan, *"A People's Contest": The Union and the Civil War* (1989)

Heather Cox Richardson, *The Greatest Nation on Earth: Republican Economic Policies During the Civil War* (1997)

Reconstruction: An Unfinished Revolution

CHAPTER 16

1865–1877

CHAPTER OUTLINE

Wartime Reconstruction

The Meanings of Freedom

Johnson's Reconstruction Plan

The Congressional Reconstruction Plan

Reconstruction Politics and Economy in the South

Retreat from Reconstruction

> **LINKS TO THE WORLD:**
> The Grants' Tour
> of the World

Summary

> **LEGACY FOR A PEOPLE
> AND A NATION:** The Lost
> Cause

The lower half of secession's seedbed, Charleston, South Carolina, lay in ruin when most of the white population evacuated on February 18, 1865. A prolonged bombardment by Union forces around Charleston harbor destroyed many of the low-country planters' town homes. Fires broke out everywhere, ignited in bales of cotton stockpiled in public squares. To many observers, the flames were the funeral pyres of a dying civilization.

The Union's Twenty-first U.S. Colored Regiment received Charleston's surrender from its mayor. For black Charlestonians, most of whom were former slaves, this was a time to celebrate freedom and rebirth. The city's freedpeople converted Confederate ruin into a vision of Reconstruction based on Union victory and black liberation.

During the war's final year, the Confederates transformed the planters' Race Course, a horseracing track, and its famed Jockey Club, into a prison. Kept outdoors in the middle of the track, 257 Union soldiers died of exposure and disease and were buried in a mass grave behind the judges' stand. After the city fell, in April more than twenty black workmen reinterred the dead in marked graves. On the archway over the cemetery's entrance they painted the inscription Martyrs of the Race Course.

On May 1, 1865, ten thousand people marched around the planters' Race Course, led by three thousand children carrying roses and singing "John Brown's Body." Black women with baskets of flowers and wreaths, came next and then black men. The parade concluded with black and white Union regiments and white missionaries and teachers. At the gravesite, five black ministers read from Scripture, and a black children's choir sang "America," "We'll Rally 'Round the Flag," "The Star-Spangled

This icon will direct you to interactive activities and study materials on A People And A Nation, Brief Edition
website: **www.cengage.com/history/norton/ peoplenationbrief8e**

Chronology

1865	Johnson begins rapid and lenient Reconstruction.	**1871**	Congress passes the second Enforcement Act and Ku Klux Klan Act.
	Confederate leaders regain power.		Treaty with England settles the *Alabama* claims.
	White southern governments pass restrictive black codes.	**1872**	Amnesty Act frees almost all remaining Confederates from restrictions on holding office.
	Congress refuses to seat southern representatives.		Grant is reelected.
	Thirteenth Amendment, abolishing slavery, is ratified.	**1873**	*Slaughter-House* cases limit the power of the Fourteenth Amendment.
1866	Congress passes the Civil Rights Act and renewal of the Freedmen's Bureau over Johnson's veto.		Panic of 1873 leads to widespread unemployment and labor strife.
	Congress approves the Fourteenth Amendment.	**1874**	Democrats win a majority in the House of Representatives.
	Most southern states reject the Fourteenth Amendment.	**1875**	Several Grant appointees are indicted for corruption.
	In *Ex parte Milligan* the Supreme Court reasserts its influence.		Congress passes a weak Civil Rights Act.
1867	Congress passes the First Reconstruction Act and Tenure of Office Act.		Democratic Party increases control of the southern states with white supremacy campaigns.
	Seward arranges the purchase of Alaska.	**1876**	*U.S. v. Cruikshank* further weakens the Fourteenth Amendment.
	Constitutional conventions called in the southern states.		Presidential election is disputed.
1868	House impeaches and Senate acquits Johnson.	**1877**	Congress elects Hayes president.
	Most southern states readmitted to the Union under the Radical plan.		"Home rule" returns to three remaining southern states not yet controlled by Democrats; Reconstruction is considered over.
	Fourteenth Amendment is ratified.		
	Grant is elected president.		
1869	Congress approves the Fifteenth Amendment (ratified in 1870).		

Banner," and Negro spirituals. When the ceremony ended, the crowd retired to the Race Course for speeches, picnics, and military festivities.

African Americans founded this Decoration Day—now Memorial Day—as a day to remember those who perished in the war. In their vision, it was the Independence Day of a Second American Revolution.

The Civil War and its aftermath wrought unprecedented changes in American society, law, and politics, but the underlying realities of economic power, racism, and judicial conservatism limited Reconstruction's revolutionary potential. The nation had to determine the nature of federal-state relations, whether confiscated land could be redistributed, and how to bring justice to freedpeople and aggrieved white southerners. Americans also had to heal psychologically from a bloody and fratricidal war. How they negotiated the relationship between healing and justice would determine the extent of change during Reconstruction.

The turmoil wrought by Reconstruction was most evident in national politics, as Lincoln's successor, Andrew Johnson, fought with Congress over Reconstruction policies. Although a southerner, Johnson disliked the South's wealthy planters, and his early moves suggested that he would be tough on "traitors." By late 1865, however, Johnson became the protector of southern interests. Jefferson Davis stayed in prison for two years, but Johnson pardoned other rebel leaders and allowed them to occupy high offices. He also ordered plantations returned to the original owners, including the abandoned coastal lands of Georgia and South Carolina on which forty thousand freed men and women settled early in 1865, by order of General William Tecumseh Sherman.

Johnson imagined a rapid restoration of the South to the Union rather than the fundamental reconstruction that Republican congressmen favored. Between 1866 and 1868, the president and the Republican leadership in Congress battled over how to put the United States back together again. Before it ended, Congress impeached the president and enfranchised freed men and gave them a role in reconstructing the South. The nation also adopted the Fourteenth and Fifteenth Amendments, ensuring equal protection of the law, citizenship, and universal manhood suffrage. But the cause of equal rights for African Americans fell almost as fast as it had risen.

By 1869 the Ku Klux Klan employed extensive violence to thwart Reconstruction and undermine black freedom. As white Democrats in the South took over state governments, they encountered little opposition. Moreover, the wartime industrial boom created new opportunities and priorities. The West, with its seemingly limitless potential and its wars against Indians, drew American resources as never before. Political corruption became a nationwide scandal, and bribery a way of doing business.

The white South's desire to reclaim control of its states and of race relations overwhelmed the national interest in stopping it. Thus Reconstruction became a revolution eclipsed, leaving legacies with which the nation has struggled ever since.

- Should the Reconstruction era be considered the Second American Revolution? By what criteria should we make such a judgment?
- What were the origins and meanings of the Fourteenth Amendment in the 1860s? What is its significance today?
- Reconstruction is judged to have ended in 1877. Over the course of the 1870s, what caused its end?

WARTIME RECONSTRUCTION

Reconstruction of the Union was an issue in 1863, well before the war ended. Specifically, four vexing problems compelled early thinking and would haunt the Reconstruction era. First, who would rule in the South once it was defeated? Second, who would rule in the federal government—Congress or the president? Third, what were the dimensions of black freedom, and what rights under law would freed men enjoy? And fourth, would Reconstruction be a preservation of the old republic or a second revolution, inventing a new republic?

Lincoln's 10 Percent Plan

Abraham Lincoln had never been antisouthern. His worst fear was that the war would collapse into guerrilla warfare by surviving bands of Confederates. Lincoln insisted on leniency for southern soldiers once they surrendered. In his Second Inaugural Address, delivered a month before his assassination, Lincoln promised "malice toward none; with charity for all."

Lincoln planned early for a swift and moderate Reconstruction process. In his 1863 Proclamation of Amnesty and Reconstruction, he proposed to replace majority rule with "loyal rule" to reconstruct southern state governments, and to pardon ex-Confederates except the highest-ranking military and civilian officers. Once 10 percent of a given state's voting population in the 1860 general election had taken an oath to the United States and established a government, the new state would be recognized. Lincoln did not consult Congress in these plans, and "loyal" assemblies (known as Lincoln governments) were created in Louisiana, Tennessee, and Arkansas in 1864, states largely occupied by Union troops on which they depended for survival.

Congress and the Wade-Davis Bill

Congress responded with hostility to Lincoln's moves to readmit southern states quickly. Led by Pennsylvania's Thaddeus Stevens in the House and Massachusetts's Charles Sumner in the Senate, Radical Republicans were strong proponents of emancipation and aggressive prosecution of the war and now proposed a longer and harsher Reconstruction. Stevens advocated a conquered provinces theory, arguing that southerners organized as a foreign nation to make war on the United States. They, therefore, must be treated as conquered foreign lands and returned to the status of unorganized territories before their readmission could be entertained.

In July 1864, the Wade-Davis bill, sponsored by Ohio senator Benjamin Wade and Maryland congressman Henry W. Davis, emerged from Congress with three specific conditions for southern readmission.

1. There had to be a majority of white male citizens participating in the creation of a new government.
2. To vote or be a delegate to constitutional conventions, men had to take an iron-clad oath declaring that they never aided the Confederate war effort.
3. All officers above the rank of lieutenant and all civil officials in the Confederacy would be disfranchised and deemed "not a citizen of the United States."

Lincoln pocket-vetoed the bill and issued a conciliatory proclamation that he would not be inflexibly committed to any one plan of Reconstruction.

This exchange occurred when the war's outcome and Lincoln's reelection were still in doubt. On August 5, Radical Republicans issued the "Wade-Davis Manifesto" to newspapers, accusing Lincoln of usurpation of presidential powers and disgraceful leniency toward an eventually conquered South. Lincoln saw Reconstruction as a means of weakening the Confederacy and winning the war; the Radicals saw it as a transformation of the nation's political and racial order.

Thirteenth Amendment

In early 1865, Congress and Lincoln joined in two important measures that recognized slavery's centrality to the war. On January 31, Congress passed the Thirteenth Amendment, which first, abolished involuntary servitude and second, declared that Congress shall have the power to enforce this outcome by appropriate legislation. When the measure passed by 119 to 56, just 2 votes more than the necessary two-thirds, Congress rejoiced.

The Thirteenth Amendment emerged from congressional debate and considerable petitioning and public advocacy. One of the first and most remarkable petitions for a constitutional amendment abolishing slavery was submitted in 1864 by Elizabeth Cady Stanton, Susan B. Anthony, and the Women's Loyal National League. Women throughout the Union accumulated thousands of signatures. It was a long road from the Emancipation Proclamation to the Thirteenth Amendment, through treacherous constitutional theory about individual property rights, beliefs that the sacred document (the Constitution) ought never be altered, and partisan politics.

Freedmen's Bureau

On March 3, 1865, Congress created the Bureau of Refugees, Freedmen, and Abandoned Lands—the Freedmen's Bureau, an unprecedented federal agency of social uplift. With thousands of refugees in the South, the government continued what private freed men's aid societies started in 1862. In its four-year existence, the Freedmen's Bureau supplied food and medical services, built several thousand schools and some colleges, negotiated several hundred thousand employment contracts between freed men and their former masters, and tried to manage confiscated land.

The bureau was a controversial aspect of Reconstruction. Southern whites hated it, and politicians divided over its constitutionality. Some bureau agents were devoted to freed men's rights; others exploited the chaos of the postwar South. The war prompted an eternal question of republics: what are the social welfare obligations of the state toward its people, and what do people owe their governments in return? Apart from conquest and displacement of the eastern Indians, Americans were inexperienced at the Freedmen's Bureau's task—social reform through military occupation.

Ruins and Enmity

In 1865, with the war's devastation, America was a land with ruins. Some of its cities lay in rubble; large stretches of the southern countryside were depopulated and defoliated; and thousands of people, white and black, were refugees. Many white refugees faced starvation. Of the approximately 18,300,000 rations distributed across the South in the first three years of the Freedmen's Bureau, 5,230,000 went to whites.

In October 1865, after a five-month imprisonment in Boston, former Confederate vice president Alexander H. Stephens rode a train southward. When he reached northern Georgia, his native state, he expressed shock: "War has left a terrible impression. . . . Fences gone, fields all a-waste, houses burnt." A northern journalist visiting Richmond that fall observed a city "mourning for her sins . . . in dust and ashes." Every northern traveler experienced hatred from white southerners. A North Carolina innkeeper told a journalist that Yankees killed his sons, burned his house, and stole his slaves and left him "one inestimable privilege . . . to hate 'em."

THE MEANINGS OF FREEDOM

Black southerners entered life after slavery with hope and circumspection. A Texas man recalled his father's telling him, "Our forever was going to be spent living among the Southerners, after they got licked." Often the changes freed men and women valued most were personal—alterations in employer or living arrangements.

The Armed Slave, William Sprang, oil on canvas, c. 1865. This remarkable painting depicts an African American veteran soldier, musket with fixed bayonet leaning against the wall, cigar in hand indicating a new life of safety and leisure, and reading a book to demonstrate his embrace of education and freedom. The man's visage leaves the impression of satisfaction and dignity. (Civil War Museum of Philadelphia)

The Feel of Freedom

For America's former slaves, Reconstruction meant a chance to explore freedom. Former slaves remembered singing into the night after federal troops, who confirmed rumors of their emancipation, reached their plantations. A few people gave in to the desire to do what was forbidden before. One angry grandmother dropped her hoe and confronted her mistress with, "I'm free! Ain't got to work for you no more!" Another man recalled that he and others "started on the move," either to search for family members or just to start fresh.

As slaves they learned to expect hostility from white people; they did not presume it would instantly disappear. Many freedpeople evaluated potential employers carefully. After searching for better circumstances, a majority of blacks eventually settled as agricultural workers on their former farms or plantations. But they relocated their houses and tried to control the conditions of their labor.

Reunion of African American Families

Throughout the South, former slaves focused on reuniting their families, separated during slavery by sale or hardship and during the war by dislocation and emancipation. By relying on the black community for help and by placing ads in black newspapers well into the 1880s, some succeeded, while others searched in vain.

Husbands and wives who belonged to different masters could finally establish homes together and raise their own children. When her old master claimed a right to whip her children, a mother informed him that "he warn't goin' to brush none of her chilluns no more." Freed men and women were tired of punishment.

Blacks' Search for Independence

Many black people wanted to minimize contact with whites because, as Reverend Garrison Frazier told General Sherman in January 1865, "There is a prejudice against us . . . that will take years to get over." As such, blacks abandoned slave quarters and fanned out to distant corners of the land they worked. Some described moving "across the creek" or building a "saplin house . . . back in the woods." Other rural dwellers established small, all-black settlements that still exist along the South's back roads.

Freedpeople's Desire for Land

In addition to a fair employer, freed men and women most wanted to own land, which represented self-sufficiency and compensation for generations of bondage. General Sherman's special Field Order Number 15, issued in February 1865, set aside 400,000 acres in the Sea Islands for exclusive settlement by freedpeople. Hope swelled among ex-slaves as forty-acre plots and mules were promised. But President Johnson ordered them removed in October and the land returned to its original owners under army enforcement. The U.S. government eventually sold thousands of acres in the Sea Islands, 90 percent of which went to wealthy northern investors.

Most members of both political parties opposed land redistribution to the freed men. Even northern reformers who administered the Sea Islands during the war showed little sympathy for black aspirations. The former Sea Island slaves wanted to establish small, self-sufficient farms. Northern soldiers, officials, and missionaries of both races brought education and aid to the freed men but also insisted that they grow cotton. They emphasized profit, cash crops, and competitive capitalism.

Black Embrace of Education

Blacks hungered for education that previously belonged only to whites. With freedom, they started schools, and on log seats and dirt floors, freed men and women studied in old almanacs and discarded dictionaries. Young children brought infants to school with them, and adults attended at night or after "the crops were laid by." Despite their poverty, many blacks paid tuition, typically $1 or $1.50 a month—which constituted major portions of a person's agricultural wages and totaled more than $1 million by 1870.

In its brief life, the Freedmen's Bureau founded over four thousand schools, and northern reformers established others through private philanthropy. The Yankee schoolmarm—selfless and religious—became an agent of progress in many southern communities. By 1877, more than 600,000 African Americans broke with their past by enrolling in elementary school.

Blacks and their white allies also established colleges and universities to train teachers, ministers, and future leaders. The American Missionary Association founded seven colleges, including Fisk and Atlanta Universities, between 1866 and 1869. The Freedmen's Bureau helped establish Howard University in Washington, D.C., and northern religious groups, such as the Methodists, Baptists, and Congregationalists, supported seminaries and teachers' colleges.

During Reconstruction, African American leaders were often highly educated members of the prewar elite of free people of color. Francis Cardozo, who held various offices in South Carolina, attended universities in Scotland and England. P. B. S. Pinchback, who became lieutenant governor of Louisiana, was the son of a planter who sent him to school in Cincinnati.

Growth of Black Churches

Freed from slavery's restrictions, blacks could build their own institutions. The secret churches of slavery came into the open; in communities throughout the South, ex-slaves started a *brush arbor*—a shelter with leaves for a roof, where freed men and women worshiped.

Within a few years, independent branches of the Methodist and Baptist denominations attracted most black Christians in the South. By 1877 in South Carolina, the African Methodist Episcopal (A.M.E.) Church had one thousand ministers, forty-four thousand members and a school of theology, while the A.M.E. Zion Church had forty-five thousand members. In these churches, some of which became the wealthiest and most autonomous institutions in black life, freedpeople created enduring communities.

Rise of the Sharecropping System Since most former slaves lacked money to buy land, they preferred the next best thing: renting. But the South had few sources of credit, and few whites would rent to blacks.

Consequently, black farmers and white landowners turned to sharecropping, a system in which a landlord or merchant furnished food and supplies, such as draft animals and seed, to farmers who worked the land. The owners and merchants were repaid with part of the crops. Although landowners tried to set the laborers' share at a low level, sharecroppers would resist or move from year to year. As the system matured during the 1870s and 1880s, most sharecroppers worked on *halves*—half for the owner and half for themselves.

The sharecropping system, which materialized as early as 1868, originated as a compromise between former slaves and white landowners. It eased landowners' problems with cash and credit and provided a permanent, dependent labor force; blacks accepted it because it freed them from daily supervision. But sharecropping proved to be a disaster. Owners and merchants developed a monopoly over the agricultural economy, as sharecroppers faced ever-increasing debt.

The fundamental problem was that southern farmers still concentrated on cotton. In freedom, black women often stayed away from cotton picking to concentrate on domestic chores, especially given the diminishing incentives of the cotton system. By 1878 the South recovered its prewar share of British cotton purchases. But even as southerners grew more cotton, their reward diminished. Cotton prices began a long decline, as world demand fell off.

Thus southern agriculture slipped into depression. Black sharecroppers struggled under growing debt which bound them to landowners and to furnishing merchants almost as oppressively as slavery had bound them to masters. Many white farmers gradually lost their land and became sharecroppers. By the end of Reconstruction, over one-third of all southern farms were worked by sharecropping tenants, white and black.

JOHNSON'S RECONSTRUCTION PLAN

Many people expected President Andrew Johnson's Reconstruction policies to be harsh. Throughout his career in Tennessee he criticized wealthy planters and championed small farmers. When an assassin's bullet thrust Johnson into the presidency, former slaveowners feared their treatment in Johnson's hands. When northern Radicals suggested the exile or execution of ten or twelve leading rebels, Johnson replied, "How are you going to pick out so small a number?"

Andrew Johnson of Tennessee

Like Lincoln, Johnson moved from obscurity to power. With no formal education, he became a tailor's apprentice. But from 1829, while in his twenties, he held nearly every office in Tennessee politics: alderman, state representative, congressman, two terms as governor, and U.S. senator by 1857. Although elected as a Democrat, Johnson was the only senator from a seceded state who refused to leave the Union. Lincoln appointed him war governor of Tennessee in 1862, hence his symbolic place on the ticket in the president's 1864 bid for reelection.

Although a Unionist, Johnson's political beliefs made him an old Jacksonian Democrat. Before the war, he supported tax-funded public schools and homestead legislation, fashioning himself as a champion of the common man. Johnson advocated limited government and was an ardent states' rightist. His philosophy toward Reconstruction may be summed up his slogan: "The Constitution as it is, and the Union as it was."

Through 1865 Johnson alone controlled Reconstruction policy; Congress recessed before he became president in April and did not reconvene until December. Johnson formed new state governments in the South by using his power to grant pardons and extended easy terms to former Confederates.

Johnson's Racial Views

Johnson had owned house slaves, although he was not a planter. He accepted emancipation but did not believe that black suffrage could be imposed on a southern state by the federal government; this set him on a collision course with the Radicals. Johnson was a thoroughgoing white supremacist. He declared in his annual message of 1867 that blacks possessed less "capacity for government than any other race of people. . . . Wherever they have been left to their own devices they have shown a constant tendency to relapse into barbarism."

Such racial views affected Johnson's policies. Where whites were concerned, however, Johnson proposed rules that would keep the wealthy planter class at least temporarily out of power.

Johnson's Pardon Policy

White southerners were required to swear an oath of loyalty to gain amnesty, but Johnson barred from the oath former federal officials, high-ranking Confederate officers, and political leaders or graduates of West Point or Annapolis who joined the Confederacy. He also added ex-Confederates whose taxable property was worth more than $20,000. These individuals had to apply to the president for pardon. The president, it seemed, sought revenge on the old planter elite and the promotion of a new yeoman leadership.

Johnson appointed provisional governors, who began the Reconstruction process by calling state constitutional conventions. The delegates had to draft new constitutions that eliminated slavery and invalidated secession. After ratification, new governments could be elected, and states would be restored to the Union. But only southerners who had taken the oath of amnesty and were eligible to vote on the day the state seceded could participate. Thus unpardoned whites and former slaves were ineligible.

Presidential Reconstruction	The old white leadership proved resilient; prominent Confederates won elections and turned up in appointive offices. Then Johnson started pardoning planters and

leading rebels. By September 1865, hundreds of pardons were issued in one day. These pardons, plus the return of planters' abandoned lands, restored the old elite to power and made Johnson seem the South's champion.

Why did Johnson allow the planters to regain power? He may have enjoyed turning proud planters into pardon seekers. He also sought a rapid Reconstruction to deny the Radicals an opportunity for more thorough racial and political changes in the South. Plus, Johnson needed southern support in the 1866 elections; hence, he declared Reconstruction complete only eight months after Appomattox. In December 1865, many Confederate congressmen claimed seats in the U.S. Congress, including former Confederate vice president Alexander Stephens, who was now Georgia's senator-elect.

Black Codes	Furthermore, to define the status of freed men and women and control their labor, some legislatures substituted the word *freedmen* for *slaves* in the old slave codes.

These new black codes compelled former slaves to carry passes, observe a curfew, and live in housing provided by a landowner. Vagrancy laws and restrictive labor contracts bound freedpeople to plantations, and antienticement laws punished anyone luring these workers to other employment. State-supported schools and orphanages excluded blacks.

It seemed to northerners that the South was intent on returning African Americans to servitude and that Johnson's Reconstruction policy held no one responsible for the war. Thus the Republican majority in Congress halted Johnson's plan, and the House and Senate did not admit newly elected southern representatives. Instead, they challenged the president's authority and established a joint committee to investigate a new direction for Reconstruction.

THE CONGRESSIONAL RECONSTRUCTION PLAN

The Constitution mentioned neither secession nor reunion, but it gave Congress the primary role in admitting states. Moreover, the Constitution declared that the United States shall guarantee to each state a "republican form of government." This provision, legislators believed, gave them the authority to devise Reconstruction policies.

The key question: What had rebellion done to the relationship between southern states and the Union? Congressmen who favored vigorous Reconstruction measures argued that the war had broken the Union and that the South was subject to the victor's will. Moderate congressmen held that states forfeited their rights through rebellion and thus came under congressional supervision.

The Radicals	Northern Democrats, weakened by their opposition to the war in its final year, denounced racial equality and supported Johnson's policies. Conservative Republicans,

despite their party loyalty, favored a limited federal role in Reconstruction. Although a minority, the Radical Republicans, led by Thaddeus Stevens, Charles Sumner, and George Julian, sought to democratize the South, establish public education, and ensure freedpeople's rights. They favored black suffrage and some land confiscation and redistribution and were willing to exclude the South from the Union for years to achieve their goals.

The Radicals brought a new civic vision to American life; they wanted to create an activist federal government and the beginnings of racial equality. A large group of moderate Republicans, led by Lyman Trumbull, opposed Johnson's leniency but wanted to restrain the Radicals. They were, however, committed to federalizing the enforcement of civil, if not political, rights for the freedmen.

With the 1866 elections looming, Johnson and the Democrats sabotaged the possibility of a conservative coalition by refusing to cooperate with conservative or moderate Republicans. They insisted that Reconstruction was over, that the new state governments were legitimate, and that southern representatives should be admitted to Congress. The Radicals' influence grew with Johnson's intransigence.

Congress Versus Johnson

Republicans believed they reached a compromise with Johnson in spring 1866 in which Johnson would modify his program by extending the Freedmen's Bureau for another year and passing a civil rights bill to counteract the black codes. This would force southern courts to practice equality under scrutiny of the federal judiciary. Its

In 1866, as Congress reviewed the progress of Reconstruction, news from the South had a considerable impact. Violence against black people, like the riot in Memphis depicted here, helped convince northern legislators that they had to modify President Johnson's policies. (Library of Congress)

provisions applied to public, not private, acts of discrimination. The Civil Rights Bill of 1866 was the first statutory definition of the rights of American citizens.

Johnson, however, vetoed both bills; they became law when Congress overrode his veto. Because the civil rights bill defined U.S. citizens as native-born persons who were taxed, Johnson claimed that it discriminated against "large numbers of intelligent, worthy, and patriotic foreigners . . . in favor of the negro."

All hope of presidential-congressional cooperation was dead. In 1866 newspapers reported daily violations of blacks' rights in the South and carried alarming accounts of antiblack violence. In Memphis, forty blacks were killed and twelve schools burned by white mobs, and in New Orleans, the toll was thirty-four African Americans dead and two hundred wounded. Violence convinced Republicans and the northern public that more needed to be done. A new Republican plan focused on the Fourteenth Amendment to the Constitution.

Fourteenth Amendment

Of the five sections of the Fourteenth Amendment, the first would have the greatest legal significance. It conferred citizenship on "all persons born or naturalized in the United States" and prohibited states from abridging their constitutional "privileges and immunities" (see the appendix for the Constitution and all amendments). It also barred states from taking a person's life, liberty, or property "without due process of law" and from denying "equal protection of the laws." These phrases have become powerful guarantees of African Americans' civil rights and the rights of all citizens, except Indians, who were not granted citizenship rights until 1924.

Republicans almost universally agreed on the amendment's second and third sections. The fourth declared the Confederate debt null and void and guaranteed the United States' war debt. Northerners rejected paying taxes to reimburse those who financed a rebellion, and business groups agreed on the necessity of upholding the U.S. government's credit. The second and third sections barred Confederate leaders from holding state and federal office. Only Congress, by a two-thirds vote of each house, could remove the penalty, thereby guaranteeing some punishment for Confederate leaders.

The second section of the amendment also dealt with representation and embodied the compromises that produced the document. Northerners disagreed about whether blacks should have the right to vote. In truth, public will, North and South, lagged behind the amendment's egalitarian spirit. Many northern states still maintained black disfranchisement laws during Reconstruction.

Emancipation ended the three-fifths clause for the purpose of counting blacks, which would have increased southern representation. Thus the postwar South stood to gain power in Congress, and if white southerners did not allow blacks to vote, former secessionists would derive the political benefit from emancipation. Consequently, Republicans determined that, if a southern state did not grant black men the vote, their representation would be reduced proportionally.

The Fourteenth Amendment specified for the first time that voters were male. As such, it damaged the women's rights movement. Advocates of women's equality worked with abolitionists for decades, often subordinating their cause to the slaves'. During the drafting of the Fourteenth Amendment, however, some leaders, such as

Elizabeth Cady Stanton and Susan B. Anthony, ended their alliance with abolitionists and fought for women, infusing new life into the women's rights movement. Other women activists, however, argued that it was "the Negro's hour." Many former male abolitionists, white and black, were willing to delay woman's suffrage to secure freed men the vote.

The South's and Johnson's Defiance

Johnson tried to block the Fourteenth Amendment. He urged state legislatures in the South to vote against ratification, and all but Tennessee rejected the amendment by a wide margin.

To present his case to northerners, Johnson organized a National Union Convention. He boarded a special train for a "swing around the circle" that carried his message into the Northeast, the Midwest, and then back to Washington. Increasingly, audiences rejected his views, jeering at him. Johnson handed out American flags with thirty-six rather than twenty-five stars, declaring the Union already restored, and he labeled the Radicals traitors for attempting to take over Reconstruction.

In the 1866 elections radical and moderate Republicans whom Johnson denounced won reelection by large margins, and the Republican majority grew to two-thirds of both houses of Congress. The North had spoken clearly: Johnson's policies of states' rights and white supremacy were giving the advantage to rebels and traitors. Thus Republican congressional leaders won a mandate to pursue their Reconstruction plan.

But nothing could be accomplished as long as the Johnson governments existed and the southern electorate remained exclusively white. Republicans resolved to form new state governments in the South and enfranchise the freed men.

Reconstruction Acts of 1867–1868

After embittered debate, the First Reconstruction Act passed in March 1867. This plan, under which the southern states were readmitted to the Union, incorporated only part of the Radical program. Union generals, commanding small garrisons and charged with supervising elections, assumed control in five military districts in the South (see Map 16.1). Confederate leaders designated in the Fourteenth Amendment were barred from voting until new state constitutions were ratified and freed men were guaranteed the right to vote. In addition, each southern state was required to ratify the Fourteenth Amendment and its new constitution by majority vote and submit that constitution to Congress for approval (see Table 16.1).

The Second, Third, and Fourth Reconstruction Acts, passed between March 1867 and March 1868, provided the details for voter registration boards, the adoption of constitutions, and the administration of good faith oaths by white southerners.

Failure of Land Redistribution

The Radicals halted Johnson, but they had hoped Congress could do much more. Thaddeus Stevens, for example, argued that economic opportunity was essential to the freedmen. He drew up a plan for extensive confiscation and redistribution of land, but it was never realized.

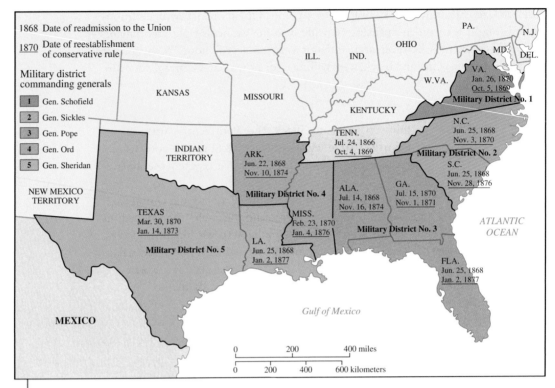

Map 16.1 The Reconstruction

This map shows the five military districts established when Congress passed the Reconstruction Act of 1867. As the dates within each state indicate, conservative Democratic forces quickly regained control of government in four southern states. So-called Radical Reconstruction was curtailed in most of the others, as factions within the weakened Republican Party began to cooperate with conservative Democrats.

TABLE 16.1 Plans for Reconstruction Compared

	Johnson's Plan	Radicals' Plan	Fourteenth Amendment	Reconstruction Act of 1867
Voting	Whites only can vote; high-ranking Confederate leaders must seek pardons.	Give vote to black males.	Southern whites may decide but can lose representation if they deny black suffrage.	Black men gain vote; whites barred from office by Fourteenth Amendment cannot vote while new state governments are being formed.
Officeholding	Many prominent Confederates regain power.	Only loyal white and black males are eligible.	Confederate leaders barred until Congress votes amnesty.	Fourteenth Amendment in effect.
Time Out of Union	Brief.	Several years; until South is thoroughly democratized.	Brief.	3–5 years after war.
Other Change in Southern Society	Little; gain of power by yeomen not realized; emancipation grudgingly accepted, but no black civil or political rights.	Expand public education; confiscate land and provide farms for freedmen; expansion of activist federal government.	Probably slight, depending on enforcement.	Considerable, depending on action of new state governments.

Racial fears and an American obsession with the sanctity of private property made land redistribution unpopular. Thus black farmers were forced to seek work in a hostile environment in which landowners opposed their acquisition of land.

Constitutional Crisis

To restrict Johnson's influence and safeguard its plan, Congress passed several controversial laws. First, it limited Johnson's power over the army by requiring the president to issue military orders through the general of the army, Ulysses S. Grant. Then Congress passed the Tenure of Office Act, which gave the Senate power to approve changes in the president's cabinet. Designed to protect Secretary of War Stanton, a Radical sympathizer, this law violated the tradition of presidents controlling cabinet appointments. All of these measures, along with the Reconstruction Acts, were passed by a two-thirds override of presidential vetoes.

In response, Johnson limited the power of military commanders in the South and increased the powers of the civil governments he created in 1865. Then he removed military officers who were enforcing Congress's new law, preferring commanders who allowed disqualified Confederates to vote. Finally, he tried to remove Secretary of War Stanton, pushing the confrontation to its climax.

Impeachment of President Johnson

Impeachment is a political procedure provided for in the Constitution as a remedy for crimes or serious abuses of power by presidents, federal judges, and other high government officials. Those who are impeached (judged or politically indicted) in the House are then tried in the Senate. Twice in 1867, the House Judiciary Committee considered impeachment of Johnson, first rejecting it and then recommending it by a 5-to-4 vote, which was defeated by the House. After Johnson tried to remove Stanton, however, a third attempt to impeach him carried in early 1868. The indictment concentrated on his violation of the Tenure of Office Act, though modern scholars regard his efforts to obstruct enforcement of the Reconstruction Act of 1867 as a more serious offense.

Johnson's trial in the Senate lasted more than three months. The prosecution, led by Radicals, attempted to prove that Johnson was guilty of "high crimes and misdemeanors." But they also argued that the trial was a means to judge Johnson's performance. The Senate rejected such reasoning, which could have made removal from office a political weapon against any chief executive who disagreed with Congress. The prosecution fell one vote short of the necessary two-thirds majority needed to convict Johnson. He remained in office, politically weakened.

Election of 1868

In the 1868 presidential election, Ulysses S. Grant, running as a Republican, defeated Horatio Seymour, a New York Democrat. Grant was not a Radical, but his platform supported congressional Reconstruction and endorsed black suffrage in the South. (Significantly, Republicans stopped short of endorsing black suffrage in the North.) The Democrats denounced Reconstruction and preached white supremacy, conducting the most openly racist campaign in American history. Both

A Republican Party brass band in action during the 1868 election campaign in Baton Rouge, Louisiana. The Union regimental colors and soldiers' caps demonstrate the strong federal presence in the South at this pivotal moment in radical Reconstruction.
(Andrew D. Lytle Collection, Louisiana and Lower Mississippi Valley Collections, LSU Libraries, Louisiana State University, Baton Rouge, Louisiana)

sides waved the "bloody shirt," blaming each other for the war's sacrifices. By associating with rebellion and Johnson's repudiated program, the Democrats were defeated in all but eight states, though the popular vote was close. Blacks voted en masse for General Grant.

In office Grant vacillated in dealing with the southern states, sometimes defending Republican regimes and sometimes currying favor with Democrats. Occasionally Grant called out federal troops to stop violence or enforce Congressional acts, but he never imposed a military occupation on the South. Rapid demobilization reduced a federal army of more than 1 million to fifty-seven thousand within a year of the surrender at Appomattox. Thereafter, the number of troops in the South declined until in 1874 there were only four thousand in southern states outside Texas. The legend of military rule, so important to southern claims of victimization during Reconstruction, was steeped in myth.

Fifteenth Amendment In 1869 the Radicals pushed through the Fifteenth Amendment, the final major measure in Reconstruction's constitutional revolution. It forbade states to deny the right to vote "on account of race, color, or previous condition of servitude." Such wording did not guarantee the right to vote and left states free to restrict suffrage on other grounds. Northern states could deny suffrage to women and certain men—Chinese immigrants, illiterates, and those too poor to pay poll taxes. With passage of the Fifteenth Amendment in 1870, many Americans, especially northerners, considered Reconstruction completed.

RECONSTRUCTION POLITICS AND ECONOMY IN THE SOUTH

From the start, white southerners resisted Reconstruction and opposed emancipation, as evident in the black codes. The former planter class proved especially unbending because of their tremendous financial loss in slaves. For many poor whites who never owned slaves, destitution, plummeting agricultural prices, disease, and the uncertainties of a growing urban industrialization drove them off land, toward cities, and into hatred of black equality.

White Resistance Some planters attempted to postpone freedom by denying or misrepresenting events. Former slaves reported that their owners didn't tell them it was freedom or wouldn't let them go. To hold onto their workers, some landowners claimed control over black children and used guardianship and apprentice laws to bind black families to the plantation. While a few planters divided up plots among their slaves, most condemned the notion of blacks as landowners.

Adamant resistance by whites soon manifested itself in other ways, including violence. A local North Carolina magistrate clubbed a black man on a public street, and in several states bands of Regulators terrorized blacks who displayed any independence. After President Johnson encouraged the South to resist congressional Reconstruction, many white conservatives captured the new state governments, while others boycotted the polls to defeat Congress's plans.

Black Voters and the Southern Republican Party Enthusiastically blacks went to the polls, voting Republican, as one man said, to "stick to the end with the party that freed me." Illiteracy did not keep them (or uneducated whites) from making intelligent choices. Mississippi's William Henry could read only "a little," but he said, "We saw D. Sledge vote; he owned half the county. We knowed he voted Democratic so we voted the other ticket so it would be Republican." Women, who could not vote, encouraged husbands and sons, and preachers exhorted congregations to use the franchise.

Thanks to a large black turnout and the restrictions on prominent Confederates, a new southern Republican Party came to power in the 1868–1870 constitutional conventions. Republican delegates consisted of a sizable black contingent (265 of the more than 1,000 delegates throughout the South), northerners who moved to the South, and native southern whites seeking change. The new constitutions they drafted were more democratic than anything previously adopted in the South. They eliminated property qualifications for voting and holding office, turned many appointed offices into elective posts, and provided for public schools and institutions to care for the mentally ill, the blind, the deaf, the destitute, and the orphaned.

The conventions broadened women's rights in property holding and divorce. Usually the goal was not equality but providing relief to thousands of suffering debtors. Since husbands usually contracted the debts, giving women legal control over their own property provided some protection for their families.

Triumph of Republican Governments

Under these new constitutions, southern states elected Republican-controlled governments. For the first time, state legislators in 1868 included black southerners. Contrary to what white southerners later claimed, Republican state governments did not disfranchise ex-Confederates as a group. James Lynch, a leading black politician from Mississippi, saw disfranchising whites as foolish. Landless former slaves "must be in friendly relations with the great body of the whites in the state," he explained. "Otherwise . . . peace can be maintained only by a standing army." Despised and lacking power, southern Republicans strove for safe ways to gain a foothold in a depressed economy.

Far from being vindictive toward the race that enslaved them, most southern blacks appealed to whites to be fair. Hence, the South's Republican Party condemned itself to defeat if white voters would not cooperate. Within a few years most fledgling Republican parties in the southern states would be struggling for survival against violent white hostility.

Industrialization and Mill Towns

Reconstruction governments promoted industry via loans, subsidies, and short-term exemptions from taxation. The southern railroad system was rebuilt and expanded, and coal and iron mining made possible Birmingham's steel plants. Between 1860 and 1880, the number of manufacturing establishments in the South nearly doubled.

This emphasis on big business, however, produced higher state debts and taxes, drew money away from schools and other programs, and multiplied possibilities for corruption. The alliance between business and government often operated at the expense of farmers and laborers. It also doomed Republicans to failure in building support among poorer whites.

Poverty remained the lot of many southern whites. The war caused a massive loss of income-producing wealth, such as livestock, and a steep decline in land values. From 1860 to 1880, the South's share of per capita income fell to 51 percent of the national average. In many regions the old planter class still had the best land and access to credit or markets.

As poor whites and blacks found farming less tenable, they moved to cities and mill towns. Industrialization did not sweep the South as it did the North, but it laid deep roots. Attracting textile mills to southern towns became a competitive crusade. In 1860 the South counted some 10,000 mill workers; by 1880, the number grew to 16,741; and by century's end to 97,559. Many poor southerners moved from farmer to mill worker or other low-income urban wage earner job.

Republicans and Racial Equality

Whites who controlled the southern Republican Party were reluctant to allow blacks a share of offices proportionate to their electoral strength. Aware of their weakness, black leaders did not push hard for revolutionary change. Instead, they led efforts to establish public schools, though without pressing for integrated facilities. In 1870 South Carolina passed the first comprehensive school law in the South. By 1875, 50 percent of that state's black school-age children were enrolled in school, and approximately one-third of the three thousand teachers were black.

Those African American politicians who did fight for civil rights and integration were typically from cities such as New Orleans or Mobile, where large populations of light-skinned free blacks existed before the war. Their experience made them sensitive to issues of status. Laws requiring equal accommodations were passed but often went unenforced.

Economic progress, particularly land ownership, was a major concern for most freedpeople. Land reform failed because in most states whites were the majority, and former slaveowners controlled the best land and financial resources. Much land did fall into state hands for nonpayment of taxes and was sold in small lots. But most freedmen had too little cash to bid against investors or speculators. Any widespread redistribution of land had to arise from Congress, which never supported such action.

Myth of Negro Rule

Within a few years, white hostility to congressional Reconstruction increasingly prevailed. Conservatives who long wanted to fight Reconstruction through economic pressure and racist propaganda began to do so. Charging that the South had been turned over to ignorant blacks, conservatives used black domination as a rallying cry for a return to white supremacy.

Such attacks were part of the growing myth of Negro rule, which would become a central theme in battles over the memory of Reconstruction. African Americans participated in politics but hardly dominated. They were a majority in only two of ten state constitutional conventions. In the state legislatures, only in South Carolina's lower house did blacks constitute a majority. Sixteen blacks won seats in Congress before Reconstruction was over. Only eighteen served in a high state office, such as lieutenant governor, treasurer, superintendent of education, or secretary of state, but none became governor.

Some four hundred blacks served in political office during the Reconstruction era, an enormous achievement. Elected officials, such as Robert Smalls in South Carolina, labored for cheaper land prices, better healthcare, access to schools, and the enforcement of civil rights. In this way, the black politicians of Reconstruction took heroic first steps in America's long civil rights movement.

Carpetbaggers and Scalawags

Conservative propaganda also assailed the allies of black Republicans. They denounced northern whites as *carpetbaggers*, greedy crooks planning to pour stolen tax revenues into their luggage made of carpet material.

In fact, most northerners who settled in the South had come seeking business opportunities, as schoolteachers, or to find a warmer climate; most never entered politics. Those who did generally wanted to democratize the South and introduce northern ways, such as industry and public education.

In addition to tagging northern interlopers as carpetbaggers, conservatives invented the term *scalawag* to discredit native white southerners cooperating with the Republicans, as many, including wealthy men, did. Most scalawags were yeoman farmers from mountain areas and nonslaveholding districts who were Unionists under the Confederacy. They hoped to benefit from the education and opportunities Republicans promoted. Sometimes joining with freed men, they pursued common class interests to make headway against long-dominant planters. Initially promising, over time most of these black-white coalitions floundered due to racism.

Tax Policy and Corruption as Political Wedges

Republicans wanted to repair the war's destruction, stimulate industry, and support such new ventures as public schools, all of which required tax monies. But the Civil War damaged the South's tax base. Hundreds of thousands of citizens lost much of their property—slaves, money, livestock, and buildings—to the war. Tax increases (sales, excise, and property) were necessary for even traditional services. Inevitably, Republican tax policies aroused strong opposition, especially among yeomen.

Corruption charges also plagued Republicans. Many carpetbaggers and black politicians engaged in fraudulent schemes or sold their votes, participating in what scholars recognize as a nationwide corruption surge in an age ruled by spoilsmen. Corruption crossed party lines, but the Democrats pinned the blame on unqualified blacks and greedy carpetbaggers among southern Republicans.

Ku Klux Klan

Republican leaders also allowed factionalism along racial and class lines to undermine party unity. At the same time, the Ku Klux Klan, a secret veterans' club that began in Tennessee in 1866, spread through the South, quickly becoming a terrorist organization. Klansmen sought to frustrate Reconstruction and keep the freed men in subjection with ongoing nighttime harassment, whippings, beatings, rapes, and murders.

Although the Klan tormented blacks, its main purpose was political. Lawless nightriders targeted active Republicans, killing leading whites and blacks in several states. After freed men who worked for a South Carolina scalawag started voting, terrorists visited the plantation and, as one victim noted, "whipped every . . . [black] man they could lay their hands on." Klansmen also attacked Union League clubs—Republican organizations that mobilized the black vote—and schoolteachers who aided freed men.

Specific social forces shaped and directed Klan violence, with Alamance and Caswell Counties in North Carolina receiving the worst of it. Slim Republican majorities there rested on cooperation between black voters and white yeomen. Together, these black and white Republicans ousted long-entrenched officials. The wealthy and powerful men who lost their accustomed political control were the Klan's county officers and local chieftains. By intimidation and murder, the Klan weakened the Republican coalition and restored a Democratic majority.

Klan violence injured Republicans across the South. One of every ten black delegates to the 1867–1868 state constitutional conventions was attacked, seven fatally. In one judicial district of North Carolina, the Ku Klux Klan was responsible for twelve murders, over seven hundred beatings, along with many cases of rape and arson. A single attack on Republicans in Eutaw, Alabama, left four blacks dead and fifty-four wounded. According to historian Eric Foner, the Klan "made it virtually impossible for Republicans to campaign or vote in large parts of Georgia."

Thus Republican mistakes, racial hostility, and terror brought down the Republican regimes. In most states, Radical Reconstruction lasted only a few years (see Map 16.1). The most enduring failure of Reconstruction, however, was that it did not alter the South's social structure or its distribution of wealth and power.

RETREAT FROM RECONSTRUCTION

During the 1870s, northerners lost the political will to sustain Reconstruction, as they confronted vast economic and social transformations in their region and the West. Radical Republicans like Albion Tourgée, a former Union soldier who moved to North Carolina and was elected a judge, condemned Congress's timidity. He and many African Americans believed that, during Reconstruction, the North "threw all the Negroes on the world without any way of getting along." As the North lost interest in the South's dilemmas, Reconstruction collapsed.

Political Implications of Klan Terrorism

Whites in the old Confederacy referred to this decline of Reconstruction as southern redemption. During the 1870s, "redeemer" Democrats claimed to be the South's saviors from alleged black domination and carpetbag rule, as the party regained control of the South.

Meanwhile, in 1870 and 1871 the Ku Klux Klan's violent campaigns forced Congress to pass two Enforcement Acts and an anti-Klan law. These laws made actions by individuals against the civil and political rights of others a federal criminal offense. They also provided for election supervisors and permitted martial law and suspension of the writ of habeas corpus to combat murders, beatings, and Klan threats. In 1872 and 1873, Mississippi and the Carolinas saw many prosecutions; but in other states, the laws were ignored. Southern juries sometimes refused to convict Klansmen; less than half of the 3,310 cases ended in convictions. Although many Klansmen fled their state to avoid prosecution, and the Klan officially disbanded, paramilitary organizations known as Rifle Clubs and Red Shirts often took the Klan's place.

Still, there were ominous signs that the North's commitment to racial justice was fading, as some influential Republicans opposed the anti-Klan laws. Rejecting other Republicans' arguments that the Thirteenth, Fourteenth, and Fifteenth Amendments made the federal government the protector of citizens' rights, dissenters charged that Congress was infringing on states' rights. This foreshadowed a general revolt within Republican ranks in 1872.

Industrial Expansion and Reconstruction in the North

Immigration and industrialization surged in the North. Between 1865 and 1873, 3 million immigrants entered the country, most settling in the industrial cities of the North and West. In that eight-year period, industrial production increased by 75 percent. For the first time, nonagricultural workers outnumbered farmers, and wage earners outnumbered independent craftsmen. Government policies encouraged this rapid growth, as low taxes on investment and high tariffs on manufactured goods helped create a new class of powerful industrialists, especially railroad entrepreneurs.

From 1865 to 1873, 35,000 miles of new track were laid; this fueled the banking industry and made Wall Street the center of American capitalism. Eastern railroad magnates, such as Thomas Scott of the Pennsylvania Railroad, created economic empires with the assistance of huge government subsidies of cash and land. Railroad corporations also bought up mining operations, granaries, and lumber companies. Big business now employed lobbyists to curry favor with government. Corruption ran rampant, with some congressmen and legislators paid retainers of major companies.

As captains of industry amassed unprecedented fortunes, gross economic inequality polarized American society. The workforce, worried a prominent Massachusetts business leader, was in a "transition state . . . living in boarding houses" and becoming a "permanent factory population." In New York and Philadelphia, workers increasingly lived in unhealthy tenement housing. Thousands would list themselves on the census as common laborer or general jobber. Concerned, in 1868 Republicans passed an eight-hour workday bill that applied to federal workers. The labor question (see Chapter 18) now preoccupied northerners far more than the southern or the freed men question.

Then the Panic of 1873 ushered in over five years of economic contraction. Three million people lost their jobs, especially in cities. Workers and farmers desperately needed cash and sought easy-money policies to spur economic expansion. Businessmen, disturbed by the strikes and industrial violence that accompanied the panic, defended property rights and demanded sound money policies. The chasm between wealthy industrialists and farmers and workers widened.

Liberal Republican Revolt

Disenchanted with Reconstruction, a largely northern group calling itself the Liberal Republicans bolted the party in 1872 and nominated Horace Greeley, editor of the New York Tribune, for president. A varied group, Liberal Republicans included foes of corruption and advocates of a lower tariff. Two popular and widespread issues united them: distaste for federal intervention in the South and an elitist desire to let market forces and the "best men" determine policy.

The Grants' Tour of the World

On May 17, 1877, two weeks after his presidency ended, Ulysses S. Grant and his wife Julia embarked from Philadelphia on a twenty-six month world tour. Portrayed as a private vacation, the trip was meant to help dissipate the taint of corruption in Grant's second term. The small entourage included John Russell Young, a reporter for the *New York Herald* who recorded the journey in the two-volume, illustrated *Around the World with General Grant*.

The Grants spent months in England attending an array of banquets, one with Queen Victoria. In Newcastle, thousands of workingmen conducted a massive parade in Grant's honor. Grant was viewed as the savior of the American nation, the liberator of slaves, and a celebrity.

Every royal or republican head of a European state hosted the Grants, including the heads of state of Belgium, France, Switzerland, Italy, Russia, Poland, Austria, and Spain. The Grants next went to Egypt and then traveled by train to the Indian Ocean, where they embarked for India. They encountered British imperialism in Bombay, and that of the French in Saigon. The grand excursion went to China and Japan. The Grants enjoyed a rare audience with Japan's Emperor Mutsuhito and found Japan "beautiful beyond description."

The Grants landed in San Francisco in late June 1879. The reason for the prolonged trip: Grant sought publicity abroad to convince his countrymen back home that they should reelect him president in 1880. But he developed no compelling reason why Americans should choose him again. He spent his final years a war hero and a national symbol. No American president would again establish such personal links to the world until Woodrow Wilson after World War I.

On their tour of the world, Ulysses and Julia Grant sat with companions and guides in front of the Great Hypostyle Hall at the Temple of Amon-Ra in Karnak at Luxor, Egypt, 1878. The Grants' extraordinary tour included many such photo opportunities, often depicting the plebeian American president's presence in exotic places with unusual people. Whether he liked it or not, Grant was a world celebrity. (Library of Congress)

The Democrats also nominated Greeley in 1872, but it was not enough to keep Grant from reelection. Greeley's campaign for North-South reunion was a harbinger of the future in American politics. Organized Blue-Gray fraternalism (gatherings of Union and Confederate veterans) began as early as 1874. Grant continued to avoid confrontation with white southerners and in 1875 refused a desperate request from Mississippi's governor for troops to quell racial and political terrorism there.

Grant made several poor appointments that fueled public dissatisfaction with his administration. His secretary of war, his private secretary, and officials in the Treasury and Navy Departments were involved in bribery or tax-cheating scandals. Instead of exposing the corruption, Grant defended the culprits. In 1874, the Democrats recaptured the House of Representatives, signaling the end of the Radical Republican vision of Reconstruction.

General Amnesty

Democratic gains in Congress weakened legislative resolve on southern issues. Congress already lifted the political disabilities of the Fourteenth Amendment from many former Confederates. In 1872 it adopted an Amnesty Act, which pardoned most of the remaining rebels. In 1875 Congress passed a Civil Rights Act, partly in tribute to the recently deceased Charles Sumner, purporting to guarantee black people equal accommodations in public places, but the bill was watered down and contained no enforcement provisions. (The Supreme Court later struck down this law;)

Democrats regained control of four state governments before 1872 and eight by late January 1876 (see Map 16.1). In the North, Democrats successfully stressed the failure and scandals of Reconstruction governments. Sectional reconciliation now seemed crucial for commerce. The nation was expanding westward, and the South was a new investment frontier.

The West, Race, and Reconstruction

As the Fourteenth Amendment and other enactments granted blacks the beginnings of citizenship, other non-whites faced continued persecution. Across the West, the federal government pursued a containment policy against Native Americans. In California, where white farmers and ranchers often forced Indians into captive labor, some civilians practiced Indian hunting. By 1880, thirty years of violence left an estimated forty-five hundred California Indians dead at the hands of white settlers.

In California and other states of the Far West, few whites objected to the Chinese immigrants who did the dangerous work of building railroads through the Rocky Mountains. But when the Chinese competed for urban, industrial jobs, conflict erupted. Anticoolie clubs appeared in California in the 1870s seeking laws against Chinese labor, inciting racism, and organizing brutal attacks on Chinese workers and the factories that employed them. Western politicians sought white votes by pandering to prejudice, and in 1879 the new California constitution denied Chinese the vote.

Viewing America from coast to coast, the Civil War and Reconstruction years dismantled racial slavery and fostered a volatile new racial complexity, especially in the West. Some African Americans, despite generations of mixture with Native Americans, asserted that they were more like whites than uncivilized Indians, while others, like the Creek freed men of Indian Territory, sought an Indian identity. In Texas, whites, Indians, blacks, and Hispanics had mixed for decades, and by the 1870s forced reconsideration in law and custom of who exactly who was white.

America was undergoing what one historian has called a reconstruction of the concept of race itself. The turbulence of the expanding West reinforced the new nationalism and the reconciliation of North and South based on a resurgent white supremacy.

Foreign Expansion

In 1867 new expansion pressures led Secretary of State William H. Seward to purchase Alaska from Russia, adding vast new territory to the United States (see Chapter 22). Opponents ridiculed Seward's $7.2 million venture, but Seward convinced important congressmen of Alaska's economic potential, and other lawmakers favored the dawning of friendship with Russia.

Also in 1867 the United States took control of the Midway Islands, a thousand miles northwest of Hawai'i. Through diplomacy, Seward and his successor, Hamilton Fish, resolved wartime grievances with Great Britain by arranging a financial settlement for damage done by the *Alabama* and other cruisers built in England and sold to the Confederacy. Sectional reconciliation in Reconstruction America would serve new ambitions for world commerce and expansion.

Judicial Retreat from Reconstruction

Meanwhile, the Supreme Court played its part in the northern retreat from Reconstruction. During the Civil War, the Court was cautious and inactive. Reaction to the *Dred Scott* decision (1857) was so vehement and the Union's wartime emergency so great, that the Court had avoided interference with government actions. But that changed in 1866 when *Ex parte Milligan* reached the Court.

Lambdin P. Milligan of Indiana plotted to free Confederate prisoners of war and overthrow state governments. Consequently, a military court sentenced Milligan, a civilian, to death. Milligan challenged the military tribunal's authority, claiming he was entitled to a civil trial. The Supreme Court declared that military trials were illegal when civil courts were functioning. It seemed the Court intended to reassert its authority.

In the 1870s the Court renewed its challenge to Congress's actions when it narrowed the meaning of the Fourteenth Amendment. The *Slaughter-House* cases (1873) began in 1869, when the Louisiana legislature granted one company a monopoly on livestock slaughtering in New Orleans. Rival butchers sued, and their attorney, former Supreme Court justice John A. Campbell, argued that Louisiana violated the rights of some citizens in favor of others. The Fourteenth Amendment, Campbell contended, had brought individual rights under federal protection.

But in the *Slaughter-House* decision, the Supreme Court dealt a blow to the scope of the Fourteenth Amendment. It declared state citizenship and national citizenship separate. National citizenship involved only matters such as the right to travel freely from state to state, and only such narrow rights, held the Court, were protected by the Fourteenth Amendment.

Shrinking from a role as "perpetual censor upon all legislation of the States, on the civil rights of their own citizens," the Court's majority declared that the framers of the recent amendments had not intended to "destroy" the federal system, in which the states exercised "powers for domestic and local government, including the regulation of civil rights." Thus the justices severely limited the amendment's potential for safeguarding the rights of black citizens—its original intent.

The next day the Court decided *Bradwell v. Illinois,* a case in which Myra Bradwell, a female attorney, was denied the right to practice law in Illinois because she was married woman, and hence not a free agent. Using the Fourteenth Amendment, Bradwell's attorneys contended that the state had unconstitutionally abridged her "privileges and immunities" as a citizen. The Supreme Court disagreed, declaring it was a woman's "paramount destiny . . . to fulfill the noble and benign offices of wife and mother."

In 1876 the Court further weakened the Reconstruction era amendments. In *U.S. v. Cruikshank* the Court overruled the conviction under the 1870 Enforcement Act of Louisiana whites who attacked a meeting of blacks and conspired to deprive them of their rights. The justices ruled that the Fourteenth Amendment did not give the federal government power to act against these whites. The duty of protecting citizens' equal rights, the Court said, "rests alone with the States." Such judicial conservatism blunted the revolutionary potential in the Civil War amendments into the next century.

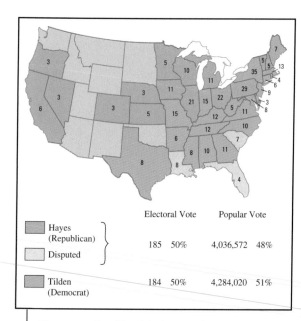

	Electoral Vote	Popular Vote
Hayes (Republican)	185 50%	4,036,572 48%
Disputed		
Tilden (Democrat)	184 50%	4,284,020 51%

Map 16.2   Presidential Election of 1876 and the Compromise of 1877

In 1876 a combination of solid southern support and Democratic gains in the North gave Samuel Tilden the majority of popular votes, but Rutherford B. Hayes won the disputed election in the electoral college, after a deal satisfied Democratic wishes for an end to Reconstruction.

Disputed Election of 1876 and Compromise of 1877

The results of the disputed presidential election of 1876 confirmed that economic issues predominated and that the North was no longer pursuing the goals of reconstruction. Samuel J. Tilden, the Democratic governor of New York, ran strongly in the South and needed one electoral vote to triumph over Rutherford B. Hayes, the Republican nominee. Nineteen electoral votes from Louisiana, South Carolina, and Florida (the only southern states not yet under Democratic rule) were disputed; both Democrats and Republicans claimed to have won those states despite fraud committed by their opponents (see Map 16.2).

To resolve this unprecedented situation, Congress established a fifteen-member electoral commission, balanced between Democrats and Republicans. Because Republicans held the majority in Congress, they prevailed, 8 to 7, on every attempt to count the returns. Hayes would become president if Congress accepted the commission's findings.

But Democrats controlled the House and could filibuster to block action on the vote. Many citizens worried about another civil war, as some southerners vowed "Tilden or Fight!" Finally, Democrats acquiesced in the election of Hayes based on a deal cut between Hayes's supporters and southerners who wanted federal aid to railroads, internal improvements, and removal of troops from southern states. Northern and southern Democrats simply decided not to contest the election of a Republican who was not going to continue Reconstruction.

Southern Democrats rejoiced that Reconstruction was over, but African Americans grieved over the betrayal of their hopes for equality. In a Fourth of July speech in Washington, D.C., in 1875, Frederick Douglass looked back on fifteen years of unparalleled change for his people and worried about the hold of white supremacy on America's historical memory: "If war among the whites brought peace and liberty to the blacks, what will peace among the whites bring?"

Summary

Reconstruction was an era of tragic aspirations and failures but also of unprecedented legal, political, and social change. The Union victory brought increased federal power, stronger nationalism, sweeping federal intervention in the southern states, and landmark constitutional amendments. But northern commitment to make these changes eroded, leaving the revolution unfinished. The early promise for new lives and liberties among freedpeople had fallen, at least temporarily, by the wayside.

The North had embraced emancipation, black suffrage, and constitutional alterations strengthening the central government, primarily to defeat the rebellion. As wartime pressures declined, Americans, especially northerners, retreated from Reconstruction. The American people and the courts maintained a preference for state authority and a distrust of federal power, while free-labor ideology stressed respect for property and individual self-reliance. Racism transformed into Klan terror and theories of black degeneration.

New challenges to American society gradually overwhelmed the aims of Reconstruction. Industrialization promised prosperity but also wrought increased exploitation of labor. Moreover, industry laid the foundation for an enlarged American role in international affairs.

In the wake of the Civil War, Americans faced two profound tasks—healing and dispensing justice. Making sectional reunion compatible with black freedom and equality overwhelmed American politics, and the nation faced much of this dilemma more than a century later.

The Lost Cause

All major wars compel a struggle over their memory. After the Civil War, white southerners and their northern allies constructed a Lost Cause tradition, a potent and racially exclusive version of the war and Reconstruction which persists today.

The Lost Cause emerged among ex-Confederates as a mourning ritual and a psychological response to the trauma of defeat. But it also took root in selective reinterpretations of the war's causes; southern resistance to Reconstruction; doctrines of white supremacy; and a mythic, nostalgic popular culture among northerners and southerners. Lost Cause advocates—from high-ranking officers to common soldiers—argued that the war had never been about slavery, that Confederates only lost to Yankee numbers and resources, and that the nation should reconcile by equally honoring southern and northern sacrifice. In the industrial, urban, multiethnic America of the emerging twentieth century, images of benevolent Southern masters and faithful slaves and of Robert E. Lee as America's truest Christian soldier provided a sentimentalized road to reunion. These images reverberated in Jim Crow America, and they endure in modern tastes for Civil War memorabilia and uses of the Confederate flag to oppose civil rights and affirmative action.

From 1865 to the 1880s, this Confederate legend was forged by wartime participants determined to vindicate the Confederacy. By the 1890s, however, Lost Cause culture emerged especially with the United Daughters of the Confederacy. Elite southern white women built monuments, lobbied congressmen, delivered lectures, ran contests for schoolchildren, and strove to control the content of history textbooks in the service of an exalted South. Above all, Lost Causers advocated what one historian has called a "victory narrative." This new victory was the nation's triumph over the racial revolution and constitutional transformations of Reconstruction.

In his 1881 memoir, Jefferson Davis declared the Lost Cause not lost: "Well may we rejoice in the regained possession of self-government. . . . This is the great victory . . . a total non-interference by the Federal government in the domestic affairs of the States."

Chapter Review

WARTIME RECONSTRUCTION

Which two political acts recognized the centrality of slavery to the war?

Passage of the Thirteenth Amendment and establishment of the Freedmen's Bureau in early 1865 sent a clear signal that slavery was a major cause for the Civil War. The Thirteenth Amendment first abolished slavery ("involuntary servitude") and second gave Congress the power to enforce it. Then, a few months later in March, Congress established the Bureau of Refugees, Freedmen and Abandoned Lands, known as the Freedmen's Bureau, to help former slaves. During its four years as a federal agency, it supplied food and medical services, built thousands of schools and colleges, negotiated job contracts between former slaves and masters, and managed confiscated lands.

THE MEANINGS OF FREEDOM

How did blacks exert their newfound freedom?

With emancipation, former slaves sought to reunite families broken apart through slave sales. Community also became important, as they built their own churches that ultimately served to unify racial ties. Seeking greater control over their work lives, African Americans wanted fairer employers and hoped to own land; when that was not possible, they rented land from former masters under the sharecropping system, in which they paid for supplies and rent by giving owners' half their crops on average. Former slaves also embraced the education that had been denied them under slavery and started schools, colleges, and universities throughout the South or attended those launched by the Freedman's Bureau.

JOHNSON'S RECONSTRUCTION PLAN

What was Johnson's vision for Reconstruction?

Johnson's approach to Reconstruction could be summed up in a single quote: "The Constitution as it is, and the Union as it was." As president, he controlled Reconstruction policy through 1865, pardoning former Confederates and reestablishing state governments in the South. Despising the planter class, he initially insisted that ex-Confederates with property worth more than $20,000 apply directly to him for pardons. Gradually, Johnson pardoned planters, too, which restored the former elite to power, possibly because he wanted to block Radical Republicans from implementing extensive and racial political changes in the South. Deeply racist, Johnson remained silent when southern states implemented black codes to restrict former slaves' freedom by requiring them to carry passes, obey curfew laws, and live in housing provided by a landowner. Nonetheless, after just eight months, Johnson declared Reconstruction was completed.

THE CONGRESSIONAL RECONSTRUCTION PLAN

What made Radical Reconstruction different from Johnson's plan?

Radical Republicans in Congress were upset at Johnson's moderate approach, which seemed to hold no one responsible for the war and re-established racial hierarchies and the southern elite. Initially a minority, the Radicals' popularity grew as Johnson increasingly dug in his heels. Radicals wanted to democratize the South through black suffrage, civil rights, and land confiscation and redistribution. They secured passage of the Fourteenth Amendment, which conferred citizenship on "all persons born or naturalized in the United States," and granted voting rights to males. They also passed four strident Reconstruction acts with strict and detailed plans for readmitting southern states to the Union. They barred ex-Confederates from voting until freedmen could and outlined the rules for voter registration boards and the adoption of state constitutions. Unpopular, land redistribution never materialized, but in 1869, Radicals pushed through their final measure, the Fifteenth Amendment, which prohibited states from denying the vote based on "race, color, or previous condition of servitude."

RECONSTRUCTION POLITICS AND ECONOMY IN THE SOUTH

> **How did black voters in the early days of Reconstruction transform the South?**

With a large black voter turnout and prominent confederates barred from the polls and political positions, a new southern variant on the Republican Party came to power during the 1868 to 1870 state constitutional conventions. Their constitutions were highly democratic, eliminating property qualifications for voting and political office, shifting some appointed offices to elected ones, and establishing public schools. They also gave women greater rights in terms of property-holding and divorce. Blacks became state legislators for the first time in 1868. Angry whites charged they were being ruled by negroes, and some resorted to violent resistance. In truth, while blacks did play a greater role in government, they remained a minority.

RETREAT FROM RECONSTRUCTION

> **What led the North to lose interest in reconstructing the South?**

First, northerners became disillusioned with Reconstruction, including some who thought federal expansion had cut too far into states rights. Second, economic and social changes in the North and West forced legislators to focus on their regional concerns. While immigration and industrialization made northern economies boom from 1865 to 1873, it also widened the gap between the richest and the poorest and created a powerful new class of industrialists. But when the Panic of 1873 brought hard times and job losses, interest in Reconstruction faded beside regional economic concerns. The Supreme Court also played a role, challenging congressional Reconstruction in several decisions. The Court ultimately narrowed the meaning of the Fourteenth Amendment by declaring state and national citizenship as separate issues and limited the amendment's ability to safeguard black citizens, as it was intended to do.

SUGGESTIONS FOR FURTHER READING

David W. Blight, *Race and Reunion: The Civil War in American Memory* (2001)

W. E. B. Du Bois, *Black Reconstruction in America* (1935)

Eric Foner, *Reconstruction: America's Unfinished Revolution, 1863–1877* (1988)

William Gillette, *Retreat from Reconstruction, 1869–1879* (1980)

Steven Hahn, *A Nation Under Our Feet: Black Political Struggles in the Rural South from Slavery to the Great Migration* (2003)

Gerald Jaynes, *Branches Without Roots: The Genesis of the Black Working Class in the American South, 1862–1882* (1986)

Michael Perman, *The Road to Redemption* (1984)

George Rable, *But There Was No Peace* (1984)

Heather Richardson, *The Death of Reconstruction* (2001)

Elliot West, "Reconstructing Race," *Western Historical Quarterly* (Spring 2003)

CHAPTER 17

The Development of the West

CHAPTER OUTLINE

The Economic Activities of Native Peoples

The Transformation of Native Cultures

The Extraction of Natural Resources

Irrigation and Transportation

LINKS TO THE WORLD:
The Australian Frontier

Farming the Plains

The Ranching Frontier

Summary

LEGACY FOR A PEOPLE AND A NATION: The Myth of the Cowboy

I n 1893 the young historian Frederick Jackson Turner delivered a stunning lecture at the Columbian Exposition in Chicago that shaped views of the American West for several generations. Titled "The Significance of the Frontier in American History," the paper argued that "free land, its continuous recession, and the advancement of American settlement westward" created a distinctively American spirit of democracy and egalitarianism. The settlement of several frontier Wests from colonial times onward explained American progress and character.

Across the street, the folk character Buffalo Bill Cody dramatized the conquest of frontiers in a stage extravaganza called "The Wild West." Whereas Turner described a peaceful settlement of empty western land, Cody portrayed violent conquest of territory occupied by savage Indians. Turner's heroes were farmers who tamed the wilderness with plows. Buffalo Bill's heroes were scouts who braved danger and vanquished Indians with firepower. Turner used log cabins, wagon trains, and wheat fields to argue that the frontier fashioned a new, progressive people. Cody depicted the West as a place of brutal aggression and heroic victory.

The American West inspired material progress, and it witnessed the forceful domination of one group over another and over the environment. Both Turner and Cody believed that by the 1890s the frontier era had ended. Over time, Turner's theory was abandoned (even by Turner himself) as too simplistic, and Buffalo Bill was relegated to the gallery of rogues and showmen. Yet both Wests persisted in the romance of American history, even while they obscured the complex story of western development in the late nineteenth century.

Much of the West was never empty, and its inhabitants utilized its resources differently. On the Plains, for example, the

 This icon will direct you to interactive activities and study materials on A People And A Nation, Brief Edition website: **www.cengage.com/history/norton/peoplenationbrief8e**

Chronology

1862	Homestead Act grants free land to citizens who live on and improve the land.	**1881–82**	Chinese Exclusion Acts prohibit Chinese immigration to the United States.
	Morrill Land Grant Act gives states public land to sell in order to finance agricultural and industrial colleges.	**1883**	National time zones are established.
		1884	U.S. Supreme Court defines Indians as wards under government protection.
1864	Chivington's militia massacres Black Kettle's Cheyennes at Sand Creek.	**1887**	Dawes Severalty Act ends communal ownership of Indian lands and grants land allotments to individual native families.
1869	First transcontinental railroad is completed.		
1872	Yellowstone becomes first national park.		Hatch Act provides for agricultural experiment stations in every state.
1873	Barbed wire is invented, enabling western farmers to enclose and protect fields cheaply.		California passes law permitting farmers to organize into water districts.
1876	Lakotas and Cheyennes ambush Custer's federal troops at Little Big Horn, Montana.	**1887–88**	Devastating winter on Plains destroys countless livestock and forces farmers into economic hardship.
1877	Nez Percé Indians led by Young Joseph surrender to U.S. troops.		
1878	Timber and Stone Act allows citizens to buy timberland cheaply but also enables large companies to acquire huge tracts of forest land.	**1890**	Final suppression of Plains Indians by U.S. Army at Wounded Knee occurs.
			Census Bureau announces closing of the frontier.
1879	Carlisle School for Indians is established in Pennsylvania.		Yosemite National Park is established.
		1892	Muir helps found Sierra Club.
1880–81	Manypenny's *Our Indian Wards* and Jackson's *A Century of Dishonor* influence public conscience about poor government treatment of Indians.	**1896**	Rural Free Delivery is made available.
		1902	Newlands Reclamation Act is passed.

Pawnee Indians planted crops in the spring, left their fields in summer to hunt buffalo, and then returned for harvesting. They sometimes battled with Cheyennes and Arapahos over access to hunting grounds and crops. Usually, Plains Indians developed and used natural resources in limited ways. In what now is the American Southwest, natives coexisted and sometimes integrated with Hispanic people, who were descendants of Spanish colonists and typically farmed small plots or worked for large landowners.

As white immigrants built new communities in the West in the late nineteenth century, they often exploited the environment for profit. They excavated the earth for minerals, felled forests for construction, built railroads, dammed rivers, and plowed soil with crop machines. Their goal included buying and selling in regional, national, and international markets. As they transformed the landscape, the triumph of their market economies transformed the nation.

The West, by 1870 spanned from the Mississippi River to the Pacific Ocean and consisted of several regions of varying economic potential. Abundant rainfall along the northern Pacific coast fed huge forests. South, California's woodlands and grasslands provided fertile valleys for vegetables and orange groves. Eastward, from the Cascades and the Sierra Nevada to the Rocky Mountains, gold, silver, and other minerals lay buried. East of the Rockies, the Great Plains divided into a semiarid western region of trees and buffalo grass and an eastern region of ample rainfall and tall grasses, which could support grain crops and livestock.

Before contact with whites, Indian peoples moved around the region, warring, trading, and negotiating with one another as they searched for food and shelter. In the Southwest, Hispanics moved north and south between Mexican and American territory, establishing towns, farms, and ranches. After the Civil War, white American migration overwhelmed the Indian and Hispanic people, swelling the population from 7 million to nearly 17 million between 1870 and 1890.

The West's abundance of exploitable land and raw materials made white Americans believe that anyone persistent enough could succeed. This confidence was based on the notion that white people were superior and asserted itself at the expense of people of color and the environment.

By 1890 farms, ranches, mines, towns, and cities existed in almost every corner of the present-day continental United States, but vast stretches of land remained unsettled. Although symbolically important to Frederick Jackson Turner, the fading frontier had little impact on people's behavior. Pioneers who failed in one locale tried again elsewhere. A surplus of seemingly uninhabited land led Americans to believe they would always have a second chance. This belief, more than Turner's theory of frontier democracy or Cody's "heroic" enactments left a deep imprint on the American character.

- How did the interaction between people and the environment shape the physical landscape of the West and the lives of the region's inhabitants?
- How did the U.S. government's relations with Native Americans change over time throughout the late nineteenth century?
- Describe the societal and technological changes that revolutionized the lives of farmers and ranchers on the Great Plains.

THE ECONOMIC ACTIVITIES OF NATIVE PEOPLES

Native Americans settled the West long before other Americans migrated there from the East. Neither passive nor powerless, Indians shaped their environment—for better and for worse—for centuries. Nevertheless, several factors contributed to the weakening of almost all native economic systems in the late nineteenth century.

Subsistence Cultures

Western Indian communities varied. Some natives inhabited permanent settlements, others temporary camps. Most Indians were both participants and recipients in a large-scale flow of goods, culture, language, and disease carried by migrating bands. Indian economies were based in differing degrees on four activities: crop growing; livestock raising; hunting, fishing, and gathering; and trading and raiding. Corn was the most common crop; sheep and horses, acquired from Spanish colonizers and other Indians, were the livestock; and buffalo (American bison) were the primary prey of hunts. Indians raided one another for food, tools, and hides. They subsisted on crops when a buffalo hunt failed, and hunted buffalo, traded livestock, or stole food and horses when crops failed.

For Indians on the Great Plains, daily life centered on the buffalo. They cooked and preserved buffalo meat; fashioned hides into clothing, shoes, and blankets; used sinew for thread and bowstrings; and carved tools from bones and horns. Buffalo were so valuable that the Pawnees and Lakotas often fought over access to herds. Plains Indians periodically set fire to tall-grass prairies, which burned away dead plants, facilitating the growth of new grasses so horses could feed all summer.

In the Southwest, Indians herded sheep, goats, and horses. Old Man Hat, a Navajo, explained, "The herd is money. . . . You know that you have some good clothing; the sheep gave you that. And you've just eaten different kinds of food; the sheep gave that food to you. Everything comes from the sheep." He was not speaking of money in a business sense but rather as status and security. Like many Indians, Navajos emphasized generosity and distrusted private property. Within the family, sharing was expected; outside the family, gifts and reciprocity governed relationships. Southwestern Indians, too, altered the environment, building elaborate irrigation systems to maximize the use of scarce water supplies.

What buffalo were to Plains Indians and sheep were to southwestern Indians, salmon were to northwestern Indians. Before the mid-nineteenth century, the Columbia River and its tributaries supported the densest native population in North America. The Clatsops, Klamathets, and S'Klallams developed technologies of stream diversion, platform construction, and special baskets to harvest fish. They traded salmon for horses, buffalo robes, beads, cloth, and knives.

Slaughter of Buffalo

On the Plains and parts of the Southwest, this native world gradually dissolved after 1850, when whites competed with Indians for natural resources. Perceiving buffalo and Indians as hindrances, whites endeavored to eliminate both. The U.S. Army refused to enforce treaties that reserved hunting grounds for exclusive Indian use, so railroads sponsored hunts in which eastern sportsmen shot at buffalo from slow-moving trains.

Neither Indians nor whites realized that a combination of circumstances doomed the buffalo before the slaughter of the late 1800s. Indians depleted herds by increasing their kills to trade with whites and other Indians. Also, in the generally dry years of the 1840s and 1850s Indians relocated to fertile river basins and forced bison out of this grazing territory to face starvation. Whites, too, settled in basin areas, further pushing buffalo out. At the same time, lethal animal diseases, such as anthrax and brucellosis, brought by white-owned livestock, decimated buffalo already weakened by malnutrition and drought. Increased numbers of horses, oxen, and sheep, owned by white newcomers and some Indians, devoured grasses that buffalo needed. The mass killing struck the final blow. By the 1880s only a few hundred remained of the 25 million buffalo estimated on the Plains in 1820.

Decline of Salmon

In the Northwest, salmon, suffered a similar fate. White commercial fishermen and canneries moved into the Columbia and Willamette River valleys during the 1860s and 1870s, and by the 1880s had greatly diminished the salmon runs. By the early

1900s, the construction of dams on the Columbia and its tributaries further impeded salmon reproduction. The U.S. government protected Indian fishing rights, and hatcheries restored some of this supply, but dams built to provide power, combined with overfishing and pollution, diminished salmon stocks.

THE TRANSFORMATION OF NATIVE CULTURES

Buffalo slaughter and salmon reduction undermined Indian subsistence, but demographic changes also contributed. Throughout the nineteenth century, white migrants were overwhelmingly single males in their twenties and thirties, the age when they were most prone to violent behavior. In 1870 white men outnumbered white women by three to two in California, two to one in Colorado, and two to one in the Dakota Territory. By 1900, the preponderance of men remained throughout these places. Indians were most likely to come into contact first with white explorers, traders, trappers, soldiers, prospectors, and cowboys, nearly all of whom had guns and no qualms about using them on animals and humans who got in their way.

Western Men

Moreover, these men subscribed to prevailing attitudes that Indians were primitive, lazy, devious, and cruel. Such contempt made exploiting and killing them easier, further "justified" by claims of preempting threats to life and property. When Indians raided white settlements, they sometimes mutilated bodies, burned buildings, and kidnapped women, acts that were embellished in campfire stories, pamphlets, and popular fiction—to reinforce images of Indians as savages. In saloons and cabins, men boasted about fighting Indians and showed off trophies of scalps and other body parts taken from victims.

Indian warriors, too, were young, armed, and prone to violence. Valuing bravery, they similarly boasted of fighting white interlopers. But Indian communities contained a large number of women and children, making native bands less mobile and more vulnerable. They also were susceptible to the bad habits of white bachelor society, copying their binges on whiskey and prostitution. The syphilis and gonorrhea that Indian men contracted from Indian women infected by whites killed many and hindered reproduction, which their populations, already dwindling from smallpox and other white diseases, could not afford. Thus the age and gender structure of the white frontier population, combined with an attitude of contempt toward Indians, threatened Indian existence in the West.

Lack of Native Unity

Government policy reinforced efforts to remove Indians. North American natives were organized not into tribes, as whites believed, but into bands, confederacies, and villages. Two hundred distinct languages and dialects separated these groups, making it difficult for Indians to unite against white invaders. Although a language group could be defined as a tribe, separate bands and clans had different leaders, and it was seldom that a tribal chief held widespread power. Moreover, bands often spent more time quarreling among themselves than with white settlers.

Territorial Treaties

After the Treaty of Greenville in 1795, American officials considered Indian tribes as nations with which they could make treaties, ensuring peace and definite land boundaries. But the government did not understand that a chief who agreed to a treaty did not speak for everyone and that the group might not abide by it. Moreover, whites seldom accepted treaties as guarantees of Indians' future land rights. In the Northwest, whites considered treaties protecting Indians' fishing rights on the Columbia River as nuisances and ousted Indians from the best locations. On the Plains, whites settled wherever they wished, often commandeering choice farmland.

Reservation Policy

Prior to the 1880s, the federal government tried to force western Indians onto reservations, where they might be "civilized." Reservations usually consisted of areas in a group's previous territory that were least desirable to whites. The government promised protection from white encroachment, along with food, clothing, and other necessities.

The reservation policy helped make way for the market economy. In the early years, trade benefited both Indians and whites equally. Indians acquired clothing, guns, and horses from whites in exchange for furs, jewelry, and, sometimes, military assistance against other Indians. Over time, Indians became more dependent, and whites increasingly dictated trade. For example, white traders persuaded Navajo weavers in the Southwest to produce heavy rugs suitable for eastern customers and to alter designs and colors to boost sales. Meanwhile, Navajos raised fewer crops and were forced to buy food. Soon they were selling land and labor to whites, and their dependency made it easier to force them onto reservations.

Indians had no say over their own affairs on reservations. Supreme Court decisions in 1884 and 1886 defined them as wards (falling, like helpless children, under government protection) and denied them U.S. citizenship. Thus they were unprotected by the Fourteenth and Fifteenth Amendments, which extended citizenship to African Americans. Second, pressure from white farmers, miners, and herders who sought Indian lands made it difficult for the government to preserve reservations intact. Third, the government ignored native history, even combining on the same reservation Indian bands that habitually warred against each other. Rather than serving as civilizing communities, reservations weakened Indian life.

Native Resistance

Not all Indians succumbed to market forces and reservation restrictions. Apaches in the Southwest battled whites even after being forced onto reservations. Pawnees in the Midwest resisted disadvantageous deals. In the Northwest, Nez Percé Indians escaped reservations by fleeing to Canada in 1877, until 1,800 miles later in Montana, their leader, Young Joseph, ended the flight. Sent to a reservation, Joseph unsuccessfully petitioned the government for a return of his ancestral lands.

Indian Wars

Whites responded to western Indian defiance with military aggression. In 1860, Navajos reacted to U.S. military pressure by raiding Fort Defiance in Arizona Territory.

Plains Indians did not write books or letters as whites did, but they did tell stories and spread news through art. They painted scenes in notebooks and on hides, like this one which depicts the Indians' annihilation of General George A. Custer's soldiers at Little Big Horn in 1876.

(National Anthropological Archives, Smithsonian Institution NAA Ms. 2367A, 08583500)

The army attacked and starved the Navajo into submission, and in 1863–1864 forced them to a reservation at Bosque Redondo in New Mexico. In 1864, in the Sand Creek region of Colorado, a militia led by Methodist minister John Chivington attacked a Cheyenne band under Black Kettle, killing almost every Indian. In 1879, four thousand U.S. soldiers forced a surrender from Utes who were resisting further concessions after giving up most of their land.

The most publicized Indian battles occurred in June 1876, when 2,500 Lakotas and Cheyennes led by Chiefs Rain-in-the-Face, Sitting Bull, and Crazy Horse surrounded and annihilated 256 government troops led by Colonel George A. Custer near the Little Big Horn River in southern Montana. Although Indians demonstrated military skill, supply shortages and relentless pursuit by U.S. soldiers eventually overwhelmed armed Indian resistance. Native Americans were not so much conquered as they were harassed and starved into submission.

Reform of Indian Policy

In the 1870s and 1880s, officials and reformers sought more purposely to "civilize" and "uplift" natives through landholding and education. This meant outlawing customs deemed savage and barbarous and pressuring Indians to adopt American values of ambition, thrift, and materialism. In doing so, the United States copied other nations' imperialist policies, such as France, which banned native religious ceremonies in its Pacific island colonies. Other groups argued for sympathetic treatment. Reform treatises, such as George Manypenny's *Our Indian Wards* (1880) and Helen Hunt Jackson's *A Century of Dishonor* (1881), aroused the American conscience.

In the United States, the two most active Indian reform organizations were the Women's National Indian Association (WNIA) and the Indian Rights Association

(IRA). The WNIA, composed mainly of white women using domestic skills to help the needy, urged gradual Indian assimilation. The IRA, which had few Native American members, advocated citizenship and landholding. Most white reformers believed Indians were culturally inferior and could succeed economically only by embracing middle-class values of diligence and education.

Reformers particularly deplored Indians' sexual division of labor. Women seemed to do all the work—tending crops, raising children, cooking, curing hides, making tools and clothes—while being servile to men, who hunted but were otherwise idle. WNIA and IRA wanted Indian men to bear more responsibilities, treat Indian women respectfully, and resemble male heads of white middle-class households. But when Indian men and women adopted the model of white society, Indian women lost much of the economic independence and power over daily life that they once had.

Zitkala-Sa

Indians like Zitkala-Sa ("Red Bird") used white-controlled education to their advantage. Born on South Dakota's Pine Ridge reservation in 1876, at age twelve this Yankton Sioux girl attended an Indiana Quaker boarding school and later Earlham College and the Boston Conservatory of Music. Her major contribution was writing on behalf of her people's needs and advocating cultural preservation. In 1901 Zitkala-Sa published *Old Indian Legends,* translating Sioux oral tradition into written stories. Zitkala-Sa became known as Gertrude Bonnin when she married a Sioux who had taken the name Ray Bonnin. Subsequently, she was elected the first Indian secretary of the Society of American Indians.

Dawes Severalty Act

In 1887 Congress reversed its reservation policy and passed the Dawes Severalty Act, which authorized the dissolution of community-owned Indian property and granted land to individual Indian families. The government held that land in trust for twenty-five years, so families could not sell their allotments. The law also awarded citizenship to those accepting allotments (a 1906 act of Congress delayed citizenship for those Indians who had not yet taken their allotment). It also entitled the government to sell unallocated land to whites.

Indian policy, under the Interior Department, now pursed two main tactics to assimilate Indians into white American culture. First, the government distributed reservation land to individual families in the belief that the American institution of private property would integrate Indians into the larger society as productive citizens. Second, officials believed that Indians would abandon their "barbaric" habits more quickly if their children were educated in boarding schools.

The Dawes Act reflected a Euro-American and Christian world-view that a society of families headed by men was ideal. Government agents, reformers, and educators used schools to create a patriotic, industrious citizenry. Following Virginia's Hampton Institute, founded in Virginia in 1869 to educate newly freed slaves, teachers established the Carlisle School in Pennsylvania in 1879 as the flagship of the government's Indian school system. Boarding schools imposed white-defined sex roles: boys learned farming and carpentry, while girls were taught sewing, cleaning, and cooking.

Ghost Dance

With active resistance suppressed, Lakotas and others turned to the Ghost Dance as a spiritual means of preserving native culture. The Ghost Dance involved movement in a circle until the dancers reached a trancelike state and envisioned dead ancestors. As they engaged in days of dancing and meditation, Ghost Dancers embraced a messianic vision of the future when buffalo would return to the Plains and all elements of white civilization, including guns and whiskey, would be buried.

Ghost Dancers forswore violence, but as the religion spread, government agents worried about possible new Indian uprisings. Charging that the cult was anti-Christian, they arrested Ghost Dancers. Late in 1890, the government sent Custer's old regiment, the Seventh Cavalry, to detain Lakotas moving toward Pine Ridge, South Dakota. Although the Indians were starving, the army assumed they were armed for revolt. Overtaking the band at Wounded Knee Creek, the troops massacred an estimated three hundred men, women, and children in the snow.

The Losing of the West

The Indian wars and the Dawes Act effectively accomplished what whites wanted and Indians feared: it reduced native land control. Between 1887 and the 1930s, Indian landholdings dwindled from 138 million acres to 52 million. Land-grabbing whites were particularly cruel to the Ojibwas of the northern plains. In 1906 Senator Moses E. Clapp of Minnesota attached a rider to an Indian appropriations bill declaring that mixed-blood adults on the White Earth reservation were competent (meaning educated in white ways) enough to sell their property without the Dawes Act's twenty-five-year waiting period. When the bill became law, speculators duped many Ojibwas into signing away their land in return for counterfeit money and worthless merchandise. The Ojibwas lost more than half their original holdings and were ruined economically.

Ultimately, political and ecological crises overwhelmed most western Indians. Buffalo extinction, enemy raids, and disease, along with white military force, hobbled subsistence culture until Native Americans could only yield their lands to market-oriented whites. Believing themselves superior, whites determined to transform Indians by teaching them about private property and American ideals and eradicating their "backward" languages, lifestyles, and religions. Indians tried to retain their culture, but by the century's end, they lost control of their land and faced increasing pressure to shed their group identity.

THE EXTRACTION OF NATURAL RESOURCES

Unlike Indians, who used natural resources to meet subsistence needs and small-scale trading, most whites who migrated to the West and the Great Plains saw a vast territory as an untapped source of wealth (see Map 17.1). Extracting its resources advanced settlement and created new markets at home and abroad and fueled revolutions in transportation, agriculture, and industry across the United States in the late nineteenth century. This same extraction of nature's wealth led to environmental wastefulness and fed racial and sexual oppression.

Map 17.1 The Development and Natural Resources of the West

By 1890, mining, lumbering, and cattle ranching had penetrated many areas west of the Mississippi River and railroad construction had linked together the western economy. These activities, along with the spread of mechanized agriculture, altered both the economy and the people who were involved in them.

Mining and Lumbering

In the mid-1800s, the mining frontier drew thousands of people to Nevada, Idaho, Montana, Utah, and Colorado seeking gold, silver, copper, and other treasures. California's gold rush helped the thriving state by 1850 and furnished many of the miners traveling to nearby states. Others followed traditional routes from the East to the West.

Prospectors climbed mountains and trekked across deserts seeking precious metals. They shot game for food and financed their explorations by convincing merchants to advance credit for equipment in return for a share of the as-yet-undiscovered lode. Unlucky prospectors whose credit ran out took jobs and saved up to try again.

Digging for and transporting minerals was expensive, so prospectors who made discoveries sold their claims to large mining syndicates, such as the Anaconda Copper

Company. Financed by eastern capital, these companies brought in engineers, heavy machinery, railroad lines, and work crews, making western mining as corporate as eastern manufacturing. Although discoveries of gold and silver first drew attention to the West and its resources, mining companies usually exploited equally lead, zinc, tin, quartz, and copper.

Unlike mining, cutting trees for lumber to satisfy demand for construction and heating materials required vast tracts of forest land to be profitable. As tree supplies in the upper Midwest and South became depleted, lumber corporations moved into northwestern forests. The 1878 Timber and Stone Act sought to stimulate settlement in California, Nevada, Oregon, and Washington by allowing private citizens to buy inexpensive 160-acre plots "valuable chiefly for timber." Lumber companies grabbed millions of acres by hiring seamen from waterfront boarding houses to register claims to timberland and then transfer them to the companies. By 1900 private citizens had purchased more than 3.5 million acres, but most of it belonged to corporations.

Around the same time, oil companies began drilling in the Southwest. In 1900 petroleum came from the Appalachians and the Midwest, but rich oil reserves were discovered in southern California and eastern Texas, turning Los Angeles and Houston into boom cities. Although oil and kerosene were used primarily for lubrication and lighting, Southwest oil later became a vital new fuel source.

Complex Communities The West became a multiracial society, including Native Americans, native-born white migrants, Mexicans, African Americans, and Asians. A crescent borderland from western Texas through New Mexico and Arizona to northern California supported Mexicano ranchers and sheepherders, descendants of early Spanish settlers. In New Mexico, Spaniards mixed with Indians to form a *mestizo* population. Across the Southwest, Mexican immigrants moved into American territory to find work. Some returned to Mexico seasonally. Although the Treaty of Guadalupe Hidalgo (1848) guaranteed property rights to Hispanics, Anglo (the Mexican name for a white American) miners, speculators, and railroads used fraud to steal Hispanic landholdings. Consequently, Mexicanos relocated to cities like San Antonio and Tucson and became wage laborers.

Before the Chinese Exclusion Act of 1882 prohibited them from immigrating, some 200,000 Chinese—mostly young, single males—came to the United States, building communities in California, Oregon, and Washington. Many came with five-year labor contracts for railroad construction; others worked in the fields. By the 1870s, the Chinese composed half of California's agricultural work force, often working in citrus groves. In cities like San Francisco, they labored in textile and cigar factories.

Japanese and European immigrants also toiled in mining and agricultural communities. The region consequently developed its own migrant economy, with workers relocating to take short-term jobs.

Many African Americans were "exodusters" who built all-black western towns. Nicodemus, Kansas, for example, was founded in 1877 by black migrants from Lexington, Kentucky. Despite challenges, the town developed newspapers, shops, churches, a hotel, and a bank, but declined when businesses left after it failed to obtain railroad connections. The major exodus occurred in 1879, when six thousand blacks, including many former slaves, moved from the South to Kansas, aided by the Kansas Freedmen's Relief Association. Other migrants, encouraged by newspaper editors and land speculators, went to the Oklahoma Territory, where they founded thirty-two all-black communities in the 1890s and early 1900s.

Western Women

Unmarried men dominated the frontier, but many white women headed west to similarly find fortune. They usually accompanied a husband or father, however. Using their labor as a resource, women earned money cooking, laundering, and sometimes as sex workers in houses of prostitution. In the Northwest, they worked in canneries, cleaning and salting fish.

Many white women helped bolster family and community life by participating in the home mission movement. They broke from traditional male-dominated Protestant missions and, in the mid-nineteenth century, sought to help women wherever polygamy and female infanticide existed. Using the slogan "Woman's work for women," they established missionary societies aiding women—unmarried mothers, Mormons, Indians, and Chinese—who they believed had fallen prey to men or had not yet adopted Christian virtue.

Significance of Race

For white settlers, race became an important means to control labor and social relations. They classified people into five races: Caucasians (themselves), Indians, Mexicans (both Mexican Americans, who had originally inhabited western lands, and Mexican immigrants), *Mongolians* (a term applied to the Chinese), and Negroes. In doing so, whites imposed racial distinctions on people who, with the possible exception of African Americans, never before considered themselves a race, and then deemed them permanently inferior. In 1878, for example, a federal judge in California ruled that Chinese could not become U.S. citizens because they were not "white persons."

Racial minorities occupied the bottom half of a two-tiered labor system and experienced prejudice as whites tried to reserve for themselves the West's riches. Whites dominated the top tier of managerial and skilled labor positions, while Irish, Chinese, Mexican, and African American laborers held unskilled positions. Anti-Chinese violence erupted during hard times. When the Union Pacific Railroad tried to replace white workers with lower-waged Chinese in Rock Springs, Wyoming, in 1885, whites burned down the Chinese part of town, killing twenty-eight. Mexicans, many of whom were the original landowners in California and elsewhere, saw their property claims ignored or their land stolen by whites.

Because so many white male migrants were single, intermarriage with Mexican and Indian women was common. Such intermarriage was acceptable for white men, but not for white women, especially with Asian immigrants. Most miscegenation laws passed by western legislatures were intended to prevent Chinese and Japanese men from marrying white women.

Conservation Movement

Questions about natural resources caught Americans between a desire for progress and a fear of spoiling nature. After the Civil War, people eager to protect the natural landscape organized a conservation movement. Sport hunters, concerned about loss of wildlife for them to kill for recreation, lobbied state legislatures to pass hunting regulations. Artists and tourists in 1864 persuaded Congress to preserve the Yosemite Valley by granting it to California for public use. In 1872, Congress designated the Yellowstone River region in Wyoming as the first national park. And in 1891 conservationists, led by naturalist John Muir, pressured Congress to authorize President Benjamin Harrison to create forest reserves—public lands protected from private-interest cutting.

Despite Muir's activism and efforts by the Sierra Club (which Muir helped found in 1892) and corporations supporting resource development, opposition was loudest in the West, where people remained eager to exploit nature. By prohibiting trespass in areas such as Yosemite and Yellowstone, conservation policy deprived Indians and white settlers of wildlife, water, and firewood previously available on federal lands.

Admission of New States

The development of mining and forest regions, along with farms and cities, brought western territories to the threshold of statehood. In 1889 Republicans seeking to solidify control of Congress passed an omnibus bill granting statehood to North Dakota, South Dakota, Washington, and Montana. Wyoming and Idaho, which allowed women to vote, were admitted the following year. Congress denied statehood to Utah until 1896, wanting assurances from the Mormons, a majority of the territory's population and leaders, that they would give up polygamy.

Western states' varied communities spiced American folk culture and fostered a go-getter optimism that distinguished the American spirit. The lawlessness of places like Deadwood, in the Dakota Territory, and Tombstone, in the Arizona Territory, gave the West notoriety and romance. Legends grew about characters whose lives magnified the western experience, and promoters like Buffalo Bill enhanced western folklore's appeal.

Arizona's mining towns, with their free-flowing cash and loose law enforcement, attracted gamblers, thieves, and opportunists who came to represent the Wild West. Near Tombstone, the infamous Clanton family and their partner John Ringgold (known as Johnny Ringo) were smugglers and cattle rustlers. The Earp brothers—Wyatt, Jim, Morgan, Virgil, and Warren—and their friends William ("Bat") Masterson and John Henry ("Doc") Holliday operated on both sides of the law as gunmen, gamblers, and politicians. A feud between the Clantons and the Earps climaxed on October 26, 1881, in a shootout at the OK Corral, where three Clantons were killed and Holliday and Morgan Earp were wounded.

Writers Mark Twain, Bret Harte, and others captured the flavor of western life, and characters like Buffalo Bill, Annie Oakley, Wild Bill Hickok, and Poker Alice became folk heroes. But in reality, miners and lumbermen worked long hours, often for corporations, and had little time, energy, or money for gambling, carousing, or gunfights. Women worked hard, too, as teachers, laundresses, storekeepers, and

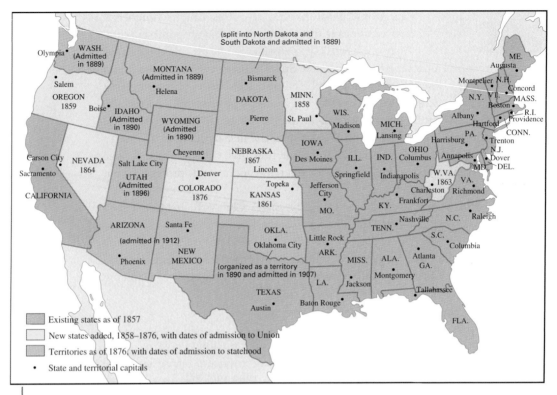

Map 17.2   The United States, 1876–1912

A wave of admissions between 1889 and 1912 brought remaining territories to statehood and marked the final creation of new states until Alaska and Hawai'i were admitted in the 1950s.

housewives. Only a few were sharpshooters or dance-hall queens. For most, western life was a struggle for survival.

IRRIGATION AND TRANSPORTATION

Western economic development is the story of how public and private interests used technology and organization to develop the region's river basins and make the arid land agriculturally productive.

For centuries, Indians irrigated southwestern lands for subsistence farming. When the Spanish arrived, they irrigated farms in southwest Texas and New Mexico. Later they channeled water to San Diego and Los Angeles, California. The Mormons were the first Americans of northern European ancestry to practice extensive irrigation. Arriving in Utah in 1847, they diverted streams and rivers into canals, enabling them to farm the hard-baked soil. By 1890 Utah boasted over 263,000 irrigated acres supporting more than 200,000 people.

Rights to Water

Efforts at land reclamation through irrigation in Colorado and California sparked conflict over rights to the precious streams that flowed through the West. Americans inherited the English common-law principle of riparian rights, which held that the stream

Water, aided by human resolve, coaxed crops from the dry soil and helped make the West habitable for whites. On this Colorado farm, a windmill pumps water for irrigation. (Longmont Museum, Longmont, Colorado)

belonged to God; those who lived nearby could take water as needed but should not diminish the river. Intended to protect nature, this principle discouraged economic development by prohibiting property owners from damming or diverting water at the expense of others who lived downstream.

Western settlers rejected riparianism and embraced prior appropriation, which awarded a river's water to the first person claiming it. Westerners, taking cues from eastern Americans who diverted waterways to power mills and factories, asserted that water existed to serve human needs and advance profits. Anyone intending a reasonable (economically productive) use of river water should have the right to appropriation. The courts generally agreed.

Under appropriation, those who dammed and diverted water often reduced its flow downstream. People disadvantaged by such action could either sue or establish a public authority to regulate water usage. Thus, in 1879 Colorado created several water divisions. In 1890 Wyoming inserted a constitutional provision declaring that the state's rivers were public property subject to state supervision.

Destined to become the most productive agricultural state, California maintained a mixed legal system that upheld riparianism while allowing for some appropriation. This system disadvantaged irrigators, who sought to change state law. In 1887 the legislature passed a bill permitting farmers to organize into districts that would construct and operate irrigation projects. An irrigation district could use its public authority to purchase water rights, seize private property for irrigation canals, and finance projects through taxation or by issuing bonds. As a result, California became the nation's leader in irrigated acreage, with more than 1 million irrigated acres by 1890, making it the nation's most profitable agricultural state.

Newlands Reclamation Act

Even so, the federal government owned most western land in the 1890s. Prodded by land-hungry developers, states wanted part of the public domain lands, claiming they could make them profitable through reclamation and irrigation. Congress generally

The Australian Frontier

Australia, founded like the United States as a European colony, had a frontier society that resembled the American West in its mining development, folk society, and treatment of indigenous people. Australia experienced a gold rush in 1851, two years after the United States, and large-scale mining companies quickly moved into its western regions to extract lucrative mineral deposits.

A promise of mineral wealth lured thousands of mostly male immigrants to Australia in the late nineteenth century, many from China. As in the United States, anti-Chinese riots erupted, and beginning in 1854, Australia passed laws restricting Chinese immigration. When the country became an independent British federation in 1901, it implemented a literacy test that terminated Chinese immigration for over fifty years.

While Australians celebrate folk heroes symbolizing white masculinity, they also considered indigenous peoples, whom they called Aborigines, savages. Christian missionaries viewed aborigines as pagans and tried to convert them. In 1869 the government of Victoria Province passed an Aborigine Protection Act, encouraging the removal of native children from their families to learn European customs in white schools. Aborigines adapted in their own ways, or, if they had light skin, sometimes told census takers they were white. In the end, Australians resorted to reservations. Like the Americans, white Australians could not find a place for indigenous people in their land of opportunity.

Much like the American counterpart, the Australian frontier was populated by natives before Anglo colonists arrived. The Aborigines, as the Australian natives were called, lived in villages and utilized their own culture to adapt to the environment. This photo shows a native camp in the Maloga Reserve. (National Library of Australia)

refused such assignments because of potential controversies. If one state sponsored irrigation, who would regulate waterways that flowed through more than one state? If, for example, California controlled the Truckee River, which flowed westward over the California-Nevada border, how would Nevadans ensure that California would give them sufficient water? Only the federal government had the power to regulate regional water development.

In 1902, after years of debate, Congress passed the Newlands Reclamation Act. It allowed the federal government to sell western public lands to individuals in parcels less than 160 acres and to use the proceeds to finance irrigation. Often identified as sensitive to natural-resource conservation, the Newlands Reclamation Act in fact represented a decision by the federal government to aid the agricultural and general economic development of the West.

Railroad Construction
Between 1865 and 1890, railroad track grew from 35,000 to 200,000 miles, mostly west of the Mississippi River (see Map 17.1). By 1900 the United States contained one-third of all railroad track in the world. The Central Pacific employed thousands of Chinese to build its tracks; the Union Pacific used mainly the Irish. Workers lived in shacks and tents that were dismantled, loaded on flatcars, and relocated each day.

After 1880, when steel replaced iron rails, railroads helped push the nation's steel industry to international leadership. Railroad expansion also spawned related industries—coal production, passenger- and freight-car manufacture, and depot construction. Railroads also gave important impetus to western urbanization. Transporting people and freight, lines like the Union Pacific and the Southern Pacific accelerated the growth of hubs, such as Chicago, Omaha, Kansas City, Cheyenne, Los Angeles, Portland, and Seattle.

Railroad Subsidies
Railroads received some of the largest government subsidies in American history. Promoters argued that, because railroads were a public benefit, the government should give them land from the public domain, which they could then sell to finance construction. During the Civil War, Congress, dominated by business-minded Republicans, granted railroad corporations over 180 million acres, mostly for interstate routes. Railroads funded construction by using the land as security for bonds or by selling it. State legislators, many of whom had financial interests in railroads, granted some 50 million acres. Cities and towns also assisted, usually through loans or by purchasing railroad bonds or stocks.

Without public help, few railroads could have prospered sufficiently to attract private investment. Railroads sometimes pressured governments into offering it. The Southern Pacific, for example, threatened to bypass Los Angeles unless the city paid a bonus and built a depot. Some laborers and farmers fought subsidies, arguing that companies like the Southern Pacific would become too powerful. Many communities boomed, however, as railroads attracted investment into the West and drew farmers into the market economy.

Standard Gauge, Standard Time
Railroad construction triggered important technological and organizational reforms. By the late 1880s, almost all lines had adopted standard-gauge rails allowing their tracks to connect. Air brakes, automatic car couplers, standardized handholds on freight cars, and other devices made rail transportation safer and efficient. The need for gradings, tunnels, and bridges spurred the growth of the American engineering profession. Organizational advances included systems for coordinating passenger and freight schedules, and the adoption of uniform freight-classification systems.

Railroads also reinforced racism by segregating black and white passengers on cars and in stations.

Railroads altered conceptions of time and space. First, instead of expressing distance in miles, people referred to the time it took to travel from place to place. Second, railroad scheduling required the nationwide standardization of time. Before railroads, local church bells and clocks struck noon when the sun was directly overhead, and people set clocks accordingly. But because the sun was not overhead at the same moment everywhere, time varied from place to place. Boston's clocks differed from those in New York by almost twelve minutes. In 1883, without authority from Congress, the railroads established four standard time zones for the country. Railroad time became national time.

FARMING THE PLAINS

Western agriculture in the late nineteenth century exemplified two important achievements: the transformation of arid prairies into crop-producing land and the transformation of agriculture into big business via mechanization, long-distance transportation, and scientific cultivation. The climate and terrain of the Great Plains presented formidable challenges. Irrigation and the mechanization of agriculture enabled farmers to feed the nation's burgeoning population and turned the United States into the world's breadbasket.

Settlement of the Plains

During the 1870s and 1880s, more acres were farmed in states such as Kansas, Nebraska, and Texas than in the entire country during the previous 250 years. The number of farms tripled from 2 million to over 6 million between 1860 and 1910, as hundreds of thousands of hopeful farmers headed to the Plains. The Homestead Act of 1862 and other measures drew settlers with cheap or free plots for those who would live there and improve their property. Land-rich railroads advertised cheap land, arranged credit terms, and offered reduced fares to would-be settlers, while company agents—often former immigrants—traveled to Denmark, Sweden, Germany, and other European nations to recruit settlers.

To most migrating families, the West seemed to promise a chance at a better life. Railroad expansion enabled remote farmers to ship produce to market, and the construction of grain elevators eased storage problems. Worldwide and national population growth sparked the demand for farm products, and the prospects for commercial agriculture became increasingly favorable.

Hardship on the Plains

Farm life was harder than advertisements and railroad agents insinuated. Migrants often encountered scarcities of essentials they once enjoyed. Open prairies contained insufficient lumber, so pioneer families built houses of sod and burned buffalo dung for heat. Water was sometimes scarce also. Machinery for drilling wells was expensive, as were windmills for drawing water to the surface.

The weather posed a formidable challenge. The climate between the Missouri River and the Rocky Mountains divides along a line running from Minnesota

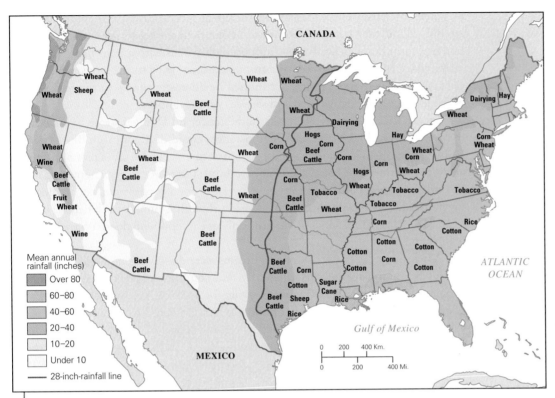

Map 17.3   Agricultural Regions of the United States, 1890

In the Pacific Northwest and east of the twenty-eight-inch-rainfall line, farmers could grow a greater variety of crops. Territory west of the line was either too mountainous or too arid to support agriculture without irrigation. The grasslands that once fed buffalo herds could now feed beef cattle.

southwest through Oklahoma, then south, bisecting Texas. West of this line, annual rainfall averages less than twenty-eight inches, not enough for most crops and even that rain was unreliable.

Weather was unpredictable. Weeks of torrid summer heat and parching winds suddenly gave way to violent storms that washed away crops and property. Winter blizzards piled up snowdrifts that halted outdoor movement. Melting snow swelled streams, and floods threatened millions of acres. In fall, a rainless week turned dry grasslands into tinder, and the slightest spark could ignite a prairie fire. A severe Texas drought between 1884 and 1886 drove many farmers off the land.

Nature could be cruel even under good conditions. Weather that was favorable for crops also bred insects. In the 1870s and 1880s, grasshopper swarms devoured everything: plants, tree bark, and clothing. One farmer lamented, the "hoppers left behind nothing but the mortgage."

Social Isolation

Settlers also faced isolation. New England and European farmers lived in villages, traveling daily to nearby fields. In the Plains, the Far West, and the South, peculiarities of land division compelled rural dwellers to live far apart. Because most plots were rectangular—usually encompassing 160 acres—at most four families could live near by, but only if they congregated around their shared four-corner intersection. In practice, farm families lived away from boundary lines with a half-mile separating farmhouses. Men might find escape from occasional trips to sell crops or buy supplies. Women were more isolated, confined by domestic chores to the household, with rare trips to exchange food and services with neighbors.

Letters that the young Nebraska homesteader Ed Donnell wrote to his family in Missouri reveal how time and circumstances could dull optimism. In fall 1885, Donnell rejoiced to his mother, "I like Nebr first rate. . . . I have saw a pretty tuff time a part of the time since I have been out here, but I started out to get a home and I was determined to win or die in the attempt. . . . Have got a good crop of corn, a floor in my house and got it ceiled overhead." Already, though, Donnell was lonely. "There is lots of other bachelors here but I am the only one I know who doesn't have kinfolks living handy."

A year and a half later, Donnell's dreams were dissolving, and still a bachelor, he was beginning to look elsewhere. By fall, conditions had worsened. Donnell lamented, "We have been having wet weather for 3 weeks. . . . My health has been so poor this summer and the wind and the sun hurts my head so. I think if I can sell I will . . . move to town for I can get $40 a month working in a grist mill and I would not be exposed to the weather." Thousands shared Donnell's hardships, and their cityward migration fueled late-nineteenth-century urban growth (see Chapter 19).

Mail-Order Companies and Rural Free Delivery

Farm families organized churches and clubs to ease isolation. By 1900 two developments brought rural settlers into closer contact with modern consumer society.

First, mail-order companies, such as Montgomery Ward and Sears, Roebuck, made new products widely attainable by the 1870s and 1880s. Letters to Ward and Sears reported family news and sought advice on needs from gifts to childcare. A Washington man wrote, "As you advertise everything for sale that a person wants, I thought I would write you, as I am in need of a wife, and see what you could do for me."

Second, after farmers petitioned Congress for extension of the postal service, in 1896 the government made Rural Free Delivery (RFD) widely available. Farmers who previously picked up mail in town, could receive letters, newspapers, and catalogues in a roadside mailbox almost daily. In 1913 the postal service inaugurated parcel post, making shipping costs much cheaper.

Mechanization of Agriculture

Machinery drove the agricultural revolution. When the Civil War drew men away from farms in the upper Mississippi River valley, women and older men who remained behind began using reapers and other mechanical implements. After the war, continued demand encouraged farmers to utilize machines, and inventors developed new implements. Seeders, combines, binders, mowers, and rotary plows improved grain production on the Plains and in California, while the centrifugal cream separator, patented in 1879, sped the skimming of cream from milk.

TABLE 17.1   Summary: Government Land Policy

Railroad land grants (1850–1871)	Granted 181 million acres to railroads to encourage construction and development
Homestead Act (1862)	Gave 80 million acres to settlers to encourage settlement
Morrill Act (1862)	Granted 11 million acres to states to sell to fund public agricultural colleges
Other grants	Granted 129 million acres to states to sell for other educational and related purposes
Dawes Act (1887)	Allotted some reservation lands to individual Indians to promote private property and weaken tribal values among Indians and offered remaining reservation lands for sale to whites (By 1906, some 75 million acres had been acquired by whites.)
Various laws	Permitted direct sales of 100 million acres by the Land Office

Source: Goldfield, David, et al., *The American Journey,* 3d ed. (Upper Saddle River, NJ: Prentice Hall, 2004).

For centuries, farmers planted only what they could harvest by hand. Machines—driven first by animals, then by steam—significantly increased productivity. Before mechanization, a farmer working alone could harvest about 7.5 acres of wheat. Using an automatic binder that cut and bundled the grain, he could harvest 135 acres. Machines made other crops more profitable as well (see Table 17.1).

Legislative and Scientific Aids

Congress and scientists worked to improve existing crops and develop new ones. The 1862 Morrill Land Grant Act gave states federal lands to sell for financing agricultural research. Consequently, new public universities were established in Wisconsin, Illinois, Minnesota, California, and other states. A second Morrill Act in 1890 aided more schools, including several all-black colleges. The Hatch Act of 1887 provided for agricultural experiment stations in every state, further encouraging farming science and technology.

Science enabled farmers to use the soil more efficiently. Researchers developed dry farming, a plowing and harrowing technique that minimized evaporation. Botanists perfected varieties of hard wheat whose seeds could withstand northern winters. Agriculturists also adapted new varieties of alfalfa from Mongolia, corn from North Africa, and rice from Asia. The horticulturist George Washington Carver, a son of slaves who became a chemist and taught at Alabama's Tuskegee Institute, created hundreds of products from peanuts, soybeans, and sweet potatoes. Other scientists combated plant and animal diseases. Technology helped American farmers expand productivity in the market economy.

THE RANCHING FRONTIER

Western commercial farming ran headlong into one of the region's most romantic industries—ranching. Beginning in the sixteenth century, Spanish landholders raised cattle in Mexico and what would become the American Southwest. They employed Indian and Mexican cowboys, known as *vaqueros*, to tend herds and round up cattle. Anglo ranchers moving into Texas and California in the early nineteenth century hired *vaqueros* to teach them roping, branding, horse training, and saddle making. About one-fourth of all cowboys were black. While they probably experienced less discrimination than other African American laborers, after work, they had to sit in separate sections in saloons and endured name-calling and mistreatment.

By the 1860s, cattle raising became increasingly profitable, as population growth boosted the demand for beef and railroads simplified food transportation. By 1870 drovers were herding thousands of Texas cattle northward to Kansas, Missouri, and Wyoming (see Map 17.1). At the northern terminus, the cattle were sold or loaded onto trains bound for Chicago and St. Louis slaughterhouses.

The long drive gave rise to romantic lore of bellowing cattle, buckskin-clad cowboys, and smoky campfires. But trekking 1,000 miles for months made cattle sinewy and tough. Herds that trespassed on Indian lands and farmers' fields were sometimes shot at. When ranchers discovered that crossing Texas longhorns with heavier Hereford and Angus breeds produced animals that were better able to survive harsh winters and were highly profitable, cattle raising expanded northward, and proliferating herds in Kansas, Nebraska, Colorado, Wyoming, Montana, and the Dakotas crowded out declining buffalo.

The Open Range

Cattle raisers minimized costs by buying a few acres bordering a stream and turning their herds loose on adjacent public domain that no one wanted because it lacked water access. Called open-range ranching, a cattle raiser could utilize thousands of acres by owning much less. Neighboring ranchers often formed associations and allowed herds to graze together, burning an identifying brand into each animal's hide. But as cattle production rose, cattle began to overrun the range, and other groups challenged ranchers over use of the land.

Sheepherders from California and New Mexico were also using the public domain, sparking territorial clashes. Ranchers complained that sheep ruined grassland by eating to the roots and that cattle refused to graze where sheep had been. Occasionally ranchers and sheepherders resorted to violence rather than settle disagreements in court, where a judge might discover that both were using public land illegally.

More important, the farming frontier generated new land demands. Lacking sufficient timber and stone for traditional fencing, western settlers could not easily define their property. Tensions flared when farmers accused cattle raisers of letting herds trespass on cropland and when herders charged that farmers should fence their property.

Barbed Wire

The solution was barbed wire. Invented in 1873 by Joseph F. Glidden, a DeKalb, Illinois, farmer, this inexpensive and mass-produced fencing consisted of wires held in place by sharp spurs twisted around them. It enabled Plains homesteaders to protect their farms from grazing cattle. It also ended open-range ranching and made roundups unnecessary, as large-scale ranchers enclosed herds within private property. Similarly, the development of the round silo for storing and making feed (silage) enabled cattle raisers to feed herds without grazing.

A group of cowboys prepare for a roundup. Note the presence of African Americans, who, along with Mexicans, made up one-fourth of all cowboys. Though they rarely became trail bosses or ranch owners, black cowboys enjoyed an independence on the trails that was unavailable to them on tenant farms and city streets. (Nebraska State Historical Society, RG 2608-PH-O-2167-a. Copy and reuse restrictions apply.)

Ranching as Big Business

By 1890 big businesses were taking over the cattle industry and applying scientific methods of breeding and feeding. Corporations also used technology to squeeze larger returns from meatpacking. Every part of a cow had uses: half was meat, but larger profits came from hides for leather, blood for fertilizer, hooves for glue, fat for candles and soap, and the rest for sausages. Cattle processing harmed the environment, as meatpackers and leather tanners dumped unsold goods into waterways. By the late nineteenth century, the Chicago River created a powerful stench that made nearby residents ill.

Open-range ranching made beef a staple of the American diet and created a few fortunes, but it could not survive the rush of history. Overgrazing destroyed Plains grass supplies, and the brutal winter of 1886–1887 destroyed 90 percent of some herds and drove small ranchers out of business. By 1890, large-scale ranchers owned or leased the land they used. Cowboys formed labor organizations and struck for higher pay. The myth of the cowboy's freedom and individualism lived on, but ranching became a corporate business.

Summary

The landscape of the American West exerted a lasting influence on the complex mix of people there. Living mostly in small groups, Indians, the original inhabitants, hunted, farmed, and depended on delicate resources, such as buffalo herds and salmon runs. When they came into contact with commerce-minded European Americans, their resistance to the market economy, diseases, and violence that whites brought failed.

Mexicans, Chinese, African Americans, and Anglos discovered a reciprocal relationship between human activities and the environment, too. Miners, timber cutters, farmers, and builders extracted raw minerals for eastern factories, used irrigation and mechanization to yield agricultural abundance, filled pastures with cattle and

The Myth of the Cowboy

The cowboy has been a distinctive American icon, yet actual American cowboys, whose heyday lasted only from about 1865 to 1890, were poorly paid, poorly fed, illiterate young men who sometimes stole employers' cattle. Of about thirty-five thousand cowboys, 25 percent were black and another 15 percent were Mexican, Indian, and Chinese, all of whom were treated worse by employers than their white counterparts. Often unemployed, some white and nonwhite cowboys joined unions and went on strike for job security and better wages. Mostly, cowboys got drunk more often than they engaged in gunfights, enforced the law, or defended a woman's honor.

Still, the apparently independent, masculine, outdoor existence that cowboys led fueled romantic notions that they symbolized the true American. Buffalo Bill Cody was one of the first to create this image in his Wild West shows through a cattle herder named Buck Taylor, whom Cody glamorized as King of the Cowboys. Writers and artists began depicting cowboys as valiant characters. Owen Wister's bestselling novel, *The Virginian* (1902), helped reinforce the image of a rugged, self-reliant individualist who took the law into his own hands. Myriad films, radio and television programs, and music similarly turned this common laborer into a hero. Roy Rogers, who acted in hundreds of movies and TV shows between 1938 and 1964, was one of many who enlarged the myth Gone were the ill-fitting, makeshift clothing, now replaced by fancy boots, Stetson hats, and blue jeans.

Equally important, the low-life reality was replaced by a lawman battling evil. President Ronald Reagan embellished his image by wearing western clothing and being photographed on horseback. And President George W. Bush, a Texan, assumed the role of "good cowboy" after September 11, 2001, while opponents of his Iraq invasion criticized America's "bad cowboy" tactics of reckless violence. The cowboy myth has consequently left a legacy of images and actions.

sheep to expand food sources, and constructed railroads to tie the nation together. But the environment exerted power through climate, insects and predators, undesirable plant growth, and impenetrable barriers to agriculture.

The West's settlers employed force, violence, and greed that sustained discrimination within a multiracial society, left many farmers feeling cheated, provoked contests over water and pastures, and sacrificed environmental balance for market profits. The region's raw materials and agricultural products improved living standards and hastened the industrial progress of the Machine Age, but not without costs.

Chapter Review

THE ECONOMIC ACTIVITIES OF NATIVE PEOPLES

What contributed to the weakening of Native Americans' economic systems in the late nineteenth century?

The Native American economic system was increasingly eroded after 1850 by a number of factors, some natural and some resulting from increasing interaction with, and encroachment by, whites. Southwestern Indian economies were devastated by the declining buffalo herd due to drought, diseases brought by white-owned livestock, excessive Native American hunting and trade, white settlement on Indian lands used for grazing, and whites' efforts to eliminate the buffalo to make way for railroads. Northwestern Indian economies, which relied on salmon fishing, similarly suffered when white commercial fisheries diminished salmon supplies and dammed up rivers and tributaries that were vital for fishing stocks.

THE TRANSFORMATION OF NATIVE CULTURES

How did the U.S. government's reservation policy make way for the market economy in the West?

U.S. reservation policy before the 1880s forced Indians onto western reservations, promising to protect this territory from white encroachment. Once on reservations, Indians' dependency on whites for trade goods such as clothing, guns, horses, and food made it easier for whites to control Indian affairs. The 1887 Dawes Severalty Act dissolved community-owned Indian land, granting it instead to qualifying individual Indian families. The land was held in trust for twenty-five years and allowed the U.S. government to sell unassigned allotments (typically to whites). The goal of this was to assimilate Indians into white culture via private property, but in truth it reduced their land holdings by more than half and made way for land sales and further white settlement of the West.

THE EXTRACTION OF NATURAL RESOURCES

What sparked the rise of the conservation movement?

Mining for precious metals, cutting trees for lumber, and drilling for oil drew thousands of people to the West seeking fortune and a better life. It also transformed the natural landscape, contributed to environmental wastefulness and sparked a debate over the desire for progress and the need to preserve nature. This gave rise to a conservation movement after the Civil War. Hunters lobbied legislatures for hunting regulations; artists and tourists pressured Congress to protect Yosemite Valley by granting it to California for public use; and in 1862, the Yellowstone River region in Wyoming became the first national park. Congress also authorized President Benjamin Harrison to create forest reserves, at the urging of a group led by activist John Muir, who founded the environmental group the Sierra Club in 1892.

IRRIGATION AND TRANSPORTATION

How did government policies aid the development of the West?

Two ways: first, during the Civil War era, government subsidies for railroad construction—among the largest in U.S. history—included massive land grants, which companies could use for interstate routes or sell to finance construction. Federal land grants topped 180 million acres, while states handed over another 50 million acres, and cities and towns helped by offering loans or buying railroad stocks. Second, through the Newlands Reclamation Act (1902), Congress supported the sale of western lands in parcels smaller than 160 acres to individuals, with the funds being used to finance irrigation projects in the region. That, in turn, facilitated the agricultural and economic development.

FARMING THE PLAINS

What helped ease the hardships farmers faced when settling the West?

Migrant families hoped to find a better life in the West, but often experienced loneliness, isolation, the lack of essential products and services they previously knew, and even shortages of lumber needed to build homes. But the arrival of the railroad, the extension of the postal service into the West, and the advent of the mail order business ended some of their problems by bringing products and people to the region. New technology and mechanization also made farming easier, and the creation of social clubs and other organizations helped ease the isolation.

THE RANCHING FRONTIER

How did ranching shift from small, individual-owned endeavors to big business?

With the increasing demand for beef and expansion of herds, ranchers overgrazed the land, which destroyed grass supplies that fed Plains herds. A brutal winter in 1886 to 1887 killed off 90 percent of some ranchers' herds and drove many out of business. By 1890, big business took over the cattle industry and used scientific methods for breeding and feeding to eliminate dependency on grass and grazing lands.

SUGGESTIONS FOR FURTHER READING

William Cronon, *Nature's Metropolis: Chicago and the Great West* (1991)

Albert L. Hurtado and Peter Iverson, *Major Problems in American Indian History: Documents and Essays,* 2d ed. (2001)

Karl Jacoby, *Crimes Against Nature: Squatters, Poachers, Thieves and the Hidden History of American Conservation* (2001)

Patricia Nelson Limerick, *The Legacy of Conquest: The Unbroken Past of the American West* (1987)

Eugene P. Moehring, *Urbanism and Empire in the Far West, 1840–1890* (2004)

Alan Trachtenberg, *The Incorporation of America: Culture and Society in the Gilded Age* (1982)

Robert M. Utley, *The Indian Frontier of the American West, 1846–1890* (1984)

Richard White, *"It's Your Misfortune and None of My Own": A New History of the American* (1991)

CHAPTER 18

The Machine Age | 1877–1920

CHAPTER OUTLINE

Technology and the Triumph
of Industrialization

>   **LINKS TO THE WORLD:**
>   The Atlantic Cable

Mechanization and the Changing Status
of Labor

Labor Violence and the Union
Movement

Standards of Living

The Corporate Consolidation
Movement

The Gospel of Wealth and Its Critics

Summary

>   **LEGACY FOR A PEOPLE
>   AND A NATION:** Technology
>   of Recorded Sound

In 1911 iron molders at the Watertown Arsenal, a government weapons factory near Boston, went on strike after a fellow worker was fired. Joseph Cooney objected to having an efficiency expert time his work with a stopwatch, and the molders feared management would impose new labor standards. The iron molders' union president John Frey explained, "The workman believes when he goes on strike that he is defending his job." The molders felt a property right to their labor, that jobs could not be changed or taken away without their consent.

The army officers who ran the factory thought they owned the molders' labor and that output was "one-half what it should be." To increase production, they hired Dwight Merrick, an expert in a new field called scientific management, to time workers and speed performance.

The day Merrick began his study, a molder named Perkins secretly timed the same task. Merrick reported that the job should take twenty-four minutes and that the workers were wasting time and materials; Perkins found that the job required fifty minutes and that there was no waste. That evening, the molders discussed how to respond to the discrepancy between Merrick's report and theirs. Cooney argued for resisting scientific management; the workers drew up a petition and were ready to walk out.

Eventually, the molders and their bosses compromised, but this incident reveals an important consequence of the industrialization that made countless new products available in the late 1800s, as a new consumer society emerged. To increase production, factory owners harnessed technology and divided work routines into minute, repetitive tasks organized by the clock. Workers who had long felt valued for their skills, now struggled to avoid becoming slaves to machines. Defenders of the new

This icon will direct you to interactive
activities and study materials on
A People And A Nation, Brief Edition
website: **www.cengage.com/history/norton/
peoplenationbrief8e**

Chronology

1869	Knights of Labor is founded.
1873–78	Economy declines.
1876	Bonsack invents machine for rolling cigarettes.
1877	Widespread railroad strikes protest wage cuts.
1878	Edison Electric Light Company is founded.
1879	George's *Poverty and Progress* argues for taxing unearned wealth.
1881	First federal trademark law begins spread of brand names.
1882	Standard Oil Trust is founded.
1884–85	Economy declines.
1886	Haymarket riot in Chicago protests police brutality against labor demonstrations. American Federation of Labor (AFL) is founded.
1888	Bellamy's *Looking Backward* depicts utopian world free of monopoly and class divisions.
1890	Sherman Anti-Trust Act outlaws "combinations in restraint of trade."
1892	Homestead (Pennsylvania) steelworkers strike against Carnegie Steel Company.
1893–97	Economic depression causes high unemployment and business failures.

1894	Workers of Pullman Palace Car Company strike.
1895	*U.S. v. E. C. Knight Co.* limits Congress's power to regulate manufacturing.
1896	*Holden v. Harcy* upholds law regulating miners' working hours.
1898	Taylor promotes scientific management as efficiency measure in industry.
1901–03	U.S. Steel Corporation is founded. E. I. du Pont de Nemours and Company is reorganized. Ford Motor Company is founded.
1903	Women's Trade Union League (WTUL) is founded.
1905	*Lochner v. New York* overturns law limiting bakery workers' working hours and limits labor protection laws. Industrial Workers of the World (IWW) is founded.
1908	*Muller v. Oregon* upholds law limiting women to ten-hour workday. First Ford Model T is built.
1911	Triangle Shirtwaist Company fire in New York City leaves 146 workers dead.
1913	Ford begins moving–assembly-line production.
1919	Telephone operators strike in New England.

system devised theories to justify it, while laborers tried to combat what they thought were abuses of power.

In the mid-nineteenth century, an industrial revolution swept through parts of the United States, and its mechanization powered a second round in the late 1800s and early 1900s. Three technological developments characterized this new stage: electricity, the internal-combustion engine, and new applications in the use of chemicals. Electricity provided a needed alternative to less efficient steam engines. The demand for transportation beyond railroads spurred progress in automobile manufacture. And the textile industry's experiments with dyes, bleaches, and cleaning agents advanced chemical research.

In 1860 one-fourth of the American labor force worked in manufacturing and transportation; by 1900 over half did. As the twentieth century dawned, the United States was the world's largest producer of raw materials and food, and the most productive industrial nation (see Map 18.1). Between 1877 and 1920 (see Chapter 19), labor-saving machines boosted productivity. Innovations in business organization and marketing also fueled the drive for profits.

These developments had momentous effects on living standards and everyday life, as goods that had once been accessible to a few became available to many.

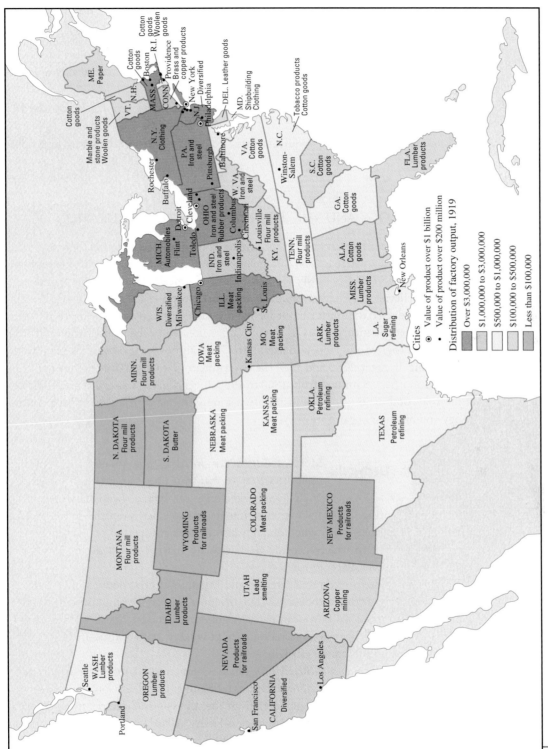

Map 18.1   Industrial Production, 1919

By the early twentieth century, each state could boast at least one kind of industrial production. Although the value of goods produced was still highest in the Northeast, states like Minnesota and California had impressive dollar values of outputs.

(*Source:* Data from U.S. Bureau of the Census, *Fourteenth Census of the United States, 1920*, Vol. 9, *Manufacturing* [Washington, DC: U.S. Government Printing Office, 1921].)

Industrialization furthered the extraction of natural resources and the expansion of agriculture (see Chapter 17). These processes combined people, the environment, and technology in ways that were both constructive and destructive.

- How did mechanization affect the lives of average workers and the makeup of the labor force?
- In what ways did technological innovation alter the American standard of living?
- What ideas did some Americans use to justify industrialization, and how did others criticize it?

TECHNOLOGY AND THE TRIUMPH OF INDUSTRIALIZATION

In 1876 Thomas Edison and his associates opened an invention factory in Menlo Park, New Jersey, where Edison said he hoped to create "a minor invention every ten days and a big thing every six months or so." If Americans wanted new products, Edison believed, they had to organize and work purposefully toward progress. His attitude reflected the spirit that propelled inventiveness and industrialization in the late nineteenth century. The U.S. Patent Office, created by the Constitution to "promote the Progress of science and useful Arts," reveals how innovative Americans were becoming. Between 1790 and 1860 the government granted 36,000 patents, and registered another 1.5 million from 1860 to 1930. Inventions in areas such as electricity, internal combustion, and chemistry often sprang from a marriage between technology and business organization.

Birth of the Electrical Industry

Most of Edison's more than one thousand inventions used electricity to transmit light, sound, and images. In 1878 he embarked on a search for a cheap, efficient means of indoor lighting. After tedious experiments, Edison perfected the incandescent bulb. His Edison Electric Light Company also devised a system of power generation and distribution to widely provide electricity. To market his ideas, at Christmas 1880, he illuminated Menlo Park.

Edison's system of direct current could transmit electric power only a mile or two, losing voltage the farther it traveled. Inventor George Westinghouse solved the problem. He purchased European patent rights to generators that used alternating current and transformers that reduced high-voltage power, thus making long-distance transmission more efficient.

Other entrepreneurs utilized new business practices to market Edison's and Westinghouse's technological breakthroughs. Samuel Insull, Edison's private secretary, organized Edison power plants nationwide, amassing an electric utility empire. In the late 1880s and early 1890s, financiers Henry Villard and J. P. Morgan bought up patents in electric lighting and merged small equipment-manufacturing companies into the General Electric Company. General Electric and Westinghouse Electric established research laboratories to create electrical products for everyday use.

Individual inventors continued to work independently and sell their handiwork and patents to manufacturers. Granville T. Woods, an engineer sometimes called the

The Atlantic Cable

During the late nineteenth century, as American manufacturers expanded their markets overseas, their ability to communicate with customers and investors improved immeasurably as a result of telegraph cable beneath the Atlantic Ocean. The telegraph was an American invention, and Cyrus Field, who thought up the idea of laying cable across the ocean, was an American. Yet most of the engineers and capitalists involved were British. In 1851 a British company laid the first successful undersea telegraph cable from Dover, England, to Calais, France, proving that an insulated wire could carry signals underwater. Its effectiveness inspired British and American businessmen to attempt a larger project across the Atlantic.

The first attempts failed, but in 1866 a British ship, funded by British investors, successfully laid a telegraph wire that operated without interruption. Thereafter, England and the United States grew more closely linked in diplomatic relations, and citizens of both nations developed greater concern for each other. When American president James Garfield was assassinated in 1881, the news traveled almost instantly to Great Britain, and Britons mourned the death profusely.

Some people lamented the stresses that near-instant international communications now created. But financially savvy individuals experienced welcome benefits. Rapid availability of stock quotes helped the New York and London stock exchanges boom. Newspaper readers enjoyed learning about events on the other side of the ocean the next day, instead of a week later. By 1902 underwater cables circled the globe. The age of global telecommunications had begun.

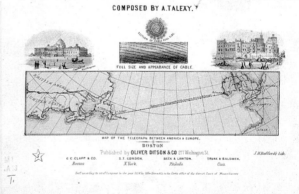

Laid by British ships across the ocean in 1866, the Atlantic cable linked the United States with England and continental Europe so that telegraph communications could be sent and received much more swiftly than ever before. Now Europeans and Americans could exchange news about politics, business, and military movements almost instantly, whereas previously such information could take a week or more to travel from one country to another.

(Library of Congress)

black Edison, patented thirty-five devices vital to electronics and communications. Most were sold to companies like General Electric, including an automatic circuit breaker, an electromagnetic brake, and instruments to aid communications between railroad trains.

Henry Ford and the Automobile Industry

European inventors made early innovations in the technology of the internal-combustion engine. In 1885 a German engineer, Gottlieb Daimler, built a lightweight engine driven by vaporized gasoline. In the 1890s, Henry Ford, an electrical engineer in Detroit's Edison Company, experimented with Daimler's engine to power a vehicle. Applying organizational genius to this invention, Ford spawned a massive industry.

Ford had a scheme as well as a product, declaring in 1909, "I am going to democratize the automobile. When I'm through, everybody will be able to afford one." Ford planned to mass-produce thousands of identical cars, and engineers set up assembly lines that drastically reduced the time and production costs. Instead of performing numerous tasks, each worker did just one, repeatedly, assembling the entire car along a conveyor belt.

In 1913 the Ford Motor Company's first assembly line opened in Highland Park inside Detroit, Michigan, and the next year, Ford sold 248,000 cars. Soon, other manufacturers entered the field. Rising automobile output created jobs, higher earnings, and greater profits for related industries, such as oil, paint, rubber, and glass, as well; this in turn necessitated increased resources from the West and abroad. Moreover, assembly-line production would not have been possible without precision machine tools to create standardized and finely tuned parts.

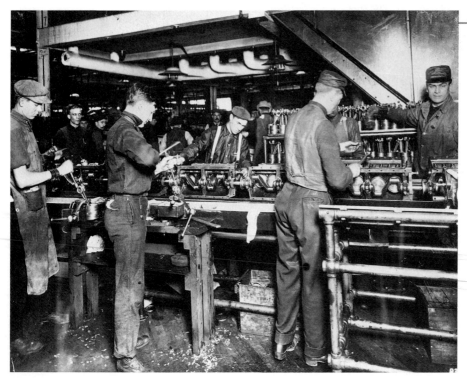

The assembly line broke the production process down into simple tasks that individual workers could efficiently repeat hour after hour. Here, around 1914 assembly-line workers at the Ford plant in Highland Park, Michigan, outside Detroit, are installing pistons in engines of the Model T. (From the Collections of The Henry Ford Museum and Greenfield Village)

By 1914 a Ford car cost $490, one-fourth of the price a decade earlier. But that was too expensive for many workers, who earned at best $2 a day. That year, Ford tried to spur productivity, reduce labor turnover, head off unionization, and better enable his workers to buy the cars they produced through his Five-Dollar-Day plan—a combination of wages and profit sharing.

The du Ponts and the Chemical Industry

The du Pont family similarly transformed the chemical industry. In 1902, fearing antitrust prosecution for the company's near monopoly of the explosives industry, three cousins, Alfred, Coleman, and Pierre, took over E. I. du Pont de Nemours and Company and broadened production into fertilizers, dyes, and other chemical products. In 1911 du Pont scientists and engineers in the nation's first corporate research laboratory adapted cellulose to produce such consumer goods as photographic film, lacquer, textile fibers, and plastics. In 1914 Pierre du Pont invested $25 million in General Motors, helping that company compete with Ford. The du Pont company also pioneered methods of management, accounting, and reinvestment of earnings, which contributed to efficient production, better recordkeeping, and higher profits.

Technology and Southern Industry

The South's major staple crops, tobacco and cotton, helped industrialize the region after the Civil War. Before the 1870s, Americans used tobacco mainly for snuff, cigars, and chewing. But in 1876 James Bonsack, an eighteen-year-old Virginian, invented a cigarette-rolling machine. Sales soared after 1885 when the North Carolinian James B. Duke mass-produced cigarettes with Bonsack's machine and enticed consumers with free samples, trading cards, and billboard ads. By 1900 his American Tobacco Company was a global business, employing black and white workers (including women), though in separate workrooms.

New technology helped relocate the textile industry to the South. Factories with electric looms were more efficient than New England's water-powered mills, required fewer skilled workers, and expanded production hours. Investors built new plants in southern communities, where cheap labor was plentiful. By 1900 the South had more than four hundred textile mills, with 4 million spindles. Women and children earned 50 cents a day for twelve or more hours—about half the wages of northern workers. Most mills hired black workers only as janitors. Companies built villages around their mills, where they controlled housing, stores, schools, and churches and banned company criticism and union organization.

Northern and European investors financed other southern industries. During the 1880s, northern capitalists developed southern iron and steel manufacturing, much of it in Birmingham, Alabama. Between 1890 and 1900, northern lumber syndicates moved into the pine forests of the Gulf states, boosting production 500 percent. Southern wood production advanced the construction industry and relocated furniture and paper production from the North to the South. Challenging the power of the planter class, a business class of manufacturers, merchants, and financiers heralded the emergence of a New South with southern cities as the nerve centers of a new economic order (see Chapter 19).

Consequences of Technology

Machines broadly altered everyday life. Telephones and typewriters made face-to-face communication less important and facilitated correspondence and recordkeeping in growing insurance, banking, and advertising firms. Electric sewing machines made mass-produced clothing. Refrigeration enabled the preservation and shipment of meat, fruit, vegetables, and dairy products. Cash registers and adding machines revamped accounting and created new clerical jobs. At the same time, American universities established programs in engineering.

Profits resulted from higher production at lower costs. As technological innovations made large-scale production more economical, owners replaced small factories with larger ones. Between 1850 and 1900, average capital investment in a manufacturing firm increased by 250 percent. Only large companies could afford to buy complex machines. And large companies received discounts for buying raw materials and shipping in bulk—advantages economists call economies of scale.

Profitability also depended on how production was organized. Where once workers controlled the methods and timing of production, by the 1890s engineers and managers with scientific knowledge planned every task to increase output. Through standardization, they reduced the need for workers' skills, boosting profits at the expense of worker independence.

Frederick W. Taylor and Efficiency

The most influential advocate of efficient production was Frederick W. Taylor. As foreman and engineer for the Midvale Steel Company in the 1880s, Taylor concluded companies could best reduce costs and increase profits by applying studies of "how quickly the various kinds of work . . . ought to be done." This meant producing more for lower cost per unit, usually by eliminating unnecessary workers.

In 1898 Taylor took his stopwatch to the Bethlehem Steel Company to illustrate his principles of scientific management. His experiments required studying workers and devising "a series of motions which can be made quickest and best." For shoveling ore, Taylor designed fifteen kinds of shovels and prescribed the proper motions for each, thereby reducing a crew of 600 men to 140. Soon other companies, including the Watertown Arsenal, applied Taylor's theories.

Consequently, time, as much as quality, became the measure of acceptable work, and management dictated how things were done. As elements of the assembly line, employees feared they were becoming another interchangeable part.

MECHANIZATION AND THE CHANGING STATUS OF LABOR

By 1900, the status of labor shifted dramatically. Technological innovation and assembly-line production created new jobs, but because most machines were labor saving, fewer workers could produce more in less time. Instead of producers, the working class now consisted mainly of employees who worked for hire. Producers were paid on the basis of the quality of what they produced; employees received wages for time spent on the job.

Mass Production

Manufacturing being subdivided into small tasks, workers repeated the same standardized operation all day every day. One investigator found that a worker became "a mere machine." Workers no longer decided when to begin and end the workday or what tools and techniques to use. The clock regulated them. As a Massachusetts factory laborer testified in 1879, "During working hours the men are not allowed to speak to each other . . . on pain of instant discharge. Men are hired to watch and patrol the shop."

Workers such as the Watertown iron molders struggled to retain autonomy. Artisans—glass workers and coopers (barrel makers)—caught in the transition from hand labor to machine production, fought to preserve their work customs, for example, by appointing a fellow worker to read a newspaper aloud while they worked. Immigrant factory workers tried to persuade foremen to hire their relatives and friends. After work, workers enjoyed drinking and holiday celebrations, ignoring employers' attempts to control their social lives.

Concerned with efficiency, employers wanted behavior standards upheld. Ford Motor Company required workers to meet the company's behavior code before becoming eligible for the Five-Dollar-Day plan. To increase worker incentives, some employers established piecework rates, paying per item produced rather than per hour worked. Efforts to increase productivity tried to make workers perform like the machines they operated.

Restructuring of the Work Force

As machines reduced the need for skilled workers, employers cut labor costs by hiring women and children and paying them low wages. Between 1880 and 1900, the numbers of employed women soared from 2.6 million to 8.6 million (see Figure 18.1). The proportion of women in domestic service (maids, cooks, laundresses)—the most common and lowest-paid female employment—dropped as jobs opened in other sectors. In manufacturing, women usually held menial positions in textile mills and food-processing plants that paid $1.56 for a seventy-hour week. (Unskilled men received $7 to $10.) Although the number of female factory hands tripled between 1880 and 1900, the proportion of women workers remained the same.

Expansion of the clerical and retail sectors boosted the numbers and percentages of women who were typists, bookkeepers, and sales clerks—previously male jobs. Inventions, such as the typewriter, cash register, and adding machine, simplified these tasks. By 1920, women filled nearly half of all clerical jobs; in 1880 only 4 percent were women. Although poorly paid, women were attracted to sales jobs because of the respectability, pleasant surroundings, and contact with affluent customers these positions offered. Nevertheless, sex discrimination persisted. In department stores, only male cashiers took in cash and made change. Women held some low-level supervisory positions, but males dominated the managerial ranks.

Meanwhile, the number of children in nonagricultural occupations tripled between 1870 and 1900. In 1890 over 18 percent of children between ages ten and

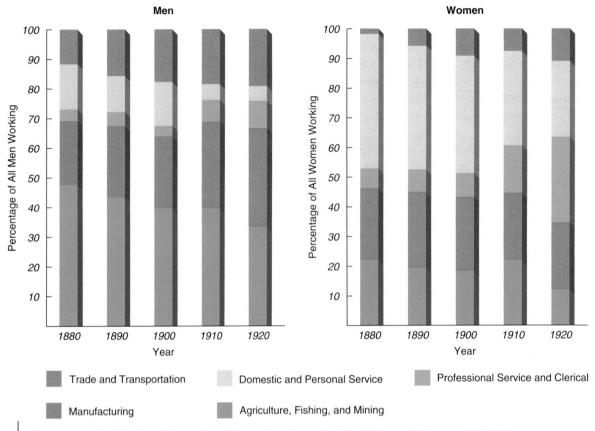

Men   **Women**

Trade and Transportation   Domestic and Personal Service   Professional Service and Clerical

Manufacturing   Agriculture, Fishing, and Mining

Figure 18.1 Distribution of Occupational Categories Among Employed Men and Women, 1880–1920
The changing lengths of the bar segments of each part of this graph represent trends in male and female employment. Over the forty years covered by this graph, the agriculture, fishing, and mining segment for men and the domestic service segment for women declined the most, whereas notable increases occurred in manufacturing for men and professional services (especially store clerks and teachers) for women. (*Source:* U.S. Bureau of the Census, *Census of the United States, 1880, 1890, 1900, 1910, 1920* [Washington, DC: U.S. Government Printing Office].)

fifteen were gainfully employed (see Figure 18.2), particularly in textile and shoe factories. Mechanization created numerous light tasks, such as running errands, which children could handle cheaply. Conditions were especially hard for child laborers in the South, where mill owners induced desperate white sharecroppers and tenant farmers to bind their children to factories at miserably low wages.

Several states, especially in the Northeast, passed laws specifying minimum ages and maximum hours for child labor. But statutes regulated only firms operating within state borders, not those engaged in interstate commerce. Enforcing age requirements proved difficult because many parents, needing income, lied about their children's ages. After 1900, state laws and automation, along with compulsory school attendance laws, reduced the number of children employed in manufacturing, and Progressive era reformers sought federal legislation restricting child labor (see Chapter 21). Still, many children continued to work at street trades—shining shoes and peddling—while poor children scavenged the streets for coal and wood and discarded clothing and furniture.

Industrial Accidents

Repetitive tasks using high-speed machinery dulled concentration, and the slightest mistake could cause serious injury. Industrial accidents rose steadily before 1920, killing or maiming hundreds of thousands of people annually. In 1913, after factories installed safety devices, 25,000 people died in industrial mishaps and 1 million were injured. There was no disability insurance to replace lost income, and families suffered acutely.

The most notorious tragedy was a fire at New York City's Triangle Shirtwaist Company in 1911, which killed 146 workers, mostly teenage immigrant women trapped in locked workrooms. Despite public clamor, prevailing free-market views hampered the passage of legislation regulating working conditions, and employers denied responsibility for employees' well-being.

Freedom of Contract

To justify their treatment of workers, employers asserted the principle of freedom of contract, claiming wages and working conditions resulted from supply and demand. Employers asserted that since workers entered into a contract with bosses, workers could seek another job if they did not like the wages or hours. Employers used supply and demand to set wages as low as laborers would accept. Employees felt trapped. A factory worker told Congress in 1879, "The market is glutted, and . . . the pay is cut down; our tasks are increased, and if we remonstrate, we are told our places can be filled."

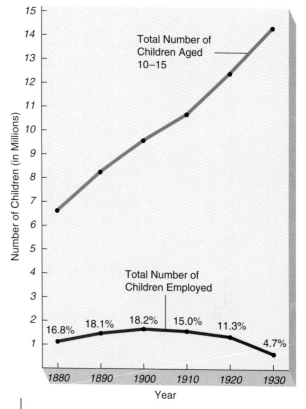

Figure 18.2   Children in the Labor Force, 1880–1930

The percentage of children in the labor force peaked around the turn of the century. Thereafter, the passage of state laws requiring children to attend school until age fourteen and limiting the ages at which children could be employed caused child labor to decline.

(*Source:* Data from *The Statistical History of the United States from Colonial Times to the Present* [Stamford, CT: Fairfield Publishers, 1965].)

Court Rulings on Labor Reform

Reformers and union leaders lobbied for laws regulating working conditions, but the Supreme Court limited such legislation by narrowly defining which jobs were dangerous and which workers needed protection. In *Holden v. Hardy* (1896), the Court upheld a law regulating miners' working hours because overly long workdays increased potential injuries. In *Lochner v. New York* (1905), however, the Court voided a law that limited bakery workers to a sixty-hour week and ten-hour day. It ruled that baking was not a dangerous enough occupation to justify restricting workers' right to sell their labor freely. Such restriction, according to the Court, violated the Fourteenth Amendment's guarantee that no state could "deprive any person of life, liberty, or property without due process of law."

In *Muller v. Oregon* (1908), the Court used a different rationale to uphold limiting laundry women to a ten-hour workday. It set aside its *Lochner* argument to assert that a woman's well-being "becomes an object of public interest and care in order to preserve the strength and vigor of the race." The case represented a victory for labor reformers seeking government regulation of women's hours and working conditions. But on the basis of the *Muller* decision, later laws barred women from occupations, such as in printing and transportation, that required heavy lifting, long hours, or night work, further confining women to low-paying, dead-end jobs.

LABOR VIOLENCE AND THE UNION MOVEMENT

Workers adjusted to mechanization as best they could, but anxiety over lost independence and a desire for better wages, hours, and working conditions drew disgruntled workers into unions. Trade unions for skilled workers in crafts like printing and iron molding dated from the early 1800s, but their influence was limited. The National Labor Union, founded in 1866, claimed 640,000 members from various industries, but it collapsed in 1873 after legislative failures.

Railroad Strikes of 1877

In the economic slump that followed the Panic of 1873, railroad managers cut wages, increased workloads, and laid off workers, especially union members. Workers responded with strikes and riots. The year 1877 marked a crisis. In July, unionized railroad workers organized strikes to protest wage cuts. Violence spread from Pennsylvania and West Virginia to the Midwest, Texas, and California, derailing trains and burning rail yards. State militia, organized and commanded by employers, broke up picket lines and fired into crowds. Factory workers, wives, and merchants aided the strikers, while railroads enlisted strikebreakers to replace union men.

Pittsburgh experienced the worst violence. On July 21 state troopers bayoneted and fired on rock-throwing demonstrators, killing ten and wounding many more. Infuriated, the mob drove the troopers into a roundhouse and set fires that destroyed 39 buildings, 104 engines, and 1,245 freight and passenger cars. The next day, the troopers shot their way out and killed twenty more citizens before fleeing. After a month, President Rutherford B. Hayes sent in federal soldiers—the first significant use of the army to quell labor unrest.

Knights of Labor

About the same time as the railroad strike, the Knights of Labor tried to attract a broad base of laborers. Founded in 1869 by Philadelphia garment cutters, the Knights began recruiting other workers in the 1870s. In 1879 Terence V. Powderly, a machinist and the mayor of Scranton, Pennsylvania, was elected grand master. Under his guidance, Knights' membership grew, peaking at 730,000 in 1886. In contrast to most craft unions, Knights welcomed unskilled and semiskilled workers, including women, immigrants, and African Americans (but not Chinese).

The Knights sought a workers' alliance offering an alternative to profit-oriented industrial capitalism. They intended to eliminate conflict between labor and management by establishing a cooperative society in which laborers, not capitalists, owned factories, mines, and railroads. The goal, argued Powderly, was to "eventually make every man his own master—every man his own employer."

The cooperative idea, attractive in the abstract, was unattainable because employers could out-compete laborers who might try to establish businesses. Strikes might achieve immediate goals, but Powderly and other Knights leaders argued that strikes diverted attention from the long-term goal of a cooperative society and that workers lost more by striking.

Some Knights, however, supported militant action. In 1886 the railroad magnate Jay Gould refused to negotiate when Knights demanded higher wages and union recognition from Southwest Railroad. A strike began in Texas and spread to Kansas, Missouri, and Arkansas. As violence increased, Powderly met with Gould and called off the strike, hoping for a settlement. But Gould rejected concessions, and the Knights gave in. Militant craft unions deserted the Knights, upset by Powderly's compromise.

After the Haymarket riot (see below), Knights' membership dwindled, although the union made a brief attempt to unite with Populists in the 1890s (see Chapter 20). Craft unions replaced the Knights' broad-based but often vague appeal, and labor unity faded.

Haymarket Riot

While the Knights were striking, other groups calling for an eight-hour workday generated the largest labor demonstration in the country's history. On May 1, 1886, in Chicago, some 100,000 workers turned out, including anarchists who believed in using violence. Chicago police, fearing that European radicals were transplanting their tradition of violence to the United States, mobilized. The day passed calmly, but two days later, police stormed an area near the McCormick reaper plant and broke up a battle between striking unionists and nonunion strikebreakers, killing two unionists and wounding others.

The next evening, laborers protested police brutality at Haymarket Square near downtown Chicago. As police approached, a bomb exploded, killing seven policemen and injuring sixty-seven. Authorities made mass arrests, and a court convicted eight anarchists of the bombing, despite questionable evidence. Four were executed, and one committed suicide in prison. The remaining three were pardoned in 1893 by Illinois governor John P. Altgeld.

The Haymarket bombing, like the 1877 railroad strikes, drew attention to labor's growing discontent and heightened the fear of radicalism. The participation of anarchists and socialists, many of them foreign-born, heightened the urgency that law and order act swiftly to prevent social turmoil. Private Chicago donors helped establish a military base outside the city. Elsewhere, governments strengthened police forces and armories. Employer associations countered labor militancy by circulating blacklists of union activists whom they would not employ and by hiring private detectives to suppress strikes.

American Federation of Labor

Founded in 1886, the American Federation of Labor (AFL) emerged from that year's upheavals as the major workers' organization. An alliance of national craft unions, the AFL had about 140,000 members, mostly skilled workers. Led by Samuel Gompers, former head of the Cigar Makers' Union, the AFL pressed for higher wages, shorter hours, and the right to bargain collectively. Unlike the Knights, the AFL accepted capitalism and worked to improve conditions within it. The AFL avoided party politics, adhering instead to Gompers's dictum to support labor's friends and oppose its enemies, regardless of party.

AFL membership grew to 1 million by 1901 and 2.5 million by 1917, when it consisted of 111 national unions and 27,000 locals. Member unions organized by craft and had little interest in recruiting unskilled workers or women. Of 6.3 million employed women in 1910, fewer than 2 percent belonged to unions. Male unionists rationalized women's exclusion by insisting that women should not be employed. According to one labor leader, "The mental and physical makeup of woman is in revolt against wage service. She is competing with the man who is her father or husband or is to become her husband." Mostly, unionists worried that, because women were paid less, men's wages would be lowered or their jobs given to cheaper female laborers.

Influenced by nativism and racism, organized labor excluded most immigrant and African American workers, fearing they, too, would depress wages. A few trade unions welcomed skilled immigrants. Blacks were prominent in the coal miners' union and were partially unionized in such trades as construction, barbering, and dock work, where large numbers of African American worked. But they could belong only to segregated local unions in the South, and most northern AFL unions had exclusion policies. Long-held prejudices were reinforced when blacks and immigrants, eager for work, replaced striking whites.

Homestead Strike

The AFL and the labor movement suffered setbacks in the early 1890s, when labor violence stirred public fears. In July 1892 the AFL-affiliated Amalgamated Association of Iron and Steelworkers went on strike against pay cuts in Homestead, Pennsylvania. Henry C. Frick, president of Carnegie Steel Company, closed the plant. Shortly thereafter, Frick hired three hundred guards from the Pinkerton Detective Agency to protect the factory and snuck them in by barge at night. Lying in wait, angry workers attacked and routed the Pinkertons. State troops intervened, and after five months the strikers gave in. By then public opinion turned against the union.

Pullman Strike

In 1894 workers at the Pullman Palace (railroad passenger) Car Company walked out over exploitative policies at the company town near Chicago. The paternalistic owner, George Pullman, provided everything for the twelve thousand residents of the so-called model town named after him. His company controlled all land and buildings, the school, the bank, and the water and gas systems. It paid wages, fixed rents, and spied on disgruntled employees.

One thing Pullman would not do was negotiate with workers. When hard times hit in 1893, Pullman protected profits by cutting wages 25 to 40 percent while holding firm on rents and prices. Hard-pressed workers sent a committee to Pullman to protest. He reacted by firing three committee members. Enraged workers called a strike; Pullman closed the factory. The union, led by Eugene V. Debs, refused to handle Pullman cars attached to any trains. Pullman rejected arbitration, and the railroad owners' association enlisted aid from U.S. Attorney General Richard Olney, a former railroad lawyer, who obtained a court injunction to prevent the union from "obstructing the railways and holding up the mails." President Grover Cleveland ordered federal troops to Chicago. Within a month strikers gave in, and Debs was jailed for defying the injunction. The Supreme Court upheld Debs's six-month sentence, arguing that the federal government could legally remove obstacles to interstate commerce.

IWW

Colorado miners engaged in several bitter struggles. In 1905 they helped form a new, radical labor organization, the Industrial Workers of the World (IWW). Like the Knights, it strove to unite all laborers of all races. Its motto was "An injury to one is an injury to all." But the Wobblies, as IWW members were known, exceeded the Knights by espousing violence and sabotage.

Embracing the rhetoric of class conflict and socialism, Wobblies believed workers should seize and run the nation's industries. Mary "Mother" Jones, an Illinois coalfield union organizer; Elizabeth Gurley Flynn, a fiery orator known as the "Joan of Arc of the labor movement"; Italian radical Carlo Tresca; and William D. ("Big Bill") Haywood, the brawny, one-eyed founder of the Western Federation of Miners, headed a series of strikes. Although the Wobblies' anticapitalist goals and aggressive tactics attracted publicity, IWW membership probably never exceeded 150,000. The organization collapsed during World War I when federal prosecution sent many of its leaders to jail and local police violently harassed IWW members.

Women Unionists

Despite exclusion from unions, some women organized and fought employers as strenuously as men. The Uprising of the 20,000 in New York City, a 1909 strike by male and female immigrant members of the International Ladies' Garment Workers' Union (ILGWU), was one of the country's largest strikes. Female trade-union membership swelled during the 1910s, but men monopolized national leadership.

Women did dominate the Telephone Operators' Department of the International Brotherhood of Electrical Workers. Organized in Montana and San Francisco early in the twentieth century, the union spread throughout the Bell system, the nation's monopolistic telephone company and single largest employer of women. To promote solidarity among their mostly young members, union leaders organized dances, excursions, bazaars, and educational programs. The union resisted scientific management and rigid supervision. In 1919 several militant union branches paralyzed the phone service in five New England states, but the union collapsed after a failed strike there in 1923.

A key organization promoting laboring women's interests was the Women's Trade Union League (WTUL), founded in 1903 and patterned after a similar organization in England. The WTUL sought workplace protection legislation and reduced hours for female workers, sponsored educational activities, and campaigned for woman suffrage. It helped telephone operators organize, and in 1909 it supported the ILGWU's massive strike against New York City sweatshops. Initially the union's highest officers were middle-class women, but control shifted in the 1910s to forceful working-class leaders, notably Agnes Nestor, a glove maker, and Rose Schneiderman, a cap maker. The WTUL advocated opening apprenticeship programs to women and training female workers for leadership. It served as a vital link between the labor and women's movements into the 1920s.

The Experience of Wage Work

Dramatic strikes aside, only a small fraction of American wage workers belonged to unions. In 1900 about 1 million out of a total of 27.6 million workers were unionized. By 1920 union membership had grown to 5 million, only 13 percent of the work force. Unionization was strong in construction trades, transportation, communications, and, to a lesser extent, manufacturing. For many workers, getting and keeping a job took priority over higher wages and shorter hours. Job instability and the seasonal nature of work seriously hindered union organizing. Few companies employed workers year-round; most hired during peak seasons and laid workers off during slack periods.

The millions of men, women, and children who were not unionized tried to cope with machine age pressures. Many native-born and immigrant workers joined fraternal societies, such as the Polish Roman Catholic Union, the African American Colored Brotherhood and Sisterhood of Honor, and the Jewish B'nai B'rith. For small contributions, these organizations provided members with life insurance, sickness benefits, and burial costs.

During the machine age, industrial wages rose between 1877 and 1914, boosting purchasing power and creating a mass market for standardized goods. Yet in 1900 most employees worked sixty hours a week at wages averaging 20 cents an hour for skilled work and 10 cents an hour for unskilled. Even as wages rose, living costs increased faster.

STANDARDS OF LIVING

American ingenuity combined with mass production and mass marketing to make available myriad goods that previously had not existed or had been the province of the wealthy. The new material well-being, symbolized by canned foods, ready-made clothing, and appliances, blended Americans of differing status into consumer communities and accentuated differences between those who could afford goods and services and those who could not.

Commonplace Luxuries

If a society's affluence is measured by how it converts luxuries into commonplace articles, the United States was becoming affluent between 1880 and 1920. By 1899 manufactured goods and perishable foodstuffs had become increasingly available. That year Americans bought 2 billion machine-produced cigarettes and 151,000 pairs of silk stockings, consumed 100 crates of oranges for every 1,000 people, and spent an average of 63 cents per person on soap. By 1921 Americans smoked 43 billion cigarettes (403 per person), bought 217 million pairs of silk stockings, ate 248 crates of oranges per 1,000 people, and spent $1.40 on soap per year.

Data for the period show that incomes rose broadly, spawning massive fortunes and creating a new industrial elite. By 1920 the richest 5 percent of the population received almost one-fourth of all earned income. Incomes also rose among the middle

TABLE 18.1   American Living Standards, 1890–1910

	1890	1910
Income and Earnings		
Annual income		
Clerical worker	$848	$1,156
Public school teacher	256	492
Industrial worker	486	630
Farm laborer	233	336
Hourly wage		
Soft-coal miner	0.18[*]	0.21
Iron worker	0.17[*]	0.23
Shoe worker	0.14[*]	0.19
Paper worker	0.12[*]	0.17
Labor Statistics		
Number of people in labor force	28.5 million	41.7 million[†]
Average workweek in manufacturing	60 h	51 h

[*]1892.
[†]1920.

class. Average pay for clerical workers rose 36 percent between 1890 and 1910 (see Table 18.1). At the turn of the century, federal employees averaged $1,072 a year (around $25,000 in modern dollars). The middle class could afford comfortable housing. A six- or seven-room house cost around $3,000 to buy (about $65,000 in current dollars) and from $15 to $20 per month ($400 to $500 in current dollars) to rent.

Although hourly wages for industrial employees increased, workers had to expend a disproportionate amount on necessities. Average, annual wages of factory laborers rose about 30 percent, from $486 in 1890 (about $12,000 in modern dollars) to $630 in 1910 (about $15,500 in current dollars). In industries with large female work forces, hourly pay rates remained lower than in male-dominated industries. Nevertheless, as Table 18.1 shows, most wages moved upward.

Cost of Living

Wage increases mean little, however, if living costs rise as fast or faster. The weekly cost of living for a typical family of four rose over 47 percent between 1889 and 1913. Goods that cost $68 in 1889 increased, after a slight dip in the mid-1890s, to $100 by 1913 (about $2,157 in current dollars).

How, then, could working-class Americans afford goods and services? Many could not. The daughter of a textile worker, recalling her school days, described how "some of the kids would bring bars of chocolate, others an orange. . . . I suppose they were richer than a family like ours. My father used to buy a bag of candy and a bag of peanuts every payday. . . . And that's all we'd have until the next payday."

Supplements to Family Income

Still, a family could raise its income and partake modestly in consumer society by sending children and women into the labor market. Where a father alone might earn $600 a year, wages of other family members could lift total household income to $900. Many families also rented rooms to boarders, yielding up to $200 annually. Between 1889 and 1901, working-class families markedly increased expenditures for life insurance and new leisure activities (see Chapter 19), improving their living standard.

More than ever, working Americans lived within a money economy. Between 1890 and 1920, the labor force increased by 50 percent, from 28 million workers to 42 million. These figures represent a change in the nature of work as much as increases in available jobs. In the rural households of the nineteenth century, women and children performed crucial tasks of cooking, cleaning, planting, and harvesting—labor absent from employment figures because they earned no wages. As the nation industrialized and the agricultural sector declined, paid employment became more common. The proportion of Americans who worked probably did not increase markedly. What was new was the increase in paid employment, making consumer goods and services more affordable.

Higher Life Expectancy

Medical advances, better diets, and improved housing sharply reduced death rates and extended life. Between 1900 and 1920, life expectancy rose by six years, and the death rate dropped by 24 percent. Notable declines occurred in deaths from typhoid, diphtheria, influenza (except for a harsh pandemic in 1918 and 1919), tuberculosis, and intestinal ailments. There were, however, significantly more deaths from cancer, diabetes, and heart disease, afflictions of an aging population and of new environmental factors, such as smoke and chemical pollution. Homicides and automobile-related deaths also increased dramatically.

Not only were luxuries more attainable, but upward mobility seemed more accessible, too. Public education, aided by the construction of new schools and laws requiring children to stay in school to age fourteen, equipped young people to achieve a higher living standard than their parents. The creation of managerial and sales jobs in service industries helped counter downward mobility when mechanization pushed skilled workers from their crafts. And mass production added greater convenience to workers' lives.

Flush Toilets and Other Innovations

At the vanguard of a revolution in lifestyles stood the toilet. The chain-pull, washdown water closet, invented in England around 1870, reached the United States in the 1880s. Shortly after 1900, the flush toilet appeared. Before 1880 only luxury hotels and wealthy families had private indoor bathrooms. By the 1890s the germ theory of disease was raising fears about carelessly disposed human waste as a source of infection and water contamination. Americans combined cleanliness with convenience, installing modern toilets in middle-class urban houses. By the 1920s, they were prevalent in working-class homes, too. Edward and Clarence Scott, who manufactured white tissue in perforated rolls, provided Americans a more convenient form of toilet tissue than the rough paper they previously used. Bodily functions took on an unpleasant image, and the home bathroom became a place of utmost privacy.

Before the mid-nineteenth century, Americans typically ate only foods in season. Drying, smoking, and salting could preserve meat for a short time, but the availability of fresh meat and milk was limited due to spoilage. A French inventor developed the cooking-and-sealing process of canning around 1810, and in the 1850s an American man named Gail Borden devised a means of condensing and preserving milk. Sales of canned goods and condensed milk increased during the 1860s, but there were production problems. In the 1880s, inventors fashioned machines to peel fruits and vegetables, process salmon, and mass-produce cans from tin plate. Now, people everywhere could consume tomatoes, milk, oysters, and other alternatives to previously monotonous diets.

Other inventions broadened Americans' diets. Growing urban populations created demands for more produce. Railroad refrigerator cars enabled growers and meatpackers to ship perishables farther and preserve them longer. By the 1890s, northern city dwellers could enjoy southern and western strawberries, grapes, and tomatoes for several months. Home iceboxes enabled middle-class families to store perishables, and by 1900 the nation had two thousand ice plants, many making home deliveries.

Dietary Reform

The availability of new foods also inspired health advocates to reform American diets. In the 1870s, John H. Kellogg, nutritionist and manager of the Western Health Reform Institute in Battle Creek, Michigan, began serving patients health foods, including peanut butter and wheat flakes. Years later, his brother, William K. Kellogg, invented corn flakes, and another nutritionist, Charles W. Post, introduced Grape-Nuts, replacing breakfast eggs, potatoes, and meat with supposedly healthier cereal. Growing numbers of published cookbooks and cooking schools reflected the heightened interest in food and its possibilities for health and enjoyment.

As in the past, the poorest people still consumed cheap foods, heavy in starches and carbohydrates, and little meat. Now, though, many could purchase previously unavailable fruits, vegetables, and dairy products. Workers spent almost half of a breadwinner's wages on food, but they never suffered the malnutrition that plagued other developing nations.

Using color, large-scale scenes, and fanciful images, manufacturers of consumer goods advertised their products to a public eager to buy. This ad from the W. K. Kellogg Company, maker of breakfast foods, shows the increasingly common practice of using an attractive young woman to capture attention. (Picture Research Consultants and Archives)

Ready-Made Clothing

The sewing machine and standardized sizes sparked a revolution in clothing. Invented in Europe but refined in the mid-nineteenth century by Americans Elias Howe Jr. and Isaac M. Singer, the sewing machine was used in clothing and shoe manufacture. Demand for uniforms during the Civil War boosted the ready-made clothing industry, and by 1890 annual retail sales reached $1.5 billion. Mass production enabled manufacturers to turn out quality apparel at low cost and to standardize sizes. By 1900 only the poorest families could not afford ready-to-wear clothes. Tailors and seamstresses were relegated to repair work. Many women continued to make clothing at home, but commercial dress patterns simplified the process and injected another form of standardization into everyday life.

Mass-produced garments altered clothing styles and tastes. As women's participation in work and leisure activities increased, dress designers shifted from burdensome Victorian designs to more comfortable styles. In the 1890s, hemlines raised and high-boned collars disappeared. By the 1920s a dress required three yards of material instead of ten.

Men's clothes, too, became lightweight. Before 1900, men in the middle and well-off working classes would have owned two suits: one for Sundays and special occasions and one for everyday. After 1900, however, manufacturers produced inexpensive garments from seasonal fabrics. Men replaced derbies with felt hats, and stiff collars and cuffs with soft ones; somber, dark-blue serge gave way to lighter shades and more intricate weaves.

Department and Chain Stores

Department stores and chain stores helped create and serve this new consumerism. Between 1865 and 1900, Macy's Department Store in New York, Wanamaker's in Philadelphia, Marshall Field in Chicago, and Rich's in Atlanta became urban landmarks. Previously, working classes bought goods in stores with limited inventories, and wealthier people patronized fancy shops; prices, quality of goods, and social custom discouraged each from shopping at the other's shops. Now, department stores, with their open displays, caused a merchandising revolution, offering home deliveries, exchange policies, and charge accounts.

Meanwhile, the Great Atlantic Tea Company, founded in 1859, became the first grocery chain. Renamed the Great Atlantic & Pacific Tea Company in 1869 (known as A&P), the stores bought in volume and sold to the public at low prices. By 1915 there were eighteen hundred A&P stores, and twelve thousand more over the next ten years.

Advertising

In the late nineteenth century, companies that mass-produced consumer goods hired advertisers to create brand loyalty. In 1881 Congress passed a trademark law enabling producers to protect brand names. Thousands of companies registered products as varied as Hires Root Beer, Uneeda Biscuits, and Carter's Little Liver Pills. Advertising agencies—a service pioneered by N. W. Ayer and Son of Philadelphia—offered expert advice on cultivating consumer loyalty. In 1865 retailers spent about $9.5 million on advertising, $95 million by 1900, and nearly $500 million by 1919. Newspapers served as the prime instrument for advertising, as people read them to find out what was for sale as well as what was happening.

Outdoor billboards and electric signs were also important selling devices. Billboards on city buildings, in railroad stations, and alongside roads promoted such products as Gillette razors, Kodak cameras, Wrigley chewing gum, and Budweiser beer. In the mid-1890s, electric lights made billboards exciting. The flashing electric signs on New York City's Broadway gave the street its label: the Great White Way.

THE CORPORATE CONSOLIDATION MOVEMENT

Neither new products nor new marketing techniques could mask unsettling economic factors. The huge capital investment for new technology meant that factories had to operate near capacity to recover costs. But the more manufacturers produced, the more they had to sell, which meant spending more on advertising and cutting prices. To compensate, they further expanded production and often reduced wages. To expand, they borrowed money. And to repay loans, they had to produce and sell even more. This spiraling process strangled small firms and thrust workers into constant uncertainty.

In this environment, optimism could dissolve at the hint that debtors could not meet their obligations. Economic downturns occurred regularly—1873, 1884, and 1893. Some business leaders blamed overproduction, others, underconsumption; still others blamed lax credit and investment practices. Still, businesspeople wanted to combat the uncertainty of boom-and-bust business cycles. Many adopted centralized forms of business organization, notably corporations, pools, trusts, and holding companies.

Rise of Corporations

Industrialists never questioned the capitalist system. They sought new ways to build on the base of state laws of the early 1800s, encouraging commerce and industry. Under such laws, anyone could start a company and raise money by selling stock to investors. Stockholders shared in profits without personal risk, because laws limited their liability for company debts to the amount of their own investment. Responsibility for company administration rested with its managers.

By 1900 two-thirds of all U.S. manufactured goods were produced by corporations like General Electric and the American Tobacco Company. In the 1880s and 1890s, the Supreme Court ruled that corporations, like individuals, are protected by the Fourteenth Amendment. States could not deny corporations equal protection under the law and could not deprive them of rights or property without due process of law. Such rulings shielded corporations from government interference.

Pools

To combat downward business cycles, corporations sought larger economic concentration. Between the late 1880s and early 1900s, business consolidation produced massive conglomerates that have since dominated the nation's economy. At first such alliances were informal, consisting of cooperative agreements among firms making the same product or offering the same service. Through these arrangements, called pools, competing companies tried to control the market by agreeing how much each should produce and sharing profits. Used by railroads, steel producers, and whiskey distillers, pools depended on their members' honesty. During slow periods, however, pool members secretly reduced prices or sold more than the agreed quota to boost profits. Pools' usefulness was fading when the Interstate Commerce Act of 1887 outlawed them among railroads.

Trusts and Holding Companies

John D. Rockefeller, founder of Standard Oil, considered pools weak. In 1879 his lawyer, Samuel Dodd, devised another means of dominating the market. Because state laws prohibited one corporation from holding stock in another, Dodd utilized an old device called a trust, a legal arrangement whereby a responsible individual would manage the financial affairs of another person who was unwilling or unable to do so. Dodd reasoned that one company could control an industry by luring stockholders of smaller companies to yield control of their stock "in trust" to the larger company's board of trustees. This allowed Rockefeller to achieve horizontal integration—the acquisition of similar companies—of the profitable petroleum industry in 1882 by combining his corporation with other refineries.

In 1888 New Jersey adopted laws allowing corporations chartered there to own property in other states and stock in other corporations. (This facilitated the creation of the holding company, which owned a partial or complete interest in other companies.) Holding companies could merge their assets (buildings, equipment, inventory, and cash) as well as their management. Rockefeller's holding company, Standard Oil, merged forty independents. By 1898 Standard Oil refined 84 percent of all oil produced in the nation, controlled most pipelines, and engaged in natural-gas production and ownership of oil-producing properties.

To dominate their markets, many holding companies sought control over all aspects of the industry, including raw materials, manufacturing, and distribution. A model of such vertical integration, which fused related businesses under unified management, was Gustavus Swift's Chicago meat-processing operation. During the 1880s, Swift invested in livestock, slaughterhouses, refrigerator cars, and marketing to ensure profits from beef sales at prices he could control.

Mergers provided order and profits. Between 1889 and 1903, three hundred combinations were formed, mostly trusts and holding companies. The most spectacular was U.S. Steel Corporation, financed by J. P. Morgan in 1901. Made up of iron-ore properties, freight carriers, wire mills, and other firms, it was capitalized at over $1.4 billion (more than $35 billion in current dollars). In 1896 fewer than a dozen corporations were worth over $10 million; by 1903 three hundred were worth that, and seventeen had assets exceeding $100 million. These huge companies ruthlessly put thousands of small firms out of business.

Financiers

The merger movement created a new species of businessman, whose vocation was financial organizing. Shrewd investors sought opportunities for combination, formed a holding company, then persuaded producers to sell their firms to the new company. These financiers raised money by selling stock and borrowing from banks. Investment bankers like J. P. Morgan and Jacob Schiff piloted the merger movement, inspiring awe with their financial power.

Corporate growth turned stock and bond exchanges into hubs of activity. In 1886 trading on the New York Stock Exchange passed 1 million shares daily. By 1914 the number of industrial stocks traded reached 511, compared with 145 in 1869. Between 1870 and 1900, foreign investment in American companies rose from $1.5 billion to $3.5 billion. Assets of savings banks, concentrated in the Northeast and on the West Coast, rose by 700 percent between 1875 and 1897. States loosened regulations to enable banks to invest in railroads and industrial enterprises.

THE GOSPEL OF WEALTH AND ITS CRITICS

Business leaders used corporate consolidation to minimize competition and justified their tactics with the doctrine of Social Darwinism. This theory loosely grafted Charles Darwin's theory of survival of the fittest onto laissez faire, the doctrine that government should not interfere in private economic matters. Social Darwinists reasoned that in a free-market economy, wealth would flow naturally to those most capable of handling it. In this view, large corporations represented the natural accumulation of economic power by those best suited for it.

Social Darwinists reasoned, too, that wealth carried moral responsibilities. Steel baron Andrew Carnegie asserted the Gospel of Wealth—that as guardians of society's wealth, he and other industrialists had a duty to serve society. Carnegie donated more than $350 million to libraries, schools, peace initiatives, and the arts. Such philanthropy, however, enabled benefactors to define what was good for society; it did not translate into paying workers decent wages.

Government Assistance to Business Leaders in the corporate consolidation movement extolled initiative but also pressed for government assistance. Denouncing efforts to legislate maximum working hours or factory conditions as interference, they nonetheless lobbied for public subsidies, loans, and tax relief to encourage business growth. Grants to railroads (see Chapter 17) were one form of such assistance. Tariffs, which benefited American products by placing import taxes on imported products, were another. Industrialists argued that tariff protection encouraged the development of new products and new enterprises. But tariffs also forced consumers to pay artificially high prices.

Dissenting Voices Critics charged that trusts and other big businesses stifled opportunity and originated from greed. Such charges by farmers, workers, and intellectuals reflected an ardent fear of monopoly—the domination of an economic activity (such as oil refining) by one powerful company (such as Standard Oil). Those who feared monopoly believed that large corporations fixed prices, exploited workers by cutting wages, destroyed opportunity by crushing small businesses, and threatened democracy by corrupting politicians.

By the mid-1880s, some intellectuals increasingly challenged Social Darwinism and laissez-faire economics. In *Dynamic Sociology* (1883), the sociologist Lester Ward argued that a system guaranteeing survival only to the fittest was wasteful and brutal. Instead, Ward reasoned, cooperative activity fostered by government intervention was fairer. The economists Richard Ely, John R. Commons, and Edward Bemis denounced laissez faire and praised the assistance government could offer ordinary people.

Others questioned why the United States had to have so many poor people while a few became wealthy. Henry George was a struggling San Francisco printer with a seventh-grade education but an avid reader of economic theory. He believed that economic inequality stemmed from the ability of a few to profit from rising land values, which made landowners rich from ever-higher rents as demand for living and working space especially in cities, skyrocketed. To prevent profiteering, George proposed replacing all taxes with a single tax on the unearned increment—the rise in property values caused by increased demand rather than owners' improvements. Argued in *Progress and Poverty* (1879), George's popular plan almost won him the mayoralty of New York City in 1886.

Novelist Edward Bellamy believed that competitive capitalism promoted waste and proposed that government own the means of production. In his popular novel, *Looking Backward* (1888), he depicted Boston in the year 2000 as a peaceful community run by benevolent elders managing the economy with scientific principles that assured everyone a job. Bellamy hoped that a "principle of fraternal cooperation" would replace vicious competition and wasteful monopoly. Dubbed Nationalism, his vision sparked Nationalist clubs across the country and kindled popular appeals for political reform, social welfare measures, and government ownership of railroads and utilities.

Antitrust Legislation   Several states took steps to prohibit monopolies and regulate business. By 1900 twenty-seven states banned pools, and fifteen had constitutional provisions outlawing trusts (see Chapter 20). But state governments lacked the staff and judicial support for an effective attack on big business, and corporations found ways to evade restrictions.

Congress moved hesitantly toward such legislation but in 1890 passed the Sherman Anti-Trust Act. Introduced by Senator John Sherman of Ohio, the law made illegal "every contract, combination in the form of trust or otherwise, or conspiracy in the restraint of trade." Those found guilty of violating the law faced fines and jail terms, and those wronged by illegal combinations could sue for triple damages. However, the law was watered down when rewritten by pro-business eastern senators. It did not clearly define restraint of trade and consigned the interpretation of its provisions to the often business-friendly courts.

Judges used the law's vagueness to blur distinctions between reasonable and unreasonable restraints of trade. When in 1895 the federal government prosecuted the so-called Sugar Trust for owning 98 percent of sugar-refining capacity, eight of nine Supreme Court justices ruled in *U.S. v. E. C. Knight Co.* that control of manufacturing did not necessarily mean control of trade. According to the Court, the Constitution empowered Congress to regulate interstate commerce but not manufacturing.

Between 1890 and 1900, the federal government prosecuted only eighteen cases under the Sherman Anti-Trust Act. The most successful involved railroads directly involved in interstate commerce. Ironically, the act equipped the government to break up labor unions: courts that did not consider monopolistic production a restraint on trade willingly applied antitrust provisions to boycotts encouraged by striking unions.

Summary

Mechanization and new inventions thrust the United States into the vanguard of industrial nations and immeasurably altered daily life. By the early twentieth century, American industrial output surpassed that of Great Britain, France, and Germany

Technology of Recorded Sound

Today's iPods and digital recorders derive from technology, chemistry, and human resourcefulness that first united in the late nineteenth century. In 1877, Thomas Edison devised a way to preserve and reproduce his voice by storing it on indentations in tin foil. Edison intended his "speaking machine" to help businesses store dictation. But in 1878, a rivalry with the telephone inventor Alexander Graham Bell, who was working on a similar device, drew Edison to invent a phonograph for recorded music. By the 1890s, audiences paid to hear recorded sounds from these machines.

By 1901, companies like the Columbia Phonograph Company produced machines that played music recorded on cylinders molded from a durable wax compound. Over the next ten years, various inventors improved the phonograph so sound played from a stylus (needle) vibrating in grooves of a shellac disc. Records' playing time increased from two minutes to four.

Phonograph records now replaced sheet music as the most popular music medium, but soon radio emerged and boosted record sales. Radio's popularity was only possible via another electronic acoustic technology: the microphone. This new device achieved vastly improved sound quality over megaphones. As phonograph prices declined and sound quality rose, more records became available.

The 1938 invention of the idler wheel, which enabled a turntable to spin a phonograph at speeds at which the stylus could accurately pick up sound, brought an important advance. Shortly thereafter, significant improvements in recording, such as the magnetic tape recorder, allowed for greater manipulation of sound in the recording studio. In 1963 Philips, a Dutch electronics firm, introduced the compact audio cassette. Two decades later, Philips joined with the Japanese corporation Sony to adapt the digital laser discs, invented by an American for video storage, to hold music. The compact disc (CD) was born, and from there it was a short step for the Apple Computer Company to create the iPod, storing music on an internal hard drive.

combined. By 1900, factories, stores, and banks converted America from a debtor agricultural nation into an industrial, financial, and exporting power.

But aggressive industrial consolidation changed the nature of work from individual activity by skilled producers to mass production by wage earners. Laborers fought to retain control of their work and struggled to organize unions. The outpouring of products created a mass society based on consumerism and dominated by technology and the communications media.

The problems of enforcing the Sherman Anti-Trust Act reflected the uneven distribution of power. Corporations consolidated to control resources, production, and politics. Laborers and reformers benefited from new and less expensive mass-produced goods, but they accused businesses of acquiring influence and profits at their expense. Some people celebrated the economic transformation; others struggled with the dilemma of industrialism: whether the new accumulations of wealth would undermine the republican ideal of democracy and equality.

Industrial expansion proved impossible to stop because so many people were benefiting from it. Moreover, the waves of newcomers pouring into the nation's cities increasingly furnished workers and consumers for America's expanding productive capacity.

Chapter Review

TECHNOLOGY AND THE TRIUMPH OF INDUSTRIALIZATION

How did technological innovations transform American industry?

New inventions and technological advances made production of goods and services faster and cheaper, which in turn fueled the rise of mass production and consumption. Thomas Edison's system for inexpensively distributing electricity facilitated the emergence of countless other inventions in the late nineteenth and early twentieth centuries. Henry Ford built on a European invention for engines to create his assembly-line process that would mass produce thousands of identical cars, making them affordable to many Americans by the early twentieth century. The du Pont family similarly revolutionized the chemical industry; electric looms advanced textile production and relocated it from North to South; while North Carolinian James B. Duke mass-produced cigarettes and remade the tobacco industry.

MECHANIZATION AND THE CHANGING STATUS OF LABOR

How did mechanization and new systems of management change the nature and status of work?

Innovation created new jobs, but labor-saving machines also meant that fewer workers could produce more in less time. Instead of doing many different tasks, workers now did only one task repeatedly. As workers rather than producers, they lost control over their work days and were regulated by the time clock and the production mandates of bosses. Skill became less important, and as the need for skilled workers declined, manufacturers turned to women and children, whom they could pay much less. The advent of typewriters and other office machines opened clerical and white collar jobs to women, as well. But in manufacturing, long days and harsh and often hazardous working conditions led to increasing number of accidents as well as labor unrest.

LABOR VIOLENCE AND THE UNION MOVEMENT

How did employers and others respond to increasing strikes and labor unrest in the late nineteenth century?

After the Haymarket bombing and other strikes, labor violence and the increasing participation of socialists and anarchists in the labor movement heightened public fear and demands for the government to get involved. Governments strengthened police forces and armories; employer associations circulated blacklists of union activists, whom they agreed not to employ, and hired private detectives to suppress strikes. State and federal governments also sent in troops, as in the case of the Homestead and Pullman strikes, to break the strikes.

STANDARDS OF LIVING

How did the rise of consumer culture widen the gap between the haves and have-nots?

While items once deemed luxuries became affordable to mainstream Americans, workers' wages did not always keep pace with the cost of goods. To afford these increasingly expensive necessities, working families often began to rely on additional sources of income from wives and children, either via factory work or taking in borders. Even while advances in nutrition and medical science helped Americans to live longer and healthier lives, those at the lowest rungs of society still ate diets high in carbohydrates and starches with little meat, and often spent half of the breadwinner's wages even on this meager diet.

THE CORPORATE CONSOLIDATION MOVEMENT

What led corporations to increasingly consolidate in the late nineteenth century?

Big companies saw consolidation as a way to control downward economic cycles—they believed the more they pooled resources to set prices and influence profits by determining how much to supply the market, the more they could manage a downturn. Until the 1880s, however, laws made it illegal for companies to own stock in another firm. Instead, businessmen such as John D. Rockefeller turned to trusts, luring stockholders of smaller companies to yield control of their stock "in trust" to the larger company's board of trustees. Once states allowed companies within their borders to own stock in corporations in other states, holding companies emerged, where one firm would own partial or complete interest in another and merge their assets and resources. Holding companies also found it easier to dominate their markets by controlling all aspects of an industry from raw materials to manufacturing to distribution.

THE GOSPEL OF WEALTH AND ITS CRITICS

How did business leaders use Social Darwinism to justify their mergers and consolidations?

Social Darwinism applied Charles Darwin's theory of survival of the fittest to laissez-faire economics, which stressed that government should let the economy manage itself. Social Darwinists argued that in a free-market economy, wealth would flow to those most capable of handling it, and that corporations represented that accumulation of power in the best hands. On the flip side, they also believed those with wealth had a moral obligation to use it to improve society; hence, they donated to the arts, education, and other worthy causes. It did not, however, translate into better wages or working conditions for their employees.

SUGGESTIONS FOR FURTHER READING

Edward L. Ayers, *The Promise of the New South: Life After Reconstruction* (1992)

Ileen A. DeVault, *United Apart: Gender and the Rise of Craft Unionism* (2004)

Steven J. Diner, *A Very Different Age: Americans of the Progressive Era* (1998)

John F. Kasson, *Civilizing the Machine: Technology and Republican Values in America, 1776–1900* (1976)

Alice Kessler-Harris, *Out to Work: A History of Wage-Earning Women in the United States* (2003)

T. J. Jackson Lears and Richard W. Fox, eds., *The Culture of Consumption: Critical Essays in American History, 1880–1980* (1983)

David Montgomery, *The Fall of the House of Labor: The Workplace, the State and American Labor Activism, 1865–1925* (1987)

Jeffrey Sklansky, *The Soul's Economy: Market Society and Selfhood in American Thought, 1820–1920* (2002)

The Vitality and Turmoil of Urban Life

CHAPTER OUTLINE

Growth of the Modern City

Urban Neighborhoods

Living Conditions in the Inner City

Managing the City

Family Life

The New Leisure and Mass Culture

    LINKS TO THE WORLD:
    Japanese Baseball

    **LEGACY FOR A PEOPLE
    AND A NATION:** Ethnic Food

Summary

Crowds on the street gasped as they looked up. A man bound in a straitjacket was hanging by his heels high above New York's Times Square. Suddenly, he wriggled wildly, and in seconds Harry Houdini, the early twentieth century's most celebrated showman, had escaped. As he had done many times, Houdini fed the public's taste for suspense, courage, and entertainment with a death-defying feat.

Born as Erich Weiss in Hungary in 1874, Houdini and his family emigrated to the United States in 1878. After Erich's father lost his job as a rabbi in Wisconsin, the family moved to New York City, where father and son worked in a necktie factory. Erich's father died in 1892, and the young man became an entertainer. He spent a few years as a magician, before discovering his true talent as an illusionist and escape artist. He changed his name to Harry Houdini and became one of America's most enthralling performers.

By the early 1900s, the Great Houdini was a feature in vaudeville, a new form of urban entertainment. His specialty was escaping from elaborate and dangerous confinements: ropes, manacles, padlocked crates, and jail cells. Houdini was a skillful self-publicist, promoting his act with posters and leaflets. Around 1913 Houdini introduced his famous Chinese water torture cell escape, in which he extracted himself from being bound and suspended upside down in a water-filled, locked glass-and-steel cabinet. Houdini escaped by manipulating his five-foot-five frame in unusual ways and also by concealing picks and keys, which he sometimes regurgitated. Although he constantly defied death on stage, Houdini could not escape the abdominal infection that took his life in 1926.

Like many people in the late nineteenth and early twentieth centuries, the Weiss family were immigrants who fled poverty

This icon will direct you to interactive activities and study materials on A People And A Nation, Brief Edition website: **www.cengage.com/history/norton/ peoplenationbrief8e**

Chronology

1867	First law regulating tenements passes in New York State.	**1895**	Hearst buys the *New York Journal,* which becomes another popular yellow-journalism newspaper.
1870	One-fourth of Americans live in cities.		
1876	National League of Professional Baseball Clubs is founded.	**1898**	Race riot erupts in Wilmington, North Carolina.
1880s	"New" immigrants from eastern and southern Europe begin to arrive in large numbers.	**1900–10**	Immigration reaches its peak. Vaudeville rises to popularity.
1883	Brooklyn Bridge is completed.	**1903**	Boston beats Pittsburgh in baseball's first World Series.
	Pulitzer buys *New York World,* creating a major publication for yellow journalism.	**1905**	Intercollegiate Athletic Association, forerunner of National Intercollegiate Athletic Association (NCAA), is formed, restructuring the rules of football.
1885	Safety bicycle is invented.		
1886	First settlement house opens in New York City.	**1915**	Griffith directs *The Birth of a Nation,* one of first major technically sophisticated movies.
1889	Edison invents the motion picture and a viewing device.	**1919**	Race riot erupts in East St. Louis, Illinois.
1890s	Electric trolleys replace horse-drawn mass transit.	**1920**	Majority (51.4 percent) of Americans live in cities.
1893	Columbian Exposition opens in Chicago.		

and tried to remake themselves in a burgeoning American city. They faced daunting challenges of where to live and work, how to deal with a cash-based economy, how to preserve their ethnic consciousness amid bigotry, and how to achieve independence and respectability. These challenges made cities places of hope, frustration, achievement, and conflict.

Not until the 1880s did the United States begin to become an urban nation. The technological innovations and industrialization of the late nineteenth century sparked widespread economic and geographical expansion, funneling millions of people into cities. By 1920, the census showed for the first time that a majority of Americans (51.4 percent) lived in cities (settlements with more than 2,500 people).

Urban dwellers patronized dance halls, theatrical performances, vaudeville, movies, and sporting events in record numbers. By idolizing Houdini, sports heroes, and movie celebrities or by benefiting from the largesse of a political boss, ordinary working- and middle-class people could believe in the potential for individuals to free themselves from the constraints of an emerging technological and urban society. At the same time, poverty and discrimination haunted the lives of countless urban dwellers, combining the era's opportunities with persistent inequality and prejudice. How people built cities and adjusted to the urban environment shaped modern American society.

- **What were the most important factors contributing to the urban growth of the period 1877–1920?**
- **How did immigrants adjust to and reshape their adopted homeland?**
- **How did industrialization and urbanization affect patterns of family life and leisure time?**

GROWTH OF THE MODERN CITY

Initially commercial centers, cities became the main arenas for industrial growth in the late nineteenth century. As labor, transportation, and communication hubs, cities supplied everything factories needed. Capital accumulated by urban mercantile enterprises fed industrial investment. Residents also acted as consumers for new products. The further industrialization advanced, the more opportunities it created for jobs and investment, which, in turn, drew more people to cities. As workers and consumers, they fueled yet more industrialization.

Industrial Development

While industrial enterprises varied, cities increasingly specialized. Mass production of clothing concentrated in New York City, the shoe industry in Philadelphia, and textiles in New England cities. Other cities created goods derived from surrounding agricultural regions: flour in Minneapolis, cottonseed oil in Memphis, and beef and pork in Chicago. Still others processed natural resources: gold and copper in Denver, fish and lumber in Seattle, coal and iron in Pittsburgh and Birmingham, and oil in Houston and Los Angeles. Such activities increased cities' magnetic attraction for people seeking steady employment.

At the same time, the compact city of the early nineteenth century, where residences mingled among shops, factories, and warehouses, expanded past the original settlement. No longer did different social groups live close together. Instead, cities subdivided into distinct districts: working-class neighborhoods, downtown, and a ring of suburbs. Two forces were responsible for this: mass transportation, which propelled people and enterprises outward, and, economic change, which drew human and material resources inward.

Mechanization of Mass Transportation

Mass transportation moved people faster and farther. By the 1870s, horse-drawn vehicles shared city streets with motor-driven conveyances. At first, commuter railroads carried passengers to and from outlying communities; then in the 1880s, cable cars were introduced. In the 1890s, electric-powered streetcars began replacing horse cars and cable cars in nearly every large city. In a few cities, companies raised track onto trestles, enabling elevated vehicles (trains, called els) to travel above jammed downtown streets. In Boston, New York, and Philadelphia, transit firms solved the traffic problem by digging underground subway tunnels. Because el and subway construction was costly, they appeared only in cities with enough riders to ensure profits.

Urban Sprawl

Mass transit launched urban dwellers into remote neighborhoods and created a commuting public. Streetcar lines serviced districts that promised the most riders and would increase company revenues. Working-class families, who needed every cent, found streetcars unaffordable. But the growing middle class who could pay the fare—usually 5 cents a ride—could escape to quiet, tree-lined neighborhoods on the outskirts and commute to the inner city for work, shopping, and entertainment.

When consumers moved outward, businesses followed, locating near mass transit. Department stores and banks joined groceries, theaters, taverns, and shops to create neighborhood shopping centers. Meanwhile, the urban core became a work zone, where tall buildings loomed over streets clogged with people, horses, and, increasingly, vehicles.

Population Growth

Between 1870 and 1920, the number of Americans living in cities increased from 10 million to 54 million. During this period, the number of cities with more than 100,000 people swelled from fifteen to sixty-eight; the number with more than 500,000 rose from two to twelve (see Map 19.1).

American urban growth derived from the annexation of bordering land and people and net migration (excess of in-migrants over out-migrants). The most notable enlargement occurred in 1898, when New York City, previously only Manhattan and the Bronx, merged with Brooklyn, Staten Island, and part of Queens and doubled to 3 million people. Suburbs often desired annexation for the schools, water, fire protection, and sewer systems that cities provided.

Urban In-Migration

In-migration from the countryside and immigration from abroad made the greatest contribution to urban population growth. Urban newcomers arrived from two major sources: the American countryside and Europe. Asia, Canada, and Latin America also supplied smaller numbers of immigrants.

Rural populations declined as urban populations burgeoned. Low crop prices and high debts drove white farmers toward opportunities that cities seemly offered. These migrations filled major cities, such as Detroit, Chicago, and San Francisco but also secondary cities, such as Indianapolis, Salt Lake City, Nashville, and San Diego. Farm boys escaped economic hardship, but for every four men who migrated cityward, five women did the same, often to escape unhappy homes and enjoy the independence that urban employment offered.

In the 1880s and 1890s, thousands of rural African Americans also moved cityward, seeking better employment and fleeing crop liens, ravages of the boll weevil on cotton crops, racial violence, and political oppression. Although black migration accelerated after 1915, thirty-two cities already had more than ten thousand black residents by 1900. Because few factories would employ African Americans, most found jobs in the service sector—cleaning, cooking, and driving. Since these were traditionally female jobs, black women outnumbered black men in cities like New York, Baltimore, and New Orleans. In the South, blacks migrating from the countryside became an important source of unskilled labor in the region's growing cities. By 1900, almost 40 percent of the total population of Atlanta, Georgia, and Charlotte, North Carolina, was black.

In the West, many Hispanics also moved into cities. They took unskilled construction jobs previously held by Chinese laborers who had been driven from Southern California cities. In some Texas cities, native Mexicans (called *Tejanos*) held most of the unskilled jobs. In Los Angeles and other cities, males often left home to take temporary agricultural jobs, leaving behind female heads of household.

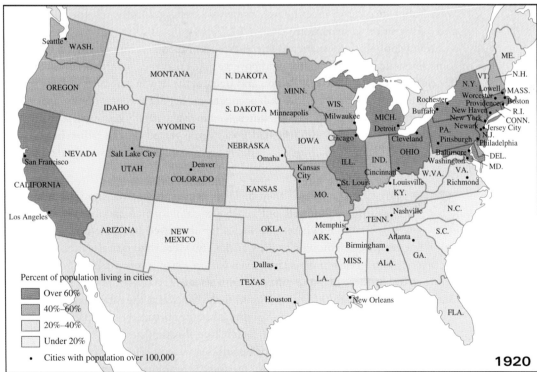

Map 19.1   Urbanization, 1880 and 1920

In 1880 the vast majority of states were still heavily rural. By 1920 only a few had less than 20 percent of their population living in cities.

Foreign Immigration

Foreign immigrants fleeing villages and cities in Europe, Asia, Canada, and Latin America flooded into the United States. Many wanted only to make enough money to return home and live in greater comfort. For every hundred foreigners who entered the country, thirty ultimately left. Still, like Houdini's family, most of the 26 million immigrants arriving between 1870 and 1920 remained, settling largely in cities.

The New Immigration

Population pressures, land redistribution, and industrialization induced millions of peasants, small landowners, and craftsmen to leave Europe and Asia for Canada, Australia, Brazil, and Argentina, as well as the United States. Religious persecution, too, particularly the merciless pogroms and military conscription that Jews suffered in eastern Europe, forced people to escape across the Atlantic. Late-nineteenth-century advances in communications and transportation spread the news of overseas opportunities and made travel cheaper.

Immigrants from northern and western Europe had long made the United States their destination, but after 1880 economic and demographic changes propelled immigrants from other regions. Increased numbers came from eastern and southern Europe, plus smaller bands from Canada, Mexico, and Japan. Between 1900 and 1909, two-thirds of the immigrants came from Italy, Austria-Hungary, and Russia. By 1910 arrivals from Mexico outnumbered arrivals from Ireland, and numerous Japanese moved to the West Coast and Hawai'i. Foreign-born blacks, chiefly from the West Indies, also came. (See the web site www.census.gov to search for population and immigration information.)

Many long-settled Americans feared these so-called new immigrants, whose customs, Catholic and Jewish faiths, and poverty made them seem particularly alien. Unlike earlier groups from Great Britain and Ireland, the new immigrants did not speak English and often worked in low-skill occupations. Yet old and new immigrants both made family the focus of all undertakings. New arrivals usually knew where to go and how to get there from relatives who had already immigrated. Workers often helped kin obtain jobs, and family members pooled resources to improve their standard of living.

Geographic and Social Mobility

Once they arrived, in-migrants and immigrants rarely stayed put. Each year millions of families moved elsewhere. The Weiss family stayed in Appleton, Wisconsin, only a few years before moving to New York City. More than half the families residing in a city were gone ten years later. Even within a city, it was not uncommon for a family to live at three or more different addresses over a ten- or fifteen-year period. One in every three or four families moved each year (today the rate is one in five).

Migration offered an escape to improved opportunity; occupational shifts offered another. An advance up the social scale through better jobs was available mostly to white males. Thousands of businesses were needed to supply goods and services to burgeoning urban populations, and as corporations grew and centralized operations, they required new managerial personnel. An aspiring merchant could open a saloon or shop for a few hundred dollars. Knowledge of accounting could qualify workers for white-collar jobs with higher incomes than manual labor.

Such advancement occurred often, but very few could accumulate large fortunes. Most of the era's wealthiest businessmen began their careers with distinct advantages: American birth, Protestant religion, education, and relatively affluent parents. Yet considerable movement occurred along the road from poverty to moderate success, from manual to nonmanual work.

Rates of upward occupational mobility were slow but steady between 1870 and 1920. In fast-growing cities like Atlanta, Los Angeles, and Omaha, approximately one in five white manual workers rose to white-collar or owner's positions within ten years. In older cities like Boston and Philadelphia, upward mobility averaged closer to one in six workers in ten years. Some men slipped from a higher to a lower rung, but rates of upward movement usually were double those of downward movement. Immigrants generally experienced less upward and more downward mobility than the native-born, yet the odds of a white male holding a higher-status job than his father were good.

The definition of a better job, however, depended on one's perspective. People who took pride in working with their hands neither desired nonmanual jobs nor encouraged their children to seek them. As one Italian tailor explained, "I learned the tailoring business in the old country. Over here, in America, I never have trouble finding a job. . . . I want that my oldest boy learn my trade because I tell him that you could always make at least enough for the family."

Failure rates were high among saloon owners and other small proprietors in working-class neighborhoods because customers' low incomes made profits uncertain. Many manual workers sought security rather than mobility, preferring a steady wage to the risks of ownership.

Many women held paying jobs, but since their standing was defined by the men in their lives, their chief means of upward mobility came from marrying men with wealth or potential. Laws limited what women could inherit; educational institutions blocked their training in such professions as medicine and law; and prevailing assumptions attributed higher aptitude for manual skills and business to men. Assigned to the lowest-paying occupations by prejudice, African Americans, American Indians, Mexican Americans, and Asian Americans could make fewer gains.

A person might achieve social mobility by acquiring property, which was not easily accomplished. Banks and savings-and-loan institutions had strict lending practices, and mortgage loans carried high interest rates and short repayment periods. Nevertheless, many families were able to amass a down payment on property. Ownership rates varied regionally—higher in western cities, lower in eastern cities—but 36 percent of all urban American families owned their homes in 1900, the highest homeownership rate of any western nation except Denmark, Norway, and Sweden.

Many who migrated, particularly unskilled workers, did not improve their status; they simply floated from one low-paying job to another. Others found greener pastures. The possibilities for upward mobility tempered people's dissatisfaction with the tensions and frustrations of city life. For every story of rags to riches, there were a multitude of small triumphs mixed with dashed hopes and discrimination. Although the gap between the very rich and the very poor widened, for those in between, the expanding economies of American cities created room.

URBAN NEIGHBORHOODS

American cities were characterized by collections of subcommunities where people, most of whom had migrated from somewhere else, coped with daily challenges to their cultures. Rather than yield completely to assimilation, migrants and immigrants interacted with the urban environment to retain their identity while altering their outlook and the social structure of cities.

Cultural Retention and Change

In their new surroundings, immigrants first anchored their lives to what they knew best: their culture. Old World customs persisted in immigrant districts of Italians from the same province, Japanese from the same island district, and Russian Jews from the same *shtetl*. Newcomers re-created mutual aid societies they knew in their homeland. For example, the Japanese transferred *ken* societies, which organized social celebrations and relief services. The Chinese used loan associations, called *whey*, which raised money to help members acquire businesses, and village associations called *fongs*, which rented apartments to homeless members. Southern Italians transplanted the system whereby a *padrone* (boss) found jobs for unskilled workers by negotiating with—and receiving a payoff from—an employer.

Urban Borderlands

In large cities, such as Chicago, Philadelphia, and Detroit, European immigrants initially clustered in inner-city neighborhoods where low-skill jobs and cheap housing were most available. These districts often were multiethnic, urban borderlands, where diverse people coexisted. Even within districts identified with a certain group, such as Little Italy, Jewtown, Polonia, or Greektown, rapid mobility constantly undermined homogeneity, as newcomers moved in and former inhabitants left. Even as population diversified, businesses and institutions, such as bakeries, churches, and club headquarters—operated by and for one ethnic group—gave a neighborhood its identity.

For first- and second-generation immigrants, their neighborhoods acted as havens until individuals were ready to move into the majority society. But borderland experiences often dissolved. The expansion of mass transportation and factories enabled people to move to other neighborhoods, where they interspersed with families of their own socioeconomic class but not necessarily their ethnicity. European immigrants encountered prejudice, such as the exclusion of Jews from certain neighborhoods, professions, and clubs, but discrimination rarely was systematic. For people of color, however—African Americans, Asians, and Mexicans—discrimination kept the borderlands from becoming multiethnic.

Racial Segregation and Violence

Although small numbers of African Americans may have lived near or interspersed with urban whites in the eighteenth and early nineteenth centuries, by the late nineteenth century racial discrimination forced them into highly segregated ghettos. By 1920 in Chicago, Detroit, Cleveland, and other cities, two-thirds or more of the total

African American population inhabited only 10 percent of the residential area. Within their neighborhoods, African Americans nurtured cultural institutions to cope with city life: shops, schools, clubs, theaters, dance halls, newspapers, and saloons. Churches, particularly the Baptist and African Methodist Episcopal (A.M.E.) branches of Protestantism, were especially influential. Membership in Cincinnati's black Baptist churches doubled between 1870 and 1900. In Louisville, blacks built their own theological institute. Black religious activity dominated urban local life and represented cooperation across class lines.

The only way blacks could relieve overcrowding from increased migration was to expand residential borders into surrounding, previously white neighborhoods, a process often resulting in harassment and attacks by white residents who feared that blacks would reduce property values. Moreover, blacks increased presence in cities, as well as their competition with whites for housing, jobs, and political influence, sparked race riots. In 1898 white citizens of Wilmington, North Carolina, resenting African Americans' involvement in local government and incensed by an African American newspaper editorial accusing white women of loose sexual behavior, rioted and killed dozens of blacks. White supremacists then overthrew the city government, expelling black and white officeholders, and instituted restrictions to prevent blacks from voting. An influx of unskilled black strikebreakers into East St. Louis, Illinois, heightened racial tensions in 1917, triggering a riot in which nine whites and thirty-nine blacks were killed and over three hundred buildings were destroyed.

Asians also encountered discrimination and isolation. Although Chinese immigrants often preferred to live apart from Anglos in Chinatowns of San Francisco, Los Angeles, and New York City, creating their own business, government, and social institutions, Anglos also tried to keep them separated. Using the slogan "The Chinese must go," Irish immigrant Denis Kearney and his followers intimidated San Francisco employers into refusing to hire Chinese and drove hundreds of Asians out of the city. San Francisco's government prohibited Chinese laundries from locating in white neighborhoods and banned the wearing of queues, the traditional Chinese hair braid. In 1882 Congress passed the Chinese Exclusion Act, which suspended Chinese immigration and prohibited naturalization of Chinese already residing in the United States. And in 1892 Congress approved the Geary Act, which extended immigration restriction and required Chinese Americans to carry certificates of residence issued by the Treasury Department. The U.S. Supreme Court upheld the Geary Act in 1893 in *Fong Yue Ting v. United States*. Similarly prevented from becoming American citizens, Japanese immigrants, called Issei, also developed separate communities.

Mexican Barrios   Mexicans in southwestern cities experienced more complex residential patterns. In places like Los Angeles, Santa Barbara, and Tucson, Mexicans had been the original inhabitants, and Anglos were migrants who pushed Mexicans out, so they became increasingly isolated in districts called barrios. Frequently, real-estate covenants kept Mexican families isolated as they pledged whites not to sell homes to Mexicans (or to African Americans or Jews). Instead, they were confined in areas away from central-city multiethnic borderlands housing European immigrants.

Although Chinese immigrants, like other immigrants, struggled to succeed in American society, they often faced severe discrimination because of their different lifestyle. As this photo of a San Francisco grocery shows, Chinese looked, dressed, and ate differently than white Americans did. Occasionally, they suffered from racist violence that caused them to fear not only for their personal safety but also for the safety of establishments like this one that might suffer damage from resentful mobs.   (The Bancroft Library, University of California)

Cultural Adaptation

Virtually everywhere immigrants lived, Old World culture mingled with New World realities. Although many foreigners identified themselves by their village or region of birth, native-born Americans categorized them simply by nationality. People from County Cork and County Limerick, for example, were merged into Irish, those from Calabria and Campobasso into Italians. Immigrant institutions, such as newspapers and churches, ultimately had to appeal to the entire nationality to survive.

Moreover, the diversity of American cities prompted foreigners to modify their habits and old ways of life. Although many immigrants tried to preserve their language, English, taught in schools and needed on the job, soon penetrated nearly every community. Foreigners fashioned homeland styled garments, but used American rather than traditional fabrics. Italians went to American doctors but still carried amulets to ward off evil spirits. Music especially revealed adaptations. Polka bands blended American and Polish folk music. Mexican ballads now described border crossing and hardships in the United States.

The influx of so many immigrants between 1870 and 1920 transformed the United States from a basically Protestant nation into a diverse collection of Protestants, Catholics, Orthodox Christians, Jews, Buddhists, and Muslims. Newcomers from Italy, Hungary, Polish lands, and Slovakia joined Irish and Germans to boost the proportion of Catholics in many cities. German and Russian immigrants gave New York City one of the largest Jewish populations in the world.

Many Catholics and Jews tried to accommodate their faiths to the new environment. Catholic and Jewish leaders from earlier immigrant groups supported liberalizing trends—use of English in services, the phasing out of such Old World rituals as saints' feasts, and a preference for public over religious schools. As long as new immigrants continued to arrive, however, these trends met stiff resistance.

Newcomers usually held onto familiar practices, whether the folk Catholicism of southern Italy or the Orthodox Judaism of eastern Europe. Despite church attempts to make American Catholicism more uniform, bishops acceded to pressures from predominantly Polish congregations for Polish priests. Eastern European Jews, convinced that Reform Judaism sacrificed too much to American ways, established the Conservative branch, which retained traditional ritual but abolished the segregation of women in synagogues and allowed English prayers. But second-generation Catholics and Jews marrying coreligionists of other ethnic groups—an Italian Catholic wedding a Polish Catholic—kept religious identity strong while undercutting ethnic identity.

The cities nurtured rich cultural variety: American folk music and literature, Italian and Mexican cuisine, Irish comedy, Yiddish theater, African American jazz and dance, and much more. Newcomers changed their environment as much as they were changed by it.

LIVING CONDITIONS IN THE INNER CITY

The central sections of American cities were plagued by poverty, disease, crime, and the tensions resulting when large numbers of people live close together. City dwellers coped, and technology, private enterprise, and public authority achieved some remarkable successes.

Inner-City Housing

In spite of massive construction in the 1880s and early 1900s, population growth outpaced housing supplies. Lack of inexpensive housing especially afflicted working-class families who, because of low wages, had to rent homes. Landlords took advantage of shortages by splitting up existing buildings to house more people, constructing multiple-unit tenements, and hiking rents. Low-income families adapted to high costs and short supply by sharing space and expenses. A one-family apartment was typically occupied by two or three families, or by a single family plus several boarders.

The result was unprecedented crowding. In 1890 New York City's immigrant-packed Lower East Side averaged 702 people per acre, one of the highest population densities in the world. Conditions were harsh. The largest rooms were barely ten feet wide, and interior rooms either lacked windows or opened onto narrow shafts that bred vermin and rotten odors. Few buildings had indoor plumbing; residents used privies (outdoor toilets) in the yard or basement. Often, the only heat source was dangerous, polluting coal-burning stoves.

Housing Reform

Housing problems sparked widespread reform campaigns. New York State led with laws in 1867, 1879, and 1901 that established light, ventilation, and safety codes for new tenement buildings. Reformers, such as journalist Jacob Riis and humanitarian Lawrence Veiller, advocated model tenements, with spacious rooms and better facilities for low-income families. Model tenements meant lower profits, a sacrifice few landlords would make. Reformers and public officials opposed government financing, fearing it would undermine private enterprise. Still, housing codes and regulatory commissions strengthened local government's power to oversee construction.

New Home Technology

Technology revolutionized home life. Advanced systems of central heating (furnaces), artificial lighting, and indoor plumbing created more comfort, first for middle-class households and later for most others. Whereas formerly families bought coal or chopped wood for cooking and heating, made candles for light, and hauled bath water, their homes were increasingly connected to outside pipes and wires for gas, electricity, and water. Moreover, these utilities helped create new attitudes about privacy. Middle-class bedrooms and bathrooms became private retreats.

Scientific and technological advances eventually enabled city dwellers and the nation to live healthier. By the 1880s, doctors began to accept the theory that microorganisms (germs) cause disease. Cities established more efficient water purification and sewage disposal, which helped control such dread diseases as cholera, typhoid fever, and diphtheria.

Meanwhile, street paving, modernized firefighting equipment, and electric street lighting spread rapidly across urban America. Steel-frame construction, which uses a metal skeleton rather than masonry walls for building support, made possible the erection of skyscrapers, and thus more efficient vertical use of scarce urban land. Steel-cable suspension bridges, developed by John A. Roebling and epitomized by his Brooklyn Bridge (completed in 1883), linked metropolitan sections more closely.

Poverty Relief

None of these improvements, however, lightened the burden of poverty. Since colonial days Americans have disagreed about public responsibility for poor relief. According to traditional beliefs, still widespread in the early twentieth century, anyone could escape poverty through hard work and clean living; moral weakness caused indigence. Such reasoning bred fear that aiding the poor encouraged them to rely on public support rather than their own efforts. As business cycles fluctuated and poverty increased, this attitude hardened, and city governments discontinued grants of food, fuel, and clothing to needy families. Instead, cities provided relief in return for work on public projects and sent special cases to state-run almshouses, orphanages, and homes for the blind, deaf, and mentally ill.

Between 1877 and 1892, philanthropists in ninety-two cities formed Charity Organization Societies to make social welfare (like business) more efficient by merging disparate charities into coordinated units. Believing poverty to be caused by personal defects, such as alcoholism and laziness, these organizations visited poor families to determine if they were deserving and encouraged them to be thriftier and more virtuous. Close observation of the poor, however, prompted some humanitarians to conclude that people's environments, not their shortcomings, caused poverty and that society should help improve social conditions. They believed they could reduce poverty through better housing, education, sanitation, and job opportunities. This fueled campaigns for building codes, factory regulations, and public health measures in the Progressive era of the early twentieth century (see Chapter 21). Still, most middle- and upper-class Americans embraced the creed that only the unfit were poor and that poverty relief should be tolerated but never encouraged.

Crime and Violence

Crime and disorder, as much as crowding and poverty, nurtured fears that cities, especially their slums, threatened the nation. While homicide rates declined in other industrialized nations, America's rose from: 25 murders per million people in 1881 to 107 per million in 1898. Domestic violence, muggings, and gang fights made cities turbulent, as did pickpockets, swindlers, and burglars. Urban outlaws, such as Rufus Minor, acquired as much notoriety as western desperadoes. Short and bald, Minor resembled a shy clerk, but a police chief labeled him "one of the smartest bank sneaks in America." Minor was implicated in bank heists in New York City, Cleveland, Detroit, Providence, Philadelphia, Albany, Boston, and Baltimore between 1878 and 1882.

Urban crime may simply have become more conspicuous rather than more prevalent. Certainly concentrations of wealth and the mingling of different peoples provided opportunities for larceny, vice, and assault. But urban lawlessness probably did not exceed that of backwoods mining camps and southern plantations. Nativists were quick to blame immigrants for crime, but the law-breaker population included native-born Americans and foreigners.

MANAGING THE CITY

Burgeoning populations, business expansion, and technological change created urgent needs for sewers, police and fire protection, schools, parks, and other services. Such needs strained municipal resources and city governments beyond their capacities. In addition to a mayor and a city council, independent boards administered health regulations, public works, poverty relief, and other functions. Philadelphia at one time had thirty such boards. State governments also interfered in local matters, appointing board members and limiting cities' abilities to levy taxes and borrow money.

Water Supply and Sewage Disposal

Finding sources of clean water and a way to dispose of waste became increasingly pressing challenges. In the early nineteenth century, urban households used privies to dispose of human excrement, and factories dumped untreated sewage into rivers, lakes, and bays. By the late nineteenth century, the installation of sewer systems and flush toilets, plus the use of water as a coolant in factories, overwhelmed waterways and contaminated drinking-water sources. The stench of rivers was often unbearable, and pollution bred disease. Memphis and New York experienced severe yellow-fever epidemics in the 1870s and 1880s, and typhoid fever threatened many cities.

Acceptance in the 1880s of the germ theory of disease prompted cities to reduce chances that human waste and other pollutants would endanger water supplies. Some states legally prohibited discharging raw sewage into rivers and streams, and a few cities began the expensive process of chemically treating sewage. Gradually, water managers installed mechanical filters, and cities, led by Jersey City, began purifying water supplies by adding chlorine. These efforts dramatically reduced deaths from typhoid fever.

But waste disposal remained a thorny problem. Experts in 1900 estimated that every New Yorker generated annually 160 pounds of garbage (food and bones), 1,200 pounds of ashes (from stoves and furnaces), and 100 pounds of rubbish. Solid waste from factories and businesses included tons of scrap metal and wood. Each of the estimated 3.5 million horses in American cities in 1900 daily dropped about 20 pounds of manure and a gallon of urine that rain washed into nearby water sources. By the twentieth century this refuse was a health and safety hazard.

Urban Engineers

Citizens' groups, led by women's organizations, began discussing these dilemmas in the 1880s, and by the turn of the century urban governments began to hire sanitary engineers to design garbage collection systems, disposing of it in incinerators and landfills. The American engineering profession developed new systems and standards of worldwide significance that made cities more livable, such as street lighting, bridge and street construction, and fire protection. Elected officials depended on engineers' expertise in aiding urban expansion. Insulated within bureaucratic agencies from tumultuous party politics, engineers made lasting contributions to urban management.

This scene, captured by a Philadelphia photographer sent to record the extent of trash that was littering city streets and sidewalks, illustrates the problems of disposal confronting inner-city, immigrant neighborhoods and the necessity for some form of public service to remove the refuse. Seemingly oblivious to the debris, the residents pose for the photographer.   (Philadelphia City Archives, Department of Records, Photo Negative #10716)

Law Enforcement

After the mid-nineteenth century, urban dwellers increasingly depended on professional police to protect life and property, but law enforcement became complicated and controversial, as various groups differed about how laws should be enforced. Ethnic and racial minorities were more likely to be arrested, and police officers applied the law less harshly to members of their own ethnic groups and to people in power or offering bribes.

Often poorly trained and prone to corruption, police were caught between demands for swift and severe action on the one hand and leniency on the other. Some people clamored for police crackdowns on saloons, gambling halls, and houses of prostitution, while those who profited from and patronized such establishments favored loose law enforcement. Achieving a balance between criminal law and individual freedom grew increasingly difficult.

Political Machines

Out of the apparent confusion surrounding urban management arose political machines, organizations whose main goals were the rewards—money, influence, and prestige—of getting and keeping power. Machine politicians routinely used fraud and bribery to further their ends. But they also provided relief, security, and services to voters.

Machines bred leaders, called bosses, who built power bases among urban working classes, especially new immigrants. Most bosses had immigrant backgrounds and grew up in the inner city. They knew their constituents' needs firsthand and gained power by tending to the problems of everyday life. In return for votes, bosses provided jobs, built parks and bathhouses, distributed food and clothing to the needy, and helped when someone ran afoul of the law. New York's Big Tim Sullivan, for example, gave out free shoes and sponsored annual picnics. Bosses, moreover, made politics a full-time profession; they attended weddings and wakes, joined clubs, and held open houses in saloons where neighborhood folk could speak to them personally. According to George Washington Plunkitt, a neighborhood boss in New York City, "As a rule [the boss] . . . plays politics every day and night in the year and his headquarters bears the inscription, 'Never closed.'"

To finance their activities and election campaigns, bosses exchanged favors for votes and money. Power over local government enabled machines to control who received public contracts, utility and streetcar franchises, and city jobs. Recipients were expected to repay the machine with a portion of their profits or salaries and to cast supporting votes. Critics called this process graft; bosses called it gratitude.

Bosses like Philadelphia's Duke Vare, Kansas City's Tom Pendergast, and New York's Richard Croker lived like kings, though their official incomes were slim. Yet machines were rarely as dictatorial or corrupt as critics charged. Rather, several machines evolved into tightly structured operations, such as New York's Tammany Hall organization (named after a society that began as a patriotic fraternal club), which wedded public accomplishments with personal gain. The system rested on a popular base and was held together by loyalty and service. Most machines were coalitions of smaller organizations that derived power directly from inner-city neighborhoods. Machine-led governments constructed urban infrastructure—public buildings, sewer systems, schools, bridges, and mass-transit lines—and expanded urban services—police, firefighting, and health departments.

Machine politics, however, was rarely neutral. Racial minorities and new immigrant groups, such as Italians and Poles, received only token jobs and nominal favors, if any. And bribes and kickbacks made machine projects and services costly to taxpayers. Cities could not ordinarily raise enough revenue for construction projects from taxes and fees, so they financed expansion with loans from the public in the form of municipal bonds, which caused public debts, and then taxes, to soar. And payoffs from gambling, prostitution, and illicit liquor traffic became important sources of machine revenue. But bosses were no guiltier of discrimination and self-interest than were business leaders who exploited workers, spoiled the environment, and manipulated government in pursuit of profits.

Civic Reform

Many middle- and upper-class Americans feared that immigrant-based political machines menaced democracy and wasted municipal finances. Anxious over the poverty, crowding, and disorder that accompanied city growth and convinced that urban services were making taxes too high, civic reformers organized to install more responsible leaders who would run government efficiently like a business.

To implement business principles in government, civic reformers supported structural changes, such as city-manager and commission forms of government, which would place administration in the hands of experts rather than politicians, and nonpartisan citywide rather than neighborhood-based election of officials. Reformers believed they could cleanse city government of party politics and weaken bosses' power bases.

A few reform mayors also addressed social problems. Hazen S. Pingree of Detroit, Samuel "Golden Rule" Jones of Toledo, and Tom Johnson of Cleveland worked to provide jobs to poor people, reduce charges by transit and utility companies, and promote government responsibility for citizens' welfare. They also supported public ownership of gas, electric, and telephone companies, quasi-socialist reforms that alienated their business allies. But Pingree, Jones, and Johnson were exceptions; civic reformers achieved some successes but rarely held office for very long.

Social Reform

Social reformers—mostly young and middle class—also wanted to solve urban problems. Housing reformers pressed local governments for building codes ensuring safety in tenements. Educational reformers sought to use public schools to prepare immigrant children for citizenship by teaching them American values.

Perhaps the most ambitious urban reform movement was the settlement house, a place located in inner-city neighborhoods and established mostly by young, middle-class women who lived and worked among the poor. The first American settlement, patterned after London's Toynbee Hall, opened in New York City in 1886, and others quickly followed, including Hull House, founded in Chicago in 1889. To help immigrants adjust, settlements offered vocational classes, English lessons, childcare, and programs to improve nutrition and housing.

Settlement-house workers like Jane Addams and Florence Kelley of Chicago and Lillian Wald of New York broadened their scope to fight for school nurses, factory safety codes, and public playgrounds. Their efforts to involve national and local governments in the solution of social problems made them key contributors to the Progressive era, when a reform spirit swept the nation (see Chapter 21). Moreover, settlement-house programs created new professional opportunities for women in social work, public health, and child welfare. These professions enabled female reformers to influence social policy and make valuable contributions to national and inner-city life.

But settlement houses were segregated. White female reformers lobbied for government programs to aid mostly white immigrant and native-born working classes. Black women reformers, excluded from white settlements, raised funds and aided their race by founding schools, old-age homes, and hospitals, as well as protecting black women from sexual exploitation. Their ranks included Jane Hunter, who founded a home for unmarried black working women in Cleveland in 1911 and inspired the establishment of similar homes in other cities.

The City Beautiful Movement

Male reformers similarly worked to improve cities by organizing the City Beautiful movement. Inspired by the Columbian Exposition of 1893, a dazzling world's fair held in Chicago, architects and planners urged the construction of civic centers, parks, and boulevards that would make cities economically efficient and beautiful. Projects were underway in Chicago, San Francisco, and Washington, D.C., in the early 1900s. Yet neither government nor private businesses could finance large-scale projects, and planners disagreed among themselves and with social reformers over whether beautification would solve urban problems.

Urban reformers wanted to save cities, but they often failed to understand cities' diverse populations and people's varying visions of reform. To civic reformers, appointing government workers on the basis of civil service exams rather than party loyalty meant progress, but to working-class men, civil service signified reduced employment opportunities. Moral reformers believed that restricting alcoholic beverages would prevent working-class breadwinners from squandering wages, but immigrants saw it as interference. Planners saw new streets and buildings as modern necessities, but such structures often displaced the poor. Well-meaning humanitarians criticized immigrant mothers for the way they dressed, did housework, and raised children, without regard for their income limitations. Thus urban reform merged idealism with naiveté and insensitivity.

FAMILY LIFE

Urbanization and industrialization strained family life. New institutions—schools, social clubs, political organizations, unions—increasingly competed with the family to provide nurture and education. Clergy and journalists warned that the growing separation between home and work, rising divorce rates, the entrance of women into the work force, and the loss of parental control over children spelled peril for home and family. Yet the family remained a cushion in an uncertain world.

Family and Household Structures

In previous eras, most American households (75 to 80 percent) consisted of nuclear families—usually a married couple, with or without children. About 15 to 20 percent of households consisted of extended families—usually a married couple, their children, and one or more relatives. About 5 percent of households had people living alone. Despite slight variations, this pattern held constant among ethnic, racial, and socioeconomic groups.

Several factors explain this pattern. Because immigrants tended to be young, the American population as a whole was young. In 1880 the median age was under twenty-one, and by 1920 it was still only twenty-five. (Median age at present is above thirty-five.) Moreover, in 1900 the death rate among people aged forty-five to sixty-four was double what it is today. Only 4 percent of the population was sixty-five or older, versus almost 13 percent today. Thus few families could form extended three-generation households, and fewer children than today had living grandparents. Migration split up many families, and the ideal of a home ownership encouraged nuclear household organization.

Declining Birth Rates   Most of Europe and North America experienced falling birth rates in the nineteenth century. In 1880 the birth rate was forty live births per one thousand people; by 1900 it had dropped to thirty-two; by 1920, to twenty-eight. Although birth rates were higher among black, immigrant, and rural women, birth rates of all groups fell.

Several factors explain this decline. First, as the United States became more urbanized, the economic value of children lessened. On farms, each child born represented an addition to the family labor force. In the wage-based urban economy, children could not contribute significantly to the family income for years, and a new child represented a draw on family income. Second, infant mortality fell as diet and medical care improved, and families did not have to bear as many children to ensure that some would survive.

Perhaps most importantly, as American society industrialized and urbanized, the idea of a child as an innocent being who needed shelter from society's corruptions spread, first among the middle class and gradually to the working class. A mother's care and attention could be more effective if she had fewer children. That seems to have stimulated decisions to limit family size, either by abstaining from sex or using contraception. Families with six or eight children became rare; three or four became more usual. Birth-control technology—diaphragms and condoms—had been utilized for centuries, but in this era new materials made these devices more convenient and dependable.

Stages of Life   Before the late nineteenth century, stages of life were less distinct than they are today. Childhood, for instance, was regarded as a period during which young people prepared for adulthood by gradually assuming more responsibilities. Subdivisions of youth—toddlers, schoolchildren, teenagers, and the like—were not defined. Because married couples had more children over a longer time span, active parenthood occupied most of adult life. Older children might begin parenting before reaching adulthood by caring for younger siblings. And older people were not isolated from other age groups. By the late nineteenth century, however, decreasing birth rates shortened the period of parental responsibility, so more middle-aged couples experienced an empty nest when children grew up and left home. Longer life expectancy and a tendency by employers to force aged workers to retire separated the old from the young.

New patterns of childhood also emerged. To be sure, youngsters in working-class families still helped out—working in factories, scavenging streets for scraps of wood and coal, and peddling newspapers. But as states passed compulsory school attendance laws in the 1870s and 1880s, education occupied more of children's daily time than ever, filling nine months of the year until they were teenagers. Schools strengthened peer rather than family influence over behavior. Researchers like G. Stanley Hall and Luther H. Gulick advocated that teachers and parents should match education and play activities to children's changing developmental stages.

The Unmarried

Although marriage rates were high, large numbers of city dwellers were unmarried. In 1890 almost 42 percent of adult American men and 37 percent of women were single, nearly twice as high as in 1960 but slightly lower than today. About half still lived with parents, but others inhabited boarding houses. Mostly young, these men and women constituted a separate subculture that supported institutions like dance halls, saloons, cafés, and the Young Men's Christian Association (YMCA) and Young Women's Christian Association (YWCA).

Some unmarried people were part of the homosexual populations that thrived in large cities like New York, San Francisco, and Boston. Although numbers are difficult to estimate, gay men had their own subculture of clubs, restaurants, coffee-houses, theaters, and support networks. A number of same-sex couples, especially women, formed lasting marital-type relationships, sometimes called Boston marriages. People in this subculture were categorized more by how they acted—men acting like women, women acting like men—than by who their sexual partners were. The term *homosexual* was not used. Men who dressed and acted like women were called fairies. Gay women remained mostly hidden, and a lesbian subculture did not develop until the 1920s.

Boarding and Lodging

In every city, boarding houses and lodging hotels were common, but families also took in boarders for rooms vacated by grown children and for additional income. By 1900 as many as 50 percent of city residents, including Erich Weiss's family, lived either as, or with, boarders at some point. Housing reformers charged that boarding and lodging caused overcrowding and loss of privacy. For people on the move, boarding or lodging was a transitional stage, providing a quasi-family environment until they set up their own households. Especially in communities where housing was expensive or scarce, newlyweds sometimes lived temporarily with one spouse's parents. Families also took in widowed parents or unmarried siblings.

Functions of Kinship

At a time when welfare agencies were scarce, the family was the institution to which people turned when in need. Relatives often resided nearby and helped with childcare, meals, advice, and consolation. They also obtained jobs for each other. According to one new arrival, "After two days my brother took me to the shop he was working in and his boss saw me and he gave me the job."

But kinship obligations were not always welcome. Immigrant families pressured last-born daughters to stay home to care for aging parents, a practice that stifled opportunities for education, marriage, and independence. Generational tensions also developed, such as when immigrant parents and American-born children clashed over the abandonment of Old World ways or the amount of wages employed children should contribute. Nevertheless, kinship helped people cope with the stresses of urban-industrial society.

Thus, by 1900, family life and functions were both changing and holding firm. New institutions were assuming tasks formerly performed by the family. Schools made education a community responsibility. Employment agencies, personnel offices, and labor unions took responsibility for employee recruitment and job security. Age-based peer groups exerted greater influence over people's values and activities. Migration and divorce seemed to be splitting families apart. Yet, kinship remained a dependable though not always appreciated institution.

Holiday Celebrations   An emphasis on family togetherness became especially visible at holiday celebrations. Middle-class moralists helped make Thanksgiving, Christmas, and Easter special times for family reunion and child-centered activities. Birthdays, too, took on an increasingly festive quality as a milestone for measuring the age-related norms that accompanied life stages. In 1914 President Woodrow Wilson signed a proclamation designating the second Sunday in May as Mother's Day, capping a six-year campaign by the schoolteacher Anna Jarvis, who believed grown children neglected their mothers. Ethnic and racial groups adapted national celebrations to their cultures, preparing special ethnic foods and engaging in special ceremonies.

THE NEW LEISURE AND MASS CULTURE

On December 2, 1889, as workers paraded through Worcester, Massachusetts, seeking shorter working hours, carpenters hoisted a banner proclaiming "Eight Hours for Work, Eight Hours for Rest, Eight Hours for What We Will." That last

SHOOTING THE CHUTES, CONEY ISLAND, N. Y.

Amusement centers like Luna Park, at Coney Island in New York City, became common and appealing features of the new leisure culture. One of the most popular Coney Island attractions was a ride called Shooting the Chutes, which resembled modern-day giant water slides. In 1904 Luna Park staged an outrageous stunt of an elephant sliding down the chute. The creature survived, apparently unfazed. (Picture Research Consultants and Archives)

phrase laid claim to a segment of daily life by the individual. Increasingly, leisure activities filled this time.

Increase in Leisure Time

Mechanization and labor-saving assembly-line production cut the average manufacturing workweek from sixty-six hours in 1860 to sixty in 1890 and forty-seven in 1920. This meant shorter workdays and freer weekends. White-collar employees spent eight to ten hours a day on the job and often worked only half a day or not at all on weekends. As the economy shifted from production to consumption, more Americans engaged in recreation, and a substantial segment of the economy provided for—and profited from—leisure.

Amusement became a commercial activity, as games, toys, and musical instruments were sold for indoor family entertainment. Improvements in printing and paper production and the rise of manufacturers like Milton Bradley and Parker Brothers increased the popularity of board games. Significantly, board games shifted from moral lessons to topics involving transportation, finance, and sports. Middle-class families were buying mass-produced pianos and sheet music which made singing popular songs a common form of home entertainment. The vanguard of new leisure pursuits, however, was sports. Formerly a fashionable indulgence of elites, organized sports became a favored pastime of all classes.

Baseball

The most popular sport was baseball. Derived from older bat, ball, and base-circling games, in 1845 the Knickerbocker Club of New York standardized the rules of play. By 1860 at least fifty baseball clubs existed, and youths played informal games in fields and city lots nationwide. The National League of Professional Baseball Clubs, founded in 1876, gave the sport a businesslike structure, but as early as 1867 a color line excluded blacks from professional teams. By the 1880s professional baseball was big business. In 1903 the National League and the competing American League (formed in 1901) began a World Series between their championship teams. The Boston Red Sox beat the Pittsburgh Pirates in that first series.

Croquet and Cycling

Baseball appealed mostly to men. But croquet, also nationally popular, attracted both sexes. Middle- and upper-class people held croquet parties and night contests that increased opportunities for social contact between the sexes.

Meanwhile, cycling achieved a popularity rivaling baseball, especially after 1885, when the cumbersome velocipede, with its huge front wheel and tall seat, gave way to safety bicycles with pneumatic tires and identical-size wheels. By 1900 Americans owned 10 million bicycles, and clubs petitioned state governments to build more paved roads. African American cyclists were allowed to compete, and one rider, Major Taylor became famous in Europe and the United States between 1892 and 1910. Moreover, the bicycle helped free women from the constraints of Victorian fashions. To ride the dropped-frame female models, women had to wear divided skirts and simple undergarments. As the 1900 census declared, "Few articles . . . have created so great a revolution in social conditions as the bicycle."

Japanese Baseball

Baseball, the American pastime, was one of the new leisure-time pursuits that Americans brought to different parts of the world. The Shanghai Base Ball Club was founded by Americans in China in 1863, but was denounced by the Imperial Court as spiritually corrupting. However, when Horace Wilson, an American teacher, taught the rules of baseball to Japanese students around 1870, the game received an enthusiastic reception as a reinforcement of traditional virtues and became a part of Japanese culture.

During the 1870s, scores of Japanese high schools and colleges sponsored baseball, and in 1883 Hiroshi Hiraoka, a railroad engineer who had studied in Boston, founded the first official local team, the Shimbashi Athletic Club Athletics.

Before baseball, the Japanese had no team sports or recreational athletics. Once they learned about baseball, they found that the idea of a team sport fit their culture well. But to them, baseball was serious business, involving often brutal training. Practices at Ichiko, one of Japan's great high school baseball teams in the late nineteenth century, were dubbed "Bloody Urine" because many players passed blood after a day of drilling. There was a spiritual quality as well, linked to Buddhist values. According to one Japanese coach, "Student baseball must be the baseball of self-discipline, or trying to attain the truth, just as in Zen Buddhism." This attitude prompted the Japanese to consider baseball as a new method to pursue the spirit of Bushido, the way of the samurai.

When Americans played baseball in Japan, the Japanese admired their talent but found them lacking in discipline and respect. Americans insulted the Japanese by refusing to remove their hats and bow when they stepped up to bat. An international dispute occurred in 1891 when William Imbrie, an American professor at Tokyo's Meijo University, arrived late for a game and climbed over a locked fence. Japanese fans considered this sacrilege and attacked Imbrie, who suffered facial injuries. The American embassy lodged a formal complaint. Americans assumed that their game would encourage the Japanese to become like westerners, but the Japanese transformed baseball into a uniquely Japanese expression of team spirit, discipline, and nationalism.

Replete with bats, gloves, and uniforms, this Japanese baseball team of 1890 very much resembles its American counterpart of that era. The Japanese adopted baseball soon after Americans became involved in their country but also added their cultural qualities to the game. (Japanese Baseball Hall of Fame and Museum)

Football

American football, as an intercollegiate competition, initially attracted mostly players and spectators wealthy enough to have access to higher education. By the late nineteenth century, however, the game appealed to a broader audience. The 1893 Princeton-Yale game drew fifty thousand spectators, and informal games were played throughout the country. Soon, however, football became a national scandal because of its violence and use of "tramp athletes," nonstudents hired to help teams win. Critics accused football of mirroring undesirable features of American society. An editor of *The Nation* charged in 1890 that "the lack of moral scruple which pervades the struggles of the business world meets with temptations equally irresistible in the miniature contests of the football field."

The scandals climaxed in 1905, when 18 players died from game-related injuries and 159 were seriously injured. President Theodore Roosevelt, a strong advocate of athletics, convened a White House conference to discuss ways to eliminate brutality. The gathering founded the Intercollegiate Athletic Association (renamed the National College Athletic Association in 1910) to police college sports. In 1906 the association altered the game to make it less violent and more open.

As more women enrolled in college, they participated in such sports as rowing, track, and swimming. Invented in 1891 as a winter sport for men, basketball—soon women's most popular sport—received women's rules (which limited dribbling and running and encouraged passing) from Senda Berenson of Smith College.

Show Business

Three branches of American show business—popular drama, musical comedy, and vaudeville—matured with the growth of cities. Theatrical performances offered audiences escape into melodrama, adventure, and comedy. For urban people unfamiliar with the frontier, popular plays made the mythical Wild West and Old South come alive through stories of Davy Crockett, Buffalo Bill, and the Civil War. Virtue and honor triumphed in melodramas like *Uncle Tom's Cabin* and *The Old Homestead,* reinforcing faith that in an uncertain world goodness would prevail.

The American musical derived from Europe's lavishly costumed operettas. George M. Cohan, a singer, dancer, and songwriter born into an Irish family of entertainers, became the master of American musical comedy after the turn of the century. Drawing on patriotism and traditional values in songs like "Yankee Doodle Boy" and "You're a Grand Old Flag," Cohan bolstered morale during World War I. Initially, American comic operas imitated European musicals, but by the early 1900s composers like Victor Herbert were writing for American audiences.

Probably the most popular mass entertainment in early-twentieth-century America, vaudeville offered something for everyone. Shows included jugglers, magicians, puppeteers, acrobats, comedians, singers, dancers, and specialty acts like Houdini's escapes. Around 1900, the number of vaudeville theaters and troupes skyrocketed, and operators like Tony Pastor and the partnership of Benjamin Keith and Edward Albee consolidated theaters and acts under their management. Producer Florenz Ziegfeld brilliantly packaged stylish shows—the Ziegfeld Follies—and gave the nation a new model of femininity, the Ziegfeld Girl, whose graceful dancing and alluring costumes suggested a haunting sensuality.

Opportunities for Women and Minorities

Show business provided social mobility to female, African American, and immigrant performers, but it also encouraged stereotyping and exploitation. The comic opera diva Lillian Russell, the vaudeville singer-comedienne Fanny Brice, and the burlesque queen Eva Tanguay attracted loyal fans and handsome fees. In contrast to the demure Victorian female, they conveyed pluck and independence. There was something both shocking and confident about Eva Tanguay singing, "It's All Been Done Before but Not the Way I Do It." But lesser female performers and showgirls (called soubrettes) were often exploited by male promoters and theater owners, who wanted to profit by titillating the public with scantily clad women.

Before the 1890s, the chief form of commercial entertainment employing African Americans was the minstrel show, but vaudeville opened new opportunities. Pandering to the prejudices of white audiences, composers ridiculed blacks, and black performers were forced to portray demeaning characters. In songs like "He's Just a Little Nigger, But He's Mine All Mine" blacks were degraded on stage as they were in society. Burt Williams, a talented black comedian and dancer, achieved success by wearing blackface (black makeup) and playing stereotypical roles of a smiling fool, but the humiliation tormented him.

Like Houdini, many performers were immigrants, and their acts reflected the everyday difficulties they faced. Vaudeville utilized ethnic humor and exaggerated dialects. Skits and songs were fast paced, replicating the tempo of factories, offices, and the streets. Performances reinforced ethnic stereotypes, but such distortions were more sympathetic than those directed at blacks. A typical scene involving Italians, for example, highlighted a character's uncertain grasp of English, which caused him to confuse *diploma* with *the plumber* and *pallbearer* with *polar bear*. Such scenes allowed audiences to laugh with, rather than at, foibles of the human condition.

Movies

Shortly after 1900, live entertainment gave way to the more accessible motion pictures. Perfected by Thomas Edison in the 1880s, movies began as slot-machine peepshows in arcades and billiard parlors. Eventually, images were projected onto a screen for large audiences. Producers, many of them from Jewish immigrant backgrounds, soon discovered that a film could tell a story in exciting ways. Using themes of patriotism and working-class experience, early filmmakers helped shift American culture away from its straitlaced Victorian values.

Movies presented controversial social messages as well as innovative technology and styles of expression. The film *The Birth of a Nation* (1915), by the director D. W. Griffith, a stunning epic about the Civil War and Reconstruction, fanned racial prejudice by depicting African Americans as threats to white moral values. The National Association for the Advancement of Colored People (NAACP), formed in 1909, led protests against it. But the film's ground-breaking techniques—close-ups, fade-outs, and battle scenes—heightened its drama.

Technology and entrepreneurship also made news a mass consumer product. Using high-speed printing presses, cheaply produced paper, and profits from growing advertisement revenues, shrewd publishers created an in-demand medium. Increased leisure time seemed to nurture a fascination with the sensational, and from the 1880s onward popular urban newspapers increasingly whetted that appetite.

Yellow Journalism

Joseph Pulitzer, a Hungarian immigrant who bought the *New York World* in 1883, pioneered journalism by making news a mass commodity. Pulitzer filled the *World* with stories of disasters, crimes, and scandals and featured screaming headlines set in large, bold type. *World* reporter Nellie Bly (real name, Elizabeth Cochrane) faked her way into a mental asylum and wrote a brazen exposé of the sordid conditions she found. Other reporters staged stunts and wrote heart-rending human-interest stories. Pulitzer also popularized comics, and the yellow ink in which they were printed gave rise to the term *yellow journalism* as a synonym for *sensationalism*.

In one year the *World*'s circulation increased from 20,000 to 100,000, and by the late 1890s it reached 1 million. Other publishers, such as William Randolph Hearst, who bought the *New York Journal* in 1895 and started a newspaper empire, adopted Pulitzer's techniques. Pulitzer, Hearst, and their rivals boosted circulation further by featuring sports and women's news. Newspapers previously reported sporting events, but yellow-journalism papers gave such stories greater prominence with separate, expanded sports pages. For women, newspapers added special sections devoted to household tips, fashion, etiquette, and club news.

Other Mass-Market Publications

By the early twentieth century, mass-circulation magazines overshadowed expensive elitist journals of earlier eras. Publications like *McClure's, Saturday Evening Post,* and *Ladies' Home Journal* offered human-interest stories, muckraking exposés, fiction, photographs, colorful covers, and eye-catching ads. Meanwhile, the total number of published books more than quadrupled between 1880 and 1917, reflecting the growing literacy. Between 1870 and 1920, the proportion of Americans over age ten who could not read or write fell from 20 to 6 percent.

Other forms of communication also expanded. In 1891 there was fewer than 1 telephone for every 100 people in the United States; by 1901 the number reached 2.1, and by 1921 it swelled to 12.6. In 1900 Americans used 4 billion postage stamps; in 1922 they bought 14.3 billion. More than ever before, people in different parts of the country knew about and discussed the same news event. America was becoming a mass society where the same products, the same technology, and the same information dominated everyday life.

To some extent, cities' new amusements and media had a homogenizing influence, allowing ethnic and social groups to share common experiences. Yet different groups adapted parks, ball fields, vaudeville shows, movies, and the feature sections of newspapers and magazines to their own cultural needs. To the dismay of reformers who hoped that public recreation and holidays would assimilate newcomers, immigrants used parks for ethnic gatherings and converted picnics and Fourth of July celebrations into occasions for boisterous drinking and sometimes violent behavior. Young working-class men and women resisted parents' and moralists' warnings and frequented urban dance halls, where they explored forms of courtship and sexual behavior. Thus, leisure—like work and politics—was shaped by the pluralistic forces that thrived in urban life.

Ethnic Food

Today, an American might eat a bagel for breakfast, a gyro sandwich for lunch, and wonton soup, shrimp creole, and rice pilaf for dinner. These items, each identified with a different ethnic group, serve as tasty reminders that immigrants have made influential and lasting contributions to the nation's culinary culture.

The American taste for ethnic food has a complicated history. Since the nineteenth century, the food business has offered immigrant entrepreneurs lucrative opportunities, many involving products unrelated to their own ethnic background. The industry is replete with success stories such as Hector Boiardi (Chef Boyardee), William Gebhardt (Eagle Brand chili and tamales), Jeno Paulucci (Chun King), and Alphonse Biardot (Franco-American), all of whom immigrated to the United States in the late nineteenth or early twentieth century. But Americans have also supported unheralded local immigrant merchants and restaurateurs offering regional fare—German, Chinese, Italian, Tex-Mex, Thai, or soul food—in every era.

The evolution of American eating habits has been peaceful. Occasionally criticisms developed, such as when dietitians and reformers in the early twentieth century charged that the rich foods of eastern European Jews made them overly emotional and less capable of assimilating. But relatively conflict-free sharing has characterized American food ways far more than intolerance. And mass marketers have been quick to capitalize.

As each wave of immigrants entered the nation—and especially as these newcomers occupied cities, where cross-cultural contact has been inevitable—food has given them ways of becoming American, of finding group acceptance, while confirming their identity. And those who already thought of themselves as Americans have made the newcomers' gastronomic legacy their own.

Summary

People and technology made the late nineteenth and early twentieth century the age of the city. Flocking cityward, migrants already in America and those from foreign lands remade themselves, like Houdini, and remade the urban environment as well. They brought cultures that in turn enriched American culture. They found escape in new forms of mass leisure and entertainment.

American cities experienced unheralded triumph by the early 1900s. Amid corruption and political conflict, engineers modernized sewer, water, and lighting services, and urban governments made cities safer by expanding professional police and fire departments. When native inventiveness met the traditions of European, African, and Asian cultures, a new society emerged. The jumble of social classes, ethnic and racial groups, and political and professional organizations sometimes lived in harmony, sometimes not.

Optimists envisioned the American nation as a melting pot, where various nationalities would fuse into a unified people. Instead, many ethnic groups proved unmeltable, and racial minorities got burned on the bottom of the pot. Instead, the United States became a pluralistic society in which cultural influences moved in both directions: imposed from above by people with power and influence and adopted from below through the traditions brought to cities by disparate peoples.

By 1920, immigrants and their offspring outnumbered the native-born in many cities, and the national economy depended on these new workers and consumers.

Migrants and immigrants transformed the United States into an urban nation. They gave American culture a varied texture and, like Harry Houdini, helped change the course of entertainment and consumerism. Together, they laid the foundations for the liberalism that would characterize American politics in the twentieth century.

Chapter Review

GROWTH OF THE MODERN CITY

What fueled urban growth in the late nineteenth century?

Cities grew two ways: by annexing areas that bordered them, as New York City did when it merged with Brooklyn, Staten Island, and parts of Queens, doubling its population to 3 million. Cities also expanded via in-migration from rural areas and immigration from abroad. Within the United States, low crop prices and heavy debts pushed some people from the country to the city; in other cases, young men sought to escape economic hardship for the excitement of cities while young women left unhappy homes for greater independence. Similarly, African Americans headed to cities for better jobs and to escape crop liens and racial violence. Population pressures, land redistribution, industrialization, and religious persecution pushed many immigrants to leave Europe, Asia, Canada, and Latin America for the United States, with most hoping to make enough money to return to their native countries and live more comfortably.

URBAN NEIGHBORHOODS

How did immigrants adapt to their new lives in U.S. cities?

While most immigrants sought to hang on to old world traditions, once in the United States, those former folkways were changed by, and also helped change, American cities. Traditions held on longer in neighborhoods with immigrants from the same region or district. Immigrants recreated the mutual aid societies, newspapers, and churches that existed in their homelands. While immigrants tried to hold fast to their native languages, English—which children learned in schools—soon dominated ethnic neighborhoods. Foreigners adapted their traditional garments to American fabrics, and their music evolved as well to include American influences or tales of their adjustment to life here. Catholics and Jews sought to merge their faiths with their new surroundings by liberalizing or eliminating some old world rituals.

LIVING CONDITIONS IN THE INNER CITY

What made cities seem particularly threatening/dangerous?

Overcrowding and housing shortages in inner cities, along with poverty and crime led to fears that cities were dangerous places filled with violence, muggings, gang fights, and even murder. While murder rates did increase fourfold from 1881 to 1898, crime in cities was not greater than that in backwoods mining camps or southern plantations. The high concentrations of people, particularly those of different classes and ethnic/racial backgrounds, mingling in cities simply made urban crime more visible, which in turn made cities seem scarier.

MANAGING THE CITY

What facilitated the rise of political machines in cities?

Political machines emerged in typically working class and immigrant neighborhoods to provide relief, security, and services to voters in exchange for votes, money, influence, and prestige. Each machine had a leader, or boss, who helped his constituents obtain jobs, clothing, or legal assistance. The power they exerted over local government meant machines could control which firms or individuals got public contracts and city jobs, and insist that those receiving these awards repay the machine with a share of their profits or salaries. Machine-led governments did build sewer systems, schools, bridges, and transportation lines and expand police and fire, but the bribes and kickbacks they commanded made their projects expensive to taxpayers.

FAMILY LIFE

What factors led to declining birth rates in the late nineteenth century United States?

As more people left farms for city life, the need for big families where children could help with heavy farm work diminished. Improvements in health, medicine, and diet meant that more babies lived past infancy into childhood so that families didn't need to bear more children in the hopes that some might survive. And as the United States became increasingly urbanized, the notion of children needing protection from the city's harsh realities meant that mothers could be more effective caregivers if they had fewer children to raise. New technology led to better materials for condoms, diaphragms, and other birth control devices, which made them more convenient and reliable.

THE NEW LEISURE AND MASS CULTURE

What fueled the rise of commercial leisure?

Mechanization and new, more efficient means of production, along with labor activism, led to shorter work weeks and hours—which, in turn, gave workers more time to use as they saw fit. New mass entertainment arose to fill this need, and included baseball and football leagues, bicycling, and other outdoor activities, as well as theater, vaudeville, and later film. Vaudeville was among the most popular entertainment because its shows tried to appeal to the broadest audiences with jugglers, magicians, comedians, singers, and dancers. Vaudeville, like other forms of show business, also provided new work opportunities for blacks, immigrants, and women.

SUGGESTIONS FOR FURTHER READING

John Bodnar, *The Transplanted: A History of Immigrants in Urban America* (1985)

Howard P. Chudacoff and Judith E. Smith, *The Evolution of American Urban Society*, 6th ed. (2005)

John D'Emilio and Estelle Freedman, *Intimate Matters: A History of Sexuality in America* (1988)

Nancy Foner and George M. Frederickson, eds., *Not Just Black and White: Historical and Contemporary Perspectives on Immigration, Race, and Ethnicity in the United States* (2004)

Kenneth T. Jackson, *The Crabgrass Frontier: The Suburbanization of the United States* (1985)

Matthew Frye Jacobson, *Whiteness of a Different Color: European Immigrants and the Alchemy of Race* (1998)

Erika Lee, *At America's Gates: Chinese Immigration During the Exclusion Era, 1882–1943* (2003)

Martin V. Melosi, *The Sanitary City: Urban Infrastructure in America from Colonial Times to the Present* (2000)

Robyn Muncy, *Creating a Female Dominion in American Reform, 1890–1935* (1991)

Kathy Peiss, *Cheap Amusements: Working Women and Leisure in Turn-of-the-Century New York* (1986)

CHAPTER 20

Gilded Age Politics 1877–1900

CHAPTER OUTLINE

The Nature of Party Politics

Issues of Legislation

Tentative Presidents

Discrimination, Disfranchisement, and Responses

Agrarian Unrest and Populism

LINKS TO THE WORLD: Russian Populism

The Depression and Protests of the 1890s

The Silver Crusade and the Election of 1896

Summary

LEGACY FOR A PEOPLE AND A NATION: Interpreting a Fairy Tale

Known to friends as the People's Joan of Arc and to enemies as the Kansas Pythoness, sharp-tongued Mary Elizabeth Lease was an electrifying orator, who, noted one observer, could "set a crowd hooting and harrahing at her will." Born in 1853 in Pennsylvania, she lived most of her adult life in Kansas. Married at age twenty, she bore five children and studied law while she took in washing, pinning her notes above her washtub.

In 1885 Lease became the first woman admitted to the Kansas bar and became an activist. Joining the Woman's Christian Temperance Union and the Farmers' Alliance, she served as spokesperson for the new Populist Party, making over 160 speeches in 1890 on behalf of downtrodden rural folk and laborers. She later ran for the U.S. Senate. Lease also spoke out for prohibition, woman suffrage, and birth control. She proclaimed, "This is a nation of inconsistencies. . . . We fought England for our liberty and put chains on four million blacks. We wiped out slavery and [then] by our tariff laws and national banks began a system of white wage slavery worse than the first." Although she denied making the oft-quoted suggestion that Kansas farmers should "raise less corn and more hell," she thought it was good advice.

Lease's turbulent career paralleled an eventful era characterized by three themes: special interest ascendancy, legislative accomplishment, and political exclusion. Her fiery speeches voiced the growing dissatisfaction with greed and the abuses of power exerted by wealthy individuals and corporations. The era's wealth obsession seemed so widespread that, when Mark Twain and Charles Dudley Warner satirized America as a land of shallow money grubbers in their novel *The Gilded Age* (1874), the name stuck as a historical characterization of the late nineteenth century.

This icon will direct you to interactive activities and study materials on A People And A Nation, Brief Edition website: **www.cengage.com/history/norton/peoplenationbrief8e**

Chronology

1873	Congress ends coinage of silver dollars.
1873–78	Economic hard times hit.
1876	Hayes is elected president.
1877	Georgia passes poll tax, disfranchising most African Americans.
1878	Bland-Allison Act requires Treasury to buy between $2 and $4 million in silver each month.
1880	Garfield becomes president.
1881	Garfield is assassinated; Arthur assumes presidency.
1883	Pendleton Civil Service Act introduces merit system.
	Supreme Court strikes down 1883 Civil Rights Act.
1884	Cleveland is elected president.
1886	*Wabash* case declares that only Congress can limit interstate commerce rates.
1887	Farmers' Alliances are formed.
	Interstate Commerce Commission begins regulating rates and practices of interstate shipping.
1888	B. Harrison is elected president.
1890	McKinley Tariff raises tariff rates.
	Sherman Silver Purchase Act commits Treasury to buying 4.5 million ounces of silver each month.
	Mississippi Plan uses poll taxes and literacy tests to prevent African Americans from voting.
	National Woman Suffrage Association is formed.
1890s	Jim Crow laws, discriminating against African Americans in legal treatment and public accommodations, are passed by southern states.
1892	Populist convention in Omaha draws up a reform platform.
	Cleveland is elected president for the second time.
1893	Sherman Silver Purchase Act is repealed.
1893–97	Major economic depression hits the United States.
1894	Wilson-Gorman Tariff passes.
	Coxey's Army marches on Washington, D.C.
1895	Cleveland makes a deal with bankers to save gold reserves.
1896	McKinley is elected president.
	Plessy v. Ferguson establishes separate-but-equal doctrine.
1898	Louisiana implements "grandfather clause," restricting voting by African Americans.
1899	*Cummings v. County Board of Education* applies the separate-but-equal doctrine to schools.
1900	Gold Standard Act requires all paper money to be backed by gold.
	McKinley is reelected president.

At the same time, Lease's rhetoric obscured economic and political accomplishments at national and state levels. Between 1877 and 1900, large corporations and business allies influenced politics and government, yet Congress achieved legislative landmarks in railroad regulation, tariff and currency reform, and civil service despite partisan and regional rivalries. Meanwhile, the judiciary countered reform by supporting big business and defending property rights against state and federal regulation. The presidency was occupied by respectable men who attempted to assert their authority. Still, exclusion prevented the majority of Americans—women, southern blacks, Indians, uneducated whites, and unnaturalized immigrants—from voting.

Until the 1890s, a stable party system and a balance of power among geographic sections kept politics in a delicate equilibrium. Then, in the 1890s, rural discontent rumbled through the West and South, and a deep economic depression revealed flaws in the industrial system. Mary Lease and others like her helped awaken the rural masses, and the 1896 presidential campaign further stirred Americans. A new party arose, old parties split, sectional unity dissolved, and fundamental disputes about the nation's future climaxed.

- What were the functions of government in the Gilded Age, and how did they change?
- How did policies of exclusion and discrimination make their mark on the political culture of the age?
- How did the economic climate give rise to the Populist movement?

THE NATURE OF PARTY POLITICS

Public interest in elections reached an all-time high between 1870 and 1896. Around 80 percent of eligible voters (white and black males in the North, somewhat lower rates among mostly white males in the South) consistently voted. (Fewer than 50 percent typically vote today.) Featuring parades, picnics, and speeches, politics became recreation, more popular than baseball or circuses.

Cultural-Political Alignments

In the Gilded Age, party loyalty was fierce. With some exceptions, people who opposed government interference in personal liberty identified with the Democratic Party; those who believed government could be an agent of reform identified with the Republicans. Democrats included immigrant and second-generation Catholics and Jews; Republicans consisted mostly of native-born Protestants. Democrats would restrict government power. Republicans believed in direct government action.

There was also a geographic dimension to these divisions. Well into the 1880s, northern Republicans capitalized on bitter memories of the Civil War by "waving the bloody shirt" at Democrats. Northern Democrats focused more on urban and economic issues, but southern Democratic candidates waved their own bloody shirt and called Republicans traitors to white supremacy and states' rights.

Adherents battled over how much government should control people's lives. The most contentious issues were over leisure time and the celebration of Sunday, the Lord's day. Protestant Republicans tried to keep the Sabbath holy through legislation that closed bars, stores, and commercial amusements on Sundays. Immigrant Democrats, accustomed to feasting after church, fought saloon closings and other restrictions.

Allegiances to national parties and candidates were so evenly divided that no faction gained control for long. Between 1877 and 1897, Republicans held the presidency for three terms, Democrats for two. Rarely did one party control the presidency and Congress simultaneously. From 1876 through 1892, presidential elections were close. The outcome often hinged on a few populous northern states—Connecticut, New York, New Jersey, Ohio, Indiana, and Illinois. Both parties tried to gain advantages by nominating candidates from these states (and also by committing vote fraud).

Party Factions

Factional quarrels split both the Republican and the Democratic Parties. Among Republicans, New York's pompous senator Roscoe Conkling led the faction known as Stalwarts and worked the spoils system to win government jobs for supporters.

Their rivals were the Half Breeds, led by James G. Blaine, who also blatantly pursued influence. On the sidelines stood more idealistic Republicans, or Mugwumps (supposedly an Indian term meaning "mug on one side of the fence, wump on the other"). Mugwumps, such as Senator Carl Schurz of Missouri, believed that only righteous men should govern. Meanwhile, Democrats subdivided into white-supremacist southerners, immigrant-stock, and working-class supporters of urban political machines, business-oriented advocates of low tariffs and the gold standard, and debtor-oriented advocates of free silver.

In each state, one party usually dominated, and often the state boss was a senator who parlayed his state power into national influence. Until the Seventeenth Amendment to the Constitution was ratified in 1913, state legislatures elected U.S. senators. As such, senators had enormous power, which they exercised brazenly.

ISSUES OF LEGISLATION

In Congress, sectional controversies, patronage abuses, railroad regulation, tariffs, and currency provoked heated debates. From the end of the Civil War into the 1880s, Congress struggled with soldiers' pensions. The Grand Army of the Republic, an organization of 400,000 Union Army veterans, allied with the Republican Party and cajoled Congress into generous pensions for former Union soldiers and their widows. Many were deserved: Union troops were poorly paid. The Union Army spent $2 billion fighting the Civil War, but veterans' pensions cost $8 billion, one of the largest welfare commitments the federal government ever made. By 1900 soldiers' pensions accounted for roughly 40 percent of the federal budget. Confederate veterans were excluded, though some southern states funded small pensions and built old-age homes for ex-soldiers.

Civil Service Reform
Few politicians dared oppose war pensions, but some attempted to dismantle the spoils system, the practice of awarding government jobs to party devotees (regardless of their qualifications). During the Civil War, the federal government expanded considerably, and the spoils system increasingly flourished, particularly after the war. As the postal service, diplomatic corps, and other government agencies grew, the number of federal jobs tripled, from 53,000 in 1865 to 166,000 in 1891. Elected officials scrambled to control these jobs to benefit themselves and their party. In return for short hours and high pay, appointees to federal positions pledged votes and part of their earnings to their patrons.

Shocked by such corruption, especially after the scandals in the Grant administration, some reformers began advocating appointments based on merit—civil service. Support for change accelerated in 1881 with the formation of the National Civil Service Reform League. The assassination of President James Garfield that year by a distraught job seeker hastened the drive for reform. The Pendleton Civil Service Act, passed by Congress in 1882, created the Civil Service Commission to oversee competitive examinations for government positions. The act gave the commission jurisdiction over only 10 percent of federal jobs, though the president could expand the list. Because the Constitution barred Congress from interfering in state affairs, civil service at state and local levels developed more haphazardly.

Economic policy was the Gilded Age's main issue. Railroads particularly provoked controversy. In their quest for customers, railroads launched rate wars and angered shippers with inconsistent freight charges. On noncompetitive routes, railroads often boosted charges to compensate for unprofitably low rates on competitive routes. Railroads also played favorites, reducing rates to large shippers and offering free passenger passes to preferred customers and politicians.

Railroad Regulation

Such favoritism stirred farmers, small merchants, and reform politicians to demand rate regulation. By 1880 fourteen states established commissions to limit freight and storage charges of state-chartered lines. Railroads fought back, arguing that the Fourteenth Amendment to the Constitution guaranteed them freedom to acquire and use property without government restraint. But in 1877, in *Munn v. Illinois,* the Supreme Court upheld state regulation, declaring that grain warehouses owned by railroads acted in the public interest and therefore must submit to regulation for "the common good."

Only the federal government could regulate interstate lines, as affirmed by the Supreme Court in the *Wabash* case of 1886. In 1887, Congress passed the Interstate Commerce Act, which prohibited pools, rebates, and long-haul/short-haul rate discrimination. It also created the Interstate Commerce Commission (ICC), the nation's first regulatory agency, to investigate railroad rate making and issue cease-and-desist orders against illegal practices. The legislation's weak provisions for enforcement, however, left railroads room for evasion, and federal judges chipped away at ICC powers. In the *Maximum Freight Rate* case (1897), the Supreme Court ruled that the ICC lacked power to set rates, and in the *Alabama Midlands* case (1897), it overturned prohibitions against long-haul/short-haul discrimination. Still, regulation, though weakened, remained in force.

Tariff Policy

From 1789 onward, Congress created tariffs, which levied duties (taxes) on imported goods, to protect American products from European competition. But tariffs quickly became a tool special interests used to enhance profits. By the 1880s these interests succeeded in obtaining tariffs on more than four thousand items. A few economists and farmers argued for free trade, but most politicians insisted that tariffs were necessary to support industry and preserve jobs.

The Republican Party put protective tariffs at the core of its agenda. Democrats complained that tariffs made prices artificially high by keeping out less expensive foreign goods, thereby benefiting domestic manufacturers while hurting consumers and farmers whose crops were not protected. During the Gilded Age, revenues from tariffs and other levies created a federal budget surplus. Most Republicans liked that the government was earning more than it spent and hoped to keep the extra money as a Treasury reserve or use it for projects that would aid commerce. Democrats acknowledged a need for protection of some manufactured goods and raw materials, but they favored lower tariff duties to encourage foreign trade and reduce the Treasury surplus.

Manufacturers and their congressional allies firmly controlled tariff policy. The McKinley Tariff of 1890 boosted already-high rates another 4 percent. When House Democrats passed a bill to trim tariffs in 1894, Senate Republicans, aided by southern Democrats, added six hundred amendments restoring most cuts (Wilson-Gorman Tariff). In 1897 the Dingley Tariff raised rates further. Attacks on duties made tariffs a symbol of privileged business in the public mind.

Monetary Policy

Monetary policy inflamed stronger emotions than tariffs. When increased industrial and agricultural production caused prices to fall after the Civil War, debtors and creditors had opposing reactions. Farmers suffered because their incomes dropped and because high demand for a limited supply of available money raised interest rates on loans, making it costly to borrow to repay mortgages and other debts. They favored coinage of silver to increase the amount of currency in circulation. This, they reasoned, would reduce interest rates. Small businessmen, also in need of loans, agreed. Large businesses and bankers favored a stable, limited money supply backed by gold, fearing currency fluctuations that would threaten investors' confidence in the U.S. economy.

Creditor-debtor tension translated into class divisions between haves and have-nots. The debate also reflected sectional cleavages: western silver-mining areas and agricultural regions of the South and West against the industrial Northeast.

Taking advantage of the new fad of bicycling (see Chapter 19), a cartoonist in an 1886 issue of the humor magazine *Puck* illustrated the controversy over silver coinage. Depicting two uncoordinated wheels, one a silver coin and the other a gold coin, the illustration conveys the message of how hard it was to proceed with conflicting kinds of currency. (Picture Research Consultants and Archives)

By the 1870s, the currency controversy boiled down to whether gold or silver should back national paper money. Previously, the government bought both, setting a ratio that made a gold dollar worth sixteen times more than a silver dollar. The gold rush of 1848, however, increased gold supply and lowered its market price relative to silver. Consequently, silver dollars disappeared from circulation as owners hoarded them. In 1873 Congress officially stopped coining them. The United States and many of its trading partners unofficially adopted the gold standard.

But within a few years, new mines in the American West began flooding the market with silver, and its price dropped. Gold now was relatively less plentiful, worth more than sixteen times the value of silver (the ratio reached twenty to one by 1890). Silver producers wanted the government to resume buying silver at the old sixteen-to-one ratio, which amounted to a subsidy. Congress tried to compromise. The Bland-Allison Act (1878) authorized the Treasury to buy $2 million to $4 million worth of silver monthly, and the Sherman Silver Purchase Act (1890) increased the government's silver purchase by specifying weight (4.5 million ounces) rather than dollars. Neither measure satisfied the different interest groups. Creditors wanted the government to stop buying silver, whereas for debtors, the legislation failed to expand the money supply satisfactorily. The issue would intensify during the 1896 presidential election.

Legislative Accomplishments

Members of Congress worked under difficult conditions. They earned small salaries yet had to maintain two residences: in their home district and in Washington. Weather was sweltering in summer, and most Congressmen had no private offices, worked long hours, wrote their own speeches, and paid their staff themselves. Still, they managed to pass significant legislation.

TENTATIVE PRESIDENTS

Operating under the cloud of Andrew Johnson's impeachment, Grant's scandals, and doubts about the legitimacy of the 1876 election (see Chapter 16), American presidents between 1877 and 1900 moved to restore authority to their office. Proper and honest, Presidents Rutherford Hayes (1877–1881), James Garfield (1881), Chester Arthur (1881–1885), Grover Cleveland (1885–1889 and 1893–1897), Benjamin Harrison (1889–1893), and William McKinley (1897–1901) tried to act as legislative and administrative leaders. Each president initiated legislation and used vetoes to guide national policy.

Hayes, Garfield, and Arthur

Rutherford B. Hayes had been a Union general and an Ohio congressman and governor before his disputed presidential election, which prompted opponents to label him Rutherfraud. Hayes served as conciliator, emphasizing national harmony over sectional rivalry and opposing racial violence. He tried to overhaul the spoils system by appointing the civil service reformer Carl Schurz to his cabinet and battling New York's patronage king, Senator Conkling.

When Hayes declined to run for reelection in 1880, Republicans nominated another Ohio congressman and Civil War hero, James A. Garfield, who won by just 40,000 votes out of 9 million cast. By winning the pivotal states of New York and Indiana, however, Garfield carried the electoral college by 214 to 155. Garfield hoped to reduce the tariff and develop economic relations with Latin America, and he rebuffed Conkling's patronage demands. But his chance to make lasting contributions ended in July 1881 when Charles Guiteau shot him in a Washington railroad station. Garfield lingered for seventy-nine days before dying September 19.

Garfield's successor was Vice President Chester A. Arthur, the New York spoilsman whom Hayes fired in 1878. Arthur became a temperate executive. He signed the Pendleton Civil Service Act, urged Congress to modify outdated tariff rates, and supported federal regulation of railroads. But congressional partisans frustrated his plans for reducing the tariff and strengthening the navy. Arthur lost the 1884 Republican presidential nomination to James G. Blaine.

Democrats named New York governor Grover Cleveland, a bachelor who fathered an out-of-wedlock son—which he admitted during the campaign. Cleveland beat Blaine by only 29,000 popular votes; his tiny margin of 1,149 votes in New York secured that state's 36 electoral votes for a 219-to-182 victory in the electoral college. Cleveland may have won New York thanks to remarks of a Protestant minister, who equated Democrats with "rum, Romanism, and rebellion." Democrats publicized the slur among New York's large Irish-Catholic population, urging voters to support Cleveland.

Cleveland and Harrison

Cleveland, the first Democratic president since James Buchanan (1857–1861), expanded the civil service, vetoed hundreds of private pension bills, and urged Congress to cut tariff duties. When advisers worried about his chances for reelection, the president retorted, "What is the use of being elected or reelected, unless you stand for something?" When Democrats renominated Cleveland in 1888, businessmen convinced him to moderate his attacks on high tariffs.

Republicans in 1888 nominated Benjamin Harrison, a former Indiana senator and grandson of President William Henry Harrison (1841). Bribery and multiple voting helped him win Indiana by 2,300 votes and New York by 14,000. (Democrats also indulged in such cheating, but Republicans proved more successful at it.) Although Cleveland outpolled Harrison by 90,000 popular votes, Harrison carried the electoral college by 233 to 168.

The first president since 1875 whose party had majorities in both Congressional houses, Harrison influenced legislation with everything from threats of vetoes to informal dinners and consultations with politicians. Partly in response, the Congress of 1889–1891 passed 517 bills, 200 more than the average passed by Congresses between 1875 and 1889. Harrison showed support for the civil service by appointing the reformer Theodore Roosevelt as civil service commissioner. But pressured by special interests, Harrison signed the Dependents' Pension Act, which provided pensions for disabled Union veterans, and widows and children—doubling the number of welfare recipients from 490,000 to 966,000.

The Pension Act and other appropriations in 1890 pushed the federal budget past $1 billion for the first time. Democrats blamed the Billion-Dollar Congress on spendthrift Republicans, and in 1890, voters unseated seventy-eight Republican congressmen. Capitalizing on voter unrest, Democrats nominated Grover Cleveland to run against Harrison in 1892. With large business contributions, Cleveland beat Harrison by 370,000 popular votes (3 percent of the total), easily winning the electoral vote.

In office again, Cleveland addressed currency, tariffs, and labor unrest, but his actions reflected political weakness and a narrow orientation toward business. Cleveland promised sweeping tariff reform, but Senate protectionists undercut his efforts. And when 120,000 boycotting railroad workers paralyzed commerce in the 1894 Pullman strike, Cleveland bowed to requests from railroad managers and Attorney General Richard Olney (a former railroad lawyer) to send in troops.

DISCRIMINATION, DISFRANCHISEMENT, AND RESPONSES

Despite speeches about freedom during the Gilded Age, policies of discrimination haunted more than half the nation's population. Racial issues shaped politics in the South, home to the majority of African Americans. Southern white farmers and workers feared that newly enfranchised African American men would challenge their political and social superiority (real and imagined). Wealthy landowners and merchants fanned these fears, keeping blacks and whites from uniting to protest their economic subjugation.

Violence Against African Americans

In 1880, 90 percent of southern blacks farmed or worked in personal and domestic service, just as they had as slaves. The New South, moreover, proved as violent for blacks as the Old South had been. Between 1889 and 1909, more than seventeen hundred African Americans were lynched in the South, often in sparsely populated districts where whites felt threatened by an influx of migrant blacks. Most lynching victims were accused of assault—rarely proved—on a white woman.

Blacks did not suffer such violence silently, however. The most notable activist was Ida B. Wells, a Memphis schoolteacher, who was removed from a railroad car in 1884 when she refused to give up her seat to a white man. In 1889 Wells became a partner of a Memphis newspaper, the *Free Speech and Headlight*, in which she published attacks against white injustice, especially in the case of three black grocers lynched in 1892 after defending themselves against whites. She herself fled to England to escape death threats, but soon returned and wrote *A Red Record* (1895), which tabulated statistics on racial lynchings and served as a foundation for further protest campaigns.

Disfranchisement

Southern leaders, eager to reassert authority and racial superiority, instituted measures to prevent blacks from voting and keep them legally segregated. Despite threats and intimidation, blacks still formed the backbone of the southern Republican Party and won numerous elective positions. In North Carolina, for example, eleven African Americans served in the state Senate and forty-three in the House between 1877 and 1890. In response, beginning with Tennessee in 1889 and Arkansas in 1892, southern states levied $1 to $2 on all voters—prohibitive to most blacks, who were poor and in debt. Other schemes disfranchised—or deprived voting rights to—blacks who could not read.

The Supreme Court determined in *U.S. v. Reese* (1876) that Congress had no control over local and state elections other than upholding the Fifteenth Amendment, which prohibits states from denying the vote "on account of race, color, or previous condition of servitude." State legislatures found ways to exclude black voters, however. An 1890 state constitutional convention established the Mississippi Plan, requiring voters to pay a poll tax eight months before each election, present the tax receipt at election time, and prove that they could read and interpret the state constitution. Registration officials applied stiffer standards to blacks than to whites, even declaring black college graduates ineligible due to illiteracy.

Such restrictions proved highly effective. In South Carolina, 70 percent of eligible blacks voted in the 1880 presidential election; by 1896 the rate dropped to 11 percent. By the 1900s African Americans effectively lost political rights in the South. Disfranchisement also affected poor whites, few of whom could meet poll tax, property, and literacy requirements. Thus the total number of eligible voters in Mississippi shrank from 257,000 in 1876 to 77,000 in 1892.

Legal Segregation

In a series of cases during the 1870s, the Supreme Court opened the door to racial discrimination by ruling that the Fourteenth Amendment protected citizens' rights only against infringement by state governments—but not from individuals or organizations. If blacks wanted legal protection from private sector discrimination, the Court said, they must seek it from state laws because under the Tenth Amendment states retained all powers not specifically assigned to Congress. These rulings climaxed in 1883 when the Court struck down the 1875 Civil Rights Act, which prohibited segregation in public facilities, such as streetcars, theaters, and parks.

States could legally segregate on a "separate-but-equal" basis, as upheld by the Supreme Court in the case of *Plessy v. Ferguson* (1896). This case began in 1892 when a New Orleans organization of prominent African Americans chose Homer Plessy, a dark-skinned Creole who was only one-eighth black (but considered black by Louisiana law), to sit in a whites-only railroad car. Plessy was arrested, and the appeal of his conviction reached the U.S. Supreme Court in 1896. The Court, however, affirmed that a state law providing for separate facilities for blacks and whites was reasonable because it preserved "public peace and good order." To the court, a law separating the races did not necessarily "destroy the legal equality of the races." Although the ruling did not use the phrase "separate but equal," it made legal separate facilities for black and white people as long as they were equal. In 1899 the Court legitimated school segregation in *Cummins v. County Board of Education,* until it was overturned by *Brown v. Board of Education* in 1954.

Segregation laws—known as Jim Crow laws—multiplied throughout the South, reminding African Americans of their inferior status. State and local statutes passed in the 1890s restricted blacks to the rear of streetcars, separate public drinking fountains and toilets, and separate sections of hospitals and cemeteries. A Birmingham, Alabama, ordinance required that the races be "distinctly separated . . . by well defined physical barriers" in "any room, hall, theatre, picture house, auditorium, yard, court, ballpark, or other indoor or outdoor place."

African American Activism

African American women and men challenged prejudice. Some boycotted discriminatory businesses; others considered moving to Africa. Still others promoted Negro enterprise. In 1898, the Atlanta University professor John Hope urged blacks to become their own employers and support Negro Business Men's Leagues. In the optimistic days following Reconstruction, many blacks saw higher education as a means to elevate their status. In all-black teachers' colleges, men and women sought opportunities for themselves and their race.

While disfranchisement pushed African American men out of public life, African American women used traditional roles as mothers, educators, and moral guardians to uplift the race and seek better services. They successfully lobbied southern governments for cleaner city streets, improved public health, expanded charity services, and vocational education. While black and white women sometimes united to achieve their goals, white women often sympathized with men in white-supremacist campaigns.

Woman Suffrage

In the North, white women pursued the vote with limited success. Prior to 1870, each state determined voting qualifications. That year, the Fifteenth Amendment forbade states from denying the vote "on account of race, color or previous condition" but omitted reference to sex. For the next twenty years, two organizations, the National Woman Suffrage Association (NWSA) and the American Woman Suffrage Association (AWSA), crusaded for female suffrage. The NWSA, led by Elizabeth Cady Stanton and Susan B. Anthony, advocated women's rights in courts, workplaces, and the ballot box. The AWSA, led by the former abolitionists Lucy Stone and Thomas Wentworth Higginson, focused narrowly on suffrage. Anthony's effort to get a constitutional amendment for woman suffrage never received support, with senators claiming suffrage would interfere with women's family obligations.

While the NWSA fought for suffrage on the national level, the AWSA worked to amend state constitutions. (The groups merged in 1890, forming the National American Woman Suffrage Association.) Between 1870 and 1910, eleven states (mostly in the West) legalized limited woman suffrage. By 1890 nineteen states allowed women to vote on school issues, and three granted suffrage on tax and bond issues. The right to vote in national elections awaited a later generation, but women like Mary Lease, Ida B. Wells, Susan B. Anthony, and Lucy Stone proved that women could be politically active even without the vote.

AGRARIAN UNREST AND POPULISM

Economic inequities sparked a mass movement. Despite rapid industrialization and urbanization in the late nineteenth century, the United States remained an agrarian society, with 64 percent of the population living in rural areas in 1890. The expression of farmers' discontent—a mixture of strident rhetoric, nostalgic dreams, and hard-headed egalitarianism—began in Grange organizations in the early 1870s and accelerated when Farmers' Alliances formed in Texas later in the decade and across the Cotton Belt and Great Plains in the 1880s. The movement flourished where tenancy, debt, weather, and insects endangered struggling farmers.

Sharecropping and Tenant Farming in the South

Southern agriculture did not benefit much from mechanization (see Chapter 17). Tobacco and cotton, the principal southern crops, required constant hoeing and weeding by hand. Tobacco leaves matured at different rates and stems were too fragile for machines. Also, mechanical devices were not precise enough to pick cotton. Thus, after the Civil War, southern agriculture remained labor-intensive, and landlords replaced slaves with sharecroppers and tenant farmers.

Sharecropping and tenant farming—where farmers rented rather than owned land—entangled millions of black and white southerners in webs of debt and humiliation, at whose center loomed the crop lien. Too poor to have ready cash, most farmers borrowed to buy necessities, offering future crops as collateral. To get supplies, a farmer dealt with a furnishing merchant, who would exchange them for a lien, or legal claim, on the farmer's forthcoming crop. After the crop was harvested and brought to market, the merchant collected the portion of the crop that would repay the loan. Often, however, the debt exceeded the crop's value. The farmer could pay off only part of the debt, but borrowed more for food and supplies for the coming year, sinking deeper into debt.

Merchants frequently took advantage by inflating prices and charging excessive interest on advances farmers received. Suppose, for example, that a farmer needed a 20-cent bag of seed. The furnishing merchant would sell it to him on credit but for 28 cents; by year's end, that loan would have accumulated interest of 50 percent or more. The farmer, pledging more than his crop's worth against such debts, fell behind and never recovered. In the southern backcountry, after the Civil War, farmers shifted from diversified agriculture to commercial farming, namely cotton production. Consequently, yeoman began purchasing supplies such as flour, potatoes, and corn that they previously grew themselves. This move to the market economy came about for two reasons: constant debt forced farmers to grow crops that would net cash, and railroads enabled them to transport cotton to market more easily than before. As backcountry yeomen devoted more acres to cotton and less to subsistence crops, they found themselves more frequently at the mercy of merchants.

Hardship in the Midwest and West

In the Midwest, as growers cultivated more land, as mechanization boosted productivity, and as foreign competition increased, supplies of agricultural products exceeded national and worldwide demand, leading to steady price drops for staple crops. A bushel of wheat that sold for $1.45 in 1866 brought only 80 cents in the mid-1880s and 49 cents by the mid-1890s. Meanwhile, transportation and storage fees remained high relative to other prices. To buy necessities and pay bills, farmers had to produce more, but the more they produced, the lower crop prices dropped (see Figure 20.1).

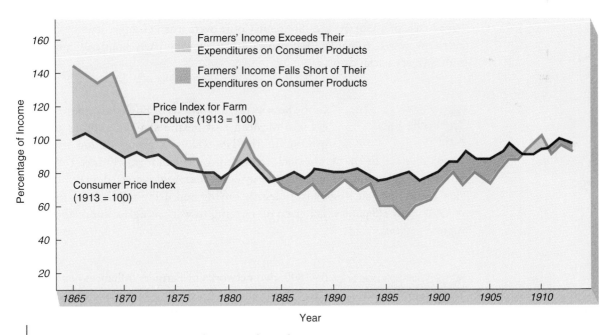

Figure 20.1   Consumer Prices and Farm Product Prices, 1865–1913

Until the late 1870s, in spite of falling farm prices, farmers were able to receive from their crops more income than they spent on consumer goods. But beginning in the mid-1880s, consumer prices leveled off and then rose, while prices for farm products continued to drop. As a result, farmers found it increasingly difficult to afford consumer goods, a problem that plagued them well into the twentieth century.

The West suffered from special hardships. In Colorado, absentee capitalists seized control of the access to transportation and water, and the concentration of technology by large mining companies pushed out small firms. Charges of monopolistic behavior by railroads echoed among farmers, miners, and stockmen in Wyoming and Montana. In California, Washington, and Oregon, wheat and fruit growers found their opportunities blocked by railroads' control of transportation and storage rates.

Grange Movement

With aid from Oliver H. Kelley, a clerk in the Department of Agriculture, farmers in almost every state during the 1860s and 1870s founded local organizations called Granges, dedicated to improving economic conditions. By 1875 the Grange had twenty thousand branches and a million members. Strongest in the Midwest and South, Granges sponsored meetings and educational events to relieve the loneliness of farm life. Family-oriented local Granges welcomed women's participation.

As membership flourished, Granges turned to economic and political action. Local Grange branches formed cooperative associations to buy supplies and to market crops and livestock. A few Grangers operated farm-implement factories and insurance companies. Most enterprises failed, however, because farmers lacked capital for large-scale buying and because large manufacturers and dealers undercut them. Granges declined in the late 1870s, after convincing states to establish agricultural colleges, electing sympathetic legislators, and pressing state legislatures for so-called Granger laws to regulate transportation and storage rates. But in the *Wabash* case of 1886, the U.S. Supreme Court overturned Granger laws by denying states the power to regulate railroad rates. Disavowing party politics, Granges became farmers' social clubs.

The White Hats

In the Southwest, migrations of English-speaking ranchers into Mexican pastureland sparked another agrarian protest. In the late 1880s, a group calling itself Las Gorras Blancas, or the White Hats, struggled to control formerly ancestral lands, harassing Anglo ranchers and destroying fences that Anglos erected on public land. They could not halt Anglos from legally buying and using public land, however; by 1900 many Hispanics had given up farming to work as agricultural laborers or migrate to cities.

Farmers' Alliances

By 1890, two networks of Farmers' Alliances—one in the Great Plains and one in the South—became the center of rural activism. The first Farmers' Alliances arose in Texas, where hard-pressed farmers rallied against crop liens, merchants, railroads, and money power. Using traveling lecturers to recruit members, Alliance leaders extended the movement into other southern states, boasting 2 million southern Alliance members by 1889. A separate Colored Farmers' National Alliance claimed 1 million black members. In the late 1880s, the Plains movement similarly organized 2 million members in Kansas, Nebraska, and the Dakotas.

To bypass corporate power and to control markets, Alliances, like the Grange, proposed that farmers form cooperatives, joining together to sell crops and livestock and buy supplies and manufactured goods. By pooling resources, Alliances reasoned, farmers could exert greater economic pressure and share the benefits of their work rather than competing with each other. They also encouraged women's participation and invited the Knights of Labor to join their "struggle against monopolistic oppression."

To relieve the most serious rural problem, shortages of cash and credit, Alliances proposed a government aid system called a subtreasury. The plan first called for the federal government to construct warehouses where farmers could store nonperishable crops while awaiting higher market prices; the government would then loan farmers Treasury notes amounting to 80 percent of the market price of the stored crops. Farmers could use these notes for debts and purchases. Once the crops were sold, farmers would repay the loans plus small interest and storage fees, thereby avoiding the exploitative crop-lien system.

The subtreasury plan's second part would provide low-interest government loans to farmers to buy land. These loans, along with the Treasury notes for stored crops, would inject cash into the economy and encourage the kind of inflation that advocates hoped would raise crop prices without raising other prices.

Problems in Achieving Alliance Unity

If Farmers' Alliances had been able to unite politically, they could have been a formidable force; but racial and sectional differences and personality clashes thwarted their merger efforts. Racial voting restrictions weakened Alliance voter strength, and racism impeded acceptance of blacks by white Alliances. Some southern leaders, such as Georgia's Senator Tom Watson, tried to unite distressed black and white farmers, but whites held fast to prejudices. Many came from families that had previously owned slaves; they considered African Americans inferior and took comfort that there would always be people worse off than they were. Regional politics also predominated. Northern farmers favored protective tariffs to keep out foreign grain, whereas white southerners wanted low tariffs to hold down costs of imports. However, both northern and southern alliances favored government regulation of railroads, equitable taxation, currency reform, an end to alleged election frauds that perpetuated special interests in office, and prohibition of landownership by foreign investors.

Rise of Populism

Expanding membership drew Alliances into politics. By 1890, farmers elected several sympathetic officeholders, especially in the South, where Alliances controlled four governorships, eight state legislatures, and forty-seven seats in Congress (forty-four in the House, three in the Senate). In the Midwest, Alliance candidates often ran on third-party tickets, such as the Greenback Party, with some success in Kansas, Nebraska, and the Dakotas. Leaders crisscrossed the country to recruit support for a new party. In summer 1890, the Kansas Alliance held a convention of the people and nominated candidates who swept the state's fall elections. Formation of this People's, or Populist, Party gave a title to Alliance political activism. (Populism is the

Russian Populism

Before American Populism, a different form of populism emerged in another largely rural country: Russia. Whereas American Populism came from the Alliance farm organizations, Russian populism was created by intellectuals seeking to educate peasants to agitate for social and economic freedom.

Russian society began to modernize in the mid-nineteenth century. Town governments were given control of local taxation and education became more widespread. Perhaps most importantly, in 1861 Czar Alexander II signed an Edict of Emancipation, freeing Russian serfs (slaves attached to specific lands) and granting them compensation to buy land. The reforms progressed slowly, prompting some educated Russians to press for more radical solutions, including socialism. The reformers became known as *narodniki*, or populists, from *narod*, the Russian term for "peasant."

Narodniki envisioned a society of self-governing village communes, somewhat like the cooperatives proposed by American Farmers' Alliances. One of their leaders, Peter Lavrov, believed that intellectuals must get closer to the people and help the masses improve their lives. Russian populists believed that only an uprising against the czar could realize their goals. When Alexander instituted repressive policies against the *narodniki* in the late 1870s, many turned to terrorism, culminating in Alexander II's assassination in 1881.

Russian peasants remained tied to tradition and could not abandon their loyalty to the czar. Government arrests and imprisonments after Alexander's assassination discouraged populists' efforts, and the movement declined. Nevertheless, the ideas of Russian populism became the cornerstone of the 1917 Russian Revolution and of Soviet social and political ideology that followed.

Russian peasants, like American tenant farmers and owners of small landholdings, suffered from poverty and pressures of the expanded market economy. The plight of struggling Russian farm families stirred up empathy from young populist intellectuals, who adopted radical solutions, but did not stir up as much political fervor among farmers as American Populism did.

(© Bettmann/Corbis)

political doctrine that asserts the rights and powers of common people versus elites.) By 1892, southern Alliance members joined their northern counterparts in summoning a People's Party convention in Omaha, Nebraska, on July 4 to draft a platform and nominate a presidential candidate.

Charging that inequality (between white classes) threatened to splinter society, the new party's platform declared, "The fruits of the toil of millions are boldly stolen to build up colossal fortunes for a few" and that "wealth belongs to him that creates it." The document addressed three sources of rural unrest: transportation, land, and money. Frustrated with weak regulation, Populists demanded government ownership of railroad and telegraph lines. The monetary plank called for the government to make more money available for farm loans and restore free and unlimited coinage of silver. Other planks advocated a graduated income tax, postal savings banks, direct election of U.S. senators, and a shorter workday. As its presidential candidate, the party nominated James B. Weaver of Iowa, a former Union general and supporter of an expanded money supply.

Populist Spokespeople

The Populist campaign featured dynamic personalities such as Mary Lease and Sockless Jerry Simpson, an unschooled but canny rural reformer who got his nickname after he ridiculed silk-stockinged wealthy people, causing a reporter to muse that Simpson probably wore no stockings. The South produced leaders such as Texas's Charles W. Macune, Georgia's Tom Watson, and North Carolina's Leonidas Polk. Minnesota's Ignatius Donnelly, a pseudoscientist and writer of apocalyptic novels, became chief visionary of the northern plains and penned the Omaha platform's thunderous language. Not since 1856 had a third party done so well in its first national effort. In 1892 Weaver garnered 8 percent of the popular vote, majorities in four states, and twenty-two electoral votes. Nevertheless, the party faced a dilemma of whether to stand by its principles or compromise to gain power. Populist candidates were successful only in the West. The vote-rich Northeast ignored Weaver, and Alabama was the only southern state that gave Populists as much as one-third of its votes.

Still, Populism gave southern and western rural dwellers faith in a future based on American ideals, as they looked toward the 1896 presidential election. Amid hardship and desperation, millions came to believe that a cooperative democracy in which government would ensure equal opportunity could overcome corporate power.

THE DEPRESSION AND PROTESTS OF THE 1890S

In 1893, shortly before Grover Cleveland's second presidency began, the Philadelphia and Reading Railroad, once a thriving and profitable line, went bankrupt. Like other railroads, it borrowed heavily to lay track and build stations and bridges. Overexpansion cut into profits, and ultimately the company could not pay its debts.

Similar problems beset manufacturers. Output at McCormick farm machinery factories was nine times greater in 1893 than in 1879, but revenues had only tripled. The company bought more equipment and squeezed more work out of fewer laborers, but it only increased debt and unemployment. Jobless workers also could not pay their bills. Banks suffered when customers defaulted. The failure of the National Cordage Company in May 1893 sparked a chain reaction of business and bank closings. Between 1893 and 1897, the nation suffered a devastating economic depression.

Nearly 20 percent of the labor force was jobless during the depression. Falling demand caused prices to drop between 1892 and 1895, but layoffs and wage cuts more than offset declining living costs. Many people could not afford basic necessities. The New York police estimated that twenty thousand homeless and jobless people roamed the city's streets.

Continuing Currency Problems

As the depression deepened, the currency dilemma reached a crisis. The Sherman Silver Purchase Act of 1890 committed the government to use Treasury notes (silver certificates) to buy 4.5 million ounces of silver each month. Recipients could redeem these certificates for gold, at the ratio of one ounce of gold for every sixteen ounces of silver. But a western mining boom increased silver supplies, causing its market value to fall and prompting holders of Sherman silver notes and Civil War greenbacks to exchange their notes for more valuable gold. As a result, the nation's gold reserve dwindled, falling below $100 million in early 1893.

If investors believed that the country's gold reserve was disappearing, they would lose confidence in America's economic stability and refrain from investing. British capitalists, for example, owned some $4 billion in American stocks and bonds and were likely to stop investing if dollars were to depreciate. The lower the gold reserve dropped, the more people rushed to redeem their money. Panic spread, causing more bankruptcies and unemployment.

To protect the gold reserve, President Cleveland called a special session of Congress to repeal the Sherman Silver Purchase Act. Repeal passed in late 1893, but the run on gold continued through 1894. In early 1895, reserves fell to $41 million, and Cleveland desperately accepted an offer of 3.5 million ounces of gold for $65 million in federal bonds from a banking syndicate led by financier J. P. Morgan. When the bankers resold the bonds, they made a $2 million profit. Cleveland claimed that he had saved the reserves, but discontented farmers, workers, silver miners, and some of Cleveland's Democratic allies saw only humiliation in the president's deal with big businessmen.

The deal between Cleveland and Morgan did not end the depression. After improving slightly in 1895, the economy plunged again. Farm income, declining since 1887, continued to slide; factories closed; banks restricted withdrawals. The tight money supply depressed housing construction and dried up jobs. Cities like Detroit encouraged citizens to cultivate potato patches on vacant land to alleviate food shortages. Urban police stations filled up nightly with homeless persons who had no place to stay.

Consequences of the Depression

In the final years of the century, gold discoveries in Alaska, good harvests, and industrial growth brought relief. But the downturn hastened the crumbling of the old economic system and emergence of a new one. The American economy expanded beyond sectional bases; when farmers in the West fell into debt, they affected the economic health of railroads, farm-implement manufacturers, and banks in other sections. Moreover, the corporate consolidation that characterized the new business system tempted many companies to expand too rapidly. When contraction occurred, their reckless debts dragged them down, and they pulled other industries down with them.

A new global marketplace was emerging, forcing American farmers to contend with discriminatory transportation rates and falling crop prices at home, along with Canadian and Russian wheat growers, Argentine cattle ranchers, Indian and Egyptian cotton manufacturers, and Australian wool producers. Consequently, one country's economy affected that of other countries. With the glutted domestic market, American businessmen sought new markets abroad (see Chapter 22).

Depression-Era Protests

The depression exposed fundamental tensions in the industrial system. Technological and organizational changes had been widening the gap between employees and employers for half a century. Labor protest began with the railroad strikes of 1877. Their vehemence and support from working-class people raised fears that the United States would experience a popular uprising like one in France in 1871, which had briefly overturned the government and introduced communist principles. The Haymarket riot of 1886, a general strike in New Orleans in 1891, and a prolonged strike at the Carnegie Homestead Steel plant in 1892 heightened anxieties. In 1892 violence erupted at a silver mine in Coeur d'Alene, Idaho, when striking miners, angered by wage cuts and a lockout, seized the mine and battled federal troops.

In 1894, there were over thirteen hundred strikes and countless riots. Contrary to accusations by businessmen, few protesters were anarchists or communists. Rather, they were men and women who believed that in a democracy their voices should be heard.

Socialists

Small numbers of socialists participated in these and other confrontations. Some socialists believed workers should control factories and businesses; others supported government ownership. All, however, opposed the private enterprise of capitalism. Their ideas derived from Karl Marx (1818–1883), a German philosopher and the father of communism, who contended that whoever controls the means of production determines how well people live. Marx wrote that industrial capitalism generates profits by paying workers less than the value of their labor and that mechanization and mass production alienate workers from their labor. According to Marx, only by abolishing the return on capital—profits—could labor receive its true value, possible only if workers owned the means of production. Marx predicted that workers worldwide would revolt and seize factories, farms, banks, and transportation lines. This revolution would establish a socialist order of justice and equality. Marx's vision appealed to some workers because it promised independence and to some intellectuals because it promised to end class conflict and crass materialism.

In America, socialism suffered from disagreement over how to achieve Marx's vision. Much of the movement consisted of ideas brought by immigrants—first Germans, later Russian Jews, Italians, Hungarians, and Poles. It splintered into small groups, such as the Socialist Labor Party, which failed to attract the mass of laborers because it often focused on doctrine rather than workers' everyday needs. Social mobility and the philosophy of individualism also undermined socialist aims. Workers hoped that they would benefit through education and the acquisition of property; most American workers sought individual betterment rather than the betterment of all.

Eugene V. Debs

In 1894, a new and inspiring Socialist leader emerged. The Indiana-born Eugene V. Debs headed the newly formed American Railway Union which carried out that year's strike against the Pullman Company. Jailed for defying an injunction against the strike, Debs read Karl Marx's works in prison. Once released, he became the leading spokesman for American socialism, combining visionary Marxism with Jeffersonian and Populist antimonopolism. Debs captivated audiences with attacks on the free-enterprise system. "Many of you think you are competing," he would lecture. "Against whom? Against Rockefeller? About as I would if I had a wheelbarrow and competed with the Santa Fe [railroad] from here to Kansas City." By 1900 the group soon to be called the Socialist Party of America was uniting around Debs.

Coxey's Army

In 1894, however, a quiet businessman named Jacob Coxey from Massillon, Ohio, captured public attention. Coxey believed that, to aid debtors, the government should issue $500 million of legal tender paper money and make low-interest loans to local governments, which would use the funds to pay the unemployed to build roads and other public works. He planned to publicize his scheme by leading a march from Massillon to Washington, D.C., gathering unemployed workers along the way. Coxey's army, about two hundred strong, left in March 1894. Moving across Ohio into Pennsylvania, the marchers received food and housing in depressed industrial towns and rural villages and added new recruits. A dozen similar processions from places such as Seattle, San Francisco, and Los Angeles also headed eastward. Sore feet prompted some marchers to commandeer trains, but most marches were law-abiding.

Coxey's band of five hundred, including women and children, entered Washington on April 30. The next day (May Day, the anniversary of the Haymarket violence), the group, armed with "war clubs of peace," advanced to the Capitol. When Coxey and a few others vaulted the wall surrounding the Capitol grounds, mounted police routed the demonstrators. Police dragged Coxey away. As arrests and clubbings continued, Coxey's dream of a demonstration of 400,000 jobless workers dissolved.

Unlike socialists, who wished to replace the capitalist system, Coxey's troops merely wanted more jobs and better living standards. The brutal reactions of officials, however, reveal how threatening dissenters like Coxey and Debs seemed to the existing social order.

THE SILVER CRUSADE AND THE ELECTION OF 1896

Social protest and economic depression made the 1896 presidential election seem pivotal. Debates over money and power were climaxing, Democrats and Republicans battled to control Congress and the presidency. The key question, however, was whether voters would abandon old party loyalties for the Populist Party.

Free Silver

The Populist crusade against money power settled on the issue of silver, which many believed would solve the nation's complex ills. To them, free coinage of silver symbolized an end to special privileges for the rich and the return of government to the people by lifting common people out of debt, increasing the cash in circulation, and reducing interest rates.

As the election of 1896 approached, Populists had to decide whether to join with sympathetic factions of the major parties, thus risking a loss of identity, or remain an independent third party. Except in mining areas of the Rocky Mountain states, where free coinage of silver had strong support, Republicans were unlikely allies because their support for the gold standard and big business represented what Populists opposed.

Alliance with northern and western Democrats was more plausible since the party there retained vestiges of antimonopoly ideology and sympathy for a looser currency system, despite the influence of "gold Democrats," such as President Cleveland and Senator David Hill of New York. Linking with Southern Democrats seemed less viable since candidates' failure to have carried out their promises left southern farmers feeling betrayed. Whichever they chose, Populists ensured that the 1896 election would be the most issue oriented since 1860.

Republican Nomination of McKinley

Both major parties were divided. For a year, the Ohio industrialist Marcus A. Hanna maneuvered to win the Republican nomination for Ohio's governor, William McKinley, and had corralled enough delegates to succeed. The Republicans' only distress occurred when they adopted a moderate platform supporting the gold standard, rejecting a prosilver stance proposed by Colorado senator Henry M. Teller. Teller, a party founder forty years earlier, left in tears, taking a small group of silver Republicans with him.

At the Democratic convention, prosilver delegates wearing silver badges and waving silver banners paraded through the Chicago Amphitheatre. A *New York World* reporter remarked that "all the silverites need is a Moses." They found one in William Jennings Bryan.

William Jennings Bryan

Bryan, age thirty-six, arrived at the Democratic convention as a member of a contested Nebraska delegation. A former congressman whose support for the coinage of silver annoyed President Cleveland, Bryan found the depression's impact on midwestern farmers distressing. Shortly after the convention seated Bryan, he joined

THE LOCKOUT IS ENDED; HE HOLDS THE KEY.

During the 1896 presidential campaign, Republicans depicted their candidate, William McKinley, as holding the key to prosperity for both the working man and the white-collar laborer, shown here raising their hats to the candidate. Republicans successfully made this economic theme, rather than the silver crusade of McKinley's unsuccessful opponent, William Jennings Bryan, the difference in the election's outcome. (Collection of David J. and Lanice L. Frent)

the resolutions committee and helped write a platform calling for unlimited coinage of silver. Bryan's now-famous closing words ignited the delegates.

> Having behind us the producing masses of this nation and the world, supported by the commercial interests, the laboring interests, and the toilers everywhere, we will answer [the wealthy classes'] demand for a gold standard by saying to them: You shall not press down upon the brow of labor this crown of thorns, you shall not crucify mankind upon a cross of gold.

After that speech, it took five ballots to win Bryan the nomination, but the magnetic Boy Orator proved irresistible. In accepting the silverite goals of southerners and westerners and repudiating Cleveland's policies, the Democratic Party became more attractive to discontented farmers. But it, too, alienated a minority wing, who withdrew and nominated their own candidate.

Bryan's nomination presented the Populist Party convention with a dilemma. Should Populists join Democrats in support of Bryan or nominate their own candidate? Some reasoned that supporting a separate candidate would split the anti-McKinley vote and guarantee a Republican victory. The convention compromised, first naming Tom Watson as its vice-presidential nominee to preserve party identity (Democrats had nominated the Maine shipping magnate Arthur Sewall) and then nominating Bryan for president.

The campaign, as the Kansas journalist William Allen White observed, "took the form of religious frenzy." Bryan preached that "every great economic question is in reality a great moral question." Republicans countered Bryan's attacks on privilege by predicting chaos if he won. Hanna invited thousands of people to McKinley's home in Canton, Ohio, where the candidate plied them with homilies on moderation and prosperity, promising something for everyone. In an appeal to working-class voters, Republicans stressed the new jobs that a protective tariff would create.

Election Results

The election revealed that the political standoff had finally ended. McKinley, symbol of urban and corporate ascendancy, beat Bryan by 600,000 popular votes and won in the electoral college by 271 to 176 (see Map 20.1).

Bryan worked hard to rally the nation, but their obsession with silver prevented Populists from building the urban-rural coalition that would have expanded their political appeal. Urban workers, who might have benefited from Populist goals, feared that silver coinage would shrink the value of their wages. Labor leaders, such as the AFL's Samuel Gompers, though partly sympathetic, would not commit fully because they viewed farmers as businessmen, not workers. And socialists denounced Populists as retrograde because they believed in free enterprise. Thus the Populist crusade collapsed. Although Populists and fusion candidates won a few state and congressional elections, the Bryan-Watson ticket of the Populist Party polled only 222,600 votes nationwide.

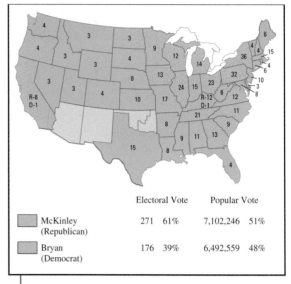

	Electoral Vote		Popular Vote	
McKinley (Republican)	271	61%	7,102,246	51%
Bryan (Democrat)	176	39%	6,492,559	48%

Map 20.1   Presidential Election, 1896
William Jennings Bryan had strong voter support in the South and West, but the numerically superior industrial states, plus California, created majorities for William McKinley.

The McKinley Presidency

As president, McKinley reinforced his support of business by signing the Gold Standard Act (1900), requiring that all paper money be backed by gold. A seasoned politician, McKinley had guided passage of record-high tariff rates as a congressman in 1890. He accordingly supported the Dingley Tariff of 1897, which raised duties even higher. A believer in opening new markets abroad to sustain profits at home, McKinley encouraged imperialistic ventures in Latin America and the Pacific. Good times and victory in the Spanish-American War enabled him to beat Bryan again in 1900.

Summary

Politicians during the Gilded Age prepared the nation for the twentieth century. Laws encouraging economic growth with some principles of regulation, measures expanding government agencies while reducing patronage, and federal intervention in trade and currency issues evolved during the 1870s and 1880s.

True to Mary Lease's characterization, the United States remained a "nation of inconsistencies." Those who supported disfranchisement of African Americans and

Interpreting a Fairy Tale

The Wizard of Oz, one of the most popular movies of all time, began as a work of juvenile literature penned by the journalist L. Frank Baum in 1900. Originally titled The Wonderful Wizard of Oz, the story used memorable characters to create an adventurous quest.

Adults, however, have searched for hidden meanings. In 1964 one scholar, Henry M. Littlefield, asserted that Baum really intended to write a Populist parable about the conditions of overburdened farmers and laborers. Dorothy, he theorized, symbolized the well-intentioned common person; the Scarecrow, the struggling farmer; the Tin Man, the industrial worker. Hoping for a better life, these friends, along with the Cowardly Lion (William Jennings Bryan), followed a yellow brick road (the gold standard) that led nowhere. The Emerald City was presided over by a wizard, who tried to be all things to all people, but Dorothy revealed him as a fraud. Dorothy was able to leave this muddled society and return to her simple Kansas farm family of Aunt Em and Uncle Henry by using her magical silver slippers (representing coinage of silver, though the movie made them red).

Subsequent theorists identified additional symbols, such as Oz being the abbreviation for ounces (oz.), the chief measurement of gold. The Wicked Witch of the East—who, Baum wrote, kept the little people (Munchkins) "in bondage"—could represent industrial capitalism.

But in 1983 the historian William R. Leach asserted that Baum's tale actually was a celebration of urban consumer culture. Its language exalted the opulence of Emerald City, which to Leach resembled the "White City" of the Chicago World's Fair of 1893. Baum's career supported this new interpretation. Before he was a writer, he designed display windows and was involved in theater—activities that gave him an appreciation of modern urban life.

The real legacy of The Wonderful Wizard of Oz has been its ability to provoke differing interpretations. Baum's fairy tale, the first truly American work of this sort, has bequeathed many fascinating images about the diversity and contradictions of American culture.

continued discrimination against both blacks and women still dominated politics. People in power could not tolerate radical views like socialism or Populism, but many of those ideas continued to find supporters in the new century.

The 1896 election realigned national politics. The Republican Party, founded in the 1850s amid a crusade against slavery, became the majority party by emphasizing government aid to business, drawing the urban middle class, and playing down moralism. The Democratic Party miscalculated on the silver issue but held its traditional support in the South and in urban political machines. At the national level, however, loyalties lacked their former potency, as suspicion of party politics increased and voter participation declined. The Populists tried to energize a third-party movement, but their success was fleeting.

Still, by 1920 many Populist goals had been incorporated by the major parties, including regulation of railroads, banks, and utilities; shorter workdays; a variant of the subtreasury plan; a graduated income tax; and direct election of senators. These reforms succeeded because various groups supported them. Immigration, urbanization, and industrialization had transformed the United States into a pluralistic society in which compromise had become a political fact of life. As the Gilded Age ended, business was still in the ascendancy, and large segments of the population remained excluded from political and economic opportunity. But the winds of dissent and reform had begun to blow more strongly.

Chapter Review

THE NATURE OF PARTY POLITICS

How did regional and factional disputes complicate party politics in the Gilded Age?

Most Democrats sought to restrict government power and included immigrants and Catholics, while most Republicans were native-born Protestants who believed government should play a bigger role in reforming society. Both parties were ultimately divided by factional rifts that kept them from simultaneously controlling the presidency and Congress or holding power in either for very long. Republican factions included Stalwarts and Half Breeds, who each sought to wield influence and jobs toward supporters; and Mugwumps who thought only the most upstanding men should be allowed in government. Democrats split into white-supremacist southerners, immigrant and working-class advocates of urban political machines, businessmen who sought lower tariffs and the gold standard, and those who embraced free silver. Such divisions within parties made unity difficult.

ISSUES OF LEGISLATION

What was at issue in the debate over the gold standard versus free silver?

The debate over gold versus free silver was in many ways a struggle between debtors and creditors in the late nineteenth century. Farmers and small businessmen (debtors) pushed for silver coinage, which they believed would put more money in circulation and lower interest rates, thereby making it easier for them to repay mortgages and other debts. Large businesses (creditors) preferred money backed by gold, because they considered it more stable, and therefore likely to maintain foreign investors' confidence in the U.S. economy. In effect, the debate became a class struggle, as well as a sectional one: those in the West and South where mining and agriculture dominated, favored silver; those in the industrial Northeast, gold.

TENTATIVE PRESIDENTS

What actions did American presidents between 1877 and 1900 take to restore authority to their office?

After Andrew Johnson's impeachment and the scandals plaguing both the Grant administration and the 1876 election, the presidency was tarnished. Presidents Rutherford Hayes (1877–1881), James Garfield (1881), Chester Arthur (1881–1885), Grover Cleveland (1885–1889 and 1893–1897), Benjamin Harrison (1889–1893), and William McKinley (1897–1901) sought to bring integrity back to federal government through various legislative initiatives. They all supported Civil Service (and its expansion) as a means to end the corruption of the spoils system. With varying success, they addressed currency, tariffs, railroad regulation, and labor unrest.

DISCRIMINATION, DISFRANCHISEMENT, AND RESPONSES

> **How did southerners find legal means to discriminate against newly enfranchised African Americans in the decades following the Civil War?**

First, southern leaders instituted measures such as poll taxes, which most blacks could not afford, and literacy tests to keep them from voting. These measures were upheld in the Supreme Court, which noted that the Fifteenth Amendment could only prohibit states from denying the vote based on "race, color, or previous condition of servitude," but could not control the local election process. Similarly, Jim Crow, or segregation laws, confined African Americans to separate areas in public places such as streetcars, hospitals, and parks, thereby deliberately reminding them of their inferior status. These laws were upheld by the Supreme Court in *Plessey v. Ferguson*, which allowed that states could legally segregate on a "separate-but-equal" basis.

AGRARIAN UNREST AND POPULISM

> **How did farmers' discontent crystallize in the Grange movement and Farmers' Alliances?**

As farm prices dropped, farmers found it increasingly difficult to earn a living from their land. Those conditions were made worse by the fact that as smallholders, most could not compete with large firms, which could negotiate lower costs for transportation and supplies by virtue of their size. In response, farmers founded local organizations called Granges in the 1860s and 1870s partly as social clubs and partly to enable them to join forces in cooperatives where they could get the same competitive advantage as larger firms. Granges declined in the late 1870s, replaced a decade later by Farmers' Alliances, which rallied against crop liens, merchants, railroads, and money power. Along with cooperatives, Alliances sought a government aid system called a subtreasury which they hoped would provide low-interest loans to farmers seeking to buy land and would assist farmers in warehousing crops until market prices increased.

THE DEPRESSION AND PROTESTS OF THE 1890S

> **Why did socialism fail to take hold amid the labor activism of the late nineteenth century?**

The depression and thousands of strikes beginning with the 1877 railroad strike revealed general worker dissatisfaction that certainly created the conditions ripe for socialism to flourish, particularly once its charismatic leader Eugene V. Debs came to the fore in the 1890s. But American socialists could not agree on how best to implement Marxist strategies for worker control of the means of production and the end of capitalism's inequities. Socialism was also thwarted by that distinctly American celebration of social mobility and individual achievement. While workers found some aspects of socialism attractive, their ultimate aim was individual advancement, which they were unwilling to sacrifice for the greater good of all workers.

THE SILVER CRUSADE AND THE ELECTION OF 1896

How did Bryan's focus on free silver undermine his presidential campaign and the Populist Party?

Populists embraced the issue of silver because they believed it would end special privileges for the rich by lifting mainstream Americans from debt, increasing the money in circulation and lowering interest rates. Populists fused these ideas to the Democratic Party by joining forces with them behind William Jennings Bryan for president in 1896. Bryan was singularly focused on silver, but this cost him votes from urban workers, who feared silver coinage would cut their wages. Labor leaders equated farmers with businessmen, and as such, could not join forces with Populists on this issue. Bryan received only 222,600 votes nationwide, and while Populists continued to influence elections, the party itself collapsed.

SUGGESTIONS FOR FURTHER READING

Edward L. Ayers, *The Promise of the New South: Life After Reconstruction* (1992)

Nancy Cohen, *The Reconstruction of American Liberalism, 1865–1914* (2002)

Glenda Elizabeth Gilmore, *Gender and Jim Crow: Women and the Politics of White Supremacy in North Carolina, 1896–1920* (1996)

Steven Hahn, *A Nation Under Our Feet: Black Political Struggles in the Rural South, from Slavery to the Great Migration* (2003)

Michael Kazin, *The Populist Persuasion: An American History* (1995)

Jean V. Matthews, *The Rise of the New Woman: The Women's Movement in America, 1875–1930* (2003)

Nick Salvatore, *Eugene V. Debs: Citizen and Socialist* (1992)

CHAPTER 21

The Progressive Era | 1895–1920

CHAPTER OUTLINE

The Varied Progressive Impulse

LINKS TO THE WORLD:
Workers' Compensation

Government and Legislative Reform

New Ideas in Social Institutions

Challenges to Racial and Sexual Discrimination

Theodore Roosevelt and the Revival of the Presidency

Woodrow Wilson and the Extension of Progressive Reform

LEGACY FOR A PEOPLE AND A NATION: Margaret Sanger, Planned Parenthood, and the Birth Control Controversy

Summary

What Ben Lindsey saw made him furious. As a young Colorado lawyer in the 1890s, a judge asked him to defend two boys, about twelve years old, arrested on burglary charges. The boys had been imprisoned for sixty days without a trial and did not understand what *burglary* meant or how the justice system worked. Visiting them in jail, Lindsey found the youngsters playing poker with two older cellmates—a safe cracker and a horse thief. Outraged that children were housed with hardened criminals, Lindsey later wrote, "Here were two boys, neither of them serious enemies of society, who were about to be convicted of burglary and have felony records. . . . I had made up my mind to smash the system that meant so much injustice to youth."

In 1901 Lindsey ran for county judge and began fighting for juvenile protection from criminal prosecution, exploitative labor practices, and the burdens of poverty. He and his wife, Henrietta, spread the ideas of a separate juvenile court system and of aiding families with children at risk of becoming criminals. They wrote reform laws, adopted by many states and foreign countries. The Lindseys' efforts to abolish injustice showed compassion and middle-class bias as part of a broader movement seeking solutions to modern America's social and economic problems.

During the 1890s, economic depression, labor violence, political upheaval, and foreign entanglements shook the nation. Great numbers of Americans continued to suffer from poverty and disease. Business and politics seemed out of control. Tensions created by urbanization and industrialization fragmented society into conflicting interest groups.

By 1900, the previous decade's political tumult had calmed, and economic depression seemed to be over. The nation emerged victorious from a war against Spain (see Chapter 22), and a new

This icon will direct you to interactive activities and study materials on A People And A Nation, Brief Edition
website: **www.cengage.com/history/norton/peoplenationbrief8e**

Chronology

1895	Booker T. Washington gives Atlanta Compromise speech. National Association of Colored Women is founded.
1898	*Holden v. Hardy* upholds limits on miners' working hours.
1900	McKinley is reelected.
1901	McKinley is assassinated; T. Roosevelt assumes the presidency.
1904	T. Roosevelt is elected president. *Northern Securities* case dissolves railroad trust.
1905	*Lochner v. New York* removes limits on bakers' working hours. NCAA is founded.
1906	Hepburn Act tightens ICC control over railroads. Meat Inspection Act is passed. Pure Food and Drug Act is passed.
1908	Taft is elected president. *Muller v. Oregon* upholds limits on women's working hours.
1909	NAACP is founded.
1910	Mann-Elkins Act reinforces ICC powers. White Slave Traffic Act (Mann Act) prohibits transportation of women for "immoral purposes." Taft fires Pinchot.
1911	Society of American Indians is founded.
1912	Wilson is elected president.
1913	Sixteenth Amendment, legalizing income tax, is ratified. Seventeenth Amendment, providing for direct election of senators, is ratified. Underwood Tariff institutes income tax. Federal Reserve Act establishes central banking system.
1914	Federal Trade Commission is created to investigate unfair trade practices. Clayton Anti-Trust Act outlaws monopolistic business practices.
1916	Wilson is reelected. Adamson Act mandates eight-hour workday for railroad workers.
1919	Eighteenth Amendment, establishing prohibition of alcoholic beverages, is ratified.
1920	Nineteenth Amendment, giving women the vote in federal elections, is ratified.

era of dynamic political leaders, such as Theodore Roosevelt and Woodrow Wilson, was dawning. A sense of renewal both intensified anxiety over continuing problems and raised hopes that democracy could be reconciled with capitalism.

Between 1895 and 1920, a complex reform movement emerged, aiming to renovate or restore American society, values, and institutions. By the 1910s, reformers from Republican and Democratic Parties were calling themselves Progressives; in 1912 Progressives formed their own party. Historians have used the term *Progressivism* to refer to the era's spirit, while disagreeing over its meaning and over which groups and individuals actually were Progressive.

The reform impulse had many sources. Industrial capitalism created awesome technology, unprecedented productivity, and copious consumer goods. But it also brought overproduction, domineering monopolies, labor strife, and the destruction of natural resources. Burgeoning cities facilitated the distribution of goods and services but also bred poverty, disease, and crime. Rising immigration and a new professional class reconfigured the social order. And the depression of the 1890s forced leading citizens to realize what working people already knew: America's central promise, equality of opportunity, was elusive.

Reformers organized around three goals. First, they sought to end abuses of power. Progressives broadened the offensive to make trustbusting, consumers' rights, and good government compelling issues.

Second, Progressives like Ben Lindsey wished to supplant corrupt power with humane institutions, such as schools, courts, and medical clinics. They abandoned conceptions that hard work and good character guaranteed success and that the poor were to blame for their plight. Instead, Progressives acknowledged that society had a responsibility to improve individual lives, and they believed that government must protect the common good and elevate public interest above self-interest. They challenged entrenched views on women's roles, race relations, education, legal and scientific thought, and morality.

Third, Progressives wanted to establish bureaus of experts who would end wasteful competition and promote social and economic order. Just as corporations applied scientific management to achieve economic efficiency, Progressives advocated expertise and planning to achieve social and political efficiency.

Progressives had faith in humankind's ability to create a better world. Rising incomes, new educational opportunities, and increased availability of goods and services inspired confidence that social improvement would follow. Judge Ben Lindsey expressed the Progressive creed when he wrote, "In the end the people are bound to do the right thing, no matter how much they fail at times."

- **What were the major characteristics of Progressivism?**
- **In what ways did Progressive reform succeed, and in what ways did it fail?**
- **How did women and racial minorities challenge previous ways of thinking about American society?**

THE VARIED PROGRESSIVE IMPULSE

After the heated election of 1896, party loyalties eroded and voter turnout declined. In northern states, voter participation in presidential elections dropped from the 1880s' levels of 80 percent to less than 60 percent. In southern states, where poll taxes and literacy tests excluded most African Americans and many poor whites from voting, it fell below 30 percent. At the same time, new interest groups, which championed their own special causes, gained influence.

National Associations and Foreign Influences   Many formerly local organizations spread nationwide after 1890. These included professional associations, such as the American Bar Association; women's organizations, such as the National American Woman Suffrage Association; issue-oriented groups, such as the National Consumers League; civic-minded clubs, such as the National Municipal League; and minority-group associations, such as the National Negro Business League and the Society of American Indians. Because they were usually independent from political parties, these groups made politics more fragmented and issue focused than in earlier eras.

Reformers adapted foreign models. Some were introduced by Americans who were exposed to reforms while studying in England, France, and Germany; others, by foreigners visiting the United States. Americans copied from England the settlement house, in which reformers live among and aid the urban poor, and workers' compensation for victims of industrial accidents. Other European reforms, such as old-age insurance, subsidized workers' housing, city planning, and rural reconstruction, were modified in America. Although Populist rural-based goals of moral regeneration, political democracy, and antimonopolism continued, the Progressive quest for social justice, labor laws, educational and legal reform, and government streamlining had a largely urban bent.

The New Middle Class and Muckrakers

Progressive goals—ending abuse of power, protecting the welfare of all classes, reforming social institutions, and promoting bureaucratic and scientific efficiency—existed across society. But a new middle class—men and women in law, medicine, engineering, social service, religion, teaching, and business—formed the reform vanguard. Offended by inefficiency and immorality in business, government, and human relations, they determined to apply the rational techniques of their professions to social problems. They also believed that they could create a unified society by Americanizing immigrants and Indians through education and programs stressing middle-class customs.

Progressive views were voiced by journalists whom Theodore Roosevelt dubbed muckrakers (after a character in the Puritan allegory *Pilgrim's Progress,* who, rather than looking heavenward at beauty, looked downward and raked the muck). Muckrakers fed public tastes for scandal by exposing social, economic, and political wrongs. Investigative articles in popular magazines attacked adulterated foods, fraudulent insurance, prostitution, and political corruption. Lincoln Steffens hoped his exposés of bosses' misrule in *McClure's* (later published as *The Shame of the Cities* in 1904) would inspire mass outrage and reform. Other well-known muckraking works included Upton Sinclair's *The Jungle* (1906), exposing outrages of the meatpacking industry; and Ida M. Tarbell's disparaging history of Standard Oil (first published in *McClure's,* 1902–1904).

Progressives advocated nonpartisan elections to prevent fraud and bribery bred by party loyalties, and promoted direct primaries instead of party caucuses. To make officeholders more responsible, they urged adoption of the initiative, which permitted voters to propose laws; the referendum, which enabled voters to accept or reject a law; and the recall, which allowed voters to remove offending officials from office.

Upper-Class Reformers

The Progressive spirit also stirred some businessmen and wealthy women. Executives like Alexander Cassatt of the Pennsylvania Railroad supported some government regulation and political reforms to protect their interests from more radical reformers. Others, like E. A. Filene, founder of a Boston department store, were humanitarians who worked for social justice. Business-dominated organizations like the Municipal Voters League and the U.S. Chamber of Commerce thought that running schools, hospitals, and local government like businesses would stabilize society. Elite women led organizations like the Young Women's Christian Association (YWCA), which aided unmarried working women, and they joined middle- and working-class women in the Woman's Christian Temperance Union (WCTU), the largest women's organization of its time.

Working-Class Reformers

But also vital elements of what became modern American liberalism derived from working-class urban experiences. By 1900 many urban workers were pressing for bread-and-butter reforms, such as safe factories, shorter workdays, workers' compensation, and better housing. Politicians who embraced such causes trained in machine politics, and their constituents supported political bosses. Yet bossism was not necessarily at odds with humanitarianism. Big Tim Sullivan, an influential boss in New York City's Tammany Hall political machine, said he supported shorter workdays for women because "I had seen me sister go out to work when she was only fourteen and I know we ought to help these gals by giving 'em a law which will prevent 'em from being broken down while they're still young." Working-class advocates opposed prohibition, Sunday closing laws, civil service, and nonpartisan elections, but joined with other reformers to pass laws aiding labor and promoting social welfare.

The Social Gospel

Much of Progressive reform rested on religious values. A movement known as the Social Gospel, led by the Protestant ministers Walter Rauschenbusch, Washington Gladden, and Charles Sheldon countered competitive capitalism by interjecting Christian churches into worldly matters, such as arbitrating industrial harmony and improving the environment of the poor. Believing that helping others provided the way to individual salvation, Social Gospelers governed their lives by asking, "What would Jesus do?"

Those who believed in service to others tried to Americanize immigrants and Indians by expanding educational, economic, and cultural opportunities. But imposing their values on people of different cultures undermined their efforts to help. Catholic and Jewish immigrants sometimes rejected the Americanization efforts of Social Gospelers, settlement-house workers, and other reformers. Working-class families, too, resented reformers' interference in child rearing.

Socialists

Disillusioned immigrant intellectuals, industrial workers, Populists, miners, and women's rights activists desired a different society altogether and turned to socialism. They wanted the United States to follow the example of Germany, England, and France, where the government sponsored low-cost housing, workers' compensation, old-age pensions, public ownership of municipal services, and labor reform. By 1912, the Socialist Party of America, a merger of several groups and founded in 1901, claimed 150,000 members, and 700,000 subscribers to its newspaper. But American socialism had difficulty sustaining widespread acceptance.

Politically, many socialists united behind Eugene V. Debs, the American Railway Union organizer who drew nearly 100,000 votes as the Socialist presidential candidate in 1900. A spellbinding orator who appealed to urban immigrants and western farmers alike, Debs won 400,000 votes in 1904 and 900,000 in 1912, at the pinnacle of his and his party's career. Some Progressives joined the Socialist Party, but most had too much at stake in capitalism to want it overthrown. Municipal ownership of public utilities represented their limit of drastic change.

Workers' Compensation

At the dawn of the twentieth century, accident rates on American railroads and in mines and factories far exceeded those in Great Britain and Germany, the other two major industrial nations, and muckraking journalists wrote about them extensively. In 1911 one study concluded that the accident rate in the nation's industries "equals the average yearly casualties of the American Civil War, plus all of those of the Philippine War, plus all of those of the Russo-Japanese War." American legal theory protected employers from liability and prevented workers from recovering medical costs and lost income from job-related injuries. Progressives argued that employers, guided by government, should shoulder the obligation.

The principle that employers should be legally responsible for compensating victims of industrial accidents emerged most strongly in Germany and Britain in the late nineteenth century. Germany required employers and wage earners to contribute to quasi-public funds to cover those injured at work, while England compelled employers to pay them through insurance company contributions or their own funds. Variations later appeared in Denmark, France, and Italy. But not until 1907 did President Theodore Roosevelt advocate for employers' liability legislation. The next year, two different Progressive organizations, the social reform–minded Russell Sage Foundation and the business-oriented National Civic Foundation, took up the cause.

Most American Progressives favored the German system because it operated more under government administration than the British method. But states, not the federal government, assumed responsibility for the form of a program. By 1911, Ohio and Washington had state-administered insurance funds into which employers made contributions, and between 1911 and 1913, twenty other states enacted some form of workers' compensation laws. By 1919, the majority of workers' compensation funds were handled by private insurance firms. American legislators, propelled by Progressive arguments, had borrowed an insurance system from abroad, but applied their imprint of private enterprise.

A SUCCESSFUL WORKMAN

This man who lost an arm in an industrial accident in Cleveland, invented a good substitute arm, wears it at work, and uses it in earning his living. He has made good by his own unaided efforts. The average man, however, needs a lift in the way of training.

In the early twentieth century, industrial accidents continued to kill and maim thousands of workers. Without insurance to support them when they were disabled, some employees created aids to enable them to continue on the job. This man, who lost an arm in a factory mishap, invented his own artificial limb. Other victims of misfortune, however, were not so handy and could receive compensation only if their state or their employer adopted the European model and instituted a workers' insurance program. (Library of Congress)

Southern and Western Progressivism

Progressive reform in the South focused on railroad and utility regulation, factory safety, pure food and drug legislation, and moral reform. The South pioneered some political reforms: the direct primary originated in North Carolina; the city-commission plan arose in Galveston, Texas; and the city-manager plan began in Staunton, Virginia. Like their northern counterparts, Progressive governors introduced business regulation, educational expansion, and other reforms.

In the West, several politicians championed humanitarianism and regulation, putting the region at the forefront of efforts to expand federal and state government functions. Nevada's Progressive senator Francis Newlands advocated federal control of water resources. California governor Hiram Johnson fought for regulation of children's and women's labor, workers' compensation, a pure food and drug act, and education reform.

Southern and western women, white and black, made notable contributions to Progressive causes. In western states, women could vote on state and local matters, but the more effective women's reform occurred outside politics in racially distinctive ways. White women crusaded against child labor, founded social service organizations, and challenged unfair wages. African American women, using a guise as homemakers and religious leaders—which whites found more acceptable than political activism—advocated for street cleaning, better education, and health reforms.

Opponents of Progressivism

It would be incorrect to assume that all of America was captivated by the Progressive spirit between 1895 and 1920. Defenders of free enterprise opposed regulatory measures, believing government programs undermined the initiative and competition basic to a free-market system. "Old-guard" Republicans, such as Senator Nelson W. Aldrich of Rhode Island and House Speaker Joseph Cannon of Illinois, championed this ideology.

Moreover, prominent Progressives were not always progressive. Governor Hiram Johnson promoted discrimination against Japanese Americans, and most southern governors rested their power on appeals to white supremacy. Settlement houses in northern cities kept blacks and whites apart in separate programs and buildings.

Progressive reformers generally occupied the center of the ideological spectrum, believing on the one hand that laissez faire was obsolete and on the other that a radical departure from free enterprise was dangerous. Like Thomas Jefferson, they expressed faith in the will of the people; like Alexander Hamilton, they desired a strong central government to act in the interest of conscience.

GOVERNMENT AND LEGISLATIVE REFORM

Mistrust of tyranny traditionally prompted Americans to believe that democratic government should be small, interfere in private affairs only in unique circumstances, and withdraw quickly. In the late 1800s this viewpoint weakened when economic problems led corporations to pursue government aid and protection. Discontented farmers sought government regulation of railroads and other monopolistic businesses. City dwellers, accustomed to favors from political machines, expected government to act on their behalf. Before 1900, state governments had been concerned largely with railroads and economic growth; the federal government had focused primarily on tariffs and the currency.

Restructuring Government

Middle-class Progressive reformers rejected the laissez-faire principle of government, reasoning that in a complex age, public authority needed to counteract inefficiency and exploitation. But to tap this power, activists would have to reclaim government from politicians whose greed they believed soiled the democratic system.

Prior to the Progressive era, reformers attacked corruption in cities by trying to regulate government through such structural reforms as civil service, nonpartisan elections, and close scrutiny of public expenditures. After 1900, campaigns to make cities more efficient resulted in city-manager and commission forms of government, in which urban officials were chosen for professional expertise rather than for political connections.

At the state level, Progressives supported several skillful governors. In the West, California governor Hiram Johnson attacked business and political corruption and inspired state laws regulating utilities and child labor and initiating workers' compensation for state employees. In the South, Georgia's Hoke Smith achieved railroad regulation, juvenile courts, and better-funded public education, though he also supported voting restrictions that disfranchised blacks.

Wisconsin's Robert M. La Follette was one of the most dynamic Progressive governors. A small-town lawyer, La Follette rose through the state Republican Party to become governor in 1900. There, he initiated direct primaries, more equitable taxes, and railroad regulation. After three terms as governor, La Follette became a U.S. senator. Battling Bob displayed a rare ability to approach reform scientifically, proclaiming that his goal was "not to 'smash' corporations, but to drive them out of politics."

Crusades against corrupt politics made the system more democratic. Political reformers achieved a major goal in 1913 with the adoption of the Seventeenth Amendment to the Constitution, which provided for the direct election of U.S. senators, replacing election by state legislatures. But party bosses were still able to control elections, and special-interest groups spent large sums to influence voting.

Labor Reform

At the instigation of middle-class–working-class coalitions, many states enacted factory inspection laws, and by 1916 nearly two-thirds of the states required compensation for victims of industrial accidents. Some legislatures granted aid to mothers with dependent children. Under pressure from the National Child Labor Committee, nearly every state set a minimum age for employment (varying from twelve to sixteen) and limited the hours that children could work. Labor laws were imperfect, however. They seldom provided for the close inspection of factories that enforcement required. And families needing extra income falsified their children's ages to employers.

Several groups also united to achieve restricted working hours for women and aided retirees. After the Supreme Court, in *Muller v. Oregon,* upheld Oregon's ten-hour limit in 1908, more states passed laws protecting female workers. In 1914 the American Association for Old Age Security secured old-age pensions in Arizona. Judges struck down the law, but the demand for pensions continued and in the 1920s many states enacted such laws.

Prohibition

Reformers did not always agree about whether laws should regulate drinking habits and sexual conduct. The Anti-Saloon League (formed in 1893) allied with the Woman's Christian Temperance Union (founded in 1874) to publicize alcoholism's role in health problems like liver disease. The league successfully shifted attention from the immorality of drunkenness to the alleged link between drinking and accidents, poverty, and poor productivity.

The war on saloons prompted many states and localities to restrict liquor consumption. By 1900 almost one-fourth of the nation's population lived in dry communities, prohibiting liquor sales. But alcohol consumption increased after 1900, convincing prohibitionists that a nationwide ban was needed. In 1918 Congress passed the Eighteenth Amendment (ratified in 1919 and implemented in 1920), outlawing the manufacture, sale, and transportation of intoxicating liquors. Not all prohibitionists were Progressive reformers, and vice versa. Nevertheless, the Eighteenth Amendment embodied the Progressive goal to protect family and workplace through reform legislation.

Controlling Prostitution

Moral outrage erupted when muckraking journalists charged that international gangs were kidnapping young women and forcing them into prostitution, a practice called white slavery. Accusations were exaggerated, but they alarmed moralists who falsely perceived a link between immigration and prostitution. Reformers prodded governments to investigate and pass corrective legislation. The Chicago Vice Commission undertook a "scientific" survey of dance halls and illicit sex and published its findings as *The Social Evil in Chicago* in 1911. The report concluded that poverty, gullibility, and desperation drove women into prostitution.

Such investigations found rising numbers of prostitutes but failed to prove that criminal organizations lured women into the trade. Reformers nonetheless believed they could attack prostitution by punishing those who promoted and practiced it. In 1910 Congress passed the White Slave Traffic Act (Mann Act), prohibiting interstate and international transportation of a woman for immoral purposes. By 1915 nearly every state outlawed brothels and solicitation of sex.

Like prohibition, the Mann Act reflected growing sentiment that government could improve behavior by restricting it. Middle-class reformers believed that the source of evil was not human nature but the social environment. The working classes, however, resented such unwarranted attempts to control them. Thus, when Chicagoans voted on a referendum to make their city dry before the Eighteenth Amendment was passed, three-fourths of the city's immigrant voters opposed it, and the measure was defeated.

NEW IDEAS IN SOCIAL INSTITUTIONS

Preoccupation with efficiency and scientific management infiltrated education, law, religion, and the social sciences. Darwin's theory of evolution challenged belief in a God-created world; immigration created complex social diversity; and technology made old production habits obsolete. Professionals grappled with how to embrace progress yet preserve the best from the past.

John Dewey and Progressive Education

As late as 1870, when families needed children to do farm work, Americans attended school only a few months a year for four years on average. By 1900, however, the urban-industrial economy and its expanding middle class advanced the goal of sheltering youngsters from society's dangers by protecting their physical and emotional growth. That meant ensuring that youngsters were exposed to age-appropriate educational materials and activities.

Thus schools shared with, and even replaced, the home as the best environment for promoting children's development and producing adult citizens and workers. In the 1870s and 1880s, laws required children to attend school to age fourteen. The number of public high schools grew from five hundred in 1870 to ten thousand in 1910. By 1900 educational reformers, such as the psychologist G. Stanley Hall and the philosopher John Dewey, asserted that schools needed to prepare children for a modern world by making personal development the focus of the curriculum.

Progressive education, based on Dewey's *The School and Society* (1899) and *Democracy and Education* (1916), stressed that learning should involve real-life problems and that children should be taught to use ingenuity to control their environments. Dewey and his wife, Alice, tested their theories that children should learn by experience not rote memorization in their Laboratory School at the University of Chicago.

Growth of Colleges and Universities

A more practical curriculum similarly drove higher education reform. Previously, American colleges resembled their European counterparts in training a select few for careers in law, medicine, and religion. But in the late 1800s, institutions of higher learning multiplied via state and federal grants. Between 1870 and 1910, American colleges and universities grew from 563 to nearly 1,000. Curricula expanded to make learning more appealing and to keep pace with technological and social changes. Harvard University, under President Charles W. Eliot, pioneered new teaching methods and substituted electives for required courses. Many schools considered athletics vital to a student's growth, and men's intercollegiate sports became a permanent feature.

Southern states created segregated land-grant colleges for blacks and whites. Although African Americans continued to suffer from inferior educational opportunities, they found intellectual stimulation in all-black colleges and used their education to help uplift their race.

Between 1890 and 1910, the number of women in colleges swelled from 56,000 to 140,000. Roughly 106,000 attended coeducational institutions (mostly state universities); the rest enrolled in women's colleges. By 1920, 283,000 women attended college, accounting for 47 percent of total enrollment. But women were encouraged (and usually sought) to take home economics and education courses, and most medical schools refused to admit women. Separate women's medical schools, such as the Women's Medical College of Philadelphia, trained numerous female physicians, but most of these schools were absorbed or put out of business by larger, male-dominated institutions.

By 1920, 78 percent of children ages five to seventeen were enrolled in public schools; another 8 percent attended private and parochial schools. There were 600,000 college and graduate students in 1920, compared with only 52,000 in 1870. Yet critical analysis seldom tested the faith that schools could promote equality as well as personal growth and responsible citizenship.

Progressive Legal Thought

The Harvard law professor Roscoe Pound and Oliver Wendell Holmes Jr., associate justice of the Supreme Court between 1902 and 1932, led the attack on the traditional view of law as universal and unchanging. Their argument that law should reflect society's needs challenged the practice of invoking inflexible legal precedents. Louis D. Brandeis, a lawyer who later joined Holmes on the Supreme Court, insisted that judges' opinions be based on scientifically gathered information about social realities. Brandeis collected extensive data on the harmful effects of long working hours to convince the Supreme Court, in *Muller v. Oregon* (1908), to uphold Oregon's ten-hour limit to women's workday.

Judges raised on laissez-faire economics and a strict interpretation of the Constitution overturned laws that Progressives thought necessary for reform. Thus, in 1905 the Supreme Court, in *Lochner v. New York,* revoked a New York law limiting bakers' working hours. The Court's majority argued that the Fourteenth Amendment protected an individual's right to make contracts without government interference.

Several decisions, beginning with *Holden v. Hardy* (1898), in which the Supreme Court sustained a Utah law regulating miners' working hours, confirmed the use of state police power to protect health, safety, and morals. Judges also affirmed federal police power and Congress's authority over interstate commerce by upholding federal legislation, such as the Pure Food and Drug Act, the Meat Inspection Act, and the Mann Act.

But even if one agreed that laws should address society's needs, whose needs should prevail in a mixed nation? In many localities a native-born Protestant majority imposed Bible reading in public schools (offending Catholics and Jews), required businesses to close on Sundays, limited women's rights, restricted religious practices of Mormons and others, prohibited interracial marriage, and enforced racial segregation. Justice Holmes asserted that laws should be made for "people of fundamentally differing views," but how to accomplish that continues to spark debate today.

Social Science

Social science—the study of society and its institutions—underwent changes. Economics scholars used statistics to argue that laws governing economic relationships were not timeless but should reflect prevailing social conditions. A new breed of sociologists led by Lester Ward, Albion Small, and Edward A. Ross agreed, adding that citizens should work to cure social ills.

Meanwhile, the historians Frederick Jackson Turner, Charles A. Beard, and Vernon L. Parrington examined the past to explain present American society. Beard, like other Progressives, believed that the Constitution was a flexible document. His *Economic Interpretation of the Constitution* (1913) argued that a group of merchants and business-oriented lawyers created the Constitution to defend private property. If the Constitution served special interests in one age, he believed, it could be changed to serve broader interests in another.

In public health, organizations such as the National Consumers League (NCL), founded in 1899 by Florence Kelley, joined physicians and social scientists to secure far-reaching Progressive reforms. NCL activities included the protection of female and child laborers and the elimination of potential health hazards. Local branches united with women's clubs to advance consumer protection measures, such as the licensing of food vendors and the inspection of dairies. They urged city governments to fund neighborhood clinics providing medical care to the poor.

Eugenics

The Social Gospel was a response to Social Darwinism, the application of biological natural selection and survival of the fittest to human interactions. But another movement, eugenics, sought to apply Darwinian principles more intrusively. The brainchild of Francis Galton, an English statistician and cousin of Charles Darwin, eugenics rested on the belief that human character and habits could be inherited, specifically bad traits, such as criminality, insanity, and feeblemindedness. Eugenicists believed society had an obligation to prevent the reproduction of the mentally defective and the criminally inclined, by prohibiting such people from marrying and, in extreme cases, by sterilizing them. Inevitably such ideas targeted immigrants and people of color. Supported by such American notables as Alexander Graham Bell, Margaret Sanger, and W. E. B. Du Bois, eugenics was discredited, especially after it became a linchpin of Nazi racial policies.

Some reformers endorsed eugenics; others embraced immigration restriction to control the composition of American society. Madison Grant's *The Passing of the Great Race* (1916) bolstered theories that immigrants from southern and eastern Europe threatened to weaken American society because they were inferior mentally and morally to earlier Nordic immigrants. Thus, many people, including some Progressives, sought new laws to curtail the influx of Poles, Italians, Jews, and other eastern and southern Europeans, and Asians. In the 1920s, restrictive legislation closed the door to "new" immigrants.

CHALLENGES TO RACIAL AND SEXUAL DISCRIMINATION

The white male reformers of the Progressive era dealt primarily with politics and institutions and ignored issues affecting former slaves, nonwhite immigrants, Native Americans, and women. Yet these groups caught the Progressive spirit and made strides toward advancement themselves. Their efforts, however, posed a dilemma. Should women and nonwhites aim to be on a par with white men? Or was there something unique about racial and sexual cultures worth preserving at the risk of broader gains?

Continued Discrimination for African Americans

In 1900 nine-tenths of African Americans lived in the South, where repressive Jim Crow laws multiplied in the 1880s and 1890s. In 1910 only 8,000 out of 970,000 high-school-age blacks in the South were enrolled in high schools. And blacks met with violence from lynching and acts of intimidation. Consequently, many African Americans moved northward in the 1880s, accelerating their migration after 1900. Although conditions in places like Chicago and Detroit represented improvement, job discrimination, inferior schools, and segregated housing prevailed.

African American leaders differed over how—and whether—to assimilate. After emancipation, ex-slave Frederick Douglass urged "ultimate assimilation through self-assertion." Others supported emigration to Africa or the establishment of all-black communities in the Oklahoma Territory and Kansas. Still others advocated militancy.

Booker T. Washington and Self-Help

Most blacks could neither escape nor conquer white society. Self-help, a strategy articulated by educator Booker T. Washington, offered one popular alternative. Born into slavery in Virginia in 1856, Washington obtained an education and in 1881 founded the Tuskegee Institute, an all-black vocational school, in Alabama. There he developed a philosophy that blacks' best hopes lay in at least temporarily accommodating to whites. Rather than fighting for rights, Washington counseled African Americans to work hard, acquire property, and prove they were worthy of respect. "Dignify and glorify common labor," he urged in a speech at the 1895 Atlanta Exposition that

Booker T. Washington's Tuskegee Institute helped train young African Americans in useful crafts, such as shoemaking and shoe repair, as illustrated here. At the same time, however, Washington's intentions and the Tuskegee curriculum reinforced what many whites wanted to believe: that blacks were unfit for anything except manual labor.

(Tuskegee University Library)

became known as the Atlanta Compromise. Washington observed that "in all things that are purely social we can be as separate as the fingers, yet one as the hand in all matters essential to mutual progress."

Because he said what they wanted to hear, white businesspeople, reformers, and politicians regarded Washington as representing all African Americans. Washington never argued that blacks were inferior to whites; rather, he asserted that they could enhance their dignity through self-improvement.

Some blacks, however, concluded that Washington endorsed second-class citizenship. In 1905 a group of anti-Bookerites convened near Niagara Falls and pledged militant pursuit of unrestricted voting, economic opportunity, integration, and equality before the law. Representing the Niagara movement was W. E. B. Du Bois, an outspoken critic of the Atlanta Compromise.

W. E. B. Du Bois and the Talented Tenth

A New Englander and the first black to receive a Ph.D. degree from Harvard, Du Bois was both a Progressive and a member of the black elite. While a faculty member at Atlanta University, Du Bois compiled sociological studies of black urban life and wrote in support of civil rights. He treated Washington politely but could not accept accommodation. Du Bois believed that an intellectual vanguard of cultured blacks, the Talented Tenth, could use their skills to pursue racial equality. In 1909 he joined with white liberals similarly discontented with Washington's accommodationism to form the National Association for the Advancement of Colored People (NAACP). The organization aimed to end racial discrimination, prevent lynching, and obtain voting rights through legal redress in the courts. By 1914 the NAACP had fifty branch offices and six thousand members.

African Americans struggled with questions about their place in white society. Du Bois voiced this dilemma, observing that "one ever feels his twoness—an American, a Negro, two souls, two thoughts, two unreconciled strivings, two warring ideals in one dark body." As Du Bois wrote in 1903, a black "would not bleach his Negro soul in a flood of white Americanism, for he knows that Negro blood has a message for the world. He simply wishes to make it possible for a man to be both a Negro and an American."

Society of American Indians

In 1911, however, middle-class Indians broke with white-led organizations and formed their own association, the Society of American Indians (SAI), to work for better education, civil rights, and healthcare. It also sponsored American Indian Days to cultivate pride and offset the images of savage peoples promulgated in Wild West shows.

SAI's emphasis on racial pride, however, was squeezed between pressures for assimilation and tribal allegiance. Its small membership did not fully represent the diverse and unconnected Indian nations. Individual hard work was not enough to overcome white prejudice, and attempts to redress grievances through legal action faltered for lack of funds. Ultimately, SAI had little effect on poverty-stricken Indians who seldom knew that the organization existed. Torn by internal disputes, the association folded in the early 1920s.

The Woman Movement

Women's groups faced similar quandaries about the tactics they should use to achieve rights. Should they try to achieve equality within a male-dominated society or use female qualities to create new roles for themselves within society?

The answers that women found involved a subtle but important shift in their politics. Before 1910, women's rights activists called themselves the woman movement. Often middle-class, these women strived to move beyond the household into higher education and paid professions. They claimed that women's special, even superior, traits as guardians of family and morality would humanize the broader society. Settlement-house founder Jane Addams, for example, endorsed woman suffrage by asking, "If women have in any sense been responsible for the gentler side of life which softens and blurs some of its harsher conditions, may not they have a duty to perform in our American cities?"

Women's Clubs

Originating as literary and educational organizations, women's clubs began taking stands on public affairs in the late nineteenth century. They asserted traditional female responsibilities for home and family as the rationale for reforming society through an enterprise that historians have called social housekeeping. These female reformers worked for factory inspection, regulation of children's and women's labor, improved housing and education, and consumer protection.

African American women had their own club movement, including the Colored Women's Federation, which sought to establish a training school for "colored girls." Founded in 1895, the National Association of Colored Women was the nation's first African American social service organization; it concentrated on establishing nurseries, kindergartens, and retirement homes. Black women also developed reform organizations within Black Baptist and African Methodist Episcopal churches.

Feminism

Around 1910 some of those concerned with women's place in society began using the term *feminism* to represent their ideas. Whereas the woman movement spoke of moral purity and duty to society, feminists emphasized women's rights and self-development. Charlotte Perkins Gilman, a major figure in the movement, declared in her book *Women and Economics* (1898) that domesticity was obsolete, and attacked men's monopoly on economic opportunity. Arguing that paid employees should handle domestic chores, Gilman asserted that modern women must take jobs in industry and the professions to be independent.

Margaret Sanger's Crusade

Several feminists joined the birth-control movement led by Margaret Sanger. A former visiting nurse who believed in women's rights, Sanger helped reverse state and federal Comstock laws—named after a nineteenth-century New York moral reformer—which had banned the distribution of information about sex and contraception. Although Sanger later gained acceptance, she initially aroused opposition from those who saw birth control as a threat to family and morality. In 1921 she formed the American Birth Control League, enlisting physicians and social workers to convince judges to allow the distribution of birth-control information. Most states still prohibited the sale of contraceptives, but Sanger provoked public debate.

Woman Suffrage

During the Progressive era, a generation of feminists, represented by Harriot Stanton Blatch, daughter of the nineteenth-century suffragist Elizabeth Cady Stanton, carried on women's battle for the vote. Blatch's chief goal was the improvement of women's working conditions. Declaring that every woman worked, for wages or unpaid housework, Blatch believed that all women's efforts contributed to society's betterment. Thus women should exercise the vote to promote and protect their economic roles.

Nine states, all in the West, allowed women to vote in state and local elections by 1912 (see Map 21.1). Their tactics ranged from moderate but persistent letter-writing and publications of the National American Woman Suffrage Association, led by Carrie Chapman Catt, to spirited meetings and militant marches of the National Woman's Party, led by Alice Paul and Harriot Stanton Blatch. More decisive, however, was women's service during World War I as factory laborers, medical volunteers, and municipal workers. Legislators could no longer deny women's ability to shoulder public responsibilities and passed the national suffrage amendment (the Nineteenth) in 1920.

Map 21.1   Woman Suffrage Before 1920

Before Congress passed and the states ratified the Nineteenth Amendment, woman suffrage already existed, but mainly in the West. Several midwestern states allowed women to vote only in presidential elections, but legislatures in the South and Northeast generally refused such rights until forced to do so by constitutional amendment.

During the Progressive era, leaders like Blatch, Paul, and Catt helped clarify issues that concerned women, but winning the vote was a step, not a conclusion. Discrimination in employment, education, and the law continued to shadow women for decades to come, and feminists, women's clubs, and suffragists failed to unite to overcome men's political, social, and economic control. As the feminist Crystal Eastman observed after the suffrage crusade: "Men are saying perhaps, 'Thank God, this everlasting women's fight is over!' But women, if I know them, are saying, 'Now at last we can begin.' . . . Now they can say what they are really after, in common with all the rest of the struggling world, is freedom."

THEODORE ROOSEVELT AND THE REVIVAL OF THE PRESIDENCY

The Progressive era's reform spirit focused on the federal government as the foremost agent of change. Although the federal government had notable accomplishments during the Gilded Age, its role was mainly to support rather than control economic expansion. Then, in September 1901, the assassination of President William McKinley by the anarchist Leon Czolgosz vaulted Theodore Roosevelt, the young vice president, into the White House. As governor of New York, Roosevelt angered state Republican bosses by showing sympathy for regulatory legislation. He would become the nation's most forceful president since Lincoln, one who bestowed the office with much of its twentieth-century character.

Theodore Roosevelt

Driven throughout his life by an obsession to overcome the physical limitations of asthma and nearsightedness of his youth, Roosevelt exerted a zest for action and display of courage that contemporaries called manliness. In his teens he became an expert marksman and horseman, and later competed on Harvard's boxing and wrestling teams. In the 1880s he lived on a Dakota ranch, roping cattle and brawling with cowboys. Roosevelt had wealth, but he also inherited a sense of civic responsibility which guided him into public service. He served three terms in the New York State Assembly, sat on the federal Civil Service Commission, served as New York City's police commissioner, was assistant secretary of the navy, and earned a reputation as a combative, crafty leader. In 1898 he thrust himself into the Spanish-American War by organizing a volunteer cavalry brigade, called the Rough Riders, to fight in Cuba. Although his dramatic act had little impact on the war's outcome, it made him a media hero.

When he assumed the presidency, Roosevelt carried his youthful exuberance into the White House. A Progressive, he concurred with allies that a small, uninvolved government would not suffice in the industrial era. Instead, economic progress necessitated a government powerful enough to guide national affairs broadly. Especially in economic matters, he wanted the government to decide when big business was good and when it was bad.

Regulation of Trusts

The federal regulation of business that characterized twentieth-century America began with Roosevelt's presidency. Although labeled a trustbuster, Roosevelt actually considered business consolidation an efficient means to material progress. He believed in distinguishing between good and bad trusts and preventing bad ones from manipulating markets. Thus he instructed the Justice Department to use antitrust laws to prosecute railroad, meatpacking, and oil trusts, which he believed unscrupulously exploited the public. Roosevelt's policy triumphed in 1904 when the Supreme Court ordered the breakup of the Northern Securities Company, the huge railroad combination created by J. P. Morgan and his business allies. Roosevelt did not attack other trusts, such as U.S. Steel, another of Morgan's creations.

When prosecution of Northern Securities began, Morgan reportedly asked Roosevelt, "If we have done anything wrong, send your man to my man and they can fix it up." The president refused but was more sympathetic to cooperation between business and government than it might seem. He urged the Bureau of Corporations (part of the newly created Department of Labor and Commerce) to assist companies in merging and expanding. Through investigation and consultation, the administration cajoled businesses to regulate themselves.

Roosevelt also supported regulatory legislation. After a year of wrangling, Roosevelt persuaded Congress to pass the Hepburn Act (1906), which gave the Interstate Commerce Commission (ICC) greater authority to set railroad freight rates and extend that authority over ferries, express companies, storage facilities, and oil pipelines. The Hepburn Act still allowed courts to overturn ICC decisions, but it now required shippers to prove they had not violated regulations, rather than making the government demonstrate violations.

Pure Food and Drug Laws

Roosevelt was willing to compromise to secure pure food and drug legislation. For decades reformers urged government regulation of processed meat and patent medicines. Public outrage flared in 1906 when Upton Sinclair published *The Jungle,* a fictionalized exposé of Chicago meatpacking plants. Sinclair, a socialist who sought to improve working conditions, shocked the public with his vivid descriptions.

> There would be meat stored in great piles in rooms; and the water from the leaky roofs would drip over it, and thousands of rats would race about on it. It was too dark in these storage places to see well, but a man could run his hand over these piles of meat and sweep off handfuls of dried dung of rats . . . the packers would put poisoned bread out for them; they would die, and then rats, bread, and meat would go into the hoppers together.

Roosevelt ordered an investigation, and finding Sinclair's descriptions accurate, he supported the Meat Inspection Act (1906). This law required government agents to monitor the quality of processed meat. But as part of a compromise with meatpackers and their congressional allies, the government had to finance inspections, and meatpackers could appeal adverse decisions. Nor were companies required to provide date-of-processing information on canned meats. Most large meatpackers benefited because the legislation helped them force out smaller competitors and restore foreign confidence in American meat products.

The Pure Food and Drug Act (1906) also addressed abuses in the patent medicine industry. Makers of tonics and pills had long been making undue claims about their products' effects and liberally using alcohol and narcotics as ingredients. The law required that labels list the ingredients—a goal consistent with Progressive confidence that with the truth, people would make wiser purchases.

Makers of unregulated patent medicines advertised that their products had exorbitant abilities to cure almost any ailment and remedy any unwanted physical condition. Loring's Fat-Ten-U tablets and Loring's Corpula were two such products. The Pure Food and Drug Act of 1906 did not ban these items but tried to prevent manufacturers from making unsubstantiated claims.
(© Bettmann/Corbis)

Roosevelt's approach to labor resembled his compromises with business. When the United Mine Workers struck against Pennsylvania coal-mine owners in 1902 over their demand for an eight-hour workday and higher pay, the president employed investigation and arbitration. Owners refused to recognize the union or arbitrate grievances. As winter approached and fuel shortages loomed, Roosevelt threatened to use federal troops to reopen the mines, thus forcing management to accept arbitration. The arbitration commission supported higher wages and reduced hours and required management to deal with miners' grievance committees, but it did not mandate recognition of the union. The settlement embodied Roosevelt's belief that the president or his representatives should determine which labor demands were legitimate and which were not.

Race Relations

Although he invited Booker T. Washington to the White House to discuss racial matters, Roosevelt believed in white superiority and was neutral toward blacks only when it helped him politically. Case in point: in 1906 the army transferred African American soldiers from Nebraska to Brownsville, Texas. Anglo and Mexican residents resented their presence and banned them from parks and businesses. On August 14, a battle between blacks and whites broke out, and a white man was killed. Brownsville residents blamed soldiers, but soldiers refused to help investigators or name names. Consequently, Roosevelt discharged 167 black soldiers without a hearing and prevented them from receiving pay and pensions. Black leaders were outraged. To gain black support for Republican candidates in the 1906 elections, Roosevelt waited until after the elections to sign discharge papers.

Conservation

Roosevelt's Progressive impulse for efficiency and love for the outdoors inspired lasting contributions to resource conservation. Government establishment of national parks began in the late nineteenth century. Roosevelt advanced the movement by favoring *conservation* over *preservation*. Thus he not only exercised presidential power to protect such natural wonders as the Grand Canyon in Arizona by declaring them national monuments, but also backed a policy of wise use of forests, waterways, and other resources. Previously, the government transferred ownership of natural resources on federal land to the states and private interests. Roosevelt, however, believed effective resource conservation demanded that the federal government manage the lands that remained in the public domain.

Roosevelt exerted federal authority over resources by protecting waterpower sites from sale to private interests and charging permit fees for users who wanted to produce hydroelectricity. He also supported the Newlands Reclamation Act of 1902, which controlled the sale of irrigated federal land in the West. Roosevelt tripled the number of national forests and supported conservationist Gifford Pinchot in creating the U.S. Forest Service.

Gifford Pinchot

As principal advocate of the wise use policy, Pinchot promoted scientific management of the nation's woodlands. He obtained Roosevelt's support for transferring management of the national forests from the Interior Department to his bureau in the Agriculture Department. The Forest Service charged fees for grazing livestock within the national forests, supervised bidding for the cutting of timber, and hired university-trained foresters as federal employees.

Pinchot and Roosevelt did not seek to preserve resources permanently; rather, they wanted to conserve their efficient use and make companies profiting from using public lands pay the government. Many involved in natural-resource exploitation welcomed such a policy because it enabled them to better control products, such as when Roosevelt and Pinchot encouraged large lumber companies to engage in reforestation.

Panic of 1907

In 1907 a financial panic caused by reckless speculation forced some New York banks to close to prevent frightened depositors from withdrawing money. J. P. Morgan helped stem the panic by persuading financiers to stop dumping their stocks. In return for Morgan's aid, Roosevelt approved a deal allowing U.S. Steel to absorb the Tennessee Iron and Coal Company—a deal at odds with Roosevelt's trustbusting aims.

During his last year in office, Roosevelt retreated from the Republican Party's friendliness to big business. He supported stronger business regulation and heavier taxation of the rich. Promising he would not seek reelection, Roosevelt backed Secretary of War William Howard Taft in 1908. Taft easily defeated three-time Democratic nominee William Jennings Bryan by 1.25 million popular votes and a 2-to-1 margin in the electoral college.

Taft Administration

Taft faced political problems that Roosevelt had postponed, foremost, extremely high tariffs. Honoring Taft's pledge to cut rates, the House passed a bill providing numerous reductions. Protectionists in the Senate prepared to amend the bill and revise rates upward. But Senate Progressives attacked the tariff for benefiting special interests, trapping Taft between reformers who claimed to be preserving Roosevelt's antitrust campaign and protectionists who dominated the Republican Party. In the end, Senator Nelson Aldrich of Rhode Island restored many of the cuts, and Taft signed what became known as the Payne-Aldrich Tariff (1909). To Progressives, Taft failed to fill Roosevelt's shoes.

In reality Taft was as sympathetic to reform as Roosevelt was. He prosecuted more trusts than Roosevelt; expanded national forest reserves; signed the Mann-Elkins Act (1910), which bolstered regulatory powers of the ICC; and supported such labor reforms as shorter work hours and mine safety legislation. The Sixteenth

Amendment, which legalized the federal income tax, and the Seventeenth Amendment, which provided for direct election of U.S. senators, were initiated during Taft's presidency (and ratified in 1913). Like Roosevelt, Taft compromised with big business, but unlike Roosevelt, he lacked the ability to manipulate the public with spirited rhetoric. Roosevelt expanded presidential power; Taft, by contrast, believed in the strict restraint of law. He had been a successful lawyer and judge, and returned to the bench as chief justice of the United States between 1921 and 1930.

Candidates in 1912

In 1910, when Roosevelt returned from a trip to Africa, he found his party torn and tormented. Reformers formed the National Progressive Republican League and rallied behind Robert La Follette for president in 1912, though many hoped Roosevelt would run. Another wing of the party remained loyal to Taft. Disappointed by Taft, Roosevelt spoke out for the welfare of the people and stronger regulation of business. When La Follette became ill early in 1912, Roosevelt, proclaiming himself fit as a bull moose, sought the Republican presidential nomination.

Taft's supporters controlled the Republican convention and nominated him for a second term. In protest, Roosevelt's supporters formed a third party—the Progressive, or Bull Moose, Party—and nominated the former president. Meanwhile, Democrats took forty-six ballots to select their candidate, New Jersey's Progressive governor Woodrow Wilson. Socialists, by now a growing party, again nominated Eugene V. Debs.

New Nationalism Versus New Freedom

Central to Theodore Roosevelt's campaign was a scheme called the New Nationalism, which envisioned an era of national unity in which government would coordinate and regulate economic activity. Roosevelt asserted that he would establish regulatory commissions to protect citizens' interests and ensure wise use of economic power.

Wilson offered a more idealistic proposal, the New Freedom. He argued that concentrated economic power threatened individual liberty and that monopolies should be broken up to ensure a free marketplace. But he would not restore laissez faire. Like Roosevelt, Wilson would enhance government authority to protect and regulate. "Without the watchful . . . resolute interference of the government, there can be no fair play between individuals and such powerful institutions as the trust," he declared. Wilson stopped short, however, of advocating the cooperation between business and government inherent in Roosevelt's New Nationalism.

Roosevelt and Wilson stood closer together than their rhetoric implied. Both believed in individual freedom. Both supported equality of opportunity (chiefly for white males), conservation of natural resources, fair wages, and social betterment for all. Neither would hesitate to expand government activity through strong leadership and bureaucratic reform.

In the election, the popular vote was inconclusive. The victorious Wilson won just 42 percent, though he did capture 435 out of 531 electoral votes. Roosevelt received 27 percent of the popular vote. Taft polled 23 percent of the popular vote and only 8 electoral votes. Debs won 6 percent of the total but no electoral votes. Three-quarters of the electorate supported alternatives to Taft's view of restrained government.

WOODROW WILSON AND THE EXTENSION OF PROGRESSIVE REFORM

Woodrow Wilson

Born in Virginia in 1856 and raised in the South, Wilson was the son of a Presbyterian minister. He earned a B.A. degree at Princeton University, studied law at the University of Virginia, received a Ph.D. degree from Johns Hopkins University, and became a professor of history, jurisprudence, and political economy at Princeton University. Between 1885 and 1908, he published several respected books on American history and government.

Wilson was a superb orator who could inspire loyalty with religious imagery and eloquent expressions of American ideals. In 1902 he became president of Princeton and initiated curricular reforms and battles against aristocratic elements. But his racism kept him from admitting blacks to the college. In 1910 New Jersey's Democrats nominated Wilson for governor. Once elected, Wilson repudiated party bosses and promoted Progressive legislation. A poor administrator, he often lost his temper and was uncooperative, but his accomplishments nevertheless won him the Democratic presidential nomination in 1912.

Wilson's Policy on Business Regulation

As president, Wilson blended New Freedom competition with New Nationalism regulation, setting the direction of future federal economic policy. The corporate merger movement made restoration of open competition impossible. Hence, Wilson sought to prevent abuses by expanding government regulation. He supported congressional passage in 1914 of the Clayton Anti-Trust Act and a bill creating the Federal Trade Commission (FTC). The Clayton Act corrected deficiencies of the Sherman Anti-Trust Act of 1890 by outlawing such practices as price discrimination (lowering prices in some regions but not others) and interlocking directorates (management of two or more competing companies by the same executives). The act also aided labor by exempting unions from its anticombination provision, thereby making peaceful strikes, boycotts, and picketing less vulnerable to government interference. The FTC could investigate companies and issue cease-and-desist orders against unfair practices to protect consumers.

Wilson expanded banking regulation with the Federal Reserve Act (1913), which established the nation's first central banking system since 1836. To break the power of banking syndicates, like the power that J. P. Morgan's syndicate held over the money supply, the act created twelve district banks to hold reserves of member banks nationwide. The district banks, supervised by the Federal Reserve Board, would lend money to member banks at a low interest rate called the discount rate. By adjusting this rate (and thus the amount a bank could afford to borrow), district banks could increase or decrease the amount of money in circulation, enabling the Federal Reserve Board to loosen or tighten credit, thereby making interest rates fairer.

Tariff and Tax Reform

Wilson and Congress attempted to restore competition with the Underwood Tariff of 1913. By the 1910s, prices for some consumer goods had become unnaturally high because tariffs discouraged the importation of cheaper foreign goods. By reducing or eliminating certain tariff rates, the Underwood Tariff encouraged imports. To replace revenues lost because of tariff reductions, the act levied a graduated income tax on U.S. residents. Incomes under $4,000 were exempt; thus almost all factory workers and farmers escaped taxation. Individuals and corporations earning between $4,000 and $20,000 had to pay a 1 percent tax; thereafter rates rose gradually to a maximum of 6 percent on earnings over $500,000.

The outbreak of World War I (see Chapter 23) and the approaching 1916 presidential election prompted Wilson to support stronger reforms. He backed the Federal Farm Loan Act, which created twelve federally supported banks that could lend money at moderate interest to farmers who belonged to credit institutions—a watered-down version of the Populists' subtreasury plan proposed a generation earlier.

To forestall railroad strikes, Wilson in 1916 pushed passage of the Adamson Act, which mandated eight-hour workdays and time-and-a-half overtime pay for railroad laborers. He pleased Progressives by appointing Brandeis, the people's advocate, to the Supreme Court, though an anti-Semitic backlash almost blocked Senate approval of the Court's first Jewish justice. Wilson also backed laws regulating child labor and providing workers' compensation for federal employees who suffered work-related injuries or illness.

But Wilson never overcame his racism. Although in 1918 he tried to appoint W. E. B. Du Bois as an army officer to keep race relations calm (Du Bois, age fifty, failed the physical), Wilson fired several black federal officials. His administration also preserved racial separation in restrooms, restaurants, and government office buildings. When the pathbreaking but inflammatory film about the Civil War and Reconstruction, *The Birth of a Nation*, was released in 1915, Wilson allowed a showing at the White House.

Election of 1916

Republicans snubbed Theodore Roosevelt as their candidate in 1916, choosing Charles Evans Hughes, Supreme Court justice and former reform governor of New York. Aware of public anxiety over the world war raging in Europe since 1914, Wilson ran on a platform of neutrality and Progressivism, using the slogan "He Kept Us Out of War." The election was close. Wilson received 9.1 million votes to Hughes's 8.5 million and barely won in the electoral college, 277 to 254. The Socialist candidate drew only 600,000 votes, largely because Wilson's reforms won over some Socialists and because the ailing Eugene Debs was no longer the party's standard-bearer.

During Wilson's second term, U.S. involvement in World War I increased government regulation of the economy. Mobilization and war, he came to believe, required greater coordination of production and cooperation between the public and private sectors. The War Industries Board exemplified this cooperation: private businesses submitted to the board's control on condition that their profit motives would be satisfied. After the war, Wilson's administration dropped these measures, including farm price supports, guarantees of collective bargaining, and high taxes. This retreat from regulation, prompted in part by the election of a Republican Congress in 1918, stimulated a new era of business ascendancy in the 1920s.

Margaret Sanger, Planned Parenthood, and the Birth-Control Controversy

Some reforms of the Progressive era illustrate how earnest intentions to help can become tangled in divisive issues of morality. Such is the legacy of the birth-control advocate Margaret Sanger. In 1912 Sanger produced a column on sex education in the *New York Call* entitled "What Every Girl Should Know." Moralists accused her of writing obscene literature because she publicly discussed venereal disease and contraception. She counseled poor women on New York's Lower East Side about how to avoid the pain of frequent childbirth, miscarriage, and bungled abortion. In 1914 Sanger launched *The Woman Rebel*, a monthly newspaper advocating a woman's right to birth control. Indicted for distributing obscenity through the mails, she fled to England, where she gave speeches promoting family planning and enjoying sexuality without fear of pregnancy.

Returning to the United States, Sanger opened the country's first birth-control clinic in Brooklyn in 1916. She was arrested, but when a court exempted physicians from a law prohibiting distribution of contraceptive information, she set up a doctor-run clinic in 1923. Staffed by female doctors and social workers, the Birth Control Clinical Research Bureau became a model for other clinics. Sanger organized the American Birth Control League (1921) and tried to win support from medical and social reformers, even from the eugenics movement, for legalized birth control. After a falling out with some allies, she resigned from the American Birth Control League in 1928.

The movement continued, however, and in 1938 the American Birth Control League and the Birth Control Clinical Research Bureau merged to form the Birth Control Federation of America, renamed the Planned Parenthood Federation of America (PPFA) in 1942. The organization's name defined its mission to strengthen the family and stabilize society rather than focus on the right to voluntary motherhood. Throughout the 1940s, the PPFA emphasized family planning through making contraceptives more accessible. In 1970 it began receiving federal funds.

In the 1960s, the emergence of new feminist agitation for women's rights and rising concerns about overpopulation moved birth control and abortion into an arena of passionate controversy. Although the PPFA had initially dissociated itself from abortion, the debate between a woman's choice and a fetus's right to life drew the organization into the fray, especially after 1973, when the Supreme Court validated women's right to abortion in *Roe v. Wade*. PPFA fought legislative and court attempts to make abortions illegal and helped organize a women's march on Washington in 1989. Some Latino and African American groups attacked the PPFA's stance, charging that abortion was a kind of eugenics program meant to reduce births among nonwhite races.

Because of the PPFA's involvement in abortion politics, several of its clinics have been targets of picketing and even violence by those who believe abortion is immoral. The PPFA now operates nearly nine hundred health centers providing medical services and education. But birth control's legacy to a people and a nation includes disagreement over whose rights and whose morality should prevail.

Summary

By 1920 a quarter-century of reform had wrought momentous changes. Progressives established the principle of public intervention to ensure fairness, health, and safety. Concern over poverty and injustice reached new heights, but reformers could not sustain their efforts indefinitely. Although Progressive values lingered after World War I, a mass-consumer society refocused people's attention from reform to materialism.

Multiple and sometimes contradictory goals characterized the Progressive era because there was no single Progressive movement. Programs on the national level ranged from Roosevelt's faith in big government as a coordinator of big business to Wilson's promise to dissolve economic concentrations and legislate open competition. At state and local levels, reformers pursued causes as varied as neighborhood improvement, government reorganization, public ownership of utilities, and better working conditions. A new consciousness about identity confronted women and African Americans, and although women made some inroads into public life, both groups still found themselves in confined social roles.

Successes aside, the failure of many Progressive initiatives indicates the strength of the opposition, as well as weaknesses within the reform movements. As issues such as Americanization, eugenics, prohibition, education, and general moral uplift illustrate, social reform often merged into social control—attempts to impose white values on all of society. Courts asserted constitutional and liberty-of-contract doctrines in striking down key Progressive legislation, notably the federal law prohibiting child labor. Federal regulatory agencies rarely had enough resources for thorough investigations; they had to depend on information from the very companies they policed. In 1920, as in 1900, government remained under the influence of business.

Yet Progressive era reforms reshaped the national outlook. Trustbusting, however faulty, made industrialists more sensitive to public opinion. Progressive legislation equipped government with tools to protect consumers against price fixing and dangerous products. Social reformers relieved some ills of urban and industrial life. Although the questions they raised about American life remained unresolved, Progressives made the nation acutely aware of its principles and promises.

Chapter Review

THE VARIED PROGRESSIVE IMPULSE

How did Progressive reform cut across class lines?

The impulse to improve society at the turn of the twentieth century had variants in the working, middle, and wealthier classes. An emerging class of educated male and female professionals stood at the vanguard of Progressivism and sought to apply the techniques of professions such as law, engineering, medicine, social service, and teaching to end the abuse of power and inefficiency in business and government, and protect the welfare of all classes. They also believed they could unify disparate factions of society, particularly new immigrants, through education and Americanization programs. Wealthy businessmen and elite women also embraced humanitarian causes. Workers, too, pressed for reforms to improve safety and housing and to include workers' compensation for injuries on the job. There was even a religious component as Protestant ministers sought to counter the negative impact of competitive capitalism and industrialization with a message of Christian salvation known as the "Social Gospel."

GOVERNMENT AND LEGISLATIVE REFORM

According to Progressives, what was the government's role in improving society?

Unlike earlier generations of Americans who believed in a limited role for government, Progressives felt the government not only had an obligation to improve society but could protect people and families by restricting behavior. Progressives pushed officials to adopt regulations that would end labor abuses (notably, factory inspection laws), compensation for injured workers, minimum age and wage laws, child labor laws, and protective legislation regulating the hours women could work. Next, Progressives focused on ending vice, pushing for the passage of state laws and later a constitutional amendment (the Eighteenth Amendment, implemented in 1920) banning the manufacture and sale of alcohol—which they believed contributed to accidents, poverty, and poor productivity. Inspired by muckraking articles about gangs forcing women into prostitution (dubbed "white slavery"), Progressives called for government investigations and laws. Congress passed the Mann Act in 1910, prohibiting the interstate and international transportation of women for immoral purposes. By 1915 nearly every state outlawed brothels and solicitation of sex.

NEW IDEAS IN SOCIAL INSTITUTIONS

What was the impact of Progressive education reforms?

Increasing concerns about the social impact of industrialization, along with a penchant for scientific management and efficiency, drove Progressive approaches to education. Reformers such as John Dewey not only wanted to ensure that children were exposed to age appropriate materials, but they also focused on preparing children for the modern world by teaching them to use their ingenuity to solve real-life problems. College curricula shifted from its previous nearly exclusive focus on preparing primarily white men for a few professions such as medicine, religion, and law, to a focus on learning that kept pace with technological and social changes. Regarded as vital to a student's growth, athletics became a permanent feature. The number of colleges expanded, including all-black land grant colleges and women's colleges.

CHALLENGES TO RACIAL AND SEXUAL DISCRIMINATION

What strategies did women use in their quest for equality in the early twentieth century?

Women's organizations had long struggled over whether to focus on their shared humanity with men—their "samenesss"—or accentuate their unique female qualities—their "difference"—in pursuit of equality and new social roles for women. Calling themselves "the woman movement" before 1910, they played up women's special, even superior, traits as guardians of the family and morality. After that date, activists adopted the term *feminism,* emphasizing women's right to citizenship. Activist styles ranged from moderate to radical, but all saw the vote as a first and vital step to influencing the laws affecting them, be it improving women's working conditions or assuring their economic roles. Women's participation in the war effort also showed their ability and willingness to serve their country and made it impossible for legislators to continue to justify denying them the vote (which women finally received in 1920).

THEODORE ROOSEVELT AND THE REVIVAL OF THE PRESIDENCY

Theodore Roosevelt was known as a trustbuster, but was he?

Yes and no. As a Progressive, Roosevelt believed government should guide national affairs and economic development and determine when business was a positive or negative force. But he also thought there were times when business consolidation and mergers could aid economic progress and urged the Bureau of Consolidation to assist them in these efforts. At the same time, he was willing to step in when business consolidation led to corruption and market manipulation, as he did when he had the Justice Department use antitrust laws to prosecute railroad, meatpacking, and oil trusts, which he believed exploited the public. Roosevelt similarly supported regulatory legislation over interstate commerce and the quality of food and drugs. While Roosevelt supported the breakup of J. P. Morgan's Northern Securities Company, he did not break up the huge U.S. Steel Corp., and actually allowed it to acquire additional companies during the economic panic of 1907.

WOODROW WILSON AND THE EXTENSION OF PROGRESSIVE REFORM

How did participation in World War I alter Wilson's position on business?

In his first term as president, Wilson was disheartened by the corporate merger movement that seemed to weaken the prospects of fair business competition. To restore that, he increased government regulation of the business sector, supporting the Clayton Antitrust Act and the establishment of the Federal Trade Commission to ensure fair business practices and protect labor. He also established banking regulation with the Federal Reserve Act of 1913 and similarly supported tariff reform and farm loans. With war mobilization a priority in his second term, Wilson sought greater cooperation between the private and public sector. Businesses agreed to submit to the federal War Industry Board's directives in exchange for the promise of profits. After the war, Wilson retreated from the regulation that had been his pre-war policy, dropping farm supports, collective bargaining guarantees for labor, and high taxes, thereby inaugurating a new era of big business in the 1920s.

SUGGESTIONS FOR FURTHER READING

Francis L. Broderick, *Progressivism at Risk: Electing a President in 1912* (1989)

Nancy F. Cott, *The Grounding of Modern Feminism* (1987)

Steven J. Diner, *A Very Different Age: Americans of the Progressive Era* (1998)

Glenda Gilmore, *Who Were the Progressives?* (2002)

Hugh D. Hindman, *Child Labor: An American History* (2002)

Alice Kessler-Harris, *Out to Work: A History of Wage-Earning Women in the United States*, 20th anniversary ed. (2003)

Michael McGerr, *A Fierce Discontent: The Rise and Fall of the Progressive Movement in America, 1870–1920* (2003)

Patricia A. Schecter, *Ida B. Wells and American Reform, 1880–1930* (2001)

David Tyack, *Seeking Common Ground: Public Schools in a Diverse* (2003)

CHAPTER 22

The Quest for Empire

1865–1914

CHAPTER OUTLINE

Imperial Dreams

   LINKS TO THE WORLD:
   National Geographic

Ambitions and Strategies

Crises in the 1890s: Hawai'i, Venezuela, and Cuba

The Spanish-American War and the Debate over Empire

Asian Encounters: War in the Philippines, Diplomacy in China

TR's World

   LEGACY FOR A PEOPLE AND A NATION: Guantánamo Bay

Summary

"Foreign devil!" they shouted at Lottie Moon. The Southern Baptist missionary, half a world away from home, braced herself against the cries of the Chinese crowd she sought to convert to Christianity in the 1880s. She walked steadily and persistently through the hecklers, silently vowing to win their acceptance and their souls.

Born in 1840 in Virginia and educated at what is now Hollins College, Charlotte Diggs Moon volunteered in 1873 for woman's work in northern China. There she taught and proselytized, largely among women and children, until her death in 1912.

In the 1870s and 1880s, Lottie Moon (Mu Ladi or 幕拉第) made sometimes dangerous evangelizing trips to isolated Chinese hamlets. Curious peasant women pinched her, pulled on her skirts, purring, "How white her hand is!" They asked: "How old are you?" "Where do you get money to live on?" Speaking in Chinese, Lottie held a picture book about Jesus Christ, drawing attention to the foreign doctrine that she hoped would displace Confucianism, Buddhism, and Taoism.

In the 1890s, a storm of persecution against foreigners swept China, and missionaries became targets. One missionary conceded that, in believing in Jesus, girls and women alarmed men who worried that "disobedient wives and daughters" would no longer "worship the idols when told." In the Shaling village in early 1890, Lottie Moon's Christian converts were beaten. Fearing for her life, she left China for several months in 1900, during the violent Boxer Rebellion.

Lottie Moon and thousands of missionaries converted to Christianity only a small minority of Chinese people. Although she, like other missionaries, probably never shed the view that western religion and culture was superior, she felt affection for the Chinese. In letters and articles for a U.S. audience, she lobbied

This icon will direct you to interactive activities and study materials on A People And A Nation, Brief Edition
website: **www.cengage.com/history/norton/ peoplenationbrief8e**

Chronology

1861–69	Seward sets expansionist course.	**1899**	Treaty of Paris enlarges U.S. empire.
1867	United States acquires Alaska and Midway.		United Fruit Company is formed and becomes influential in Central America.
1876	Pro-U.S. Díaz begins thirty-four-year rule in Mexico.		Philippine insurrection breaks out, led by Emilio Aguinaldo.
1878	United States gains naval rights in Samoa.	**1901**	McKinley is assassinated; Theodore Roosevelt becomes president.
1885	Strong's *Our Country* celebrates Anglo-Saxon destiny of dominance.	**1903**	Panama grants canal rights to United States.
1887	United States gains naval rights to Pearl Harbor, Hawai'i.		Platt Amendment subjugates Cuba.
1890	Mahan publishes *The Influence of Sea Power upon History.*	**1904**	Roosevelt Corollary declares United States a hemispheric police power.
	McKinley Tariff hurts Hawaiian sugar exports.	**1905**	Portsmouth Conference ends Russo-Japanese War.
1893	Economic crisis leads to business failures and mass unemployment.	**1906**	San Francisco School Board segregates Asian schoolchildren.
	Pro-U.S. interests stage successful coup against Queen Lili'uokalani of Hawai'i.		United States invades Cuba to quell revolt.
1895	Cuban revolution against Spain begins.	**1907**	Great White Fleet makes world tour.
	Japan defeats China in war, annexes Korea and Formosa (Taiwan).	**1910**	Mexican revolution threatens U.S. interests.
1898	United States formally annexes Hawai'i.	**1914**	U.S. troops invade Mexico.
	U.S. battleship *Maine* blows up in Havana harbor.		World War I begins.
	United States defeats Spain in Spanish-American War.		Panama Canal opens.

to recruit Christian women to stir up "a mighty wave of enthusiasm for Woman's Work for Woman."

Like many Americans who went overseas in the late nineteenth and early twentieth centuries, Lottie Moon helped spread American culture abroad. Other peoples sometimes adopted and sometimes rejected American ways. American participants likewise were transformed. Lottie Moon, for example, strove to understand the Chinese and learn their language. She assumed their dress and abandoned such derogatory phrases as "heathen Chinese." She reminded less sensitive missionaries that the Chinese rightfully took pride in their ancient history.

Lottie Moon also changed—in her own words—from "a timid self-distrustful girl into a brave self-reliant woman." As she questioned the Chinese confinement of women, most conspicuous in arranged marriages, foot binding, and sexual segregation, she advanced women's rights. She understood that she could not convert Chinese women unless they had the freedom to listen to her appeals. She also challenged the male domination of America's religious missions. When the Southern Baptist Foreign Mission Board denied woman missionaries the right to vote in meetings, she resigned. The board soon reversed itself.

Decades later, critics labeled missionaries' activities as cultural imperialism, accusing the missionaries of subverting indigenous traditions and sparking cultural clashes. Defenders of missionary work have celebrated their efforts to break down cultural barriers. Either way, Lottie Moon's story illustrates how Americans in the late nineteenth century interacted with the world, how the categories domestic and foreign intersected, and how Americans expanded abroad not only to seek land, trade, investments, and strategic bases but also to promote American culture.

Between the Civil War and World War I, an expansionist United States joined the great world powers. Before the Civil War, Americans repeatedly extended the frontier: they bought and annexed territories, pushed Indians out of the path of white migration, seized California and other western areas from Mexico, and acquired southern parts of present-day Arizona and New Mexico from Mexico (the Gadsden Purchase). Americans also developed a lucrative foreign trade with most of the world and promoted American culture everywhere.

By the 1870s, most of Europe's powers were carving up Africa and large parts of Asia and Oceania for themselves. By 1900 they had conquered more than 10 million square miles and 150 million people. As the century turned, France, Russia, and Germany were spending heavily on modern steel navies, challenging an overextended Great Britain. In Asia, a rapidly modernizing Japan was expanding at the expense of China and Russia.

Engineering advances altered the world's political geography through the Suez Canal (1869), the British Trans-Indian railroad (1870), and the Russian Trans-Siberian Railway (1904), while steamships, machine guns, telegraphs, and malaria drugs facilitated the imperialists' task. Simultaneously, Europe's optimism in the 1850s and 1860s gave way to a pessimistic sense of impending warfare informed by notions of racial conflict and survival of the fittest.

Observant Americans argued that the United States risked being left behind if it failed to join the scramble for territory and markets. Republican senator Henry Cabot Lodge of Massachusetts argued that "civilization and the advancement of the [Anglo-Saxon] race" were at stake. Such thinking enticed Americans to reach beyond the continental United States for land, markets, cultural penetration, and power.

By 1900 the United States emerged as a great power with particular clout in Latin America, especially as Spain declined and Britain disengaged from the Western Hemisphere. In the Pacific, the new U.S. empire included Hawai'i, American Samoa, and the Philippines. In the decade that followed, President Theodore Roosevelt would seek to consolidate this power.

Most Americans applauded expansionism—the outward movement of goods, ships, dollars, people, and ideas. But many became uneasy whenever expansionism gave way to imperialism—the imposition of control over other peoples, undermining their sovereignty. Abroad, native nationalists, commercial competitors, and other imperial nations tried to block the spread of U.S. influence.

- **What accounts for the increased importance of foreign policy concerns in American politics in the closing years of the nineteenth century?**
- **What key arguments were made by American anti-imperialists?**
- **How did late-nineteenth-century imperialism transform the United States?**

IMPERIAL DREAMS

Foreign policy assumed a new importance for Americans at the end of the nineteenth century. Internal matters such as industrialization, the construction of the railroads, and the settlement of the West still preoccupied many, but political and business leaders now began to advocate an activist approach to world affairs. Their motives were complex, but all emphasized the supposed benefits to the country's domestic health.

Leaders who guided America's expansionist foreign relations also guided the economic development of the machine age, forged the transcontinental railroad, built America's bustling cities and giant corporations, and shaped a mass culture. They unabashedly believed the United States was an exceptional nation, different from and superior to others because of its Anglo-Saxon heritage and its God-favored and prosperous history.

Along with exceptionalism, American leaders were influenced by nationalism, capitalism, Social Darwinism, and a paternalistic attitude toward foreigners. "They are children and we are men in these deep matters of government," future president Woodrow Wilson announced in 1898. His words reveal the gender and age bias of American attitudes. Where these attitudes intersected with foreign cultures, the result was a mix of adoption, imitation, and rejection.

Foreign Policy Elite

Foreign policy is usually dominated by what scholars have labeled the foreign policy elite—opinion leaders in politics, journalism, business, agriculture, religion, education, and the military. Better read and traveled than most Americans and more politically active in the post–Civil War era, they believed that U.S. prosperity and security depended on the exertion of U.S. influence abroad. Increasingly in the late nineteenth century, the expansionist-minded elite urged formal and informal imperialism. They often met in Washington, D.C., at the homes of the historian Henry Adams and the writer and diplomat John Hay (who became secretary of state in 1898) or at the Metropolitan Club. They talked about building a bigger navy and digging a canal across Panama, Central America, or Mexico; establishing colonies; and selling surpluses abroad. Among them was Theodore Roosevelt, appointed assistant secretary of the navy in 1897; Senator Henry Cabot Lodge, who joined the Foreign Relations Committee in 1896; and the corporate lawyer Elihu Root, who later served as secretary of war and secretary of state.

These American leaders believed that selling, buying, and investing in foreign marketplaces were important to the United States. Why? One reason was profits from foreign sales. Another was the belief that foreign markets might offset American overproduction and unemployment since the nation's farms and factories produced more than Americans could consume. This was especially true during the depression of the 1890s. Economic ties also enabled Americans to exert political influence abroad and helped spread the American way of life, especially capitalism.

Foreign Trade Expansion

Foreign trade figured prominently in the United States' tremendous economic growth after the Civil War. Foreign commerce stimulated the building of a larger navy, the

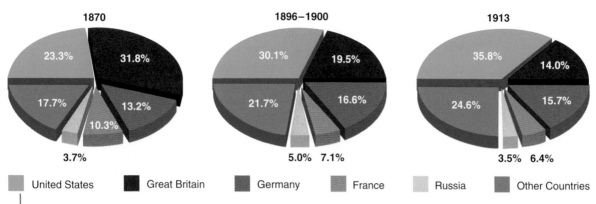

Figure 22.1   The Rise of U.S. Economic Power in the World

These pie charts showing percentage shares of world manufacturing production for the major nations of the world demonstrate that the United States came to surpass Great Britain in this significant economic measurement of power.   (*Source:* League of Nations data presented in Aaron L. Friedberg, *The Weary Titan: Britain and the Experience of Relative Decline, 1895–1905* [Princeton, NJ: Princeton University Press, 1988], 26.)

professionalization of the foreign service, calls for more colonies, and a more interventionist foreign policy. In 1865 U.S. exports totaled $234 million; by 1900 they reached $1.5 billion (see Figure 22.1). By 1914, exports hit $2.5 billion. In 1874 the United States reversed its historically unfavorable balance of trade (importing more than it exported) and began to enjoy a long-term favorable balance. Most of America's products went to Britain, continental Europe, and Canada, but increasing amounts flowed to new markets in Latin America and Asia. Meanwhile, American investments abroad reached $3.5 billion by 1914, placing the United States among the top four investor countries.

Agricultural goods accounted for about three-fourths of total exports in 1870 and about two-thirds in 1900, with grain, cotton, meat, and dairy products topping the list. Farmers' livelihoods thus became tied to world-market conditions and foreign wars. Wisconsin cheesemakers shipped to Britain; the Swift and Armour meat companies exported refrigerated beef to Europe.

In 1913, manufactured goods led U.S. exports for the first time (see Figure 22.1). Much of America's steel, copper, and petroleum were sold abroad, making many workers in those industries dependent on American exports.

Race Thinking and the Male Ethos

In expanding U.S. influence overseas, officials championed a nationalism based on notions of American supremacy. Some found justification for expansionism in racist theories then permeating western thought. For decades, the western scientific establishment classified humankind by race, and students of physical anthropology drew on phrenology and physiognomy—the analysis of skull size and facial features—to produce a hierarchy of superior and inferior races. One French researcher claimed that blacks represented a female race and "like the woman, the black is deprived of political and scientific intelligence."

The language of U.S. leaders was also weighted with words like *manliness* and *weakling.* Theodore Roosevelt viewed people of color (or "darkeys," as he called them) as effeminate weaklings who were unable to govern themselves and could not cope with world politics. Americans debased Latin Americans by referring to them as half-breeds needing supervision or distressed damsels begging for manly rescue. The gendered imagery prevalent in U.S. foreign relations joined racial thinking to place women, people of color, and nations weaker than the United States low in the hierarchy of power and, hence, in a dependent status justifying U.S. dominance.

"As America goes, so goes the world," declared Reverend Josiah Strong, author of the influential *Our Country* (1885), which celebrated an Anglo-Saxon race destined to lead others. Social Darwinists saw Americans as a superior people certain to overcome competition. Secretary of State Thomas F. Bayard (1885–1889) applauded the "overflow of our population and capital" into Mexico to "saturate those regions with Americanism."

Racial thinking—popularized in magazine photos and cartoons, world's fairs, postcards, school textbooks, museums, and political orations—reinforced notions of American greatness, influenced the way U.S. leaders dealt with other peoples, and obviated the need to think about the subtle textures of other societies. *National Geographic,* which began publication in 1888, pictorially chronicled America's new overseas involvements in Asia and the Pacific, regularly featuring images of exotic, premodern peoples who had not become western. Fairs also put so-called uncivilized people of color on display in the freak or midway section. Dog-eating Filipinos aroused comment at the 1904 St. Louis World's Fair. Such racism downgraded diplomacy and justified domination and war.

Similar thinking permeated attitudes toward immigrants, whose entry into the United States was first restricted in these years. Although the Burlingame Treaty (1868) provided for free immigration between the United States and China, riots against Chinese immigrants continuously erupted in the American West. An 1880 treaty permitted Congress to suspend Chinese immigration to the United States. Tensions continued: in 1885, white coal miners and railway workers in Rock Springs, Wyoming, massacred at least twenty-five Chinese.

In 1906 the San Francisco School Board ordered Chinese, Koreans, and Japanese segregated in special schools. Tokyo protested, and President Roosevelt quieted the crisis by striking a gentleman's agreement with Tokyo restricting Japanese immigration. Relations with Tokyo worsened again in 1913 when the California legislature denied Japanese residents the right to own property.

The "Civilizing" Impulse

Expansionists believed that empire benefited Americans and those who came under their control. When the United States intervened in weaker states, Americans claimed they were extending liberty and prosperity to less fortunate people. William Howard Taft, as civil governor of the Philippines (1901–1904), described the United States' mission in its new colony as lifting Filipinos up "to a point of civilization" that will make them "call the name of the United States blessed." Later, Taft said about the Chinese that "the more civilized they become . . . the wealthier they become, and the better market they become for us."

Missionaries dispatched to Africa and Asia, like Lottie Moon, helped spur the transfer of American culture and power abroad—"the peaceful conquest of the world,"

National Geographic

In early 1888, thirty-three members of Washington, D.C.'s elite Cosmos Club considered "organizing a society for the increase and diffusion of geographical knowledge." The result was the National Geographic Society, the world's largest nonprofit scientific and educational institution.

At the heart of the enterprise was *National Geographic Magazine*, which debuted in October 1888. Early issues were brief and visually bland, and sales lagged. When Alexander Graham Bell became the society's president in 1898, he shifted emphasis from newsstand sales to society membership, reasoning correctly that the notion of a distinguished fellowship would draw members. He also appointed a talented new editor, Gilbert H. Grosvenor, age twenty-three, who commissioned general interest articles and filled eleven pages with photographs.

Early photos showed people posed in their native costumes, displayed as anthropological specimens. By 1908 pictures occupied 50 percent of the magazine. In 1910 the first color photographs appeared in a twenty-four-page spread on Korea and China—then, the largest collection of color photographs published in a single magazine. *National Geographic*'s other photographic firsts included the first natural-color photos of Arctic life, the stratosphere, and the undersea world.

The society also sponsored expeditions, such as Robert Peary's and Matthew Henson's 1909 journey to the North Pole and, later, Jacques Cousteau's oceanic explorations and Jane Goodall's observations of wild chimpanzees. These adventures then appeared in the magazine's pages. By the end of Grosvenor's tenure as editor, in 1954, circulation topped 2 million.

Less admirably, Grosvenor's editors pressured photographers for pictures of pretty girls. One photographer recalled, "Hundreds of bare-breasted women, all from poorer countries, were published at a time of booming subscription rates." Editors also developed a well-earned reputation for presenting a rosy world-view. An article about Berlin published before the start of World War II, for example, contained no criticism of the Nazi regime and no mention of its persecution of Jews. Recently, the magazine has featured more newsworthy topics—AIDS, stem cell research, Hurricane Katrina, global warming—but in measured tones.

Throughout, the society expanded its reach, producing books, atlases, globes, and television documentaries. Targeting overseas readers, the society in 1995 launched a Japanese-language edition and later twenty-five other foreign editions. *National Geographic*, after a century linking Americans to faraway places, now connected readers around the globe to the United States.

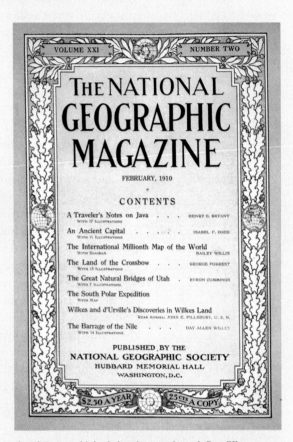

National Geographic had already gone through five different cover formats when Robert Weir Crouch, an English-born Canadian decorative artist, came up with a design that cemented the magazine's visual identity. Singular and immediately recognizable, the oak-and-laurel frame on the cover of the February 1910 issue would remain largely unchanged for nearly half a century, though the buff-colored border would be replaced with a golden one. Even today, the gold border and the crown of laurels remain.

(National Geographic Society Image Collection)

as Reverend Frederick Gates put it. In 1915, 10,000 American missionaries worked overseas. In China by 1915, more than 2,500 mostly female American Protestant missionaries taught, preached the gospel, and administered medical care.

AMBITIONS AND STRATEGIES

The U.S. empire grew gradually, as American leaders defined guiding principles and built institutions to support overseas ambitions. William H. Seward, one of its chief architects, argued for extension of the American frontier as a senator from New York (1849–1861) and secretary of state (1861–1869). Seward envisioned a large U.S. empire encompassing Canada, the Caribbean, Cuba, Central America, Mexico, Hawai'i, Iceland, Greenland, and the Pacific islands. This empire would result from a natural process of gravitation toward the United States. Commerce would hurry the process, as would a canal across Central America, a transcontinental American railroad, and a telegraph system to speed communications.

Seward's Quest for Empire

Most of Seward's grandiose plans did not reach fruition in his lifetime. In 1867, his efforts for a treaty with Denmark to buy the Danish West Indies (Virgin Islands), was scuttled by Senate foes and a hurricane that wrecked St. Thomas. The Virgin Islanders, who voted for annexation, would wait until 1917 for official U.S. status. Seward's scheme with unscrupulous Dominican Republic leaders to gain a Caribbean naval base at Samaná Bay also failed. The corruption surrounding this deal foiled President Ulysses S. Grant's initiative in 1870 to buy the island nation.

Anti-imperialism blocked Seward. Senator Carl Schurz and E. L. Godkin, editor of the magazine *The Nation,* argued that creating a showcase of democracy and prosperity on unsettled land at home would best persuade other peoples to adopt American ways. Some anti-imperialists, sharing the era's racism, opposed the annexation of territory populated by dark-skinned people.

Seward enjoyed some successes. In 1866, citing the Monroe Doctrine, he sent troops to the Mexico border and demanded that France abandon its puppet regime there. Also facing angry Mexican nationalists, Napoleon III abandoned the Maximilian monarchy that he forcibly installed three years earlier. In 1867 Seward paid Russia $7.2 million for the 591,000 square miles of Alaska—land twice the size of Texas. That same year, Seward claimed the Midway Islands (two small islands and a coral atoll northwest of Hawai'i).

International Communications

In 1866, through the efforts of financier Cyrus Field, an underwater transatlantic cable linked European and American telegraph networks. Backed by J. P. Morgan, the communications pioneer James A. Scrymser strung telegraph lines to Latin America, entering Chile in 1890. In 1903 a submarine cable spanned the Pacific to the Philippines; three years later, it reached Japan and China. Wire telegraphy—like radio (wireless telegraphy) later—shrank the globe. Nellie Bly, a reporter for the *New York World,* accented the impact of the new technology in 1890 when she completed a well-publicized trip around the world in seventy-two days. Drawn closer through improved communications and transportation, nations found that faraway events had greater impact on their prosperity and security.

Increasingly, American diplomats negotiated with their European counterparts as equals, signaling the United States' arrival on the international stage. Seward's successor, Hamilton Fish (1869–1887), for example, achieved a diplomatic victory in resolving the knotty problem of the *Alabama* claims. Great Britain built the ship and other vessels for the Confederacy during the Civil War to prey on Union shipping. Senator Charles Sumner demanded that Britain pay $2 billion in damages or cede Canada to the United States. But in 1871 Fish negotiated the Washington Treaty, whereby the British apologized and agreed to the creation of a tribunal which later awarded the United States $15.5 million.

Washington officials also confronted European powers over Samoa, South Pacific islands 4,000 miles from San Francisco on the trade route to Australia. In 1878 the United States gained the exclusive right to a coaling station at Samoa's coveted port of Pago Pago. Eyeing the same prize, Britain and Germany began cultivating ties with Samoan leaders. Tensions grew, and war seemed possible. Britain, Germany, and the United States met in Berlin in 1889 and, without consulting the Samoans, devised a three-part protectorate that limited Samoa's independence. Ten years later, the three powers partitioned Samoa: the United States received Pago Pago through annexation of part of the islands (now called American Samoa), Germany took what is today independent Western Samoa, and Britain obtained the Gilbert Islands and Solomon Islands.

Alfred T. Mahan and Navalism Calling attention to the naval buildup by European powers, notably Germany, U.S. expansionists argued for a bigger, modernized navy, adding the "blue water" command of the seas to its traditional role of "brown water" coastline defense. Captain Alfred Thayer Mahan, a popularizer of this New Navy, argued that because foreign trade was essential, the nation required an efficient navy to protect its shipping; in turn, a navy required colonies for bases. Mahan's ideas were published as *The Influence of Sea Power upon History* (1890). Theodore Roosevelt and Henry Cabot Lodge consulted Mahan, sharing his belief in the links between trade, navy, and colonies and his alarm over Germany's aggressive military spirit.

Moving toward naval modernization, Congress in 1883 authorized construction of the first steel-hulled warships. American factories produced steam engines, high-velocity shells, powerful guns, and precision instruments. The navy shifted from sail power to steam and from wood construction to steel. New Navy ships, such as the *Maine, Oregon,* and *Boston,* earned the United States naval prominence.

CRISES IN THE 1890S: HAWAI'I, VENEZUELA, AND CUBA

In the depression-plagued 1890s, crises in Hawai'i and Cuba—and the belief that the frontier at home had closed—reinforced the expansionist argument. In 1893 the historian Frederick Jackson Turner postulated that the ever-expanding continental frontier, which shaped the American character, was gone. He did not say that a new frontier had to be found overseas, but he did claim that "American energy will continually demand a wider field for its exercise."

Annexation of Hawai'i

Hawai'i, the Pacific Ocean archipelago of eight major islands located 2,000 miles from the U.S. West Coast, emerged as America's new frontier. The Hawaiian Islands had long commanded American attention—commercial, missionary religious, naval, and diplomatic. By 1881 Secretary of State James Blaine already declared the Hawaiian Islands "essentially a part of the American system." By 1890 Americans owned about three-quarters of Hawai'i's wealth and subordinated its economy to that of the United States through sugar exports that entered the U.S. marketplace duty-free.

In Hawai'i's multiracial society, Chinese and Japanese nationals far outnumbered Americans, who represented a mere 2.1 percent of the population. Prominent Americans on the islands organized secret clubs and military units to contest the royal government. In 1887 they forced the king to accept a constitution that allowed foreigners to vote and shifted decision making from the monarchy to the legislature. The same year, Hawai'i granted the United States naval rights to Pearl Harbor. Many native Hawaiians believed that the *haole* ("foreigners")—especially Americans—were taking their country from them.

The native government was further undermined when the McKinley Tariff of 1890 eliminated the duty-free status of Hawaiian sugar exports in the United States. Suffering declining sugar prices and profits, the American island elite pressed for annexation by the United States, thereby classifying their sugar as domestic. When Princess Lili'uokalani assumed the throne in 1891, she sought to roll back the political power of the *haole*. The next year, the white oligarchy formed the subversive Annexation Club.

The annexationists struck in January 1893 in collusion with John L. Stevens, America's chief diplomat in Hawai'i, who dispatched troops from the USS *Boston* to occupy Honolulu. The queen, arrested and confined, surrendered. Rather than yield to the new provisional regime, headed by Sanford B. Dole, son of missionaries and a prominent attorney, she relinquished authority to the U.S. government. President Benjamin Harrison hurriedly sent an annexation treaty to the Senate.

Sensing foul play, incoming President Grover Cleveland ordered an investigation, which confirmed a conspiracy and noted that most Hawaiians opposed annexation. But when Hawai'i proved a strategic and commercial way station to Asia and the Philippines during the Spanish-American War, President William McKinley maneuvered annexation through Congress on July 7, 1898. Under the Organic Act of June 1900, the people of Hawai'i became U.S. citizens. Statehood came in 1959.

Venezuelan Boundary Dispute

The Venezuelan crisis of 1895 also saw the United States in an expansive mood. For decades Venezuela and Great Britain had quarreled over the border between Venezuela and British Guiana, a territory containing rich gold deposits and a commercial gateway to northern South America via the Orinoco River. Venezuela sought U.S. help, and in July 1895, Secretary of State Richard Olney brashly lectured the British that the Monroe Doctrine prohibited European powers from denying self-government to nations in the Western Hemisphere. With almost no Venezuelan input, in 1896 an Anglo-American arbitration board divided the disputed territory between Britain and Venezuela. Thus the United States displayed a typical imperialist trait: disregard for the rights of small nations.

In 1895 Cuba was the site of another crisis. From 1868 to 1878 the Cubans battled Spain for their independence, winning only the end of slavery. While the Cuban economy suffered, repressive Spanish rule continued. Insurgents committed to *Cuba libre* waited for another chance, and José Martí, one of the heroes of Cuban history, collected money, arms, and men in the United States.

Revolution in Cuba

Cuban and U.S. culture intersected as Cubans settled in Baltimore, New York, Boston, and Philadelphia. Prominent Cubans on the island sent their children to schools in the United States. When Cuban expatriates returned home, many spoke English, had American names, played baseball, and jettisoned Catholicism for Protestant denominations.

The Cuban and U.S. economies were also intertwined. American investments of $50 million, mostly in sugar, dominated the island. Over 90 percent of Cuba's sugar was exported to the United States, and most island imports came from the United States. Havana's famed cigar factories relocated to Key West and Tampa to evade U.S. tariff laws. Martí, however, feared that "economic union means political union," for "the nation that buys, commands" and "the nation that sells, serves."

Martí's fears of a conquering U.S. policy were prophetic. In 1894 the Wilson-Gorman Tariff imposed a duty on Cuban sugar. The Cuban economy, highly dependent on exports, plunged into crisis, hastening the island's revolution against Spain and its further incorporation into the American system.

From American soil, Martí launched a revolution against Spain in 1895. Rebels burned sugar-cane fields and razed mills. U.S. investments evaporated, and Cuban-American trade dwindled. To separate insurgents from supporters, Spanish general Valeriano Weyler instituted a policy of reconcentration. Some 300,000 Cubans were herded into fortified towns and camps, where starvation and disease caused tens of thousands of deaths. As reports of atrocity and destruction became headline news in the United States, Americans sympathized with the insurrectionists. In late 1897, a new government in Madrid modified reconcentration and promised some autonomy for Cuba, but the insurgents continued to gain ground.

Sinking of the *Maine*

President William McKinley took office as an imperialist who advocated foreign bases for the New Navy, the export of surplus production, and U.S. supremacy in the Western Hemisphere. Vexed by Cuba's turmoil, he explored purchasing Cuba from Spain for $300 million. In January 1898, when antireform pro-Spanish loyalists and army rioted in Havana, Washington ordered the battleship *Maine* to Havana harbor to demonstrate U.S. concern and to protect American citizens.

On February 15 an explosion ripped the *Maine*, killing 266 of 354 American officers and crew. A week earlier, William Randolph Hearst's inflammatory *New York Journal* published a stolen private letter written by the Spanish minister in Washington, Enrique Dupuy de Lôme, belittling McKinley and suggesting that Spain would fight on. Congress complied unanimously with McKinley's request for $50 million in

On July 1, 1898, U.S. troops stormed Spanish positions on San Juan Hill near Santiago, Cuba. Both sides suffered heavy casualties. A *Harper's* magazine correspondent reported a "ghastly" scene of hundreds killed and thousands wounded. The American painter William Glackens (1870–1938) put to canvas what he saw. Because Santiago surrendered on July 17, propelling the United States to victory in the war, and because the Rough Rider Theodore Roosevelt fought at San Juan Hill and later gave a self-congratulatory account of the experience, the human toll has often gone unnoticed.   (Wadsworth Atheneum Museum of Art, Hartford, Connecticut. Gift of Henry Schnakenberg)

defense funds. Vengeful Americans blamed Spain. (Later, official and unofficial studies attributed the sinking to an accidental internal explosion.)

Mckinley's Ultimatum and War Decision

Though reluctant to go to war, McKinley sent Spain an ultimatum: accept an armistice, end reconcentration, and designate McKinley as arbiter. Madrid made concessions. It abolished reconcentration and rejected, then accepted, an armistice. The president would no longer tolerate chronic disorder 90 miles off the U.S. coast. On April 11, McKinley asked Congress for authorization to use force "to secure a full and final termination of hostilities between . . . Spain and . . . Cuba, and to secure in the island the establishment of a stable government, capable of maintaining order."

McKinley listed the reasons for war: the "cause of humanity"; the protection of American life and property; the "very serious injury to the commerce, trade, and business of our people"; and, referring to the destruction of the *Maine,* the "constant menace to our peace." On April 19, Congress declared Cuba free and independent and directed the president to use force to remove Spanish authority. The legislators also passed the Teller Amendment, which disclaimed U.S. intention to annex Cuba or control the island except to ensure its "pacification." McKinley blocked a congressional amendment to recognize the rebel government, arguing they were not ready for self-government.

THE SPANISH-AMERICAN WAR AND THE DEBATE OVER EMPIRE

By the time the Spanish concessions were on the table, prospects for compromise appeared dim. Cuban insurgents wanted full independence, and no Spanish government could have given up and remained in office. Nor did the United States welcome a truly independent Cuban government that might attempt to reduce U.S. interests.

Motives for War

McKinley's April message expressed a humanitarian impulse to stop the bloodletting and a concern for commerce and property. Republican politicians wanted the Cuba question solved to secure their party's victory in the upcoming congressional elections. Many businesspeople and farmers believed that ejecting Spain would open new markets for surplus production.

Imperialists saw the war as an opportunity to fulfill expansionist dreams, while conservatives, alarmed by Populism and labor strikes, welcomed war as a national unifier. One senator commented that "internal discord" was disappearing in the "fervent heat of patriotism." Theodore Roosevelt and others too young to remember the Civil War looked on war as adventure.

More than 263,000 regulars and volunteers served in the army, and another 25,000 in the navy during the war. Most, however, never left the United States. The typical volunteer was young (early twenties), white, unmarried, native-born, and working class. Deaths numbered 5,462, mostly from a typhoid epidemic in Tennessee, Virginia, and Florida. Only 379 died in combat. About 10,000 African American troops in segregated regiments found no relief from racism, even though black troops were central to the victorious battle for Santiago de Cuba. For all, food, sanitary conditions, and medical care were bad. Still, Roosevelt could hardly contain himself. Although Roosevelt's Rough Riders, a motley unit of Ivy Leaguers and cowboys, proved undisciplined and ineffective, Roosevelt's self-serving publicity efforts ensured they received good press.

Dewey in the Philippines

The first war news came from faraway Asia, from the Spanish colony of the Philippine Islands, where Filipinos were also seeking independence. On May 1, 1898, Commodore George Dewey's New Navy ship *Olympia* led an American squadron into Manila Bay and wrecked the Spanish fleet. Dewey received orders from Washington to attack the islands if war broke out. Manila was a choice harbor, and the Philippines sat en route to China's potentially huge market.

Facing Americans and rebels in Cuba and the Philippines, Spanish resistance collapsed rapidly. U.S. ships blockaded Cuban ports and insurgents cut off supplies from the countryside, causing starvation and illness for Spanish soldiers. American troops landed near Santiago de Cuba on June 22 and laid siege to the city. On July 3, U.S. warships sank the Spanish Caribbean squadron in Santiago harbor. American forces then assaulted the Spanish colony of Puerto Rico, winning another Caribbean naval base and pushing Madrid to defeat.

Treaty of Paris

On August 12, 1898, Spain and the United States signed an armistice ending the war, and in December they agreed on peace terms: independence for Cuba and cession of the Philippines, Puerto Rico, and the Pacific island of Guam to the United States for $20 million. The U.S. empire now stretched deep into Asia, and the annexation of Wake Island (1898), Hawai'i (1898), and Samoa (1899) gave American traders, missionaries, and naval promoters other steppingstones to China.

During the war, the *Washington Post* detected that "The taste of empire is in the mouth of the people." But anti-imperialists such as the author Mark Twain, Nebraska politician William Jennings Bryan, reformer Jane Addams, and industrialist Andrew Carnegie argued against annexation of the Philippines. Their concern that a war to free Cuba had led to empire, stimulated debate over American foreign policy.

Anti-Imperialist Arguments

Imperial control could be imposed either formally (by military occupation, annexation, or colonialism) or informally (by economic domination, political manipulation, or the threat of intervention). Anti-imperialist ire focused mostly on formal imperial control. Some critics cited the Declaration of Independence and the Constitution, arguing that the conquest of people against their will violated the right of self-determination.

Other anti-imperialists feared that the American character was being corrupted by imperialist zeal. Jane Addams, seeing children playing war games on Chicago streets, noted that they were not freeing Cubans but slaying Spaniards. Hoping to build a distinct foreign policy constituency from women's organizations, prominent women championed peace and an end to imperial conquest.

Some anti-imperialists protested that the United States was practicing a double standard—"offering liberty to the Cubans with one hand, cramming liberty down the throats of the Filipinos with the other, but with both feet planted upon the neck of the negro," as an African American politician from Massachusetts put it. Still other anti-imperialists warned that annexing people of color would undermine Anglo-Saxon purity and supremacy at home.

For Samuel Gompers and other anti-imperialist labor leaders, the issue was jobs. Might not the new colonials be imported as cheap contract labor to drive down American wages? Would not exploitation of the weak abroad become contagious and lead to further exploitation at home? The anti-imperialists, however, never launched an effective campaign. Although they organized the Anti-Imperialist League in November 1898, they differed so profoundly on domestic issues that they found it difficult to speak with one voice on a foreign question.

Imperialist Arguments

The imperialists appealed to patriotism, destiny, and commerce. They envisioned American merchant ships plying the waters to boundless Asian markets, naval vessels protecting America's Pacific interests, and missionaries uplifting inferior peoples. It was America's duty, they insisted, quoting a then-popular Rudyard Kipling poem, to "take up the white man's burden." Furthermore, Filipino insurgents were beginning to resist U.S. rule, and it seemed cowardly to pull out under fire, especially with Germany and Japan ready to seize the islands.

In February 1899, by a 57-to-27 vote , the Senate passed the Treaty of Paris, ending the war with Spain. Most Republicans voted yes and most Democrats no. An amendment promising independence once the Filipinos formed a stable government lost by only the tie-breaking ballot of the vice president.

ASIAN ENCOUNTERS: WAR IN THE PHILIPPINES, DIPLOMACY IN CHINA

The Philippine crisis was far from over. Emilio Aguinaldo, the Philippine nationalist leader who battled the Spanish for years, believed that American officials promised independence for his country. But after the victory, U.S. officers ordered Aguinaldo out of Manila. In early 1899, he proclaimed an independent Philippine Republic and took up arms.

Philippine Insurrection and Pacification
Both sides fought viciously; American soldiers burned villages and tortured captives, while Filipino forces staged brutal hit-and-run guerilla ambushes. U.S. troops introduced a variant of the Spanish reconcentration policy; in the province of Batangas, for instance, U.S. troops forced residents to live in designated zones to separate insurgents from local supporters. Poor sanitation, starvation, and malaria and cholera killed thousands. Outside secure areas, Americans destroyed food supplies to starve out the rebels. At least one-quarter of the population of Batangas died or fled.

Before the Philippine insurrection was suppressed in 1902, some 20,000 Filipinos died in combat, and 600,000 succumbed to starvation and disease. More than 4,000 Americans lay dead. Resistance to U.S. rule, however, continued. When the fiercely independent, often violent Muslim Filipinos of Moro Province refused to knuckle under, the U.S. military threatened extermination. In 1906, 600 Moros, including women and children, were slaughtered at the Battle of Bud Dajo.

U.S. officials soon tried to Americanize the Philippines, instituting a new education system with English as the main language. The architect Daniel Burnham, leader of the City Beautiful movement, planned modern Manila. The Philippine economy grew as an American satellite, and a sedition act sent U.S. critics to prison. In 1916 the Jones Act vaguely promised independence once the Philippines established a "stable government." But the United States did not end its rule until 1946.

China and the Open Door Policy
In China, McKinley successfully focused on a policy emphasizing negotiation. Outsiders had pecked away at China since the 1840s. Taking advantage of the Qing (Manchu) dynasty's weakness, the major imperial powers carved out spheres of influence (regions over which they claimed political control and exclusive commercial privileges): Germany in Shandong, Russia in Manchuria, France in Yunnan and Hainan, and Britain in Kowloon and Hong Kong. Then, in 1895, Japan claimed victory over China in a short war and assumed control of Formosa and Korea and parts of China proper (see Map 22.1). American religious and business leaders petitioned Washington to halt the dismemberment of China before they were closed out.

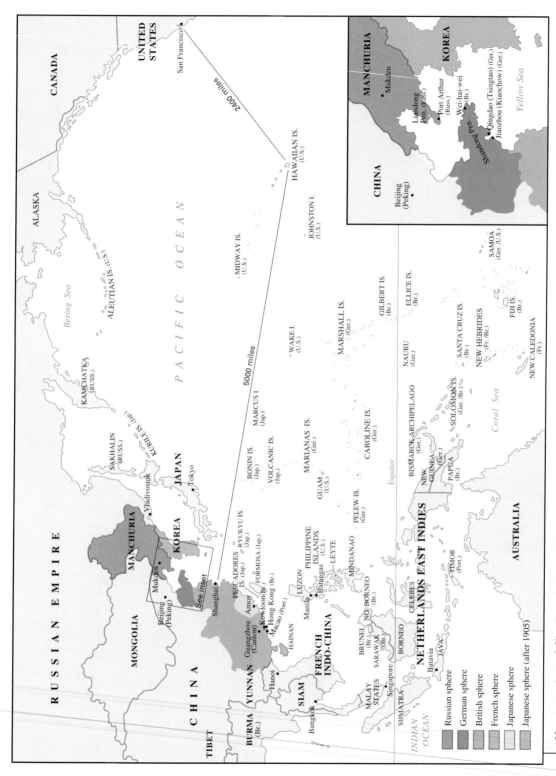

Map 22.1   Imperialism in Asia: Turn of the Century

China and the Pacific region had become imperialist hunting grounds by the turn of the century. The European powers and Japan controlled more areas than the United States, which nonetheless participated in the imperial race by annexing the Philippines, Wake, Guam, Hawai'i, and Samoa; announcing the Open Door policy; and expanding trade. As the spheres of influence in China demonstrate, that besieged nation succumbed to outsiders despite the Open Door policy.

Secretary of State John Hay knew that missionaries like Lottie Moon had become targets of Chinese nationalist anger and that American oil and textile companies had been disappointed with their investments there. Thus, in September 1899, Hay sent nations with spheres of influence in China a note seeking their respect for the principle of equal trade opportunity—an Open Door. The recipients sent evasive replies, privately complaining that the United States was seeking, for free, the trade rights in China that they had gained at considerable cost.

The next year, the Boxers, a Chinese secret society, (so named in the western press because some members were martial artists) sought to expel foreigners. They rioted, killing many outsiders and laying siege to the foreign legations in Beijing. The United States joined the other imperial powers in sending troops. Hay also sent a second Open Door note instructing other nations to preserve China's territorial integrity and honor "equal and impartial trade." China continued for years to be fertile soil for foreign exploitation, especially by the Japanese.

The Open Door policy became a cornerstone of U.S. diplomacy. While the United States had long opposed barriers to international commerce, after 1900, when the U.S. emerged emerge as the premier world trader, the Open Door policy became an instrument first to pry open markets and then to dominate them. The Open Door also developed as an ideology with several tenets: first, that America's domestic well-being required exports; second, that foreign trade would suffer interruption unless the United States intervened abroad; and third, that the closing of any area to American products, citizens, or ideas threatened the survival of the United States.

TR's World

Theodore Roosevelt played an important role in shaping U.S. foreign policy in the McKinley administration. As assistant secretary of the navy (1897–1898), as a Spanish-American War hero, and then as vice president in McKinley's second term, Roosevelt worked to make the United States a great power. Long fascinated by power, he also relished hunting and killing. After an argument with a girlfriend in his youth, he vented his anger by shooting a neighbor's dog. Roosevelt justified the slaughtering of American Indians, if necessary, and took his Rough Riders to Cuba, desperate to get in on the fighting.

Like many Americans of his day, Roosevelt took for granted the superiority of Protestant Anglo-American culture and believed in using American power to shape world affairs. In Roosevelt's view, there were civilized and uncivilized nations; the former, primarily white and Anglo-Saxon or Teutonic, had a right and a duty to intervene in the affairs of the latter (generally nonwhite, Latin, or Slavic, and therefore "backward") to preserve order, even if that meant using violence.

Presidential Authority Roosevelt's love of the good fight caused many to rue his ascension to the presidency after McKinley's assassination in September 1901. But the cowboy was also an astute analyst of foreign policy. Roosevelt understood that American power, though growing, remained limited and that in many parts of the world the United States would have to rely on diplomacy to achieve satisfactory outcomes.

Roosevelt sought to centralize foreign policy in the White House, believing the president should lead foreign relations as he did domestic affairs. Congress was too large and unwieldy, and he saw public opinion as "the voice of the devil, or what is still worse, the voice of the fool." Most presidents after Roosevelt shared the notion that foreign policy belonged primarily in the executive branch.

Roosevelt's first efforts were focused on Latin America, where U.S. economic and power towered (see Map 22.2). He also focused on Europe, where repeated disputes persuaded Americans to develop friendlier relations with Great Britain while avoiding the continent's troubles, which Americans blamed on Germany.

As U.S. economic interests expanded in Latin America, so did U.S. political influence. Exports to Latin America rose from over $50 million in the 1870s to more than $120 million in 1901 and $300 million in 1914. Investments by U.S. citizens in Latin America climbed to $1.26 billion in 1914. In 1899 two large banana importers merged to form the United Fruit Company, owning much of the land in Central America (more than a million acres in 1913) and the railroad and steamship lines.

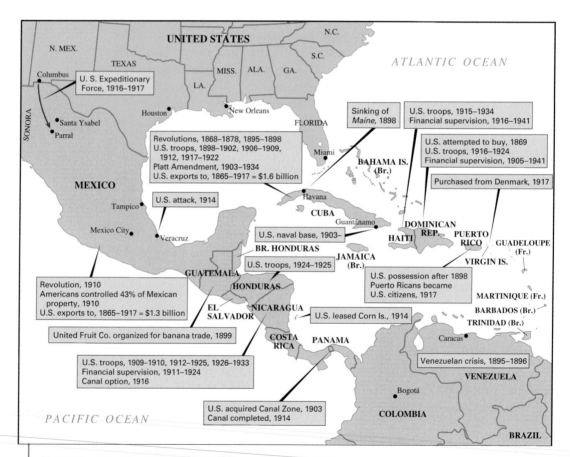

Map 22.2   U.S. Hegemony in the Caribbean and Latin America

Through many interventions, territorial acquisitions, and robust economic expansion, the United States became the predominant power in Latin America in the early twentieth century. The United States often backed up the Roosevelt Corollary's declaration of a police power by dispatching troops to Caribbean nations, where they met nationalist opposition.

Cuba and the Platt Amendment

After the war in Cuba, U.S. business interests continued to dominate the island's economy, controlling the sugar, mining, tobacco, and utilities industries, and most of the rural lands. Private U.S. investments grew from $50 million before the revolution to $220 million by 1913, and U.S. exports to the island rose from $26 million in 1900 to $196 million in 1917. The Teller Amendment outlawed the annexation of Cuba, but Washington officials used its call for pacification to justify U.S. control and maintenance of American troops there until 1902.

U.S. authorities restricted voting rights to propertied Cuban males, excluding two-thirds of adult men and all women. American officials also forced Cubans to add the Platt Amendment to their constitution. This prohibited Cuba from making treaties that might impair its independence; in practice, this meant all treaties required U.S. approval. Most important, the Platt Amendment granted the United States "the right to intervene" to preserve the island's independence and maintain domestic order. Finally, it required Cuba to lease a naval base to the United States (at Guantánamo Bay, still under U.S. jurisdiction today). Formalized in a 1903 treaty, the amendment governed Cuban-American relations until 1934.

Cubans widely protested the Platt Amendment, and a rebellion in 1906 prompted another U.S. invasion. The marines stayed until 1909, returned briefly in 1912 and again from 1917 to 1922. U.S. officials helped develop a transportation system, expand the public school system, found a national army, and increase sugar production. When Dr. Walter Reed's experiments, based on the theory of the Cuban physician Carlos Juan Finlay, proved that mosquitoes transmitted yellow fever, sanitary engineers eradicated the disease.

Puerto Rico, the Caribbean island taken as a spoil of war in the Treaty of Paris, first welcomed the United States as an improvement over Spain. But the U.S. military governor, General Guy V. Henry, regarded Puerto Ricans as children who needed "kindergarten instruction in controlling themselves without allowing them too much liberty." Some residents warned against the "Yankee peril"; others applauded the "Yankee model" and futilely anticipated statehood.

Panama Canal

Panama, meanwhile, became the site of a bold U.S. expansionist venture. In 1869 the world marveled when the newly completed Suez Canal facilitated travel between the Indian Ocean and Mediterranean Sea and enhanced the British Empire's power. Surely that feat could be duplicated in the Western Hemisphere, possibly in Panama, a province of Colombia. Business interests joined politicians, diplomats, and navy officers in insisting that the United States control such an interoceanic canal.

But the Clayton-Bulwer Treaty with Britain (1850) provided for joint control of a canal. The British, recognizing their diminishing influence in the region and cultivating friendship with the United States as a counterweight to Germany, permitted a solely U.S.-run canal in the Hay-Pauncefote Treaty (1901). When Colombia resisted Washington's terms, Roosevelt encouraged Panamanian rebels to declare independence and ordered American warships to back them.

In 1903 the new Panama awarded the United States a canal zone and long-term rights to its control. The treaty guaranteed Panama its independence. (In 1922 the

United States paid Colombia $25 million in conscience money but did not apologize.) A technological achievement, the Panama Canal was completed in 1914.

In a suit and hat, President Theodore Roosevelt occupies the controls of a ninety-five-ton power shovel at a Panama Canal worksite. Roosevelt's November 1906 trip to inspect the massive project was the first time a sitting president left the United States.   (AP Images)

Roosevelt Corollary

Worried that Latin American nations' defaults on debts owed to European banks were provoking European intervention, Theodore Roosevelt in 1904 issued the Roosevelt Corollary to the Monroe Doctrine. He warned Latin Americans to stabilize their politics and finances or risk "intervention by some civilized nation." Roosevelt's declaration provided the rationale for frequent U.S. interventions in Latin America.

From 1900 to 1917, U.S. presidents ordered American troops to Cuba, Panama, Nicaragua, the Dominican Republic, Mexico, and Haiti to quell civil wars, thwart challenges to U.S. influence, gain ports and bases, and forestall European meddling (see Map 22.2). U.S. authorities ran elections, trained national guards, and shifted foreign debts to U.S. banks. They also controlled tariff revenues and government budgets (as in the Dominican Republic, from 1905 to 1941).

U.S.-Mexican Relations

U.S. officials focused particular attention on Mexico, where long-time dictator Porfirio Díaz (1876–1910) aggressively recruited foreign investors through tax incentives and land grants. American capitalists came to own Mexico's railroads and mines and invested heavily in petroleum and banking, thereby dominating Mexico's foreign trade in the early 1890s. By 1910 Americans controlled 43 percent of Mexican property and produced more than half of the country's oil. The Mexican revolutionaries who ousted Díaz in 1910 wanted to end their economic dependence on the United States.

The revolution descended into a bloody civil war with strong anti-Yankee overtones, and the Mexican government intended to nationalize American-owned properties. President Woodrow Wilson twice ordered troops onto Mexican soil: once in 1914, at Veracruz, to overthrow President Victoriano Huerta, and again in 1916, in northern Mexico, where General John J. "Black Jack" Pershing spent months pursuing Mexican rebel Pancho Villa for raiding an American border town. Failing to capture Villa and facing another nationalistic government, U.S. forces departed in January 1917.

As the United States demonstrated its power to enforce the Monroe Doctrine, European nations reluctantly honored U.S. hegemony in Latin America. In turn, the

United States continued to stand outside European embroilments. Theodore Roosevelt did help settle a Franco-German clash over Morocco by mediating a settlement at Algeciras, Spain (1906), but he drew American criticism for this involvement. Americans endorsed the Hague peace conferences (1899 and 1907) and negotiated arbitration treaties, but generally remained outside the European arena, except for trade.

Peacemaking in East Asia

In East Asia, Roosevelt and his successor, William Howard Taft, sought to preserve the Open Door and to contain Japan's rising power. The United States gradually made concessions to Japan to protect the Philippines and sustain the Open Door policy. Japan continued to plant interests in China and then smashed the Russians in the Russo-Japanese War (1904–1905). President Roosevelt mediated the negotiations at the Portsmouth Conference in New Hampshire and won the Nobel Peace Prize for helping to preserve a balance of power in Asia.

In 1905, in the Taft-Katsura Agreement, the United States conceded Japanese hegemony over Korea in return for Japan's respect for the U.S. position in the Philippines. Three years later, in the Root-Takahira Agreement, Washington recognized Japan's interests in Manchuria, and Japan again pledged the security of U.S. Pacific possessions and endorsed the Open Door in China. Roosevelt deterred the Japanese with reinforced naval power; in late 1907 he sent the navy's Great White Fleet on a world tour. Impressed, the Japanese expanded their navy.

Dollar Diplomacy

President Taft hoped to counter Japanese advances in Asia through dollar diplomacy—the use of private funds to serve American diplomatic goals while garnering profits for American financiers and bringing reform to developing countries. Taft induced American bankers to join an international consortium to build a railway in China. But it seemed only to embolden Japan to solidify its holdings in China.

In 1914, when World War I broke out in Europe, Japan seized Shandong and some Pacific islands from the Germans. In 1915 Japan issued its Twenty-One Demands, insisting on hegemony over China. The United States lacked power in Asia to block Japan's imperialism. A new president, Woodrow Wilson, worried about how the "white race" could blunt the rise of "the yellow race."

Anglo-American Rapprochement

British officials shared this concern, though their attention was focused on rising tensions in Europe. Anglo-American cooperation blossomed during the Roosevelt-Taft years. The intense German-British rivalry and the rise of the United States to world power furthered London's quest for friendship with Washington. The two nations shared a common language and respect for private property rights, and Americans appreciated British support in the 1898 war and the Hay-Pauncefote Treaty, London's virtual endorsement of the Roosevelt Corollary, and the withdrawal of British warships from the Caribbean.

British-American trade and U.S. investment in Britain also secured ties. By 1914 more than 140 American companies operated in Britain, including H. J. Heinz's

Guantánamo Bay

Four hundred miles from Miami, near the southeastern corner of Cuba, sits the U.S. naval base Guantánamo Bay (Gitmo). The oldest American base outside the United States, it is the only one in a country with which Washington does not have an open political relationship. The United States has occupied Guantánamo since the aftermath of the Spanish-American War, leasing it from Cuba for $4,085 annually (originally $2,000 in gold coins).

Cuban leaders were dissatisfied with the deal early on, and after Fidel Castro's communist takeover in 1959, Guantánamo fueled tensions between the two countries. Castro called it "a dagger pointed at Cuba's heart" and refused to cash the rent checks. That he cashed the very first check, however, enabled Washington to argue that Castro's government accepts the lease.

Since late 2001 Gitmo has contained a detainment camp for alleged combatants captured in Afghanistan and, later, Iraq and elsewhere. By late 2005, there were over five hundred detainees from more than forty countries. The George W. Bush administration called the detainees "unlawful enemy combatants" but promised to follow the Geneva accords governing prisoners of war. Soon there were allegations of abuse and complaints that holding detainees without trial, charges, or prospect of release was unlawful. Some detainees committed suicide. For critics the camp became an international symbol of American heavy-handedness and harmful to America's image abroad.

In June 2006, the U.S. Supreme Court ruled that President Bush overstepped his power in establishing procedures for the Guantánamo detainees without congressional authority—and that the procedures violated the Uniform Code of Military Justice and the Geneva accords. Bush said he would like to close the Guantánamo camp but some prisoners were too "darned dangerous" to release or deport. The question for a people and a nation remained: how would the United States balance security with due process and the rule of law?

processed foods and F. W. Woolworth's "penny markets." Many decried an Americanization of British culture. Such exaggerated fears, however, gave way to cooperation, especially in 1917 when the United States entered World War I supporting Britain against Germany.

Summary

By 1914 Americans held extensive economic, strategic, and political interests worldwide. The outward reach of U.S. foreign policy from Seward to Wilson sparked opposition from domestic critics, other imperialist nations, and foreign nationalists, but expansionists prevailed, and the trend toward empire endured.

Economic and strategic needs motivated and justified expansion. The belief that the United States needed foreign markets to absorb surplus production joined missionary zeal in reforming other societies through American products and culture. Notions of racial and male supremacy and appeals to national greatness also fed the appetite for foreign adventure. The greatly augmented navy became a primary means for satisfying America's expansionist desires.

Revealing the diversity of America's intersection with the world, missionaries like Moon, generals, companies, and politicians carried American ideas, guns, and goods abroad to a mixed reception. When world war broke out in August 1914, the United States' self-proclaimed greatness and political isolation from Europe were tested.

Chapter Review

IMPERIAL DREAMS

| **What drove U.S. expansion overseas in the late nineteenth century?**

| A new group of elite leaders and intellectuals believed the nation's future prosperity and security depended on greater U.S. influence over world affairs. They believed foreign trade could prevent future downturns by shipping surplus products overseas. Leaders also embraced the notion of American "exceptionalism"— that the United States was unique and superior to other regions because of its heritage and God-favored prosperity. Nationalism, capitalism, Social Darwinism, and a paternalistic racism also provided rationales for U.S. expansion and imperialism in the late nineteenth and early twentieth centuries. Together, these theories depicted Latin Americans, Filipinos, and others as less advanced and less human than their U.S. counterparts; hence, expansionists argued that when they intervened in these regions, they were helping to bring prosperity and liberty to weaker, less fortunate peoples.

AMBITIONS AND STRATEGIES

| **What happened to Seward's vision of an American empire?**

| Secretary of State William Seward longed for a U.S. empire that would extend the frontier to include Canada, the Caribbean, Cuba, Central America, Mexico, Hawai'i, Iceland, Greenland, and the Pacific islands. He anticipated these areas would naturally gravitate to—and easily become enveloped by—the United States, and that foreign trade and certain infrastructure developments—such as a transcontinental U.S. railroad, a canal across Central America, and a telegraph system—would speed things along. Most of his vision never came to pass, blocked by anti-imperialists, political foes, and failed schemes. He had a few successes, however, including chasing the French puppet government from Mexico in 1866, purchasing Alaska from the Russians in 1867, and claiming the Midway Islands for the United States that year.

CRISES IN THE 1890S: HAWAI'I, VENEZUELA, AND CUBA

| **What typically imperialist actions did the United States take in its dealings with Hawai'i and Venezuela?**

| In both cases, the United States showed disregard for the rights of small nations. Hawai'i was annexed despite the objections of its queen and most Hawaiians because it proved strategically and commercially important to the United States—particularly during the Spanish-American War, when it served as a way station to Asia and the Philippines. Venezuela, also a small nation, sought U.S. assistance in its border dispute with Great Britain over where its boundary with British Guiana should lie. The Anglo-American arbitration board divided up the territory, which was rich with gold and provided a commercial gateway to South America, between Britain and Venezuela, with almost no input from the latter.

THE SPANISH-AMERICAN WAR AND THE DEBATE OVER EMPIRE

What were the U.S. justifications for entering a war with Spain?

Among his reasons for the war, President McKinley listed protecting "American life and property," particularly in the wake of the destruction of the *Maine*. Many American business people and farmers believed opening up the regions held by Spain—initially Cuba and later the Philippines—would open up new markets for US surplus production. Imperialists looked to the war to fulfill expansionist dreams by adding new U.S. territories, while conservatives, alarmed by Populism and labor strikes, hoped the war could unify the nation behind a single cause.

What were the anti-imperialist arguments against U.S. annexation of the Philippines after the Spanish-American War?

Anti-imperialists expressed a wide range of concerns about the potential annexation of the Philippines. For many it seemed hypocritical for Americans to fight a war for Cuban liberation, only to acquire another small nation in the process. Some argued that it violated the fundamental right of a people to self-determination that Americans themselves embraced in the Declaration of Independence and Constitution. Prominent women felt imperialist zeal corrupted the American character. Racists saw the annexation of non white nation as a potential threat to Anglo-Saxon purity and supremacy, while labor leaders feared the new colonists might become a cheap labor force to drive down American wages.

ASIAN ENCOUNTERS: WAR IN THE PHILIPPINES, DIPLOMACY IN CHINA

What made the Open Door policy a key component of U.S. diplomacy?

The Open Door Policy originated in the late nineteenth century as a solution to U.S. trade difficulties in China. The concept called for nations with spheres of influence in turbulent China to respect the principle of equal trade opportunity. After 1900, when the United States became the world's preeminent trader, the Open Door became the tool by which it could first enter new markets and then dominate them. As it developed, the Open Door included the following tenets: that America's economy required exports to remain strong; that trade abroad could be interrupted unless the United States intervened; and that keeping U.S. citizens, products, or ideas from other regions threatened U.S. survival.

TR's WORLD

What solidified U.S.-British ties heading into World War I?

Aside from their shared language and respect for private property rights, England and the United States were united by several other factors. Both were concerned about growing Japanese influence in Asia. U.S. investment in Britain, along with increased trade, further strengthened their bonds. British support for the Roosevelt Corollary to Monroe doctrine (granting the United States hegemony in the Western Hemisphere) and the withdrawal of British ships from the

Caribbean made relations easier, as did England's respect for the United States's growing status as a world power. Increased tensions between Germany and England, along with British support for the 1898 war, increased cooperation between the two countries and ensured the United States would take England's side in the impending global conflict.

SUGGESTIONS FOR FURTHER READING

Robert L. Beisner, *Twelve Against Empire: The Anti-Imperialists, 1898–1900* (1968)

Kristin L. Hoganson, *Fighting for American Manhood: How Gender Politics Provoked the Spanish-American and Philippine-American Wars* (1998)

Michael H. Hunt, *Ideology and U.S. Foreign Policy* (1987)

Paul A. Kramer, *The Blood of Government: Race, Empire, the United States, and the Philippines* (2006)

Walter LaFeber, *The American Search for Opportunity, 1865–1913* (1993)

Brian M. Linn, *The Philippine War, 1899–1902* (2000)

Eric T. Love, *Race over Empire: Racism and U.S. Imperialism, 1865–1900* (2004)

Stuart Creighton Miller, *"Benevolent Assimilation": The American Conquest of the Philippines, 1899–1903* (1982)

John Offner, *An Unwanted War: The Diplomacy of the United States and Spain over Cuba, 1895–1898* (1992)

Louis A. Perez Jr., *The War of 1898: The United States and Cuba in History and Historiography* (1998)

CHAPTER 23

Americans in the Great War

CHAPTER OUTLINE

Precarious Neutrality

The Decision for War

Winning the War

LINKS TO THE WORLD: The Influenza Pandemic of 1918

Mobilizing the Home Front

Civil Liberties Under Challenge

Red Scare, Red Summer

The Defeat of Peace

Summary

LEGACY FOR A PEOPLE AND A NATION: Freedom of Speech and the ACLU

On May 7, 1915, Secretary of State William Jennings Bryan was lunching with cabinet members in Washington when he received a bulletin: the luxurious British ocean liner *Lusitania* had been sunk, apparently by a German submarine. He rushed to his office, and at 3:06 P.M. received confirmation from London: "THE LUSITANIA WAS TORPEDOED OFF THE IRISH COAST AND SANK IN HALF AN HOUR." In fact, the giant vessel sank in eighteen minutes; 1,198 people perished, including 128 Americans. With Europe at war, Bryan feared such a calamity. Britain imposed a naval blockade on Germany, and the Germans responded with submarine warfare against Allied shipping, proclaiming the North Atlantic a danger zone, then sinking British and Allied ships. As a passenger liner, the *Lusitania* was supposed to be spared, but German officials warned Americans in newspaper notices that they traveled on British or Allied ships at their own risk; passenger liners suspected of carrying munitions or contraband were subject to attack. For weeks Bryan urged President Woodrow Wilson to stop Americans from booking passage on British ships; Wilson refused.

The *Lusitania*, it soon emerged, *was* carrying munitions. Desperate to keep the United States out of the war, Bryan urged Wilson to condemn Germany and Britain and ban Americans from traveling on belligerent ships. Others, including former president Theodore Roosevelt, called the sinking "an act of piracy" and pressed for war. Wilson did not want war, but disagreed with Bryan. He sent a strong note to Berlin, insisting Germany end its submarine warfare.

As Bryan pressed his case, he became increasingly isolated within the administration. When in early June Wilson refused to ban Americans from travel on belligerent ships and sent a second protest note to Germany, Bryan resigned.

This icon will direct you to interactive activities and study materials on *A People And A Nation*, Brief Edition
website: **www.cengage.com/history/norton/peoplenationbrief8e**

Chronology

1914	World War I begins in Europe.
1915	Germans sink the *Lusitania* off the coast of Ireland.
1916	After torpedoing the *Sussex,* Germany pledges not to attack merchant ships without warning.
	National Defense Act expands the U.S. military.
1917	Germany declares unrestricted submarine warfare.
	Russian Revolution ousts the tsar; Bolsheviks take power later.
	United States enters World War I.
	Selective Service Act creates the draft.
	Espionage Act limits First Amendment rights.
	Race riot breaks out in East St. Louis, Illinois.
1918	Wilson announces Fourteen Points for a new world order.
	Sedition Act further limits free speech.

	U.S. troops at Château-Thierry help blunt the German offensive.
	U.S. troops intervene in Russia against Bolsheviks.
	Spanish flu pandemic kills 20 million people worldwide.
	Armistice ends World War I.
1919	Paris Peace Conference punishes Germany and launches the League of Nations.
	May Day bombings help instigate the Red Scare.
	American Legion organizes for veterans' benefits and antiradicalism.
	Wilson suffers a stroke after a speaking tour.
	Senate rejects the Treaty of Versailles and U.S. membership in the League of Nations.
	Schenck v. U.S. upholds the Espionage Act.
1920	Palmer Raids round up suspected radicals.

Americans were similarly divided over Europe's war. Eastern newspapers charged Bryan with stabbing the country in the back. In the Midwest and South, Bryan won praise from pacifists and German American groups. A few weeks later, speaking to fifteen thousand people at Madison Square Garden, Bryan was applauded when he warned against "war with any of the belligerent nations." Although many Americans agreed with Wilson that honor ranked above peace, others shared Bryan's position that some sacrifice of neutral rights was reasonable to keep the country out of war.

To many, full-scale war seemed unthinkable. The new machine guns, howitzers, submarines, and dreadnoughts were awesome death engines; one social reformer lamented that using them would mean "civilization is all gone, and barbarism come."

For almost three years President Wilson kept America out of the war, while protecting U.S. trade interests and improving the nation's military posture. But American property, lives, and neutrality fell victim to British and German naval warfare. When, two years after the *Lusitania* went down, the president asked Congress for a declaration of war, he insisted America would not just win but "make the world safe for democracy."

A year and a half later, the Great War would be over. Some 10 million soldiers perished. Europeans experienced the destruction of ideals, confidence, and goodwill. Economically, too, the damage was immense. The Great War toppled four empires of the Old World—the German, Austro-Hungarian, Russian, and Ottoman Turkish—and left two others, the British and French, drastically weakened.

Losses for the United States were comparatively small, yet American involvement tipped the scales in favor of the Allies by contributing troops, supplies, and loans. The war years also witnessed a massive international transfer of wealth from Europe across the Atlantic, as the United States went from the world's largest debtor nation to its largest creditor. The conflict marked the United States as a world power.

At home, World War I intensified social divisions. Racial tensions accompanied the northward migration of southern blacks, and pacifists and German Americans were harassed. The federal government trampled on civil liberties to promote patriotism and silence critics. After Russia's communist revolution, a Red Scare in America repressed radicals and tarnished America's democratic image. Although reformers continued to address issues like prohibition and woman suffrage, the war splintered the Progressive movement.

Abroad, Americans who marched to battle grew disillusioned with the peace process. They recoiled from victors squabbling over the spoils, and they chided Wilson for failing to deliver his promised "peace without victory." Americans again debated about foreign policy. After negotiating the Treaty of Versailles at Paris following World War I, the president urged U.S. membership in the new League of Nations, which he believed would reform world politics. The Senate rejected his appeal (the League nonetheless organized without U.S. membership), because many Americans feared that the League might threaten the U.S. empire and entangle Americans in Europe's problems.

- **Why did the United States try to remain neutral and then enter the European war in 1917?**
- **How was American society changed by the war?**
- **What were the main elements of Woodrow Wilson's postwar vision, and why did he fail to realize them?**

PRECARIOUS NEUTRALITY

The war that erupted in August 1914 grew from years of European competition over trade, colonies, allies, and armaments. Two powerful alliance systems had formed: the Triple Alliance of Germany, Austria-Hungary, and Italy and the Triple Entente of Britain, France, and Russia. All had imperial holdings and wanted more. But as Germany challenged Great Britain for world leadership, many Americans saw Germany as an excessively militaristic nation that threatened U.S. interests in the Western Hemisphere.

Outbreak of the First World War

Crises in the Balkans triggered a chain of events that shattered Europe's delicate balance of power. Slavic nationalists sought to enlarge independent Serbia by annexing regions such as Bosnia, then a province of the Austro-Hungarian Empire. On June 28, 1914, Archduke Franz Ferdinand, heir to the Austro-Hungarian throne, was assassinated by a Serbian nationalist while visiting Sarajevo, the capital of Bosnia. Austria-Hungary consulted its Triple Alliance partner Germany, which urged toughness. When Serbia called on its Slavic friend Russia for help, Russia enlisted France and began mobilizing its armies.

Germany struck first, declaring war against Russia on August 1 and against France two days later. When German forces slashed into neutral Belgium to get to France, London declared war against Germany on August 4. Eventually Turkey (the

Ottoman Empire) joined Germany and Austria-Hungary as the Central Powers, and Italy (switching sides) and Japan teamed up with Britain, France, and Russia as the Allies. Japan seized Shandong, Germany's area of influence in China.

President Wilson at first distanced America by proclaiming neutrality—the traditional U.S. policy toward European wars. Privately, the president worried that without neutrality, "our mixed populations would wage war on each other."

| **Taking Sides** | Despite Wilson's appeal for unity at home, ethnic groups did take sides. Many German Americans and anti-British Irish Americans (Ireland was then trying to break free |

from British rule) cheered for the Central Powers. Americans with roots in Allied nations, championed the Allied cause. Germany's attack on Belgium confirmed for many that Germany was the archetype of unbridled militarism.

The pro-Allied sympathies of Wilson's administration also weakened the U.S. neutrality proclamation. Wilson shared the conviction with British leaders that a German victory would destroy free enterprise and government by law. If Germany won the war, he prophesied, "it would change the course of our civilization and make the United States a military nation."

U.S. economic links with the Allies also rendered neutrality difficult, if not impossible. England, a long-time customer, flooded America with new orders, especially for arms. Sales to the Allies helped end an American recession. Between 1914 and 1916, American exports to England and France grew 365 percent, from $753 million to $2.75 billion. Largely because of Britain's naval blockade, exports to Germany dropped by more than 90 percent, from $345 million to only $29 million. Loans to Britain and France from private American banks—totaling $2.3 billion during neutrality—financed much of U.S. trade with the Allies. Germany received only $27 million in the same period.

To Germans, the links between the U.S. economy and the Allies meant that the United States had become the Allied arsenal and bank. Americans, however, worried that cutting their economic ties with Britain would constitute a nonneutral act in favor of Germany. Under international law, Britain—which controlled the seas—could buy contraband (war-related goods) and noncontraband from neutrals. It was Germany's responsibility, not America's, to stop such trade as international law prescribed by blockading the enemy's territory, seizing contraband from neutral (U.S.) ships, or confiscating goods from belligerent (British) ships.

| **Wilsonianism** | Wilsonianism, the cluster of ideas that Wilson espoused, consisted of traditional American principles (such as democracy and the Open Door) and a vision of the United |

States as a beacon of freedom. Only the United States could lead the convulsed world into a peaceful era of unobstructed commerce, free-market capitalism, democratic politics, and open diplomacy. "America had the infinite privilege of fulfilling her destiny and saving the world," Wilson claimed. Critics, however, charged that Wilson often violated his own credos while forcing them on others—as his military interventions in Mexico in 1914, Haiti in 1915, and the Dominican Republic in 1916 testified. Nonetheless, his ideals served U.S. commercial purposes.

To say that U.S. neutrality was never a real possibility given ethnic loyalties, economic ties, and Wilsonian preferences is not to say that Wilson sought to enter the war. In early 1917, the president remarked that "we are the only one of the great white nations that is free from war today, and it would be a crime against civilization for us to go in." But go in the United States finally did. Why?

Violations of Neutral Rights

The short answer is that Americans got caught in the Allied–Central Power crossfire. The British sought to cripple the German economy by severing neutral trade. They declared a blockade of water entrances to Germany and mined the North Sea. They seized cargoes and defined a broad list of contraband (including foodstuffs) that they prohibited neutrals from shipping to Germany. Furthermore, to counter German submarines, the British flouted international law by arming their merchant ships and flying neutral (sometimes U.S.) flags. Wilson frequently protested British violations of neutral rights, but London deflected Washington's criticism by paying for confiscated cargoes, while German provocations made British behavior appear less offensive in comparison.

Germany looked for victory at sea by using submarines. In February 1915, Berlin declared a war zone around the British Isles, warned neutral vessels to stay out so as not to be mistakenly attacked, and advised passengers to stay off Allied ships. Wilson informed Germany it would be held accountable for any losses of American life and property.

Wilson held to a strict interpretation of international law and expected Germans to warn passenger or merchant ships before attacking, so that passengers and crew could disembark safely into lifeboats. The Germans thought that surfacing

Initially underestimated as a weapon, the German U-boat proved to be frighteningly effective against Allied ships. At the beginning of the war, Germany had about twenty operational submarines in its High Seas Fleet, but officials moved swiftly to speed up production. This photograph shows a German U-boat under construction in 1914. (Bibliothek fuer Zeitgeschichte, Stuttgart, Germany)

its slender and sluggish *Unterseebooten* (U-boats) would risk their advantage and leave them vulnerable to attack. Berlin protested that Wilson was denying it the one weapon that could break the British economic stranglehold, disrupt the Allies' substantial connection with U.S. producers and bankers, and win the war. To British, Germans, and Americans, naval warfare became a matter of life and death.

THE DECISION FOR WAR

In early 1915, German U-boats sank ship after ship, notably the *Lusitania* on May 7. Germany's subsequent brief promise to refrain from attacking passenger liners ended in mid August when another British vessel, the *Arabic,* was sunk off Ireland. Three Americans died. The Germans quickly pledged that an unarmed passenger ship would never again be attacked without warning. But the *Arabic* incident led critics to ask: why not require Americans to sail on American craft? From August 1914 to March 1917, after all, only 3 Americans died on an American ship (the tanker *Gulflight,* sunk by a German U-boat in May 1915), versus 190 killed on belligerent ships.

Peace Advocates

In March 1916, a U-boat attack on the *Sussex,* a French vessel crossing the English Channel, injured four Americans and brought the United States closer to war. Wilson threatened Berlin that the United States would sever diplomatic relations if the attacks continued. Again the Germans retreated. At the same time, U.S.-British relations soured after Britain's crushing response to the Easter Rebellion in Ireland and further British restriction of U.S. trade with the Central Powers.

As the United States became more entangled in the Great War, many Americans urged Wilson to keep the nation out. In early 1915, Jane Addams, Carrie Chapman Catt, and other suffragists helped found the Woman's Peace Party, the U.S. section of the Women's International League for Peace and Freedom. Later that year, some pacifist Progressives organized an antiwar coalition, the American Union Against Militarism. The businessmen Andrew Carnegie and Henry Ford financed peace efforts, standing alongside the socialist Eugene Debs.

Antiwar advocates emphasized that war drained a nation of its youth, resources, and reform impulse; that it fostered repression at home; that it violated Christian morality; and that wartime business barons reaped huge profits at the expense of the people. Militarism and conscription, Addams pointed out, were what millions of immigrants left behind in Europe. Although the peace movement was splintered, it articulated several ideas that Wilson, who campaigned on a peace platform in the 1916 election, shared. Wilson futilely labored once again to bring the belligerents to the conference table, urging them in early 1917 to temper their acquisitive war aims and embrace "peace without victory."

Unrestricted Submarine Warfare

In Germany, Wilson's overture went unheeded. Since August 1916, German leaders debated whether to resume the unrestricted U-boat campaign. Opponents feared a break with the United States, but proponents claimed that only through an all-out attack on Britain's supply shipping could Germany win the war. True, the United States might enter the war, but victory might be achieved before U.S. troops crossed the Atlantic. Consequently, in early February 1917, Germany launched unrestricted submarine warfare, attacking all warships and merchant vessels—belligerent or neutral—in the declared war zone. Wilson quickly broke diplomatic relations with Berlin.

In late February, British intelligence intercepted and passed to U.S. officials a telegram addressed to the German minister in Mexico from German foreign secretary Arthur Zimmermann. Its message: If Mexico joined an alliance against the United States, Germany would help Mexico recover the territories it lost in 1848. Zimmermann hoped to "set new enemies on America's neck—enemies which give them plenty to take care of over there."

Although Mexico rejected Germany's offer, Wilson judged Zimmermann's telegram "a conspiracy against this country." The prospect of a German-Mexican collaboration helped turn the tide of opinion in the American Southwest, where antiwar sentiment had been strong.

Soon afterward, Wilson asked Congress for "armed neutrality" to defend U.S. lives and commerce, seeking authority to arm U.S. merchant ships, for example. In the midst of the debate, Wilson released Zimmermann's telegram to the press. Americans were outraged. The antiwar senators Robert M. La Follette and George Norris, among others, saw the armed-ship bill as a blank check for the president to move the country to war, and they filibustered it to death. Wilson armed U.S. commercial vessels anyway, but acted too late to prevent the sinking of several U.S. ships. War cries escalated. In late March, Wilson called Congress into special session.

War Message and War Declaration

On April 2, 1917, the president stepped before a hushed Congress and enumerated U.S. grievances: Germany's violation of freedom of the seas, disruption of commerce, interference with Mexico, and breach of human rights by killing innocent Americans. Congress declared war against Germany on April 6 by a vote of 373 to 50 in the House and 82 to 6 in the Senate. (This vote was for war against Germany only; a declaration of war against Austria-Hungary came months later, on December 7.) Montana's Jeannette Rankin, the first woman in Congress, cast a ringing no vote.

For principle, for morality, for honor, for commerce, for security, for reform—for all of these reasons, Wilson took the United States into the Great War. The submarine was certainly the culprit that drew a reluctant president and nation into the maelstrom. Critics blamed Wilson's rigid definition of international law and his contention that Americans should be entitled to travel anywhere, even on a belligerent ship loaded with contraband. Most Americans came to accept Wilson's view that the Germans had to be checked to ensure an open, orderly world in which U.S. principles and interests would be safe.

The United States went to war to reform world politics, not to destroy Germany. By early 1917 the president concluded that the United States would not be able to claim a seat at the postwar peace conference unless it became a combatant. At the peace conference, Wilson intended to promote the principles he thought essential to a stable world order, to advance democracy and the Open Door, and to outlaw revolution and aggression. In designating the United States an "Associated" rather than an Allied nation, Wilson tried to preserve part of his country's neutrality, but to no avail.

WINNING THE WAR

Even before the U.S. declaration of war, the Wilson administration strengthened the military under the banner of "preparedness." The National Defense Act of 1916 provided for increases in the army and National Guard, and for summer training camps modeled on the one in Plattsburgh, New York, where some of America's social and economic elite trained in 1915 as "citizen-soldiers." The Navy Act of 1916 started the largest naval expansion in American history.

The Draft and the Soldier

To raise an army, Congress in May 1917 passed the Selective Service Act, requiring all males between the ages of twenty-one and thirty (later changed to eighteen and forty-five) to register. National service, proponents believed, would prepare the nation for battle and instill patriotism and respect for democracy and personal sacrifice. Critics feared it would lead to the militarization of American life.

On June 5, 1917, more than 9.5 million men signed up for the "great national lottery." By war's end, 24 million men had been registered by local draft boards. The typical soldier was in his early to mid-twenties, white, single, American-born, and poorly educated (most had not attended high school, and perhaps 30 percent could not read or write). Tens of thousands of women enlisted in the army Nurse Corps, served as "hello girls" (volunteer bilingual telephone operators) in the army Signal Corps, and became clerks in the navy and Marine Corps.

Some 400,000 African Americans also served in the military. Many southern politicians feared arming African Americans, but the army drafted them into segregated units and assigned them to menial labor. They endured miserable conditions. Ultimately more than 40,000 blacks would see combat in Europe, and several black units served with distinction in the French army. The all-black 369th Infantry Regiment spent more time in the trenches—191 days—and received more medals than any other American outfit.

Although French officers had their share of racial prejudice and often treated the soldiers from their own African colonies poorly, black Americans serving with the French reported a degree of respect lacking in the American army. The irony was not lost on African American leaders, such as W. E. B. Du Bois, who endorsed the National Association for the Advancement of Colored People's (NAACP) support for the war and urged blacks to volunteer to help make the world safe for democracy.

Approximately 3 million men evaded draft registration. Some were arrested, others fled to Mexico or Canada, but most stayed home and were never discovered. Another 338,000 men who registered never showed up for induction. Nearly 65,000 draftees applied for conscientious-objector (CO) status (refusing to bear arms for religious or pacifist reasons), but some changed their minds or failed preinduction examinations. Quakers and Mennonites were numerous among the 4,000 inductees classified as COs. COs who refused noncombat service, such as in the medical corps, faced imprisonment.

Trench Warfare

U.S. general John J. Pershing, head of the American Expeditionary Forces (AEF), insisted that his "sturdy rookies" remain a separate army. He refused to turn over his "doughboys" (so termed, apparently, because the large buttons on American uniforms in the 1860s resembled a deep-fried bread of that name) to Allied commanders, who favored deadly trench warfare. Since fall 1914, zigzag trenches fronted by barbed wire and mines stretched across France. Between the muddy, stinking trenches lay "no man's land," denuded by artillery fire. When ordered out, soldiers would charge enemy trenches, only to face machine gun fire and poison gas.

First used by the Germans in April 1915, chlorine gas stimulated overproduction of fluid in the lungs, leading to death by drowning. Gas in a variety of forms (mustard and phosgene, in addition to chlorine) would be used throughout the war, sometimes blistering, sometimes incapacitating, often killing.

The death toll in trench warfare was overwhelming. At the Battle of the Somme in 1916, the British and French suffered 600,000 dead or wounded to earn only 125 square miles; the Germans lost 400,000 men. At Verdun that year, 336,000 Germans perished, and at Passchendaele in 1917 more than 370,000 British men died to gain about 40 miles of mud and barbed wire.

Shell Shock

Not long after arriving on the French front, U.S. units faced the horrors caused by advanced weaponry. Some suffered shell shock, a mental illness also known as war psychosis. Symptoms included a fixed, empty stare; violent tremors; paralyzed limbs; listlessness; jabbering; screaming; and haunting dreams. The illness could strike anyone; even soldiers who appeared courageous cracked after days of incessant shelling and inescapable human carnage. Providing some relief were Red Cross canteens, staffed by women volunteers, which offered haircuts, food, and recreation.

In Paris, where forty large houses of prostitution thrived, venereal disease became such a problem that French prime minister Georges Clemenceau offered licensed, inspected prostitutes in special houses to the U.S. army. Still, by war's end, about 15 percent of America's soldiers contracted venereal disease, costing the army $50 million and 7 million days of active duty. Periodic inspections, chemical prophylactic treatments, and the threat of court-martial for infected soldiers kept the problem from being greater.

American Units in France

In France, soldiers filled their diaries and letters with descriptions of local customs and "ancient" architecture and noted how the war-torn French countryside bore little resemblance to the groomed landscapes in paintings. "Life in France for the American soldier meant marching in the dirt and mud, living in cellars in filth, being wet and cold and fighting," the chief of staff of the Fourth Division remarked. "He had come to help . . . but these French people did not seem to appreciate him at all."

With both sides exhausted, the Americans tipped the balance toward the Allies. But not right away. Initially, the U.S. Navy battled submarines and escorted troop carriers, and pilots in the U.S. Air Service, flying mostly British and French aircraft, saw limited action. American flying aces like Eddie Rickenbacker defeated their German counterparts in aerial dogfights and became heroes in France and their own country. But only ground troops could make a decisive difference, and U.S. units did not engage in much combat until after the harsh winter of 1917–1918.

The Bolshevik Revolution

The military and diplomatic situation changed dramatically as a result of the Bolshevik Revolution in Russia. In November 1917, the liberal-democratic government of Aleksander Kerensky, which had led the country since the tsar's abdication early in the year, was overthrown by V. I. Lenin's radical socialists. Lenin vowed to change world politics and end imperial rivalries on terms that challenged Wilson's. To Lenin, the war signaled the impending end of capitalism and the rise of a global revolution of workers. For western leaders, the prospect of Bolshevik-style revolutions worldwide was too frightening to contemplate.

In the weeks following their takeover, the Bolsheviks attempted to embarrass the capitalist governments and incite world revolution by publishing several Allied secret agreements for dividing up the colonies and other territories of the Central Powers if Allies were victorious. Wilson confided to Colonel House that he really wanted to tell the Bolsheviks to "go to hell," but he accepted the colonel's argument that he would have to address Lenin's claims that there was little to distinguish the two warring sides and that socialism represented the future.

Fourteen Points

In the Fourteen Points, unveiled in January 1918, Wilson reaffirmed America's commitment to an international system governed by laws and renounced territorial gains as a legitimate war aim. The first five points called for diplomacy "in the public view," freedom of the seas, lower tariffs, armament reductions, and the decolonization of empires. The next eight points specified the evacuation of foreign troops from Russia, Belgium, and France and appealed for self-determination for nationalities in Europe, such as the Poles. For Wilson, the fourteenth point was the mechanism for achieving the others: "a general association of nations," or League of Nations.

Lenin was unimpressed and called for an immediate end to the fighting, the eradication of colonialism, and self-determination for all peoples. Lenin also made a separate peace with Germany—the Treaty of Brest-Litovsk, signed on March 3, 1918. The deal erased centuries of Russian expansion, as Poland, Finland, and the Baltic states were taken from Russia and Ukraine was granted independence. One of Lenin's motives was to allow Russian troops loyal to the Bolsheviks to return home to fight anti-Bolshevik forces attempting to oust his government.

Americans in Battle

In March 1918, the Germans launched a major offensive, and by May they were within 50 miles of Paris. U.S. First Division troops helped blunt the German advance at Cantigny (see Map 23.1). In June the Third Division and French forces held positions along the Marne River at Château-Thierry, and the Second Division attacked the Germans in the Belleau Wood. U.S. soldiers won the battle after three weeks, but thousands died or were wounded in sacrificial frontal assaults against German machine guns.

Allied victory in the Second Battle of the Marne in July 1918 stemmed German advances. In September, French and American forces took St. Mihiel in a ferocious battle. Then, in the Meuse-Argonne offensive, over 1 million Americans joined British and French troops in weeks of combat; some 26,000 Americans died before

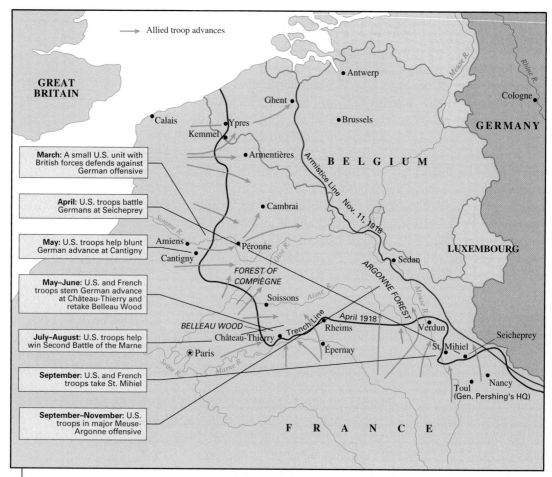

March: A small U.S. unit with British forces defends against German offensive

April: U.S. troops battle Germans at Seicheprey

May: U.S. troops help blunt German advance at Cantigny

May–June: U.S. and French troops stem German advance at Château-Thierry and retake Belleau Wood

July–August: U.S. troops help win Second Battle of the Marne

September: U.S. and French troops take St. Mihiel

September–November: U.S. troops in major Meuse-Argonne offensive

Map 23.1 American Troops at the Western Front, 1918

America's 2 million troops in France met German forces head-on, ensuring the defeat of the Central Powers in 1918.

the Allies claimed the Argonne Forest on October 10. For Germany—its ground and submarine war stymied, its troops and cities mutinous, its allies Turkey and Austria dropping out, its Kaiser abdicating—peace became imperative. The Germans accepted a punishing armistice effective November 11, 1918.

Casualties

The cost of the war is impossible to compute: the belligerents counted 10 million soldiers and 6.6 million civilians dead and 21.3 million people wounded. Fifty-three thousand American soldiers died in battle and another 62,000 from disease, mainly a virulent strain of influenza that ravaged the world in late 1918. Economic damage was colossal, and output dwindled, contributing to widespread starvation in Europe in the winter of 1918–1919.

The German, Austro-Hungarian, Ottoman, and Russian empires were gone. For a time it appeared the Bolshevik Revolution might spread westward, as communist

The Influenza Pandemic of 1918

In summer and fall 1918, a terrible influenza outbreak swept the earth. It claimed more than twice as many lives as the Great War, between 25 and 40 million people. In the United States, 675,000 people died.

The first cases were identified in midwestern military camps in early March. At Fort Riley, Kansas, forty-eight men died. Soldiers shipped out to Europe in large numbers (84,000 in March), some unknowingly carrying the virus. The illness appeared on the western front in April. By June, an estimated 8 million Spaniards were infected, giving the disease its name, the Spanish flu.

In August, a second, deadlier form of the influenza erupted simultaneously in three cities on three continents: Freetown, Sierra Leone; Brest, France; and Boston, Massachusetts. In September, the disease swept down the East Coast, killing twelve thousand Americans.

People could be healthy at the start of the weekend and dead by the end of it. Some experienced a rapid accumulation of fluid in the lungs and literally drowned. Others died slowly. Mortality rates were highest for twenty- to twenty-nine-year-olds—the same group as those dying in the trenches.

In October, the epidemic hit full force, spreading to Japan, India, Africa, and Latin America. In the United States, 200,000 perished. There was a nationwide shortage of caskets and gravediggers, and funerals were limited to fifteen minutes. Bodies were left in gutters or on front porches, to be picked up by trucks that drove the streets.

Suddenly, in November, for reasons still unclear, the epidemic eased, though the dying continued into 1919. In England and Wales, the final toll was 200,000, while in India the epidemic may have claimed 20 million. It was, in the historian Roy Porter's words, "the greatest single demographic shock mankind has ever experienced." World War I had helped spread the disease. Americans, accustomed to thinking that two great oceans isolated them, were reminded that they were immutably linked to the rest of humankind.

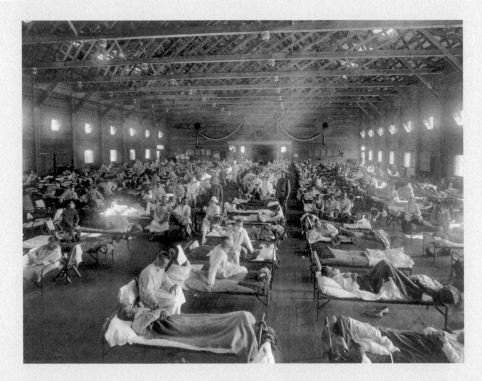

The influenza pandemic of 1918 perhaps started in earnest here, at Camp Funston, Kansas, in the spring of that year. Soldiers were struck with a debilitating illness they called "knock me down fever."
(National Museum of Health and Medicine, Armed Forces Institute of Pathology)

uprisings shook Germany and parts of central Europe. Before the armistice, revolutionaries temporarily took power in the German cities of Bremen, Hamburg, and Lübeck. In Moscow, meanwhile, the new Soviet state sought to consolidate its power.

MOBILIZING THE HOME FRONT

The war had a tremendous impact on America. The federal government expanded its power over the economy to meet war needs and intervened in American life as never before. The enlarged Washington bureaucracy managed the economy, labor force, military, and public opinion. The government spent more than $760 million a month from April 1917 to August 1919. As tax revenues lagged, the administration resorted to deficit spending (see Figure 23.1). To Progressives of the New Nationalist persuasion, the wartime expansion and centralization of government power were welcome, but others worried about the dangers of concentrated federal power.

Business-Government Cooperation

The federal government and private business became partners during the war. Early on, the government relied on industrial committees for advice on purchases and prices. But evidence of self-interested businesspeople cashing in on the national interest aroused public protest. The head of the aluminum advisory committee, for example, was also president of the largest aluminum company. Consequently, the committees were replaced in July 1917 with a single manager, the War Industries Board. The

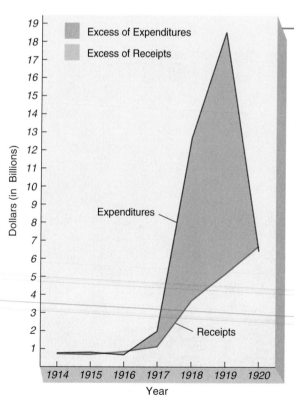

Figure 23.1   The Federal Budget, 1914–1920

During World War I, the federal government spent more money than it received from increased taxes. It borrowed from banks or sold bonds through Liberty Loan drives. To meet the mounting costs of the war, in other words, the federal government had to resort to deficit spending. Expenditures topped receipts by more than $13 billion in 1919. Given this wartime fiscal pattern, moreover, the U.S. federal debt rose from $1 billion in 1914 to $25 billion in 1919.

(*Source:* U.S. Department of Commerce, *Historical Statistics of the United States: Colonial Times to 1957* [Washington, DC: Bureau of the Census, 1960], 711.)

government also suspended antitrust laws and signed cost-plus contracts, guaranteeing companies healthy profits and a means to head off labor strikes with higher wages. Competitive bidding was virtually abandoned, and big business grew bigger.

Hundreds of new government agencies, staffed primarily by businesspeople, used economic controls to shift the nation's resources to the Allies, the AEF, and war-related production. The Food Administration, led by the engineer and investor Herbert Hoover, urged Americans to grow victory gardens and eat meatless meals on Mondays and wheatless meals on Wednesdays. It also regulated prices and distribution. The Railroad Administration took over the railway industry. The Fuel Administration controlled coal supplies and rationed gasoline. When strikes threatened the telephone and telegraph companies, the federal government seized and ran them.

The largest of the superagencies was the War Industries Board (WIB), headed by the financier Bernard Baruch. This Wall Streeter told Henry Ford that he would dispatch the military to seize his plants unless the automaker accepted WIB limits on car production. Designed as a clearing-house to coordinate the national economy, the WIB made purchases, allocated supplies, and fixed prices at levels that business requested. The WIB also ordered the standardization of goods to streamline production. The varieties of automobile tires, for example, were reduced from 287 to 3.

Economic Performance About one-quarter of American production was diverted to war needs. As farmers enjoyed boom years, they put more acreage into production and mechanized. Gross farm income from 1914 to 1919 increased more than 230 percent. Although manufacturing output leveled off in 1918, wartime demand fueled substantial growth for industries such as steel, which reached peak production of 45 million tons in 1917, twice the prewar figure. Overall, the gross national product in 1920 stood 237 percent higher than in 1914.

Mistakes happened in the rush to production. Weapons deliveries fell short, and the bloated bureaucracy of the War Shipping Board failed to build enough ships. In the severe winter of 1917–1918, coal companies reduced production to raise prices; railroads did not have enough coal cars; and harbors froze, closing out coal barges. People died from pneumonia and freezing. To pay its wartime bills, the government hiked taxes. The Revenue Act in 1916 started by raising the surtax on high incomes and corporate profits, imposing a federal tax on large estates, and significantly increasing the tax on munitions manufacturers. Still, taxation financed only one-third of the war. The other two-thirds came from loans, including Liberty bonds sold to the American people. The War Revenue Act of 1917 provided a steeply graduated personal income tax, a corporate income tax, an excess-profits tax, and increased excise taxes on alcoholic beverages, tobacco, and luxury items.

Although taxes curbed excessive corporate profiteering, there were loopholes. Sometimes companies inflated costs to conceal profits. Corporate net earnings for 1913 totaled $4 billion; in 1917 they reached $7 billion; and in 1918, after the tax bite and the war's end, they still stood at $4.5 billion. The abrupt cancellation of billions of dollars' worth of contracts at war's end, however, caused a brief downturn, a short boom, and then an intense decline (see Chapter 24).

Labor Shortage

For American workers, the full-employment wartime economy increased earnings. With the higher cost of living, however, workers saw minimal improvement. Turnover rates escalated as workers switched jobs for better pay and conditions. Some employers sought to overcome labor shortages by expanding welfare and social programs and establishing personnel departments.

To meet the labor crisis, the Department of Labor's U.S. Employment Service matched laborers with job vacancies, attracting workers from the South and Midwest to war industries in the East. The department also temporarily relaxed the literacy-test and head-tax provisions of immigration law to attract farm labor, miners, and railroad workers from Mexico. As workers crammed into cities, the U.S. Housing Corporation and Emergency Fleet Corporation built row houses in Newport News, Virginia, and Eddystone, Pennsylvania.

The tight wartime labor market meant new job opportunities for women. In Connecticut, a special motion picture, *Mr. and Mrs. Hines of Stamford Do Their Bit,* appealed to housewives' patriotism, urging them to take factory jobs. Although the total number of women in the work force increased slightly, the real story was that many moved into formerly male jobs. Some white women left domestic service for factories, shifted from clerking in department stores to stenography and typing, or departed textile mills for firearms plants. At least 20 percent of employees in the wartime electrical-machinery, airplane, and food industries were women. For the first time, department stores employed African American women as elevator operators and cafeteria waitresses. But most working women were single and remained in the sex-segregated occupations of typists, nurses, teachers, and domestic servants.

Women also participated in the war effort as volunteers, making clothing for refugees and soldiers, serving at Red Cross facilities, and teaching French to nurses assigned to the war zone. Many worked for the Women's Committee of the Council of National Defense, a network of state and local organizations publicizing government mobilization programs, encouraging home gardens, sponsoring drives to sell Liberty bonds, and promoting social welfare reforms. This patriotic work improved prospects for passing the Nineteenth Amendment granting woman suffrage. "We have made partners of women in this war," Wilson said as he endorsed woman suffrage in 1918. "Shall we admit them only to a partnership of suffering and sacrifice . . . and not to a partnership of privilege and right?"

War mobilization encouraged a great migration of southern African Americans to northern cities to work in railroad yards, packing houses, steel mills, shipyards, and coal mines. Between 1910 and 1920, Cleveland's African American population swelled by more than 300 percent, Detroit's by more than 600 percent, and Chicago's by 150 percent. All told, about a half-million African Americans moved to the North, with families pooling savings or selling household goods to fund the journey. Most migrants were unmarried and skilled or semiskilled males in their early twenties. Northern wartime jobs provided an escape from low wages, sharecropping, tenancy, crop liens, debt peonage, lynching, and political disfranchisement. One African American wrote to a friend in Mississippi: "I just begin to feel like a man. . . . I don't have to humble to no one. . . . Will vote the next election."

National War Labor Board

To keep factories running smoothly, Wilson instituted the National War Labor Board (NWLB) in early 1918. The NWLB discouraged strikes and lockouts and urged management to negotiate with existing unions. In July, after the Western Union Company fired eight hundred union members for trying to organize the firm's workers, the president nationalized the telegraph lines and put the laborers back to work. But in September the NWLB ordered striking Bridgeport, Connecticut, machinists back to munitions factories, threatening to revoke the draft exemptions they received for working in an essential industry.

Labor leaders hoped the war would lead to recognition and better pay through partnership with government. Samuel Gompers threw the AFL's loyalty to Wilson, promising to deter strikes. He and other moderate labor leaders accepted appointments to federal agencies. The antiwar Socialist Party blasted the AFL for becoming a "fifth wheel on [the] capitalist war chariot," but union membership climbed from roughly 2.5 million in 1916 to more than 4 million in 1919.

The AFL, however, could not curb strikes by the radical Industrial Workers of the World (IWW, also known as Wobblies) or rebellious AFL locals, especially those controlled by socialists. In the nineteen war months, more than six thousand strikes expressed workers' demands for a living wage and improved working conditions. Unions sought to create industrial democracy, a more representative workplace with labor helping to determine job categories and content. Defying the AFL, labor parties had sprung up in twenty-three states by 1920.

CIVIL LIBERTIES UNDER CHALLENGE

Wilson and his advisers enjoyed the support of newspapers, religious leaders, and public officials. They were less certain, however, about ordinary Americans. An official and unofficial campaign soon began to silence dissenters who questioned Wilson's decision for war or who protested the draft. The Wilson administration compiled one of the worst civil liberties records in American history.

The targets of government and quasi-vigilante repression included hundreds of thousands of Americans and aliens: pacifists, conscientious objectors, socialists, radical labor groups, the debt-ridden Oklahoma tenant farmers who staged the Green Corn Rebellion against the draft, the Non-Partisan League, reformers like Robert La Follette and Jane Addams, and others. In the wartime debate over democratic free speech, the concept of civil liberties emerged for the first time as a major public policy issue (see Legacy for a People and a Nation, page 623).

The Committee on Public Information

Spearheading the administration's war campaign was the Committee on Public Information (CPI), formed in April 1917 and headed by the Progressive journalist George Creel. Employing talented writers and scholars, the CPI used propaganda to mobilize public opinion. Pamphlets and films demonized the Germans, and CPI "Four-Minute Men" spoke at movie theaters, schools, and churches to pump up patriotism. Encouraged by the CPI, film companies and the National Association of the Motion Picture Industry produced documentaries, newsreels, and anti-German movies, such as The Kaiser, the Beast of Berlin (1918).

The committee also urged the press to practice self-censorship and encouraged people to spy on neighbors. Ultrapatriotic groups, such as the Sedition Slammers and the American Defense Society, used vigilantism. In Hilger, Montana, citizens burned history texts mentioning Germany. To avoid trouble, the Kaiser-Kuhn grocery in St. Louis changed its name to Pioneer Grocery. The townspeople in Berlin, Iowa, henceforth hailed from Lincoln. The German shepherd became the Alsatian shepherd.

Towns had Liberty Loan quotas and sometimes bullied slackers into purchasing bonds. Nativist advocates of "100% Americanism" exploited the atmosphere to exhort immigrants to throw off their Old World cultures. Companies offered English language and naturalization classes and refused jobs and promotions to those who did not learn English. Even institutions that had long prided themselves on tolerance became contaminated. Wellesley College economics professor Emily Greene Balch was fired for her pacifist views (she won the Nobel Peace Prize in 1946). Three Columbia University students were apprehended in mid-1917 for circulating an antiwar petition. Columbia fired Professor J. M. Cattell, a distinguished psychologist, for his antiwar stand. His colleague Charles Beard, a historian with a prowar perspective, resigned in protest. Local school boards also dismissed teachers who questioned the war.

Espionage and Sedition Acts

The Wilson administration guided through an obliging Congress the Espionage Act (1917) and the Sedition Act (1918), giving the government wide latitude to crack down on critics. The first statute forbade "false statements" designed to impede the draft or promote military insubordination, and it banned from the mails materials considered treasonous. The Sedition Act made it unlawful to obstruct the sale of war bonds and to use "disloyal, profane, scurrilous, or abusive" language to describe the government, the Constitution, the flag, or the military uniform. More than two thousand people were prosecuted under the acts, with many others intimidated into silence.

Progressives and conservatives used the war emergency to throttle the Industrial Workers of the World and the Socialist Party. Government agents raided IWW meetings, and the army put down IWW strikes. By war's end, most of the union's leaders were in jail. In summer 1918, the Socialist Party leader Eugene V. Debs was arrested by federal agents for an oration extolling socialism and freedom of speech—including the freedom to criticize Wilson on the war. Debs told the court what many thought of the Espionage Act: it was "a despotic enactment in flagrant conflict with democratic principles and with the spirit of free institutions." Handed a ten-year sentence, Debs remained in prison until he was pardoned in late 1921.

The Supreme Court endorsed such convictions. In Schenck v. U.S. (1919), the Court upheld the conviction of a Socialist Party member who mailed pamphlets urging draft resistance. In wartime, Justice Oliver Wendell Holmes wrote, the First Amendment could be restricted when words "are of such a nature as to create a clear and present danger that they will bring about the substantial evils that Congress has a right to prevent."

RED SCARE, RED SUMMER

The line between wartime suppression of dissent and the postwar Red Scare is not easily drawn. Together they stabbed at the Bill of Rights and wounded radicalism in America. But while wartime fears focused on subversion, after the armistice it was revolution; and while the prewar target was often German Americans, in 1919 it was frequently organized labor. Alarmed by the Russian Revolution and the communist uprisings in Europe, American fears grew in 1919 when the Soviet leadership formed the Communist International (or Comintern) to export revolution worldwide. Terrified conservatives sought out pro-Bolshevik sympathizers (or Reds, from the red flag used by communists) in the United States, especially in immigrant groups and labor unions.

Labor Strikes

Labor union leaders emerged out of the war determined to secure higher wages and retain wartime bargaining rights. Employers instead rescinded benefits they were forced to grant during the war, including recognition of unions. The result was more than 3,300 strikes involving 4 million laborers in 1919. On May 1, a day of celebration for workers worldwide, bombs were sent to prominent Americans, though most were intercepted and dismantled. Police never captured the conspirators, but many blamed anarchists and others bent on destroying the American way of life. When the Boston police went on strike in September, some claimed a Bolshevik conspiracy, but others thought it ridiculous to label Boston's Irish American, Catholic cops radicals.

Unrest in the steel industry in September stirred more ominous fears. Many steelworkers worked twelve hours a day, seven days a week, and lived in squalid housing, counting on the National Committee for Organizing Iron and Steel Workers to improve their lives. When postwar unemployment in the industry climbed and the U.S. Steel Corporation refused to meet with committee representatives, some 350,000 workers walked off the job, demanding the right to collective bargaining, a shorter workday, and a living wage. The steel barons hired strikebreakers and sent agents to club strikers. The strike collapsed in early 1920.

Political and business leaders dismissed the steel strike as a foreign threat orchestrated by American radicals. There was no conspiracy, and the American left was badly splintered. Two defectors from the Socialist Party, John Reed and Benjamin Gitlow, founded the Communist Labor Party in 1919. The rival Communist Party of the United States of America, composed largely of aliens, was launched the same year. But their combined membership did not exceed seventy thousand, and in 1919 the harassed Socialist Party could muster barely thirty thousand members.

American Legion

Although divisiveness signified radicals' weakness, Progressives and conservatives interpreted the rise of new parties as strengthening the radical menace. Organized in May 1919 to lobby for veterans' benefits, the American Legion soon preached an antiradicalism that fueled the Red Scare. By 1920, 843,000 Legion members, mostly middle- and upper-class, embraced an impassioned Americanism demanding conformity.

Wilson's attorney general, A. Mitchell Palmer, also insisted that Americans think alike. A Progressive reformer, Quaker, and ambitious politician, Palmer appointed J. Edgar Hoover to head the Radical Division of the Department of Justice. Hoover compiled index cards naming allegedly radical individuals and organizations. During 1919, agents jailed IWW members; Palmer made sure that 249 alien radicals, including anarchist Emma Goldman, were deported to Russia.

States passed peacetime sedition acts and arrested hundreds of people. Vigilante groups and mobs flourished once again, their numbers swelled by returning veterans. In November 1919, in Centralia, Washington, American Legionnaires broke from a parade to storm the IWW hall. Several were wounded, others were arrested, and one ex-soldier was taken from jail by a mob, then beaten, castrated, and shot. The New York State legislature expelled five elected Socialist Party members in early 1920.

Palmer Raids

The Red Scare reached a climax in January 1920 in the Palmer Raids. Planned and directed by J. Edgar Hoover, government agents in thirty-three cities broke into meeting halls and homes without search warrants, jailing four thousand people without counsel. In Boston some four hundred people were detained on bitterly cold Deer Island; two died of pneumonia, one leaped to his death, and another went insane. Because of court rulings and the courageous efforts of Assistant Secretary of Labor Louis Post, most of the arrestees were released, although in 1920–1921 nearly six hundred were deported.

Palmer's disregard for elementary civil liberties drew criticism, with many charging that his tactics violated the Constitution. When Palmer called for a peacetime sedition act, he alarmed both liberal and conservative leaders. His dire prediction that pro-Soviet radicals would incite violence on May Day 1920 proved mistaken; no disturbances occurred anywhere. Palmer, who called himself the Fighting Quaker, was jeered as the Quaking Fighter.

Racial Unrest

Palmer also blamed communists for the racial violence that gripped the nation, though the charge was equally baseless. African Americans realized well before the war ended that their participation did little to change discriminatory white attitudes. The Ku Klux Klan was reviving, and racist films like D. W. Griffith's *The Birth of a Nation* (1915) fed prejudice with its celebration of the Klan and its demeaning depiction of blacks. Despite wartime declarations of humanity, between 1914 and 1920, 382 blacks were lynched, some of them in military uniform.

Northern whites who resented "the Negro invasion" rioted, as in East St. Louis, Illinois, in July 1917 and a month later in Houston. During the bloody Red Summer of 1919 (so named by African American author James Weldon Johnson for the blood that was spilled), race riots rocked two dozen cities and towns. The worst violence occurred in Chicago, a favorite destination for migrating African Americans. In the very hot days of July 1919, an African American youth swimming at a segregated white beach was hit by a thrown rock and drowned. Soon African Americans and whites were battling each other. Stabbings, burnings, and shootings continued for days until state police restored some calm. Thirty-eight people died, twenty-three African Americans and fifteen whites.

A disillusioned W. E. B. Du Bois vowed a struggle: "We return from fighting. We return fighting." Or, as the poet Claude McKay put it after the Chicago riot in his poem "If We Must Die,"

> Like men we'll face the murderous cowardly pack.
> Pressed to the wall, dying, but fighting back.

African American Militancy

Du Bois and McKay reflected a newfound militancy among African American veterans and northern African American communities. Editorials in African American newspapers subjected white politicians to increasingly harsh criticism and implored readers to embrace their own prowess and beauty. The NAACP stepped up its campaign for civil rights and equality, vowing in 1919 to publicize the terrors of lynching and seek legislation against it. Other blacks, doubting the potential for equality, turned instead to the charismatic Jamaican immigrant Marcus Garvey, who called on African Americans to seek a separate black nation.

The crackdown on laborers and radicals and the resurgence of racism in 1919 dashed wartime hopes. Although the passage of the Nineteenth Amendment in 1920, guaranteeing women the right to vote, showed that reform could happen, it was the exception. Unemployment, inflation, racial conflict, labor upheaval, and a campaign against free speech inspired disillusionment in the immediate postwar years.

THE DEFEAT OF PEACE

President Wilson seemed focused on confronting the threat of radicalism more abroad than at home. In mid-1918, Wilson revealed his ardent anti-Bolshevism when he ordered five thousand American troops to northern Russia and ten thousand more to Siberia, where they joined other Allied contingents in fighting what was now a Russian civil war. Wilson did not consult Congress. He said the military expeditions would guard Allied supplies and Russian railroads from German seizure, and would also rescue Czechs who wished to fight the Germans.

Seeking to smash the infant Bolshevik government, Wilson backed an economic blockade of Russia, sent arms to anti-Bolshevik forces, and refused to recognize Lenin's government. The United States also secretly passed military information to anti-Bolshevik forces and used food relief to shore up Soviet opponents in the Baltic region. Later, at the Paris Peace Conference, Soviets were denied a seat. U.S. troops did not leave Russia until spring 1920, after the Bolsheviks demonstrated their staying power.

Wilson faced a monumental task in securing a postwar settlement, though some observers suggested that he underestimated his task. During the 1918 congressional elections, Wilson misstepped in suggesting that patriotism required the election of a Democratic Congress; Republicans blasted the president for questioning their love of country and gained control of both houses. This created problems because a peace treaty would require approval from a potentially hostile Senate and because the election results at home diminished Wilson's stature before foreign leaders. Wilson aggravated his political problems by not naming a senator to his advisory

American Peace Commission and refusing to take any prominent Republicans with him to, or to consult with the Senate Foreign Relations Committee before, the Paris Peace Conference.

Wilson was greeted by adoring crowds in Paris, London, and Rome, but their leaders—Georges Clemenceau of France, David Lloyd George of Britain, and Vittorio Orlando of Italy (with Wilson, the Big Four)—became formidable adversaries. After four years of horrible war, the Allies were not going to be cheated out of the fruits of victory. The late-arriving Americans had not suffered the way the peoples of France and Great Britain had. Germany would have to pay big for the calamity it caused.

Paris Peace Conference

The Big Four tried to work out an agreement, mostly behind closed doors. The victors demanded that Germany (which had been excluded from the proceedings) pay a huge reparations bill. Wilson instead called for a small indemnity, fearing that an economically hobbled Germany might turn to Bolshevism. Unable to moderate the Allied position, the president reluctantly agreed to a clause blaming the war on Germany and to the creation of a commission to determine reparations (later set at $33 billion). Wilson acknowledged that the peace terms were hard, but he also came to believe that "the German people must be made to hate war."

As for dismantling empires and the principle of self-determination, Wilson could only achieve some of his goals. Creating a League-administered mandate system, Japan gained authority over Germany's Pacific colonies, while the French obtained what became Lebanon and Syria and the British received the three former Ottoman provinces that became Iraq. Britain also secured Palestine, on the condition that it promote "the establishment in Palestine of a national home for the Jewish people" without prejudice to "the civil and religious rights of existing non-Jewish communities"—the so-called Balfour Declaration of 1917.

Elsewhere in Europe, Wilson's prescriptions fared better. Out of Austria-Hungary and Russia came the newly independent states of Austria, Hungary, Yugoslavia, Czechoslovakia, and Poland. Wilson and his colleagues also built a *cordon sanitaire* (buffer zone) of new westward-looking nations (Finland, Estonia, Latvia, and Lithuania) around Russia, to quarantine the Bolshevik contagion.

League of Nations and Article 10

Wilson worked hardest on the charter for the League of Nations, the centerpiece of his plans for the postwar world. He envisioned the League as having power over all disputes among states; as such, it could transform international relations. Even so, the great powers would have preponderant say: the organization would have an influential council of five permanent members and elected delegates from smaller states, an assembly of all members, and a World Court.

Wilson identified Article 10 as the "kingpin" of the League covenant: "The Members of the League undertake to respect and preserve as against external aggression the territorial integrity and existing political independence of all Members of the League." Wilson insisted that there could be no future peace with Germany without a league to oversee it.

German representatives at first refused to sign the punitive treaty but submitted in June 1919. They gave up 13 percent of Germany's territory, 10 percent of its population, all of its colonies, and a huge portion of its national wealth. Many people wondered how the League could function in the poisoned postwar atmosphere of humiliation and revenge.

Critics of the Treaty

In March 1919, thirty-nine senators (enough to deny the treaty the necessary two-thirds vote) signed a petition stating that the League's structure did not adequately protect U.S. interests. Wilson denounced his critics as having pygmy minds, but persuaded the peace conference to exempt the Monroe Doctrine and domestic matters from League jurisdiction. Wilson would budge no more. Could his critics not see that League membership would give the United States leadership in the world?

By summer, criticism intensified: Wilson had bastardized his own principles. He conceded Shandong to Japan and killed a provision affirming the racial equality of all peoples. The treaty ignored freedom of the seas, and tariffs were not reduced. Reparations promised to be punishing on Germany. Critics on the left protested that the League would perpetuate empire. Conservative critics feared that the League would limit American freedom of action in world affairs, stymie U.S. expansion, and intrude on domestic questions. And Article 10 raised serious questions: Would the United States be *obligated* to use armed force to ensure collective security? And would the League feel compelled to crush colonial rebellions, such as in Ireland or India?

Henry Cabot Lodge of Massachusetts led the Senate opposition. A Harvard-educated Ph.D. and partisan Republican who intensely disliked Wilson, Lodge packed the Foreign Relations Committee with critics and introduced several reservations to the treaty, most importantly that Congress had to approve any obligation under Article 10.

In September 1919 Wilson embarked on a speaking tour of the United States. Growing more exhausted, he dismissed antagonists as "contemptible quitters." While doubts about Article 10 multiplied, Wilson highlighted neglected features of the League charter—such as the arbitration of disputes and an international conference to abolish child labor. In Colorado, the president awoke to nausea and uncontrollable facial twitching. A few days later, he suffered a massive stroke that paralyzed his left side. He became peevish and more stubborn, increasingly unable to conduct presidential business. Advised to placate Lodge and other senatorial critics so the Versailles treaty might receive Congressional approval, Wilson rejected "dishonorable compromise."

Senate Rejection of the Treaty and League

Twice in November the Senate rejected the Treaty of Versailles and thus U.S. membership in the League. In March 1920 the Senate again voted; this time, a majority (49 for and 35 against) favored the treaty with reservations, but the tally fell short of the two-thirds needed. Had Wilson permitted Democrats to compromise—to accept reservations—he could have achieved his goal of membership in the League, which, despite the U.S. absence, came into being.

At the core of the debate lay a basic foreign policy issue: whether the United States would endorse collective security or continue the more solitary path articulated in George Washington's Farewell Address and the Monroe Doctrine. In a world dominated by imperialist states unwilling to subordinate their strategic ambitions to an international organization, Americans preferred their traditional nonalignment and freedom of choice over binding commitments to collective action. Wilson countered that the League promised something better than the status quo for the United States and the world: collective security in place of the frail protection of alliances and the instability of a balance of power.

An Unsafe World

World War I did not make the world safe for democracy, but it did make the United States an even greater world power. By 1920 the United States was the world's leading economic power, producing 40 percent of its coal, 70 percent of its petroleum, and half of its pig iron. It also ranked first in world trade. American companies used the war to nudge Germans and British out of foreign markets, especially in Latin America. Meanwhile, the United States shifted from a debtor to a creditor nation, becoming the world's leading banker.

After the disappointment of Versailles, the peace movement revitalized, and the military became more professional. The Reserve Officers Training Corps (ROTC) became permanent; military colleges provided upper-echelon training; and the Army Industrial College, founded in 1924, pursued business-military cooperation in logistics and planning. The National Research Council, created in 1916 with government money and Carnegie and Rockefeller funds, continued a defense research alliance. Tanks, quick-firing guns, armor-piercing explosives, and oxygen masks for high-altitude-flying pilots were among the technological advances emerging from World War I.

The international system born in these years was unstable. Nationalist leaders active during World War I, such as Ho Chi Minh of Indochina and Mohandas K. Gandhi of India, vowed independence for their people. Communism became a disruptive force in world politics, and the Soviets bore a grudge against those who tried to thwart their revolution. The new states in central and eastern Europe proved weak. Germans bitterly resented the harsh peace settlement, and German war debts and reparations problems dogged international order for years.

Summary

The war years marked the emergence of the United States as a world power, and Americans could take justifiable pride in their contribution to the Allied victory. But the war exposed deep divisions among Americans: white versus African American, nativist versus immigrant, capital versus labor, men versus women, radical versus Progressive and conservative, pacifist versus interventionist, and nationalist versus internationalist.

During the war, the federal government intervened in the economy and influenced people's everyday lives as never before. Although the Wilson administration shunned reconversion plans (war housing projects, for example, were sold to private

Freedom of Speech and the ACLU

Before World War I, those with radical views often received harsh treatment for exercising their freedom of speech. During the war, however, the Wilson administration's suppression of dissidents led some Americans to reformulate the traditional definition of allowable speech. Roger Baldwin, a conscientious objector, and Crystal Eastman, a woman suffrage activist, were among the first to advance the idea that the content of political speech could be separated from the identity of the speaker and that patriotic Americans could—indeed should—defend the right of others to express political beliefs abhorrent to their own. After defending conscientious objectors, Baldwin and Eastman—joined by activists such as Jane Addams, Helen Keller, and Norman Thomas—formed the American Civil Liberties Union (ACLU).

Since 1920 the ACLU, which today has some 300,000 members, has aimed to protect the basic civil liberties of all Americans. It has been involved in almost every major civil liberties case in U.S. courts, among them the landmark *Brown v. Board of Education* case (1954) which ended federal tolerance of racial segregation. More recently, the ACLU was involved in the 1997 Supreme Court case, ruling that the 1996 Communications Act banning "indecent speech" violated First Amendment rights.

Conservatives have criticized the ACLU for its opposition to official prayers in public schools and its support of legal abortion, as well as its decisions on whose free speech to defend. ACLU proponents countered that it had also defended those on the right, such as Oliver North, a key figure in the 1980s Iran-contra scandal.

Either way, the principle of free speech is today broadly accepted by Americans, so that even ACLU bashers take it for granted. Membership in the ACLU has skyrocketed since the September 11, 2001, terrorist attacks, due to concern about government policies eroding privacy and legal protections for Americans and foreign detainees at Guantánamo Bay. Ironically, the Wilson administration's crackdown on dissent produced an expanded commitment to freedom of speech for a people and a nation.

investors) and quickly dismantled the many government agencies, the World War I experience of the activist state served as guidance for 1930s reformers battling the Great Depression (see Chapter 25). The partnership of government and business in managing the wartime economy advanced the development of a mass society through the standardization of products and the promotion of efficiency. Wilsonian wartime policies also nourished the concentration of corporate ownership by suspending antitrust laws. Business power dominated the next decade, while labor entered lean years.

Although the disillusionment evident after Versailles did not cause the United States to adopt isolationism (see Chapter 26), skepticism about America's ability to right wrongs abroad marked the postwar American mood. People recoiled from photographs of shell-shocked faces and bodies dangling from barbed wire. American soldiers, tired of idealism, craved regular jobs. Many Progressives lost their enthusiasm for crusades, disgusted by the bickering of the victors.

By 1920 idealism faded at home and abroad. Americans were unsure what their country's newfound status as a leading world power meant for the nation. With uneasiness and a mixed legacy from the Great War, the country entered the new era of the 1920s.

Chapter Review

PRECARIOUS NEUTRALITY

How viable was U.S. neutrality during World War I?

President Woodrow Wilson, like most Americans, not only embraced neutrality, he took pride in being one of the few western nations to be free from the war for its first three years. Still, U.S. economic links with Allied nations and Wilson's shared belief with the British that a German victory would spell the end of free enterprise, made pure neutrality less believable to the outside world and less possible. The United States relied on sales to Allied nations to end a recession. It was also difficult to claim U.S. neutrality while banks here made extensive loans to Britain and France. Indirectly, or at least via commerce, the United States had taken sides.

THE DECISION FOR WAR

How did the Zimmerman telegram lead Americans to abandon neutrality?

For months in early 1917, Germany had launched a submarine attack on both warships and commercial vessels regardless of stated neutrality. Americans were already outraged by this when British intelligence passed on to the United States an intercepted telegram in which the German minister in Mexico, Arthur Zimmerman, promised to help Mexico regain the territories it lost to the United States in 1848 if it united with Germany against the United States. Wilson released the telegram to the press, which led many Americans to shed their anti-war position. When several American ships were sunk shortly thereafter, war cries heightened, and Wilson asked Congress to declare war against Germany.

WINNING THE WAR

What was the impact of modern, trench warfare on soldiers?

Aside from an increased risk of casualty or fatality, trench warfare was mentally debilitating. Battles would be fought in zigzag, muddy, vile-smelling trenches fronted by barbed wire and mines across France. Soldiers would charge enemy trenches, often facing machine gun fire or poison gas. Many surviving soldiers suffered a mental illness dubbed "shell shock." Though not labeled as such, its victims faced a kind of post-traumatic stress disorder, with symptoms including a fixed stare, violent tremors, paralyzed limbs, listlessness, jabbering, screaming, and nightmares.

MOBILIZING THE HOME FRONT

How did wartime labor shortages create new opportunities for American workers?

A full employment economy during the war not only meant that workers saw salaries increase (albeit sometimes only slightly ahead of inflation), but they also could easily leave jobs with low salaries or harsh conditions for something better.

Worker shortages also enabled women to move into higher-paying, formerly male jobs, trading domestic service for factories, shifting from clerking in department stores to stenography and typing, or leaving textile mills for firearms plants. Blacks made gains, too, as war mobilization pushed a half million African Americans to migrate to northern cities, leaving behind low-paid sharecropping and tenant farming for better wages in railroad yards, packing houses, steel mills, shipyards, and coal mines.

CIVIL LIBERTIES UNDER CHALLENGE

How did free speech come under fire during World War I and the years that followed?

President Wilson worried about mainstream Americans' feelings regarding the war and the draft and launched a campaign to silence those who disagreed with him. His Committee on Public Information launched propaganda films and pamphlets to mobilize support for the war. Ultrapatriotic groups employed vigilantism, burning textbooks that mentioned Germany or bullying people to buy war bonds. Professors who articulated pacifist views found themselves fired or forced to resign. Labor unions were similarly quashed. Passage of the Espionage Act (1917) and the Sedition Act (1918) empowered the federal government to legally prosecute its critics (nearly 20,000 were prosecuted), while others were intimidated into silence. Federal agents arrested Socialist Party leader Eugene V. Debs when he spoke out about socialism and freedom of speech, including the freedom to criticize Wilson's move to war.

RED SCARE, RED SUMMER

How did the postwar Red Scare dash wartime hopes?

Fears of a communist invasion began shortly after the Bolshevik Revolution and heightened when the Communist Party promised to spread its message worldwide. As membership in both the Socialist and Communist Parties in the United States grew, nationwide crackdowns began against radicals, with labor a particular target. The passage of the nineteenth amendment granting women the right to vote in 1920 provided a glimmer of hope for postwar social improvement, but it was the rare exception. Instead, violations of the Bill of Rights and freedom of speech combined with unemployment, inflation, resurgent racism, and a revitalized Ku Klux Klan to dampen hopes for a more promising postwar America.

THE DEFEAT OF PEACE

What kept the United States out of the League of Nations?

While the League of Nations was Wilson's brainchild, the United States never joined. To Wilson, the League promised a balance of power and solid international allies. But the notion of the League's collectivity was problematic for Americans accustomed to being in world politics. Critics on the left feared that the League would perpetuate empire. Conservative critics worried that it might limit America's freedom to act as it saw fit in world affairs, block U.S. expansion, and intrude on domestic concerns. Worse, critics at home worried about being compelled to participate in collective action deemed necessary by the League.

SUGGESTIONS FOR FURTHER READING

John Milton Cooper Jr., *Breaking the Heart of the World: Woodrow Wilson and the Fight for the League of Nations* (2001)

David S. Foglesong, *America's Secret War Against Bolshevism* (1995)

James B. Grossman, *Land of Hope: Chicago, Black Southerners, and the Great Migration* (1989)

Michael Kazin, *A Godly Hero: The Life of William Jennings Bryan* (2006)

Jennifer D. Keene, *Doughboys, the Great War, and the Remaking of America* (2001)

David M. Kennedy, *Over Here: The Home Front in the First World War* (1980)

Thomas J. Knock, *To End All Wars: Woodrow Wilson and the Quest for a New World Order* (1992)

Margaret Macmillan, *Paris 1919: Six Months That Changed the World* (2002)

John A. Thompson, *Woodrow Wilson* (2002)

Robert H. Zieger, *America's Great War: World War I and the American Experience* (2000)

CHAPTER 24

The New Era | 1920–1929

CHAPTER OUTLINE

Big Business Triumphant

Politics and Government

A Consumer Society

Cities, Migrants, and Suburbs

LINKS TO THE WORLD:
Pan American Airways

New Rhythms of Everyday Life

Lines of Defense

The Age of Play

Cultural Currents

The Election of 1928 and the End of the New Era

Summary

LEGACY FOR A PEOPLE AND A NATION:
Intercollegiate Athletics

Beth and Robert Gordon were not compatible marriage partners. Beth was frumpy and demanding; Robert liked to party. One evening at a nightclub, he met Sally Clark, who liked to party, too. When Robert came home smelling of perfume, he and Beth argued, and then subsequently divorced. Soon, however, Robert missed Beth's intellect. Meanwhile, Beth bought new clothes and makeup, becoming a glamorous beauty. The couple coincidentally visited the same summer resort and rekindled their romance. When Robert was injured in an accident, Beth nursed him back to health, much to Sally's disappointment, and in the end, Beth and Robert remarried.

This story is the plot of the 1920 motion picture *Why Change Your Wife?*—one of dozens of films directed by Cecil B. DeMille. DeMille gave audiences what they wanted to see and fantasized about doing. Beth, Robert, and Sally dressed stylishly, went out dancing, listened to phonograph records, rode in cars, and visited resorts. Although DeMille's films and others of the 1920s usually ended by reinforcing marriage, ruling out premarital sex, and supporting the work ethic, they also exuded a new morality. Both male and female characters shed old-style values for the pursuit of luxury, fun, and the trappings of sexual freedom, just as actors such as the stars of *Why Change Your Wife?*—*Gloria* Swanson and Thomas Meighan—were doing in their off-screen lives. In this way, the film was a harbinger of a new era.

During the 1920s, consumerism flourished. Although poverty beset small farmers, workers in declining industries, and nonwhites in inner cities, most other people enjoyed a high standard of living relative to previous generations. Spurred by advertising and installment buying, Americans acquired radios, automobiles, real estate, and stocks. As in the Gilded Age, the federal government maintained a favorable climate for business.

This icon will direct you to interactive activities and study materials on A People And A Nation, Brief Edition website: **www.cengage.com/history/norton/ peoplenationbrief8e**

Chronology

1920	Volstead Act implements prohibition (Eighteenth Amendment).
	Nineteenth Amendment, legalizing the vote for women in federal elections, is ratified.
	Harding is elected president.
	KDKA transmits the first commercial radio broadcast.
1920–21	Postwar deflation and depression occur.
1921	Federal Highway Act funds the national highway system.
	Emergency Quota Act establishes immigration quotas.
	Sacco and Vanzetti are convicted.
	Sheppard-Towner Act allots funds to states to set up maternity and pediatric clinics.
1922	Economic recovery raises the standards of living.
	Coronado Coal Company v. United Mine Workers rules that strikes could be illegal actions in restraint of trade.
	Bailey v. Drexel Furniture Company voids restrictions on child labor.

	Federal government ends strikes by railroad shop workers and miners.
	Fordney-McCumber Tariff raises rates on imports.
1923	Harding dies; Coolidge assumes the presidency.
	Adkins v. Children's Hospital overturns a minimum wage law affecting women.
1923–24	Government scandals (Teapot Dome) are exposed.
1924	Snyder Act grants citizenship to all Indians not previously citizens.
	National Origins Act revises immigration quotas.
	Coolidge is elected president.
1925	Scopes trial highlights the battle between religious fundamentalists and modernists.
1927	Lindbergh pilots the first solo transatlantic flight.
	Ruth hits sixty home runs.
	The Jazz Singer, the first movie with sound, is released.
1928	Stock market soars.
	Hoover is elected president.
1929	Stock market crashes; the Great Depression begins.

In contrast to the Progressive era, few people worried about abuses of power. Still, state and local governments undertook important reforms.

It was an era in which people embraced new technology while trying to preserve long-held values. New forms of leisure coincided with creativity in the arts and advances in science and technology. Changes in work habits, family responsibilities, and healthcare fostered new uses of time and new attitudes about behavior, including encouragements to "think young." While many people experienced material bounty, others continued to endure hardship. The decade's modernism and materialism were appealing to many but unsettling to those who held tightly to traditional beliefs.

The glitter of consumer culture that dominated DeMille's films blinded Americans to rising debt and uneven prosperity. A devastating depression would bring the era to a close.

- How did developments in technology and the workplace stimulate social change during the 1920s?
- What were the benefits and costs of consumerism, and how did people deal with challenges to old-time values?
- What caused the stock market crash and the ensuing deep depression that signaled the end of the era?

BIG BUSINESS TRIUMPHANT

The 1920s began with economic decline. After World War I, industrial output dropped as wartime orders dried up. In the West, railroads and the mining industry suffered, and layoffs spread through New England as textile companies abandoned outdated factories for the South's convenient raw materials and cheap labor. When demobilized soldiers flooded the work force, unemployment, around 2 percent in 1919, passed 12 percent in 1921. Consumer spending dwindled, causing more contraction and joblessness.

New Economic Expansion

Electric energy prompted a recovery in 1922 that continued unevenly until 1929. Electric motors replaced steam engines, producing goods more cheaply and efficiently. Most urban households now had electric service, enabling them to utilize the new appliances, such as refrigerators and vacuum cleaners. The growing economy gave Americans more spending money for new services, too, such as restaurants, beauty salons, and movie theaters. Installment, or time-payment, plans drove the new consumerism. Of 3.5 million automobiles sold in 1923, 80 percent were bought on credit.

Although Progressive era trustbusting had reined in big business, it had not eliminated oligopoly, the control of an entire industry by one or a few large firms. By the 1920s, a few sprawling companies, such as U.S. Steel and General Electric, dominated basic industries, and oligopolies controlled marketing, distribution, and finance.

Associations and "New Lobbying"

Business and professional organizations also expanded in the 1920s. Retailers and manufacturers formed trade associations to swap information. Farm bureaus promoted scientific agriculture and tried to stabilize markets. These special-interest groups participated in what is called the "new lobbying." With government playing an increasingly influential role, hundreds of organizations sought to convince legislators to support their interests. Government policies helped business thrive, and legislators depended on lobbyists' expertise. Prodded by lobbyists, Congress cut taxes on corporations and wealthy individuals in 1921 and passed the Fordney-McCumber Tariff Act in 1922. Presidents Warren G. Harding, Calvin Coolidge, and Herbert Hoover appointed cabinet officers who were favorable toward business. Regulatory agencies, such as the Federal Trade Commission and the Interstate Commerce Commission, cooperated with corporations more than they regulated them.

Key Supreme Court decisions sheltered business from government regulation and hindered organized labor. In *Coronado Coal Company v. United Mine Workers* (1922), Chief Justice and former president William Howard Taft ruled that a striking union, like a trust, could be prosecuted for illegal restraint of trade. Yet in *Maple Floor Association v. U.S.* (1929), the Court decided that trade associations that distributed anti-union information were not acting in restraint of trade. The Court also voided restrictions on child labor (*Bailey v. Drexel Furniture Company,* 1922), and overturned a minimum wage law affecting women because it infringed on liberty of contract (*Adkins v. Children's Hospital,* 1923).

Setbacks for Organized Labor

Public opinion turned against organized labor in the 1920s, linking it with communism brought to America by radical immigrants. Using Red Scare tactics, the Harding administration in 1922 obtained a sweeping court injunction to quash a strike by 400,000 railroad workers. State and federal courts issued injunctions to prevent other strikes and permitted businesses to sue unions for damages suffered from labor actions.

Some companies imposed yellow dog contracts which made refusal to join a union a condition of employment. Companies also countered the appeal of unions by offering pensions, profit sharing, and company-sponsored picnics and sporting events—a policy known as welfare capitalism. State legislators aided employers by prohibiting closed shops (workplaces where union membership was mandatory) and permitting open shops (where employers could hire nonunion employees). As a result of court action, welfare capitalism, and ineffective leadership, union membership fell from 5.1 million in 1920 to 3.6 million in 1929.

Languishing Agriculture

Agriculture languished during the 1920s, as farmers faced international competition and and went into debt when they tried to increase productivity by investing in new machines, such as harvesters and tractors. Irrigation and mechanization made large-scale farming so efficient that fewer farmers could produce more crops. As a result, crop prices plunged, big agribusinesses took over, and small landholders and tenants struggled when incomes plummeted and debts rose.

POLITICS AND GOVERNMENT

A series of Republican presidents extended Theodore Roosevelt's government-business cooperation, but they made government a compliant coordinator rather than the active manager Roosevelt advocated. President Warren G. Harding, elected in 1920, was a symbol of government's good will toward business. He captured 16 million popular votes to 9 million for the Democratic nominee, Ohio governor James M. Cox. (The total vote in the 1920 presidential election was 36 percent higher than in 1916, reflecting the first-time participation of women voters.)

A small-town newspaperman and senator from Ohio, Harding appointed assistants who promoted business growth, notably Secretary of State Charles Evans Hughes, Secretary of Commerce Herbert Hoover, Secretary of the Treasury Andrew Mellon, and Secretary of Agriculture Henry C. Wallace. Harding also backed reforms such as the Budget and Accounting Act of 1921 to streamline federal spending, and he supported antilynching legislation (rejected by Congress) and bills assisting farm cooperatives and liberalizing farm credit.

Scandals of the Harding Administration

Harding, however, had personal weaknesses, among them his extramarital affairs. In 1917 he began a relationship with Nan Britton, thirty-one years his junior, that resulted in a daughter in 1919. Britton reputedly visited Harding in the White House, although Harding never acknowledged his illegitimate offspring.

Of greater consequence, Harding appointed cronies who used office holding for personal gain. Charles Forbes, head of the Veterans Bureau, went to federal prison, convicted of fraud and bribery in government contracts. Most notoriously, a congressional inquiry in 1923 and 1924 revealed that Secretary of the Interior Albert Fall accepted bribes to lease government property to oil companies. Fall was fined $100,000 and spent a year in jail for his role in the so-called Teapot Dome scandal, named for the Wyoming oil reserve he handed to the Mammoth Oil Company.

By mid-1923, Harding had become disillusioned. On a speaking tour, he became ill and died in San Francisco on August 2. Although his death preceded revelation of the Teapot Dome scandal, some speculated that Harding committed suicide to avoid impeachment or was poisoned by his wife. Most evidence, however, points to death from natural causes, probably heart disease.

Vice President Calvin Coolidge, who became president, was less outgoing than Harding. As governor of Massachusetts, Coolidge had attracted national attention in 1919 with his stand against striking Boston policemen and won business support and the vice-presidential nomination in 1920.

Coolidge Prosperity

Respectful of private enterprise and aided by Andrew Mellon, who was retained as treasury secretary, Coolidge's administration reduced federal debt, lowered income-tax rates (especially for the wealthy), and began construction of a national highway system. With farm prices falling, Congress twice passed bills to establish government-backed price supports for staple crops (the McNary-Haugen bills of 1927 and 1928). Resembling the 1890s Farmers' Alliances subtreasury scheme, these bills would have established a system whereby the government would buy surplus farm products and either hold them until prices rose or sell them abroad. Coolidge, however, vetoed the measures as improper government interference in the market economy.

"Coolidge prosperity" was the decisive issue in the 1924 presidential election. Both major parties ran candidates who favored private initiative over government intervention. At their convention, Democrats voted 542 to 541 against condemning the revived Ku Klux Klan and deadlocked for 103 ballots between southern prohibitionists, who supported former treasury secretary William G. McAdoo, and antiprohibition easterners, who backed New York's governor Alfred E. Smith. They compromised on John W. Davis, a New York corporate lawyer.

Remnants of the Progressive movement, along with farm, labor, and socialist groups, formed a new Progressive Party and nominated Robert M. La Follette, the aging Wisconsin reformer. The new party stressed public ownership of railroads and power plants, conservation of natural resources, aid to farmers, rights for organized labor, and regulation of business. Coolidge beat Davis by 15.7 million to 8.4 million popular votes and 382 to 136 electoral votes. La Follette received 4.8 million popular votes and 13 electoral votes.

Extensions of Progressive Reform

The urgency for political and economic reform that inspired the previous Progressive generation faded in the 1920s. Much reform, however, occurred at state and local levels. Following pre–World War I initiatives, thirty-four states instituted or expanded workers' compensation laws and public welfare programs in the 1920s. By

1926 every major city and many smaller ones had planning and zoning commissions to harness physical growth to the common good. A new generation of reformers who later influenced national affairs acquired valuable experience in statehouses, city halls, and universities.

Indian Affairs and Politics

Organizations such as the Indian Rights Association, the Indian Defense Association, and the General Federation of Women's Clubs worked to obtain justice and social services for Native Americans, including better education and the return of tribal lands. But like other minorities, Indians generally met discrimination and pressure to assimilate. Severalty, the policy created by the Dawes Act of 1887 of allotting land to individuals rather than to tribes, failed to make Indians self-supporting. Deeply attached to their land, they showed little inclination to move to cities. Whites still hoped to convert native peoples into "productive" citizens, typically ignoring indigenous cultures. Reformers were especially critical of Indian women, who refused to adopt middle-class homemaking habits and balked at sending their children to boarding schools.

Citizenship remained unclear. The Dawes Act had conferred citizenship on Indians who accepted land allotments, but not those who remained on reservations. After several court challenges, Congress passed an Indian Citizenship Act (Snyder Act) in 1924, granting citizenship to all Indians. President Hoover reinforced this measure's intent by stating that citizenship was the best means for Indians to assimilate.

Women and Politics

Ratification of the Nineteenth Amendment in 1920 gave women the vote, but they remained excluded from local and national power structures. Instead, they worked through voluntary organizations to lobby legislators on issues such as birth control, peace, education, Indian affairs, or opposition to lynching.

In 1921 women's groups persuaded Congress to pass the Sheppard-Towner Act, allotting funds to states to create maternity and pediatric clinics to reduce infant mortality. (The measure ended in 1929, when Congress, pressured by physicians, canceled funding.) The Cable Act of 1922 reversed the law under which an American woman who married a foreigner assumed her husband's citizenship, allowing her to retain U.S. citizenship. At the state level, women achieved some rights, such as the ability to serve on juries.

As new voters, however, women pursued diverging goals. Women in the National Association of Colored Women, for example, fought for the rights of minorities. Other groups, such as the National Woman's Party, pressed for an equal rights amendment to ensure women's equality under the law. But such activity alienated the National Consumers League, the Women's Trade Union League, the League of Women Voters, and other organizations that supported special protective legislation to limit hours and improve conditions for employed women.

A CONSUMER SOCIETY

The consumerism depicted in *Why Change Your Wife?* reflected important economic changes affecting the nation. Between 1919 and 1929, the gross national product— the total value of all goods and services produced in the United States—swelled by

TABLE 24.1   Consumerism in the 1920s

1900	
2 bicycles	$ 70.00
Wringer and washboard	5.00
Brushes and brooms	5.00
Sewing machine (mechanical)	25.00
Total	$ 105.00
1928	
Automobile	$ 700.00
Radio	75.00
Phonograph	50.00
Washing machine	150.00
Vacuum cleaner	50.00
Sewing machine (electric)	60.00
Other electrical equipment	25.00
Telephone (per year)	35.00
Total	$1,145.00

Source: From an article in *Survey Magazine* in 1928 reprinted in *Another Part of the Twenties,* by Paul Carter. Copyright 1977 by Columbia University Press. Reprinted with permission of the publisher.

40 percent. Wages and salaries also grew (though not as drastically), while the cost of living remained relatively stable. People had more purchasing power (see Table 24.1). By 1929, two-thirds of all Americans had electricity, compared to one-sixth in 1912. In 1929 one-fourth of all families owned vacuum cleaners. Many could afford such goods as radios, beauty products, and movie tickets, because several family members worked or because the breadwinner took a second job. Nevertheless, new products and services were available to more than just the rich.

Effects of the Automobile

During the 1920s, automobile registrations soared from 8 million to 23 million, and by 1929 there was one car for every five Americans. Mass production and competition made cars affordable. A Ford Model T cost less than $300, and a Chevrolet sold for $700 by 1926—when factory workers earned about $1,300 a year and clerical workers about $2,300. At those prices, people could consider the car a necessity rather than a luxury.

Cars altered American life. Streets became cleaner as autos replaced the horses that daily dumped tons of manure. Women who learned to drive achieved newfound independence. By 1927 most autos were enclosed (they previously had open tops), creating new private space for courtship and sex. Most important, the car was the ultimate social equalizer. As one writer observed in 1924, "It is hard to convince Steve Popovich, or Antonio Branca, or plain John Smith that he is being ground into the dust by Capital when at will he may drive the same highways . . . and get as much enjoyment from his trip as the modern Midas."

After World War I, motorists joined farmers and bicyclists in their decades-old campaign for improved roads. In 1921 Congress passed the Federal Highway Act, providing funds for state roads, and in 1923 the Bureau of Public Roads planned a national highway system. Road building inspired such technological developments as mechanized road graders and concrete mixers. The oil-refining industry, which produced gasoline, became vast and powerful. In 1920 the United States produced about 65 percent of the world's oil. Public officials paid more attention to traffic control, with General Electric Company producing the first timed stop-and-go traffic light in 1924.

Advertising

By 1929 more money was spent on advertising than on formal education. Blending psychological theory with practical cynicism, advertising theorists asserted that people's tastes could be manipulated. For example, cosmetics manufacturers like Max Factor, Helena Rubenstein, and African American entrepreneur Madame C. J. Walker used movie stars and beauty advice in magazines to entice female customers. The baseball star Babe Ruth was hired to endorse food and sporting goods.

Radio

Radio became an influential advertising medium. By 1929 over 10 million Americans owned radios, spending $850 million annually on radio equipment. In the early 1920s, Congress decided that broadcasting should be a private enterprise, not a tax-supported public service as in Great Britain. American programming focused on entertainment rather than educational content, because entertainment attracted larger audiences and therefore higher advertising profits. Station KDKA in Pittsburgh, owned by Westinghouse Electric Company, pioneered commercial radio in 1920. In 1922, an AT&T-run station in New York City broadcast advertisements—commercials. Other stations followed; by late 1922 there were 508 commercial stations.

Radio transformed American society. In 1924, both political parties broadcast their presidential nominating conventions, enabling candidates to reach more Americans. And radio's mass marketing and standardized programming blurred ethnic boundaries and created—at least in one way—a homogeneous American culture, which television and other mass media expanded throughout the twentieth century.

CITIES, MIGRANTS, AND SUBURBS

The 1920 federal census revealed that, for the first time, a majority of Americans lived in urban areas (defined as places with 2,500 or more people). Growth in manufacturing and services helped propel urbanization. Industries like steel, oil, and auto production energized Birmingham, Houston, and Detroit; services and retail trades boosted expansion in Seattle, Atlanta, and Minneapolis.

During the 1920s, 6 million Americans left their farms for the city. Young farm people traded seemingly staid rural life for the flashy openness of cities, relocating to regional centers like Kansas City and Indianapolis or to the West. Between 1920 and 1930, California's population increased 67 percent, and California became a highly urbanized state while retaining its status as a leading agricultural producer.

African American Migration

African Americans, in what is called the Great Migration, made up a sizable portion of people on the move during the 1920s. Pushed from cotton farming by a boll weevil plague and lured by industrial jobs, 1.5 million African Americans moved, doubling the African American populations of New York, Chicago, Detroit, and Houston.

Forced by low wages and discrimination to seek cheap housing, African American newcomers squeezed into low-rent ghettos like Chicago's South Side. The only way to expand their housing opportunities was to spill into nearby white neighborhoods, which sparked resistance and violence. Fears of such invasion prompted neighborhood associations to adopt restrictive covenants, whereby white homeowners pledged not to sell or rent property to African Americans.

Marcus Garvey

In response to discrimination and violence, thousands of urban African Americans joined movements that glorified racial independence. The most influential of these black nationalist groups was the Universal Negro Improvement Association (UNIA), led by Marcus Garvey, a Jamaican immigrant who believed blacks should separate from corrupt white society. His newspaper, *Negro World,* preached black independence, and Garvey promoted black-owned businesses that would manufacture and sell products to black consumers, establishing the Negro Factories Corporation to fund such enterprises. He also founded the Black Star steamship line to transport products among black businesses in North America, the Caribbean and Africa.

The UNIA declined in the mid-1920s after mismanagement forced dissolution of the Negro Factories Corporation, and Garvey was deported for mail fraud involving the bankrupt Black Star line. His prosecution, however, was politically motivated. Middle-class African American leaders, such as W. E. B. Du Bois, opposed the UNIA, fearing that its extremism would undermine their efforts. The U.S. Bureau of Investigation monitored Garvey's radical activities since 1919, and in 1923 eight prominent African Americans petitioned the attorney general to deport Garvey. Nevertheless, for years the UNIA attracted a large following (contemporaries estimated 500,000; Garvey claimed 6 million), and Garvey's speeches instilled in many African Americans a heightened sense of racial pride.

Newcomers from Mexico and Puerto Rico

The newest immigrants to U.S. cities came from Mexico and Puerto Rico, where declining fortunes pushed people off the land. During the 1910s, Anglo farmers' associations encouraged Mexican immigration to provide cheap agricultural labor, and by the 1920s Mexican migrants constituted three-fourths of farm labor in the U.S. West. Growers treated Mexican laborers as slaves, paying them extremely low wages. Although some achieved middle-class status, most crowded into low-rent districts plagued by poor sanitation, poor police protection, and poor schools. Mexicans moved back and forth across the border, creating a way of life that Mexicans called *sin fronteras*—without borders.

The 1920s also witnessed an influx of Puerto Ricans to the mainland. as a shift in the island's economy from sugar to coffee production created a labor surplus. Attracted by contracts from employers seeking cheap labor, they created *barrios* (communities) and found jobs in factories, hotels, restaurants, and domestic service. Like Mexicans, Puerto Ricans maintained traditional customs and developed businesses—*bodegas* (grocery stores), cafés, boarding houses—and social organizations to help them adapt to American society. Educated elites—doctors, lawyers, and business owners—became community leaders.

Pan American Airways

Air transportation and airmail service between the United States and Latin America began in the 1920s, but anti-American hostility in the region made establishing connections difficult. In 1926 the U.S. government, fearful that German aircraft might bomb the Panama Canal in future conflicts, signed a treaty with Panama giving American airplanes exclusive rights to Panamanian airports. Charles Lindbergh and a formerly obscure pilot, Juan Trippe, played key roles in expanding American air service throughout Latin America.

With help from his father-in-law, a banking partner of J. P. Morgan, Trippe established Pan American Airways (informally known as Pan Am) in 1927 and won a contract to carry mail between Florida and Cuba. In December of that year, Lindbergh charmed the Mexicans into accepting airline links to the United States. The next year, Lindbergh joined Pan Am and began flying company planes to Central and South America, helping Trippe initiate mail and passenger service to Panama, Mexico, and other Latin American countries. By 1929 Trippe advertised to wealthy Americans the opportunity to escape prohibition and enjoy Caribbean beaches on Pan Am.

Pan Am built airports that became essential connections between Latin America and the rest of the world. Trippe's employees created aerial maps that provided navigational aids. Pan Am not only linked Latin America with the United States but also helped unite parts of Latin America that were previously divided by impenetrable mountain ranges. Yet Pan Am would resort to almost any tactic to build an airport: it cooperated with unsavory dictators, engaged in bribery, and violated human rights, in one case helping Bolivian police corral local Indians behind barbed wire for days in order to clear a new airport.

Still, Pan Am enabled Americans (mostly the wealthy) to travel abroad and brought more foreigners to the United States. In 1942 its aircraft became the first to fly around the world. In the 1940s, the company began offering flights to Europe and Africa. Until its demise in 1991, Pan Am provided a leading link between the United States and the rest of the world.

Providing air transport connections to the Caribbean, Central America, and South America, Pan American Airways established the first major passenger and cargo links between the United States and other nations. By the early 1930s, flights were so numerous that the timetable announced in this illustration consisted of twelve pages. (The Pan American Heritage Web Site)

Over half a million Mexicans immigrated to the United States during the 1920s. Many of them traveled in families and worked together in the fields and orchards of California and other western states. This family is shown pitting apricots in Los Angeles County in 1924.   (Seaver Center for Western History Research, Natural History Museum of Los Angeles County)

Growth of Suburbs

Prosperity and automobile transportation in the 1920s made suburbs more accessible to those wishing to flee congested urban neighborhoods. Between 1920 and 1930, suburbs of Chicago (such as Oak Park and Evanston), Cleveland (Shaker Heights), and Los Angeles (Burbank and Inglewood) grew five to ten times faster than nearby central cities. Los Angeles builders alone erected 250,000 suburban homes. Most suburbs were middle- and upper-class bedroom communities; some, like Highland Park (near Detroit) were industrial satellites.

Suburbanites wanted to escape big-city crime, grime, and taxes, and they fought to preserve control over their own police, schools, and water and gas services. Particularly in the Northeast and Midwest, the suburbs' independence prevented central cities from accessing the resources and tax bases of wealthier suburban residents. Population dispersal spread the environmental problems of city life—trash, pollution, noise—across the metropolitan area.

Most of the consumers who jammed shops, movie houses, and sporting arenas and who embraced fads like crossword puzzles and miniature golf, lived in or around cities. People defied morals by patronizing speakeasies (illegal saloons during prohibition), wearing outlandish clothes, and dancing to jazz, while others reminisced about the simplicity of a world gone by.

NEW RHYTHMS OF EVERYDAY LIFE

Amid changes, people increasingly split their day into distinct time compartments: work, family, and leisure. For many, mechanization and higher productivity enabled employers to shorten the workweek for many industrial laborers from six days to five and a half. White-collar employees often worked a forty-hour week, enjoyed the weekend off, and received annual vacations.

Family size decreased between 1920 and 1930 as birth control became more widely practiced. Over half the women married in the 1870s and 1880s had five or more children; only 20 percent of their counterparts marrying in the 1920s had that birth pattern. The divorce rate jumped from 1 divorce for every 7.5 marriages in 1920 to 1 in 6 by 1929.

Household Management

Although housework remained time-consuming, machines now lightened some household tasks. Especially in middle-class households, electric irons and washing machines simplified wives' chores. Gas- and oil-powered central heating and hot-water heaters eliminated the hauling of wood, coal, and water; maintaining a kitchen fire; and removing ashes.

But technology and economic change also created new demands on women's time. Daughters of working-class families stayed in school longer, making them less available for housework. The availability of washing machines, hot water, vacuum cleaners, and commercial soap put greater pressure on housewives to keep everything clean. No longer a producer of food and clothing as her ancestors were, a housewife instead became the chief shopper. And the automobile also made her the family's chauffeur. One survey found that urban housewives spent seven and one-half hours per week driving to shop and transport children.

Health and Life Expectancy

Nutrition added a scientific dimension to housewives' responsibilities. With the discovery of vitamins between 1915 and 1930, nutritionists advocated certain foods to prevent illness, and giant companies advertised their products as filled with vitamins and minerals. Producers of milk, canned fruits and vegetables, and other foods made claims that were hard to dispute because little was known about these invisible, tasteless ingredients. Welch's Grape Juice, for example, avoided mentioning its excess sugars when it advertised that it was "Rich in Health Values."

Better diets and improved hygiene made Americans healthier. Life expectancy at birth increased from fifty-four to sixty years between 1920 and 1930, and infant mortality decreased by two-thirds. Public sanitation and research in bacteriology reduced life-threatening diseases such as tuberculosis and diphtheria. But infant mortality rates were 50 to 100 percent higher among nonwhites, and tuberculosis in inner-city slums remained alarmingly common. Nevertheless, the total population over age sixty-five grew 35 percent between 1920 and 1930.

Older Americans and Retirement

Industrialism put premiums on youth and agility, pushing older people into poverty from forced retirement and reduced income. Most European countries established state-supported pension systems in the early 1900s. Many Americans, however, believed that pensions smacked of socialism and that individuals should prepare for old age by saving in their youth.

Most inmates in state poorhouses were older people, and almost one-third of Americans age sixty-five and older depended financially on someone else. Few employers, including the federal government, provided for retired employees. Resistance to pension plans finally broke at the state level in the 1920s. Led by the physician Isaac Max Rubinow and the journalist Abraham Epstein, reformers persuaded voluntary associations, labor unions, and legislators to endorse old-age assistance. By 1933 almost every state provided at least minimal support to the needy elderly, opening the door to a national program of old-age insurance.

Social Values

New influences altered habits and values. Women and men wore more casual and gaily colored styles than their parents' generation. The line between acceptable and inappropriate behavior blurred as smoking, drinking, and frankness about sex became fashionable. Birth control gained a large following in respectable circles. Newspapers, magazines, motion pictures, and popular songs (such as "Hot Lips" and "Burning Kisses") made certain that Americans did not suffer from sex starvation.

Because state child-labor laws and compulsory-attendance rules kept children in school longer, peer groups played a more influential role in socializing youngsters. Graded school classes, sports, and clubs constantly brought together children of the same age, separating them from the company and influence of adults. Meanwhile, parents relied less on traditions of childcare and more on experts who wrote manuals on successful child rearing.

Between 1890 and the mid-1920s, ritualized middle- and upper-class courtship, consisting of men's formally calling on women and chaperoned social engagements, faded in favor of dating without supervision. Employed unmarried young people, living away from family restraints, were eager to go on dates to new commercial amusements, such as movies and nightclubs. Automobiles made dating even more extensive. A woman's job, however, seldom provided sufficient income for entertainments, but she could enjoy them if a man treated her. Companionship, romance, and, at times, sexual exploitation accompanied the practice, especially when a woman was expected to trade sexual favors for being treated. Under the courtship system, a woman controlled who could call on her, but reliance on a man's money for entertainment presented difficult moral choices.

Women in the Work Force

After World War I, women continued to stream into the labor force. By 1930, 10.8 million women held paying jobs, an increase of 2 million since war's end. Although the proportion of women working in agriculture shrank, their proportion in categories of urban jobs grew or held steady (see Figure 24.1). Sex segregation persisted; most women took jobs that men seldom sought. Thus, over 1 million women worked as

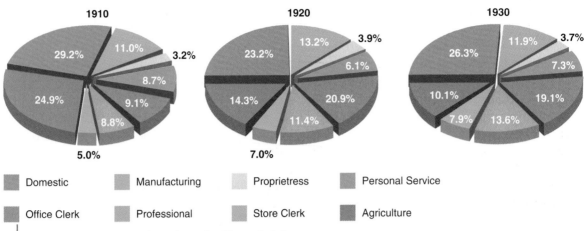

Figure 24.1   Changing Dimensions of Paid Female Labor, 1910–1930

These charts reveal the extraordinary growth in clerical and professional occupations among employed women and the accompanying decline in agricultural labor in the early twentieth century. Notice that manufacturing employment peaked in 1920 and that domestic service fluctuated as white immigrant women began to move out of these jobs and were replaced by women of color.

teachers and nurses. Some 2.2 million women were typists, bookkeepers, and filing clerks, a tenfold increase since 1920. Another 736,000 were store clerks, and growing numbers were personal service workers, such as waitresses and hairdressers. Although almost 2 million women worked in manufacturing, their numbers grew little over the decade. Women's wages seldom exceeded half of those paid to men.

Family economic needs were paramount among women's reasons for working. Consumerism tempted working- and middle-class families to live beyond their means or expand their incomes with women's wages. Although the majority of married women did not hold paying jobs (only 12 percent were employed in 1930), married women as a proportion of the work force rose by 30 percent during the 1920s, and the number of employed married women swelled from 1.9 million to 3.1 million.

Employment of Minority Women

The proportion of nonwhite women in paid labor was double that of white women. Often they entered the work force because their husbands were unemployed or underemployed. The majority of employed African American women held domestic jobs doing cooking, cleaning, and laundry. The few who held factory jobs performed the least desirable, lowest-paying tasks. Some opportunities opened for educated African American women in social work, teaching, and nursing, but these women also faced discrimination and low incomes.

Next to African American women, Japanese American women were the most likely to hold paying jobs, similarly working as field hands and domestics, facing racial bias and low pay. Economic necessity also drew thousands of Mexican American women into the labor force, although their tradition resisted female employment. Most worked as domestic servants, operatives in garment factories, and agricultural laborers.

Alternative Images of Femininity

Women remade the image of femininity, casting aside the heavy, floor-length dresses and long hair of previous generations. Instead, many opted for the independence and sexual freedom of the 1920s flapper with her short skirts and bobbed hair. Although few women lived the flapper life, office workers, store clerks, and college coeds adopted the look. As Cecil B. DeMille's movies showed, new female icons included movie temptresses, such as Clara Bow, known as the It Girl, and Gloria Swanson, notorious for torrid love affairs on and off the screen. Many women were asserting a new social equality with men. One observer described the new woman as intriguingly independent.

> She takes a man's point of view as her mother never could. . . . She'll drive you from the station . . . in her own little sports car. . . . She'll dive as well as you, perhaps better, she'll dance as long as you care to, and she'll take everything you say the way you mean it.

Gay and Lesbian Culture

The era's sexual openness enabled the underground homosexual culture to surface somewhat. In nontraditional city neighborhoods, such as New York's Greenwich Village, cheap rents and a relative tolerance attracted gay men and lesbians, who patronized dance halls, speakeasies, and cafés. Still, gay establishments remained targets for police raids, demonstrating that there was little acceptance from the rest of society.

These trends represented a break with the nineteenth century's more restrained culture. But social change rarely proceeds smoothly. As the decade advanced, groups mobilized to defend older values.

LINES OF DEFENSE

Early in 1920, the leader of a newly formed organization hired two public relations experts, Edward Clarke and Elizabeth Tyler. They canvassed the South, Southwest, and Midwest, where they found countless people eager to pay a $10 membership fee and $6 for a white uniform. Clarke and Tyler pocketed $2.50 from each membership and secured 5 million members by 1923.

Ku Klux Klan

This was the Ku Klux Klan, a revived version of the hooded order that terrorized southern communities after the Civil War. The new KKK vowed to protect female, racial, and ethnic purity. As one pamphlet declared, "Every criminal, every gambler, every thug, every libertine, every girl ruiner, every home wrecker, every wife beater, every dope peddler, every moonshiner, every white slaver, every Rome-controlled newspaper, every black spider—is fighting the Klan. . . . Which side are you on?"

Reconstituted in 1915 by William J. Simmons, an Atlanta, Georgia, evangelist and insurance salesman, the Klan adopted the hoods, intimidating tactics, and mystical terminology of its forerunner (its leader was the Imperial Wizard; its book of rituals, the Kloran). But the new Klan fanned outward from the Deep South, wielding power in places as diverse as Oregon, where Portland's mayor was a Klan member, and Indiana, where Klansmen held the governorship and several legislative seats. Members included many from the urban middle class who feared losing social and economic gains and were nervous about a new youth culture that eluded family control.

One phrase summed up Klan goals: "Native, white, Protestant supremacy." *Native* meant no immigration, no mongrelization of American culture. According to Imperial Wizard Hiram Wesley Evans, "The world has been so made that each race must fight for its life, must conquer, accept slavery, or die." Evans accused the Catholic Church of discouraging assimilation and enslaving people to priests and a foreign pope.

Using threatening assemblies, violence, and political and economic pressure, the Klan meted out vigilante justice to suspected bootleggers, wife beaters, and adulterers; forced schools to stop teaching evolution; campaigned against Catholic and Jewish political candidates; and fueled racial tensions against Mexicans in Texas border cities. Klan women promoted native white Protestantism but also worked for moral reform and prohibition. Because the KKK vowed to protect women's virtue, housewives sometimes appealed to the Klan to punish abusive or irresponsible husbands when legal authorities would not intervene. The Klan's method of justice was flogging.

By 1925, however, scandal undermined the Klan's moral base. Indiana grand dragon David Stephenson was convicted of second-degree murder after he kidnapped and raped a woman who later died. Eventually, the Klan's negative, exclusive brand of patriotism and purity could not compete in a pluralistic society.

Intolerance pervaded American society in the 1920s. Nativists charged that Catholic and Jewish immigrants clogged city slums, flouted community norms, and stubbornly embraced alien religious and political beliefs. Fear of immigrant radicals also fueled the dramatic 1921 trial of two Italian anarchists, Nicola Sacco and Bartolomeo Vanzetti, convicted of murdering a paymaster and guard in Braintree, Massachusetts, though the evidence was flimsy.

Immigration Quotas

Efforts to restrict immigration gathered support. Labor leaders warned that aliens would depress wages and raise unemployment. Business executives, who formerly desired cheap immigrant laborers, now realized that mechanization would keep wages low. Drawing support from such groups, Congress set yearly immigration allocations for each nationality in the Emergency Quota Act of 1921. By restricting annual immigration of a given nationality to 3 percent of the number of immigrants from that nation residing in the United States in 1910, the Act favored Anglo-Saxon Protestant immigrants. It discriminated against Catholics and Jews from southern and eastern Europe, whose numbers were comparatively small in 1910.

In 1924 Congress replaced the Quota Act with the National Origins Act. This law limited annual immigration to 150,000 people and set quotas at 2 percent of each nationality residing in the United States in 1890, except for Asians, who were banned completely. The act further restricted southern and eastern Europeans, since fewer of those groups lived in the United States in 1890 than in 1910, although it allowed wives and children of U.S. citizens to enter as nonquota immigrants. In 1927 a revised National Origins Act redefined quotas to be distributed among European countries in proportion to the national origins (country of birth or descent) of

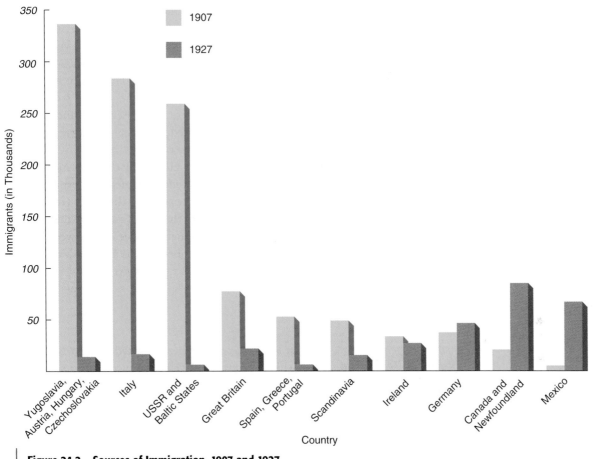

Figure 24.2   Sources of Immigration, 1907 and 1927

Immigration peaked in 1907 and 1908, when newcomers from southern and eastern Europe poured into the United States. After immigration restriction laws were passed in the 1920s, the greatest number of immigrants came from the Western Hemisphere (Canada and Mexico), which was exempted from the quotas, and the number coming from eastern and southern Europe shrank.

American inhabitants in 1920. People from the Western Hemisphere did not fall under the quotas (except for those whom the Labor Department defined as potential paupers) and became the largest immigrant groups (see Figure 24.2).

Fundamentalism

The pursuit of spiritual purity stirred religious fundamentalists, as millions sought salvation from what they perceived as the irreverence of a materialistic, hedonistic society. Resolutely believing that God's miracles created the world, they condemned the theory of evolution as heresy. Wherever fundamentalists constituted a majority of a community, they sought to determine what schools taught. Their enemies were modernists, who used social sciences, such as psychology, to interpret behavior. To modernists, God was important to the study of culture and history, but science advanced knowledge.

Scopes Trial

In 1925 Christian fundamentalism clashed with modernism in Dayton, Tennessee. The Tennessee legislature had banned public schools from teaching the theory that humans evolved from lower forms of life rather than descending from Adam and Eve. The high school teacher John Thomas Scopes volunteered to serve as a test case and was arrested for violating the law. William Jennings Bryan, former secretary of state and three-time presidential candidate, argued for the prosecution, and civil liberties lawyers headed by Clarence Darrow represented Scopes. News correspondents crowded into town, and radio stations broadcast the trial.

Although Scopes was convicted—clearly he had broken the law—modernists claimed victory. The testimony, they believed, showed fundamentalism to be illogical. The trial's climax was when Bryan testified as an expert on the Bible. He asserted that Eve really had been created from Adam's rib, that the Tower of Babel was responsible for the diversity of languages, and that Jonah had been swallowed by a big fish. Spectators in Dayton cheered Bryan, but the liberal press mocked him. Nevertheless, fundamentalists continued to pressure schools to stop teaching evolution and created an independent subculture of schools, camps, radio ministries, and missionary societies.

Religious Revivalism

Urban Pentecostal churches attracted African Americans and whites struggling with economic insecurity, nervous about modernism's attack on old-time religion, and swayed by their depiction of a personal Savior. Using modern advertising and elaborately staged radio broadcasts, magnetic preachers, such as Aimee Semple McPherson of Los Angeles, the former baseball player Billy Sunday, and Father Divine (an African American who amassed an interracial following) stirred revivalist fervor.

Clergy and teachers of all faiths condemned dancing, new dress styles, and sex in movies. Many urban dwellers supported prohibition, believing that it would win the battle against poverty, vice, and corruption. Yet most Americans sincerely sought balance as they tried to adjust to the modern order. Few refrained from the radio and movies like *Why Change Your Wife?*—activities that proved less corrupting than critics feared. Americans sought fellowship in civic organizations, such as Rotary, Elks, and women's clubs. Perhaps most important, people were finding release in recreation and leisure time.

THE AGE OF PLAY

Americans in the 1920s embraced commercial entertainment, spending $2.5 billion on leisure in 1919; by 1929 spending topped $4.3 billion. Spectator amusements—movies, music, and sports—accounted for 21 percent of the 1929 total; the rest involved participatory recreation, such as games, hobbies, and travel. Entrepreneurs fed an appetite for fads and spectacles. Early in the 1920s, mahjong, a Chinese tile game, was the craze. In the mid-1920s, devotees popularized crossword puzzles, printed in mass-circulation newspapers and magazines. By 1930 the nation boasted thirty thousand miniature golf courses. Dance crazes like the Charleston and recorded music on radio boosted the growing popularity of jazz.

Movies and Sports

Americans also enjoyed watching movies and sports. In total capital investment, motion pictures became one of the nation's leading industries. In 1922 movies attracted 40 million viewers weekly; by decade's end, nearly 100 million—at a time when the nation's population was 120 million and total weekly church attendance was 60 million. Between 1922 and 1927, the Technicolor Corporation developed a means of producing movies in color. That, along with the introduction of sound in 1927's *The Jazz Singer*, made movies more exciting.

Although DeMille's romantic comedies like *Why Change Your Wife?* were entertaining, his most popular films—*The Ten Commandments* (1923) and *The King of Kings* (1927)—were biblical. Lurid dramas like *Souls for Sale* (1923) and *A Woman Who Sinned* (1924) also drew big audiences, as did slapstick comedies starring Harold Lloyd and Charlie Chaplin. In 1927 producers, bowing to pressure from legislators and religious leaders, instituted self-censorship, forbidding nudity, rough language, and plots that did not end with justice and morality triumphant.

Spectator sports drew millions every year. In an age when technology and mass production robbed experiences of their uniqueness, sports provided the unpredictability that people craved. Newspapers and radio magnified this tension, glorifying events with such dramatic narrative that promoters did not need advertising.

Baseball's drawn-out suspense, variety of plays, and potential for keeping statistics attracted a huge following. After the 1919 Black Sox scandal, when eight members of the Chicago White Sox were banned for allegedly throwing the World Series to the Cincinnati Reds (even though a jury acquitted them), baseball transformed itself. Discovering that home runs excited fans, the leagues redesigned the ball. A record 300,000 people attended the six-game 1921 World Series between the New York Giants and New York Yankees. Millions enjoyed professional games on the radio. Although African American ballplayers were prohibited from the major leagues, they formed their own teams, and in 1920 the first successful Negro League was founded in Kansas City, Missouri.

Sports Heroes

As technology and mass society made the individual less significant, people clung to heroic athletes as a means of identifying with the unique. Bill Tilden in tennis, Gertrude Ederle in swimming (in 1926 she became the first woman to swim across the English Channel), and Bobby Jones in golf were famous. But boxing, football, and baseball produced the most popular sports heroes. Heavyweight champion Jack Dempsey, the Manassa (Colorado) Mauler, attracted the first of several-million-dollar gates in his fight with Georges Carpentier in 1921.

Baseball's foremost hero was George Herman "Babe" Ruth, who began his career as a pitcher but broke records hitting home runs. Ruth hit twenty-nine homers in 1919, fifty-four in 1920 (the year the Boston Red Sox traded him to the New York Yankees), fifty-nine in 1921, and sixty in 1927—each year a record. His talent and boyish grin endeared him to millions. Known for overindulgence in food, drink, and sex, he charmed fans with public appearances and visiting hospitalized children.

Movie Stars and Public Heroes

Americans fulfilled their yearning for romance and adventure through movie idols. One of the decade's most adored movie personalities was Rudolph Valentino, whose image exploited the era's sexual liberalism. In his most famous film, Valentino played a passionate sheik who carried away beautiful women to his tent, combining the roles of abductor and seducer. When he died at thirty-one of complications from ulcers and appendicitis, the press turned his funeral into a public extravaganza.

The era's most celebrated hero was Charles A. Lindbergh, who in May 1927 flew a plane solo from New York to Paris. The flight riveted America, as newspaper and telegraph reports followed Lindbergh's progress. After the pilot landed successfully, President Coolidge dispatched a warship to bring Lucky Lindy home, where he was greeted with a triumphant parade. Among countless prizes, Lindbergh received the Distinguished Flying Cross and the Congressional Medal of Honor. Promoters offered him millions of dollars to tour the world and $700,000 for a movie contract. Although his flight symbolized the merger of technology and mass culture in the 1920s, Lindbergh epitomized individual achievement and courage—old-fashioned values that attracted public allegiance.

Prohibition

The Eighteenth Amendment (1919) and subsequent federal law (the Volstead Act of 1920) prohibited the manufacture, sale, and transportation of alcoholic beverages. It worked well at first. Per capita consumption of liquor dropped, as did arrests for drunkenness. But it was barely enforced: in 1922 Congress gave the Prohibition Bureau less than $7 million for nationwide enforcement, and by 1927 most state budgets omitted funds to enforce prohibition.

After 1925, prohibition broke down as thousands made their own wine and gin illegally and bootleg importers evaded the few patrols that existed. Moreover, drinking was a business with willing customers, and criminal organizations capitalized on public demand. The most notorious of such mobs belonged to Al Capone, who seized control of illegal liquor and vice in Chicago, maintaining power over politicians and the vice business through intimidation, bribery, and violence. Americans wanted liquor, and until 1931, when a federal court convicted and imprisoned Capone for income-tax evasion (the only charge for which authorities could obtain hard evidence), he supplied them.

CULTURAL CURRENTS

Intellectuals were quick to expose the era's hypocrisies. Writers and artists felt at odds with society, and their rejection of materialism and conformity was biting and bitter.

Literature of Alienation

Several writers from the so-called Lost Generation, including the novelist Ernest Hemingway and the poets Ezra Pound and T. S. Eliot, abandoned the United States for Europe. Others, like the novelists William Faulkner and Sinclair Lewis, remained in America but expressed disillusionment with the materialism that they witnessed.

F. Scott Fitzgerald's novels *This Side of Paradise* (1920) and *The Great Gatsby* (1925) and Eugene O'Neill's plays scorned Americans' preoccupation with money. Edith Wharton explored the clash of old and new moralities in novels such as *The Age of Innocence* (1920). Hemingway's *A Farewell to Arms* (1929) interwove antiwar sentiment with critiques of the emptiness in modern relationships.

Harlem Renaissance

Discontent inspired a new generation of African American artists. Middle-class, educated, and proud of their African heritage, African American writers rejected white culture and exalted the militantly assertive New Negro. In the Negro Mecca of New York's Harlem, African American intellectuals and artists, aided by a few white patrons, celebrated African American culture during what became known as the Harlem Renaissance.

The popular 1921 musical comedy *Shuffle Along* is often credited with launching the Harlem Renaissance and showcased talented African American artists, such as the composer Eubie Blake and the singer Josephine Baker. Harlem in the 1920s also fostered gifted writers, including Langston Hughes, Countee Cullen, Zora Neale Hurston, Jessie Fauset, and Alain Locke.

Though cherishing their African heritage and black folk culture of the slave South, these artists and intellectuals realized that African Americans had to come to terms with being free Americans. Langston Hughes wrote, "We younger Negro artists who create now intend to express our individual dark-skinned selves without fear or shame. If white people are pleased, we are glad. If they are not, it doesn't matter. We know we are beautiful."

Jazz

The Jazz Age, as the 1920s is sometimes called, owes its name to the music of the African American culture. Evolving from African and African American folk music, early jazz communicated exuberance, humor, and autonomy that African Americans seldom experienced in their public and political lives. Jazz's emotional rhythms and improvisation blurred the distinction between composer and performer. Urban dance halls and nightclubs, some of which included interracial audiences, featured performers like the trumpeter Louis Armstrong and the blues singer Bessie Smith. Music recorded by African American artists and aimed at African American consumers (sometimes called "race records") gave African Americans a place in commercial culture. More important, jazz endowed America with its own distinctive art form.

In many ways the 1920s were the nation's most creative years. Painters such as Georgia O'Keeffe, Aaron Douglas, and John Marin forged a uniquely American style of visual art. Composer Henry Cowell pioneered electronic music, and Aaron Copland built orchestral works around native folk motifs. George Gershwin blended jazz rhythms, classical forms, and folk melodies in serious works (*Rhapsody in Blue*, 1924, and *Piano Concerto in F*, 1925) and hit tunes, such as "The Man I Love." In architecture, skyscrapers drew worldwide attention to American forms. The "emotional and aesthetic starvation" that essayist Harold Stearns lamented early in the decade were gone by 1929.

THE ELECTION OF 1928 AND THE END OF THE NEW ERA

Intellectuals' uneasiness about materialism seldom affected the confident rhetoric of politics. Herbert Hoover voiced that confidence when he accepted the Republican nomination for president in 1928. "We in America today," Hoover boasted, "are nearer to the final triumph over poverty than ever before in the history of any land."

Herbert Hoover

As the Republican candidate in 1928 (Coolidge chose not to seek reelection) Hoover fused the tradition of individual hard work with the modern emphasis on corporate action. A Quaker from Iowa, orphaned at age ten, Hoover put himself through Stanford University and became a wealthy mining engineer. During and after World War I, he distinguished himself as a U.S. food administrator.

As secretary of commerce under Harding and Coolidge, Hoover promoted associationalism. Recognizing that nationwide associations dominated commerce and industry, Hoover sought business and government cooperation. He made the Commerce Department a center for the promotion of business, encouraging trade associations, holding conferences, and issuing reports, all aimed at improving productivity and profits.

Al Smith

In sharp contrast, Democrats in 1928 chose New York's governor Alfred E. Smith. Hoover had rural, native-born, Protestant, and business roots but had never run for public office. Smith was an urbane politician of Irish stock with a career embedded in New York City's Tammany Hall political machine. He relished the give-and-take of city streets.

Smith was the first Roman Catholic to run for president on a major party ticket. His religion enhanced his appeal among urban ethnics, who increasingly voted, but intense anti-Catholic sentiments lost him southern and rural votes. Smith had a strong record on Progressive reform and civil rights, but his campaign stressed issues unlikely to unite these groups, particularly his opposition to prohibition.

Hoover, who emphasized national prosperity under Republican administrations, won the popular vote by 21 million to 15 million and the electoral vote by 444 to 87. Smith carried the nation's twelve largest cities, formerly Republican strongholds, and he lured millions of foreign-stock voters to the polls for the first time. For the next forty years, the Democratic Party solidified this urban base, which when combined with its traditional strength in the South, made the party a formidable force in national elections.

Hoover's Administration

At his inaugural, Hoover proclaimed a New Day, "bright with hope." His cabinet featured mostly businessmen, including six millionaires. To lower ranking posts, Hoover appointed young professionals who agreed that a scientific approach could solve national problems. Like Hoover, Americans widely believed that individual effort led to success and that poverty suggested personal weakness. Prevailing opinion also held that fluctuations of the business cycle were natural and therefore not to be tampered with by government.

Stock Market Crash

This trust dissolved on October 24, 1929, later known as Black Thursday, when stock market prices suddenly plunged, wiping out $10 billion in value (worth around $100 billion today). Panic set in. Prices of many stocks hit record lows; some sellers could find no buyers. At noon, leading bankers put up $20 million and ceremoniously began buying stocks. The mood brightened, and some stocks rallied.

But as news spread, frightened investors sold off stocks to avoid further losses. On Black Tuesday, October 29, prices plummeted again. Hoover assured Americans that "the crisis will be over in sixty days." He shared the popular assumption that the economy was strong enough to endure until the market righted itself. Instead, the crash unleashed a devastating worldwide depression.

In hindsight, the depression began long before the stock market crash. Prosperity in the 1920s was not as widespread as optimists believed. Agriculture had languished for decades, and many areas, especially in the South, were outside the new bounty of consumer society. Industries such as mining and textiles failed to sustain profits throughout the decade, and even the automotive and household goods industries had been stagnant since 1926. The fever of speculation included rash investment in California and Florida real estate, as well as in the stock market, and masked what was unhealthy in the national economy.

Declining Demand

The economic weakness that underlay the Great Depression had several interrelated causes. Since mid-1928, demand for new housing faltered, reducing sales of building materials and increasing unemployment. Growth industries, such as automobiles and electric appliances, saw demand level off, so factory owners cut back production and workers. Retailers had amassed large inventories that were going unsold and started ordering less. Farm prices continued to sag, leaving farmers with less income for new machinery and goods. As wages and employment fell, families could not afford to buy consumer goods. Thus by 1929 a sizable population of underconsumers was causing serious repercussions.

As the rich grew richer, middle- and lower-income Americans barely made modest gains. Although average per capita disposable income (income after taxes) rose about 9 percent between 1920 and 1929, income of the wealthiest 1 percent rose 75 percent. Much of this increase was put into stock market investments, not consumer goods.

Corporate Debt and Stock Market Speculation

Furthermore, many businesses overloaded themselves with debt. To obtain loans, they misrepresented their assets in ways that hid their inability to repay. Such practices, overlooked by lending agencies, put the nation's banking system on a precarious footing.

Risky stock market speculation also precipitated the depression. Individuals and corporations bought millions of stocks on margin, meaning that they invested with a down payment of only a fraction of a stock's price and then used these partially paid-for stocks as collateral for more stock purchases. When stock prices stopped rising, people tried to unload what they bought on margin. But with numerous investors selling simultaneously, prices dropped. Brokers then demanded full payment for stocks bought on margin. Bankers pressured businesses to pay back their loans, tightening the vise further. The more obligations went unmet, the more the system tottered. Inevitably, banks and investment companies collapsed.

International Economic Troubles

International economic conditions also contributed to the Depression. During and after World War I, Americans loaned billions to European nations. By the late 1920s, however, American investors instead kept their money in the lucrative U.S. stock market. Europeans, unable to borrow more or sell goods in the American market because of high tariffs, bought less from the United States. Moreover, the Allied nations depended on German war reparations to pay their debts to the United States, and the German government depended on American bank loans to pay those reparations. When the crash choked off American loans, the western economy ground to a halt.

Failure of Federal Policies

The government refrained from regulating speculation. In supporting business expansion, the Federal Reserve Board pursued easy credit policies, charging low discount rates (interest rates on its loans to member banks) even though such loans were financing the speculative mania.

Neither experts nor people on the street realized what really happened in 1929. Conventional wisdom, based on previous depressions, held that economic problems had to run their course. So in 1929 people waited for the tailspin to ease, never realizing that the new era had ended and that the economy, politics, and society would have to be rebuilt.

Summary

Two critical events, the end of World War I and the beginning of the Great Depression, marked the boundaries of the 1920s. After the war, traditional customs weakened as women and men sought new forms of self-expression and gratification. Modern science and technology touched rich and poor alike through mass media, movies, sports, automobiles, and electric appliances. Moreover, the decade's freewheeling consumerism enabled ordinary Americans to emulate wealthier people by purchasing more and engaging in stock market speculation.

Beneath the new era's materialism, prejudice and ethnic tensions tainted the American dream. Prohibitionists, Klansmen, and immigration restrictionists encouraged discrimination against racial minorities and ethnic groups. Meanwhile, the distinguishing forces of twentieth-century life—technological change, bureaucratization, mass culture, and growth of the middle class—accelerated, making the decade truly new.

Intercollegiate Athletics

In 1924 brutality, academic fraud, and illegal payments to recruits prompted the Carnegie Foundation for the Advancement of Higher Education to undertake a five-year investigation of college sports. Its 1929 report recommended the abolition of football and condemned coaches and alumni but had minimal effect. Football was immensely popular, and colleges and universities built stadiums to attract spectators, bolster alumni allegiance, and enhance revenues.

For most of the twentieth century and into the twenty-first, intercollegiate athletics ranked as a major commercial entertainment. Still, American institutions have struggled to reconcile conflicts between the commercialism of athletic competition and the ideals of scholarship and amateurism. The economic potential of college sports coupled with expanding athletic departments—elaborate facilities as well as staffs—has created programs that compete with and sometimes overshadow an institution's academic mission.

Since the 1920s, recruiting scandals, academic fraud, and felonious behavior sparked controversy in college sports. In 1952, after revelations of point-shaving (fixing the outcome) of basketball games at several colleges, the American Council on Education undertook its own study. Its recommendations, including the elimination of football bowl games, went largely unheeded. In 1991 further abuses prompted the Knight Foundation Commission on Intercollegiate Athletics to urge college presidents to reform intercollegiate athletics. Few significant changes resulted, even after a follow-up study in 2001.

The most sweeping reforms followed court rulings in the 1990s, mandating that women's sports be treated equally with men's under Title IX of the Educational Amendments Act of 1972. Enforcement, however, provoked a backlash that resulted in efforts to prevent men's teams from being cut to satisfy Title IX. In recent years, the National College Athletic Association (NCAA) has attempted to regulate academic standards in college athletics, but its success depends on cooperation from member institutions. With millions of dollars involved, the system established in the 1920s has withstood most pressures for change.

Chapter Review

BIG BUSINESS TRIUMPHANT

What triggered the post–World War I economic recovery?

Two factors helped turn the initial postwar recession into recovery: the advent of electric energy in 1922 and new government pro-business initiatives. Electricity enabled goods to be produced more inexpensively, thereby driving consumer demand and stimulating the economy across the board. New installment or credit plans for purchasing big items such as cars also drove consumption. As business organizations used lobbying to influence government, new federal policies emerged to aid business growth and development. Congress cut taxes on corporations and wealthy individuals in 1921, and passed the Fordney-McCumber Tariff Act (1922). The Federal Trade Commission and the Interstate Commerce Commission tended to cooperate with corporations rather than regulate them. And several Supreme Court decisions sheltered business from government regulation and hindered organized labor.

POLITICS AND GOVERNMENT

What happened to Progressive reform in the 1920s?

While Progressivism faded on a national level, its reform spirit continued to inspire local and state initiatives, as well as those by women and ethnic groups. After the war, many states adopted or expanded workers' compensation laws and public welfare programs. Native American groups worked for better education and return of tribal lands, while white reformers held out hope of getting Indians to adopt white middle-class standards of work, family, and citizenship. Although women got the right to vote in 1920, their voluntary organizations became the tools for lobbying for various issues from birth control to protective labor legislation to questions of citizenship and equality.

A CONSUMER SOCIETY

How did the emergence of a consumer society change American life?

In the 1920s, incomes increased, while new mass production methods kept the price of goods stable or made them more affordable. Consequently, greater numbers of Americans could afford products such as automobiles that once were the province of the wealthy. Car ownership led consumers to join with farmers in seeking improved roadways. At the same time, the emergence of advertising as a tool helped manipulate purchases and increasingly erased ethnic differences to create a more homogenous consumer society. And the growth of the radio, with its mass marketing and standardized programs, further blurred differences and heightened "Americanization."

CITIES, MIGRANTS, AND SUBURBS

What fueled the growth of cities in the 1920s?

In 1920, for the first time in U.S. history, more people lived in urban areas than rural areas. In part, the shift was driven by young people, who left farms for the more exciting and varied life of cities. The demographic change was also driven by the migration of African Americans from poverty on southern farms to seek better paying factory jobs in the North. Immigrants from Mexico and Puerto Rico were similarly pushed off their land due to agricultural changes to find better opportunities in America. Many Mexicans became underpaid and exploited farm laborers in the West, while Puerto Ricans found jobs in factories and restaurants or as domestic servants.

NEW RHYTHMS OF EVERYDAY LIFE

How did technological advances impact social life in America in the 1920s?

First, improved productivity and mechanization led to shorter workweeks, permitting the expansion of leisure activities and greater freedom, especially for young people. Industrialism privileged youth and agility over experience and forced older people to retire, which often meant economic hardship or poverty. Second, new appliances made housework less arduous and time-consuming and shifted women's roles from producer within the home to consumer for the family. Third, advances in nutrition helped people live longer and healthier lives. Birth control also enabled families to separate sexuality from reproduction, and family size decreased. Finally, as products and services became more widely available, an increasing number of married women moved into the work force to expand their families' purchasing power.

LINES OF DEFENSE

How did various groups defend an older version of America against the tide of change in the 1920s?

Troubled by the liberal social influences of the era, several groups emerged seeking to restore what they considered to be traditional American values. The Ku Klux Klan was reconstituted in 1915 to re-establish native white American supremacy in the face of increasing immigration and black migration and to protect white women's virtue against so-called corrupting influences. They were joined in their anti-immigration sentiment by other nativist groups, who pressed Congress to establish immigration quotas. Similarly, fundamentalist Christian groups sought to replace the modern emphasis on science with a renewed centrality of God's role in creation and daily life. Hence, the Tennessee legislature banned the teaching of the theory of evolution, resulting in the pivotal Scopes trial in 1925. Religious revivalism likewise condemned the new social practices of dating, dancing, and fashion and the hint of sex in movies.

THE AGE OF PLAY

Why did movie and sports heroes become so pivotally important during the 1920s?

As mechanization and mass consumption took hold, Americans felt robbed of a sense of individual distinctiveness and sense of purpose. Prohibition added to their sense of restricted personal freedom. To recover that lost sensibility, Americans gravitated toward leisure activities that celebrated individual achievement or that inspired a sense of adventure or romance. Sports provided drama, unpredictability, and a chance to celebrate a particular player's talent. Motion pictures not only let viewers live vicariously through the exciting lives of characters, but also inspired the hope for adventure in their own lives. Finally, national heroes such as aviator Charles Lindbergh made the possibility of greatness seem real and attainable, even if most Americans would never personally experience it for themselves.

CULTURAL CURRENTS

How did discontent with 1920s conformity give rise to important creative cultural movements?

Many artists and writers felt disillusioned with the materialism and preoccupation with money they witnessed in America during this age of mass consumption and innovation. While some, like Ernest Hemingway, left for Europe, others remained in the United States and transformed these feelings into novels and other creative works that explored the problems of modern society or proffered a particular political view. Middle-class, educated African Americans rejected white culture and celebrated their heritage in novels, poems, plays, and art, creating the literary and artistic movement known as the Harlem Renaissance. Black culture also produced the Jazz Age, creating a distinctly American musical form.

THE ELECTION OF 1928 AND THE END OF THE NEW ERA

What were the early signs that the prosperity of the 1920s was coming to an end?

While the 1929 stock market crash put a definitive ending on the era's seeming prosperity, in truth, the seeds of recession were sown many years before. First, so-called prosperity had never reached farmers; agriculture had lagged for decades. Mining, textiles, and other industries did not remain profitable the entire decade, and even the automobile industry was stagnant after 1926. As demand faltered, factories cut back on production and workers, which in turn meant less disposable income to purchase consumer goods, triggering further cutbacks in retail orders and production. Housing demand dropped off after mid-1928, and at the same time, businesses were overloaded with debt. Together, this made for a perfect economic storm when the market crashed in 1929.

SUGGESTIONS FOR FURTHER READING

Lynn Dumenil, *The Modern Temper: American Culture and Society in the 1920s* (1995)

James R. Grossman, *Land of Hope: Chicago, Black Southerners, and the Great Migration* (1989)

Maury Klein, *Rainbow's End: The Crash of 1929* (2003)

Roland Marchand, *Advertising the American Dream: Making Way for Modernity, 1920–1940* (1985)

David Montgomery, *The Fall of the House of Labor: The Workplace, the State, and American Activism, 1865–1925* (1987)

Mae M. Ngai, *Impossible Subjects: Illegal Aliens and the Making of Modern America* (2004)

George Sanchez, *Becoming Mexican American: Ethnicity, Culture and Identity in Chicano Los Angeles, 1900–1945* (1993)

Susan Thistle, *From Marriage to the Market: The Transformation of Women's Lives and Work* (2006)

Michael Miller Topp, *The Sacco and Vanzetti Case: A Brief History With Documents* (2005)

CHAPTER 25

The Great Depression and the New Deal

CHAPTER OUTLINE

Hoover and Hard Times, 1929–1933

Franklin D. Roosevelt and the Launching of the New Deal

Political Pressure and the Second New Deal

Labor

Federal Power and the Nationalization of Culture

    LINKS TO THE WORLD:
The 1936 Olympic Games

The Limits of the New Deal

Summary

    LEGACY FOR A PEOPLE AND A NATION: Social Security

I n 1931 the rain stopped in the Great Plains. Montana and North Dakota became as arid as the Sonora Desert, and temperatures reached 115 degrees in Iowa. Farmers watched rich black dirt turn to gray dust.

Then the winds began to blow. In the 1920s farmers stripped the Plains of native grasses to put millions of acres into production. Now, with nothing to hold the earth, it began to blow away. The dust storms began in 1934 and worsened in 1935. Cattle, blinded by blowing grit, ran in circles until they died. Boiling clouds of dust filled the skies in Kansas, Colorado, Oklahoma, Texas, and New Mexico—the Dust Bowl.

In late 1937, on a farm near Stigler, Oklahoma, Marvin Montgomery counted his assets: $53 and a 1929 Hudson automobile he had just bought. On December 29, 1937, Montgomery, his wife, and four children—along with their furniture, bedding, pots, and pans—squeezed into the Hudson. Traveling west on Route 66, the Montgomerys headed for California.

At least a third of the farms in the Dust Bowl were abandoned in the 1930s, and many families headed west, lured by advertisements promising work in California fields. Some 300,000 people migrated to California in the 1930s; many were white-collar workers seeking opportunity in California's cities. But the plight of families like the Montgomerys, captured in federal government-sponsored Farm Security Administration (FSA) photographs, came to represent the human suffering of the Great Depression.

The Montgomerys ran out of money in Arizona and worked the cotton fields there for five weeks before they moved on. In California, wages were low, and migrant families found little welcome. Because they took over the agricultural labor formerly done by Mexicans and Mexican Americans, they forfeited their

This icon will direct you to interactive activities and study materials on A People And A Nation, Brief Edition website: **www.cengage.com/history/norton/peoplenationbrief8e**

Chronology

1929	Stock market crashes (October); Great Depression begins.
1930	Hawley-Smoot Tariff raises rates on imports.
1931	Scottsboro Boys are arrested in Alabama.
1932	Banks fail throughout the nation.
	Bonus Army marches on Washington.
	Hoover's Reconstruction Finance Corporation tries to stabilize banks, insurance companies, and railroads.
	F. D. Roosevelt is elected president.
1933	13 million Americans are unemployed.
	During its First Hundred Days, the Roosevelt administration offers major legislation for economic recovery and poor relief.
	National bank holiday halts run on banks.
	Agricultural Adjustment Act (AAA) encourages decreased farm production.
	National Industrial Recovery Act (NIRA) attempts to spur industrial growth.
	Tennessee Valley Authority (TVA) is established.
1934	Long starts Share Our Wealth Society.
	Townsend proposes old-age pension plan.

	Indian Reorganization (Wheeler-Howard) Act restores lands to tribal ownership.
1935	National Labor Relations (Wagner) Act guarantees workers' right to unionize.
	Social Security Act establishes insurance for the aged, the unemployed, and needy children.
	Works Progress Administration (WPA) creates jobs in public works projects.
	Revenue (Wealth Tax) Act raises taxes on business and the wealthy.
1936	9 million Americans are unemployed.
	United Auto Workers win sit-down strike against General Motors.
1937	Roosevelt's "Court-packing" plan fails.
	Memorial Day massacre of striking steelworkers occurs.
	"Roosevelt recession" begins.
1938	10.4 million Americans are unemployed.
	80 million movie tickets are sold each week.
1939	Marian Anderson performs at the Lincoln Memorial.
	Social Security amendments add benefits for spouses and widows.

"whiteness" in the eyes of many Californians. "Negroes and 'Okies' upstairs," read a sign in a San Joaquin valley movie theater.

Most migrants to rural California lived in squalid makeshift camps, but the Montgomerys secured housing provided by the Farm Security Administration. The FSA camp had 240 tents and 40 small houses. For nine months the Montgomery family lived in a fourteen-by-sixteen-foot tent, which rented for 10 cents a day plus four hours of volunteer labor a month. Then they proudly moved into an FSA house, "with water, lights, and everything, yes sir; and a little garden spot furnished." Soon many employment opportunities emerged in California in aircraft factories and shipyards mobilizing for World War II.

Between 1929 and 1933, the U.S. gross national product was cut in half. Corporate profits fell from $10 billion to $1 billion; 100,000 businesses closed. Four million workers were unemployed in January 1930; by November the number jumped to 6 million. When President Herbert Hoover left office in 1933, 13 million workers—about one-fourth of the labor force—were idle, and millions had only part-time work. There was no national safety net: no welfare system, no unemployment compensation, no Social Security. And, as thousands of banks failed, with no federally guaranteed deposit insurance, families' savings disappeared.

Herbert Hoover, who was elected president in the prosperous late 1920s, looked first to private enterprise for solutions. By the end of his term, he extended the federal government's role in managing an economic crisis further than his predecessors had. Still, the depression deepened, and Americans felt increasingly desperate. The economic catastrophe exacerbated existing racial and class tensions in the United States, while in Germany, the international economic crisis propelled Adolf Hitler to power. By late 1932 many feared the depression was a crisis of capitalism, even of democracy itself.

In 1932 voters replaced Hoover with a man who promised a New Deal. Franklin Delano Roosevelt's programs did not end the depression (only the massive mobilization for World War II did that), but they did alleviate suffering. For the first time, the federal government assumed responsibility for the nation's economy and its citizens' welfare, thus strengthening its power in relation to states.

As it transformed the role of the federal government, however, the New Deal maintained America's existing economic and social systems. Although some Americans saw the depression as an opportunity for major economic change—even revolution— Roosevelt's goal was to save capitalism. New Deal programs increased federal government regulation without altering the existing capitalist system or the distribution of wealth. And, despite pressure to attack racial discrimination, Roosevelt never directly challenged legal segregation in the South—in part because he relied on southern white Democrats to pass New Deal legislation.

Despite its limits, the New Deal preserved America's democratic experiment through uncertainty and crisis. By decade's end, a world war shifted America's focus from domestic to foreign policy. But the changes set in motion by the New Deal continued to transform the United States for decades to come.

- How did economic hard times during the 1930s affect Americans, and what differences were there in the experiences of specific groups and regions?

- How and why did the power of the federal government expand during the Great Depression?

- What were the successes and the failures of the New Deal?

HOOVER AND HARD TIMES, 1929–1933

As the depression deepened in the early 1930s, tens of millions of Americans were desperately poor. In the cities, the hungry ate at soup kitchens or scratched through garbage cans for food. In West Virginia and Kentucky, widespread hunger and limited resources led the American Friends Service Committee to distribute food only to those weighing 10 percent less than the normal weight for their height. In November 1932, *The Nation* told readers that one-sixth of the American population risked starvation over the coming winter.

Families, unable to pay rent, were evicted. The new homeless poured into shantytowns, called Hoovervilles in ironic tribute to the formerly popular president. Over a million men took to the road or rails in search of work. The average marriage age rose by more than two years during the 1930s. People delayed having children, and in 1933 the birth rate sank below the replacement rate.

Farmers and Industrial Workers

The agricultural sector, which employed almost one-quarter of American workers and missed the good times of the 1920s, was hit hard by the depression. As urbanites cut spending and foreign competitors dumped agricultural surpluses into the global market, farm prices hit bottom. Farmers tried to compensate for lower prices by producing more, thus adding to the surplus and further depressing prices. By 1932, a bushel of wheat that cost North Dakota farmers 77 cents to produce brought only 33 cents. Cash-strapped farmers could not pay property taxes or mortgages. Banks, facing their own ruin, foreclosed. In Mississippi, on a single day in April 1932, approximately one-fourth of all farmland was auctioned off to meet debts. By the middle of the decade, the ecological crisis of the Dust Bowl would drive thousands of farmers from their land.

America's industrial workers had seen their standard of living improve during the 1920s, and their consumer spending bolstered the nation's growth. But as incomes declined, sales of manufactured goods plummeted and factories closed— more than seventy thousand were out of business by 1933. As car sales dropped from 4.5 million in 1929 to 1 million in 1933, Ford laid off more than two-thirds of its Detroit workers. Almost one-quarter of industrial workers were unemployed, and those with jobs saw the average wage fall by almost one-third.

Marginal Workers

For workers on the lowest rungs of the employment ladder, the depression was a crushing blow. In the South, jobs that many white men had considered below their dignity— bellhop, garbage collector—now seemed desirable. In 1930 a short-lived fascist-style organization, the Black Shirts, recruited forty thousand members with the slogan "No Jobs for Niggers Until Every White Man Has a Job!" Northern African Americans did not fare much better. An Urban League survey of 106 cities found African American unemployment rates averaged 30 to 60 percent higher than rates for whites. By 1932, African American unemployment reached almost 50 percent.

Mexican Americans and Mexican nationals in the Southwest also felt the twin impacts of depression and racism. Their wages on California farms fell from a miserable 35 cents an hour in 1929 to 14 cents an hour by 1932. Throughout the Southwest, campaigns against foreigners hurt not only Mexican immigrants but also American citizens of Hispanic background whose families lived in the Southwest for centuries, long before the land belonged to the United States. In 1931 the Labor Department announced plans to deport illegal immigrants to free jobs for American citizens. This policy fell hardest on people of Mexican origin. Even those who immigrated legally often lacked full documentation. Officials often ignored that children born in the United States were U.S. citizens. The U.S. government deported 82,000 Mexicans between 1929 and 1935, but a half a million people repatriated to Mexico during the 1930s. Some left voluntarily, but many were tricked into believing they had no choice.

Even before the depression, women were barred from many jobs and paid significantly less than men. With widespread male unemployment, many believed that women who worked took jobs from men. In fact, men laid off from U.S. Steel would not have been hired as elementary school teachers, secretaries, "salesgirls," or

This 1939 photograph, titled "Mother and Children on the Road," was taken in Tule Lake, California, by Farm Security Administration photographer Dorothea Lange. The FSA used photos like this one to build public support for New Deal programs to assist migrant workers and the rural poor.   (Library of Congress)

maids. Nonetheless, when a 1936 Gallup poll asked whether wives should work if their husbands had jobs, 82 percent of respondents (including 75 percent of the women) answered no. Such beliefs became policy. In 1930 and 1931, 77 percent of urban school systems refused to hire married women as teachers, and 63 percent fired female teachers who married.

At first, women lost jobs faster than men. Women in low-wage manufacturing jobs were laid off before male employees. Almost one-quarter of women in domestic service—many of them African American—lost jobs as middle-class families economized by dispensing with household help. Despite discrimination and a poor economy, the number of women working outside the home rose during the 1930s. Women's jobs, such as teaching and clerical work were not hit as hard as men's jobs in heavy industry, and women increasingly sought employment to keep their families afloat during hard times. Still, by 1940 only 15.2 percent of married women were employed.

Middle-Class Workers and Families

Although unemployment climbed to 25 percent, most Americans did not lose their homes or jobs during the depression. Professional and white-collar workers did not fare as badly as industrial workers and farmers. Many middle-class families, however, made do with less. Housewives economized, using cheap ingredients to make food go further (cracker-stuffed cabbage). Although most families' income fell, the impact was cushioned by the decreasing cost of consumer goods. Even for the relatively affluent, the psychological impact of the depression was inescapable. The human toll of the depression was visible everywhere, and no one took economic security for granted any more.

Hoover's Limited Solutions

Although Herbert Hoover, the Great Engineer, had a reputation as a problem solver, no one knew what to do about the crisis. Experts disagreed about the depression's causes and the proper course of action. Many business leaders believed that financial panics and depressions, no matter how painful, were part of a natural and ultimately beneficial business cycle. Economic depressions, according to this theory, brought down inflated prices and cleared the way for economic growth.

Herbert Hoover disagreed. "The economic fatalist," he said, "believes that these crises are inevitable. . . . I would remind these pessimists that exactly the same thing was once said of typhoid, cholera, and smallpox." Hoover had faith in associationalism: business and professional organizations, coordinated by the federal government, working together to solve the nation's problems. The federal government's role was limited to a clearing-house for ideas that state and local governments, along with private industry, could voluntarily implement.

While many Americans thought Hoover was doing nothing to fight the downturn, in truth he stretched his beliefs about the role of government to their limit. He tried voluntarism, exhortation, and limited government intervention. First, he sought voluntary pledges from hundreds of business groups to keep wages stable and renew economic investment. But when businessmen looked at their own bottom lines, few could live up to those promises.

As unemployment climbed, Hoover continued to encourage voluntary responses, creating the President's Organization on Unemployment Relief (POUR) to generate private contributions to aid the destitute. Although 1932 saw record charitable contributions, they were inadequate. By mid-1932 one-quarter of New York's private charities, funds exhausted, closed their doors. State and city officials found their treasuries drying up, too.

Hoover feared that government relief would destroy self-reliance in the poor. Thus he authorized federal funds to feed the drought-stricken livestock of Arkansas farmers but rejected a smaller grant providing food for impoverished farm families. Many Americans became angry at Hoover's seeming insensitivity. Two years after his election, Hoover was the most hated man in America.

Hoover eventually endorsed limited federal action to combat the crisis, but it was too little. Federal public works projects, such as the Grand Coulee Dam in Washington, created some jobs. The Federal Farm Board, established in 1929, supported crop prices by lending money to cooperatives to buy crops and keep them off the market. But the board soon ran short of money, and unsold surpluses jammed warehouses.

Hoover also signed the Hawley-Smoot Tariff (1930) to support American farmers and manufacturers by raising import duties to a staggering 40 percent. Instead it hampered international trade as other nations created their own protective tariffs. And, as other nations sold less to the United States, they had less money to repay their U.S. debts or buy U.S. products. Fearing the collapse of the international monetary system, Hoover in 1931 announced a moratorium on the payment of World War I debts and reparations.

In January 1932, the administration took its most forceful action. The Reconstruction Finance Corporation (RFC) provided federal loans to banks, insurance companies, and railroads, which Hoover hoped would shore up those industries and halt disinvestment in the U.S. economy. Here, Hoover compromised his principles: this was direct government intervention, not voluntarism. If he would support direct assistance to private industries, why not relief to the millions of unemployed?

Protest and Social Unrest

Increasingly, Americans asked that same question. As the depression worsened, social unrest and violence surfaced. Increasing violence raised the specter of popular revolt, and Chicago mayor Anton Cermak told Congress that, if the federal government did not send his citizens aid, it would have to send troops instead.

Tens of thousands of farmers nationwide took the law into their own hands. Angry crowds forced auctioneers to accept just a few dollars for foreclosed property, and then returned it to the original owners. In August 1932, a new group, the Farmers' Holiday Association, encouraged farmers to withhold agricultural products to limit supply and drive prices up. In the Midwest, farmers barricaded roads to stop other farmers' trucks, and then dumped the contents in roadside ditches.

In the cities, the most militant actions came from Unemployed Councils, local groups for unemployed workers that were created and led by Communist Party members. Communist leaders believed that the depression demonstrated capitalism's failure and offered an opportunity for revolution. Few of the quarter-million Americans joining the local Unemployed Councils sought revolution, but they did demand action. "Fight, Don't Starve," read banners in a Chicago demonstration.

As social unrest spread, so did racial violence. Vigilante committees offered bounties to force African Americans off the Illinois Central Railroad's payroll: $25 for maiming and $100 for killing African American workers. Ten men were murdered and at least seven wounded. The Ku Klux Klan reemerged, and at least 140 attempted lynchings were recorded between January 1930 and February 1933. In most cases local authorities were able to prevent the lynchings, but white mobs tortured, hanged, and mutilated thirty-eight African American men during the depression's early years. Outside the South, lynchings also took place in Pennsylvania, Minnesota, Colorado, and Ohio.

Bonus Army

The worst public confrontation happened in summer 1932. More than fifteen thousand unemployed World War I veterans and their families converged on the nation's capital as Congress debated a bill authorizing immediate payment of cash bonuses that veterans were scheduled to receive in 1945. Calling themselves the Bonus Army, they set up a sprawling Hooverville shantytown across the river from the Capitol. Concerned about the impact on the federal budget, President Hoover opposed the bonus bill, and the Senate voted it down.

Most of the Bonus Marchers left Washington, but several thousand stayed. Calling them insurrectionists—though many were simply destitute—the president set a deadline for their departure. On July 28, Hoover sent in General Douglas MacArthur and four infantry companies, four troops of cavalry, a machine gun squadron, and six tanks. What followed shocked the nation: men and women chased by horsemen, children tear-gassed, shacks set afire. The next day, newspapers carried photographs of U.S. troops attacking their own citizens.

Many Americans worried about the growing disillusionment with democracy, for as the depression worsened the appeal of a strong leader—someone who would take decisive action, unencumbered by constitutionally mandated checks and balances—grew. In February 1933 the U.S. Senate passed a resolution calling for newly elected president Franklin D. Roosevelt to assume "unlimited power." The rise of Hitler and his National Socialist Party in depression-ravaged Germany is an obvious parallel.

FRANKLIN D. ROOSEVELT AND THE LAUNCHING OF THE NEW DEAL

In the presidential campaign of 1932, Democratic challenger Franklin Delano Roosevelt insisted that the federal government had to play a much greater role than Hoover's limited intervention. Roosevelt supported direct relief payments for the unemployed, declaring that such governmental aid was "a matter of social duty." During the campaign, he was never very explicit about the outlines of his New Deal. His most concrete proposals, in fact, were sometimes contradictory. But he had committed to use the power of the federal government to combat the paralyzing economic crisis. Roosevelt's 22.8 million popular votes outdistanced Hoover's

15.8 million. Third-party Socialist candidate Norman Thomas drew nearly 1 million votes.

Franklin Roosevelt, the twentieth-century president most beloved by America's common people, was born into upper-class privilege. After graduating from Harvard College and Columbia Law School, he married Eleanor Roosevelt, Theodore Roosevelt's niece and his own fifth cousin, once removed. He served in the New York State legislature, was appointed assistant secretary of the navy by Woodrow Wilson, and at the age of thirty-eight, ran for vice president in 1920 on the Democratic Party's losing ticket.

In 1921, Roosevelt was stricken with polio and was bedridden for two years. He lost the use of his legs but gained, according to his wife Eleanor, a new strength of character. By 1928 Roosevelt was sufficiently recovered to run for—and win—the governorship of New York, and then to accept the Democratic Party's presidential nomination in 1932.

Elected president in November 1932, Roosevelt would not take office until March 4, 1933. (The Twentieth Amendment to the Constitution shifted future inaugurations to January 20.) In this long interregnum, the American banking system reached the verge of collapse.

Banking Crisis

The origins of the banking crisis lay in the flush years of World War I and the 1920s, when American banks made risky loans. After real-estate and stock market bubbles burst in 1929 and agriculture prices collapsed, many of these loans soured, leaving many banks without sufficient funds to cover customers' deposits. Fearful of losing their savings, depositors pulled money out of banks and put it into gold or under mattresses. Bank runs, in which crowds of frightened customers demanded their money, became common.

By the 1932 election, the bank crisis was escalating rapidly. Hoover, the lame-duck president, refused to take action without Roosevelt's support, while Roosevelt refused to endorse actions he could not control. By Roosevelt's March 4 inauguration, every state had either suspended banking operations or restricted depositors' access to their money. The new president understood that the total collapse of the U.S. banking system would threaten the nation's survival.

Standing in a cold rain on the Capitol steps, Roosevelt vowed in his inaugural address to face the crisis "frankly and boldly." The lines best remembered from his speech are words of comfort: "The only thing we have to fear is fear itself—nameless, unreasoning, unjustified terror." But the only loud cheers came when Roosevelt asserted that, if need be, "I shall ask the Congress for the one remaining instrument to meet the crisis—broad Executive power to wage a war against the emergency, as great as the power that would be given to me if we were in fact invaded by a foreign foe."

The next day Roosevelt, using powers legally granted by the World War I Trading with the Enemy Act, closed the nation's banks for a four-day "holiday" and summoned Congress to an emergency session. He immediately introduced the Emergency Banking Relief Bill, which was passed sight unseen by a unanimous House vote, approved 73 to 7 in the Senate, and signed into law the same day. It provided federal authority to reopen solvent banks and reorganize the rest and authorized federal money to shore up private banks. Roosevelt attacked "unscrupulous money changers," and many critics of the failed banking system hoped he planned to remove the banks from private hands. Instead, Roosevelt's banking policy was much like Hoover's— a fundamentally conservative approach that upheld the status quo.

The banking bill could save the U.S. banking system only if Americans were confident enough to deposit money in the reopened banks. In the first of his radio Fireside Chats, Roosevelt asked Americans for support. "We have provided the machinery to restore our financial system," he said. "It is up to you to support and make it work." The next morning, when the banks opened, people lined up—this time, most waited to deposit money.

First Hundred Days

During the ninety-nine-day-long special session of Congress, dubbed by journalists the First Hundred Days, the federal government took on dramatically new roles. Roosevelt , aided by advisers—lawyers, university professors, and social workers collectively nicknamed the Brain Trust—and by the enormously capable First Lady, sought to revive the American economy. These New Dealers had no single plan, and Roosevelt fluctuated between attempts to balance the budget and massive deficit spending (spending more than is taken in in taxes and borrowing the difference). But with a strong mandate for action and the support of a Democrat-controlled Congress, the administration produced a flood of legislation. Two basic strategies emerged during the First Hundred Days. New Dealers experimented with national economic planning, and they created a range of relief programs for the needy.

National Industrial Recovery Act

At the heart of the New Deal experiment were the National Industrial Recovery Act (NIRA) and the Agricultural Adjustment Act (AAA). The NIRA was based on the belief that destructive competition worsened industry's economic woes. Skirting antitrust regulation, the NIRA authorized competing businesses to cooperate in crafting industrywide codes. Thus automobile manufacturers, for example, would cooperate to limit production and establish industrywide prices and wages. With wages and prices stabilized, the theory went, consumer spending would increase, thus allowing industries to rehire workers. Participation in this National Recovery Administration (NRA) program was voluntary, so though it was larger than previous government-private sector cooperation, it was not very different from Hoover-era associationalism.

As small-business owners feared, big business easily dominated the NRA-mandated cartels. Often NRA staff were unable to stand up to corporate representatives. The twenty-six-year-old NRA staffer who oversaw the creation of the petroleum industry code was "helped" by twenty highly paid oil industry lawyers. The majority of the 541 codes approved by the NRA reflected the interests of major corporations, not small-business owners, labor, or consumers. Most fundamentally, the NRA did not deliver economic recovery. In 1935 the Supreme Court put an end to the fragile, floundering system when it found that the NRA extended federal power past its constitutional bounds.

Agricultural Adjustment Act

The Agricultural Adjustment Act (AAA) had a more enduring effect. Establishing a national system of crop controls, it offered subsidies to farmers who agreed to limit production of specific crops. (Overproduction drove crop prices down.) In 1933, the nation's farmers destroyed 8.5 million piglets and plowed under crops in the fields. Millions of hungry Americans found it difficult to understand this waste of food.

Government crop subsidies proved a disaster for tenant farmers and sharecroppers, who were turned off the land as landlords cut production. In the South the number of sharecropper farms dropped by almost one-third between 1930 and 1940. The result was a homeless population of dispossessed Americans—many of them African American—heading to cities and towns. But subsidies did help many. In the Dakotas, government payments accounted for almost three-quarters of the total farm income for 1934.

In 1936 the Supreme Court found that the AAA, like the NRA, was unconstitutional. But the AAA (unlike the NRA) was too popular with its constituency, American farmers, to disappear. The legislation was rewritten to meet the Supreme Court's objections, and farm subsidies continued into the twenty-first century.

Relief Programs

Roosevelt moved quickly to implement poor relief: $3 billion in federal dollars was allocated in 1935. New Dealers, like many other Americans, disapproved of direct relief payments. Thus New Deal programs emphasized work relief. By January 1934, the Civil Works Administration hired 4 million people, most earning $15 a week. And the Civilian Conservation Corps (CCC) paid unmarried young men, segregated by race, $1 a day to do hard outdoor labor: building dams and reservoirs, creating trails in national parks. By 1942 the CCC employed 2.5 million men, including 80,000 Native Americans working on western Indian reservations.

Work relief programs rarely included poor women. Mothers of young children were usually classified as unemployable and offered mother's-aid grants, which historian Linda Gordon explains, were miniscule compared to wages in federal works program jobs. And while federal relief programs rejected the poor-law tradition that distinguished between the "deserving" and the "undeserving" poor, local officials often did not. "The investigators, they were like detectives," complained one woman who had requested relief.

The Public Works Administration (PWA), created by Title II of the National Industrial Recovery Act, appropriated $3.3 billion in 1933. PWA workers built the Grand Coulee Dam (begun during Hoover's administration) and the Triborough Bridge in New York City, as well as hundreds of public buildings. But the PWA's main purpose was to pump federal money into the economy. This huge appropriation shows the Roosevelt administration's willingness to use controversial deficit spending to stimulate the economy.

In the three months until Congress adjourned on June 16, 1933, Roosevelt delivered fifteen messages to Congress proposing major legislation, and Congress passed fifteen significant laws (see Table 25.1). The United States rebounded from near collapse. As New Deal programs were implemented, unemployment fell from

TABLE 25.1 New Deal Achievements

Year	Labor	Agriculture and Environment	Business and Industrial Recovery	Relief	Reform
1933	Section 7(a) of NIRA	Agricultural Adjustment Act Farm Credit Act	Emergency Banking Relief Act Economy Act Beer-Wine Revenue Act Banking Act of 1933 (guaranteed deposits) National Industrial Recovery Act	Civilian Conservation Corps Federal Emergency Relief Act Home Owners Refinancing Act Public Works Administration Civil Works Administration	TVA Federal Securities Act
1934	National Labor Relations Board	Taylor Grazing Act			Securities Exchange Act
1935	National Labor Relations (Wagner) Act	Resettlement Administration Rural Electrification Administration		Works Progress Administration National Youth Administration	Social Security Act Public Utility Holding Company Act Revenue Act (wealth tax)
1937		Farm Security Administration		National Housing Act	
1938	Fair Labor Standards Act	Agricultural Adjustment Act of 1938			

Source: Adapted from Charles Sellers, Henry May, and Neil R. McMillen, *A Synopsis of American History*, 6th ed. Copyright © 1985 by Houghton Mifflin Company. Reprinted by permission.

13 million in 1933 to 9 million in 1936. Farm prices rose, along with wages and salaries, and business failures abated (see Figure 25.1).

POLITICAL PRESSURE AND THE SECOND NEW DEAL

The unprecedented popular and congressional support for Roosevelt's New Deal did not last. The seeming unity of the First Hundred Days masked deep divides within the nation, and once the immediate crisis was averted, the struggle over solutions began in earnest. Some tried to stop the expansion of government power; others pushed for increased governmental action to combat continuing poverty and inequality.

Business Opposition

As the economy partially recovered, many wealthy business leaders criticized the New Deal. They condemned government regulation and taxation, along with the use of deficit financing. In 1934 several corporate leaders joined former presidential candidate

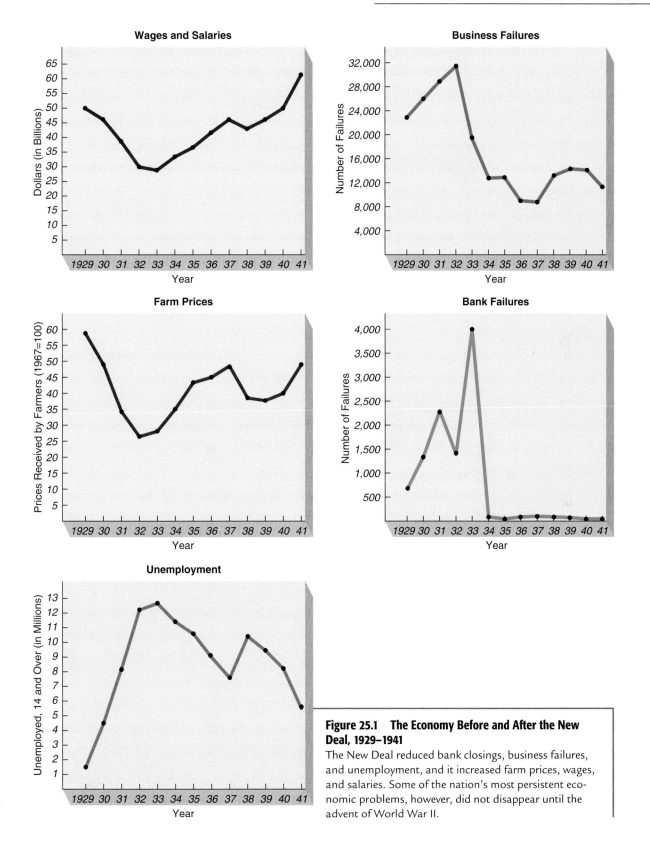

Figure 25.1   The Economy Before and After the New Deal, 1929–1941
The New Deal reduced bank closings, business failures, and unemployment, and it increased farm prices, wages, and salaries. Some of the nation's most persistent economic problems, however, did not disappear until the advent of World War II.

Al Smith and disaffected conservative Democrats to establish the American Liberty League and campaign against New Deal "radicalism." Hoping to turn southern whites against the New Deal and splinter the Democratic Party, the Liberty League also secretly channeled funds to a racist group in the South, which circulated incendiary pictures of the First Lady with African Americans.

Demagogues and Populists

Other Americans (sometimes called populists) thought the government favored business over the common people. Unemployment had decreased—but 9 million people were still jobless. In 1934 a wave of strikes hit the nation, affecting 1.5 million workers. In 1935 enormous dust storms enveloped the southern plains, killing livestock and driving families like the Montgomerys from their land. As dissatisfaction mounted, so did the appeal of demagogues, who played to people's prejudices.

Father Charles Coughlin, a Roman Catholic priest whose weekly radio sermons reached 30 million listeners, spoke to those who felt they had lost control of their lives to distant elites. Increasingly anti–New Deal, he was also anti-Semitic, telling listeners that an international conspiracy of Jewish bankers caused their problems.

Another challenge came from Dr. Francis E. Townsend, a public health officer in Long Beach, California, who lost his job at age sixty-seven with only $100 in savings. His situation was common. With social welfare left to the states, only about 400,000 of the 6.6 million elderly Americans received any state-supplied pensions. As employment and savings disappeared with the depression, many older people fell into poverty.

Townsend proposed that Americans over the age of sixty should receive a government pension of $200 a month, financed by a new transaction (sales) tax. Townsend's plan was fiscally impossible (almost three-quarters of working Americans earned $200 a month or less) and profoundly regressive (because sales tax rates are the same for everyone, they take a larger share of income from those who earn least). Nonetheless, 20 million Americans, or 1 in 5 adults, signed petitions supporting this plan.

Then, there was Huey Long, perhaps the most successful populist demagogue in American history. As a U.S. senator, Long initially supported the New Deal but soon decided that Roosevelt had fallen captive to big business. Long countered in 1934 with the Share Our Wealth Society, advocating the seizure (by taxation) of all income exceeding $1 million a year and wealth in excess of $5 million per family. From these funds, the government would provide each American family an annual income of $2,000 and a one-time homestead allowance of $5,000. By mid-1935 Long's movement claimed 7 million members. But Long was killed by a bodyguard's bullet during an assassination attempt in September 1935.

Left-Wing Critics

The political left also gained ground. In Wisconsin, the left-wing Progressive Party reelected Robert La Follette to the Senate in 1934 and provided seven of the state's ten representatives to Congress. Disclaiming any intention of overthrowing the U.S. government, the Communist Party proclaimed that "Communism Is Twentieth Century Americanism" and cooperated with left-wing labor unions, student groups, and writers' organizations in a Popular Front against fascism abroad and racism at home. In the late 1920s, the Communist Party established the League of Struggle for Negro Rights to fight lynching and, from 1931 on, provided legal and financial support to the Scottsboro Boys, who were falsely accused of raping two white women in Alabama. In 1938, the party had 55,000 members.

Shaping the Second New Deal

It was not only external critics who pushed Roosevelt to focus on social justice. Due to Eleanor Roosevelt's influence, the president's administration included many progressive activists. Frances Perkins, America's first woman cabinet member, came from a social work background, as did Roosevelt's close adviser Harold Ickes. Women social reformers who coalesced around the First Lady played important roles, and African Americans had an unprecedented voice in this White House. By 1936 at least fifty African Americans held relatively important positions in New Deal agencies and cabinet-level departments. Journalists called these officials—who met on Friday evenings at the home of Mary McLeod Bethune, Director of Negro Affairs for the National Youth Administration—the black cabinet.

As Roosevelt faced the 1936 election, he knew he had to appeal to seemingly contradictory desires. Americans hit hard by the depression looked to the New Deal for help. Those with a tenuous hold on the middle class feared continued chaos and disorder. They wanted security and stability. Still others, frightened by the populist promises of people like Long and Coughlin, wanted the New Deal to preserve American capitalism. With this in mind, Roosevelt took the initiative once more.

During the period historians call the Second New Deal, Roosevelt introduced progressive programs aimed at providing "greater security for the average man than he has ever known before in the history of America." The first triumph of the Second New Deal was a law that Roosevelt called the Big Bill. The Emergency Relief Appropriation Act provided $4 billion in new deficit spending, primarily for massive public works programs for the jobless. It also established the Resettlement Administration, which resettled destitute families and organized rural homestead communities and suburban greenbelt towns for low-income workers; the Rural Electrification Administration, which brought electricity to isolated rural areas; and the National Youth Administration, which sponsored work-relief programs for young adults.

Works Progress Administration

The largest and best-known program was the Works Progress Administration (WPA), later renamed the Work Projects Administration. The WPA employed more than 8.5 million people who built 650,000 miles of highways and roads and 125,000 public buildings, as well as bridges, reservoirs, irrigation systems, sewage treatment plants, parks, playgrounds, and swimming pools nationwide.

The WPA also employed artists, musicians, writers, and actors in cultural programs. The WPA's Federal Theater Project brought vaudeville, circuses, and theater, including African American plays and Yiddish plays, to cities and towns. Its Arts Project hired painters and sculptors to teach in rural schools and commissioned artists to decorate post office walls with murals depicting life in America. Perhaps the most ambitious program, the WPA's Federal Writers' Project (FWP) hired authors such as John Steinbeck and Richard Wright to create guidebooks for every state and write about the people of the United States. More than two thousand elderly former slaves told their stories to FWP writers as slave narratives. Life stories of sharecroppers and textile workers were published as *These Are Our Lives* (1939). WPA arts projects were controversial, for many of the artists, performers, and writers sympathized with the political struggles of workers and farmers and some were communists.

Social Security Act

Big Bill programs were part of a short-term emergency strategy, but Roosevelt's long-term strategy centered on the Social Security Act. This measure created, for the first time, a federal system to provide for the social welfare of American citizens. Its key provision was a pension system in which eligible workers paid mandatory Social Security taxes on their wages and their employers contributed an equivalent amount; these workers then received federal retirement benefits. The Social Security Act also created several welfare programs, including a cooperative federal-state system of unemployment compensation and Aid to Dependent Children (later renamed Aid to Families with Dependent Children, AFDC) for needy children in families without fathers present.

Compared with the national systems of social security in most western European nations, the U.S. system was fairly conservative. First, the government did not pay for old-age benefits; workers and their bosses did. Second, the tax was regressive in that the more workers earned, the less they were taxed proportionally. Finally, the law did not cover agricultural labor, domestic service, and "casual labor not in the course of the employer's trade or business" (for example, janitorial work at a hospital). Thus a disproportionately high number of people of color, who worked as farm laborers or domestic servants or in service jobs, received no benefits. The act also excluded public-sector employees, so many teachers, nurses, librarians, and social workers (mostly women) went uncovered. (Although the original Social Security Act provided no retirement benefits for spouses or widows of covered workers, Congress added these benefits in 1939.) Despite these limitations, the federal government took some responsibility for the economic security of the aged, the temporarily unemployed, dependent children, and people with disabilities.

Roosevelt's Populist Strategies

As the 1936 election approached, Roosevelt adopted the populist language of his critics. Denouncing the "unjust concentration of wealth and power," he proposed that government should "cut the giants down to size" through antitrust suits and heavy corporate taxes. He also supported the Wealth Tax Act, which helped slightly redistribute income by raising the wealthy's income taxes (see Figure 25.2). It imposed a new tax on business profits and increased taxes on inheritances, large gifts, and profits from the sale of property.

Roosevelt won by a landslide, defeating Republican nominee Governor Alf Landon of Kansas by 27.8 to 16.7 million votes. The Democrats also won majorities in the House and Senate. The Democrats forged a powerful New Deal coalition, consisting of the urban working class (especially immigrants from southern and eastern Europe), organized labor, the eleven states of the Confederacy (the Solid South), and northern African Americans. African Americans in northern cities now constituted

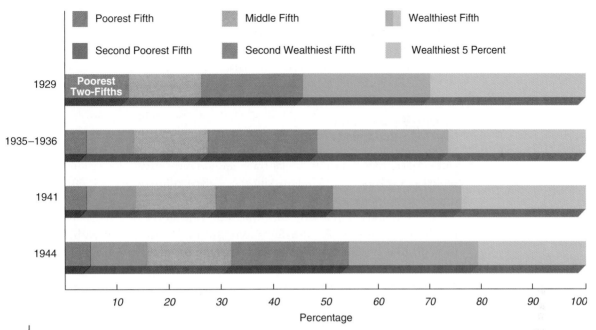

Figure 25.2 Distribution of Total Family Income Among the American People, 1929–1944 (percentage)

Although the New Deal provided economic relief to the American people, it did not, as its critics so often charged, significantly redistribute income downward from the rich to the poor.   (*Source:* Adapted from U.S. Bureau of the Census, *Historical Statistics of the United States, Colonial Times to 1970,* 2 parts [Washington, DC: U.S. Government Printing Office, 1975], Part 1, p. 301.)

voting blocks, and New Deal benefits drew them away from the Republican Party, which they had long supported as the party of Lincoln. This New Deal coalition ensured Democrats would occupy the White House for most of the next thirty years.

LABOR

During the worst years of the depression, American workers continued to struggle for the rights of labor. Management, however, resisted unionization vigorously, with some employers refusing to recognize unions, and others hiring armed thugs to intimidate workers. When workers walked off the job, employers replaced them with strikebreakers. Workers tried to keep strikebreakers from crossing picket lines, and the situation often turned violent. Local police or National Guard troops frequently intervened for management. As strikes spread, violence erupted in the steel, automobile, and textile industries, among lumber workers in the Pacific Northwest, and among teamsters in the Midwest.

The Roosevelt administration provided support for labor with the 1935 National Labor Relations (Wagner) Act. It guaranteed workers the right to organize unions and bargain collectively. It outlawed "unfair labor practices," such as firing workers who joined unions, prohibited management from sponsoring company unions, and required employers to bargain with labor's elected union representatives on wages, hours, and working conditions. Critically important, the Wagner Act created an enforcement mechanism: the National Labor Relations Board (NLRB). By decade's end, the NLRB played a key role in mediating disputes. With federal protection, union membership grew from 3.6 million in 1929 to more than 7 million in 1938. The business-sponsored Liberty League insisted—incorrectly—that the Supreme Court would find the Wagner Act unconstitutional.

Rivalry Between Craft and Industrial Unions

The rapid growth and increasing militancy of the labor movement exacerbated an existing division between craft and industrial unions. Craft unions represented labor's elite—skilled workers in a particular trade, such as carpentry. Industrial unions represented all workers, skilled and unskilled, in a given industry. In the 1930s, industrial unions grew dramatically.

Craft unions dominated the American Federation of Labor, the powerful umbrella organization for specific unions. Most AFL leaders offered little support for industrial organizing. Many looked down on the industrial workers, disproportionately immigrants from southern and eastern Europe—"the rubbish at labor's door," in the words of the Teamsters' president. Skilled workers had economic interests different from those of the great mass of unskilled workers, and more conservative craft unionists were alarmed by what they saw as the radicalism of industrial unions.

In 1935 John L. Lewis, head of the United Mine Workers and the nation's most prominent labor leader, resigned as vice president of the AFL. He and other industrial unionists created the Committee for Industrial Organization (CIO); the AFL then suspended all CIO unions. In 1938 the slightly renamed Congress of Industrial Organizations had 3.7 million members, slightly more than the AFL's 3.4 million. Unlike the AFL, the CIO included women and people of color, giving these marginal workers greater employment security and the benefits of collective bargaining.

Sit-Down Strikes

The most decisive labor conflict came when the United Auto Workers (UAW) demanded recognition from General Motors (GM), Chrysler, and Ford. When GM refused, workers at the Fisher Body plant in Flint, Michigan, responded on December 30, 1936 with a sit-down strike, *inside* the factory. Refusing to leave, they immobilized a key part of the GM production system. GM tried to force them out by turning off the heat. The police used tear gas; strikers turned the plant's water hoses on the police.

As the sit-down strike spread to adjacent plants, auto production plummeted. General Motors obtained a court order to evacuate the plant, but strikers stood firm, risking imprisonment and fines. Michigan's governor refused to send in the National Guard. After forty-four days, GM agreed to recognize the union, and Chrysler followed. Ford held out until 1941.

Memorial Day Massacre

On the heels of this triumph, however, came a grim reminder of the costs of labor's struggle. On Memorial Day 1937, picnicking workers and their families marched toward the Republic Steel plant in Chicago, intending to support strikers there. Police ordered them to disperse. One marcher threw something, and the police attacked. Ten men were killed, seven shot in the back. Thirty marchers were wounded, including a woman and three children. Many Americans, fed up with labor strife and violence, showed little sympathy for the workers. Gradually violence receded, as the National Labor Relations Board successfully mediated disputes. Unionized workers—about 23 percent of the nonagricultural work force—saw their standard of living rise. By 1941 the average steelworker could afford to buy a pair of shoes for each of his children every other year.

FEDERAL POWER AND THE NATIONALIZATION OF CULTURE

In the 1930s, both national media and the federal government played an increasingly important role in the lives of Americans from different regions, classes, and ethnic backgrounds. In 1930, with the single exception of the post office, Americans had little direct contact with the federal government. By the end of the 1930s, almost 35 percent of the population received some federal benefit, whether crop subsidies through the federal AAA or a WPA job. Americans now expected the federal government to play a major role in the life of the nation.

New Deal in the West   The New Deal changed the American West more than any other region, as the federally sponsored construction of dams and other public works projects reshaped the region's economy and environment. During the 1930s, the federal Bureau of Reclamation, an obscure agency created by the Newlands Reclamation Act of 1902, expanded its mandate dramatically to build large multipurpose dams that controlled river systems. The Boulder Dam (later renamed for Herbert Hoover) harnessed the Colorado River, providing water to southern California municipalities and using hydroelectric power to produce electricity for Los Angeles and southern Arizona.

The water from these dams opened new areas to agriculture and allowed western cities to expand; the cheap electricity they produced attracted industry. After the completion of Washington State's Grand Coulee Dam in 1941, the federal government controlled a great deal of water and hydroelectric power in the region, which effectively meant control over the region's future.

The federal government also brought millions of acres of western land under its control in the 1930s. To combat the environmental disaster of the Dust Bowl and keep agriculture prices from falling further, federal programs worked to limit production. In 1934 the Taylor Grazing Act imposed new restrictions on ranchers' use of public lands for grazing stock. Federal livestock reduction programs probably saved the western cattle industry, but they destroyed the traditional economy of the Navajos by forcing them to reduce the size of their sheep herds on federal reservation lands. The large farms and ranches of the West benefited from federal subsidies and crop supports through the AAA, but such programs also increased federal control in the region.

New Deal for Native Americans   New federal activism also extended to the West's people. Previous federal policies toward Native Americans, especially those on western Indian reservations, were disastrous. The

Bureau of Indian Affairs (BIA) was riddled with corruption; in its attempts to assimilate Native Americans, it separated children from parents, suppressed native languages, and outlawed tribal religious practices. The division of tribal lands, however, failed to promote individual land ownership. In the early 1930s, Native Americans were the poorest group in the nation, with an infant mortality rate twice that of white Americans.

In 1933 Roosevelt named one of the BIA's most vocal critics to head the agency. John Collier, founder of the American Indian Defense Agency, meant to completely reverse the course of America's Indian policy. The Indian Reorganization Act (1934) worked toward ending forced assimilation and restoring Indian lands to tribal ownership. Indian tribes regained their status as semisovereign nations, guaranteed "internal sovereignty" in all matters not limited by acts of Congress.

Some Indians denounced the IRA as a "back-to-the-blanket" measure based on romantic notions of "authentic" Indian culture. The tribal government structure specified by the IRA was culturally alien to tribes such as the Papagos, whose language had no word for "representative." The Navajo nation also refused to ratify the IRA, especially since the vote was timed during the federally mandated destruction of Navajo sheep herds. Eventually, however, 181 tribes organized under the IRA, which laid the groundwork for future economic development and limited political autonomy among native peoples.

New Deal in the South New Dealers did not set out to transform the American West, but they did intend to transform the American South. Well before the Great Depression, the South was mired in debilitating poverty. In 1929 the South's per capita income of $365 per year was less than half of the West's $921. More than half of southern farm families were tenants or sharecroppers with no land of their own. Almost 15 percent of South Carolina's people could not read or write.

The largest federal intervention in the South was the Tennessee Valley Authority (TVA), authorized by Congress during Roosevelt's First Hundred Days. The TVA was created to develop a water and hydroelectric power project similar to the multipurpose dams of the West. However, confronted with the poverty of the Tennessee River Valley region (which included parts of Virginia, North Carolina, Tennessee, Georgia, Alabama, Mississippi, and Kentucky), the TVA expanded to promote economic development, bring electricity to rural areas, restore fields worn out from overuse, and fight malaria.

Although it benefited many southerners, the TVA proved to be a monumental environmental disaster. TVA strip mining caused soil erosion. Its coal-burning generators released sulfur oxides, which combined with water vapor to produce acid rain. Above all, the TVA degraded the water by dumping untreated sewage, toxic chemicals, and metal pollutants from strip mining into streams and rivers.

Southern senators benefited from the flow of federal dollars to their states, but they were suspicious of federal intervention. When federal action threatened the South's racial hierarchy, they resisted passionately. As the nation's poorest and least educated region, the South would not easily be integrated into the national culture and economy. But New Deal programs began that process and improved the lives of at least some of the region's people.

Mass Media and Popular Culture

America's national popular culture helped break down regional boundaries and foster national connections. Radio filled the days and nights of the depression era. As cheaper models became available, by 1937 Americans were buying radios at the rate of twenty-eight a minute. By decade's end, 27.5 million households owned radios, and families listened on average five hours a day. Roosevelt used radio to speak directly to the American people with Fireside Chats.

In a time of uncertainty, radio gave citizens immediate access to the political news and the actual voices of their elected leaders. During hard times, radio offered escape: for children, the adventures of *Flash Gordon* and *Jack Armstrong, The All-American Boy;* for housewives, new soap operas, such as *The Romance of Helen Trent* and *Young Widder Brown.* Families gathered to listen to the comedy of the ex-vaudevillians George Burns and Gracie Allen, and Jack Benny.

Listeners were carried to New York City for performances of the Metropolitan Opera on Saturday afternoons, to the Moana Hotel on the beach at Waikiki through the live broadcast of *Hawaii Calls,* and to major league baseball games (begun by the St. Louis Cardinals in 1935) in distant cities. Millions shared the horror of the kidnapping of aviator Charles Lindbergh's son in 1932; African Americans in the urban North and rural South shared the triumphs of African American boxer Joe Louis (the Brown Bomber). Radio lessened the isolation of individuals and helped create a more homogeneous mass culture across class and regional lines.

The shared popular culture of 1930s America also centered on Hollywood movies. The film industry suffered in the initial years of the depression, but it rebounded after 1933. In a nation of fewer than 130 million people, 80 to 90 million tickets were sold weekly by the mid-1930s, as Americans sought escape at the movies. Comedies were especially popular, from the slapstick of the Marx Brothers to the sophisticated banter of *My Man Godfrey*.

Yet as gangster movies (including *Little Caesar* and *Scarface*) drew crowds in the early 1930s, many Americans worried about their glamorization of crime. Faced with a boycott organized by the Roman Catholic Legion of Decency, in 1934 the film industry established a production code that would determine what American film audiences saw—and did not see—for decades.

Finally, in an unintended consequence, federal policies intended to channel jobs to male heads of households strengthened the power of national popular culture. During Roosevelt's first two years in office, 1.5 million youths lost jobs; many young people who would have gone to work at the age of fourteen in better times decided to stay in school. By the end of the decade, three-quarters of

King Kong broke all box-office records in 1933, as Americans flocked to see the giant ape fighting off airplanes from the top of New York's new Empire State Building—the tallest building in the world. (The Granger Collection, New York)

The 1936 Olympic Games

The 1936 Olympic Games scheduled in Berlin, under the Nazi regime, created a dilemma for the United States and other nations. Would participation in the Nazi-orchestrated spectacle lend credence to Hitler? Or would victories by other nations undermine Hitler's claims about the superiority of Germany's "Aryan race"?

From the first modern Olympic Games in 1896, international politics were always near the surface. Germany was excluded in 1920 and 1924 following its World War I defeat. The International Olympic Committee's choice (in 1931) of Berlin for the XI Olympiad was intended to welcome Germany back into the world community. However, with Hitler's rise to power in 1933, Germany determined to use the games as propaganda for the Nazi state. Soon thereafter, campaigns to boycott the Berlin Olympics emerged in several nations, including the United States.

Americans were divided over the boycott. Some U.S. Jewish groups led campaigns against U.S. participation in Berlin, and Jewish athletes decided individually whether to attend. But the debate over the Berlin Olympics revealed pockets of American anti-Semitism. The president of the American Olympic Committee, Avery Brundage, attributed the boycott movement to a "conspiracy of Jews and communists." African Americans opposed the boycott and looked forward to demonstrating in Berlin how wrong Hitler's notions of Aryan superiority were.

The United States sent 312 athletes to Berlin; 18 were African Americans, who won 14 medals, almost one-quarter of the U.S. total of 56. Track and field star Jesse Owens earned 4 gold medals. Jewish athletes won 13 medals.

Despite the controversy, the XI Olympiad was a public relations triumph for Germany. The *New York Times*, impressed by the games and Germans' hospitality, proclaimed that the XI Olympiad put Germany "back in the fold of nations." Still, the idealistic vision of nations linked in peaceful athletic competition hit a low point at the 1936 Olympics. The 1940 Olympic Games, scheduled for Tokyo, were cancelled because of the escalating world war.

GERMANY
XIᵗʰ OLYMPIC GAMES
1936
1ˢᵗ—16ᵗʰ AUGUST
BERLIN

The eleventh summer Olympic Games in Berlin were carefully crafted as propaganda for the Nazi state. And the spectacle of the 1936 games, as represented in this poster, was impressive. But on the athletic fields, Nazi claims of Aryan superiority were challenged by athletes such as African American Jesse Owens, who is shown breaking the Olympic record in the 200-meter race.

(Above: © Leonard de Selva/Corbis; left: © Bettmann/ Corbis)

American youth went to high school—up from one-half in 1920—and graduation rates doubled. As more young people went to high school, more participated in that national youth culture, increasingly listening to the same music and adopting similar clothing, dance, and speech. Paradoxically, the hard times of the depression caused youth culture to spread more widely among America's young.

THE LIMITS OF THE NEW DEAL

Roosevelt began his second term with a strong mandate for reform. Almost immediately, however, the president's own actions undermined his New Deal agenda. Labor strife and racial issues divided America. As the world inched toward war, domestic initiatives lost ground to foreign affairs and defense. By late 1938, New Deal reform ground to a halt.

Court-Packing Plan

Following his landslide in 1936, Roosevelt set out to safeguard his progressive agenda. He saw the Supreme Court as its greatest threat. In ruling both the National Industrial Recovery Act (in 1935) and the Agricultural Adjustment Act (in 1936) unconstitutional, the Court not only rejected specific legislative provisions but also the expansion of presidential and federal power this legislation entailed. Only three of the nine justices were consistently sympathetic to New Deal emergency measures, and Roosevelt was convinced the Court would invalidate most of the Second New Deal legislation. Citing the advanced age and heavy workload of the nine justices, he asked Congress for authority to appoint up to six new justices. But in an era that had seen the rise of Hitler, Mussolini, and Stalin, many Americans saw Roosevelt's plan as an attack on constitutional government. Congress rebelled, and Roosevelt experienced his first major congressional defeat.

Ironically, during the long debate over court packing, key swing-vote justices began to vote for pro–New Deal rulings. The Court upheld both the Social Security Act and the Wagner Act (*NLRB v. Jones & Laughlin Steel Corp.*), extending Congress's power to regulate interstate commerce to production of goods for interstate commerce. Moreover, a new judicial pension program encouraged older judges to retire, and the president appointed seven new associate justices. In the end, Roosevelt got what he wanted from the Supreme Court, but the court-packing plan damaged his political credibility.

Roosevelt Recession

Another New Deal setback was the recession of 1937–1939, sometimes called the Roosevelt recession. In 1937, confident that the depression had ebbed, Roosevelt reduced government spending. At the same time, the Federal Reserve Board, concerned about a 3.6 percent inflation rate, tightened credit. These actions sent the economy into a tailspin: unemployment climbed from 7.7 million in 1937 to 10.4 million in 1938.

New Dealers struggled over the direction of liberal reform. Some urged trust-busting; others advocated the resurrection of national economic planning. But Roosevelt instead chose deficit financing to stimulate consumer demand and create jobs. And in 1939, with conflict over the world war in Europe commanding more of the nation's attention, the New Deal came to an end. Roosevelt sacrificed further domestic reforms in return for conservative support for his programs of military rearmament and preparedness.

Election of 1940

No president had ever served more than two terms, and Americans speculated about whether Franklin Roosevelt would seek a third term in 1940. Roosevelt seemed undecided until spring, when Adolf Hitler's military advances in Europe convinced him to stay on. In the 1940 campaign, Roosevelt promised Americans, "Your boys are not going to be sent into any foreign wars."

Roosevelt did not win this election in a landslide, but the New Deal coalition held. Roosevelt again won in the cities, supported by blue-collar workers, ethnic Americans, and African Americans. He also carried every southern state.

Race and the Limits of the New Deal

While the New Deal benefited many Americans, it fell short of equality for people of color. Implemented at the local level, national programs were subjected to local custom. In the South, that meant African Americans received lower relief payments than whites and were paid less for WPA jobs. In Tucson, Arizona, Federal Emergency Relief Agency officials divided applicants into four groups—Anglos, Mexican Americans, Mexican immigrants, and Indians—and allocated relief payments in descending order.

Such discriminatory practices were rooted not only in racism but also in the economic interests of whites, or Anglos. The majority of African American and Mexican American workers were paid so poorly that they *earned* less than impoverished whites got for relief. Why would these workers take low-paying private jobs if government relief or government work programs provided more income? Local communities understood that federal programs threatened a political, social, and economic system based on racial hierarchies.

The case of the Scottsboro Boys illustrates the power of racism in the conflict between local and national power in 1930s America. One night in March 1931, two white women riding the rails on a Southern Railroad freight train claimed that young black hobos on this train had raped them. Medical evidence later showed that the women were lying. But within two weeks, eight of the so-called Scottsboro Boys were convicted of rape by all-white juries and sentenced to death. The ninth, a boy of thirteen, was saved from the death penalty by one vote. The case—clearly a product of southern racism—became a cause célèbre, both nationally and, through the efforts of the Communist Party, around the world.

The Supreme Court intervened, ruling that Alabama deprived black defendants of equal protection under the law by systematically excluding African Americans from juries and denying the defendants counsel. Alabama, however, staged new trials, convicting five of the young men (four would be paroled by 1950, and one escaped from prison). On issues of race, the South would not yield easily to federal power.

Second, the gains made by people of color under the New Deal were limited by the political realities of southern resistance. For example, in 1938 southern Democrats blocked an antilynching bill with a six-week-long filibuster in the Senate. Roosevelt refused to use his political capital to break the filibuster and pass the bill. He knew African Americans would not desert the Democratic Party, but without southern senators, his legislative agenda was dead. Roosevelt wanted all Americans to enjoy the benefits of democracy, but he had no strong commitment to civil rights.

African American Support

Why, then, did African Americans support Roosevelt? Because, despite discriminatory policies, the New Deal helped African Americans. By 1939, almost one-third of African American households survived on income from a WPA job. African Americans held significant positions in the Roosevelt administration, and the First Lady publically showed her commitment to racial equality. When the Daughters of the American Revolution refused to allow acclaimed African American contralto Marian Anderson to perform in Washington's Constitution Hall, Eleanor Roosevelt arranged for Anderson to sing at the Lincoln Memorial instead. Nonetheless, given the limits of New Deal reform, some African Americans concluded that self-help and direct-action movements were a surer alternative. In 1934 African American tenant farmers and sharecroppers joined with poor whites to form the Southern Tenant Farmers' Union. In the North, African American consumers boycotted white merchants who refused to hire African Americans. Their slogan was "Don't Buy Where You Can't Work." And the Brotherhood of Sleeping Car Porters, under the astute leadership of A. Philip Randolph, fought for African American workers. Such actions helped improve the lives of African Americans during the 1930s.

An Assessment of the New Deal

Assessments of Roosevelt varied widely during his presidency: he was passionately hated and passionately loved. When he spoke to Americans in his Fireside Chats, hundreds of thousands wrote to him, asking for help and offering advice.

Eleanor Roosevelt played an unprecedented role in the Roosevelt administration. As First Lady, she worked for social justice, bringing reformers, trade unionists, and advocates for the rights of women and African Americans to the White House. Sometimes described as the conscience of the New Deal, she took public positions—especially on African American civil rights—far more progressive than those of her husband's administration. She served as a lightning rod, deflecting conservative criticism from her husband to herself. And she cemented the allegiance of groups such as African Americans to the New Deal.

Most historians consider Franklin Roosevelt a truly great president, citing his courage, his willingness to experiment, and his capacity to inspire the nation. Some, who see the New Deal as a squandered opportunity for "true" change, charge that Roosevelt lacked vision. They judge Roosevelt by goals that were not his own: Roosevelt was a pragmatist whose goal was to preserve the system. But even critics agree he transformed the presidency. Some find this transformation troubling, tracing the roots of the imperial presidency to the Roosevelt administration.

During his more than twelve years in office, Roosevelt strengthened the presidency and the federal government. Through New Deal programs, the government expanded its regulatory responsibilities, including overseeing the nation's financial systems. For the first time the federal government offered relief to the jobless and used deficit spending to stimulate the economy. Millions of Americans benefited from government programs that are still operating today, among them Social Security.

However, as late as 1939, more than 10 million men and women remained jobless, and the nation's unemployment rate stood at 19 percent. It was not until1941, as the nation mobilized for war, that unemployment fell to 10 percent. By1944, only 1 percent of the labor force was unemployed. World War II, not the New Deal, reinvigorated the American economy.

Summary

In the 1930s, a major economic crisis threatened the nation. By 1933 almost one-quarter of American workers were unemployed. Millions were homeless and hungry. Herbert Hoover, elected president in 1928, believed government should play only a limited role in managing the economy. He tried to solve the nation's economic problems through associationalism, a voluntary partnership of businesses and the federal government. In the 1932 presidential election, voters turned to the candidate who promised them a New Deal, Franklin Delano Roosevelt.

The New Deal was a liberal reform program that developed within the parameters of America's capitalist and democratic system. It expanded the power of the federal government. New Deal reforms forced banks, utilities, stock markets, farms, and most businesses to adhere to federal guidelines. The government guaranteed the workers' right to join unions, and federal law required employers to negotiate with workers' unions on wages, hours, and working conditions. Many unemployed workers, elderly and disabled Americans, and dependent children were protected by a national welfare system administered through the federal government.

The New Deal had its detractors. Business leaders attacked the New Deal for its new regulation and support of organized labor. As the federal government expanded its role, tensions between national and local authority sometimes flared, and differences in regional ways of life and in social and economic structures challenged national policymakers. Both the West and the South were transformed by federal government action, but citizens of both regions were suspicious of federal intervention, and white southerners resisted challenges to the racial system of Jim Crow. The political realities of a fragile New Deal coalition and strong opposition shaped—and limited—New Deal programs of the 1930s. But the New Deal fundamentally changed the way that the U.S. government would deal with future economic downturns and with the needs of its citizens in good times and in bad.

Social Security

The New Deal's Social Security system created a secure old age for millions of Americans. Although Social Security initially excluded some of America's neediest citizens, such as farm and domestic workers, amendments expanded eligibility. At present, almost 99 percent of American workers are covered by Social Security.

Today's Social Security system faces an uncertain future. Its troubles are partly due to decisions made during the 1930s. President Franklin Roosevelt did not want Social Security to be confused with poor relief. Instead he created a system financed by payments from workers and their employers. This system, however, presented a short-term problem. If benefits came from their own contributions, workers who began receiving Social Security payments in 1940 would have received less than $1 a month. Therefore, Social Security payments from current workers paid the benefits of those already retired.

Over time, this financing system has become increasingly unstable. In 1935, average life expectancy was under sixty-five years, the age one could collect benefits. Today, American men live almost sixteen years past retirement age, and women close to twenty years past retirement age. In 1935 there were 16 current workers paying into the system for each person receiving retirement benefits. In 2000 there were fewer than 3.5 workers per retiree. Unless the system is reformed, many argue, the retirement of 77 million baby boomers born in the 1940s, 1950s, and 1960s could bankrupt the system.

When the stock market rose dramatically during the 1990s, some proposed that, because Social Security paid only a fraction of what individuals might have earned by investing their Social Security tax payments in the stock market, let Americans do just that. Opponents declared this proposal too risky; others asked if current workers kept their money to invest, where would benefits for current retirees come from? With the stock market's huge decline in the first years of the twenty-first century (and the losses sustained by private pension funds), President George W. Bush's privatization initiative gained little congressional support. But, with the oldest baby boomers beginning to retire, questions about the future of Social Security will become increasingly important.

Chapter Review

HOOVER AND HARD TIMES, 1929–1933

Why was Hoover so reluctant to implement relief programs during the Great Depression?

Hoover was afraid that government hand-outs would create dependency among the struggling and poor. When he made federal funds available to feed livestock, but not people, he was reviled by Americans everywhere. By the time he finally initiated federal programs, it was too late to change public opinion or make much difference in the crisis. His public works projects, such as the Grand Coulee Dam, created some jobs, but nowhere near enough to have an impact. While the Federal Farm Board, established in 1929, supported farm prices and lent money to coops, it was poorly funded. Hoover's most direct government program—the Reconstruction Finance Corporation implemented at the end of his presidency in 1932—offered relief to businesses, but still provided nothing for the unemployed.

FRANKLIN D. ROOSEVELT AND THE LAUNCHING OF THE NEW DEAL

> **How did the government take on new roles during the period dubbed "The First Hundred Days"?**

During this special session of Congress, Roosevelt sought to revive the flagging economy through two types of federal initiatives: national economic planning and relief programs. The planning portion of this "New Deal" focused on the National Industrial Recovery Act (NIRA) and the Agricultural Adjustment Act (AAA). The NIRA encouraged industries to adopt wage and price standards that could erase competition and increase consumer spending and, therefore, demand for workers. The AAA established crop controls and offered farm subsidies. Roosevelt also spent $3 billion on work relief programs, such as the Civilian Conservation Corps, which hired young men to help build dams, reservoirs, and trails in national parks; and the Public Works Administration, whose workers completed the Grand Coulee Dam and built New York City's Triborough Bridge and hundreds of other public facilities. All tolled, fifteen laws were passed, helping the United States to recover and unemployment to drop from 13 million in 1933 to 9 million in 1936.

POLITICAL PRESSURE AND THE SECOND NEW DEAL

> **What were the hallmarks of the Second New Deal?**

Roosevelt's goal for the Second New Deal was more far-reaching than his initial efforts. First, the Emergency Relief Appropriation Act allocated $4 billion in deficit spending to provide public works jobs through the Works Progress Administration (WPA)—building roads, bridges, and parks and renovating schools and hospitals. It also implemented initiatives to teach illiterate Americans to read and write and employed artists, writers and actors to put on plays, create original artwork, produce guidebooks for every state, and collect stories about the American people, including those of former slaves. The Resettlement Administration relocated poor families and organized homestead communities, while the Rural Electrification Administration brought electricity to rural areas. But Roosevelt's long-term strategy was the Social Security Act, a federal pension system taxing workers' wages and providing retirement benefits. The SSA included an unemployment compensation program, as well as welfare for needy families without fathers present under Aid to Dependent Children.

LABOR

> **How did Roosevelt provide support for labor?**

Labor unrest and dissatisfaction with dwindling wages and harsh working conditions increased throughout the 1930s. Public support for strikes waned as violence escalated throughout the decade. But Roosevelt bolstered labor with the 1935 National Labor Relations (Wagner) Act, which guaranteed workers the right to organize unions and bargain collectively. It made it illegal for businesses to fire workers who joined unions and banned management from sponsoring company unions. It also required firms to bargain with union representatives about wages, hours, and working conditions and created a National Labor Relations Board to mediate disputes. As the NLRB took hold, violence dissipated and workers' wages increased.

FEDERAL POWER AND THE NATIONALIZATION OF CULTURE

How did the Depression cause youth culture to spread?

Government policies focused on channeling jobs to the male heads of household. That meant that young boys who, at age 14, under normal economic conditions would have gone to work, could not find jobs. Hence, they stayed in school longer, and high school graduation rates by the end of the decade doubled. As young people spent more time in school, they were influenced more greatly by their peers than by parents as well as by a shared youth culture in music, clothing, and manner of speaking.

THE LIMITS OF THE NEW DEAL

How did Roosevelt undermine his New Deal agenda and, ultimately, his legacy?

Roosevelt made two moves with serious consequences for the New Deal. First, since the Supreme Court had ruled unconstitutional both the NIRA and the AAA, Roosevelt considered the Court an adversary and sought to pack it with sympathetic justices. He asked Congress to give him the authority to appoint six new justices, arguing that the present nine were getting old and were overworked. Congress refused, and although he ultimately was able to name seven new associate justices when a new pension program encouraged older judges to retire, Roosevelt's political credibility was damaged by his court-packing scheme. Second, in 1937, Roosevelt reduced government spending, certain that the depression was winding down. That, combined with the Federal Reserve's move to tighten credit, triggered a two-year recession.

SUGGESTIONS FOR FURTHER READING

Anthony J. Badger, *The New Deal: The Depression Years, 1933–1940* (1989)

Alan Brinkley, *The End of Reform: New Deal Liberalism in Recession and War* (1995)

Alan Brinkley, *Voices of Protest: Huey Long, Father Coughlin, and the Great Depression* (1982)

Lizabeth Cohen, *Making a New Deal: Industrial Workers in Chicago* (1990)

Blanche Wiesen Cook, *Eleanor Roosevelt,* Vols. 1 and 2 (1992, 1999)

Sidney Fine, *Sitdown: The General Motors Strike of 1936–37* (1969)

James E. Goodman, *Stories of Scottsboro* (1994)

David M. Kennedy, *Freedom from Fear: The American People in Depression and War* (1999)

Robert McElvaine, The *Great Depression: America, 1929–1941* (1984)

Donald Worster, *Dust Bowl: The Southern Plains in the 1930s* (2004)

CHAPTER 26

The United States in a Troubled World

1920–1941

CHAPTER OUTLINE

Searching for Peace and Order in the 1920s

The World Economy, Cultural Expansion, and Great Depression

U.S. Dominance in Latin America

The Course to War in Europe

Japan, China, and a New Order in Asia

U.S. Entry into World War II

LINKS TO THE WORLD: Radio News

Summary

LEGACY FOR A PEOPLE AND A NATION: Presidential Deception of the Public

In 1921 the Rockefeller Foundation dedicated several million dollars for projects to control yellow fever in Latin America, beginning in Mexico. Carried by mosquitoes, the virus caused severe headaches, vomiting, jaundice (yellow skin), and often death. Learning from the pioneering work of Carlos Juan Finlay of Cuba, Oswaldo Cruz of Brazil, and U.S. Army surgeon Walter Reed, scientists sought to destroy the mosquito in its larval stage, before it became an egg-laying adult.

U.S. diplomats, military officers, and business executives agreed that the disease threatened public health, and this in turn disturbed political and economic order. When outbreaks occurred, ports were closed and quarantined, disrupting trade and immigration. The infection struck U.S. officials, merchants, investors, and soldiers stationed abroad and incapacitated workers. Throughout Latin America, insufficient official attention to yellow-fever epidemics stirred public discontent against regimes the United States supported. When the Panama Canal opened in 1914, leaders feared that the disease would spread, even reinfecting the United States, which had suffered its last epidemic in 1905.

Gradually overcoming strong local anti-U.S. feelings, Rockefeller personnel inspected breeding places and deposited larvae-eating fish in public waterworks. In 1924 La Fundación Rockefeller declared yellow fever eradicated in Mexico. Elsewhere in Latin America, the foundation's antimosquito campaign proved successful in maritime and urban areas but less so in rural and jungle regions. Politically, Rockefeller Foundation efforts in the 1920s and 1930s strengthened central governments by providing a public health infrastructure and diminished anti-U.S. sentiment.

The Rockefeller Foundation's campaign offers insights into Americans' fervent but futile effort to build a stable international

This icon will direct you to interactive activities and study materials on A People And A Nation, Brief Edition

website: **www.cengage.com/history/norton/ peoplenationbrief8e**

Chronology

1921–22	Washington Conference limits naval arms. Rockefeller Foundation begins the battle against yellow fever in Latin America.
1922	Mussolini comes to power in Italy.
1924	Dawes Plan eases German reparations.
1928	Kellogg-Briand Pact outlaws war.
1929	Great Depression begins. Young Plan reduces German reparations.
1930	Hawley-Smoot Tariff raises duties.
1931	Japan seizes Manchuria.
1933	Adolf Hitler becomes chancellor of Germany. United States extends diplomatic recognition to the Soviet Union. United States announces the Good Neighbor policy for Latin America.
1934	Batista comes to power in Cuba.
1935	Italy invades Ethiopia. Congress passes the first Neutrality Act.
1936	Germany reoccupies the Rhineland. Spanish Civil War breaks out.
1937	Sino-Japanese War breaks out. Roosevelt makes Quarantine Speech against aggressors.
1938	Mexico nationalizes U.S.-owned oil companies. Munich Conference grants part of Czechoslovakia to Germany.
1939	Germany and the Soviet Union sign a nonaggression pact. Germany invades Poland; World War II begins.
1940	Germany invades Denmark, Norway, Belgium, the Netherlands, and France. Selective Training and Service Act starts the first U.S. peacetime draft.
1941	Lend-Lease Act gives aid to the Allies. Germany attacks the Soviet Union. United States freezes Japanese assets. Roosevelt and Churchill sign the Atlantic Charter. Japanese flotilla attacks Pearl Harbor, Hawai'i; United States enters World War II.

order after World War I. Despite the isolationist tag sometimes applied to U.S. foreign relations during the interwar decades, Americans remained active in world affairs in the 1920s and 1930s—from gunboats on Chinese rivers, to negotiations in European financial centers, to marine occupations in Haiti and Nicaragua, to oil wells in the Middle East, to campaigns against diseases in Africa and Latin America. President Wilson rightly said after World War I that the United States had "become a determining factor in the history of mankind."

The most apt description of interwar U.S. foreign policy is independent internationalism. Notwithstanding the nation's overseas projects—colonies, spheres of influence, naval bases, investments, trade, missionary activity, humanitarian projects—many Americans regarded themselves as isolationists, meaning that they wanted no part of Europe's political squabbles or military alliances or the League of Nations, which might drag them into war. Internationalist-minded Americans, including most senior officials, also wanted to stay out of future European wars but were more willing than isolationists to attempt to reshape the world.

A stable world would better facilitate American prosperity and security. In the interwar years, American diplomats increasingly sought to exercise U.S. power through conferences, humanitarian programs, cultural penetration (Americanization), moral lectures and calls for peace, nonrecognition of disapproved regimes, arms control, and economic and financial ties under the Open Door principle.

But a stable world order proved elusive. Public health projects saved lives but could not address staggering poverty around the globe. World War I debts and reparations bedeviled the 1920s. The Great Depression shattered world trade and threatened America's prominence in international markets. It also spawned political extremism, militarism, and war in Europe and Asia. As Nazi Germany marched to war, the United States adopted a neutrality policy. The United States sought to defend its interests in Asia against Japanese aggression by invoking the Open Door policy.

After the outbreak of European war in September 1939, many Americans came to agree with President Franklin D. Roosevelt that Germany and Japan imperiled U.S. interests because they were building self-sufficient spheres of influence on the basis of military and economic domination. Roosevelt first pushed for U.S. military preparedness and then favored aiding Britain and France. A German victory, he reasoned, would destroy traditional economic ties, threaten U.S. influence in the Western Hemisphere, and place at the pinnacle of European power Adolf Hitler, whose ambitions and barbarities seemed limitless.

Meanwhile, Japan seemed determined to dismember the United States' Asian friend China, destroy the Open Door principle, and endanger a U.S. colony—the Philippines. To deter the Japanese, the United States cut off supplies of vital U.S. products, such as oil. Japan's surprise attack on Pearl Harbor, Hawai'i, in December 1941 brought the United States into World War II.

- Why and by what means did Americans try to facilitate a stable world order in the interwar period?
- How did the Roosevelt administration respond to the growing Nazi German threat in the second half of the 1930s?
- Why did the United States enter World War II?

SEARCHING FOR PEACE AND ORDER IN THE 1920S

World War I left Europe in shambles. Between 1914 and 1921, Europe suffered tens of millions of casualties from world war, civil wars, massacres, epidemics, and famine. Germany and France lost 10 percent of their workers. The American Relief Administration and private charities delivered food to needy Europeans, including Russians wracked by famine in 1921 and 1922. Through food relief, Americans hoped to dampen any appeal political radicalism might have overseas. Secretary of State Charles Evans Hughes and other leaders expected U.S. economic expansion to promote international stability, believing prosperity would eliminate ideological extremes, revolution, arms races, aggression, and war.

Collective security, as envisioned by Woodrow Wilson, elicited little enthusiasm among Republican leaders. Senator Henry Cabot Lodge gloated in 1920 that "we have destroyed Mr. Wilson's League of Nations." The Geneva-headquartered League of Nations, envisioned as a peacemaker, proved feeble, not just because the United States did not join but also because members failed to utilize it to settle disputes. Still, starting in the mid-1920s, U.S. officials participated discreetly in League meetings on public health, prostitution, drug and arms trafficking, counterfeiting of currency, and other questions. The Rockefeller Foundation donated $100,000 a year to the League's public health ventures.

Peace Groups

During the interwar years, peace groups drew widespread support. Women gravitated to their own organizations because they lacked influence in the male-dominated groups and because of the popular assumption that women—as nurturing mothers—had a unique aversion to war. Carrie Chapman Catt's moderate National Conference on the Cure and Cause of War, formed in 1924, and the U.S. section of the Women's International League for Peace and Freedom (WILPF), organized in 1915 by Jane Addams and Emily Greene Balch, became the largest women's peace groups. When Addams won the Nobel Peace Prize in 1931, she transferred her award money to the League of Nations.

Peace groups differed over strategies to ensure world order. Some urged cooperation with the League of Nations and the World Court. Others championed arbitration, disarmament and arms reduction, the outlawing of war, and strict neutrality during wars. The WILPF called for an end to U.S. economic imperialism, which, it claimed, compelled the United States to intervene militarily in Latin America to protect U.S. business interests. The Women's Peace Union (organized in 1921) lobbied for a constitutional amendment requiring a national referendum on a declaration of war. Quakers, YMCA officials, and Social Gospel clergy in 1917 created the American Friends Service Committee to identify pacifist alternatives to warmaking.

Washington Naval Conference

Peace advocates influenced Warren G. Harding's administration to convene the Washington Naval Conference of November 1921–February 1922. Delegates from Britain, Japan, France, Italy, China, Portugal, Belgium, and the Netherlands joined a U.S. team led by Secretary of State Hughes to discuss limiting naval armaments. American leaders worried that huge military spending endangered economic rehabilitation and that an expansionist Japan, with the world's third largest navy, would overtake the United States's, ranked second behind Britain.

Secretary of State Hughes opened the conference with the stunning proposal to scrap thirty major U.S. ships, totaling 846,000 tons. He urged the British and Japanese delegations to do away with smaller amounts. The final limit was 500,000 tons each for the Americans and the British, 300,000 tons for the Japanese, and 175,000 tons each for the French and the Italians. These limits were agreed to in the Five-Power Treaty, which also set a ten-year moratorium on building capital ships (battleships and aircraft carriers). The governments further pledged not to build new fortifications in their Pacific possessions (such as the Philippines).

Next, the Nine-Power Treaty reaffirmed the Open Door in China, recognizing Chinese sovereignty. Finally, in the Four-Power Treaty, the United States, Britain, Japan, and France agreed to respect one another's Pacific possessions. These treaties did not limit submarines, destroyers, or cruisers and did not provide enforcement powers for the Open Door. Still, Hughes achieved arms limitation and improved America's strategic position vis-à-vis Japan in the Pacific.

Kellogg-Briand Pact

Peace advocates welcomed the Locarno Pact of 1925, several agreements among European nations that sought to reduce tensions between Germany and France, and the

Kellogg-Briand Pact of 1928. In the latter document, sixty-two nations agreed to "condemn recourse to war for the solution of international controversies, and renounce it as an instrument of national policy." The Kellogg-Briand Pact passed the U.S. Senate 85 to 1, but it lacked enforcement provisions. It did reflect popular opinion that war was barbaric. But arms limitations, peace pacts, and efforts by peace groups failed to muzzle the dogs of war, which fed on the economic troubles that upended world order.

THE WORLD ECONOMY, CULTURAL EXPANSION, AND GREAT DEPRESSION

While Europe struggled to recover after World War I, the international economy wobbled and collapsed. The Great Depression set off a political chain reaction that carried the world to war. Cordell Hull, U.S. secretary of state from 1933 to 1944, argued that political extremism and militarism sprang from maimed economies. Hull proved right.

Economic and Cultural Expansion Due to World War I, the United States became a creditor nation and the financial capital of the world (see Figure 26.1). From 1914 to 1930, private investments abroad grew fivefold, to more than $17 billion. By the late 1920s, the United States produced nearly half of the world's industrial goods and ranked first among exporters ($5.2 billion worth of shipments in 1929). Britain and Germany lost ground to American businesses in Latin America, where Standard Oil operated in eight nations and the United Fruit Company became a huge landowner.

America's economic prominence facilitated the export of American culture. Hollywood movies saturated the global market and stimulated interest in all things American. Although some foreigners warned against Americanization, others aped American mass-production methods and emphasis on efficiency and modernization. Coca-Cola opened a bottling plant in Essen, Germany; Ford built an automobile assembly plant in Cologne.

Germans marveled at Henry Ford's industrial techniques (*Fordismus*). In the 1930s, Nazi leader Adolf Hitler sent German car designers to Detroit before launching the Volkswagen. The Phelps-Stokes Fund further advertised the American capitalist model, exporting to black Africa Booker T. Washington's Tuskegee philosophy of education, while the Rockefeller Foundation supported colleges to train doctors in Lebanon and China and funded medical research in Europe.

The U.S. government assisted this expansion. The Webb-Pomerene Act (1918) excluded from antitrust prosecution those combinations set up for export trade, the Edge Act (1919) permitted U.S. banks to open foreign-branch banks, and overseas offices of the Department of Commerce distributed market information. The federal government also stimulated foreign loans by American investors. U.S. government support for expansion of the telecommunications industry helped International Telegraph and Telephone (IT&T), Radio Corporation of America (RCA), and the Associated Press (AP) become international giants by 1930.

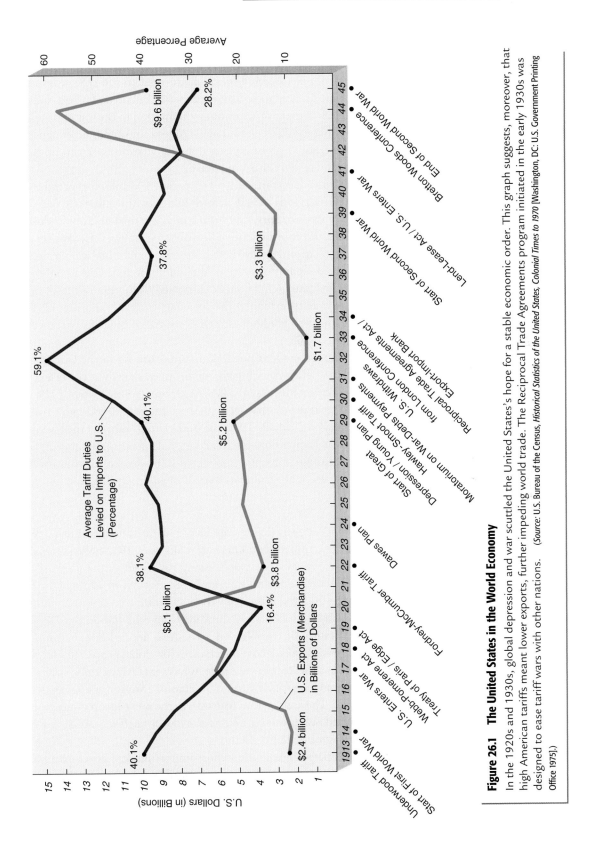

Figure 26.1   The United States in the World Economy
In the 1920s and 1930s, global depression and war scuttled the United States's hope for a stable economic order. This graph suggests, moreover, that high American tariffs meant lower exports, further impeding world trade. The Reciprocal Trade Agreements program initiated in the early 1930s was designed to ease tariff wars with other nations.   *(Source:* U.S. Bureau of the Census, *Historical Statistics of the United States, Colonial Times to 1970* [Washington, DC: U.S. Government Printing Office 1975].)

War Debts and German Reparations

Europeans branded the United States stingy for its handling of World War I debts and reparations. Twenty-eight nations became entangled in inter-Allied government debts totaling $26.5 billion ($9.6 billion of them owed to the U.S. government). Europeans owed private American creditors another $3 billion and urged Americans to erase government debts as a magnanimous contribution to the war effort. During the war, they angrily charged, Europe bled while America profited. American leaders insisted on repayment, some pointing out that the victorious European nations gained vast territory and resources as war spoils.

The debts question became linked to Germany's $33 billion reparations bill, which some believed Germany could afford but was unwilling to pay. When Germany defaulted on its payments, American bankers loaned millions of dollars to keep the nation afloat and forestall the radicalism that might thrive on economic troubles. A triangular relationship developed: American investors' money flowed to Germany, Germany paid reparations to the Allies, and the Allies then paid some of their debts to the United States. The American-crafted Dawes Plan of 1924 reduced Germany's annual payments, extended the repayment period, and provided more loans. The United States also gradually scaled down Allied obligations, cutting the debt by half during the 1920s.

But everything hinged on continued German borrowing in the United States, and in 1928 and 1929 American lending abroad dropped sharply in the face of more lucrative stock market opportunities. The U.S.-negotiated Young Plan of 1929, which reduced Germany's reparations, salvaged little as the world economy collapsed following the stock market crash. By 1931, the Allies had paid back only $2.6 billion. Staggered by the Great Depression—an international catastrophe—they defaulted on the rest. Annoyed, Congress in 1934 passed the Johnson Act, which forbade U.S. government loans to foreign governments in default to the United States.

Decline in Trade

As the depression deepened, tariff wars revealed a reinvigorated economic nationalism. By 1932 twenty-five nations retaliated against rising American tariffs (created in the Fordney-McCumber Act of 1922 and the Hawley-Smoot Act of 1930) by imposing higher rates on foreign imports. From 1929 to 1933, world trade declined by 40 percent. Exports of American merchandise slumped from $5.2 billion to $1.7 billion.

For Secretary of State Hull, the solution to the crisis depended on reviving world trade; this he insisted would also boost the chances for global peace. He successfully pressed Congress to pass the Reciprocal Trade Agreements Act in 1934, empowering the president to reduce U.S. tariffs by up to 50 percent through special agreements with foreign countries. The act's central feature was the most-favored-nation principle, whereby the United States was entitled to the lowest tariff rate set by any nation with which it had an agreement.

In 1934 Hull also helped create the Export-Import Bank, a government agency providing loans to foreigners purchasing American goods. The bank stimulated trade and became a diplomatic weapon, allowing the United States to exact concessions by approving or denying loans. In the short term, Hull's ambitious programs brought mixed results.

U.S. Recognition of the Soviet Union

The Roosevelt administration's move to extend diplomatic recognition to the Soviet Union was also economically inspired. Throughout the 1920s the Republicans refused diplomatic relations with the Soviet government, which failed to pay $600 million for confiscated American-owned property and repudiated preexisting Russian debts. Nonetheless, in the late 1920s American businesses, such as General Electric and International Harvester, entered the Soviet marketplace, and Henry Ford signed a contract to build an automobile plant there. By 1930 the Soviet Union was the largest buyer of American farm and industrial equipment.

Roosevelt speculated that closer Soviet-American relations might help the economy while deterring Japanese expansion. In 1933 Roosevelt granted U.S. diplomatic recognition to the Soviet Union in return for Soviet agreement to discuss its debts, forgo subversive activities in the United States, and grant Americans in the Soviet Union religious freedom and legal rights.

U.S. Dominance in Latin America

Through the Platt Amendment, the Roosevelt Corollary, the Panama Canal, military intervention, and economic preeminence, the United States had thrown an imperial net over Latin America in the early twentieth century. U.S. dominance in the hemisphere grew after World War I. A prominent State Department officer patronizingly remarked that Latin Americans were of their "low racial quality" and "easy people to deal with if properly managed."

U.S.-made schools, roads, telephones, and irrigation systems dotted Caribbean and Central American nations. American "money doctors" in Colombia and Peru helped reform tariff and tax laws and invited U.S. companies to build public works. Washington forced private high-interest loans on the Dominican Republic and Haiti. Republican administrations curtailed U.S. military intervention in the hemisphere, withdrawing troops from the Dominican Republic (1924) and Nicaragua (1925). But marines returned to Nicaragua in 1926 to end fighting between conservative and liberal Nicaraguans and protect American property. In Haiti, the U.S. troop commitment lasted from 1915 until 1934, with soldiers there to keep pro-Washington governments in power.

U.S. Economic Muscle

By 1929 direct U.S. investments in Latin America (excluding bonds and securities) totaled $3.5 billion, and U.S. exports dominated the region's trade. Country after country experienced the repercussions of U.S. economic and political decisions. For example, the price that Americans set for Chilean copper determined the health of Chile's economy.

Latin American nationalists protested that their resources were being drained away by U.S. companies, leaving many nations in a disadvantageous position. Unapologetic Americans believed they were bringing material improvements and the blessings of liberty to Latin American neighbors.

Criticism of U.S. imperialism in the region mounted in the interwar years. In 1928, at the Havana Inter-American conference, U.S. officials unsuccessfully tried to kill a resolution stating that "no state has a right to intervene in the internal affairs of another." Two years later, a Chilean newspaper warned that the U.S. Colossus had "financial might" without "equal in history" and that its aim was "Americas for the Americans—of the North." In the United States, Senator William Borah of Idaho urged that Latin Americans be granted the right to decide their own futures. Business leaders feared that Latin American nationalists would direct their anti-Yankee feelings against U.S.-owned property.

Good Neighbor Policy

Renouncing unpopular military intervention, the United States tried new methods to maintain its influence in Latin America: Pan-Americanism (a fifty-year-old concept strengthening ties between North and South America), support for strong local leaders, the training of national guards, economic and cultural penetration, Export-Import Bank loans, financial supervision, and political subversion. Dubbed the Good Neighbor policy by Roosevelt in 1933, it meant that the United States would be less blatant in its domination—less willing to defend exploitative business practices and to launch military expeditions and less reluctant to consult with Latin Americans.

Most notably, Roosevelt ordered home the U.S. military forces stationed in Haiti (since 1915) and Nicaragua (since 1912, with a hiatus in 1925–1926), and he restored some sovereignty to Panama and increased that nation's income from the canal. Roosevelt's popularity in Latin America grew when, in a series of pan-American conferences, he joined in pledging that no nation in the hemisphere would intervene in the "internal or external affairs" of any other.

Roosevelt promised more than he could deliver. His administration continued to bolster dictators in the region, believing that they would preserve U.S. economic interests. When a revolution brought a radical government to power in Cuba in 1933, FDR instructed the American ambassador in Havana to work with conservative Cubans to replace the new government with one friendlier to U.S. interests. With Washington's support, army sergeant Fulgencio Batista took power in 1934.

During the Batista era, which lasted until Fidel Castro ousted Batista in 1959, Cuba protected U.S. investments and aligned itself with U.S. foreign policy. In return, the United States provided military aid and Export-Import Bank loans, abrogated the unpopular Platt Amendment, and gave Cuban sugar a favored position in the U.S. market. American tourists flocked to Havana's nightlife of rum, rhumba, prostitution, and gambling. Nationalistic Cubans protested that their nation had become a mere extension of the United States.

Clash with Mexican Nationalism

In Mexico, Roosevelt again showed the restraint his predecessors had lacked. Since Woodrow Wilson sent troops to Mexico in 1914 and 1916, U.S.-Mexican relations struggled as the two governments wrangled over U.S. economic interests. Still, by 1934, the United States accounted for 61 percent of Mexico's imports and received 52 percent of its exports. That year, however, a new government under Lázaro Cárdenas pledged "Mexico for the Mexicans" and strengthened trade unions to strike against foreign corporations.

In 1937 workers struck foreign oil companies for higher wages and recognition, but the companies, including Standard Oil, rejected union appeals, hoping to send a message across the hemisphere that economic nationalism could never succeed. The following year, the Cárdenas government expropriated the property of all foreign-owned petroleum companies, calculating that the approaching war in Europe would restrain the United States from attacking Mexico. The United States countered by reducing purchases of Mexican silver and promoting a multinational business boy-cott. But Roosevelt rejected appeals to intervene militarily, fearing that Mexicans would increase oil sales to Germany and Japan. Tense negotiations led to a 1942 agreement whereby the United States conceded that Mexico owned and controlled its raw materials, and Mexico compensated the companies for their lost property.

While the United States remained the dominant power in the hemisphere, the Good Neighbor policy filled Latin Americans with hope that a new era had dawned. The sober-minded nationalists in the region knew that deepening tensions in Europe and Asia might have influenced Washington's restraint. But these threats also created a sense that nations in the Western Hemisphere should stand together.

THE COURSE TO WAR IN EUROPE

On March 5, 1933, one day after Roosevelt's inauguration, Germany's parliament granted dictatorial powers to the new chancellor, Adolf Hitler, leader of the Nazi Party. It was a stunning rise to power for Hitler, whose Nazis probably would have remained a fringe party had the Great Depression not hit Germany so hard. Produc-tion plummeted 40 percent, and unemployment ballooned to 6 million, meaning that two out of five people were jobless. A disintegrating banking system, which robbed millions of their savings, and widespread German resentment over the Versailles peace settlement fueled mass discontent. While the communists preached a workers' revolution, German businessmen and property owners supported Hitler and the Nazis, believing they could manipulate him once he had thwarted the com-munists. They were wrong.

Like Benito Mussolini, who gained control of Italy in 1922, Hitler was a fascist. Fascism (called Nazism, or National Socialism, in Germany) celebrated supremacy of the state over the individual, dictatorship over democracy, authoritarianism over freedom of speech, a state-regulated economy over a free market, and militarism over peace. The Nazis vowed to revive Germany, cripple communism and "purify" the German "race" by destroying Jews and others, such as homosexuals and Gypsies, whom Hitler deemed inferior. The Nuremberg Laws of 1935 stripped Jews of citi-zenship and outlawed Jewish intermarriage with Germans. Half of all German Jews were without work.

German Aggression Under Hitler
Determined to get out from under the Versailles treaty, Hitler withdrew Germany from the League of Nations, ended reparations payments, and began to rearm. While secretly laying plans to conquer neighboring states, he watched admiringly as Mussolini's troops invaded Ethiopia in 1935. The next year Hitler ordered his troops into the Rhineland, an area demilitarized by the Versailles treaty.

In 1936 Italy and Germany formed an alliance called the Rome-Berlin Axis. Shortly thereafter, Germany and Japan united against the Soviet Union in the Anti-Comintern Pact. Britain and France responded with a policy of appeasement, hoping to curb Hitler's expansionism by permitting him a few territorial nibbles. Instead, the German leader continually raised his demands.

The Spanish Civil War in 1936 upped the ante for Hitler. Beginning in July, about three thousand American volunteers, known as the Abraham Lincoln Battalion of the International Brigades, joined Spanish Loyalists in defending Spain's elected republican government against Francisco Franco's fascist movement. The Soviet Union also aided the Loyalists. Hitler and Mussolini sent military aid to Franco, who won in 1939, tightening fascism's grip on the European continent.

Early in 1938, Hitler again tested European tolerance when he sent soldiers to annex his birth nation, Austria. In September, he seized the Sudeten region of Czechoslovakia. France and Britain, without consulting the Czechs, agreed to allow Hitler this territorial bite, in exchange for a pledge that he would not take more. British prime minister Neville Chamberlain returned home to proclaim "peace in our time." In March 1939 Hitler swallowed the rest of Czechoslovakia (see Map 26.2).

Isolationist Views in the United States

Many Americans sought to distance themselves from Europe's tumult by embracing isolationism, because they either hated war or opposed U.S. alliances with other nations. Americans learned powerful negative lessons from World War I: that war damages reform movements, undermines civil liberties, dangerously expands federal power, disrupts the economy, and accentuates racial and class tensions. In a 1937 Gallup poll nearly two-thirds thought U.S. participation in World War I was a mistake.

Conservative isolationists feared higher taxes and increased executive power if the nation went to war. Liberal isolationists worried that domestic problems might go unresolved with increased military spending. Many isolationists predicted that, in attempting to spread democracy, Americans would lose freedoms at home. The vast majority of isolationists opposed fascism, but they did not think the United States should do what Europeans refused to do: block Hitler.

Nye Committee Hearings

A congressional committee headed by Senator Gerald P. Nye held hearings from 1934 to 1936 on the role of business in the U.S. decision to enter World War I. The Nye committee did not prove that American munitions makers dragged the nation into war, but it uncovered evidence that corporations bribed foreign politicians to bolster arms sales in the 1920s and 1930s.

Isolationists grew suspicious of American business ties with Nazi Germany and fascist Italy. Twenty-six of the top American corporations, including DuPont, Standard Oil, and General Motors, had contracts in 1937 with German firms. After Italy attacked Ethiopia in 1935, American petroleum, copper, scrap iron, and steel exports to Italy increased substantially, despite Roosevelt's call for a moral embargo. Other businesses, such as the Wall Street law firm of Sullivan and Cromwell, severed lucrative ties with Germany to protest the Nazi persecution of Jews.

Roosevelt signed a series of neutrality acts. Congress meanwhile outlawed the kinds of contacts that had compromised U.S. neutrality during World War I. The Neutrality Act of 1935 prohibited arms shipments to either side in a war, once the president declared the existence of belligerency. The Neutrality Act of 1936 forbade loans to belligerents and introduced the cash-and-carry principle which required warring nations to pay cash for nonmilitary purchases and carry goods from U.S. ports in their own ships. The act also forbade Americans from traveling on the ships of belligerent nations.

Roosevelt's Evolving Views

President Roosevelt shared isolationist views in the early 1930s. Although prior to World War I he was an expansionist and interventionist, during the interwar period FDR talked more about the horrors of war. In a speech in August 1936 at Chautauqua, New York, Roosevelt appealed to pacifist voters in the upcoming election. The United States, he promised, would remain unentangled in the European conflict. During the crisis over Czechoslovakia in 1938, Roosevelt endorsed appeasement.

Meanwhile, Roosevelt grew troubled by the arrogance of Germany, Italy, and Japan—aggressors that he called the three bandit nations. He condemned Nazi persecution of the Jews and Japan's expansionist actions in East Asia. In November 1938, Hitler launched *Kristallnacht* ("Crystal Night," named for the shattered glass that littered the streets after the attack on Jewish synagogues, businesses, and homes) and sent tens of thousands of Jews to concentration camps. Shocked, Roosevelt recalled the U.S. ambassador to Germany and allowed fifteen thousand refugees on visitor permits to remain longer in the United States. But he would not break trade relations with Hitler or push Congress to loosen immigration laws. Congress rejected all measures, including a bill to admit twenty thousand children under age fourteen. Motivated by economic concerns and widespread anti-Semitism, more than 80 percent of Americans supported Congress's decision to uphold immigration restrictions.

Even the tragic voyage of the *St. Louis* did not change government policy. The vessel left Hamburg in mid-1939 carrying 930 desperate Jews. Denied entry to Havana, the *St. Louis* headed for Miami, where Coast Guard cutters prevented it from docking and forced its return to Europe. Some refugees took shelter in countries that later were overrun by Hitler's legions.

Quietly, Roosevelt began readying for war. In early 1938 he successfully pressured the House of Representatives to defeat a constitutional amendment that would require a majority vote in a national referendum before a congressional declaration of war could take effect (unless the United States were attacked). Later, in the wake of the Munich crisis, Roosevelt asked Congress for funds to fortify the air force, which he believed essential to deter aggression. In January 1939 the president secretly decided to sell bombers to France. Although these five hundred combat planes did not deter war, French orders spurred the growth of the U.S. aircraft industry.

Hitler's swallowing of Czechoslovakia in March 1939 proved a turning point for Western leaders. Until now, they could explain away Hitler's actions by saying he was only trying to reunite German-speaking peoples. They realized it would take force to stop him. When Hitler began eyeing Poland, London and Paris stood by the Poles.

Undaunted, Berlin signed a nonaggression pact with Moscow in August 1939, including a top-secret protocol that carved eastern Europe into German and Soviet zones and let the Soviets grab the eastern half of Poland and the Baltic states of Lithuania, Estonia, and Latvia, formerly part of the Russian Empire.

Poland and the Outbreak of World War II   Early on September 1, 1939, German tanks rolled into Poland. German fighter planes covered the advance, thereby launching a new type of warfare, the *blitzkrieg* ("lightning war")—highly mobile land forces and armor combined with tactical aircraft. Within forty-eight hours, Britain and France declared war on Germany.

When Europe descended into war in September 1939, Roosevelt declared neutrality and pressed for repeal of the arms embargo. After much debate, Congress in November lifted the embargo on contraband and approved cash-and-carry exports of arms. Using methods short of war, Roosevelt thus began to aid the Allies. Hitler sneered that a "half Judaized . . . half Negrified" United States was "incapable of conducting war."

JAPAN, CHINA, AND A NEW ORDER IN ASIA

Asia suffered the aggressive march of Japan. The United States had interests at stake in Asia: the Philippines and Pacific islands, religious missions, trade and investments, and the Open Door in China. In missionary fashion, Americans believed that they were China's friend and protector. Pearl Buck's bestselling novel and subsequent film, *The Good Earth* (1931), countered prevailing images of the "heathen Chinee" by representing the Chinese as noble, persevering peasants. By contrast, the aggressive Japan loomed as a threat to American interests. The Tokyo government seemed bent on subjugating China and unhinging the Open Door doctrine of equal trade and investment.

The Chinese were uneasy about the U.S. presence in Asia and shared Japan's desire to reduce Western influence. The Chinese Revolution of 1911 still rumbled in the 1920s, as antiforeign riots damaged American property and imperiled American missionaries. Chinese nationalists criticized the American imperialist practice of extraterritoriality (the exemption of foreigners from Chinese legal jurisdiction) and demanded an end to this affront.

Jiang Jieshi   In the late 1920s, civil war broke out in China when Jiang Jieshi (Chiang Kai-shek) ousted Mao Zedong from the ruling Guomindang Party. Americans applauded this anti-Bolshevism and Jiang's conversion to Christianity in 1930. Jiang's new wife, American-educated Soong Meiling, won their hearts with her flawless English and western fashion. Warming to Jiang, U.S. officials signed a treaty in 1928 restoring control of tariffs to the Chinese. U.S. gunboats and marines still remained in China to protect American citizens and property.

Japan grew suspicious of U.S. ties with China. In the early twentieth century, Japanese-American relations deteriorated as Japan gained influence in Manchuria,

Shandong, and Korea. The Japanese sought to dominate Asian territories that produced the raw materials that their import-dependent island nation required. The Japanese also resented the discriminatory immigration law of 1924, which excluded them from emigrating to the United States. Secretary Hughes called the law "a lasting injury" to Japanese-American relations. Despite the Washington Conference treaties, naval competition continued, as did commercial rivalry. In the United States the importation of inexpensive Japanese goods spawned Buy America campaigns.

Manchurian Crisis

Relations further soured in 1931 after the Japanese military seized Manchuria from China (see Map 26.1). Larger than Texas, Manchuria served Japan both as a buffer against the Soviets and as a vital source of coal, iron, timber, and food. More than half of Japan's foreign investments rested in Manchuria. Although the seizure of Manchuria violated the Nine-Power Treaty and the Kellogg-Briand Pact, the

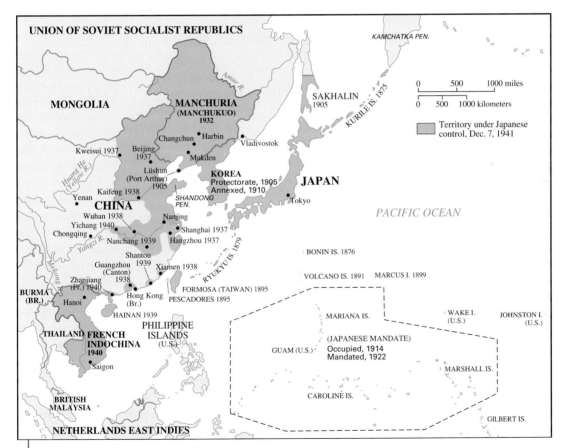

Map 26.1   Japanese Expansion Before Pearl Harbor

The Japanese quest for predominance began at the turn of the century and intensified in the 1930s. China suffered the most at the hands of Tokyo's military. Vulnerable U.S. possessions in Asia and the Pacific proved no obstacle to Japan's ambitions for a Greater East Asia Co-Prosperity Sphere.

United States lacked the power to compel Japanese withdrawal, and the League of Nations merely condemned the Tokyo government. The American response came as a moral lecture known as the Stimson Doctrine: the United States would not recognize any impairment of China's sovereignty or of the Open Door policy, Secretary Stimson declared in 1932.

Japan continued to pressure China, triggering the Sino-Japanese War in mid-1937. Japanese forces seized Beijing and several coastal cities. The bombing of Shanghai intensified anti-Japanese sentiment in the United States. To help China by permitting it to buy American arms, Roosevelt refused to declare the existence of war, thus avoiding activation of the Neutrality Acts.

Roosevelt's Quarantine Speech   On October 5, 1937, the president called for a quarantine to curb the "epidemic of world lawlessness." People who thought Washington had been too gentle with Japan cheered. Isolationists warned that Roosevelt was edging toward war. On December 12, Japanese aircraft sank the American gunboat *Panay,* an escort for Standard Oil Company tankers on the Yangtze River, killing two American sailors. Roosevelt was relieved when Tokyo apologized and offered to pay for damages.

Japan's declaration of a New Order in Asia, in the words of one American official, "banged, barred, and bolted" the Open Door. Alarmed, the Roosevelt administration during the late 1930s gave loans and sold military equipment to Jiang's Chinese government. In mid-1939 the United States abrogated its trade treaty with Tokyo, yet Americans continued to ship oil, cotton, and machinery to Japan. The administration hesitated to initiate economic sanctions because it might spark a Japanese-American war at a time when Germany posed a more serious threat and the United States was unprepared for war. When war broke out in Europe in late summer 1939, Japanese-American relations were stalemated.

U.S. ENTRY INTO WORLD WAR II

A stalemate was fine with many Americans if it kept the United States out of war. Roosevelt remarked in 1939 that the United States could not "draw a line of defense around this country and live completely and solely to ourselves." Polls showed that Americans favored the Allies and supported aid to Britain and France, but the great majority emphatically wanted the United States to remain at peace. Troubled by this conflicting advice—oppose Hitler, aid the Allies, but stay out of the war—the president gradually moved the nation from neutrality to undeclared war against Germany and then, after the Japanese attack on Pearl Harbor, to full-scale war.

Unprecedented numbers of Americans spoke out on foreign affairs and joined organizations that addressed the issues. The widespread use of radio, the nation's chief news source, helped stimulate public interest. So did ethnic affiliations with the various belligerents and victims. The American Legion, the League of Women Voters, labor unions, and local chapters of the Committee to Defend America by Aiding the Allies and the isolationist America First Committee provided outlets for citizen participation in the national debate. African American churches organized anti-Italian boycotts to protest Mussolini's pummeling of Ethiopia.

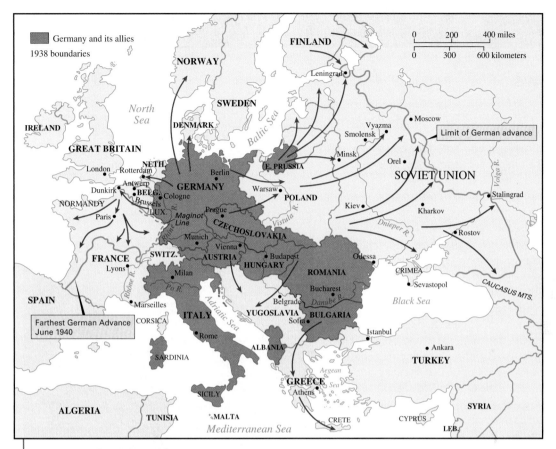

Map 26.2   The German Advance

Hitler's drive to dominate Europe pushed German troops deep into France and the Soviet Union. Great Britain took a beating but held on with the help of American economic and military aid before the United States itself entered World War II in late 1941.

In March 1940, the Soviet Union invaded Finland. In April, Germany conquered Denmark and Norway (see Map 26.2). On May 10, 1940, Germany attacked Belgium, the Netherlands, and France, ultimately pushing French and British forces back to the English Channel. At Dunkirk, France, between May 26 and June 6, more than 300,000 Allied soldiers frantically escaped to Britain on a flotilla of small boats. The Germans occupied Paris a week later. A new French government in the town of Vichy collaborated with the Nazis and, on June 22, surrendered France to Berlin. The German Luftwaffe (air force) launched massive bombing raids against Great Britain.

Alarmed by the swift defeat of one European nation after another, Americans shed their isolationism. Insisting that New Deal reforms would not be sacrificed for military preparedness, the president aided the beleaguered Allies to prevent the fall of Britain. In May 1940 he ordered the sale of old surplus military equipment to Britain and France. In July he cultivated bipartisan support by naming the Republicans Henry L. Stimson and Frank Knox, backers of aid to the Allies, to be secretaries of war and the navy, respectively. In September, the president traded fifty over-age American destroyers for leases to eight British military bases, including Newfoundland, Bermuda, and Jamaica.

Radio News

In radio's early years, network executives believed their job was to entertain Americans, and that left current affairs to newspapers. Yet radio could report news events as they happened, something no previous medium could do.

Franklin Roosevelt was among the first to grasp radio's potential. As governor of New York, he occasionally went on the air, and after becoming president, he commenced his Fireside Chats, reassuring Americans during the depression that the government was working to help them. The broadcasts were so successful that one journalist remarked, "The President has only to look toward a radio to bring Congress to terms."

Across the Atlantic, Adolf Hitler also used the radio to carry speeches directly to the German people. His message: Germany had been wronged by enemies abroad and by Marxists and Jews at home. But under Hitler, the Nazis promised to restore the country's former greatness. As *Sieg Heil!* thundered over the airwaves, millions of Germans saw Hitler as their salvation.

In 1938, as events in Europe escalated, American radio networks increased news coverage. When Hitler annexed Austria in March, NBC and CBS broke into scheduled programs to deliver bulletins. Then, on March 13, CBS broadcast the first international news roundup, a half-hour show featuring live reports. A new era in American radio was born. In the words of author Joseph Persico, what made the broadcast revolutionary "was the listener's sensation of being on the scene" in far-off Europe. When leaders from France and Britain met with Hitler in Munich later that year, millions of Americans listened intently to live radio updates.

Correspondents became well known, none more than CBS's Edward R. Murrow. During the Nazi air blitz of London in 1940–1941, Murrow's understated, nicotine-scorched voice kept Americans spellbound, as he tried to "report suffering to people [Americans] who have not suffered."

Undoubtedly, Murrow's reports strengthened the interventionist voices in Washington by emphasizing Winston Churchill's greatness and England's bravery. And radio reports from Europe made Americans feel closely linked to people living an ocean away.

Edward R. Murrow at his typewriter in wartime London.
(Library of Congress)

First Peacetime Military Draft

Two weeks later, Roosevelt signed the hotly debated and narrowly passed Selective Training and Service Act, the first peacetime military draft in American history. The law called for the registration of all men between the ages of twenty-one and thirty-five; more than 16 million men signed up. Meanwhile, Roosevelt won reelection in November 1940 with promises of peace: "Your boys are not going to be sent into any foreign wars."

Roosevelt claimed that the United States could avoid war by enabling the British to win. In January 1941, Congress debated the president's Lend-Lease bill. Because Britain was broke, the president explained, the United States should lend rather than sell weapons. In March 1941, with pro-British sentiment running high, the House passed the Lend-Lease Act by 317 votes to 71; the Senate followed with a 60-to-31 tally. The initial appropriation was $7 billion, but by war's end, it reached $50 billion, more than $31 billion of it for Britain.

To ensure delivery of Lend-Lease goods, Roosevelt ordered the U.S. Navy to patrol halfway across the Atlantic, and he sent American troops to Greenland. In July, the president dispatched marines to Iceland, arguing that it was essential for safeguarding the Western Hemisphere. He also sent Lend-Lease aid to the Soviet Union, which Hitler attacked in June (thereby shattering the 1939 Nazi-Soviet nonaggression pact). If the Soviets could hold off two hundred German divisions in the east, Roosevelt calculated, Britain would gain some breathing time.

Atlantic Charter

In August 1941, Churchill and Roosevelt met for four days on a British battleship off the coast of Newfoundland. The two leaders issued the Atlantic Charter, a set of war aims reminiscent of Wilsonianism: collective security, disarmament, self-determination, economic cooperation, and freedom of the seas. Churchill later recalled that the president told him that he could not ask Congress to declare war against Germany, but "he would wage war" and "become more and more provocative."

On September 4, a German submarine launched torpedoes at (but did not hit) the American destroyer *Greer*. Henceforth, Roosevelt said, the U.S. Navy would fire first when under threat. He also made good on a promise to Churchill: American warships would convoy British merchant ships across the ocean. Thus the United States entered into an undeclared naval war with Germany. When in early October the destroyer *Reuben James* went down with the loss of more than one hundred American lives, Congress scrapped the cash-and-carry policy and further revised the Neutrality Acts to permit transport of munitions to Britain on armed American merchant ships. The United States was edging close to being a belligerent.

U.S. Demands on Japan

It seems ironic that World War II came to the United States by way of Asia. Roosevelt wanted to avoid war with Japan to concentrate on defeating Germany. In September 1940, after Germany, Italy, and Japan signed the Tripartite Pact (to form the Axis powers), Roosevelt slapped an embargo on shipments of aviation fuel and scrap metal to Japan. After Japanese troops occupied French Indochina in July 1941, Washington froze Japanese assets in the United States, virtually ending trade (including oil) with Japan. "The oil gauge and the clock stood side by side" for Japan, wrote one observer.

Tokyo recommended a summit meeting between President Roosevelt and Prime Minister Prince Konoye, but American officials insisted that the Japanese first agree to respect China's sovereignty and honor the Open Door policy. Roosevelt supported Secretary Hull's hard line against Japan's pursuit of the Greater East Asia Co-Prosperity Sphere—the name Tokyo gave to the vast Asian region it intended to dominate.

Roosevelt told his advisers to string out ongoing Japanese-American talks to gain time to fortify the Philippines and check the fascists in Europe. By deciphering intercepted messages through Operation MAGIC, American officials learned that Tokyo's patience with diplomacy was fast dissipating. In late November, the Japanese rejected American demands to withdraw from Indochina. An intercepted message on December 3 instructed the Japanese embassy in Washington to burn codes and destroy cipher machines—a step suggesting that war was coming.

Surprise Attack on Pearl Harbor

In a daring raid on Pearl Harbor in Hawai'i, an armada of sixty Japanese ships, including six carriers bearing 360 airplanes, crossed 3,000 miles of the Pacific Ocean. To avoid detection, they maintained radio silence. Early on December 7, some 230 miles northwest of Honolulu, the carriers unleashed their planes, dropping torpedoes and bombs on an unsuspecting American naval base and nearby airfields.

The battleship USS *Arizona* fell victim to a Japanese bomb that ignited explosives below deck, killing more than 1,000 sailors. The USS *Nevada* tried to escape by heading out to sea, but was hit in a second aerial attack. Altogether the invaders sank or damaged eight battleships, many smaller vessels, and more than 160 aircraft on the ground. A total of 2,403 died; 1,178 were wounded. The Pearl Harbor tragedy, from the perspective of the war's outcome, amounted to a military inconvenience more than a disaster.

Explaining Pearl Harbor

American cryptanalysts may have broken the Japanese diplomatic code, but the intercepted messages never revealed naval or military plans and never mentioned Pearl Harbor specifically. Roosevelt did not, as some critics charged, conspire to leave

The stricken USS *West Virginia* was one of eight battleships caught in the surprise Japanese attack at Pearl Harbor, Hawai'i, on December 7, 1941. In this photograph, sailors mount a launch attempt to rescue a crew member from the water as oil burns around the sinking ship.   (U.S. Army)

the fleet vulnerable to attack so that the United States could enter World War II through the back door of Asia. The base at Pearl Harbor was not on red alert because a message from Washington warning of the imminence of war was transmitted by a slow method and arrived too late. Base commanders believed Hawai'i too far from Japan to be a target. Like Roosevelt's advisers, they expected an assault on British Malaya, Thailand, or the Philippines (see Map 26.1). The Pearl Harbor calamity stemmed from mistakes and insufficient information, not from conspiracy.

On December 8, referring to the previous day as "a date which will live in infamy," Roosevelt asked Congress for a declaration of war against Japan. He noted that the Japanese had also attacked Malaya, Hong Kong, Guam, the Philippines, Wake, and Midway. A unanimous vote in the Senate and a 388-to-1 vote in the House thrust America into war. Representative Jeannette Rankin of Montana voted against war, as she had for World War I. Britain declared war on Japan, but the Soviet Union did not. Three days later, Germany and Italy, honoring the Tripartite Pact they had signed with Japan in September 1940, declared war against the United States.

A fundamental clash of systems explains why war came. Germany and Japan preferred a world divided into closed spheres of influence. The United States sought a liberal capitalist world. American principles manifested respect for human rights; fascists in Europe and militarists in Asia did not. The United States prided itself on democracy; Germany and Japan embraced authoritarian regimes. When the United States protested against German and Japanese expansion, Berlin and Tokyo charged that Washington conveniently ignored its sphere of influence in Latin America and its history of military and economic aggrandizement. Such incompatible objectives obstructed diplomacy and made war likely.

Summary

In the 1920s and 1930s, Americans could not create a peaceful and prosperous world order. The Washington Conference treaties failed to curb a naval arms race or protect China, and both the Dawes Plan and the Kellogg-Briand Pact proved ineffective. U.S. trade policies, shifting from protectionist tariffs to reciprocal trade agreements, only minimally improved U.S. or international commerce during the Great Depression. Recognition of the Soviet Union barely improved relations. Most ominous, the aggressors Germany and Japan ignored repeated U.S. protests. Even where U.S. policies seemed to satisfy Good Neighbor goals in Latin America, nationalist resentments simmered and Mexico challenged U.S. dominance.

During the late 1930s and early 1940s, President Roosevelt hesitantly but steadily moved the United States from neutrality to aiding the Allies, to belligerency, and finally to war after the attack on Pearl Harbor. Congress gradually revised and retired the Neutrality Acts in the face of growing danger.

World War II offered yet another opportunity for Americans to set things right in the world. As the publisher Henry Luce wrote in the *American Century* (1941), the United States must "exert upon the world the full impact of our influence." Isolationists joined the president's call for victory, when he said, "We are going to win the war, and we are going to win the peace that follows."

Presidential Deception of the Public

Before U-652 launched two torpedoes at the *Greer*, heading for Iceland on September 4, 1941, the U.S. destroyer had stalked the German submarine for hours. After the attack, which missed its mark, the *Greer* also released depth charges. But when President Roosevelt described the encounter in a radio Fireside Chat on September 11, he declared that the German submarine fired the first shot and accused Germany of violating freedom of the seas.

Roosevelt misled the American people about the events of September 4. The incident had little to do with freedom of the seas, which related to merchant ships, not U.S. warships in a war zone. Roosevelt's words were a call to arms, yet he never asked Congress for a declaration of war against Germany. The president believed that deceiving Americans would move them toward war as noble and necessary. The practice worked: polls showed that most Americans approved Roosevelt's shoot-on-sight policy following the *Greer* incident.

Over time, even those who agreed that Germany had to be stopped, questioned Roosevelt's methods as dangerous to the democratic process, which cannot work in an environment of dishonesty and a usurping of congressional powers. In the 1960s, during the Vietnam War, Senator J. William Fulbright of Arkansas recalled the *Greer* incident: "FDR's deviousness in a good cause made it easier for LBJ to practice the same kind of deviousness in a bad cause." In the mid-1980s, Reagan administration officials consciously lied about U.S. arms sales to Iran and covert aid to the Nicaraguan rebels. After the March 2003 U.S. invasion of Iraq, there were charges that President George W. Bush and his aides did the same in claiming that Iraq had weapons of mass destruction, which its leader, Saddam Hussein, intended to use. Bush, critics charged, had used "weapons of mass deception" to justify the invasion of Iraq.

Following Roosevelt, presidents have found it easier to distort, withhold, or lie about foreign relations to shape public opinion. One result: the growth of the imperial presidency—grabbing power from Congress and using questionable means to reach presidential objectives. The practice of deception, even for a noble end, was one of Roosevelt's legacies for a people and a nation.

Chapter Review

SEARCHING FOR PEACE AND ORDER IN THE 1920S

How did the peace movement influence U.S. foreign policy in the interwar years?

In the wake of World War I, several peace organizations—some formed by female activists—emerged to ensure world order and prevent another war. Their strategies varied: some embraced alliances with the League of Nations and the World Court; others looked to arbitration, disarmament, arms reduction, making wars illegal, and observing strict neutrality. Peace activism led President Warren Harding to convene the Washington Naval Conference from November 1921 to February 1922 in which delegates from Britain, Japan, France, Italy, China, Portugal, Belgium, and the Netherlands agreed to limit naval armaments and set a ten-year moratorium on ship-building. Other important policy developments included the Nine-Power Treaty, which reaffirmed the Open Door in

China and recognized Chinese sovereignty; the Locarno Pact of 1925, which sought to reduce tensions between Germany and France; and the Kellogg-Briand Pact of 1928, in which sixty-two nations agreed to condemn war as the solution to international disputes.

THE WORLD ECONOMY, CULTURAL EXPANSION, AND GREAT DEPRESSION

How did the Great Depression help push the world to the brink of war?

Economic tensions existed between the United States and Europe after World War I. The United States emerged as a creditor nation and Europeans—particularly Germany—largely as debtors. Europeans often accused the United States of stinginess and profiting from their hardships. While the United States did gradually scale down Allied debts and reduce Germany's payments, still, much depended on loan repayments. When the stock market crashed in 1929, Europeans defaulted on a large portion of what they owed. The Great Depression not only created an international economic crisis, it also inspired economic nationalism in countries that were already pushed financially to the edge. Secretary of State Charles Hull aptly predicted that maimed economies inspired militarism and extremism, and no country's economy was as hard-pressed as Germany's.

U.S. DOMINANCE IN LATIN AMERICA

How was Roosevelt's Good Neighbor policy different from past dealings in Latin America?

Prior to Roosevelt, the U.S. strategy for maintaining its influence in Latin America focused on military intervention. The Good Neighbor policy took a more subtle approach: it centered on building friendship ties through Pan-Americanism; supporting strong local leaders; training national guards; penetrating the region through economic and cultural means; providing financial supervision and loans; and relying on political subversion. Roosevelt withdrew troops from Haiti and Nicaragua and restored some sovereignty to Panama and increased that nation's income from the canal. While the administration-backed dictators who seemed supportive of U.S. economic interests, the Good Neighbor policy nonetheless convinced Latin Americans that a new era of friendship had begun.

THE COURSE TO WAR IN EUROPE

Why did most Americans support isolationism for much of World War II?

Americans had long embraced isolationism largely because of their aversion to war and because of a long legacy of political independence that did not allow for alliances with other nations. That was fortified by the experience of World War I, which damaged reform movements at home, disrupted the U.S. economy, and expanded federal power. In fact, two-thirds of Americans surveyed thought entry into World War I had been a mistake. Americans similarly feared tax increases, the loss of freedom at home, and the shift of federal funds away from domestic problems toward military spending. They also distrusted the role of business in pushing the nation toward war.

JAPAN, CHINA, AND A NEW ORDER IN ASIA

How did the United States perceive its interests to be threatened by Japanese expanisionism?

As Japan moved to lessen—and eliminate—western influence in the East and to dominate Asian territories producing beneficial raw materials, the United States worried about what this would mean to its interests in Asia, notably, the Philippines and Pacific islands, religious missions, trade and investments, and the Open Door doctrine in China of equal trade and investment. They feared it portended Japanese control of China. The Japanese resented the United States's discriminatory immigration law of 1924, which excluded them from emigrating to the United States. U.S. leaders acknowledged, and were sometimes frustrated that, its immigration policies thwarted efforts toward friendly relations with Japan, and the two nations remained locked in a stalemate as World War II loomed.

U.S. ENTRY INTO WORLD WAR II

In what way did Roosevelt gradually move Americans into World War II?

Like most Americans, Roosevelt remained an isolationist, but as one European nation after another was defeated, staying out of the conflict in Europe proved increasingly difficult. Concerned about events overseas, Americans slowly shed their isolationism. Roosevelt was horrified by Germany's treatment of Jews and Japan's expansionism in East Asia, but Hitler's 1939 takeover of Czechoslovakia proved the turning point. Roosevelt quietly began preparing for war, even while hoping that he could keep the United States out of it by ensuring that Britain did not fall. The president secretly sold bombers to France, and in May 1940 he ordered the sale of surplus military equipment to Britain and France. Because England had no money to pay for weapons, the president urged Congress to let them borrow the necessary arms. He also signed the Selective Training and Service Act, the first peacetime military draft.

SUGGESTIONS FOR FURTHER READING

Patrick Cohrs, *The Unfinished Peace After World War I: America, Britain and the Stabilization of Europe, 1919–1932* (2006)

Frank Costigliola, *Awkward Dominion: American Political, Economic, and Cultural Relations with Europe* (1984)

Robert Dallek, *Franklin D. Roosevelt and American Foreign Policy* (1995)

Justus D. Doenecke, *Storm on the Horizon: The Challenge to American Intervention, 1939–1941* (2000)

Akira Iriye, *The Origins of the Second World War in Asia and the Pacific* (1987)

David M. Kennedy, *Freedom from Fear: The American People in Depression and War, 1929–1945* (1999)

Walter LaFeber, *Inevitable Revolutions: The United States in Central America*, 2d and extended ed. (1993)

Fredrick B. Pike, *FDR's Good Neighbor Policy* (1995)

Emily S. Rosenberg, *Spreading the American Dream: American Economic and Cultural Expansion, 1890–1945* (1982)

Linda A. Schott, *Reconstructing Women's Thoughts: The Women's International League for Peace and Freedom Before World War II* (1997)

CHAPTER 27

The Second World War at Home and Abroad

CHAPTER OUTLINE

The United States at War

The Production Front and American Workers

Life on the Home Front

The Limits of American Ideals

LINKS TO THE WORLD:
War Brides

Life in the Military

Winning the War

Summary

LEGACY FOR A PEOPLE AND A NATION:
Nuclear Proliferation

W illiam Dean Wilson was sixteen in 1942 when U.S. Marine Corps recruiters came to Shiprock, New Mexico, where he attended the Navajo boarding school. Five years too young to be drafted and a year too young to volunteer, he lied about his age and removed the note reading, "Parents will not consent" from his recruiting file.

Wilson was recruited for one of the most important projects of the war. Battles were won or lost because nations broke the codes enemies used to transmit messages, and the Marines wanted a code based on Diné, the highly complex Navajo language. In 1942 there was no written form and fewer than thirty non-Navajos worldwide—none of them Japanese—understood it. This code promised to be unbreakable. Navajo words represented the first letter of their English translations; thus *wol-la-chee* ("ant") stood for the letter *A*. Each operator also memorized Navajo words that represented 413 basic military terms and concepts. *Dah-he-tih-hi* ("hummingbird") meant fighter plane, *ne-he-mah* ("our mother") was the United States, and *beh-na-ali-tsosie* ("slant-eye") stood for Japan.

Beginning with the Battle of Guadalcanal, Wilson and others of the 420 code talkers participated in every Marine assault in the Pacific. Usually, two code talkers were assigned to a battalion, one going ashore with assault forces and the other receiving messages on ship. Often under hostile fire, code talkers set up their equipment and transmitted enemy sightings or directed shelling by American detachments. "Were it not for the Navajos," declared Major Howard Conner, Fifth Marine Division signal officer, "the Marines would never have taken Iwo Jima. The entire operation was directed by Navajo code. They sent and received over eight hundred messages without an error."

This icon will direct you to interactive activities and study materials on *A People And A Nation, Brief Edition* website: **www.cengage.com/history/norton/peoplenationbrief8e**

Chronology

1941	Government war-preparedness study concludes United States will not be ready for war before June 1943.
	Roosevelt issues Executive Order No. 8802, forbidding racial discrimination by the defense industry.
	Japan attacks Pearl Harbor.
	United States enters World War II.
1942	War Production Board is created to oversee the conversion to military production.
	Millions of Americans move to take jobs in war industries.
	Allies are losing the war in the Pacific to Japan; U.S. victory at Battle of Midway in June is the turning point.
	Office of Price Administration creates a rationing system for food and consumer goods.
	United States pursues Europe First war policy; Allies reject Stalin's demands for a second front in Europe and invade North Africa.
	West Coast Japanese Americans are relocated to internment camps.
	Manhattan Project is set up to create an atomic bomb.
	Congress of Racial Equality is established.

1943	Soviet army defeats German troops at Stalingrad.
	Congress passes War Labor Disputes (Smith-Connally) Act following coal miners' strike.
	"Zoot suit riots" occur in Los Angeles; race riots break out in Detroit, Harlem, and other cities.
	Allies invade Italy.
	Roosevelt, Churchill, and Stalin meet at the Teheran Conference.
1944	Allied troops land at Normandy on D-Day, June 6.
	Roosevelt is elected to fourth term as president.
	United States retakes the Philippines.
1945	Roosevelt, Stalin, and Churchill meet at the Yalta Conference.
	British and U.S. forces firebomb Dresden, Germany.
	Battles of Iwo Jima and Okinawa result in heavy Japanese and U.S. losses.
	Roosevelt dies; Truman becomes president.
	Germany surrenders; Allied forces liberate Nazi death camps.
	Potsdam Conference calls for Japan's unconditional surrender.
	United States uses atomic bombs on Hiroshima and Nagasaki.
	Japan surrenders.

Wartime service changed the Navajo code talkers' lives, broadening their horizons and often deepening their ambitions. William Dean Wilson later became a tribal judge. From "the service," recalled Raymond Nakai, a navy veteran who became chairman of the Navajo nation, "the Navajo got a glimpse of what the rest of the world is doing." But in 1945 most Navajo war veterans were happy to return to their homes and traditional culture. World War II marked a turning point in the lives of Americans and in the history of the United States.

Although the war began badly for the United States, by mid-1942 the Allies halted the Axis powers' advance. In June 1944, U.S. troops, together with Canadian, British, and Free French units, launched a massive invasion across the English Channel, landing at Normandy and pushing into Germany the following spring. Battered by bombing raids, leaderless after Adolf Hitler's suicide, and pressed by a Soviet advance, the Nazis capitulated in May 1945. In the Pacific, Americans drove Japanese forces back, island by island, toward Japan. America's devastating conventional bombing of Japanese cities, followed by the atomic bombs that demolished Hiroshima and Nagasaki in August 1945, led to Japan's surrender. Throughout the war, the Grand Alliance—Britain, the Soviet Union, and the United States—united to defeat Germany but disagreed about how best to fight and how to shape the postwar world. Prospects for postwar international cooperation seemed bleak, and the advent of the atomic age frightened everyone.

The war was fought far from the United States, but it had a major impact on American society. America's leaders committed the United States to become the arsenal of democracy, producing vast quantities of arms. All sectors of the economy were mobilized. America's big businesses got even bigger, as did its central government, labor unions, and farms. The federal government had the monumental task of coordinating these spheres and two new ones: higher education and science.

During the war, nearly one of every ten Americans moved to another state. Most headed for war-production centers, especially cities in the North and on the West Coast. Japanese Americans were rounded up by the army and placed in internment camps. And while the war encouraged African Americans to demand citizenship rights, competition for jobs and housing sparked race riots. For women, the war offered new job opportunities in the armed forces and war industries.

On the home front, Americans supported the war effort by collecting scrap iron, rubber, and newspapers for recycling, and planting "victory gardens." At war's end, although many Americans grieved for lost loved ones and worried about the postwar order, the United States had unprecedented power and prosperity.

- **What military, diplomatic, and social factors influenced decisions about how to fight World War II?**
- **Was the generation of Americans that fought World War II the greatest generation?**
- **How did World War II transform the United States?**

THE UNITED STATES AT WAR

As Japanese bombs fell on the U.S. territory of Hawai'i, American antiwar sentiment evaporated. Franklin Roosevelt declared war with Japan on December 8. When Germany declared war on the United States three days later, America joined British and Soviet Allied nations in battling the Axis powers of Japan, Germany, and Italy. The American public's shift from caution—even isolationism—to fervent support for war was dramatic. As the world went to war, the United States had not been idle. America's embargo of shipments to Japan and refusal to accept Japan's expansionist policies brought the two nations to the brink of war. The United States was also involved in an undeclared naval war with Germany well before Japan's attack on Pearl Harbor. By December 1941, Roosevelt had already instituted an unprecedented peacetime draft, created war mobilization agencies, and commissioned war plans for simultaneous struggle in Europe and the Pacific.

A Nation Unprepared   Still, the nation was not ready for war. Throughout the 1930s, military funding was a low priority. In September 1939 (when Hitler invaded Poland and began World War II), the U.S. Army ranked forty-fifth in size among the world's armies and could fully equip only one-third of its 227,000 men. A peacetime draft instituted in 1940 expanded the U.S. military to 2 million men, but Roosevelt's 1941 survey of war preparedness estimated that the United States could not be ready to fight before June 1943.

In December 1941, the Allies were losing the war (see Map 26.1). Hitler claimed Austria, Czechoslovakia, Poland, the Netherlands, Denmark, and Norway. Romania was lost, then Greece and Bulgaria. France fell in 1940. Britain fought on, but German planes rained bombs on London. More than 3 million German-led soldiers penetrated the Soviet Union and Africa. German U-boats controlled the Atlantic from the Arctic to the Caribbean. Within months of America's entry into the war, German submarines sank 216 vessels—some so close to American shores that people could see the glow of burning ships.

War in the Pacific

In the Pacific, the war was largely America's. The Soviets had not declared war on Japan, and there were too few British troops protecting England's Asian colonies to make much difference. By late spring 1942 Japan had captured most European colonial possessions in Southeast Asia. The Japanese attacked the Philippines hours after Pearl Harbor and destroyed U.S. air capability in the region. American and Filipino troops retreated to the Bataan Peninsula, hoping to hold the main island, Luzon, but Japanese forces were superior. In March 1942, General Douglas MacArthur, the commander of U.S. forces in the Far East, departed the Philippines, proclaiming, "I shall return."

Left behind were almost eighty thousand American and Filipino troops. Starving and weakened by disease, they held on for almost another month before surrendering. The Japanese troops, lacking supplies, were unprepared to deal with this large number of prisoners, and most believed the prisoners forfeited honorable treatment by surrendering. In what came to be known as the Bataan Death March, the Japanese force-marched their captives to prison camps 80 miles away, denying them food and water and bayoneting or beating to death those who fell behind. Ten thousand Filipinos and six hundred Americans died on the march.

The United States struck back. On April 18, sixteen American B-25s appeared over Japan. The Doolittle raid (named after the mission's leader) did little harm, but pushed Japanese commander Yamamoto to bold action. Japan moved to lure the weakened United States into a decisive battle. The target was Midway—two tiny islands about 1,000 miles northwest of Honolulu, where the U.S. Navy had a base. If Japan could take Midway—not implausible, given Japan's string of victories—it would secure a defensive perimeter far from the home islands (see Map 27.1). By using Guam, the Philippines, and even Australia as hostages, Japan believed, it could negotiate a favorable peace agreement with the United States.

General Yamamoto did not know that America's MAGIC code-breaking machines could decipher Japanese messages. When the Japanese fleet arrived, it found the U.S. Navy lying in wait. The Battle of Midway in June 1942 was a turning point in the Pacific war. Japan's hope to force the United States to withdraw, leaving Japan to control the Pacific, vanished. Now Japan was on the defensive.

Europe First Strategy

Despite the importance of these early Pacific battles, America's war strategy was Europe First. American war planners believed that if Germany conquered the Soviet Union, it might directly threaten the United States. Roosevelt also feared that the

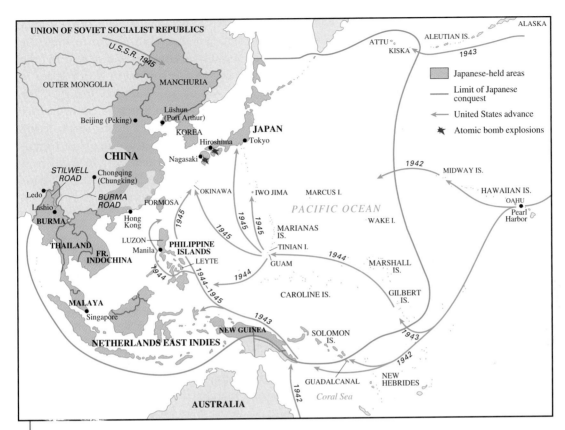

Map 27.1 The Pacific War

The strategy of the United States was to island-hop, from Hawai'i in 1942 to Iwo Jima and Okinawa in 1945. Naval battles were also decisive, notably the Battles of the Coral Sea and Midway in 1942. The war in the Pacific ended with Japan's surrender on August 15, 1945 (V-J Day). (*Source:* Thomas G. Paterson, J. Garry Clifford, Kenneth J. Hagan, *American Foreign Policy: A History,* Vol. 2, 3d ed. Copyright © 1991 by D. C. Heath Company. Used by permission of Houghton Mifflin Company.)

Soviet Union, suffering heavy losses against Hitler, might pursue a separate peace with Germany and so undo the Allied coalition. Therefore, the United States would work with Britain and the Soviet Union to defeat Germany, then deal with an isolated Japan.

British Prime Minister Winston Churchill and Soviet Premier Joseph Stalin disagreed over strategy. By late 1941, German troops nearly reached Moscow and Leningrad (present-day St. Petersburg) and slashed into Ukraine, taking Kiev and claiming the lives of over a million Soviet soldiers. Stalin pressed for British and American troops to attack Germany from the west to draw Germans away from the Soviet front. Roosevelt agreed and promised to open a second front before the end of 1942. Churchill, however, blocked this plan. Churchill wanted to win control of the North Atlantic shipping lanes first and promoted air attacks on Germany and a smaller, safer attack on Axis positions in North Africa. He believed halting the Germans there would protect British imperial possessions in the Mediterranean and the oil-rich Middle East.

Against his advisers' advice, Roosevelt accepted Churchill's plan. The U.S. military was not yet ready for a major campaign, and Roosevelt needed to show the American public some success in the European war. Thus, instead of rescuing the Soviet Union, the British and Americans made a joint landing in North Africa in November 1942, winning quick victories in Algeria and Morocco. In Egypt, the British confronted General Erwin Rommel and his Afrika Korps in a struggle over the Suez Canal and the Middle East oil fields, with Rommel's army surrendering after six months. Meanwhile, the Soviet army hung on. The Soviet Union lost 1.1 million men in the Battle of Stalingrad, but defeated the German Sixth Army there in early 1943. By spring 1943, Germany, like Japan, was on the defensive. But relations among the Allies remained precarious as the United States and Britain continued to resist Stalin's demand for a second front.

THE PRODUCTION FRONT AND AMERICAN WORKERS

Although the war would be fought on the battlefields of Europe and the Pacific, America's strategic advantage lay on the production front at home. By making the machines that would win the war for the Allies, the United States would prevail through a "crushing superiority of equipment," Roosevelt told Congress.

Goals for military production were staggering. In 1940, American factories built 3,807 airplanes. Following Pearl Harbor, Roosevelt wanted 60,000 aircraft in 1942 and twice that in 1943. Plans called for the manufacture of 16 million tons of shipping and 120,000 tanks. The military needed supplies for a force that would reach almost 16 million men. During the war, military production superseded the manufacture of civilian goods. Automobile plants built tanks and airplanes instead of cars; dress factories sewed military uniforms. The War Production Board, established in early 1942, allocated resources and coordinated production among thousands of independent factories.

Businesses, Universities, and the War Effort During the war, American businesses overwhelmingly cooperated with government war-production plans. Patriotism was one reason, but generous incentives were another. In 1940, as the United States produced armaments for the Allies, the U.S. economy began to recover from the depression. Rising consumer spending built industrial confidence. Auto manufacturers, for example, expected to sell 25 percent more in 1941 than in 1939. The massive retooling necessary to produce planes or tanks would be expensive and leave manufacturers dependent on a single client—the federal government.

The federal government, however, paid for retooling and factory expansions; it guaranteed profits by allowing corporations to charge it production costs plus a fixed profit. It created generous tax write-offs and exemptions from antitrust laws. Consequently, corporations doubled their net profits between 1939 and 1943. Most military contracts went to the United States's largest corporations, which had the facilities to guarantee rapid production. From mid-1940 through September 1944 the government awarded contracts totaling $175 billion, with about two-thirds going to the top hundred corporations. General Motors received 8 percent of the total. This approach made sense for a nation that wanted enormous quantities of war goods manufactured in the shortest possible time; most small businesses lacked the necessary capacity. However, wartime government contracts further consolidated U.S. manufacturing in the hands of a few giant corporations.

Manhattan Project

Wartime needs also created a new relationship between science and the U.S. military. Millions of dollars went to fund university research programs. Such federally sponsored research programs developed new technologies of warfare, such as vastly improved radar systems. The most important government-sponsored scientific research program was the Manhattan Project, a $2 billion secret effort to build an atomic bomb. Roosevelt was convinced by scientists fleeing the Nazis in 1939 that Germany was developing an atomic weapon, and he resolved to do it first. The Manhattan Project achieved the world's first sustained nuclear chain reaction in 1942 at the University of Chicago, and in 1943 the federal government established a secret community for atomic scientists and their families at Los Alamos, New Mexico, to develop the weapon that would change the world.

New Opportunities for Workers

The United States's new defense factories required millions of workers. At first workers were plentiful: 9 million Americans were still unemployed in 1940 when war mobilization began. But the armed forces took almost 16 million men, forcing industry to look elsewhere for workers. Women, African Americans, Mexican Americans, and poor whites from Appalachia and the Deep South streamed into defense plant jobs.

Still, many industries refused to hire African Americans. A. Philip Randolph, head of the Brotherhood of Sleeping Car Porters, proposed a march on Washington, D.C., to demand equal access to defense jobs. Roosevelt, fearing race riots, offered the March on Washington movement a deal. In exchange for canceling the march, he issued Executive Order No. 8802, which prohibited discrimination in war industries and government jobs. Although enforcement was uneven, hundreds of thousands of African Americans migrated from the South to northern and western industrial cities on the strength of this official guarantee of job equality.

Mexican workers also filled wartime jobs in the United States. About 200,000 Mexican farm workers, or *braceros,* were offered short-term agricultural contracts as Americans sought well-paid war work. Mexican and Mexican American workers faced discrimination and segregation, but they seized these new economic opportunities. In 1941 there were no Mexican Americans working in the Los Angeles shipyards; by 1944, 17,000 were employed there.

Women at Work

Initially, employers insisted that women were not suited for industrial jobs. But as labor shortages loomed, employers did an about-face. Posters and billboards urged women to "Do the Job HE Left Behind." The government's War Manpower Commission glorified the invented worker Rosie the Riveter, who was featured on posters, in magazines, and in recruitment jingles.

Rosie the Riveter was an inspiring, albeit inaccurate, image of working women. Only 16 percent of women workers had jobs in defense plants, and only 4.4 percent held skilled jobs (such as riveting). Nonetheless, during the war, more than 6 million women entered the labor force, and the number of working women increased by 57 percent. More than 400,000 African American women left domestic service for higher-paying industrial jobs, often with union benefits. Seven million women moved to war-production areas, such as southern California. Women workers in all fields kept the U.S. economy going.

Workers in defense plants were often expected to work ten days for every day off or to accept difficult night shifts. Businesses and the federal government provided workers new support to keep them on the job. The West Coast Kaiser shipyards offered high pay, but also childcare, subsidized housing, and healthcare: the Kaiser Permanente Medical Care Program, a forerunner of the health maintenance organization (HMO). The federal government also funded childcare centers and before- and after-school programs, with 130,000 preschoolers and 320,000 school-age children enrolled during peak years.

Organized Labor During Wartime

The federal government attempted to ensure that labor strikes, so common in the 1930s, would not interrupt production. Days after Pearl Harbor, a White House labor-management conference agreed to a no-strike/no-lockout pledge. In 1942 Roosevelt created the National War Labor Board (NWLB) to settle disputes. The NWLB forged a temporary compromise between union demands for a closed shop, in which only union members could work, and management's desire for an open shop, in which union and nonunion workers could work. Workers could not be required to join a union, but unions could enroll as many members as possible. Between 1940 and 1945, union membership ballooned from 8.5 million to 14.75 million.

The government did restrict union power if it threatened war production. When coal miners in the United Mine Workers union went on strike in 1943, following an NWLB attempt to limit wage increases to a cost-of-living adjustment, lack of coal halted railroads and shut down steel mills. Congress responded with the War Labor Disputes (Smith-Connally) Act, granting the president authority to seize and operate any strike-bound plant deemed necessary to national security.

Success on the Production Front

For nearly four years, U.S. factories operated twenty-four hours a day, seven days a week, turning out roughly 300,000 airplanes, 102,000 armored vehicles, 77,000 ships, 20 million small arms, 40 billion bullets, and 6 million tons of bombs. By war's end, the United States was producing 40 percent of the world's weaponry. This feat depended on transforming formerly skilled work into assembly-line mass production. Henry Ford, now seventy-eight years old, created a massive bomber plant outside Detroit with assembly lines almost a mile long producing one B-24 Liberator bomber every hour. On the West Coast, William Kaiser cut construction time for Liberty ships—the huge, 440-foot-long cargo ships transporting tanks, guns, and bullets overseas—from 355 to 56 days. The ships were not well made; welded hulls sometimes split in rough seas. However, as the United States struggled to produce cargo ships faster than German U-boats could sink them, production was more important than quality.

LIFE ON THE HOME FRONT

The United States was protected by two oceans from its enemies and spared the war that other nations experienced. Americans grieved the loss of loved ones abroad, but bombs did not fall on U.S. cities; invading armies did not burn and rape and kill. Instead, war mobilization ended the Great Depression and brought prosperity. American civilians experienced the paradox of good times amid global conflagration.

Supporting the War Effort

Still the war was a constant presence for Americans on the home front. Civilians supported the war efforts, though Americans were never as committed to shared sacrifice as images of the greatest generation—widely circulated in early twenty-first century popular history and culture—suggest. During the war, however, families planted 20 million victory gardens to free up food supplies for the military. Housewives saved cooking fat and returned it to butchers because it yielded glycerin to make black powder used in shells or bullets. Children collected scrap metal: the iron in one old shovel blade could make four hand grenades.

Many consumer goods were rationed or unavailable. To save wool for military use, the War Production Board redesigned men's suits, narrowing lapels, shortening jackets, and eliminating vests and pant cuffs. Bathing suits, the WPB specified, must shrink by 10 percent. When silk and nylon were diverted from stockings to parachutes, women used makeup on their legs. The Office of Price Administration (OPA), created by Congress in 1942, established a nationwide rationing system for such goods as sugar, coffee, and gasoline. By early 1943, every citizen—regardless of age—received two ration books each month. Sugar was tightly rationed, and people saved for months to make a birthday cake. A black market existed, but most Americans understood that sugar produced alcohol for weapons manufacture and meat fed our boys overseas.

Propaganda and Popular Culture

Despite near-unanimous support for the war, government leaders worried that, over time, public willingness to sacrifice might lag. In 1942 Roosevelt created the Office of War Information (OWI), which hired Hollywood filmmakers and New York copywriters to sell the war at home. OWI posters exhorted Americans to save and sacrifice and reminded them to watch what they said, for "loose lips sink ships."

Popular culture also reinforced wartime messages. A *Saturday Evening Post* advertisement for vacuum cleaners (unavailable for the duration) urged women war workers to fight "for freedom and all that means to women everywhere. You're fighting for a little house of your own, and . . . the right to bring up your children without the shadow of fear." Songs urged Americans to "Remember December 7th" or to "Accentuate the Positive." Others made fun of America's enemies ("You're a sap, Mr. Jap/Uncle Sam is gonna spanky").

DECEMBER 7, 1941

In the days following the attack on Pearl Harbor, the Japanese were often pictured as subhuman—buck-toothed, nearsighted rodents and other vermin. Racial stereotyping would affect how both the Americans and the Japanese waged war. The Americans badly underestimated the Japanese, leaving themselves open for the surprise attack on Pearl Harbor and American forces in the Philippines. And the Japanese, believing Americans were barbarians who lacked a sense of honor, mistakenly expected that the United States would withdraw from East Asia once confronted with Japanese power and determination. (*Collier's,* December 12, 1942)

Movies drew 90 million viewers a week in 1944—out of a total population of 132 million. Hollywood sought to meet Eleanor Roosevelt's challenge to "Keep 'em laughing." *A WAVE, a WAC, and a Marine* promised "no battle scenes, no message, just barrels of fun." Others, such as *Bataan* or *Wake Island,* portrayed actual—if sanitized—events in the war. Even in comedies, the war was always present. Theaters held plasma premieres, offering free admission to those who donated a half-pint of blood to the Red Cross. Audiences rose to sing "The Star Spangled Banner," then watched newsreels with censored combat footage. In movie theaters Americans saw the horror of Nazi death camps in May 1945.

Wartime Prosperity

The war demanded sacrifices from Americans, but between 1939 and the end of the war, per capita income rose from $691 to $1,515. Price controls kept inflation down so that wage increases did not disappear to higher costs. With little to buy, savings rose.

World War II cost approximately $304 billion (more than $3 trillion in today's dollars), which the United States financed through deficit spending, borrowing money by selling war bonds. The national debt skyrocketed, from $49 billion in 1941 to $259 billion in 1945 (and was not paid off until 1970). However, wartime revenue acts increased the number of Americans paying personal income tax from 4 million to 42.6 million—at rates ranging from 6 to 94 percent—and introduced a new system where employers withheld taxes from employee paychecks. For the first time, individual Americans paid more in taxes than corporations.

A Nation in Motion

Despite hardships and fears, the war offered home-front Americans new opportunities. More than 15 million civilians moved during the war. Seven hundred thousand African Americans left the South during the war. People who never traveled farther than the next county found themselves on the other side of the country or of the world.

The rapid influx of war workers to cities and small towns strained community resources. Migrants crowded into substandard housing—even woodsheds, tents, or cellars—and into trailer parks without adequate sanitary facilities. Disease spread: scabies and ringworm, polio, tuberculosis. Many long-term residents found the newcomers, especially the unmarried male war workers, a rough bunch.

In and around Detroit, where car factories now produced tanks and planes, established residents called war workers freshly arrived from southern Appalachia hillbillies and white trash. Many migrants knew little about urban life. One man from rural Tennessee, unfamiliar with traffic lights and street signs, navigated by counting the trees between his home and the war plant where he worked. Some Appalachian trailerites appalled their neighbors by building outdoor privies or burying garbage in their yards.

Racial Conflicts

As people from different backgrounds confronted one another, tensions rose and racism flared. In 1943 almost 250 racial conflicts exploded in forty-seven cities. In Detroit in June, white mobs, undeterred by police, roamed the city attacking African Americans. African Americans hurled rocks at police and dragged white passengers off streetcars. After thirty hours of rioting, twenty-five African Amerians and nine whites lay dead.

In Los Angeles in 1943, young Mexican American gang members, or *pachucos,* wore zoot suits: long jackets with wide padded shoulders, loose pants pegged below the knee, wide-brimmed hats, and dangling watch chains. With cloth rationed, wearing pants requiring five yards of fabric was a purposeful rejection of wartime sacrifice. Although a high percentage of Mexican Americans served in the military, many white servicemen believed otherwise. Racial tensions fueled rumors that *pachucos* attacked white sailors, triggering violence. For four days, mobs of white men—mainly soldiers and sailors—attacked and stripped zoot suiters. Los Angeles outlawed zoot suits, but the riots only ended when naval personnel left.

Families in Wartime

War profoundly transformed families. Despite policies exempting married men and fathers from the draft, almost 3 million families were broken up. The divorce rate of 16 per 1,000 marriages in 1940 almost doubled to 27 per 1,000 in 1944. Still, the number of marriages rose from 73 per 1,000 unmarried women in 1939 to 93 in 1942. Some couples scrambled to marry before the man was sent overseas; others sought military deferments. Total births rose from 2.4 million in 1939 to 3.1 million in 1943. Many were goodbye babies, conceived to guarantee the family's continuation if the father died in the war.

On college campuses, women complained, along with the song lyrics, "There is no available male." But other young women found plenty of male company, sparking concern about wartime threats to sexual morality. *Youth in Crisis,* a 1943 newsreel, featured a girl with "experience far beyond her age" necking with a soldier on the street. These victory girls were said to support the war by giving their all to men in uniform. Many young men and women behaved as they never would in peacetime, which often meant hasty marriages to strangers, especially if a baby was on the way. Wartime mobility increased opportunities for young people to explore same-sex attraction, and gay communities grew in such cities as San Francisco.

In many ways, the war reinforced traditional gender roles weakened during the depression, when men often lost the breadwinner role. Now, while men defended their nation, women "kept the home fires burning," sometimes filling jobs vacated by soldiers. Women who worked were frequently blamed for neglecting their children and creating an epidemic of juvenile delinquency. Nonetheless, millions of women took on new responsibilities and enjoyed greater independence. Many husbands returned to find that their families' lives seemed complete without them.

THE LIMITS OF AMERICAN IDEALS

The U.S. government worked hard to explain to its citizens the reasons for their wartime sacrifices. In 1941 Roosevelt pledged the United States to defend four essential human freedoms—freedom of speech, freedom of religion, freedom from want, and freedom from fear—and government-sponsored films contrasted democracy and totalitarianism, freedom and fascism, equality and oppression.

As the United States fought the totalitarian regimes of the Axis powers, the nation confronted tough questions. What limits on civil liberties were justified in the interest of national security? How freely could information flow without revealing military secrets and costing American lives? How could the United States protect itself against spies or saboteurs, especially from German, Italian, or Japanese citizens living in the United States? And what about the United States's ongoing race problem? The answers revealed tensions between the nation's democratic ideals and its wartime practices.

Regarding civil liberties, U.S. leaders embraced a strategy of truth, declaring that citizens required a truthful accounting of the war's progress. However, the government closely controlled military information, as even seemingly unimportant details might tip off enemies about troop movements. While government-created propaganda sometimes dehumanized the enemy, such hate mongering was used much less frequently than during World War I.

More complex was how to handle dissent and guard against the possibility that enemy agents were operating within the nation's borders. The 1940 Alien Registration (Smith) Act made it unlawful to advocate the overthrow of the U.S. government by force or violence. After Pearl Harbor, the government arrested thousands of Germans, Italians, and other Europeans as suspected spies and potential traitors. The government interned 14,426 Europeans in Enemy Alien Camps and prohibited ten thousand Italian Americans from living or working in restricted zones along the California coast.

Internment of Japanese Americans

In March 1942, Roosevelt ordered that all 112,000 foreign-born Japanese and Japanese Americans living in California, Oregon, and the state of Washington (the vast majority of the mainland population) be removed from the West Coast to relocation centers. There were no individual charges, as was the case with Italians and Germans; Japanese and Japanese Americans were imprisoned solely because they were of Japanese descent.

Anger at Japan's sneak attack on Pearl Harbor fueled calls for internment, as did fears that West Coast cities might come under attack. Long-standing racism also played a major role, as people in economic competition with Japanese Americans strongly supported internment. Although Japanese nationals were forbidden U.S. citizenship or property ownership, American-born Nissei (second generation) and

Links to the World

War Brides

During and immediately after World War II, more than sixty thousand U.S. servicemen married women from other nations. The U.S. government promised servicemen that it would deliver their wives and babies to the United States free of charge.

Beginning in Britain in 1946, the U.S. Army's Operation War Bride eventually transported more than seventy thousand women and children. The first group—455 British women and their 132 children—arrived in the United States on February 4, 1946. As the former World War II transport *Argentina* sailed into New York harbor in the predawn darkness, the Statue of Liberty was specially illuminated. Women who sang, "There'll Always Be an England" as they set sail from Southampton, England, gathered on deck to attempt "The Star-Spangled Banner."

These women, many of them teenagers, left their homes and families behind to join their new husbands in a strange land.

Women from war-destroyed cities were impressed by America's material abundance and the warm welcome they received. But America's racial prejudice shocked Shanghai native Helen Chia Wong, wife of Staff Sergeant Albert Wong, when she and her husband were refused rental of a house with the explanation "The neighbors wouldn't like it." It was not always easy, but most of the war brides settled into their new communities, becoming part of their new nation and helping to forge an intimate link between the United States and other nations of the world.

The army's Operation War Bride (sometimes called Operation Mother-in-Law or the Diaper Run) began in Britain in early 1946. Employing eleven former World War II troopships, including the *Queen Mary,* the U.S. government relocated the wives and babies of U.S. servicemen from dozens of nations to the United States. These English war brides, with babies their fathers had not yet seen, were waiting to be reunited with their husbands in Massachusetts, Missouri, and Iowa.

(© Bettmann/Corbis)

Sansei (third generation), all U.S. citizens, were increasingly successful in business and agriculture. The relocation order forced Japanese Americans to sell property valued at $500 million for a fraction of its worth.

The internees were sent to flood-damaged lands at Relocation, Arkansas, to the intermountain terrain of Wyoming and the desert of western Arizona, and to other desolate spots in the West. The camps were bleak: behind barbed wire, entire families lived in a single room furnished only with cots, blankets, and a bare light bulb. Toilets and dining and bathing facilities were communal. People nonetheless attempted to sustain community life, setting up schools and clubs.

Betrayed by their government, almost 6,000 internees renounced U.S. citizenship and demanded to be sent to Japan. Some sought legal remedy, but the Supreme Court upheld the government's action in *Korematsu v. U.S.* (1944). Others sought to demonstrate their loyalty. The all–Japanese American 442nd Regimental Combat Team, drawn heavily from internees, was the most decorated unit of its size, receiving a Congressional Medal of Honor, 47 Distinguished Service Crosses, 350 Silver Stars, and more than 3,600 Purple Hearts. In 1988 Congress publically apologized and paid $20,000 to each of the 60,000 surviving Japanese American internees.

African Americans and Double V

Meanwhile, African American leaders wanted the nation to confront the parallels between the Nazi racist doctrines and the persistence of Jim Crow segregation in the United States. Proclaiming a Double V campaign (victory at home and abroad), groups such as the National Association for the Advancement of Colored People (NAACP) hoped to "persuade, embarrass, compel and shame our government and our nation . . . into a more enlightened attitude toward a tenth of its people." The NAACP, 50,000 strong in 1940, had 450,000 members by 1946. In 1942 civil rights activists founded the Congress of Racial Equality (CORE), which stressed "nonviolent direct action" and staged sit-ins to desegregate restaurants and movie theaters in Chicago and Washington, D.C.

Military service was a key issue for African Americans, who understood the traditional link between the military service and citizenship. But the U.S. military remained segregated by race and strongly resisted using African American units as combat troops. As late as 1943, less than 6 percent of the armed forces were African American. The Marines initially refused to accept African Americans at all, and the navy approximated segregation by assigning African American men to service positions in which they would rarely interact with non–African Americans as equals or superiors.

A Segregated Military

The U.S. federal government and War Department decided that the world war was no time to integrate the armed forces. The majority of Americans (approximately 89 percent of Americans were white) opposed integration. Racism was so entrenched that the Red Cross segregated blood plasma during the war Integration of military installations, the majority of which were in the South, would have provoked a crisis as federal power contradicted state law. Pointing to outbreaks of racial violence in southern training camps, government and military officials argued that wartime integration would provoke more racial violence and hinder America's war effort. Hopes for racial justice, were another casualty of the war.

Despite such discrimination, African Americans stood up for their rights. Lt. Jackie Robinson refused to move to the back of the bus at the army's Camp Hood, Texas, in 1944 and faced court-martial, even though military regulations forbade racial discrimination on military vehicles. African American sailors disobeyed orders to return to work after an explosion that destroyed two ships and killed 320 men—an explosion caused by the navy practice of assigning untrained men to load bombs onto Liberty ships. When they were court-martialed for mutiny, future Supreme Court justice and chief counsel for the NAACP Thurgood Marshall asked why only African American sailors did this work. He proclaimed, "This is the Navy on trial for its whole vicious policy toward Negroes."

African American servicemen did eventually fight on the front lines. The Marine Corps commandant in the Pacific proclaimed that "Negro Marines are . . . Marines, period." The Tuskegee Airmen, trained at the Tuskegee Institute in Alabama, saw heroic service in all-black units, such as the Ninety-ninth Pursuit Squadron, which won eighty Distinguished Flying Crosses. After the war, African Americans called on their wartime service to claim full citizenship rights. African Americans shared fully in veterans' benefits under the GI Bill. The war marked a turning point for equal rights.

America and the Holocaust

America's inaction in what we now call the Holocaust is tragic, though the consequences are clearer in retrospect than at the time. When the United States turned away refugees on the *St. Louis* (page 695) in early 1939 and refused to relax immigration quotas to admit European Jews and others fleeing Hitler's Germany, almost no one foresaw death camps like Auschwitz. While American anti-Semitism played a significant role, it was not unusual to refuse those seeking refuge, especially during a major economic crisis.

In 1942, American newspapers reported the mass slaughter of Jews and other "undesirables" (Gypsies, homosexuals, the physically and mentally handicapped) under Hitler. Many Americans, having been duped by manufactured atrocity tales during World War I, wrongly discounted these stories. But Roosevelt knew about Nazi death camps capable of killing up to two thousand people an hour using the gas Zyklon-B.

In 1943 British and American representatives met in Bermuda but took no action. Appalled, Secretary of the Treasury Henry Morgenthau Jr. charged that the State Department's foot dragging made the United States an accessory to murder. In 1944, Roosevelt created the War Refugee Board, establishing refugee camps in Europe and helping to save 200,000 Jews. But it came too late. By war's end, the Nazis had systematically murdered almost 11 million people.

LIFE IN THE MILITARY

More than 15 million men and approximately 350,000 women served in the U.S. armed forces during World War II. Eighteen percent of American families had a father, son, or brother in the armed forces. Some men (and all of the women) volunteered. But more than 10 million were draftees. By presidential order, the military stopped accepting volunteers in December 1942. Instead, the Selective Service system and the new War Manpower Commission attempted to centralize control over filling military positions while maintaining war production. The draft extended mostly equitably across the population during World War II.

Selective Service

The Selective Service Act allowed deferments, but they did not disproportionately benefit the wealthy. Almost 10,000 Princeton students or alumni served—as did all 4 of Franklin and Eleanor Roosevelt's sons. The small number of college deferments was balanced by deferments for many critical occupations, including war workers and almost 2 million agricultural workers. Most exemptions were for men deemed physically or mentally unqualified to serve. Army physicians discovered the depression's impact as draftees arrived with rotted teeth and deteriorated eyesight—signs of malnutrition. Army dentists pulled 15 million teeth; optometrists prescribed 2.5 million pairs of glasses. Up to one-third of African American draftees were functionally illiterate, while forty-six percent were classified 4-F—unfit for service.

Nonetheless, almost 12 percent of America's population served in the military. Ethnic and regional differences were profound, and northerners and southerners often could not understand one another. Although African Americans and Japanese Americans served in separate units, Hispanics, Native Americans, and Chinese Americans served in "white" units. The result was often tension, but many Americans became less prejudiced as they served with men unlike themselves.

Fighting the War

Although military service was widespread, the burdens of combat were not equally shared. Women's roles in the U.S. military were much more restricted than in the British or Soviet militaries, where women served in combat-related positions. U.S. women served as nurses, in communications offices, and as typists or cooks. The recruiting slogan for the WACs (Women's Army Corps) was "Release a Man for Combat." However, most men never saw combat either; one-quarter never left the United States. One-third of U.S. military personnel served in clerical positions, with well-educated men most likely slotted into noncombat positions. African Americans, though assigned dirty and dangerous tasks, were largely kept from combat. In World War II, lower-class, less-educated white men bore the brunt of the fighting.

Combat in World War II was horrible. Hollywood war films depicted men dying bravely, shot cleanly and comforted by buddies in their last moments. In reality, less than 10 percent of casualties were caused by bullets; most men were killed or wounded by mortars, bombs, or grenades. Seventy-five thousand American men remained missing at war's end, blown into fragments too small to identify. Combat meant sliding down a mud-slicked hill into a pile of putrid corpses and using flamethrowers that burned at 2,000 degrees Fahrenheit on other human beings. It meant steering a landing craft through floating body parts of those who went ahead, knowing that if you made it ashore you could be blown apart by artillery. Service was for the duration of the war. Only death, serious injury, or victory offered release.

Close to 300,000 U.S. servicemen died in combat, and nearly 1 million were wounded, half of them seriously. Medical advances, such as the development of penicillin and the use of blood plasma to prevent shock, helped wounded men survive, but many never fully recovered. Between 20 and 30 percent of combat casualties were psychoneurotic. The federal government strictly censored images of American combat deaths, consigning them to a secret file known as the chamber of horrors. Many men never talked about their experiences in the war.

WINNING THE WAR

Axis hopes for victory depended on a short war. German and Japanese leaders knew that, if the United States had time to fully mobilize, the war was lost. Hitler, blinded by racial arrogance, stated, "I don't see much future for the Americans. . . . It's a decayed country. . . . American society [is] half Judaized, and the other half Negrified. How can one expect a State like that to hold together?" By mid-1942 the Axis powers understood that they had underestimated American resolve and the other Allies' willingness to sacrifice their citizens to stop the Axis advance (see Map 27.2). The chance of an Axis victory grew slim as months passed, but though the outcome was virtually certain after spring 1943, two years of bloody fighting lay ahead.

Tensions Among the Allies
The Allies' suspicions of one another undermined cooperation. The Soviets continued to press Britain and the United States to open a second front to draw German troops away from the Soviet Union. The United States and Britain, however, continued to delay. With the alliance badly strained, the three Allied leaders met in Teheran, Iran, in December 1943. Stalin dismissed Churchill's proposal for another peripheral attack, this time through the Balkans to Vienna. The three agreed to launch Operation Overlord—the cross-Channel invasion of France—in early 1944. And the Soviet Union promised to aid the Allies against Japan once Germany was defeated.

War in Europe
The second front opened in the dark morning hours of June 6, 1944: D-Day. In the largest amphibious landing in history, more than 140,000 Allied troops commanded by American general Dwight D. Eisenhower scrambled ashore at Normandy, France. Landing craft and soldiers immediately encountered the enemy; they triggered mines and were pinned down by fire from cliffside pillboxes. Although heavy aerial and naval bombardment and the clandestine work of saboteurs softened the German defenses, the fighting was ferocious.

Allied troops spread across the countryside, liberating France and Belgium by the end of August and entering Germany in September. Almost 54,000 Allied troops died in the struggle, and 20,000 French civilians were killed, most by Allied bombing. German armored divisions counterattacked in Belgium's Ardennes Forest in December, hoping to reach Antwerp to halt Allied supplies through that Belgian port. After weeks of heavy fighting in the Battle of the Bulge, the Allies gained control in late January 1945.

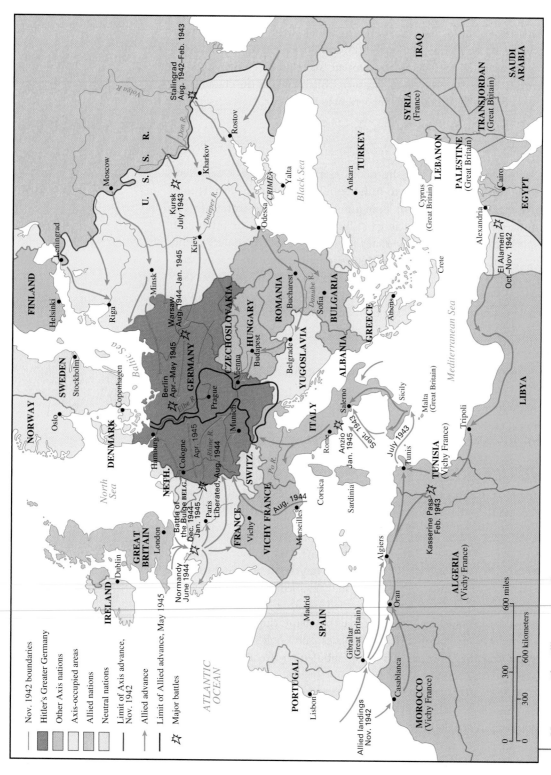

Map 27.2   The Allies on the Offensive in Europe, 1942–1945

The United States pursued a Europe First policy: first defeat Germany, then focus on Japan. U.S. military efforts began in North Africa in late 1942 and ended in Germany in 1945 on May 8 (V-E Day).

Legend:
- Nov. 1942 boundaries
- Hitler's Greater Germany
- Other Axis nations
- Axis-occupied areas
- Allied nations
- Neutral nations
- Limit of Axis advance, Nov. 1942
- Allied advance
- Limit of Allied advance, May 1945
- Major battles

By that point, strategic bombing (not nearly as precise as was publicly claimed) destroyed Germany's war production and devastated its economy. In early 1945, the British and Americans began morale bombing, killing tens of thousands of civilians in aerial attacks on Berlin and then Dresden. Meanwhile, Soviet troops marched through Poland and cut a path to Berlin. American forces crossed the Rhine River in March 1945 and captured the industrial Ruhr valley. Several units entered Austria and Czechoslovakia, where they met Soviet soldiers.

Yalta Conference

Allied leaders began planning the peace in early 1945. Franklin Roosevelt, by this time very ill, called for a summit meeting. The three Allied leaders convened at Yalta, in the Russian Crimea, in February 1945, each with definite goals for the postwar world. Britain, its formerly powerful empire now vulnerable and shrinking, sought to protect its colonial possessions and to limit Soviet power. The Soviet Union, with 21 million dead, wanted German reparations for its massive rebuilding effort. The Soviets hoped to expand their sphere of influence throughout eastern Europe and guarantee their national security; Germany, Stalin insisted, must be permanently weakened.

The three Allied leaders—Winston Churchill, Franklin D. Roosevelt, and Joseph Stalin—met at Yalta in February 1945. Having been president for twelve years, Roosevelt showed signs of age and fatigue. Two months later, he died of a massive cerebral hemorrhage.   (Franklin D. Roosevelt Library, Hyde Park, New York)

The United States also sought to expand its influence and control the peace. Roosevelt lobbied for the United Nations organization, approved in principle the previous year at Dumbarton Oaks in Washington, D.C., through which the United States hoped to exercise influence. The United States hoped to avoid the debts-reparations fiasco that plagued Europe after World War I. U.S. goals included self-determination for liberated peoples; gradual decolonization; and management of world affairs by the Soviet Union, Great Britain, the United States, and China. (Roosevelt hoped China might help stabilize Asia after the war. The United States abolished the Chinese Exclusion Act in 1943 to consolidate ties between the two nations.) The United States was also determined to limit Soviet influence in the postwar world.

Military positions during the Yalta conference helped shape the negotiations. Soviet troops occupied eastern European nations, including Poland, where Moscow had installed a pro-Soviet regime despite a British-supported Polish government-in-exile in London. With Soviet troops in place, Britain and the United States were limited in negotiating this region's future. The Big Three agreed that some eastern German territory would be transferred to Poland and the remainder divided into four zones, the fourth zone to be administered by France. Berlin, within the Soviet zone, would also be divided among the four victors. In exchange for U.S. promises to support Soviet claims on territory lost to Japan in the Russo-Japanese War of 1904–1905, Stalin agreed to a treaty of friendship with Jiang Jieshi (Chiang Kai-shek), America's ally, rather than with the communist Mao Zedong (Mao Tse-tung), and to declare war on Japan within three months of Hitler's defeat.

Harry Truman

Franklin D. Roosevelt, reelected to an unprecedented fourth term in November 1944, did not live to see the war's end. He died on April 12, and Vice President Harry S Truman became president. Truman, who replaced the former vice president Henry Wallace as Roosevelt's running mate in 1944, was inexperienced in foreign policy and was not informed about the top-secret atomic weapons project until after he became president. Eighteen days into Truman's presidency, Adolf Hitler killed himself in a bunker in bomb-ravaged Berlin. On May 8 Germany surrendered.

As the great powers jockeyed for influence after Germany's surrender, the Grand Alliance began to crumble. At the Potsdam Conference in mid-July, Truman—a novice at international diplomacy—was less patient with the Soviets than Roosevelt had been. And Truman learned during the conference that a test of the new atomic weapon had been successful. The United States no longer needed the Soviet Union's help in the Pacific war. The Allies did agree that Japan must surrender unconditionally. But with the end of the European war, the wartime bonds between the Allies were strained.

War in the Pacific

In the Pacific, the war continued. Since the Battle of Midway in June 1942, American strategy had been to island-hop toward Japan, skipping the most fortified islands whenever possible and taking the weaker ones, aiming to strand Japanese forces on their island outposts. To cut off supplies, Americans targeted the Japanese merchant marine. By 1944, Allied troops—from the United States, Britain, Australia, and New Zealand—secured the Solomon, Gilbert, Marshall, and Mariana Islands. General Douglas MacArthur landed at Leyte in the Philippines to retake them in October 1944.

In February 1945, U.S. and Japanese troops battled for Iwo Jima, a small island about 700 miles south of Tokyo. Twenty-one thousand Japanese defenders occupied the island's high ground. Hidden in caves, trenches, and underground tunnels, they were protected from U.S. aerial bombardment supporting its amphibious landing. The island offered no cover, and Marines were slaughtered as they came ashore. For twenty days, U.S. forces fought their way up Mount Suribachi, the highest and most heavily fortified point on Iwo Jima. Iwo Jima claimed 6,821 Americans and more than 20,000 Japanese lives.

A month later, U.S. troops landed on Okinawa, an island at the southern tip of Japan, from which Allied forces planned to invade the main Japanese islands. Fighting raged for two months. The monsoon rains began in May, turning battlefields into seas of mud filled with decaying corpses. The supporting fleet endured mass kamikaze ("suicide") attacks, as Japanese pilots intentionally crashed bomb-laden planes into American ships. On Okinawa, 7,374 Americans died in battle. Almost the entire Japanese garrison of 100,000 was killed. More than one-quarter of Okinawa's people, or approximately 80,000 civilians, perished.

Bombing of Japan

With American forces just 350 miles from Japan's main islands, a powerful Japanese military faction was determined to avoid the humiliation of an unconditional surrender and preserve the emperor's sovereignty. On March 9, 1945, 333 American B-29 Superfortresses dropped explosives and incendiary devices on a 4-by-3-mile area of Tokyo. They created a firestorm, a fierce blaze that sucked the oxygen from the air, creating hurricane-force winds and growing hot enough to melt concrete and steel. Almost 100,000 people were incinerated, suffocated, or boiled to death hiding in canals. Over the following five months, U.S. bombers attacked sixty-six Japanese cities, leaving 8 million people homeless, killing almost 900,000.

Japan, meanwhile, was attempting to bomb the U.S. mainland. Thousands of bomb-bearing high-altitude balloons, constructed from rice paper and potato-flour paste by schoolgirls, were launched into the jet stream. Those that reached the United States fell on unpopulated areas, occasionally starting forest fires. The only mainland U.S. casualties in the war were five children and an adult on a Sunday school picnic in Oregon who accidentally detonated a balloon bomb that they found in the underbrush.

Early in summer 1945, Japan put out peace feelers through the Soviets. Japan was not, however, willing to accept the unconditional surrender terms that Allied leaders agreed to at Potsdam, and Truman chose not to pursue a negotiated peace. U.S. troops were mobilizing to invade the Japanese home islands, factoring in the experiences of Iwo Jima and Okinawa. The Manhattan Project's success offered another option, and Truman took it. Using atomic bombs on Japan, Truman believed, would end the war quickly and save American lives.

Historians still debate Truman's decision to use the atomic bomb rather than negotiate surrender terms. Was Japan on the verge of an unconditional surrender, as some argue? Or was the antisurrender faction of Japanese military leaders strong enough to prevail? Truman knew the bomb could give the United States real and psychological power in negotiating the peace. How much did his desire to demonstrate the bomb's power to the Soviet Union influence him? Did racism or a desire for retaliation play a role? Whatever the answers, bombing (whether conventional or atomic) fit the established U.S. strategy of using machines rather than men whenever possible.

The decision to use the bomb did not seem as momentous to Truman as it does in retrospect. The moral line had already been crossed with wholesale bombing of civilian populations: the Japanese bombed Shanghai in 1937; Germans terror-bombed Warsaw, Rotterdam, and London. British and American bombers purposely created firestorms in German cities, killing, for example, 225,000 people in Dresden. The U.S. bombing of Japanese cities with conventional weapons had already killed nearly a million people. What distinguished the atomic bombs from conventional bombs was their power and their efficiency, not that they killed huge numbers of civilians in unspeakable ways.

On July 26, 1945, the Allies delivered an ultimatum to Japan: promising that the Japanese people would not be enslaved, the Potsdam Declaration called for unconditional surrender or threatened "prompt and utter destruction." Tokyo radio announced that the government would respond with *mokusatsu* (literally, "kill with silence," or ignore the ultimatum). On August 6, 1945, a B-29 bomber *Enola Gay* dropped an atomic bomb above Hiroshima, igniting a firestorm and killing 130,000 people. Tens of thousands more would suffer from radiation poisoning.

On August 8, the Soviet Union declared war on Japan. On August 9, Americans dropped a second atomic bomb on Nagasaki, killing 60,000 people. Five days later, Japan surrendered. Recent histories argue that the Soviet declaration of war played a more significant role in Japan's surrender than America's use of atomic weapons. In the end, the Allies promised that the Japanese emperor could remain as the nation's titular head. World War II was over.

Summary

Hitler once prophesied, "We may be destroyed, but if we are, we shall drag a world with us." World War II devastated much of the globe. In Asia and in Europe, people pawed through rubble, searching for food. One out of nine people in the Soviet Union had perished: at least 21 million civilian and military war dead. The Chinese lost 10 million; the Germans and Austrians, 6 million; the Japanese, 2.5 million. Almost 11 million people were murdered in Nazi death camps. Across the globe, World War II killed at least 55 million people.

War required Allied nations with different goals to cooperate. Tensions remained high, as the United States and Britain resisted Stalin's demands for a second front to draw Germans away from the Soviet Union. The United States, meanwhile, was fighting the Japanese in the Pacific. When Japan surrendered in August 1945, the

Nuclear Proliferation

Virtually from the moment of the Hiroshima and Nagasaki atomic bombings, U.S. strategists grappled with the problem of others joining the nuclear club, particularly the Soviet Union. On September 23, 1949, President Truman informed shocked Americans that the Soviets had successfully tested an atomic device.

In the years thereafter, membership in the nuclear club grew, through a combination of national investments, espionage, and a black market selling raw materials and western technologies. There were successful detonations by Great Britain (1952), France (1960), China (1964), India (1974), and Pakistan (1998). Israel crossed the nuclear weapon threshold on the eve of the 1967 Six-Day War but to this day has refused to confirm that it has the bomb. Recently, credible reports indicate that North Korea has a small nuclear arsenal and that Iran is working to get one. But in June 2008, after much pressure by an American-led initiative to halt its nuclear weapons program, North Korea destroyed the cooling tower of its main nuclear power plant, possibly signaling an initial step in that direction.

Still, the number of nuclear states is fewer than experts predicted in the 1960s, when analysts thought thirty nations might be so armed by the 1990s. The main reason it did not happen is that the five existing nuclear powers committed themselves in the mid-1960s to promoting nonproliferation. Subsequently, twenty-two of thirty-one states that started down the nuclear path changed course and renounced the bomb. By late 2006, the Treaty on the Non-Proliferation of Nuclear Weapons (NPT), enacted on July 1, 1968, had 187 signatories and was hailed as one of the great international agreements of the post-1945 era.

Skeptics took a different view, noting that three states outside the NPT (Israel, India, and Pakistan) became nuclear powers. They charged the original five with preventing others from obtaining nuclear arms while keeping large stockpiles themselves. With the world in 2007 awash in some twenty-seven thousand nuclear weapons (97 percent belonging to the United States and Russia), critics feared terrorist groups or other nonstate actors getting one or more bombs. In that nightmare scenario, they warned, the post-Nagasaki international moratorium on the use of nuclear weapons would be literally blown away.

strains between the Soviet Union and its English-speaking Allies made postwar stability unlikely.

U.S. servicemen covered the globe, while at home, Americans worked around the clock to make the weapons. Despite wartime sacrifices, many Americans found the war improved their lives. Mobilization ended the Great Depression. Americans moved to war-production centers. The influx of workers strained the resources of existing communities and sometimes led to social friction and violence. But many Americans—African Americans, Mexican Americans, women, and poor whites from the South—found new opportunities in well-paid war jobs.

The federal government became a stronger presence, regulating business and employment, overseeing military conscription, and even controlling what people could buy to eat or wear. At war's end, only the United States had the economic resources to spur international recovery; only the United States was more prosperous than when war began. In the coming international struggle to fashion a new world—the Cold War—the United States held a commanding position. For better or worse, World War II was a turning point in the nation's history.

Chapter Review

THE UNITED STATES AT WAR

Was the United States prepared for war when it finally entered World War II?

No. Aside from its long history of caution and isolationism, the United States had also made military spending a low priority, particularly as the nation struggled to pull itself out of the Great Depression. In 1939, the U.S. Army ranked forty-fifth among world armies, and there was only enough equipment for one-third of its troops. The army grew to 2 million men after the establishment of a peacetime draft in 1941, but President Roosevelt's study about U.S. preparedness determined that the country would not be up to fighting before 1943—a luxury it would not have after the December 7, 1941 attack on Pearl Harbor pulled America officially into the war.

What was America's strategy in World War II?

While the battle against Japan was a U.S.-only situation, it was not America's military priority. America's war strategy was Europe First because U.S. leaders feared that if Germany conquered the Soviet Union, it could threaten the United States. The Russians might also agree to a separate peace treaty with Germany, thereby unraveling the Allied unity. Hence, the United States made defeating Germany its first priority; once that was achieved, it would focus on Japan.

THE PRODUCTION FRONT AND AMERICAN WORKERS

How did wartime production needs create a new relationship between government and business, and government and science?

Mobilizing for war required that factories shift from producing consumer goods to wartime necessities such as uniforms, arms, tanks, and so forth. The federal government enticed businesses to cooperate by offering generous tax write-offs and exemptions from antitrust laws. It also paid to retool or expand factories and guaranteed the bottom line by allowing corporations to charge production costs plus a fixed profit, enabling companies to double their profits by 1944. The government ensured that labor strikes would not disrupt production by having the newly-formed National War Labor Board settle disputes. The government spent millions on university research programs developing new war technologies, most importantly, the $2 billion secret Manhattan Project to build an atomic bomb.

LIFE ON THE HOME FRONT

How did Roosevelt sell the war to Americans?

While Americans did not experience the ravages of war on their own soil, they felt it through loss of, or injury to, loved ones and everyday sacrifices of products and conveniences that might benefit soldiers. Housewives returned cooking fat to butchers because it could be used to make black powder for shells or bullets.

Men's suits were redesigned with narrower lapels and shorter jackets to save wool for uniforms. Items such as sugar, coffee, and gasoline were rationed, with families given ration books with points for in-demand items. While citizens considered such sacrifices part of their patriotic duty, government leaders wanted to keep that goodwill from waning, and developed, via the Office of War Information, a series of films and posters that would do the job. Even ads for everyday items reminded consumers that they were fighting for their right to live freely and without fear. Movie audiences were treated to newsreels with censored combat footage that would inspire their ongoing wartime support, and audiences rose to sing the national anthem.

THE LIMITS OF AMERICAN IDEALS

What drove the decision to intern Japanese nationals and Japanese Americans within the United States during World War II?

Within months of Japan's attack on Pearl Harbor, fears about potential enemies on U.S. shores led President Roosevelt to order that all 112,000 foreign-born Japanese and Japanese Americans in California, Oregon, and Washington state (where most resided) be moved to "relocation centers." Racism was also a factor, as those who competed with Japanese-owned businesses supported internment. Internees were forced to quickly sell their property—valued at $500 million total—which often meant huge financial losses. They were then transported to internment camps in Arkansas, Wyoming, and Arizona, which were enclosed in barbed wire and housed entire families in a single room. Almost 6,000 internees renounced U.S. citizenship and asked to return to Japan. In 1988 Congress issued a public apology, with included a $20,000 payment to each of the surviving 60,000 Japanese American internees.

LIFE IN THE MILITARY

How did racial and gender norms play out in the military during World War II?

Nearly 12 million Americans served in World War II, including women and racial minorities. The discrimination that existed throughout American society was replicated in the armed services: African Americans and Japanese Americans served in units segregated from whites (although Hispanics, Native Americans, and Chinese Americans were part of "white" units). African Americans were given the dirtiest and most dangerous assignments, although they were kept from combat for most of the war. Less-educated, lower class white men did most of the fighting. Women were similarly kept from combat and their military organizations, such as the Women's Army Corps, were treated as auxiliaries. Their primary positions were as nurses, communications officers, typists, and cooks, a military extension of their traditional helpmeet roles.

WINNING THE WAR

Why did Truman opt to use the atomic bomb to help end the war, rather than negotiate a peace with Japan?

Historians continue to debate this question. Certainly, some argue that racism was a factor. From a military standpoint, Truman had insisted on an unconditional surrender of the Japanese. Although Japan indicated to the Soviet Union its interest in negotiating peace, it was not about to accept Truman's terms. Truman believed that using the atomic bomb would end the war fast and save U.S. soldiers' lives. Because extensive bombing of Japanese civilian areas had already occurred, Truman did not see the use of the bomb as the historic turning-point it would later seem to have been. The only difference in his mind—and many leaders' minds at the time—between conventional and atomic bombs was in their power and efficiency, not their manner of killing or the huge numbers who would likely perish.

SUGGESTIONS FOR FURTHER READING

Michael C. C. Adams, *The Best War Ever: America and World War II* (1993)

Roger Daniels, *Prisoners Without Trial: Japanese Americans in World War II* (1993)

Tsuyoshi Hasegawa, *Racing the Enemy: Stalin, Truman, and the Surrender of Japan* (2005)

David M. Kennedy, *Freedom from Fear: The American People in Depression and War, 1929–1945* (1999)

Warren F. Kimball, *Forged in War: Roosevelt, Churchill, and the Second World War* (1997)

Nelson Lichtenstein, *Labor's War at Home: The CIO in World War II* (1983)

Gerald F. Linderman, *The World Within War: America's Combat Experience in World War II* (1997)

Leisa Meyers, *Creating G.I. Jane: Sexuality and Power in the Women's Army Corps During World War II* (1996)

George Roeder Jr., *The Censored War: American Visual Experience During World War II*

Ronald Takaki, *Double Victory: A Multicultural History of America in World War II* (2000)

CHAPTER 28

The Cold War and American Globalism

CHAPTER OUTLINE

From Allies to Adversaries

Containment in Action

The Cold War in Asia

The Korean War

Unrelenting Cold War

> **LINKS TO THE WORLD:**
> The People-to-People
> Campaign

The Struggle for the Third World

Summary

> **LEGACY FOR A PEOPLE
> AND A NATION:** The National
> Security State

On July 16, 1945, the Deer Team leader parachuted into northern Vietnam, near Kimlung, a village in a valley of rice paddies. Colonel Allison Thomas and five members of his Office of Strategic Services (OSS) unit could not know that the end of the Second World War was weeks away. Their mission: to work with the Vietminh, a nationalist Vietnamese organization, to sabotage Japanese forces that seized Vietnam from France in March. A banner proclaimed, "Welcome to Our American Friends." Ho Chi Minh, head of the Vietminh, offered supper to the OSS team. The next day Ho denounced the French but remarked, "We welcome 10 million Americans." "Forget the Communist Bogy," Thomas radioed OSS headquarters in China.

A communist dedicated to winning his nation's independence from France, Ho joined the French Communist Party after World War I. For the next two decades, living in China, the Soviet Union, and elsewhere, he planned and fought to free his nation from French colonialism. During World War II, Ho's Vietminh warriors harassed French and Japanese forces and rescued downed American pilots. In March 1945 Ho met with U.S. officials in China. Receiving no aid from ideological allies in the Soviet Union, Ho hoped the United States would favor his nation's quest for liberation.

Other OSS personnel soon parachuted into Kimlung, including a male nurse who diagnosed Ho's ailments as malaria and dysentery. Quinine and sulfa drugs restored his health, but Ho remained frail. Everywhere the Americans went, impoverished villagers thanked them with gifts of food and clothing, interpreting the foreigners' presence as a sign of U.S. anticolonial and anti-Japanese sentiments. In early August the Deer Team offered Vietminh soldiers weapons training. Ho hoped young

This icon will direct you to interactive activities and study materials on A People And A Nation, Brief Edition website: **www.cengage.com/history/norton/ peoplenationbrief8e**

Chronology

1945	Roosevelt dies; Truman becomes president. United States drops atomic bombs on Japan.
1946	Kennan's long telegram criticizes Soviet Union. Vietnamese war against France erupts.
1947	Truman Doctrine seeks aid for Greece and Turkey. Marshall offers Europe economic assistance. National Security Act reorganizes government.
1948	Communists take power in Czechoslovakia. Truman recognizes Israel. United States organizes Berlin airlift.
1949	NATO is founded as anti-Soviet alliance. Soviet Union explodes atomic bomb. Mao's communists win power in China.
1950	NSC-68 recommends major military buildup. Korean War starts in June; China enters in fall.
1951	United States signs Mutual Security Treaty with Japan.

1953	Eisenhower becomes president. Stalin dies. United States helps restore shah to power in Iran. Korean War ends.
1954	Geneva accords partition Vietnam. CIA-led coup overthrows Arbenz in Guatemala.
1955	Soviets create Warsaw Pact.
1956	Soviets crush uprising in Hungary. Suez crisis sparks war in Middle East.
1957	Soviets fire first ICBM and launch *Sputnik*.
1958	U.S. troops land in Lebanon. Berlin crisis occurs.
1959	Castro ousts Batista in Cuba
1960	Eighteen African colonies become independent. Vietcong are organized in South Vietnam.

Vietnamese could study in the United States and that U.S. technicians could help build an independent Vietnam.

A second OSS unit, the Mercy Team, headed by Captain Archimedes Patti, arrived in Hanoi on August 22. But, unbeknownst to these OSS members, who believed that President Franklin D. Roosevelt's sympathy for eventual Vietnamese independence remained U.S. policy, the new Truman administration wanted France to decide Vietnam's fate. That policy change explains why Ho never received answers to the letters and telegrams he sent to Washington beginning August 30, 1945.

On September 2, 1945, with OSS personnel present, an emotional Ho Chi Minh read his declaration of independence for the Democratic Republic of Vietnam: "All men are created equal; they are endowed by their Creator with certain unalienable Rights; among these are Life, Liberty, and the pursuit of Happiness." Having borrowed from the internationally renowned 1776 American document, Ho itemized Vietnamese grievances against France.

In a last meeting with Captain Patti, Ho expressed sadness that the United States armed the French to reestablish their colonial rule in Vietnam. Sure, Ho said, U.S. officials in Washington judged him a Moscow puppet because he was a communist. But Ho claimed that he drew inspiration from the American struggle for independence. Ho insisted the Vietnamese would go it alone. And they did—first against the French and eventually against more than half a million U.S. troops in what became the United States's longest war.

Because Ho Chi Minh and his nationalist followers declared themselves communists, U.S. leaders rejected their appeal. Endorsing the containment doctrine against communism, U.S. presidents from Truman to George H. W. Bush believed that a ruthless Soviet Union directed a worldwide communist conspiracy against peace, free-market capitalism, and democracy. Soviet leaders from Joseph Stalin to Mikhail Gorbachev protested that a militarized, economically aggressive United States sought world domination. This protracted contest between the United States and the Soviet Union acquired the name Cold War.

The primary feature of world affairs for more than four decades, the Cold War was fundamentally a contest between the United States and the Soviet Union over spheres of influence. The contest between the capitalist West and the communist East dominated international relations and eventually took the lives of millions, cost trillions of dollars, spawned doomsday fears, and destabilized several nations. Occasionally, the two superpowers negotiated and signed agreements to temper their dangerous arms race; at other times they went to the brink of war and armed allies to fight vicious Third World conflicts. Sometimes these allies had their own ambitions and resisted pressure from one or both superpowers.

Vietnam was part of the *Third World*, a term for nations that in the Cold War era wore neither the West (the First World) nor the East (the Second World) label. Sometimes called developing countries, Third World nations were generally nonwhite, nonindustrialized, and located in the southern half of the globe—in Asia, Africa, the Middle East, and Latin America. Many had been colonies of European nations or Japan and were vulnerable to the Cold War rivalry. U.S. leaders often interpreted their anticolonialism as Soviet inspired rather than as expressions of indigenous nationalism. Vietnam became one among many sites where Cold War fears and Third World aspirations intersected, prompting U.S. intervention and a globalist foreign policy that regarded the world as the appropriate sphere for America's influence.

Critics in the United States challenged Cold War exaggerations of threats from abroad, meddlesome interventions in the Third World, and militarization of foreign policy. But when leaders like Truman described the Cold War as a life-and-death struggle against a monstrous enemy, critics were drowned out by charges that dissenters were soft on communism, if not un-American. U.S. leaders successfully cultivated a Cold War consensus that stifled debate and shaped the mindset of generations of Americans.

- Why did relations between the Soviet Union and the United States turn hostile soon after their victory in World War II?
- When and why did the Cold War expand from a struggle over the future of Europe and central Asia to one encompassing virtually the entire globe?
- By what means did the Truman and Eisenhower administrations seek to expand the United States's global influence in the late 1940s and the 1950s?

FROM ALLIES TO ADVERSARIES

World War II unsettled the international system. Germany was in ruins. Great Britain was overstrained, France was rent by internal division, and Italy was weakened. Japan was decimated and occupied, and China was headed toward renewed civil war. Throughout Europe and Asia, factories, transportation, and communications links were reduced to rubble, and agricultural production plummeted. The United States and the Soviet Union offered different solutions. The collapse of Germany and

Japan, moreover, created power vacuums that drew the two major powers into collision as they sought influence where Axis aggressors had once held sway. For example, in Greece and China, where civil wars raged between leftists and conservative regimes, the two powers supported opposite sides.

Decolonization

With empires disintegrating, a new Third World came into being. Financial constraints and nationalist rebellions forced the imperial states to set their colonies free. Britain exited India (and Pakistan) in 1947 and Burma and Sri Lanka (Ceylon) in 1948. The Philippines gained independence from the United States in 1946. After four years of battling nationalists in Indonesia, the Dutch left in 1949. In the Middle East, Lebanon (1943), Syria (1946), and Jordan (1946) gained independence, while in Palestine, British officials faced pressure from Zionists intent on creating a Jewish homeland and from Arab leaders opposed to it. In Iraq, nationalist agitation increased against the British-installed government. Washington and Moscow saw these emerging Third World states as potential allies that might provide military bases, resources, and markets. Some new nations chose nonalignment in the Cold War.

Stalin's Aims

The United States and Soviet Union assessed their most pressing tasks differently. The Soviets, though committed to victory over capitalist countries, were most concerned about preventing another invasion of their homeland. Its land mass was three times that of the United States, but it had only 10,000 miles of seacoast, which was under ice for much of the year. Russian leaders before and after the revolution made increased maritime access a chief foreign policy aim.

Worse, the Soviet Union's geographical frontiers were hard to defend. Siberia, vital for its mineral resources, lay 6,000 miles east of Moscow and was vulnerable to encroachment by Japan and China. In the west, the border with Poland generated violent clashes since World War I, and in World War II 21 million Russians died and there was massive physical destruction. Henceforth, Soviet leaders wanted no dangers along their western borders.

Overall, however, Soviet territorial objectives were limited. Although Americans were quick to compare Stalin to Hitler, Stalin's aims were more limited and resembled those of tsars before him: he wanted to push the Soviet Union's borders to include the Baltic states of Estonia, Latvia, and Lithuania, along with the eastern part of prewar Poland. To the south, Stalin wanted a presence in northern Iran, and he pressed the Turks for naval bases and free access out of the Black Sea. Economically, the Soviets did not promote rapid rebuilding of the region's war-ravaged economies or expanded world trade.

U.S. Economic and Strategic Needs

The United States, by contrast, came out of the war secure in its borders. Separated from other world powers by two oceans, the U.S. home base was virtually immune from attack during the fighting. American casualties were fewer than any of the other major combatants. With its fixed capital intact, its resources more plentiful than ever, and in lone possession of the atomic bomb, the United States was the strongest power in the world at war's end.

But Washington officials worried about complacency. Some other power—almost certainly the Soviet Union—could take advantage of instability in war-torn Europe and Asia and seize control of these areas, with dire implications for the United States's security. Therefore, Washington sought bases overseas to keep an airborne enemy at bay. To enhance U.S. security, U.S. planners sought the quick reconstruction of nations—including former enemies Germany and Japan—and a world economy based on free trade.

The Soviets refused to join the new World Bank and International Monetary Fund (IMF), created at the July 1944 Bretton Woods Conference by forty-four nations to stabilize trade and finance. They held that the United States dominated both institutions and used them to promote private investment and open international commerce, which Moscow saw as capitalist tools. With the United States as its largest donor, the World Bank opened in 1945 and made loans to finance members' reconstruction projects; the IMF, also heavily U.S.-backed, helped members meet their balance of payments through currency loans.

Stalin and Truman

Joseph Stalin, though hostile to the western powers and capable of ruthlessness against his people (his periodic purges since the 1930s took the lives of millions), did not want war. He was aware of his country's weakness vis-à-vis the United States and believed he must try to achieve his aspirations through cooperation. Stalin believed that Germany and Japan would eventually threaten the Soviet Union, and his suspicion of capitalist powers was boundless. Many concluded that Stalin was clinically paranoid. As historian David Reynolds has noted, this alleged paranoia, coupled with Stalin's xenophobia (fear of anything foreign) and his Marxist-Leninist ideology, created in him a mental map of them versus us that influenced his approach to world affairs.

To a lesser degree, Harry Truman was also prone to a them versus us worldview. He often glossed over nuances, ambiguities, and counterevidence, preferring an either/or answer. Truman exaggerated, as when he declared in his undelivered farewell address that he "knocked the socks off the communists" in Korea. When Truman protested in 1945 during a meeting at the White House that the Soviets were not fulfilling the Yalta agreement on Poland, the Soviet commissar of foreign affairs, V. M. Molotov, stormed out. Truman self-consciously developed what he called his tough method, which became a trademark of U.S. Cold War diplomacy.

The Beginning of the Cold War

No precise start date for the Cold War can be given. It resulted from an ongoing process that arguably began in 1917 with the Bolshevik Revolution and the western powers' hostile response, but in a more meaningful sense began in mid-1945, as World War II ended. By the spring of 1947, certainly, the struggle had begun.

One of the first Soviet-American clashes came in Poland in 1945, when the Soviets blocked the Polish government-in-exile in London from becoming part of the communist government that Moscow sponsored. The Soviets also extinguished civil liberties in Romania, arguing that the United States similarly manipulated Italy. Moscow initially allowed free elections in Hungary and Czechoslovakia, but as the Cold War accelerated and U.S. influence in Europe expanded, the Soviets encouraged communist coups in Hungary (1947) and Czechoslovakia (1948). Yugoslavia was unique: its independent communist government, led by Josip Broz Tito, broke with Stalin in 1948.

To defend their actions, Moscow officials noted that the United States was reviving their traditional enemy, Germany, and was meddling in eastern Europe. The Soviets cited clandestine American meetings with anti-Soviet groups, repeated calls for elections likely to produce anti-Soviet regimes, and the use of loans to gain political influence (financial diplomacy). Moscow charged that the United States was pursuing a double standard—intervening in eastern Europe but demanding that the Soviet Union stay out of Latin America and Asia. The United States called for free elections in the Soviet sphere, Moscow noted, but not in the U.S. sphere in Latin America.

Atomic Diplomacy

The Soviets believed that the United States was practicing atomic diplomacy, maintaining a nuclear monopoly to scare the Soviets into diplomatic concessions. Secretary of State James F. Byrnes thought that the atomic bomb could deter Soviet expansion, but Secretary of War Henry L. Stimson disagreed in 1945. If Americans continued to have "this weapon rather ostentatiously on our hip," he warned Truman, the Soviets' "suspicions and their distrust of our purposes and motives will increase."

In this atmosphere, Truman refused to turn over the weapon to an international authority. In 1946 he backed the Baruch Plan, named after its author, financier Bernard Baruch, which provided for U.S. abandonment of its atomic monopoly only after the world's fissionable materials were controlled by an international agency. The Soviets retorted that it would require them to shut down their atomic-bomb development project while the United States continued its own. Washington and Moscow soon became locked in a frightening nuclear arms race.

By mid-1946, the Soviets and Americans clashed on every front. When the United States refused the Soviets a reconstruction loan but gave one to Britain, Moscow upbraided Washington for using its dollars to manipulate foreign governments. The two Cold War powers also backed different groups in Iran, where the United States helped bring the pro-West shah to the throne. Unable to agree on the unification of Germany, the former allies built up their zones independently.

Warnings from Kennan and Churchill

After Stalin gave a speech in February 1946 depicting the world as threatened by capitalist acquisitiveness, the U.S. chargé d'affaires in Moscow, George F. Kennan, sent a pessimistic long telegram to Washington. His widely circulated report fed a growing belief among U.S. officials that only toughness would work with the Soviets. The following month, in Fulton, Missouri, former British prime minister Winston Churchill warned that a Soviet-erected iron curtain cut off eastern European countries from the West. With an approving Truman nearby, Churchill called for Anglo-American partnership to resist the new menace.

The growing Soviet-American tensions had major implications for the United Nations. The delegates who gathered in San Francisco in April 1945 to sign the U.N. charter agreed on an organization that included a General Assembly of all member states and a smaller Security Council spearheading peace and security issues. Five great powers were given permanent seats on the council—the United States, the Soviet Union, Great Britain, China, and France—and each could exercise a veto against any proposed action. To be effective, therefore, the U.N. needed great-power cooperation. Of the fifty-one founding states, twenty-two came from the Americas and another fifteen from Europe, which effectively gave the United States a majority in the assembly. In retaliation, Moscow exercised its veto in the Security Council.

Some high-level U.S. officials were dismayed by the administration's harsh anti-Soviet posture. Secretary of Commerce Henry A. Wallace charged that Truman's get-tough policy substituted atomic and economic coercion for diplomacy. Wallace told a Madison Square Garden audience in September 1946 that "getting tough never brought anything real and lasting—whether for schoolyard bullies, or businessmen or world powers." Truman fired Wallace, blasting him privately as "a real Commy."

On March 5, 1946, former British prime minister Winston S. Churchill (1874–1965) delivered a speech, which he intended for a worldwide audience, at Westminster College in Fulton, Missouri. President Harry S Truman (right) had encouraged Churchill (seated) to speak on two themes: the need to block Soviet expansion and the need to form an Anglo-American partnership. Always eloquent and provocative, Churchill denounced the Soviets for drawing an iron curtain across eastern Europe. This speech became one of the landmark statements of the Cold War.
(Terry Savage / Harry S. Truman Presidential Library, Independence, Missouri)

Truman Doctrine

East-West tensions escalated further in early 1947, when the British requested American help defending their conservative client-government (a government dependent on the economic or military support of a more powerful country) in Greece in a civil war against leftists. The Republican Eightieth Congress wanted less spending, and many members had little respect for the Democratic president who voters repudiated in the 1946 elections by giving the GOP ("Grand Old Party," the Republican Party) majorities in both congressional houses. Republican senator Arthur Vandenberg of Michigan, a bipartisan leader, told the president that he would have to "scare hell out of the American people" to gain congressional approval.

Thus, the president delivered a speech laced with alarmist language staking out the United States's role in the postwar world. Truman claimed that communism imperiled the world. "If Greece should fall under the control of an armed minority," he concluded in an early version of the domino theory, "the effect upon its neighbor, Turkey, would be immediate and serious. Confusion and disorder might well spread throughout the entire Middle East." Truman articulated what became known as the Truman Doctrine: "It must be the policy of the United States to support free peoples who are resisting attempted subjugation by armed minorities or by outside pressures."

Critics correctly pointed out that the Soviet Union was little involved in the Greek civil war, that the communists in Greece were more pro-Tito than pro-Stalin, and that the resistance movement had noncommunist as well as communist members. Truman countered that, should communists gain control of Greece, they might open the door to Soviet power in the Mediterranean. The Senate approved Truman's request by 67 to 23 votes. Using U.S. dollars and military advisers, the Greek government defeated the insurgents in 1949, and Turkey became a U.S. ally on the Soviets' border.

Inevitable Cold War?   In the months after Truman's speech, the term *Cold War* slipped into the lexicon as a description of the Soviet-American relationship. Within two years of the victory over the Axis powers, the two Grand Alliance members were locked in a struggle for world dominance that would last almost half a century. Even before World War II ended, observers anticipated that the United States and the Soviet Union would seek to fill the power vacuum. The two countries had a history of hostility and were militarily powerful. Most of all, they were divided by sharply differing political economies with divergent needs and by a deep ideological chasm.

It is far less clear that the conflict had to result in a Cold War. The "cold peace" that prevailed from the revolution in 1917 through World War II could conceivably have continued into the postwar years. Neither side's leadership wanted war. Both hoped—at least initially—that cooperation could be maintained. The Cold War resulted from decisions by individuals who might have done more to maintain diplomatic dialogue and negotiate solutions to international problems. For decades, Americans would wonder if the high price they were paying for victory in the superpower confrontation was necessary.

Containment in Action

To counter Soviet and communist expansion, the Truman team chose a policy of containment. George Kennan, now at the State Department in Washington, published an influential statement of the containment doctrine. Writing as Mr. X in the July 1947 issue of *Foreign Affairs* magazine, Kennan advocated a "policy of firm containment, designed to confront the Russians with unalterable counterforce at every point where they show signs of encroaching upon the interests of a peaceful and stable world." Such counterforce, Kennan argued, would check Soviet expansion. Kennan's X article joined the Truman Doctrine as a key manifesto of Cold War policy.

Lippmann's Critique   The veteran journalist Walter Lippmann took issue with the containment doctrine in his powerful book *The Cold War* (1947), calling it a "strategic monstrosity" that failed to distinguish between areas vital and peripheral to U.S. security. Nor did Lippmann share Truman's conviction that the Soviet Union was plotting to take over the world. Ironically, Kennan agreed with much of Lippmann's critique and soon distanced himself from the doctrine he helped create.

Invoking the containment doctrine, the United States in 1947 and 1948 began to build an international economic and defensive network to protect U.S. prosperity and security and advance U.S. hegemony. In western Europe, the region of primary concern, American diplomats pursued economic reconstruction, the ouster of communists from governments, as occurred in 1947 in France and Italy, and blockage of third force, or neutralist, tendencies. U.S. officials kept the decolonization of European empires orderly. Meanwhile, American culture—consumer goods, music, consumption ethic, and production techniques—permeated European societies. Some Europeans resisted Americanization, but transatlantic ties strengthened.

Marshall Plan

Americans, who already spent billions on European relief and recovery by 1947, remembered all too well the troubles of the 1930s: global depression, political extremism, and war born of economic discontent. Such cataclysms could not be allowed to happen again; communism must not replace fascism.

Hence, in June 1947, Secretary of State George C. Marshall announced that the United States would finance a massive European recovery program. Launched in 1948, the Marshall Plan sent $12.4 billion to western Europe until 1951 (see Map 28.1). To stimulate business at home, the legislation required that Europeans spend this aid on U.S.-made products. The Marshall Plan proved a mixed success; it caused inflation, failed to solve a balance-of-payments problem, took only tentative steps toward economic integration, and further divided Europe between East and West. But the program spurred impressive western European industrial production and investment, started the region toward self-sustaining economic growth, and—from the U.S. perspective—contained communism.

National Security Act

Truman streamlined U.S. defense by working with Congress on the National Security Act of July 1947. The act created the Office of Secretary of Defense (which became the Department of Defense two years later) to oversee the armed services, the National Security Council (NSC) of high-level officials to advise the president, and the Central Intelligence Agency (CIA) to conduct spy operations and information gathering overseas. By the early 1950s the CIA expanded to include covert (secret) operations aimed at overthrowing unfriendly foreign leaders. The National Security Act gave the president increased powers regarding foreign policy.

In response, Stalin forbade communist satellite governments in eastern Europe to accept Marshall Plan aid and ordered communist parties in western Europe to work to thwart it. He also created the Cominform, an organization designed to coordinate communist activities around the world. Whereas U.S. planners saw the Marshall Plan as protecting their European friends against a potential Soviet threat, to Stalin it raised anew the specter of capitalist penetration. He tightened his grip on eastern Europe—most notably, engineering a coup in Czechoslovakia in February 1948 that ensured full Soviet control, which heightened anxiety in the United States.

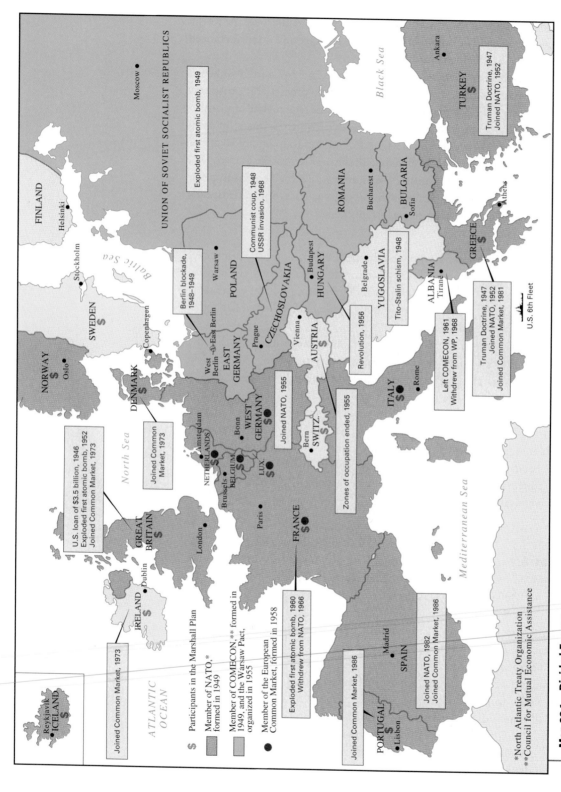

Map 28.1 Divided Europe

After World War II, Europe broke into two competing camps. When the United States launched the Marshall Plan in 1948, the Soviet Union countered with its own economic plan the following year. When the United States created NATO in 1949, the Soviet Union answered with the Warsaw Pact in 1955. On the whole, these two camps held firm until the late 1980s.

Berlin Blockade and Airlift

In June 1948, the Americans, French, and British agreed to fuse their German zones and integrate West Germany (the Federal Republic of Germany) into the western European economy. Fearing a resurgent Germany tied to the U.S. Cold War camp, the Soviets cut off western land access to the jointly occupied city of Berlin, located inside the Soviet zone. President Truman then ordered a massive airlift of food, fuel, and other supplies to Berlin. The Soviets finally lifted the blockade in May 1949 and founded the German Democratic Republic, or East Germany.

The successful airlift may have saved Truman's political career; he narrowly defeated Republican Thomas E. Dewey in the November 1948 presidential election. Truman next formalized the military alliance among the United States, Canada, and western Europe. In April 1949, twelve nations signed a mutual defense treaty, agreeing that an attack on any one of them would be considered an attack on all, and establishing the North Atlantic Treaty Organization (NATO; see Map 28.1).

Not since 1778 had the United States entered a formal European military alliance, and some critics, such as Senator Robert A. Taft, Republican of Ohio, claimed that NATO would provoke rather than deter war. Administration officials responded that should the Soviets ever probe westward, NATO would bring the full force of the United States to bear on the Soviet Union. Truman officials also hoped that NATO would keep western Europeans from embracing communism or even neutralism in the Cold War. The Senate ratified the treaty by 82 votes to 13, and the United States began to spend billions of dollars under the Mutual Defense Assistance Act.

By the summer 1949, Truman and his advisers were basking in the successes of their foreign policy. Containment was working, West Germany was on the road to recovery, the Berlin blockade had been defeated, and NATO had been formed. True, there was trouble in China, where the communists under Mao Zedong were winning a civil war. But that struggle would likely wax and wane for years to come. Just possibly, some dared to think, Harry Truman was on his way to winning the Cold War.

Twin Shocks

Then, suddenly, in late September, came the twin shocks, two momentous developments that made Americans feel in even greater danger than ever before. First, a U.S. reconnaissance aircraft detected unusually high radioactivity in the atmosphere: the Soviets had exploded an atomic device. With the U.S. nuclear monopoly erased, western Europe seemed more vulnerable. Second, the communists in China completed their conquest sooner than many expected. Now the world's largest and most populous countries were ruled by communists, and one of them had the atomic bomb.

Rejecting calls for high-level negotiations, Truman in early 1950 gave the go-ahead for production of a hydrogen bomb, the "Super." Kennan bemoaned the militarization of the Cold War and was replaced at the State Department by Paul Nitze. The National Security Council delivered to the president in April 1950 a significant top-secret document tagged NSC-68. Predicting continued tension with expansionistic communists, the report, authored primarily by Nitze, urged a much enlarged military budget and the mobilization of public support. The Cold War was about to become vastly more expensive and far-reaching.

THE COLD WAR IN ASIA

Asia gradually became ensnared in the Cold War. Indeed, the consequences of an expansive containment doctrine would exact its heaviest price on the United States, in large scale in Korea and Vietnam. Though less important to both superpowers than Europe, Asia was where the Cold War turned hot.

From the start, Japan was crucial to U.S. strategy. The United States monopolized Japan's reconstruction through a military occupation directed by General Douglas MacArthur. Truman disliked "Mr. Prima Donna, Brass Hat" MacArthur, but MacArthur wrote a democratic constitution, gave women voting rights, revitalized the economy, and destroyed the nation's weapons. U.S. authorities Americanized Japan by censoring films critical of the United States (for the destruction of Hiroshima, for example) or depicting Japanese customs, such as suicide, arranged marriages, and swordplay. In 1951 the United States and Japan signed a separate peace that restored Japan's sovereignty and ended the occupation. A Mutual Security Treaty that year provided for the stationing of U.S. forces in Japan, including a U.S. base on Okinawa.

Chinese Civil War

The administration had less success in China. The United States had long backed the Nationalists of Jiang Jieshi (Chiang Kai-shek) against Mao Zedong's communists. But after World War II, Generalissimo Jiang's government had become corrupt, inefficient, and out of touch with discontented peasants, whom the communists enlisted with promises of land reform. Jiang also subverted U.S. efforts to negotiate a cease-fire and a coalition government.

U.S. officials divided on the question of whether Mao was an Asian Tito—communist but independent—or, as most believed, part of an international communist movement that might give the Soviets a springboard into Asia. Thus, when the Chinese communists made secret overtures to the United States for diplomatic talks in 1945 and again in 1949, U.S. officials rebuffed them. Mao leaned to the Soviet side in the Cold War. Because of China's fierce independence, a Sino-Soviet schism opened.

With his victory in September 1949, Mao proclaimed the People's Republic of China (PRC). Truman hesitated to extend diplomatic recognition to the new government. U.S. officials became alarmed by the 1950 Sino-Soviet treaty of friendship and the harassment of Americans in China. Truman also chose nonrecognition because vocal Republican critics, the so-called China lobby, pinned Jiang's defeat on Truman. The president argued that despite billions of dollars in American aid, Jiang proved a poor instrument of containment. Not until 1979 did official Sino-American relations resume.

Vietnam's Quest for Independence

Mao's victory in China drew urgent U.S. attention to Indochina, the southeast Asian peninsula held by France for more than half a century. The Japanese wrested control over Indochina during World War II, but still the Vietnamese nationalist movement grew. Their leader, Ho Chi Minh, hoped to use Japan's defeat to assert Vietnamese independence and sought U.S. support. American officials rejected Ho's appeals in favor of restoring French rule, mostly to ensure France's cooperation in the emerging Soviet-American confrontation. Paris warned that U.S. support of the Vietnamese would strengthen the French Communist Party. In addition, the Truman administration feared that Ho Chi Minh was an agent of international communism who would assist Soviet and, after 1949, Chinese expansionism. Overlooking the native roots of the nationalist rebellion against French colonialism, Washington officials interpreted events in Indochina through a Cold War lens.

When war between the Vietminh and France broke out in 1946, the United States initially took a hands-off approach. But when Jiang's regime collapsed in China three years later, the Truman administration in February 1950 recognized the French puppet government of Bao Dai, a playboy and former emperor. To many Vietnamese, the United States thus became in essence a colonial power, an ally of the hated French. Second, in May, the administration agreed to send weapons and assistance to sustain the French in Indochina. From 1945 to 1954, the United States gave $2 billion of the $5 billion that France spent to keep Vietnam within its empire—to no avail (see Chapters 30 and 31). How Vietnam became the site of the United States's longest war is one of the most tragic stories of modern history.

THE KOREAN WAR

Early on June 25, 1950, a large military force of the Democratic People's Republic of Korea (North Korea) moved into the Republic of Korea (South Korea). Colonized by Japan since 1910, Korea was divided in two after Japan's defeat in 1945. Although the Soviets armed the North and the Americans armed the South (U.S. aid had reached $100 million a year), the Korean War began as a civil war. Since its division, the two parts had been skirmishing while antigovernment (and anti-U.S.) guerrilla fighting flared in the South.

Both the North's communist leader, Kim Il Sung, and the South's president, Syngman Rhee, sought to reunify their nation. Kim's military gained strength when tens of thousands returned home in 1949 after serving in Mao's army. President Truman claimed that the Soviets masterminded the North Korean attack.

Actually, Stalin reluctantly approved the attack after Kim predicted an early victory and after Mao backed Kim. When the U.N. Security Council voted to defend South Korea, the Soviet representative was not present to veto because the Soviets were boycotting the United Nations for its refusal to admit the People's Republic of China. During the war, Moscow gave limited aid to North Korea and China, reneging on promised Soviet airpower. Aware of his strategic inferiority vis-à-vis the United States, Stalin did not want war.

U.S. Forces Intervene   The president first ordered General Douglas MacArthur to send arms and troops to South Korea. He did not seek congressional approval—fearing lawmakers would initiate a lengthy debate—and thereby set the precedent of waging war on executive authority alone. After the Security Council voted to assist South Korea, MacArthur became commander of U.N. forces in Korea. Sixteen nations contributed troops, but 40 percent were South Korean and about 50 percent American. In the war's early weeks,

North Korean tanks and superior firepower sent the South Korean army into retreat. The first U.S. soldiers, taking heavy casualties, could not stop the North Korean advance. Within weeks, the South Koreans and Americans were pushed into the tiny Pusan perimeter at South Korea's tip.

General MacArthur planned a daring amphibious landing at heavily fortified Inchon, several hundred miles behind North Korean lines. After U.S. bombs pounded Inchon, marines sprinted ashore on September 15, 1950, liberating the South Korean capital of Seoul and pushing the North Koreans back. Truman meanwhile redefined the U.S. war goal from the containment of North Korea to the reunification of Korea by force.

Chinese Entry into the War

In September, U.N. forces drove deep into North Korea, and U.S. aircraft began strikes against bridges on the Yalu River, the border between North Korea and China. Mao publicly warned that China could not permit the bombing of its transportation links with Korea and would not accept the annihilation of North Korea. MacArthur shrugged off the warnings, and Washington officials agreed, confident that the Soviets were not preparing for war.

MacArthur was right about the Soviets, but wrong about the Chinese. On October 25, the Chinese sent soldiers into the war near the Yalu River. Perhaps to lure U.S. forces into a trap or to signal willingness to negotiate, they pulled back after a successful offensive against South Korean troops. Then, on November 26, tens of thousands of Chinese troops surprised U.S. forces and drove them southward. One U.S. officer described "the men of a whole United States Army fleeing from a battlefield, abandoning their wounded, running for their lives."

Truman's Firing of Macarthur

By 1951 the front had stabilized around the 38th parallel. Both Washington and Moscow welcomed negotiations, but MacArthur called for an attack on China and Jiang's return. Denouncing the concept of limited war (war without nuclear weapons, confined to one place), MacArthur hinted that the president was practicing appeasement. In April, backed by the Joint Chiefs of Staff (the heads of the various armed services), Truman fired MacArthur, who nonetheless returned home a hero. Truman's popularity sagged, but he weathered scattered demands for his impeachment.

Armistice talks began in July 1951, but the fighting continued for two years. Defying the Geneva Prisoners of War Convention (1949), U.S. officials announced that only those North Korean and Chinese prisoners of war (POWs) who wished to go home would be returned. While Americans resisted forced repatriation, the North Koreans denounced forced retention. Both sides undertook reeducation, or brainwashing, on POWs.

Peace Agreement

As the POW issue stalled negotiations, U.S. officials made deliberately vague statements about using atomic weapons in Korea. Not until July 1953 was an armistice signed. Stalin's death in March and new leaders in Moscow and Washington facilitated a settlement. The combatants agreed to hand over the POW question to a special panel of neutral nations, which later gave prisoners their choice of staying or leaving. The North Korean–South Korean borderline was set near the 38th parallel, the prewar boundary, and a demilitarized zone was created between them.

U.S. casualties totaled 54,246 dead and 103,284 wounded. Nearly 5 million Asians died: 2 million North Korean civilians and 500,000 soldiers; 1 million South Korean civilians and 100,000 soldiers; and at least 1 million Chinese soldiers—ranking Korea as one of the costliest wars of the twentieth century.

Consequences of the War

The Korean War carried major domestic political consequences. The failure to achieve victory and the public's impatience undoubtedly helped to elect Republican Dwight Eisenhower to the presidency in 1952, as the former general promised to end the war. The powers of the presidency grew as Congress repeatedly deferred to Truman. The president never asked Congress for a declaration of war, believing that, as commander-in-chief, he had the authority to send troops wherever he wished. He saw no need to consult Congress, except to get the $69.5 billion Korean War bill paid. In addition, Republican lawmakers, including Wisconsin senator Joseph McCarthy, accused Truman and Secretary of State Dean Acheson of being soft on communism; this pushed the administration into an uncompromising position in the negotiations.

The Sino-American hostility generated by the war made U.S. reconciliation with the Beijing government impossible and made South Korea and Formosa major recipients of American foreign aid. The alliance with Japan strengthened as its economy boomed after filling large U.S. procurement orders. Australia and New Zealand joined the United States in a mutual defense agreement, the ANZUS Treaty (1951). The U.S. Army sent four divisions to Europe and initiated plans to rearm West Germany. The military budget jumped from $14 billion in 1949 to $44 billion in 1953; it remained between $35 billion and $44 billion a year throughout the 1950s. The Soviet Union matched this military buildup, resulting in an arms race. Truman's legacy was a highly militarized U.S. foreign policy on a global scale.

UNRELENTING COLD WAR

President Eisenhower and Secretary of State John Foster Dulles largely sustained Truman's Cold War policies. As a World War II general, Eisenhower negotiated with world leaders. After the war, he served as army chief of staff and NATO supreme commander. Dulles had been closely involved with U.S. diplomacy since the first decade of the century.

Eisenhower and Dulles

Eisenhower and Dulles accepted the Cold War consensus about the threat of communism and the need for global vigilance. Although Democrats promoted an image of Eisenhower as a bumbling, aging hero, deferring most foreign policy matters to Dulles, the president in fact commanded the policymaking process and occasionally tamed the more hawkish proposals of Dulles and Vice President Richard Nixon. Even so, the secretary of state was influential. Few Cold Warriors rivaled Dulles's impassioned anticommunism, often expressed in biblical terms. A graduate of Princeton and George Washington Universities, Dulles assisted Woodrow Wilson at Versailles and later became a senior partner in a prestigious Wall Street law firm and an officer of the Federal Council of Churches. Dulles impressed people as arrogant and unwilling to compromise, a successful diplomatic strategy for getting others to back down. His assertion that neutrality was an "immoral and short-sighted conception" did not sit well with Third World leaders, who resented being forced to choose between East and West.

Dulles conceded much to the anticommunist McCarthyites, who claimed that the State Department was infested with communists. The State Department's chief security officer targeted homosexuals and other "incompatibles," making few distinctions between New Dealers and communists. Dulles thus forced many talented officers out of the Foreign Service, among them, Asia specialists. "The wrong done," the journalist Theodore A. White wrote, "was to poke out the eyes and ears of the State Department on Asian affairs, to blind American foreign policy."

Massive Retaliation

Considering containment too defensive, Dulles called instead for liberation, freeing eastern Europe from Soviet control. *Massive retaliation* was the administration's plan for the nuclear obliteration of the Soviet state or its assumed client, the People's Republic of China, if either one took aggressive action.

Militarily, Eisenhower and Dulles emphasized airpower and nuclear weaponry. The president's preference for heavy weapons stemmed partly from his desire to trim the federal budget (and get more bang for the buck, as the saying went). Galvanized by the successful test of the world's first hydrogen bomb in November 1952, Eisenhower oversaw a massive stockpiling of nuclear weapons—from 1,200 at the start of his presidency to 22,229 at the end. With this huge military arsenal, the United States could practice *brinkmanship*: not backing down, even if it meant taking the nation to the brink of war. Eisenhower also popularized the *domino theory*: that small, weak, neighboring nations would fall to communism like a row of dominoes unless they were supported by the United States.

CIA as Foreign Policy Instrument

Eisenhower increasingly utilized the Central Intelligence Agency as an instrument of foreign policy. The CIA put foreign leaders (such as King Hussein of Jordan) on its payroll; subsidized foreign labor unions, newspapers, and political parties; planted false stories in newspapers through disinformation projects; and trained foreign military officers in counterrevolution. It hired American journalists and professors, used business executives as fronts, and conducted experiments on unsuspecting Americans to determine the effects of mind control drugs (the MKULTRA program). The CIA also launched covert operations (including assassination schemes) to subvert Third World governments, helping to overthrow the governments of Iran (1953) and Guatemala (1954).

The U.S. intelligence community followed the principle of plausible deniability: covert operations should be conducted in such a way and the decisions that launched them concealed so well that the president could deny any knowledge of them. Thus President Eisenhower disavowed any U.S. role in Guatemala, even though he ordered the operation. He and his successor, John F. Kennedy, also denied instructing the CIA to assassinate Cuba's Fidel Castro, whose regime after 1959 became stridently anti-American.

Nuclear Buildup

Leaders in Moscow quickly became aware of Eisenhower's covert actions, as well as his stockpiling of nuclear weapons. They increased their intelligence and tested their first H-bomb in 1953. Four years later, they fired the world's first intercontinental ballistic missile (ICBM) and propelled the satellite *Sputnik* into outer space. Americans felt more vulnerable to air attack, even though in 1957 the United States had 2,460 strategic weapons and a nuclear stockpile of 5,543, compared with the Soviet Union's 102 and 650. The administration deployed intermediate-range missiles in Europe, targeted against the Soviet Union. At the end of 1960 the United States added Polaris missile–bearing submarines to its navy. To foster future technological advancement, the National Aeronautics and Space Administration (NASA) was created in 1958.

Overall, Eisenhower sought to avoid military confrontations with the Soviet Union and China, content to follow Truman's containment of communism. Eisenhower refused to use nuclear weapons and proved more reluctant than other Cold War presidents to send soldiers into battle. Convinced that the struggle against Moscow would be largely decided by international public opinion, he wanted to win the hearts and minds of people overseas. The People-to-People campaign, launched in 1956, used ordinary Americans and nongovernmental organizations to enhance the international image of the United States.

Sometimes the propaganda war was waged on the Soviets' turf. In 1959 Vice President Richard Nixon traveled to Moscow for a U.S. products fair. In the display of a modern American kitchen, Nixon extolled capitalist consumerism, while Soviet premier Nikita Khrushchev, Stalin's successor, touted the merits of communism. The encounter became famous as the kitchen debate.

Rebellion in Hungary

In February 1956, Khrushchev called for peaceful coexistence between capitalists and communists, denounced Stalin, and suggested that Moscow would tolerate different brands of communism. Testing Khrushchev's permissiveness, revolts erupted in Poland and Hungary. After a new Hungarian government in 1956 withdrew from the Warsaw Pact (the Soviet military alliance formed in 1955 with communist countries of eastern Europe), Soviet troops and tanks crushed the rebellion.

Although the Eisenhower administration's propaganda encouraged liberation efforts, U.S. officials could not aid the rebels without igniting a world war. Instead, they promised only to welcome more Hungarian immigrants than American quota laws allowed. The West could have reaped some propaganda advantage had not British, French, and Israeli troops—U.S. allies—invaded Egypt during the Suez crisis just before the Soviets smashed the Hungarian uprising.

The People-to-People Campaign

Just after the Cold War began, U.S. officials determined that the Soviet-American confrontation was as much psychological and ideological as military and economic. One result was the People-to-People campaign, a state-private venture initiated by the United States Information Agency in 1956, which aimed to win the hearts and minds of people around the world. In this program, U.S. propaganda experts used ordinary Americans, businesses, civic organizations, labor groups, and women's clubs to promote confidence abroad in American goodness. The People-to-People campaign, one USIA pamphlet said, made "every man an ambassador."

Campaign activities resembled the home-front mobilization efforts of World War II. Americans were told that $30 could send a ninety-nine-volume portable library of American books to schools and libraries overseas. Publishers donated magazines and books for free distribution to foreign countries. People-to-People committees organized sister-city affiliations and pen-pal letter exchanges, hosted exchange students, and organized traveling People-to-People delegations. The travelers were urged to behave like goodwill ambassadors and "help overcome any feeling that America is a land that thinks money can buy everything."

Camp Fire Girls in more than three thousand communities took photographs on the theme "This is our home. This is how we live. These are my People." The photographs were sent to girls in Latin America, Africa, Asia, and the Middle East. The Hobbies Committee connected people with interests in radio, photography, coins, stamps, and horticulture.

The persistence to this day of the widespread impression that Americans are a provincial, materialistic people prompts skepticism about the People-to-People campaign's success. But alongside this negative image is a positive one that sees Americans as admirably open, friendly, optimistic, and pragmatic. Whatever role the People-to-People campaign played in the larger Cold War struggle, it certainly linked ordinary Americans more closely to people around the world.

This Alice Nast painting of two girls—one from the United States and one from Taiwan—was commissioned by the Kansas City chapter of People to People and the Kansas City/Tainan Sister City Committee. The painting was presented to the mayor of Tainan in September 1994, prior to the 11th Worldwide Conference of the People-to-People International. (Courtesy of People to People International, Kansas City, Missouri, www.ptpi.org)

The turmoil barely subsided when the divided city of Berlin again became a Cold War flash point. The Soviets railed against U.S. bombers capable of carrying nuclear warheads in West Germany, and they complained that West Berlin had become an escape route for East Germans. In 1958 Khrushchev announced that the Soviet Union would recognize East German control of all of Berlin unless the United States and its allies began talks on German reunification and rearmament. The United States refused; Khrushchev backed down but promised to press the issue again.

U-2 Incident

Two weeks before a summit in Paris on May 1, 1960, a U-2 spy plane carrying high-powered cameras crashed 1,200 miles inside the Soviet Union. Moscow admitted shooting down the plane and promptly displayed captured CIA pilot Francis Gary Powers and the pictures he had snapped of Soviet military sites. Khrushchev demanded an apology for the U.S. violation of Soviet airspace. When Washington refused, the Soviets left the Paris summit.

Meanwhile, both sides kept a wary eye on the People's Republic of China. Despite evidence of a widening Sino-Soviet split, most U.S. officials treated communism as a monolithic movement. In 1954, in a dispute over Jinmen (Quemoy) and Mazu (Matsu), two tiny islands off the Chinese coast, the United States and the People's Republic of China lurched toward the brink. Taiwan's Jiang Jieshi used these islands to raid the mainland. Communist China bombarded the islands in 1954. Thinking that U.S. credibility was at stake, Eisenhower defended the outposts, hinting that he might use nuclear weapons. "Let's keep the Reds guessing," advised John Foster Dulles.

Formosa Resolution

In early 1955, Congress passed the Formosa Resolution, authorizing the president to deploy troops to defend Formosa and adjoining islands. In so doing, Congress formally surrendered to the president what it informally gave up in the 1950 Korea decision: the constitutional power to declare war. The crisis passed, but war loomed again in 1958 over Jinmen and Mazu. This time, as Jiang withdrew some troops, China relaxed its bombardments. But Eisenhower's nuclear threats persuaded the Chinese that they, too, needed nuclear arms. In 1964 China exploded its first nuclear bomb.

THE STRUGGLE FOR THE THIRD WORLD

In much of the Third World, the process of decolonization that began during World War I accelerated after World War II, when the economically wracked imperial countries proved incapable of resisting their colonies' demands for freedom. From 1943 to 1994, 125 countries became independent (including the former Soviet republics that departed the Soviet Union in 1991) (see Map 28.2). The emergence of so many new states after the 1940s shook the foundations of the international system. In the traditional U.S. sphere of influence, Latin America, nationalists once again challenged Washington's dominance.

Interests in the Third World

By the late 1940s, Soviet-American rivalry shifted increasingly to the Third World. The new nations could buy U.S. goods, supply strategic raw materials, and invite investments (more than one-third of the United States's private foreign investments were in Third World countries in 1959). Both great powers looked to these new states for votes in the United Nations and for military and intelligence bases. But many new nations sought to end the economic, military, and cultural hegemony of the West

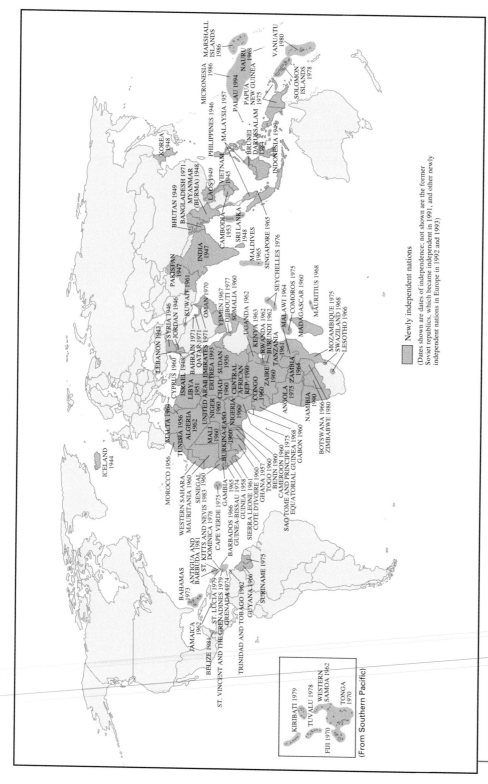

Map 28.2 The Rise of the Third World: Newly Independent Nations Since 1943

Accelerated by World War II, decolonization liberated many peoples from imperial rule. New nations emerged in the postwar international system dominated by the Cold War rivalry of the United States and the Soviet Union. Many newly independent states became targets of great-power intrigue but chose nonalignment in the Cold War.

and played the two superpowers against each other to garner more aid and arms. U.S. interventions—military and otherwise—in the Third World, American leaders believed, became necessary to impress Moscow with Washington's might and to counter other potential threats to U.S. interests.

To thwart nationalist, radical, and communist challenges, more than 90 percent of U.S. foreign aid was going to developing nations by 1961. Washington also allied with undemocratic but anticommunist regimes, meddled in civil wars, and unleashed CIA covert operations. When some of the larger Third World states—notably India, Ghana, Egypt, and Indonesia—refused to take sides in the Cold War, Secretary of State Dulles declared that neutralism was a step toward communism, insisting with Eisenhower that every nation should take sides.

American leaders argued that technologically "backward" Third World countries needed western-induced capitalist development to enjoy economic growth and political moderation. U.S. officials ascribed stereotyped race-, age-, and gender-based characteristics to Third World peoples, seeing them as emotional and irrational, and therefore dependent on the fatherly tutelage of the United States.

Racism and Segregation as U.S. Handicaps

Racism influenced U.S. relations with Third World countries. In 1955 G. L. Mehta, the Indian ambassador to the United States, was refused service in the whites-only section of a restaurant at Houston International Airport. The insult stung, as did similar indignities experienced by other Third World diplomats. Dulles apologized to Mehta and thought racial segregation in the United States was a "major international hazard," spoiling U.S. efforts to win friends in Third World countries and giving the Soviets a propaganda advantage.

Thus, as the U.S. attorney general noted, race relations "furnished grist for the Communist propaganda mills." When the Court announced its *Brown* decision in 1954, the government quickly broadcast news of the desegregation order around the world in thirty-five languages on its *Voice of America* overseas radio network. But the problem did not go away. For example, after the 1957 Little Rock crisis, Dulles remarked that racial bigotry was "ruining our foreign policy." Still, when a Department of State office countered Soviet propaganda with a 1958 World's Fair exhibit in Brussels titled "The Unfinished Work"—on U.S. strides toward desegregation—southern conservatives kicked up such a furor that the Eisenhower administration closed the display.

U.S. hostility toward revolution also obstructed the quest for influence in the Third World. In the twentieth century, the United States opposed revolutions in Mexico, China, Russia, Cuba, Vietnam, Nicaragua, and Iran, among other nations. Many Third World revolutions arose against the United States's Cold War allies and threatened American investments, markets, and military bases. Preferring to maintain the status quo, the United States usually supported its European allies or the conservative, propertied classes in the Third World.

Development and Modernization

Yet idealism inspired U.S. policy. Believing that Third World peoples craved modernization and the U.S. economic model of private enterprise, U.S. policymakers launched various development projects. Such projects promised sustained economic growth, prosperity, and stability, which the benefactors hoped would undermine radicalism. In the 1950s, the Carnegie, Ford, and Rockefeller Foundations worked with the U.S. Agency for International Development (AID) to sponsor a Green Revolution promoting agricultural production. The Rockefeller Foundation supported foreign universities' efforts to train national leaders committed to nonradical development.

To persuade Third World peoples to abandon radical doctrines, U.S. leaders created propaganda campaigns. The United States Information Agency (USIA), founded in 1953, used films, radio broadcasts, the magazine *Free World*, exhibitions, and libraries (in 162 cities worldwide by 1961) to trumpet the theme of People's Capitalism. Citing the United States's economic success—contrasted with "slave-labor" conditions in the Soviet Union—it showcased well-paid U.S. workers, political democracy, and religious freedom. To counter ugly pictures of segregation, the USIA applauded success stories of individual African Americans, such as boxers Floyd Patterson and Sugar Ray Robinson. In 1960, some 13.8 million people visited U.S. pavilions abroad.

Undoubtedly the American way of life had appeal for some Third World peoples. Hollywood movies offered enticing glimpses of middle-class materialism, and American films dominated many overseas markets. Blue jeans, advertising billboards, and soft drinks flooded foreign societies. Foreigners envied and resented Americans for wasting so much while poorer peoples went without. The people of many countries, moreover, resented the profits that U.S. corporations extracted from them. Americans were often blamed for the persistent poverty of the developing world, even though the leaders of those nations made decisions hindering their own progress, such as pouring millions of dollars into their militaries while their people needed food. Nonetheless, anti-American resentments manifested in late 1950s' attacks on USIA libraries in Calcutta, India; Beirut, Lebanon; and Bogotá, Colombia.

Intervention in Guatemala

When the more benign techniques of containment—aid, trade, and cultural relations—proved insufficient to prompt Third World nations to side with the United States in the Cold War, the Eisenhower administration pressed harder. Guatemala was an early test case. In 1951 the leftist Jacobo Arbenz Guzmán was elected president of Guatemala, a poor country where the largest land-holder was the U.S.-owned United Fruit Company (UF). It owned 3 million acres across Latin America and operated railroads, ports, ships, and telecommunications facilities. Arbenz expropriated UF's uncultivated land and offered compensation. The company charged that Arbenz posed a communist threat. The CIA began a secret plot to overthrow Arbenz, who turned to Moscow for military aid, thus reinforcing U.S. suspicions. The CIA airlifted arms into Guatemala, and in mid-1954, CIA-supported Guatemalans struck from Honduras. U.S. planes bombed the capital city, driving Arbenz from power. The new pro-American regime returned UF's land, but an ensuing civil war staggered the nation for decades.

The Cuban Revolution and Fidel Castro

Eisenhower was apprehensive as turmoil gripped Cuba in the late 1950s. In early 1959, Fidel Castro's rebels, or *barbudos* ("bearded ones"), driven by anti-American nationalism, ousted Fulgencio Batista, a long-time U.S. ally whose corrupt, dictatorial regime turned Havana into a haven for gambling, prostitution, and organized crime. Cubans resented U.S. domination since the early twentieth century, when the Platt Amendment compromised their independence. Castro sought to break the U.S. grasp on Cuban trade and roll back American business, which had invested some $1 billion on the island.

In early 1960, after Cuba signed a trade treaty with the Soviet Union, Eisenhower ordered the CIA to organize Cuban exiles to overthrow the Castro government. The agency also plotted the Cuban leader's assassination. When the president drastically cut U.S. sugar purchases, Castro seized North American–owned companies that had not yet been nationalized. Castro appealed to the Soviet Union, which offered loans and expanded trade. Before leaving office in early 1961, Eisenhower broke diplomatic relations with Cuba and advised president-elect John F. Kennedy to advance plans for the invasion, which came—and failed—in early 1961.

Arab-Israeli Conflict

In the Middle East, meanwhile, ongoing tensions between Arabs and Jews posed additional challenges (see Map 33.2). Before the end of World War II, only France and Britain had been concerned with this region of the world. But the dissolution of empires and the rise of Cold War tensions drew Washington in, as did tensions in British-held Palestine. From 1945 to 1947, Britain tried to enlist U.S. officials to help resolve how to split Palestine between Arabs and Jews. The Truman administration declined, and the British in 1947 turned the issue over to the United Nations, which voted to partition Palestine into separate Arab and Jewish states. Arab leaders opposed the decision, but in May 1948 Jewish leaders announced the creation of Israel.

The United States, which lobbied to secure the U.N. vote, extended recognition to the new state mere minutes after its founding. A moral conviction that Jews deserved a homeland after the Holocaust and that Zionism would create a democratic Israel influenced Truman, as did the belief that Jewish votes might swing some states to the Democrats in the 1948 election. These beliefs trumped concerns that Arab oil producers might turn against the United States. The Soviet Union recognized the new nation, but Israel kept Moscow at arm's length. Palestinian Arabs, displaced from land they considered theirs, joined with Israel's Arab neighbors to make immediate war on the new state. The Israelis fought for six months until a U.N.-backed truce was called.

Thereafter, U.S. Middle East policy centered on ensuring Israel's survival and cementing ties with Arab oil producers. U.S. companies produced about half of the region's petroleum in the 1950s. Oil-rich Iran, became a special friend, as its shah granted U.S. oil companies a 40 percent interest in a new petroleum consortium in return for CIA help in the successful overthrow, in 1953, of his rival, Mohammed Mossadegh.

U.S. officials faced a more formidable foe in Egypt's Gamal Abdul Nasser, a towering figure in a pan-Arabic movement who vowed to expel the British from the Suez Canal and Israelis from Palestine. The United States wished neither to anger the Arabs, for fear of losing valuable oil supplies, nor to alienate its ally Israel, supported at home by politically active American Jews. When Nasser declared neutrality in the Cold War, Dulles lost patience.

Suez Crisis

In 1956 the United States reneged on its offer to help Egypt finance the Aswan Dam, which would provide inexpensive electricity and water for Nile valley farmland. Nasser responded by nationalizing the British-owned Suez Canal, intending to use its profits to build the dam. Fully 75 percent of western Europe's oil came from the Middle East, most of it via the Suez Canal. Fearing an interruption, the British and French conspired with Israel to bring down Nasser. On October 29, 1956, the Israelis invaded Suez, joined two days later by British and French forces.

Eisenhower fumed. The United States's allies had not consulted him, and the president feared the invasion would cause Nasser to seek help from the Soviets, inviting them into the Middle East. Eisenhower sternly demanded that London, Paris, and Tel Aviv pull their troops out, and they did. Egypt took possession of the canal, the Soviets built the Aswan Dam, and Nasser became a hero. The United States countered Nasser by supporting the notoriously corrupt conservative King Ibn Saud of Saudi Arabia, who renewed America's lease of an air base.

Eisenhower Doctrine

Washington officials worried that a power vacuum existed in the Middle East and that the Soviets might fill it. To protect U.S. interests, the president proclaimed in the 1957 Eisenhower Doctrine that the United States would intervene in the Middle East if any government threatened by a communist takeover asked for help. In 1958 fourteen thousand American troops scrambled to quell an internal political dispute in Lebanon that Washington feared might be exploited by pro-Nasser groups or communists.

Cold War concerns also drove Eisenhower's policy toward Vietnam. Despite substantial U.S. aid, the French lost steadily to the Vietminh. Finally, in early 1954, Ho's forces surrounded the French fortress at Dienbienphu in northwest Vietnam (see Map 30.2). The United States had advised and bankrolled the French, but had not committed troops to the war.

Eisenhower pressed the British to help form a coalition to address the Indochinese crisis, but they refused. At home, influential members of Congress—including Lyndon Baines Johnson of Texas, who as president would wage large-scale war in Vietnam—told Eisenhower they wanted no more Koreas and warned him against any U.S. military commitment. The issue became moot on May 7, when French defenders at Dienbienphu surrendered.

Geneva Accords on Vietnam

Peace talks, already under way in Geneva, brought Cold War and nationalist contenders together—the United States, the Soviet Union, Britain, the People's Republic of China, Laos, Cambodia, and the competing Vietnamese regimes of Bao Dai and Ho Chi Minh. The 1954 Geneva accords, signed by France and Ho's Democratic Republic of Vietnam, temporarily divided Vietnam at the 17th parallel; Ho's government was confined to the North, Bao Dai's to the South. The 17th parallel was meant as a truce line, not a national boundary; the country was scheduled to be reunified after national elections in 1956. Meanwhile, neither North nor South was to join a military alliance or permit foreign bases on its soil.

Confident that the Geneva agreements would mean communist victory, the United States tried to undermine them. Soon after the conference, a CIA team entered Vietnam and undertook secret operations against the North, including commando raids across the 17th parallel. In the South, the United States helped Ngo Dinh Diem push Bao Dai aside and inaugurate the Republic of Vietnam. Diem was a dedicated nationalist and anticommunist, but he had little mass support. When Ho and world leaders pressed for national elections, Diem and Eisenhower refused, fearing that the popular Vietminh leader would win. From 1955 to 1961, the Diem government received more than $1 billion in U.S. aid, most of it military. U.S. advisers trained Diem's army, and American agriculturalists improved crops. Diem's Saigon regime became dependent on the United States for its existence.

National Liberation Front

Diem proved a difficult ally. He abolished village elections and appointed people beholden to him. He threw dissenters in jail and shut down newspapers criticizing him. Noncommunists and communists alike struck back at Diem's repressive government. In Hanoi, Ho's government in the late 1950s sent aid to southern insurgents, who assassinated hundreds of Diem's village officials. In late 1960, southern communists, acting at Hanoi's direction, organized the National Liberation Front (NLF), known as the Vietcong. The Vietcong attracted other anti-Diem groups in the South. The Eisenhower administration, aware of Diem's shortcomings, affirmed its commitment to an independent, noncommunist South Vietnam.

Summary

The United States emerged from World War II as the preeminent world power. Washington officials nevertheless worried that the unstable international system, an unfriendly Soviet Union, and the decolonizing Third World could upset U.S. plans for the postwar peace. Locked with the Soviet Union in a Cold War, U.S. leaders marshaled their nation's superior resources to influence other countries. Foreign economic aid, atomic diplomacy, military alliances, client states, covert operations, propaganda, and cultural infiltration became the instruments of the Cold War, which began as a conflict over the Europe's future but soon encompassed the globe.

The United States's international leadership was welcomed by those who feared Stalin's intentions. The reconstruction of former enemies Japan and West Germany helped those nations recover swiftly and become staunch members of the western alliance. But U.S. policy also sparked resistance. Communist countries condemned financial and atomic diplomacy, while Third World nations sought to undermine the United States's European allies and sometimes identified the United States as an imperial coconspirator. Occasionally even the United States's allies bristled at a United States that boldly proclaimed itself economic master and global policeman.

At home, critics protested that Presidents Truman and Eisenhower exaggerated the communist threat, wasting U.S. assets on immoral foreign ventures. Still, these presidents and their successors held to creating a nonradical, capitalist, free-trade international order. Determined to contain Soviet expansion, fearful of domestic

The National Security State

For decades, the United States's Cold War religion has been national security; its texts, the Truman Doctrine, the X article, and NSC-68; and its cathedral, the national security state. The word *state* in this case means "civil government." During the Cold War, embracing preparedness for total war, the U.S. government essentially transformed itself into a huge military headquarters that interlocked with corporations and universities.

Overseen by the president and his National Security Council, the national security state's core, once called the National Military Establishment, in 1949 became the Department of Defense. This department is a leading employer; its payroll by 2007 included 1.4 million people on active duty and almost 600,000 civilian personnel. Almost 700,000 of these troops and civilians served overseas in 177 countries. Although national defense spending declined after the Cold War, it never fell below $290 billion. In the aftermath of the 9/11 terrorist attacks and the invasion of Iraq, the military budget rose again, reaching $439 billion in 2007. That does not include tens of billions of dollars in supplementary funds allocated by Congress to pay for operations in Afghanistan and Iraq.

Joining the Department of Defense as instruments of national security policy were the Joint Chiefs of Staff, the Central Intelligence Agency, and dozens more government bodies. The focus of these entities was finding the best means to combat real and potential threats from foreign governments. But what about threats from within? The terrorist attacks of September 2001 made starkly clear that enemies existed who, while perhaps beholden to a foreign entity, launched their attacks from inside the nation's borders.

In 2002 President George W. Bush created the Department of Homeland Security (DHS), with 170,000 employees encompassing all or part of twenty-two agencies, including the Coast Guard, the Customs Service, the Federal Emergency Management Administration (FEMA), and the Internal Revenue Service. It would involve the biggest overhaul of the federal bureaucracy since the creation of the Department of Defense, and it signified a more expansive notion of national security. By 2006, the number of DHS employees reached 190,000.

In 1961 President Eisenhower warned against a military-industrial complex, while others feared a warfare state. Still, the national security state remained vigorous in the early twenty-first century, a lasting legacy of the initial Cold War period for a people and a nation.

charges of being soft on communism, they enlarged the U.S. sphere of influence and held the line against the Soviet Union and the People's Republic of China and against revolution everywhere. One consequence was a dramatic increase in presidential power over foreign affairs—what the historian Arthur M. Schlesinger Jr. called "the Imperial Presidency."

The United States' globalist perspective prompted Americans to interpret troubles in the developing world as Cold War conflicts, inspired by Soviet-backed communists. The intensity of the Cold War obscured for Americans the indigenous roots of most Third World troubles, as the wars in Korea and Vietnam attested. Nor could the United States abide developing nations' drive for economic independence—for controlling their own raw materials and economies. Intertwined in the global economy as importer, exporter, and investor, the United States read challenges from this periphery as threats to the American standard of living. Overall, the rise of the Third World introduced new actors to the world stage, challenging the bipolarity of the international system. All the while, the threat of nuclear war unsettled Americans and foreigners alike.

Chapter Review

FROM ALLIES TO ADVERSARIES

Was the Cold War inevitable?

Historians aren't sure that it had to be. Aside from their alliance during World War II, the United States and Soviet Union had a tense relationship dating back to the 1917 Bolshevik Revolution. Since leaders of each country did not want war, their decades-old "cold peace" could have continued and inspired future cooperation. However, some believe that each nation's desire to fill the power vacuum left by the World War II defeat of Germany and Japan, along with their disparate goals and political ideologies, led individual leaders to make decisions that exacerbated tensions to the point of Cold War. While both nations clashed on most fronts by 1946, some argue that leaders could have done more to keep diplomatic negotiations open. Both countries backed different groups in Iran, could not agree on German reunification, and took many other opposing foreign policy positions. And the United States's nuclear monopoly only escalated strife first because the Soviets believed the United States used their nuclear superiority to bully them into concessions, and later when the Soviets had their own nuclear bomb, by advancing an arms race.

CONTAINMENT IN ACTION

Was the U.S. containment policy successful?

In 1947, Truman and his aides adopted what they called the containment policy, which meant forcefully confronting the Soviets every time they attempted to spread communism beyond their borders. The policy was successful in building an international network by aiding European reconstruction and having communists removed from governments, as in Italy and France. The policy also led the United States to a twelve-nation mutual defense treaty in 1949 and the establishment of NATO (the North Atlantic Treaty Organization). Truman hoped NATO would keep Europeans from turning communist and would deter Soviets from expansion. But containment failed when China, the world's most populous nation, became communist in 1949. Containment similarly could not keep the Soviet Union from becoming a nuclear power.

THE COLD WAR IN ASIA

How did the Cold War turn "hot" in Asia?

U.S. foreign policy focused on containing Soviet communism from spreading into Asia. That often led to decisions that alienated potential allies. The United States rejected an offer for diplomatic talks with China, and later refused diplomatic recognition to the People's Republic of China in 1949, fearing the nation was ultimately a likely Soviet ally. After the Sino-Soviet treaty of friendship in 1950, U.S. policy focused on keeping Indochina from falling to the communists. Rather than recognizing tensions in Vietnam as a rebellion against French colonial rule,

Truman and his aides blamed the Soviets for stirring up insurrection to expand communism. As such, the United States lent military aid, then arms, to the French, becoming increasingly engaged in what would develop into the Vietnam War, America's longest conflict.

THE KOREAN WAR

What were the consequences of the Korean War for the United States?

Along with heavy casualties (54,246 Americans died and 103,284 were wounded), the conflict greatly influenced politics in the United States. First, the powers of the U.S. president expanded, as Truman never sought congressional permission to declare war, believing that as commander-in-chief, he could dispatch troops at will. Consequently, he only turned to Congress for funding, and Congress also deferred to Truman rather than exercise its authority. As Republicans accused Truman of being soft on communism, he took an increasingly uncompromising position in negotiations for peace. He also engaged in a contest over military buildup with the Soviet Union. But public frustration over U.S. failure in the war led to Eisenhower's election in 1952. Finally, the war generated increased hostilities between the United States and China and strengthened the U.S. alliance with Japan.

UNRELENTING COLD WAR

How did Dulles and Eisenhower raise the stakes in the Cold War?

While President Eisenhower and Secretary of State Dulles continued the containment policy, they also added more aggressive tactics to their Cold War politics. Militarily, Eisenhower preferred increasing the nuclear arsenal, seeing it as a way to get more bang for the buck. Possessing the atomic bomb and the hydrogen bomb by 1952 enabled the United States to practice brinkmanship, not backing down against the spread of communism, even to the brink of war. Eisenhower also popularized the domino theory—that small, neighboring countries would fall to communism like dominoes without U.S. assistance. Despite his aggressive stand, however, Eisenhower was less likely to engage in war than other presidents. Instead, he increasingly utilized the Central Intelligence Agency, training foreign military officers in counterrevolutions, subverting Third World governments, and attempting to influence international opinion with disinformation and pro-U.S. campaigns. Brinkmanship and espionage prompted a similar Soviet response, as they tested their own H-bomb in 1953, fired the first intercontinental ballistic missile in 1957, and increased their intelligence operations—all of which made Americans feel increasingly vulnerable to attack.

THE STRUGGLE FOR THE THIRD WORLD

How did racism in America interfere with U.S. leaders' ability to win Cold War allies among developing nations?

Racism directly influenced U.S. relations with Third World countries, whose leaders were often people of color. With segregation and discrimination persisting in the United States, it was difficult for U.S. leaders to claim a moral advantage over communism and win friends in new and developing nations. Matters were made worse when there were incidents of discrimination against visiting leaders, as when Indian ambassador G. L Mehta was refused service in the whites-only section of a Houston restaurant. To counter this image, the U.S. government broadcast the positive news of the Supreme Court's desegregation ruling in the *Brown vs. Board of Education* in 1954, using its Voice of America overseas radio network to get the word out around the world in thirty-five languages.

SUGGESTIONS FOR FURTHER READING

Campbell Craig, *Destroying the Village: Eisenhower and Thermonuclear War* (1998)

Nick Cullather, *Secret History: The CIA's Classified Account of Its Operations in Guatemala, 1952–1954* (1999)

Mary L. Dudziak, *Cold War Civil Rights: Race and the Image of American Democracy* (2000)

John Lewis Gaddis, *Strategies of Containment*, 2d ed. (2005)

Walter LaFeber, *America, Russia, and the Cold War, 1945–2006*, 10th ed. (2006)

Douglas Little, *American Orientalism: The United States and the Middle East Since 1945* (2002)

Fredrik Logevall, *The Origins of the Vietnam War* (2001)

Robert J. McMahon, *The Limits of Empire: The United States and Southeast Asia Since World War II* (1999)

Geoffrey Roberts, *Stalin's Wars: From World War to Cold War, 1939–1953* (2007)

Marc Trachtenberg, *A Constructed Peace: The Making of the European Settlement, 1945–1963* (1999)

CHAPTER 29

America at Midcentury

CHAPTER OUTLINE

Shaping Postwar America

Domestic Politics in the Cold War Era

Cold War Fears and Anticommunism

The Struggle for Civil Rights

Creating a Middle-Class Nation

Men, Women, and Youth at Midcentury

   LINKS TO THE WORLD:
Barbie

The Limits of the Middle-Class Nation

   **LEGACY FOR A PEOPLE AND
A NATION:** The Pledge
of Allegiance

Summary

E venings after supper, when the sticky heat of Georgia summer days ebbed, families on Nancy Circle enjoyed a walk. Parents chatted as children played.

In 1959 the twenty houses on Nancy Circle were a couple of years old. Each stood on land that once belonged to the Cherokees, in a development carved from the old Campbell plantation, near where Confederate troops tried to stop General William Tecumseh Sherman's Union Army from attacking Atlanta. Slaves picked cotton there a century before, but no African Americans lived in those suburban homes.

Nancy Circle was part of a new suburban development in Smyrna, Georgia, northwest of Atlanta, but few of its residents worked in the city. Instead, most traveled to the massive Lockheed Georgia airplane plant created largely by Cold War defense spending. Born of the Cold War and the baby boom, this suburb's three-bedroom homes sold for about $17,000, making them affordable to young families.

Children played in each other's houses, and women gathered to drink coffee and gossip after men left for work. There were aerospace engineers, three career military men, an auto mechanic, and a musician. Only two women held paid jobs—one with almost-grown children taught second grade; the other was a divorced secretary. People were suspicious of her. Two war brides—one Japanese and one German—lived in the neighborhood. The Japanese woman spoke little English; the German woman taught the girls in the neighborhood to crochet.

The people who lived on Nancy Circle read magazines criticizing the homogeneity and conformity of suburban life, but it didn't feel that way to them. On this street, people from deep in Appalachia lived next to people who grew up in crowded city apartments, and women who'd done graduate work baked

This icon will direct you to interactive activities and study materials on A People And A Nation, Brief Edition website: **www.cengage.com/history/norton/ peoplenationbrief8e**

Chronology

1945	World War II ends.
1946	Marriage and birth rates skyrocket, creating baby boom.
	More than 1 million veterans enroll in colleges under GI Bill.
	More than 5 million U.S. workers go on strike.
1947	Taft-Hartley Act limits power of unions.
	Truman orders loyalty investigation of 3 million government employees.
	Mass-production techniques are used to build Levittown houses.
1948	Truman issues executive order desegregating armed forces and federal government.
	Truman is elected president.
1949	Soviet Union explodes atomic bomb.
	National Housing Act promises decent housing for all Americans.
1950	Korean War begins.
	McCarthy alleges communists in government.
	Treaty of Detroit creates model for new labor-management relations.
1951	Race riots occur in Cicero, Illinois, as white residents oppose residential integration.

1952	Eisenhower is elected president.
1953	Korean War ends.
	Congress adopts termination policy for Native American tribes.
	Rosenbergs are executed as spies.
1954	*Brown v. Board of Education* decision reverses separate-but-equal doctrine.
	Senate condemns McCarthy.
1955	Montgomery bus boycott begins.
1956	Highway Act launches interstate highway system.
	Eisenhower is reelected.
	Elvis Presley appears on *Ed Sullivan Show*.
1957	King is elected first president of Southern Christian Leadership Conference.
	School desegregation crisis occurs in Little Rock, Arkansas.
	Congress passes Civil Rights Act.
	Soviet Union launches *Sputnik*.
1958	Congress passes National Defense Education Act.
1959	Alaska and Hawai'i become forty-ninth and fiftieth states.

cookies with women who had not finished high school. These new suburbanites were creating a new middle-class culture. Having grown up with the Great Depression and world war, these new suburbanites believed they had found good lives.

The United States had emerged from World War II stronger and more prosperous. Europe and Asia had been devastated, but America's farms, cities, and factories were intact. U.S. production capacity increased during the war, and the fight against fascism gave Americans a unified purpose. But memories of sixteen years of depression and war would continue to shape the choices Americans made in their private lives, domestic policies, and relations with the world.

In the postwar era, the federal government's actions and individuals' choices profoundly reconfigured American society. Postwar social policies that sent millions of veterans to college on the GI Bill, linked the nation with high-speed interstate highways, fostered the growth of suburbs and the Sunbelt, and disrupted regional isolation helped to create a middle-class culture encompassing an unprecedented majority of citizens. Countless individual decisions—to go to college, marry young, have a large family, move to the suburbs, start a business—were made possible by federal initiatives.

Americans in the postwar era defined a new American Dream—one that centered on the family, material comfort and consumption, and a shared sense of belonging to a common culture. Nonetheless, almost one-quarter of Americans did not share in postwar prosperity, and they were nearly invisible to the middle-class majority. Rural poverty continued, and inner cities became increasingly impoverished as more-affluent Americans moved to the suburbs and new migrants—poor African American and white southerners, new immigrants from Mexico and Puerto Rico, and Native Americans resettled by the federal government from tribal lands—arrived.

As class and ethnicity became less important in suburbia, race continued to divide Americans. African Americans faced discrimination nationwide, but the war was a turning point in their struggle for equal rights. African American initiatives increasingly led to important federal actions, including the Supreme Court's school desegregation decision in *Brown v. Board of Education*. In 1955 the yearlong Montgomery bus boycott launched the modern civil rights movement.

The economic boom that began with the end of the war lasted twenty-five years, bringing new prosperity to America. Although fears—of nuclear war and of returning hard times—lingered, prosperity bred complacency by the late 1950s. The most significant domestic political ferment, in fact, was a byproduct of the Cold War: a ferocious anticommunism that narrowed the boundaries of acceptable dissent. At decade's end, people sought satisfaction in their families and the consumer pleasures newly available to so many.

- **How did the Cold War affect American society and politics?**
- **How did federal government actions following World War II change the nation?**
- **During the 1950s, many people began to think of their country as a middle-class nation. Were they correct?**

SHAPING POSTWAR AMERICA

At the end of World War II, many Americans feared the economy would plunge back into depression, and in the immediate aftermath of the war, unemployment rose and a wave of strikes rocked the nation. But dire predictions were wrong: the economy flourished, and Americans' standard of living improved. The GI Bill and other new federal programs created opportunities that fundamentally changed the nation.

Postwar Economic Uncertainty

As the end of the war approached, factories began to lay off workers. Ten days after the victory over Japan, 1.8 million people nationwide received pink slips, and 640,000 filed for unemployment compensation. More than 15 million GIs awaited demobilization, raising questions about jobs for them, too.

In spring 1944—a year before V-E Day—Congress, anticipating a postwar crisis, unanimously passed the Servicemen's Readjustment Act, known as the GI Bill of Rights. It showed the nation's gratitude to servicemen, but also attempted to keep demobilized veterans from swamping the U.S. economy: year-long unemployment benefits meant they could be gradually absorbed into civilian employment, and higher-education benefits would keep men in college and out of the job market.

In winter 1945, congressional Democrats introduced the Full Employment Act guaranteeing work through public-sector employment if necessary. By the time Truman signed the full Employment Act into law in early 1946, key provisions regarding guaranteed work virtually disappeared. But the act reaffirmed the federal government's responsibility for managing the economy and created a Council of Economic Advisers to help prevent downturns.

Postwar Strikes and the Taft-Hartley Act

Conversion to a peacetime economy hit workers hard, especially as inflation skyrocketed. More than 5 million workers walked off the job. Unions shut down the coal, automobile, steel, and electric industries and halted railroad and maritime transportation. The strikes were so disruptive that Americans began hoarding food and gasoline.

By spring 1946, Americans grew impatient with the strikes. When unions threatened a national railway strike, President Truman announced that if strikers in an industry deemed vital to national security refused a presidential order to return to work, he would ask Congress to draft them into the armed forces. The Democratic Party would not offer unlimited support to organized labor.

Then, in 1947 in an effort to restrict the power of labor unions, pro-business Republicans and conservative Democrats passed the Taft-Hartley Act. It permitted states to enact right-to-work laws outlawing closed shops, in which all workers were required to join the union if a majority favored a union shop. The law also mandated an eighty-day cooling-off period before unions initiated strikes imperiling national security. These restrictions limited unions' ability to expand their membership. Truman did not want to see union power so limited, but Congress passed the act over Truman's veto.

Economic Growth

Despite initial difficulties, the economy recovered quickly, fueled by consumer spending. Although Americans brought home steady paychecks during the war, there was little on which to spend them. No new cars, for example, had been built since 1942. Americans saved for four years, and when new cars and appliances appeared at war's end, they were ready to buy. Because most factories around the world were in ruins, U.S. corporations expanded their global dominance and increased in size. The United States's ten largest corporations were in automobiles (GM, Ford, and Chrysler), oil (Standard Oil of New Jersey, Mobil, and Texaco), and electronics and communications (GE, IBM, IT&T, and AT&T).

In the agricultural sector, new machines, such as mechanical cotton, tobacco, and grape pickers, and crop-dusting planes revolutionized farming, and the increased use of fertilizers and pesticides raised the total value of farm output from $24.6 billion in 1945 to $38.4 billion in 1961. Large investors were drawn to agriculture by its increased profitability, and the average farm size increased from 195 to 306 acres.

Economic growth was also fueled by government programs. By 1949, veterans received close to $4 billion in unemployment compensation. The GI Bill offered veterans low-interest loans to buy a house or start a business and stipends to cover college or technical school tuition and expenses.

Before the war, higher education was for the affluent; only about 7.5 percent of young Americans attended college. With GI benefits, almost half of America's returning veterans sought higher education. The resulting increase in the number of well-educated or technically trained workers benefited the U.S. economy. The flood of students and federal dollars into the nation's colleges and universities brought a golden age for higher education.

Education created social mobility: children of barely literate menial laborers became white-collar professionals. The GI Bill fostered the emergence of a national middle-class culture, for as colleges exposed students to new ideas and experiences, they became less rooted in ethnic or regional cultures.

Baby Boom

The end of the war brought a boom in marriage and birth rates. In 1946 the U.S. marriage rate was higher than that of any record-keeping nation (except Hungary). The soaring birth rate reversed the downward trend of the past 150 years. "Take the 3,548,000 babies born in 1950," wrote Sylvia F. Porter in her syndicated newspaper column, "bundle them into a batch, bounce them all over the bountiful land that is America. What do you get?" Porter's answer: "Boom. The biggest, boomiest boom ever known in history. Just imagine how much these extra people, these new markets, will absorb— in food, clothing, in gadgets, in housing, in services." Although the baby boom peaked in 1957, more than 4 million babies were born every year until 1965 (see Figure 29.1). As this vast cohort grew older, it had successive impacts on housing, schools, fads, popular music, the job market, and retirement funds, including Social Security.

Scarcely any new housing had been built since the 1920s. Almost 2 million families were doubled up with relatives in 1948; 50,000 lived in Quonset huts, and housing was so tight in Chicago that 250 used trolley cars were sold as homes.

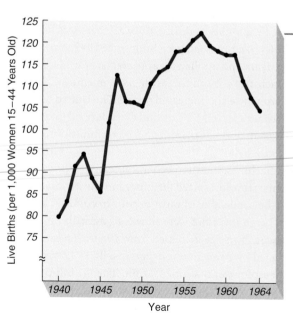

Figure 29.1   Birth Rate, 1945–1964

The birth rate began to rise in 1942 and 1943, but it skyrocketed during the post-war years beginning in 1946, reaching its peak in 1957. From 1954 to 1964, the United States recorded more than 4 million births every year. (*Source:* Adapted from U.S. Bureau of the Census, *Historical Statistics of the United States, Colonial Times to 1970*, bicentennial ed. [Washington, DC: U.S. Government Printing Office, 1975], p. 49.)

TABLE 29.1   **Geographic Distribution of the U.S. Population, 1930–1970 (in percentages)**

Year	Central Cities	Suburbs	Rural Areas and Small Towns
1930	31.8	18.0	50.2
1940	31.6	19.5	48.9
1950	32.3	23.8	43.9
1960	32.6	30.7	36.7
1970	31.4	37.6	31.0

Source: Adapted from U.S. Bureau of the Census, *Decennial Censuses, 1930–1970* (Washington, DC: U.S. Government Printing Office).

Suburbanization

In the postwar years, white Americans moved to the suburbs. Some escaped crowded cities. People from rural areas moved closer to city jobs. Some white families left urban neighborhoods because African American families were moving in. Most, however, simply wanted to own their own home, and suburban developments were affordable. Although suburban development predated World War II, the massive migration of 18 million Americans to the suburbs between 1950 and 1960 was on a wholly different scale (see Table 29.1).

In 1947 the builder William Levitt adapted Henry Ford's assembly-line methods to revolutionize home building. By 1949, instead of 4 or 5 custom homes per year, Levitt's company built 180 houses a week. They were basic—four and a half rooms on a 60-by-100-foot lot, all with identical floor plans disguised by four different exteriors. By rotating seven paint colors, Levitt guaranteed that only 1 in 28 houses would be identical. The basic house sold for $7,990. Other homebuilders quickly adopted Levitt's techniques.

Suburban development happened on such a large scale because federal policies encouraged it. The Federal Housing Administration (FHA) offered low-interest GI mortgages and loans. Congress authorized construction of a 37,000-mile chain of highways in 1947 and in 1956 passed the Highway Act to create a 42,500-mile interstate highway system. Intended to facilitate commerce and rapid mobilization of the military, new highways allowed workers to live farther from their jobs in central cities, thereby fueling suburban construction.

Inequality in Benefits

Postwar federal programs did not benefit all Americans equally. First, federal policies often assisted men at the expense of women. As industry laid off civilian workers to make room for veterans, women lost their jobs at a rate 75 percent higher than men. Many women still worked but were pushed into lower-paying jobs. Universities made room for veterans on the GI Bill by excluding qualified women students.

Inequities were also based on race. Like European American veterans, African American, Native American, Mexican American, and Asian American veterans received educational benefits and hiring preference in civil service jobs. But war workers from these groups were among the first laid off. Federal loan officers and bankers often labeled African American or racially mixed neighborhoods high risk, denying mortgages to racial minorities regardless of individual creditworthiness. This practice, called redlining because such neighborhoods were outlined in red on lenders' maps, kept African Americans and many Hispanics from experiencing the postwar economic explosion. White families who bought homes with federally guaranteed mortgages saw their investments grow dramatically over the years.

DOMESTIC POLITICS IN THE COLD WAR ERA

The United States's social and economic transformations in the postwar era were largely due to federal policies, but politically, foreign affairs were paramount given the challenges of the expanding Cold War. Domestically, Truman attempted to build on the New Deal's liberal agenda, while Eisenhower sought balanced budgets and business-friendly policies. Neither administration approached the political and legislative activism of the 1930s New Deal.

Harry S Truman and Postwar Liberalism

Harry Truman, the plainspoken former haberdasher from Missouri, had never expected to be president. In 1944, when Franklin Roosevelt asked him to be his vice-presidential candidate, he almost refused. With the war in its fourth year, the president had little time for his new vice president and left Truman in the dark about everything from the Manhattan Project to plans for postwar domestic policy. When Roosevelt died suddenly in April 1945, Truman was unprepared to take his place.

Truman stepped forward, placing a sign on his desk that proclaimed, "The Buck Stops Here." Most of Truman's presidency focused on foreign relations, as he led the nation through the end of World War II and into the Cold War with the Soviet Union. Domestically, he oversaw reconversion from war to peace and attempted to keep a liberal agenda—the legacy of Roosevelt's New Deal—alive.

In his 1944 State of the Union address, President Roosevelt had offered Americans a Second Bill of Rights: the right to employment, healthcare, education, food, and housing. This declaration of government responsibility for citizens' welfare was the cornerstone of postwar liberalism. Truman's legislative program sought to maintain the federal government's active role: he supported an increase in the minimum wage and the Full Employment Act. To pay for social welfare programs, Truman gambled that full employment would generate sufficient tax revenue and that consumer spending would fuel economic growth.

The gamble paid off, but the conservative coalition of Republicans and southern Democrats that stalled Roosevelt's New Deal legislation in the late 1930s was even less inclined to support Truman. Congress gutted the Full Employment Act, refused to raise the minimum wage, and passed the anti-union Taft-Hartley Act. With powerful congressional opposition, Truman had few legislative accomplishments. But his inexperience contributed to the political impasse. "To err is Truman," people began to joke. As Truman presided over the rocky transition from wartime to peacetime economy, he faced massive inflation (briefly hitting 35 percent), shortages of consumer goods, and postwar strikes that slowed production and drove prices up. Truman's approval rating plunged from 87 percent in late 1945 to 32 percent in 1946.

1948 Election

By 1948 it seemed that Republicans would win the White House in November, and the party nominated Thomas Dewey, the man Roosevelt defeated in 1944, as its candidate. Republicans hoped schisms in the Democratic Party would ensure victory. The former New Dealer Henry A. Wallace ran for president on the Progressive Party ticket, advocating friendly relations with the Soviet Union, racial desegregation, and nationalization of basic industries. A fourth party, the Dixiecrats (States' Rights Democratic Party), was organized by white southerners who left the 1948 Democratic convention when it adopted a pro–civil rights plank. They nominated South Carolina's fiercely segregationist governor Strom Thurmond.

Truman refused to give up. He resorted to red-baiting, denouncing "Henry Wallace and his communists." Most important, he appealed to the burgeoning population of African American voters in northern cities, becoming the first presidential candidate to campaign in Harlem. In the end, Truman prevailed, with help from African American voters. Roosevelt's New Deal coalition—African Americans, union members, northern urban voters, and most southern whites—endured.

Truman's Fair Deal

In his 1949 State of the Union message, Truman stated, "I expect to give every segment of our population a fair deal." Unlike Roosevelt, Truman pushed legislation supporting the civil rights of African Americans, including antilynching laws. He proposed a national health insurance program and federal aid for education. Southern conservatives in Congress destroyed his civil rights legislation. The American Medical Association denounced his health insurance plan as socialized medicine, and the Roman Catholic Church opposed educational assistance because it would not include parochial schools.

When Truman ordered troops to Korea in June 1950, Americans grumbled as the nation again mobilized for war. People remembered the previous war's shortages and stocked up on sugar, coffee, and canned goods. Fueled by panic buying, inflation rose. An unpopular war and charges of influence peddling by Truman's cronies pushed the president's approval rating to an all-time low of 23 percent in 1951.

Eisenhower's Dynamic Conservatism

"It's Time for a Change" was the Republican presidential campaign slogan in 1952, and voters agreed. Americans hoped that the Republican candidate Dwight D. Eisenhower, the immensely popular World War II hero, could end the Korean War. And Eisenhower appealed to moderates in both parties (the Democrats tried to recruit him as their presidential candidate).

With a Republican in the White House for the first time in twenty years, conservatives hoped to roll back New Deal liberal programs such as Social Security.

A moderate, Eisenhower adopted what he called dynamic conservatism: being "conservative when it comes to money and liberal when it comes to human beings." In 1954 Eisenhower signed amendments to the Social Security Act that raised benefits and added 7.5 million workers, mostly self-employed farmers, to its rolls. Eisenhower's administration, motivated by Cold War fears, also increased government funding for education. When the Soviet Union launched *Sputnik,* the first earth-orbiting satellite, in 1957 (and the United States's first launch exploded seconds after liftoff), improving technology and education became an issue of national security. Congress responded in 1958 with the National Defense Education Act (NDEA), which funded enrichment of school programs in mathematics, foreign languages, and the sciences and offered fellowships and loans to college students.

Growth of the Military-Industrial Complex

Overall, Eisenhower was an ally of business and industry. The Eisenhower tax reform bill raised business depreciation allowances, and the 1954 Atomic Energy Act allowed private companies to own reactors and nuclear materials to produce electricity. Eisenhower balanced only three of his eight budgets, using deficit spending to cushion the impact of three recessions (1953–1954, 1957–1958, and 1960–1961) and fund America's global activities. In 1959 federal expenditures climbed to $92 billion, about half of which went to the military, mostly for developing new weapons.

Before leaving office in 1961 after his second term, Eisenhower delivered his farewell address. Because of the Cold War, he observed, the United States had a large standing army—3.5 million men—and devoted ever-greater percentages of its budget to developing weapons. Condemning the new "conjunction of an immense military establishment and a large arms industry," Eisenhower warned, "The total influence—economic, political, even spiritual—is felt in every city, every statehouse, every office of the federal government" and threatened the nation's democratic process. Eisenhower, the former five-star general, urged Americans to "guard against . . . the military-industrial complex."

COLD WAR FEARS AND ANTICOMMUNISM

International relations had a profound influence on America's domestic politics after World War II. Americans were frightened by Cold War tensions between the United States and the Soviet Union. Their legitimate fears inspired anticommunist demagoguery and witch hunts, allowing the trampling of civil liberties, the suppression of dissent, and the persecution of innocent Americans.

Anticommunism was not new: a Red Scare swept the United States following the 1917 Russian Revolution, and opponents of the United States's labor movement used charges of communism to block unionization through the 1930s. Many saw the Soviet Union's virtual takeover of eastern Europe in the late 1940s as an alarming parallel to Nazi Germany's takeover of neighboring states. People remembered the failure of appeasement at Munich and worried about being too soft toward the Soviet Union.

Espionage and Nuclear Fears

U.S. intelligence officers in a top-secret project, code-named "Venona," decrypted almost three thousand Soviet telegraphic cables that proved Soviet spies had infiltrated U.S. government agencies and nuclear programs. (The United States also had spies in the Soviet Union.) Intelligence officials withheld this evidence from the American public even as it prosecuted Soviet spies so that the Soviets would not realize their codes had been compromised.

Fear of nuclear war also contributed to American anticommunism. In 1949 when the Soviet Union joined the United States in possessing atomic weapons, President Truman initiated a national atomic civil defense program, advising Americans, "I cannot tell you when or where the attack will come or that it will come at all. I can only remind you that we must be ready when it does come." Children practiced duck-and-cover positions in school classrooms, learning how to shield their faces from the atomic flash. *Life* magazine featured backyard fallout shelters. Americans worried that the United States was newly vulnerable to attack.

Politics of Anticommunism

American leaders did not always draw a line between prudent attempts to prevent Soviet spies from infiltrating government agencies and anticommunist scare-mongering. Republican politicians red-baited Democratic opponents, eventually targeting the Truman administration. In 1947 President Truman ordered investigations into the loyalty of more than 3 million government employees. As anticommunist hysteria grew, the government discharged people deemed security risks, among them alcoholics, homosexuals, and debtors thought susceptible to blackmail. In most cases there was no evidence of disloyalty.

Leading the anticommunist crusade was the House Un-American Activities Committee (popularly known as HUAC). Created in 1938 to investigate "subversive and un-American propaganda," the committee lost credibility by charging that film stars—including eight-year-old Shirley Temple—were Communist Party dupes. In 1947, HUAC attacked Hollywood again, using Federal Bureau of Investigation (FBI) files and the testimony of people like Screen Actors Guild president Ronald Reagan (a secret FBI informant). Screenwriters and directors known as the Hollywood Ten were sent to prison when they refused to name names of suspected communists. At least a dozen others committed suicide. Studios blacklisted actors, screenwriters, directors, even makeup artists, suspected of communist affiliations. With no evidence of wrongdoing, people's lives and careers were ruined.

McCarthyism and the Growing Witch Hunt

University professors became targets of the growing witch hunt in 1949, when HUAC demanded lists of the textbooks used at eighty-one universities. When the board of regents at the University of California, Berkeley, instituted a loyalty oath and fired twenty-six faculty members resisting on principle, protests nationwide forced the regents to back down. But many professors began to downplay controversial material in their courses. In the labor movement, the CIO expelled eleven unions, with more than 900,000 members, for alleged communist domination.

The red panic reached its nadir in February 1950, when Joseph R. McCarthy, a relatively obscure U.S. senator from Wisconsin, charged that the U.S. State Department was "thoroughly infested with Communists." Republican senator Joseph R. McCarthy of Wisconsin was not an especially credible source. He first claimed that there were 205 communists in the State Department, then 57, then 81. He had a severe drinking problem and a record of dishonesty as a lawyer and judge. But McCarthy crystallized Americans' anxieties, and anticommunist excesses came to be known as McCarthyism.

Anticommunism in Congress

In such a climate, most public figures found it risky to stand up against McCarthyist tactics. In 1950, with bipartisan support, Congress passed the Internal Security (McCarran) Act, which required members of Communist-front organizations to register with the government and prohibited them from holding government jobs or traveling abroad. In 1954 the Senate passed the Communist Control Act sponsored by Democratic senator Hubert H. Humphrey of Minnesota, which effectively made membership in the Communist Party illegal.

In 1948 Congressman Richard Nixon of California, a member of HUAC, was propelled onto the national stage when he accused the former State Department official Alger Hiss of espionage. That same year, Ethel and Julius Rosenberg were arrested for passing atomic secrets to the Soviets; they were found guilty of treason and executed in 1953. For decades, many historians believed that the Rosenbergs were victims of a witch hunt, but there was evidence of Julius Rosenberg's guilt in cables decrypted by the Venona Project. This evidence was not presented at trial for national security reasons and remained top secret until 1995, when a Clinton administration initiative opened the files.

Waning of the Red Scare

The worst excesses of Cold War anticommunism waned when Senator McCarthy was discredited on national television in 1954. McCarthy was a master at using the press, making sensational accusations front-page material just before reporters' deadlines. When McCarthy's charges proved untrue, retractions appeared in the back pages of the newspapers.

But McCarthy's crucial mistake was charging on television that the U.S. Army was shielding communists, citing the case of one army dentist. In the so-called Army-McCarthy hearings, held by a Senate subcommittee in 1954, McCarthy, apparently drunk, abused witnesses, ranted, and slurred his words. In December 1954, the Senate voted to condemn McCarthy for sullying the dignity of the Senate. He remained a senator, but exhaustion and alcohol took their toll and he died in 1957 at the age of forty-eight. With McCarthy discredited, the most virulent anticommunism had run its course. However, the use of fear tactics for political gain and the narrowing of American freedoms and liberties were chilling domestic legacies of the Cold War.

THE STRUGGLE FOR CIVIL RIGHTS

The Cold War also shaped African American struggles for social justice and the nation's responses to them. As the Soviet Union pointed out, the United States could hardly pose as the leader of the free world or condemn the denial of human rights in eastern Europe and the Soviet Union while practicing segregation. Nor could the United States convince new African and Asian nations of its dedication to human rights if African Americans were subjected to segregation, discrimination, disfranchisement, and racial violence. Many Americans viewed such criticism as a Soviet-inspired attempt to weaken the United States. The FBI and local law enforcement commonly used such anticommunist fears to justify attacking civil rights activists. In this heated environment, African Americans struggled to seize the political initiative.

Growing Black Political Power African Americans who helped win World War II were determined to enjoy better lives in the postwar United States. Politicians like Harry Truman were heeding black aspirations, especially as black voters in some urban-industrial states began to influence the political balance of power.

President Truman had compelling political reasons for supporting African American civil rights. He genuinely believed that every American, regardless of race, should enjoy full citizenship. Truman was disturbed by a resurgence of racial terrorism, as a revived Ku Klux Klan burned crosses and murdered blacks seeking civil rights after World War II. But what really horrified Truman was the report that police in Aiken, South Carolina, gouged out the eyes of a black sergeant three hours after his army discharge. In December 1946, Truman signed an executive order establishing the President's Committee on Civil Rights. Its report, *To Secure These Rights,* would become the civil rights movement agenda for the next twenty years. It called for antilynching and antisegregation legislation and for laws guaranteeing voting rights and equal employment opportunity. For the first time since Reconstruction, a president acknowledged the government's responsibility to protect African Americans and strive for racial equality.

In 1948 Truman issued two executive orders ending racial discrimination in the federal government. One proclaimed a policy of "fair employment throughout the federal establishment" and created the Employment Board of the Civil Service Commission to hear discrimination charges. The other ordered the racial desegregation of the armed forces. Segregated units were being phased out by the Korean War.

Changing social attitudes and experiences in postwar America facilitated these changes. A new and visible African American middle class emerged, composed of college-educated activists, war veterans, and union workers. White awareness of social injustice was heightened by Gunnar Myrdal's social science study *An American Dilemma* (1944) and by Richard Wright's novel *Native Son* (1940) and autobiography *Black Boy* (1945). African Americans and whites worked together in CIO unions and service organizations, such as the National Council of Churches. In 1947 a black baseball player, Jackie Robinson, broke the major league color barrier and electrified Brooklyn Dodgers fans.

Supreme Court Victories and School Desegregation

African Americans were successfully challenging racial discrimination in the courts. In 1939 the NAACP had established its Legal Defense and Educational Fund under Thurgood Marshall. By the 1940s, Marshall (who in 1967 would become the first African American Supreme Court justice) and his colleagues worked to destroy the separate-but-equal doctrine established in *Plessy v. Ferguson* (1896). In higher education, the NAACP calculated, the cost of true equality in racially separate schools would be prohibitive. "You can't build a cyclotron for one student," the president of the University of Oklahoma acknowledged. Through NAACP lawsuits, African American students won admission to professional and graduate schools at several formerly segregated state universities. The NAACP also won victories through the Supreme Court in *Smith v. Allwright* (1944), which outlawed the whites-only primaries held by the Democratic Party in some southern states; *Morgan v. Virginia* (1946), which struck down segregation in interstate bus transportation; and *Shelley v. Kraemer* (1948), which held that racially restrictive covenants (private agreements among white homeowners not to sell to African Americans) could not legally be enforced.

Even so, African Americans continued to suffer disfranchisement, job discrimination, segregation, and violence. But in 1954 the NAACP won a historic Supreme Court victory, *Brown v. Board of Education of Topeka*, which Thurgood Marshall argued, incorporated school desegregation cases from several states. Written by Chief Justice Earl Warren, the court's unanimous decision concluded that "Separate educational facilities are inherently unequal." But the ruling that overturned *Plessy v. Ferguson* did not demand immediate compliance. A year later, the Court ordered school desegregation, but only "with all deliberate speed."

Montgomery Bus Boycott

By the mid-1950s, African Americans were increasingly engaged in a grassroots struggle for civil rights. In 1955 Rosa Parks, a department store seamstress and long-time NAACP activist, was arrested when she refused to give her seat to a white man on a public bus in Montgomery, Alabama. Her arrest enabled local black women's organizations and civil rights groups to organize a boycott of the city's bus system. They selected Martin Luther King Jr., a recently ordained minister, as their leader. King launched the boycott declaring, "If we are wrong, the Constitution is wrong. If we are wrong, God Almighty is wrong. . . . If we are wrong, justice is a lie."

Martin Luther King Jr. was a twenty-six-year-old Baptist minister with a recent Ph.D. from Boston University. Schooled in the teachings of India's leader Mohandas K. Gandhi, King believed in nonviolent civil disobedience as a vehicle to focus the nation's attention on the immorality of Jim Crow.

During the year-long Montgomery bus boycott, African Americans rallied in their churches. They maintained their boycott through heavy rains and the steamy summer heat, often walking miles a day. With the bus company near bankruptcy and downtown merchants suffering from declining sales, city officials adopted harassment tactics to end the boycott. But the African American people of Montgomery persevered: thirteen months later, the Supreme Court declared Alabama's bus segregation laws unconstitutional.

For leading the movement to gain equality for African Americans riding city buses in Montgomery, Alabama, Martin Luther King Jr. (1929–1968) and other African Americans, including twenty-three other ministers, were indicted by an all-white jury for violating an old law banning boycotts. In late March 1956, King was convicted and fined $500. A crowd of well-wishers cheered a smiling King (here with his wife, Coretta) outside the courthouse, where King proudly declared, "The protest goes on!" King's arrest and conviction made the bus boycott front-page news across the United States.   (© Bettmann/Corbis)

White Resistance

White reactions to civil rights gains varied. Some communities in border states like Kansas and Maryland quietly implemented the school desegregation order, and many southern moderates advocated a gradual rollback of segregation. But others urged defiance. The Klan experienced another resurgence, and white violence against African Americans increased. In 1955, Emmett Till, a fourteen-year-old from Chicago, was murdered by white men in Mississippi who took offense at the way he spoke to a white woman. Business and professional people created White Citizens' Councils (known familiarly as uptown Ku Klux Klans) to resist school desegregation and use economic power against civil rights activists. When FBI director J. Edgar Hoover briefed President Eisenhower on southern racial tensions in 1956, he warned of communist influences among civil rights activists and even suggested that, Citizens' Councils might "control the rising tension."

White resistance also mounted in large northern cities. Chicago's African American population increased from 275,000 in 1940 to 800,000 in 1960. These newcomers found good jobs and enjoyed political power, but faced racism and housing segregation. So racially divided was Chicago that the U.S. Commission on Civil Rights in

1959 described it as "the most residentially segregated city in the nation." Other northern cities were not far behind.

Federal Authority and States' Rights   Although President Eisenhower disapproved of racial segregation, he objected to "compulsory federal law," believing instead that race relations would improve "only if [desegregation] starts locally." He also feared that ugly public confrontations likely to follow rapid desegregation would jeopardize Republican inroads in the South. Thus Eisenhower did not state forthrightly that the federal government would enforce the *Brown* decision as the nation's law.

Events in Little Rock, Arkansas, forced the president to get involved. In September 1957, Arkansas governor Orval E. Faubus defied a court-supported desegregation plan for Little Rock's Central High School, saying on television that "blood would run in the streets" if black students tried to enter the high school. Eight black teenagers tried to enter Central High on the second day of school but were turned away by the Arkansas National Guard. The ninth was surrounded by jeering whites and narrowly escaped the mob with the help of a sympathetic white woman.

The Little Rock Nine entered Central High more than two weeks later after a federal judge intervened. Television broadcast the scene to the world. Eisenhower, fearing violence, nationalized the Arkansas National Guard (placing it under federal, not state, control) and dispatched one thousand army paratroopers to guard the students for the rest of the year. Eisenhower's use of federal power was a critical step toward racial equality, for he had directly confronted the conflict between federal authority and states' rights. However, state power triumphed the following year, when Faubus closed all public high schools in Little Rock rather than desegregate them.

In 1957 Congress passed the first Civil Rights Act since Reconstruction, creating the Commission on Civil Rights to investigate systemic discrimination, such as in voting. Although this measure was not fully effective, it lent further federal recognition to civil rights. Most important, however, was growing grassroots activism. In 1957 Martin Luther King Jr. became the first president of the Southern Christian Leadership Conference (SCLC), organized to coordinate civil rights activities. With the success in Montgomery and the gains through the Supreme Court, African Americans were poised to launch a national civil rights movement.

CREATING A MIDDLE-CLASS NATION

Despite resistance to civil rights during the 1950s, the United States was becoming increasingly inclusive. National prosperity offered greater numbers of Americans material comfort and economic security through entrance into an economic middle class. Old European ethnic identities faded, as an ever-smaller percentage of Americans were first- or second-generation immigrants.

In the new suburbs, people from different backgrounds created communities. Middle-class Americans increasingly looked to national media for advice on matters ranging from how to celebrate Thanksgiving to how to raise children. New opportunities for consumption—whether teenage fads or suburban ranch-style homes—also tied disparate Americans together. In the postwar years, a new middle-class way of life transformed the United States.

Prosperity for More Americans

During the 1950s, sustained economic growth created unprecedented prosperity and economic security. In great part the boom was driven by consumer spending. Americans eagerly bought goods unavailable during the war, and industries expanded production. As the Cold War deepened, government defense spending created jobs and further stimulated the economy.

Cold War military and aerospace spending fueled the need for highly educated scientists, engineers, and other white-collar professionals. Universities received billions of dollars to fund research, expanding the place of academia in the United States. Their research went beyond military applications and transformed society: the transistor, invented in the 1950s, was used in radios and sparked the computer revolution.

A new era of labor relations helped spread prosperity to more Americans. By 1950, the United Auto Workers (UAW) and General Motors led the way for other corporations in providing workers with health insurance, pension plans, and guaranteed cost-of-living adjustments (COLAs). The 1950 agreement gave GM's workers a five-year contract, with regular wage increases tied to corporate productivity. And with wage increases tied to corporate productivity, labor cast its lot with management: workplace stability and efficiency, not strikes, would bring higher wages. During the 1950s, wages and benefits propelled union families into the ranks of the economic middle class.

Sunbelt and Economic Growth

In the 1930s, Roosevelt called the South with its poverty "the nation's No. 1 economic problem." During World War II, new defense plants and military camps channeled federal money to the region, stimulating economic growth. In the postwar era, massive defense spending continued to shift economic development to the South and Southwest—the Sunbelt (see Map 29.1). Government actions—including generous tax breaks for oil companies, siting of military bases, and defense and aerospace contracts—were crucial to the region's new prosperity.

The Sunbelt's spectacular growth was fueled by agribusiness, the oil industry, real-estate development, and recreation. Sunbelt states aggressively and successfully sought foreign investment and drew industry with lower taxes and heating bills, along with right-to-work laws banning closed shops. The development of air conditioning was also crucial, making the hottest days bearable. Houston, Phoenix, Los Angeles, San Diego, Dallas, and Miami boomed, and by 1963 California was the most populous state in the United States.

A New Middle-Class Culture

By the 1950s, it seemed that the United States was becoming a middle-class nation. Unionized blue-collar workers gained middle-class incomes, and veterans with GI Bill college educations swelled the growing managerial and professional class. In 1956,

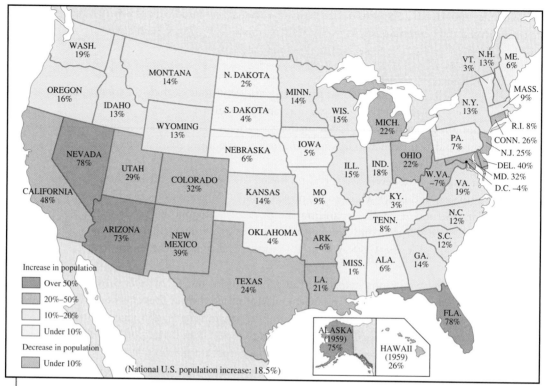

Map 29.1   Rise of the Sunbelt, 1950–1960

The years after World War II saw a continuation of the migration of Americans to the Sunbelt states of the Southwest and the West Coast.

for the first time, the United States had more white-collar than blue-collar workers, and 60 percent of families had incomes in the middle-class range (approximately $3,000 to $9,000 a year in the mid-1950s).

Paradoxically, the strength of unions in the postwar era contributed to a decline in working-class identity: as large numbers of blue-collar workers participated in suburban middle-class culture, the lines separating working class and middle class seemed less important. Increasingly, a family's standard of living mattered more than what sort of work made the standard possible. People of color did not share equally in the United States's postwar prosperity and were usually invisible in American representations of the good life. However, many middle-income African Americans, Latinos, and Asian Americans did participate in middle-class culture.

Whiteness and National Culture

The emergence of a national middle-class culture was possible in part because the United States's population was more homogeneous in the 1950s than before or since. In the nineteenth and early twentieth centuries, the United States restricted or prohibited immigration from Asia, Africa, and Latin America while accepting millions of Europeans. This large-scale European immigration was shut off in the 1920s, so by 1960 only 5.7 percent of Americans were foreign-born (compared with approximately 15 percent in 1910 and 12.4 percent in 2005). In 1950, 88 percent of Americans were of European ancestry (compared with 69 percent in 2000), 10 percent of the population was African American, 2 percent was Hispanic, and Native Americans and Asian Americans each accounted for about one-fifth of 1 percent. In 1959 the addition of two new states, Alaska and Hawai'i, brought more people of native, Asian, or Pacific origin into the U.S. population.

Although the new suburbs were peopled mostly by whites, these suburbs were more diverse than the communities from which their residents had come. The United States's small towns and urban ethnic enclaves were homogeneous and usually intolerant of challenges to tradition. In the suburbs, paradoxically, many people encountered different customs and beliefs. But new suburbanites often traded the provincial homogeneity of specific ethnic or regional cultures for a new sort of homogeneity: a national middle-class culture.

Television

Because many white Americans were new to the middle class, they were uncertain about what was expected of them. They found answers in the national mass media. Women's magazines helped housewives replace ethnic dishes with American recipes created from national brand name products, such as casseroles made with Campbell's cream of mushroom soup. Television also fostered a shared culture. Although television sets cost about $300—the equivalent of $2,000 today—almost half of American homes had TVs by 1953, and TV ownership rose to 90 percent by 1960, when more American households had a television set than a washing machine.

On television, suburban families like the Cleavers (*Leave It to Beaver*) ate dinner at a properly set dining room table. Every crisis was resolved through paternal wisdom. These popular family situation comedies reinforced the suburban middle-class ideal many American families sought.

The middle classness of television programming was due in part to advertising. Corporations buying airtime did not want to offend potential consumers. Thus, although the African American musician Nat King Cole drew millions of viewers to his NBC show, it never found a sponsor. National corporations feared that being linked to an African American performer would hurt sales among whites, especially in the South. Because African Americans made up only 10 percent of the population and many had little disposable income, they had little influence. The *Nat King Cole Show* was canceled within a year; it was a decade before the networks again anchored a show around an African American performer.

With only network television available—ABC, CBS, and NBC (and, until 1956, DuMont)—at any one time 70 percent or more of all viewers might be watching the same popular program. (In the early twenty-first century, the most popular shows might attract 12 percent of the audience.) Television gave Americans shared experiences and helped create a more homogeneous, white-focused, middle-class culture.

Consumer Culture

Americans also found common ground in a wealth of consumer goods. After decades of scarcity, Americans had a dazzling array of choices, and even utilitarian objects got two-tone paint jobs or rocket-ship details. People used purchases to express personal identities and to claim status. Cars more than anything embodied the consumer fantasies. Expensive Cadillacs were the first to develop tail fins, soon added to midrange Chevys, Fords, and Plymouths. Americans spent $65 billion on automobiles in 1955—a figure equivalent to almost 20 percent of the gross national product. To pay for cars, suburban houses and modern appliances, consumer debt rose from $5.7 billion in 1945 to $58 billion in 1961.

Religion

Church membership (primarily in mainline Christian churches) doubled between 1945 and the early 1960s. The media probably played a role, as preachers like Billy Graham created national congregations from television audiences with a message that combined the promise of salvation with Cold War patriotism. But local churches and synagogues offered new suburbanites a sense of community, celebrating life's rituals and supporting those far from their extended families.

MEN, WOMEN, AND YOUTH AT MIDCENTURY

Having survived the Great Depression and a world war, many Americans sought fulfillment in private life. They saw their familial commitment as an expression of faith in the future. Despite the satisfaction that many found in family life, both men and women felt limited by social pressures to conform to narrowly defined gender roles.

Marriage and Families

During the 1950s, few Americans remained single, and most people married young. By 1959, almost half of American brides were younger than nineteen; their husbands were usually only a year or so older. Early marriage was endorsed by experts and approved by most parents, partly to prevent premarital sex. As Americans accepted psychotherapeutic insights, they worried that premarital sex might leave the young woman pregnant or ruin her reputation, and also that it could damage her psychologically so she would never adjust to normal marital relations. One popular women's magazine argued, "When two people are ready for sexual intercourse at the fully human level they are ready for marriage. . . . And society has no right to stand in their way."

Many young couples found freedom from parental authority by marrying. Most newlyweds quickly had babies—an average of three—completing their families while still in their twenties. Birth control (condoms and diaphragms) was widely available and widely used, as couples planned family size. Two children were the American ideal in 1940; by 1960, most couples wanted four. About 88 percent of children under eighteen lived with two parents (in 2000, the figure was 69 percent), and fewer were born outside marriage; only 3.9 percent of births were to unmarried women in 1950 (compared with more than one-third of births in 2000). As late as 1960, there were only nine divorces per one thousand married couples.

Gender Roles in 1950s Families

In 1950s families, men and women usually took distinct roles, with male breadwinners and female homemakers. Contemporary commentators insisted this was based on essential differences between the sexes. In fact, the economic and social structure and the cultural values of the postwar United States determined the choices available to men and women.

During the 1950s, it was possible for many families to live in modest middle-class comfort on one (male) salary. There were strong incentives for women to stay home, especially while children were young. Good childcare was unavailable, and fewer families lived close to relatives. Childcare experts, including Dr. Spock, whose 1946 *Baby and Child Care* sold millions of copies, insisted that a mother's full-time attention was necessary for her children's well-being. Because of hiring discrimination, women who could afford to stay home often did not find the available jobs attractive enough to justify juggling cooking and housework, too. Instead, schools and religious institutions benefited immensely from women's volunteer labor.

Women and Work

Suburban domesticity left many women feeling isolated from the larger world their husbands inhabited. The popular belief that one should find complete emotional satisfaction in private life put unrealistic pressure on marriages. And despite near-universal celebration of women's domestic roles, many women were managing both job and family responsibilities (see Figure 29.2). Twice as many women were employed in 1960 as in 1940, including 39 percent of women with children between

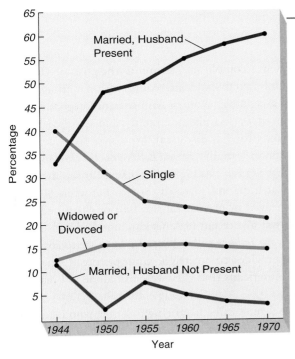

Figure 29.2   Marital Distribution of the Female Labor Force, 1944–1970

The composition of the female labor force changed dramatically from 1944 to 1970. In 1944, 41 percent of women in the labor force were single; in 1970, only 22 percent were single. During the same years, the percentage of the female labor force who had a husband in the home jumped from 34 to 59. The percentage who were widowed or divorced remained about the same from 1944 to 1970.   (*Source:* Adapted from U.S. Bureau of the Census, *Historical Statistics of the United States, Colonial Times to 1970*, bicentennial ed. [Washington, DC: U.S. Government Printing Office, 1975], p. 133.)

age six and seventeen. Most worked part-time for a specific family goal like a new car. They saw their jobs as in service to the family, not a means to independence from it.

Women faced discrimination in the work force. Want ads were divided into Help Wanted—Male and Help Wanted—Female categories. Female full-time workers earned, on average, 60 percent of what men were paid and were restricted to lower-paid "female" fields: maids, secretaries, teachers, and nurses. A popular book, *Modern Woman: The Lost Sex,* claimed that ambitious women and feminists suffered from penis envy. College psychology textbooks warned women not to compete with men; magazine articles described career women as a third sex. Medical schools limited female admission to 5 percent of each class. In 1960 less than 4 percent of lawyers and judges were female. When the future Supreme Court justice Ruth Bader Ginsburg graduated at the top of her Columbia Law School class in 1959, she could not find a job.

"Crisis of Masculinity"

Academics and mass media critics devoted equal attention to the plight of the American male. American men faced a "crisis of masculinity," proclaimed the nation's mass-circulation magazines. In a bestselling book, the sociologist William H. Whyte explained that postwar corporate employees had become organization men, succeeding through cooperation and conformity, not initiative and risk. Experts claimed women's "natural" desire for security and comfort was stifling men's instinct for adventure. Men who did not conform to standards of male responsibility— husband, father, breadwinner—were forcefully condemned. Some linked concerns about masculinity to the Cold War, arguing that, unless the United States's men recovered masculinity diminished by white-collar work or a suburban, family-centered existence, the nation's future was at risk.

Sexuality

Sexuality was complicated terrain in the postwar United States. Only heterosexual intercourse within marriage was deemed acceptable. Women who became pregnant outside marriage were often ostracized by friends and family and expelled from school. Homosexuality was grounds for job dismissal, expulsion from college, even jail. In his major works on human sexuality, *Sexual Behavior in the Human Male* (1948) and *Sexual Behavior in the Human Female* (1953), Dr. Alfred Kinsey, director of the Institute for Sex Research at Indiana University, noted that while 80 percent of his female sample disapproved of premarital sex, half of them had had premarital sex. He also reported that 37 percent of American men had had "some homosexual experience." The *Chicago Tribune* called Kinsey a "menace to society." Although Kinsey's samples did not provide a completely accurate picture of American sexual behavior, they told many Americans that they were not alone in breaking certain rules.

Another challenge to the sexual rules came from Hugh Hefner, who launched *Playboy* magazine in 1953. Within three years, it had a circulation of 1 million. Hefner saw *Playboy* as an attack on the United States's "ferocious anti-sexuality" and his nude playmates as a means for men to combat the increasingly "blurred distinctions between the sexes" in suburban culture.

Youth Culture

The sheer numbers of baby boom youth made them a force in U.S. society. As this group moved from childhood to youth, a distinctive youth culture developed. Its customs and rituals were created within peer groups and were shaped by national media—teen magazines, movies, radio, advertising, and music. The United States's corporations quickly learned the power of youth, as children's fads launched multimillion- dollar industries. Mr. Potato Head—probably the first toy advertised on television—had $4 million in sales in 1952. In the mid-1950s, when Walt Disney's television show *Disneyland* featured Davy Crockett, "King of the Wild Frontier," every child in America (and more than a few adults) just *had* to have a coonskin cap. As baby-boom children grew up, their buying power shaped American popular culture.

By 1960, the United States's 18 million teenagers were spending $10 billion a year. Seventy-two percent of movie tickets in the 1950s were sold to teenagers, and Hollywood created a flood of teen films, ranging from forgettable B-movies to controversial films such as James Dean's *Rebel Without a Cause*. Adults worried that teens would copy the delinquency romanticized in *Rebel Without a Cause,* and teenage boys did emulate Dean's rebellious look. The film, however, blamed parents for teenage confusion, drawing heavily on popular psychological theories about sexuality and the "crisis of masculinity."

Nothing defined youth culture as much as music. Young Americans were electrified by the driving energy of Bill Haley and the Comets, Chuck Berry, Little Richard, and Buddy Holly. Elvis Presley's 1956 appearance on TV's *Ed Sullivan Show* touched off a frenzy of teen adulation and a flood of letters from parents scandalized by his "gyrations." Although few white musicians acknowledged it, the roots of rock 'n' roll lay in African American rhythm and blues. The raw energy and sometimes sexually suggestive lyrics of early rock music faded as the music industry sought white performers, like Pat Boone, to do blander, more acceptable "cover," or copycat, versions of music by African American artists.

The distinct youth culture of the 1950s made adults uneasy. Parents worried that going steady might encourage teens to "go too far" sexually. Juvenile delinquency was a major concern. Crime rates for young people rose dramatically after World War II, but much juvenile delinquency was status crimes—curfew violations, sexual experimentation, underage drinking—activities that were criminal only because of the person's age. Congress held hearings on juvenile delinquency, with experts testifying to the corrupting power of youth-oriented popular culture, comic books in particular. Most youthful behavior, however, fit squarely into the consumer culture that youth shared with their parents.

Challenges to Middle-Class Culture

The growth of middle-class culture inspired pockets of cultural dissent. *Beat* (a word that suggested both down and out and beatific) writers rejected middle-class social decorum and contemporary literary conventions. The Beat Generation

Barbie

Barbie, the all-American doll, is—like many Americans—an immigrant. Although introduced in 1959 by the American toy company Mattel, Barbie's origins lie in Germany, where she was called Lilli.

The German Lilli doll was a novelty toy for adult men (as evidenced by her proportions, equivalent to 39-21-31 in human terms). She was based on a character that cartoonist Reinhard Beuthien drew for the German tabloid *Das Bild* in 1952. Lilli was so popular that she became a regular feature, later made three-dimensional as *Bild Lilli*, an eleven-and-a-half-inch-tall blonde doll with the figure Barbie would make famous.

Lilli came to the United States with Ruth Handler, one of the founders of the Mattel toy company. When she glimpsed Lilli while vacationing in Europe, Handler bought three and gave one to her daughter Barbara, after whom Lilli would be renamed. Mattel bought the rights to Lilli (the doll and the cartoon, which Mattel quietly retired) and unveiled Barbie in March 1959. Despite mothers' hesitations about a doll that looked like Barbie, within the year Mattel sold 351,000 Barbies at $3 each (or about $17 in 2000 dollars). The billionth Barbie was sold in 1997.

Within the United States, Barbie has been controversial. Some have worried that Barbie's wildly unrealistic figure fosters girls' dissatisfaction with their own body, potentially leading to eating disorders. Others claim that Barbie represents a model of empty-headed femininity. In 2002 international labor-rights groups called for a boycott of Barbie. They cited studies showing that half of all Barbies are made by exploited young women in mainland China: of the $10 retail, Chinese factories receive only 35 cents per doll to cover their costs, including labor. Saudi Arabia banned Barbie in 2003, arguing that her skimpy outfits and the values she represents are not suitable for a Muslim nation. Still, the eleven-and-a-half-inch doll remains popular worldwide, selling in more than 150 countries. For better or worse, Barbie continues to link the United States and the rest of the world.

Before Barbie became a U.S. child's toy, she was Lilli, a German sex symbol. Mattel transformed the doll into a wholesome American teenager with a new wardrobe to match. (Gareth Cattermole/Getty Images)

embraced spontaneity in their art, escape from the demands of everyday life, and enjoyed open sexuality and drug use. Perhaps the most significant beat work was Allen Ginsberg's angry poem "Howl" (1956), the subject of an obscenity trial whose verdict opened U.S. publishing to a broader range of works. The mainstream press ridiculed the beats, dubbing them *beatniks* (after *Sputnik*, suggesting their un-Americanness). Still, they laid the groundwork for the 1960s counterculture.

THE LIMITS OF THE MIDDLE-CLASS NATION

During the 1950s, the United States's popular culture and mass media celebrated new opportunities. But influential critics condemned middle-class culture as a wasteland of conformity, homogeneity, and ugly consumerism.

Critics of Conformity These critics were not lone figures crying out in the wilderness. Americans, obsessed with self-criticism even as most participated wholeheartedly in the celebratory consensus culture of their age, rushed to books, such as J. D. Salinger's *The Catcher in the Rye* and Norman Mailer's *The Naked and the Dead,* which were profoundly critical of U.S. society. Americans even made bestsellers of difficult academic works, such as David Riesman's *The Lonely Crowd* (1950) and William H. Whyte's *The Organization Man* (1955), both of which criticized conformity in U.S. life. These critiques also appeared in mass-circulation magazines like *Reader's Digest.* Steeped in cultural criticism, many Americans understood *Invasion of the Body Snatchers*—a 1956 film in which zombielike aliens grown in pods gradually replace a town's inhabitants—as criticism of suburban conformity and postwar cultural homogeneity.

Many critics were attempting to understand large-scale and significant changes in U.S. society. Americans did lose some autonomy in work as large corporations replaced smaller businesses. They experienced the homogenizing force of mass production and a national consumer culture and saw distinctions among ethnic groups and socioeconomic classes fade. Critics, however, were often elitist and antidemocratic, seeing only bland conformity and sterility in the emerging middle-class suburban culture. But identical houses did not produce identical souls; instead, inexpensive suburban housing gave healthier—possibly happier—lives to millions raised in dank tenements or ramshackle farmhouses without indoor plumbing.

Environmental Degradation The new consumer culture encouraged wasteful habits and harmed the environment. *BusinessWeek* noted that corporations need not rely on planned obsolescence, purposely designing a product to wear out. Americans replaced products because they were out of date, not because they did not work. Hence, automakers revamped designs annually. The United States's new consumer society used an ever-larger share of the world's resources. By the 1960s, the United States, with only 5 percent of the world's population, consumed more than one-third of its goods and services.

The rapid economic growth exacted environmental costs. Steel mills, coal-powered generators, and internal-combustion car engines burning lead-based gasoline polluted the atmosphere and imperiled people's health. As suburbanites commuted greater distances to work and neighborhoods were built without public transportation, Americans relied on private automobiles, consuming the nonrenewable resources of oil and gasoline and filling cities and suburbs with smog. Water was diverted from lakes and rivers to service burgeoning Sunbelt cities, including the swimming pools and golf courses that dotted parched Arizona and southern California.

Defense contractors and farmers were among the country's worst polluters. Refuse from nuclear weapons facilities at Hanford, Washington, and Colorado's Rocky Flats arsenal poisoned soil and water resources. Agriculture used pesticides and other chemicals. DDT, a chemical used on Pacific islands during the war to kill mosquitoes and lice, was used widely in the United States until after 1962, when wildlife biologist Rachel Carson indicted DDT for the deaths of mammals, birds, and fish in her bestselling book *Silent Spring.*

The nation was moving toward a postindustrial economy in which providing goods and services to consumers was more important than producing goods. Therefore, though union members prospered during the 1950s, membership grew slowly, because most new jobs were created in the union-resistant white-collar service trades. Technological advances increased productivity and also pushed people from well-paid blue-collar jobs into the growing and lower-paid service sector.

Continuing Racism   Racial discrimination stood unchallenged in most of the 1950s United States. Suburbs, both North and South, were almost always racially segregated. Many white Americans had little or no contact with people of different races, partly because the relatively small populations of nonwhite Americans were not equally dispersed nationwide. In 1960, 68 people of Chinese descent and 519 African Americans lived in Vermont; 181 Native Americans lived in West Virginia; and Mississippi had just 178 Japanese American residents. Most white Americans in the 1950s, especially those outside the South, gave little thought to race. Instead, they regarded the emerging middle-class culture not as white, but as American, marginalizing people of color in image as in reality.

In an age of abundance, more than one in five Americans still lived in poverty. One-fifth of the poor were people of color, including almost half of the nation's African Americans and more than half of all Native Americans. Two-thirds of the poor lived in households headed by a person with an eighth-grade education or less, one-fourth in households headed by a single woman. More than one-third were under age eighteen; one-fourth were over age sixty-five. Social Security payments helped, but many retirees were not yet covered, and medical costs drove many older Americans into poverty.

Poverty in an Age of Abundance

As millions of Americans (most of them white) settled in suburbs, the poor concentrated in inner cities. African American migrants from the South were joined by poor whites from the southern Appalachians, moving to Chicago, Cincinnati, Baltimore, and Detroit. Latin Americans arrived in growing numbers from Mexico, the Dominican Republic, Colombia, Ecuador, and Cuba. According to the 1960 census, over a half-million Mexican Americans migrated to the Los Angeles–Long Beach area since 1940. And New York City's Puerto Rican population exploded from 70,000 in 1940 to 613,000 in 1960.

Because of the strong economy, many newcomers gained the higher standard of living they sought. But discrimination limited their advances, and they endured crowded and decrepit housing and poor schools. Federal programs that helped middle-class Americans sometimes made the poor's lives worse. For example, the National Housing Act of 1949, passed to make available "a decent home . . . for every American family," provided for urban redevelopment. Redevelopment meant slum clearance, replacing poor neighborhoods with luxury high-rise buildings, parking lots, or highways.

The growth of large agribusinesses pushed more tenant farmers and owners of small farms off the land. From 1945 to 1961 the nation's farm population declined from 24.4 million to 14.8 million. When the harvesting of southern cotton was mechanized in the 1940s and 1950s, more than 4 million people were displaced. Southern tobacco growers dismissed tenant farmers, bought tractors, and hired migratory workers. In the West and Southwest, Mexican citizens served as cheap migrant labor under the *bracero* program. Almost 1 million Mexican workers came legally to the United States in 1959. Entire families labored, enduring conditions little better than in the Great Depression.

Native Americans were America's poorest people, with an average annual income barely half that of the poverty level. Conditions were worsened by termination, a federal policy implemented during the Eisenhower administration. Termination reversed the Indian Reorganization Act of 1934, allowing Indians to terminate their tribal status and remove reservation lands from federal protection prohibiting their sale. Sixty-one tribes were terminated between 1954 and 1960. Termination could occur only with a tribe's agreement, but pressure was sometimes intense, especially when reservation land was rich in natural resources. Enticed by cash payments, almost four-fifths of the Klamaths of Oregon voted to sell their shares of forest land. Many Indians left reservation land for the city. By the time termination ceased in the 1960s, observers compared the situation of Native Americans to the devastation their forebears had endured in the nineteenth century.

Many Americans enjoyed relative prosperity in the postwar era. But those who made it to the comfortable middle class often ignored the plight of those left behind. Their children—the baby-boom generation—would see racism, poverty, and the self-satisfaction of postwar suburban culture as a failure of American ideals.

The Pledge of Allegiance

The Pledge of Allegiance Americans recite today was shaped by the Cold War. Congress added the phrase "under God" to the pledge in 1954 to emphasize the difference between the god-fearing United States and the "godless communists" of the Soviet Union.

The Pledge of Allegiance was not always an important part of American life. The original version was written in 1892 by Francis Bellamy, editor of *The Youth's Companion*, to commemorate the four hundredth anniversary of Columbus's arrival in North America. In 1942 Congress officially adopted a revised version as an act of wartime patriotism. The Supreme Court ruled in 1943, however, that schoolchildren could not be forced to say the Pledge to the Flag.

During the Cold War years, the pledge became an increasingly important symbol of U.S. loyalty. Cold War fears fueled a campaign by the Knights of Columbus, a Catholic men's service organization, to include "under God"

in the pledge. Supporting the bill, President Eisenhower proclaimed that

in this way we shall constantly strengthen those spiritual weapons which forever will be our country's most powerful resource in peace and war. From this day forward, the millions of our schoolchildren will daily proclaim in every city and town, every village and every rural schoolhouse, the dedication of our nation and our people to the Almighty.

Some Americans, citing the doctrine of separation of church and state, have protested including "under God." In June 2002, the Ninth District Court (covering California and eight western states) sparked a controversy by ruling that the 1954 pledge was unconstitutional because it conveyed "state endorsement" of a religious belief. Questions about the proper role of religion in the United States remain controversial, a legacy for a people and a nation becoming more diverse in the twenty-first century.

Summary

In the years following World War II, Americans married and had children in record numbers. Millions of veterans used the GI Bill to attend college, buy homes, and start businesses. Although U.S. leaders feared the nation would lapse back into economic depression after wartime government spending ended, consumer spending fueled growth. Sustained economic growth lifted a majority of Americans into an expanding middle class.

The Cold War presidencies of Truman and Eisenhower focused more on international relations than on domestic politics. Within the United States, Cold War fears provoked an extreme anticommunism that stifled political dissent and diminished Americans' civil liberties and freedoms.

The continuing African American struggle for civil rights drew national attention during the Montgomery bus boycott. African Americans won victories in the Supreme Court, including the landmark *Brown v. Board of Education* decision. Truman and Eisenhower used federal power to guarantee the rights of African Americans, as a national civil rights movement coalesced.

Despite continued racial divisions, the United States became a more inclusive nation in the 1950s, as a majority of Americans participated in a national, consumer-oriented, middle-class culture. This culture largely ignored the poverty in the nation's cities and rural areas, but for the growing number in the middle-class, the American Dream seemed a reality.

Chapter Review

SHAPING POSTWAR AMERICA

What prompted the mass migration of Americans to the suburbs after World War II?

Two factors facilitated massive migration to the suburbs: first, demand for affordable, single-family homes, and second, federal policies. With the economic hardship of the Great Depression and World War II, few new homes were built, and many people moved in with relatives. But the prosperity of the postwar years joined with more economical housing developments to feed a growing demand for home ownership. At the same time, the Federal Housing Authority offered low-interest mortgages and loans, and Congress authorized the construction of major roadways and interstate highways in the late 1940s and 1950s. These roads enabled people to move further away from city jobs.

What happened to the U.S. economy after World War II?

Despite initial difficulties, the economy did not return to a depression, as many feared. Instead, it quickly recovered, driven by consumer spending. With the economic boom during the war, Americans had money to spend again, but rationing and war production meant few consumer goods to spend it on. At the end of the war, however, they were ready to buy. Manufacturing boomed as factories shifted production from war products to consumer goods. Government programs also encouraged growth. The GI Bill offered veterans low-interest loans to buy homes or launch businesses, as well as funds for education. The resulting increase in the number of well-educated or technically trained workers benefited the American economy.

DOMESTIC POLITICS IN THE COLD WAR ERA

What happened to New Deal style liberalism after World War II?

President Harry S. Truman embraced the same government responsibility for citizens' welfare that drove FDR's New Deal programs, but with limited success. He sought an increase in the minimum wage, national housing legislation offering mortgage loans, national health insurance, and federal aid for education. He additionally supported the Full Employment Act and civil rights legislation for African Americans. But conservative Republicans and southern Democrats in Congress gutted the Full Employment Act and refused to raise the minimum wage, while southern conservatives destroyed his civil rights legislation. His medical insurance and educational funding also met with resistance. A moderate Republican, Eisenhower signed amendments to the Social Security Act that increased benefits and made 7.5 million workers eligible for the program. He also increased government funding for education. Still, neither Truman nor Eisenhower came close to the liberalism of the New Deal.

COLD WAR FEARS AND ANTICOMMUNISM

How did Cold War fears inspire a Red Scare in the United States?

After World War II, Cold War tensions between the United States and the Soviet Union frightened Americans about the prospect of a communist invasion. People also prepared for nuclear attack once the Soviet Union had its own atomic weapons in 1949 by building backyard bomb shelters and teaching school children to shield their faces with duck-and-cover positions. As the hysteria grew, it fed anticommunist demagoguery and witch hunts, the trampling of civil liberties, the suppression of dissent, and the persecution of innocent Americans. The House Un-American Activities Committee (HUAC) was formed to investigate so-called subversive and un-American propaganda—even going so far as to charge that film stars (including eight-year-old Shirley Temple) were Communist Party dupes and to send ten screenwriters and directors to prison when they refused to name names of suspected communists. Studios blacklisted actors, screenwriters, directors, and makeup artists suspected of communist affiliations, and university professors were similarly targeted based on the books they used or their unwillingness to take a loyalty oath. In 1950, Senator Joseph R. McCarthy symbolized public fears when he charged that the U.S. State Department was "thoroughly infested with Communists." He was later discredited on national television.

THE STRUGGLE FOR CIVIL RIGHTS

How did changing social attitudes in the postwar era facilitate the burgeoning civil rights movement?

African Americans who helped win the World War II were determined to improve their status at home. Politicians such as President Harry S Truman agreed that they were entitled to full citizenship and equality. Truman's President's Committee on Civil Rights issued a report that would become the civil rights movement agenda for the next twenty years, calling for antilynching and antisegregation legislation, and for laws guaranteeing voting rights and equal employment opportunity. Truman also ordered desegregation of the military, which was completed by the Korean War. Cold War politics also aided the African American cause: the United States could not condemn other countries for denying human rights when it practiced segregation at home. At the same time, a new and visible black middle-class of college-educated activists, war veterans, and union workers emerged. Together this climate encouraged ongoing efforts to challenge racial discrimination through the courts and through grass roots activism.

CREATING A MIDDLE-CLASS NATION

What led to the emergence of a middle-class culture in the 1950s?

In the 1950s, the American population was more homogeneous than it had been before or would be later. Immigration restrictions in the 1920s meant that a small percent of Americans were foreign-born by the 1950s, and most Americans (88 percent) could trace their roots to Europe. The emergence of a national mass media—magazines, newspapers, film, and television—taught all Americans how to behave and live like the suburban middle-class—with American foods replacing ethnic dishes, national brands that replaced homemade products, and so on. Television shows even taught how to set the table or properly parent a child, thereby reinforcing middle-class ideals to those watching across class, racial, and ethnic lines.

MEN, WOMEN, AND YOUTH AT MIDCENTURY

How did the economic and social structure of the 1950s determine the choices and roles available to men and women?

In the 1950s, middle-class families could survive on one income, typically the man's. That enabled experts and individuals to embrace the notion that it was better for women to stay at home, especially while children were young. Women's maternal roles were celebrated, and those who considered careers were considered abnormal. While many women did work, it was often part-time and for a specific goal, such as a new car. Hiring discrimination kept women out of high-paying jobs legally. Employment ads were sex segregated into Help Wanted Male and Help Wanted Female categories, and women earned only 60 percent of what men earned. The pressure to provide restricted the options available to men, too, with many choosing safer, corporate jobs that promoted conformity rather than risk.

THE LIMITS OF THE MIDDLE-CLASS NATION

What critiques emerged about middle-class America?

Influential critics condemned middle-class culture as a wasteland of conformity, homogeneity, and crass consumerism. During the prosperity of the postwar era, an increasing number of Americans made it into the middle-class and answered the call to keep the economy thriving by partaking in an assortment of new consumer goods. Many corporations, however, built a limited lifespan into the goods they produced, designing them to wear out so they would need to be replaced, and hence continue to spark demand. Worse, critics noted as early as the 1960s that the United States, with only 5 percent of the world's population, consumed more than one-third of its goods and services. All of this production generated increased pollution and health concerns. Critics also noted that those who made it to the middle-class often failed to notice that poverty persisted, with one-fifth of Americans considered poor.

SUGGESTIONS FOR FURTHER READING

Taylor Branch, *Parting the Waters: America in the King Years, 1954–1963* (1988)

Lizabeth Cohen, *A Consumer's Republic: The Politics of Mass Consumption in Postwar America* (2003)

Stephanie Coontz, *The Way We Never Were: American Families and the Nostalgia Trap* (1992)

Mary Dudziak, *Cold War Civil Rights: Race and the Image of American Democracy* (2000)

James Gregory, *The Southern Diaspora: How the Great Migrations of Black and White Southerners Transformed the Nation* (2007)

Thomas Hine, *Populuxe* (1986)

Grace Palladino, *Teenagers* (1996)

James T. Patterson, *Grand Expectations: The United States, 1945–1974* (1996)

Ellen W. Schrecker, *Many Are the Crime: McCarthyism in America* (1998)

Thomas J. Sugrue, *The Origins of the Urban Crisis: Race and Inequality in Postwar Detroit* (1996)

CHAPTER 30

The Tumultuous Sixties

CHAPTER OUTLINE

Kennedy and the Cold War

Marching for Freedom

Liberalism and the Great Society

Johnson and Vietnam

A Nation Divided

> **LINKS TO THE WORLD:**
> The British Invasion

1968

> **LEGACY FOR A PEOPLE
> AND A NATION:** The
> Immigration Act of 1965

Summary

It was late, and Ezell Blair had an exam the next day. But he and his friends in the dormitory sat talking—as they often did—about injustice, about living in a nation that proclaimed equality for all but denied full citizenship to some because of the color of their skin. They were complaining about the do-nothing adults, condemning the African American community of Greensboro when Franklin McCain said, as if he meant it, "It's time to fish or cut bait." Joe McNeil and McCain's roommate, David Richmond, agreed. Blair hesitated. "I was thinking about my grades," he said later.

The next day, February 1, 1960, after their classes at North Carolina Agricultural and Technical College, the four freshmen walked into town. At the F. W. Woolworth's on South Elm Street, one of the most profitable stores in the national chain, each bought a few small things. Then, nervously, they sat down at the lunch counter and tried to order coffee. These seventeen- and eighteen-year-olds were prepared to be arrested, even physically attacked. But nothing happened. The counter help ignored them as long as possible; finally, one worker said, "We don't serve colored here." An elderly white woman told the boys how proud she was of them. Still nothing happened. The store closed; the manager turned out the lights. After forty-five minutes, the four men who began the sit-in movement left the store.

The next day they returned with twenty fellow students. By February 3, sixty-three of the sixty-five seats were taken. On February 4, the sit-in spread to the S. H. Kress store across the street. By February 7, there were sit-ins in Winston-Salem; by February 8, in Charlotte; on February 9, in Raleigh. By the third week in February, students were picketing Woolworth's stores in the North. On July 26, 1960, F. W. Woolworth's ended segregation in all its stores.

This icon will direct you to interactive activities and study materials on A People And A Nation, Brief Edition

website: **www.cengage.com/history/norton/ peoplenationbrief8e**

Chronology

1960	Sit-ins begin in Greensboro.
	Birth-control pill is approved for contraceptive use.
	John F. Kennedy is elected president.
	Young Americans for Freedom write Sharon Statement.
1961	Freedom Rides protest segregation in transportation.
1962	Students for a Democratic Society issues Port Huron Statement.
	Cuban missile crisis courts nuclear war.
1963	Civil rights March on Washington for Jobs and Freedom draws more than 250,000.
	South Vietnamese leader Diem is assassinated following U.S.-sanctioned coup d'état .
	John F. Kennedy is assassinated; Lyndon B. Johnson becomes president.
1964	Civil Rights Act outlaws discrimination in hiring and public accommodations.
	Race riots break out in first of the long, hot summers.
	Gulf of Tonkin Resolution is passed by Congress.
	Free Speech Movement begins at University of California, Berkeley.
	Lyndon B. Johnson is elected president.
1965	Lyndon Johnson launches Great Society programs.
	United States commits ground troops to Vietnam and initiates Rolling Thunder bombing campaign.
	Voting Rights Act outlaws practices preventing most African Americans from voting in southern states.
	Immigration and Nationality Act lowers barriers to immigration from Asia and Latin America.
	Malcolm X is assassinated.
	Watts riot leaves thirty-four dead.
1966	National Organization for Women is founded.
1967	Summer of love occurs in San Francisco's Haight-Ashbury district.
	Race riots erupt in Newark, Detroit, and other cities.
1968	Tet Offensive deepens fear of losing war in Vietnam.
	Martin Luther King Jr. is assassinated.
	Robert Kennedy is assassinated.
	Antiwar protests escalate.
	Violence erupts at Democratic National Convention.
	Richard Nixon is elected president.

The sit-in at the Greensboro Woolworth's signaled the beginning of a decade of public activism rarely matched in U.S. history. During the 1960s, millions of Americans—many of them young— marched for civil rights or against the war in Vietnam. Passion over contemporary issues revitalized democracy and threatened to tear the nation apart.

John F. Kennedy, the nation's youngest president, told Americans as he took office in 1961, "The torch has been passed to a new generation." Despite his inspirational language, Kennedy had only modest success implementing his domestic agenda. In his third year as president, however, Kennedy offered greater support for civil rights and proposed ambitious domestic policies. When he was assassinated in November 1963, his death seemed to many the end of an era of hope.

Lyndon Johnson, Kennedy's successor, invoked the memory of the martyred president to launch an ambitious civil rights program and other liberal legislation. Calling his vision the Great Society, Johnson intended to use federal power to eliminate poverty and guarantee equal rights to all Americans.

Despite liberal triumphs and civil rights gains, social tensions escalated during the mid-1960s. A revitalized conservative movement emerged, and Franklin Roosevelt's old New Deal coalition fractured as white southerners abandoned the Democratic Party. Angry that poverty and discrimination persisted despite landmark civil rights laws, many African Americans rioted. White youth culture increasingly rejected the values and lifestyle of its elders, creating what Americans have called the generation gap.

Meanwhile, after the 1962 Cuban missile crisis brought the Soviet Union and the United States close to nuclear disaster, President John F. Kennedy and the Soviet leader Nikita Khrushchev deescalated tensions in 1963 and lessened Cold War pressures in Europe. Everywhere else, however, the superpowers competed frantically. Throughout the 1960s, the United States tried various approaches—including foreign aid, CIA covert actions, military assaults, cultural penetration, economic sanctions, and diplomacy—to win the Cold War. In Vietnam, Kennedy expanded U.S. involvement significantly. Johnson increased U.S. troops there to more than half a million in 1968.

By 1968 the Vietnam War divided Americans and undermined Johnson's Great Society. With the assassinations of Martin Luther King Jr. and Robert Kennedy— two of America's brightest leaders—with cities in flames and tanks on Chicago streets in August, the fate of the nation hung in the balance.

- **What were the successes and failures of American liberalism in the 1960s?**
- **Why did the United States expand its participation in the war in Vietnam and continue in the war so long?**
- **By 1968, many believed the fate of the nation hung in the balance. What did they think was at stake? What divided Americans, and how did they express their differences?**

KENNEDY AND THE COLD WAR

Young, handsome, and intellectually curious, John F. Kennedy brought wit and sophistication to the White House. His Irish American grandfather had been mayor of Boston, and his millionaire father, Joseph P. Kennedy, served as ambassador to Great Britain. In 1946 the young Kennedy returned from World War II a naval hero (the boat he commanded was sunk by a Japanese destroyer in 1943, and Kennedy saved his crew) and campaigned to represent Boston in the U.S. House of Representatives. He served three terms in the House, and in 1952 was elected to the Senate.

John Fitzgerald Kennedy

As a Democrat, Kennedy inherited the New Deal commitment to the United States's social welfare system. He generally voted with the pro-labor sentiments of his low-income, blue-collar constituents. But he avoided controversial issues, such as civil rights and the censure of Joseph McCarthy. Kennedy won a Pulitzer Prize for his *Profiles in Courage* (1956), a study of principled politicians, but he shaded the truth in claiming sole authorship, as it was written largely by aide Theodore Sorensen (from more than one hundred pages of notes dictated by Kennedy). In foreign policy, Senator Kennedy endorsed the Cold War policy of containment. Despite an unimpressive legislative record, he enjoyed an enthusiastic following, especially after his landslide Senate reelection in 1958.

Kennedy cultivated an image as a happy and healthy family man. But he was a chronic womanizer, even after his 1953 marriage to Jacqueline Bouvier. Nor was he the picture of physical vitality: as a child he nearly died of scarlet fever and later developed severe back problems, made worse by his participation in World War II. After the war, Kennedy was diagnosed with Addison's disease, an adrenalin deficiency that required daily cortisone injections and often left him in acute pain. As president he would require plenty of bed rest and frequent therapeutic swims in the White House pool.

Election of 1960

Kennedy beat Republican Richard Nixon for president in 1960 by a narrow 118,000 votes out of nearly 69 million cast. Kennedy achieved mixed success in the South but ran well in the Northeast and Midwest. His Roman Catholic faith hurt him in states where voters feared he would take direction from the pope, but helped in states with large Catholic populations. As the sitting vice president, Nixon had to answer for sagging economic figures and the Soviet downing of a U-2 spy plane. In televised debates against the telegenic Kennedy, Nixon looked nervous, and the camera made him appear unshaven. Perhaps worse, when asked to list Nixon's significant decisions as vice president, Eisenhower replied, "If you give me a week, I might think of one."

The new president surrounded himself with mostly young advisers whom writer David Halberstam called "the best and the brightest." Secretary of Defense Robert McNamara (age forty-four) was an assistant professor at Harvard at twenty-four and later the whiz-kid president of the Ford Motor Company. Kennedy's special assistant for national security affairs, McGeorge Bundy (age forty-one) became a Harvard dean at thirty-four with only a bachelor's degree. Secretary of State Dean Rusk (fifty-two) had been a Rhodes scholar in his youth. Kennedy was only forty-three, and his brother Robert, the attorney general, was thirty-five.

Kennedy gave top priority to the Cold War. In the campaign he accused Eisenhower of unimaginative foreign policy that failed to reduce the threat of nuclear war with the Soviet Union and weakened the United States's standing in the Third World.

Nation Building in the Third World

Kennedy in office understood sooner than his advisers the limits of U.S. power abroad. More than his predecessor, he proved willing to initiate dialogue with the Soviets, sometimes using his brother Robert as a secret channel to Moscow. Yet Kennedy also sought victory in the Cold War. After the Soviet leader Nikita Khrushchev endorsed wars of national liberation, such as the one in Vietnam, Kennedy called for peaceful revolution through nation building. The administration helped developing nations with aid to improve agriculture, transportation, and communications. Kennedy thus oversaw the creation of the multibillion-dollar Alliance for Progress in 1961 to spur economic development in Latin America. That year, too, he created the Peace Corps, dispatching U.S. teachers, agricultural specialists, and health workers, many of them recent college graduates, to assist developing nations.

Cynics then and later dismissed the Alliance and the Peace Corps as Kennedy's Cold War tools for countering anti-Americanism and defeating communism in the developing world. True enough, but the programs were also born of genuine humanitarianism. As the historian Elizabeth Cobbs Hoffman has written, "the Peace Corps broached an age-old dilemma of U.S. foreign policy: how to reconcile the imperatives and temptations of power politics with the ideals of freedom and self-determination for all nations."

Although Kennedy and his aides were supportive of social revolution in the Third World, they could not see the legitimacy of communist involvement in these uprisings. Therefore, the administration also relied on counterinsurgency to defeat revolutionaries who challenged pro-U.S. Third World governments. U.S. military and technical advisers trained native troops and police to quell unrest.

The Alliance for Progress was only partly successful; infant mortality rates improved, but Latin American economies registered unimpressive growth and class divisions widened, exacerbating political unrest. Although many foreign peoples welcomed U.S. economic assistance and American material culture, they resented meddling. And because aid was usually funneled through a self-interested elite, it often never reached the poor. To people who preferred the quick solutions of a managed economy, moreover, the American emphasis on private enterprise seemed inappropriate.

Soviet-American Tensions

Nor did the new president succeed in relations with the Soviet Union. A summit meeting with the Soviet leader Nikita Khrushchev in Vienna in June 1961 went poorly, with the two leaders disagreeing over preconditions for peace and stability in the world. Consequently, the administration's first year witnessed little movement on controlling the nuclear arms race or getting a superpower ban on testing nuclear weapons in the atmosphere or underground. Instead, both superpowers accelerated their arms production. In 1961 the U.S. military budget shot up 15 percent; by mid-1964, U.S. nuclear weapons increased by 150 percent. Government advice to citizens to build fallout shelters in their backyards intensified public fear of devastating war.

If war occurred, many believed Berlin would be the cause. In mid-1961 Khrushchev demanded an end to western occupation of West Berlin and a reunification of East and West Germany, but Kennedy stood by U.S. commitment to West Berlin and West Germany. In August the Soviets, at the urging of the East German regime, erected a concrete and barbed-wire barricade to halt the exodus of East Germans into the prosperous and politically free West Berlin. The Berlin Wall inspired protests throughout the noncommunist world, but Kennedy privately sighed that "a wall is a hell of a lot better than a war."

Bay of Pigs Invasion

Kennedy knew that Khrushchev would continue to press elsewhere, and he was particularly rankled by growing Soviet assistance to Fidel Castro's Cuban government. The Eisenhower administration contested the Cuban revolution and bequeathed to the Kennedy administration a partially developed CIA plan to overthrow Castro: CIA-trained Cuban exiles would land and secure a beachhead; the Cuban people would rise up against Castro and welcome a new U.S.-backed government.

The attack took place on April 17, 1961, as twelve hundred exiles landed at the swampy Bay of Pigs in Cuba. Instead of discontented Cubans, they were greeted by Castro's troops and quickly captured. Kennedy tried to keep the U.S. participation in the operation hidden, but the CIA's role swiftly became public. Anti-American sentiment swept through Latin America. Castro, concluding that the United States might launch another invasion, looked increasingly toward the Soviet Union for military and economic assistance.

Embarrassed by the Bay of Pigs fiasco, Kennedy vowed to bring Castro down. The CIA soon hatched a project called Operation Mongoose to disrupt the island's trade, support raids on Cuba from Miami, and plot to kill Castro. The agency's assassination schemes included providing Castro with cigars laced with explosives and poison. The United States also tightened its economic blockade and undertook military maneuvers in the Caribbean. The Joint Chiefs of Staff sketched plans to spark a rebellion in Cuba that would be followed by an invasion of U.S. troops.

Cuban Missile Crisis

Both Castro and Khrushchev believed an invasion was coming, which partly explains the Soviet leader's risky decision in 1962 to secretly deploy nuclear missiles in Cuba as a deterrent. But Khrushchev also hoped the move would improve the Soviet position in the nuclear balance of power and force Kennedy to finally resolve the German problem. Khrushchev worried that Washington might provide West Germany with nuclear weapons. He thought he could prevent it by putting Soviet missiles just 90 miles off the coast of Florida. The world soon faced brinkmanship at its most frightening.

In mid-October 1962, a U-2 plane flying over Cuba photographed the missile sites. The president immediately organized a special Executive Committee (ExComm) to force the missiles and their nuclear warheads out of Cuba. Options considered ranged from full-scale invasion to limited bombing to quiet diplomacy. Defense Secretary Robert McNamara proposed a solution acceptable to the president: a naval quarantine of Cuba.

Kennedy addressed the nation on television on October 22, demanding that the Soviets retreat. U.S. warships began crisscrossing the Caribbean, while B-52s with nuclear bombs took to the skies. Khrushchev agreed to withdraw the missiles if the United States pledged never to attack Cuba and removed Jupiter missiles aimed at the Soviet Union from Turkey. For several days the world teetered on the brink of disaster. Then, on October 28, came a compromise. The United States agreed to Soviet demands in exchange for the withdrawal of Soviet offensive forces from Cuba. Fearing Castro might make matters worse, Khrushchev settled without consulting the Cubans.

Many observers then and later called it Kennedy's finest hour. Critics, however, claimed Kennedy may have caused the crisis in the first place with his anti-Cuban projects. Either way, the Cuban missile crisis was a watershed in the Soviet-American relationship. Both Kennedy and Khrushchev acted with greater prudence in its aftermath, taking steps toward improved relations. In August 1963 the adversaries signed a treaty banning nuclear tests in the atmosphere, the oceans, and outer space. They also installed a coded wire-telegraph hot line staffed around the clock to allow near-instant communication between the capitals. Both sides refrained from further confrontation in Berlin.

Together these small steps began to build much-needed mutual trust. By autumn 1963, the Cold War in Europe was fading as both sides accepted the status quo of a divided continent and a fortified border. But the arms race continued and accelerated, and the superpower competition in the Third World remained intense.

MARCHING FOR FREEDOM

President Kennedy regarded the Cold War as the most important issue Americans faced. But in the early 1960s, young civil rights activists seized the national stage and demanded that the federal government mobilize behind them.

Students and the Movement

In 1960, six years after the *Brown* decision declared separate but equal unconstitutional, only 10 percent of southern public schools had begun desegregation. Fewer than one in four adult African Americans in the South could vote, and water fountains were still labeled White Only and Colored Only. One year after the young men sat down at the all-white lunch counter in Greensboro, more than seventy thousand Americans—mostly college students—had participated in sit-ins.

The young people who created the Student Nonviolent Coordinating Committee (SNCC) in spring 1960 to coordinate the sit-in movement were committed to nonviolence. In the years to come, SNCC stalwarts would risk their lives in the struggle for social justice.

Freedom Rides and Voter Registration

On May 4, 1961, thirteen members of the Congress of Racial Equality (CORE), a nonviolent civil rights organization formed during World War II, purchased bus tickets in Washington, D.C., for a 1,500-mile trip through the South to New Orleans. Calling themselves Freedom Riders, this racially mixed group meant to demonstrate that, despite Supreme Court rulings ordering the desegregation of interstate buses, Jim Crow still ruled in the South. They knew they were risking their lives. One bus was firebombed outside Anniston, Alabama. Riders were badly beaten in Birmingham. In Montgomery, a thousand whites attacked riders with baseball bats and steel bars. Police stayed away; the police commissioner called the freedom riders troublemakers.

News of the violent attacks made headlines worldwide. Soviet commentators highlighted the "savage nature of American freedom and democracy." One southern business leader, in Tokyo promoting Birmingham as a site for international business development, saw Japanese interest evaporate when photographs of the Birmingham attacks appeared in Tokyo newspapers.

In the United States, the violence forced many to confront racial discrimination and hatred in their nation. Middle- and upper-class white southerners resisted integration following the *Brown* decision. The Freedom Rides made some think differently. The *Atlanta Journal* editorialized: "[I]t is time for the decent people . . . to muzzle the jackals." The national and international outcry pushed a reluctant President Kennedy to send federal marshals to safeguard Freedom Riders in Alabama. But bowing to white southern pressure, he allowed the Freedom Riders to be arrested in Mississippi.

Beginning in 1961, thousands of SNCC volunteers, many of them high school and college students, risked their lives encouraging African Americans in rural Mississippi and Georgia to register to vote. Some SNCC volunteers were white, some were northerners, but many were African American southerners, often from low-income families. They experienced first-hand the intersection of racism, powerlessness, and poverty.

Kennedy and Civil Rights

Kennedy was sympathetic—though not terribly committed—to the civil rights movement, and he realized that racial oppression hurt the United States in the Cold War struggle for international opinion. However, like Franklin D. Roosevelt, he knew that if he alienated conservative southern Democrats in Congress, his legislative programs would founder. Thus he appointed five die-hard segregationists to the federal bench in the Deep South and delayed issuing an executive order forbidding segregation in federally subsidized housing (a pledge made in the 1960 campaign) until late 1962. He allowed the FBI director J. Edgar Hoover to harass Martin Luther King and other activists, using wiretaps and surveillance to gather personal information and circulating rumors of communist connections and personal improprieties to discredit them.

But grassroots civil rights activism—and the violence of white mobs—forced Kennedy's hand. In September 1962, the president ordered five hundred U.S. marshals to protect James Meredith, the first African American to attend the University of Mississippi. Thousands of whites attacked the marshals with guns, gasoline bombs, bricks, and pipes, killing 2 and seriously wounding 160. Neither the marshals nor James Meredith backed down.

Birmingham and the Children's Crusade

In 1961 the Freedom Riders captured the attention of the nation and the larger Cold War world. Martin Luther King Jr., having risen through the Montgomery bus boycott to leadership in the movement, concluded that only by provoking a crisis would the civil rights struggle advance. King and the SCLC planned a 1963 campaign in the most violently racist city in the United States: Birmingham, Alabama. Anticipating a violent response, they called their plan Project C—for confrontation. King wanted all Americans to see the racist hate and violence that marred their nation.

Through April 1963, nonviolent protests in Birmingham led to hundreds of arrests. Then, on May 2, in a controversial action, King and the parents of Birmingham put children on the front lines. As about a thousand African American children, some as young as six, marched, police commissioner Eugene "Bull" Connor ordered his police to train "monitor" water guns—powerful enough to strip bark from a tree at 100 feet—on them. The water guns mowed the children down, and police loosed attack dogs as the nation watched in horror on TV. President Kennedy demanded that Birmingham's white business and political elite negotiate a settlement. The Birmingham movement had won and, more importantly, pushed civil rights to the fore of Kennedy's agenda.

"Segregation Forever!"

On June 11, defiant Alabama governor George C. Wallace fulfilled a promise to "bar the schoolhouse door" himself to prevent the desegregation of the University of Alabama. Hearing echoes of Wallace's January 1963 inaugural pledge "Segregation now, segregation tomorrow, segregation forever!" and facing a nation rocked by civil rights protests, Kennedy committed the federal government to guarantee racial justice. In a televised address on June 12, Kennedy said, "Now the time has come for this nation to fulfill its promise." Hours later, the civil rights leader Medgar Evers was murdered in his driveway in Jackson, Mississippi. The next week, the president asked Congress to pass a comprehensive civil rights bill ending legal racial discrimination.

March on Washington

On August 28, 1963, a quarter-million Americans gathered on the Washington Mall to show support for Kennedy's civil rights bill. Behind the scenes, organizers from major civil rights groups—SCLC, CORE, SNCC, the NAACP, the Urban League, and A. Philip Randolph's Brotherhood of Sleeping Car Porters—grappled with growing tensions within the movement. SNCC activists saw Kennedy's proposed legislation as too little, too late. King and other older leaders counseled moderation. The movement was splintering.

What most Americans saw, however, was a celebration of unity. Black and white celebrities joined hands; folk singers sang freedom songs. Television aired Martin Luther King Jr.'s prophesy of a day when "all God's children, black men and white men, Jews and Gentiles, Protestants and Catholics, will be able to join hands and sing in the words of the old Negro spiritual, 'Free at last! Free at last! Thank God Almighty, we are free at last!'" The 1963 March on Washington for Jobs and Freedom was a triumph, powerfully demonstrating African Americans' commitment to equality and justice. Days later, white supremacists bombed the Sixteenth Street Baptist Church in Birmingham, killing four African American girls.

Freedom Summer

During summer 1964, more than one thousand white students joined the voter mobilization project in Mississippi. They formed Freedom Schools, teaching literacy and constitutional rights, and helped organize the Mississippi Freedom Democratic Party as an alternative to the whites-only Democratic Party. SNCC organizers also believed that

A historic moment for the civil rights movement was the March on Washington of August 28, 1963. The Reverend Martin Luther King Jr. (center) joined a quarter-million black people and white people in their march for racial equality. Addressing civil rights supporters and the nation from the steps of the Lincoln Memorial, King delivered his "I Have a Dream" speech. (R.W. Kelley / Getty Images)

large numbers of white volunteers would focus national attention on Mississippi's repression and violence. Project workers were arrested over a thousand times and were shot at, bombed, and beaten. On June 21, local black activist James Cheney and two white volunteers, Michael Schwerner and Andrew Goodman, were murdered by a Klan mob. That summer, black and white activists risked their lives together.

LIBERALISM AND THE GREAT SOCIETY

By 1963, Kennedy seemed to be taking a new path. Campaigning in 1960, he promised to lead Americans into a New Frontier, with the federal government working to eradicate poverty, guarantee healthcare to the elderly, and provide decent schools for all children. But few of Kennedy's domestic initiatives were passed into law. Lacking a popular mandate in the 1960 election, fearful of alienating southern Democrats in Congress, Kennedy let his social policy agenda languish.

Instead, Kennedy focused on the economy, believing that continued prosperity would solve the United States' social problems. Kennedy's vision was perhaps best realized in the United States's space program. As the Soviets drew ahead in the space race, Kennedy vowed in 1961 to put a man on the moon before decade's end. With billions in new funding, the National Aeronautics and Space Administration (NASA) began the Apollo program. And in February 1962, astronaut John Glenn orbited the earth in the space capsule *Friendship 7*.

Kennedy Assassination On November 22, 1963, Kennedy visited Texas, the home state of his vice president, Lyndon Johnson. In Dallas, riding with his wife, Jackie, in an open-top limousine, Kennedy was cheered by thousands along the motorcade's route. Suddenly shots rang out. The president crumpled, shot in the head. Tears ran down the cheeks of the CBS anchorman Walter Cronkite as he announced that the president was dead.

That same day police captured a suspect: Lee Harvey Oswald, a former U.S. marine (dishonorably discharged) who once attempted to gain Soviet citizenship. Two days later, television cameras rolled as Oswald was shot dead by the nightclub owner Jack Ruby. Shocked Americans wondered if Ruby was silencing Oswald to prevent him from implicating others. The seven-member Warren Commission, headed by U.S. Supreme Court chief justice Earl Warren, concluded that Oswald acted alone. But debates still rage over whether Oswald was a lone assassin.

Millions of Americans watched their president's funeral on television: the brave young widow, a riderless horse, three-year-old John-John saluting his father's casket. In one awful moment in Dallas, the reality of the Kennedy presidency had been transformed into myth, the man into martyr. In the post-assassination national grief, Lyndon Johnson invoked Kennedy's memory to push through the most ambitious legislative program since the New Deal.

Johnson and the Great Society Where Kennedy came from wealth and privilege and was educated at Harvard, Johnson grew up in modest circumstances in the Texas hill country and graduated from Southwest Texas State Teachers' College. He was as earthy as Kennedy was elegant, prone to colorful curses and willing to use his physical size to his advantage. Johnson had first come to Congress in 1937. As Senate majority leader from 1954 to 1960, he learned how to manipulate people and wield power. Now, as president, he used these skills to unite the nation.

Johnson, a liberal in the style of Franklin D. Roosevelt, believed that the federal government must actively improve the lives of Americans. In a 1964 commencement address at the University of Michigan, he described his vision of "abundance and liberty for all . . . demand[ing] an end to poverty and racial injustice . . . where every child can find knowledge to enrich his mind and to enlarge his talents." Johnson called this vision the Great Society.

Civil Rights Act

Johnson signed into law the Civil Rights Act of 1964, which ended *legal* discrimination on the basis of race, color, religion, or national origin, in federal programs, voting, employment, and public accommodation. The original bill did not include sex discrimination; that was introduced by a southern congressman who hoped it would engender enough opposition to torpedo the entire bill. But a bipartisan group of women members of the House of Representatives ensured it was passed with sex as a protected category. Significantly, the Civil Rights Act of 1964 gave the government authority to withhold federal funds from public agencies or federal contractors that discriminated and established the Equal Employment Opportunity Commission (EEOC) to investigate and judge claims of job discrimination. However, the EEOC largely ignored sex discrimination, prompting women's equality activists in 1966 to form the National Organization for Women (NOW).

Many Americans did not believe that it was the federal government's job to end racial discrimination or poverty. White southerners especially resented federal intervention in local customs, and millions of conservative Americans believed that since the New Deal the federal government had overstepped its constitutional boundaries. They sought a return to local control and states' rights. In the 1964 election, this vision was championed by the Republican candidate, Arizona senator Barry Goldwater.

Election of 1964

Goldwater not only voted against the 1964 Civil Rights Act, he also opposed the national Social Security system. Like many conservatives, he believed that individual *liberty,* not equality, mattered most. Goldwater further believed that the United States needed a more powerful national military to fight communism; in campaign speeches he suggested that the United States should use tactical nuclear weapons against its enemies.

Goldwater's campaign slogan, "In your heart you know he's right," was turned against him by Lyndon Johnson supporters: "In your heart you know he's right . . . far right," one punned. Johnson campaigned on an unemployment rate below 4 percent and economic growth above 6 percent. But his civil rights support severed the New Deal coalition, and he told an aide, "delivered the south to the Republican Party for my lifetime and yours."

Tensions mounted at the 1964 Democratic National Convention. Two delegations from Mississippi demanded to be seated. The Democratic Party's official delegation was exclusively white; the Mississippi Freedom Democratic Party's

(MFDP) was racially mixed. White southern delegates threatened to leave if the MFDP delegates were seated. Johnson sought a compromise, but the MFDP declined. "We didn't come all this way for no two seats," MFDP delegate Fannie Lou Hamer said, and the delegation walked out.

Johnson won the election by a landslide, but he lost the Deep South—the first Democrat since the Civil War to do so. Voters also elected the most liberal Congress in history. With a record 61.1 percent of the popular vote, Johnson launched his Great Society. Congress passed the most sweeping reform legislation since 1935.

In late 1964, the SCLC made voting rights its top priority. Martin Luther King Jr. and other leaders turned to Selma, Alabama, seeking another public confrontation that would mobilize national support and federal action. It came on March 6, when state troopers turned electric cattle prods, chains, and tear gas against peaceful marchers. On March 15, the president offered support for a second monumental civil rights bill, the Voting Rights Act. It outlawed practices that prevented most African American citizens in the Deep South from voting and provided for federal election oversight in districts with evidence of past discrimination. Within two years, African American registered voters in Mississippi jumped from 7 percent to more than 60 percent. African American elected officials became increasingly common in southern states over the following decade.

Improving American Life

Seeking to improve the quality of American life, the Johnson administration established new student loan and grant programs to help low- and moderate-income Americans attend college and created the National Endowment for the Arts and the National Endowment for the Humanities. The Immigration Act of 1965 ended racially based quotas. And Johnson supported consumer protection legislation, including the 1966 National Traffic and Motor Vehicle Safety Act, inspired by Ralph Nader's exposé of the automobile industry, *Unsafe at Any Speed* (1965). Johnson signed preservation legislation protecting the United States's wilderness and supported laws addressing environmental pollution.

War on Poverty

At the heart of Johnson's Great Society was the War on Poverty, which included major legislation beginning in 1964 (see Table 30.1). Johnson and other liberals believed that, in a time of affluence, the nation should use its resources to end "poverty, ignorance and hunger as intractable, permanent features of American society."

Johnson's goal was "to offer the forgotten fifth of our people opportunity, not doles." Municipalities and school districts received billions of federal dollars to improve opportunities for the poverty-stricken, from preschoolers (Head Start) to high schoolers (Upward Bound) to young adults (Job Corps). The Model Cities program offered federal funds to upgrade employment, housing, education, and health in targeted urban neighborhoods, and Community Action Programs involved poor Americans in creating local grassroots antipoverty programs.

The Johnson administration also expanded the Food Stamp program and earmarked billions for constructing public housing and subsidizing rents. Two new federal programs guaranteed healthcare: Medicare for those sixty-five and older, and

TABLE 30.1   Great Society Achievements, 1964–1966

	1964	1965	1966
Civil Rights	Civil Rights Act Equal Employment Opportunity Commission Twenty-fourth Amendment	Voting Rights Act	
War on Poverty	Economic Opportunity Act Office of Economic Opportunity Job Corps Legal Services for the Poor VISTA		Model Cities
Education		Elementary and Secondary Education Act Head Start Upward Bound	
Environment		Water Quality Act Air Quality Act	Clean Water Restoration Act

**New Government
    Agencies**
		Department of
		    Housing and Urban
		    Development
		National Endowments for
		    the Arts and Humanities
			Department of
			Transportation

Miscellaneous		Medicare and Medicaid Immigration and Nationality Act	

The Great Society of the mid-1960s saw the biggest burst of reform legislation since the New Deal of the 1930s.

Medicaid for the poor. Finally, Aid to Families with Dependent Children (AFDC), the welfare program created during the New Deal, broadened benefits and eligibility.

The War on Poverty was controversial. Leftists believed that the government was doing too little to change structural inequality. Conservatives argued that Great Society programs created dependency among the United States's poor. Policy analysts noted that specific programs were ill conceived and badly implemented. Decades later, most historians judge the War on Poverty a mixed success. Its programs improved the quality of housing, healthcare, and nutrition available to the poor. Federal spending for Social Security, healthcare, welfare, and education more than doubled between 1965 and 1975, with the number of Americans receiving food stamps increasing from 600,000 to 17 million. Poverty among the elderly fell from about 40 percent in 1960 to 16 percent in 1974, due largely to increased Social Security benefits and to Medicare. The War on Poverty improved many Americans' quality of life (see Figure 30.1).

But War on Poverty programs less successfully addressed the root causes of poverty. Neither the Job Corps nor Community Action Programs showed significant results. Economic growth largely sparked the dramatic decrease in poverty rates during the 1960s—from 22.4 percent of Americans in 1959 to 11 percent in 1973. Unchanged was the fact that 11 million Americans in female-headed households remained poor in 1969—the same number as in 1963.

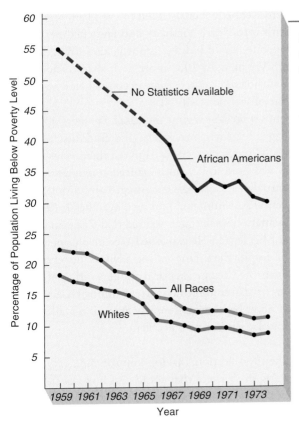

Figure 30.1   Poverty in America for Whites, African Americans, and All Races, 1959–1974

Because of rising levels of economic prosperity, combined with the impact of Great Society programs, the percentage of Americans living in poverty in 1974 was half as high as in 1959. African Americans still were far more likely than white Americans to be poor. In 1959 more than half of all African Americans (55.1 percent) were poor; in 1974 the figure remained high (30.3 percent). The government did not record data on African American poverty for the years 1960 through 1965.

Political compromises created long-term problems. For example, Congress accommodated doctors and hospitals in Medicare legislation by allowing federal reimbursements of hospitals' "reasonable costs" and doctors' "reasonable charges" in treating elderly patients. With no incentives for doctors or hospitals to hold prices down, national healthcare expenditures as a percentage of the gross national product rose by almost 44 percent from 1960 to 1971. Problems aside, Johnson's Great Society was a moment in which many Americans believed they could and should solve the problems of poverty, disease, and discrimination.

JOHNSON AND VIETNAM

In foreign policy, Johnson held firmly to ideas about U.S. superiority and the communist menace. International affairs held little interest for him, and he had little appreciation for foreign cultures. At the Taj Mahal in India, Johnson tested the monument's echo with a Texas cowboy yell. On a trip to Senegal, he ordered that an American bed, a special showerhead, and cases of Cutty Sark be sent with him. "Foreigners," Johnson quipped, only half-jokingly, "are not like the folks I am used to."

Kennedy's Legacy in Vietnam

Yet Johnson knew that foreign policy, especially regarding Vietnam, would demand his attention. Since the late 1950s, hostilities in Vietnam increased, as Ho Chi Minh's North assisted the Vietcong guerrillas in the South in reunifying the country under a communist government. President Kennedy increased aid to the Diem regime in Saigon, airdropped more raid teams into North Vietnam, and launched herbicide crop destruction to starve the Vietcong out of hiding. Kennedy also strengthened the U.S. military presence in South Vietnam: by 1963 more than sixteen thousand military advisers were there, some authorized to participate in combat alongside the U.S.-equipped Army of the Republic of Vietnam (ARVN).

Meanwhile, opposition to Diem's repressive regime increased. Peasants objected to being removed from their villages for their own safety, and Buddhist monks, protesting Roman Catholic Diem's religious persecution, ignited themselves in the streets of Saigon. Although Diem was honest, he countenanced corruption in his government and jailed critics. Eventually U.S. officials encouraged ambitious South Vietnamese generals to remove Diem. They murdered him on November 1, 1963.

The timing of Kennedy's assassination weeks later ensured that Vietnam would be the most controversial aspect of his legacy. He expanded U.S. involvement and approved a coup against Diem, but despite the urgings of top advisers, he refused to commit U.S. ground forces. Over time he became skeptical about South Vietnam's prospects and hinted he would end the U.S. commitment after winning reelection in 1964. Whether he would have can never be known. Kennedy arrived in Dallas that fateful day uncertain about how to solve the Vietnam problem.

Tonkin Gulf Incident and Resolution

Facing the 1964 election, Lyndon Johnson did not want to do anything in Vietnam that could cost him the election, so he kept Vietnam on the back burner. Yet Johnson also sought victory there, and throughout 1964 the administration secretly considered expanding the war to North Vietnam.

In early August 1964, U.S. destroyers reported coming under attack twice in three days from North Vietnamese patrol boats in the Gulf of Tonkin (see Map 30.1). Despite a lack of evidence that the second attack occurred, Johnson ordered retaliatory air strikes against North Vietnamese patrol boat bases and an oil depot. By a vote of 416 to 0 in the House and 88 to 2 in the Senate, Congress quickly passed the Gulf of Tonkin Resolution, giving the president the authority to "take all necessary measures to repel any armed attack against the forces of the United States and to prevent further aggression." In so doing, Congress essentially surrendered its war-making powers to the executive branch.

Decision for Escalation

President Johnson also appreciated how the Gulf of Tonkin affair boosted his public approval ratings and effectively removed Vietnam as a campaign issue for GOP presidential nominee Barry Goldwater. On the ground in South Vietnam, however, the outlook remained grim, as the Vietcong made gains. U.S. officials secretly planned to escalate U.S. involvement.

In February 1965, in response to Vietcong attacks on U.S. installations in South Vietnam which killed thirty-two Americans, Johnson ordered Operation Rolling Thunder, a bombing program that continued until October 1968. On March 8, the first U.S. combat battalions came ashore near Danang. The North Vietnamese responded by increasing infiltration into the South. In Saigon, meanwhile, coups and countercoups by self-serving military leaders undermined U.S. efforts.

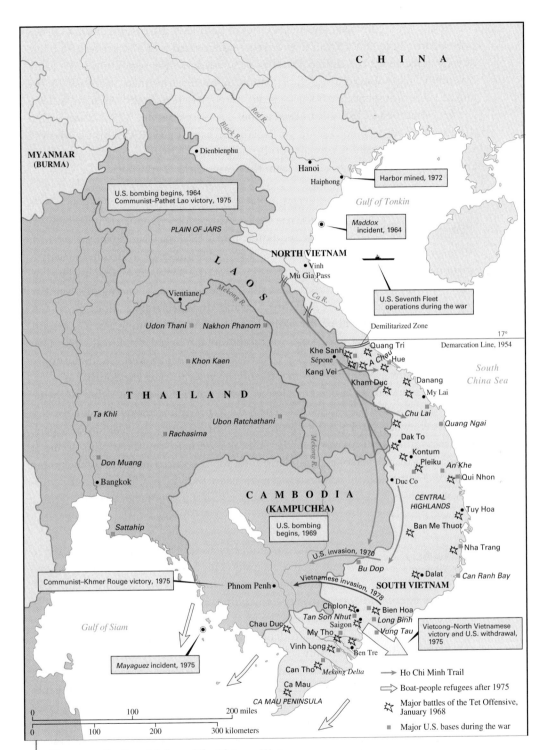

Map 30.1   Southeast Asia and the Vietnam War

To prevent communists from coming to power in Vietnam, Cambodia, and Laos in the 1960s, the United States intervened massively in Southeast Asia. The interventions failed, and the remaining U.S. troops made a hasty exit from Vietnam in 1975, as the victorious Vietcong and North Vietnamese took Saigon and renamed it Ho Chi Minh City.

In July 1965, Johnson convened a series of high-level discussions about U.S. war policy, partially so history would record that he agonized over a choice he had in fact already made about the United States's open-ended involvement. On July 28, Johnson publicly announced a significant troop increase, with others to follow. By the end of 1965, more than 180,000 U.S. ground troops were in South Vietnam. In 1966 the figure climbed to 385,000. In 1967 alone, U.S. warplanes flew 108,000 sorties and dropped 226,000 tons of bombs on North Vietnam. In 1968 U.S. troop strength reached 536,100. Each U.S. escalation brought a new North Vietnamese escalation and increased assistance to Hanoi from the Soviet Union and China.

Opposition to Americanization

Rolling Thunder and the U.S. troop commitment Americanized the war, transforming it from a civil war between North and South into a U.S. war against the communist Hanoi government. In the key months of decision, Democratic leaders in the Senate, major newspapers such as the *New York Times* and the *Wall Street Journal,* and prominent columnists such as Walter Lippmann warned against deepening involvement, as did Vice President Hubert H. Humphrey and Undersecretary of State George W. Ball. Abroad, virtually all of the United States's allies—including France, Britain, Canada, and Japan—cautioned against escalation and urged a political settlement. Remarkably, top U.S. officials knew that the odds of success were small but hoped the new measures would cause Hanoi to end the insurgency in the South.

U.S. leaders feared that if the United States failed in Vietnam, other countries would find U.S. power less credible. The Soviets and Chinese would challenge U.S. interests elsewhere, and allied governments might conclude they could not depend on Washington. Johnson worried that failure in Vietnam would harm his domestic agenda and feared personal humiliation. As for the stated objective of helping a South Vietnamese ally repulse external aggression, that did not figure into the equation as much as it would have had the Saigon government—racked with infighting and little popular support—done more in its own defense.

U.S. Soldiers in Vietnam

To minimize publicity about the war, Johnson refused to call up reserve units. This forced the military to rely heavily on the draft, which made Vietnam a young man's war; the average age of soldiers was twenty-two, compared with twenty-six in World War II. It also became a war of the poor and the working class. Through the years of heavy escalation (1965–1968), college students could get deferments, as could teachers and engineers. (In 1969 the draft was changed so that some students were called up through a lottery system.) The armed services recruited hard in poor communities, many of them heavily African American and Hispanic American, advertising the military as an avenue of training and advancement. Once in uniform, those with fewer skills were far more likely to see combat, and hence to die.

Infantrymen maneuvered into thick jungles, where booby traps and land mines were a constant threat. Boots and human skin rotted from the rains. The enemy was hard to find, often burrowed into elaborate underground tunnels or melded into the population, where any Vietnamese might be a Vietcong.

The entry of U.S. forces into the conflict in 1965 helped stave off a South Vietnamese defeat, thereby achieving Americanization's most immediate and basic

Wounded U.S. soldiers after a battle in Vietnam.
(Larry Burrows/Getty Images)

objective. But as the North Vietnamese matched each U.S. escalation with their own, the war became a stalemate. The U.S. commander, General William Westmoreland, mistakenly believed that a strategy of attrition represented the key to victory. Thus, the measure of success became the body count, the number of North Vietnamese and Vietcong corpses found after battle. But counts were manipulated by officers eager to demonstrate an operation's success. Worse, the U.S. reliance on massive military technology—including carpet bombing, napalm (jellied gasoline), and crop defoliants that destroyed forests—alienated many South Vietnamese and brought new recruits to the Vietcong.

Divisions at Home

As television coverage brought the war—its body bags, burned villages, and weeping refugees—into U.S. homes nightly, the number of opponents grew. College professors and students organized debates and lectures on U.S. policy, which became a form of protest, called teach-ins after the sit-ins of the civil rights movement. Pacifist groups, such as the American Friends Service Committee and the Women's International League for Peace and Freedom, organized early protests.

In early 1966 Senator William Fulbright held televised hearings on whether the national interest was served by pursuing the war. To the surprise of some, George F. Kennan testified that his containment doctrine was meant for Europe, not volatile Southeast Asia. The United States's preoccupation with Vietnam, Kennan asserted, was undermining its global obligations. The Fulbright hearings provoked Americans to think about the conflict and the nation's role in it and revealed deep divisions on Vietnam among public officials.

Defense secretary Robert McNamara, who championed the Americanization of the war in 1965, became increasingly troubled by the killing and destructiveness of the bombing. In November 1965 he expressed skepticism that victory could ever be achieved. U.S. credibility was suffering grievous damage, McNamara feared. But Johnson was determined to prevail in Vietnam. Although he occasionally halted the bombing to encourage Ho Chi Minh to negotiate, such pauses often were accompanied by increases in U.S. troop strength. Hanoi demanded suspension of bombing raids before negotiating. And Ho rejected U.S. terms, which amounted to abandonment of his lifelong dream of an independent, unified Vietnam.

A NATION DIVIDED

As Johnson struggled in Vietnam, his Great Society faced challenges at home. The United States was fracturing not only over Vietnam but also along many different lines: black and white, youth and age, radical and conservative.

Urban Unrest

In 1964, shortly after President Johnson signed the landmark Civil Rights Act, racial violence erupted in northern cities. Angry residents of Harlem took to the streets after a white police officer shot an African American teenager. The following summer, in the predominantly African American Watts section of Los Angeles, crowds burned, looted, and battled police for five days. The riot, which began when a white police officer attempted to arrest an African American resident on suspicion of drunken driving, left thirty-four dead. In July 1967, twenty-six people were killed in street battles between African Americans and police and army troops in Newark, New Jersey. A week later, in Detroit, forty-three died as 3 square miles of the city went up in flames. In 1967 alone, there were 167 violent outbreaks in 128 cities.

The long, hot summers of urban unrest differed from previous race riots, which were typically started by whites. Here, African American residents exploded in anger and frustration over the conditions of their lives. They looted and burned stores, most of them white-owned, while also devastating their own neighborhoods.

In 1968 the National Advisory Commission on Civil Disorders, chaired by Governor Otto Kerner of Illinois, warned that the United States was "moving towards two societies, one white, one black—separate and unequal" and blamed white racism for the riots. "What white Americans have never fully understood—but what the Negro can never forget—is that white society is deeply implicated in the ghetto. White institutions created it, white institutions maintain it, and white society condones it," concluded the Kerner Commission. Some white Americans disagreed, while others wondered why African Americans were venting their frustration just when they were making real progress in civil rights.

The answer stemmed partly from regional differences. The civil rights movement focused mostly on fighting *legal* disenfranchisement and discrimination in the South and largely ignored problems in the North. Increasingly concentrated in the deteriorating inner-city ghettos, most northern African Americans faced discrimination in housing, credit, and employment. The median income of northern African Americans was roughly half that of northern whites, and their unemployment rate was twice as high. Many northern African Americans had given up on the civil rights movement and the Great Society.

Black Power

In this climate, a new voice urged African Americans to seize freedom "by any means necessary." Malcolm X, a onetime pimp and street hustler who converted in prison to the Nation of Islam faith, offered African Americans new leadership. Members of the Nation of Islam, known as Black Muslims, espoused black pride and separatism from white society. Their faith combined traditional Islam with a belief that whites were subhuman devils whose race would soon be destroyed and emphasized sobriety, thrift, and social responsibility. By the early 1960s, Malcolm X had become the Black Muslims' chief spokesperson. But his murder in 1965 by members of the Nation of Islam who felt betrayed when he started his own, more racially tolerant organization, transformed Malcolm X into a powerful symbol of black defiance and self-respect.

A year after Malcolm X's death, Stokely Carmichael, SNCC chairman, denounced "the betrayal of black dreams by white America." To end white oppression, Carmichael proclaimed, blacks had to "stand up and take over" by electing black candidates and organizing their own schools and institutions to embrace Black Power. That year, SNCC expelled its white members and repudiated nonviolence and integration. CORE followed in 1967.

The best-known black radicals were the Black Panthers, an organization formed in Oakland, California, in 1966. Blending black separatism and revolutionary communism, the Panthers focused on destroying capitalism and its "military arm," the police. Male Panthers dressed in commando gear, carried weapons, and talked about killing "pigs" and did kill eleven police officers by 1970. Police responded in kind; most infamously, Chicago police murdered the local Panther leader Fred Hampton in his bed. However, the Panthers also worked to improve life in their neighborhoods by instituting free breakfast and healthcare programs for ghetto children, offering courses in African American history, and demanding jobs and housing. Before the end of the decade, a vocal minority of the United States's young would join in calls for revolution.

Youth and Politics

By the mid-1960s, 41 percent of the U.S. population was under the age of twenty. These young people spent more time with peers than any previous generation, as three-quarters of them graduated from high school (up from one-fifth in the 1920s) and almost half of them went to college (up from 16 percent in 1940). As this large baby-boom generation came of age, many believed they must provide democratic leadership for their nation. Inspired by the sit-in movement at African American colleges, some white college students—from both political left and right—committed themselves to changing the system.

In fall 1960, a group of conservative college students met at William F. Buckley's estate in Sharon, Connecticut, to form Young Americans for Freedom (YAF). Their manifesto, the Sharon Statement, endorsed Cold War anticommunism and a vision of limited government directly opposed to New Deal liberalism. The YAF planned to capture the Republican Party and move it to the political right; Goldwater's selection as the Republican candidate for president in 1964 demonstrated their early success.

At the other end of the political spectrum, an emerging New Left also rejected liberalism. Whereas conservatives believed liberalism's activist government encroached on individual liberty, the New Left believed that liberalism was not enough to bring equality to all Americans. Meeting in Port Huron, Michigan, in 1962, founding members of Students for a Democratic Society (SDS) drafted their Port Huron Statement, condemning racism, poverty in the midst of plenty, and the Cold War. Calling for participatory democracy, SDS sought to wrest power from the corporations, the military, and the politicians and return it to the people.

Free Speech Movement

The rise of activist white youth crystallized at the University of California, Berkeley. In the fall of 1964, the university administration banned political activity—including recruiting volunteers for civil rights work in Mississippi—from its traditional place along a university-owned sidewalk bordering the campus. When police tried to arrest a CORE worker who defied the order, four thousand students surrounded the police car. Berkeley graduate student and Mississippi Freedom Summer veteran Mario Savio encouraged the students: "You've got to put your bodies upon the levers . . . [and] you've got to indicate to the people who run it, to the people who own it, that unless you're free, the machine will be prevented from working at all."

Student political groups, left and right, united to create the Free Speech Movement (FSM). The FSM won back the right to political speech, but not before state police arrested almost eight hundred student protesters. Many saw the administration's actions as a failure of the United States's democratic promises, but the FSM's victory also demonstrated to students their potential power. By decade's end, the activism born at Berkeley would spread to hundreds of colleges and universities.

Student Activism

Student protesters sought greater control over their education, demanding more relevant class offerings, more freedom in course selection, and a greater voice in the running of universities. Students protested against the doctrine of in loco parentis, which put universities legally "in the place of parents," allowing control over student behavior that went beyond the law. In loco parentis fell heaviest on women, who had strict curfew regulations called parietals, while men did not. Along with an end to sex discrimination, protesters like those at the University of Kansas wanted administrators to explain how statements that "college students are assumed to have maturity of judgment necessary for adult responsibility" squared with the minute regulation of students' nonacademic lives. One young man complained that "a high school dropout selling cabbage in a supermarket" had more rights and freedoms than successful university students.

Youth and the War in Vietnam

It was the war in Vietnam, however, that mobilized a nationwide student movement. Believing that learning and speaking out about issues was their civic duty, in 1965 university students and faculty held teach-ins about U.S. involvement in Vietnam.

SDS sponsored the first major antiwar march that year, drawing twenty thousand protesters to Washington, D.C. On campuses everywhere, students borrowed civil rights movement tactics, picketing ROTC buildings and protesting military research and recruiting done on their campuses. Despite the antiwar protests' visibility, most students did not yet oppose the war: in 1967, only 30 percent of male students were doves on Vietnam, while 67 percent were hawks. But as the war escalated, more students distrusted the government as well as the seemingly arbitrary authority of university administrations.

Youth Culture and the Counterculture

The large baby-boom generation changed the nation's culture more than its politics. Although many protested the war and marched for social justice, most did not. Fraternity and sorority life stayed strong even as radicalism flourished. And although there was some crossover, African American, white, and Hispanic American youth had different cultural styles, clothes, and music. Nonetheless, as potential consumers, young people exercised tremendous cultural authority and drove American popular culture in the late 1960s.

The most unifying element of youth culture was music. The Beatles electrified U.S. teenagers; 73 million viewers watched their first television appearance on the *Ed Sullivan Show* in 1964. Bob Dylan promised revolutionary answers in "Blowin' in the Wind," Janis Joplin brought the sexual power of the blues to white youth, James Brown and Aretha Franklin proclaimed black pride, and the psychedelic rock of Jefferson Airplane and the Grateful Dead—along with hallucinogenic drugs—redefined reality. At the Woodstock Festival in upstate New York in 1969, more than 400,000 people reveled in music and a world of their own making, living in rain and mud for four days without shelter or violence.

Some hoped to turn youth rebellion into social revolution, rejecting what they saw as hypocritical middle-class values. They crafted an alternative way of life, or counterculture, liberated from competitive materialism and celebrating pleasure. "Sex, drugs, and rock 'n' roll" became a mantra of sorts, offering these hippies a path to a new consciousness. Many did the hard work of creating communes and intentional communities, whether in cities or in hidden stretches of the rural United States. Although the New Left criticized the counterculture as apolitical, many hippies did envision revolutionary change through mind-altering drugs, sex, or music.

The nascent counterculture first entered the national consciousness during summer 1967, when tens of thousands poured into the Haight-Ashbury district of San Francisco, the heart of the United States's psychedelic culture, for the summer of love. As an older generation of "straight" (or establishment) Americans watched with horror, white youth looked like the counterculture. Coats and ties disappeared, as did stockings and bras. Young men grew long hair, and parents complained, "You can't tell the boys from the girls." Millions used marijuana or hallucinogenic drugs, read underground newspapers, and thought of themselves as alienated from straight culture even though as high school or college students, they were not completely dropping out.

Some of the most lasting cultural changes involved attitudes about sex. The mass media were fascinated with free love, and while some youth embraced promiscuous sexuality, it was most important that premarital sex no longer destroyed a

The British Invasion

The British invasion began in earnest on February 7, 1964. Three thousand screaming American teenagers were waiting when Pan Am's *Yankee Clipper* touched down at Kennedy Airport with four British "moptops" aboard. "I Want to Hold Your Hand" was at the top of the U.S. charts, and seventy-three million people—the largest television audience in history—watched the Beatles on the *Ed Sullivan Show* the following Sunday night.

Although the Beatles led the invasion, they did not conquer the United States alone. The Rolling Stones' first U.S. hit single also came in 1964. The Dave Clark Five appeared on *Ed Sullivan* eighteen times. And there were many others: Herman's Hermits, the Animals, the Yardbirds, the Hollies, the Kinks, and Petula Clark.

The British invasion was, at least partly, the triumphal return of American music, a transatlantic exchange that reinvigorated both nations. American rock 'n' roll had lost much of its energy by the early 1960s, and the London-centered popular music industry was pumping out a saccharine version of American pop. But by the late 1950s, young musicians in England's provincial cities were listening to the music of the African American bluesmen Muddy Waters and Howlin' Wolf and the early rock 'n' roll of Buddy Holly and Chuck Berry. None of this music had a large following in the United States, where *Billboard* magazine's number one hit for 1960 was Percy Faith's "Theme from *A Summer Place*" (a movie starring Sandra Dee and Troy Donahue).

Young British musicians, including John Lennon, Eric Clapton, and Mick Jagger, re-created American musical forms and reinvented rock 'n' roll. By the mid-1960s, the British invasion bands were at the heart of a youth culture that transcended the boundaries of nations. This music connected Britain and America as well as young people throughout the world.

The Beatles perform on the *Ed Sullivan Show* in February 1964. Although Britain's Queen Mother thought the Beatles "young, fresh, and vital," U.S. parents were appalled when the long Beatles haircut swept the nation. (AP Images)

woman's reputation. The birth-control pill, widely available to single women by the late 1960s, greatly lessened the risk of unplanned pregnancy, and venereal diseases were easily cured by a course of antibiotics. The number of couples living together increased 900 percent from 1960 to 1970. While many young people no longer tried to hide that they were sexually active, 68 percent of adults disapproved of premarital sex in 1969. The adult generation that grew up in the hard decades of depression and war and saw middle-class respectability as crucial to success and stability did not understand how promising young people could risk their futures by having sex without marriage, taking drugs, or protesting the war in Vietnam.

1968

By 1968, it seemed that the nation was coming apart. Divided over the war in Vietnam, frustrated by the slow pace of social change, or angry about racial violence, Americans faced the most serious domestic crisis of the postwar era.

The Tet Offensive

On January 31, 1968, the first day of the Vietnamese New Year (Tet), Vietcong and North Vietnamese forces struck South Vietnam, capturing provincial capitals (see Map 30.1). During the carefully planned offensive, the Saigon airport, the presidential palace, and the ARVN headquarters were attacked. The U.S. embassy was occupied by Vietcong soldiers for six hours. U.S. and South Vietnamese units eventually regained ground, inflicting heavy casualties and devastating villages.

Although the Tet Offensive was not the resounding battlefield victory its strategists sought, the heavy fighting called into question U.S. military leaders' predictions that the war would soon be won. Had not the Vietcong and North Vietnamese demonstrated that they could strike when and where they wished? If the United States's airpower, dollars, and half a million troops could not now defeat the Vietcong, could they ever do so? Top presidential advisers sounded notes of despair. Clark Clifford, the new secretary of defense, told Johnson the war could not be won, even with the 206,000 additional soldiers Westmoreland requested. Aware that the nation was suffering a financial crisis prompted by rampant deficit spending, Johnson's advisors knew that taking the initiative in Vietnam would cost billions more, further derail the budget, panic foreign owners of dollars, and wreck the economy.

Johnson's Exit

Controversy over the war split the Democratic Party, just as a presidential election loomed in November. Senator Eugene McCarthy of Minnesota and Robert F. Kennedy (now a senator from New York), both strong opponents of Johnson's war policies, forcefully challenged the president in early primaries. During a March 31 television address Johnson announced a halt to most of the bombing, asked Hanoi to negotiate, and stunned his listeners by withdrawing from the presidential race. His presidency had become a casualty of the war. Peace talks began in May in Paris, but the war ground on.

Assassinations

Days after Johnson's shocking announcement, Martin Luther King Jr. was murdered in Memphis. It remains unclear why James Earl Ray, a white forty-year-old drifter and petty criminal, shot King or whether he acted alone. By 1968 King, the senior states-man of the civil rights movement, was an outspoken critic of the Vietnam War and of U.S. capitalism. Most Americans mourned his death, and African American rage and grief exploded in 130 cities. The violence provoked a backlash from whites—primarily urban, working-class people who were had no sympathy for African Americans' increasing demands. In Chicago, Mayor Richard Daley ordered police to shoot rioters.

An already shaken nation watched in disbelief only two months later when the antiwar Democratic presidential candidate Robert Kennedy was shot and killed after winning the California primary. His assassin, Sirhan Sirhan, an Arab nationalist, tar-geted Kennedy because he supported Israel.

Chicago Democratic National Convention

Violence erupted again in August at the Democratic National Convention in Chicago. Thousands of protesters converged on the city: students who'd gone Clean for Gene, cutting long hair and donning "respectable" clothes to campaign for antiwar candidate Eugene McCarthy; members of the United States's counterculture, drawn by the anarchist Yippies' promise of a Festival of Life to counter the Convention of Death; and antiwar groups. Mayor Daley assigned twelve thousand police to twelve-hour shifts and had twelve thousand army troops with bazookas, rifles, and flamethrowers as backup. Police attacked peaceful antiwar protesters and journal-ists. "The whole world is watching," chanted protesters, as police beat people.

Global Protest

Upheavals spread around the world that spring and sum-mer. In France, university students protested rigid aca-demic policies and the Vietnam War. They received support from French workers, who occupied factories and paralyzed public transport; the turmoil contributed to the collapse of Charles de Gaulle's government the following year. In Italy, Germany, England, Ireland, Sweden, Canada, Mexico, Chile, Japan, and South Korea, students held similar protest. In Czechoslovakia, hundreds of thou-sands of demonstrators flooded Prague streets, demanding democracy and an end to Soviet repression. This so-called Prague Spring developed into a full-scale national rebellion before being crushed by Soviet tanks.

Why so many uprisings occurred simultaneously is unclear. The postwar baby boom produced by the late 1960s a huge mass of young adults, many who grew up in relative prosperity with high expectations for the future. Technological advances allowed the nearly instantaneous transmittal of televised images worldwide, so protests in one country could readily inspire similar actions in others.

Nixon's Election

The 1968 presidential election did not heal the nation. The Democratic nominee Hubert Humphrey, Johnson's vice president, seemed a continuation of old politics. The Republican candidate Richard Nixon appealed to those tired of social unrest. He reached out to those he called "the great, quite forgotten majority—the nonshouters and the nondemonstrators." On Vietnam, Nixon vowed he would "end the war and win the peace." Governor George Wallace of Alabama, a segregationist who proposed using nuclear weapons on Vietnam, ran as a third-party candidate. Wallace carried

The Immigration Act of 1965

When President Johnson signed the 1965 Immigration Act in a ceremony at the Statue of Liberty, he believed its importance was that it "repair[ed] a very deep and painful flaw in the fabric of American justice" by ending national-origins quotas that all but excluded "Polynesians, orientals, and Negroes." Nevertheless, the president mistakenly saw it as primarily symbolic. In fact, this act may have had greater long-term impact on Americans than any other Great Society legislation.

The 1965 Immigration Act ended blatant discrimination against potential immigrants from Asia, Africa, and Third World nations by substituting Eastern and Western Hemispheric caps for national quotas and allowing family reunification. The architects of the Immigration Act did not expect immigration to change, but world events decreed otherwise. Political instability along with rapidly growing populations in many poorer nations, created a large pool of potential immigrants drawn by U.S. prosperity.

Immigration rates skyrocketed, and by the 1990s, immigration accounted for almost 60 percent of the United States's population growth. By 2000, more Americans were foreign-born than at any time since the 1930s. The majority came from Mexico, the Philippines, Vietnam, China, the Dominican Republic, Korea, India, the Soviet Union, Jamaica, and Iran.

More than two-thirds of the new immigrants settled in six states—New York, California, Florida, New Jersey, Illinois, and Texas. By the late twentieth century, Spanish-language signs appeared in South Carolina, and Hmong farmers from the mountains of southeast Asia offered their produce at the farmers' market in Missoula, Montana. The legacy of the 1965 Immigration Act was unintended but profound: the Unites States is much more diverse than it otherwise would have been.

five southern states, drawing almost 14 percent of the popular vote, and Nixon was elected with the slimmest of margins.

On Christmas Eve 1968, *Apollo 8* entered lunar orbit. Looking down on a troubled world, the astronauts broadcast photographs of a fragile blue orb floating in darkness and read aloud the opening passages of Genesis, "In the beginning, God created the heaven and the earth . . . and God saw that it was good." Many listeners found themselves in tears.

Summary

The 1960s began with high hopes for a more democratic United States. Civil rights volunteers, often risking their lives, carried the quest for racial equality across the nation. The 1964 Civil Rights Act and the 1965 Voting Rights Act were major milestones. The United States was shaken by the assassination of President John Kennedy in 1963, but under President Johnson, the liberal vision of government working to improve citizens' lives inspired legislation designed to create a Great Society.

The Cold War between the United States and the Soviet Union intensified during the 1960s, and a nuclear war nearly happened in the 1962 Cuban missile crisis. Determined not to let Vietnam fall to communists, the United States sent military forces to prevent the victory of communist Vietnamese nationalists led by Ho Chi Minh. By 1968 there were more than half a million U.S. ground troops in Vietnam, which divided the United States at home, undermined Great Society domestic programs, and destroyed Lyndon Johnson's presidency.

Despite civil rights gains, many African Americans turned away from the movement, seeking more immediate change. Poor African American neighborhoods burned as riots spread through the nation. Vocal young people and some of their elders questioned whether democracy truly existed in the United States. Large numbers of the nation's white youth rebelled by embracing a counterculture that rejected white middle-class respectability. 1968 was a year of crisis, assassinations, and violence in the streets. The decade that started with promise ended in fierce political polarization.

Chapter Review

KENNEDY AND THE COLD WAR

How was the Cuban missile crisis a watershed in U.S.–Soviet relations?

Like his predecessors and his Soviet counterpart, President Kennedy wanted to win the Cold War. As such, he and Soviet leader Nikita Khrushchev disagreed over preconditions for peace and ultimately escalated (rather than controlled) nuclear arms production. Concerns about Khrushchev's relationships in Cuba tipped the balance toward war first in 1961 when Kennedy initiated a failed attempt in the Bay of Pigs to establish a U.S. beachhead in Cuba and spark an uprising. But in 1963 when the Soviets placed nuclear missiles in Cuba, just 90 miles from the Florida coast, these Cold War rivals were on the brink of a nuclear disaster. While Kennedy's steady handling eventually led the Soviets to remove the missiles, the event forced both leaders to take important small steps toward improving their relationship and operating with greater trust. In August 1963, they signed a treaty banning nuclear tests in the atmosphere, oceans, and outer space.

MARCHING FOR FREEDOM

What was Kennedy's reaction to growing civil rights activism?

President Kennedy was sympathetic to civil rights and recognized that U.S. racism damaged the nation's international reputation. But he also worried about alienating southern white Democrats in Congress. He initially thwarted civil rights by appointing segregationist judges to federal courts in the Deep South and held off an executive order forbidding segregation in federally subsidized housing. He also permitted the FBI to harass civil rights leaders—Martin Luther King Jr. in particular—with wiretaps, surveillance, and efforts to damage their reputations. But increasing grass roots activism in the form of sit-ins, the Freedom Rides, Freedom Summer, and the Montgomery Bus Boycott forced Kennedy to finally and formally support civil rights. He not only ordered U.S. marshals to protect James Meredith, the first African American to attend the University of Mississippi, but in 1963, he asked Congress to pass a comprehensive civil rights bill.

How did the protest in Birmingham make civil rights a priority for Kennedy?

Before Martin Luther King Jr. organized the 1963 protest against racism in Birmingham, Alabama, President Kennedy took a lukewarm position on civil rights. He thought the cause of equality was worthwhile, but did not want to alienate southern white voters. Then, in 1963, civil rights leader Martin Luther King Jr. and the SCLC planned a nonviolent campaign in one of the nation's most violently racist cities, Birmingham, Alabama, hoping to give Americans a true picture of the face of racial hatred. What made this protest different was that King and African American parents put young black children on the front lines of the march. When the children were mowed down by police using high-force water guns, the nation watched in horror on TV. From that point on, civil rights moved to the top of Kennedy's agenda, and he asked Congress to pass a comprehensive bill ending racial discrimination.

LIBERALISM AND THE GREAT SOCIETY

What made the War on Poverty controversial?

As part of his Great Society programs, President Johnson believed he could use the nation's prosperity to end poverty once and for all. War on Poverty programs included public housing and subsidized rents, Medicare and Medicaid, Food Stamps, Head Start, Job Corps, and Community Action Programs to involve the poor in creating antipoverty efforts. While a noble idea, the War on Poverty triggered intense reactions on both sides of the political spectrum. Those on the left felt the government had treated the surface-level problems resulting from poverty, without analyzing poverty's causes or addressing the structural inequalities that caused it in the first place. Those on the right feared the programs would create dependency rather than inspire initiative among the poor. Analysts, too, thought many of the programs were poorly implemented.

JOHNSON AND VIETNAM

How did the war in Vietnam become Americanized?

Two factors transformed the conflict in Vietnam from a civil war between the North and South into an American war against communism. First, Johnson dramatically expanded the number of U.S. troops from 180,000 to 385,000 in 1966 and 536,100 by 1968. Second, in 1965, Johnson responded to Vietcong attacks on American installations in South Vietnam with Operation Rolling Thunder, a bombing program that lasted for three years. As the U.S. presence grew, so did the response from North Vietnam, as well as assistance to that country from the Soviet Union and China.

A NATION DIVIDED

How did disillusionment with civil rights and the Great Society fuel political unrest in the sixties?

By the mid-1960s, a new breed of activist emerged, less willing to embrace the nonviolent, integrationist agenda of the past. Many northern blacks saw both civil rights and the Great Society as failing to eradicate inequality, especially with their unemployment rates for African Americans that were double that of whites while blacks', incomes were nearly half. Instead, these new African American leaders—among them Malcolm X, and later Stokely Carmichael and the Black Panthers—urged African Americans to seize freedom, expelled white members from civil rights organizations, and repudiated nonviolence and integration. At the same time, 41 percent of the population was under age twenty, and many young people, inspired by sit-ins and civil rights, wanted to change their country. This in turn fueled student movements on college campuses nationwide, among them the free speech movement, antiwar movement, and Students for a Democratic Society. By 1967, a youth counterculture emerged first in the Haight-Ashbury district of San Francisco, seeking to replace middle-class materialism with free love and a higher consciousness achieved through music and mind-altering drugs.

1968

What made 1968 unique?

Around the world, 1968 was a year of violent protest and political disillusionment. The heavy fighting during the Tet Offensive in Vietnam not only had leaders seriously doubting whether the war could be won quickly, but it also sparked antiwar protests. Two national leaders—Martin Luther King and Robert Kennedy—were assassinated, dousing the hopes held by African Americans, political activists, and young voters for a different, more progressive America. Protests at the Democratic National Convention in Chicago turned violent, as police and army troops attacked peaceful antiwar protesters and journalists. In France, students protested the war and rigid school policies, supported by workers who occupied factories and shut down public transportation. Within a year, similar student rebellions occurred in Italy, Germany, England, Ireland, Sweden, Canada, Mexico, Chile, Japan, and South Korea, while in Prague, Czechoslovakia, protesters democracy and an end to Soviet repression.

SUGGESTIONS FOR FURTHER READING

Beth Bailey, *Sex in the Heartland* (1999)

Lawrence Freedman, *Kennedy's Wars: Berlin, Cuba, Laos, and Vietnam* (2000)

David Farber, *Chicago '68* (1988)

George C. Herring, *LBJ and Vietnam: A Different Kind of War* (1994)

Michael Kazin and Maurice Isserman, *America Divided: The Civil War of the 1960s* (1999)

Fredrik Logevall, *Choosing War: The Lost Chance for Peace and the Escalation of War in Vietnam* (1999)

Lisa McGirr, *Suburban Warriors: The Origins of the New American Right* (2001)

Charles Payne, *I've Got the Light of Freedom: The Organizing Tradition and the Mississippi Freedom Struggle* (1995)

CHAPTER 31

Continuing Divisions and New Limits

CHAPTER OUTLINE

The New Politics of Identity

The Women's Movement and Gay Liberation

The End in Vietnam

Nixon, Kissinger, and the World

   LINKS TO THE WORLD: OPEC and the 1973 Oil Embargo

Presidential Politics and the Crisis of Leadership

Economic Crisis

An Era of Cultural Transformation

Renewed Cold War and Middle East Crisis

   LEGACY FOR A PEOPLE AND A NATION: The All-Volunteer Force

Summary

In 1969 Daniel Ellsberg was a thirty-eight-year-old former aide to Assistant Secretary of Defense John McNaughton. At the Pentagon, Ellsberg worked on a top-secret study of U.S. decision making in Vietnam. When he left office after Richard Nixon's election, he accessed a copy of the study stored at the Rand Corporation, where he would resume his pre-government research career. He spent the next six months poring over the seven thousand pages that made up the Pentagon Papers.

Initially supportive of U.S. military intervention in Vietnam, Ellsberg had grown disillusioned. A Harvard-trained Ph.D., former marine officer, and Cold Warrior, he spent from 1965 to 1967 in South Vietnam, assessing the war's progress for Washington. He had gone on combat patrols and interviewed military officials, U.S. diplomats, and Vietnamese leaders. The war, he concluded, was in military, political, moral respects a lost enterprise.

Loyal to the president, Ellsberg was initially reluctant to act on that conviction. But when in 1969 it became clear that Nixon had no intention of ending the war, Ellsberg boldly decided to risk imprisonment by making the Pentagon Papers public. The study, he believed, showed that presidents had escalated the United States's commitment in Vietnam despite pessimistic estimates from their advisers and that they had repeatedly lied to the public about their actions and the results. Ellsberg hoped disclosing this information would generate sufficient uproar to force a dramatic policy change.

Aided by a Rand colleague, Ellsberg surreptitiously photocopied the study, then spent months pleading with antiwar senators and representatives to release it. When they refused, he went to the press. On June 13, 1971, the *New York Times* published a front-page article on the Pentagon Papers. Other newspapers soon published excerpts as well.

This icon will direct you to interactive activities and study materials on A People And A Nation, Brief Edition website: **www.cengage.com/history/norton/ peoplenationbrief8e**

Chronology

1969	Stonewall Inn uprising begins gay liberation movement.
	Apollo 11 Astronaut Neil Armstrong becomes first person to walk on moon's surface.
	National Chicano Liberation Youth Conference is held in Denver.
	Indians of All Tribes occupy Alcatraz Island.
	Nixon administration begins affirmative-action plan.
1970	United States invades Cambodia.
	Students at Kent State and Jackson State Universities shot by National Guard troops.
	First Earth Day is celebrated.
	Environmental Protection Agency is created.
1971	Pentagon Papers are published.
1972	Nixon visits China and Soviet Union.
	CREEP stages Watergate break-in.
	Congress approves ERA and passes Title IX, which creates growth in women's athletics.
1973	Peace agreement in Paris ends U.S. involvement in Vietnam.
	OPEC increases oil prices, creating U.S. energy crisis.
	Roe v. Wade legalizes abortion.
	Agnew resigns; Ford is named vice president.
1974	Nixon resigns under threat of impeachment; Ford becomes president.
1975	In deepening economic recession, unemployment hits 8.5 percent.
	New York City is saved from bankruptcy by federal loan guarantees.
	Congress passes Indian Self-Determination and Education Assistance Act in response to Native American activists.
1976	Carter is elected president.
1978	*Regents of the University of California v. Bakke* outlaws quotas but upholds affirmative action.
	California voters approve Proposition 13.
1979	Three Mile Island nuclear accident raises fears.
	Camp David accords signed by Israel and Egypt.
	American hostages are seized in Iran.
	Soviet Union invades Afghanistan.
	Consumer debt doubles from 1975 to hit $315 billion.

Ellsberg's leak became controversial. Nixon tried to stop the papers' publication—the first efforts to muzzle the press since the American Revolution—and to discredit Ellsberg and deter other leakers through the illegal actions of petty operatives. Many saw Ellsberg as a hero who acted to shorten an illegitimate war. To others, he was a publicity-seeking traitor.

The 1970s would be, for Americans, a decade of division and an age of limits. The chaos of 1968 continued in Nixon's early presidency. Antiwar opposition became more extreme, and, as government deceptions were exposed, Americans were increasingly divided over Vietnam. The movements for racial equality and social justice also became more radical by the early 1970s. Although some continued to work for racial integration, many embraced cultural nationalism, which sought separatist cultures and societies. Even the women's movement, the strongest social movement of the 1970s, had a polarizing effect. Opponents, many of them women, understood feminism as an attack on their way of life and mobilized a conservative grassroots movement that would gain political importance in subsequent decades.

This divided United States faced great challenges abroad. Richard Nixon and his national security adviser, Henry Kissinger, understood that the United States and the Soviet Union, weakened by the costs of their competition and challenged by other nations, faced a world where power was diffused. Accordingly, Nixon and Kissinger sought improved relations with the People's Republic of China and the Soviet Union to maintain world order.

Ultimately, Richard Nixon's illegal acts in the political scandal known as Watergate shook the faith of Americans. By the time Nixon, under threat of impeachment, resigned, Americans were cynical about politics. Neither of Nixon's successors, Gerald Ford or Jimmy Carter could restore that lost faith. Carter's presidency was undermined by international events beyond his control. In the Middle East—a region of increasing importance in U.S. foreign policy—Carter helped broker peace between Egypt and Israel but proved powerless to end a lengthy hostage crisis in Iran. Meanwhile, the Soviet invasion of Afghanistan in 1979 revived Cold War tensions.

A deepening economic crisis added to Carter's woes. In the 1970s, middle-class Americans saw their savings disappear to double-digit inflation, and unemployment skyrocketed. The downturn was largely caused by changes in the global economy and international trade, worsened by the oil embargo launched by Arab members of the Organization of Petroleum Exporting Countries in 1973. Americans realized their vulnerability to decisions made in far-off lands.

- **How did U.S. foreign policy change as a result of involvement in Vietnam?**
- **Why did Americans see this era as an age of limits?**
- **Some historians describe the period between 1968 and 1980 as a time when many Americans lost faith—in their government, in the possibility of joining together in a society that offered equality to all, in the possibility of consensus instead of conflict. Do you agree, or were the struggles and divisions of this era similar to those of previous decades?**

THE NEW POLITICS OF IDENTITY

By the end of the 1960s, divisions among Americans deepened. The civil rights movement, begun in a quest for equal rights and integration, splintered, as many young African Americans, rejected integration in favor of separatism and embraced a distinct African American culture. Mexican Americans and Native Americans, inspired by the civil rights movement, created powerful Brown Power and Red Power movements by the early 1970s. They too demanded equal rights and cultural recognition. These movements fueled a new identity politics, which saw group identity as the basis for political action and argued that social policy should be based on the needs not of individuals but of different identity-based groups.

African American Cultural Nationalism

By 1970, most African American activists no longer sought political power and racial justice by emphasizing the shared humanity of all people. Instead, they attracted a large following by highlighting the distinctiveness of black culture. Many African Americans, disillusioned by the racism that outlasted the end of legal segregation, believed that integration would mean subordination in a white-dominated society.

In the early 1970s, though mainstream groups such as the NAACP continued to seek equality through the courts and ballot boxes, many African Americans looked to culture for social change. Rejecting European American standards of beauty, young people let their hair grow into "naturals" and Afros. Seeking strength in their own histories, African American college students and faculty fought successfully to create black studies departments in American universities. African traditions were reclaimed or sometimes created. The new holiday, Kwanzaa, created in 1966 by Maulana Karenga, professor of black studies at California State University, Long Beach, celebrated African heritage.

Mexican American Activism

In 1970, the nation's 9 million Mexican Americans (4.3 percent of the United States's population) were concentrated in the Southwest and California. Although the federal census counted all Hispanics as white, discrimination in hiring, pay, housing, schools, and the courts was commonplace. Almost half of Mexican Americans were functionally illiterate, and in 1974, only 21 percent of Mexican American males graduated high school. Although more Mexican Americans were middle class, almost one-quarter remained below the poverty level in the 1970s.

The national Mexican American movement for social justice began with migrant farm workers. From 1965 through 1970, the labor organizers César Chávez and Dolores Huerta led migrant workers in a strike (*huelga*) against large grape growers in California's San Joaquin Valley. Chávez and the AFL-CIO–affiliated United Farm Workers (UFW) drew national attention to the working conditions of migrant laborers, who received 10 cents an hour (the minimum wage in 1965 was $1.25) and were often lodged by employers in squalid housing without running water or indoor toilets. A national consumer boycott of table grapes brought the growers to the bargaining table, and in 1970 the UFW won better wages and working conditions. The union resembled nineteenth-century Mexican *mutualistas,* or cooperative associations. Its members founded cooperative groceries, a Spanish-language newspaper, and a theater group.

Chicano Movement

During the same period, in northern New Mexico, Reies Tijerina created the Alianza Federal de Mercedes (Federal Alliance of Grants). The group wanted the return of land it claimed belonged to local *hispano* villagers, whose ancestors occupied the territory before the United States annexed it under the 1848 Treaty of Guadalupe Hidalgo. In Denver, former boxer Rudolfo "Corky" Gonzáles drew more than one thousand Mexican Americans for the National Chicano Liberation Youth Conference in 1969. They adopted a manifesto, *El Plan Espiritual de Aztlán,* condemning the "brutal 'Gringo' invasion of our territories."

These young activists called for the liberation of *La Raza* (from *La Raza de Bronze,* "the brown people") from oppressive U.S. society, not for equal rights. They also rejected a hyphenated Mexican-American identity. The "Mexican American," they explained in *El Plan Espiritual de Aztlán,* "lacks respect for his culture." Instead, they called themselves Chicanos or Chicanas—barrio slang associated with *pachucos,* the hip and sometimes criminal young men who symbolized much of what "respectable" Mexican Americans despised.

Many middle-class Mexican Americans and members of the older generations never embraced the term *Chicano* or the separatist agenda of *el movimiento.* Younger activists succeeded in introducing Chicano studies into local high school and college curricula and creating a unifying cultural identity for Mexican American youth. Politically, La Raza Unida (RUP), a Southwest-based political party, registered tens of thousands of voters and won local elections. Although never as influential as the

African American civil rights movement, the Chicano movement effectively challenged discrimination locally and created a basis for political action.

Native American Activism

Between 1968 and 1975, Native American activists forced American society to hear their demands and reform U.S. government policies toward native peoples. Young Native American activists were greatly influenced by cultural nationalist beliefs. Seeking a return to the old ways, they joined with traditionalists to challenge tribal leaders advocating assimilation.

In November 1969 a small group of activists, calling themselves Indians of All Tribes, occupied Alcatraz Island in San Francisco Bay, demanding that the land be returned to native peoples for an Indian cultural center. The protest, which lasted nineteen months and eventually involved more than four hundred people from fifty different tribes, marked the consolidation of pan-Indian activism. Before Alcatraz, protests were reservation-based and local. Although the protesters did not reclaim Alcatraz Island, they drew national attention to the growing Red Power movement. In 1972 the radical U.S. Indian Movement occupied a Bureau of Indian Affairs office in Washington, D.C., and then in 1973 a trading post in Wounded Knee, South Dakota, where U.S. Army troops massacred three hundred Sioux men, women, and children in 1890.

Meanwhile, moderate activists, working through such pan-tribal organizations as the National Congress of American Indians and the Native American Rights Fund, lobbied Congress for greater resources to govern themselves. In response, Congress and the federal courts returned millions of acres of land, and in 1975 Congress passed the Indian Self-Determination and Education Assistance Act. Still, during the 1970s and 1980s, American Indians had a higher rate of tuberculosis, alcoholism, and suicide than any other group. Nine of ten lived in substandard housing, with nearly 40 percent unemployment.

Calling their movement Red Power, these American Indian activists dance in 1969 "reclaiming" Alcatraz Island in San Francisco Bay. Arguing that an 1868 Sioux treaty entitled them to possession of unused federal lands, the group occupied the island until mid-1971.   (Ralph Crane / Getty Images)

Affirmative Action

As activists made Americans aware of discrimination and inequality, policymakers struggled to frame remedies. As early as 1965, President Johnson acknowledged the limits of civil rights legislation, calling for "not just legal equality . . . but equality as a fact and equality as a result." Johnson joined his belief that the federal government must help *individuals* attain competitive skills to a new concept: equality could be measured by *group* outcomes.

Practical issues also contributed to the shift from individual opportunity to group outcomes. The 1964 Civil Rights Act outlawed discrimination but seemingly stipulated that action could be taken only when an employer "intentionally engaged" in discrimination against an individual. The tens of thousands of cases filed with the

Equal Employment Opportunity Commission (EEOC) suggested a pervasive pattern of racial and sexual discrimination in education and employment, but each required proof of intentional actions against an individual. Some people argued that it was possible, instead, to prove discrimination by results—by the relative number of African Americans or women an employer hired or promoted.

In 1969 the Nixon administration implemented the first major government affirmative-action program. The Philadelphia Plan (so called because it targeted government contracts in that city) required businesses contracting with the federal government to show "affirmative action to meet the goals of increasing minority employment" and set specific numerical goals, or quotas, for employers. Affirmative action for women and racial and ethnic minorities was soon required by all major government contracts, and many corporations and educational institutions began their own programs.

Supporters saw affirmative action as a remedy for the effects of past discrimination. Critics argued that creating proportional representation for women and minorities meant discrimination against others who had not created past discrimination and that group-based remedies violated the principle that individuals should be judged on their merits. As affirmative action affected hiring and university admissions, bringing members of underrepresented groups into college classrooms, law firms, and firehouses nationwide, a deepening recession made jobs scarce. Thus increasing the number of minorities and women hired often meant reducing the number of white men, which triggered resentment.

THE WOMEN'S MOVEMENT AND GAY LIBERATION

During the 1960s, a second wave of the U.S. women's movement emerged, and by the 1970s, mainstream and radical activists waged a multi-front battle for women's liberation. In 1963, the popularity of Betty Friedan's *The Feminine Mystique* signaled that there was energy for a revived women's movement. Writing as a housewife and mother (though she had a long history of political activism), Friedan described "the problem with no name," the dissatisfaction of educated, middle-class wives and mothers, who—looking at their homes and families—wondered guiltily if that was all there was to life. Instead of blaming women for failing to adapt to women's proper role, as 1950s magazines often did, Friedan blamed the role itself and the society that created it.

Liberal and Radical Feminism
The organized, liberal wing of the women's movement emerged in 1966 with the founding of the National Organization for Women (NOW). Consisting primarily of educated, professional women, NOW was a lobbying group seeking to pressure the EEOC to enforce the 1964 Civil Rights Act. With racial discrimination the EEOC's focus, sex discrimination became a low priority. By 1970, NOW had one hundred chapters with more than three thousand members nationwide.

Another strand of the women's movement developed from the nation's increasingly radical social justice movements. Many women working for civil rights or against the Vietnam War were treated as second-class citizens, making coffee, not policy. As they analyzed inequality, these women recognized women's oppression, too. In 1968 a group of women protested the "degrading mindless-boob girlie symbol" represented by the Miss America Pageant in Atlantic City. Although nothing was burned, the pejorative term for feminists, *bra-burners*, came from this event, in which women threw items of "enslavement" (girdles, high heels, curlers, and bras) into a Freedom Trashcan.

Second-wave feminism was never a single set of beliefs. Most radical feminists, however, practiced personal politics, believing that "there is no private domain of a person's life that is not political, and there is no political issue that is not ultimately personal." In the early 1970s, women meeting in suburban kitchens, college dorm rooms, and churches or synagogues, created consciousness-raising groups, where they explored topics such as power relationships in marriage, sexuality, abortion, healthcare, work, and family.

Accomplishments of the Women's Movement

During the 1970s, the women's movement claimed significant achievements: the right of a married woman to obtain credit in her own name, the right of an unmarried woman to obtain birth control, the right of women to serve on juries, the end of sex-segregated help-wanted ads. At the state and local level, they challenged understandings of rape that blamed the victim for the attack. By decade's end, activists established rape crisis centers, educated police and hospital officials about procedures for protecting survivors of rape, and changed laws.

In 1971, the Boston Women's Health Collective published *Our Bodies, Ourselves* to help women understand and take charge of their sexual and reproductive health. And women who sought the right to safe and legal abortions won a major victory in 1973 when the Supreme Court, in a 7-to-2 decision on *Roe v. Wade,* ruled that privacy rights protected a woman's choice to end a pregnancy.

Women's organizations united to revive the 1920s Equal Rights Amendment ending discrimination on the basis of sex. On March 22, 1972, Congress approved the amendment, which stated that "equality of rights under the law shall not be denied or abridged by the United States or by any State on account of sex." By the end of the year, twenty-two states (of the thirty-eight necessary to amend the Constitution) ratified the ERA. Also in 1972, Congress passed Title IX of the Higher Education Act, which barred federal funds from colleges or universities discriminating against women. Universities then began channeling money to women's athletics, and women's participation in sports boomed.

Women's applications to graduate programs also boomed. In 1970 only 8.4 percent of medical school graduates and 5.4 percent of law school graduates were women. By 1979, those figures climbed to 23 percent and 28.5 percent respectively. Colleges and universities established women's studies departments, and by 1980 more than thirty thousand college courses focused on women or gender relations. Women also increased their roles in religious organizations, and some denominations began to ordain women.

Opposition to the Women's Movement

The women's movement met with powerful opposition, much of it from women. Many had no desire to be equal if that meant giving up traditional gender roles in marriage or working at low-wage jobs. African and Hispanic American women, many of whom were active in movements for the liberation of their people and some of whom helped create second-wave feminism, often regarded feminism as a white movement that ignored their cultural traditions and diverted attention from the fight for racial equality.

Organized opposition to feminism came primarily from conservative, often religiously motivated men and women. As one conservative Christian writer claimed, "The Bible clearly states that the wife is to submit to her husband's leadership." Such beliefs, along with fears about changing gender roles, fueled the STOP-ERA movement led by Phyllis Schlafly, a lawyer and conservative political activist. Schlafly attacked the women's movement as "a total assault on the role of the American woman as wife and mother." Schlafly's group argued that the ERA would decriminalize rape, force Americans to use unisex toilets, and make women subject to the military draft.

In fighting the ERA, tens of thousands of women became politically experienced; they fed a growing grassroots conservative movement that would blossom in the 1980s. By the mid-1970s, the STOP-ERA movement stopped the Equal Rights Amendment. Despite Congress's deadline extension, the amendment fell three states short of ratification and expired in 1982.

Gay Liberation

In the early 1970s, gay men and lesbians faced widespread discrimination. Consensual same-sex sexual intercourse was illegal in almost every state, and until 1973 homosexuality was labeled a mental disorder by the American Psychiatric Association. Homosexual couples did not receive partnership benefits, such as health insurance; they could not marry or adopt children. Gay men and women remained targets of discrimination in hiring and endured public ridicule, harassment, and physical attacks.

There were small homophile organizations, such as the Mattachine Society and the Daughters of Bilitis, that worked for gay rights since the 1950s. But the symbolic beginning of the gay liberation movement came on June 28, 1969, when New York City police raided the Stonewall Inn, a gay bar in Greenwich Village, for violating a city law that made it illegal for more than three homosexual patrons to occupy a bar at the same time. That night, patrons stood up to the police, and hundreds joined them. The next morning, New Yorkers found a new slogan spray-painted on neighborhood walls: Gay Power.

Inspired by the Stonewall riot, some men and women worked openly and militantly for gay rights. They focused on a dual agenda: legal equality and the promotion of Gay Pride. Some rejected the notion of fitting into straight (heterosexual) culture and created distinctive gay communities. By 1973, there were about eight hundred gay organizations in the United States. Centered in big cities and on college campuses, most organizations created supportive environments for gay men and lesbians to come out of the closet and push for reform. By decade's end, gay men and lesbians were a political force in cities including New York, Miami, and San Francisco.

THE END IN VIETNAM

No issue divided Americans as pervasively as the Vietnam War. Although Richard Nixon said he was going to end the war fast so it would not ruin his political career as it had Johnson's, he did not. Like Johnson, he feared that a precipitous withdrawal would harm U.S. credibility on the world stage. Anxious to get U.S. troops out of Vietnam, Nixon was equally committed to preserving an independent, noncommunist South Vietnam. Hence, he adopted a policy that at once contracted and expanded the war.

Invasion of Cambodia

Nixon's policy centered on Vietnamization—building up South Vietnamese forces to replace U.S. forces. Accordingly, the president decreased U.S. troops from 543,000 in the spring of 1969 to 156,800 by the end of 1971, and to 60,000 by the fall of 1972. Vietnamization helped limit domestic dissent, but it did not end the stalemate in the Paris peace talks underway since 1968. Therefore, Nixon intensified the bombing of North Vietnam and enemy supply depots in neighboring Cambodia, hoping to pound Hanoi into concessions (see Map 30.2 on page 000).

The bombing of neutral Cambodia commenced in March 1969. For fourteen months, B-52 pilots flew 3,600 missions and dropped over 100,000 tons of bombs, initially in secret. When the North Vietnamese refused to buckle, Nixon turned up the heat: in April 1970 South Vietnamese and U.S. forces invaded Cambodia. The president announced that he would not allow "the world's most powerful nation" to act "like a pitiful, helpless giant."

Protests and Counterdemonstrations

Instantly, the antiwar movement emerged, as students on about 450 college campuses went out on strike and hundreds of thousands of demonstrators in various cities protested the administration's policies. The crisis atmosphere intensified on May 4, when National Guardsmen in Ohio fired into a crowd of fleeing students at Kent State University, killing four and wounding eleven. Ten days later, police armed with automatic weapons blasted a women's dormitory at the historic African American Jackson State University in Mississippi, killing two and wounding nine students. Police claimed they had been shot at, but no such evidence could be found. Nixon's widening of the war sparked congressional outrage, and in June the Senate terminated the 1964 Tonkin Gulf Resolution. After two months, U.S. troops withdrew from Cambodia.

Although a majority of Americans told pollsters they thought the original troop commitment to Vietnam was a mistake, 50 percent said they believed Nixon's claim that the Cambodia invasion would shorten the war, and some were angered by antiwar protests. In Washington, an Honor America Day program attracted 200,000 people who heard Billy Graham and Bob Hope laud administration policy. Nevertheless, the tumult over the invasion reduced Nixon's options on the war. Henceforth, solid majorities opposed any new missions for U.S. ground troops in Southeast Asia.

Morale Problems in Military

Equally troubling was that morale and discipline among troops was declining even before Nixon took office. There were growing reports of drug addiction, desertion, racial discord, even the murder of unpopular officers by enlisted men (called fragging). The 1971 court-martial and conviction of Lieutenant William Calley, charged with overseeing the killing of more than three hundred unarmed South Vietnamese civilians in My Lai in 1968, got particular attention when an army photographer captured the horror in graphic pictures.

Paris Peace Accords

The Nixon administration, meanwhile, stepped up its efforts to pressure Hanoi into a settlement. When the North Vietnamese launched a major offensive into South Vietnam in March 1972, Nixon responded with a massive aerial onslaught. In December 1972, after an apparent peace agreement collapsed, the United States launched another air strike on the North—the so-called Christmas bombing.

A diplomatic agreement was close, however. Months earlier, Kissinger and his North Vietnamese counterpart, Le Duc Tho, resolved many of the outstanding issues. Most notably, Kissinger agreed that North Vietnamese troops could remain in the South after the settlement, while Tho abandoned Hanoi's insistence that the Saigon government of Nguyen Van Thieu be removed. On January 27, 1973, Kissinger and Le Duc Tho signed a cease-fire agreement, and Nixon compelled a reluctant Thieu to accept it by threatening to cut off U.S. aid. The United States promised to withdraw its troops within sixty days. North Vietnamese troops could stay in South Vietnam, and a coalition government that included the Vietcong would be formed in the South.

The United States pulled its troops out of Vietnam, leaving behind some military advisers. Soon, full-scale war erupted again. Just before the South Vietnamese surrendered, hundreds of Americans and Vietnamese who had worked with the Americans were hastily evacuated from Saigon. On April 29, 1975, the South Vietnamese government collapsed, and Vietnam was reunified under a communist government in Hanoi. Saigon was renamed Ho Chi Minh City for the persevering patriot who died in 1969.

Costs of the Vietnam War

More than 58,000 Americans and between 1.5 and 2 million Vietnamese died in the war. Civilian deaths in Cambodia and Laos reached hundreds of thousands. The war cost the United States at least $170 billion, and billions more in subsequent veterans' benefits. With funds shifted from domestic programs during the war, the nation suffered inflation, political schism, and abuses of executive power. The war also delayed accommodation with the Soviet Union and the People's Republic of China, fueled friction with allies, and alienated Third World nations.

In 1975 communists established repressive governments in Vietnam, Cambodia, and Laos, but beyond Indochina the domino effect once predicted by U.S. officials never occurred. Acute hunger afflicted the people of those devastated lands. Soon refugees—boat people—crowded aboard unsafe vessels to escape. Many emigrated to the United States, where they were received with mixed feelings by Americans reluctant to be reminded of defeat and their responsibility for the plight of the southeast Asian peoples.

Debate over the Lessons of Vietnam

As the historian William Appleman Williams observed, Americans had had their overseas sphere of influence pushed back and were suffering from "empire shock."

Hawkish observers claimed that failure in Vietnam undermined the nation's credibility. They pointed to a Vietnam syndrome—an American suspicion of foreign entanglements—which they feared would inhibit the future exercise of U.S. power. The United States lost in Vietnam, they asserted, because Americans lost their guts at home.

Dovish analysts blamed the war on an imperial presidency that permitted strong-willed men to act without restraint and a weak Congress that conceded too much power to the executive branch. Make the president adhere to the checks-and-balances system—make him go to Congress for a declaration of war—these critics counseled. This view found expression in the War Powers Act of 1973, which limited the president's war-making freedom and required congressional approval before committing U.S. forces to combat lasting more than sixty days.

Vietnam Veterans   Veterans' calls for help in dealing with posttraumatic stress disorder, which afflicted thousands of the 2.8 million Vietnam veterans, stimulated public discussion. Doctors reported that the disorder, which included nightmares and extreme nervousness, stemmed from the soldiers' having seen many children, women, and elderly killed. Some GIs inadvertently killed these people; some killed them vengefully and later felt guilt. Other veterans publicized their deteriorating health from defoliant Agent Orange and other herbicides they had handled or were accidentally sprayed with in Vietnam.

NIXON, KISSINGER, AND THE WORLD

The difficulties of the Vietnam war signified to Nixon and Kissinger that U.S. power was limited and, in relative terms, in decline. This reality necessitated a new approach to the Cold War. In particular, they believed the United States had to adapt to a new, multipolar international system no longer defined simply by the Soviet-American rivalry. Western Europe was becoming a major player in its own right, as was Japan. The Middle East loomed increasingly large. Above all, Americans had to come to grips with China by rethinking the policy of hostile isolation.

They were an unlikely duo—the reclusive, ambitious Californian, born of Quaker parents, and the sociable, dynamic Jewish intellectual who fled Nazi Germany as a child. Nixon, ten years older, was a career politician, while Kissinger made his name as a Harvard professor and foreign policy consultant. What the two men shared was a paranoia about rivals and a capacity to think in large conceptual terms about the United States's place in the world.

Nixon Doctrine   In July 1969 Nixon and Kissinger acknowledged the limits of U.S. power and resources in the Nixon Doctrine. The United States, they said, would provide economic aid to allies, but these allies should not count on U.S. troops. Washington could no longer afford to sustain its overseas commitments and would have to rely on regional allies, including authoritarian regimes, to maintain an anticommunist world order. Nixon's doctrine partially retreated from the 1947 Truman Doctrine's promise to support noncommunist governments facing threats.

Détente

The other pillar of the new foreign policy was détente: measured cooperation with the Soviets through negotiations within an environment of rivalry. Détente's primary purpose, like that of the containment doctrine, was to check Soviet expansion and limit the Soviet arms buildup, but through diplomacy and mutual concessions. The second part of the strategy sought to curb revolution and radicalism in the Third World to quash threats to U.S. interests. More specifically, expanded trade with friendlier Soviets and Chinese might reduce the huge U.S. balance-of-payments deficit. And improving relations with both communist giants, at a time when Sino-Soviet tensions were increasing, might weaken communism.

The Soviet Union too found that the Cold War drained its resources, with defense needs and consumer demands at odds. Improved ties with Washington would allow the Soviet Union to focus on its increasingly fractious relations with China and might generate serious progress on outstanding European issues, including the status of Germany and Berlin. In May 1972 the United States and the Soviet Union agreed in the ABM Treaty to slow the arms race by limiting intercontinental ballistic missiles and antiballistic missile defenses.

Opening to China

Meanwhile, the United States took dramatic steps to end two decades of Sino-American hostility. The Chinese wanted to spur trade and hoped that friendlier Sino-American relations would make their onetime ally and now enemy, the Soviet Union, more cautious. In early 1972 Nixon made a historic trip to Red China, where he and the venerable Chinese leaders Mao Zedong and Zhou Enlai agreed to disagree on many issues, except one: the Soviet Union should not be permitted to make gains in Asia. Sino-American relations improved slightly, and official diplomatic recognition came in 1979.

The opening to communist China and the policy of détente with the Soviet Union reflected Nixon's and Kissinger's belief in the importance of maintaining stability among the great powers. In the Third World, too, Nixon and Kissinger sought stability, though there they hoped to get it by maintaining the status quo. As it happened, events in the Third World would provide the Nixon-Kissinger approach with its greatest test.

Wars in the Middle East

In the Middle East the situation grew more volatile after the Arab-Israeli Six-Day War in 1967. Israel scored victories against Egypt and Syria, seizing the Sinai Peninsula and the Gaza Strip from Egypt, the West Bank and East Jerusalem from Jordan, and the Golan Heights from Syria (see Map 33.2). Israel gained 28,000 square miles and could henceforth defend itself against invading forces. But with Gaza and the West Bank as the ancestral home to hundreds of thousands of Palestinians (see Chapter 28), Israel found itself governing people who wanted to see it destroyed. When the Israelis established Jewish settlements in their newly won areas, Arab resentment grew. Terrorists associated with the Palestinian Liberation Organization (PLO) made hit-and-run raids on Jewish settlements, hijacked jetliners, and murdered Israeli athletes at the 1972 Olympic Games in Munich, West Germany. The Israelis retaliated by assassinating PLO leaders.

OPEC and the 1973 Oil Embargo

If one date can mark the decline of U.S. power in the Cold War era and the arrival of the Arab nations of the Middle East as important players on the world stage, it would be October 20, 1973. That day, the Arab members of the Organization of Petroleum Exporting Countries (OPEC)—Saudi Arabia, Iraq, Kuwait, Libya, and Algeria—imposed an embargo on oil shipments to the United States and other Israeli allies. The move was in retaliation against U.S. support of Israel in the two-week-old Yom Kippur War. The embargo followed an OPEC price hike days earlier from $3.01 to $5.12 per barrel. In December, the five Arab countries, joined by Iran, raised prices again, to $11.65 per barrel, almost a fourfold increase from early October.

Gasoline prices surged across the United States, and some dealers ran low on supplies. Frustrated Americans endured endless lines at the pumps and shivered in underheated homes. When the embargo was lifted in April 1974, oil prices stayed high, and the aftereffects of the embargo would linger through the decade. It confirmed how much the United States's economic destiny was outside its control.

Just twenty years before, in the early 1950s, Americans produced at home all the oil they needed. By the early 1960s, the picture changed, as Americans depended on foreign sources for one out of every six barrels of oil. By 1972, the figure increased to about two out of six, or more than 30 percent. Few Americans worried, and all Americans were later shocked by the embargo. As author Daniel Yergin put it, "The shortfall struck at fundamental beliefs in the endless abundance of resources, . . . that a large part of the public did not even know, up until October 1973, that the United States imported any oil at all."

When the embargo ended, Americans resumed their wastefulness, but in a changed world. The United States had become a dependent nation, its economic future linked to decisions by Arab leaders half a world away.

In 1976 OPEC sharply raised the price of oil a second time, prompting this editorial cartoon by Don Wright of the Miami News.

(© Tribune Media Services, Inc. All Rights Reserved. Reprinted with permission)

In October 1973, on the Jewish High Holy Day of Yom Kippur, Egypt and Syria attacked Israel, primarily seeking revenge for the 1967 defeat. Surprised, Israel reeled before launching an effective counteroffensive. To punish the United States for its pro-Israel stance, the Organization of Petroleum Exporting Countries (OPEC), a group of mostly Arab nations that united to raise oil prices, embargoed oil shipments to the United States and other Israeli supporters. An energy crisis rocked the nation. Kissinger arranged a cease-fire in the war, but OPEC did not lift the oil embargo until March 1974. The next year Kissinger persuaded Egypt and Israel to accept a U.N. peacekeeping force in the Sinai. But Arabs still vowed to destroy Israel, and Israelis built more Jewish settlements in occupied lands.

Antiradicalism in Latin America and Africa In Latin America, the Nixon administration thwarted radical leftist challenges to authoritarian rule. When voters in Chile elected a Marxist president, Salvador Allende, in 1970 the CIA secretly encouraged military officers to stage a coup. In 1973 a military junta ousted Allende and installed an authoritarian regime under General Augusto Pinochet. (Allende was subsequently murdered.) Washington publicly denied any role.

In Africa, too, Washington preferred the status quo, backing the white-minority regime in Rhodesia (now Zimbabwe) and activated the CIA in a failed effort to defeat a Soviet- and Cuban-backed faction in Angola's civil war. In South Africa, Nixon tolerated the white rulers who imposed segregationist apartheid on blacks and mixed-race "coloureds" (85 percent of the population), keeping them poor, disfranchised, and ghettoized in prisonlike townships. After the leftist government came to power in Angola, however, Washington paid attention to Africa, building economic ties and sending arms to friendly black nations, such as Kenya and the Congo, while distancing the United States from the white governments of Rhodesia and South Africa.

PRESIDENTIAL POLITICS AND THE CRISIS OF LEADERSHIP

Richard Nixon's foreign policy accomplishments were overshadowed by his domestic failures. He betrayed the public trust and broke laws. That, combined with Americans' belief that their leaders had lied repeatedly about the war in Vietnam, shook their faith in government. This new mistrust joined with conservatives' traditional suspicion of big, activist government to create a crisis of leadership and undermine liberal policies that had governed since the New Deal. Nixon's successors, Gerald Ford and Jimmy Carter, were limited by the public's suspicion of government.

Nixon's Domestic Agenda Richard Nixon was brilliant, driven, politically cunning, yet also crude, prejudiced against Jews and African Americans, happy to use dirty tricks and presidential power against his enemies, and driven by a resentment that bordered on paranoia. The son of a grocer from an agricultural region of southern California, Nixon loathed the liberal establishment, which loathed him back, and his presidency was driven by that as much as by any strong philosophical commitment to conservative principles.

Much of Nixon's domestic policy initiatives seem liberal. The Nixon administration pioneered affirmative action. It doubled the budgets of the new National

Endowment for the Humanities (NEH) and National Endowment for the Arts (NEA). Nixon supported the ERA, signed major environmental legislation, created the Occupational Safety and Health Administration (OSHA), actively used deficit spending to manage the economy, and proposed a guaranteed minimum income for all Americans.

At the same time, Nixon pursued a conservative agenda that involved devolution, shifting federal government authority to states and localities. He promoted revenue-sharing programs that distributed federal funds back to the states, thus appealing to those who saw high taxes as supporting liberal giveaway programs for poor and minority Americans. Nixon worked to equate the Republican Party with law and order and the Democrats with permissiveness, crime, drugs, radicalism, and the hippie lifestyle. He used his outspoken vice president, Spiro Agnew, to attack war protesters and critics as "naughty children." He appointed four conservative justices to the Supreme Court: Warren Burger, Harry Blackmun, Lewis Powell Jr., and William Rehnquist.

But most of Nixon's liberal agenda was not so much liberal as it was tricky—a term commonly applied to Nixon at the time. Instead of attacking liberal programs and the entrenched government bureaucracies that administered them, he attempted to undermine them while appearing to offer support. For example, when the Nixon administration proposed a guaranteed minimum income for all Americans, his larger goal was to dismantle the federal welfare system and destroy its liberal bureaucracy of social workers.

Nixon additionally sought to attract white southerners to the Republican Party. He nominated two southerners to the Supreme Court, one of whom had a segregationist record. When Congress declined to confirm either nominee, Nixon protested angrily. After the Supreme Court upheld a school desegregation plan requiring a highly segregated North Carolina school system to achieve racial integration by busing both African American and white children throughout the county (*Swann v. Charlotte-Mecklenburg*, 1971), Nixon denounced busing.

Enemies and Dirty Tricks

Nixon was almost sure of reelection in 1972. His Democratic opponent was George McGovern, a progressive senator from South Dakota and strong opponent of the Vietnam War, who appealed to the left. Alabama governor George Wallace, running on a third-party ticket, withdrew from the race after an assassination attempt left him paralyzed. The Nixon campaign, however, took no chances. On June 17, five men from the Committee to Re-elect the President, known as CREEP, were caught breaking into the Democratic National Committee's offices at the Watergate apartment and office complex in Washington, D.C. The break-in got little attention, and Nixon was swept into office in November with 60 percent of the popular vote. McGovern carried only Massachusetts and the District of Columbia. But as Nixon triumphed, his downfall began.

From the beginning of his presidency, Nixon obsessively believed he was surrounded by enemies. He made enemies lists, hundreds of names long, that included all African American members of Congress and the presidents of most Ivy League universities. On Nixon's order, his aide Charles Colson formed a secret group called the Plumbers. Their first job was to break into the office of the psychiatrist treating

Daniel Ellsberg, the former Pentagon employee who made the Pentagon Papers public, looking for material to discredit him. During the 1972 presidential campaign, the Plumbers bugged phones, infiltrated campaign staffs, and wrote anonymous letters falsely accusing Democratic candidates of sexual misconduct. They were going back to plant more surveillance equipment at the Democratic National Committee offices when they were caught by the D.C. police at the Watergate complex.

Watergate Cover-Up and Investigation

Nixon was not directly involved in the Watergate affair. But instead of distancing himself and firing those responsible, he covered up their connection to the break-ins. He had the CIA stop the FBI's investigation, claiming national security. At this point, Nixon obstructed justice—a felony and an impeachable crime—but he also halted the investigation. However, two relatively unknown reporters for the *Washington Post*, Carl Bernstein and Bob Woodward, stayed on the story. Aided by an anonymous, highly placed government official whom they code-named Deep Throat (the title of a notorious 1972 X-rated film), they followed a money trail leading straight to the White House. (W. Mark Felt, second in command at the FBI in the early 1970s, identified himself as Watergate's Deep Throat in 2005.)

From May to August 1973, the Senate held televised hearings on the Watergate affair. White House Counsel John Dean, fearful that he was becoming the fall guy for the Watergate fiasco, gave damning testimony. On July 13, a White House aide told the Senate Committee that Nixon regularly recorded his conversations in the Oval Office. Nixon refused to turn the tapes over to Congress.

Impeachment and Resignation

Nixon faced scandals on other fronts. In October 1973, Vice President Spiro Agnew resigned, following charges that he accepted bribes while governor of Maryland. Nixon appointed and Congress approved Michigan's Gerald Ford, the House minority leader, as Agnew's replacement. Meanwhile, Nixon's staff was increasingly concerned about his excessive drinking and seeming mental instability. Then, on October 24, 1973, the House of Representatives began impeachment proceedings.

Under court order, Nixon released edited portions of the Oval Office tapes. Although the first tapes revealed nothing criminal, the public was shocked by Nixon's obscenities and racist slurs. In July 1974, the Supreme Court ruled that Nixon must release all the tapes. Despite erasures on two key tapes, the House Judiciary Committee found evidence to impeach Nixon on three grounds: obstruction of justice, abuse of power, and contempt of Congress. On August 9, 1974, facing certain impeachment and conviction, Richard Nixon became the first president of the United States to resign.

The Watergate scandal shook Americans' confidence in government yet further and prompted Congress to pass several bills aimed at restricting presidential power, including the War Powers Act.

Ford's Presidency

Gerald Ford, the nation's first unelected president, faced a cynical nation. The presidency was discredited. The economy was in decline. Ford was an honorable man who tried to end the long national nightmare. But when he issued a full pardon to Richard Nixon, his approval ratings plummeted from 71 to 41 percent. Some suggested, with no evidence, that he struck a deal with Nixon.

Ford accomplished little domestically during his two and a half years in office. The Democrats gained a large margin in the 1974 congressional elections, and after Watergate, Congress was willing to exercise its power. Ford almost routinely vetoed its bills—thirty-nine in one year—but Congress often overrode his veto. Ford was often portrayed as a buffoon and klutz in political cartoons, comedy monologues, and especially on the new hit television show *Saturday Night Live*. Ford caught the fallout of disrespect that Nixon's actions had unleashed. No longer would respect for the presidency prevent the media from reporting presidential stumbles or misconduct.

Carter as Outsider President

Jimmy Carter, who was elected in 1976 by a slim margin, initially benefited from Americans' suspicion of politicians. Carter was a one-term governor of Georgia, one of the new southern leaders committed to racial equality. He grew up on his family's peanut farm in the rural Plains, Georgia; graduated from the Naval Academy, then served as an engineer in the navy's nuclear submarine program. Carter, a born-again Christian, promised the United States, "I will never lie to you," underscoring his distance from Washington's recent political corruption.

From his inauguration, when he broke with the convention of a motorcade and walked down Pennsylvania Avenue holding hands with his wife and close adviser, Rosalynn, and their young daughter, Amy, Carter emphasized his populist, outsider appeal. But that status proved a problem as president. Though an astute policymaker, he scorned the deal making that was necessary to pass legislation in Congress.

Carter faced problems that would have challenged any leader: continued economic decline, unabated energy shortages, and public distrust of government. More than any other postwar U.S. leader, Carter was willing to tell Americans things they did not want to hear. As shortages of natural gas forced schools and businesses to close during the bitterly cold winter of 1977, Carter, wearing a cardigan sweater, called for sacrifice and implemented energy conservation measures at government buildings. In the defining speech of his presidency, Carter told Americans that the nation suffered from a crisis of the spirit. He talked about the false lures of self-indulgence and consumption. He called for a "new commitment to the path of common purpose." But he offered few solutions for the national malaise.

Resigning in disgrace as impeachment for his role in the Watergate cover-up became a certainty, Richard Nixon flashed the V for victory sign as he left the White House for the last time.
(Nixon Presidential Materials Project, National Archives and Records Administration)

Carter did ease burdensome government regulations without destroying consumer and worker safeguards and created the Departments of Energy and Education. He also established a $1.6 billion superfund to clean up abandoned chemical-waste sites and placed more than 100 million acres of Alaskan land under federal protection as national parks, forests, and wildlife refuges.

ECONOMIC CRISIS

Since World War II, except for a few brief downturns, prosperity dominated American life. Prosperity made possible the great liberal initiatives of the 1960s and improved the lives of the United States's poor and elderly. But in the early 1970s, that long period of economic expansion ended. In 1974 alone, the gross national product dropped 2 percentage points. Industrial production fell 9 percent. Inflation—the increase in costs of goods and services—skyrocketed, and unemployment grew.

Stagflation and Its Causes

Throughout most of the 1970s, the U.S. economy floundered in what economists dubbed stagflation: a stagnant economy characterized by high unemployment combined with out-of-control inflation. Stagflation was almost impossible to manage with traditional economic remedies. When the federal government increased spending to stimulate the economy and reduce unemployment, inflation grew. When it tried to control inflation by cutting government spending or tightening the money supply, the recession deepened and unemployment escalated.

The causes of the economic crisis were complex. President Johnson created inflationary pressure by waging an expensive war in Vietnam while greatly expanding domestic spending in his Great Society programs. But fundamental problems also came from the United States' changing role in the global economy. By the early 1970s, both of the United States's wartime adversaries, Japan and Germany, had become major economic powers and competitors in global trade that the United States once dominated. In 1971, for the first time since the nineteenth century, the United States imported more than it exported, beginning an era of U.S. trade deficits.

Corporate actions also contributed to the growing trade imbalance. During the years of global dominance, few U.S. companies improved production techniques or educated workers. Consequently, U.S. productivity—the average output of goods per hour of labor—declined. But wages rarely did. The combination of falling productivity and high labor costs meant that U.S. goods became increasingly expensive. Worse, U.S. companies allowed the quality of their goods to decline. From 1966 to 1973, for example, U.S. car and truck manufacturers recalled almost 30 million vehicles because of serious defects.

The United States's global economic vulnerability was driven home by the energy crisis in 1973. The country depended on imported oil for almost one-third of its energy. When OPEC cut off shipments to the United States, prices rose 350 percent and increased heating costs, shipping costs, and manufacturing costs, as well as the cost of goods and services. Inflation jumped from 3 percent in 1973 to 11 percent in 1974. Sales of gas-guzzling U.S. cars plummeted as people switched to energy-efficient subcompacts from Japan and Europe. GM laid off 6 percent of its domestic work force and put larger numbers on rolling unpaid leaves. As the ailing automobile industry quit buying steel, glass, and rubber, manufacturers of these goods laid off workers, too.

Attempts to Fix the Economy

U.S. leaders tried desperately to manage the economic crisis, but their actions often exacerbated it instead. As the United States's rising trade deficit undermined international confidence in the dollar, the Nixon administration ended the dollar's link to the gold standard; free-floating exchange rates increased the price of foreign goods in the United States and stimulated inflation. Following monetary theory, which held that, with less money available to chase the supply of goods, price increases would slow, ending the inflationary spiral, Ford curbed federal spending and encouraged the Federal Reserve Board to tighten credit, prompting the worst recession in forty years. In 1975 unemployment climbed to 8.5 percent.

Carter's larger economic policies, including his 1978 deregulation of airline, trucking, banking, and communications industries, would eventually foster economic growth, but not soon enough. After almost a decade of decline, Americans were losing faith in the economy and the ability of their leaders to manage it.

Impacts of the Economic Crisis

The economic crisis of the 1970s accelerated the transition from an industrial to a service economy. During the 1970s, the United States deindustrialized, as automobile companies laid off workers and steel plant closings left communities devastated. Other manufacturing concerns moved overseas, seeking lower labor costs and fewer government regulations. New jobs were created—27 million of them—overwhelmingly in what economists called the service sector: retail sales, restaurants, and other service providers. These jobs—such as warehouse work or retail sales, for example—paid much lower wages than union manufacturing positions and often lacked healthcare and other benefits.

Formerly successful blue-collar workers saw their middle-class standards of life slipping away. More married women joined the work force because they had to. High school or college graduates in the 1970s, raised with high expectations, found limited possibilities, if they found jobs at all.

As the old industrial regions of the North and Midwest declined, people headed for the Sunbelt, which was booming (see Map 31.1). The federal government invested heavily in the South and West during the postwar era, especially in military and defense industries. The Sunbelt was primed for the rapid growth of modern industries and services—aerospace, defense, electronics, transportation, research, banking and finance, and leisure. City and state governments competed for business dollars, partly by preventing the growth of unions. Atlanta, Houston, and other southern cities marketed themselves as cosmopolitan and racially tolerant; they bought sports teams and built museums.

The population shift south and west created disaster in northern and midwestern cities. New York City, near financial collapse by late 1975, was saved only when the House and Senate Banking Committees approved federal loan guarantees. Cleveland defaulted on its debts in 1978, the first major city to do so since Detroit declared bankruptcy in 1933.

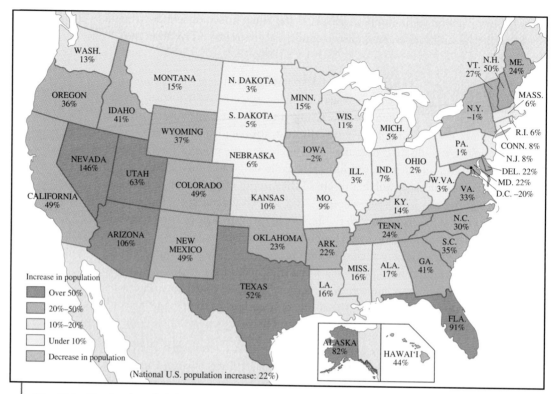

Map 31.1   The Continued Shift to the Sunbelt in the 1970s and 1980s

Throughout the 1970s and 1980s, Americans continued to leave economically declining areas of the North and East in pursuit of opportunity in the Sunbelt. States in the Sunbelt and in the West had the largest population increases.   (*Source:* "Shift to the Sunbelt," *Newsweek,* September 10, 1990.)

Tax Revolts

Meanwhile, a tax revolt movement emerged in the West. In California, inflation had driven property taxes up rapidly, hitting middle-class taxpayers hard. Instead of calling for wealthy citizens and major corporations to pay a larger share, voters rebelled against taxation itself. California's Proposition 13, passed by a landslide in 1978, rolled back property taxes and restricted future increases. Thirty-seven states similarly cut property taxes, and twenty-eight lowered their state income taxes.

The impact of Proposition 13 and similar initiatives was initially cushioned by state budget surpluses, but as those turned to deficits, states cut services—closing fire stations and public libraries and ending or limiting mental health services and programs for the disabled. Public schools were hit especially hard.

Credit and Investment

Before the runaway inflation of the 1970s, home mortgages and auto loans were the only major debt most Americans had. National credit cards had become common only in the late 1960s, and few Americans—especially those who remembered the Great Depression—were willing to spend money they did not have. In the 1970s, however, double-digit inflation rates made it economically smarter to buy goods before prices went up, even if it meant borrowing the money. Because debt was paid off later with devalued dollars, the consumer came out ahead. In 1975 consumer debt hit a high of $167 billion; it almost doubled to $315 billion by 1979.

In the 1970s, Americans became investors rather than savers. Because banking regulations capped interest paid on individual savings accounts, with inflation, a savings account bearing 5 percent interest actually *lost* more than 20 percent of its value from 1970 through 1980. That same money, invested at market rates, would have grown dramatically. Fidelity Investments, a mutual fund company, saw an opportunity: its money market accounts combined many smaller investments to purchase large-denomination Treasury bills and certificates of deposit, thus providing small investors the high interest rates normally available only to major investors. Money market investments grew from $1.7 billion in 1974 to $200 billion in 1982. Deregulation of the New York Stock Exchange spawned discount brokerage houses, whose low commission rates were affordable for middle-class investors.

AN ERA OF CULTURAL TRANSFORMATION

As Americans struggled with economic recession, governmental betrayal, and social division, major strands of late-twentieth-century culture were developed. The current environmental movement, the growth of technology, the rise of born-again Christianity and a therapeutic culture, contemporary forms of sexuality and the family, and the United States's emphasis on diversity all have roots in this odd decade sandwiched between the political vibrancy of the 1960s and the conservatism of the 1980s.

Environmentalism

A series of ecological crises drove home the fragility of the environment. In 1969 a major oil spill took place off the coast of Santa Barbara, California; that same year, the polluted Cuyahoga River, flowing through Cleveland, caught fire. In 1979 human error contributed to a nuclear accident at the Three Mile Island nuclear power plant near Harrisburg, Pennsylvania, and in 1980 President Carter declared a federal emergency at New York State's Love Canal, a dump site for a local chemical manufacturer, after it was discovered that 30 percent of local residents had suffered chromosome damage. Public activism produced major environmental initiatives, from the Environmental Protection Agency (EPA), created (under strong public pressure) in 1970 by the Nixon administration, to eighteen major environmental laws enacted by Congress during the decade.

When almost 20 million Americans—half of them schoolchildren—celebrated the first Earth Day on April 22, 1970, they signaled the triumph of a new understanding of environmentalism. Central to this movement was a recognition that the earth's resources were finite and must be conserved and protected. Many also identified rapid global population growth as a problem, and state public health offices frequently dispensed contraceptives to stem this new "epidemic."

Technology

During these years, Americans became increasingly uneasy about the science and technology that had been one source of the United States's might. Americans watched with pride as the astronaut Neil Armstrong stepped onto the lunar surface on July

20, 1969, saying, "That's one small step for a man, one giant step for mankind." But technology seemed unable to cope with earthbound problems of poverty, crime, pollution, and urban decay. The failure of technological warfare to deliver victory in Vietnam came as antiwar protesters were questioning the morality of such technology. But in the 1970s, the foundation was laid for the United States's computer revolution, with the creation of the integrated circuit in 1970, and by 1975 the MITS Altair 8800, boasting 256 bytes of memory and requiring thirty hours to assemble.

Religion and the Therapeutic Culture

Americans increasingly sought spiritual fulfillment. Methodist, Presbyterian, and Episcopalian churches lost members during this era, while evangelical and fundamentalist Christian churches grew dramatically. Protestant evangelicals, describing themselves as born again, emphasized the immediate, daily presence of God in their lives. Even some Catholics, such as the Mexican Americans who embraced the *cursillo* movement (a "little course" in faith), sought a more personal relationship with God. The New Age movement, which drew from and combined non-western spiritual and religious practices, including Zen Buddhism, yoga, and shamanism, along with insights from western psychology and spiritually oriented environmentalism, also drew adherents.

During the 1970s, the United States saw the emergence of a therapeutic culture. Although some were disgusted with the self-centeredness of the Me-Decade, bestselling books by therapists and self-help gurus insisted that individual feelings offered the ultimate measure of truth. Self-help books with titles like *I'm OK—You're OK* made up 15 percent of all bestselling books.

Sexuality and the Family

Sex became much more visible in U.S. culture during the 1970s, as network television loosened its regulation of sexual content. Early in the 1960s, married couples in television shows were required to occupy twin beds; in the 1970s, hit television shows included *Three's Company*, a situation comedy based on the then-scandalous premise that a single man shared an apartment with two female roommates and got away with it by pretending that he was gay. Donna Summers's 1975 disco hit "Love to Love You Baby" contained sixteen minutes of sexual moaning. And though few Americans participated in heterosexual orgies at New York City's Plato's Retreat, many read about them in *Time* magazine.

Sexual behaviors also changed. The seventies were the era of singles bars and gay bathhouses, but for most Americans, the sexual revolution meant a broader public acceptance of premarital sex and a limited acceptance of homosexuality, especially among more educated Americans. More heterosexual young people lived together without marriage during the 1970s; the census bureau even coined the term *POSSLQ* (persons of opposite sex sharing living quarters) to describe the relationship.

Changes in sexual mores and in women's roles altered the U.S. family as well. Men and women married later and had fewer children. By 1979, the birth rate had dropped almost 40 percent from its 1957 peak. Almost one-quarter of young single women in 1980 said they did not plan to have children. And a steadily rising percentage of babies were born to unmarried women, as the number of families headed by never-married women rose 400 percent. The divorce rate also rose, in part because states implemented no-fault divorce, which did not require evidence of adultery, physical cruelty, abandonment, or other wrongdoing. Americans also developed a greater acceptance of various family forms, symbolized by the blended family of television's *Brady Bunch*.

Diversity

The racial justice and identity movements of the late 1960s and 1970s made Americans more aware of differences among the nation's peoples—an awareness strengthened by new immigrants from Latin America and Asia. The challenge was figuring out how to acknowledge the new importance of difference in public policy. The 1970s solution was the idea of diversity. Difference was not a problem but a strength; the nation should seek to foster the diversity of its schools, workplaces, and public culture.

The 1978 Supreme Court decision in *Regents of the University of California v. Bakke* was a crucial early step. Allan Bakke, a thirty-three-year-old white man with a strong academic record, was denied admission to the medical school of the University of California at Davis. Bakke sued, charging that he had been denied equal protection because the medical school's affirmative-action program reserved 16 percent of its slots for racial-minority candidates, who were held to lower standards than other applicants. In 1978 the Supreme Court, in a split decision, decided in favor of Bakke. Four justices argued that any race-based decision violated the Civil Rights Act of 1964; four saw affirmative-action programs as constitutionally acceptable. The deciding vote, though for Bakke, contained an important qualification. A "diverse student body," Justice Lewis Powell wrote, is "a constitutionally permissible goal for an institution of higher education." To achieve diversity, educational institutions could consider race in admissions.

RENEWED COLD WAR AND MIDDLE EAST CRISIS

When Jimmy Carter took office in 1977, he asked Americans to abandon their "inordinate fear of Communism." Carter vowed to reduce the U.S. military presence overseas, to cut back arms sales, and slow the nuclear arms race. More than 400,000 U.S. military personnel were stationed abroad, the United States had military links with ninety-two nations, and the CIA was active on every continent. Carter promised to avoid new Vietnams and give more attention to environmental issues. He especially determined to improve human rights abroad—the freedom to vote, worship, travel, speak out, and get a fair trial. Like his predecessors, however, Carter identified revolutionary nationalism as a threat to the United States's global prominence.

Carter's Divided Administration

Carter spoke and acted inconsistently, partly because in the post-Vietnam years no consensus existed in foreign policy and partly because his advisers squabbled among themselves. One source of the problem was the stern-faced Zbigniew Brzezinski, a Polish-born political scientist who became Carter's national security adviser. An old-fashioned Cold Warrior, Brzezinski blamed foreign crises on Soviet expansionism. Carter gradually listened more to Brzezinski than to Secretary of State Cyrus Vance, an experienced public servant who advocated quiet diplomacy.

Under Carter, détente deteriorated and the Cold War deepened. Initially, Carter maintained fairly good relations with Moscow and secured some foreign policy successes. The United States signed two treaties with Panama in 1977. One provided for the return of the Canal Zone to Panama in 2000, and the other guaranteed the United States the right to defend the canal after that time. With conservatives denouncing the deal as a sellout, the Senate narrowly endorsed both agreements in 1978. The majority agreed with Carter's argument that relinquishing the canal would improve U.S. relations with Latin America.

Camp David Accords

The crowning accomplishment of Carter's presidency was the Camp David accords, the first mediated peace treaty between Israel and an Arab nation. In September 1978, the president persuaded Israel and Egypt to agree to a peace treaty, gained Israel's promise to withdraw from the Sinai Peninsula, and forged a provisional agreement that provided for continued negotiations on the future status of Palestinians living in the occupied territories of Jordan's West Bank and Egypt's Gaza Strip. Other Arab states denounced the agreement for not requiring Israel to relinquish all occupied territories and not guaranteeing a Palestinian homeland. But the accord, signed on March 26, 1979, by Israeli prime minister Menachem Begin and Egyptian president Anwar al-Sadat, at least ended warfare along one frontier.

Soviet Invasion of Afghanistan

Meanwhile, relations with Moscow deteriorated. U.S. and USSR officials sparred over the Kremlin's reluctance to lift restrictions on Jewish emigration and over the Soviet decision to deploy new intermediate-range ballistic missiles aimed at western Europe. Then, in December 1979, the Soviets invaded Afghanistan, a remote country whose strategic position made it a source of great-power conflict. Following World War II, Afghanistan struggled with ongoing ethnic and factional squabbling; in the 1970s, it spiraled into anarchy. In late 1979, the Red Army entered Afghanistan to shore up a faltering communist government under siege by Muslim rebels. Moscow officials calculated they could be in and out of the country before anyone noticed, including the Americans.

Carter not only noticed but reacted forcefully. He suspended shipments of grain and high-technology equipment to the Soviet Union, withdrew a major arms control treaty from Senate consideration, and initiated an international boycott of the 1980 Summer Olympics in Moscow. He also secretly authorized the CIA to distribute aid, including arms and military support, to the Mujahidin (Islamic guerillas) fighting the communist government and sanctioned military aid to their backer, Pakistan. Announcing the Carter Doctrine, the president asserted that the United States would intervene, unilaterally and militarily, should Soviet aggression threaten the petroleum-rich Persian Gulf. Carter warned aides that the Soviets, unless checked, would likely attack elsewhere in the Middle East, but declassified documents confirm what contemporary critics said: that the Soviet invasion was limited and did not presage a push into the Persian Gulf.

Iranian Hostage Crisis

Carter simultaneously faced a tough foreign policy test in neighboring Iran. The shah, long favored by the United States, was dethroned by a coalition of Iranians, who resented the dislocation of their traditional ways by the shah's attempts at modernization. Riots led by anti-American Muslim clerics erupted in late 1978. The shah went into exile, and in April 1979 Islamic revolutionaries, led by the Ayatollah Khomeini, an elderly cleric who denounced the United States as the stronghold of capitalism and western materialism, proclaimed a Shi'ite Islamic Republic. In November, with the exiled shah in the United States for medical treatment, mobs stormed the U.S. embassy in Teheran. They took American personnel as hostages, demanding the return of the shah to stand trial. The Iranians eventually released a few American prisoners, but fifty-two others suffered solitary confinement, beatings, and terrifying mock executions.

Unable to gain the hostages' freedom through diplomatic intermediaries, Carter took steps to isolate Iran economically, freezing Iranian assets in the United States. When the hostage takers paraded their blindfolded captives before television cameras, Americans felt taunted and humiliated. In April 1980, Carter broke diplomatic relations with Iran and ordered a daring rescue mission. But equipment failed and two aircraft collided, killing eight American soldiers. The hostages were not freed until January 1981, after Carter left office.

The Iranian revolution, together with the rise of the Mujahidin in Afghanistan, signified the emergence of Islamic fundamentalism as a force in world affairs. Socialism and capitalism, the answers that the two superpowers offered to the problems of modernization, failed to solve the problems in Central Asia and the Middle East. Consequently, Islamic orthodoxy found growing support for its message: that secular leaders such as Nasser in Egypt and the shah in Iran had taken their people down the wrong path, necessitating a return to conservative Islamic values and Islamic law. The Iranian revolution expressed a complex mixture of discontents within Islamic societies.

Rise of Saddam Hussein

U.S. officials took some consolation from the avowedly secular government in neighboring Iraq. Ruled by the Ba'athist Party, Iraq won favor in Washington for its pursuit and execution of Iraqi communists. When a Ba'athist leader named Saddam Hussein took over as president of Iraq in 1979 and threatened the Teheran government, U.S. officials thought Saddam could offset the Iranian danger in the Persian Gulf. As border clashes between Iraqi and Iranian forces escalated into war in 1980, Washington policymakers were officially neutral but soon tilted toward Iraq.

Carter earned some diplomatic successes in the Middle East, Africa, and Latin America, but the revived Cold War and prolonged Iranian hostage crisis hurt the administration politically. Contrary to Carter's goals, more U.S. military personnel were stationed overseas in 1980 than in 1976; the defense budget climbed and arms sales grew to $15.3 billion in 1980. On human rights, the president practiced a double standard, applying the human-rights test to some nations (the Soviet Union, Argentina, and Chile) but not to U.S. allies (South Korea, the shah's Iran, and the Philippines). Still, Carter's human-rights policy saved the lives of some political prisoners and institutionalized concern for human rights worldwide. But his inability to restore economic and military dominance dashed his reelection prospects. He lost in 1980 to the hawkish Ronald Reagan, former Hollywood actor and governor of California.

The All-Volunteer Force

On In 1973, the United States ended the draft and turned to an all-volunteer force (AVF). The draft had been in effect, with only a brief interruption in the late 1940s, since the United States began mobilizing for World War II. Never before had the United States had a peacetime draft. But as the country embraced global leadership and faced a heightened Cold War, the draft became an accepted part of American life. By 1973 more than 50 million American men had been inducted into the military since World War II.

Richard Nixon promised to end the draft during his 1968 presidential campaign, realizing that the draft was a focus for widespread protest against the Vietnam War. Ending the draft was not feasible during the war, but Nixon began planning for an all-volunteer force once in office. Many Americans supported the shift because they believed a president could not rely on a draft to compel people to fight a war they did not support.

The military, however, disliked Nixon's plan. The war in Vietnam shattered morale and left the military, particularly the army, in disarray. With public opinion of the military at an all-time low, how would it attract volunteers?

The largest of the four services, the army required the most volunteers. To draw volunteers, the army ended make-work ("chickenshit") tasks and enhanced military professionalism. It also turned to market research and advertising. Discovering that many young men were afraid to lose their individuality, the army launched a campaign that told potential volunteers, "Today's Army Wants to Join You."

The army needed about 225,000 recruits annually (compared to about 80,000 per year in 2006) and had difficulty attracting them. Within a decade, however, the United States's military boasted a higher rate of high school graduates than the comparable age population. During an era of relative peace, many young people found opportunities for education and training through military service, particularly the economically disadvantaged—a high percentage of whom were African American.

The military understood that, without a draft, it would need women to fill the ranks. The proportion of women in the military increased from 1.9 percent in 1972 to about 15 percent currently, with a wider range of available roles. The nation's understanding of military service changed from an obligation of (male) citizenship to a voluntary choice. The implications seemed less urgent in peacetime. But in wartime, the volunteer force raises the question: What does it mean when only a small number of volunteers bears the burden of warfare and most Americans do not have to consider the possibility of going to war?

Summary

From the crisis year of 1968 on, Americans were highly polarized—over the war in Vietnam, over the best path to racial equality and equal rights, over the meaning of the United States itself. As many activists turned to cultural nationalism, or group-identity politics, notions of American unity seemed a relic of the past. And though a new women's movement won victories against sex discrimination, powerful opposition arose in response.

During this era, Americans became increasingly disillusioned with politics and presidential leadership. Richard Nixon's abuses of power in the Watergate scandal and cover-up, combined with growing awareness that the administration had lied repeatedly about the United States's role in Vietnam, produced a profound suspicion of government. A major economic crisis ended the post–World War II expansion, and Americans struggled with the effects of stagflation: rising unemployment rates coupled with high inflation.

Overseas, a string of setbacks—defeat in Vietnam, the oil embargo, and the Iranian hostage crisis—signified the waning of U.S. power. Détente with the Soviet Union had flourished for a time; however, by 1980 Cold War tensions escalated. And the Middle East became an increasing focus of U.S. foreign policy.

Plagued by political, economic, and foreign policy crises, at the end of the 1970s, the United States's age of liberalism was over; the elements for a conservative resurgence were in place.

Chapter Review

THE NEW POLITICS OF IDENTITY

What defined political activism in the late 1960s and 1970s?

A new identity politics, in which groups stressed and celebrated their racial and ethnic differences, became the hallmark of activism by the 1970s. African Americans no longer sought equality via their shared humanity with white society. Instead, they—as well as Native Americans and Mexican Americans—looked to first validate what made them culturally unique and use that as the starting point for their demands for social and political equality. Through the Black Power movement, African Americans embraced a black standard of beauty, celebrated their heritage, and founded black studies programs in universities. Native Americans began a Red Power movement similarly to seek the return of native lands, validate tribal customs, and ensure greater power to self-govern. Hispanics likewise embraced their cultural distinctiveness while seeking better pay and conditions for migrant farm workers and establishing cooperative societies and ethnically-focused businesses.

THE WOMEN'S MOVEMENT AND GAY LIBERATION

What were the successes of the women's movement?

The women's movement made major gains in the 1960s and 1970s: the right of a married woman to obtain credit in her own name; the right of an unmarried woman to obtain birth control; the right to serve on juries; and the end of sex-segregated help wanted ads. Activists established rape crisis centers, educated law enforcement, and challenged definitions of rape that blamed the victim for the attack. They worked for legalized abortion at the state level and won a major victor with the 1973 Supreme Court decision in *Roe v. Wade,* which ruled that privacy rights protected a woman's decision not to continue a pregnancy. The women's movement also achieved greater opportunities for women in sports via passage of Title IX of the Higher Education Act, which barred federal funds from colleges or universities discriminating against women. Likewise, the movement sparked the creation of women's studies programs in colleges nationwide.

THE END IN VIETNAM

What kept Nixon from ending the Vietnam War as quickly as he had hoped?

Nixon's policy in Vietnam was driven by a goal to end the war fast, partly so that it would not ruin his political career as it had Johnson's. But at the same time, he did not want to hurt American credibility as a world leader, and he refused to allow South Vietnam to fall to the communists. Consequently, although he dramatically decreased the number of American troops from 543,000 in 1969 to 60,000 in 1970, he increased bombing of North Vietnam and neutral Cambodia, hoping to force the enemy into concessions. This failed even after invading Cambodia. A cease-fire was agreed to in 1973, and shortly after U.S. troops left, a full-scale war developed between North and South Vietnam, with the latter falling and the two countries reunifying as a communist nation in 1975.

NIXON, KISSINGER, AND THE WORLD

How did Vietnam influence Nixon's approach to foreign policy?

The failure in Vietnam forced Nixon to rethink the Cold War containment policy of providing military aid to anticommunist revolutions and wars. Instead, he adopted the Nixon Doctrine, which said the United States would provide economic aid but not troops to allies. Second, he implemented détente, a policy of minimizing Soviet expansion and arms buildup through diplomacy and mutual concessions. Détente also focused on improving trade relations with the Soviets and other communist giants, such as China, to help minimize communism's reach. And Chinese leaders Mao Zedong and Zhou Enlai agreed with Nixon that the Soviet Union should be kept from making gains in Asia.

PRESIDENTIAL POLITICS AND THE CRISIS OF LEADERSHIP

How did Watergate bring down the Nixon administration?

Sometimes paranoid, Nixon kept long lists of so-called enemies and directed aide Charles Colson to form a secret group called the Plumbers to dig up dirt on various groups and individuals. During Nixon's 1972 reelection campaign, the Plumbers were arrested while breaking into the Democratic National Campaign headquarters in the Watergate complex to plant surveillance equipment. While Nixon was not directly involved in this effort, he made the mistake of blocking the CIA and FBI investigations into it—which constituted an obstruction of justice. He also initially refused to turn over his audiotape conversations to congressional hearings. Eventually, he relinquished the tapes, although several contained significant gaps. Congress began impeachment hearings, and facing certain conviction and impeachment, Nixon became the first U.S. president to resign on August 9, 1974.

ECONOMIC CRISIS

What were the long-term effects of the 1970s recession?

The 1970s recession accelerated the nation's shift from an industrial to a service-based economy. As manufacturers in leading industries, such as automobiles and steel, laid off large numbers of workers or shifted to cheaper production, new jobs opened in the lower-paid service sector, such as cashiers and waiters. Increasing numbers of married women went to work to keep their families afloat. Older industrial cities suffered decay, while the Sunbelt was well-positioned to prosper with the growth of modern industries such as defense, aerospace and finance. Double-digit inflation in the 1970s led people to buy up goods before prices would rise, often on credit, fueling a major rise in consumer indebtedness. Finally, with interest rates capped on savings accounts, people increasingly shifted to investments via mutual funds and the stock market.

AN ERA OF CULTURAL TRANSFORMATION

How did the openness of the 1970s impact family life?

The tolerance and openness about sex in the 1970s facilitated major changes in traditional notions of what constituted a family. As norms against premarital sex ebbed, more young couples were opting to live together rather than get married. Those who wed, tended to do so later in life and had fewer children. By decade's end, the birth rate dropped nearly 40 percent from its all-time high, and nearly 25 percent of single women said they did not intend to have children at all. Divorce rates also shot up as a result of new no fault laws that enabled couples to end bad relationships without proving adultery, abandonment, or other cause.

RENEWED COLD WAR AND MIDDLE EAST CRISIS

What was Carter's record regarding the Middle East?

On the one hand, Carter achieved great success in mediating a peace treaty between Israel and Egypt in 1978. While the move was a major first step toward future negotiations, Arab states felt it fell short in not providing a Palestinian homeland and allowing Israel to maintain some of its occupied territories. On the other hand, Carter aided Islamic guerillas to fight Soviets in Afghanistan, which he mistakenly feared was the communist country's first step toward the Persian Gulf. Second, Carter angered Iranians when he provided protection for the exiled shah in the United States to seek medical treatment. Mobs stormed the U.S. embassy in Iran and took hostages to press for the shah to stand trial. While some were released, fifty-two other hostages were imprisoned and beaten or paraded before television cameras for the world to see. Carter's inability to free the U.S. hostages contributed to his political downfall and defeat in his reelection bid in 1980.

SUGGESTIONS FOR FURTHER READING

Donald T. Critchlow, *Phyllis Schlafly and Grassroots Conservatism: A Woman's Crusade* (2005)

Daniel Ellsberg, *Secrets: A Memoir of Vietnam and the Pentagon Papers* (2002)

David Farber, *Taken Hostage: The Iran Hostage Crisis and America's First Encounter with Radical Islam* (2004)

Ian F. Haney-Lopez, *Racism on Trial: The Chicano Fight for Justice* (2003)

Richard Reeves, *President Nixon: Alone in the White House* (2001)

Ruth Rosen, *The World Split Open: How the Modern Women's Movement Changed America* (2000)

Hal Rothman, *The Greening of a Nation: Environmentalism in the U.S. Since 1945* (1997)

Bruce Schulman, *The Seventies: The Great Shift in American Culture, Society, and Politics* (2001)

John D. Skrentny, *The Minority Rights Revolution* (2002)

Odd Arne Westad, *The Global Cold War: Third World Interventions and the Making of Our Times* (2005)

CHAPTER 32

Conservatism Revived

CHAPTER OUTLINE

Reagan and the Conservative Resurgence

Reaganomics

Reagan and the World

American Society in the 1980s

The End of the Cold War and Global Disorder

> **LINKS TO THE WORLD:** CNN

Summary

> **LEGACY FOR A PEOPLE AND A NATION:** The Americans with Disabilities Act

"It was hot and there was a lot of desert," Luisa Orellana remembered about crossing the Mexican border into the United States in the early 1980s. "All of us started running, each one with a child in our arms. . . . It rained so hard we couldn't see where we were going, but it helped because the Border Patrol couldn't see us either."

Three months earlier Luisa's father was murdered. Tanis Stanislaus Orellana worked in El Salvador with Archbishop Óscar Romero, the most powerful critic of the ruling military dictatorship whose death squads killed thirty thousand Salvadorans between 1979 and 1981. In 1980 Romero was shot and killed as he consecrated the Eucharist during Mass. The civil war that followed lasted twelve years, leading an estimated 1 million Salvadorans to seek refuge elsewhere from the torture, rape, and murder increasingly commonplace in their homeland.

After Orellana's murder, his widow fled with their children, leaving almost everything behind. They took the bus through Guatemala, crossed illegally into Mexico, and, sheltered by churches, made their way from Chiapas to Mexico City to Agua Prieta, on the U.S.-Mexico border.

There, Luisa and her family ran 2 miles through blinding rain. Cold, hungry, and scared, they were met in Douglas, Arizona, by the Sanctuary movement, Americans who believed that the U.S. government's refugee policy, which offered asylum to those fleeing violent repression and possible death or torture, must include people who escaped the deadly civil wars ravaging Central America in the 1980s. Officially, the U.S. government designated them economic refugees and denied them asylum.

The originators of the U.S. Sanctuary movement used church networks and human-rights groups throughout Central America to investigate refugees' stories of abuse and murder. Their mission

This icon will direct you to interactive activities and study materials on *A People And A Nation*, Brief Edition
website: **www.cengage.com/history/norton/peoplenationbrief8e**

Chronology

1980	Reagan is elected president.		**1986**	Iran-contra scandal erupts.
1981	AIDS is first observed in United States.		**1987**	Stock market drops 508 points in one day.
	Economic problems continue; prime interest rate reaches 21.5 percent.			Palestinian *intifada* begins.
	Reagan breaks air traffic controllers' strike.		**1988**	George H. W. Bush is elected president.
	Reaganomics plan of budget and tax cuts is approved by Congress.		**1989**	Tiananmen Square massacre occurs in China.
				Berlin Wall is torn down.
1982	Unemployment reaches 10.8 percent, highest rate since Great Depression.			U.S. troops invade Panama.
	ERA dies after Stop-ERA campaign prevents ratification in key states.			Gulf between rich and poor is at highest point since 1920s.
1983	Reagan introduces SDI.		**1990**	Americans with Disabilities Act is passed.
	Terrorists kill U.S. Marines in Lebanon.			Communist regimes in eastern Europe collapse.
	U.S. invasion of Grenada occurs.			Iraq invades Kuwait.
1984	Reagan aids contras despite congressional ban.			South Africa begins to dismantle apartheid.
	Economic recovery; unemployment rate drops and economy grows without inflation.		**1991**	Persian Gulf War occurs.
	Reagan is reelected.			Soviet Union dissolves into independent states.
	Gorbachev promotes reforms in Soviet Union.			United States enters recession.
			1992	Annual federal budget deficit reaches high of $300 billion at end of Bush presidency.

was to protect human rights and to save those they could from torture and death. Many members belonged to faith-based communities, although secular institutions, including some universities and the state of New Mexico, also participated. Some movement members went to prison, charged with transporting or harboring fugitives.

Luisa and her family moved from the sanctuary offered by Tucson churches, which were at the center of the movement, to live in the basement of a Spokane, Washington, Catholic church. In 1989 the U.S. government granted protection and work permits to Central American refugees. Luisa stayed in Washington, where she became a teacher of English as a second language.

Luisa Orellana and her family were part of the new immigration that began in the early 1970s and grew throughout the 1980s, as record numbers of immigrants came to the United States from Asia, Mexico, Central and South America, and the Caribbean. Many from Central America, Vietnam, the Soviet Union, and Cuba were political refugees. The Orellanas found safety and peace in the United States, but not all immigrants—or all Americans—fared so well in the 1980s, when divisions between rich and poor widened dramatically. While the urban poor struggled with social problems—drugs, violence, homelessness, the growing AIDS epidemic— those on the other side of the economic divide enjoyed an era of luxury and ostentation.

The election of Ronald Reagan in 1980 began twelve years of Republican rule, as Reagan was succeeded by his vice president, George Bush, in 1988. Reagan was a popular president who seemed to restore the confidence shaken by the social, economic, and political crises of the 1970s. Wealthy people liked Reagan's pro-business economic policies; the religious New Right shared his vision of God's America; white middle- and working-class Americans admired Reagan's charisma and embrace of old-fashioned values.

Reagan supported New Right social issues: he was anti-abortion, embraced prayer in schools, and reversed the GOP's support of the Equal Rights Amendment. Most important, Reagan appointed Supreme Court and federal judges whose rulings strengthened social-conservative agendas. Reagan's primary focus was on the conservative issues of reducing the size and power of the federal government and creating favorable conditions for business. The U.S. economy recovered from the 1970s stagflation and boomed through much of the 1980s. But corruption flourished in financial institutions freed from government oversight. By the end of the Reagan-Bush era, a combination of tax cuts and massive increases in defense caused the budget deficit to jump fivefold.

In a single decade, the Cold War intensified, then ended. The key figure in the intensification was Reagan, who promised to stand up to the Soviet Union. The key figure in ending the Cold War was Soviet leader Mikhail Gorbachev, who came to power in 1985 determined to end the Soviet Union's economic decline, which required a more amicable superpower relationship. Gorbachev hoped to reform the Soviet system, but lost control of events as revolutions in eastern Europe toppled one communist regime after another. In 1991 the Soviet Union disappeared, and the Persian Gulf War demonstrated the United States's unrivaled world power and the unprecedented importance of the Middle East.

- Ronald Reagan, campaigning for president in 1984, told voters, "It's morning again in America." How would Americans from different backgrounds judge the accuracy of his claim?

- What issues, beliefs, backgrounds, and economic realities divided Americans in the 1980s, and how did those divisions shape the culture and politics of contemporary America?

- Why did the Cold War intensify and then wane during the decade of the 1980s?

REAGAN AND THE CONSERVATIVE RESURGENCE

The 1970s were hard for Americans: defeat in Vietnam, the resignation of a president in disgrace, the energy crisis, economic stagflation, and the Iranian hostage crisis. In 1980, President Carter's approval rating stood at 21 percent, lower than Richard Nixon's during the Watergate crisis. The time was ripe for a challenge to Carter's leadership, the Democratic Party, and the liberalism that had basically governed the United States since Franklin Roosevelt's New Deal.

Ronald Reagan   In 1980 several conservative Republican politicians ran for the White House, including Ronald Reagan, former movie star and two-term California governor. In the 1940s, as president of the Hollywood Screen Actors Guild, Reagan was a New Deal Democrat. But in the 1950s, as a corporate spokesperson for General Electric, he became increasingly conservative. In 1964 Reagan's televised speech supporting Republican presidential candidate Barry Goldwater catapulted him to the forefront of conservative politics.

Elected governor of California two years later, Reagan became known for his right-wing rhetoric: The United States should "level Vietnam, pave it, paint stripes on it, and make a parking lot out of it." And in 1969, when student protestors occupied People's Park near the University of California in Berkeley, he threatened a "bloodbath," dispatching National Guard troops. Reagan was often pragmatic; he denounced welfare but presided over reform of the state's social welfare bureaucracy. And he signed one of the nation's most liberal abortion laws.

The New Conservative Coalition

In the 1980 election, Reagan contrasted Carter with an optimistic vision for the United States's future. With his Hollywood charm, he forged different kinds of conservatives into a new coalition. Strongly anticommunist, many wanted to strengthen national defense, limit federal power and roll back the liberal programs of the 1930s New Deal and 1960s Great Society. Reagan similarly attracted economic conservatives who sought deregulation and tax policies benefiting corporations, wealthy investors, and entrepreneurs. He also drew neoconservatives, a small but influential group of intellectuals—typically former Democrats disillusioned with the party after Vietnam.

Reagan further tapped into the sentiments that fueled the tax revolt of the 1970s, drawing voters from traditionally Democratic constituencies, such as labor unions and urban ethnic groups. Many middle- and working-class whites resented what they saw as tax-funded welfare for people who did not work. These Reagan Democrats found the Republican critique of tax-funded social programs and big government appealing, even though Reagan's policies would benefit the wealthy at their expense.

Finally, Reagan drew the increasingly powerful, religiously based New Right. "When political conservative leaders began to . . . strike an alliance with social conservatives—the pro-life people, the anti-ERA people, the evangelical and born-again Christians, the people concerned about gay rights, prayer in the schools, sex in the movies or whatever," explained conservative fundraiser Richard Viguerie, "that's when this whole movement began to come alive."

Reagan's Conservative Agenda

Reagan won with 51 percent of the popular vote. Jimmy Carter carried only six states. Reagan served two terms as president, and, like Franklin Roosevelt, defined the era over which he presided. Reagan was not especially focused on the details of governing. When Carter briefed him on foreign and domestic policy, Reagan took no notes. Critics argued that his lack of knowledge could prove dangerous—as when he insisted that intercontinental ballistic missiles carrying nuclear warheads could be called back once launched.

But supporters insisted that Reagan focused on the big picture. When he spoke to the American people, he offered what seemed to be simple truths. While even supporters winced at his willingness to reduce complex policy issues to basic (and often misleading) stories, Reagan was to most Americans the Great Communicator. He won admiration for his courage after he was seriously wounded in an assassination attempt sixty-nine days into his presidency. Most important, Reagan had a clear vision for the

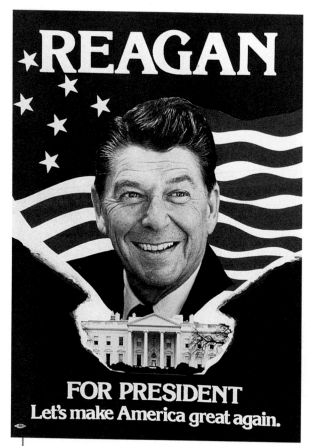

REAGAN

FOR PRESIDENT
Let's make America great again.

Ronald Reagan, the Republican presidential candidate in 1980, campaigned for family values, an aggressive anti-Soviet foreign and military policy, and tax cuts. He also exuded optimism and appealed to Americans' patriotism. This poster issued by the Republican National Committee included Reagan's favorite campaign slogan, "Let's make America great again." (Collection of David J. and Janice L. Frent)

United States's future. He wanted to roll back the liberalism of the past fifty years that made government responsible for the nation's economic health and the social welfare of its citizens.

Attacks on Social Welfare Programs

Reagan, like traditional conservatives, believed that the federal government could not solve social problems. He also tapped into a backlash against Great Society social programs. Many Americans who struggled to make ends meet during the economic crises of the 1970s and early 1980s resented paying taxes that, they believed, funded government handouts. Lasting racial tensions also fueled public resentment: Reagan fed a stereotype of welfare recipients as unwed, black, teenage mothers who kept having babies to collect larger checks.

In 1981 the administration cut social welfare funding by $25 billion. But welfare programs benefiting the poor (Aid to Families with Dependent Children and food stamp programs) were small compared with Social Security and Medicare—welfare programs benefiting Americans across income levels. The Reagan administration did shrink the *proportion* of the federal budget devoted to social welfare programs (including Social Security and Medicare) from 28 to 22 percent by the late 1980s, but only because of a $1.2 trillion increase in defense spending.

Pro-Business Policies and the Environment

Reagan also attacked federal environmental, health, and safety regulations as reducing business profits and discouraging economic growth. Administration officials claimed that removing government regulation would restore the creativity of the United States's free-market system. However, they did not so much end government's role as deploy government power to aid corporate America. The president even appointed opponents of federal regulations to head agencies charged with enforcing them.

Environmentalists were appalled when Reagan appointed James Watt, a well-known antienvironmentalist, as secretary of the interior. Watt was a leader in the Sagebrush Rebellion, which sought the return of publicly owned lands in the West, such as national forests, to state control. The federal government controlled more than half of western lands, including 83 percent of the land in Nevada, 66 percent in Utah, and 50 percent in Wyoming. But state control was not the sole issue; Watt's group wanted to open western public lands to businesses for logging, mining, and ranching.

Telling Congress in 1981, "I don't know how many generations we can count on until the Lord returns," Watt dismissed concerns about protecting resources and public lands for future generations and allowed private corporations to acquire oil, mineral, and timber rights to federal lands for minuscule payments. He was forced to resign in 1983 after he referred to a federal advisory panel as "a black . . . a woman, two Jews, and a cripple." Even before Watt's resignation, his appointment backfired, as his actions reenergized the nation's environmental movement and even provoked opposition from business leaders who understood that uncontrolled strip-mining and clear-cut logging could destroy lucrative tourism and recreation industries in western states.

Attacks on Organized Labor
The pro-business Reagan administration undercut organized labor's ability to negotiate wages and working conditions. Union power was already waning; labor union membership declined in the 1970s as jobs in heavy industry disappeared and efforts to unionize the high-growth electronics and service sectors of the economy failed. Reagan intervened in an August 1981 strike by the Professional Air Traffic Controllers Organization (PATCO). The air traffic controllers—federal employees, for whom striking was illegal—protested working conditions they believed compromised the safety of air travel. Forty-eight hours later, Reagan fired the 11,350 strikers, stipulating they could never be rehired by the Federal Aviation Administration.

With the support of Reagan appointees to the National Labor Relations Board, businesses took an increasingly hard line with labor during the 1980s, and unions failed to mount effective opposition. Yet roughly 44 percent of union families voted for Reagan in 1980, drawn to his espousal of old-fashioned values and vigorous anticommunist rhetoric.

The New Right
It is surprising that the religious New Right was drawn to Reagan, a divorced man without strong ties to religion or, seemingly, his own children. But Reagan supported New Right social issues: the anti-abortion cause and prayer in public schools.

Reagan's judicial nominations also pleased the religious New Right. The Senate, in a bipartisan vote, refused to confirm Supreme Court nominee Robert Bork. Congress eventually confirmed Anthony M. Kennedy. Reagan also appointed Anton Scalia, who would become a key conservative force, and Sandra Day O'Connor (the first woman appointee), and elevated Nixon appointee William Rehnquist to chief justice.

These appointments made the Court more conservative. In 1986, for example, the Supreme Court upheld a Georgia law that punished consensual anal or oral sex between men with up to twenty years in jail (*Bowers v. Hardwick*); in 1989 justices ruled that a Missouri law restricting the right to an abortion was constitutional (*Webster v. Reproductive Health Services*), thus encouraging further challenges to *Roe v. Wade*. Overall, however, the Reagan administration did not push a conservative social agenda as strongly as some in the new Republican coalition hoped.

REAGANOMICS

The centerpiece of Reagan's domestic agenda was the economic program that took his name: Reaganomics. The U.S. economy was faltering in the early 1980s. Stagflation proved resistant to traditional remedies: when the government increased spending to stimulate the economy, inflation skyrocketed; when it cut spending or tightened the money supply to reduce inflation, the economy plunged deeper into recession, and unemployment increased.

Reagan offered a simple answer. Instead of focusing on the complexities of global competition, deindustrialization, and OPEC's control of oil, Reagan argued that U.S. economic problems were caused by intrusive government regulation of business and industry, expensive social programs, high taxes, and deficit spending—in short, government itself. Reagan sought to unshackle the free-enterprise system from government regulation, slash social programs, and balance the budget by reducing the role of the federal government.

Supply-Side Economics   Reagan's economic policy was based largely on supply-side economics, the theory that tax cuts (rather than government spending) stimulate growth. Economist Arthur Laffer proposed one hypothesis—his soon-to-be-famous Laffer curve. It stated that at some point rising tax rates discourage people from engaging in taxable activities (such as investing). As people invest less, the economy slows, and there is less tax revenue to collect. Cutting taxes, in contrast, reverses the cycle.

Although economists accepted the larger principle behind Laffer's curve, almost none believed U.S. tax rates approached the point of disincentive. Even conservative economists were suspicious of supply-side principles. Reagan and his staff, however, sought a massive tax cut, arguing that U.S. corporations and individuals would invest funds freed up by lower tax rates, producing new plants, new jobs, and new products. And as prosperity returned, the profits at the top would trickle down to the middle classes and even the poor.

David Stockman, head of the Office of Management and Budget, proposed a five-year plan to balance the federal budget through economic growth (created by tax cuts) and deep spending cuts, primarily in social programs. Congress cooperated with a three-year, $750 billion tax cut, the largest in American history. Stockman's plan assumed $100 billion in cuts from government programs, including Social Security and Medicare, which Congress rejected. Reagan, meanwhile, canceled out gains from domestic spending cuts by dramatically increasing defense spending.

With major tax cuts, big increases in defense spending, and small cuts in social programs, the federal budget deficit exploded, from $59 billion in 1980 to more than $100 billion in 1982 to almost $300 billion by the end of George W. H. Bush's presidency in 1992. The federal government borrowed money to make up the difference, transforming the United States from the world's largest creditor to its largest debtor (see Figure 32.1). The national debt grew to almost $3 trillion.

Harsh Medicine for Inflation   In 1981, the Federal Reserve Bank, an autonomous federal agency, raised interest rates for bank loans to an unprecedented 21.5 percent, battling inflation by tightening the money supply and slowing the economy. The nation plunged into recession. By year's end, the gross national product (GNP) fell 5 percent, and sales of cars and houses dropped sharply. Unemployment soared to 8 percent.

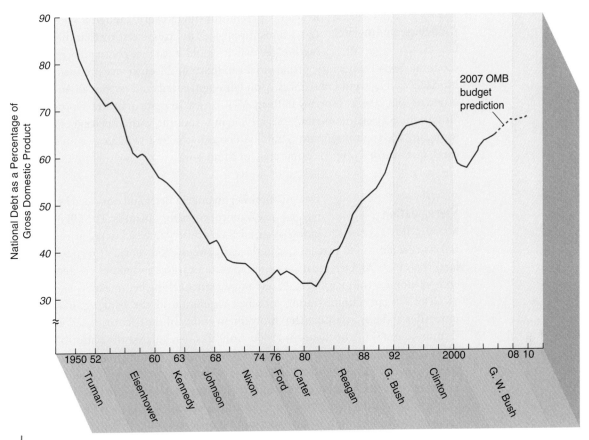

Figure 32.1   The United States's Rising National Debt, 1974–1989

The United States's national debt, which rose sporadically throughout the 1970s, soared to record heights during the 1980s. Under President Reagan, large defense expenditures and tax cuts caused the national debt to grow by $1.5 trillion.   (*Source:* Adapted from U.S. Bureau of the Census, *Statistical Abstract of the United States* [Washington, DC: U.S. Government Printing Office, 1992], p. 315.)

By late 1982, unemployment reached 10.8 percent, the highest rate since 1940. For African Americans, it was 20 percent. Reagan promised that consumers would lift the economy from the recession by spending their tax cuts. But as late as April 1983, unemployment remained at 10 percent, and people were angry. Along with industries such as steel and automobiles, agriculture, too, was faltering as farmers suffered from falling crop prices, floods, droughts, and burdensome debts at high interest rates. Many lost their property through mortgage foreclosures; others filed for bankruptcy. As the recession deepened, poverty rose to its highest level since 1965.

It was harsh medicine, but the Federal Reserve Bank's plan to end stagflation worked. High interest rates helped drop inflation from 12 percent in 1980 to less than 7 percent in 1982. The economy also benefited from OPEC's 1981 decision to increase oil production, thus lowering prices. In 1984 the GNP rose 7 percent, the sharpest increase since 1951, and midyear unemployment fell to a four-year low of 7 percent.

"Morning in America" Reagan got credit for the recovery, though it had little to do with his supply-side policies. Insisting that the escalating budget deficit would have dire consequences for the economy, 1984 Democratic presidential candidate and former vice president Walter Mondale said he would raise taxes. Mondale emphasized fairness; not all Americans, Mondale said, were prospering in Reagan's America. Reagan, in contrast, proclaimed, "It's morning again in America." Reagan won in a landslide, with 59 percent of the vote. Mondale, with running mate Geraldine Ferraro—the first woman vice-presidential candidate—carried only his home state of Minnesota.

Deregulation Deregulation, begun under Carter and expanded by Reagan, created new opportunities for business. The 1978 deregulation of the airline industry lowered ticket prices; airline tickets cost almost 45 percent less in the early twenty-first century (in constant dollars) than in 1978. Deregulation of telecommunications industries created serious competition for the giant AT&T, and long-distance calling became inexpensive.

The Reagan administration loosened regulation of the banking and finance industries and purposely cut the enforcement ability of the Securities and Exchange Commission (SEC). In the early 1980s, Congress deregulated the nation's savings-and-loan institutions (S&Ls), organizations previously required to invest depositors' savings in thirty-year, fixed-rate mortgages secured by property within a 50-mile radius of the S&L's main office. By ending government oversight of investment practices, while covering losses from bad S&L investments, Congress left no penalties for failure. S&Ls increasingly put depositors' money into high-risk investments and engaged in shady—even criminal—deals.

Junk Bonds and Merger Mania Risky investments typified Wall Street as well, as Michael Milken, a reclusive bond trader, pioneered the junk bond industry and created lucrative investment possibilities. Milken offered financing to debt-ridden corporations unable to get traditional, low-interest bank loans, using bond issues that paid investors high interest rates because they were high-risk (thus junk bonds). Many of these corporations were attractive targets for takeover by other corporations or investors, who, in turn, could finance takeovers with junk bonds. Such predators could use the first corporation's existing debt as a tax write-off, sell off unprofitable units, and lay off employees to create a more profitable corporation.

By the mid-1980s, hundreds of major corporations, including giants Walt Disney and Conoco—fell prey to merger mania and hostile takeovers. Profits for investors were staggering, and by 1987 Milken, the guru of junk bonds, was earning $550 million a year, about $1,046 a minute.

Deregulation helped smaller corporations challenge the virtual monopolies of giant corporations in fields like telecommunications. And the U.S. economy boomed. Although the stock market plunged 508 points on a single day in October 1987—losing 22.6 percent of its value, or almost double the loss of value in the 1929 crash—it rebounded quickly. But the high-risk boom of the 1980s had significant costs. Corporate downsizing meant layoffs for white-collar workers and management personnel, many of whom had difficulty finding comparable positions. The wave of mergers and takeovers left U.S. corporations increasingly burdened by debt. It also helped consolidate sectors of the economy, such as the media, under the control of fewer players.

The Rich Get Richer The 1980s boom, furthermore, was rotten with corruption. By the late 1980s, insider trading scandals, in which people used inside information not available to the public to make huge profits trading stocks, rocked financial markets and sent some of the most prominent Wall Street figures to jail. Savings and loans lost billions in bad investments, sometimes turning to fraud to cover them up. Scandal reached to the White House: Vice President Bush's son Neil was involved in shady S&L deals. The Reagan-Bush administration's bailout of the S&L industry cost taxpayers half a trillion dollars.

During the 1980s, the rich got richer, and the poor got poorer (see Figure 32.2). The number of Americans reporting an annual income of $500,000 increased tenfold between 1980 and 1989. The average compensation of corporate executive officers increased from 35 times an average worker's pay in 1978 to 71 times workers' average pay in 1989 (in 2005 the ratio was 262 to 1). In 1987 the United States had forty-nine billionaires—up from one in 1978. Middle-class incomes, however, remained stagnant.

Reagan's economic policies benefited the wealthy at the expense of other Americans. Reagan's tax policies decreased the total effective tax rates—income taxes plus Social Security taxes—for the top 1 percent of American families by 14.4 percent. But they increased taxes for the poorest 20 percent of families by 16 percent. By 1990, the richest 1 percent controlled 40 percent of the nation's wealth; with 80 percent of wealth controlled by the top 20 percent.

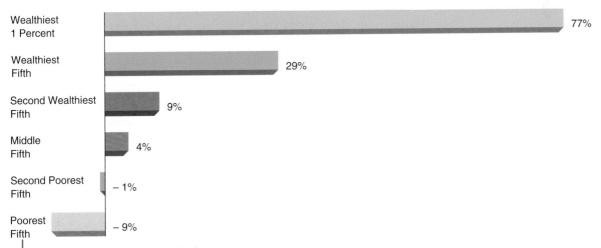

Percentage Increase in Pretax Income, 1977–1989

Wealthiest 1 Percent	77%
Wealthiest Fifth	29%
Second Wealthiest Fifth	9%
Middle Fifth	4%
Second Poorest Fifth	– 1%
Poorest Fifth	– 9%

Figure 32.2   Poverty in America by Race.
Between 1977 and 1989, the richest 1 percent of American families reaped most of the gains from economic growth. In fact, the average pretax income of families in the top 1 percent rose 77 percent. At the same time, the typical family saw its income edge up only 4 percent. And the bottom 40 percent of families had actual declines in income. (*Source:* Data from the *New York Times,* March 5, 1992)

REAGAN AND THE WORLD

A key element in Reagan's winning strategy in the 1980 election was his call for the United States to assert itself in the world. Though lacking a firm grasp of world issues, history, and geography, Reagan adhered to a few core principles. One was a deep anticommunism; a second was an underlying optimism about the United States's power and ability to positively affect the world. Together, these elements help explain Reagan's aggressive anticommunist foreign policy and his positive response in his second term to Soviet leader Mikhail Gorbachev's call for "new thinking" in world affairs.

Soviet-American Tension

Initially embracing the strident anticommunism of early Cold War foreign policy, Reagan rejected Nixon's détente and Carter's focus on human rights. Where Nixon and Carter perceived an increasingly multipolar international system, the Reagan team reverted to a bipolar perspective defined by the Soviet-American relationship. When Poland's pro-Soviet leaders in 1981 cracked down on an independent labor organization, Solidarity, Washington restricted Soviet-American trade and hurled angry words at Moscow. In March 1983, Reagan told evangelical Christians in Florida that the Soviets were "an evil empire." That year, Reagan restricted commercial flights to the Soviet Union after a Soviet fighter pilot mistakenly shot down a South Korean commercial jet straying 300 miles off course into Soviet airspace, and killed 269 passengers.

Reagan believed that substantial military buildup would thwart the Soviet threat. Accordingly, the administration launched the largest peacetime arms buildup in history. In 1985, when the military budget hit $294.7 billion (a doubling since 1980), the Pentagon spent an average $28 million an hour. Assigning low priority to arms control talks, Reagan announced in 1983 his desire for a space-based defense shield against incoming ballistic missiles: the Strategic Defense Initiative (SDI). His critics tagged it Star Wars and said such a system could never work; some enemy missiles would get through. Moreover, critics warned, SDI would elevate the arms race to dangerous levels. SDI research and development ultimately consumed tens of billions of dollars.

Reagan Doctrine

Because he attributed Third World disorders to Soviet intrigue, the president declared the Reagan Doctrine: the United States would openly support anticommunist movements—freedom fighters battling the Soviets or Soviet-backed governments. In Afghanistan, Reagan continued providing covert assistance, through Pakistan, to the Mujahidin rebels fighting Soviet occupation. When the Soviets stepped up the war in 1985, the Reagan administration sent more high-tech weapons, particularly anti-aircraft Stinger missiles. Easily transportable and fired by a single soldier, the Stingers turned the tide in Afghanistan by making Soviet jets and helicopters vulnerable below fifteen thousand feet.

Senior officials believed that the Soviets and Castro's Cuba were fomenting disorder in the region (see Map 32.1). In October 1983 the president sent troops into the tiny Caribbean island of Grenada to oust a pro-Marxist government. In El Salvador, he provided military and economic assistance to a military-dominated government

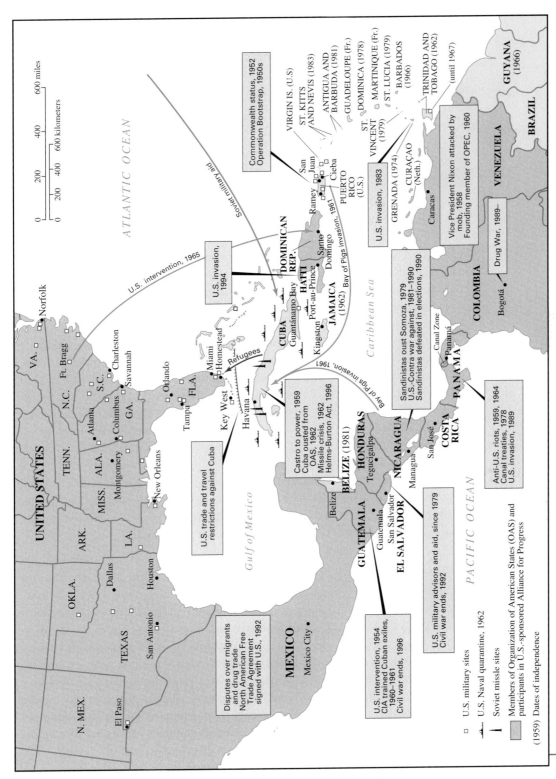

Map 32.1 The United States in the Caribbean and Central America

The United States has often intervened in the Caribbean and Central America. Geographic proximity, economic stakes, political disputes, security links, trade in illicit drugs, and Cuba's alliance with the Soviet Union and defiance of the United States have kept North American eyes fixed on events in the region.

Map labels (clockwise/by region):

- Commonwealth status, 1952 Operation Bootstrap, 1950s
- VIRGIN IS. (U.S)
- ST. KITTS AND NEVIS (1983)
- ANTIGUA AND BARBUDA (1981)
- GUADELOUPE (Fr.)
- DOMINICA (1978)
- MARTINIQUE (Fr.)
- ST. LUCIA (1979)
- BARBADOS (1966)
- TRINIDAD AND TOBAGO (1962)
- GUYANA (1966)
- BRAZIL
- ST. VINCENT (1979)
- ST. DOMINICA (1979) (until 1967)
- GRENADA (1974)
- CURAÇAO (Neth.)
- VENEZUELA
- U.S. invasion, 1983
- Vice President Nixon attacked by mob, 1958 Founding member of OPEC, 1960
- Caracas
- San Juan
- Cieba
- Ramey
- PUERTO RICO (U.S.)
- COLOMBIA
- Bogotá
- Drug War, 1989–
- U.S. intervention, 1965
- U.S. invasion, 1994
- DOMINICAN REP.
- Santo Domingo
- HAITI
- Port-au-Prince
- Guantánamo Bay
- JAMAICA (1962) Bay of Pigs invasion, 1961
- Kingston
- Caribbean Sea
- Sandinistas oust Somoza, 1979 U.S.-Contra war against, 1981–1990 Sandinistas defeated in elections, 1990
- Canal Zone
- PANAMÁ
- Panamá
- PANAMA
- Anti-U.S. riots, 1959, 1964 Canal treaties, 1978 U.S. invasion, 1989
- COSTA RICA
- San José
- NICARAGUA
- Managua
- U.S. military advisors and aid, since 1979 Civil war ends, 1992
- HONDURAS
- Tegucigalpa
- BELIZE (1981)
- Belize
- GUATEMALA
- Guatemala
- San Salvador
- EL SALVADOR
- PACIFIC OCEAN
- U.S. intervention, 1954 CIA trained Cuban exiles, 1960–1961 Civil war ends, 1996
- MEXICO
- Mexico City
- Disputes over migrants and drug trade North American Free Trade Agreement signed with U.S., 1992
- N. MEX.
- El Paso
- TEXAS
- San Antonio
- Houston
- Dallas
- OKLA.
- ARK.
- LA.
- New Orleans
- MISS.
- ALA.
- Montgomery
- TENN.
- GA.
- Columbus
- Atlanta
- S.C.
- N.C.
- Charleston
- Savannah
- VA.
- Ft. Bragg
- Norfolk
- UNITED STATES
- Gulf of Mexico
- FLA.
- Tampa
- Orlando
- Miami
- Homestead
- Key West
- Refugees
- Havana
- CUBA
- Castro to power, 1959 Cuba ousted from OAS, 1962 Missile crisis, 1962 Helms-Burton Act, 1996
- U.S. trade and travel restrictions against Cuba
- Bay of Pigs invasion, 1961
- Soviet military aid
- ATLANTIC OCEAN
- Scale: 0–600 miles / 0–600 kilometers

Legend:
- □ U.S. military sites
- ⟙ U.S. Naval quarantine, 1962
- | Soviet missile sites
- ▨ Members of Organization of American States (OAS) and participants in U.S.-sponsored Alliance for Progress
- (1959) Dates of independence

struggling with left-wing revolutionaries. The regime used right-wing death squads, from which Luisa Orellana and her family fled. By decade's end, the death squads had killed forty thousand dissidents and citizens, as well as several U.S. missionaries. By the late 1980s, the United States spent more than $6 billion there in a counterinsurgency war. In January 1992 the Salvadoran combatants negotiated a U.N.-sponsored peace.

Contra War in Nicaragua

The Reagan administration also meddled in the Nicaraguan civil war. In 1979 leftist insurgents in Nicaragua overthrew Anastasio Somoza, a long-time U.S. ally. The revolutionaries called themselves Sandinistas in honor of César Augusto Sandino, who headed the anti-imperialist Nicaraguan opposition against U.S. occupation in the 1930s and was finally assassinated by Somoza supporters. When the Sandinistas aided rebels in El Salvador, bought Soviet weapons, and invited Cubans to help reorganize the Nicaraguan army, Reagan officials charged that Nicaragua was becoming a Soviet client. In 1981 the CIA began to train, arm, and direct more than ten thousand counterrevolutionaries, known as contras, to overthrow the Nicaraguan government.

Many Americans, including Democratic leaders in Congress, were skeptical about the communist threat and warned that Nicaragua could become another Vietnam. Congress in 1984 voted to stop U.S. military aid to the contras. Secretly, the Reagan administration lined up other countries, including Saudi Arabia, Panama, and South Korea, to funnel money and weapons to the contras, and in 1985 Reagan imposed an economic embargo against Nicaragua. Reagan rejected a plan by Costa Rica's president Oscar Arias Sánchez in 1987 to obtain a cease-fire in Central America through negotiations and cutbacks in military aid to rebel forces. (Arias won the 1987 Nobel Peace Prize.) Three years later, Central American presidents brokered a settlement; in the national election that followed, the Sandinistas lost to a U.S.-funded party. After nearly a decade of civil war, thirty thousand Nicaraguans were dead and the ravaged Nicaraguan economy was one of the poorest in the hemisphere.

Iran-Contra Scandal

Reagan's obsession with defeating the Sandinistas almost caused his political undoing. In November 1986 it became known that the president's national security adviser, John M. Poindexter, and an aide, Marine lieutenant colonel Oliver North, in collusion with CIA director Casey, covertly sold weapons to Iran in an unsuccessful attempt to win the release of Americans held hostage by Islamic fundamentalist groups. Washington condemned Iran as a terrorist nation and demanded that America's allies cease trading there. More damaging was the revelation that money from the Iran arms deal had been illegally diverted to the contras. North later admitted that he illegally destroyed government documents and lied to Congress to keep the operation clandestine.

Although Reagan survived the scandal, his popularity declined, and Congress reasserted its authority over foreign affairs. In late 1992, outgoing president George W. H. Bush pardoned several former government officials convicted of lying to Congress. Critics smelled a cover-up, for Bush himself, as vice president, participated in high-level meetings on Iran-contra deals. As for North, his conviction was overturned on a technicality.

U.S. Interests in the Middle East

U.S. foreign policy placed increased importance on the Middle East and terrorism (see Map 33.2). The main U.S. goals in the Middle East were preserving access to oil and supporting its ally Israel, while checking Soviet influence. In the 1980s, though, American leaders faced new pressures from a deepened Israeli-Palestinian conflict and an anti-American and anti-Israeli Islamic fundamentalist movement that spread after the ouster of the shah of Iran in 1979.

The 1979 Camp David accords between Israel and Egypt raised hopes of a lasting settlement involving self-government for the Palestinian Arabs living in the Israeli-occupied Gaza Strip and West Bank. Instead, Israel and the Palestinian Liberation Organization (PLO) remained at odds. In 1982, in retaliation for Palestinian shelling of Israel from Lebanon, Israeli troops invaded Lebanon. The beleaguered PLO and various Lebanese factions called on Syria to contain the Israelis. Thousands of civilians died. Soon after Reagan sent Marines to Lebanon to join a peacekeeping force, U.S. troops became embroiled in a war between Christian and Muslim factions. In October 1983, terrorist bombs demolished a barracks, killing 241 U.S. servicemen. Four months later, Reagan pulled the remaining Marines out.

Terrorism

The attack on the Marine barracks showed the growing danger of terrorism to the United States and other western countries. In the 1980s, numerous otherwise powerless groups, many of them associated with the Palestinian cause or with Islamic fundamentalism, relied on terrorism to further their aims. Often they targeted U.S. citizens and property, because of Washington's support of Israel and U.S. involvement in the Lebanese civil war. Of the 690 hijackings, kidnappings, bombings, and shootings around the world in 1985, for example, 217 were against Americans, most originating in Iran, Libya, Lebanon, and the Gaza Strip. Three years later, a Pan American passenger plane was destroyed over Scotland, and many suspected pro-Iranian terrorists.

Washington proposed peace plans for the Israelis to give back occupied territories and the Arabs to stop trying to push the Jews out of the Middle East. As the peace process stalled in 1987, Palestinians living in the West Bank began an *intifada* (Arabic for "uprising") against Israeli forces. Israel refused to negotiate, but the United States talked with PLO chief Yasir Arafat after he renounced terrorism and accepted Israel's right to live in peace. For the PLO to recognize Israel and the United States to recognize the PLO were major developments in the Arab-Israeli conflict.

In South Africa, too, American diplomacy became more aggressive. At first, the Reagan administration followed a policy of constructive engagement, asking the increasingly isolated government to reform its white supremacist apartheid system. But many Americans demanded cutting off imports from South Africa and pressuring 350 U.S. companies to cease operations there. Some U.S. cities and states passed divestment laws, withdrawing dollars from U.S. companies active in South Africa.

Public protest and congressional legislation forced the Reagan administration in 1986 to impose economic restrictions. Within two years, about half of the U.S. companies in South Africa left.

Enter Gorbachev

Many on the right disliked the South Africa sanctions policy; they believed the main black opposition group, the African National Congress (ANC), was dominated by communists, and they doubted the efficacy of sanctions. They also balked when Reagan, his popularity declining, entered negotiations with the Soviet Union. At a 1985 Geneva summit meeting, Reagan agreed in principle with new Soviet leader Mikhail S. Gorbachev's contention that strategic weapons should be substantially reduced, and at a 1986 Reykjavik, Iceland, meeting, they came close to a major reduction agreement. SDI stood in the way: Gorbachev insisted it should be shelved, and Reagan refused.

But Reagan and Gorbachev got along well. As General Colin Powell commented, though the Soviet leader was far superior to Reagan in mastery of specifics, he understood that Reagan was, as Powell put it, "the embodiment of his people's down-to-earth character, practicality, and optimism." And Reagan toned down his strident anti-Soviet rhetoric.

Perestroika and *Glasnost*

The turnaround in Soviet-American relations stemmed more from changes abroad than from Reagan's decisions. Under Gorbachev, a younger generation of Soviet leaders came to power in 1985. They modernized the highly bureaucratized, decaying economy through a reform program known as *perestroika* ("restructuring") and liberalized the authoritarian political system through *glasnost* ("openness"). For these reforms to work, Soviet military expenditures had to be reduced.

In 1987 Gorbachev and Reagan signed the Intermediate-Range Nuclear Forces (INF) Treaty banning all land-based intermediate-range nuclear missiles in Europe. About 2,800 missiles were destroyed. Gorbachev also reduced his nation's armed forces, helped settle regional conflicts, and began the withdrawal of Soviet troops from Afghanistan. The Cold War was coming to an end.

AMERICAN SOCIETY IN THE 1980s

As the Cold War waned, the belief in a United States united by shared middle-class values also lost its force. By the 1980s, after years of social struggle and division, few Americans believed in the reality of that vision; many rejected it as undesirable. Although the 1980s were never as contentious as the 1960s and 1970s, deep social divides split Americans. A newly powerful group of Christian conservatives challenged the secular majority. A growing class of affluent Americans seemed a society apart from the urban poor, whom sociologists and journalists began calling the underclass. And the composition of the U.S. population was changing dramatically, as people immigrated to the United States from more and different nations than ever before.

Growth of the Religious Right

Since the 1960s, the United States's liberal Protestant churches—Episcopalian, Presbyterian, Methodist—had been losing members, while Southern Baptists and other denominations offering the experience of being born again through belief in Jesus Christ and the literal truth of the Bible (fundamentalism) grew rapidly. Fundamentalist preachers reached out through television: by the late 1970s, televangelist Oral Roberts was drawing 3.9 million viewers. Nearly 20 percent of Americans self-identified as fundamentalist Christians in 1980.

Most fundamentalist Christian churches stayed out of the social and political conflicts of the 1960s and early 1970s. But in the late 1970s, some influential preachers mobilized for political struggle against the United States's increasing permissiveness. In a 1980 Washington for Jesus rally, fundamentalist leader Pat Robertson told crowds, "We have enough votes to run the country." The Moral Majority, founded in 1979 by Jerry Falwell, sought to create a Christian America, partly by supporting political candidates. Falwell's defense of socially conservative family values and his condemnation of feminism (he called NOW the National Order of Witches), homosexuality, pornography, and abortion resonated with many Americans.

Throughout the 1980s, conservative Christians known as the New Right campaigned against the United States's secular culture. Rejecting multiculturalism—that different cultures and lifestyles were equally valid—the New Right wanted God's law to be the basis for American society. Concerned Women for America, founded by Beverly LaHayes in 1979, wanted elementary school readers containing "unacceptable" religious beliefs (including excerpts from *The Diary of Anne Frank* and *The Wizard of Oz*) removed from classrooms. The Reagan administration frequently turned to James Dobson, founder of the conservative Focus on the Family organization, for policy advice. Conservative Christians also joined with Roman Catholics, Mormons, and other groups in the anti-abortion, or prolife, movement.

Culture Wars

Many Americans vigorously opposed the New Right's seeming intolerance and threat to basic freedoms, including freedom of religion for those whose beliefs differed from the conservative Christianity of the New Right. In 1982 politically progressive television producer Norman Lear, influential former congresswoman Barbara Jordan, and other prominent figures from the fields of business, religion, politics, and entertainment founded People for the American Way to support American civil liberties, the separation of church and state, and the values of tolerance and diversity. The struggle between the religious right and their opponents for the nation's future came to be known as the culture wars.

Many beliefs of Christian fundamentalists ran counter to the way most Americans lived, especially regarding women's roles. By the 1980s, a generation of girls had grown up with the gains of the women's movement, expecting freedoms and opportunities that their mothers never had. Legislation such as the Civil Rights Act of 1964 and Title IX opened academic and athletic programs to females. By 1985, more than half of married women with children under three worked outside the home, many from economic necessity. The religious right's insistence that women's place was in the home, subordinated to her husband, contradicted the gains made toward sexual equality and the reality of many women's lives.

The New Inequality

A 1988 national report on race relations looked back to the 1968 Kerner Commission report to claim, "America is again becoming two separate societies," white and black. It argued that African Americans endured poverty, segregation, and crime in inner-city ghettos while whites lived comfortably in suburbia. The majority of the United States's poor were white, and the black middle class was expanding. But people of color were disproportionately poor. In 1980, 33 percent of African Americans and 26 percent of Hispanic Americans lived in poverty, compared with 10 percent of whites (see Figure 32.3).

Reasons for poverty varied. The legacies of racism played a role. The changing job structure was partly responsible, as well-paid jobs decreased, replaced by lower-paid service jobs. In addition, families headed by a single mother were five times more likely to be poor than families maintained by a married couple. By 1992, 59 percent of African American children and 17 percent of white children lived in female-headed households, and almost half of African American children lived in poverty.

Social Crises in American Cities

In impoverished inner-city neighborhoods, violent crime—particularly homicides and gang warfare—grew alarmingly, as did school dropout rates, crime rates, and child abuse. Some people sought escape in hard drugs, especially crack, a derivative of cocaine, which first struck New York City's poorest neighborhoods in 1985. Gang shootouts over drugs were deadly: the toll in Los Angeles in 1987 was 387 deaths, more than half

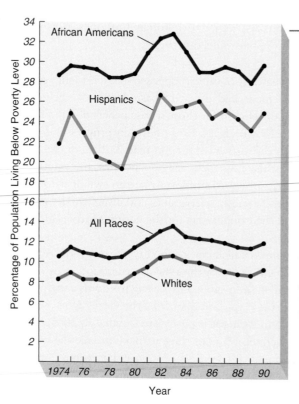

Figure 32.3 Poverty in the United States by Race, 1974–1990

Poverty in the United States rose in the early 1980s but subsided afterward. Many people of color, however, experienced little relief during the decade. Notice that the percentage of African Americans living below the poverty level was three times higher than that for whites. It was also much higher for Hispanic Americans. (*Source:* Adapted from U.S. Bureau of the Census, *Statistical Abstract of the United States* [Washington, DC: U.S. Government Printing Office, 1992], p. 461.)

of them innocent bystanders. Many states instituted mandatory prison sentences for possessing small amounts of crack equivalent to those for 100 grams of cocaine, the drug favored by more affluent, white Americans. Such policies increased the United States's prison population almost fourfold from 1980 to the mid-1990s, with African and Hispanic American youth arrested in disproportionate numbers. By 2000, young African American men were more likely to have been arrested than to have graduated from college.

Homelessness also grew during the 1980s. Some homeless were impoverished families; many had drug or alcohol problems. About one-third of the homeless were former psychiatric patients. By 1985, 80 percent of the beds in state mental hospitals were eliminated on the claim that neighborhood programs would serve people better. Such local programs never materialized. Consequently, many of the United States's mentally ill citizens wandered the streets.

In the 1980s there was an alarming spread of sexually transmitted diseases, especially acquired immune deficiency syndrome (AIDS). Campaigns for safe sex, such as this New York City subway ad, urged people to use condoms.   (Sandro Tucci/Time Life Pictures/Getty Images)

The AIDS Epidemic

Another social crisis in the 1980s was the global spread of acquired immune deficiency syndrome, or AIDS. Caused by the human immunodeficiency virus (HIV), AIDS leaves its victims susceptible to deadly infections and cancers. The human immunodeficiency virus is spread through the exchange of blood or body fluids, often through sexual intercourse or needle sharing by intravenous drug users.

AIDS was first diagnosed in the United States in 1981. Between 1981 and 1988, of the 57,000 AIDS cases reported, nearly 32,000 resulted in death. Politicians were slow to devote resources to AIDS, partly because it was initially perceived as a gay man's disease. "A man reaps what he sows," declared the Reverend Jerry Falwell of the Moral Majority. AIDS, along with other sexually transmitted diseases, such as genital herpes and chlamydia, ended an era defined by penicillin and the pill, in which sex was freed from the threat of serious disease or unwanted pregnancy.

An Era of Ostentation

For the rich, the 1980s were an era of ostentation. "Greed is all right," the Wall Street financier Ivan Boesky told students at the University of California, Berkeley, the center of 1960s campus protest, and he was met with cheers and laughter. The New York entrepreneur Donald Trump's $29 million yacht had gold-plated bathroom fixtures. The publisher Malcolm Forbes flew eight hundred guests to Morocco for his seventieth birthday; the party cost $2 million.

Nineteen eighty-four was the Year of the Yuppie—Young Urban Professional—proclaimed *Newsweek* magazine. A derogatory term, *Yuppie* (and *Buppie,* for Black Urban Professional) described ambitious and successful young Americans in demanding careers who enjoyed a consumer-driven lifestyle: BMWs, Armani suits, Häagen-Dazs ice cream. Americans seemed fascinated with the superrich (making *Dallas* a top-rated television show) and with Yuppie lifestyles. But Yuppies also represented those who got ahead without caring about those left behind. As Yuppies gentrified urban neighborhoods, displacing poorer residents, graffiti, like "Die, Yuppie Scum," appeared in New York.

New Immigrants from Asia

Social divisions were further complicated by the arrival of new immigrants from regions barely represented in the United States. Between 1970 and 1990 the United States absorbed more than 13 million new arrivals, most from Latin America and Asia. Before the 1965 immigration reforms Americans of Asian ancestry made up less than 1 percent of the population; by 1990 that figure tripled.

Before 1965, most Asian Americans were of Japanese ancestry (about 52 percent in 1960), followed by Chinese and Filipino. In the 1960s and 1970s, the highest rates of immigration were from nations not previously represented in the U.S. population. There were only 603 Vietnamese residents of the United States in 1964. By 1990, the United States absorbed almost 800,000 refugees from Indochina, casualties of the Vietnam War. Immigrants flooded in from South Korea, Thailand, India, Pakistan, Bangladesh, Indonesia, Singapore, Laos, Cambodia, and Vietnam. Japanese Americans were now only 15 percent of the Asian American population.

Immigrants from Asia were typically either highly skilled or unskilled. Unsettled conditions in the Philippines in the 1970s and 1980s created an exodus of well-educated Filipinos to the United States. India's overabundance of physicians and healthcare workers increasingly emigrated, as did educated, skilled workers from Korea, Taiwan, and China. Other Chinese immigrants, however, had few job skills and spoke little English. Many crowded into neighborhoods like New York City's Chinatown, where women worked under terrible conditions in the city's nonunion garment industry. But even highly educated immigrants had limited options. A 1983 study found that Korean Americans owned three-quarters of the approximately twelve hundred greengroceries in New York City. Though often cited as a success story, Korean greengrocers usually descended the professional ladder: 78 percent had college or professional degrees.

The Growing Hispanic American Population

Unprecedented immigration coupled with a high birth rate made Hispanic Americans the fastest-growing group of Americans. In 1970 Hispanic Americans made up 4.5 percent of the nation's population; that jumped to 9 percent by 1990, when one out of three Los Angelenos and Miamians were Hispanic. Mexican Americans, concentrated in California and the Southwest, made up most of this population, but Puerto Ricans, Cubans, Dominicans, and other Caribbean immigrants also lived in the United States, clustered principally in East Coast cities.

During the 1980s, people from Guatemala and El Salvador, like Luisa Orellana, fled civil war and government violence for the United States. Although the U.S. government commonly refused them political asylum (about 113,000 Cubans received political refugee status during the 1980s, compared with fewer than 1,400 El Salvadorans), a national Sanctuary movement of Christian churches defied the law to protect refugees from deportation. Economic troubles in Mexico and throughout

Central and South America also produced a flood of undocumented workers who crossed the poorly guarded 2,000-mile border between the United States and Mexico, seeking economic opportunities. Some were sojourners, who moved back and forth across the border. A majority meant to stay.

Many Americans believed new arrivals threatened jobs and economic security, and nativist violence and bigotry increased. In 1982 twenty-seven-year-old Vincent Chin was beaten to death in Detroit by an unemployed auto worker and his uncle. U.S. automobiles were losing to Japanese imports, and the two men seemingly mistook the Chinese American Chin for Japanese. In New York, Philadelphia, and Los Angeles, inner-city African Americans boycotted Korean groceries. Riots broke out in Los Angeles schools between African American students and newly arrived Mexicans. In Dade County, Florida, voters passed an antibilingual measure that removed Spanish-language signs on public transportation, while at the state and national level people debated declaring English the official U.S. language. Concerned about illegal aliens, Congress passed the Immigration Reform and Control (Simpson-Rodino) Act in 1986. The act's purpose was to discourage illegal immigration by imposing sanctions on employers who hired undocumented workers, but it also provided amnesty to millions who immigrated illegally before 1982.

THE END OF THE COLD WAR AND GLOBAL DISORDER

The end of Ronald Reagan's presidency coincided with world events that brought the dawn of a new international system. Reagan's vice president, George Herbert Walker Bush, would become president and oversee the transition. The scion of a Wall Street banker and U.S. senator from Connecticut, Bush attended an exclusive boarding school and then Yale. He had the advantage in seeking the Republican presidential nomination in having been a loyal vice president. And he possessed a formidable résumé, including ambassador to the United Nations, chairman of the Republican Party, special envoy to China, and director of the CIA. He had also been a war hero, flying fifty-eight combat missions in the Pacific in World War II and receiving the Distinguished Flying Cross.

George Herbert Walker Bush

Bush entered the 1988 presidential campaign trailing his Democratic opponent, Massachusetts governor Michael Dukakis. Republicans turned that around by waging one of the most negative campaigns in U.S. history. Most notoriously, the Bush camp aired a television commercial featuring an African American convicted murderer, Willie Horton, who terrorized a Maryland couple, raping the woman, while on weekend furlough from prison—a temporary release program begun under Dukakis's Republican predecessor but attributed in the ad to Dukakis's being soft on crime. The Republicans also falsely suggested that Dukakis had a history of psychiatric problems. Dukakis, while not personally attacking Bush, ran an uninspired campaign. Bush won by 8 percentage points in the popular vote and received 426 electoral votes to Dukakis's 112. The Democrats, however, retained control of both houses of Congress.

Bush focused on foreign policy, though naturally cautious and reactive in world affairs, much to the chagrin of neoconservatives. Mikhail Gorbachev's reforms in the Soviet Union were now stimulating reforms in eastern Europe that ultimately led to revolution. In 1989 thousands in East Germany, Poland, Hungary, Czechoslovakia, and Romania startled the world by repudiating their communist governments and staging mass protests for increased freedom. In November 1989, Germans scaled the Berlin Wall and tore it down; the following October, the two Germanys reunited. By then other eastern European communist governments had fallen or were near collapse.

Pro-Democracy Movements

Other communist challenges were less successful. In June 1989, Chinese armed forces slaughtered hundreds—perhaps thousands—of unarmed students and citizens holding peaceful pro-democracy rallies in Beijing's Tiananmen Square. The Bush administration, anxious to preserve influence in Beijing, simply denounced the action, allowing the Chinese government to emphatically reject political liberalization.

Elsewhere, however, democratization efforts proved too powerful to resist. In South Africa, a new government under F. W. de Klerk began a cautious retreat from apartheid. In February 1990, de Klerk legalized all political parties in South Africa, including the ANC, and released Nelson Mandela, a hero to black South Africans, after a twenty-seven-year imprisonment. Then, the government repealed its apartheid laws over several years, allowing all citizens to vote. Mandela, who became South Africa's first black president in 1994, called the transformation a small miracle.

Collapse of Soviet Power

In 1990 the Soviet Union began to disintegrate. First the Baltic states of Lithuania, Latvia, and Estonia declared independence from Moscow. The following year, the Soviet Union ceased to exist, disintegrating into successor states—Russia, Ukraine, Tajikistan, and many others (see Map 32.2). Muscled aside by Russian reformers who thought he was moving too slowly toward democracy and free-market economics, Gorbachev lost power. The breakup of the Soviet empire, the dismantling of the Warsaw Pact (the Soviet military alliance formed in 1955 with communist countries of eastern Europe), the repudiation of communism by its leaders, German reunification, and a significantly reduced risk of nuclear war signaled the end of the Cold War.

The United States and its allies had won. The containment policy followed by nine presidents—from Truman through Bush—had many critics over the years, but succeeded at containing communism for four-plus decades without blowing up the world or obliterating freedom at home. Over time, the Soviet socialist economy proved less able to compete with the U.S. free-market one, less able to cope with the demands of the Soviet and eastern European citizenry.

Yet the Soviet empire might have survived longer had it not been for Gorbachev, one of the most influential figures of the twentieth century. Through unexpected overtures and decisions, Gorbachev fundamentally transformed the superpower relationship in ways that could scarcely have been anticipated before. Ronald Reagan's role was less central but still important because of his later willingness to negotiate and treat Gorbachev more as a partner than as an adversary. Just as personalities mattered in starting the Cold War, they mattered in ending it.

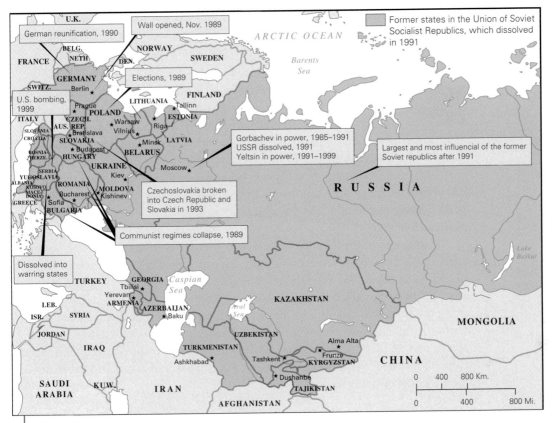

Map 32.2   The End of the Cold War in Europe

When Mikhail Gorbachev came to power in the Soviet Union in 1985, he initiated reforms that ultimately undermined the communist regimes in eastern Europe and East Germany and led to the breakup of the Soviet Union itself, ensuring an end to the Cold War.

Costs of Victory

The victory in the Cold War elicited little celebration among Americans. The confrontation may never have become a hot war globally, but the period after 1945 nevertheless witnessed numerous Cold War–related conflicts claiming millions of lives. In the Vietnam War alone, up to 2 million people died, more than 58,000 of them Americans. Military budgets ate up billions of dollars, shortchanging domestic programs. Some Americans wondered whether the communist threat was ever as grave as officials had claimed.

Bush proclaimed a new world order and signed important arms reduction treaties with the Soviet Union in 1991 and with the post-breakup Russia in 1993. But the United States sustained a large defense budget and stationed large numbers of military forces overseas. As a result, Americans were denied the peace dividend that they hoped would reduce taxes and free up funds for domestic problems.

In Central America, the Bush administration cooled the zeal with which Reagan meddled, but showed no reluctance to intervene to further U.S. aims. In December 1989, U.S. troops invaded Panama to oust military leader Manuel Noriega. A long-time drug trafficker, Noriega stayed in Washington's favor in the mid-1980s by providing logistical support for the Nicaraguan contras. In the early 1990s, exposés of his sordid record changed Bush's mind. Noriega was captured and taken to Miami, where, in 1992, he was convicted of drug trafficking and imprisoned. Devastated Panama, meanwhile, became increasingly dependent on the United States.

Saddam Hussein's Gamble

The strongest test of Bush's foreign policy came in the Middle East. The Iran-Iraq War ended inconclusively in August 1988, after eight years and almost 400,000 dead. The Reagan administration assisted the Iraqis with weapons and intelligence, as had many NATO countries. In mid-1990 Iraqi president Saddam Hussein, facing massive war debts, invaded neighboring Kuwait, hoping to enhance his regional power and oil revenues. George Bush condemned the invasion and vowed to defend Kuwait, partly fearing that Iraq might threaten U.S. oil supplies in Kuwait and petroleum-rich Saudi Arabia.

Within weeks, Bush convinced every important government, including most Arab and Islamic states, to economically boycott Iraq. Then, in Operation Desert Shield, Bush dispatched more than 500,000 U.S. forces to the region, joined by more than 200,000 from allied countries. Likening Saddam to Hitler and declaring it the first post–Cold War "test of our mettle," Bush rallied a deeply divided Congress to authorize "all necessary means" to oust Iraq from Kuwait (a vote of 250 to 183 in the House and 52 to 47 in the Senate). Many Americans believed that economic sanctions should be given more time to work, but Bush would not wait. Victory would come swiftly and cleanly.

Operation Desert Storm

Operation Desert Storm began on January 16, 1991, with the greatest air armada in history pummeling Iraqi targets. U.S. missiles reinforced round-the-clock bombing raids on Baghdad, Iraq's capital. It was a television war, in which CNN reporters broadcast live from a Baghdad hotel as bombs fell. In late February, coalition forces under General Norman Schwartzkopf launched a ground war that quickly routed the Iraqis from Kuwait. When the war ended on March 1, at least 40,000 Iraqis had been killed, while allied troops lost 240 (148 of them Americans).

Bush rejected suggestions from advisers to take Baghdad and topple Hussein's regime. Coalition members would not have agreed to such a plan, and it was unclear who would replace Iraq's dictator. So Saddam Hussein remained, though with his authority curtailed. The United Nations maintained an arms and economic embargo, and the Security Council issued Resolution 687, demanding full disclosure of Iraq's program to develop weapons of mass destruction and ballistic missiles. In Resolution 688, the Security Council condemned the Iraqi regime's brutal crackdown against Kurds in northern Iraq and Shi'ite Muslims in the south and demanded access for humanitarian groups. The United States, Britain, and France seized on Resolution 688 to create a northern no-fly zone, prohibiting Iraqi aircraft flights. A similar no-fly zone was set up in southern Iraq in 1992 and expanded in 1996.

Domestic Problems

Although many would later question President Bush's decision to stop short of Baghdad, initially there were few objections. In the wake of Desert Storm, the president's

CNN

When Ted Turner launched CNN, his Cable News Network, on June 1, 1980, few people took it seriously. With a staff of three hundred—mostly young, mostly inexperienced—CNN operated from the basement of a converted Atlanta country club. CNN was initially known for its on-air errors, as when a cleaning woman emptied anchor Bernard Shaw's trash during his live newscast. But by 1992, CNN was seen in more than 150 nations, and *Time* magazine named Ted Turner its Man of the Year.

Throughout the 1980s, CNN built relations with local news outlets worldwide. CNN reported live from Tiananmen Square and from the Berlin Wall in 1989. Millions watched as CNN reporters broadcast live from Baghdad in the 1991 Gulf War. When the Soviet Union wanted to denounce the 1989 U.S. invasion of Panama, officials called CNN's Moscow bureau instead of the U.S. embassy. During the Gulf War, Saddam Hussein reportedly kept televisions in his bunker tuned to CNN, and U.S. generals used its broadcasts to judge the effectiveness of missile attacks. Despite its global mission, CNN's U.S. origins were often apparent. During the U.S. invasion of Panama, CNN cautioned correspondents not to refer to the U.S. military forces as "our" troops. What CNN offered was a global experience: people throughout the world watching the major moments in contemporary history as they unfolded. The United States's CNN created new links among the world's people. But, as *Time* magazine noted (while praising Turner as the Prince of the Global Village), such connections "did not produce instantaneous brotherhood, just a slowly dawning awareness of the implications of a world transfixed by a single TV image."

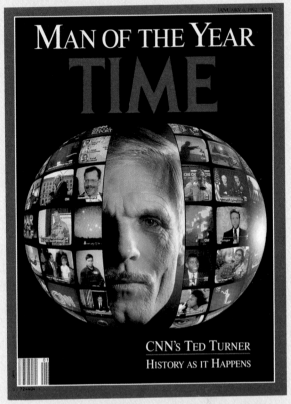

"I am the right man in the right place at the right time," Ted Turner declared at the time of CNN's founding in 1980. "Not me alone, but all the people who think the world can be brought together by telecommunications." Just over a decade later, Turner was rewarded for his visionary ideas by being named *Time* magazine's Man of the Year for 1991.
(Time Life Pictures/Getty Images)

popularity soared to 91 percent, beating the record 89 percent set by Harry Truman in June 1945 after Germany surrendered. Cocky advisers thought Bush could ride his popularity through the 1992 election.

Bush could also claim domestic achievements that seemed to affirm his pledge to lead a "kinder, gentler nation." In 1990, for example, Bush signed the Americans with Disabilities Act. Also in 1990, the president signed the Clean Air Act, which sought to reduce acid rain by limiting factory and automobile emissions.

Yet Bush's poll numbers started falling and kept falling, largely because of his ineffectual response to the weakening economy. He was slow to grasp the implications of the heavy national debt and massive federal deficit. When the nation entered into a full-fledged recession after the Gulf War, Bush merely proclaimed that things were not *that* bad.

Business shrank, despite low interest rates that theoretically should have encouraged investment. Real-estate prices plummeted. U.S. products faced tougher overseas competitors, especially in Japan and elsewhere in Asia. As unemployment climbed to 8 percent, consumer confidence sank. By late 1991, fewer than 40 percent of the American people felt comfortable about the nation's direction.

Clarence Thomas's Nomination

Bush's credibility was diminished further in fall 1991 by the confirmation hearings for Clarence Thomas, his Supreme Court nominee. The Bush administration hoped that those who opposed the nomination of another conservative to the high court might support an African American justice. But in October, Anita Hill, an African American law professor at the University of Oklahoma, charged that Thomas had sexually harassed her when she worked for him during the early 1980s. The televised Judiciary Committee hearings turned ugly, and some Republican members suggested that Hill was either lying or mentally ill. Thomas described himself as the "victim" of a "high-tech lynching." However, Hill's testimony focused the nation's attention on issues of power, gender, race, and the workplace. And the Senate's confirmation of Thomas, along with the attacks on Hill, angered many, further increasing the gender gap in American politics.

Summary

When Ronald Reagan left the White House in 1988, the *New York Times* wrote: "Ronald Reagan leaves no Vietnam War, no Watergate, no hostage crisis. But he leaves huge question marks—and much to do." George H. W. Bush met the foreign policy promises of the 1980s, as the Soviet Union collapsed and the United States won the Cold War. He also led the United States into war with Iraq, which ended swiftly and left Saddam Hussein in power.

During the 1980s, the United States moved from recession to economic prosperity. However, deep tax cuts and massive increases in defense spending increased the national debt from $994 billion to more than $2.9 trillion. Pro-business policies, such as deregulation, created opportunities for economic growth but also opened the door for corruption. Policies that benefited the wealthy at the expense of middle-class or poor Americans widened the gulf between the very rich and everyone else. Drug addiction, crime, and violence grew, especially in the most impoverished areas. The 1980s also saw the beginning of culture wars between fundamentalist Christians who sought to "restore" America to God and those who championed separation of church and state. The nation shifted politically to the right, though the coalitions of economic and social conservatives who supported Reagan were fragile.

Finally, during the 1980s, the nation's Hispanic population grew. New immigrants from Asia arrived in large numbers, too. During the Reagan-Bush years, the United States became both more divided and more diverse.

The Americans with Disabilities Act

The Americans with Disabilities Act (ADA), passed by large bipartisan majorities in Congress and signed into law by President George H. W. Bush on July 26, 1990, built on the legacy of the United States's civil rights movement. Beyond prohibiting discrimination, it mandated that public and private entities—schools, stores, restaurants and hotels, government buildings, and public transportation authorities—provide "reasonable accommodations" allowing people with disabilities to participate fully in their communities and the nation.

The equal-access provisions of the ADA have changed the U.S. landscape. Steep curbs and stairs once blocked access to wheelchair users; now ramps and lifts are common. Buses "kneel" for passengers with limited mobility; crosswalks and elevators use audible signals for the sight-impaired; colleges and universities offer qualified students a wide range of assistance. People with various disabilities have traveled into the Grand Canyon and other parks, thanks to the National Park Service's accessibility programs.

At the same time, ADA employment regulations have generated difficult legal questions. Which conditions are covered by the ADA? (The Supreme Court ruled that asymptomatic HIV infection is a covered disability and carpal tunnel syndrome is not.) Employers may not discriminate against qualified people who can, with "reasonable" accommodation, perform the "essential" tasks of a job—but what is "reasonable" and what is "essential"? The specific provisions of the ADA will likely continue to be contested and redefined in the courts. But as Attorney General Janet Reno noted, as she celebrated the ADA's tenth anniversary, its true legacy is the determination "to find the best in everyone and to give everyone equal opportunity."

Chapter Review

REAGAN AND THE CONSERVATIVE RESURGENCE

How did Ronald Reagan unify conservatives into a powerful political coalition?

In his 1980 and 1984 presidential campaigns (and as president), Ronald Reagan appealed to, and ultimately united, a broad range of previously fragmented groups nationwide, transforming them into a strong, unified conservative Republican base. First, Reagan drew those who wanted to strengthen the military, minimize federal power, and weaken liberal social programs of the 1930s New Deal and 1960s Great Society. Second, Reagan attracted economic conservatives with his stand on deregulation, weaker unions, and tax policies benefiting corporations and investors. Third, Reagan drew support from disillusioned Democrats—intellectual neoconservatives who fell away from the party after Vietnam and members of unions and ethnic groups who resented their hard-earned tax dollars funding welfare handouts to those who did not work. Finally, though divorced, Reagan also drew the religious New Right into his coalition by embracing causes that were important to them: the anti-abortion cause and prayer in public schools.

REAGANOMICS

Which policies helped transform the economic recession into an economic boom?

Reaganomics—President Ronald Reagan's supply-side economic policy—is often credited with ending stagflation and promoting economic recovery. This theory held that by cutting taxes, businesses and the wealthy would invest in the economy, and the growth produced by this investment would, in turn, ultimately trickle down to benefit all Americans. In truth, Federal Reserve policies actually deserve the credit for ending stagflation and reversing the downturn. This autonomous governmental body raised interest rates on loans to an all-time high of 21.5 percent and tightened money supply. While this policy initially took the nation deeper into a slump, as foreclosures, bankruptcy, and unemployment rates skyrocketed, it ultimately lowered inflation and raised the Gross National Product, triggering an economic resurgence by 1984.

Why was the 1980s' economic boom a mixed blessing?

On the one hand, by 1984, the Federal Reserve's policy of increasing interest rates and tightening money supply ended stagflation and reversed the economic downturn. And President Reagan's pro-business policies and deregulation helped smaller companies make inroads into fields previously dominated by major corporations. On the other hand, deregulation allowed many businesses—particularly the financial services industry—to operate without accountability to governing authorities such as the SEC. Consequently, corruption was widespread, as some investors became rich via insider trading, the illegal practice of buying stocks with information not available to the public. Shady deals in the savings and loan industry caused its collapse and required a federal bail-out of half a trillion dollars. The high-risk investment climate of the latter half of the decade not only fueled a stock market crash in 1987, but also led to corporate downsizing and layoffs for middle managers. Finally, Reagan's tax cuts and other policies benefited the rich at the expense of other Americans, enabling the rich to get richer while the poor became poorer.

REAGAN AND THE WORLD

What characterized Reagan's approach to foreign policy?

In foreign policy, Reagan was both aggressive and optimistic. In dealing with the Soviets, he initially adopted a strident anticommunist position, implementing the Reagan Doctrine to aid anticommunist freedom fighters around the world. He even branded the Soviet Union as "an evil empire" and helped arm counter-revolutionaries to overthrow the Nicaraguan government when he thought it was becoming communist. Believing that a solid defense would thwart the Soviet threat, Reagan launched the largest peacetime arms buildup in U.S. history, spending $294.7 billion in 1985 (twice as much as in 1980). But his optimism about the power of the United States to positively affect world events also led him in his second term to accept Soviet leader Mikhail Gorbachev's call for disarmament and new thinking in world affairs that led to the end of the Cold War.

AMERICAN SOCIETY IN THE 1980S

What divided Americans in the 1980s?

Americans continued to feel the tug of unresolved racial and ethnic tensions, especially as the immigrant groups who arrived in the 1960s and 1970s (particularly Asians and Hispanics) began to claim their place in society. In addition, a growing class of rich Americans were farther removed from the so-called underclass, as journalists referred to urban poor. New lines were also being drawn between secular and religious forces, as a powerful new group of Christian conservatives sought to reverse what they regarded as society's increased permissiveness, restore conservative family values, and shape the nation's future around their core Christian beliefs. The resulting battle, dubbed the culture wars, pitted those who supported the separation of church and state and celebrated tolerance and diversity against the religious right's seeming intolerance, antifeminism, and homophobia.

THE END OF THE COLD WAR AND GLOBAL DISORDER

What were the highs and lows of Bush's presidency?

George H. W. Bush's popularity ratings soared to 91 percent after the United States's success in Operation Desert Storm. He scored kudos for passing the Americans with Disabilities Act, banning job discrimination against those with disabilities who can reasonably perform a job's task with minor accommodations. He also signed the Clean Air Act in 1990, which sought to reduce acid rain by restricting factory and auto emissions. But his blind-spot about the weakening economy and recession that emerged after the Gulf War turned voters off. He dismissed the rising jobless rates, shrinking number of businesses, and plummeting real estate prices as not that bad, leading many Americans to distrust the nation's future in Bush's hands.

SUGGESTIONS FOR FURTHER READING

Elijah Anderson, *Streetwise: Race, Class, and Change in an Urban Community* (1992)

A. J. Bacevich et al., *The Gulf War of 1991 Reconsidered* (2003)

Lou Cannon, *President Reagan: The Role of a Lifetime* (2000)

Robert M. Collins, *Transforming America: Politics and Culture During the Reagan Years* (2006)

Jack F. Matlock, *Reagan and Gorbachev: How the Cold War Ended* (2004)

John Micklethwait and Adrian Wooldridge, *The Right Nation: Conservative Power in America* (2004)

James A. Morone, *Hellfire Nation: The Politics of Sin in American History* (2003)

James Patterson, *The Restless Giant: The United States from Watergate to Bush vs. Gore* (2005)

For a more extensive list for further reading, go to college.cengage.com/pic/norton8e.

CHAPTER 33

Into the Global Millennium

CHAPTER OUTLINE

Social Strains and New Political Directions

The New Economy and Globalization

Paradoxes of Prosperity

September 11 and the War on Terrorism

War and Occupation in Iraq

Americans in the First Decade of the New Millennium

> **LINKS TO THE WORLD:**
> The Global AIDS Epidemic

> **LEGACY FOR A PEOPLE AND A NATION:** The Internet

Summary

At 8:46 A.M. on that fateful Tuesday morning, Jan Demczur, a window washer, stepped into an elevator in the North Tower of the World Trade Center in New York City. Before the elevator reached its next landing, one of the six occupants recalled, "We felt a muted thud. The whole building shook. And the elevator swung from side to side like a pendulum." None of the occupants knew it, but American Airlines Flight 175 had just crashed into the building at 440 miles per hour.

The elevator started plunging. Someone pushed the emergency stop button. Then a voice came over the intercom: there had been an explosion. As smoke seeped into the elevator, several men used the wooden handle of Demczur's squeegee to force open the doors but discovered they were on the fiftieth floor, where this elevator did not stop. In front of them was a wall.

Demczur, a Polish immigrant who once worked as a builder, saw that the wall was made of Sheetrock, a plasterboard that could be cut. Using the squeegee, the six men took turns scraping and poking, and finally burst through to a men's bathroom. Startled firefighters guided them to a stairwell. They finally reached the street at 10:23 A.M. Five minutes later the tower collapsed.

It was September 11, 2001.

Later that day Demczur learned that terrorists had hijacked four airliners and turned them into missiles. Two were flown into the World Trade Center; one slammed into the Pentagon in Washington, D.C.; and one crashed in a Pennsylvania field after passengers tried to retake the plane from the hijackers. Both World Trade Center towers collapsed, killing nearly three thousand people.

It was the deadliest attack the United States ever suffered on its soil, and it would dramatically change American life. The events sent shock waves around the globe, revealing how

This icon will direct you to interactive activities and study materials on A People And A Nation, Brief Edition
website: **www.cengage.com/history/norton/peoplenationbrief8e**

Chronology

1992	Violence erupts in Los Angeles over Rodney King verdict.		Antiglobalization demonstrators disrupt World Trade Organization (WTO) meeting in Seattle.
	Major economic recession occurs.	**2000**	Nation records longest economic expansion in its history.
	Clinton is elected president.		Supreme Court settles contested presidential election in favor of Bush.
	United States sends troops to Somalia.		
1993	Congress approves North American Free Trade Agreement (NAFTA).	**2001**	Economy dips into recession; period of low growth and high unemployment begins.
	United States withdraws from Somalia.		Bush becomes president.
1994	Contract with America helps Republicans win majorities in House and Senate.		Al Qaeda terrorists attack World Trade Center and Pentagon.
	Genocide occurs in Rwanda.		PATRIOT Act is passed by Congress.
	U.S. intervenes in Haiti.		United States attacks Al Qaeda positions in Afghanistan, topples ruling Taliban regime.
1995	Domestic terrorist bombs Oklahoma City federal building.	**2003**	United States invades Iraq, ousts Saddam Hussein regime.
	U.S. diplomats broker peace for Bosnia.	**2004**	Bush is reelected.
1996	Welfare reform bill places time limits on welfare payments.	**2005**	Hurricane Katrina strikes Gulf Coast.
	Clinton is reelected.	**2006**	Iraq War continues; by end of year U.S. deaths reach three thousand.
1998	House votes to impeach Clinton.		Democrats take both houses of Congress in midterm elections.
1999	Senate acquits Clinton of impeachment charges.		
	NATO bombs Serbia over Kosovo crisis.		

interconnected the world had become in the early twenty-first century. At the World Trade Center, almost five hundred foreigners from more than eighty countries perished: sixty-seven Britons, twenty-one Jamaicans, twenty-seven Japanese, seventeen Mexicans, thirty-four Indians, sixteen Canadians, fifteen Australians, and seven Haitians. Many of the victims were, like Demczur, immigrants who came to New York seeking a better life; others were on temporary work visas. But all made the World Trade Center a kind of global city within a city, where some 50,000 people worked and another 140,000 visited daily.

A symbol of U.S. financial power, the World Trade Center towers also represented the globalization of world trade that marked the 1980s and 1990s. The towers housed the offices of more than four hundred businesses, including some of the world's leading financial institutions—Bank of America, Switzerland's Credit Suisse Group, Germany's Deutsche Bank, and Japan's Dai-Ichi Kangyo Bank.

Globalization was a 1990s buzzword and went beyond trade and investment to include connections in commerce, communications, and culture. While the terrorists—tied to the radical Islamic group Al Qaeda—sought to bring down that globalization, their attack used the same international technological, economic, and travel infrastructure that fueled global integration. Cell phones, computers, intercontinental air travel—all instruments of globalization—were crucial in the terrorists plot to turn four jetliners into lethal weapons.

Islamic militants had struck the World Trade Center before, bombing its underground parking garage in 1993. But Americans at the time paid only fleeting attention. President Bill Clinton took office in 1993 and concentrated less on foreign policy and more on domestic issues such as healthcare and deficit reduction. Clinton also sought to harness globalization to the United States's benefit.

For most Americans, the 1990s brought good times. The stock market soared, unemployment dropped, and more Americans owned homes. But the 1990s were also marked by violence and cultural conflict—the first multiethnic uprising in Los Angeles, domestic terrorism in Oklahoma City, school shootings, and hate crimes.

These were also politically volatile years. Republicans blocked the Democrats' legislative programs. With a conservative agenda of limited government and family values, the GOP routed Democrats in the 1994 midterm elections. But Republicans alienated voters by shutting down the federal government during the winter of 1995–1996 in a budget standoff, and Clinton was reelected in 1996. However, scandal plagued the Clinton White House, and in 1999 the House of Representatives voted to impeach Clinton, alleging he committed perjury and obstructed justice. The Senate failed to convict him, and his popularity remained high, but his leadership was compromised.

Clinton's successor, George W. Bush, successful in an extremely controversial election, responded to the 9/11 attacks by declaring a war on terrorism. Bush ordered U.S. forces into large-scale military action, first in Afghanistan, where Al Qaeda was headquartered with the blessing of the Taliban regime, then in Iraq to oust Saddam Hussein's government. Militarily, the Taliban and Iraqi governments were quickly beaten. Al Qaeda, however, remained a threat, and in Iraq, U.S. occupying forces battled a large-scale insurgency. Bush's high approval ratings dropped, and though he won reelection in 2004, his second term was undermined by continued bloodshed in Iraq and scandal at home.

- What was the New Economy of the 1990s, and how did it contribute to the globalization of business?
- Did the attacks of September 11, 2001, change the United States in fundamental ways? Explain
- Why did the United States invade Iraq in 2003, and why did its occupying forces subsequently face a drawn-out and bloody insurgency?

SOCIAL STRAINS AND NEW POLITICAL DIRECTIONS

Although the 1990s would be remembered for relative peace and prosperity, the decade did not start that way. Scourges of drugs, homelessness, and crime plagued U.S. cities. Racial tensions worsened; the gulf between rich and poor became more pronounced. The economy tipped into recession. Public disillusionment with political leaders ran strong. As the 1992 presidential election began, Americans wanted a change.

Violence in Los Angeles

Racial tensions erupted in Los Angeles in 1992. A jury (with no African American members) acquitted four white police officers charged with beating an African American man, Rodney King, who fled a pursuing police car at speeds exceeding 110 miles per hour. A bystander's video of the beating played so often on CNN, the new twenty-four-hour news network, that the local event became major national news. Within hours of the verdict, fires were burning in South Central Los Angeles.

The roots of this violence, however, went deeper. Well-paid jobs disappeared in the deindustrialization of the 1970s and 1980s, as more than a hundred manufacturing and industrial plants shut their doors. By the early 1990s, almost one-third of South Central residents lived in poverty—a rate 75 percent higher than the entire city.

Tensions increased as new immigrants arrived—Hispanics from Mexico and Central America, who competed with African Americans for scarce jobs, and Korean immigrants, who established small businesses such as grocery stores. Street gangs struggled over territory in South Central as the crack epidemic further decimated the neighborhood and homicide rates soared. Many African and Hispanic American residents saw high prices in Korean-owned shops as exploitation, while Korean shopkeepers complained of frequent shoplifting, robberies, and even beatings.

The violence in Los Angeles left at least fifty-three people dead. Almost a billion dollars in property was destroyed, including 2,300 stores owned by Koreans or Korean Americans. More than sixteen thousand people were arrested, many of them recent immigrants.

Economic Troubles and the 1992 Election

During the Bush administration, the economy grew slowly or not at all. Some city and thirty state governments faced bankruptcy. In 1978 California's Proposition 13—the first in a series of tax revolts nationwide—cut property taxes while the population boomed, and the state government, out of money in mid-1992, paid workers and bills in IOUs. Many businesses closed down or cut back. Factory employment plummeted, and corporate downsizing cost well-educated white-collar workers their jobs as well. In 1991 median household incomes hit the most severe decline since the 1973 recession; in 1992 the number of poor people in America reached the highest level since 1964.

As economic woes continued, President George H. W. Bush's approval rating fell to half of its high of 91 percent after the Persian Gulf War. Despite the credit Bush gained for ending the Cold War and the quick victory in the Gulf War, economic woes and the belief that he was out of touch with the problems most Americans faced left him vulnerable in the 1992 presidential election.

The Democratic nominee, Arkansas governor Bill Clinton, offered a profound contrast to Bush. Clinton's campaign headquarters bore signs with the four-word reminder "It's the economy stupid." In a town hall–format presidential debate, a woman asked how the economic troubles affected each candidate, and Clinton replied, "Tell me how it's affected you again?" George Bush was caught on camera looking at his watch.

On election day, Americans denied George Bush a second term. Ross Perot, a Texas billionaire who claimed he would bring economic common sense to the federal government, claimed almost 20 percent of the popular vote—the highest percentage for a third-party candidate in eighty years—but did not carry a single state. Clinton, with 43 percent of the popular vote, swept New England, the West Coast, and much of the industrial Midwest, even making inroads into the South and drawing Reagan Democrats back to the fold. Although Democrats controlled both houses, incumbents did not fare well. The 103rd Congress had 110 new representatives and 11 new senators.

William Jefferson Clinton

A journalist described the paradoxical Bill Clinton in a 1996 *New York Times* article as "one of the biggest, most talented, articulate, intelligent, open, colorful characters ever to inhabit the White House," while also noting that Clinton can be "an undisciplined, fumbling, obtuse, defensive, self-justifying rogue." Larger than life, Clinton was a born politician from a small town called Hope who wanted to be president most of his life. At Georgetown University in Washington, D.C., during the 1960s he protested the Vietnam War and maneuvered to keep himself out of it. Clinton won a Rhodes scholarship to Oxford, earned his law degree from Yale, and returned to his home state of Arkansas, where he was elected governor in 1978 at age thirty-two.

In 1975 Clinton married Hillary Rodham, whom he met when both were law students at Yale. Rodham Clinton was the first First Lady to have a significant career of her own, and she spoke of balancing her professional and family life. Rodham Clinton was attacked by conservatives and antifeminists. After she told a hostile interviewer, "I suppose I could have stayed home and baked cookies and had teas," the *New York Post* called her "a buffoon, an insult to most women."

A New Democrat's Promise and Pitfalls

Politically, Bill Clinton was a new Democrat, advocating a more centrist—though still socially progressive—position for the Democratic Party. Clinton and his colleagues emphasized private-sector economic development, focusing on job training and other policies to promote opportunity, not dependency. Some Democrats found Clinton too conservative. However, the political right vehemently attacked Clinton, making the political struggles of the 1990s exceptionally partisan.

Clinton began his presidency with an ambitious program of reform and revitalization, including appointing a cabinet that "looks like America" in all its diversity. But Republicans, determined not to allow Clinton the traditional honeymoon period, maneuvered him into fulfilling his pledge to end the ban on gays in the military before he secured congressional or military support. Amid great controversy, Clinton accepted a "don't ask, don't tell" compromise that alienated liberals and conservatives, the gay community and the military.

Clinton's major goal was to make healthcare affordable and accessible for all Americans. But special interests mobilized in opposition: the insurance industry worried about lost profits; the business community feared higher taxes; the medical community worried about more regulation, lower government reimbursement rates, and reduced healthcare quality. The healthcare task force, cochaired by Hillary Rodham Clinton, could not defeat these forces. Within a year, the centerpiece of Clinton's fledgling presidency failed.

Republican Revolution

New-style Republicans challenged the beleaguered new Democrat. In September 1994, more than three hundred Republican candidates for the House of Representatives endorsed the Contract with America. Developed under the leadership of Georgia representative Newt Gingrich, the Contract promised "the end of [big] government . . . [and] the beginning of a Congress that respects the values and shares the faith of the American family." It called for a balanced-budget amendment to the Constitution, reduction of the capital gains tax, a two-year limit on welfare payments (while making unmarried mothers under eighteen ineligible), and increased defense spending.

In the midterm elections, the Republican Party mobilized socially conservative voters and took control of both houses of Congress for the first time since 1954. Ideological passions ran high, and many Republicans believed that their attempts to weaken federal power and to dismantle the welfare state would succeed.

Although many Americans applauded cutting government spending, they opposed cuts to specific programs, including Medicare and Medicaid, education and college loans, highway construction, farm subsidies, veterans' benefits, and Social Security. Republicans made a bigger mistake when they issued Clinton an ultimatum on the federal budget and forced the government to suspend all nonessential action during the winter of 1995–1996.

Political Compromise and the Election of 1996

Such struggles led Clinton to make compromises that moved U.S. politics to the right. For example, he signed the 1996 Personal Responsibility and Work Opportunity Act, a welfare reform measure that eliminated cash assistance for poor children (Aid to Families with Dependent Children). The law mandated that heads of families on welfare must find work within two years—though states could exempt 20 percent of recipients—and limited welfare benefits to five years over an individual's lifetime. The Telecommunications Act of 1996, signed by Clinton, reduced diversity in media by permitting companies to own more television and radio stations.

Clinton was reelected in 1996 (defeating Republican Bob Dole and Reform Party candidate Ross Perot), partly because Clinton stole some of the conservatives' thunder. He declared that "the era of big government is over" and invoked family values, a centerpiece of the Republican campaign. Sometimes Clinton's actions were true compromises; other times he attempted to reclaim issues from the conservatives, as when he redefined family values as "fighting for the family-leave law." And despite scandal and gridlock, Clinton's election-year promise to "build a bridge to the future" seemed plausible as prosperity increased.

THE NEW ECONOMY AND GLOBALIZATION

Just how much credit Clinton deserved for the improved economy is debatable. The roots of the 1990s boom were in the 1970s, when U.S. corporations began investing in new technologies, retooling plants to become more energy-efficient, and cutting labor costs. Specifically, companies reduced the influence of organized labor by moving operations to the union-weak South and West and to countries such as China and Mexico, where labor was cheap and pollution controls were lax.

Digital Revolution

The rapid development of what came to be called information technology—computers, fax machines, cell phones, and the Internet—had a huge economic impact in the 1980s and 1990s. New companies and industries sprang up, many headquartered in the Silicon Valley near San Francisco. By the second half of the 1990s, the *Forbes* list of the 400 Richest Americans featured high-tech leaders such as Microsoft's Bill Gates, who became the wealthiest person in the world with worth approaching $100 billion, as his company produced the operating software for most personal computers. The high-tech industry had considerable spillover effects, generating improved productivity, new jobs, and sustained economic growth.

The heart of this technological revolution was the microprocessor. Introduced in 1970 by Intel, the microprocessor miniaturized the central processing unit of a computer, meaning small machines could now perform calculations previously requiring large machines. Computing chores that took a week in the early 1970s took only a minute by 2000; the cost of storing one megabyte of information fell from more than $5,000 in 1975 to $.17 in 1999.

Analysts dubbed this technology-driven sector the New Economy, and it would have emerged no matter who was in the White House. Yet Clinton and his advisers had some responsibility for the dramatic upturn. With the U.S. budget deficit topping $500 billion, they made the politically risky move of abandoning the middle-class tax cut and making deficit reduction a top priority. White House officials rightly concluded that, if the deficit could be brought under control, interest rates would drop and the economy would rebound. And that is what happened. The budget deficit decreased (by 1997 it had been erased); this lowered interest rates, and this boosted investment. Stock prices soared, and the gross national product rose by an average of 3.5 to 4 percent annually.

Globalization of Business

Clinton perceived early on that the technology revolution would make the world more interconnected. He was convinced that, with the demise of Soviet communism, capitalism—or at least the introduction of market forces, freer trade and deregulation—was spreading around the globe.

The journalist Thomas L. Friedman asserted that the post–Cold War world was the age of globalization, characterized by the integration of markets, finance, and technologies. U.S. officials lowered trade and investment barriers, completing the North American Free Trade Agreement (NAFTA) with Canada and Mexico in 1993, and in 1994 concluding the Uruguay Round of the General Agreement on Tariffs and Trade (GATT), which lowered tariffs for the seventy member nations that accounted for about 80 percent of world trade. The administration also endorsed the 1995 creation of the World Trade Organization (WTO), to administer and enforce agreements made at the Uruguay Round. Finally, the president formed a National Economic Council to promote trade missions around the world.

Multinational corporations were the hallmark of this global economy. By 2000 there were 63,000 parent companies worldwide and 690,000 foreign affiliates. Some, such as Nike and Gap, Inc., subcontracted production of certain merchandise to whichever developing countries had the lowest labor costs. Such arrangements created a new international division of labor and generated a boom in world exports, which, at $5.4 trillion in 1998, had doubled in two decades. U.S. exports reached $680 billion in 1998, but imports rose even higher, to $907 billion (for a trade deficit of $227 billion). Sometimes the multinationals affected foreign policy, as when Clinton in 1995 extended full diplomatic recognition to Vietnam under pressure from such corporations as Coca-Cola, Citigroup, General Motors, and United Airlines, which wanted to enter that emerging market.

Critics of Globalization While the administration promoted open markets, labor unions argued that free-trade agreements exacerbated the trade deficit and exported U.S. jobs. Average real wages for U.S. workers declined steadily after 1973, from $320 per week to $260 by the mid-1990s. Other critics maintained that globalization widened the gap between rich and poor countries, creating a mass of "slave laborers" in poor countries working under conditions that would never be tolerated in the West. Environmentalists charged that globalization also exported pollution to countries unprepared to deal with it. Still other critics warned about the power of multinational corporations and the global financial markets over traditional cultures.

Antiglobalization fervor reached a peak in fall 1999, when thousands of protesters disrupted the WTO meeting in Seattle. In the months that followed, there were sizable protests at meetings of the International Monetary Fund (IMF) and the World Bank. In July 2001, fifty thousand demonstrators protested an IMF and World Bank meeting in Genoa, Italy.

Target: McDonald's Activists also targeted corporations, such as the Gap, Starbucks, Nike, and, especially, McDonald's, which by 1995 was serving 30 million customers daily in twenty thousand franchises in over one hundred countries. Critics assailed the company's slaughterhouse techniques, alleged exploitation of workers, its high-fat menu, and its role in creating an increasingly homogeneous and sterile world culture. For six years starting in 1996, McDonald's endured hundreds of often-violent protests, including bombings in Rome, Prague, London, Macao, Rio de Janeiro, and Jakarta.

Protesting that the World Trade Organization (WTO) possessed the dangerous power to challenge any nation's environmental laws if the WTO deemed them barriers to trade, chanting demonstrators marched in the streets of Seattle on November 30, 1999. Critics of the WTO claimed that sea turtles and dolphins have already been victimized by the WTO. Demonstrators identified the WTO as an example of globalization gone wrong. The WTO meeting went on, but the results proved meager because nations could not agree on rules governing dumping, subsidies for farm goods, genetically altered foods, and lower tariffs on high-tech goods. (Beth A. Keiser/AP Images)

Others decried the violence and the underlying arguments of the antiglobalization campaigners. True, some economists acknowledged, statistics showed that global inequality had grown in recent years. But if one included quality-of-life measurements, such as literacy and health, global inequality had declined. Some studies found that wage and job losses for U.S. workers were caused not primarily by globalization factors, such as imports, production outsourcing, and immigration, but by technological change that made production more efficient, that used less labor. Other researchers saw no evidence that governments' sovereignty had been seriously compromised or that there was a "race to the bottom" in environmental standards from globalization.

As for creating a homogeneous global culture, McDonald's, others said, tailored its menu and operating practices to local tastes. And although American movies, TV programs, music, computer software, and other intellectual property often dominated world markets, foreign competition also arrived in the United States. Millions of American children were gripped by the Japanese fad Pokemon, and satellite television established a worldwide following for European soccer teams.

Clinton's Diplomacy

Still, it remained true that the United States occupied a uniquely powerful position on the world stage. The demise of the Soviet Union created a one-superpower world, in which the United States stood far above other powers in political, military, and economic might. Yet in his first term Clinton was more wary in traditional aspects of foreign policy—great-power diplomacy, arms control, regional disputes—than in facilitating American cultural and trade expansion. Recalling the public's impatience in the Vietnam debacle, he was deeply suspicious of foreign military involvements.

Clinton's mistrust of foreign interventions was cemented by the difficulties he inherited from Bush in Somalia. In 1992 Bush sent U.S. Marines to the East African nation as part of a U.N. effort to ensure that humanitarian supplies reached starving Somalis. But in summer 1993, when Americans came under deadly attack, Clinton withdrew U.S. troops. And he did not intervene in Rwanda, where in 1994 the majority Hutus butchered 800,000 of the minority Tutsis in a brutal civil war.

Balkan Crisis

Many administration officials argued for using the United States's power to contain ethnic hatreds, support human rights, and promote democracy worldwide. Humanitarian intervention faced a test in the Balkans, where Bosnian Muslims, Serbs, and Croats were killing one another. Clinton talked tough against Serbian aggression and atrocities in Bosnia-Herzegovina, especially the Serbs' ethnic cleansing of Muslims through massacres and rape camps. He occasionally ordered air strikes, but he primarily emphasized diplomacy. In late 1995, U.S. diplomats brokered a fragile peace.

But Yugoslav president Slobodan Milosevic continued the anti-Muslim and anti-Croat fervor. When Serb forces moved to violently rid Kosovo of its majority ethnic Albanians, reports of Serbian atrocities and a major refugee crisis stirred world opinion and pressed Clinton to intervene. In 1999 U.S.-led NATO forces launched a massive aerial bombardment of Serbia. Milosevic withdrew from Kosovo, where U.S. troops joined a U.N. peacekeeping force.

Agreements in the Middle East

In the Middle East, Clinton took an active role in trying to bring the PLO and Israel together to settle their differences. In September 1993 the PLO's Yasir Arafat and Israel's prime minister Yitzhak Rabin signed an agreement at the White House for Palestinian self-rule in the Gaza Strip and the West Bank's Jericho. The following year Israel signed a peace accord with Jordan, further reducing the chances of another full-scale Arab-Israeli war. Radical anti-Arafat Palestinians, however, continued terrorist attacks on Israelis, while extremist Israelis killed Palestinians and, in November 1995, Rabin himself. With American-conducted negotiations and renewed violence in the West Bank, Israel agreed in early 1997 to withdraw troops from the Palestinian city of Hebron. Thereafter, the peace process alternately lagged and spurted.

International environmentalism also gathered pace in the 1990s. The George H. W. Bush administration had opposed many provisions of the 1992 Rio de Janeiro Treaty protecting the diversity of plant and animal species and resisted stricter rules to reduce global warming. Clinton, urged on by his environmentalist vice president Al Gore, signed the 1997 Kyoto protocol, which aimed to combat emissions of carbon dioxide and other gases. But facing strong opposition, Clinton never submitted the protocol for ratification to the Republican-controlled Senate.

Bin Laden and Al Qaeda

Meanwhile, the administration was increasingly concerned about the threat to U.S. interests by Islamic fundamentalism. Senior officials worried Al Qaeda (Arabic for "the base"), an international terrorist network led by Osama bin Laden, wanted to purge Muslim countries of what it considered the profane influence of the West.

The son of a Yemen-born construction tycoon in Saudi Arabia, bin Laden supported the Afghan Mujahidin—also backed by the United States—against Soviet occupation. He then founded Al Qaeda and financed terrorist projects with his substantial inheritance. U.S. officials grew more concerned, particularly as bin Laden focused on U.S. targets. In 1995 a car bomb in Riyadh killed 7 people, 5 of them Americans. In 1998 simultaneous bombings at the American embassies in Kenya and Tanzania killed 224 people, including 12 Americans. In Yemen in 2000, a boat laden with explosives hit the destroyer USS *Cole,* killing 17 American sailors. Although bin Laden masterminded and financed these attacks, he eluded U.S. attempts to apprehend him. In 1998 Clinton approved a plan to assassinate bin Laden, but it failed.

PARADOXES OF PROSPERITY

For most Americans, the late 1990s marked unprecedented peace and prosperity, fueled by the dizzying rise of the stock market. Between 1991 and 1999, the Dow Jones Industrial Average climbed from 3,169 to a high of 11,497. The booming market benefited the middle class and the wealthy, as mutual funds, 401(k) plans, and other new investment vehicles drew a majority of Americans into the stock market. In 1952 only 4 percent of U.S. households owned stocks; by 2000, almost 60 percent did.

At the end of the 1990s, the unemployment rate stood at 4.3 percent. That made it easier to implement welfare reform, and welfare rolls declined 50 percent. Both the richest 5 percent and the least well-off 20 percent of U.S. households saw their incomes rise almost 25 percent. But that translated to an average $50,000 gain for the top 5 percent and only $2,880 for the bottom, further widening the gap between rich and poor. Still, by decade's end, more than two-thirds of Americans were homeowners—the highest proportion in history.

Oklahoma City Bombing

New crises emerged. On April 19, 1995, 168 people were killed in a bomb blast that destroyed the nine-story Alfred P. Murrah Federal Building in Oklahoma City. At first, many blamed Middle Eastern terrorists. But a charred piece of truck axle two blocks away, with the vehicle identification number still legible, revealed that the bomber was Timothy McVeigh, a white American and Persian Gulf War veteran. He sought revenge for the deaths of Branch Davidian religious sect members, whom he believed the FBI had deliberately slaughtered in a standoff over firearms charges two years before in Waco, Texas.

In subsequent months, reporters and investigators discovered militias, tax resisters, and white-supremacist groups nationwide. United by distrust of the federal government, many saw gun control laws as a dangerous usurpation of citizens' right to bear arms. They believed that the federal government was controlled by sinister forces, including Zionists, cultural elitists, Queen Elizabeth, and the United Nations.

Violence and Hate Crimes

On April 20, 1999, eighteen-year-old Eric Harris and seventeen-year-old Dylan Klebold opened fire on classmates and teachers at Columbine High School in Littleton, Colorado, killing thirteen before killing themselves. No clear reason why two academically successful students in a middle-class suburb would commit mass murder ever emerged. Students in Paducah, Kentucky; Springfield, Oregon; and Jonesboro, Arkansas, also massacred classmates.

In the late 1990s, two hate crimes shocked the nation. In 1998 James Byrd Jr., a forty-nine-year-old African American, was murdered by three white supremacists who dragged him with a chain from the back of a pickup truck in Jasper, Texas. Later that year, Matthew Shepherd, a gay college student, was beaten unconscious and left tied to a wooden fence in freezing weather outside Laramie, Wyoming. His killers said they were humiliated when he flirted with them at a bar. To some, these murders signified the strength of racism and homophobia in the United States. Others saw the horror Americans expressed at these murders as a sign of positive change.

Scandal in the Clinton White House

Scandals plagued the Clinton White House. The independent counsel would eventually spend $72 million investigating allegations of wrongdoing by Hillary and Bill Clinton. Independent counsel Kenneth Starr, a conservative Republican and former judge, was originally charged with investigating Whitewater, a 1970s Arkansas real-estate deal in which the Clintons had invested. He never found any evidence against the Clintons, but expanded the range of his investigation.

Early in Clinton's presidency, former Arkansas state employee Paula Jones brought charges of sexual harassment against him, which were eventually dropped.

But when asked before a grand jury whether he had sexual relations with twenty-two-year-old White House intern Monica Lewinsky, Clinton said no. Speaking to the American people, Clinton angrily declared, "I did not have sexual relations with that woman, Miss Lewinsky." Starr produced DNA evidence: a navy blue dress of Lewinsky's, stained with Clinton's semen.

Impeachment

In a 445-page report to Congress, Starr outlined eleven possible grounds for impeachment, accusing Clinton of lying under oath, obstruction of justice, witness tampering, and abuse of power. On December 19, 1998, the House voted on four articles of impeachment; largely along party lines, the House passed two of the articles, one alleging the president committed perjury in his grand jury testimony, the other that he obstructed justice. Clinton became only the second president to face a trial in the Senate, which has the constitutional responsibility to decide (by two-thirds vote) whether to remove a president from office.

But the American people did not want Clinton removed from office. Polls showed that large majorities approved of his job performance, even while condemning his personal behavior. And many did not believe that his actions constituted "high crimes and misdemeanors" (normally acts such as treason) required by the Constitution for impeachment. The Republican-controlled Senate, responding partly to popular opinion, voted against the charges of perjury and obstructing justice, thus clearing Clinton.

Political Partisanship, the Media, and Celebrity Culture

Clinton was not the first president to engage in illicit sex. President John F. Kennedy had numerous and well-known sexual affairs, including one with a nineteen-year-old intern. But after the 1970s Watergate scandals, the mass media no longer turned a blind eye to presidential misconduct. The fiercely competitive news networks relied on scandal, spectacle, and crisis to lure viewers.

The 1990s partisan political wars created a take-no-prisoners climate. Both Republican Speaker of the House Newt Gingrich and his successor, Robert Livingston, resigned when evidence of their extramarital affairs surfaced. Finally, as the former Clinton aide Sidney Blumenthal writes, the impeachment struggle was part of the culture wars: "a monumental battle over . . . cultural mores and the position of women in American society, and about the character of the American people."

Clinton's Legislative Record

Clinton's legislative accomplishments during his two terms included the Family and Medical Leave Act, guaranteeing 91 million workers the right to take time off to care for ailing relatives or newborn children. The Health Insurance Portability and Accountability Act ensured that, when Americans changed jobs, they would not lose health insurance because of preexisting medical conditions. The federal government operated efficiently with 365,000 fewer employees. Clinton created national parks and monuments that protected 3.2 million acres of U.S. land and made unprecedented progress cleaning up toxic waste dumps.

The Bush-Gore Race

Vice President Al Gore was the favorite in the 2000 presidential election. The son of a prominent senator from Tennessee, Gore graduated cum laude from Harvard in 1969 and served in Vietnam despite his reservations about the war. He had served six terms in Congress and played a greater role than any vice president in American history. After eight years of prosperity and relative peace, he had a strong platform. Earnest and highly intelligent, Gore appeared to be a policy wonk rather than a charismatic leader.

Gore's Republican opponent was the son of George H. W. Bush, the forty-first president of the United States. An indifferent student, George W. Bush graduated from Yale in 1968 and pulled strings to jump ahead of a one-and-a-half-year waiting list for the Texas Air National Guard, thus avoiding service in Vietnam. He had a rocky career in the oil business. At age forty, after years of hard drinking, Bush gave up alcohol and embraced Christianity. In 1994 he was elected to the first of two terms as governor of Texas.

As a presidential candidate, Bush made up for his limited foreign policy knowledge, often garbled syntax, and lack of interest in the intricacies of public policy with a confident style that connected with many Americans. Bush spoke of his relationship with God and his commitment to conservative social values, styling himself a "compassionate conservative." Supported by Republican business leaders, Bush amassed the largest campaign war chest in history ($67 million, compared with Gore's $28 million).

The consumer rights activist Ralph Nader ran on the Green Party ticket. Condemning globalization and environmental despoliation, he attacked Bush and Gore, calling them Tweedledee and Tweedledum. Nader drew support from left-liberal voters who might have voted for Gore and so possibly helped tip some states to Bush.

The Contested Election of 2000

On election day 2000, Al Gore narrowly won the popular vote, but not the presidency. It all came down to Florida (where Bush's brother Jeb was governor) and its twenty-five electoral votes. According to the initial tally, Bush narrowly edged Gore out in Florida, but by a close margin that legally required a recount. In several heavily African American counties, tens of thousands of votes went uncounted because voters failed to fully dislodge the chads, small perforated squares, when punching the paper ballots. Lawyers struggled over whether hanging chads (partially detached) and pregnant chads (punched but not detached) were sufficient signs of voter intent. In Palm Beach County, many elderly Jewish residents were confused by a poorly designed ballot and accidentally selected the allegedly anti-Semitic Pat Buchanan instead of Gore. After thirty-six days, with court cases at the state and federal levels, the Supreme Court voted 5 to 4 along narrowly partisan lines to end the recount process. Florida's electoral votes—and the presidency—went to George Bush.

Gore won the West Coast, Northeast, and industrial Midwest. The South, Rocky Mountain West (except New Mexico), and heartland went to Bush. More than 90 percent of African American voters selected Gore, as did 63 percent of Hispanic Americans and 55 percent of Asian Americans. Bush won 60 percent of the white vote, and, overall, 95 percent of his supporters were white. The gender gap was 12 points: 54 percent of women voted for Gore, 42 for Bush. The struggles over the election outcome further polarized the nation.

SEPTEMBER 11 AND THE WAR ON TERRORISM

With the close election and bitter controversy, many believed Bush would govern from the center. Some also thought he, like his father, moved to the right during the election only to secure conservative evangelical Christian voters. But Bush governed from the right, arguably further to the right than any other modern administration.

Bush's Tax Plan

The centerpiece of the Bush agenda was a massive tax cut, to be financed by the predicted budget surplus. Critics believed that a massive cut would wipe out the surplus and that the Bush plan favored the wealthy, but Bush used his party's control of Congress to push through the largest tax cut in U.S. history—$1.3 trillion. To the dismay of environmentalists, he also reiterated his plan to drill for oil in America's last wilderness, the Arctic National Wildlife Refuge.

In international affairs, the administration charted a unilateralist course. Given the United States's preponderant power, senior Bush officials reasoned, it did not need other countries' help. Accordingly, Bush withdrew the United States from the 1972 Anti-Ballistic Missile Treaty with Russia to develop a National Missile Defense system similar to Reagan's Star Wars. The White House also renounced the 1997 Kyoto protocol on controlling global warming and opposed a carefully negotiated protocol to strengthen the 1972 Biological and Toxin Weapons Convention. These decisions and the administration's hands-off policy toward the Israeli-Palestinian peace process caused consternation in Europe.

9/11

Then came September 11. On that sunny Tuesday morning, nineteen hijackers seized control of four commercial jets departing from East Coast airports. At 8:46 A.M. one plane crashed into the 110-story North Tower of the World Trade Center in New York City. At 9:03 A.M., a second plane flew into the South Tower. In less than two hours, both buildings collapsed, killing thousands of office workers, firefighters, and police officers. At 9:43, a third plane crashed into the Pentagon, leaving a huge hole in its west side. The fourth plane was also headed toward Washington, but several passengers, learning of the World Trade Center attacks through cell-phone conversations, stormed the cockpit; in the scuffle, the plane crashed in Somerset County, Pennsylvania, killing all aboard.

More than three thousand people died in the deadliest act of terrorism in history. The hijackers—fifteen Saudi Arabians, two Emiratis, one Lebanese, and, leading them, an Egyptian—had ties to Al Qaeda, Osama bin Laden's radical Islamic organization. Some officials in the Clinton and Bush administrations warned that an Al Qaeda attack was inevitable, but neither administration made counterterrorism a foreign policy priority.

Afghanistan War

September 11 made counterterrorism priority number one. President Bush responded quickly with military force. Al Qaeda operated out of Afghanistan with the blessing of the ruling Taliban, a repressive Islamic fundamentalist group that gained power in 1996. In early October, the United States launched a sustained bombing campaign against Taliban and Al Qaeda positions and sent special operations forces to help a resistance organization in northern Afghanistan. Within two months, the Taliban was driven from power, although bin Laden and top Taliban leaders eluded capture.

As administration officials acknowledged, military victory did not end the terrorist threat. Bush spoke of a long struggle against evil forces, in which the nations of the world were either with the United States or against it. Some questioned whether a war on terrorism could ever be won in a meaningful sense, given that the foe was a nonstate actor with little to lose. Most Americans, however, were ready to believe. Stunned by September 11, they experienced a renewed sense of national unity and pride. Flag sales soared, and Bush's approval ratings skyrocketed.

PATRIOT Act

But the new patriotism had a dark side. Congress passed the USA PATRIOT Act (Uniting and Strengthening America by Providing Appropriate Tools Required to Intercept and Obstruct Terrorism), making it easier for law enforcement to conduct searches, wiretap telephones, and obtain electronic records on individuals. Attorney General John Ashcroft approved giving FBI agents new powers to monitor the Internet, mosques, and rallies. Civil libertarians charged that the Justice Department overstepped, and some judges ruled against the tactics. Yet, according to a June 2002 Gallup poll, 80 percent of Americans were willing to exchange some freedoms for security.

In surveys weeks after the attacks, 71 percent of respondents said that they felt depressed, and one-third had trouble sleeping. The discovery of anthrax-laden letters in several East Coast cities heightened fears, particularly after post offices and government buildings were closed and five people died. Investigators found no evidence to connect the letters to the 9/11 hijackings, but also no good clues as to who the perpetrator might be.

Yet people continued shopping in malls, visiting amusement parks, and working in skyscrapers. Although airline bookings dropped significantly in the early weeks (causing severe problems for many airlines), people still took to the skies. In Washington, the partisanship that disappeared after 9/11 returned, as Democrats and Republicans sparred over judicial appointments, energy policy, and the proposed new Department of Homeland Security. Approved by Congress in November 2002, the department incorporated parts of eight cabinet departments and twenty-two agencies to coordinate intelligence and defense against terrorism.

Economic Uncertainty

Economically, the months before September 11 witnessed a collapse of the dot-coms, Internet companies that were the darlings of Wall Street in the 1990s. In 2001 some five hundred dot-coms declared bankruptcy or closed. There were other economic warning signs as well, notably a meager 0.2 percent growth rate in goods and services for the second quarter. Corporate revenues were also down.

Economic concerns deepened after 9/11 with a four-day closing of Wall Street and a subsequent sharp drop in stock prices. The Dow Jones Industrial Average plunged 14.26 percent. The markets eventually rebounded, but questions remained about the economy's overall health. Neither economic uncertainty nor the failure to capture Osama bin Laden and top Taliban leaders dented Bush's post-9/11 popularity. In the 2002 midterm elections, Republicans retook the Senate and increased their majority in the House.

International Responses

Immediately after September 11, there was an outpouring of support from people everywhere. "We are all Americans now," said the French newspaper *Le Monde* after the attacks. Governments worldwide announced they would work with Washington against terrorism. But within a year, attitudes changed dramatically. Bush's good-versus-evil stance put off foreign observers, but they initially swallowed their objections. When the president hinted that the United States might unilaterally strike Saddam Hussein's Iraq or deal forcefully with North Korea or Iran—Bush's "axis of evil"— many allied governments strongly objected.

Bush and other top officials argued that in an age of terrorism, the United States would not wait for a potential security threat to become real; henceforth, it would strike first. Americans, Bush declared had to be "ready for preemptive action when necessary to defend our liberty and to defend our lives." Critics, among them many world leaders, called it recklessly aggressive and contrary to international law.

The attacks on 9/11 brought forth an outpouring of sympathy for the victims and their families, and for the United Sates generally, from people around the world. Here firefighters in Taipei, Taiwan, attend a prayer service during a global day of mourning. (Sam Yeh/Getty Images)

WAR AND OCCUPATION IN IRAQ

But Bush was determined, particularly on Iraq. Several of his top advisers, including Secretary of Defense Donald Rumsfeld and Vice President Dick Cheney, wanted to oust Saddam Hussein since the end of the Gulf War in 1991. After the Twin Towers fell, they folded Iraq into the larger war on terrorism even though counterterrorism experts saw no link between Saddam and Al Qaeda. For a time, Secretary of State Colin Powell, the first African American in that post, kept the focus on Afghanistan, but gradually the thinking in the White House shifted. In November 2001 Bush ordered the Pentagon to initiate war planning for Iraq; by spring 2002 a secret consensus was reached: Saddam Hussein would be removed by force.

Why Iraq?
In September 2002 Bush challenged the United Nations to enforce its resolutions against Iraq, or the United States would act on its own. In subsequent weeks, he and his aides offered shifting reasons for getting tough with Iraq. They said Saddam was a major threat to the United States and its allies, a leader who possessed and would use banned biological and chemical "weapons of mass destruction" (WMDs) and who sought to acquire nuclear weapons. They claimed, contrary to intelligence estimates, that he had ties to Al Qaeda and could be linked to the 9/11 attacks.

Beneath the surface lurked other motivations. Neoconservatives claimed that ousting Saddam would enhance the security of Israel, the United States's key Middle East ally, and start a chain reaction that would extend democracy throughout the region. White House political strategists believed a swift removal of a hated dictator would assure Bush's reelection. And Bush wanted to prevent an Iraq armed with WMDs from destabilizing an oil-rich region.

Congressional Approval
Bush claimed he did not need congressional authorization for military action against Iraq but sought it anyway. In early October 2002, the House of Representatives voted 296 to 133 and the Senate 77 to 23 to authorize him to use force against Iraq. Many who voted in favor were unwilling to defy a president so close to a midterm election, even though they opposed military action without U.N. sanction. Critics complained that the president had not presented evidence that Saddam Hussein constituted an imminent threat or was connected to the 9/11 attacks. Bush switched to a less hawkish stance, and in early November, the U.N. Security Council unanimously approved Resolution 1441, imposing rigorous new arms inspections on Iraq.

But the Security Council was divided over the next move. In late January 2003, the weapons inspector's report castigated Iraq for failing to complete "the disarmament that was demanded of it" but also said it was too soon to tell whether inspections would succeed. Whereas U.S. and British officials said the time for diplomacy was up, France, Russia, and China called for more inspections. As the U.N. debate continued, Bush sent about 250,000 soldiers to the region. Britain sent about 45,000 troops.

Fall of Baghdad

In late February, the United States floated a draft resolution to the United Nations that proposed issuing an ultimatum to Iraq, but only three of the fifteen Security Council members affirmed support. Bush abandoned the resolution and diplomatic efforts on March 17, when he ordered Saddam Hussein to leave Iraq within forty-eight hours or face an attack. Saddam ignored the ultimatum, and on March 19 the United States and Britain launched an aerial bombardment of Baghdad and other areas. A ground invasion followed (see Map 33.1). The Iraqis initially offered stiff resistance, but on April 9, Baghdad fell.

The military victory was swift, the result of sixteen months of planning. But senior policymakers showed scant interest in readying for postwar Iraq. Top officials who voiced worst-case scenarios in urging war, emphasized best-case outcomes in preparing for peace, expecting that Iraqis would embrace "liberation" with joy, that stability would emerge quickly, and that few U.S. troops would be required to secure the country.

Insurgency

Thus, when violence and lawlessness soon erupted, U.S. planners seemed powerless to respond. The plight of ordinary Iraqis deteriorated as the occupation authority proved unable to maintain order. In Baghdad, electricity worked only a few hours each day, and telephone service was nonexistent. Decisions by the Coalition Governing Council (CPA), headed by Ambassador Paul Bremer, made matters worse, notably Bremer's move in May to disband the Iraqi army. A multisided insurgency of Saddam loyalists, Iraqi nationalists, and foreign Islamic revolutionaries took shape; soon, U.S. occupying forces faced frequent ambushes. By October 2003 more troops had died from these attacks than had perished in the initial invasion.

The chaos in Iraq and the failure to find weapons of mass destruction had critics questioning the war's validity. Sanctions and U.N. inspections had clearly been successful. Prewar claims of a "rush to war" resounded again. Even defenders of the invasion castigated the administration for its failure to anticipate the occupation problems. In spring 2004, photos showing Iraqi detainees being abused by American guards at Abu Ghraib prison were broadcast worldwide, generating international condemnation.

Election of 2004

Facing reelection, President Bush expressed disgust at Abu Ghraib and fended off charges that he and his top aides condoned the abuse. The White House also claimed the dissolution of the CPA in late June and the transfer of sovereignty to an interim Iraqi government would flatten the insurgency. Bush's Democratic opponent, Senator John Kerry of Massachusetts, a Vietnam veteran who had voted for the Iraq resolution, never articulated a clear alternative strategy on the war. Bush won reelection with 51 percent of the popular vote to Kerry's 48 percent and 279 electoral votes to Kerry's 252. The GOP also increased its majorities in the House and Senate.

Bush and his aides took the victory as a mandate to make major domestic policy changes, including partially privatizing Social Security. This plan failed, as Democrats and Republicans in Congress argued that it would not work. The president succeeded, however, in reshaping the Supreme Court. The conservative U.S. Circuit Court judge John Roberts was confirmed as chief justice following the death of Chief Justice

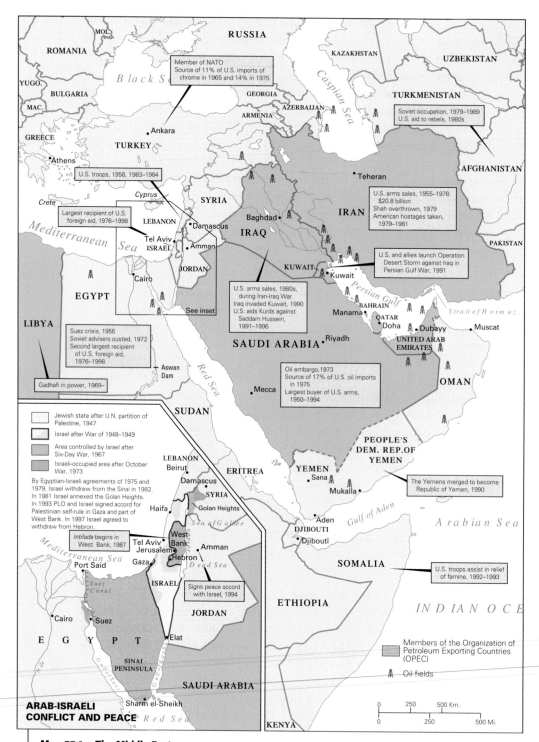

Map 33.1   The Middle East

Extremely volatile and often at war, the nations of the Middle East maintained precarious relations with the United States. To protect its interests, the United States extended large amounts of economic and military aid and sold huge quantities of weapons to the area. At times, Washington ordered U.S. troops to the region. The Arab-Israeli dispute particularly destabilized order, although the peace process moved forward intermittently.

William Rehnquist, and another strong conservative, Samuel Alito, became junior associate justice following the resignation of Sandra Day O'Connor.

The increasing evidence that the war in Iraq had little chance of success undermined Americans' confidence in President Bush. Growing perceptions of administrative incompetence were exacerbated when Hurricane Katrina, the sixth most powerful Atlantic hurricane on record, hit the Gulf Coast and New Orleans in late August 2005. The high winds and storm surge destroyed the levees that kept low-lying parts of New Orleans from being swamped by Lake Pontchartrain and surrounding canals. Floodwaters covered 80 percent of the city, and more than eighteen hundred people died.

Tens of thousands of people who lacked the resources to evacuate the city sought shelter at the Superdome. Food and water supplies quickly ran low, and toilets backed up; people wrapped the dead in blankets and waited for rescue. Those outside the Gulf region, watching the suffering of poor, African American New Orleanians, discussed what Democratic Party leader Howard Dean called the ugly truth: that poverty remains linked to race. The public also worried about administrative mismanagement and the president's seeming indifference. Despite the federal government's failure in handling the crisis, President Bush told Federal Emergency Management Association (FEMA) director Michael Brown, "Brownie, you're doing a heck of a job." Within a few weeks, Brown resigned amid criticism, and Bush distanced himself from him.

America Isolated
Internationally, too, Bush faced criticism because of Iraq, Abu Ghraib, and his administration's lack of engagement in the Israeli-Palestinian dispute. The White House, critics said, rightly sought to prevent North Korea and Iran from joining the nuclear club but seemed incapable of working imaginatively and multilaterally to make it happen. In Europe, Bush continued to be depicted as a gun-slinging cowboy whose aggressive policies threatened world peace.

The bill for the Iraq war now exceeded $1 billion per week. In March 2005, the U.S. war dead reached 1,500; in December 2006, it reached 3,000; in September 2008, it topped 4,100. Meanwhile by mid-2006, estimates of Iraqi civilian deaths since the invasion ranged from 60,000 to 655,000. These Iraqi casualties resulted from insurgent suicide attacks, U.S. bombing of suspected insurgent hideouts, and increased sectarian violence between Sunnis and Shi'ites.

The Bush administration denied that Iraq had degenerated into civil war or that the struggle had become a Vietnam-like quagmire, but it seemed uncertain how to end the fighting. Far from reducing the terrorist threat, the Iraq invasion seemed to have increased it, as the Al Qaeda presence in the United States (nonexistent before the war) became pronounced.

In Congress and the press, calls for withdrawal from Iraq multiplied, but skeptics cautioned it could make things worse, triggering sectarian bloodshed and a collapse of the Baghdad government. The power and regional influence of neighboring Iran would increase, and U.S. credibility would be undermined throughout the Middle East. Some commentators instead called for a major increase of U.S. forces in Iraq. The 2006 midterm election was partly a referendum on the war, and the voters were clear: 55 percent voted for Democratic candidates, and the party seized control of both houses of Congress.

AMERICANS IN THE FIRST DECADE OF THE NEW MILLENNIUM

At the beginning of the twenty-first century, the United States is a nation of extraordinary diversity. Immigration reform in the mid-1960s opened U.S. borders to people from a wider variety of nations than previously. New technologies—the Internet and cable and satellite television—replaced mass markets with niche markets. Everything from television shows to cosmetics to cars could be targeted toward specific groups defined by age, ethnicity, class, gender, or lifestyle choices. These changes helped to make Americans' understandings of identity more fluid and complex.

Race and Ethnicity in Recent America

In the 2000 U.S. government census, for the first time Americans could identify themselves as belonging to more than one race. The change acknowledged the growing number of Americans born to parents of different racial backgrounds. Critics, however, worried that, because census data are used to gather information about social conditions to allocate resources, the new multiracial option would reduce the clout of minority groups. Thus, the federal government counted those who identified both as white and as a racial or ethnic minority as belonging to the minority group. Consequently, the official population of some groups increased. Others rejected racial and ethnic categories: 20 million people identified themselves simply as American.

On October 17, 2006, the United States passed the 300 million population mark (100 million in 1915 and 200 million in 1967). During the 1990s, the population of people of color grew twelve times as fast as the white population, fueled by immigration and birth rates. In 2003 Hispanic Americans passed African Americans to become the second largest ethnic or racial group (after non-Hispanic whites) (see Figure 33.1). Immigration from Asia also remained high, and in 2006, 5 percent of the U.S. population was Asian or Asian American.

These rapid demographic changes have altered the face of the United States. At a Dairy Queen in the far southern suburbs of Atlanta, teenage children of Indian and

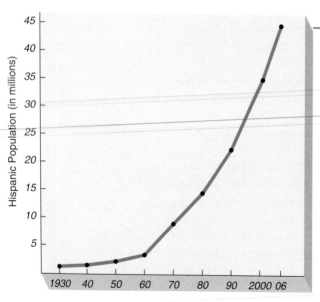

Figure 33.1   The Growth of the U.S. Hispanic Population
The Hispanic category combines people from a wide variety of national origins or ancestries—including all the nations of Central and South America, Mexico, Cuba, Puerto Rico, the Dominican Republic, and Spain—as well as those who identify as Californio, Tejano, Nuevo Mexicano, and Mestizo.   (*Source:* Adapted from the U.S. Department of Commerce, Economics and Statistics Information, Bureau of the Census, 1993 report "We, the American . . . Hispanics"; also recent census bureau figures for the Hispanic population)

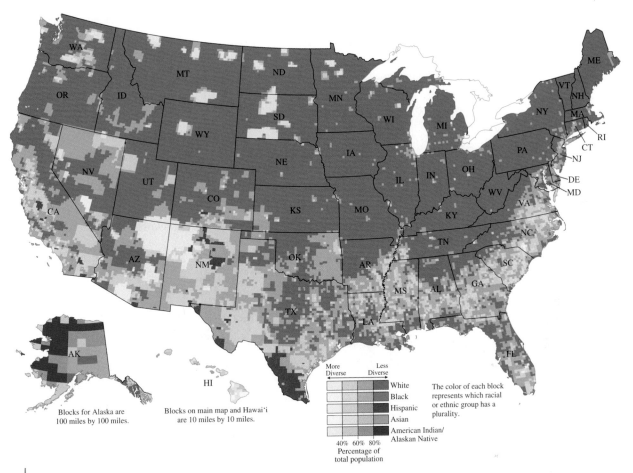

Map 33.2   Mapping the United States's Diversity

Aggregate figures (more than 12 percent of the U.S. population was African American and about 4 percent Asian American in 2000, for example) convey the United States's ethnic and racial diversity. However, as this map shows, members of racial and ethnic groups are not distributed evenly throughout the nation.   (*Source:* Adapted from the *New York Times* National Edition, April 1, 2001, "Portrait of a Nation," p. 18. Copyright © 2001 by The New York Times Co. Reprinted with permission.)

Pakistani immigrants serve Blizzards. In the small town of Ligonier, Indiana, the formerly empty main street now boasts three Mexican restaurants; Mexican immigrants cross paths with the newest immigrants, Yemenis, some in traditional dress, and with Amish families in horse-drawn buggies.

American popular culture embraced this new multiethnic population. Hispanic Americans' buying power exceeded $798 billion in 2006, and average income for Asian American households topped all other ethnic groups. But audiences also crossed racial and ethnic lines. Golfer Tiger Woods became a symbol of this new hybrid, multiethnic nation: of African, European, Native American, Thai, and Chinese descent, he calls himself Cablinasian (CAucasian-BLack-INdian-ASIAN).

The Changing American Family

Americans were divided over the meaning of changing family structure (see Figure 33.4). The median age at marriage continued to rise, reaching 27.1 for men and 25.8 for

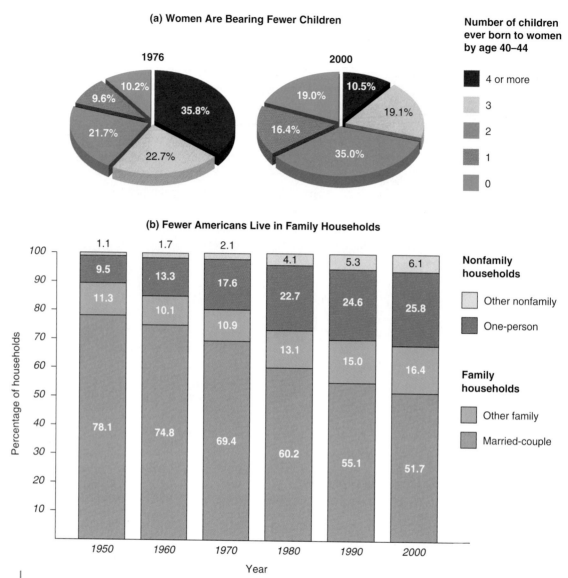

Figure 33.4   The Changing American Family

American households became smaller in the latter part of the twentieth century, as more people lived alone and women had, on average, fewer children.   (*Source:* Adapted from U.S. Bureau of the Census, http://www.census.gov/prod/2002pubs/censr-4.pdf and http://www.census.gov/population/pop-profile/2000/chap04.pdf.)

women in 2006. In 2006, when households composed of married couples slipped below 50 percent for the first time, unmarried, opposite-sex partners were about 5 percent of households, and same-sex couples accounted for just under 1 percent. One-third of female-partner households and one-fifth of male-partner households had children, and in 2002 the American Academy of Pediatrics endorsed adoption by gay couples. A vocal antigay movement coexisted with support for the legal equality of gay, lesbian, transgendered, and bisexual Americans. Although many states and corporations extended domestic-partner benefits to gay couples, the federal Defense of Marriage Act, passed in 1996, defined marriage only as a union between one man and one woman.

Early in the twenty-first century, one-third of all children and more than two-thirds of African American children were born to unmarried women. In the majority of married-couple families with children under eighteen, both parents held jobs. Although almost one-third of families with children had only one parent present—usually the mother—children also lived in blended families created by second marriages. For couples marrying in the mid-1990s, the woman's educational level was the clearest predictor of divorce: if the woman graduated from a four-year college, the couple had a 25 percent likelihood of divorce; if she had not, the rate jumped to 50 percent.

In 2006 the leading edge of the baby-boom generation turned sixty. As life expectancy increases, the growing number of elderly Americans will put enormous pressure on the nation's healthcare system and family structure and strain the Social Security and Medicare systems.

More than 65 percent of American adults are now overweight or obese—conditions linked to hypertension, cardiovascular disease, and diabetes. In 1995 no state had an adult obesity rate that hit 20 percent. By 2005, only four states were under that 20 percent marker. Cigarette smoking continues to slowly decline. About one-fifth of U.S. adults smoked in 2005, down from about one-third of adults in 1980. Approximately 440,000 people die annually from smoking-related illnesses, and medical costs and lost productivity total about $157 billion a year. Local governments have increasingly banned smoking in public spaces.

Medicine, Science, and Religion

Rapid advances in biogenetics offer great new possibilities and raise ethical conundrums. During in vitro fertilizations—in which sperm and egg combine in a sterile dish and the fertilized egg or eggs are then transferred to the uterus—five- or six-cell blastocytes are formed. These blastocytes contain stem cells, unspecialized cells that can be induced to become cells with specialized functions. For example, stem cells might become insulin-producing cells of the pancreas, and thus a cure for diabetes.

President Bush in 2001 called embryonic stem cell research "the leading edge of a series of moral hazards," because extracting stem cells destroys the blastocyte's "potential for life," and limited federally funded research to the existing seventy-eight stem cell lines, most of which proved not viable for research. In 2006 he vetoed a bipartisan congressional bill that expanded the number of stem cell lines available for federally funded research. Often treated as a conflict between religion and science, stem cell research is supported by most Americans, who believe the moral good of curing diseases outweighs preserving the potential life of blastocytes.

Still, many Americans see a conflict between religious belief and scientific study. Fundamentalist Christians sought to prevent the teaching of evolution in the nation's science classes or to introduce parallel instruction of biblical creationism or intelligent design, which hold that an intelligent creator is behind the development

of life on earth. The percentage of Americans who accept scientific evidence for evolution is lower than that in any other major nation except Turkey.

Century of Change

The twentieth century witnessed momentous changes, some bringing enormous benefits, others threatening the existence of the human species. Research in the physical and biological sciences provided insight into the structure of matter and the universe. Technology—the application of science—made startling advances that benefited Americans in nearly every aspect of life.

Consequently, Americans at the start of the new century were more connected to other people worldwide than ever before. This was perhaps the most powerful result of globalization. The world had shrunk to the size of an airplane ticket. In 1955, 51 million people a year traveled by plane. By the turn of the century, 1.6 billion were airborne annually, and 530 million—about 1.5 million each day—crossed international borders. This permeability of national boundaries brought many benefits, as did the integration of markets and the global spread of information that occurred with it.

Globalization and World Health

On the flip side, the rapid increase in international air travel was a potent force for the spread of global disease, as flying enabled people to reach the other side of the world in less time than the incubation period for many ailments. In early 2003, a respiratory illness known as severe acute respiratory syndrome (SARS) emerged in China and threatened to spread across the globe. Thirteen labs in ten countries worked to map the genome, followed by efforts to devise a diagnostic test for it. SARS did not develop into a worldwide epidemic, but health authorities recognized that international cooperation would be essential to combat the health threats intensified by globalization.

In 2003 the World Health Organization (WHO) estimated that nearly one-quarter of the global burden of disease and injury was related to environmental disruption and decline. For example, some 90 percent of diarrheal diseases (such as cholera), which were killing 3 million people a year, resulted from contaminated water. WHO also noted that in the final two decades of the twentieth century, more than thirty infectious diseases were identified in humans for the first time—including AIDS, Ebola virus, hantavirus, and hepatitis C and E. Environmentalists insisted that the growing global interaction was having a deleterious impact on the ecosystem through climate change, ozone depletion, hazardous waste, and damage to fisheries.

Confronting Terrorism

In diplomatic terms, the 9/11 attacks brought home what Americans had previously only dimly perceived: that globalization shrunk the natural buffers that distance and two oceans provided the United States. Al Qaeda used the increasingly open, globalized world to give itself new power and reach. It had shown that small terrorist cells could become transnational threats without a state sponsor or home base. According to U.S. intelligence, Al Qaeda operated in more than ninety countries.

The Global AIDS Epidemic

AIDS, first reported in the United States in 1981, has become a global epidemic. Researchers now believe that the first infection with HIV, the human immunodeficiency virus that causes AIDS, may have appeared in West Africa around 1930. HIV/AIDS spread rapidly in the late 1970s, partly as a byproduct of globalization. Increased international travel allowed for sexual transmission of HIV between populations; the international heroin trade stimulated intravenous drug use, another means of transmission; and the international circulation of blood for medical transfusions also contributed to the virus's spread. In 2003 the World Health Organization estimated that 58 million people worldwide were living with HIV/AIDS and 23 million had died from the disease.

Globally, AIDS claims 350 lives per hour, and though altered behavior and new drug therapies have slowed the disease's progress in North America and western Europe, infection and death rates continue to escalate in sub-Saharan Africa, Thailand, eastern Europe and the former Soviet Union, and Latin America, especially the Caribbean. In the African nation of Malawi, one in six adults is HIV-positive, and the nation expects to lose almost one-quarter of its work force to AIDS in the next decade.

U.S. worries about the global spread of AIDS are not solely humanitarian. In 2000 the U.S. National Intelligence Council concluded that "these diseases will endanger U.S. citizens at home and abroad, threaten U.S. armed forces deployed overseas, and exacerbate social and political instability in key countries and regions in which the United States has significant interests." In nations already facing shortages of food and clean water and rife with conflict, AIDS has further undermined government ability to cope with crisis, triggering political instability.

In 2002 U.N. secretary general Kofi Annan estimated that between $7 billion and $10 billion are needed annually to combat the spread of AIDS and tuberculosis and malaria, which have reemerged as threats to world health. President Bush called for increases in U.S. AIDS spending internationally, but many believe the United States should do more. With globalization, diseases do not stop at borders. The links between Americans and the rest of the world cannot be denied.

Activists protest outside Parliament in Cape Town, South Africa, calling on South African president Thabo Mbeki to make the struggle against AIDS a national priority. An estimated 20 percent of South Africans between the ages of fifteen and forty-nine are HIV-positive.

(Benny Goo/AP Images)

903

How would one go about vanquishing such a foe? Was a decisive victory even possible? These remained open questions five years after the World Trade Center collapsed. Unchallenged militarily, the United States felt few constraints about intervening in Afghanistan and then Iraq. It continued to spend colossal sums on its military. (In 2006 the Pentagon spent more than $500 billion, or roughly $60 million per hour.) The United States had military commitments around the globe, from the Balkans and Iraq to Afghanistan and Korea (see Table 33.1).

TABLE 33.1   U.S. Military Personnel on Active Duty in Foreign Countries, 2005*

Region/Country[†]	Personnel	Region/Country[†]	Personnel
United States and Territories		**North Africa, Near East, and South Asia**	
Continental U.S.	894,921	Bahrain	1,482
Alaska	18,980	Diego Garcia	773
Hawai'i	33,816	Egypt	424
Guam	2,931	Iraq	207,000
Puerto Rico	211	Israel	43
		Oman	36
Europe		Pakistan	195
Belgium[‡]	1,388	Qatar	387
Bosnia and Herzegovina	261	Saudi Arabia	269
France[‡]	56	United Arab Emirates	72
Germany[‡]	66,000		
Greece[‡]	431	**Sub-Saharan Africa**	
Greenland[‡]	144	Kenya	32
Iceland[‡]	1,257	South Africa	33
Italy[‡]	11,428		
Macedonia	40	**Western Hemisphere**	
Netherlands[‡]	579	Brazil	39
Norway[‡]	74	Canada	145
Portugal[‡]	990	Chile	29
Russia	44	Colombia	96
Serbia (includes Kosovo)	1,909	Cuba (Guantanamo)	950
Spain[‡]	1,634	Honduras	416
Turkey[‡]	1,738	Peru	36
United Kingdom[‡]	10,536	Venezuela	21
East Asia and Pacific		Total foreign countries[†]	271,381
Australia	140	Ashore	247,341
China (includes Hong Kong)	71	Afloat	24,040
Japan	35,050	Total worldwide[†]	1,605,414
Korea, Rep. of	29,982	Ashore	1,249,616
Philippines	44	Afloat	128,398
Singapore	159		
Thailand	116		

*Only countries with 35 or more U.S. military personnel are listed.
[†]Includes all regions/countries, not simply those listed.
[‡]NATO countries.

Source: U.S. Department of Defense, Defense Manpower Data Center.

The Internet

"Google it"—the phrase, essentially unknown before the new century, had within its first years become a household expression. Google was the hugely popular Internet search engine that went from obscurity in the mid-1990s to responding almost instantly to 200 million queries daily from around the world—almost 40 percent of all Internet searches.

While widespread use of the Internet was a recent phenomenon, its history went back four decades. In the mid-1960s, the U.S. military's Advanced Research Projects Agency (ARPA) wanted a communications network for government and university researchers across the nation. In 1969 early portions of the experimental system, called ARPANET, went online at UCLA; the University of California, Santa Barbara; Stanford Research Institute; and the University of Utah. By 1971, twenty-three computers were connected, and the numbers reached nearly a thousand by 1984. Renamed the Internet, this system transmitted only words, but in 1990 computer scientists developed the World Wide Web to send graphic and multimedia information. Then in 1993 the first commercial browser for Web navigation hit the market, followed in 1994 and 1995 by two superior browsers: Netscape and Internet Explorer.

By 2003, there were almost half a billion Internet users worldwide, including 140 million Americans. Thanks to technological advances and to new forms of broadband access with high-speed connections, users could send and receive e-mail, join online discussion groups, read newspapers, book vacations, download movies and music, shop, and even do their banking—all through a small computer at home. For Americans in the new globally connected millennium, the Internet was a fitting legacy of the twentieth century.

Election of 2008

On many levels, the 2008 election proved historic. During primary season, it looked like Americans might get their first female presidential party nominee when New York Senator and former First Lady Hillary Rodham Clinton made a strong showing for the Democrats. While she fought until the end of the primaries in June 2008, newcomer and little-known Illinois Senator Barrack Obama garnered more of the necessary delegates and advanced to the general election, making him the first African American presidential candidate from either party. He selected popular Delaware Senator Joseph Biden as his running mate. The Republicans made history, too, nominating long-time Arizona Senator and Vietnam veteran and POW John McCain, who, at age 72, would have become the nation's oldest elected president if he should win, and his running mate, Alaska Governor Sarah Palin, the country's first woman vice president.

The nation's economic turmoil soon surpassed the War in Iraq as the number one issue. Until September, McCain was leading in the polls, but with one Wall Street firm after another in trouble, the stock market tumbling, a banking and credit crisis looming, unemployment increasing, and housing foreclosures at record numbers, Americans feared an impending depression worse than the Great Depression of the 1930s. Two missteps by McCain—telling reporters that "the fundamentals of the nation's economy are strong" and

Newly elected President of the United States, Barack Obama, and Vice President-Elect, Joe Biden.
(© Jason Reed/Reuters/Corbis)

promising to put his campaign on hold until a $700 billion bailout plan could be approved—made many question his leadership. That, combined with Palin's poor showing in several television interviews and incumbent president George Bush's record low approval rating of 25%, undermined McCain's candidacy. Obama, meanwhile, merged his skills as a community organizer with the Internet age to marshal support and win young voters. He turned away from public financing to build a massive private campaign fund of over $600 million, which enabled him to run a half-hour infomercial during the World Series, and he convinced many middle and working class voters that McCain was out of touch with their economic anxieties. Record numbers of voters (roughly 125 million or 61.7%*) turned out to elect Barack Obama with 365 electoral votes to McCain's 173. The popular vote totals were 66,882,230 (53%) for Obama and 58,343,671 (46%) for McCain. Obama would take his oath of office in January 2009 on the Capitol steps that were installed by African slaves over 200 years ago. But the significance of his election went beyond race: along with being America's first African American president, Obama is also the first post-Vietnam generation president. At age 47, he was too young to have served there, and his election makes military service in that war unlikely to be a necessary credential for future presidential candidates.

Summary

The 1990s were good times for most Americans. A digitized revolution in communications and information generated prosperity and transformed life in the United States and worldwide. The longest economic expansion in U.S. history—from 1991 to 2001—meant that most Americans who wanted jobs had them, that the stock market boomed, that the nation had a budget surplus, and that more Americans owned homes. And with no other formidable rival, the United States stood as the world's lone superpower.

Yet, unsettling events troubled the nation. Ethnic conflicts in the Balkans, the Middle East, Central Asia, and Africa crowded the international agenda, as did human rights and the environment. At home, violence—the 1995 domestic terrorist attack in Oklahoma City and a rash of school shootings—captured headlines, even as the crime rate dropped. And scandal further undermined Americans' faith in their government, as President Bill Clinton was caught lying about having a sexual relationship with an intern, and later the House of Representatives voted to impeach him.

Minutes before midnight on December 31, 1999, President Clinton had called on Americans not to fear the future, but to "welcome it, create it, and embrace it." The challenges ahead would include the contested presidential election in 2000 that was decided by the Supreme Court in a partisan 5-to-4 vote, and in 2001 the end of the ten-year economic expansion.

Then, on September 11, 2001, radical Islamic terrorists attacked the World Trade Center and the Pentagon, killing thousands. The new president, George W. Bush,

---

* While the number of voters broke records this year, the percentage of eligible voters did not. The record was set in 1960, when 67% of voters cast their ballots.

declared a war on terrorism. While U.S. forces went after targets in Afghanistan, Congress created the Department of Homeland Security and passed the PATRIOT Act, expanding the federal government's surveillance powers. In March 2003, Bush initiated a war in Iraq, not expecting an insurgency by disaffected Iraqis against U.S. occupying forces and sectarian violence between Sunnis and Shi'ites. To counter a troubled economy, Bush pushed through tax cuts each of his first three years in office.

The world that Americans found in the first years of the twenty-first century was different from the one they imagined for the new millennium. The horror of the September 11 terror attacks made people declare that life would never be the same. But, their resilience saw them through, as they continued to struggle over the nation's future with the passion and commitment that keeps democracy alive.

Chapter Review

SOCIAL STRAINS AND NEW POLITICAL DIRECTIONS

What undermined Bill Clinton's first presidency?

As a "New Democrat" or centrist, Bill Clinton faced members of his own party who found some of his policies—such as his emphasis on private sector economic development—too conservative. Worse, from the start, a new breed of conservative Republicans challenged many of Clinton's campaign goals, and ultimately took control of both houses of Congress after the mid-term elections in 1994. This group successfully blocked Clinton's attempts at nationalized healthcare and ending the ban on gays in the military. These increasing partisan roadblocks led the beleaguered president to make compromises that pushed the nation further to the right—most notably, signing the 1996 Personal Responsibility and Work Opportunity Act (also known as "Welfare Reform") which limited federal assistance for the needy to two years, and the Telecommunications Act, which allowed greater concentration of media ownership in fewer hands.

"THE NEW ECONOMY" AND GLOBALIZATION

What concerns did critics raise about globalization?

The so-called "age of globalization" that emerged in the late 1990s was characterized by greater worldwide integration of markets, finance and technology. Labor unions feared losing jobs to less expensive overseas production, while critics argued that globalization widened the gap between rich and poor nations. Environmentalists charged that globalization resulted in greater pollution of developing countries, and others feared the power of multinational corporations over traditional cultures. Anti-global protests targeted McDonalds as symbolizing the creation of a homogeneous global culture, and demonstrations turned violent at World Trade Organization meetings in 1999 and those of the International Monetary Fund in 2001.

PARADOXES OF PROSPERITY

Why was the presidential election in 2000 so hotly contested?

While vice president Al Gore narrowly won the popular vote, in the end, it all came down to Florida. Republican George W. Bush had a slight lead there, which, by state law, required a recount. Because of a flawed paper ballot, tens of thousands of African American votes went uncounted, and Jewish voters in Palm Beach County accidentally voted for anti-Semitic candidate Pat Buchanan. After thirty-six days with no president and legal challenges pending, the Supreme Court voted 5 to 4 along partisan lines to give the state's 25 electoral votes—and thereby the election—to George W. Bush. Some people also felt that third party candidate Ralph Nader drew support from left-liberal voters who might have voted for Gore.

SEPTEMBER II AND THE WAR ON TERRORISM

How did the events of Sept. II change America's relationship to the world?

The terrorist attacks in which hijackers forced two planes to deliberately crash into each of the twin World Trade Center towers claimed more than 3000 American lives. Another plane targeted the Pentagon and a fourth plane crashed in rural Pennsylvania when passengers attempted to wrest control of it away from hijackers. Initially, the world community united in support of the United States. But within a year, as President Bush took a hard line in the battle against terrorism that dictated countries were either with the US or against it, he began to alienate former allies. International relations further soured when he hinted he might strike Saddam Hussein's Iraq or deal forcefully with North Korea or Iran.

WAR AND OCCUPATION IN IRAQ

What challenges did the War in Iraq pose?

The U.S. and Britain moved forward (with some support from a few other countries) in March 2003 with an attack on Iraq, claiming that the country harbored biological and chemical weapons of mass destruction (WMD) and that— despite intelligence reports to the contrary—it provided refuge for Al Qaeda terrorists. Other countries and the United Nations felt diplomacy and weapons inspections were working and wanted to hold off on military action. While U.S. and British forces won the early military battle within a few months, they did not anticipate the insurgency and anti-Western ambushes it would inspire among Iraqis on the ground. Five years later, the war cost $1 billion a week, with no end in sight. Bush also faced sharp international criticism for Iraq and the US military's abuse of war prisoners at Abu Ghraib.

AMERICANS IN THE FIRST DECADE OF THE NEW MILLENNIUM

What demographic changes are Americans beginning to face in the 21st century?

As the American population reached the 300 million mark in 2006, the country was more racially and ethnically diverse than ever. The population of people of color grew 12 times faster than that of whites. Family structure has become increasingly varied, with households composed of arried couples representing less than 50% of the population, and one third of all children are born to single women. The country also faces an aging population, as the leading edge of the baby boom generation turned 60 in 2006. That, combined with greater life expectancy, presents new concerns of healthcare and additional family pressures. Meanwhile, debates about medical technology and balancing science and religion—particularly over the question of stem cell research—continues to divide the nation.

SUGGESTIONS FOR FURTHER READING

Daniel Benjamin and Steven Simon, *The Sacred Age of Terror* (2002)

Barbara Ehrenreich, *Nickled and Dimed: On (Not) Getting by in America* (2002)

David Halberstam, *War in a Time of Peace: Bush, Clinton, and the Generals* (2001)

John F. Harris, *The Survivor: Bill Clinton in the White House* (2005)

Jennifer L. Hochschild, *Facing up to the American Dream: Race, Class, and the Soul of the Nation* (1995)

James Mann, *Rise of the Vulcans: The History of Bush's War Cabinet* (2004)

Alejandro Portes and Reuben G. Rumbaut, *Immigrant America: A Portrait,* 3d ed. (2006)

Thomas E. Ricks, *Fiasco: The American Military Adventure in Iraq* (2006)

Joseph E. Stiglitz, *Globalization and Its Discontents* (2002)

For a more extensive list for further reading, go to college.cengage.com/ pic/norton8e.

DECLARATION OF INDEPENDENCE
IN CONGRESS, JULY 4, 1776

When, in the course of human events, it becomes necessary for one people to dissolve the political bonds which have connected them with another, and to assume, among the powers of the earth, the separate and equal station to which the laws of nature and of nature's God entitle them, a decent respect to the opinions of mankind requires that they should declare the causes which impel them to the separation.

We hold these truths to be self-evident: That all men are created equal; that they are endowed by their Creator with certain unalienable rights; that among these are life, liberty, and the pursuit of happiness; that, to secure these rights, governments are instituted among men, deriving their just powers from the consent of the governed; that whenever any form of government becomes destructive of these ends, it is the right of the people to alter or to abolish it, and to institute new government, laying its foundation on such principles, and organizing its powers in such form, as to them shall seem most likely to effect their safety and happiness. Prudence, indeed, will dictate that governments long established should not be changed for light and transient causes; and accordingly all experience hath shown that mankind are more disposed to suffer, while evils are sufferable, than to right themselves by abolishing the forms to which they are accustomed. But when a long train of abuses and usurpations, pursuing invariably the same object, evinces a design to reduce them under absolute despotism, it is their right, it is their duty, to throw off such government, and to provide new guards for their future security. Such has been the patient sufferance of these colonies; and such is now the necessity which constrains them to alter their former systems of government. The history of the present King of Great Britain is a history of repeated injuries and usurpations, all having in direct object the establishment of an absolute tyranny over these states. To prove this, let facts be submitted to a candid world.

He has refused his assent to laws, the most wholesome and necessary for the public good.

He has forbidden his governors to pass laws of immediate and pressing importance, unless suspended in their operation till his assent should be obtained; and, when so suspended, he has utterly neglected to attend to them.

He has refused to pass other laws for the accommodation of large districts of people, unless those people would relinquish the right of representation in the legislature, a right inestimable to them, and formidable to tyrants only.

He has called together legislative bodies at places unusual, uncomfortable, and distant from the depository of their public records, for the sole purpose of fatiguing them into compliance with his measures.

He has dissolved representative houses repeatedly, for opposing, with manly firmness, his invasions on the rights of the people.

He has refused for a long time, after such dissolutions, to cause others to be elected; whereby the legislative powers, incapable of annihilation, have returned to the people at large for their exercise; the state remaining, in the mean time, exposed to all the dangers of invasions from without and convulsions within.

He has endeavored to prevent the population of these states; for that purpose obstructing the laws for naturalization of foreigners; refusing to pass others to encourage their migration hither, and raising the conditions of new appropriations of lands.

He has obstructed the administration of justice, by refusing his assent to laws for establishing judiciary powers.

He has made judges dependent on his will alone, for the tenure of their offices, and the amount and payment of their salaries.

He has erected a multitude of new offices, and sent hither swarms of officers to harass our people and eat out their substance.

He has kept among us, in times of peace, standing armies, without the consent of our legislatures.

He has affected to render the military independent of, and superior to, the civil power.

He has combined with others to subject us to a jurisdiction foreign to our constitution, and unacknowledged by our laws, giving his assent to their acts of pretended legislation:

For quartering large bodies of armed troops among us;

For protecting them, by a mock trial, from punishment for any murders which they should commit on the inhabitants of these states;

For cutting off our trade with all parts of the world;

For imposing taxes on us without our consent;

For depriving us, in many cases, of the benefits of trial by jury;

For transporting us beyond seas, to be tried for pretended offenses;

For abolishing the free system of English laws in a neighboring province, establishing therein an arbitrary government, and enlarging its boundaries, so as to render it at once an example and fit instrument for introducing the same absolute rule into these colonies;

For taking away our charters, abolishing our most valuable laws, and altering fundamentally the forms of our governments;

For suspending our own legislatures, and declaring themselves invested with power to legislate for us in all cases whatsoever.

He has abdicated government here, by declaring us out of his protection and waging war against us.

He has plundered our seas, ravaged our coasts, burned our towns, and destroyed the lives of our people.

He is at this time transporting large armies of foreign mercenaries to complete the works of death, desolation, and tyranny already begun with circumstances of cruelty and perfidy scarcely paralleled in the most barbarous ages, and totally unworthy the head of a civilized nation.

He has constrained our fellow-citizens, taken captive on the high seas, to bear arms against their country, to become the executioners of their friends and brethren, or to fall themselves by their hands.

He has excited domestic insurrection among us, and has endeavored to bring on the inhabitants of our frontiers the merciless Indian savages, whose known rule of warfare is an undistinguished destruction of all ages, sexes, and conditions.

In every stage of these oppressions we have petitioned for redress in the most humble terms; our repeated petitions have been answered only by repeated injury. A prince, whose character is thus marked by every act which may define a tyrant, is unfit to be the ruler of a free people.

Nor have we been wanting in our attentions to our British brethren. We have warned them, from time to time, of attempts by their legislature to extend an unwarrantable jurisdiction over us. We have reminded them of the circumstances of our emigration and settlement here. We have appealed to their native justice and magnanimity; and we have conjured them, by the ties of our common kindred, to disavow these usurpations, which would inevitably interrupt our connections and correspondence. They, too, have been deaf to the voice of justice and of consanguinity. We must, therefore, acquiesce in the necessity which denounces our separation, and hold them, as we hold the rest of mankind, enemies in war, in peace friends.

We, therefore, the representatives of the United States of America, in General Congress assembled, appealing to the Supreme Judge of the world for the rectitude of our intentions, do, in the name and by the authority of the good people of these colonies, solemnly publish and declare, that these United Colonies are, and of right ought to be, FREE AND INDEPENDENT STATES; that they are absolved from all allegiance to the British crown, and that all political connection between them and the state of Great Britain is, and ought to be, totally dissolved; and that, as free and independent states, they have full power to levy war, conclude peace, contract alliances, establish commerce, and do all other acts and things which independent states may of right do. And for the support of this declaration, with a firm reliance on the protection of Divine Providence, we mutually pledge to each other our lives, our fortunes, and our sacred honor.

ARTICLES OF CONFEDERATION

(The text of the Articles of Confederation can be found at cengage.com/ history/norton/peoplenationbrief8e)

CONSTITUTION OF THE UNITED STATES OF AMERICA AND AMENDMENTS*

Preamble

We the people of the United States, in order to form a more perfect union, establish justice, insure domestic tranquillity, provide for the common defense, promote the general welfare, and secure the blessings of liberty to ourselves and our posterity, do ordain and establish this Constitution for the United States of America.

Article I

Section 1 All legislative powers herein granted shall be vested in a Congress of the United States, which shall consist of a Senate and a House of Representatives.

---

* Passages no longer in effect are printed in italic type.

Section 2 The House of Representatives shall be composed of members chosen every second year by the people of the several States, and the electors in each State shall have the qualifications requisite for electors of the most numerous branch of the State Legislature.

No person shall be a Representative who shall not have attained to the age of twenty-five years, and been seven years a citizen of the United States, and who shall not, when elected, be an inhabitant of that State in which he shall be chosen.

Representatives and direct taxes shall be apportioned among the several States which may be included within this Union, according to their respective numbers, *which shall be determined by adding to the whole number of free persons, including those bound to service for a term of years and excluding Indians not taxed, three-fifths of all other persons.* The actual enumeration shall be made within three years after the first meeting of the Congress of the United States, and within every subsequent term of ten years, in such manner as they shall by law direct. The number of Representatives shall not exceed one for every thirty thousand, but each State shall have at least one Representative; *and until such enumeration shall be made, the State of New Hampshire shall be entitled to choose three, Massachusetts eight, Rhode Island and Providence Plantations one, Connecticut five, New York six, New Jersey four, Pennsylvania eight, Delaware one, Maryland six, Virginia ten, North Carolina five, South Carolina five, and Georgia three.*

When vacancies happen in the representation from any State, the Executive authority thereof shall issue writs of election to fill such vacancies.

The House of Representatives shall choose their Speaker and other officers; and shall have the sole power of impeachment.

Section 3 The Senate of the United States shall be composed of two Senators from each State, *chosen by the legislature thereof,* for six years; and each Senator shall have one vote.

Immediately after they shall be assembled in consequence of the first election, they shall be divided as equally as may be into three classes. The seats of the Senators of the first class shall be vacated at the expiration of the second year, of the second class at the expiration of the fourth year, and of the third class at the expiration of the sixth year, so that one-third may be chosen every second year; *and if vacancies happen by resignation or otherwise, during the recess of the legislature of any State, the Executive thereof may make temporary appointments until the next meeting of the legislature, which shall then fill such vacancies.*

No person shall be a Senator who shall not have attained to the age of thirty years, and been nine years a citizen of the United States, and who shall not, when elected, be an inhabitant of that State for which he shall be chosen.

The Vice-President of the United States shall be President of the Senate, but shall have no vote, unless they be equally divided.

The Senate shall choose their other officers, and also a President *pro tempore,* in the absence of the Vice-President, or when he shall exercise the office of President of the United States.

The Senate shall have the sole power to try all impeachments. When sitting for that purpose, they shall be on oath or affirmation. When the President of the United States is tried, the Chief Justice shall preside: and no person shall be convicted without the concurrence of two-thirds of the members present.

Judgment in cases of impeachment shall not extend further than to removal from the office, and disqualification to hold and enjoy any office of honor, trust or profit under the United States: but the party convicted shall nevertheless be liable and subject to indictment, trial, judgment and punishment, according to law.

Section 4 The times, places and manner of holding elections for Senators and Representatives shall be prescribed in each State by the legislature thereof; but the Congress may at any time by law make or alter such regulations, except as to the places of choosing Senators.

The Congress shall assemble at least once in every year, and such meeting *shall be on the first Monday in December, unless they shall by law appoint a different day.*

Section 5 Each house shall be the judge of the elections, returns and qualifications of its own members, and a majority of each shall constitute a quorum to do business; but a smaller number may adjourn from day to day, and may be authorized to compel the attendance of absent members, in such manner, and under such penalties, as each house may provide.

Each house may determine the rules of its proceedings, punish its members for disorderly behavior, and with the concurrence of two-thirds, expel a member.

Each house shall keep a journal of its proceedings, and from time to time publish the same, excepting such parts as may in their judgment require secrecy; and the yeas and nays of the members of either house on any question shall, at the desire of one-fifth of those present, be entered on the journal.

Neither house, during the session of Congress, shall, without the consent of the other, adjourn for more than three days, nor to any other place than that in which the two houses shall be sitting.

Section 6 The Senators and Representatives shall receive a compensation for their services, to be ascertained by law and paid out of the treasury of the United States. They shall in all cases except treason, felony and breach of the peace, be privileged from arrest during their attendance at the session of their respective houses, and in going to and returning from the same; and for any speech or debate in either house, they shall not be questioned in any other place.

No Senator or Representative shall, during the time for which he was elected, be appointed to any civil office under the authority of the United States, which shall have been created, or the emoluments whereof shall have been increased, during such time; and no person holding any office under the United States shall be a member of either house during his continuance in office.

Section 7 All bills for raising revenue shall originate in the House of Representatives; but the Senate may propose or concur with amendments as on other bills.

Every bill which shall have passed the House of Representatives and the Senate, shall, before it become a law, be presented to the President of the United States; if he approve he shall sign it, but if not he shall return it with objections to that house in which it originated, who shall enter the objections at large on their journal, and proceed to reconsider it. If after such reconsideration two-thirds of that house shall agree to pass the bill, it shall be sent, together with the objections, to the other house, by which it shall likewise be reconsidered, and, if approved by two-thirds of that house, it shall become a law. But in all such cases the votes of both houses shall be determined by yeas and nays, and the names of the persons voting for and against the bill shall be entered on the journal of each house respectively. If any bill shall not be returned by the President within ten days (Sundays excepted) after it shall have been presented to him, the same shall be a law, in like manner as if he had signed it, unless the Congress by their adjournment prevent its return, in which case it shall not be a law.

Every order, resolution, or vote to which the concurrence of the Senate and House of Representatives may be necessary (except on a question of adjournment) shall be presented to the President of the United States; and before the same shall take effect, shall be approved by him, or being disapproved by him, shall be repassed by two-thirds of the Senate and House of Representatives, according to the rules and limitations prescribed in the case of a bill.

Section 8 The Congress shall have power

To lay and collect taxes, duties, imposts, and excises, to pay the debts and provide for the common defense and general welfare of the United States; but all duties, imposts and excises shall be uniform throughout the United States;

To borrow money on the credit of the United States;

To regulate commerce with foreign nations, and among the several States, and with the Indian tribes;

To establish an uniform rule of naturalization, and uniform laws on the subject of bankruptcies throughout the United States;

To coin money, regulate the value thereof, and of foreign coin, and fix the standard of weights and measures;

To provide for the punishment of counterfeiting the securities and current coin of the United States;

To establish post offices and post roads;

To promote the progress of science and useful arts by securing for limited times to authors and inventors the exclusive right to their respective writings and discoveries;

To constitute tribunals inferior to the Supreme Court;

To define and punish piracies and felonies committed on the high seas and offenses against the law of nations;

To declare war, grant letters of marque and reprisal, and make rules concerning captures on land and water;

To raise and support armies, but no appropriation of money to that use shall be for a longer term than two years;

To provide and maintain a navy;

To make rules for the government and regulation of the land and naval forces;

To provide for calling forth the militia to execute the laws of the Union, suppress insurrections, and repel invasions;

To provide for organizing, arming, and disciplining the militia, and for governing such part of them as may be employed in the service of the United States, reserving to the States respectively the appointment of the officers, and the authority of training the militia according to the discipline prescribed by Congress;

To exercise exclusive legislation in all cases whatsoever, over such district (not exceeding ten miles square) as may, by cession of particular States, and the acceptance of Congress, become the seat of government of the United States, and to exercise like authority over all places purchased by the consent of the legislature of the State, in which the same shall be, for erection of forts, magazines, arsenals, dockyards, and other needful buildings;—and

To make all laws which shall be necessary and proper for carrying into execution the foregoing powers, and all other powers vested by this Constitution in the government of the United States, or in any department or officer thereof.

Section 9 The migration or importation of such persons as any of the States now existing shall think proper to admit shall not be prohibited by the Congress prior to the year 1808; but a tax or duty may be imposed on such importation, not exceeding $10 for each person.

The privilege of the writ of habeas corpus shall not be suspended, unless when in cases of rebellion or invasion the public safety may require it.

No bill of attainder or ex post facto law shall be passed.

No capitation, or other direct, tax shall be laid, unless in proportion to the census or enumeration herein before directed to be taken.

No tax or duty shall be laid on articles exported from any State.

No preference shall be given by any regulation of commerce or revenue to the ports of one State over those of another; nor shall vessels bound to, or from, one State, be obliged to enter, clear, or pay duties in another.

No money shall be drawn from the treasury, but in consequence of appropriations made by law; and a regular statement and account of the receipts and expenditures of all public money shall be published from time to time.

No title of nobility shall be granted by the United States: and no person holding any office of profit or trust under them, shall, without the consent of the Congress, accept of any present, emolument, office, or title, of any kind whatever, from any king, prince, or foreign state.

Section 10 No State shall enter into any treaty, alliance, or confederation; grant letters of marque and reprisal; coin money; emit bills of credit; make anything but gold and silver coin a tender in payment of debts; pass any bill of attainder, ex post facto law, or law impairing the obligation of contracts, or grant any title of nobility.

No State shall, without the consent of Congress, lay any imposts or duties on imports or exports, except what may be absolutely necessary for executing its inspection laws: and the net produce of all duties and imposts, laid by any State on imports or exports, shall be for the use of the treasury of the United States; and all such laws shall be subject to the revision and control of the Congress.

No State shall, without the consent of Congress, lay any duty of tonnage, keep troops or ships of war in time of peace, enter into any agreement or compact with another State, or with a foreign power, or engage in war, unless actually invaded, or in such imminent danger as will not admit of delay.

Article II

Section 1 The executive power shall be vested in a President of the United States of America. He shall hold his office during the term of four years, and, together with the Vice-President, chosen for the same term, be elected as follows:

Each State shall appoint, in such manner as the legislature thereof may direct, a number of electors, equal to the whole number of Senators and Representatives to which the State may be entitled in the Congress; but no Senator or Representative, or person holding an office of trust or profit under the United States, shall be appointed an elector.

The electors shall meet in their respective States, and vote by ballot for two persons, of whom one at least shall not be an inhabitant of the same State with themselves. And they shall make a list of all the persons voted for, and of the number of votes for each; which list they shall sign and certify, and transmit sealed to the seat of government of the United States, directed to the President of the Senate. The President of the Senate shall, in the presence of the Senate and House of Representatives, open all the certificates, and the votes shall then be counted. The person having the greatest number of votes shall be the President, if such number be a majority of the whole number of electors appointed; and if there be more than one who have such majority, and have an equal number of votes, then the House of Representatives shall immediately choose by ballot one of them for President; and if no person have a majority, then from the five highest on the list said house shall in like manner choose the President. But in choosing the President the votes shall be taken by States, the representation from each State having one vote; a quorum for this purpose shall consist of a member or members from two-thirds of the States, and a majority of all the States shall be necessary to a choice. In every case, after the choice of the President, the person having the greatest number of votes of the electors shall be the Vice-President. But if there should remain two or more who have equal votes, the Senate shall choose from them by ballot the Vice-President.

The Congress may determine the time of choosing the electors and the day on which they shall give their votes; which day shall be the same throughout the United States.

No person except a natural-born citizen, *or a citizen of the United States at the time of the adoption of this Constitution,* shall be eligible to the office of President; neither shall any person be eligible to that office who shall not have attained to the age of thirty-five years, and been fourteen years a resident within the United States.

In cases of the removal of the President from office or of his death, resignation, or inability to discharge the powers and duties of the said office, the same shall devolve on the Vice-President, and the Congress may by law provide for the case of removal, death, resignation, or inability, both of the President and Vice-President, declaring what officer shall then act as President, and such officer shall act accordingly, until the disability be removed, or a President shall be elected.

The President shall, at stated times, receive for his services a compensation, which shall neither be increased nor diminished during the period for which he shall have been elected, and he shall not receive within that period any other emolument from the United States, or any of them.

Before he enter on the execution of his office, he shall take the following oath or affirmation:—"I do solemnly swear (or affirm) that I will faithfully execute the office of the President of the United States, and will to the best of my ability preserve, protect and defend the Constitution of the United States."

Section 2 The President shall be commander in chief of the army and navy of the United States, and of the militia of the several States, when called into the actual service of the United States; he may require the opinion, in writing, of the principal officer in each of the executive departments, upon any subject relating to the duties of their respective offices, and he shall have power to grant reprieves and pardons for offenses against the United States, except in cases of impeachment.

He shall have power, by and with the advice and consent of the Senate, to make treaties, provided two-thirds of the Senators present concur; and he shall nominate, and by and with the advice and consent of the Senate, shall appoint ambassadors, other public ministers and consuls, judges of the Supreme Court, and all other officers of the United States, whose appointments are not herein otherwise provided for, and which shall be established by law: but Congress may by law vest the appointment of such inferior officers, as they think proper, in the President alone, in the courts of law, or in the heads of departments.

The President shall have power to fill up all vacancies that may happen during the recess of the Senate, by granting commissions which shall expire at the end of their next session.

Section 3 He shall from time to time give to the Congress information of the state of the Union, and recommend to their consideration such measures as he shall judge necessary and expedient; he may, on extraordinary occasions, convene both houses, or either of them, and in case of disagreement between them, with respect to the time of adjournment, he may adjourn them to such time as he shall think proper; he shall receive ambassadors and other public ministers; he shall take care that the laws be faithfully executed, and shall commission all the officers of the United States.

Section 4 The President, Vice-President and all civil officers of the United States shall be removed from office on impeachment for, and on conviction of, treason, bribery, or other high crimes and misdemeanors.

Article III

Section 1 The judicial power of the United States shall be vested in one Supreme Court, and in such inferior courts as the Congress may from time to time ordain and establish. The judges, both of the Supreme and inferior courts, shall hold their offices during good behavior, and shall, at stated times, receive for their services a compensation which shall not be diminished during their continuance in office.

Section 2 The judicial power shall extend to all cases, in law and equity, arising under this Constitution, the laws of the United States, and treaties made, or which shall be made, under their authority;—to all cases affecting ambassadors, other public ministers and consuls;—to all cases of admiralty and maritime jurisdiction;—to controversies to which the United States shall be a party;—to controversies between two or more States;—*between a State and citizens of another State;*—between citizens of different States;—between citizens of the same State claiming lands under grants of different States, and between a State, or the citizens thereof, and foreign states, citizens or subjects.

In all cases affecting ambassadors, other public ministers and consuls, and those in which a State shall be party, the Supreme Court shall have original jurisdiction. In all the other cases before mentioned, the Supreme Court shall have appellate jurisdiction, both as to law and fact, with such exceptions, and under such regulations, as the Congress shall make.

The trial of all crimes, except in cases of impeachment, shall be by jury; and such trial shall be held in the State where said crimes shall have been committed; but when not committed within any State, the trial shall be at such place or places as the Congress may by law have directed.

Section 3 Treason against the United States shall consist only in levying war against them, or in adhering to their enemies, giving them aid and comfort. No person shall be convicted of treason unless on the testimony of two witnesses to the same overt act, or on confession in open court.

The Congress shall have power to declare the punishment of treason, but no attainder of treason shall work corruption of blood, or forfeiture except during the life of the person attainted.

Article IV

Section 1 Full faith and credit shall be given in each State to the public acts, records, and judicial proceedings of every other State. And the Congress may by general laws prescribe the manner in which such acts, records, and proceedings shall be proved, and the effect thereof.

Section 2 The citizens of each State shall be entitled to all privileges and immunities of citizens in the several States.

A person charged in any State with treason, felony, or other crime, who shall flee from justice, and be found in another State, shall on demand of the executive authority of the State from which he fled, be delivered up, to be removed to the State having jurisdiction of the crime.

No person held to service or labor in one State, under the laws thereof, escaping into another, shall, in consequence of any law or regulation therein, be discharged from such service or labor, but shall be delivered up on claim of the party to whom such service or labor may be due.

Section 3 New States may be admitted by the Congress into this Union; but no new State shall be formed or erected within the jurisdiction of any other State; nor any State be formed by the junction of two or more States, or parts of States, without the consent of the legislatures of the States concerned as well as of the Congress.

The Congress shall have power to dispose of and make all needful rules and regulations respecting the territory or other property belonging to the United States; and nothing in this Constitution shall be so construed as to prejudice any claims of the United States, or of any particular State.

Section 4 The United States shall guarantee to every State in this Union a republican form of government, and shall protect each of them against invasion; and on application of the legislature, or of the executive (when the legislature cannot be convened), against domestic violence.

Article V

The Congress, whenever two-thirds of both houses shall deem it necessary, shall propose amendments to this Constitution, or, on the application of the legislatures of two-thirds of the several States, shall call a convention for proposing amendments, which, in either case, shall be valid to all intents and purposes, as part of this Constitution, when ratified by the legislatures of three-fourths of the several States, or by conventions in three-fourths thereof, as the one or the other mode of ratification may be proposed by the Congress; provided *that no amendments which may be made prior to the year one thousand eight hundred and eight shall in any manner affect the first and fourth clauses in the ninth section of the first article;* and that no State, without its consent, shall be deprived of its equal suffrage in the Senate.

Article VI

All debts contracted and engagements entered into, before the adoption of this Constitution, shall be as valid against the United States under this Constitution, as under the Confederation.

This Constitution, and the laws of the United States which shall be made in pursuance thereof; and all treaties made, or which shall be made, under the authority of the United States, shall be the supreme law of the land; and the judges in every State shall be bound thereby, anything in the Constitution or laws of any State to the contrary notwithstanding.

The Senators and Representatives before mentioned, and the members of the several State legislatures, and all executive and judicial officers, both of the United States and of the several States, shall be bound by oath or affirmation to support this Constitution; but no religious test shall ever be required as a qualification to any office or public trust under the United States.

Article VII

The ratification of the conventions of nine States shall be sufficient for the establishment of this Constitution between the States so ratifying the same.

Done in Convention by the unanimous consent of the States present, the seventeenth day of September in the year of our Lord one thousand seven hundred and eighty-seven and of the Independence of the United States of America the twelfth. In witness whereof we have hereunto subscribed our names.

AMENDMENTS TO THE CONSTITUTION*

Amendment I

Congress shall make no law respecting an establishment of religion, or prohibiting the free exercise thereof; or abridging the freedom of speech, or of the press; or the right of the people peaceably to assemble, and to petition the government for a redress of grievances.

Amendment II

A well-regulated militia being necessary to the security of a free State, the right of the people to keep and bear arms shall not be infringed.

Amendment III

No soldier shall, in time of peace, be quartered in any house without the consent of the owner, nor in time of war, but in a manner to be prescribed by law.

Amendment IV

The right of the people to be secure in their persons, houses, papers, and effects, against unreasonable searches and seizures, shall not be violated, and no warrants shall issue but upon probable cause, supported by oath or affirmation, and particularly describing the place to be searched, and the persons or things to be seized.

---

*The first ten Amendments (the Bill of Rights) were adopted in 1791.

Amendment V

No person shall be held to answer for a capital, or otherwise infamous crime, unless on a presentment or indictment of a grand jury, except in cases arising in the land or naval forces, or in the militia, when in actual service in time of war or public danger; nor shall any person be subject for the same offense to be twice put in jeopardy of life or limb; nor shall be compelled in any criminal case to be a witness against himself, nor be deprived of life, liberty, or property, without due process of law; nor shall private property be taken for public use without just compensation.

Amendment VI

In all criminal prosecutions, the accused shall enjoy the right to a speedy and public trial, by an impartial jury of the State and district wherein the crime shall have been committed, which district shall have been previously ascertained by law, and to be informed of the nature and cause of the accusation; to be confronted with the witnesses against him; to have compulsory process for obtaining witnesses in his favor, and to have the assistance of counsel for his defense.

Amendment VII

In suits at common law, where the value in controversy shall exceed twenty dollars, the right of trial by jury shall be preserved, and no fact tried by a jury shall be otherwise reexamined in any court of the United States, than according to the rules of the common law.

Amendment VIII

Excessive bail shall not be required, nor excessive fines imposed, nor cruel and unusual punishments inflicted.

Amendment IX

The enumeration in the Constitution, of certain rights, shall not be construed to deny or disparage others retained by the people.

Amendment X

The powers not delegated to the United States by the Constitution, nor prohibited by it to the States, are reserved to the States respectively, or to the people.

Amendment XI

[Adopted 1798]

The judicial power of the United States shall not be construed to extend to any suit in law or equity, commenced or prosecuted against one of the United States by citizens of another State, or by citizens or subjects of any foreign state.

Amendment XII

[Adopted 1804]

The electors shall meet in their respective States, and vote by ballot for President and Vice-President, one of whom, at least, shall not be an inhabitant of the same State with themselves; they shall name in their ballots the person voted for as President, and in distinct ballots the person voted for as Vice-President, and they shall make distinct lists of all persons voted for as President, and of all persons voted for as Vice-President, and of the number of votes for each, which lists they shall sign and certify, and transmit sealed to the seat of government of the United States, directed to the President of the Senate;—the President of the Senate shall, in the presence of the Senate and House of Representatives, open all the certificates and the votes shall then be counted;—the person having the greatest number of votes for President shall be the President, if such number be a majority of the whole number of electors appointed; and if no person have such majority, then from the persons having the highest numbers not exceeding three on the list of those voted for as President, the House of Representatives shall choose immediately, by ballot, the President. But in choosing the President, the votes shall be taken by States, the representation from each State having one vote; a quorum for this purpose shall consist of a member or members from two-thirds of the States, and a majority of all the States shall be necessary to a choice. And if the House of Representatives shall not choose a President whenever the right of choice shall devolve upon them, before *the fourth day of March* next following, then the Vice-President shall act as President, as in the case of the death or other constitutional disability of the President.

The person having the greatest number of votes as Vice-President shall be the Vice-President, if such number be a majority of the whole number of electors appointed; and if no person have a majority, then from the two highest numbers on the list the Senate shall choose the Vice-President; a quorum for the purpose shall consist of two-thirds of the whole number of Senators, and a majority of the whole number shall be necessary to a choice. But no person constitutionally ineligible to the office of President shall be eligible to that of Vice-President of the United States.

Amendment XIII

[Adopted 1865]

Section 1 Neither slavery nor involuntary servitude, except as a punishment for crime whereof the party shall have been duly convicted, shall exist within the United States, or any place subject to their jurisdiction.

Section 2 Congress shall have power to enforce this article by appropriate legislation.

Amendment XIV

[Adopted 1868]

Section 1 All persons born or naturalized in the United States, and subject to the jurisdiction thereof, are citizens of the United States and of the State wherein they reside. No State shall make or enforce any law which shall abridge the privileges or immunities of citizens of the United States; nor shall any State deprive any person of life, liberty, or property, without due process of law; nor deny to any person within its jurisdiction the equal protection of the laws.

Section 2 Representatives shall be apportioned among the several States according to their respective numbers, counting the whole number of persons in each State, excluding Indians not taxed. But when the right to vote at any election for the choice of Electors for President and Vice-President of the United States, Representatives in Congress, the executive and judicial officers of a State, or the members of the legislature thereof, is denied to any of the male inhabitants of such State, being twenty-one years of age and citizens of the United States, or in any way abridged, except for participation in rebellion, or other crime, the basis of representation therein shall be reduced in the proportion which the number of such male citizens shall bear to the whole number of male citizens twenty-one years of age in such State.

Section 3 No person shall be a Senator or Representative in Congress, or Elector of President and Vice-President, or hold any office, civil or military, under the United States, or under any State, who, having previously taken an oath, as a member of Congress, or as an officer of the United States, or as a member of any State legislature, or as an executive or judicial officer of any State, to support the Constitution of the United States, shall have engaged in insurrection or rebellion against the same, or given aid or comfort to the enemies thereof. Congress may, by a vote of two-thirds of each house, remove such disability.

Section 4 The validity of the public debt of the United States, authorized by law, including debts incurred for payment of pensions and bounties for services in suppressing insurrection or rebellion, shall not be questioned. But neither the United States nor any State shall assume or pay any debt or obligation incurred in aid of insurrection or rebellion against the United States, or any claim for the loss of emancipation of any slave; but all such debts, obligations, and claims shall be held illegal and void.

Section 5 The Congress shall have power to enforce, by appropriate legislation, the provisions of this article.

Amendment XV

[Adopted 1870]

Section 1 The right of citizens of the United States to vote shall not be denied or abridged by the United States or by any State on account of race, color, or previous condition of servitude.

Section 2 The Congress shall have power to enforce this article by appropriate legislation.

Amendment XVI

[Adopted 1913]

The Congress shall have power to lay and collect taxes on incomes, from whatever source derived, without apportionment among the several States, and without regard to any census or enumeration.

Amendment XVII

[Adopted 1913]

Section 1 The Senate of the United States shall be composed of two Senators from each State, elected by the people thereof, for six years; and each Senator shall have one vote. The electors in each State shall have the qualifications requisite for electors of [voters for] the most numerous branch of the State legislatures.

Section 2 When vacancies happen in the representation of any State in the Senate, the executive authority of such State shall issue writs of election to fill such vacancies: Provided, that the Legislature of any State may empower the executive thereof to make temporary appointments until the people fill the vacancies by election as the Legislature may direct.

Section 3 This amendment shall not be so construed as to affect the election or term of any Senator chosen before it becomes valid as part of the Constitution.

Amendment XVIII

[Adopted 1919; Repealed 1933]

Section 1 After one year from the ratification of this article the manufacture, sale, or transportation of intoxicating liquors within, the importation thereof into, or the exportation thereof from the United States and all territory subject to the jurisdiction thereof, for beverage purposes, is hereby prohibited.

Section 2 The Congress and the several States shall have concurrent power to enforce this article by appropriate legislation.

Section 3 This article shall be inoperative unless it shall have been ratified as an amendment to the Constitution by the legislatures of the several States, as provided by the Constitution, within seven years from the date of the submission thereof to the States by the Congress.

Amendment XIX

[Adopted 1920]

Section 1 The right of citizens of the United States to vote shall not be denied or abridged by the United States or by any State on account of sex.

Section 2 The Congress shall have power to enforce this article by appropriate legislation.

Amendment XX

[Adopted 1933]

Section 1 The terms of the President and Vice-President shall end at noon on the 20th day of January, and the terms of Senators and Representatives at noon on the 3rd day of January, of the years in which such terms would have ended if this article had not been ratified; and the terms of their successors shall then begin.

Section 2 The Congress shall assemble at least once in every year, and such meeting shall begin at noon on the 3d day of January, unless they shall by law appoint a different day.

Section 3 If, at the time fixed for the beginning of the term of the President, the President-elect shall have died, the Vice-President–elect shall become President. If a President shall not have been chosen before the time fixed for the beginning of his term, or if the President-elect shall have failed to qualify, then the Vice-President–elect shall act as President until a President shall have qualified; and the Congress may by law provide for the case wherein neither a President-elect nor a Vice-President–elect shall have qualified, declaring who shall then act as President, or the manner in which one who is to act shall be selected, and such persons shall act accordingly until a President or Vice-President shall have qualified.

Section 4 The Congress may by law provide for the case of the death of any of the persons from whom the House of Representatives may choose a President whenever the right of choice shall have devolved upon them, and for the case of the death of any of the persons from whom the Senate may choose a Vice-President whenever the right of choice shall have devolved upon them.

Section 5 Sections 1 and 2 shall take effect on the 15th day of October following the ratification of this article.

Section 6 This article shall be inoperative unless it shall have been ratified as an amendment to the Constitution by the Legislatures of three-fourths of the several States within seven years from the date of its submission.

Amendment XXI
[Adopted 1933]

Section 1 The eighteenth article of amendment to the Constitution of the United States is hereby repealed.

Section 2 The transportation or importation into any State, Territory, or Possession of the United States for delivery or use therein of intoxicating liquors, in violation of the laws thereof, is hereby prohibited.

Section 3 This article shall be inoperative unless it shall have been ratified as an amendment to the Constitution by conventions in the several States, as provided in the Constitution, within seven years from the date of submission thereof to the States by the Congress.

Amendment XXII
[Adopted 1951]

Section 1 No person shall be elected to the office of President more than twice, and no person who has held the office of President, or acted as President, for more than two years of a term to which some other person was elected President shall be elected to the office of President more than once. But this article shall not apply to any person holding the office of President when this article was proposed by the Congress, and shall not prevent any person who may be holding the office of President, or acting as President, during the term within which this article becomes operative from holding the office of President or acting as President during the remainder of such term.

Section 2 This article shall be inoperative unless it shall have been ratified as an amendment to the Constitution by the legislatures of three-fourths of the several States within seven years from the date of its submission to the States by the Congress.

Amendment XXIII

[Adopted 1961]

Section 1 The District constituting the seat of Government of the United States shall appoint in such manner as the Congress may direct:

A number of electors of President and Vice-President equal to the whole number of Senators and Representatives in Congress to which the District would be entitled if it were a State, but in no event more than the least populous State; they shall be in addition to those appointed by the States, but they shall be considered for the purposes of the election of President and Vice-President, to be electors appointed by a State; and they shall meet in the District and perform such duties as provided by the twelfth article of amendment.

Section 2 The Congress shall have the power to enforce this article by appropriate legislation.

Amendment XXIV

[Adopted 1964]

Section 1 The right of citizens of the United States to vote in any primary or other election for President or Vice-President, for electors for President or Vice-President, or for Senator or Representative in Congress, shall not be denied or abridged by the United States or any State by reason of failure to pay any poll tax or other tax.

Section 2 The Congress shall have the power to enforce this article by appropriate legislation.

Amendment XXV

[Adopted 1967]

Section 1 In case of the removal of the President from office or of his death or resignation, the Vice-President shall become President.

Section 2 Whenever there is a vacancy in the office of the Vice-President, the President shall nominate a Vice-President who shall take office upon confirmation by a majority vote of both Houses of Congress.

Section 3 Whenever the President transmits to the President pro tempore of the Senate and the Speaker of the House of Representatives his written declaration that he is unable to discharge the powers and duties of his office, and until he transmits to them a written declaration to the contrary, such powers and duties shall be discharged by the Vice-President as Acting President.

Section 4 Whenever the Vice-President and a majority of either the principal officers of the executive departments or of such other body as Congress may by law provide, transmit to the President pro tempore of the Senate and the Speaker of the House of Representatives their written declaration that the President is unable to discharge the powers and duties of his office, the Vice-President shall immediately assume the powers and duties of the office as Acting President.

Thereafter, when the President transmits to the President pro tempore of the Senate and the Speaker of the House of Representatives his written declaration that no inability exists, he shall resume the powers and duties of his office unless the Vice-President and a majority of either the principal officers of the executive department[s] or of such other body as Congress may by law provide, transmit within four days to the President pro tempore of the Senate and the Speaker of the House of Representatives their written declaration that the President is unable to discharge the powers and duties of his office. Thereupon Congress shall decide the issue, assembling within forty-eight hours for that purpose if not in session. If the Congress, within twenty-one days after receipt of the latter written declaration, or, if Congress is not in session, within twenty-one days after Congress is required to assemble, determines by two-thirds vote of both Houses that the President is unable to discharge the powers and duties of his office, the Vice-President shall continue to discharge the same as Acting President; otherwise, the President shall resume the powers and duties of his office.

Amendment XXVI

[Adopted 1971]

Section 1 The right of citizens of the United States, who are eighteen years of age or older, to vote shall not be denied or abridged by the United States or by any State on account of age.

Section 2 The Congress shall have power to enforce this article by appropriate legislation.

Amendment XXVII

[Adopted 1992]

No law, varying the compensation for the services of the Senators and Representatives, shall take effect, until an election of Representatives shall have intervened.

Presidential Elections

Year	Number of States	Candidates	Parties	Popular Vote	% of Popular Vote	Electoral Vote	% Voter Participation[a]
1789	10	**George Washington**	No party designations			69	
		John Adams				34	
		Other candidates				35	
1792	15	**George Washington**	No party designations			132	
		John Adams				77	
		George Clinton				50	
		Other candidates				5	
1796	16	**John Adams**	Federalist			71	
		Thomas Jefferson	Democratic-Republican			68	
		Thomas Pinckney	Federalist			59	
		Aaron Burr	Democratic-Republican			30	
		Other candidates				48	
1800	16	**Thomas Jefferson**	Democratic-Republican			73	
		Aaron Burr	Democratic-Republican			73	
		John Adams	Federalist			65	
		Charles C. Pinckney	Federalist			64	
		John Jay	Federalist			1	
1804	17	**Thomas Jefferson**	Democratic-Republican			162	
		Charles C. Pinckney	Federalist			14	
1808	17	**James Madison**	Democratic-Republican			122	
		Charles C. Pinckney	Federalist			47	
		George Clinton	Democratic-Republican			6	
1812	18	**James Madison**	Democratic-Republican			128	
		DeWitt Clinton	Federalist			89	
1816	19	**James Monroe**	Democratic-Republican			183	
		Rufus King	Federalist			34	
1820	24	**James Monroe**	Democratic-Republican			231	
		John Quincy Adams	Independent Republican			1	

Presidential Elections (*continued*)

Year	Number of States	Candidates	Parties	Popular Vote	% of Popular Vote	Electoral Vote	% Voter Participation[a]
1824	24	**John Quincy Adams**	Democratic-Republican	108,740	30.5	84	26.9
		Andrew Jackson	Democratic-Republican	153,544	43.1	99	
		Henry Clay	Democratic-Republican	47,136	13.2	37	
		William H. Crawford	Democratic-Republican	46,618	13.1	41	
1828	24	**Andrew Jackson**	Democratic	647,286	56.0	178	57.6
		John Quincy Adams	National Republican	508,064	44.0	83	
1832	24	**Andrew Jackson**	Democratic	701,780	54.2	219	55.4
		Henry Clay	National Republican	484,205	37.4	49	
		Other candidates		107,988	8.0	18	
1836	26	**Martin Van Buren**	Democratic	764,176	50.8	170	57.8
		William H. Harrison	Whig	550,816	36.6	73	
		Hugh L. White	Whig	146,107	9.7	26	
1840	26	**William H. Harrison**	Whig	1,274,624	53.1	234	80.2
		Martin Van Buren	Democratic	1,127,781	46.9	60	
1844	26	**James K. Polk**	Democratic	1,338,464	49.6	170	78.9
		Henry Clay	Whig	1,300,097	48.1	105	
		James G. Birney	Liberty	62,300	2.3		
1848	30	**Zachary Taylor**	Whig	1,360,967	47.4	163	72.7
		Lewis Cass	Democratic	1,222,342	42.5	127	
		Martin Van Buren	Free Soil	291,263	10.1		
1852	31	**Franklin Pierce**	Democratic	1,601,117	50.9	254	69.6
		Winfield Scott	Whig	1,385,453	44.1	42	
		John P. Hale	Free Soil	155,825	5.0		
1856	31	**James Buchanan**	Democratic	1,832,955	45.3	174	78.9
		John C. Frémont	Republican	1,339,932	33.1	114	
		Millard Fillmore	American	871,731	21.6	8	
1860	33	**Abraham Lincoln**	Republican	1,865,593	39.8	180	81.2
		Stephen A. Douglas	Democratic	1,382,713	29.5	12	
		John C. Breckinridge	Democratic	848,356	18.1	72	
		John Bell	Constitutional Union	592,906	12.6	39	
1864	36	**Abraham Lincoln**	Republican	2,206,938	55.0	212	73.8
		George B. McClellan	Democratic	1,803,787	45.0	21	
1868	37	**Ulysses S. Grant**	Republican	3,013,421	52.7	214	78.1
		Horatio Seymour	Democratic	2,706,829	47.3	80	

Presidential Elections (*continued*)

Year	Number of States	Candidates	Parties	Popular Vote	% of Popular Vote	Electoral Vote	% Voter Participation[a]
1872	37	**Ulysses S. Grant**	Republican	3,596,745	55.6	286	71.3
		Horace Greeley	Democratic	2,843,446	43.9	[b]	
1876	38	**Rutherford B. Hayes**	Republican	4,036,572	48.0	185	81.8
		Samuel J. Tilden	Democratic	4,284,020	51.0	184	
1880	38	**James A. Garfield**	Republican	4,453,295	48.5	214	79.4
		Winfield S. Hancock	Democratic	4,414,082	48.1	155	
		James B. Weaver	Greenback-Labor	308,578	3.4		
1884	38	**Grover Cleveland**	Democratic	4,879,507	48.5	219	77.5
		James G. Blaine	Republican	4,850,293	48.2	182	
		Benjamin F. Butler	Greenback-Labor	175,370	1.8		
		John P. St. John	Prohibition	150,369	1.5		
1888	38	**Benjamin Harrison**	Republican	5,447,129	47.9	233	79.3
		Grover Cleveland	Democratic	5,537,857	48.6	168	
		Clinton B. Fisk	Prohibition	249,506	2.2		
		Anson J. Streeter	Union Labor	146,935	1.3		
1892	44	**Grover Cleveland**	Democratic	5,555,426	46.1	277	74.7
		Benjamin Harrison	Republican	5,182,690	43.0	145	
		James B. Weaver	People's	1,029,846	8.5	22	
		John Bidwell	Prohibition	264,133	2.2		
1896	45	**William McKinley**	Republican	7,102,246	51.1	271	79.3
		William J. Bryan	Democratic	6,492,559	47.7	176	
1900	45	**William McKinley**	Republican	7,218,491	51.7	292	73.2
		William J. Bryan	Democratic; Populist	6,356,734	45.5	155	
		John C. Wooley	Prohibition	208,914	1.5		
1904	45	**Theodore Roosevelt**	Republican	7,628,461	57.4	336	65.2
		Alton B. Parker	Democratic	5,084,223	37.6	140	
		Eugene V. Debs	Socialist	402,283	3.0		
		Silas C. Swallow	Prohibition	258,536	1.9		
1908	46	**William H. Taft**	Republican	7,675,320	51.6	321	65.4
		William J. Bryan	Democratic	6,412,294	43.1	162	
		Eugene V. Debs	Socialist	420,793	2.8		
		Eugene W. Chafin	Prohibition	253,840	1.7		
1912	48	**Woodrow Wilson**	Democratic	6,296,547	41.9	435	58.8
		Theodore Roosevelt	Progressive	4,118,571	27.4	88	
		William H. Taft	Republican	3,486,720	23.2	8	
		Eugene V. Debs	Socialist	900,672	6.0		
		Eugene W. Chafin	Prohibition	206,275	1.4		

Presidential Elections (*continued*)

Year	Number of States	Candidates	Parties	Popular Vote	% of Popular Vote	Electoral Vote	% Voter Participation[a]
1916	48	**Woodrow Wilson**	Democratic	9,127,695	49.4	277	61.6
		Charles E. Hughes	Republican	8,533,507	46.2	254	
		A. L. Benson	Socialist	585,113	3.2		
		J. Frank Hanly	Prohibition	220,506	1.2		
1920	48	**Warren G. Harding**	Republican	16,143,407	60.4	404	49.2
		James M. Cox	Democratic	9,130,328	34.2	127	
		Eugene V. Debs	Socialist	919,799	3.4		
		P. P. Christensen	Farmer-Labor	265,411	1.0		
1924	48	**Calvin Coolidge**	Republican	15,718,211	54.0	382	48.9
		John W. Davis	Democratic	8,385,283	28.8	136	
		Robert M. La Follette	Progressive	4,831,289	16.6	13	
1928	48	**Herbert C. Hoover**	Republican	21,391,993	58.2	444	56.9
		Alfred E. Smith	Democratic	15,016,169	40.9	87	
1932	48	**Franklin D. Roosevelt**	Democratic	22,809,638	57.4	472	56.9
		Herbert C. Hoover	Republican	15,758,901	39.7	59	
		Norman Thomas	Socialist	881,951	2.2		
1936	48	**Franklin D. Roosevelt**	Democratic	27,752,869	60.8	523	61.0
		Alfred M. Landon	Republican	16,674,665	36.5	8	
		William Lemke	Union	882,479	1.9		
1940	48	**Franklin D. Roosevelt**	Democratic	27,307,819	54.8	449	62.5
		Wendell L. Willkie	Republican	22,321,018	44.8	82	
1944	48	**Franklin D. Roosevelt**	Democratic	25,606,585	53.5	432	55.9
		Thomas E. Dewey	Republican	22,014,745	46.0	99	
1948	48	**Harry S Truman**	Democratic	24,179,345	49.6	303	53.0
		Thomas E. Dewey	Republican	21,991,291	45.1	189	
		J. Strom Thurmond	States' Rights	1,176,125	2.4	39	
		Henry A. Wallace	Progressive	1,157,326	2.4		
1952	48	**Dwight D. Eisenhower**	Republican	33,936,234	55.1	442	63.3
		Adlai E. Stevenson	Democratic	27,314,992	44.4	89	
1956	48	**Dwight D. Eisenhower**	Republican	35,590,472	57.6	457	60.6
		Adlai E. Stevenson	Democratic	26,022,752	42.1	73	
1960	50	**John F. Kennedy**	Democratic	34,226,731	49.7	303	62.8
		Richard M. Nixon	Republican	34,108,157	49.5	219	
1964	50	**Lyndon B. Johnson**	Democratic	43,129,566	61.1	486	61.7
		Barry M. Goldwater	Republican	27,178,188	38.5	52	
1968	50	**Richard M. Nixon**	Republican	31,785,480	43.4	301	60.6
		Hubert H. Humphrey	Democratic	31,275,166	42.7	191	
		George C. Wallace	American Independent	9,906,473	13.5	46	

Presidential Elections (*continued*)

Year	Number of States	Candidates	Parties	Popular Vote	% of Popular Vote	Electoral Vote	% Voter Partici-pation[a]
1972	50	Richard M. Nixon	Republican	47,169,911	60.7	520	55.2
		George S. McGovern	Democratic	29,170,383	37.5	17	
		John G. Schmitz	American	1,099,482	1.4		
1976	50	James E. Carter	Democratic	40,830,763	50.1	297	53.5
		Gerald R. Ford	Republican	39,147,793	48.0	240	
1980	50	Ronald W. Reagan	Republican	43,904,153	50.7	489	52.6
		James E. Carter	Democratic	35,483,883	41.0	49	
		John B. Anderson	Independent	5,720,060	6.6		
		Ed Clark	Libertarian	921,299	1.1		
1984	50	Ronald W. Reagan	Republican	54,455,075	58.8	525	53.3
		Walter F. Mondale	Democratic	37,577,185	40.6	13	
1988	50	George H. W. Bush	Republican	48,886,097	53.4	426	50.1
		Michael S. Dukakis	Democratic	41,809,074	45.6	111[c]	
1992	50	William J. Clinton	Democratic	44,909,326	43.0	370	55.2
		George H. W. Bush	Republican	39,103,882	37.4	168	
		H. Ross Perot	Independent	19,741,048	18.9		
1996	50	William J. Clinton	Democratic	47,402,357	49.2	379	49.1
		Robert J. Dole	Republican	39,196,755	40.7	159	
		H. Ross Perot	Reform	8,085,402	8.4		
		Ralph Nader	Green	684,902	0.7		
2000	50	George W. Bush	Republican	50,455,156	47.9	271	51.2
		Albert Gore	Democratic	50,992,335	48.4	266	
		Ralph Nader	Green	2,882,955	2.7		
2004	50	George W. Bush	Republican	62,039,073	50.7	286	55.3
		John F. Kerry	Democratic	59,027,478	48.2	251	
		Ralph Nader	Independent	240,896	0.2		
2008	50	Barack Obama	Democratic	66,882,230	53.0	365	61.7
		John McCain	Republican	58,343,671	46.0	173	
		Ralph Nader	Independent	705,200	0.55		

Candidates receiving less than 1 percent of the popular vote have been omitted. Thus the percentage of popular vote given for any election year may not total 100 percent.
 Before the passage of the Twelfth Amendment in 1804, the electoral college voted for two presidential candidates; the runner-up became vice president.
 Before 1824, most presidential electors were chosen by state legislatures, not by popular vote.

[a]Percent of voting-age population casting ballots.
[b]Greeley died shortly after the election; the electors supporting him then divided their votes among minor candidates.
[c]One elector from West Virginia cast her electoral college presidential ballot for Lloyd Bentsen, the Democratic Party's vice-presidential candidate.

Presidents and Vice Presidents

1. President	George Washington	1789–1797		18. President	Ulysses S. Grant	1869–1877
Vice President	John Adams	1789–1797		Vice President	Schuyler Colfax	1869–1873
2. President	John Adams	1797–1801		Vice President	Henry Wilson	1873–1877
Vice President	Thomas Jefferson	1797–1801		19. President	Rutherford B. Hayes	1877–1881
3. President	Thomas Jefferson	1801–1809		Vice President	William A. Wheeler	1877–1881
Vice President	Aaron Burr	1801–1805		20. President	James A. Garfield	1881
Vice President	George Clinton	1805–1809		Vice President	Chester A. Arthur	1881
4. President	James Madison	1809–1817		21. President	Chester A. Arthur	1881–1885
Vice President	George Clinton	1809–1813		Vice President	None	
Vice President	Elbridge Gerry	1813–1817		22. President	Grover Cleveland	1885–1889
5. President	James Monroe	1817–1825		Vice President	Thomas A. Hendricks	1885–1889
Vice President	Daniel Tompkins	1817–1825		23. President	Benjamin Harrison	1889–1893
6. President	John Quincy Adams	1825–1829		Vice President	Levi P. Morton	1889–1893
Vice President	John C. Calhoun	1825–1829		24. President	Grover Cleveland	1893–1897
7. President	Andrew Jackson	1829–1837		Vice President	Adlai E. Stevenson	1893–1897
Vice President	John C. Calhoun	1829–1833		25. President	William McKinley	1897–1901
Vice President	Martin Van Buren	1833–1837		Vice President	Garret A. Hobart	1897–1901
8. President	Martin Van Buren	1837–1841		Vice President	Theodore Roosevelt	1901
Vice President	Richard M. Johnson	1837–1841		26. President	Theodore Roosevelt	1901–1909
9. President	William H. Harrison	1841		Vice President	Charles Fairbanks	1905–1909
Vice President	John Tyler	1841		27. President	William H. Taft	1909–1913
10. President	John Tyler	1841–1845		Vice President	James S. Sherman	1909–1913
Vice President	None			28. President	Woodrow Wilson	1913–1921
11. President	James K. Polk	1845–1849		Vice President	Thomas R. Marshall	1913–1921
Vice President	George M. Dallas	1845–1849		29. President	Warren G. Harding	1921–1923
12. President	Zachary Taylor	1849–1850		Vice President	Calvin Coolidge	1921–1923
Vice President	Millard Fillmore	1849–1850		30. President	Calvin Coolidge	1923–1929
13. President	Millard Fillmore	1850–1853		Vice President	Charles G. Dawes	1925–1929
Vice President	None			31. President	Herbert C. Hoover	1929–1933
14. President	Franklin Pierce	1853–1857		Vice President	Charles Curtis	1929–1933
Vice President	William R. King	1853–1857		32. President	Franklin D. Roosevelt	1933–1945
15. President	James Buchanan	1857–1861		Vice President	John N. Garner	1933–1941
Vice President	John C. Breckinridge	1857–1861		Vice President	Henry A. Wallace	1941–1945
16. President	Abraham Lincoln	1861–1865		Vice President	Harry S Truman	1945
Vice President	Hannibal Hamlin	1861–1865		33. President	Harry S Truman	1945–1953
Vice President	Andrew Johnson	1865		Vice President	Alben W. Barkley	1949–1953
17. President	Andrew Johnson	1865–1869		34. President	Dwight D. Eisenhower	1953–1961
Vice President	None			Vice President	Richard M. Nixon	1953–1961

35. President	John F. Kennedy	1961–1963
Vice President	Lyndon B. Johnson	1961–1963
36. President	Lyndon B. Johnson	1963–1969
Vice President	Hubert H. Humphrey	1965–1969
37. President	Richard M. Nixon	1969–1974
Vice President	Spiro T. Agnew	1969–1973
Vice President	Gerald R. Ford	1973–1974
38. President	Gerald R. Ford	1974–1977
Vice President	Nelson A. Rockefeller	1974–1977
39. President	James E. Carter	1977–1981
Vice President	Walter F. Mondale	1977–1981

40. President	Ronald W. Reagan	1981–1989
Vice President	George H. W. Bush	1981–1989
41. President	George H. W. Bush	1989–1993
Vice President	J. Danforth Quayle	1989–1993
42. President	William J. Clinton	1993–2001
Vice President	Albert Gore	1993–2001
43. President	George W. Bush	2001–2009
Vice President	Richard Cheney	2001–2009
44. President	Barack Obama	2009–
Vice President	Joseph Biden	2009–

For a complete list of Presidents, Vice Presidents, and Cabinet Members, go to cengage.com/history/norton/peoplenationbrief8e

Justices of the Supreme Court

	Term of Service	Years of Service	Life Span		Term of Service	Years of Service	Life Span
John Jay	1789–1795	5	1745–1829	William Strong	1870–1880	10	1808–1895
John Rutledge	1789–1791	1	1739–1800	Joseph P. Bradley	1870–1892	22	1813–1892
William Cushing	1789–1810	20	1732–1810	Ward Hunt	1873–1882	9	1810–1886
James Wilson	1789–1798	8	1742–1798	Morrison R. Waite	1874–1888	14	1816–1888
John Blair	1789–1796	6	1732–1800	John M. Harlan	1877–1911	34	1833–1911
Robert H. Harrison	1789–1790	–	1745–1790	William B. Woods	1880–1887	7	1824–1887
James Iredell	1790–1799	9	1751–1799	Stanley Mathews	1881–1889	7	1824–1889
Thomas Johnson	1791–1793	1	1732–1819	Horace Gray	1882–1902	20	1828–1902
William Paterson	1793–1806	13	1745–1806	Samuel Blatchford	1882–1893	11	1820–1893
John Rutledge*	1795	–	1739–1800	Lucius Q. C. Lamar	1888–1893	5	1825–1893
Samuel Chase	1796–1811	15	1741–1811	Melville W. Fuller	1888–1910	21	1833–1910
Oliver Ellsworth	1796–1800	4	1745–1807	David J. Brewer	1890–1910	20	1837–1910
Bushrod Washington	1798–1829	31	1762–1829	Henry B. Brown	1890–1906	16	1836–1913
Alfred Moore	1799–1804	4	1755–1810	George Shiras Jr.	1892–1903	10	1832–1924
John Marshall	1801–1835	34	1755–1835	Howell E. Jackson	1893–1895	2	1832–1895
William Johnson	1804–1834	30	1771–1834	Edward D. White	1894–1910	16	1845–1921
H. Brockholst Livingston	1806–1823	16	1757–1823	Rufus W. Peckham	1895–1909	14	1838–1909
Thomas Todd	1807–1826	18	1765–1826	Joseph McKenna	1898–1925	26	1843–1926
Joseph Story	1811–1845	33	1779–1845	Oliver W. Holmes	1902–1932	30	1841–1935
Gabriel Duval	1811–1835	24	1752–1844	William D. Day	1903–1922	19	1849–1923
Smith Thompson	1823–1843	20	1768–1843	William H. Moody	1906–1910	3	1853–1917
Robert Trimble	1826–1828	2	1777–1828	Horace H. Lurton	1910–1914	4	1844–1914
John McLean	1829–1861	32	1785–1861	Charles E. Hughes	1910–1916	5	1862–1948
Henry Baldwin	1830–1844	14	1780–1844	Willis Van Devanter	1911–1937	26	1859–1941
James M. Wayne	1835–1867	32	1790–1867	Joseph R. Lamar	1911–1916	5	1857–1916
Roger B. Taney	1836–1864	28	1777–1864	Edward D. White	1910–1921	11	1845–1921
Philip P. Barbour	1836–1841	4	1783–1841	Mahlon Pitney	1912–1922	10	1858–1924
John Catron	1837–1865	28	1786–1865	James C. McReynolds	1914–1941	26	1862–1946
John McKinley	1837–1852	15	1780–1852	Louis D. Brandeis	1916–1939	22	1856–1941
Peter V. Daniel	1841–1860	19	1784–1860	John H. Clarke	1916–1922	6	1857–1945
Samuel Nelson	1845–1872	27	1792–1873	William H. Taft	1921–1930	8	1857–1930
Levi Woodbury	1845–1851	5	1789–1851	George Sutherland	1922–1938	15	1862–1942
Robert C. Grier	1846–1870	23	1794–1870	Pierce Butler	1922–1939	16	1866–1939
Benjamin R. Curtis	1851–1857	6	1809–1874	Edward T. Sanford	1923–1930	7	1865–1930
John A. Campbell	1853–1861	8	1811–1889	Harlan F. Stone	1925–1941	16	1872–1946
Nathan Clifford	1858–1881	23	1803–1881	Charles E. Hughes	1930–1941	11	1862–1948
Noah H. Swayne	1862–1881	18	1804–1884	Owen J. Roberts	1930–1945	15	1875–1955
Samuel F. Miller	1862–1890	28	1816–1890	Benjamin N. Cardozo	1932–1938	6	1870–1938
David Davis	1862–1877	14	1815–1886	Hugo L. Black	1937–1971	34	1886–1971
Stephen J. Field	1863–1897	34	1816–1899	Stanley F. Reed	1938–1957	19	1884–1980
Salmon P. Chase	1864–1873	8	1808–1873	Felix Frankfurter	1939–1962	23	1882–1965

	Term of Service	Years of Service	Life Span		Term of Service	Years of Service	Life Span
William O. Douglas	1939–1975	36	1898–1980	Abe Fortas	1965–1969	4	1910–1982
Frank Murphy	1940–1949	9	1890–1949	Thurgood Marshall	1967–1991	24	1908–1993
Harlan F. Stone	1941–1946	5	1872–1946	*Warren C. Burger*	1969–1986	17	1907–1995
James F. Byrnes	1941–1942	1	1879–1972	Harry A. Blackmun	1970–1994	24	1908–1998
Robert H. Jackson	1941–1954	13	1892–1954	Lewis F. Powell Jr.	1972–1987	15	1907–1998
Wiley B. Rutledge	1943–1949	6	1894–1949	*William H. Rehnquist*	1972–2005	33	1924–2005
Harold H. Burton	1945–1958	13	1888–1964	John P. Stevens III	1975–	–	1920–
Fred M. Vinson	1946–1953	7	1890–1953	Sandra Day O'Connor	1981–	–	1930–
Tom C. Clark	1949–1967	18	1899–1977	Antonin Scalia	1986–	–	1936–
Sherman Minton	1949–1956	7	1890–1965	Anthony M. Kennedy	1988–	–	1936–
Earl Warren	1953–1969	16	1891–1974	David H. Souter	1990–	–	1939–
John Marshall Harlan	1955–1971	16	1899–1971	Clarence Thomas	1991–	–	1948–
William J. Brennan Jr.	1956–1990	34	1906–1997	Ruth Bader Ginsburg	1993–	–	1933–
Charles E. Whittaker	1957–1962	5	1901–1973	Stephen Breyer	1994–	–	1938–
Potter Stewart	1958–1981	23	1915–1985	John G. Roberts	2005–	–	1955–
Byron R. White	1962–1993	31	1917–	Samuel A. Alito, Jr.	2006–	–	1950–
Arthur J. Goldberg	1962–1965	3	1908–1990				

Note: Chief justices are in italics.

*Appointed and served one term, but not confirmed by the Senate.

A

A Brief and True Report of the New Found Land of Virginia (Harriot), **2,** 23
A Century of Dishonor (Jackson), **440,** 445
Abenakis, 64
Abolition of Negro Slavery (Dew), **231**
Abolitionism
  opposition to, 299–300
Activism
  of women, 127
  students and, 812
Adams, Abigail, **155,** 160
Adams, John, 107–109, 123, 133
Adams, Quincy, 237
Adams, Samuel, 133, 175
Adams-Onís Treaty, **204,** 222
Adamson Act, **549**
Addams, Jane, 508, 615
Adkins v. Children's Hospital, **628**
Adolf Hitler, 685
Advertising, 634
Affirmative Action, 825–826
Afghanistan
  Soviet invasion of, 844
Afghanistan War, 891–892
Africa
  involuntary migrants of, 82–84
  origination of human beings, 3
  Portuguese trading posts in, 13
  slavery in, 25
African Americans
  activism among, 531
  and double V, 720
  cultural nationalism, 823
  discrimination against, 560
  migration of, 634–635
  militancy of, 619
  population of, **162**
  reunion of families, 414
  support of, 679
  violence against, 530
African enslavement
  in Chesapeake, 68–69
  in South Carolina, 69
African Methodist Episcopal (A.M.E.), 501
  growth of, 416
African slavery
  reasons for, 65–66
Africans
  origins and destinations of, **83**
Agricultural Adjustment Act, 665
Agriculture

  languishing, 630
  mechanization of, 458–459
Agricultural Adjustment Act (AAA), **656**
AIDS epidemic, 867, 903
Al Qaeda, 879, 887, 894
Alabama Midlands, 526
Alaska
  acquired by U.S., **576**
  becomes a state, **763**
  purchase of, **410**
Albany Congress, **108,** 110–111
Albee, Edward, 515
Algonquian
  English cultural differences and, 38–40
Alien Acts, 193, 201
All-Volunteer Force (AVF), 846
Alliance unity
  problems in achieving, 535
Allies
  tensions among, 723
Altgeld, John P., 477
Álvares Cabral, Pedro, 16
America
  European explorations in, **14**
  relations with England, 151
  tensions with Soviet Union, 796, 860
America, 1841, 234
American Antislavery Society, 299, 300
American Bar Association, 550x
American Board of Customs Commissioners, 121, 122–125
American Civil Liberties Union (ACLU), 623
American Federation of Labor (AFL), **466,** 477
American Friends Service Committee, 809
American Indian Defense Agency, 674
American Legion, 617–618
American Missionary Association, 415
American Railway Union, 540
American Revolution, 139
  consequences of, 132
American Revolutions
  forming of other nations, 139
American Society for the Promotion of Temperance, **290,** 293
American Tobacco Company, 471, 485
Americanization
  opposition to, 808
Americans with Disabilities Act, 851, 875
Amistad case, 237
Amnesty Act, **410,** 432

Andros, Edmund, 73
Animals, 814
Annapolis Convention
  meeting of, **155**
Anthony, Susan B., 301, 413, 532
Anti-federalists
  versus federalists, 180
Anti-Saloon League, 556
Anticommunism, 770–772
  politics of, 771
Antimasonry, 306
Antislavery movement
  international, 298
Antitrust legislation, 488
Apaches
  as servants, 96–97
Apartheid, **851**
Appeal . . . to the Colored Citizens, 296–297
Appleton, Nathan, 219
Appomattox
  surrender at, 424
Arab-Israeli conflict, 755
Arbella, 46
Armed Slave, The, 414
Arnold, Benedict, 146
Arthur, Chester A., 528
Articles of Confederation, 165
  ratification of, **155**
Arts
  virtue and, 157–159
Asia
  cold war in, 744–745
  imperialism in, **590**
  new immigrants from, 868
Assassinations, 815–816
Asylums, 293
Atlantic Cable, 469
Atlantic Charter, 701
  signed, **685**
Atlantic Creoles, 61
Atlantic slave trade, 66–67
Atlantic trading system, 78
  routes for, **66**
Atomic Energy Act, 770
Australia
  and American Revolution, 139
Automobile
  effects of, 633
Avery, William Waightstill, 247–248
Awakening
  impact of, 102
Ayer, N.W., 484
Aztecs, 4–5

B

Baby and Child Care (Spock), 781
Baby boom, 766–767
Bacon's Rebellion, **56**, 65, 77
Baghdad
    fall of, 895
Bailey v. Drexel, **628**
Balafo, 69–70
Balkan Crisis, 886
Banking crisis, 663–664
Banks
    chartering, 200
    first in United States, 187
Banneker, Benjamin, 163
Baptisms
    by missionaries, 47–48
Baptists
    in Old South, 233
Barbados
    founding of, **31**
Barbed wire
    invented, 460
Barbie, 784
Barrow, Bennet, 246–247
Bartram, John, 92
Bartram, William, 92
Baseball, 513
    Japanese, 514
Battle of Bunker Hill, 140, 157
Battle of Concord, 132, 140
Battle of Fallen Timbers, 195
Battle of Horseshoe Bend, **204**
Battle of Lexington, 132, 140
Battle of New Orleans, **204,**
        217, 303
Battle of Princeton, 144
Battle of Tippecanoe, 211–212
Baum, L. Frank, 544
Bay of Pigs invasion, 796–797
Bayard, Thomas F., 580
Beatles, The, 813, 814
Beaver Wars, 62
Beecher, Lyman, 291–292, 297
Bell, Alexander Graham, 559
Bemis, Edward, 487
Bennitt, James, 244
Berenson, Senda, 515
Berkeley, John Lord, 59
Berkeley, William, 65
Berlin Blockade, 743
Berlin crisis, **734**
Berlin, Ira, 61
Bernard, Francis, 121
Berry, Chuck, 814
Bethlehem Steel Company, 472
Biardot, Alphonse, 518
Bibb, Henry, 299
Bible belt, 311
Biddle, Nicholas, 305
Big Turtle, 131

Bill of Rights, 175–176, 183
    purpose of, 200
    ratified, **182**
Bin Laden, Osama, 887
Birney, James G., 300, 309
Birth control
    in United States, 571, 780
    pill approved, 793
Birth of a Nation, The, **494,** 516
Birth rates
    declining, 510
Black churches
    growth of, 415–416
Black codes, 418
Black Death, 11
Black Muslims, 811
Black Panthers, 811
Black Robes, 31–32
Black voters
        Southern Republican Party and, 425–426
Blackfish, 131
Blacks. *See also* Jim Crow laws; Segregation;
        Slavery
    free, 245–246
    new freedom of, 437
    political power, 773
    religion and, 415–416
Blackwell, Henry, 301
Blaine, James G., 525
Blair, Ezell, 792
Bland-Allison Act, **523,** 527
Bleeding Kansas, 361
Blight of Benin, 82
Blue Laws, 51
Board of Trade and Plantations
    establishment of, **56**
Boarding, 511
Boiardi, Hector, 518
Boleyn, Anne, 36
Bolshevik Revolution, 609
Bonaparte, Napoleon, 194
Bondspeople
    dilemma during Revolution, 138
Bonnin, Gertrude, 446
Bonnin, Ray, 446
Book of Mormon, 296
Boone, Daniel, 131
Borden, Gail, 483
Border Ruffians, 361
Boston
    British evacuation of, 141–142
    confrontations in, 122–125, 129
Boston Committee of Correspondence
    formed, **108**
Boston Manufacturing Company, 204, 219
Boston Massacre, **108,** 122–125, **124**
Boston Tea Party, **108**
Boudinot, Elias, 240
Bouquet, Henry, 114

Boycotts
    opinions on, 122
Boykin, Mary, 248–249
Boylston, Zabdiel, 93
Braddock Edward, 112
Bradwell v. Illinois, 434
Bradwell, Myra, 434
Brant, Joseph, 144–145
Brant, Mary, 144–145
Breckinridge, John C., 366
Breckinridge, Lucy, 249
Breed's Hill, 140
Brezezinski, Zbigniew, 843
Brice, Fanny, 516
Britain
    loyalty to, 118
British and Foreign Anti-Slavery
        Society, 298
Britton, Nan, 630
Brooklyn Bridge
    completed, **494**
Brooks, Preston, 362
Brown v. Board of Education, 531, 623,
        763, 764
Brown, Albert G., 360
Brown, James, 813
Brown, Sterling, 252
Brown, William Hill, **155**
Brown, William Wells, 298
Bryan, Joseph, 230
Bryan, William Jennings, 541
Bryant, William Cullen, 362
Buffalo
    slaughter of, 442
Burgoyne, John, 144
Burma
    decolonization of, 736
Burns, Anthony, 356
Burr, Aaron, 199
Burroughs, George, 74
Bush, George H. W., 869–870
    elected president, 851
Bush, George W., 596, 758
    race with Al Gore, 890
    reelected, **879**
    tax plan of, 891
Business
    globalization of, 884–885
Business-government cooperation, 612
Butler, Andrew P., 362
Butler, William, 351
Byrnes, James F., 738

C

Cabboto, Zuan, 16
Cabeza de Vaca, Alvar Nuñez, 1–2
Cable Act, The, 632
Cabot, John, 20–23
    explorations of, 16
Cabrera, Miguel, 97

Calhoun, John C., 215, 302, 304–305
Callender, James, 193
Calley, William, 829–830
Calvert, Cecilius, 41
Calvert, George, 41
Calvin, John, 36
Cambodia
    invasion of, 829
    United States invasion of, **822**
Camp David Accords, 844
Campaign of 1777, 144
Campbell, John, 234
Canada
    and American Revolution, 139
    invasion of, 216
Candidates
    in 1912, 568
Capitals
    burning, 216–217
Caribbean, 33–35, 136–137, 147–148
    and New England, 67–68
    trade in, 67–68
    warfare in, 35
Carlisle riots, 154
Carnegie Homestead Steel, 539
Carnegie Steel Company, 478
Carnegie, Andrew, 103
Carolina, 90–91
    chartered, **56**
Caroline affair, **290**
Carpetbaggers, 428
Carreta, Vincent, 103
Carter, Jimmy
    elected president, **822**
    presidency of, 837–838
Carteret, George, 59
Cartier, Jacques, 30–31
Cass, Lewis, 351
Cassatt, Alexander, 551
Castro, Fidel, 596, 749, 797
    and Cuban revolution, 754–755
Casualties
    in Great War, 610–611
Catherine of Aragón, 36
Catholic Church
    authority of, 10
    conversion to, 15
    converting to, 73
    differences with Protestants, 294
    immigrants and, 503
    Indians and, 18
Causation, 369
Cavelier de LaSalle, René-Robert, 62
Cayugas
    as part of Iroquois Confederacy, 62–63
    in Iroquois Confederacy, 62–63
Central Intelligence Agency (CIA), 741
    as foreign policy instrument, 748–749
Ceylon
    decolonization of, 736

Chaplin, Charlie, 645
Chapman, Maria, 299
Charles I, 41
    as king, **29**
    execution of, **56**
Charles II, 60–61
Charles River Bridge v. Warren Bridge, 221
Charlotte Temple (Rowson), 158
Chase, Samuel, 207
Château-Thierry, 601
Checks and balances, 174–175
Cheney, Dick, 894
Cherokees
    background of, 239
    versus Georgia, 239–240
Chesapeake, 41–43
    African enslavement in, 68–69
    middle colonies and, 89–90
Chicago Democratic National
        Convention, 816
Chicano movement, 824–825
    term discussed, 824
Chickasaws, 63
Chief Coacoochee, 241
Child, Lydia Maria, 299
China
    civil war in, 744
    open door policy of, 589
Chinese Exclusion Acts, **440,** 449, 726
Chippewas
    alliance with Pontiac, 114
Chisholm v. Georgia, 184
Chocolate
    in colonies, 76
Choctaws, 63
Christianity
    as dominant European religion, 10
    slaves and, 259
Church
    separation from state, 205
Church of Jesus Christ of Latter-Day
        Saints, 296
Churchill, Winston, 711
    Cold War and, 738
Cigar Makers' Union, 477
Cincinnati Freeman, 363
City Beautiful movement, 509
City life, 98–99
    managing, 505
City-dwellers
    unmarried, 511
Civic reform, 508
Civic rituals, 94–95
Civil Rights
    riots and unrest and, 810–811
Civil Rights Act, 410, 432, 531, **763, 793,**
        802, 865
Civil service
    reform, 525–526
Clapp, Moses E., 447

Clapton, Eric, 814
Clarissa (Richardson), 158
Clark, Petula, 814
Clark, William, 210
Class
    tensions in antebellum South, 259
Clay, Henry, 215, 224, 226, 297, 302, 352
Clayton Anti-Trust Act, 569
Clayton-Bulwer Treaty, 593
Cleveland, Grover, 479, 528
    William Henry Harrison and, 529
Clinton, DeWitt, 215
Clinton, Henry, 147–148
Clinton, William Jefferson, 882
    elected president, **879**
    legislative record, 889–890
CNN (Cable News Network), 873
Cobbett, William, 181
Cody, Buffalo Bill, 439, 451
Coercive Acts, 126, 130
Coffee
    in colonies, 76
Cohan, George M., 515
Cold Peace, 740
Cold War, 747–751
    and national security, 758
    beginning of, 737–738
    domestic politics, 768–780
    end in Europe, 871
    John F. Kennedy and, 794–801
Cold War, The (Lippmann), 740–741
College of William and Mary, 234
Colleges
    growth of, 557–558
Collier, John, 674
Colonial assemblies, 99
Colonial autonomy
    challenges to, 73
Colonization, 296–297
    English interest in, 35–37
    lessons of, 13, 25
    models of, 26
    Spanish, 17–18
Colored Women's Federation, 562
Columbian exchange
    major items in, **19**
Columbus
    observations of, 14–16
    ships of, 14
    voyage of, 14
Commercial reform, 170
Committee for Relief of the Black
        Poor, 139
Committee on Public Information,
        615–616
Committees of Correspondence
    Samuel Adams and, 124–125
Committees of Observation, 134
Common Sense (Paine), **132,** 142, 152
Commons, John R., 487

Commonwealth period, 57, 75
Communications
    international, 582
Communism, 749
Compromise of 1850, 347, 353–354, 371
Compromise of 1877, 434
Concerned Women for America, 127
Confederation
    trials of, 165–168
Confederation Congress, 165
Confessions of Nat Turner, The, 256
Congregationalism, 49
Congress
    anticommunism in, 772
    bans slave importation, **204**
    debates over, 172–173
Congress of Racial Equality, **708,** 720, 798
Congressional powers, 174–175
Congressional Reconstruction Plan,
        418–425
Conkling, Roscoe, 524–525
Connecticut
    founding of, 29, **31**
Conservation movement, 566–567
    rise of, 463
*Considerations on the Propriety of Imposing Taxes
        on the British Colonies* (Dulany), 118
Constitution
    interpreting, 187
    Madison and, 172
    slavery and, 173–174, 179
    the word "slavery" in, 358
Constitutional Convention
    delegates to, 171–172
Constitutional Crisis, 423
Constitutions
    of states, 164
Consumer culture
    in the United States, 779
Consumption
    rituals of, 95
Continental Army, 145–146
    staffing, 152–153
Continental Association, 133
Contra War
    in Nicaragua, 862
Contrast, The (Tyler), **155,** 157–159
Convention of 1800, 194
Cook, James, 139
Cooney, Joseph, 465
Corn Laws, 223–224
*Coronado Coal Company v. United Mine
        Workers,* **628**
Corps of Discovery, 210
Corruption
    as political wedge, 428
Cortés, Hernán, 17
Cotton, 257–258
    global economy and, 248–249
Cotton gin, 208
Cotton trade, **231**

Cotton, John, 50
Coureurs de bois, 63
Covey, James, 237
Cowboys
    myth of, 462
Coxey's Army, 540
Crane, Timothy B., 289
Crawford, William H., 302
Crazy Horse, 445
Credit, 840–841
Crime, 505
Crisis, The (Paine), 143–144
Crispus Attucks, 123
Crittenden, John J., 366
Crockett, Davy, 515
Croker, Richard, 507
Cromwell, Oliver, 57
Crops
    cultivation of, **2**
Croquet, 513
Crummwell, Alexander, 298
Cuba
    annexation of, 360
    invaded by U.S., **576**
    Platt Amendment and, 593
    revolution in, 585, 754–755
Cuban missile crisis, 797
Cultural adaptation, 502–503
Cultural expansion, 688
Culture
    genteel, 91–92
    retention of, 500
Cummings v. County Board of Education,
        523, 531
Currency, 165–167
    depreciation of, **167**
Currency Act, **108,** 116
Custis, Martha, 141
Cycling, 513

D

da Gama, Vasco, 13
da Verrazzano, Giovanni, 16
Daley, Richard, 816
Darrow, Clarence, 64
Dartmouth (ship), 126
Darwin, Charles, 559
Daughters of Liberty, 121, 127
Dave Clark Five, The, 814
Davis, Henry W., 412
Davis, Jefferson, 361, 367, 436
Davis, John W., 631
Dawes Severalty Act, **440**
Dawes, William, 140
de Baude de Frontenac, Louis, 62
de Champlain, Samuel, 30, 34
de Grasse, François, 148
de la Palma, Resaca, 349
de León, Ponce, **2,** 17
de Rasière, Isaac, 34
de Tocqueville, Alexis, 247

de Zaldívar, Juan, 30
Dean, Howard, 897
Debs, Eugene V., 478–479, 540, 552, 616
Debts
    national and state, 186
Declaration of Independence
    Jefferson's words in, 155
    language of, 150
    Thomas Jefferson and, 142–143
Declaration of Rights and Grievances, 132
    crucial clauses in, 133
Declaratory Act, 108, 120
Decolonization, 736
Delaware
    as restoration colony, 57–62
Delawares, 60
    alliance with Pontiac, 114
Demagogues, 668
Democracy and Education (Dewey), 557
Democratic party
    split of, 347
Democratic societies, 189
Democrats, 303–304
    differences with Whig party, 313
Demographic patterns
    in New England, 44
Deposit Act of 1836, 306
Depression
    of 1890s, 537–538
Desertion
    punishments for, 146–147
Détente, 832
deTocqueville, Alexis, 238, 240
Dew, Thomas R., 234
Dewey, John 557
Dewey, Thomas E., 743
Dias, Bartholomew, 13, **15**
Díaz del Castillo, Bernal, 17
Dickinson, John (quoted), 156
Diet
    of Americans, 483
Digital revolution, 884
Discrimination
    sexual and racial, 559
Disease, 146–147
Disunion, 364–365
Diversity, 843
Dixon, Archibald, 357
Doctrine of the Covenant, 46
Doegs, 65
Donnell, Ed, 458
Doolittle raid, 710
Douglas, Stephen A., 346, 352, 364, 435
Douglass, Frederick, **231,** 298, 299
Drake, Francis, 22
Dred Scott v. Sanford, **347,** 363
Du Bois, W.E.B., 561, 607, 619
Duke's Laws, The, 59
Duke, James B., 471
Dulany, Daniel, 118
Dulles, John Foster (quoted), 751

Dutch West India Company, 33, 59
Dylan, Bob, 813
Dynamic Sociology (Ward), 487

E

Earp brothers, 451
East Asia
    peacemaking in, 595
Economic crisis
    impacts of, 839
Economic growth, 87, 629, 688, 765–766
    U.S. muscle, 691
Economy
    attempts to fix, 839
    in postwar America, 764
    slave trade and, 56, 149
Ed Sullivan Show, The, 813, 814
Edison Electric Light Company, 468
    founded, **466**
Edison, Thomas, 468, 516
Education
    blacks and, 415
    reform, 159
Eighteenth Amendment, **549**
Eisenhower
    becomes president, **734**
Eisenhower Doctrine, 756
Eisenhower, Dwight D.
    Cold War and, 747–748
    conservatism, 769–770
    elected president, **763**
El Plan Espiritual de Aztlán, 824
Election of 1796, 192
Election of 1800, 197–199
Election of 1808, 214
Election of 1824, 302
Election of 1828, 302
Election of 1836, 308
Election of 1840, 309–310
Election of 1860, 365
Election of 1868, 423–425
Election of 1876, 434
Election of 1916,
Election of 1928, 648
Election of 1940, 678
Election of 1948, 769
Election of 1960, 795
Election of 1964, 802–803
Election of 1992, 881
Election of 1996, 883
Election of 2000, 890
Election of 2004, 895–896
Electoral college, 173–174
Electrical industry
    birth of, 468
Eliot, Charles W., 557
Elizabeth I
    as queen, **29**
Ellmaker, Amos, 306
Ellsberg, Daniel, 821

Ely, Richard, 487
Emancipation
    racism and, 160–163
Embargo Act, 204
Embargo of 1807, 213
Embargoes
    War of 1812, **204**
Emerson, Ralph Waldo, 365
    American renaissance and, 295
Emigration
    from England and Scotland, **85**
Encomienda system, 18
Encomiendas, 63–64
Enforcement Act
    passed, **410**
England
    contest with Spain, 22
    relations with America, 151
English Catholic Church, 36
English Civil War, 61–62
English Reformation, 36–37
Enlightenment, The, 92–93
    of rationalism, 92
Enslavement
    in North, 71
    term discussed, 123–124
Environment
    degradation of, 785–786
Environmental Protection Agency
        (EPA), 40
*Economics Interpretation of the
        Constitution,* 559
Equiano, Olaudah, 103
Era of Good Feelings, 221
Ericsson, Leif, 16
Erie Canal
    constructed, **204**
Eries, 70–71
Espionage Act, **601**
Essay Concerning Human Understanding
        (Locke), **81**, 92
Ethnic diversity, 82–86
Ethnic food, 518
Eugenics, 559
European colonies
    founding of, **31**
    in Eastern North America, **32**
    Indians and, **111**
Europeans
    trade with Indians, 21–22
    warfare with Indians, 109–112
Europe
    division of, **742**
Environmentalism, 841
Ex parte Milligan, 410
Experiments and Observations on Electricity
        (Franklin), **81**, 92
Exploration
    motives for, 11–12
Exposition and Protest, 304

F

Faith, Percy, 814
Falwell, Jerry, 865
Families, 509–510
    African American, 97–98
    and sexuality, 842
    changing American, 899–900
    colonial, 96–99
    European American, 97
    in Chesapeake, 42
    in slavery, 254–255
    in the United States, 780
Farmers, 658
Farmers' alliances, 534–535
Faubus, Orval E., 776
Federal Highway Act, **628**
Federal policies
    failure of, 650
Federal Reserve Act, **549**
Federal Trade Commission, **549**
Federalist, The (Hamilton), **155,** 176, 186
Federalists
    and New England merchants, 191
    versus anti-federalists, 180
Female Moral Reform Society, 292
Female sachems, 8
Femininity
    alternate images of, 641
Feminism, 562, 826–827
Ferdinand of Aragón, 11
Field, Cyrus, 469
Fifteenth Amendment, 425
    ratified, **410**
Fifteenth Century
    technological change in, 11
Filene, E. A., 551
Fillmore, Millard, 351–352
Financial affairs, 165–167
Financiers, 486
Finney, Charles, 292
First Barbary War, 212
First Congress, 183
First Continental Congress, **108,** 132, 133
First Great Awakening, 101
First Navigation Act
    passed, **56**
First Reconstruction Act, **410**
First World War
    outbreak of, 602–603
Fitzhugh, George, **231,** 234
Fleming, Samuel, 247
Flintoff, John F., 243–244
Florida
    founding of, **31**
Floyd, John, 306
Food crops
    cultivation of, **2**
Football, 515
Ford Motor Company, 470
    founded, **466**

Ford, Gerald
    presidency of, 836–837
Ford, Henry, 470
Fordney-McCumber Tariff,
    628, 690
Foreign affairs, 167–168
Foreign war
    and popular imagination, 349–350
Fort Rosalie, 63
Fort Sumter, 368
    attack on, **347**
Four Minute Men, 615
Fourier, Charles, 295
Fourierists, 295
Fourteen Points, 609
Fourteenth Amendment, 420–421, 434
    Slaughter-House cases, **410**
France
    American units in, 608
    declaration of war on Britain, **182**
Franco-American Alliance of 1778, 145
Franklin, Aretha, 813
Franklin, Benjamin, 103, 114, 142,
    149–150, 184
Franklin, Benjamin (quoted), 174
Frazier, Garrison, 414
Free blacks, 245–246
    communities, 246
    growth of population of, 161
Free silver, 541
Free Speech Movement (FSM), 812
Free World (magazine), 754
Free-Soil Party, 347, **352**
Freedom
    meaning of, 413–416
Freedom of Contract, 475
Freedom Rides, **793**
Freedom schools, 800
Freemasonry, 306
Freedpeople's
    lives of, 161–162
Frémont, John C., 350, 362
French and Indian War, **109**
French Protestants, 86
French Revolution, 189
    start of, **182**
Frey, John, 465
Frick, Henry C., 478
Friedman, Thomas L., 884
Fries's Rebellion, 196, 197
Fries, John, 197
Fugitive Slave Act, 298, 354–355, 356
    opposition to, 358
Fuller, Margaret
    American renaissance and, 295
Fundamental Constitutions of Carolina,
    The, 60
Fundamental Orders of Connecticut,
    46
Fundamentalism, 643

G

Gabriel's Rebellion, 196, 197, 256
Gag rule, 308
Gage, Thomas, 138
Galloway, Joseph, 133
Gandy, Moses, 298
Garden, Forest, 289
Garfield, James, 52, 525
Garrison, William Lloyd, 297,
    298, 300
Garvey, Marcus, 635
Gaspée, 123
Gates, Horatio, 148
Gay culture, 641
Gay liberation, 828
Gebhardt, William, 518
Gender roles
    in 1950s families, 781
    in West Africa, 9
General Electric, 470, 485
Genêt, Edmond, 189
Geneva Accords
    on Vietnam, 756
Geneva Prisoners of War Convention,
    746
Genizaros, 96
George III, 133
Georgia, 90–91
    founded, **81**
    versus Cherokees, 239–240
German Lilli doll, 784
Germans, 84–86
    identity of, 86
Ghost Dance, 447
GI Bill, **763**
Gibbons v. Ogden, 221–222
Gibbs, Jacob, 355–356
Gibbs, Josiah, 237
Gilded age, 524
Gilded Age, The, 522
Gilmore, William, 219
Glackens, William, 586
Gladden, Washington, 552
Glasnost, 864
Glidden, Joseph F., 460
Globalization, 879
    critics of, 885
    world health and, 902
Glorious Revolution, 117
    deposition of James II, **56**
    in America, **56,** 73
Goerge, Henry, 487
Gold
    Spain's decline and, 18
Gold Standard Act, **523,** 543
Goldman, Emma, 618
Gompers, Samuel, 477–478
Gonorrhea, 443
Good Neighbor Policy, 692
Gorbachev, Mikhail, 851–852

Gore, Al
    race with George W. Bush, 890
Gottlieb Daimler, 470
Gould, Jay, 477
Grange movement, 534
Grant, Madison, 559
Grant, Ulysses, 423, 431
Grateful Dead, The, 813
Gray, Thomas R., 256
Great Atlantic Tea Company, 484
Great Awakening, 101
Great society, 801
Great War for the Empire, 113
Great White Fleet, **576**
Greeley, Horace, 361
Green Corn Rebellion, 615
Greene, Nathanael, 148–149
Grenville, George, 115, **120**
Grier, Robert, 363
Grimké, Sarah, 300
Guantánamo Bay, 596
Guatemala
    U.S. intervention in, 754
Guinea, 9–10
Gulf of Tonkin Resolution, **793**
Gurley Flynn, Elizabeth, 479
Guzmán, Jacobo Arbenz, 754

H

Hale, Stephen, 368
Hall, G. Stanley, 557
Hamilton, Alexander, 176,
    185–186, 193
    domestic policy under, 184–188
    financial plan of, 186
    killed by Burr, **204**
Hammond, James Henry, 234
Hanna, Marcus A., 541
Harding administration
    scandals of, 630–631
Harding, Warren G., 629
Harmar, Josiah, 195
Harpers Ferry raid, **347,** 365, 370
Harriot, Thomas, 23
Harrison, Benjamin, 451
    elected president, **523**
Harrison, William Henry, 308
    Grover Cleveland and, 529
Harte, Bret, 451
Hartford Convention of 1814, 194
Hatch Act, **440**
Hawaii
    annexation of, 584
    becomes a state, **763**
Hawkins, John, 22
Hawley-Smoot Tariff, **656,** 685
Hawthorne, Nathaniel, 295
    American renaissance and, 295
Hay, John, 591
Hay-Pauncefote Treaty, 593

Hayes, Rutherford B., 434
    elected president, 523
Haymarket riot, **466, 477**
Hayne, Robert Y., 304–305
Health Insurance Portability and
        Accountability Act, 889
Hearst, William Randolph, 517
Hefner, Hugh, 782–783
Helper, Hinton R., **231**
Henry VII
    divorces Catherine of Aragón, 29
    Tudor dynasty and, 11
Henry, Patrick, 114, 117–118, 129, 133, 175
Henry, Richard, 175
Hepburn Act, **549**
Herbalism
    slavery and, 250
Herbert, Victor, 515
Herman's Hermits, 814
Hickok, Wild Bill, 451
Highland Scots, 80, 84–86
    identity of, 86
Hill, David, 541
Hiroshima, 708
Hispanic
    population growth in U.S., 868–869
Hitler, Adolph
    German aggression under, 693
Ho Chi Minh, 733–735, 744–745
Hohokam, 4
Holden v. Hardy, **466,** 475–476, **549,** 558
Holidays
    celebration of, 512–513
Hollies, The, 814
Holly, Buddy, 814
Holmes, Oliver Wendell Jr., 558, 616
Holocaust
    America and, 721
Homestead Act, 440, 456, **459**
Homestead strike, 478
Homosexuality
    in the United States, 782
Hoover, Herbert, 648, 660
Hoover, J. Edgar
    racial tensions and, 775
Hope, John, 531
Horses, 20
Hostages
    seized in Iran, **822**
Hostilities
    on frontier, 136
Houdini, Harry, 493
House of Burgesses
    support of, 114
House, Callie, 257
Housing reform, 504
Houston, Sam, 360
Howard University, 415
Howe, Elias Jr., 483–484
Howe, William, 143

Hudson River land riots, **81**
Hudson, Henry, 33
Huguenots, 86
Huitzilopochtli, 4–5
Hull, William, 216
Hundred Years' War, 10
Hungary
    rebellion in, 749–750
Hurons
    alliance with Pontiac, 114
Hurricane Katrina, **879**
Hurricanes
    Caribbean and, 35
Hussein, Saddam, 872
    rise of, 845
Hutchinson, Anne, 50
Hutchinson, Thomas, 126
Hylton v. U.S., 184

I

Ice Age, 3
Immigrants
    Americanizing, 294
Immigration, 498
    quotas for, 642–643
Immigration Act of 1965, 817
Immigration and Nationality Act, **793**
Impeachment, 836, 889
Impending Crisis, The (Helper), **231**
Imperial reorganization, 72–77, 78
Imperialist
    arguments for, 588–589
Indentured servitude
    myths of, 53
India
    decolonization of, 736
Indian
    assaults, 40
    treaty making, 236
Indian accommodation, 236–238
Indian affairs
    politics and, 632
Indian Defense Association, 632
Indian enslavement
    in the Carolinas, 70–71
Indian policy
    reform of, 445–446
Indian relations, 169
Indian Removal Act, 239
Indian Reorganization Act, 674
Indian Right Association, 632
Indian Trade and Intercourse Act of
        1793, 196
Indians
    Catholicism and, 18
    civilizing, 196
    European settlements and, **111**
    federal policy and, 238–239
    trade with Europeans, 21–22
    warfare with Europeans, 109–112

Indigo, 69–70
Industrial accidents, 475
Industrial development, 495
Industrial production, **467**
Industrial workers, 658
Industrial Workers of the World
        (IWW), 479
    founded, **466**
Industrialization
    mill towns and, 426–427
Influence of Sea Power upon History
        (Mahan), **576**
Influenza Pandemic of 1918, 611
Inner-city housing, 503
Innovations, 482, 490
Insull, Samuel, 468
Insurrection
    of Nat Turner, 256
Intercollegiate Athletic Association,
        494, 515
Interesting Narrative, 103
Internet, 905
Internment
    of Japanese Americans, 718–720
Intolerable Acts, 126, 130
Investment, 840–841
Iran-Contra Scandal, 862
Iran-Contra scandal, **851**
Iranian Hostage Crisis, 844–845
Irish
    identity of, 86
Iroquois
    neutrality of, 109–110
Iroquois Confederacy, 62, 144–145
    Cayugas in, 62–63
    Mohawks in, 62–63
    Oneidas in, 62–63
    Onondagas in, 62–63
    Senecas in, 62–63
    Tuscaroras in, 62–63
Irrigation, 452
Isabelle of Castile, 11

J

Jackson, Helen Hunt, 445
Jacksonianism, 301–304
Jagger, Mick, 814
James I, 40
    coronation, 29, **56**
James II, 73
James, Nancy, 244
Jamestown, 38
Japan
    bombing of, 727–728
Jarvis, Anna, 512
Jay Treaty, **182**
    debate, 190–191
Jay, John, 133, 176, 190
Jazz, 647
Jefferson Airplane, 813

Jefferson, Thomas, 114, 142, 155, 205, 226, 297, 360
  election of, 196
  inaugurated, 204
  on blacks, 163
  quoted, 176, 250–251
Jennings, William, 600
Jerry, Ginney, 246–247
Jesuit missions
  in New France, 31–32
Jesuits
  Native Americans and, 52
Jewett, William, 292
Jewish faith
  immigrants and, 503
Jews
  identity of, 86
Jiang Jieshi, 696–697
Jim Crow laws, **523**
Johnson, Andrew, 410
  impeachment of, 423, 528
  pardon policy, 417
  political beliefs of, 417
  racial views of, 417
  reconstruction plan, 416–418
  versus congress, 419–420
Johnson, Hiram, 555
Johnson, Lyndon B.
  elected president, **793**
Johnson, Michael, 256
Johnson, Richard M., 308
Jolliet, Louis, 62
Jones, Mary "Mother," 479
Joplin, Janis, 813
Journalism
  yellow, 517
Judiciary Act of 1789, 183, 208
Jungle, The (Sinclair), 551
Junk bonds, 858
Justice Act, 126

K

Kaiser, The (movie), 616
Kansas-Nebraska Act, **347**
  slavery expansion and, 354–355
  vote on, **357**
Kaskaskia, 63
Kearny, Stephen, 350
Keith, Benjamin, 515
Keller, Helen, 623
Kelley, Florence, 508
Kelley, Oliver H., 534
Kellogg, William K., 483
Kellogg-Briand Pact, 685, 687–688
Kemble, Fanny, 230
Kennedy, John F., 794–795
  assassination of, 801
  CIA and, 749
  civil rights and, 799
Kennedy, Robert, 816
Kentucky Resolution, **182,** 194

Kerensky, Aleksander, 609
Kerner, Otto, 810
Kerry, John, 895
Key, Francis Scott, 217
Khrushchev, Nikita, 749
  Cuban missile crisis and, 797
Kim Il Sung, 745
King Andrew I, 304
King George's War, **81,** 100, 109–110
  New England and, 88–89
King Henry VII, 16
King John I of Portugal, 13
King Kong, 675
King Philip's War, 55, 64
King William's War, **56,** 74, **109**
King's Mountain, 149
King, Martin Luther Jr., 774, 776, **800**
  assassinated, 793
King, Rodney
  verdict, 879
King, Rufus, 208, 221
Kinks, The, 814
Kinsey, Alfred, 782
Kinship
  functions of, 511
Knights of Labor, 476–477
  founded, 466
Know-Nothings, **352**
  anti immigrant fears of, 358–359
Knox, Henry, 196
Korea War, **734**
Korean War, 745–747
Ku Klux Klan Act, **410,** 428–430, 618–619, 631, 641–642, 775

L

L'Ouverture, Toussaint, 198
La Follette, Robert M., 555, 615
Labor, 671–673
  gender division of, 5
  shortage, 614
  strikes, 617
Labor reform, 555–556
  court rulings on, 475–476
Laborers
  demand for, 41
Land
  desire for, 415
Land Ordinance 1785, **155,** 177
Land redistribution
  failure of, 421–423
Lane Debates, 297
Las Gorras Blancas, 534
Lavrov, Peter, 536
Law enforcement, 507
Le Duc Tho, 830
Le Moyne, Jacques, **7**
le pays de Illinois, 63
League of Nations, **601**
  article 10, 620–621
Lease, Mary Elizabeth, 522

Lecompton Constitution, 347
Lee, Henry, 306
Lee, Richard Henry, 133, 142
Lee, Robert E., 436
Leflore, Greenwood, 247
Legal rights
  of women, 300–301
Leisler, Jacob, 73
Lenapes, 60
Lend-Lease Act, 685
Lennon, John, 814
Lesbian culture, 641
Leisure time
  increase in, 513
Letters from a Farmer in Pennsylvania, 121
Letters from a Federal Farmer, 176
Levitt, William, 767
Lew, Barzillai, 146
Lewis and Clark expedition, 210–211
Lewis, John L., 672
Lewis, Meriwether, 210
Liberty Party, **352**
Life expectancy, 482, 638–639
Life of Washington (Weems), **155,** 157–159
Liberator, The, 297
Lilli (German doll), 784
Lincoln, Abraham, 346
  slave power and, 364
  ten percent plan, 411
Lincoln, Benjamin, 148
Lincoln-Douglas debates, **347**
Lindsey, Ben, 548
Lippmann, Walter, 740–741
Little Rock Nine, 776
Little Turtle, 195
Littlefield, Henry M., 544
Livingston, Robert, 221
Lochner v. New York, **466,** 475–476, 558
Locke, John, 60–61, 115
Lodge, Henry Cabot, 578, 621
Lodging, 511
Log Cabin, The, 310
Logan Act, 181
Logan, Deborah Norris, 181
Long, Huey, 668
Looking Backward (Bellamy), **466**
Lord Cornwallis, 147
Lord Dunmore, 135, 147
Lord Hillsborough, 121
Lord North, **120**
Lord Rockingham, **120**
Los Angeles
  violence in, 880
Lost Cause, 436
Lost Generation, 646
Lotteries, 165–167
Louis, Joe, 675
Louisiana Purchase, **209,** 227
Lovejoy, Elijah P., 300
Lowell, Francis Cabot, 219, 223
Loyal Nine, 118–119

Lumbering, 448
Lusitania, 600
Luther, Martin, 36
Lynch, James, 426
Lyons, Matthew, 193

M

MacArthur, Douglass, 744
Macune, Charles W., 537
Madeira, 95
Madison, Dolley, 214, 217
Madison, James, 172, 176, 183, 187, 209,
        226, 297
    constitution and, 172
    elected president, **204**
    last year as president, 220
Mail-order companies, 458
Maine
    founding of, **31**
Maine
    sinking of, 585–586
Maine (battleship), **576**
Maize, 21
    drawing of, **21**
Malcolm X, 811
Male ethos, 579–580
Manchurian crisis, 697
Manhattan project, 713
Mann, Horace, 294
Mann-Elkins Act, **549**
Manufactures
    report on, 187–188
Manumission, 160–161
Marbury v. Madison, **204,** 207–208
Marcellus, Henricus, 15
March on Washington, 800
Marco Polo, **2,** 11
Market expansion
    government promotion of, 221
Marquette, Jacques, 62
Marriage
    in the United States, 779
Married Women's Property Act, **231**
Marshall Plan, 741
Marshall, George C., 741
Marshall, John, 199, 240
Marshall, Thurgood, 774
Marx, Karl, 539
Maryland
    founding of, 29, **31**
Maryland's Act of Religious
        Toleration, 41
Marshall Court, 207
Mass media, 675
Mass production, 473
Mass transportation
    mechanization of, 495
Mass-market publications, 517
Massachusetts
    charter issued, **56**

Massachusetts Bay
    founded, **29,** 31
Massachusetts Bay Company, 45
Mather, Cotton, **75,** 93
Maximum Freight Case, 526
Mayas, 3–4
Mayflower, 45
Mayhew, Thomas, 48
McAdoo, William G., 631
McAllister, Alexander (quoted), 80
McCarthy, Eugene, 815
McCarthyism, 771–772, 772–773
McCulloch v. Maryland, **204,** 221
McDonald's, 885–886
McGowan v. Maryland, 51
McKinley Tariff, **523,** 527
McKinley, William
    assassinated, **549, 576**
    presidency, 543
    Republican nomination of, 541
    war decision, 586
McNamara, Robert, 797
McNaughton, John, 821
McNeil, Joe, 792
Meat Inspection Act, **549**
Medicine, 901
Mediterranean Atlantic
    islands in, 12–13
Mehta, G.L., 753
Melville, Herman, 349
    American renaissance and, 295
Memorial Day Massacre, 672–673
Menéndez de Avilés, Pedro, 30
Mercantilism
    Navigation Acts and, 72–73
Merrick, Dwight, 465
Mesoamerica, 3
Mestizos, 96–97, 449
Methodists
    in Old South, 233
Métis, 63, 96–97
Mexica, 4–5
Mexican American
    activism, 824
Mexican barrios, 501
Mexico
    clash with nationalism, 692–693
    conquest and, 350
    invaded by U.S., **576**
    newcomers from, 635
    relations with United States, 594–595
    Treaty of Guadalupe Hidalgo, 350
    war with, 348–352
Michilimackinac, 63
Middle class
    challenges to, 783–784
    conformity in, 785
    culture of, 777–778
Middle colonies
    Chesapeake and, 89–90

Middle East, **896**
    agreements in, 887
    U.S. Interests in, 863
    wars in, 832–834
Middle ground
    rituals on, 95–96
Midvale Steel Company, 472
Migration
    by Southern whites, 258
Military
    morale problems in, 829
    segregated, u20
Milken, Michael, 858–859
Mill towns
    industrialization and, 426–427
Mingoes
    alliance with Pontiac, 114
Mining, 448
Minorities
    opportunities for, 516
Minority women
    employment of, 640
Missionaries
    activities of, 47–48
Mississippi Plan, **523**
Missouri
    application for statehood, **204**
Missouri Compromise, **204,** 224, 362
    State of the Union and, **225**
Modern Woman: The Lost Sex, 782
Modernization
    and Third World, 753
Mogollon, 4
Mohawks
    as part of Iroquois Confederacy, 62–63
    in Iroquois Confederacy, 62–63
Monetary policy, 527
Mongolians, 450
Monroe Doctrine, **204,** 222
Monroe, James, 213, 221, 238–239, 297
Montgomery Bus Boycott, 774
Montoya, Pablo, 350
Montreal, 30–31
    founded, **29**
Moon, Lottie, 575
Morgan, Daniel, 149
Morgan, J.P., 468, 486, 565
Morgan, Lewis, 28
Mormons, 294, 296
Morrill Act, **459**
Morris, Robert, 167
Mossadegh, Mohammed, 755
Motecuhzoma, 4–5
Mott, Lucretia, 300
Movies, 516, 645
*Mr. and Mrs. Hines of Stamford Do Their
        Bit,* 614
Muckrakers, 551
Muguet, Peter, 76
Muller v. Oregon, **466,** 475–476, **549,** 558

Municipal Voters League, 551
Munn v. Illinois, 526
Murray, Judith Sargent, 159
Murray, William Vans, 194
Music
    of slaves, 253
Mutual Defense Assistance Act, 743
Mutual Security Treaty, **734**

N

Nader, Ralph, 890
NAFTA (North America Free Trade
    Agreement), 884
Nagasaki, 708
Narragansetts, 64
*Narrative of the Life of Frederick Douglass,
    An American Slave, Written by
    Himself,* **231**
Nasser, Gamal Abdul, 755
Natchez Indians, 71
National Aeronautics and Space
    Administration (NASA), 749
National American Woman Suffrage
    Association, 550
National Anti-Slavery Standard, 299
National Association for the Advancement
    of Colored People (NAACP),
    516–517, **549,** 607
National Association of Colored
    Women, 632
National Civil Service Reform League, 525
National Consumers League, 550, 559
National Cordage Company, 538
National debts, 186
National Defense Education Act, **763,** 770
National Ex-Slave Pension and Bounty
    Association, 257
National Geographic, 581
National Housing Act, **763**
National Industrial Recovery Act, 664, 665
National Intelligencer, 206
National Labor Relations Act, **656,** 671
National League Professional Baseball
    Clubs, **494,** 513
National Liberation Front, 757
National Organization for Women
    (NOW), **793**
National Recovery Administration
    (NRA), 664
National Reparation Coordinating
    Committee, 257
National Research Council, 622
National Security Act, 741–742
National Security Council (NSC), 741
National time zones
    established, **440**
National Union Convention, 421
National War Labor Board, 615, 714
National Woman Suffrage Association,
    523, 532

National Women's Political Caucus, 127
Native American
    activism, 825
    term examined, 24
Native American Graves Protection and
    Repatriation Act (NAGPRA), 24
Native Americans
    and European American
        newcomers, 135
Native cultures
    gender dimensions of, 25
    map of, **6**
    polytheism in, 8
    social organization of, 4–5
    war and politics, 7–8
NATO
    founded, **734**
Natural resources
    development of West, **448**
    extraction of, 447–452
Naturalization Act of 1798, 207
Navajos
    as servants, 96–97
    raiding Fort Defiance, 444–445
Naval battles, 216
Navalism
    Alfred T. Mahan, 583
Navigation Acts, 116
    Mercantilism and, 72–73
    trade restrictions of, 75
Negro rule
    myth of, 427
Neolin, 114
Neutral rights
    violation of, 604–605
Neutrality Act, 685
Neutrals, 137
New Conservative Coalition, 853
New Deal
    assessment of, 679–680
    economy before and after, **667**
    for Native Americans, 673–674
    in the South, 674
    in the West, 673
    launch of, 662–666
    limits of, 677–680
    second, 669
New England
    Caribbean and, 67
    families in, 48–49
    founding of, 44–48
    King George's War and, 88–89
    life in, 48–50
    merchants and federalists, 191
    religion in, 49
    towns of, 46–47
    trade in, 67–68
New France
    founding of, **31**
    Jesuit missions in, 31

New freedom
    versus new nationalism, 568
New Hampshire
    founding of, **31**
New Haven
    founding of, **31**
New Jersey
    as restoration colony, 57–62
New Jersey plan, 172
New Left, 813
New Mexico, 30
    founding of, **31**
New nationalism
    versus new freedom, 568
New Netherlands
    founding of, **31**
New Orleans
    founded, **56**
New Right, 855
    under Ronald Reagan, 852
New York
    as restoration colony, 57–62
    slave rebellions in, 100
New-York Evening Post, 206
Newlands Reclamation Act, **440,**
    453, 454
Nez Percé Indians, 444
Niña, 14
9/11 attacks, 199
Nineteenth Amendment, **549**
Nipmucks, 64
Nixon Doctrine, 831
Nixon, Richard M., 749, **793,** 821
    domestic agenda, 834
    election, 816
    resignation of, **822**
Non–Importation Act, 212–213
Non-Intercourse Act, 215
North
    similarity with South, 232
North America
    Europeans in, 20–23
North American Free Trade Agreement
    (NAFTA), 879
North Briton, The, 121
North Carolina
    as restoration colony, 57–62
Northwest Ordinance,
    169–170, 179
Northwest Territory
    war in, 194–196
Nova Scotia, 136–137
Noyes, John Humphrey, 295
Nuclear proliferation, 729
    espionage and, 771
Nullification, 304–305
    controversy over, 313
Núñez de Balboa, Vasco, 17
Nye Committee Hearings,
    694–695

O

Oakley, Annie, 451
Office of Price Administration, 715
Ojibwas, 447
Old Indian Legends, 446
Old South
    characteristics of, 233
    term discussed, 235
Olmec civilization, **2**
Olney, Richard, 529
Olympic Games 1963, 676
Oneidas
    as part of Iroquois Confederacy, 62–63
    in Iroquois Confederacy, 62–63
Onondagas
    as part of Iroquois Confederacy, 62–63
    in Iroquois Confederacy, 62–63
OPEC (Organization of Oil Exporting Companies), 833
Opechancanough, 40
Operation Desert Storm, 872
Operation War Bride, 719
Oral cultures, 94
Ordinance of 1785
Oregon, 348–349
Oregon Treaty, 34
Organized Labor
    during wartime, 714
    setbacks for, 630
Organized labor
    attacks on, 855
Osages, 63
Ostend Manifesto, 360
Otis, Harrison Gray, 214
Otis, James, 116–117
Our Country (Strong), **576,** 580
Our Indian Ward (Manypenny), 440, 445
Owen, Robert Dale, 295

P

P.B.S. Pinchback, 415
Pacific War, **711**
Paine, Thomas, **132,** 142, 143–144, 152
Pakistan
    decolonization of, 736
Paleo-Indians
    as first Americans, 3
    migration from Asia, **2**
Palmer Raids, **601,** 618
Pamela (Richardson), 158
Pan American Airways, 636
Panama Canal, 593–594
Panic of 1819, 223–224, 305
Panic of 1907, 567
Paris Peace Accords, 830
Paris Peace Conference, 298, 620
Parks, Rosa, 774
Parliament's Navigation Acts, 72–73
Partisan politics, 188–190

Partisanship
    bases of, 191
Pastor, Tony, 515
Patch, Sam, 289, 293–294, 307–308
Paternalism, 248–249, 259
PATRIOT Act, 879, 892
Payne-Aldrich Tariff, 567
Peace groups, 687
Peale, Charles Wilson, 144
Pearl Harbor, **716**
    explaining, 702–703
    surprise attack on, 702
Peirce, Franklin, 356
Pendergadst, Tom, 507
Pendleton Civil Service Act, 525, 528
Penitentiaries, 293
Penn, William, 60, 78
Pennington, J.W.C., 298
Pennsylvania
    as restoration colony, 57–62
    chartered, **56**
Pennsylvania Journal, 123
Pentagon Papers, **822**
People-to-People Campaign, 750
Pequot War, **29,** 47
Perestroika, 864
Perot, Ross, 881
Perry, Oliver Hazard, 216
Persian Gulf War, **851**
Peters, Samuel, 51
Philadelphia Railroad, 537
Philippine insurrection
    pacification and, 589
Pickering, John, 207
Pilgrim's Progress, 551
Pilgrims
    in New England, 45
Pinchot, Gifford, 567
Pinckney Cotesworth, Charles, 199, 208
Pinckney's Treaty, **182,** 191
Pinckney, Thomas, 191
Pinckney, William, 213
Pinta, 14
Pitt, William, 112, **120**
Pizarro, Francisco, 17
Plague
    effects of, 11
Plan of Union, 110–111
Planned Parenthood, 571
Planter's values
    social status and, 247–248
Planters
    marriage and family and, 249
Platt Amendment
    Cuba and, 593
Playboy (magazine), 782–783
Pledge of Allegiance, The, 788
Plessy v. Ferguson, 523, 531, 774
Plymouth colony
    founding of, 29, **31**
Pocahontas, 38

Pokanokets
    in New England, 45
Political factions
    rise of, 201
Political machines, 507–508
Political rights
    of women, 301
Politics
    in Chesapeake, 43
Polk, James K., 348
Polk, Leonidas, 537
Polygyny
    in West Africa, 9
Polytheism
    in native cultures, 8
Pontiac
    alliances, 114
Popé, 63–64
Pope Alexander VI, 16
Population growth, 82–86, 87, 496
Populism
    rise of, 535–537
Populist
    Roosevelt's strategies, 670
Populists, 668
Porter, Sylvia F., 766
Portsmouth
    slaves in, 160
Postwar era
    in America, 763–768
Postwar trade, **168**
Potawatomis
    alliance with Pontiac, 114
Pound, Roscoe, 558
Poverty, 87–88, 787
    by race, **859**
    in United States, **866**
    war on, 803–805
Poverty and Progress (George), **466**
Poverty relief, 504
Powderly, Terence V., 476
Powell, Colin, 894
Power of Sympathy, The (Brown), **155**
Powers, Francis Gary, 751
Powhatan Confederacy
    attacks Virginia, **29**
Praying Towns, 47–48
Prescott, Samuel, 140
Presidential powers, 174–175
Presley, Elvis, **763**
Prigg v. Pennsylvania, 352–353
Prince Henry the Navigator, 13
Princeton University
    founded, **81**
Proclamation of 1763, 114, 135
Progress and Poverty, 488
Progressive education, 557
Progressive reform, 631–632
Progressivism
    opponents of, 554
    Southern and Western, 554

Prohibition, 556, 646
Propaganda
    popular culture and, 715
Proslavery argument
    in South, 233–234
Prostitution
    controlling, 556
Protestant Reformation, 36
Protestants
    differences with Catholics, 294
Protests, 661
    of 1890s, 537–538
Provincial Conventions, 134–135
Public Works Administration, 665
Pueblos
    as servants, 96–97
Puerto Rico
    newcomers from, 635
Pullman Strike, 478–479
Pure Food and Drug Act, **549,** 558, 565–566
Puritans
    codes of conduct of, 49

Q

Quakers, 60, 355–356
    as pacifists, 137–138
Quebec, 30–31
    founded, **29**
Quebec Acts, 126
Queen Anne's War, 75, **109**
Queen Elizabeth I
    birthright of, 10
Quincy, Josiah Jr., 123

R

Race
    conflicts about, 717
    riots in Illinois, **763**
    significance of, 450
Race relations, 566
Race riots, **494**
Racism
    as U.S. handicap, 753
    continuing, 786–787
    growth of, 160–163, 178
Racist theory
    development of, 162
Radicals, 418–419
Radio, 634
Radio News, 700
Railroad
    construction of, 455
    regulation of, 526
    strikes of 1877, 476
    subsidies, 455
Railroad land grants, **459**
Rain-in-the-Face, 445
Raleigh, Walter, 22, **39**
Rape
    by white masters, 254

Rauschenbusch, Walter, 552
Ray, James Earl, 816
Reading Railroad, 537
Reagan, Ronald, 462
    conservative agenda, 853–854
    elected president, **851**
Reaganomics, 855–856
Real Whigs, 115
    ideology of, 175
Reconstruction, **422,** 432–433
    industrial expansion, 430
    Johnson's vision for, 437
    presidential, 418
    wartime, 411–413
Reconstruction Acts of 1867–1868, 421
Reconstruction plan
    Andrew Johnson, 416–418
Recorded sound
    technology of, 489
Red Record, A, 530
Red scare, 618, 770–772. *See also*
            Anticommunism; Communism
Reformers
    upper-class, 551
    working class, 552
Regan Doctrine, 860
Regents of the University of California v. Bakke,
    822, 843
Regulation of Trusts, 564–565
Relief programs, 665
Religion, 901
    impact in New England, 49, 53–54
    in the United States, 779
    of native cultures, 8
    of slaves, 253
    rituals of, 94–95
    therapeutic culture and, 842
Religious patterns
    in New England, 44
Religious right
    growth of, 865
Report on Public Credit (Hamilton), **182,** 186
Republican governments
    designing, 163–165, 178
Republican Party, **352**
    formed, **347,** 358
    ideology of, 359–361
Republicanism
    defined, 154
    varieties of, 156–157
Republicans
    as subversive foreign agents, 193
    liberal revolt, 430–432
    racial equality and, 427
Resignations, 836
Resistance
    forms of, 98
    strategies of, 255–256
Restoration colonies, 57
Retirement
    of older Americans, 639

*Return to Africa of the Amistad Captives,
    The,* 237
Revenue Act of 1789, 183
Revenue Act of 1916, 613
Revere, Paul, 121, 140
Revivals, 291–292, 311, 644
Revolution of 1800, 206
Revolutionary War
    beginnings of, 131
Rhode Island
    founding of, **31**
Rice, 69–70
Richardson, Samuel, 158
Richmond, David, 792
Rights of the British Colonies (Otis),
    116–117
Ringgold, John, 451
Ripley, George, 295
Rituals
    of consumption, 95
    on middle ground, 95–96
    religious and civic, 94–95
Rituals of Resistance, 121
Roanoke, 22
Robertson, Pat, 865
Rockefeller Foundation, 684
Rockefeller, John D., 103
Rodney, George, 148
Rodriguez Miró, Esteban, 198
Roe v. Wade, 822
Rogers Clark, George, 136
Rolfe, John, 38
Roman Catholicism, 126
Romero, Tomás, 350
Roosevelt
    death of, **734**
Roosevelt corollary, 594
Roosevelt, Theodore, 515, 551
    evolving views of, 695
    quarantine speech, 698
    revival of presidency and, 564
Root, Elihu, 578
Ross, John, 239, 240
Rowlandson, Joseph, 55
Rowlandson, Mary, 55, 64
Rowson, Susanna, 158
Royal Navy, 148
Rudyerd, William, 28
Ruggles, David, 355–356
Rum
    in colonies, 76
Rumsfeld, Donald, 894
Rural Free Delivery, **440,** 458
Rush, Benjamin (quoted), 160
Rush-Bagot Treaty, **204,** 222
Russell, Lillian, 516

S

Sabbath Day, 524
Sabbath laws, 308
Sacagawea, 210

Safety bicycle
 invented, **494**
Sailing
 in Mediterranean Atlantic, 12
Salem Village, 74
Salmon
 decline of, 442
Samuel Adams
 Committees of Correspondence and, 124–125
Sanger, Margaret, 562–563, 571
Santa Fe
 founded, **29**
Santa Maria, 14
Scalawags, 428
Schaw, Janet, 107–109, 122
Schiff, Jacob, 486
Schlafly, Phyllis, 828
School and Society, The (Dewey), 557
Schuyler, Elizabeth, 186
Science, 901
Scopes trial, 644
Scots-Irish, 84–86
Scott, Dred, 362
Scott, Winfield, 356
Second Bank of the United States
 chartered, 220
Second Barbary War, 218
Second Continental Congress, 132, 135, 141, **155,** 163–165
Second Great Awakening, **290,** 291, 294, 312
Sedition Act, **182,** 193, 207, **601,** 616
 purpose of, 201
Sedition Act of 1798, 199
Segregation
 as U.S. handicap, 753
 legal, 530–531
 racial, 500–501
Selective service, 722
Selective Service Act, **601**
Seminole Wars, 241–242, 356
Senecas
 as part of Iroquois Confederacy, 62–63
 in Iroquois Confederacy, 62–63
Separatists
 in New England, 44
 South Carolina and, 305
September 2001, 758, 891
Sergeant, John, 306
Serres, Dominic, 113
Servitude
 conditions of, 41–42
Seven Years' War, 81, **108,** 112, 113, 128, 141
 British victory in, 136
 financing, 115
Seventeenth Amendment, 549
Sewage disposal, 505–506
Seward, William H., 433
 quest for empire, 582

Sexual abuse
 by white masters, 254
Sexual activity
 interracial, 163
Sexual Behavior in the Human Female (Kinsey), 782
Sexual Behavior in the Human Male (Kinsey), 782
Sexuality
 and the family, 842
 in United States, 782–783
Seymour, Horatio, 423
Shakers, 294
Sharecropping, 532–533
 rise of, 416
Shawnees
 alliance with Pontiac, 114
Shays's Rebellion, **155,** 171
Shays, Daniel, 171
Sheldon, Charles, 552
Sheltowee, 131
Sherman Anti-Trust Act, **466,** 488
Sherman Silver Purchase Act, **523,** 527
Sherman, John, 488
Show business, 515
Shuffle Along, 647
Sierra Leone
 and American Revolution, 139
Silver
 Spain's decline and, 18
Silver dollars, **523**
Sinclair, Upton, 551
Singer, Isaac M., 483–484
Sino-Japanese War, 685
Sir Charles Grandison (Richardson), 158
Sirhan Sirhan, 816
Sitting Bull, 445
Sixteenth Amendment
Slater, Samuel, 219, 223
Slave
 as a term, 173
 demographics on, **368**
 relationships with masters, 251–253
 society of, 234–235
Slave doctors, 250
Slave Power, 363
Slave rebellion
 in Virginia, **231**
Slave trade
 Atlantic, 66–67
 domestic, 255
 economy and, 56
 in West Africa, 67
 international, 213
 voyages in, 68
Slaveowners
 worst fears of, 138
Slavery, 352–353
 African, 65–66
 as a term, 173
 black families and, 254–255

collapse of party system, 371
 constitution and, 173–174
 debate over, 184
 domestic, 255
 in Guinea, 9–10
 party system and, 357
 South's argument for, 233–234
Slaves, 138
 America-born, 84
 auction for, 230
 culture and resistance, 252–257
 economy and, 149
 in Spanish and French North America, 71
 life and labor, 249–252
 rebellions, 100
 relationships with masters, 259
 religion and music, 253
 resistance of, 72
 runaways, 149
 violence and intimidation against, 251
Smallpox, 19–20
 inoculation for, 93
Smallpox epidemic, **81**
Smith, Al, 648
Smith, John, 38
Smith, William, 69
Sumner, Charles, 419
Snyder Act, **628**
Social Darwinism, 491
Social Gospel, 552
Social mobility, 498
Social organization
 in native cultures, 5–6
Social reform, 508
Social Security Act, 670, 681
Social unrest, 661
Social values, 639
Social welfare programs
 attacks on, 854
Socialists, 539
Society of Friends, 60
Society of American Indians, 561
 founded, **549**
Society of Cincinnati, 159
Society of Friends, 60
Society of Jesus (Jesuits), 31–32
Sons of Liberty
 composition of, 119
 formed, **108**
Sound
 recorded, 489
South
 proslavery argument in, 233–234
 similarity with North, 232
 victory in, 147–150
South Carolina, 147–148
 African enslavement in, 69
 as restoration colony, 57–62
 secedes from Union, 347
 slave rebellions in, 100

South Carolina Gazette, 123
Southern Democrats, 361
Southern Republican Party
    black voters and, 425–426
Southern Thought (Fitzhugh), **231**
Sovereignty
    threats to, 212
Sovereignty and Goodness of God, The
        (Rowlandson), 55
Soviet Union. *See also* Cold War
    tensions with America, 796, 860
Spain
    contest with England, 22
    decline of, 18
Specie, 165–167
Specie Circular, 307
Spiritualism
    slavery and, 250
Sports, 645
Sprang, William, 414
Sputnik, 749
Sri Lanka
    decolonization of, 736
St. Clair, Arthur, 194–196
St. Kitts
    founding of, **31**
St. Mary's Mutual Benevolence Total
        Abstinence Society, 293–294
Stagflation
    causes of, 838
Stalin, Joseph, 711, 736
Stamp Act, **108,** 128
    boycotts to, 122
    crisis, 116–120, 129
    demonstrations against, 118
    opposition to, 120
Standard of living
    in Chesapeake, 42
Standard Oil Trust
    founded, **466**
Stanton, Elizabeth Cady, 300, 413, 532
Staple crops
    postwar restrictions on, 170
Star Spangled Banner, 217
State
    separated from Church, 205
State constitutions, 164
    revising, 164–165
State debts, 186
State governments
    limiting, 164
Steel, Ferdinand L., 243–244
Stephens, Alexander H., 413, 418
Stevens, Judith Sargent, 159
Stevens, Thaddeus, 419
*Still Life of Harriet Tubman with Bible and
        Candle,* 356
Still, William, 355–356
Stimson, Henry L., 738
Stock market
    crash of 1929, 649
    speculation on, 649–650

Stolle, J.M., 86
Stone, Lucy, 301
Stonewall Inn uprising, **822**
Stono Rebellion, **81,** 100
Stout, Harry, 101
Stowe, Harriet Beecher, 355
Strait, Davis, 16
Strikes
    sit-down, 672
Stuart Monarchs of England
    restored, 57
Stuart, Gilbert, 217
Submarine warfare, 605–606
Suburbanization, 767
Suburbs
    growth of, 637–638
Suez crisis, 756
Suffrage, **290,** 522, 531–532
    of women, 160
Sugar, 20
    cultivation on Barbados, **29,** 35
Sugar Act, **108,** 116
Sullivan, Tim, 507
Sully, Lawrence, 117
Summer, Donna, 842
Sumner, Charles, 362
Sunbelt
    rise of, 777–778
    shifts to, **840**
Supply-side economics, 856
Supreme Court
    first decade of, 184
Susquehannocks, 65
Swift, Gustavus, 486
Syphilis, 443

T

Taft administration, 567
Taft, Robert A., 743
Taft-Hartley Act, **763,** 765
Taft-Katsura Agreement, 595
Tallmadge, James Jr., 224
Taney, Roger B., 363
Tanguay, Eva
Taos Revolt, 350
Tarbell, Ida M., 551
Tariff of Abominations, **290**
Tarleton's Legion, 149
Tariff policy, 526–527
Tariff of 1816, 220
Tariff reform, 569–570
Tax policy
    as political wedge, 428
    revolts, 840
Tax reform, 569–570
Taxes, 165–167
Taylor, Frederick W., 472
Taylor, Zachary, 216, 351–352
Tea, 95, 130
    in colonies, 76
Tea Act, **108**
    reactions to, 125

Technology, 841–842
    consequences of, 472
    new home, 504
Tecora, 237
Tecumseh, William, **204,** 211, 762
Television
    in the United States, 779
Teller, Henry M., 541
Temperance, 293–294
Ten percent plan, 411
Tennessee Valley Authority (TVA), 656
Tenochtitlán
    capture of, 17
Tenskwatawa, **204,** 211
Tenure of Office Act, **410,** 423
Teotihuacán, 3–4
    influence of, **2**
Terrorism
    confronting, 902–904
Terrorist attacks, 863–864
    on United States, 758, 878–880
Tet Offensive, The, 815
Theories of representation, 115
Third World
    nation building in, 795–796
    rise of, **752**
Thirteenth Amendment, 412–413
Thomas, Clarence
    nomination to Supreme Court, 874
Thomas, Will, 24
Thoreau, Henry David, 365
    American renaissance and, 295
Three Mile Island
    nuclear accident on, **822**
Tiananmen Square, 851
Tilden, Samuel J., 434
Till, Emmett, 775
Timber and Stone Act, **440,** 449
Tobacco, 20, 40
Tompkins, Daniel, 221
Tonkin Gulf Incident, 806
Townshend Acts, **108,** 124, 128
    Massachusetts assembly and, 121
    resistance to, 120–125, 129
    resistance to, 122
Townshend, Charles, **120,** 120–125
*Tractatus De Poto Caphe, Chinesium The et de
        Chocolata,* 76
Trade
    decline in, 690
Trade routes
    in Atlantic, **66**
Trading
    patterns in Chesapeake, 90
    patterns in Lower South, **91**
    patterns in New England, **88**
Traditions
    of Native Americans, 53
Trail of Tears, The, **242**
Transcontinental railroad, **440**
Transportation, 452
    mechanization of, 495

Travels (Polo), **2**, 11
Treaty of 1778, 194
Treaty of Aix-la-Chapelle, 89
Treaty of Alliance, 145, 153, 189
Treaty of Ghent, 217, 218, 226
    ends War of 1812, **204**
Treaty of Greenville, 195, 444
Treaty of Guadalupe Hidalgo, 347, 350, 449
Treaty of New Echota, 240
Treaty of Paris, **108**, 112, **132**, 149–150, 576, 588
    provisions for, 168–169
    signed, **155**
Treaty of Payne's Landing, 241
Treaty of Tordesillas, **2**, 16
Treaty of Versailles, **601**
    senate rejection of, 621–622
Triangle Shirtwaist Company
    fire at, 475
Tribes
    in North America, **32**
Tripoli War, 204
Truman Doctrine, **734**, 739–740
Truman, Harry, 726
    fires MacArthur, 746
    postwar liberalism and, 768–769
Trumbull, John, 157
Truth, Sojourner, 299
Tsenacomoco, 38
Tubman, Harriet, 299
Tudor dynasty
    founded by Henry VII, 11
Turner, Frederick Jackson, 439, 583
Turner, Nat, 234, 291–292
    insurrection, 256
Turner, Ted, 873
Tuscarora War, **56**
Tuscaroras
    as part of Iroquois Confederacy, 62–63
    in Iroquois Confederacy, 62–63
Twain, Mark, 451, 522
Twelfth Amendment
    adoption of, 199
Two Treatises of Government, 92
Tyler, John, 309–310
Tyler, Royall, **155**, 157

U

U-2 incident, 751
U.S. Chamber of Commerce, 551
U.S. Patent Office
    created, 468
U.S. Steel Corporation
    founded, **466**
U.S. v. Cruikshank, **410**, 434
U.S. v. E.C. Knight Co., 488
U.S. v. Reese, 530
Uncle Tom's Cabin (Stowe), 347, 515
Underground Railroad, 256, 355–356
Underwood Tariff, **549**, 569
United Auto Workers (UAW), 777

United States
    as "league of friendship," 165
    relations with Mexico, 594–595
    rising national debt, 857
Universal Negro Improvement Association
    (UNIA), 635
Universities
    growth of, 557–558
Urban engineers, 506
Urban sprawl, 495–496
Urbanization, **497**
USA Patriot Act, 199
USS Chesapeake, 213
USS Wasp, 216
Utopian awakening, 294–295, 312

V

Van Buren, Martin, 237, 305
    elected president, **290**
Vaqueros, 459
Vare, Duke, 507
Vassa, Gustavus, 103
Venezuela
    boundary dispute, 584
Verelst, John, 63
Vermont
    slavery banned in, 160–161
Vesey, Denmark, 256
Vespucci, Amerigo, 15
Vietnam
    independence and, 744–745
    John F. Kennedy and, 805–806
    U.S. soldiers in, 808–809
Vietnam War
    and Southeast Asia, **807**
    veterans, 831
    youth and, 812–813
Villard, Henry, 468
Violence, 505
    against African Americans, 530
    and segregation, 500–501
    hate crimes and, 888
Virginia
    founding of, **31**, 37–40
    population of, **43**
    slave rebellion in, **231**
Virginia Baptists, 102
Virginia Company
    end of, 40
Virginia plan, 172
Virginia Resolution, **182**, 194
Virginia Stamp Act Resolves, 117–118
Virginian, The (Wister), 462
Virtue
    arts and, 157–159
Volstead Act, **628**
Voter registration
    freedom rides and, 798
Voyages
    for slave trade, 68
    of Columbus, 14

W

Wabash, 526
Wade, Benjamin, 412
Wade-Davis Bill
    congress and, 412
Wage work, 480
Wald, Lillian, 508
Waldo, Samuel, 292
Waldseemüller, Martin, 15
Walker, David, 296–297
Wallace, George C., 799, 816, 835–836
Wampanoags, 64
Wampum, 34
War
    fighting in, 722
    in Europe, 723
    in Pacific, 710, 726–727
    motives for, 587
War brides, 719
War of 1812, 215, 218, 222
    consequences of, 228
    embargoes and, **204**
    ended by Treaty of Ghent, **204**
    reasons for, 227
    surge westward, 224
War of the Spanish Succession, 75
Ward, Artemas, 140
Ware v. Hylton, 184
Warfare
    Caribbean and, 35
    effects of, 11
    unrestricted submarine, 605–606
Warner, Charles Dudley, 522
Warsaw Pact, **734**, 749–750
Wartime
    families in, 717
    prosperity in, 716
Washington Naval Conference, 687
Washington, Booker T., **549**, 560
Washington, George, 114, 132, 133, 141, 144
    domestic policy under, 184–188
    farewell address, 191
    inaugurated, **182**
Washington, Martha, 293–294
Water
    rights to, 452–453
Water supply, 505–506
Watergate, 832, 836. *See also* Nixon, Richard M.
Watson, Tom, 535, 537
Watt, James, 854
Wayne, Anthony, 195
Wealth, 87–88
Webb-Pomerene Act, 688
Webster, Daniel, 304, 310
Weems, Mason Locke, 157
Weld, Theodore, 297, 300
Weapons of Mass Destruction (WMD), 894
West Africa, 9–10
    slave trade in, 67

West, Benjamin, 114
Wester, Daniel, 308
Western land
    claims and cessions, **166**
Westinghouse, George, 468
Westos, 70
Whig party, 290
    differences with Democrats, 313
    economic expansion and,
        307–308
Whiskey Rebellion, **182,** 188
White Hats, 534
White House
    scandals in, 888
White resistance, 425, 775–776
White, Hugh, 308
White, John, 22, **39**
White, Richard, 95–96
White, William Allen, 542
Whitefield, George, **81**
Whites
    landless, 244
Whitney, Eli, 208
Wilkinson, James, 208
Williams, Burt, 516
Williams, Roger, 49–50
Williams, Wiliam Appleman, 830
Wilmot Proviso, 347, 351, 363
Wilmot, David, 351
Wilson, William Dean, 707
Wilson, Woodrow, 512, 569, 619
    elected president, **549**
    policy on business regulation, 569
    Wilsonianism and, 603–604
Wilson-GormanTariff, **523**
Winthrop, John, 45–46, 48
Wirt, William, 306
Wister, Owen, 462

Witchcraft
    1692 crisis, 74
    in Salem, **56**
Wizard of Oz, 544
Wolfe, James, 112
Woman movement, 562
Woman suffrage, 563
Woman's Christian Temperance Union
        (WCTU), 551, 556
Women
    at work, 713
    in the workforce, 639–640
    opportunities for, 516
    politics and, 214–215, 632
    suffrage, 160, **290**
    the republic and, 159–160
    work and, 781–782
Women's Christian Temperance Union, 522
Women's clubs, 562
Women's International League for Peace
        and Freedom, 809
Women's Loyal National League, 413
Women's movement
    accomplishments of, 827
    opposition to, 827–828
    rise of, 312
Women's rights, 300
Women's Rights Convention, 301
Women's Trade Union League (WTUL), 479
Wonders of the Invisible World, The, 75
Woods, Granville T., 468
Woodstock, 813
Worcester v. Georgia, 240
Work force
    middle-class, 660
    restructuring of, 473
Workers'
    marginal, 658

Workers' Compensation, 553
Works Progress Administration, 669–670
World Health Organization
    smallpox and, 93
World War II
    end of, **763**
    Poland and outbreak, 696
    U.S. entry, 708

X

XYZ Affair, 192

Y

Yalta Conference, 725
Yamasee War, **56**
Yardbirds, 814
Yellow journalism, 517
Yellowstone Park, **440**
Yeoman Farmers
    livelihoods of, 243–244
    white class relations and, 244–245
Yorktown
    surrender at, 149
Yosemite National Park
    established, **440**
Young Men's Christian Association
        (YMCA), 511
Young Women's Christian Association
        (YWCA), 511, 551
Young, John Russell, 431
Youth culture
    in the United States, 783
Yuppies, 867–868

Z

Zenger, John Peter, **81,** 99
Zimmermann, Arthur, 606
Zitkala-Sa, 446